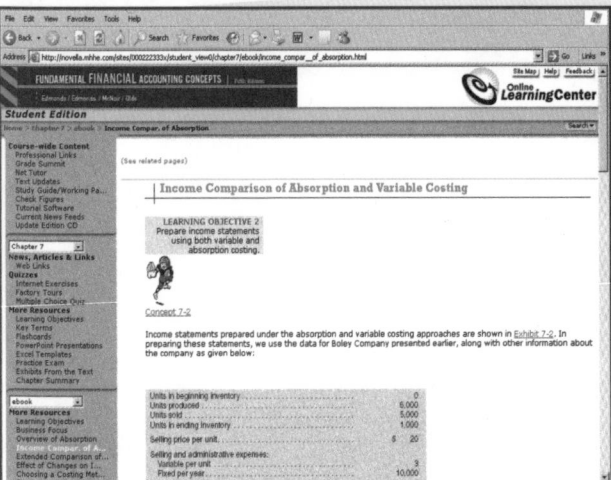

Interactive Online Version
of the Textbook

Online LearningCenter

In addition to the textbook, students can rely on this online version of the text for a convenient way to study. The interactive content is integrated with Homework Manager to give students quick access to relevant content as they work through problems, exercises, and practice quizzes.

Features:
- online version of the text is integrated with Homework Manager
- students referred to sections of the online book as they tackle an assignment or take a practice quiz

Homework Manager helps you

McGraw-Hill's
Homework
Manager

Assign coursework online

Problems and exercises from the book as well as questions from the testbank have been integrated into Homework Manager to give you many options as you deliver assignments and quizzes to students online. You can choose from static or algorithmic questions and have graded results automatically stored in your gradebook.

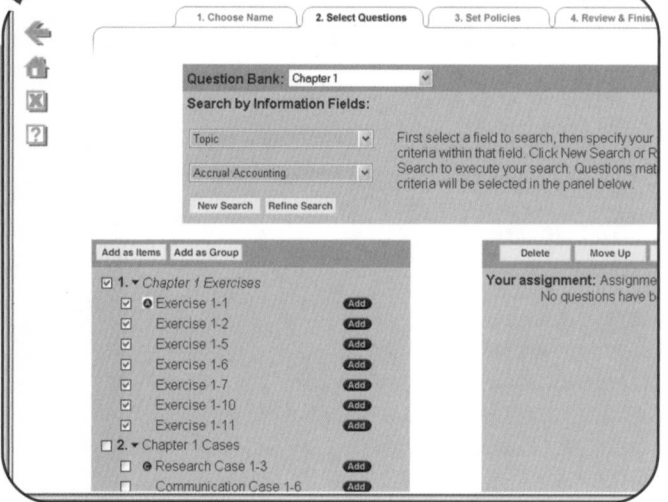

Problem 2-13: (Appendix 2A) Classification of Labor Costs [LO8]

Lynn Bjorland is employed by Southern Laboratories, Inc., and is directly involved in preparing the company's
half (i.e., $36 per hour) for any work in excess of 40 hours per week.

Required:

1. Suppose that in a given week Lynn works 45 hours. Compute Lynn's total wages for the week. How much
2. Suppose in another week that Lynn works 50 hours but is idle for 4 hours during the week due to equip
    allocated to direct labor cost? To manufacturing overhead cost?
3. Southern Laboratories has an attractive package of fringe benefits that costs the company $8 for each
    but is idle for 3 hours due to material shortages. Compute Lynn's total wages and fringe benefits for the
    Lynn's wages and fringe benefits for the week would be allocated to direct labor cost? To manufacturin
4. Refer to the data in (3) above. If the company treats that part of fringe benefits relating to direct labor
    to direct labor cost? To manufacturing overhead cost?

1. Total wages for the week:

Regular time: 40 hours × $24 per hour		$ 960
Overtime: 5 hours × $36 per hour		180
Total Wages		1140

Allocation of total wages:

Direct labor: 45 hours × $24 per hour		$
Manufacturing overhead: 5 hours × $12 per hour		

Question 1: *Score 6.5/8*

Your response	Correct response

Exercise 2-1: Using Cost Terms [LO2, LO5, LO7]

Following are a number of cost terms introduced in the chapter:

Period cost	Fixed cost
Variable cost	Prime cost
Opportunity cost	Conversion cost
Product cost	Sunk cost

Choose the cost term or terms above that most appropriately describe the costs identified in each of the following situations. A cost term can be used more than once.

1. Crestline Books, Inc., prints a small book titled *The Pocket Speller* . The paper going into the manufacture of the book would be called direct materials and classified as a Product cost (6%). In terms of cost behavior, the paper could also be described as a Product cost (0%) with respect to the number of books printed.
2. Instead of compiling the words in the book, the author hired by the company could have earned considerable fees consulting with business organizations. The consulting fees forgone by the author would be called Opportunity cost (6%).
3. The paper and other materials used in the manufacture of the book, combined with the direct labor cost involved, would be called Prime cost (6%).
4. The salary of Crestline Books' president would be classified as a Product cost (0%), and the salary will appear on the income statement as an expense in the time period in which it is incurred.
5. Depreciation on the equipment used to print the book would be classified by Crestline Books as a Product cost (6%). However, depreciation on any equipment used by the company in selling and administrative activities would be classified as a Period cost (6%). In terms of cost behavior, depreciation would probably be classified as a Fixed cost (6%) with respect to the number of books printed.
6. A Product cost (6%) is also known as an inventoriable cost,

---

Exercise 2-1: Using Cost Terms [LO2, LO5, LO7]

Following are a number of cost terms introduced in the chapter:

Period cost	Fixed cost
Variable cost	Prime cost
Opportunity cost	Conversion cost
Product cost	Sunk cost

Choose the cost term or terms above that most appropriately describe the costs identified in each of the following situations. A cost term can be used more than once.

1. Crestline Books, Inc., prints a small book titled *The Pocket Speller* . The paper going into the manufacture of the book would be called direct materials and classified as a Product cost. In terms of cost behavior, the paper could also be described as a variable cost with respect to the number of books printed.
2. Instead of compiling the words in the book, the author hired by the company could have earned considerable fees consulting with business organizations. The consulting fees forgone by the author would be called Opportunity cost.
3. The paper and other materials used in the manufacture of the book, combined with the direct labor cost involved, would be called Prime cost.
4. The salary of Crestline Books' president would be classified as a Period cost, and the salary will appear on the income statement as an expense in the time period in which it is incurred.
5. Depreciation on the equipment used to print the book would be classified by Crestline Books as a Product cost. However, depreciation on any equipment used by the company in selling and administrative activities would be classified as a Period cost. In terms of cost behavior, depreciation would probably be classified as a Fixed cost with respect to the number of books printed.
6. A Product cost is also known as an inventoriable cost, since

INCOR

efficiently manage your class.

Control how content is presented.

Homework Manager gives you a flexible and easy way to present coursework to students. You determine which questions to ask and how much help students will receive as they work through assignments. For example, you can determine the number of attempts a student can make with each problem; provide hints and feedback with each question, including references to the online version of the text; and much more.

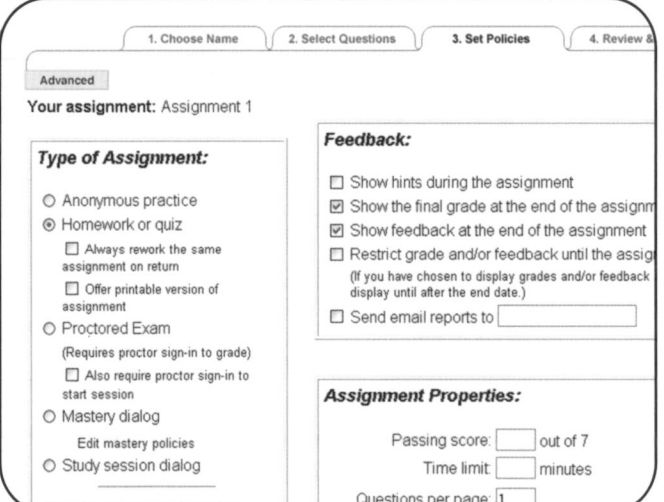

Track student progress.

Assignments are graded automatically, with the results stored in your private gradebook. Detailed results let you see at a glance how each student does on an assignment or an individual problem. You can even see how many attempts it took them to solve it. You can monitor how the whole class does on each problem, and even exactly where individual students might need extra help.

FIFTH EDITION

Fundamental Financial
ACCOUNTING
Concepts

Thomas P. Edmonds
University of Alabama–Birmingham

Cindy D. Edmonds
University of Alabama-Birmingham

Frances M. McNair
Mississippi State University

Philip R. Olds
Virginia Commonwealth University

Nancy W. Schneider
Lynchburg College

McGraw-Hill
Irwin

Boston   Burr Ridge, IL   Dubuque, IA   Madison, WI   New York   San Francisco   St. Louis
Bangkok   Bogotá   Caracas   Kuala Lumpur   Lisbon   London   Madrid   Mexico City
Milan   Montreal   New Delhi   Santiago   Seoul   Singapore   Sydney   Taipei   Toronto

McGraw-Hill
Irwin

FUNDAMENTAL FINANCIAL ACCOUNTING CONCEPTS

Published by McGraw-Hill/Irwin, a business unit of The McGraw-Hill Companies, Inc., 1221 Avenue of the Americas, New York, NY, 10020. Copyright © 2006, 2003, 2000, 1998, 1996 by The McGraw-Hill Companies, Inc. All rights reserved. No part of this publication may be reproduced or distributed in any form or by any means, or stored in a database or retrieval system, without the prior written consent of The McGraw-Hill Companies, Inc., including, but not limited to, in any network or other electronic storage or transmission, or broadcast for distance learning.

Some ancillaries, including electronic and print components, may not be available to customers outside the United States.

This book is printed on acid-free paper.

1 2 3 4 5 6 7 8 9 0 VNH/VNH 0 9 8 7 6 5 4

ISBN 0-07-298943-2

Editorial director: *Brent Gordon*
Publisher: *Stewart Mattson*
Sponsoring editor: *Steve Schuetz*
Managing developmental editor: *Gail Korosa*
Marketing manager: *Richard Kolasa*
Media producer: *Elizabeth Mavetz*
Lead project manager: *Pat Frederickson*
Senior production supervisor: *Michael R. McCormick*
Senior designer: *Mary E. Kazak*
Photo research coordinator: *Jeremy Cheshareck*
Photo researcher: *David Tietz*
Supplement producer: *Matthew Perry*
Senior digital content specialist: *Brian Nacik*
Cover design: *Lodge Design*
Cover image: © *Joseph Sohm; ChromoSohm Inc./Corbis*
Interior design: *Ellen Pettengell*
Typeface: *10/12 Times*
Compositor: *Cenveo*
Printer: *Von Hoffmann Corporation*

Library of Congress Cataloging-in-Publication Data

Fundamental financial accounting concepts / Thomas P. Edmonds . . . [et al.] — 5th ed.
    p. cm.
  Includes index.
  ISBN 0-07-298943-2
  1. Accounting. I. Edmonds, Thomas P.
HF5635.F95 2006
657—dc22   20004509257

www.mhhe.com

NOTE FROM THE AUTHORS

Over the past 15 years, major changes in accounting education have impacted the way most college and university professors teach introductory accounting. We are gratified that our concepts approach has been so effective it has become a market leader in the change movement. The concepts approach takes traditional accounting to the next level. We not only cover debits and credits, but more importantly explain how those debits and credits impact financial statements.

How have we become market leaders in the introductory accounting course?

We look at ourselves as **innovative traditionalists**. We don't aim to radically transform accounting education, but instead to make it more effective. Students who use this text follow a different path toward the accomplishment of a conventional set of learning objectives. However, the path is easier to walk; and students complete the journey with a far greater understanding of accounting.

In contrast to traditional textbooks, **this is a concepts-based text that focuses on the big picture**. Recording procedures and other details are presented after a conceptual foundation has been established. This approach enables students to understand rather than memorize. Just as a stable house rests on a solid foundation, technical competence and decision making skills must be supported by a strong conceptual framework.

What do we mean by a concepts-based textbook? We mean the text stresses the relationships between business events and financial statements. The primary objective is to develop students who can explain how any given business event affects the income statement, balance sheet, and statement of cash flows. Do assets increase, decrease, or remain unchanged? What effect does the event have on liabilities, equity, revenue, expense, gains, losses, net income, and dividends? Furthermore, how does the event affect cash flows? In summary, **the focus is on learning how business events affect financial statements**.

Balance Between Theory and Practice

This text addresses the issues raised by advocates for change in accounting education. The big picture approach enables professors to focus on developing skills as well as covering content. Students who understand concepts are better able to communicate ideas and more effective at solving unstructured problems. Students who understand concepts are also better prepared to learn technical content. Students using this text will learn the basics of double-entry bookkeeping including debits and credits, journal entries, T-accounts, and trial balances. This text maintains an appropriate balance between skill development and technical competence.

This is not a user or preparer approach. Indeed, the concepts approach serves both users and preparers. In order to function effectively in today's business world both preparers and users must understand event/statement relationships. By teaching concepts, you no longer have to choose between the interests of accounting majors and those of other business students. The concepts-approach serves both groups.

Implementing the concepts approach is surprisingly simple.

Instead of teaching students to record transactions in journals or T-accounts, teach them to record transactions directly into financial statements. While this shift is easy for instructors, it represents a dramatic change from how students have traditionally studied accounting. Making a direct connection between business events and financial statements encourages students to analyze conceptual relationships rather than memorize procedures. Early in the course students develop a conceptual framework that supports critical thinking and communication. Students become interested in accounting issues and are motivated to learn.

But don't take our word for it.

With over 200 colleges and universities successfully making the change to the concepts approach, we feel confident you will experience the same success as many of your colleagues have across the country. We would like to thank all of those who have been supportive of our teaching philosophy, and we highly encourage you to contact the author team or your local McGraw-Hill/Irwin representative to learn more about our texts.

Tom Edmonds • Cindy Edmonds • Frances McNair • Phil Olds • Nancy Schneider

> "The text is well organized, covers the critical topics, achieves the advertised balance between theory and practice, and is an appropriate introductory financial accounting text for BOTH the future accounting major and non-accounting major. It gets away from the historic "pure preparer's approach but doesn't go off the "deep end." "
> **Robert Derstine – Villanova University**

> "It has totally changed my attitude about teaching the first accounting course. Subject matter is much more "teachable" and easier to learn."
> **Elizabeth V. Mulig – Columbus State University**

ABOUT THE

Thomas P. Edmonds

Dr. Edmonds holds the Friends and Alumni Professorship in the Department of Accounting at the University of Alabama at Birmingham (UAB). He has been actively involved in teaching accounting principles throughout his academic career. Dr. Edmonds has **coordinated the accounting principles courses at the University of Houston and UAB.** He currently teaches introductory accounting in mass sections that frequently include more than 180 students. Dr. Edmonds has received five prestigious teaching awards including the UAB President's Excellence in Teaching Award and the distinguished Ellen Gregg Ingalls Award for excellence in classroom teaching. He has written a number of articles for many publications including *Issues in Accounting;* the *Journal of Accounting Education; Advances in Accounting Education; Accounting Education: A Journal of Theory, Practice and Research;* the *Accounting Review; Advances in Accounting;* the *Journal of Accountancy; Management Accounting;* the *Journal of Commercial Bank Lending;* the *Banker's Magazine;* and the *Journal of Accounting, Auditing, and Finance.* He has published four textbooks, five practice problems (including two computerized problems), and a variety of supplemental materials including study guides, working papers, and solutions manuals. Dr. Edmonds' writing is influenced by a wide range of business experience. He was a successful entrepreneur, worked as a management accountant for Refrigerated Transport, a trucking company, and worked in the not-for-profit sector as a commercial lending officer for the Federal Home Loan Bank. In addition, he has acted as a consultant to major corporations including First City Bank of Houston, AmSouth Bank in Birmingham, Texaco, and Cortland Chemicals. Dr. Edmonds began his academic training at Young Harris Community College in Young Harris, Georgia. He received a B.B.A. degree with a major in finance from Georgia State University in Atlanta, Georgia. He obtained an M.B.A. degree with a concentration in finance from St. Mary's University in San Antonio, Texas. His Ph.D. degree with a major in accounting was awarded by Georgia State University. Dr. Edmonds' work experience and academic training have enabled him to bring a unique user perspective to this textbook.

Cindy D. Edmonds

Cindy D. Edmonds, Ph.D., is an Associate Professor of Accounting at the University of Alabama at Birmingham. She serves as the coordinator of the introductory accounting courses at UAB. Dr. Edmonds received the 2001 Loudell Ellis Robinson Excellence in Teaching Award. Also, in 2000 and 2001 she was one of two School of Business faculty members nominated for the Ellen Gregg Ingalls Award for excellence in classroom teaching. She has written a variety of supplemental text materials including practice problems, a study guide, work papers, and test banks. Dr. Edmonds' articles appear in numerous publications including *Advances in Accounting Education, Journal of Education for Business, Journal of Accounting Regulation, Advances in Accounting, Management Accounting, CMA Journal, Disclosures,* and *Business & Professional Ethics Journal.* Her manuscript "Running a City on a Shoe String" received a certificate of merit award from the Institute of Management Accountants. The manuscript was used by the City of Vestavia in its application for Moody's Municipal Bond Rating. Dr. Edmonds is heavily involved in service activities. She is the 2001 president of the Birmingham Chapter of the American Society of Women Accountants. Dr. Edmonds has worked in the insurance industry, in a manufacturing company, and in a governmental agency. This work experience has enabled her to bring a real-world flavor to her writing. Dr. Edmonds holds a B.S. degree from Auburn University, an M.B.A degree from the University of Houston and a Ph.D. degree from the University of Alabama.

AUTHORS

Frances M. McNair

Dr. McNair holds the KPMG Peat Marwick Professorship in Accounting at Mississippi State University (MSU). She has been involved in teaching principles of accounting for the past 12 years and currently serves as the **coordinator for the principles of accounting courses at MSU.** She joined the MSU faculty in 1987 after receiving her Ph.D. from the University of Mississippi. The author of various articles that have appeared in the *Journal of Accountancy, Management Accounting, Business and Professional Ethics Journal, The Practical Accountant, Taxes,* and other publications, she also coauthored the book *The Tax Practitioner* with Dr. Denzil Causey. Dr. McNair is currently serving on committees of the American Taxation Association, the American Accounting Association, and the Institute of Management Accountants as well as numerous School of Accountancy and MSU committees.

Philip R. Olds

Professor Olds is Associate Professor of Accounting at Virginia Commonwealth University (VCU). He serves as the **coordinator of the introduction to accounting courses at VCU.** Professor Olds received his A.S. degree from Brunswick Junior College in Brunswick, Georgia (now Costal Georgia Community College). He received a B.B.A. in Accounting from Georgia Southern College (now Georgia Southern University) and his M.P.A. and Ph.D. degrees are from Georgia State University. After graduating from Georgia Southern, he worked as an auditor with the U.S. Department of Labor in Atlanta, Georgia. A CPA in Virginia, Professor Olds has published articles in various professional journals and presented papers at national and regional conferences. He also served as the faculty adviser to the VCU chapter of Beta Alpha Psi for five years. In 1989, he was recognized with an Outstanding Faculty Vice-President Award by the national Beta Alpha Psi organization.

Nancy W. Schneider

Professor Schneider is Associate Professor of Accounting at Lynchburg College in central Virginia where she has served for many years as the lead instructor for the accounting principles courses. Since attending graduate school she has participated in the writing, reviewing, editing, checking, and revising of college-level accounting and finance textbooks, textbook supplements, and related teaching materials. She has a deep personal commitment to student learning and to finding and sharing ways to improve college teaching. She is a recipient of the Sydnor Award for Teaching Excellence in Business at Lynchburg College and is frequently nominated by students for the College Excellence in Teaching Award. Professor Schneider initiated and organizes a highly popular annual symposium in which professors across all disciplines at the College exchange good teaching ideas. She has made numerous presentations at local and regional conferences, often related to teaching strategies, and is the coauthor of articles published in professional journals. Professor Schneider's professional activities also include active membership on the board of her local chapter of the Institute of Management Accountants where she regularly involves students in professional accounting educational meetings. Prior to teaching accounting, she was an auditor with an international public accounting firm in Atlanta and an internal auditor for a large integrated oil and gas company in Houston. Professor Schneider has maintained an active license to practice as a certified public accountant since 1980, and became a certified management accountant in 1992. She is a member of the American Institute of Certified Public Accountants and the Virginia Society of Certified Public Accountants. Professor Schneider received a Bachelor's degree in Mathematics Education with High Honors from the University of Florida in 1973, and a Master's degree in Professional Accountancy from Georgia State University in 1978.

HOW DOES THE BOOK HELP

STUDENTS SEE THE BIG PICTURE?

"Greatly benefited our students. They learn how business transactions affect financial position of a business without the debit/credits nuances. I think this is a great learning tool for intro students. They have no difficulty making the transition to Dr/Cr later in Chapter 4."
Peter Theuri – Northern Kentucky University

"I am a big supporter of the horizontal model! It is amazing what students know only by the end of chapter three. If a student were to drop the course at that point, they still would have a good foundational understanding of the four basic financial statements and accounting events."
Linda Bell – William Jewell College

PRINCIPAL FEATURES

Horizontal Financial Statements Model

A horizontal financial statements model replaces the accounting equation as the predominant teaching platform in this text. The model arranges the balance sheet, income statement and statement of cash flows horizontally across a single line of text as shown below.

Assets	=	Liabilities	+	Stockholders' Equity	Revenue	–	Expense	=	Net Income	Cash Flow

The statements model approach enables students to more clearly see how accounting relates to real-world decision making. Under the traditional approach students learn to journalize a series of events and to present summarized information in financial statements. They never see how individual transactions affect financial statements. In contrast, when students record transactions into a statements model, they see a direct connection between business events and financial statements. Most business people think "if I take this particular action, how will it affect my financials," not "if I do these fifteen things how will they be journalized." Accordingly, the statements model approach provides a learning experience that is more intuitive and relevant than the one provided by traditional teaching methodology.

Establishing the Conceptual Framework

Chapter 1 introduces the key components of the conceptual framework for financial accounting. Accruals are introduced in Chapter 2, deferrals in Chapter 3. The first three chapters use only non-technical terms (increase/decrease rather than debit/credit) to discuss the effects of events on the financial statements. Chapter 4 introduces recording procedures, including debits and credits. By the end of the first four chapters, students using this text will have been exposed to the same accounting content as those who use traditional books.

After Chapter 4, the text demonstrates both the conceptual structure and the recording procedures in tandem. For example, the purchase of treasury stock would be shown as follows:

Assets	=	Liabilities	+	Equity	Revenue	_	Expense	=	Net Income	Cash Flow
(1,000)		n/a		(1,000)	n/a		n/a		n/a	(1,000) FA

Account Title	Debit	Credit
Treasury Stock	1,000	
Cash		1,000

The Effects of Cash Flows Are Shown Through the Entire Text

The statement of cash flows is introduced in the first chapter and included throughout the text. Students learn to prepare a statement of cash flows in the first chapter by learning to analyze each increase and decrease in the cash account. They can prepare a statement of cash flows by classifying each entry in the cash account as an operating, investing, or financing activity.

Effects on Financial Statements Over Multiple Accounting Cycles

The text also uses a vertical statements model that shows financial statements from top to bottom on a single page. This model displays financial results for consecutive accounting cycles in adjacent columns, thereby enabling the instructor to show how related events are reported *over multiple accounting cycles*.

Exhibit 2
Elden Enterprises
Financial Statements Under Double-declining-balance

Income Statements

	2003	2004	2005	2006	2007
Rent Revenue	$15,000	$ 9,000	$ 5,000	$ 3,000	$ -0-
Depreciation Expense	12,000	6,000	2,000	-0-	-0-
Operating Income	$ 3,000	$ 3,000	$ 3,000	$ 3,000	$ -0-
Gain on sale of Van	-0-	-0-	-0-	-0-	500
Net Income	$ 3,000	$ 3,000	$ 3,000	$ 3,000	$ 500

Balance Sheets

Assets:					
Cash	$16,000	$25,000	$30,000	$33,000	$37,500
Van	24,000	24,000	24,000	24,000	-0-
Accumulated Depreciation	(12,000)	(18,000)	(20,000)	(20,000)	-0-
Total Assets	$28,000	$31,000	$34,000	$37,000	$37,500
Stockholders' Equity					
Common Stock	$25,000	$25,000	$25,000	$25,000	$25,000
Retained Earnings	3,000	6,000	9,000	12,000	12,500
Total Stockholders' Equity	$28,000	$31,000	$34,000	$37,000	$37,500

Statements of Cash Flows

Operating Activities					
Inflow from Customers	$15,000	$ 9,000	$ 5,000	$3,000	$ -0-
Investing Activities					
Outflow to Purchase Van	(24,000)				
Inflow from Sale of Van					4,500
Financing Activities					
Inflow from Stock Issue	25,000				
Net Change in Cash	$16,000	$ 9,000	$ 5,000	$ 3,000	$ 4,500
Beginning Cash Balance	0	16,000	25,000	30,000	33,000
Ending Cash Balance	$16,000	$25,000	$30,000	$33,000	$37,500

"For the most part students are very visual and it is important to see how events impact the various statements. As stated, this approach is simplified, but I can see that it would be easier for a student to understand a concept like buying and depreciating an asset using this format as opposed to having to look at several complete financial statements."
Patricia Lopez – Valencia Community College

"This is absolutely the best way to teach the SCF."
Paul Clikeman – University of Richmond

"Great; very logical. SCF is the least understood and appreciated by students. This focus keeps cash flows ever present and helps show the relationship to other financial statements."
George R. Violette – University of Southern Maine

"Excellent! Many books don't talk about cash flows until the end of the book."
James M. Lukawitz – University of Memphis

"It is easy for students to follow and presents the information in a natural approach."
Bruce Chase – Radford University

"I agree with it completely. This is how it should be taught. You cannot understand accrual accounting without comparing/contrasting cash flow."
Irvin T. Nelson – Utah State University

WHAT'S NEW THIS EDITION?

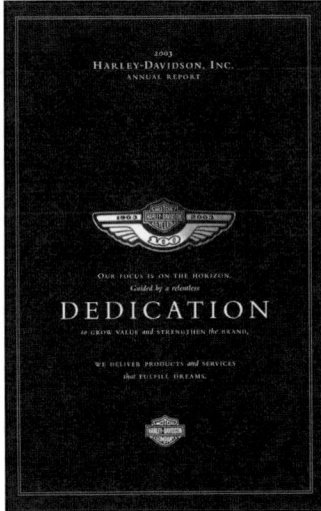

Topps Annual Report 2003

"The new manuscript exhibits a more personal approach in its writing style. This makes a big difference in it being "readable." I compare it to the difference between reading a factual and informative textbook, to reading a personal letter or even an interesting novel."
Steve Muller, Valencia Community College

Revisions for Fundamental Financial Accounting Concepts are in response to extensive feedback from instructors and students. Through formal reviews, instructor and student comments and suggestions, and focus groups, we have responded with constructive changes. There are three significant features.

Annual Report Projects

Two annual reports accompany the text.

- The 2003 annual report for Harley-Davidson, Inc. is packaged separately with the text.

- The 2003 annual report for The Topps Company, Inc. is printed in Appendix B.

In the Annual Report and Financial Statement Analysis Projects section (Appendix D) projects for each of these companies are included as well as a general purpose annual report project instructors can assign for any company's annual report.

Comprehensive Problem to Integrate Concepts Across Chapters

Chapters 5 through 11 include a comprehensive problem designed to integrate concepts across chapters. These problems help students understand interrelationships between various accounting concepts. The problem builds in each successive chapter, with the ending account balances in one chapter becoming the beginning account balances in the next chapter.

User-Friendly Writing Style

Every chapter of the text has been completely rewritten in an easy to read and easy to comprehend writing style. The revised, student-friendly writing style is designed to encourage students to read the book.

Overall revisions

- The presentation of material has been simplified.
- We have expanded coverage of the matching concept throughout the text.
- The text has been thoroughly updated to include all relevant changes in authoritative pronouncements.
- The exercises and problems have been thoroughly revised.
- Financial statement analysis is highlighted in each chapter under the heading *The Financial Analyst*.
- All real world data have been updated to reflect information contained in the companies' most recent annual reports.
- There is an ethics case in the *Analyze, Think, Communicate* section of the end-of-chapter materials for each chapter.
- Check figures added to Problems for Series A.

Chapter specific changes

Chapter 1
Curious Accountant vignette now features Coca-Cola Company.
Coverage of the closing process and the vertical statements model moved from Chapter 1 to Chapter 2.

Chapter 2
Curious Accountant vignette features Union Pacific Railroad.
Coverage of the closing process and the vertical statements model moved from Chapter 1 to Chapter 2.
We have included coverage of the Sarbanes-Oxley Act.
New Reality Bytes on Enron Corporation.

Chapter 3
Revised end-of-chapter material.

Chapter 4
Change of title from The Recording Process to The Double-Entry Accounting System.
We have included coverage of the Sarbanes-Oxley Act.
New Reality Bytes on filing Form 8-K with the SEC related to American Airlines and September 11 World Trade Center attacks.

Chapter 5
We have changed the coverage of cash discounts from the gross method to the net method. While most texts use the gross method, the net method is more intuitive and theoretically preferable, not to mention that it is the method used more frequently in practice.
We have moved coverage of the periodic method to the appendix. As a result of advances in technology, the perpetual method is the dominent approach used in practice today.

Chapter 6 (Formerly chapter 8)
Chapter 5 is now followed immediately by coverage of advanced inventory topics (cost flow methods, lower of cost or market, and inventory errors). This change facilitates the growing practice of covering these two subjects back-to-back.
Innocent inventory errors that are material in amount are highly unlikely in today's business environment. We have changed the write-up on inventory errors so as to couch the subject in terms of fraud prevention.

Chapter 7 (Formerly chapter 6)
Curious Accountant vignette now features WorldCom.

Chapter 8 (Formerly chapter 7)
Change in title from Advanced Topics: Receivables and Payables to Advanced Topics Related to Receivables.
Curious Accountant now features Costco and Procter & Gamble.
Coverage of accounting for discount notes moved to the appendix. Reviewers suggested that this subject is too technical for most professors to cover in an introductory accounting course.

Chapter 9
New Reality Byes on Hewlett-Packard Company and Compaq Computer Corporation.

Chapter 10
Curious Accountant now features Time Warner.

Chapter 11
New Realty Bytes on Sarbanes-Oxley Act.

Chapter 12
Updated Priceline Exhibit 12-3.

New Appendix B Topps Company Annual Report
New Appendix C Summary of Financial Ratios
New Appendix D Annual Report and Financial Statement Analysis Projects

HOW DOES THE BOOK

Real World Examples

The Edmonds' text provides a variety of thought-provoking, real-world examples of financial accounting as an essential part of the management process. There are descriptions of accounting practices from real organizations such as Coca-Cola, Union Pacific Railroad, Enron, General Motors, JCPenney, and Amazon.com. These companies are highlighted in blue in the text.

The Curious Accountant

Each chapter opens with a short vignette that sets the stage and helps pique student interest. These vignettes pose a question about a real-world accounting issue related to the topic of the chapter. The answer to the question appears in a separate sidebar a few pages further into the chapter.

Focus on International Issues

These boxed inserts expose students to international issues in accounting.

Check Yourself

These short question/answer features occur at the end of each main topic and ask students to stop and think about the material just covered. The answer follows to provide immediate feedback before students go on to a new topic.

"These are very effective and I have used some of them for class discussions – these boxes capture the interest of the students since they see the application to the real world."
Jacqueline Burke – Hofstra University

THE *curious* ACCOUNTANT

If a person wishes to subscribe to *Reader's Digest* for one year (12 issues), the subscriber must pay for the magazines before they are actually published. Suppose Paige Long sends $12 to the Reader's Digest Association in September 2007 for a one-year subscription; she will receive her first issue in October.

How should Reader's Digest account for the receipt of this cash? How would this event be reported on Reader's Digest's December 31, 2007, financial statements? (Answers on page 115.)

CHAPTER *opening*

*In Chapter 2, we defined accruals as the recognition of revenue and expense before the receipt or payment of cash. In this chapter, you will learn that accrual accounting involves deferrals and allocations as well as accruals. A **deferral** involves recognizing a revenue or expense at some later time after cash has been collected or paid. For example, if a business collects cash in 2001 for services it will perform in 2002, the revenue is recognized in 2002 even though the ...accrual. When ...*

focus on INTERNATIONAL ISSUES

Is There Global GAAP?

As explained in this chapter, financial reporting is a measurement and communication discipline based on rules referred to as generally accepted accounting principles. The accounting rules described in this text are based on GAAP used in the United States. Not all economies throughout the world use the same accounting rules. Although there are many similarities among the accounting principles used in different countries, there also are major differences. Accountants have made attempts to create international accounting standards, but individual countries have retained the authority to establish their own GAAP. Simply put, each country has its own GAAP; there is no single "global GAAP." Examples of how financial reporting in other countries differs from that in the United States are presented throughout this book.

Accounting rules differ among countries for a variety of reasons, including the economic and legal environments in each country and how the GAAP in that country is established. Generally accepted accounting principles in the United States are primarily established by the Financial Accounting Standards Board (FASB). The FASB is a nongovernment rule-making body established by the accounting profession. In countries such as Germany and Japan, for example, the GAAP is established by government bodies. In these countries GAAP is established more like the way federal laws and regulations are established in the United States.

Furthermore, in the United States any connection between GAAP established by the FASB and tax accounting rules established by Congress and the Internal Revenue Service (IRS) is coincidental, not deliberate. In some countries there is a close connection between tax accounting rules and GAAP.

$1,500 of the $18,000 cash received is recognized as revenue in 2006 ($1,500 is included in the $168,500 of revenue reported on the income statement) but the entire $18,000 is reported in the operating activities section of the statement of cash flows ($18,000 is included in the $147,000 cash receipts from customers). Trace the effects of these transactions to the financial statements.

On January 1, 2002, Lambert Company paid $28,000 cash to purchase office furniture. The furniture has a $3,000 salvage value and a five-year useful life. Explain how Lambert would report this asset purchase on the 2002 statement of cash flows. Also, determine the amount of depreciation expense and accumulated depreciation Lambert would report in the *2004* financial statements.

Answer Lambert would report a $28,000 cash outflow in the investing activities section of the 2002 statement of cash flows. During 2004 and every other year of the asset's useful life, Lambert would report $5,000 ([$28,000 − $3,000] ÷ 5) of depreciation expense on the income statement. The accumulated depreciation would increase by $5,000 each year of the asset's useful life. As of December 31, 2004, Lambert would report accumulated depreciation on the balance sheet of $15,000 (3 years × $5,000 per year).

Check Yourself 3-3

THE FINANCIAL ANALYST

MOTIVATE STUDENTS?

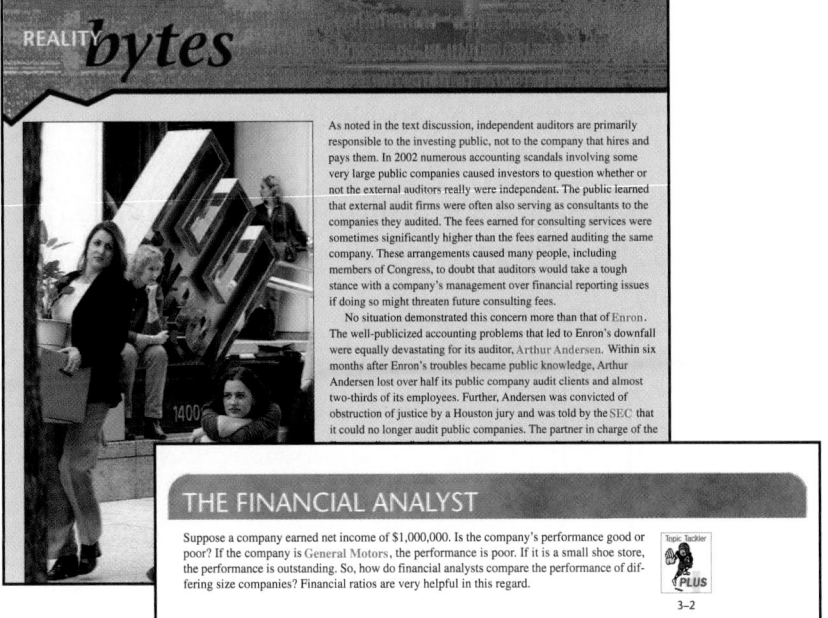

REALITY *bytes*

As noted in the text discussion, independent auditors are primarily responsible to the investing public, not to the company that hires and pays them. In 2002 numerous accounting scandals involving some very large public companies caused investors to question whether or not the external auditors really were independent. The public learned that external audit firms were often also serving as consultants to the companies they audited. The fees earned for consulting services were sometimes significantly higher than the fees earned auditing the same company. These arrangements caused many people, including members of Congress, to doubt that auditors would take a tough stance with a company's management over financial reporting issues if doing so might threaten future consulting fees.

No situation demonstrated this concern more than that of Enron. The well-publicized accounting problems that led to Enron's downfall were equally devastating for its auditor, Arthur Andersen. Within six months after Enron's troubles became public knowledge, Arthur Andersen lost over half its public company audit clients and almost two-thirds of its employees. Further, Andersen was convicted of obstruction of justice by a Houston jury and was told by the SEC that it could no longer audit public companies. The partner in charge of the

THE FINANCIAL ANALYST

Suppose a company earned net income of $1,000,000. Is the company's performance good or poor? If the company is General Motors, the performance is poor. If it is a small shoe store, the performance is outstanding. So, how do financial analysts compare the performance of differing size companies? Financial ratios are very helpful in this regard.

Topic Tackler
PLUS
3–2

a look
back

This chapter introduced the role of accounting in society and business: to provide information helpful to operating and evaluating the performance of organizations. Accounting is a measurement discipline. To communicate effectively, users of accounting must agree on the rules of measurement. *Generally accepted accounting principles (GAAP)* constitute the rules used by the accounting profession in the United States to govern financial reporting. GAAP is a work in progress that continues to evolve.

This chapter has discussed eight elements of financial statements: *assets, liabilities, equity, common stock (contributed capital), revenue, expenses, dividends (distributions),* and *net income.* The elements represent broad classifications reported on financial statements. Four basic financial statements appear in the reports of public companies: the *balance sheet,* the *income statement,* the *statement of changes in stockholders' equity,* and the *statement of cash flows.* The chapter discussed the form and content of each statement as well as the interrelationships among the statements.

income statement, the *statement of changes in stockholders' equity,* and the *statement of cash flows.* The chapter discussed the form and content of each statement as well as the interrelationships among the statements.

This chapter introduced a *horizontal financial statements model* as a tool to help you understand how business events affect a set of financial statements. This model is used throughout the text. You should carefully study this model before proceeding to Chapter 2.

a look
forward

To keep matters as simple as possible and to focus on the interrelationships among financial statements, this chapter considered only cash events. Obviously, many real-world events do not involve an immediate exchange of cash. For example, customers use telephone service throughout the month without paying for it until the next month. Such phone usage represents an expense in one month with a cash exchange in the following month. Events such as this are called *accruals.* Understanding the effects that accrual events have on the financial statements is the subject of Chapter 2.

Reality Bytes
This feature provides examples or expansions of the topics presented by highlighting companies and showing how they use the accounting concepts discussed in the chapter to make business decisions.

The Financial Analyst
Financial statement analysis is highlighted in each chapter under this heading.

Topic Tackler Plus
A logo indicates a topic explained on the Topic Tackler Plus DVD. The DVD includes two hard-to-learn topics for each chapter explained with video, PowerPoint, practice quizzes, self tests, and a demonstration problem walkthrough.

A Look Back/A Look Forward
Students need a roadmap to make sense of where the chapter topics fit into the whole picture. A Look Back reviews the chapter material and a Look Forward introduces new material to come in the next chapter.

HOW CAN TECHNOLOGY

Our technology resources help students and instructors focus on learning success. By using the Internet and multimedia students get book-specific help at their convenience. Compare our technology to those of any other book and we're confident you'll agree that *Fundamental Financial Accounting Concepts* has the best in the market.

Teaching aids make in-class presentations easy and stimulating. These aids give you more power than ever to teach your class the way you want.

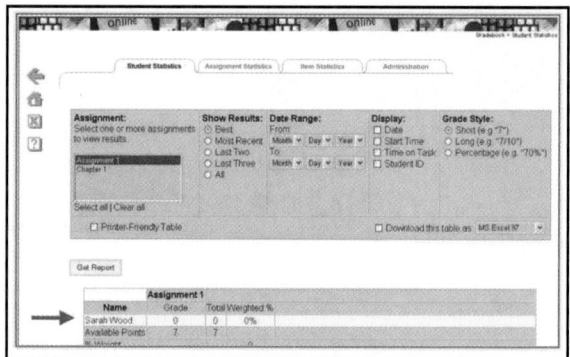

OnePass

McGraw-Hill/Irwin offers a complete range of technology to support and complement Fundamental Financial Accounting Concepts. OnePass integrates all of the text's multimedia resources. With just one access code, students can obtain state of the art study aids, including Homework Manager, Net Tutor and an online version of the text.

McGraw-Hill's Homework Manager is a

Web-based supplement that duplicates problem structures directly from the end-of-chapter material in your textbook, using algorithms to provide a limitless supply of online self-graded assignments that can be used for student practice, homework, or testing. Each assignment has a unique solution. Say goodbye to cheating in your classroom; say hello to the power and flexibility you've been waiting for in creating assignments. All Exercises and Problems in Series A are available with Homework Manager.

 McGraw-Hill's Homework Manager is also a useful grading tool. All assignments can be delivered over the Web and are graded automatically, with the results stored in your private grade book. Detailed results let you see at a glance how each student does on an assignment or an individual problem—you can even see how many tries it took them to solve it.

Students receive full access to McGraw-Hill's Homework Manager when they purchase One Pass.

HELP STUDENT SUCCESS?

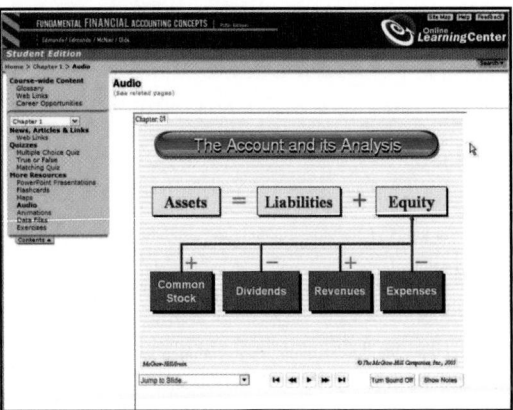

Topic Tackler Plus DVD

This software is a complete tutorial focusing on areas in the course that give students the most trouble. It provides help on two key topics for each chapter by use of

- Video clips
- PowerPoint slide shows
- Interactive exercises
- Self-grading quizzes

The DVD also includes the Self-Study Review Problems in the book presented in an audio-narrated PowerPoint slide presentation.

A logo in the text marks the topic given further coverage in Topic Tackler Plus.

Online Learning Center (OLC)

www.mhhe.com/edmonds5e

More and more students are studying online. That's why we offer an Online Learning Center (OLC) that follows Fundamental Financial Accounting Concepts chapter by chapter. The OLC now includes the following:

- Excel Spreadsheets
- Spreadsheet Tips
- Text Updates
- Glossary
- Key Term Flashcards
- Chapter Learning Objectives
- Interactive Quizzes
- E Lectures (audio-narrated PowerPoints)
- Additional Check Figures
- Mobile Resources
- Topic Tackler Plus

For instructors, the book's secured OLC contains essential course materials. You can pull all of this material into your PageOut course syllabus or use it as part of another online course management system. It doesn't require any building or maintenance on your part. It's ready to go the moment you type in the URL.

- Instructor's Manual
- Solutions Manual
- Solutions to Excel Template Assignments
- Sample Syllabi
- Transition Notes
- Text Updates

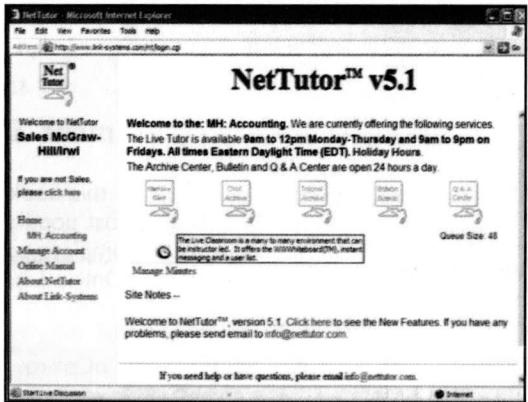

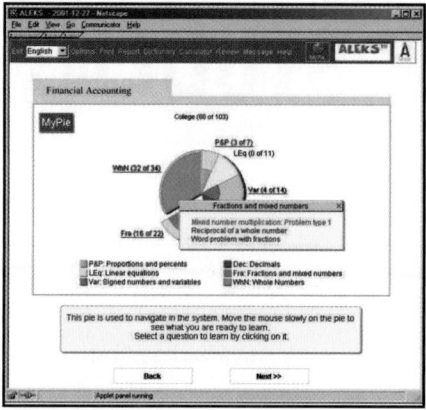

NetTutor

Many students work or have other commitments outside of class, making it difficult for them to get help with their questions during regular school hours. NetTutor is a breakthrough program that connects your students with qualified tutors online so they can get help at their convenience.

Students can communicate with tutors in a variety of ways:

- The Live Tutor Center, where students can view tutor-created spreadsheets, T-accounts, and instant responses to their questions

- The Q&A Center, which allows students to submit questions anytime and receive answers within 24 hours.

- The Archive Center that lets students browse for answers to previously asked questions. They can also search for questions pertinent to a particular topic.

With OnePass, students receive unlimited access to NetTutor for the length of the course.

ALEKS

ALEKS for the Accounting Cycle and ALEKS for Financial Accounting

ALEKS (Assessment and Learning in Knowledge Spaces) provides precise assessment and individualized instruction in the fundamental skills your students need to succeed in accounting. ALEKS motivates your students because it can tell what a student knows, doesn't know, and is most ready to learn next. ALEKS uses an artificial intelligence engine to exactly identify a student's knowledge of accounting.

To learn more about adding ALEKS to your accounting course, visit *www.business.aleks.com*.

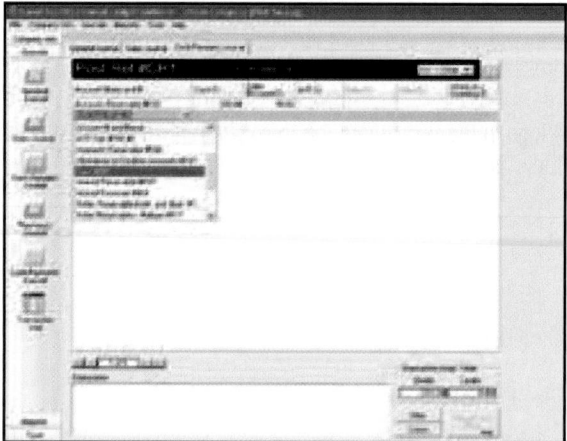

Carol Yacht's General Ledger & Peachtree Complete 2005 CD

The CD-ROM includes fully functioning versions of McGraw-Hill's General Ledger Application software as well as Peachtree Complete 2005. Problem templates are included that allow you to assign text problems for working in either Yacht's General Ledger or Peachtree Complete 2005. These problems are indicated by the GL logo.

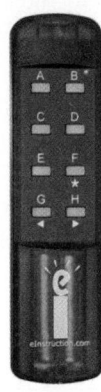

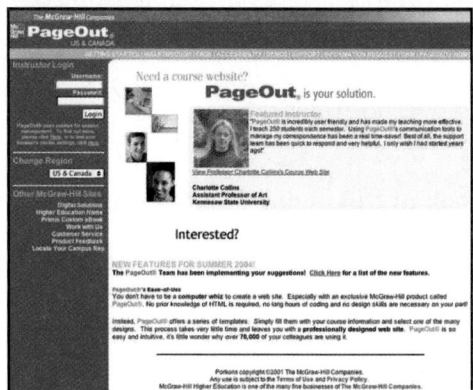

e Instruction®

CPS Classroom Performance System

This is a revolutionary system that brings ultimate interactivity to the classroom. CPS is a wireless response system that gives you immediate feedback from every student in the class. CPS units include easy-to-use software for creating and delivering questions and assessments to your class. With CPS you can ask subjective and objective questions. Then every student simply responds with their individual, wireless response pad, providing instant results. CPS is the perfect tool for engaging students while gathering important assessment data.

Instructor's Resource CD

This CD includes electronic versions of the Instructor's Manual, Solutions Manual, Test Bank, and Computerized Test Bank, as well as PowerPoint slides, video clips, and all exhibits in the text in a PowerPoint format.

  Bb
Blackboard
www.blackboard.com

Online Course Management
WebCT, eCollege, and Blackboard

We offer *Fundamental Financial Accounting Concepts* content for complete online courses. You can customize the Online Learning Center content and author your own course materials. No matter which online course solution you choose, you can count on the highest level of support. Our specialists offer free training and answer any question you have through the life of your adoption.

PageOut

McGraw-Hill's Course Management System
Pageout is the easiest way to create a Website for your accounting course. Just fill in a series of boxes with plain English and click on one of our professional designs. In no time your course is online with a Website that contains your syllabus. If you need help, our team of specialists is ready to take your course materials and build a custom website to your specifications. To learn more visit *www.pageout.net.*

Knowledge Gateway

Knowledge Gateway is an all-purpose service and resource center for instructors teaching online. While training programs from WebCT and Blackboard will help teach you their software, only McGraw-Hill/Irwin has services to help you actually manage and teach your online course, as well as run and maintain the software. To see how these platforms can assist your online course, visit *www.mhhe.com/solutions.*

HOW ARE CHAPTER

Regardless of the instructional approach, there is no shortcut to learning accounting. Students must practice to master basic accounting concepts. The text includes a prodigious supply of practice materials and exercises and problems.

Self-Study Review Problem

These representative example problems include a detailed, worked-out solution and provide another level of support for students before they work problems on their own. These review problems are included on the Topic Tackler Plus DVD in an animated audio presentation.

Exercise Series A & B and Problem Series A & B

There are two sets of problems and exercises, Series A and B. Instructors can assign one set for homework and another set for classwork.

• Check figures

The figures provide a quick reference for students to check on their progress in solving the problem. These are included for all problems in Series A.

• Excel

Many exercises and problems can be solved using the Excel™ spreadsheet templates contained on the text's Online Learning Center. A logo appears in the margins next to these exercises and problems for easy identification.

• General Ledger and Peachtree Software

If a problem can be solved using our General Ledger or Peachtree software, a logo is shown.

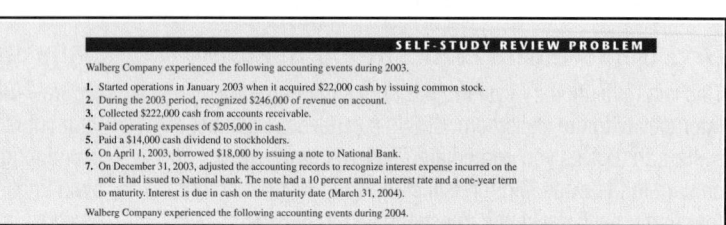

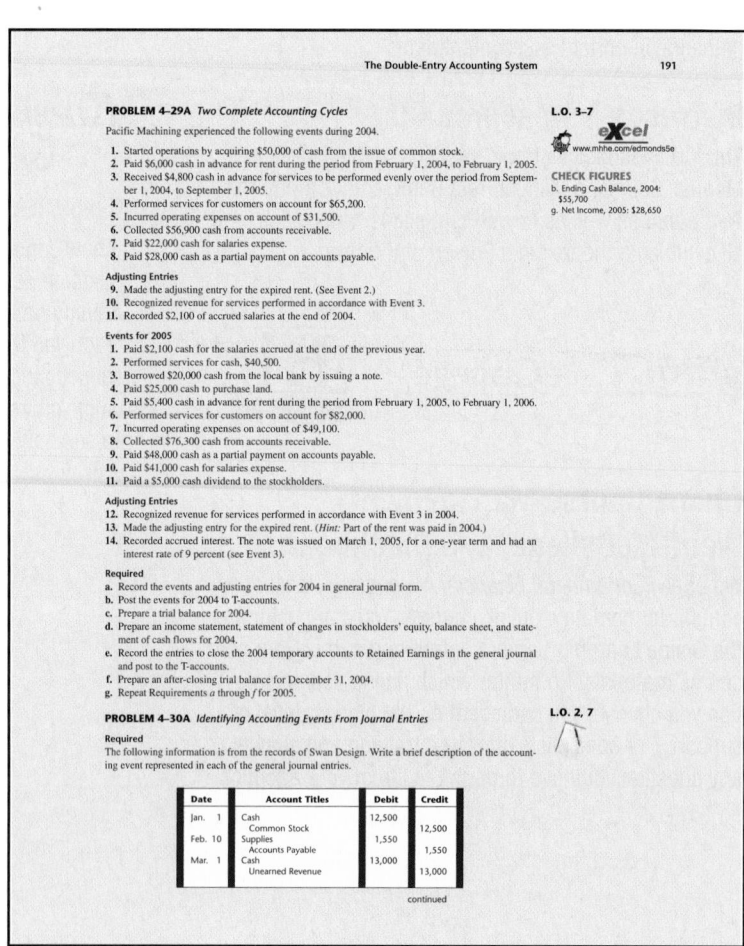

CONCEPTS REINFORCED?

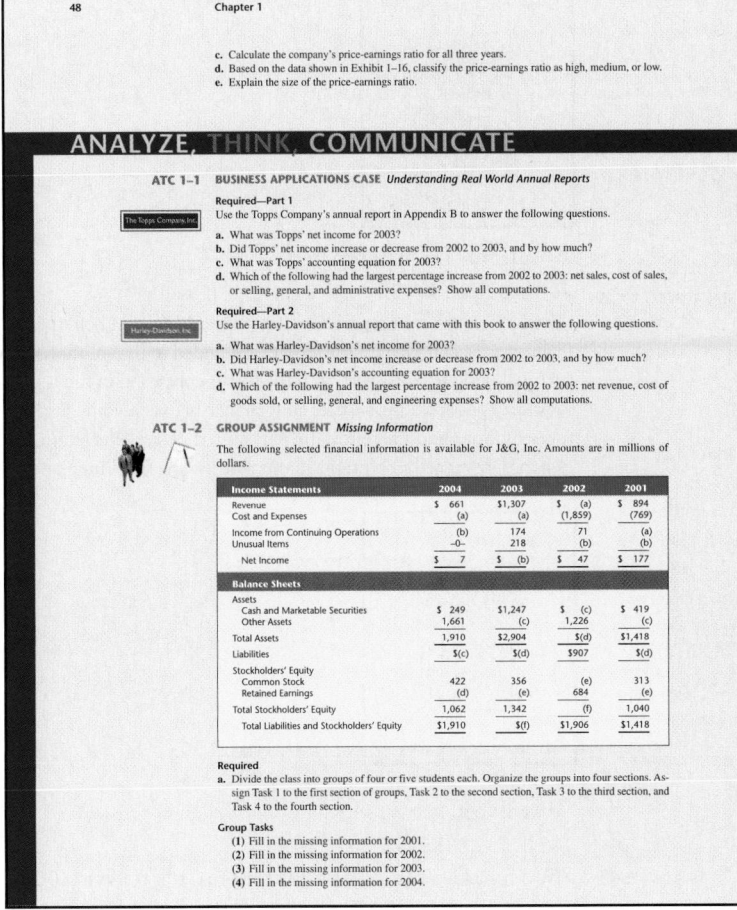

48   Chapter 1

c. Calculate the company's price-earnings ratio for all three years.
d. Based on the data shown in Exhibit 1–16, classify the price-earnings ratio as high, medium, or low.
e. Explain the size of the price-earnings ratio.

ANALYZE, THINK, COMMUNICATE

ATC 1–1   BUSINESS APPLICATIONS CASE *Understanding Real World Annual Reports*

Required—Part 1
Use the Topps Company's annual report in Appendix B to answer the following questions.

a. What was Topps' net income for 2003?
b. Did Topps' net income increase or decrease from 2002 to 2003, and by how much?
c. What was Topps' accounting equation for 2003?
d. Which of the following had the largest percentage increase from 2002 to 2003: net sales, cost of sales, or selling, general, and administrative expenses? Show all computations.

Required—Part 2
Use the Harley-Davidson's annual report that came with this book to answer the following questions.

a. What was Harley-Davidson's net income for 2003?
b. Did Harley-Davidson's net income increase or decrease from 2002 to 2003, and by how much?
c. What was Harley-Davidson's accounting equation for 2003?
d. Which of the following had the largest percentage increase from 2002 to 2003: net revenue, cost of goods sold, or selling, general, and engineering expenses? Show all computations.

ATC 1–2   GROUP ASSIGNMENT *Missing Information*

The following selected financial information is available for J&G, Inc. Amounts are in millions of dollars.

Income Statements	2004	2003	2002	2001
Revenue	$ 661	$1,307	$ (a)	$ 894
Cost and Expenses	(a)	(a)	(1,859)	(769)
Income from Continuing Operations	(b)	174	71	(a)
Unusual Items	–0–	218	(b)	(b)
Net Income	$ 7	$ (b)	$ 47	$ 177

Balance Sheets				
Assets				
Cash and Marketable Securities	$ 249	$1,247	$ (c)	$ 419
Other Assets	1,661	(c)	1,226	(c)
Total Assets	1,910	$2,904	$(d)	$1,418
Liabilities	$(c)	$(d)	$907	$(d)
Stockholders' Equity				
Common Stock	422	356	(e)	313
Retained Earnings	(d)	(e)	684	(e)
Total Stockholders' Equity	1,062	1,342	(f)	1,040
Total Liabilities and Stockholders' Equity	$1,910	$(f)	$1,906	$1,418

Required
a. Divide the class into groups of four or five students each. Organize the groups into four sections. Assign Task 1 to the first section of groups, Task 2 to the second section, Task 3 to the third section, and Task 4 to the fourth section.

Group Tasks
(1) Fill in the missing information for 2001.
(2) Fill in the missing information for 2002.
(3) Fill in the missing information for 2003.
(4) Fill in the missing information for 2004.

COMPREHENSIVE PROBLEM

The following information is available for Pacilio Security Systems Sales and Service for 2005, its first year of operations. Pacilio sells security systems and provides 24-hour alarm monitoring service. Pacilio sells two types of alarm systems, standard and deluxe. The following summary transactions occurred during 2005. (Round calculations to the nearest whole dollar.)

1. Acquired $50,000 cash from the issue of common stock.
2. Rented a building for a period of 12 months. On March 2, 2005, paid $6,000 for one year's rent in advance.
3. Purchased $800 of supplies with cash to be used over the next several months by the business.
4. Purchased 50 standard alarm systems for resale at a list price of $12,245 and 20 deluxe alarm systems at a list price of $10,204. The alarm systems were purchased on account with the terms 2/10 n/30.

Analyze, Think, Communicate (ATC)

Each chapter includes an innovative section entitled Analyze, Think, Communicate (ATC). This section contains:

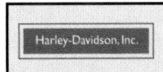 

- Business application cases related to the annual reports from Harley-Davidson and Topps Company

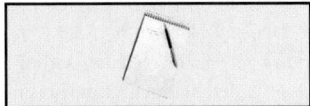

- Writing assignments

- Group exercises

- Ethics cases

- Internet assignments

- Excel spreadsheet applications

Comprehensive Problem

Beginning in Chapter 5, a comprehensive problem builds in each successive chapter, with the ending account balances in one chapter becoming the beginning account balances in the next chapter.

SUPPLEMENTS for Instructors

Instructor's Resource CD
ISBN 0072989513
This CD includes electronic versions of the Instructor's Manual, Solutions Manual, Test Bank, and computerized Test Bank, as well as PowerPoint slides, video clips, all exhibits in the text in PowerPoint, and spreadsheet templates with solutions. This CD-ROM makes it easy for instructors to create multimedia presentations.

Instructor's Transition CD
ISBN 0072993448
How do I get started teaching with this innovative material? We've provided help with this transition CD-ROM. It includes a video of Tom Edmonds explaining how he teaches the course and uses the horizontal statements model. It also demonstrates how to integrate the technology available with the text, and provides transition notes on how to convert your notes from other financial texts.

Instructor's Manual
ISBN 0072989505
(Also available on the password-protected Instructor Online Learning Center (OLC) and Instructor's Resource CD.)
This comprehensive manual includes step-by-step, explicit instructions on how the text can be used to implement alternative teaching methods. It also provides guidance for instructors who use the traditional lecture method. The guide includes lesson plans and demonstration problems with student work papers, as well as solutions. It was prepared by Tom Edmonds and Nancy Schneider.

Solutions Manual
ISBN 0072989467
(Also available on the password-protected Instructor Online Learning Center (OLC) and Instructor Resource CD)
Prepared by the authors, the manual contains complete solutions to all the text's end-of-chapter exercises, problems, and cases.

Solutions Transparencies
ISBN 0072989483
Transparencies are prepared in easy-to-read 14-point bold type. They are exact images of the answers provided in the solutions manual and are consistent with the forms contained in the working papers. This ensures congruence between your class presentations and the follow-up exposure that students attain when they view the solutions manual or use the working papers.

Test Bank
ISBN 0072989475
(Also available on the Instructor's Resource CD)
This test bank in Word™ format contains multiple-choice questions, essay questions, and short problems. Each test item is coded for level of difficulty and learning objective. In addition to an expansive array of traditional test questions, the test bank includes new types of questions that focus exclusively on how business events affect financial statements. It was prepared by Steve Muller of Valencia Community College.

Computerized Test Bank
(Available on the Instructor's Resource CD)
This test bank utilizes McGraw-Hill's testing software to quickly create customized exams. This user-friendly program allows instructors to sort questions by format; edit existing questions or add new ones. It also can scramble questions for multiple versions of the same test.

PowerPoint Presentation
(Available on the Online Learning Center and Instructor's Resource CD-ROM)
These audio-narrated slides can serve as interactive class discussions and were prepared by Jon A. Booker and Charles W. Caldwell of Tennessee Technological University and Susan Galbreath of David Lipscomb University.

SUPPLEMENTS for Students

One Pass

One Pass integrates all of the text's multimedia resources. With just one access code, students can obtain state of the art study aids, including Homework Manager, NetTutor and an online version of the text.

Homework Manager

This web-based software duplicates problem structures directly from the end-of-chapter material in the textbook. It uses algorithms to provide a limitless supply of self-graded practice for students. It shows students where they made errors. All Exercises and Problems in Series A are available with Homework Manager.

Study Guide

ISBN 0072989459

Each chapter contains a review and explanation of the chapter's learning objectives, as well as multiple-choice problems and short exercises. Unique to this Study Guide is a series of problems that require students to indicate how accounting events affect the elements of financial statements. The guide includes appropriate working papers and a complete set of solutions.

Working Papers

ISBN 0072989440

Working papers are available to direct students in solving text assignments.

Computerized Practice Sets

Wheels Exquisite, Level 1
Student ISBN 0072428457
Instructor ISBN 0072427531

Gold Run Snowmobile
Student ISBN 0072957883
Instructor ISBN 0072947683

Granite Bay Jet Ski, Level 2
Student ISBN 0072426950
Instructor ISBN 0072426209

Topic Tackler Plus DVD

This tutorial offers a virtual helping hand in understanding the most challenging topics in the financial accounting course. Through a step-by-step sequence of video clips, PowerPoint slides, interactive practice exercises, and self tests, Topic Tackler Plus offers help on two key topics for each chapter. These topics are indicated by a logo in the text. Another component on the DVD takes the Self-Study Review Problem in the book and demonstrates how to solve it in an animated audio presentation.

Carol Yacht's General Ledger & Peachtree Complete 2005 CD

ISBN 0072992239

This software package includes both an easy-to-use general ledger software tool and a real-world accounting package on one CD-ROM. It will help students learn how to record transactions and create financial statements. Logos in the text highlight selected end-of-chapter problems where both the general ledger software and Peachtree Complete 2005 software are available to help students work through the problem.

Excel Templates

(Available on the Online Learning Center (OLC))
These templates allow students to develop spreadsheet skills to solve selected assignments identified by an icon in the end-of-chapter material.

E Lectures

(Available on the Online Learning Center (OLC))
These PowerPoint slides cover key chapter topics in an audio-narrated presentation sure to help students learn. These were prepared by Jon A. Booker and Charles W. Caldwell of Tennessee Technological University and Susan Galbreath of David Lipscomb University.

ALEKS for Financial Accounting

ISBN 0072841966

ALEKS for the Accounting Cycle

ISBN 0072975326

Online Learning Center (OLC)

www.mhhe.com/edmonds5e

See page xiii for details

ACKNOWLEDGEMENTS

Our grateful appreciation is extended to those who reviewed previous editions:

Special thanks to the talented people who prepared the supplements. These take a great deal of time and effort to write and we appreciate their efforts. Steve Muller of Valencia Community College prepared the Test Bank and Self-Review Problem PowerPoint slides. Leonard Stokes of Siena College wrote the online quizzes. Linda Schain of Hofstra University developed the Topic Tackler Plus DVD. Jack Terry of ComSource Associates prepared the Excel templates and General Ledger Accounting Software. Carol Yacht prepared the Peachtree templates. Jon Booker and Charles W. Caldwell both of Tennessee Technological University, and Susan C. Galbreath of David Lipscomb University did the PowerPoint presentation. We also thank our accuracy checkers for checking the text manuscript and solutions manual. They include Kim Temme of Maryville University and Nina Collum of Mississippi University for Women. A special thanks to Linda Bell of William Jewell College for her contribution to the Financial Statement Analysis material that appears in Appendix D.

We are deeply indebted to our sponsoring editor, Steve Schuetz. His direction and guidance have added clarity and quality to the text. We especially appreciate the efforts of our developmental editor, Gail Korosa. Gail has coordinated the exchange of ideas among our class testers, reviewers, copy editor, and error checkers; she has done far more than simply pass along ideas. She has contributed numerous original suggestions that have enhanced the quality of the text. Our editors have certainly facilitated our efforts to prepare a book that will facilitate a meaningful understanding of accounting. Even so, their contributions are to no avail unless the text reaches its intended audience. We are most grateful to Rich Kolasa and Jackie Powers and the sales staff for providing the informative advertising that has so accurately communicated the unique features of the concepts approach to accounting educators. Many others at McGraw-Hill/Irwin at a moment's notice redirected their attention to focus their efforts on the development of this text. We extend our sincere appreciation to Pat Fredrickson, Elizabeth Mavetz, Michael McCormick, Mary Kazak, Jeremy Cheshareck, Matt Perry and Erwin Llereza. We deeply appreciate the long hours that you committed to the formation of a high-quality text.

Thomas P. Edmonds • Cindy D. Edmonds • Frances M. McNair • Philip R. Olds • Nancy W. Schneider

---

We would like to express our appreciation to the people who have provided assistance in the development of this textbook.

We express our sincere thanks to the following individuals who provided extensive reviews for the fifth edition:

Reviewers

Mary Allen, Boise State University
Charles Baril, James Madison University
Linda Bell, William Jewell College
Rodger Brannan, University of Minnesota, Duluth
Radie Bunn, Southwest Missouri State University
Jacqueline Burke, Hofstra University
Bruce Chase, Radford University
Ginger Clark, University of Cincinnati
Paul Clikeman, University of Richmond
Wagih Dafashy, College of William & Mary
Laura DeLaune, Louisiana State University
Robert Derstine, Villanova University
Lola Dudley, Eastern Illinois University
David Fordham, James Madison University
Ken Fowler, San Jose State University
Lucille Genduso, Nova Southeastern University
John Gould, Western Carolina University
Jan Holmes, Louisiana State University
Scott Jerris, San Francisco State University.
William Link, University of Missouri, St. Louis
Patricia Lopez, Valencia Community College
James Lukawitz, University of Memphis
Dwight McIntyre, Clemson University
Dawn McKinley, William Rainey Harper College

Elizabeth Minbiole, Northwood University
Elizabeth Mulig, Columbus State University
Steven Muller, Valencia Community College
Carol Murphy, Quinsigamond Community College
Irvin Nelson, Utah State University
Ashton Oravetz, Tyler Junior College
Craig Reeder, Florida A&M University
Patricia Robinson, Johnson and Wales University
Cindy Seipel, New Mexico State University
Talitha Smith, Auburn University
Barbara Squires, Corning Community College
Sue Stickland, University of Texas, Arlington
Ellen Sweatt, Georgia Perimeter College
Peter Theuri, Northern Kentucky University
Donna Ulmer, St. Louis Community College, Meramec
Denise Dickins Veitch, Florida Atlantic University
George Violette, University of Southern Maine
Sharon Walters, Morehead State University
Andrea Weickgenannt, Northern Kentucky University
T. Sterling Wetzel, Oklahoma State University, Stillwater
Alan Winters, Clemson University
Gail Wright, Bryant College
Haiwen Zhang, University of Minnesota

Past Edition Reviewers

Our grateful appreciation is extended to those who reviewed previous editions:

Charles Richard Aldridge, Western Kentucky University
Sheila Ammons, Austin Community College
Debra Barbeau, Southern Illinois University-Carbondale
Beryl Barkman, University of Massachusetts-Dartmouth
Jim Bates, Mountain Empire Community College
Linda Bell, William Jewell College
Wilbur Berry, Jacksonville State University
Nancy Bledsoe, Millsaps College
Cendy Boyd, Northeast Louisiana State
Arthur Boyett, Francis Marion University
Cassie Bradley, Troy State University
Gregory Bushong, Wright State University
Judith Cadle, Tarleton State University
James Cahsell, Miami University
Scott Cairns, Shippensburg College
Eric Carlsen, Kean University
Frederic J. Carlson, LeTourneau University
Joan Carroll, SUNY-College at Oswego
Alan Cherry, Loyola Marymount University
Ronald Colley, State University of West Georgia
William Cress, University of Wisconsin-La Cross
Walter Doehring, Genesee Community College
George Dow, Valencia Community College
Melanie Earls, Mississippi State University
M. J. Edwards, Adirondack Community College
Ruth Epps, Virginia Commonwealth University
Ralph Fritzsch, Midwestern State University
Lou Fowler, Missouri Western State College
Mary Anne Gaffney, Temple University
David Ganz, University of Missouri-Saint Louis
Michael Garner, Salisbury State University
William T. Geary, College of William and Mary
Frank Gersich, Gustavus Adolphus College
Claudia Gilbertson, North Hennepin Community College
Lorraine Glasscock, University of North Alabama
Diane Glowacki, Tarrant County College
Larry Hagler, East Carolina University
Penny Hanes, Virginia Tech University
Leon Hanouille, Syracuse University
Phillip Harsha, Southwest Missouri State University
Charles Hart, Copiah-Lincoln Community College
Inez Heal, Youngstown State University
Kenneth Hiltebeitel, Villanova
Nitham Hindi, Shippensburg College
Karen Hull, Kansas Wesleyan University
Richard Hulme, California State Polytechnic University-Pomona
Pamela Jones, Mississippi State University
Khondkar Karim, Monmouth University
Nathan Kranowski, Radford University
Helen LaFrancois, University of Massachusetts-Dartmouth
Robert Landry, Massasoit Community College

William Lathen, Boise State University
David Law, Youngstown State University
William Link, University of Missouri-Saint Louis
Larry Logan, University of Massachusetts- Dartmouth
Catherine Lumbattis, Southern Illinois University-Carbondale
Joseph Marcheggiani, Butler University
Herb Martin, Hope College
Alan Mayer-Sommer, Georgetown University
Nancy Meade, Radford University
George Minmier, University of Memphis
Cheryl Mitchem, Virginia State University
Lu Montondon, Southwest Texas State University
Tim Nygaard, Madisonville Community College
Brian O'Doherty, East Carolina University
Joseph Onyeocha, South Carolina State University
Lawrence Ozzello, University of Wisconsin-Eau Claire
Eileen Peacock, Oakland University
Kathy Perdue, DeVry Institute of Technology at Decatur
Thomas Phillips, Jr., Louisiana Tech University
Cathy Pitts, Highline Community College
Mary Raven, Mount Mary College
Jane Reimers, Florida State University
Michael Riordan, James Madison University
Ken Ruby, Idaho State University
Nancy Schneider, Lynchburg College
Jeffrey Schwartz, Montgomery College
Suzanne Sevalstad, University of Nevada-Las Vegas
Kim Shaughnessy, James Madison University
John Shaver, Louisiana Tech University
Lewis Shaw, Suffolk University
Jill Smith, Idaho State University
Paul E. Solomon
John Sperry, Virginia Commonwealth University
Paul Steinbart, Saint Louis University-Saint Louis
Tim Stephens, DeVry Institute of Technology at Addison
Mary Stevens, University of Texas-El Paso
Leonard Stokes, Siena College
Janice Swanson, Southern Oregon University
James Swayze, University of Nevada, Las Vegas
Maurice Tassin, Louisiana Tech University
Kim Temme, Maryville University
Bor-Yi Tsay, University of Alabama-Birmingham
Suneel Udpa, St. Mary's College of California
Beth Vogel, Mount Mary College
J.D. Weinhold, Concordia College
Judith Welch, University of Central Florida
Sterling Wetzel, Oklahoma State University
Thomas Whitacre, University of South Carolina
Macil C. Wilkie, Jr., Grambling State University
Stephen Willits, Bucknell University
Marie Winks, Lynchburg College
Kenneth Winter, University of Wisconsin-La Cross.

This book is dedicated to our students whose questions have so frequently caused us to reevaluate our method of presentation that they have, in fact, become major contributors to the development of this text.

BRIEF CONTENTS

CONTENTS

Chapter 6 Accounting for Merchandising Businesses—Advanced Topics 266

Chapter 7 Internal Control and Accounting for Cash 314

Chapter 12 Statement of Cash Flows 560

CHAPTER *one*

ELEMENTS OF FINANCIAL STATEMENTS

LEARNING *objectives*

After you have mastered the material in this chapter you will be able to:

1 Explain the role of accounting in society.

2 Distinguish among the different accounting entities involved in business events.

3 Name and define the major elements of financial statements.

4 Describe the relationships expressed in the accounting equation.

5 Record business events in general ledger accounts organized under an accounting equation.

6 Explain how the historical cost and reliability concepts affect amounts reported in financial statements.

7 Classify business events as asset source, use, or exchange transactions.

8 Use general ledger account information to prepare four financial statements.

9 Record business events using a horizontal financial statements model.

10 Explain how to use the price-earnings ratio and growth percentage analysis to assess the market value of common stock.

11 Identify three types of business organizations and some of the technical terms they use in their real world financial reports.

CREATING NEW VALUE

THE COCA-COLA COMPANY 2002 ANNUAL REPORT

THE *curious* ACCOUNTANT

Who owns **Coca-Cola**? Who owns the **American Heart Association** (AHA)? In addition to owners, many people and organizations are interested in the operations of Coke and the AHA. These parties are called *stakeholders.* Among others, they include lenders, employees, suppliers, customers, benefactors, research institutions, hospitals, doctors, patients, lawyers, bankers, financial analysts, and government agencies such as the Internal Revenue Service and the Securities and Exchange Commission. Organizations communicate information to stakeholders through *financial reports.*

How do you think the financial reports of Coke differ from those of the AHA? (Answer on page 9.)

CHAPTER *opening*

Why should you study accounting? You should study accounting because it can help you succeed in business. In fact, your chances of success are pretty dismal if you are ignorant about accounting. Imagine playing football or Monopoly without knowing how to keep score. In business, accounting is how you keep score. Business is highly competitive. If you do not know the rules of the game, you will be severely disadvantaged.

Accounting provides information that helps individuals and business managers make better decisions. Do not underestimate the importance of reliable information. If you could predict which companies will succeed and which will fail, you could become a very wealthy Wall Street investor.

The users of accounting information include a variety of people and organizations. These users are commonly referred to as stakeholders because they have either direct or indirect interests in the entities that issue accounting reports. The fortunes of a business directly affect such stakeholders as owners, managers, creditors, suppliers, and employees. For example, owners and employees of a business prosper when the business makes money and suffer when the business loses money. In contrast, the fortunes of a business do not directly affect such stakeholders as financial analysts, brokers, attorneys, government regulators, and news reporters. For example, financial analysts use accounting reports to advise clients to buy or sell stock of companies but the performance of the companies they recommend does not personally affect the analysts.

Accounting is a dynamic discipline. It affects a wide range of individuals and organizations. Accounting is so important that it is often called the language of business. *In fact, accounting affects not only individual businesses but also society as a whole.*

Role of Accounting in Society

LO1 Explain the role of accounting in society.

How much should society emphasize producing food versus developing a cure for cancer? Should we devote more time and energy to making computers or cars? Should you invest your money in IBM or General Motors? Accounting provides information that is useful in answering such resource allocation questions.

Market-Based Allocations

Suppose you want to start a business. You may have heard "you have to have money to make money." In fact, you will need more than just money to operate a business. You will likely need such resources as equipment, land, materials, employees, and so on. If you do not have these resources, how can you get them? In the United States, you would compete for resources in open markets.

A **market** is a group of people or entities organized to exchange things of value. The market for business resources involves three distinct participants: consumers, conversion agents, and resource owners. *Consumers* are resource users. Resources, however, are frequently not in a form that consumers want. For example, nature provides trees but consumers want furniture. *Conversion agents* (businesses) transform resources such as trees into desirable products such as furniture. *Resource owners* control the distribution of resources to conversion agents.

Resource owners expect rewards for providing resources to conversion agents. Conversion agents (businesses) can reward resource owners because the transformation process adds value to the resources they obtain. The outputs (goods and services) are *more valuable* than the inputs (resources) because they are more useful to consumers after transformation. For example, a house is more valuable than the materials and labor used in its construction. Labor or materials alone do not provide shelter. By transforming labor and materials into a house, the conversion agent produces an output (a house) more valuable than the sum of the inputs (labor and materials). A house that cost $220,000 to build could have a market value of $250,000.

Common terms for the added value created in the transformation process include **profit, income,** or **earnings.** Accountants measure the added value as the difference between the cost of a product or service and the selling price of that product or service. For example, the profit on the house described earlier is $30,000, the difference between its $220,000 cost and $250,000 market value. Conversion agents who successfully satisfy consumer preferences efficiently (at low cost) are rewarded with high earnings. These earnings are shared with resource owners, so conversion agents who exhibit high earnings potential are more likely to compete successfully for resources. Return to the original question. If you want to start a business, how do you get necessary resources? To get resources, you must go to open markets and convince resource owners that you can produce profits.

To summarize, resource owners, conversion agents, and consumers create open markets. The resource owners and conversion agents *supply* goods and services in response to consumer demand. Consumers motivate resource providers and conversion agents to satisfy

Exhibit 1–1 *Market Trilogy for the Allocation of Resources*

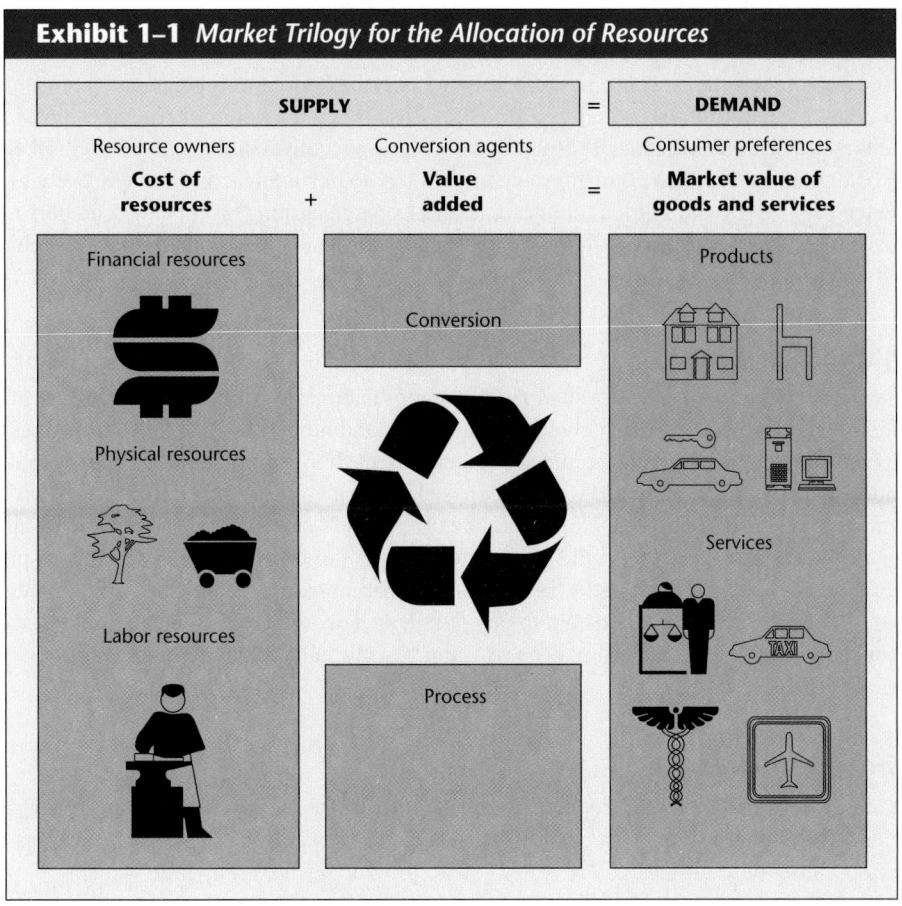

their demands by paying prices that result in profits. As a result, consumer demand determines the allocation of resources. Exhibit 1–1 illustrates the market trilogy involved in resource allocation. The following section of the text discusses specific types of resources that businesses commonly use to satisfy consumer demand.

Financial Resources

Conversion agents need **financial resources** (money) to establish and operate their businesses. *Investors* and *creditors* are two primary providers of financial resources. **Investors** provide resources in exchange for ownership interests in a business. Ownership interests entitle investors to share in the distribution of income. If a business prospers, investors can receive handsome rewards. If it fails, investors can lose the resources they provided. Investors allocate resources to businesses based on their assessment of how profitable they expect a business to be. **Creditors** provide financial resources to businesses on a lending basis. Instead of accepting the risks and rewards of ownership in a business, creditors expect businesses to repay borrowed resources at a future date.

   If a business fails, any resources (assets) it still has are returned to the resource providers (investors and creditors). The process of dividing remaining assets and returning them to resource providers is called business **liquidation.** Normally, creditors have a priority claim on assets in business liquidations. In other words, assets are distributed to creditors first. After creditor claims have been satisfied, any remaining assets are distributed to investors (owners). Suppose a business acquired $100 cash from investors and $200 cash from creditors. Assume the business lost $75 and returned the remaining $225 ($300 − $75) to the resource providers. The creditors would receive $200; the owners would receive only $25. If the business lost $120, the creditors would receive only $180 ($300 − $120); the investors would receive nothing. In other words, both creditors and investors can lose resources when businesses fail.

Creditors, however, are in a more secure position than investors because their resources are returned first.

Because of their more secure position, creditors normally do not share business profits. Instead, they receive **interest,** which is a fixed fee based on the amount of resources provided. Creditors prefer to lend financial resources to businesses (conversion agents) with high earnings potential because such companies are more likely to pay interest and are less likely to experience bankruptcy and liquidation. Also, less risky (high earning) companies can borrow at lower interest rates because creditors are more confident that such companies will be able to satisfy their obligations.

Physical Resources

In their most primitive form, **physical resources** are natural resources. The process of transforming natural resources can include several stages and numerous independent businesses. One conversion agent's output becomes another's input. For example, most furniture makers do not produce lumber. They use wood purchased from sawmills to make their products. The sawmills likely bought harvested logs from the timberlands' owner. Physical resources, therefore, are natural resources that could be at different stages of transformation. Owners of physical resources seek to sell those resources to profitable businesses because profitable businesses are more likely to be able to pay for them. The ability of a business to add value (produce income) in the conversion process is the basis for allocation of physical as well as financial resources.

Labor Resources

Labor resources include intellectual as well as physical labor. Like other resource providers, workers seek relationships with businesses (conversion agents) that have high earnings potential because these businesses are better able to provide rewards (pay high wages).

Accounting Provides Information

How do resource owners (financial, physical, and labor) identify those conversion agents (businesses) with the high profit potential to pay competitive prices for the resources? This is where accounting enters the picture. *Accounting* provides information useful in evaluating a conversion agent's profit potential and relative risk. Accounting plays a major role in determining how resources are assigned to conversion agents.

Types of Accounting Information

External resource providers, such as investors and creditors, are viewed as entities separate from the business. Accounting information focused on the needs of these *external users* is called **financial accounting.** Another branch of accounting, **managerial,** provides information useful to managers and employees who work inside a business, *internal users.* The information needs of external and internal users frequently overlap. For example, both external and internal users are interested in the amount of income a business earns. Managerial accounting information, however, is usually more detailed than financial accounting reports. Whereas an investor is interested in whether Wendy's or Burger King produces more overall income relative to risk, a Wendy's regional manager is interested in the store-by-store earnings of the restaurants she controls. In fact, a regional manager is also interested in nonfinancial measures, such as the number of employees needed to operate a restaurant, the times at which customer demand is high versus low, and measures of cleanliness and customer satisfaction.

Nonbusiness Resource Allocations

The United States economy is not *purely* market based. Many factors other than profitability affect the allocation of resources. For example, governments allocate resources for national defense, the redistribution of wealth, or environmental protection. Foundations, religious

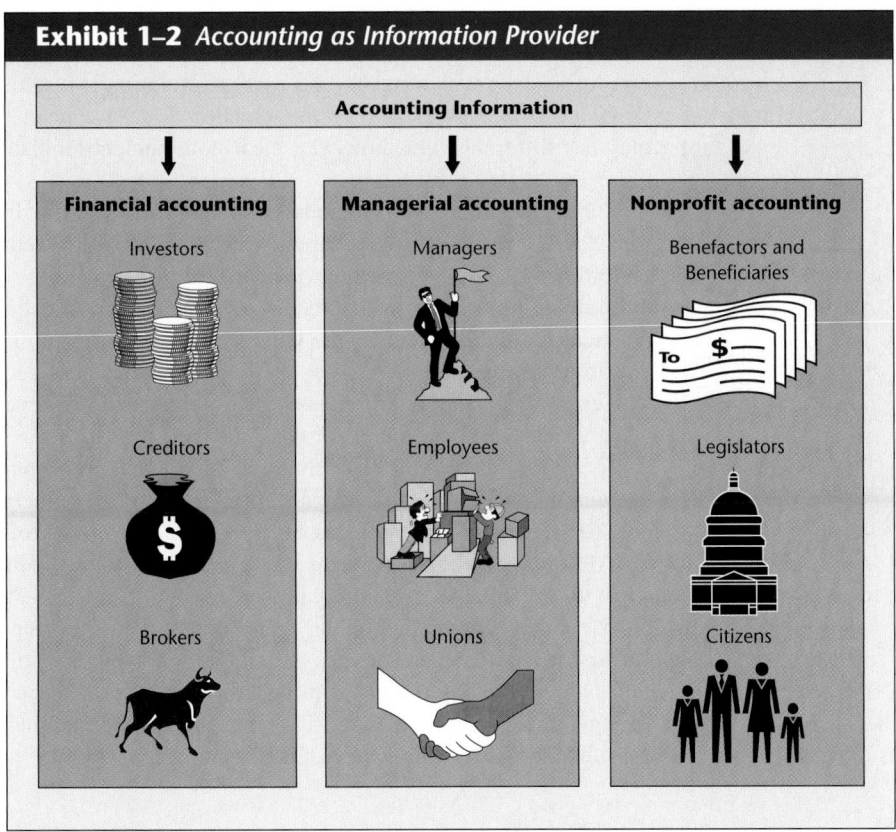

Exhibit 1–2 *Accounting as Information Provider*

Accounting Information

Financial accounting	Managerial accounting	Nonprofit accounting
Investors	Managers	Benefactors and Beneficiaries
Creditors	Employees	Legislators
Brokers	Unions	Citizens

groups, the **Peace Corps**, and various benevolent organizations allocate resources based on humanitarian concerns. Other groups allocate resources to support art, music, dance, and theater. Like profit-oriented businesses, these organizations also add value through resource transformation. For example, a nonprofit soup kitchen adds value by converting raw meats and vegetables into desirable meals. The consumers who eat at a soup kitchen, however, are unable to pay the kitchen's operating costs, much less for the added value the soup kitchen provides. The soup kitchen's motivation is to meet humanitarian needs, not to earn profits. Organizations that are not motivated by profit are called **not-for-profit entities** (also called *nonprofit* or *nonbusiness entities*).

The absence of a profit motive by no means negates the need for accounting information. The accounting system can measure the cost of the goods and services a not-for-profit organization provides, its efficiency and effectiveness in providing goods and services, and its ability to continue to provide goods and services. This information is useful to a host of stakeholders, including taxpayers, contributors, lenders, suppliers, employees, managers, financial analysts, attorneys, and beneficiaries. Accounting serves the information needs of a variety of business and nonbusiness user groups. Although Exhibit 1–2 shows three distinct areas of accounting, these areas frequently overlap. For example, managers of all types of organizations use managerial accounting information.

Measurement Rules

Accountants establish measurement and reporting rules that business people use to facilitate communication. Suppose a store sells a compact disk player in December to a customer who agrees to pay for it in January. Should the business *recognize* (report) the sale as a December transaction or as a January transaction? If the storeowner uses *accrual accounting* rules, he will include the effects of the sale in the store's December profits because the customer purchased the compact disk player in December. If the storeowner uses *cash accounting* rules, he will recognize the sale in January when he collects the cash from the customer. Whether

the storeowner uses accrual accounting rules or cash accounting rules is not important as long as he also follows the rule requiring him to disclose which method he uses. Accounting rules do not eliminate diverse financial reporting practices. Because businesses may use different rules, however, clear communication also requires full and fair disclosure.

Communication would certainly be simpler if each type of business activity were reported using only one measurement method. Unfortunately, world economies have not yet evolved to the point of attaining uniformity in financial reporting. Even in highly sophisticated countries such as the United States, significant diversity in reporting methods exists. Well-educated business people can understand and interpret accounting information prepared using a variety of measurement rules.

The measurement rules used in the United States for *financial accounting* are called **generally accepted accounting principles (GAAP).** Financial reports issued to the public must follow GAAP. This textbook introduces these principles so you will be able to understand business activity presented in accounting reports issued in the USA.

It is worth mentioning that, for convenience and efficiency, many internal business reports use accounting data that conform to GAAP. Companies are not required, however, to follow GAAP when preparing *management accounting* reports. Although there is considerable overlap between financial and managerial accounting, managers are free to construct internal reports in whatever fashion best suits the effective operation of their companies.

Reporting Entities

LO2 Distinguish among the different accounting entities involved in business events.

Financial accounting reports disclose the financial activities of particular individuals or organizations described as **reporting entities.** Each entity is treated as a separate reporting unit. For example, a business, the person who owns the business, and a bank that loans money to the business are treated as three separate reporting entities. Accountants would prepare three separate sets of financial reports to describe the economic activities of each of the three entities. The first step in understanding accounting reports is identifying the reporting entity.

This text describes accounting from the perspective of business entities. This perspective may require a mental adjustment in your view of the world. You likely think from a customer perspective. For example, you think—from a customer perspective—a sales discount is a great thing. The view is different, however, from the perspective of the business granting the discount. A sales discount means an item did not sell at the expected price. To move the item, the business had to accept less money than it originally planned to accept. From this perspective, a sales discount is not a good thing. To understand accounting, train yourself to interpret transactions from the perspective of a business rather than a consumer.

Check Yourself 1–1

In a recent business transaction, land was exchanged for cash. Did the amount of cash increase or decrease?

Answer The answer depends on the reporting entity to which the question pertains. One entity sold land. The other entity bought land. For the entity that sold land, cash increased. For the entity that bought land, cash decreased.

Topic Tackler PLUS

1-1

Elements of Financial Statements

Business entities communicate information to the public through the *financial reporting* process. The central feature of external financial reporting is a set of four **financial**

Anyone who owns stock in Coke owns a part of the company. Coke has many owners. In contrast, nobody actually owns the American Heart Association (AHA). The AHA has a board of directors that is responsible for overseeing its operations, but the board is not its owner.

Ultimately, the purpose of a business entity is to increase the wealth of its owners. To this end, it "spends money to make money." The expense that Coke incurs for advertising is a cost incurred in the hope that it will generate revenues when it sells soft drinks. The financial statements of a business show, among other things, whether and how the company made a profit during the current year.

The AHA is a not-for-profit entity. It operates to provide services to society at large, not to make a profit. It cannot increase the wealth of its owners, because it has no owners. When the AHA spends money to reduce heart disease, it does not spend this money in the expectation that it will generate revenues. The revenues of the AHA come from contributors who wish to support efforts related to reducing heart disease. Because the AHA does not spend money to make money, it has no reason to prepare an *income statement* like that of Coke.

Not-for-profit entities do prepare financial statements that are similar in appearance to those of commercial enterprises. The financial statements of not-for-profit entities are called the *statement of financial position*, the *statement of activities*, and the *cash flow statement*.

---

statements: (1) an income statement, (2) a statement of changes in equity, (3) a balance sheet, and (4) a statement of cash flows. These statements have alternate names. For example, the income statement may be called *results of operations* or *statement of earnings*. The balance sheet is sometimes called the *statement of financial position*. The statement of changes in equity might be called *statement of capital* or *statement of stockholders' equity*. Since the **Financial Accounting Standards Board (FASB)**[1] called for the title *statement of cash flows,* companies do not use alternate names for that statement. Exhibit 1–3 illustrates how frequently companies use the different names.

The information reported in financial statements is organized into categories known as **elements.** Eight of the 10 financial statement elements the FASB has defined are discussed in this chapter: assets, liabilities, equity, contributed capital, revenue, expenses, distributions, and net income. The other two elements—gains and losses—are discussed in a later chapter. In practice, many different titles are used to identify the elements of financial statements. For example, business people use net income, net earnings, and net profit interchangeably to describe the same element. Contributed capital may be called common stock and equity may be called stockholders' equity, owner's capital, and partners' equity. Furthermore, the transfer of assets from a business to its owners may be called distributions, withdrawals, or dividends. Think of accounting as a language. Different terms can describe the same business event.

The elements represent broad classifications. Accountants do not identify financial statement items like cash, equipment, buildings, and land as elements, but rather as subclassifications of the element known as *assets.* The subclassifications of various elements are frequently called **accounts.** Accounts are reported in the financial statements as components of the broader classifications identified as elements. For example, the element assets includes accounts that describe specific items such as cash, equipment, buildings, and land.

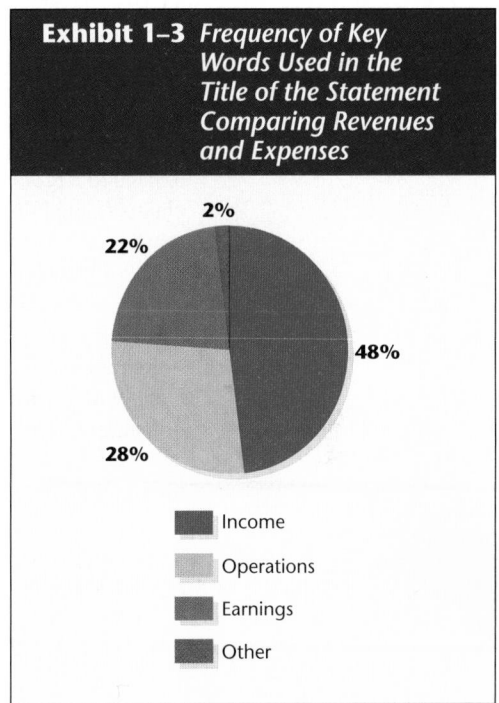

Exhibit 1–3 *Frequency of Key Words Used in the Title of the Statement Comparing Revenues and Expenses*

2%
22%
48%
28%

- Income
- Operations
- Earnings
- Other

Data Source: AICPA, *Accounting Trends and Techniques,* 2002.

LO3 Name and define the major elements of financial statements.

---

[1]The Financial Accounting Standards Board is a privately funded organization with the primary authority for establishing accounting standards in the United States. The FASB consists of seven full-time members appointed by the supporting organization, the Financial Accounting Foundation (FAF). The FAF membership is intended to represent the broad spectrum of individuals and institutions that have an interest in accounting and financial reporting. FAF members include representatives of the accounting profession, industry, financial institutions, the government, and the investing public.

How many accounts does a business use? The number depends on a company's information-gathering objectives. Companies establish the number of accounts necessary to capture the information managers need to make decisions. Some managers want very detailed information; others want highly summarized data. The number of accounts used in an accounting system varies from company to company.

Accounting Equation

LO4 Describe the relationships expressed in the accounting equation.

The resources that a business uses or will use to produce earnings are called **assets.** Examples of assets include land, buildings, equipment, materials, and supplies. In order to recognize assets in the financial statements, generally accepted accounting principles (GAAP) require that the assets must result from historical events. For example, if a business owns a truck that was purchased in a past transaction, the truck is an asset of the business. A truck that a business *plans* to purchase in the future, however, is not an asset of that business, no matter how certain the future purchase might be.

The assets of a business belong to the resource providers (creditors and investors). These resource providers have **claims** on the assets. The relationship between the assets and the providers' claims is described by the **accounting equation:**

$$\text{Assets} = \text{Claims}$$

Since the creditors have first claim on the assets, claims of the *investors (owners)* are described as a **residual interest.** This means that in the case of a business liquidation, the owners receive whatever assets are left after the debts to creditors have been paid. The following expanded accounting equation recognizes the relationship among the assets, the creditors' claims (called **liabilities**), and the investors' claims (called **equity**).

$$\text{Assets} = \underset{\text{Claims}}{\underline{\text{Liabilities} + \text{Equity}}}$$

Liabilities can also be viewed as *obligations of the enterprise.* In the future, to settle the obligations, the business will probably either relinquish some of its assets (e.g., pay off its debts with cash), provide services to its creditors (e.g., work off its debts), or accept other obligations (e.g., trade short-term debt for long-term debt).

Algebraically, the amount of total assets minus total liabilities equals the *equity.* Since equity equals the net difference between assets and liabilities, equity is also called **net assets.** *Equity, net assets,* and *residual interest* are synonyms for the ownership interest in a business. To illustrate, assume that Hagan Company has assets of $500, liabilities of $200, and equity of $300. These amounts appear in the accounting equation as follows:

$$\text{Assets} = \underset{\text{Claims}}{\underline{\text{Liabilities} + \text{Equity}}}$$
$$\$500 = \quad \$200 \quad + \quad \$300$$

Using algebra, the equity (net assets or residual interest) can be computed as follows:

$$\text{Assets} - \text{Liabilities} = \text{Equity}$$
$$\$500 - \quad \$200 \quad = \quad \$300$$

The claims side of the accounting equation (liabilities plus equity) can be viewed as listing the sources of assets. For example, consider the liability created when a business borrows assets (money) from a bank. The bank loan represents the source of the assets (money), and the bank has a claim for the future return of those assets.

Equity can also be viewed as a source of assets. In fact, equity represents two distinct sources of assets. First, businesses typically acquire assets from their owners (investors). Many businesses issue **common stock**[2] certificates to acknowledge assets received from

---

[2]This presentation assumes the business is organized as a corporation. Other forms of business organization include proprietorships and partnerships. The treatment of equity for these types of businesses is slightly different from that of corporations. A detailed discussion of the differences is included in Chapter 11.

owners. The owners of such businesses are often called **stockholders,** and the ownership interest in the business is called **stockholders' equity.**

Second, businesses usually obtain assets through their earnings activities (the business acquires assets by working for them). Assets a business has earned can either be distributed to the owners or kept in the business. The portion of assets that has been provided by earnings activities is named **retained earnings.** Since stockholders own the business, they are entitled to assets acquired through its earnings activities. Retained earnings is therefore a component of stockholders' equity. Further expansion of the accounting equation can show the three sources of assets (liabilities, common stock, and retained earnings):

$$\text{Assets} = \text{Liabilities} + \overset{\text{Stockholders' Equity}}{\overline{\text{Common Stock} + \text{Retained Earnings}}}$$

Gupta Company has $250,000 of assets, $60,000 of liabilities, and $90,000 of common stock. What percentage of the assets was provided by retained earnings?

Answer
First, using algebra, determine the dollar amount of retained earnings:
Assets = Liabilities + Common Stock + Retained Earnings
Retained Earnings = Assets − Liabilities − Common Stock
Retained Earnings = $250,000 − $60,000 − $90,000
Retained Earnings = $100,000

Second, determine the percentage:
Percentage of Assets Provided by Retained Earnings = Retained Earnings / Total Assets
Percentage of Assets Provided by Retained Earnings = $100,000 / $250,000 = 40%

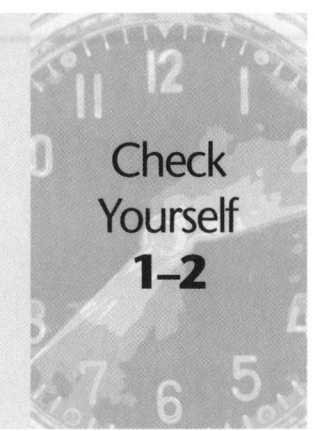

Check Yourself 1–2

Recording Business Events Under the Accounting Equation

Topic Tackler PLUS 1–2

An **accounting event** is an economic occurrence that changes an enterprise's assets, liabilities, or stockholders' equity. An event may be internal to the company, such as a reorganization. Events also may involve external parties, such as exchanges of goods or services with other companies. A **transaction** is a particular kind of event that involves transferring something of value between two entities. Examples of transactions include acquiring assets from owners, borrowing money from creditors, and purchasing or selling goods and services. The following section of the text explains how several different types of accounting events affect a company's accounting equation.

LO5 Record business events in general ledger accounts organized under an accounting equation.

Asset Source Transactions

As previously mentioned, businesses obtain assets from three sources. They acquire assets from owners (stockholders); they borrow assets from creditors; and they earn assets through profitable operations. Asset source transactions increase total assets and total claims. A more detailed discussion of the effects of asset source transactions is provided below:

Event 1 *Rustic Camp Sites (RCS) was formed on January 1, 2004, when it acquired $120,000 cash from issuing common stock.*

When RCS issued stock, it received cash and gave each investor (owner) a stock certificate as a receipt. Since this transaction provided $120,000 of assets (cash) to the business, it is an

asset source transaction. It increases the business's assets (cash account) and its stockholders' equity (common stock account).

	Assets			=	Liab.	+	Stockholders' Equity		
	Cash	+	Land	=	N. Pay	+	C. Stk.	+	Ret. Ear.
Acquired Cash through Stock Issue	120,000	+	NA	=	NA	+	120,000	+	NA

Notice the elements have been divided into accounts. For example, the element *assets* is divided into a Cash account and a Land account. Do not be concerned if these account titles are unfamiliar. They will be explained as new transactions are presented. Recall that the number of accounts a company uses depends on the nature of its business and the level of detail management needs to operate the business. For example, Sears would have an account called Cost of Goods Sold while GEICO Insurance would not. Why? Because Sears sells goods (merchandise) while GEICO does not. Also, notice that this single transaction affects the accounting equation in two places, first under an asset (cash) and second under the source of that asset (common stock). All transactions affect the accounting equation in at least two places. It is from this practice that the **double-entry bookkeeping** system derives its name.

Event 2 *RCS acquired an additional $400,000 of cash by borrowing from a creditor.*

This transaction is also classified as an asset source transaction. It increases assets (cash) and liability claims (notes payable). The account title Notes Payable is used because the borrower (RCS) is required to issue a promissory note to the creditor (a bank). A promissory note, among other things, describes the amount of interest RCS will pay and for how long it will borrow the money. The effect of the borrowing transaction on the accounting equation is indicated below.

	Assets			=	Liab.	+	Stockholders' Equity		
	Cash	+	Land	=	N. Pay	+	C. Stk.	+	Ret. Ear.
Beginning Balances	120,000	+	NA	=	NA	+	120,000	+	NA
Acquired Cash by Issuing Note	400,000	+	NA	=	400,000	+	NA	+	NA
Ending Balances	520,000	+	NA	=	400,000	+	120,000	+	NA

The beginning balances above came from the ending balances produced by the prior transaction. This practice is followed throughout the illustration.

Asset Exchange Transactions

Businesses frequently trade one asset for another asset. In such cases, the amount of one asset decreases and the amount of the other asset increases. Total assets are unaffected by asset exchange transactions. An asset exchange transaction follows.

Event 3 *RCS paid $500,000 cash to purchase land.*

This asset exchange transaction reduces the asset account Cash and increases the asset account Land. The amount of total assets is not affected. An asset exchange transaction simply reflects changes in the composition of assets. In this case, the company traded cash for land. The amount of cash decreased by $500,000 and the amount of land increased by the same amount.

	Assets			=	Liab.	+	Stockholders' Equity		
	Cash	+	Land	=	N. Pay	+	C. Stk.	+	Ret. Ear.
Beginning Balances	520,000	+	NA	=	400,000	+	120,000	+	NA
Paid Cash to Buy Land	(500,000)	+	500,000	=	NA	+	NA	+	NA
Ending Balances	20,000	+	500,000	=	400,000	+	120,000	+	NA

Another Asset Source Transaction

Event 4 *RCS obtained $85,000 cash by leasing camp sites to customers.*

Revenue represents an economic benefit a company obtains by providing customers with goods and services. In this example the economic benefit is an increase in the asset cash. Revenue transactions can therefore be viewed as *asset source transactions.* In this case, RCS's asset account Cash increased. The asset increase is balanced by an increase in the retained earnings section of stockholders' equity because producing revenue increases the amount of earnings that can be retained in the business.

	Assets		=	Liab.	+	Stockholders' Equity	
	Cash	+ Land	=	N. Pay	+ C. Stk.	+	Ret. Ear.
Beginning Balances	20,000	+ 500,000	=	400,000	+ 120,000	+	NA
Acquired Cash by Earning Revenue	85,000	+ NA	=	NA	+ NA	+	85,000
Ending Balances	105,000	+ 500,000	=	400,000	+ 120,000	+	85,000

Asset Use Transactions

Businesses use assets for a variety of purposes. For example, assets may be used to pay off liabilities or they may be transferred to owners as dividends. Assets may also be used in the process of generating earnings. All asset use transactions decrease the total amount of assets and the total amount of claims on assets (liabilities or stockholders' equity).

Event 5 *RCS paid $50,000 cash for operating expenses such as salaries, rent, and interest. (RCS could establish a separate account for each type of expense. However, the management team does not currently desire this level of detail. Remember, the number of accounts a business uses depends on the level of information managers need to make decisions.)*

In the normal course of generating revenue, a business consumes various assets and services. The assets and services consumed to generate revenue are called **expenses.** Revenue results from providing goods and services to customers. In exchange, the business acquires assets from its customers. Since the owners bear the ultimate risk and reap the rewards of operating the business, revenues increase stockholders' equity (retained earnings), and expenses decrease retained earnings. In this case, the asset account, Cash, decreased. This decrease is balanced by a decrease in the retained earnings section of stockholders' equity because expenses decrease the amount of earnings that can be retained in the business.

	Assets		=	Liab.	+	Stockholders' Equity	
	Cash	+ Land	=	N. Pay	+ C. Stk.	+	Ret. Ear.
Beginning Balances	105,000	+ 500,000	=	400,000	+ 120,000	+	85,000
Used Cash to Pay Expenses	(50,000)	+ NA	=	NA	+ NA	+	(50,000)
Ending Balances	55,000	+ 500,000	=	400,000	+ 120,000	+	35,000

Event 6 *RCS paid $4,000 in cash dividends to its owners.*

The enterprise's *net assets* had increased by $35,000 ($85,000 of revenue − $50,000 of expense) as a result of its earnings activities. Since the risks and rewards of operating a business rest with its owners, the owners are entitled to the assets generated through earnings activities. RCS can keep the additional assets in the business or transfer them to the owners. If a business transfers some or all of its earned assets to owners, the transfer is frequently called a **dividend.**

Since assets distributed to stockholders are not used for the purpose of generating revenue, *dividends are wealth transfers, not expenses.*

	Assets			=	Liab.	+	Stockholders' Equity		
	Cash	+	Land	=	N. Pay	+	C. Stk.	+	Ret. Ear.
Beginning Balances	55,000	+	500,000	=	400,000	+	120,000	+	35,000
Used Cash to Pay Dividends	(4,000)	+	NA	=	NA	+	NA	+	(4,000)
Ending Balances	51,000	+	500,000	=	400,000	+	120,000	+	31,000

Historical Cost and Reliability Concepts

LO6 Explain how the historical cost and reliability concepts affect amounts reported in financial statements.

Event 7 *The land that RCS paid $500,000 to purchase had an appraised market value of $525,000 on December 31, 2004.*

Although the appraised value of the land is higher than the original cost, RCS will not increase the amount recorded in its accounting records above the land's $500,000 historical cost. In general, accountants do not recognize changes in market value. The **historical cost concept** requires that most assets be reported at the amount paid for them (their historical cost) regardless of increases in market value.

Certainly investors would rather know what an asset is worth rather than how much it originally cost. So why do accountants maintain records and report financial information based on historical cost? Market value is elusive. Accountants rely heavily on the **reliability concept.** Information is reliable if it can be independently verified. For example, two people looking at the legal documents associated with RCS's land purchase will both conclude that RCS paid $500,000 for the land. That historical cost is a verifiable fact. The appraised value, in contrast, is an opinion. Even two persons who are experienced appraisers are not likely to come up with the same amount for the land's market value. Accountants do not report market values in financial statements because such values are not reliable.

Recap: Types of Transactions

LO7 Classify business events as asset source, use, or exchange transactions.

The transactions described above have each been classified into one of three categories: (1) asset source transactions; (2) asset exchange transactions; and (3) asset use transactions. A fourth category, claims exchange transactions, is introduced in a later chapter. To reiterate: *asset source transactions increase the total amount of assets and increase the total amount of claims.* In its first year of operation, RCS acquired assets from three sources: first, from owners (Event 1); next, by borrowing (Event 2); and finally, through earnings activities (Event 4). *Asset exchange transactions decrease one asset account and increase another asset account. The total amount of assets is unchanged by asset exchange transactions.* RCS experienced one asset exchange transaction; it used cash to purchase land (Event 3). *Asset use transactions decrease the total amount of assets and the total amount of claims.* RCS used assets to pay expenses (Event 5) and to pay dividends (Event 6). As you proceed through this text, practice classifying transactions into one of the four categories. Businesses engage in thousands of transactions every day. It is far more effective to learn how to classify the transactions into meaningful categories than to attempt to memorize the effects of thousands of transactions.

Summary of Transactions

LO5 Record business events in general ledger accounts organized under an accounting equation.

A full collection of a company's accounts is called the **general ledger.** The information in the ledger accounts is used to prepare the financial statements. The general ledger account infor-

Exhibit 1–4 *General Ledger Accounts Organized Under the Accounting Equation*

	Assets			=	Liabilities	+	Stockholders' Equity			Other
	Cash	+	Land	=	Notes Payable	+	Common Stock	+	Retained Earnings	Account Titles
Event No.	$ 0		$ 0		$ 0		$ 0		$ 0	
1	120,000						120,000			
2	400,000				400,000					
3	(500,000)		500,000							
4	85,000								85,000	Revenue
5	(50,000)								(50,000)	Expense
6	(4,000)								(4,000)	Dividend
7	NA		NA		NA		NA		NA	
	$ 51,000	+	$500,000	=	$400,000	+	$120,000	+	$31,000	

mation for RCS's 2004 accounting period is shown in Exhibit 1–4. The revenue, expense, and dividend account data appear in the retained earnings column. These account titles are shown immediately to the right of the dollar amounts listed in the retained earnings column. To help you review RCS's general ledger, the business events that the company experienced during 2004 are summarized below.

1. RCS issued common stock, acquiring $120,000 cash from its owners.
2. RCS borrowed $400,000 cash.
3. RCS paid $500,000 cash to purchase land.
4. RCS received $85,000 cash from earning revenue.
5. RCS paid $50,000 cash for expenses.
6. RCS paid dividends of $4,000 cash to the owners.
7. The land that RCS paid $500,000 to purchase had an appraised market value of $525,000 on December 31, 2004.

As indicated earlier, accounting information is normally presented to external users in four general-purpose financial statements. The information in the ledger accounts is used to prepare these financial statements. The data in the above ledger accounts are color coded to help you understand the source of information in the financial statements. The numbers in *green* are used in the *statement of cash flows*. The numbers in *red* are used to prepare the *balance sheet*. Finally, the numbers in *blue* are used to prepare the *income statement*. The numbers reported in the statement of changes in stockholders' equity have not been color coded because they appear in more than one statement. The next section explains how the information in the accounts is presented in financial statements.

Preparing Financial Statements

The financial statements for RCS are shown in Exhibit 1–5. The information used to prepare these statements was drawn from the ledger accounts. Information in one statement may relate to information in another statement. For example, the amount of net income reported on the income statement also appears on the statement of changes in stockholders' equity. Accountants use the term ***articulation*** to describe the interrelationships among the various elements of the financial statements. The key articulated relationships in RCS's financial statements are highlighted with arrows (Exhibit 1–5). A description of each statement follows.

LO8 Use general ledger account information to prepare four financial statements.

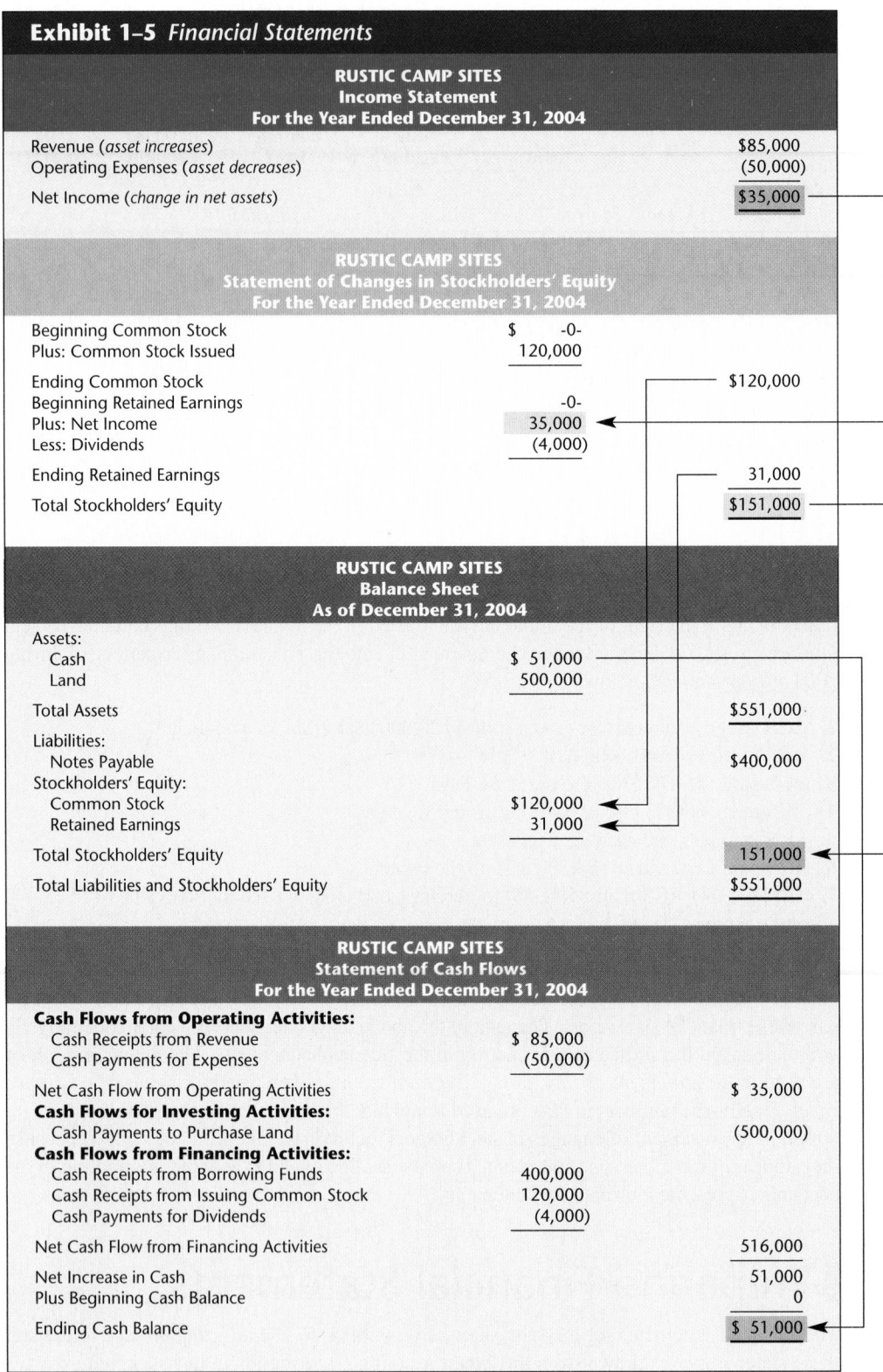

Exhibit 1–5 *Financial Statements*

RUSTIC CAMP SITES
Income Statement
For the Year Ended December 31, 2004

Revenue (*asset increases*)	$85,000
Operating Expenses (*asset decreases*)	(50,000)
Net Income (*change in net assets*)	$35,000

RUSTIC CAMP SITES
Statement of Changes in Stockholders' Equity
For the Year Ended December 31, 2004

Beginning Common Stock	$ -0-	
Plus: Common Stock Issued	120,000	
Ending Common Stock		$120,000
Beginning Retained Earnings	-0-	
Plus: Net Income	35,000	
Less: Dividends	(4,000)	
Ending Retained Earnings		31,000
Total Stockholders' Equity		$151,000

RUSTIC CAMP SITES
Balance Sheet
As of December 31, 2004

Assets:		
Cash	$ 51,000	
Land	500,000	
Total Assets		$551,000
Liabilities:		
Notes Payable		$400,000
Stockholders' Equity:		
Common Stock	$120,000	
Retained Earnings	31,000	
Total Stockholders' Equity		151,000
Total Liabilities and Stockholders' Equity		$551,000

RUSTIC CAMP SITES
Statement of Cash Flows
For the Year Ended December 31, 2004

Cash Flows from Operating Activities:		
Cash Receipts from Revenue	$ 85,000	
Cash Payments for Expenses	(50,000)	
Net Cash Flow from Operating Activities		$ 35,000
Cash Flows for Investing Activities:		
Cash Payments to Purchase Land		(500,000)
Cash Flows from Financing Activities:		
Cash Receipts from Borrowing Funds	400,000	
Cash Receipts from Issuing Common Stock	120,000	
Cash Payments for Dividends	(4,000)	
Net Cash Flow from Financing Activities		516,000
Net Increase in Cash		51,000
Plus Beginning Cash Balance		0
Ending Cash Balance		$ 51,000

Income Statement and the Matching Concept

Businesses consume assets and services in order to generate revenues, thereby creating greater quantities of other assets. For example, RCS may pay cash (asset use) to an employee who maintains the camp sites. Maintaining the sites is necessary in order to collect cash (obtain assets) from customers. The **income statement** *matches* asset increases from operating a business with asset decreases from operating the business.[3] Asset increases resulting from providing goods and services to customers in the course of normal operations are called revenues. Asset decreases resulting from consuming assets and services for the purpose of generating revenues are called expenses. If revenues are greater than expenses, the difference is called **net income.** If expenses exceed revenues, the difference is a **net loss.**

The income statement shown in Exhibit 1–5 indicates that RCS has earned more assets than it has used. Specifically, the statement shows that RCS has increased its assets by $35,000 (net income) as a result of operating its business. Observe the phrase *For the Year Ended December 31, 2004* in the heading of the income statement. Income is measured for a span of time called the **accounting period.** While accounting periods of one year are normal for external financial reporting, income can be measured weekly, monthly, quarterly, semiannually, or over any other time period that the users deem appropriate. Notice that the cash RCS paid to its stockholders (dividends) is not reported as expense. The decrease in assets for dividend payments is not incurred for the purpose of generating revenue. Instead, dividends are transfers of wealth to the owners of the business. Dividend payments are not shown on the income statement.

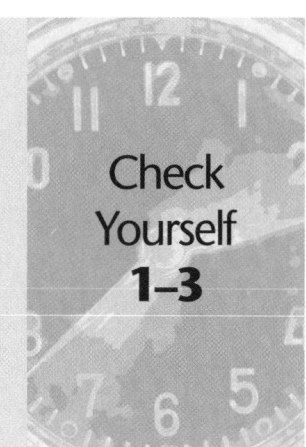

Mahoney, Inc. was started when it issued common stock to its owners for $300,000. During its first year of operation Mahoney received $523,000 cash for services provided to customers. Mahoney paid employees $233,000 cash. Advertising costs paid in cash amounted to $102,000. Other cash operating expenses amounted to $124,000. Finally, Mahoney paid a $25,000 cash dividend to its stockholders. What amount of net income would Mahoney's report on its earnings statement?

Answer The amount of net income is $64,000 ($523,000 Revenue − $233,000 Salary Expense − $102,000 Advertising Expense − $124,000 Other Operating Expenses). The cash received from issuing stock is not revenue because it was not acquired from earnings activities. In other words, Mahoney did not work (perform services) for this money; it was contributed by owners of the business. Likewise, the dividends are not expenses because the decrease in cash was not incurred for the purpose of generating revenue. Instead, the dividends represent a transfer of wealth to the owners.

Check Yourself 1–3

Statement of Changes in Stockholders' Equity

The **statement of changes in stockholders' equity** explains the effects of transactions on stockholders' equity during the accounting period. It starts with the beginning balance in the common stock account. In the case of RCS, the beginning balance in the common stock account is zero because the company did not exist before the 2004 accounting period. The amount of stock issued during the accounting period is added to the beginning balance to determine the ending balance in the common stock account.

In addition to reporting the changes in common stock, the statement describes the changes in retained earnings for the accounting period. RCS had no beginning balance in retained earnings. During the period, the company earned $35,000 and paid $4,000 in dividends to the stockholders, producing an ending retained earning balance of $31,000 ($0 + $35,000 − $4,000). Since equity consists of common stock and retained earnings, the ending total equity balance is $151,000 ($120,000 + $31,000). This statement is also dated with the phrase *For the Year Ended December 31, 2004,* because it describes what happened to stockholders equity over the year 2004.

---

[3]This description of the income statement is expanded in subsequent chapters as additional relationships among the elements of financial statements are introduced.

Balance Sheet

The **balance sheet** draws its name from the accounting equation. Specifically, total assets balances with (equals) the sources of those assets. Balance sheets are normally divided into two sections. The first section lists a company's assets. The second section shows the sources of those assets (liabilities and stockholders' equity). The balance sheet for RCS is shown in Exhibit 1–5. Note that total claims (liabilities plus stockholders' equity) are equal to total assets ($551,000 = $551,000). Also, note the order of the assets in the balance sheet. Cash appears first, followed by the land account. Assets are displayed in the balance sheet based on their level of **liquidity.** This means that assets are listed in order of how rapidly they will be converted to cash. Finally, note that the balance sheet is dated with the phrase *As of December 31, 2004,* indicating that it describes the company's financial condition on the last day of the accounting period.

Check Yourself 1–4

To gain a clear understanding of the balance sheet, try to create one that describes your personal financial condition. First list your assets, then your liabilities. Determine the amount of your equity by subtracting your liabilities from your assets.

Answer Answers for this exercise will vary depending on the particular assets and liabilities each student identifies. Common student assets include automobiles, computers, stereos, TVs, phones, CD players, clothes, and textbooks. Common student liabilities include car loans, mortgages, student loans, and credit card debt. The difference between the assets and the liabilities is the equity.

Statement of Cash Flows

The **statement of cash flows** explains how a company obtained and used *cash* during the accounting period. The sources of cash are called *cash inflows,* and the uses are *cash outflows.* The statement classifies cash receipts (inflows) and payments (outflows) into three categories: financing activities, investing activities, and operating activities.

Businesses normally start with an idea. Implementation of the idea usually requires cash. For example, suppose you decide to start an apartment rental business. First, you would need cash to finance building the apartments. Acquiring cash to start a business is a financing activity. **Financing activities** include obtaining cash (inflow) from owners or paying cash (outflow) to owners (dividends). Financing activities also include borrowing cash (inflow) from creditors and repaying the principal (outflow) to creditors. Because interest on borrowed money is an expense, however, cash paid to creditors for interest is reported in the operating activities section of the statement of cash flows.

After obtaining cash from financing activities, you would invest the money by building or buying apartments. **Investing activities** involve paying cash (outflow) for productive assets or receiving cash (inflow) from selling productive assets. **Productive assets** are sometimes called long-term assets because businesses normally use them for more than one year. Cash outflows to purchase land or cash inflows from selling a building are examples of investing activities.

After investing in the productive assets (apartments), you would engage in operating activities. Specifically, **operating activities** involve receiving cash (inflow) from revenue and paying cash (outflow) for expenses. Note that cash spent to purchase short-term assets such as office supplies is reported in the operating activities section because the office supplies would likely be used (expensed) within a single accounting period.

The primary cash inflows and outflows related to the types of business activity introduced in this chapter are summarized in Exhibit 1–6. The exhibit will be expanded as additional types of events are introduced in subsequent chapters.

The statement of cash flows for Rustic Camp Sites in Exhibit 1–5 shows that the amount of cash increased by $51,000 during the year. The beginning balance in the Cash account was

Exhibit 1–6 *Classification Scheme for Statement of Cash Flows*

Cash Flows from Operating Activities:
Cash Receipts (Inflows) from Revenue (Including Interest)
Cash Payments (Outflows) for Expenses (Including Interest)
Cash Flows from Investing Activities:
Cash Receipts (Inflows) from the Sale of Long-Term Assets
Cash Payments (Outflows) for the Purchase of Long-Term Assets
Cash Flows from Financing Activities:
Cash Receipts (Inflows) from Borrowing Funds
Cash Receipts (Inflows) from Issuing Common Stock
Cash Payments (Outflows) to Repay Borrowed Funds
Cash Payments (Outflows) for Dividends

zero; adding the $51,000 increase to the beginning balance results in a $51,000 ending balance. Notice that the $51,000 ending cash balance on the statement of cash flows is the same as the amount of cash reported in the asset section on the December 31 year-end balance sheet. Also, note that the statement of cash flows is dated with the phrase *For the Year Ended December 31, 2004,* because it describes what happened to cash over the span of the year.

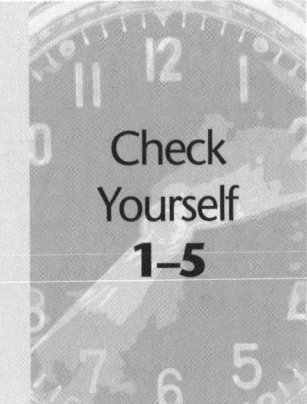

Classify each of the following items as an operating activity, investing activity, or financing activity.

1. Acquired cash from owners.
2. Borrowed cash from creditors.
3. Paid cash to purchase land.
4. Earned cash revenue.
5. Paid cash for salary expenses.
6. Paid cash dividend.
7. Paid cash for interest.

Answer (1) financing activity; (2) financing activity; (3) investing activity; (4) operating activity; (5) operating activity; (6) financing activity; (7) operating activity.

Check Yourself 1–5

The Horizontal Financial Statements Model

Financial statements are the scorecard for business activity. If you want to succeed in business, you must know how your business decisions affect your company's financial statements. This text uses a **horizontal statements model** with which you can visualize several financial statements simultaneously to help you understand how business events affect financial statements. This learning aid is so named because it models a set of financial statements horizontally across a single page of paper. The model is extremely useful for analyzing the effects of a single event on the financial statements. The balance sheet is displayed first, adjacent to the income statement, and then the statement of cash flows. Because the effects of equity transactions can be analyzed by referring to certain balance sheet columns, and because of limited space, the statement of changes in equity is not shown in the horizontal statements model.

The model frequently uses abbreviations. For example, activity classifications in the statement of cash flows are identified using OA for operating activities, IA for investing activities, and FA for financing activities. NC designates the net change in cash. The statements model uses "NA" when an account is not affected by an event. The background of the *balance sheet*

LO9 Record business events using a horizontal financial statements model.

is red, the *income statement* is blue, and the *statement of cash flows* is green. To demonstrate the usefulness of the horizontal statements model, we use it to display the seven accounting events that RCS experienced during its first year of operation (2004).

1. RCS acquired $120,000 cash from the owners.
2. RCS borrowed $400,000 cash.
3. RCS paid $500,000 cash to purchase land.
4. RCS received $85,000 cash from earning revenue.
5. RCS paid $50,000 cash for expenses.
6. RCS paid $4,000 of cash dividends to the owners.
7. The market value of the land owned by RCS was appraised at $525,000 on December 31, 2004.

Event No.	Balance Sheet							Income Statement				Statement of Cash Flows
	Assets			= Liab.	+ Stockholders' Equity							
	Cash	+	Land	= N. Pay	+ C. Stk.	+ Ret. Ear.		Rev.	− Exp.	= Net Inc.		
Beg. Bal.	0	+	0	= 0	+ 0	+ 0		0	− 0	= 0		NA
1.	120,000	+	NA	= NA	+ 120,000	+ NA		NA	− NA	= NA		120,000 FA
2.	400,000	+	NA	= 400,000	+ NA	+ NA		NA	− NA	= NA		400,000 FA
3.	(500,000)	+	500,000	= NA	+ NA	+ NA		NA	− NA	= NA		(500,000) IA
4.	85,000	+	NA	= NA	+ NA	+ 85,000		85,000	− NA	= 85,000		85,000 OA
5.	(50,000)	+	NA	= NA	+ NA	+ (50,000)		NA	− 50,000	= (50,000)		(50,000) OA
6.	(4,000)	+	NA	= NA	+ NA	+ (4,000)		NA	− NA	= NA		(4,000) FA
7.	NA	+	NA	= NA	+ NA	+ NA		NA	− NA	= NA		NA
Totals	51,000	+	500,000	= 400,000	+ 120,000	+ 31,000		85,000	− 50,000	= 35,000		51,000 NC

It is important to recognize that statements models are learning tools. Because they are very helpful in understanding how accounting events affect financial statements, they are used extensively in this book. However, the models do not represent the full, formal presentation formats used in published financial statements. For example, the horizontal model shows only a partial set of statements. Also, since the statements are presented in aggregate, the description of dates (i.e., "as of" versus "for the period ended") does not distinguish periodic from cumulative data.

THE FINANCIAL ANALYST

LO10 Explain how to use the price-earnings ratio and growth percentage analysis to assess the market value of common stock.

When you buy a share of stock, what do you really get? The stock certificate you receive is evidence of your right to share in the earnings of the company that issued the stock. The more the company earns, the more your wealth increases. This explains why investors are willing to pay higher prices for companies with higher earnings potential.

Price-Earnings Ratio

The **price-earnings ratio,** frequently called the *P/E ratio,* is the most commonly reported measure of a company's value. The P/E ratio is a company's market price per share of stock divided by the company's annual earnings per share (EPS).[4]

---

[4]The amount of earnings per share is provided in the company's annual report. In its simplest form, it is computed by dividing the company's net income (net earnings) by the number of shares of common stock outstanding.

Assume Western Company recently reported annual earnings per share of $3. Western's stock is currently selling for $54 per share. Western's stock is therefore selling at a P/E ratio of 18 ($54 market price / $3 EPS). What does a P/E ratio of 18 mean? If Western continued earning $3 per share of stock each year and paid all its earnings out to stockholders in the form of cash dividends, it would take 18 years for an investor to recover the price paid for the stock.

In contrast, assume the stock of Eastern Company, which reported EPS of $4, is currently selling for $48 per share. Eastern's P/E ratio is 12 ($48 market price / $4 EPS). Investors who buy Eastern Company stock would get their money back six years faster ($18 - 12$) than investors who buy Western Company stock.

Why would investors buy a stock with a P/E ratio of 18 when they could buy one with a P/E ratio of 12? If investors expect Western Company's earnings to grow faster than Eastern Company's earnings, the higher P/E ratio makes sense. For example, suppose Western Company's earnings were to double to $6 per share while Eastern's remained at $4 per share. Western's P/E ratio would drop to 9 ($54 market price / $6 EPS) while Eastern's remains at 12. This explains why high-growth companies sell for higher P/E multiples than do low-growth companies.

Measuring Growth Through Percentage Analysis

The income statements for Cammeron, Inc., show that earnings increased by $4.2 million from 2005 to 2006. Comparable data for Diller Enterprises indicate earnings growth of $2.9 million. Is Cammeron a better-managed company than Diller? Not necessarily; perhaps Cammeron is simply a larger company than Diller. Investors frequently use percentage analysis to level the playing field when comparing companies of differing sizes. Consider the following actual earnings data for the two companies:

	2005*	2006*	Growth†
Cammeron	$42.4	$46.6	$4.2
Diller	9.9	12.8	2.9

*Earnings data shown in millions.

†Growth calculated by subtracting 2002 earnings from 2003 earnings.

The percentage growth in earnings between 2005 and 2006 for each of the companies can be measured with the following formula:

$$\frac{\text{Alternative year earnings} - \text{Base year earnings}}{\text{Base year earnings}} = \text{Percentage Growth Rate}$$

Cammeron, Inc.:

$$\frac{\$46.6 - \$42.4}{\$42.4} = 9.9\%$$

Diller Enterprises:

$$\frac{\$12.8 - \$9.9}{\$9.9} = 29.3\%$$

This analysis shows that Cammeron is the larger company, but Diller is growing much more rapidly. If this trend continues, Diller will eventually become the larger company and have higher earnings than Cammeron. This higher earnings potential is why investors value

Exhibit 1-7 Real-World Price-Earnings Ratios and Growth Rates		
Company	P/E Ratio	Average Annual Earnings Growth 1999–2001
High growth companies:		
Cisco Systems	90	35.3
Microsoft	46	13.2
Medium growth companies:		
General Electric	20	6.2
General Mills	24	6.4
Low growth companies:		
DuPont	10	(4.2)
Sara Lee	10	1.4

fast-growing companies. The P/E ratios of real-world companies are highly correlated with their growth rates, as demonstrated in the data reported in Exhibit 1–7. The data in this exhibit are based on the closing stock prices on June 25, 2002.

LO11 Identify three types of business organizations and some of the technical terms they use in their real world financial reports.

Real-World Financial Reports

Organizations exist in many different forms. As previously indicated, two major classifications include *business* entities and *not-for-profit* entities. Business entities are typically

focus on INTERNATIONAL ISSUES

Is There Global GAAP?

As explained in this chapter, financial reporting is a measurement and communication discipline based on rules referred to as *generally accepted accounting principles.* The accounting rules described in this text are based on GAAP used in the United States. Not all economies throughout the world use the same accounting rules. Although there are many similarities among the accounting principles used in different countries, there also are major differences. Accountants have made attempts to create international accounting standards, but individual countries have retained the authority to establish their own GAAP. Simply put, each country has its own GAAP; there is no single "global GAAP." Examples of how financial reporting in other countries differs from that in the United States are presented throughout this book.

Accounting rules differ among countries for a variety of reasons, including the economic and legal environments in each country and how the GAAP in that country is established. Generally accepted accounting principles in the United States are primarily established by the Financial Accounting Standards Board (FASB). The FASB is a nongovernment rule-making body established by the accounting profession. In countries such as Germany and Japan, for example, the GAAP is established by government bodies. In these countries GAAP is established more like the way federal laws and regulations are established in the United States.

Furthermore, in the United States any connection between GAAP established by the FASB and tax accounting rules established by Congress and the Internal Revenue Service (IRS) is coincidental, not deliberate. In some countries there is a close connection between tax accounting rules and GAAP.

service, merchandising, or manufacturing companies. **Service businesses,** which include doctors, attorneys, accountants, dry cleaners, and maids, provide services to their customers. **Merchandising businesses,** sometimes called *retail* or *wholesale companies,* sell goods to customers that other entities make. **Manufacturing businesses** make the goods that they sell to their customers.

Some business operations include combinations of these three categories. For example, an automotive repair shop might change oil (service function), sell parts such as oil filters (retail function), and rebuild engines (manufacturing function). The nature of the reporting entity affects the form and content of the information reported in an entity's financial statements. For example, not-for-profit entities provide statements of revenues, expenditures, and changes in fund equity while business entities provide income statements. Similarly, income statements of retail companies show an expense item called *cost of goods sold,* but service companies that do not sell goods have no such item in their income statements. You should expect some diversity when reviewing real-world financial statements.

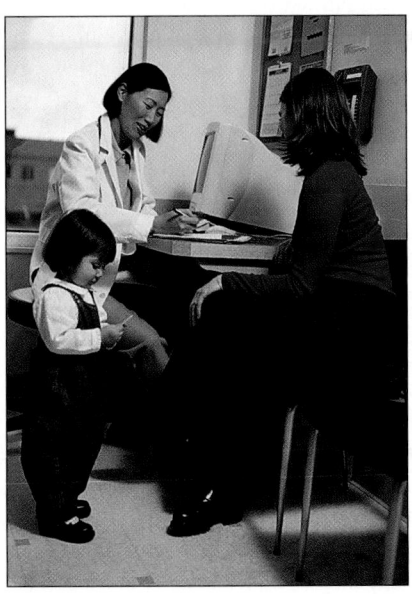  

Annual Report for The Topps Company, Inc.

Organizations normally provide information, including financial statements, to *stakeholders* yearly in a document known as an **annual report.** The annual report for Topps is reproduced in Appendix B of this text. This report includes the company's financial statements (see pages 12–15 of the report). Immediately following the statements are footnotes that provide additional details about the items described in the statements (see pages 16–30). The annual report contains the *auditors' report,* which is discussed in Chapter 2. Annual reports also include written commentary describing management's assessment of significant events that affected the company during the reporting period. This commentary, called *management's discussion and analysis* (MD&A), is explained in Chapter 4.

The U.S. Securities and Exchange Commission (SEC) requires public companies to file an annual report on a document known as a 10-K. The SEC is discussed in more detail in Chapter 4. Even though the annual report is usually flashier than the 10-K (contains more color and pictures), the 10-K is normally more comprehensive with respect to content. As a result, the 10-K report can substitute for the annual report, but the annual report cannot substitute for the 10-K. In an effort to reduce costs, some companies use the 10-K report as their annual report.

Special Terms in Real-World Reports

The financial statements of real-world companies include numerous items relating to advanced topics that are not covered in introductory accounting textbooks, especially the first chapter of an introductory accounting textbook. Do not, however, be discouraged from browsing through real-world annual reports. You will significantly enhance your learning if you look at many annual reports and attempt to identify as many items as you can. As your accounting knowledge grows, you will likely experience increased interest in real-world financial reports and the businesses they describe.

We encourage you to look for annual reports in the library or ask your employer for a copy of your company's report. The Internet is another excellent source for obtaining annual reports. Most companies provide links to their annual reports on their home pages. Look for links labeled "about the company" or "investor relations" or other phrases that logically lead to the company's financial reports. The best way to learn accounting is to use it. Accounting is the language of business. Learning the language will serve you well in almost any area of business that you pursue.

a look back

This chapter introduced the role of accounting in society and business: to provide information helpful to operating and evaluating the performance of organizations. Accounting is a measurement discipline. To communicate effectively, users of accounting must agree on the rules of measurement. *Generally accepted accounting principles (GAAP)* constitute the rules used by the accounting profession in the United States to govern financial reporting. GAAP is a work in progress that continues to evolve.

This chapter has discussed eight elements of financial statements: *assets, liabilities, equity, common stock (contributed capital), revenue, expenses, dividends (distributions),* and *net income.* The elements represent broad classifications reported on financial statements. Four basic financial statements appear in the reports of public companies: the *balance sheet,* the *income statement,* the *statement of changes in stockholders' equity,* and the *statement of cash flows.* The chapter discussed the form and content of each statement as well as the interrelationships among the statements.

This chapter introduced a *horizontal financial statements model* as a tool to help you understand how business events affect a set of financial statements. This model is used throughout the text. You should carefully study this model before proceeding to Chapter 2.

a look forward

To keep matters as simple as possible and to focus on the interrelationships among financial statements, this chapter considered only cash events. Obviously, many real-world events do not involve an immediate exchange of cash. For example, customers use telephone service throughout the month without paying for it until the next month. Such phone usage represents an expense in one month with a cash exchange in the following month. Events such as this are called *accruals.* Understanding the effects that accrual events have on the financial statements is the subject of Chapter 2.

SELF-STUDY REVIEW PROBLEM

During 2005 Rustic Camp Sites experienced the following transactions.

1. RCS acquired $32,000 cash by issuing common stock.
2. RCS received $116,000 cash for providing services to customers (leasing camp sites).
3. RCS paid $13,000 cash for salaries expenses.
4. RCS paid a $9,000 cash dividend to the owners.
5. RCS sold land that had cost $100,000 for $100,000 cash.
6. RCS paid $47,000 cash for other operating expenses.

Required

a. Record the transaction data in a horizontal financial statements model like the following one. In the Cash Flow column, classify the cash flows as operating activities (OA), investing activities (IA), or financing activities (FA). The beginning balances have been recorded as an example. They are the ending balances shown on RCS's December 31, 2004, financial statements illustrated in the chapter.

Note that the revenue and expense accounts have a zero beginning balance. Amounts in these accounts apply only to a single accounting period. Balances are not carried forward from one accounting period to the next.

Event No.	Balance Sheet							Income Statement			Statement of Cash Flows
	Assets		= Liab.	+ Stockholders' Equity							
	Cash	+ Land	= N. Pay	+ C. Stk.	+ Ret. Ear.			Rev.	− Exp.	= Net Inc.	
Bal.	51,000	+ 500,000	= 400,000	+ 120,000	+ 31,000			NA	− NA	= NA	NA

b. Explain why there are no beginning balances in the Income Statement columns.
c. What amount of net income will RCS report on the 2005 income statement?
d. What amount of total assets will RCS report on the December 31, 2005, balance sheet?
e. What amount of retained earnings will RCS report on the December 31, 2005, balance sheet?
f. What amount of net cash flow from operating activities will RCS report on the 2005 statement of cash flows?
g. Assume that RCS has 20,000 shares of common stock outstanding that is selling at a market price of $33.60 per share. Determine the company's P/E ratio. Based on the information shown in Exhibit 1–7, indicate whether investors believe RCS has a high-, medium-, or low-earnings growth potential.

Answer
a.

Event No.	Balance Sheet							Income Statement			Statement of Cash Flows
	Assets		= Liab.	+ Stockholders' Equity							
	Cash	+ Land	= N. Pay	+ C. Stk.	+ Ret. Ear.			Rev.	− Exp.	= Net Inc.	
Bal.	51,000	+ 500,000	= 400,000	+ 120,000	+ 31,000			NA	− NA	= NA	NA
1	32,000	+ NA	= NA	+ 32,000	+ NA			NA	− NA	= NA	32,000 FA
2	116,000	+ NA	= NA	+ NA	+ 116,000			116,000	− NA	= 116,000	116,000 OA
3	(13,000)	+ NA	= NA	+ NA	+ (13,000)			NA	− 13,000	= (13,000)	(13,000) OA
4	(9,000)	+ NA	= NA	+ NA	+ (9,000)			NA	− NA	= NA	(9,000) FA
5	100,000	+ (100,000)	= NA	+ NA	+ NA			NA	− NA	= NA	100,000 IA
6	(47,000)	+ NA	= NA	+ NA	+ (47,000)			NA	− 47,000	= (47,000)	(47,000) OA
Totals	230,000	+ 400,000	= 400,000	+ 152,000	+ 78,000			116,000	− 60,000	= 56,000	179,000 NC*

*The letters NC on the last line of the column designate the net change in cash.

b. The revenue and expense accounts are temporary accounts used to capture data for a single accounting period. They are closed (amounts removed from the accounts) at the end of the accounting period and therefore always have zero balances at the beginning of the accounting cycle.
c. RCS will report net income of $56,000 on the 2005 income statement. Compute this amount by subtracting the expenses from the revenue ($116,000 Revenue − $13,000 Salaries expenses − $47,000 Other operating expense).
d. RCS will report total assets of $630,000 on the December 31, 2005, balance sheet. Compute total assets by adding the cash amount to the land amount ($230,000 Cash + $400,000 Land).
e. RCS will report retained earnings of $78,000 on the December 31, 2005 balance sheet. Compute this amount using the following formula: Beginning retained earnings + Net income − Dividends = Ending retained earnings. In this case, $31,000 + $56,000 − $9,000 = $78,000.
f. Net cash flow from operating activities is the difference between the amount of cash collected from revenue and the amount of cash spent for expenses. In this case, $116,000 cash inflow from revenue − $13,000 cash outflow for salaries expenses − $47,000 cash outflow for other operating expenses = $56,000 net cash inflow from operating activities.
g. Earnings per share = Net earnings ÷ Number of shares outstanding = $56,000 ÷ 20,000 shares = $2.80 per share. Price-carnings = Market price per share ÷ Earnings per share = $33.60 ÷ $2.80 = 12. Based on the information in Exhibit 1–7, a P/E ratio of 12 indicates that investors see RCS as a company with low earnings growth potential.

KEY TERMS

Account *9*

Accounting *3*

Accounting equation *10*

Accounting event *11*

Accounting period *17*

Annual report *23*

Articulation *15*

Asset *10*

Asset source transaction *12*

Balance sheet *18*

Claims *10*

Common stock *10*

Creditor *5*

Dividend *13*

Double-entry bookkeeping *12*

Earnings *4*

Elements *9*

Equity *10*

Expense *13*

Financial accounting *6*

Financial Accounting
    Standards Board
    (FASB) *9*

Financial resources *5*

Financial statements *8*

Financing activities *18*

General ledger *14*

Generally accepted accounting
    principles (GAAP) *8*

Historical cost concept *14*

Horizontal statements
    model *19*

Income *4*

Income statement *17*

Interest *6*

Investing activities *18*

Investors *5*

Labor resources *6*

Liabilities *10*

Liquidation *5*

Liquidity *18*

Managerial accounting *6*

Manufacturing businesses *23*

Market *4*

Merchandising businesses *23*

Net assets *10*

Net income *17*

Net loss *17*

Not-for-profit entities *7*

Operating activities *18*

Physical resources *6*

Price-earnings ratio *20*

Productive assets *18*

Profit *4*

Reliability concept *14*

Reporting entities *8*

Residual interest *10*

Retained earnings *11*

Revenue *13*

Service businesses *23*

Stakeholders *3*

Statement of cash flows *18*

Statement of changes in
    stockholders' equity *17*

Stockholders *11*

Stockholders' equity *11*

Transaction *11*

Users *3*

QUESTIONS

1. Explain the term *stakeholder*. Distinguish between stakeholders with a direct versus an indirect interest in the companies that issue accounting reports.
2. Why is accounting called the *language of business?*
3. What is the primary mechanism used to allocate resources in the United States?
4. In a business context, what does the term *market* mean?
5. What market trilogy components are involved in the process of transforming resources into finished products?
6. Give an example of a financial resource, a physical resource, and a labor resource.
7. What type of income or profit does an investor expect to receive in exchange for providing financial resources to a business? What type of income does a creditor expect from providing financial resources to an organization or business?
8. How do financial and managerial accounting differ?
9. Describe a not-for-profit or nonprofit enterprise. What is the motivation for this type of entity?
10. What are the U.S. rules of accounting information measurement called?
11. How does establishing GAAP in the United States differ from establishing accounting principles in Japan and Germany?
12. What body has the primary responsibility for establishing GAAP in the United States?
13. Distinguish between elements of financial statements and accounts.
14. What is the most basic form of the accounting equation?
15. What role do assets play in business profitability?
16. To whom do the assets of a business belong?
17. What is the nature of creditors' claims on assets?
18. What does *residual interest* mean? Identify two other terms that describe the residual interest.
19. What term describes creditors' claims on the assets of a business?
20. What is the accounting equation? Describe each of its three components.
21. Who ultimately bears the risk and collects the rewards associated with operating a business?
22. What does a *double-entry bookkeeping system* mean?
23. Identify the three types of accounting transactions discussed in this chapter. Provide an example of each type of transaction, and explain how it affects the accounting equation.
24. How does acquiring capital from owners affect the accounting equation?
25. What is the difference between assets that are acquired by issuing common stock and those that are acquired using retained earnings?

26. How does earning revenue affect the accounting equation?
27. What are the three primary sources of assets?
28. What is the source of retained earnings?
29. How does distributing assets (paying dividends) to owners affect the accounting equation?
30. What are the similarities and differences between dividends and expenses?
31. What four general-purpose financial statements do business enterprises use?
32. Which of the general-purpose financial statements provides information about the enterprise at a specific designated date?
33. What causes a net loss?
34. What three categories of cash receipts and cash payments do businesses report on the statement of cash flows? Explain the types of cash flows reported in each category.
35. How are asset accounts usually arranged in the balance sheet?
36. What type of information does a business typically include in its annual report?

EXERCISES—SERIES A

All Exercises in Series A are available with McGraw-Hill's Homework Manager

EXERCISE 1–1A *Understanding Markets*

L.O. 1

Free economies use open markets to allocate resources.

Required
Identify the three participants in a free business market. Write a brief memo explaining how these participants interact to ensure that goods and services are distributed in a manner that satisfies consumers.

EXERCISE 1–2A *Distributions in a Business Liquidation*

L.O. 2

Assume that Mallory Company acquires $700 cash from creditors and $900 cash from investors (stockholders). The company then has an operating loss of $1,000 cash and goes out of business.

Required
a. Define the term *business liquidation.*
b. What amount of cash will Mallory's creditors receive?
c. What amount of cash will Mallory's investors (stockholders) receive?

EXERCISE 1–3A *Identifying the Reporting Entities*

L.O. 2

Reza Pierno recently started a business. During the first few days of operation, Mr. Pierno transferred $15,000 from his personal account into a business account for a company he named Pierno Enterprises. Pierno Enterprises borrowed $20,000 from the State Bank of Renu. Mr. Pierno's father-in-law, Edward Goebel, invested $32,000 into the business for which he received a 25% ownership interest. Pierno Enterprises purchased a building from Stokes Realty Company. The building cost $60,000 cash. Pierno Enterprises earned $28,000 in revenue from the company's customers and paid its employees $17,000 for salaries expense.

Required
Identify the entities that were mentioned in the scenario and explain what happened to the cash accounts of each entity that you identify.

EXERCISE 1–4A *Financial Statement Elements and Accounts*

L.O. 3

Required
Write a brief memo that distinguishes between the *elements* of financial statements and the *accounts* that appear on financial statements.

EXERCISE 1–5A *Titles and Accounts Appearing on Financial Statements*

L.O. 3

Annual reports normally include an income statement, a statement of changes in stockholders' equity, a balance sheet, and a statement of cash flows.

Required

Identify the financial statements on which each of the following titles or accounts would appear. If a title or an account appears on more than one statement, list all statements that would include it.

a. Common Stock
b. Land
c. Ending Cash Balance
d. Beginning Cash Balance
e. Notes Payable
f. Retained Earnings
g. Revenue
h. Dividends
i. Financing Activities
j. Salary Expense

L.O. 4   EXERCISE 1–6A *Components of the Accounting Equation*

Required

The following three requirements are independent of each other.

a. James Auto Parts has assets of $9,100 and net assets of $6,500. What is the amount of liabilities? What is the amount of claims?
b. Best Candy, Inc., has liabilities of $2,400 and equity of $5,400. What is the amount of assets? What is the amount of net assets?
c. Sam's Dive Shop has assets of $49,200 and liabilities of $21,600. What is the amount of its equity? What is the amount of its net assets?

L.O. 4   EXERCISE 1–7A *Effect of Events on the Accounting Equation*

Sun Co. experienced the following events during 2006.

1. Acquired cash from the issue of common stock.
2. Provided services to clients for cash.
3. Borrowed cash.
4. Paid operating expenses with cash.
5. Paid a cash dividend to the stockholders.
6. Purchased land with cash.

Required

Explain how each of these events affect the accounting equation by writing the letter I for increase, the letter D for decrease, and NA for no effect under each of the components of the accounting equation. The first event is shown as an example.

| | | | | Stockholders' Equity | |
Event Number	Assets	= Liabilities	+	Common Stock	+ Retained Earnings
1	I	NA		I	NA

L.O. 4, 5   EXERCISE 1–8A *Effects of Issuing Stock*

Jeter Company was started in 2009 when it acquired $18,000 cash by issuing common stock. The cash acquisition was the only event that affected the business in 2009.

Required

Write an accounting equation, and record the effects of the stock issue under the appropriate general ledger account headings.

L.O. 4, 5   EXERCISE 1–9A *Effects of Borrowing*

South Pacific Company was started in 2007 when it issued a note to borrow $8,400 cash.

Required

Write an accounting equation, and record the effects of the borrowing transaction under the appropriate general ledger account headings.

EXERCISE 1–10A *Effects of Revenue, Expense, and Dividend Events*

L.O. 3, 4, 5, 8

Epps Company was started on January 1, 2005. During 2005, the company experienced the following three accounting events: (1) earned cash revenues of $13,500, (2) paid cash expenses of $8,600, and (3) paid a $1,000 cash dividend to its stockholders. These were the only events that affected the company during 2005.

Required

a. Write an accounting equation, and record the effects of each accounting event under the appropriate general ledger account headings.

b. Prepare an income statement for the 2005 accounting period and a balance sheet at the end of 2005 for Epps Company.

EXERCISE 1–11A *Classifying Items for the Statement of Cash Flows*

L.O. 3

Required

Indicate how each of the following would be classified on the statement of cash flows as operating activities (OA), investing activities (IA), financing activities (FA), or not applicable (NA).

a. Paid $4,000 cash for salary expense.

b. Borrowed $8,000 cash from First State Bank.

c. Received $30,000 cash from the issue of common stock.

d. Purchased land for $8,000 cash.

e. Performed services for $14,000 cash.

f. Paid $4,200 cash for utilities expense.

g. Sold land for $7,000 cash.

h. Paid a cash dividend of $1,000 to the stockholders.

i. Hired an accountant to keep the books.

j. Paid $3,000 cash on the loan from First State Bank.

EXERCISE 1–12A *Effect of Transactions on General Ledger Accounts*

L.O. 3, 4, 5, 6

At the beginning of 2004, Quick Service Company's accounting records had the following general ledger accounts and balances.

QUICK SERVICE COMPANY Accounting Equation								
Event	**Assets**		**=**	**Liabilities**	**+**	**Stockholders' Equity**		**Acct. Titles for RE**
	Cash	**Land**		**Notes Payable**		**Common Stock**	**Retained Earnings**	
Balance 1/1/2004	25,000	50,000		35,000		30,000	10,000	

Quick completed the following transactions during 2004:

1. Purchased land for $12,000 cash.

2. Acquired $20,000 cash from the issue of common stock.

3. Received $65,000 cash for providing services to customers.

4. Paid cash operating expenses of $42,000.

5. Paid $20,000 cash on notes payable.

6. Paid a $3,000 cash dividend to the stockholders.

7. Determined that the market value of the land is $72,000.

Required

a. Record the transactions in the appropriate general ledger accounts. Record the amounts of revenue, expense, and dividends in the Retained Earnings column. Provide the appropriate titles for these accounts in the last column of the table.

b. Determine the amount of net income for the 2004 period.

c. What is the amount of total assets at the end of 2004? What is the amount of net assets at the end of 2004?

L.O. 3, 4, 5, 6, 8   **EXERCISE 1–13A** *Preparing Financial Statements*

Dale Company experienced the following events during 2004.

1. Acquired $30,000 cash from the issue of common stock.
2. Paid $12,000 cash to purchase land.
3. Borrowed $8,000 cash.
4. Provided services for $20,000 cash.
5. Paid $1,000 cash for rent expense.
6. Paid $12,000 cash for other operating expenses.
7. Paid a $2,000 cash dividend to the stockholders.
8. Determined that the market value of the land purchased in Event 2 is now $12,700.

Required

a. The January 1, 2004, general ledger account balances are shown in the following accounting equation. Record the eight events in the appropriate general ledger accounts. Record the amounts of revenue, expense, and dividends in the Retained Earnings column. Provide the appropriate titles for
   these accounts in the last column of the table. The first event is shown as an example.

<table>
<tr><td colspan="9" align="center">DALE COMPANY
Accounting Equation</td></tr>
<tr><td rowspan="2">Event</td><td colspan="2" rowspan="2">Assets</td><td rowspan="2">=</td><td rowspan="2">Liabilities</td><td rowspan="2">+</td><td colspan="2" rowspan="2">Stockholders' Equity</td><td rowspan="2">Acct. Titles
for RE</td></tr>
<tr></tr>
<tr><td></td><td>Cash</td><td>Land</td><td></td><td>Notes
Payable</td><td></td><td>Common
Stock</td><td>Retained
Earnings</td><td></td></tr>
<tr><td>Balance
1/1/2004</td><td>2,000</td><td>16,000</td><td></td><td>0</td><td></td><td>10,000</td><td>8,000</td><td></td></tr>
<tr><td>1.</td><td>30,000</td><td></td><td></td><td></td><td></td><td>30,000</td><td></td><td></td></tr>
</table>

b. Prepare an income statement, statement of changes in equity, year-end balance sheet, and statement
   of cash flows for the 2004 accounting period.
c. Determine the percentage of assets that were provided by retained earnings. How much cash is in the
   retained earnings account?

L.O. 7   **EXERCISE 1–14A** *Classifying Events as Asset Source, Use, or Exchange*

Foster Company experienced the following events during its first year of operations.

1. Acquired $10,000 cash from the issue of common stock.
2. Borrowed $8,000 cash from First Bank.
3. Paid $4,000 cash to purchase land.
4. Received $5,000 cash for providing boarding services.
5. Acquired an additional $2,000 cash from the issue of common stock.
6. Purchased additional land for $3,500 cash.
7. Paid $2,500 cash for salary expenses.
8. Signed a contract to provide additional services in the future.
9. Paid $1,000 cash for rent expense.
10. Paid a $1,000 cash dividend to the stockholders.
11. Determined the market value of the land to be $8,000 at the end of the accounting period.

Required

Classify each event as an asset source, use, or exchange transaction or as not applicable (NA).

L.O. 4   **EXERCISE 1–15A** *Relationship between Assets and Retained Earnings*

Eastern Company was organized when it acquired $1,000 cash from the issue of common stock. During
its first accounting period the company earned $800 of cash revenue and incurred $500 of cash expenses.
Also, during the accounting period the company paid its owners a $100 cash dividend.

Required

a. Determine the amount of the retained earnings account.
b. As of the end of the accounting period, determine what percentage of total assets were provided by
   earnings.

EXERCISE 1–16A *Historical Cost Versus Market Value*

L.O. 6

Feloma Company purchased land in April 2001 at a cost of $520,000. The estimated market value of the land is $600,000 as of December 31, 2004. Feloma purchased marketable equity securities (bought the common stock of a company that is independent of Feloma) in May 2001 at a cost of $320,000. These securities have a market value of $360,000 as of December 31, 2004. Generally accepted accounting principles require that the land be shown on the December 31, 2004 balance sheet at $520,000, while the marketable equity securities are required to be reported at $360,000.

Required

Write a brief memo that explains the contradiction regarding why GAAP requires Feloma to report historical cost with respect to the land versus market value with respect to the marketable securities. This answer may require speculation on your part. Use your knowledge about the historical cost and reliability concepts to formulate a logical response.

EXERCISE 1–17A *Relating Accounting Events to Entities*

L.O. 2, 7

Hanson Company was started in 2004 when it acquired $50,000 cash by issuing common stock to Michael Hanson.

Required

a. Was this event an asset source, use, or exchange transaction for Hanson Company?
b. Was this event an asset source, use, or exchange transaction for Michael Hanson?
c. Was the cash flow an operating, investing, or financing activity on Hanson Company's 2004 statement of cash flows?
d. Was the cash flow an operating, investing, or financing activity on Michael Hanson's 2004 statement of cash flows?

EXERCISE 1–18A *Missing Information in the Accounting Equation*

L.O. 4

Required

Calculate the missing amounts in the following table:

					Stockholders' Equity		
Company	Assets	=	Liabilities	+	Common Stock	+	Retained Earnings
A	$?		$48,000		$52,000		$36,000
B	90,000		?		25,000		40,000
C	87,000		15,000		?		37,000
D	102,000		29,000		42,000		?

EXERCISE 1–19A *Missing Information in the Accounting Equation*

L.O. 4

As of December 31, 2002, Thomas Company had total assets of $156,000, total liabilities of $85,600, and common stock of $48,400. During 2003 Thomas earned $36,000 of cash revenue, paid $22,000 for cash expenses, and paid a $1,000 cash dividend to the stockholders.

Required

a. Determine the amount of retained earnings as of December 31, 2002.
b. Determine the amount of net income earned in 2003.
c. Determine the amount of retained earnings as of December 31, 2003.
d. Determine the amount of cash that is in the retained earnings account as of December 31, 2003.

EXERCISE 1–20A *Missing Information for Determining Net Income*

L.O. 3, 4

The December 31, 2006, balance sheet for Kerr Company showed total stockholders' equity of $62,500. Total stockholders' equity increased by $53,400 between December 31, 2006, and December 31, 2007. During 2007 Kerr Company acquired $11,000 cash from the issue of common stock. Kerr Company paid an $8,000 cash dividend to the stockholders during 2007.

Required

Determine the amount of net income or loss Kerr reported on its 2007 income statement. (*Hint:* Remember that stock issues, net income, and dividends all change total stockholders' equity.)

L.O. 6, 9 **EXERCISE 1–21A** *Effect of Events on a Horizontal Financial Statements Model*

Hayes Consulting Services experienced the following events during 2006.

1. Acquired cash by issuing common stock.
2. Collected cash for providing tutoring services to clients.
3. Borrowed cash from a local government small business foundation.
4. Purchased land for cash.
5. Paid cash for operating expenses.
6. Paid a cash dividend to the stockholders.
7. Determined that the market value of the land is higher than its historical cost.

Required

Use a horizontal statements model to show how each event affects the balance sheet, income statement, and statement of cash flows. Indicate whether the event increases (I), decreases (D), or does not affect (NA) each element of the financial statements. Also, in the Cash Flows column, classify the cash flows as operating activities (OA), investing activities (IA), or financing activities (FA). The first transaction is shown as an example.

Event No.	Balance Sheet											Income Statement						Statement of Cash Flows
	Cash	+	Land	=	N. Pay	+	C. Stock.	+	Ret. Ear.			Rev.	−	Exp.	=	Net Inc.		
1.	I	+	NA	=	NA	+	I	+	NA			NA	−	NA	=	NA		I FA

L.O. 3, 9 **EXERCISE 1–22A** *Record Events in the Horizontal Statements Model*

Marshall Co. was started in 2004. During 2004, the company (1) acquired $9,000 cash from the issue of common stock, (2) earned cash revenue of $18,000, (3) paid cash expenses of $12,500, and (4) paid a $1,000 cash dividend to the stockholders.

Required

a. Record these four events in a horizontal statements model. Also, in the Cash Flows column, classify the cash flows as operating activities (OA), investing activities (IA), or financing activities (FA). The first event is shown as an example.

Event No.	Balance Sheet							Income Statement						Statement of Cash Flows
	Cash	=	N. Pay	+	C. Stock.	+	Ret. Ear.	Rev.	−	Exp.	=	Net Inc.		
1.	9,000	=	NA	+	9,000	+	NA	NA	−	NA	=	NA		9,000 FA

b. What does the income statement tell you about the assets of this business?

L.O. 6, 9 **EXERCISE 1–23A** *Effect of Events on a Horizontal Statements Model*

Tax Help, Inc., was started on January 1, 2004. The company experienced the following events during its first year of operation.

1. Acquired $30,000 cash from the issue of common stock.
2. Paid $12,000 cash to purchase land.
3. Received $30,000 cash for providing tax services to customers.
4. Paid $9,500 cash for salary expenses.
5. Acquired $5,000 cash from the issue of additional common stock.
6. Borrowed $10,000 cash from the bank.
7. Purchased additional land for $5,000 cash.
8. Paid $6,000 cash for other operating expenses.
9. Paid a $2,800 cash dividend to the stockholders.
10. Determined that the market value of the land is $18,000.

Required

a. Record these events in a horizontal statements model. Also, in the Cash Flows column, classify the cash flows as operating activities (OA), investing activities (IA), or financing activities (FA). The first event is shown as an example.

Event	Balance Sheet											Income Statement						Statement of Cash Flows	
No.	Cash	+	Land	=	N. Pay	+	C. Stock.	+	Ret. Ear.			Rev.	–	Exp.	=	Net Inc.			
1.	30,000	+	NA	=	NA	+	30,000	+	NA			NA	–	NA	=	NA		30,000	FA

b. What is the net income earned in 2004?

c. What is the amount of total assets at the end of 2004?

d. What is the net cash flow from operating activities for 2004?

e. What is the net cash flow from investing activities for 2004?

f. What is the net cash flow from financing activities for 2004?

g. What is the cash balance at the end of 2004?

h. As of the end of the year 2004, what percentage of total assets were provided by creditors, investors, and earnings?

EXERCISE 1–24A *Types of Transactions and the Horizontal Statements Model*   **L.O. 6, 7, 9**

The Shoe Shop experienced the following events during its first year of operations, 2008.

1. Acquired cash by issuing common stock.
2. Provided services and collected cash.
3. Borrowed cash from a bank.
4. Paid cash for operating expenses.
5. Purchased land with cash.
6. Paid a cash dividend to the stockholders.
7. Determined that the market value of the land is higher than the historical cost.

Required

a. Indicate whether each event is an asset source, use, or exchange transaction.

b. Use a horizontal statements model to show how each event affects the balance sheet, income statement, and statement of cash flows. Indicate whether the event increases (I), decreases (D), or does not affect (NA) each element of the financial statements. Also, in the Cash Flows column, classify the cash flows as operating activities (OA), investing activities (IA), or financing activities (FA). The first transaction is shown as an example.

Event	Balance Sheet											Income Statement						Statement of Cash Flows	
No.	Cash	+	Land	=	N. Pay	+	C. Stock.	+	Ret. Ear.			Rev.	–	Exp.	=	Net Inc.			
1.	I	+	NA	=	NA	+	I	+	NA			NA	–	NA	=	NA		I	FA

EXERCISE 1–25A *Price-Earnings Ratio*   **L.O. 10**

The following information is available for two companies.

	Henry Company	Pager Company
Earnings per share	$ 1.05	$ 4.50
Market price per share	38.50	108.00

Required

a. Compute the price-earnings ratio for each company.

b. Explain why one company would have a higher price-earnings ratio than the other.

PROBLEMS—SERIES A

All Problems in Series A are available with McGraw-Hill's Homework Manager

PROBLEM 1–26A *Accounting's Role in Not-for-Profits*   **L.O. 1**

Charles Robertson is struggling to pass his introductory accounting course. Charles is intelligent but he likes to party. Studying is a low priority for Charles. When one of his friends tells him that he is going to have trouble in business if he doesn't learn accounting, Charles responds that he doesn't plan to go into business. He says that he is arts oriented and plans someday to be a director of a museum. He is in the school of business to develop his social skills, not his quantitative skills. Charles says he won't have to worry about accounting, since museums are not intended to make a profit.

Required
a. Write a brief memo explaining whether you agree or disagree with Charles's position regarding accounting and not-for-profit organizations.
b. Distinguish between financial accounting and managerial accounting.
c. Identify some of the stakeholders of not-for-profit institutions that would expect to receive financial accounting reports.
d. Identify some of the stakeholders of not-for-profit institutions that would expect to receive managerial accounting reports.

L.O. 2   **PROBLEM 1–27A** *Accounting Entities*

The following business scenarios are independent from one another.

1. Tilly Jensen starts a business by transferring $5,000 from her personal checking account into a checking account for the business.
2. A business that Bart Angle owns earns $2,300 of cash revenue.
3. Phil Culver borrows $20,000 from the National Bank and uses the money to purchase a car from Henderson Ford.
4. Lipka Company pays its five employees $2,000 each to cover their salaries.
5. Kevin Dow loans his son Brian $5,000 cash.
6. Asthana, Inc. paid $150,000 cash to purchase land from Waterbury, Inc.
7. Moshe Liu and Chao Porat form a partnership by contributing $30,000 each from their personal bank accounts to a partnership bank account.
8. Ken Stanga pays cash to purchase $2,000 of common stock that is issued by Krishnan, Inc.
9. Omni Company pays a $42,000 cash dividend to each of its seven shareholders.
10. McCann, Inc. borrowed $5,000,000 from the National Bank.

Required
a. For each scenario create a list of all of the entities that are mentioned in the description.
b. Describe what happens to the cash account of each entity that you identified in Requirement *a*.

L.O. 3   **PROBLEM 1–28A** *Relating Titles and Accounts to Financial Statements*

Required
Identify the financial statements on which each of the following items (titles, date descriptions, and accounts) appears by placing a check mark in the appropriate column. If an item appears on more than one statement, place a check mark in every applicable column.

Item	Income Statement	Statement of Changes in Stockholders' Equity	Balance Sheet	Statement of Cash Flows
Notes payable				
Beginning common stock				
Service revenue				
Utility expense				
Cash from stock issue				
Operating activities				
For the period ended (date)				
Net income				
Investing activities				
Net loss				
Ending cash balance				

continued

Item	Income Statement	Statement of Changes in Stockholders' Equity	Balance Sheet	Statement of Cash Flows
Salary expense				
Consulting revenue				
Dividends				
Financing activities				
Ending common stock				
Interest expense				
As of (date)				
Land				
Beginning cash balance				

PROBLEM 1–29A *Preparing Financial Statements for Two Complete Accounting Cycles*

Keller Consulting experienced the following transactions for 2006, its first year of operations, and 2007. *Assume that all transactions involve the receipt or payment of cash.*

Transactions for 2006
1. Acquired $20,000 by issuing common stock.
2. Received $65,000 cash for providing services to customers.
3. Borrowed $25,000 cash from creditors.
4. Paid expenses amounting to $42,000.
5. Purchased land for $30,000 cash.

Transactions for 2007
Beginning account balances for 2007 are:

Cash	$38,000
Land	30,000
Notes Payable	25,000
Common Stock	20,000
Retained Earnings	23,000

1. Acquired an additional $24,000 from the issue of common stock.
2. Received $95,000 for providing services.
3. Paid $10,000 to creditors to reduce loan.
4. Paid expenses amounting to $71,500.
5. Paid a $6,000 dividend to the stockholders.
6. Determined that the market value of the land is $47,000.

Required
a. Write an accounting equation, and record the effects of each accounting event under the appropriate headings for each year. Record the amounts of revenue, expense, and dividends in the Retained Earnings column. Provide appropriate titles for these accounts in the last column of the table.
b. Prepare an income statement, statement of changes in stockholders' equity, year-end balance sheet, and statement of cash flows for each year.
c. Determine the amount of cash that is in the retained earnings account at the end of 2006 and 2007.
d. Examine the balance sheets for the two years. How did assets change from 2006 to 2007?
e. Determine the percentage growth in net earnings from 2006 to 2007. Based on the data shown in Exhibit 1–7, is this a high-, medium-, or low-growth company?

PROBLEM 1–30A *Interrelationships among Financial Statements*

O'Shea Enterprises started the 2002 accounting period with $30,000 of assets (all cash), $18,000 of liabilities, and $4,000 of common stock. During the year, O'Shea earned cash revenues of $48,000, paid cash expenses of $32,000, and paid a cash dividend to stockholders of $2,000. O'Shea also acquired

L.O. 3, 4, 5, 6, 8

www.mhhe.com/edmonds5e

CHECK FIGURES
a. Net Income 2006: $23,000
b. Retained Earnings 2007: $40,500

L.O. 3, 5, 8

$10,000 of additional cash from the sale of common stock and paid $6,000 cash to reduce the liability owed to a bank.

Required

a. Prepare an income statement, statement of changes in stockholders' equity, period-end balance sheet, and statement of cash flows for the 2002 accounting period. (*Hint:* Determine the amount of beginning retained earnings before considering the effects of the current period events. It also might help to record all events under an accounting equation before preparing the statements.)

b. Determine the percentage of total assets that were provided by creditors, investors, and earnings.

L.O. 4, 7   **PROBLEM 1–31A** *Classifying Events as Asset Source, Use, or Exchange*

The following unrelated events are typical of those experienced by business entities.

1. Acquire cash by issuing common stock.
2. Purchase land with cash.
3. Purchase equipment with cash.
4. Pay monthly rent on an office building.
5. Hire a new office manager.
6. Borrow cash from a bank.
7. Pay a cash dividend to stockholders.
8. Pay cash for operating expenses.
9. Pay an office manager's salary with cash.
10. Receive cash for services that have been performed.
11. Provide services for cash.
12. Acquire land by accepting a liability (financing the purchase).
13. Pay cash to purchase a new office building.
14. Discuss plans for a new office building with an architect.
15. Repay part of a bank loan.

Required

Identify each of the events as an asset source, use, or exchange transaction. If an event would not be recorded under generally accepted accounting principles, identify it as *not applicable* (NA). Also indicate for each event whether total assets would increase, decrease, or remain unchanged. Organize your answer according to the following table. The first event is shown in the table as an example.

Event No.	Type of Event	Effect on Total Assets
1	Asset source	Increase

L.O. 6, 9   **PROBLEM 1–32A** *Recording the Effect of Events in a Horizontal Statements Model*

Lighthouse Services experienced the following transactions during 2006.

1. Acquired cash by issuing common stock.
2. Received cash for performing services.
3. Paid cash expenses.
4. Borrowed cash from the local bank.
5. Purchased land for cash.
6. Paid cash to reduce the principal balance of the bank loan.
7. Paid a cash dividend to the stockholders.
8. Determined that the market value of the land is higher than its historical cost.

Required

Use a horizontal statements model to show how each event affects the balance sheet, income statement, and statement of cash flows. Indicate whether the event increases (I), decreases (D), or does not affect (NA) each element of the financial statements. Also, in the Cash Flows column, classify the cash flows as operating activities (OA), investing activities (IA), or financing activities (FA). The first transaction is shown as an example.

Event No.	Balance Sheet								Income Statement					Statement of Cash Flows
	Cash	+	Land	=	N. Pay	+	C. Stock.	+	Ret. Ear.	Rev.	−	Exp.	= Net Inc.	
1.	I	+	NA	=	NA	+	I	+	NA	NA	−	NA	= NA	I FA

PROBLEM 1–33A *Recording Events in a Horizontal Statements Model*

L.O. 4, 6, 9

CHECK FIGURES
a. Net Income: $13,000
e. Net Cash Flow from Operating
   Activities: $13,000

Flick Company was started on January 1, 2003, and experienced the following events during its first year of operation.

1. Acquired $30,000 cash from the issue of common stock.
2. Borrowed $20,000 cash from State Bank.
3. Earned cash revenues of $48,000 for performing services.
4. Paid cash expenses of $35,000.
5. Paid a $4,000 cash dividend to the stockholders.
6. Acquired an additional $20,000 cash from the issue of common stock.
7. Paid $5,000 cash to reduce the principal balance of the bank note.
8. Paid $53,000 cash to purchase land.
9. Determined that the market value of the land is $60,000.

Required

a. Record the preceding transactions in the horizontal statements model. Also, in the Cash Flows column, classify the cash flows as operating activities (OA), investing activities (IA), or financing activities (FA). The first event is shown as an example.

Event No.	Balance Sheet											Income Statement						Statement of Cash Flows	
	Cash	+	Land	=	N. Pay	+	C. Stock.	+	Ret. Ear.			Rev.	–	Exp.	=	Net Inc.			
1.	30,000	+	NA	=	NA	+	30,000	+	NA			NA	–	NA	=	NA		30,000	FA

b. Determine the amount of total assets that Flick would report on the December 31, 2003, balance sheet.
c. Identify the sources of the assets that Flick would report on the December 31, 2003, balance sheet. Determine the amount of each of these sources.
d. Determine the net income that Flick would report on the 2003 income statement. Explain why dividends do not appear on the income statement.
e. Determine the net cash flows from operating activities, financing activities, and investing activities that Flick would report on the 2003 statement of cash flows.
f. Determine the percentage of assets that were provided by investors, creditors, and earnings.

PROBLEM 1–34A *Price-Earnings Relationships*

L.O. 10

Earnings per share and market price per share data for Advantage, Inc., and Hi-Lite, Inc., follow.

Advantage, Inc.	2005	2006	2007
Earnings per share	$ 4.22	$ 4.13	$ 4.18
Market price per share	50.64	45.43	45.98

Hi-Lite, Inc.	2005	2006	2007
Earnings per share	$ 3.27	$ 4.19	$ 5.81
Market price per share	98.10	129.89	220.78

CHECK FIGURE
b. Advantage, Inc. 2005 P/E
   ratio: 12
   Hi-Lite, Inc. 2007 P/E ratio: 38

Required

a. Calculate the annual percentage growth rate in the earnings per share of each company from 2005 to 2006 and from 2006 to 2007.
b. Calculate the price-earnings ratio for each company for all three years.
c. Explain what the price-earnings ratio means.
d. Why would the price-earnings ratios of the two companies be different?

EXERCISES—SERIES B

EXERCISE 1–1B *Identifying Resources*

L.O. 1

Resource owners provide three types of resources to conversion agents that transform the resources into products or services that satisfy consumer demands.

Required

Identify the three types of resources. Write a brief memo explaining how resource owners select the particular conversion agents to which they will provide resources.

L.O. 2   EXERCISE 1–2B *Distributions in a Business Liquidation*

Assume that Clark Company acquires $800 cash from creditors and $900 cash from investors. The company then has operating losses of $600 cash and goes out of business.

Required
a. Explain the primary differences between investors and creditors.
b. What amount of cash will Clark's creditors receive?
c. What amount of cash will Clark's investors (stockholders) receive?

L.O. 2   EXERCISE 1–3B *Identifying the Reporting Entities*

Wonda DeLeo helped organize a charity fund to help cover the medical expenses of a friend of hers who was seriously injured in a bicycle accident. The fund was named Gloria Novin Recovery Fund (GNRF). Wonda contributed $500 of her own money to the fund. The $500 was paid to WRCK, a local radio station that designed and played an advertising campaign to educate the public as to the need for help. The campaign resulted in the collection of $12,000 cash. GNRF paid $10,000 to the Hillsboro Hospital to cover Gloria's outstanding hospital cost. The remaining $2,000 was contributed to the National Cyclist Fund.

Required
Identify the entities that were mentioned in the scenario and explain what happened to the cash accounts of each entity that you identify.

L.O. 3   EXERCISE 1–4B *Financial Statement Names*

Accounting reports that are issued to the public normally contain four financial statements. The same statement may have more than one name.

Required
Provide two names that are commonly used for each statement. If a statement has only one name, indicate that this is the case.

L.O. 3   EXERCISE 1–5B *Titles and Accounts Appearing on Financial Statements*

Annual reports normally include an income statement, statement of changes in equity, balance sheet, and statement of cash flows.

Required
Identify the financial statements on which each of the following titles or accounts would appear. If a title or an account appears on more than one statement, list all statements that would include it.

a. Retained Earnings
b. Revenue
c. Common Stock
d. Financing Activities
e. Salaries Expense
f. Land
g. Ending Cash Balance
h. Beginning Cash Balance
i. Notes Payable
j. Dividends

L.O. 4   EXERCISE 1–6B *Components of the Accounting Equation*

Required
The following three requirements are independent of each other.

a. Jackson Camping Supplies has assets of $8,500 and net assets of $3,200. What is the amount of liabilities? What is the amount of claims?
b. Betty's Snow Cones has liabilities of $2,400 and equity of $4,400. What is the amount of its assets? What is the amount of its net assets?
c. Petrello Company has assets of $98,300 and liabilities of $56,200. What is the amount of its equity? What is the amount of its residual interest?

EXERCISE 1–7B *Effect of Events on the Accounting Equation*

L.O. 4

Olive Enterprises experienced the following events during 2007.

1. Acquired cash from the issue of common stock.
2. Paid cash to reduce the principal on a bank note.
3. Sold land for cash at an amount equal to its cost.
4. Provided services to clients for cash.
5. Paid utilities expenses with cash.
6. Paid a cash dividend to the stockholders.

Required
Explain how each of the events would affect the accounting equation by writing the letter I for increase, the letter D for decrease, and NA for no effect under each of the components of the accounting equation. The first event is shown as an example.

Event Number	Assets	=	Liabilities	+	Stockholders' Equity Common Stock	+	Retained Earnings
1	I		NA		I		NA

EXERCISE 1–8B *Effects of Issuing Stock*

L.O. 3

Lambena Company was started in 2002 when it acquired $24,000 cash by issuing common stock. The cash acquisition was the only event that affected the business in 2002.

Required
Which financial statements would be affected by this event?

EXERCISE 1–9B *Effects of Borrowing*

L.O. 3

Southern Pacific Company was started in 2003 when it borrowed $19,500 from National Bank.

Required
Which financial statements would be affected by this event?

EXERCISE 1–10B *Effects of Revenue, Expense, and Dividend Events*

L.O. 3, 4, 5, 8

Kim Company was started on January 1, 2004. During 2004, the company completed three accounting events: (1) earned cash revenues of $12,500, (2) paid cash expenses of $8,600, and (3) paid a $1,000 cash dividend to the owner. These were the only events that affected the company during 2004.

Required
a. Write an accounting equation, and record the effects of each accounting event under the appropriate general ledger account headings.
b. Prepare an income statement for the 2004 accounting period and a balance sheet at the end of 2004 for Kim Company.

EXERCISE 1–11B *Classifying Items for the Statement of Cash Flows*

L.O. 3

Required
Indicate how each of the following would be classified on the statement of cash flows as operating activities (OA), investing activities (IA), financing activities (FA), or not applicable (NA).

a. Borrowed $8,000 cash from First State Bank.
b. Paid $5,000 cash for salary expense.
c. Signed a contract to provide services in the future.
d. Performed services for $25,000 cash.
e. Paid $9,000 cash to purchase land.
f. Paid $1,500 cash for utilities expense.
g. Sold land for $5,000 cash.
h. Paid $4,000 cash on the principal of a bank loan.
i. Paid a $2,000 cash dividend to the stockholders.
j. Received $30,000 cash from the issue of common stock.

L.O. 3, 4, 5, 6   **EXERCISE 1–12B** *Effect of Transactions on General Ledger Accounts*

At the beginning of 2001, Pete's Pest Control's accounting records had the following general ledger accounts and balances.

PETE'S PEST CONTROL **Accounting Equation**								
Event	**Assets**		**=**	**Liabilities**	**+**	**Stockholders' Equity**		**Acct. Titles for RE**
	Cash	**Land**		**Notes Payable**		**Common Stock**	**Retained Earnings**	
Balance 1/1/2001	15,000	20,000		15,000		7,000	13,000	

Pete's completed the following transactions during 2001.

1. Purchased land for $5,000 cash.
2. Acquired $25,000 cash from the issue of common stock.
3. Received $65,000 cash for providing services to customers.
4. Paid cash operating expenses of $42,000.
5. Borrowed $10,000 cash from the bank.
6. Paid a $2,500 cash dividend to the stockholders.
7. Determined that the market value of the land is $30,000.

Required

a. Record the transactions in the appropriate general ledger accounts. Record the amounts of revenue, expense, and dividends in the Retained Earnings column. Provide the appropriate titles for these accounts in the last column of the table.
b. Determine the net cash flow from financing activities.
c. What is the balance in the Retained Earnings Accounts as of January 1, 2002?

L.O. 3, 4, 5, 6, 8   **EXERCISE 1–13B** *Preparing Financial Statements*

J & A, Inc., experienced the following events during 2004.

1. Acquired $55,000 cash from the issue of common stock.
2. Paid $15,000 cash to purchase land.
3. Borrowed $5,000 cash from First Bank.
4. Provided services for $21,000 cash.
5. Paid $1,500 cash for utilities expense.
6. Paid $11,000 cash for other operating expenses.
7. Paid a $2,000 cash dividend to the stockholders.
8. Determined that the market value of the land purchased in Event 2 is $20,000.

Required

a. The January 1, 2004, general ledger account balances are shown in the following accounting equation. Record the eight events in the appropriate general ledger accounts. Record the amounts of revenue, expense, and dividends in the Retained Earnings column. Provide the appropriate titles for these accounts in the last column of the table. The first event is shown as an example.

J & A, INC. **Accounting Equation**								
Event	**Assets**		**=**	**Liabilities**	**+**	**Stockholders' Equity**		**Acct. Titles for RE**
	Cash	**Land**		**Notes Payable**		**Common Stock**	**Retained Earnings**	
Balance 1/1/2004	12,000	20,000		0		15,000	17,000	
1.	55,000					55,000		

b. Prepare an income statement, statement of changes in stockholders' equity, year-end balance sheet, and statement of cash flows for the 2004 accounting period.

c. Determine the percentage of assets that were provided by retained earnings. How much cash is in the retained earnings account?

EXERCISE 1–14B *Classifying Events as Asset Source, Use, or Exchange*   L.O. 7

Hill Company experienced the following events during its first year of operations.

1. Acquired $8,000 cash from the issue of common stock.
2. Paid $3,500 cash for salary expenses.
3. Borrowed $10,000 cash from New South Bank.
4. Paid $6,000 cash to purchase land.
5. Provided boarding services for $6,500 cash.
6. Acquired an additional $1,000 cash from the issue of common stock.
7. Paid $1,200 cash for utilities expense.
8. Paid a $1,500 cash dividend to the stockholders.
9. Provided additional services for $3,000 cash.
10. Purchased additional land for $2,500 cash.
11. The market value of the land was determined to be $12,000 at the end of the accounting period.

Required

Classify each event as an asset source, use, or exchange transaction.

EXERCISE 1–15B *Financial Statement Elements*   L.O. 3

Western Company was organized by issuing $550 of common stock and by borrowing $250. During the accounting period, the company earned and retained $200. Also during the accounting period, the company purchased land for $950.

Required

a. What asset accounts would appear on the company's balance sheet? What are the balance sheet amounts in these accounts?

b. Determine the percentage of total assets that were provided by investors, creditors, and earnings.

c. How much cash is in the retained earnings account?

EXERCISE 1 16B *Historical Cost versus Market Value*   L.O. 6

ACCO, Inc. purchased land in January 2004 at a cost of $230,000. The estimated market value of the land is $270,000 as of December 31, 2006.

Required

a. Name the December 31, 2006, financial statement(s) on which the land will be shown.

b. At what dollar amount will the land be shown in the financial statement(s)?

c. Name the key concept that will be used in determining the dollar amount that will be reported for land that is shown in the financial statement(s).

EXERCISE 1–17B *Relating Accounting Events to Entities*   L.O. 2, 7

Jackling Company sold land for $50,000 cash to Power Company in 2004.

Required

a. Was this event an asset source, use, or exchange transaction for Jackling Company?

b. Was this event an asset source, use, or exchange transaction for Power Company?

c. Was the cash flow an operating, investing, or financing activity on Jackling Company's 2004 statement of cash flows?

d. Was the cash flow an operating, investing, or financing activity on Power Company's 2004 statement of cash flows?

L.O. 4 **EXERCISE 1–18B** *Missing Information in the Accounting Equation*

Required
Calculate the missing amounts in the following table.

Company	Assets	=	Liabilities	+	Common Stock	+	Retained Earnings
					Stockholders' Equity		
A	$?		$25,000		$48,000		$25,000
B	50,000		?		15,000		30,000
C	75,000		20,000		?		42,000
D	125,000		45,000		75,000		?

L.O. 4 **EXERCISE 1–19B** *Missing Information in the Accounting Equation*

As of December 31, 2004, Stone Company had total assets of $132,000, retained earnings of $74,300, and common stock of $45,000. During 2005 Stone earned $42,000 of cash revenue, paid $21,500 for cash expenses, and paid a $600 cash dividend to the stockholders. Stone also paid $5,000 to reduce its debt during 2005.

Required
a. Determine the amount of liabilities at December 31, 2004.
b. Determine the amount of net income earned in 2005.
c. Determine the amount of total assets as of December 31, 2005.
d. Determine the amount of total liabilities as of December 31, 2005.

L.O. 3, 4 **EXERCISE 1–20B** *Missing Information for Determining Revenue*

Total stockholders' equity of Zullo Company increased by $46,500 between December 31, 2005, and December 31, 2006. During 2006 Zullo acquired $15,000 cash from the issue of common stock. The company paid a $5,000 cash dividend to the stockholders during 2006. Total expenses during 2006 amounted to $22,000.

Required
Determine the amount of revenue that Zullo reported on its 2006 income statement. (*Hint:* Remember that stock issues, net income, and dividends all change total stockholders' equity.)

L.O. 6, 9 **EXERCISE 1–21B** *Effect of Events on a Horizontal Financial Statements Model*

Lourens Auto Repair, Inc., experienced the following events during 2007.

1. Purchased land for cash.
2. Issued common stock for cash.
3. Collected cash for providing auto repair services to customers.
4. Paid a cash dividend to the stockholders.
5. Paid cash for operating expenses.
6. Paid cash to reduce the principal balance on a liability.
7. Determined that the market value of the land is higher than its historical cost.

Required
Use a horizontal statements model to show how each event affects the balance sheet, income statement, and statement of cash flows. Indicate whether the event increases (I), decreases (D), or does not affect (NA) each element of the financial statements. Also, in the Cash Flows column, classify the cash flows as operating activities (OA), investing activities (IA), or financing activities (FA). The first transaction is shown as an example.

Event No.	Balance Sheet									Income Statement					Statement of Cash Flows
	Cash	+	Land	=	N. Pay	+	C. Stock.	+	Ret. Ear.	Rev.	−	Exp.	=	Net Inc.	
1.	D	+	I	=	NA	+	NA	+	NA	NA	−	NA	=	NA	D IA

EXERCISE 1–22B *Record Events in the Horizontal Statements Model*   **L.O. 3, 9**

Eaton Boat Repairs was started in 2002. During 2002, the company (1) acquired $9,000 cash from the issue of common stock, (2) earned cash revenue of $22,000, (3) paid cash expenses of $12,800, and (4) paid an $800 cash dividend to the stockholders.

Required
a. Record these four events in a horizontal statements model. Also, in the Cash Flows column, classify the cash flows as operating activities (OA), investing activities (IA), or financing activities (FA). The first event is shown as an example.

Event No.	Cash	=	N. Pay	+	C. Stock.	+	Ret. Ear.	Rev.	−	Exp.	=	Net Inc.	Statement of Cash Flows
		Balance Sheet							**Income Statement**				
1.	9,000	=	NA	+	9,000	+	NA	NA	−	NA	=	NA	9,000 FA

b. Why is the net income different from the net increase in cash for this business?

EXERCISE 1–23B *Effect of Events on a Horizontal Statements Model*   **L.O. 6, 9**

Joyce Higgins started Computer Software Services on January 1, 2006. The company experienced the following events during its first year of operation.

1. Acquired $20,000 cash by issuing common stock.
2. Paid $5,000 cash to purchase land.
3. Received $32,000 cash for providing computer consulting services to customers.
4. Paid $12,500 cash for salary expenses.
5. Acquired $4,000 cash from the issue of additional common stock.
6. Borrowed $15,000 cash from the bank.
7. Purchased additional land for $15,000 cash.
8. Paid $14,000 cash for other operating expenses.
9. Paid a $2,500 cash dividend to the stockholders.
10. Determined that the market value of the land is $18,000.

Required
a. Record these events in a horizontal statements model. Also, in the Cash Flows column, classify the cash flows as operating activities (OA), investing activities (IA), or financing activities (FA). The first event is shown as an example.

Event No.	Cash	+	Land	=	N. Pay	+	C. Stock.	+	Ret. Ear.	Rev.	−	Exp.	=	Net Inc.	Statement of Cash Flows
1.	20,000	+	NA	=	NA	+	20,000	+	NA	NA	−	NA	=	NA	20,000 FA

b. What is the net income earned in 2006?
c. What is the amount of total assets at the end of 2006?
d. What is the net cash flow from operating activities for 2006?
e. What is the net cash flow from investing activities for 2006?
f. What is the net cash flow from financing activities for 2006?
g. What is the cash balance at the end of 2006?
h. As of the end of the year 2006, what percentage of total assets were provided by creditors, investors, and earnings?

EXERCISE 1–24B *Types of Transactions and the Horizontal Statements Model*   **L.O. 6, 7, 9**

Computer Parts experienced the following events during its first year of operations, 2007.

1. Acquired cash by issuing common stock.
2. Purchased land with cash.
3. Borrowed cash from a bank.
4. Signed a contract to provide services in the future.
5. Paid a cash dividend to the stockholders.
6. Paid cash for operating expenses.
7. Determined that the market value of the land is higher than the historical cost.

Required

a. Indicate whether each event is an asset source, use, or exchange transaction.

b. Use a horizontal statements model to show how each event affects the balance sheet, income statement, and statement of cash flows. Indicate whether the event increases (I), decreases (D), or does not affect (NA) each element of the financial statements. Also, in the Cash Flows column, classify the cash flows as operating activities (OA), investing activities (IA), or financing activities (FA). The first transaction is shown as an example.

Event No.	Balance Sheet											Income Statement						Statement of Cash Flows
	Cash	+	Land	=	N. Pay	+	C. Stock.	+	Ret. Ear.			Rev.	–	Exp.	=	Net Inc.		
1.	I	+	NA	=	NA	+	I	+	NA			NA	–	NA	=	NA		I FA

L.O. 10   EXERCISE 1–25B *Price-Earnings Ratio*

The following information is available for two companies:

	ARC Company	Pager Company
Earnings per share	$ 0.85	$ 2.25
Market price per share	46.50	75.40

Required

a. Compute the price-earnings ratio for each company.

b. Which company would you expect to have the higher earnings growth potential?

PROBLEMS—SERIES B

L.O. 1   PROBLEM 1–26B *Applying GAAP to Financial Reporting*

Kim Verhaeghe is a business consultant. She analyzed the business processes of one of her clients, Rector Companies, in November 2005. She prepared a report containing her recommendation for changes in some of the company's business practices. She presented Rector with the report in December 2005. Kim guarantees that her clients will save money by following her advice. She does not collect for the services she provides until the client is satisfied with the results of her work. In this case she received cash payment from Rector in February 2006.

Required

a. Define the acronym GAAP.

b. Assume that Kim's accountant tells her that GAAP permits Kim to recognize the revenue from Rector in either 2005 or 2006. What GAAP rule would justify reporting the same event in two different ways? Write a brief memo explaining the logic behind this rule.

c. If Kim were keeping records for managerial reporting purposes, would she be bound by GAAP rules? Write a brief memo to explain how GAAP applies to financial versus managerial reporting.

L.O. 2   PROBLEM 1–27B *Accounting Entities*

The following business scenarios are independent from one another.

1. Mary Poort purchased an automobile from Hayney Bros. Auto Sales for $9,000.
2. John Rodman loaned $15,000 to the business in which he is a stockholder.
3. First State Bank paid interest to Caleb Co. on a certificate of deposit that Caleb Co. has invested at First State Bank.
4. Parkside Restaurant paid the current utility bill of $128 to Gulf Utilities.
5. Gatemore, Inc. borrowed $50,000 from City National Bank and used the funds to purchase land from Morgan Realty.
6. Steven Wong purchased $10,000 of common stock of International Sales Corporation from the corporation.
7. Dan Dow loaned $4,000 cash to his daughter.
8. Mega Service Co. earned $5,000 in cash revenue.

9. McCloud Co. paid $1,500 for salaries to each of its four employees.

10. Shim Inc. paid a cash dividend of $3,000 to its sole shareholder, Marcus Shim.

Required

a. For each scenario, create a list of all of the entities that are mentioned in the description.

b. Describe what happens to the cash account of each entity that you identified in Requirement *a*.

PROBLEM 1–28B *Relating Titles and Accounts to Financial Statements*

L.O. 3

A random list of various financial statements components follows: (1) Retained Earnings account ending balance, (2) revenues, (3) Common Stock account beginning balance, (4) Common Stock account ending balance, (5) assets, (6) expenses, (7) operating activities, (8) dividends, (9) Retained Earnings beginning balance, (10) investing activities, (11) common stock issued during the period, (12) liabilities, and (13) financing activities.

Required

Set up a table with the following headings. Identify the financial statements on which each of the preceding components appears by placing the reference number for the component in the appropriate column. If an item appears on more than one statement, place the reference number in every applicable column. The first component is shown as an example.

Income Statement	Statement of Changes in Stockholders' Equity	Balance Sheet	Statement of Cash Flows
	1	1	

PROBLEM 1–29B *Preparing Financial Statements for Two Complete Accounting Cycles*

L.O. 3, 4, 5, 6, 8

Jim's Janitorial Services experienced the following transactions for 2007, the first year of operations, and 2008. *Assume that all transactions involve the receipt or payment of cash.*

Transactions for 2007

1. Acquired $60,000 by issuing common stock.

2. Received $100,000 for providing services to customers.

3. Borrowed $25,000 cash from creditors.

4. Paid expenses amounting to $70,000.

5. Purchased land for $40,000 cash.

Transactions for 2008

Beginning account balances for 2008 are:

Cash	$75,000
Land	40,000
Notes Payable	25,000
Common Stock	60,000
Retained Earnings	30,000

1. Acquired an additional $20,000 from the issue of common stock.

2. Received $120,000 for providing services in 2008.

3. Paid $10,000 to reduce notes payable.

4. Paid expenses amounting to $80,000.

5. Paid a $15,000 dividend to the stockholders.

6. Determined that the market value of the land is $45,000.

Required

a. Write an accounting equation, and record the effects of each accounting event under the appropriate headings for each year. Record the amounts of revenue, expense, and dividends in the Retained Earnings column. Provide appropriate titles for these accounts in the last column of the table.

b. Prepare an income statement, statement of changes in stockholders' equity, year-end balance sheet, and statement of cash flows for each year.

c. Determine the amount of cash that is in the retained earnings account at the end of 2007 and 2008.

d. Compare the information provided by the income statement with the information provided by the statement of cash flows. Point out similarities and differences.

e. Determine the percentage growth in earnings from 2007 to 2008. Based on the data shown in Exhibit 1–7, is this a high-, medium-, or low-growth company?

L.O. 3, 5, 8   PROBLEM 1–30B *Interrelationships among Financial Statements*

Best Electronics started the accounting period with $10,000 of assets, $2,200 of liabilities, and $4,550 of retained earnings. During the period, the Retained Earnings account increased by $3,565. The book-keeper reported that Best paid cash expenses of $5,010 and paid a $625 cash dividend to stockholders, but she could not find a record of the amount of cash that Best received for performing services. Best also paid $1,000 cash to reduce the liability owed to a bank, and the business acquired $2,000 of additional cash from the issue of common stock.

Required

a. Prepare an income statement, statement of changes in stockholders' equity, year-end balance sheet, and statement of cash flows for the accounting period. (*Hint:* Determine the beginning balance in the common stock account before considering the effects of the current period events. It also might help to record all events under an accounting equation before preparing the statements.)

b. Determine the percentage of total assets that were provided by creditors, investors, and earnings.

L.O. 4, 7   PROBLEM 1–31B *Classifying Events as Asset Source, Use, or Exchange*

The following unrelated events are typical of those experienced by business entities:

1. Acquire cash by issuing common stock.
2. Borrow cash from the local bank.
3. Pay office supplies expense.
4. Make plans to purchase office equipment.
5. Trade a used car for a computer with the same value.
6. Pay other operating supplies expense.
7. Agree to represent a client in an IRS audit and to receive payment when the audit is complete.
8. Receive cash from customers for services rendered.
9. Pay employee salaries with cash.
10. Pay back a bank loan with cash.
11. Pay interest to a bank with cash.
12. Transfer cash from a checking account to a money market account.
13. Sell land for cash at its original cost.
14. Pay a cash dividend to stockholders.
15. Learn that a financial analyst determined the company's price-earnings ratio to be 26.

Required

Identify each of the events as an asset source, asset use, or asset exchange transaction. If an event would not be recorded under generally accepted accounting principles, identify it as *not applicable* (NA). Also indicate for each event whether total assets would increase, decrease, or remain unchanged. Organize your answer according to the following table. The first event is shown in the table as an example.

Event No.	Type of Event	Effect on Total Assets
1	Asset source	Increase

L.O. 6, 9   PROBLEM 1–32B *Recording the Effect of Events in a Horizontal Statements Model*

Belzio Company experienced the following transactions during 2006.

1. Paid a cash dividend to the stockholders.
2. Acquired cash by issuing additional common stock.
3. Signed a contract to perform services in the future.
4. Performed services for cash.
5. Paid cash expenses.
6. Sold land for cash at an amount equal to its cost.
7. Borrowed cash from a bank.
8. Determined that the market value of the land is higher than its historical cost.

Required

Use a horizontal statements model to show how each event affects the balance sheet, income statement, and statement of cash flows. Indicate whether the event increases (I), decreases (D), or does not affect (NA) each element of the financial statements. Also, in the Cash Flows column, classify the cash flows as operating activities (OA), investing activities (IA), or financing activities (FA). The first transaction is shown as an example.

Event No.	Balance Sheet													Income Statement						Statement of Cash Flows
	Cash	+	Land	=	N. Pay	+	C. Stock.	+	Ret. Ear.				Rev.	–	Exp.	=	Net Inc.		
1.	D	+	NA	=	NA	+	NA	+	D				NA	–	NA	=	NA		D FA

PROBLEM 1–33B *Recording Events in a Horizontal Statements Model*

L.O. 4, 6, 9

Foreman Company was started January 1, 2003, and experienced the following events during its first year of operation.

1. Acquired $32,000 cash from the issue of common stock.
2. Borrowed $20,000 cash from National Bank.
3. Earned cash revenues of $42,000 for performing services.
4. Paid cash expenses of $28,000.
5. Paid a $6,000 cash dividend to the stockholders.
6. Acquired $10,000 cash from the issue of additional common stock.
7. Paid $15,000 cash to reduce the principal balance of the bank note.
8. Paid $45,000 cash to purchase land.
9. Determined that the market value of the land is $50,000.

Required

a. Record the preceding transactions in the horizontal statements model. Also, in the Cash Flows column, classify the cash flows as operating activities (OA), investing activities (IA), or financing activities (FA). The first event is shown as an example.

Event No.	Balance Sheet													Income Statement						Statement of Cash Flows
	Cash	+	Land	=	N. Pay	+	C. Stock.	+	Ret. Ear.				Rev.	–	Exp.	=	Net Inc.		
1.	32,000	+	NA	=	NA	+	32,000	+	NA				NA	–	NA	=	NA		32,000 FA

b. Determine the amount of total assets that Foreman would report on the December 31, 2003, balance sheet.
c. Identify the asset source transactions and related amounts for 2003.
d. Determine the net income that Foreman would report on the 2003 income statement. Explain why dividends do not appear on the income statement.
e. Determine the net cash flows from operating activities, investing activities, and financing activities that Foreman would report on the 2003 statement of cash flows.
f. Determine the percentage of assets that were provided by investors, creditors, and earnings.

PROBLEM 1–34B *Price-Earnings Relationships*

L.O. 10

Beta One, Inc., is a pharmaceutical company heavily involved in research leading to the development of genealogy-based medicines. While the company has several promising research studies in progress, it has brought only two viable products to market during the last decade. Earnings per share and market price per share data for the latest three years of operation follow.

Beta One, Inc.	2003	2004	2005
Earnings per share	$ 1.22	$ 1.19	$ 1.20
Market price per share	85.40	84.49	87.60

Required

a. Calculate the company's annual growth rate in earnings per share from 2003 to 2004 and from 2004 to 2005.
b. Based on the data shown in Exhibit 1–7, identify the company as a high-, medium-, or low-growth company.

c. Calculate the company's price-earnings ratio for all three years.
d. Based on the data shown in Exhibit 1–16, classify the price-earnings ratio as high, medium, or low.
e. Explain the size of the price-earnings ratio.

ANALYZE, THINK, COMMUNICATE

ATC 1–1   BUSINESS APPLICATIONS CASE *Understanding Real World Annual Reports*

Required—Part 1

Use the Topps Company's annual report in Appendix B to answer the following questions.

a. What was Topps' net income for 2003?
b. Did Topps' net income increase or decrease from 2002 to 2003, and by how much?
c. What was Topps' accounting equation for 2003?
d. Which of the following had the largest percentage increase from 2002 to 2003: net sales, cost of sales, or selling, general, and administrative expenses? Show all computations.

Required—Part 2

Use the Harley-Davidson's annual report that came with this book to answer the following questions.

a. What was Harley-Davidson's net income for 2003?
b. Did Harley-Davidson's net income increase or decrease from 2002 to 2003, and by how much?
c. What was Harley-Davidson's accounting equation for 2003?
d. Which of the following had the largest percentage increase from 2002 to 2003: net revenue, cost of goods sold, or selling, general, and engineering expenses? Show all computations.

ATC 1–2   GROUP ASSIGNMENT *Missing Information*

The following selected financial information is available for J&G, Inc. Amounts are in millions of dollars.

Income Statements	2004	2003	2002	2001
Revenue	$ 661	$1,307	$ (a)	$ 894
Cost and Expenses	(a)	(a)	(1,859)	(769)
Income from Continuing Operations	(b)	174	71	(a)
Unusual Items	–0–	218	(b)	(b)
Net Income	$ 7	$ (b)	$ 47	$ 177
Balance Sheets				
Assets				
Cash and Marketable Securities	$ 249	$1,247	$ (c)	$ 419
Other Assets	1,661	(c)	1,226	(c)
Total Assets	1,910	$2,904	$(d)	$1,418
Liabilities	$(c)	$(d)	$907	$(d)
Stockholders' Equity				
Common Stock	422	356	(e)	313
Retained Earnings	(d)	(e)	684	(e)
Total Stockholders' Equity	1,062	1,342	(f)	1,040
Total Liabilities and Stockholders' Equity	$1,910	$(f)	$1,906	$1,418

Required

a. Divide the class into groups of four or five students each. Organize the groups into four sections. Assign Task 1 to the first section of groups, Task 2 to the second section, Task 3 to the third section, and Task 4 to the fourth section.

Group Tasks

(1) Fill in the missing information for 2001.
(2) Fill in the missing information for 2002.
(3) Fill in the missing information for 2003.
(4) Fill in the missing information for 2004.

b. Each section should select two representatives. One representative is to put the financial statements assigned to that section on the board, underlining the missing amounts. The second representative is to explain to the class how the missing amounts were determined.

c. Each section should list events that could have caused the unusual item category on the income statement.

REAL-WORLD CASE *Deciding Which Company Is the Best Investment*   ATC 1–3

Following are the net earnings of four large companies for the fiscal years from 1999 to 2002. Note that these amounts are in thousands of dollars.

Company	Industry	Net Earnings in $000			
		2002	2001	2000	1999
Autozone	Automobile parts retailer	$428,148	$175,526	$267,590	$244,783
Kohl's	Department store chain	643,381	495,676	372,148	258,142
Oshkosh B'Gosh	Children's clothing	32,045	32,808	32,217	32,448
Peoplesoft	Software development	182,589	191,554	145,691	(177,765)

Required

Based on this information alone, decide which of the companies you think would present the best investment opportunity for the future and which would be the worst. Write a brief memorandum supporting your choices, and show any computations that you used to reach your conclusions. As part of your analysis, compute the annual growth rates for each company's earnings. To do this, compute by what percentage each company's earnings increased or decreased from the year before. You will not be able to compute a growth rate for 1999 since the earnings for 1998 are not given. Perform whatever additional analysis you think is useful.

BUSINESS APPLICATIONS CASE *Use of Real-World Numbers for Forecasting*   ATC 1–4

The following information was drawn from the annual report of Machine Import Company (MIC):

	For the Years	
	2001	2002
Income Statements		
Revenue	$600,000	$690,000
Operating Expenses	480,000	552,000
Income from Continuing Operations	120,000	138,000
Extraordinary Item—Lottery Win		62,000
Net Income	$120,000	$200,000
Balance Sheets		
Assets	$880,000	$880,000
Liabilities	$200,000	$ 0
Stockholders' Equity		
Common Stock	380,000	380,000
Retained Earnings	300,000	500,000
Total Liabilities and Stockholders' Equity	$880,000	$880,000

Required

a. Compute the percentage of growth in net income from 2001 to 2002. Can stockholders expect a similar increase between 2002 and 2003?

b. Assuming that MIC collected $200,000 cash from earnings (i.e., net income), explain how this money was spent in 2002.

c. Assuming that MIC experiences the same percentage of growth from 2002 to 2003 as it did from 2001 to 2002, determine the amount of income from continuing operations that the owners can expect to see on the 2003 income statement.

d. During 2003, MIC experienced a $40,000 loss due to storm damage (note that this would be shown as an extraordinary loss on the income statement). Liabilities and common stock were unchanged from 2002 to 2003. Use the information that you computed in Part c plus the additional information provided in the previous two sentences to prepare an income statement and balance sheet as of December 31, 2003.

ATC 1–5   WRITING ASSIGNMENT *Elements of Financial Statements Defined*

Bob and his sister Marsha both attend the state university. As a reward for their successful completion of the past year (Bob had a 3.2 GPA in business, and Marsha had a 3.7 GPA in art), their father gave each of them 100 shares of The Walt Disney Company stock. They have just received their first annual report. Marsha does not understand what the information means and has asked Bob to explain it to her. Bob is currently taking an accounting course, and she knows he will understand the financial statements.

Required

Assume that you are Bob. Write Marsha a memo explaining the following financial statement items to her. In your explanation, describe each of the two financial statements and explain the financial information each contains. Also define each of the elements listed for each financial statement and explain what it means.

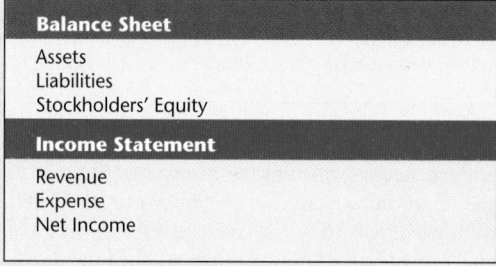

Balance Sheet
Assets
Liabilities
Stockholders' Equity
Income Statement
Revenue
Expense
Net Income

ATC 1–6   ETHICAL DILEMMA *Loyalty Versus the Bottom Line*

Assume that Jones has been working for you for five years. He has had an excellent work history and has received generous pay raises in response. The raises have been so generous that Jones is quite overpaid for the job he is required to perform. Unfortunately, he is not qualified to take on other, more responsible jobs available within the company. A recent job applicant is willing to accept a salary $5,000 per year less than the amount currently being paid to Jones. The applicant is well qualified to take over Jones's duties and has a very positive attitude. The following financial statements were reported by your company at the close of its most recent accounting period.

Required

a. Reconstruct the financial statements, assuming that Jones was replaced at the beginning of the most recent accounting period. Both Jones and his replacement are paid in cash. No other changes are to be considered.

b. Discuss the short- and long-term ramifications of replacing Jones. There are no right answers. However, assume that you are required to make a decision. Use your judgment and common sense to support your choice.

Financial Statements		
Income Statement		
Revenue		$57,000
Expense		(45,000)
Net Income		$12,000
Statement of Changes in Stockholders' Equity		
Beginning Common Stock	$20,000	
Plus: Stock issued	5,000	
Ending Common Stock		$25,000
Beginning Retained Earnings	50,000	
Net Income	12,000	
Dividends	(2,000)	
Ending Retained Earnings		60,000
Total Stockholders' Equity		$85,000

continued

Balance Sheet

Assets	
Cash	$85,000
Equity	
Common Stock	$25,000
Retained Earnings	60,000
Total Stockholders' Equity	$85,000

Statement of Cash Flows

Operating Activities		
Inflow from Customers	$57,000	
Outflow for Expenses	(45,000)	
Net Inflow from Operations		$12,000
Investing Activities		0
Financing Activities		
Inflow from Stock Issue	5,000	
Outflow for Dividends	(2,000)	
Net Inflow from Financing Activities		3,000
Net Change in Cash		15,000
Plus: Beginning Cash Balance		70,000
Ending Cash Balance		$85,000

SPREADSHEET ASSIGNMENT *Using Excel*

ATC 1–7

The financial statements for Simple Company are reported here using an Excel spreadsheet.

Required
Recreate the financial statements using your own Excel spreadsheet.

a. For each number with an arrow by it, enter a formula in that particular cell address to solve for the number shown. (Do not enter the arrow.)

b. When complete, print the spreadsheet with formulas rather than absolute numbers.

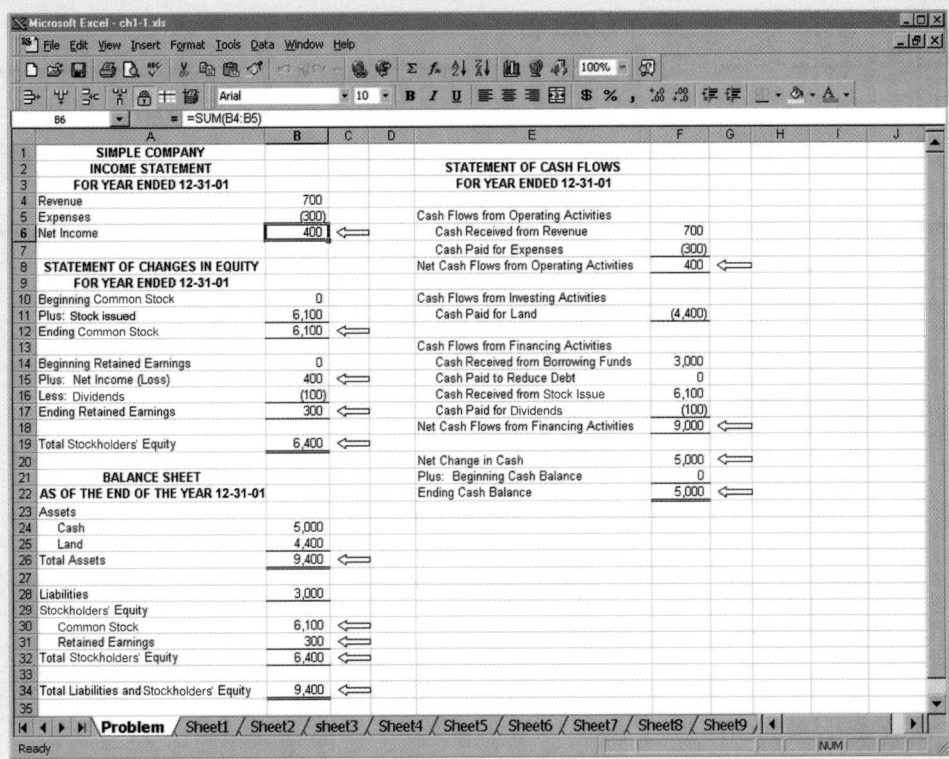

Spreadsheet Tips

   (1) Widen a column by positioning the cursor on the vertical line between two column headings until a crosshair appears. Either double click to automatically widen or click and drag the crosshair to the desired width.

   (2) Negative numbers can be parenthesized by choosing Format and then Cells. Under Category, choose Custom and under Type, choose the first option containing parentheses.

   (3) The SUM function is one way to add a series of numbers. For example, the formula for net income in cell B6 is =SUM(B4:B5).

   (4) Single and double lines can be drawn using the Borders icon.

   (5) Print a spreadsheet on one page by choosing File, Page Setup, and Fit to 1.

   (6) Print without gridlines by choosing File, Page Setup, and Sheet and uncheck Gridlines. Another option is to choose Tools and Options and uncheck Gridlines.

   (7) Print formulas by choosing Tools, Options, and Formulas.

ATC 1–8   SPREADSHEET ASSIGNMENT *Mastering Excel*

Required

a. Enter the following headings for the horizontal statements model onto a blank spreadsheet.

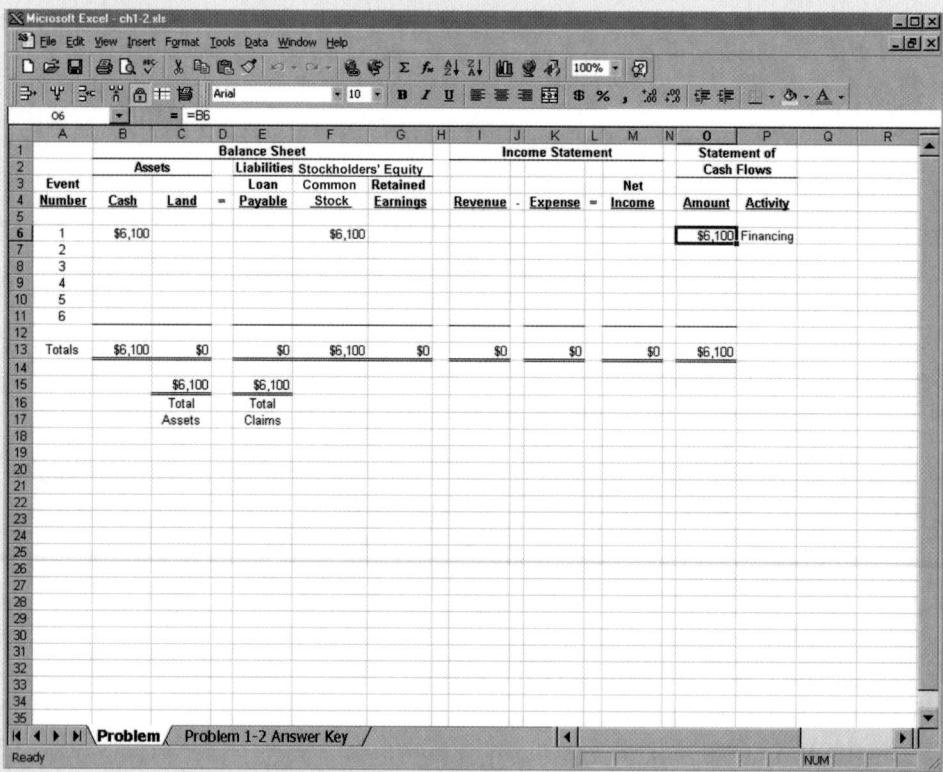

b. Under the appropriate headings, record the effects of each of the following accounting events for the first month of operations. The first event has been recorded as an example.

   (1) Acquired $6,100 from the issue of common stock.

   (2) Paid $4,400 to purchase land.

   (3) Borrowed $3,000 cash.

   (4) Provided services to customers and received $700 in cash.

   (5) Paid $300 for expenses.

   (6) Paid a $100 dividend to the stockholders.

   (*Note:* The amounts on the statement of cash flows can be referenced to the Cash account on the balance sheet. In other words, recording the cash amounts twice is not necessary. Instead enter formulas in the Statement of Cash Flows column equating those cell addresses to the respective cell in the Cash column. Notice that the formula in cell O6 (statement of cash flows) is set equal to cell B6 (cash on the balance sheet). Once the formula is completed for cell O6, it can be easily copied to cells O7 through O11.)

c. Using formulas, sum each of the quantitative columns to arrive at the end-of-month amounts reported on the financial statements.

Spreadsheet Tips

(1) Center the heading *Balance Sheet* across columns by entering the entire heading in cell B1. Position the cursor on B1 until a fat cross appears. Click and drag the cursor across B1 through G1. Click on the Merge and Center icon (it is highlighted in the screen in the computer display).

(2) Enter arithmetic signs as headings by placing an apostrophe in front of the sign. For example, to enter the equals sign in cell D4, enter ' =.

(3) Copy cells by positioning the cursor in the bottom right corner of the cell to copy from (such as cell O6) until a thin cross appears. Click and drag the cursor down through the desired locations to copy to (through cell O11).

(4) To enter the dollar sign, choose Format, Cells, and Currency.

CHAPTER *two*

ACCOUNTING FOR ACCRUALS

LEARNING *objectives*

After you have mastered the material in this chapter, you will be able to:

1 Record basic accrual events in a horizontal financial statements model.

2 Organize general ledger accounts under an accounting equation.

3 Prepare financial statements based on accrual accounting.

4 Describe the matching concept, the accounting cycle, and the closing process.

5 Record business events involving interest-bearing receivables and payables in a horizontal financial statements model.

6 Prepare a vertical financial statements model.

7 Explain how business events affect financial statements over multiple accounting cycles.

8 Describe the auditor's role in financial reporting.

9 Describe the articles of the AICPA's Code of Professional Conduct and identify the major factors that lead to unethical conduct.

10 Classify accounting events into one of four categories:
    a. asset source transactions.
    b. asset use transactions.
    c. asset exchange transactions.
    d. claims exchange transactions.

THE *curious* ACCOUNTANT

Suppose **Union Pacific** agrees to deliver goods from St. Louis, Missouri to Seattle, Washington. Further, assume that Union Pacific charges $4,500 to deliver the goods by rail. The distance between St. Louis and Seattle is approximately 2,135 miles.

When should Union Pacific recognize the $4,500 of revenue? More specifically, should the revenue be recognized before, during, or after the delivery of the goods? (Answers on page 62.)

CHAPTER *opening*

*To understand financial statements you must be able to distinguish between the terms recognition and realization. **Recognition** means showing an event in the financial statements. In contrast, **realization** refers to the collection of cash. Note carefully, that recognition and realization can occur in different accounting periods. Suppose Johnson Company provides services in 2005 but collects cash for those services in 2006. Under these circumstances, realization occurs in 2006. However, Johnson could recognize the revenue in 2005 or 2006 depending on whether the company uses the cash or the accrual basis of accounting.*

*Cash basis accounting recognizes revenues and expenses in the period in which cash is collected or paid. Under this approach Johnson would recognize revenue in 2006 when the cash is collected. In contrast, **accrual accounting** recognizes revenues and expenses in the period in which they occur regardless of when cash is collected or paid. Under* *accrual accounting Johnson would recognize the revenue in 2005 (the period in which the work was done) even though the associated cash collection is realized in 2006.*

*Accrual accounting uses both accruals and deferrals. The term **accrual** applies to events that are recognized **before** cash is exchanged. Johnson's recognition of revenue in 2005 with the cash realization in 2006 is an example of an accrual. The term deferral applies to events that are recognized **after** cash has been exchanged. This chapter introduces the most common types of accruals. Deferrals are explained in Chapter 3.*

Topic Tackler
PLUS
2–1

LO1 Record basic accrual events in a horizontal financial statements model.

Accrual Accounting

Virtually all of the major companies operating in the United States use accrual accounting. This section of the text demonstrates accrual accounting by describing seven events that relate to a company named Conner Consultants that delivers training services.

Event 1 Conner Consultants was started on January 1, 2004, when it acquired $5,000 cash by issuing common stock.

The issue of stock for cash is an **asset source transaction.** It increases the company's assets (cash) and its equity (common stock). The transaction does not affect the income statement. The cash inflow is classified as a financing activity (acquisition from owners). These effects are shown in the following financial statements model:

Assets	=	Liab.	+	C. Stk.	+	Ret. Ear.	Rev.	–	Exp.	=	Net Inc.	Cash Flow	
5,000	=	NA	+	5,000	+	NA	NA	–	NA	=	NA	5,000	FA

Event 2 During 2004 Conner Consultants provided $84,000 of consulting services to its clients. The business has completed the work and sent bills to the clients, but not yet collected any cash. This type of transaction is frequently referred to as providing services *on account.*

Accrual accounting requires companies to recognize revenue in the period in which the work is done regardless of when cash is collected. In this case, revenue is recognized in 2004 even though cash has not been realized (collected). Recall that revenue represents the economic benefit that results in an increase in assets from providing goods and services to customers. The specific asset that increases is called **Accounts Receivable.** The balance in an Account Receivable represents the amount of cash that is expected to be collected in the future. Since the revenue recognition causes assets (accounts receivable) to increase, it is classified as an asset source transaction. Its effect on the financial statements follows:

Assets			=	Liab.	+	Stockholders' Equity							
Cash	+	Accts. Rec.	=	Liab.	+	C. Stk.	+	Ret. Ear.	Rev.	–	Exp.	=	Net Inc.	Cash Flow
NA	+	84,000	=	NA	+	NA	+	84,000	84,000	–	NA	=	84,000	NA

Notice that the event affects the income statement but not the statement of cash flows. The statement of cash flows will be affected in the future when cash is collected.

Event 3 Conner collected $60,000 cash from customers in partial settlement of its accounts receivable.

The collection of an account receivable is an **asset exchange transaction.** One asset account (Cash) increases and another asset account (Accounts Receivable) decreases. The amount of total assets is unchanged. The effect of the $60,000 collection of receivables on the financial statements is as follows:

Assets			=	Liab.	+	Stockholders' Equity									
Cash	+	Accts. Rec.	=	Liab.	+	C. Stk.	+	Ret. Ear.	Rev.	−	Exp.	=	Net Inc.	Cash Flow	
60,000	+	(60,000)	=	NA	+	NA	+	NA	NA	−	NA	=	NA	60,000	OA

Notice that collecting the cash did not affect the income statement. The revenue was recognized when the work was done (see Event 2). Revenue would be double counted if it were recognized again when the cash is collected. The statement of cash flows reflects a cash inflow from operating activities.

Event 4 The instructor earned a salary of $16,000. No cash has yet been paid to the employee.

Accrual accounting requires companies to recognize expenses in the period in which they are incurred regardless of when cash is paid. In this case, Conner must recognize the expense in the period in which the employee worked even though the actual cash payment will be made later. The recognition of the salary expense decreases stockholders' equity (retained earnings) and increases a liability account called **Salaries Payable.** The balance in the Salaries Payable account represents the amount of cash that the company is obligated to pay the employee in the future. The effect of the expense recognition on the financial statements follows:

Assets			=	Liab.	+	Stockholders' Equity								
Cash	+	Accts. Rec.	=	Sal. Pay.	+	C. Stk.	+	Ret. Ear.	Rev.	−	Exp.	=	Net Inc.	Cash Flow
NA	+	NA	=	16,000	+	NA	+	(16,000)	NA	−	16,000	=	(16,000)	NA

This event is a **claims exchange transaction.** The claims of creditors (liabilities) increase by $16,000 and the claims of stockholders (retained earnings) decrease by $16,000. Total claims remain unchanged. The salary expense is recognized on the income statement. The statement of cash flows is not affected.

Be careful not to confuse liabilities with expenses. While liabilities may increase as a result of expense recognition, they are not the same thing as expenses. Liabilities are obligations. They can arise from acquiring assets as well as recognizing expenses. For example, if a business borrows money from a bank, it recognizes an increase in assets (cash) and liabilities (notes payable). The borrowing activity does not affect expenses.

Event 5 Conner paid $10,000 to the instructor in partial settlement of salaries payable.

Cash payments to creditors are **asset use transactions.** When Conner pays the instructor, the asset account Cash and the liability account Salaries Payable both decrease by $10,000. The effect of this transaction on the financial statements follows:

Assets			=	Liab.	+	Stockholders' Equity									
Cash	+	Accts. Rec.	=	Sal. Pay.	+	C. Stk.	+	Ret. Ear.	Rev.	−	Exp.	=	Net Inc.	Cash Flow	
(10,000)	+	NA	=	(10,000)	+	NA	+	NA	NA	−	NA	=	NA	(10,000)	OA

The actual cash payment does not affect the income statement. The salary expense was recognized in full at the time the employee did the work (see Event 4). The expense would be double counted if it were recognized again when Conner made the cash payment. The statement of cash flows reflects a cash outflow from operating activities.

Event 6 Conner paid $2,000 cash for advertising costs. The advertisements appeared in 2004.

Cash payments for expenses are asset use transactions. Both the asset account Cash and the equity account Retained Earnings decrease by $2,000. Recognizing the expense decreases net income on the income statement. Since the expense was paid with cash, the statement of cash flows reflects a cash outflow from operating activities. These effects on the financial statements follow:

Assets			=	Liab.	+	Stockholders' Equity				Rev.	−	Exp.	=	Net Inc.	Cash Flow
Cash	+	Accts. Rec.	=	Sal. Pay.	+	C. Stk.	+	Ret. Ear.		Rev.	−	Exp.	=	Net Inc.	Cash Flow
(2,000)	+	NA	=	NA	+	NA	+	(2,000)		NA	−	2,000	=	(2,000)	(2,000) OA

Event 7 **Conner signed contracts for $42,000 of consulting services to be performed in 2005.**

The $42,000 for consulting services to be performed in 2005 is not recognized in the 2004 financial statements. Revenue is recognized for work actually completed, *not* work expected to be completed. This event does not affect any of the financial statements.

Assets			=	Liab.	+	Stockholders' Equity				Rev.	−	Exp.	=	Net Inc.	Cash Flow
Cash	+	Accts. Rec.	=	Sal. Pay.	+	C. Stk.	+	Ret. Ear.		Rev.	−	Exp.	=	Net Inc.	Cash Flow
NA	+	NA	=	NA	+	NA	+	NA		NA	−	NA	=	NA	NA

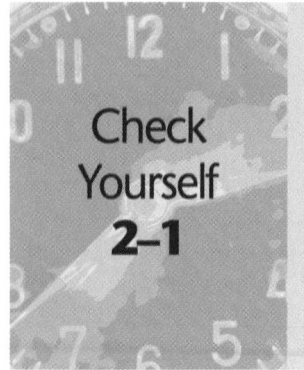

Check Yourself 2–1

During 2006, Anwar Company earned $345,000 of revenue on account and collected $320,000 cash from accounts receivable. Anwar paid cash expenses of $300,000 and cash dividends of $12,000. Determine the amount of net income Anwar should report on the 2006 income statement and the amount of cash flow from operating activities Anwar should report on the 2006 statement of cash flows.

Answer Net income is $45,000 ($345,000 revenue − $300,000 expenses). The cash flow from operating activities is $20,000, the amount of revenue collected in cash from customers (accounts receivable) minus the cash paid for expenses ($320,000 − $300,000). Dividend payments are classified as financing activities and do not affect the determination of either net income or cash flow from operating activities.

Transaction Data in Ledger Accounts

LO2 Organize general ledger accounts under an accounting equation.

Event 1 Conner Consultants acquired $5,000 cash by issuing common stock.
Event 2 Conner provided $84,000 of consulting services on account.
Event 3 Conner collected $60,000 cash from customers in partial settlement of its accounts receivable.
Event 4 Conner recognized $16,000 of salary expense on account.
Event 5 Conner paid $10,000 to its instructor in partial settlement of the salary payable.
Event 6 Conner paid $2,000 cash for 2004 advertising costs.
Event 7 Conner signed contracts for $42,000 of consulting services to be performed in 2005.

The general ledger accounts used to record the transaction data for Conner Consultants' 2004 accounting period are shown in Exhibit 2–1. Event 7 is not shown in the illustration because it does not affect any of the ledger account balances. The data in the accounts are used to prepare the financial statements. The revenue and expense accounts appear in the Retained Earnings column with their titles immediately to the right of the dollar amounts. The amounts are color coded to help you trace the data to the financial statements. Data in red appear on the balance sheet; data in blue on the income statement; and data in green on the statement of cash flows.

Exhibit 2-1   Transaction Data Recorded in Accounts

	Assets			=	Liabilities	+	Stockholders' Equity				
Event No.	Cash	+	Accounts Receivable	=	Salaries Payable	+	Common Stock	+	Retained Earnings		Other Account Titles
Beg. Bal.	0		0		0		0		0		
1	5,000						5,000				
2			84,000						84,000		Consulting Revenue
3	60,000		(60,000)								
4					16,000				(16,000)		Salary Expense
5	(10,000)				(10,000)						
6	(2,000)								(2,000)		Advertising Expense
End Bal.	53,000	+	24,000	=	6,000	+	5,000	+	66,000		

2004 Financial Statements

Conner Consultants' financial statements for the 2004 accounting period are shown in a vertical statements model in Exhibit 2–2.

LO3 Prepare financial statements based on accrual accounting.

Income Statement

The income statement illustrates several effects of accrual accounting. For example, the definition of expenses used in Chapter 1 can now be expanded. Expenses were previously defined as assets and services consumed in the process of generating revenue. In the Conner illustration, no assets were consumed when the salaries expense was recognized. Instead of a decrease in assets, Conner recorded an increase in liabilities (salaries payable). In expanded form, **expenses** can be defined as decreases in assets *or* increases in liabilities resulting from consuming assets and services to generate revenue. Similarly, revenue can be defined as increases in assets *or* decreases in liabilities from providing goods and services to customers in the normal course of operations. Specific examples of how revenue can be related to liability decreases are provided in the next chapter.

Statement of Changes in Stockholders' Equity

The statement of changes in stockholders' equity reports the effects on equity of issuing common stock, earning net income, and paying dividends to stockholders. It identifies how an entity's equity increased and decreased during the period as a result of transactions with stockholders and operating the business. In the Conner case, the statement shows that equity increased when the business acquired $5,000 cash by issuing common stock. The statement also reports that equity increased by $66,000 from earning income and that none of the $66,000 of net earnings was distributed to owners (no dividends were paid). Equity at the end of the year is $71,000 ($5,000 + $66,000).

Balance Sheet

The balance sheet discloses an entity's assets, liabilities, and stockholders' equity at a particular point in time. Conner Consultants had two assets at the end of the 2004 accounting period: cash of $53,000 and accounts receivable of $24,000. These assets are listed on the balance sheet in order of liquidity. Of the $77,000 in total assets, creditors have a $6,000 claim, leaving stockholders with a $71,000 claim.

Exhibit 2-2 *Vertical Statements Model*

CONNER CONSULTANTS
Financial Statements*

Income Statement for the Year Ended December 31, 2004

Consulting Revenue	$84,000
Salary Expense	(16,000)
Advertising Expense	(2,000)
Net Income	$66,000

Statement of Changes in Stockholders' Equity for the Year Ended December 31, 2004

Beginning Common Stock	$ 0	
Plus: Common Stock Issued	5,000	
Ending Common Stock		$ 5,000
Beginning Retained Earnings	0	
Plus: Net Income	66,000	
Less: Dividends	0	
Ending Retained Earnings		66,000
Total Stockholders' Equity		$71,000

Balance Sheet as of December 31, 2004

Assets		
Cash	$53,000	
Accounts Receivable	24,000	
Total Assets		$77,000
Liabilities		
Salaries Payable		$ 6,000
Stockholders' Equity		
Common Stock	$ 5,000	
Retained Earnings	66,000	
Total Stockholders' Equity		71,000
Total Liabilities and Stockholders' Equity		$77,000

Statement of Cash Flows for the Year Ended December 31, 2004

Cash Flows from Operating Activities		
Cash Receipts from Customers	$60,000	
Cash Payments for Salary Expense	(10,000)	
Cash Payments for Advertising Expenses	(2,000)	
Net Cash Flow from Operating Activities		$48,000
Net Cash Flow from Investing Activities		0
Net Cash Flow from Financing Activities		
Cash Receipt from Issuing Common Stock		5,000
Net Change in Cash		53,000
Plus: Beginning Cash Balance		0
Ending Cash Balance		$53,000

*In real-world annual reports, financial statements are normally presented separately with appropriate descriptions of the date to indicate whether the statement applies to the entire accounting period or a specific point in time.

Statement of Cash Flows

The statement of cash flows explains the change in cash from the beginning to the end of the accounting period. It can be prepared by analyzing the Cash account. Since Conner Consultants was established in 2004, its beginning cash balance was zero. By the end of the year, the cash balance was $53,000. The statement of cash flows explains this increase. The Cash account increased because Conner collected $60,000 from customers and decreased because Conner paid $12,000 for expenses. As a result, Conner's net cash inflow from operating activities was $48,000. Also, the business acquired $5,000 cash through the financing activity of issuing common stock, for a cumulative cash increase of $53,000 ($48,000 + $5,000) during 2004.

Notice that the amount of cash flow from operating activities ($48,000) is different from the amount of net income ($66,000). The difference results from the fact that some revenue was earned on account (cash has not been realized). Also, some of the salary expense was recognized on account (cash has not been paid). Many students enter their first accounting class with the misconception that revenue and expense items are cash equivalents. The Conner illustration clearly demonstrates that revenue or expense can be recognized without a corresponding cash collection or payment.

The Closing Process

Much of the information disclosed in a company's financial statements summarizes business activity for a specified time period. The end of one time period marks the beginning of the next time period. Each time period, which typically lasts one year, is called an **accounting cycle.** Accounting cycles follow one after the other from the time a business is formed until it is dissolved.

LO4 Describe the matching concept, the accounting cycle, and the closing process.

The amounts in balance sheet accounts (assets, liabilities, common stock, and retained earnings) at the end of an accounting cycle carry forward to the beginning of the next accounting cycle. For example, a company will begin 2005 with the same amount of cash it had at the end of 2004. Because their balances carry forward, balance sheet accounts are sometimes called **permanent accounts.**

In contrast, revenue, expense, and dividend accounts are **temporary** or **nominal accounts,** used to capture accounting information for one single accounting cycle at a time. After the financial statements have been prepared at the end of the accounting cycle, the amounts in the nominal accounts are moved to Retained Earnings, a permanent account. Accountants call the process of moving the revenue, expense, and dividend account balances to retained earnings **closing the books,** or simply **closing.** After closing, every nominal account has a zero balance and the retained earnings account is updated to reflect the earning activities and dividend distributions that took place during the accounting period.

Exhibit 2–3 shows the general ledger accounts for Conner Consultants after the revenue and expense accounts have been closed to retained earnings. The closing entry labeled Cl.1 transfers the balance in the Consulting Revenue account to the Retained Earnings account. Closing entries Cl.2 and Cl.3 transfer the balances in the expense accounts to retained earnings.

Matching Concept

Cash basis accounting can distort the measurement of net income because it sometimes fails to properly match revenues with expenses. For example, assume Chapin Company paid salaries expense of $500 cash in 2005. The work that its employees performed during 2005 produced $900 of revenue for Chapin. However, Chapin did not collect cash from its customers until 2006. If Chapin uses cash basis accounting, the company will recognize $500 of expense in 2005 and $900 of revenue in 2006. Clearly, the amount of net income is distorted in both accounting periods. The objective of accrual accounting is to improve matching. Under accrual accounting Chapin would recognize both the $500 salary expense and the corresponding $900 revenue in 2005.

The matching of revenues and expenses can be difficult even when accrual accounting is used. Returning to the Conner Consultants example, we note that the advertising expense presents a complicated matching issue. The advertising cost can generate revenue in future accounting periods as well as the present period. For example, a prospective customer could save an advertising brochure for several years before calling Conner for training services. The relationship between advertising expense and revenue generation is unclear. When the relationship between an expense and the corresponding revenue is vague, the expense is commonly matched with the period in which it is incurred. With respect to Conner's advertising cost, the entire $2,000 is matched with (recognized in) the 2004 accounting period even

ANSWERS TO THE *curious* ACCOUNTANT

Accrual accounting requires a company to recognize revenue when it is earned rather than when cash is collected. In some business operations, it is not always easy to know precisely when the revenue is earned. **Union Pacific (UNP) Corporation,** a very large transportation company, recognizes revenue on a "percentage-of-completion basis" as shipments move from origin to destination. This policy means that if UNP agrees to ship goods 2,135 miles for $4,500, it recognizes approximately $2.11 ($4,500 ÷ 2,135) of revenue for every mile the goods are

moved. If you think this must require a very sophisticated computer system, you are correct!

Notice that the "recognize-as-you-go" practice does not violate the rule that revenue cannot be recognized before it is earned. UNP cannot recognize the entire $4,500 until the goods reach their destination. However, the company can recognize the revenue in proportion to the amount of the trip that is completed. If one-half of the trip is completed, one-half of the revenue can be recognized.

Exhibit 2–3 *General Ledger Accounts for Conner Consultants*

Assets		=	Liabilities		+	Stockholders' Equity	
Cash			**Salaries Payable**			**Common Stock**	
[1]	5,000		[4]	16,000		[1]	5,000
[3]	60,000		[5]	(10,000)			
[5]	(10,000)		Bal.	6,000		**Retained Earnings**	
[6]	(2,000)					Cl.1	84,000
Bal.	53,000					Cl.2	(16,000)
						Cl.3	(2,000)
Accounts Receivable						Bal.	66,000
[2]	84,000						
[3]	(60,000)					**Consulting Revenue**	
Bal.	24,000					[2]	84,000
						Cl.1	(84,000)
						Bal.	0
						Salary Expense	
						[4]	(16,000)
						Cl.2	16,000
						Bal.	0
						Advertising Expense	
						[6]	(2,000)
						Cl.3	2,000
						Bal.	0

though some of that cost might generate revenue in future accounting periods. Expenses that are matched with the period in which they are incurred are frequently called **period costs.**

As the previous paragraph suggests, matching is not a perfect science. It would be more accurate to match expenses with revenues than with periods. Unfortunately, there is no direct connection between some expense items and the associated revenue. Accountants are frequently required to use judgment in selecting the accounting period in which revenues and expenses are to be recognized. The concept of conservatism is helpful in making such judgment calls.

Conservatism suggests that when faced with a recognition dilemma, accountants should select the alternative that produces the lowest amount of net income. Investors who base their decisions on conservative estimates of net income will be pleasantly surprised to discover later that they are better off than they thought. In contrast, investors who base their decisions on optimistic measures of income will be severely disappointed if they discover later that their investments were overpriced. Accordingly, the doctrine of conservatism concludes that is better to understate net income than to overstate it. When uncertainty exists, accountants tend to delay the recognition of revenue and to accelerate the recognition of expenses. This explains why Conner recognized all of the advertising cost in 2004 even though some of that cost may generate revenue in future accounting periods.

Second Accounting Cycle

Topic Tackler

PLUS

2–2

LO5 Record business events involving interest-bearing receivables and payables in a horizontal financial statements model.

Assume the following accounting events apply to the operations of Conner Consultants during 2005:

Event 1 Conner Consultants acquired $25,000 cash by issuing common stock.
Event 2 During the period, Conner recognized $96,000 of revenue on account.
Event 3 Conner collected $102,000 of cash from accounts receivable.
Event 4 Conner accrued $22,000 of salary expense.
Event 5 Conner paid $20,000 cash toward the settlement of salaries payable.
Event 6 Conner paid a $10,000 cash dividend to stockholders.

These events are conceptually identical to transactions explained previously. The effects of these events on the general ledger accounts are shown in Exhibit 2–4. If you do not understand these effects, review the previous material.

Event 7 On March 1, 2005, Conner invested $60,000 in a certificate of deposit (CD).

Purchasing a certificate of deposit is an asset exchange transaction. It represents an **investment** made by Conner. The event decreases the asset account Cash and increases the asset account Certificate of Deposit. Total assets remain unchanged. The income statement is not affected. The statement of cash flows shows an outflow from investing activities. The effects of this transaction on the financial statements are shown here:

Assets		= Liab. +	Stockholders' Equity					
Cash +	CD	= Liab. +	C. Stk. +	Ret. Ear.	Rev. −	Exp. =	Net Inc.	Cash Flow
(60,000) +	60,000	= NA +	NA +	NA	NA −	NA =	NA	(60,000) IA

Exhibit 2–4 Transaction Data Recorded in Accounts

Event No.		Assets			= Liabilities +	Stockholders' Equity		
	Cash +	Accounts Receivable +	Interest Receivable +	Certificate of Deposit =	Salaries Payable +	Common Stock +	Retained Earnings	Other Account Titles
Beg. Bal.	53,000	24,000	0	0	6,000	5,000	66,000	
1	25,000					25,000		
2		96,000					96,000	Consulting Revenue
3	102,000	(102,000)						
4					22,000		(22,000)	Salary Expense
5	(20,000)				(20,000)			
6	(10,000)						(10,000)	Dividends
7	(60,000)			60,000				
8			3,000				3,000	Interest Revenue
End Bal.	90,000 +	18,000 +	3,000 +	60,000 =	8,000 +	30,000 +	133,000	

Adjusting the Accounts

Event 8 **On December 31, 2005, Conner adjusted the books to recognize interest revenue earned to date on the certificate of deposit. The certificate had a 6 percent annual rate of interest and a one-year term to maturity. Interest is due in cash on the maturity date (March 1, 2006).**

When Conner invested in (purchased) the certificate of deposit, the company, in fact, loaned the bank money. In exchange for the privilege of using Conner's money, the bank will pay Conner both the money (principal) and an additional 6 percent of the principal amount (interest) one year from the date that it borrowed Conner's money. In other words, in exchange for receiving $60,000 on March 1, 2005, the bank agreed to pay Conner $63,600 (or $60,000 + [0.06 × $60,000]) on March 1, 2006. Conner will receive $3,600 (0.06 × $60,000) per year as compensation for letting the bank use its cash.

It is important to recognize that interest is earned continually even though the full amount of cash is not collected until the maturity date. In other words, the amount of interest due increases proportionally as time passes. The amount of accumulated but uncollected interest is called *accrued interest.* Without using sophisticated computer programs, recording (recognizing) accrued interest continually is impossible. Think about it; how could you record something that occurs continually?

As a practical matter, many businesses only record accrued interest when it is time to prepare financial statements. The accounts are then *adjusted* to reflect the amount of interest due as of the end of the accounting period. For example, when Conner purchased the certificate of deposit (CD) on March 1, 2005, it recorded the asset exchange immediately (see Event 7). However, Conner would not recognize the interest earned on the certificate until the balance sheet date, December 31, 2005. At that time, Conner would make an entry to recognize all of the interest that had been earned during the previous 10 months (March 1 through December 31). This entry is called an **adjusting entry** because it updates (adjusts) the account balances prior to preparing financial statements.

The amount of interest is computed by multiplying the face value (purchase price) of the CD by the annual interest rate and by the length of time for which the certificate has been outstanding.

Principal	×	Annual interest rate	×	Time outstanding	=	Interest revenue
$60,000	×	0.06	×	(10/12)	=	$3,000

The effects of the adjusting entry on the financial statements follow:

Assets			= Liab. + Stockholders' Equity							
Cash + CD + Int. Rec.			= Liab. +	C. Stk. +	Ret. Ear.		Rev. − Exp. = Net Inc.			Cash Flow
NA + NA + 3,000			= NA +	NA +	3,000		3,000 − NA = 3,000			NA

$3,000 of the CD interest is revenue in 2005 although Conner will not collect the cash until 2006. This practice is consistent with the **matching concept**. Interest revenue is recognized in (matched with) the period in which it is earned regardless of when the associated cash is collected. The adjusting entry is an asset source transaction. The asset account Interest Receivable increases, and the stockholders' equity account Retained Earnings increases. The income statement reflects an increase in revenue and net income. The statement of cash flows is not affected because cash will not be collected until the maturity date (March 1, 2006).

Mei Company purchased a $36,000 certificate of deposit (CD) from State Bank on October 1, 2004. The CD had a 5 percent annual interest rate and a two-year term to maturity. The interest is to be collected in cash on the maturity date. Determine the amount of interest revenue Mei would report on the 2004 income statement and the amount of cash flow from operating activities Mei would report on the 2004 statement of cash flows.

Answer Mei would report interest revenue of $450 on the 2004 income statement (see the following calculation). There would be no cash flow from operating activities to report on the 2004 statement of cash flows because Mei will not collect any cash for the interest until the CD matures on September 30, 2006. (Mei *would* report a $36,000 cash outflow in 2004 for the CD purchase as an investing activity, not an operating activity.)

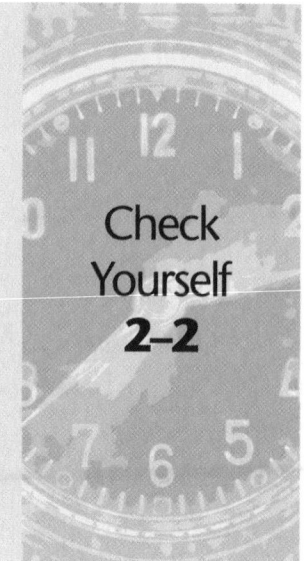

Check Yourself 2–2

Principal × Annual interest rate × Time outstanding = Interest revenue
$36,000 ×   0.05   ×   (3/12)   = $450

Because the interest rate is 5 percent *per year,* the denominator for the *time outstanding* is 12 months although the note has a 24-month term. Mei will earn 5 percent interest each year, a total of 10 percent for the full 24-month term.

Summary of 2005 Transactions

Event 1 Conner Consultants acquired $25,000 cash by issuing common stock.
Event 2 During the period, Conner recognized $96,000 of revenue on account.
Event 3 Conner collected $102,000 of cash from accounts receivable.
Event 4 Conner accrued $22,000 of salary expense.
Event 5 Cash paid $20,000 toward the settlement of salaries payable.
Event 6 Conner paid a $10,000 cash dividend to stockholders.
Event 7 On March 1, 2005, Conner invested $60,000 in a certificate of deposit (CD).
Event 8 On December 31, 2005, Conner adjusted the books to recognize interest revenue earned to date on the certificate of deposit. The certificate had a 6 percent annual rate of interest and a one-year term to maturity. Interest is due in cash on the maturity date (March 1, 2006).

LO2 Organize general ledger accounts under an accounting equation.

The general ledger account information for Conner Consultants' 2005 accounting period is shown in Exhibit 2–4. The information in the accounts is used to prepare the financial statements. The revenue, expense, and dividend account data appear in the retained earnings column. The account titles are shown immediately to the right of the dollar amounts listed in the retained earnings column. The amounts are color coded to help you understand the source of information in the financial statements. The numbers in green are used in the statement of cash flows. The numbers in blue are used to prepare the income statement. The numbers in red are used to prepare the balance sheet.

2005 Financial Statements

The financial statements prepared using ledger account information from Exhibit 2–4 are shown in Exhibit 2–5. The relationships among the statements are discussed in the following section of the chapter.

LO3 Prepare financial statements based on accrual accounting.

Income Statement

Notice that the net income of $77,000 is not equivalent to any cash figure. The cash flow from operating activities is $82,000, as the statement of cash flows reports. Although Conner recognized only $96,000 of consulting revenue in 2005, it collected from customers cash of $102,000 because some of the cash collected in 2005 related to revenue recognized in 2004. The income statement also recognizes $3,000 of interest revenue for which no cash was collected during 2005. Finally, although the amount of salary expense recognized was $22,000, Conner paid

Exhibit 2–5 *Vertical Statements Model*

CONNER CONSULTANTS
Financial Statements

Income Statement for the Year Ended December 31, 2005

Consulting Revenue	$ 96,000	
Interest Revenue	3,000	
Total Revenue		$ 99,000
Salary Expense		(22,000)
Net Income		$ 77,000

Statement of Changes in Stockholders' Equity for the Year Ended December 31, 2005

Beginning Common Stock	$ 5,000	
Plus: Common Stock Issued	25,000	
Ending Common Stock		$ 30,000
Beginning Retained Earnings	66,000	
Plus: Net Income	77,000	
Less: Dividends	(10,000)	
Ending Retained Earnings		133,000
Total Stockholders' Equity		$163,000

Balance Sheet as of December 31, 2005

Assets		
Cash	$ 90,000	
Accounts Receivable	18,000	
Interest Receivable	3,000	
Certificate of Deposit	60,000	
Total Assets		$171,000
Liabilities		
Salaries Payable		$ 8,000
Stockholders' Equity		
Common Stock	$ 30,000	
Retained Earnings	133,000	
Total Stockholders' Equity		163,000
Total Liabilities and Stockholders' Equity		$171,000

Statement of Cash Flows for the Year Ended December 31, 2005

Cash Flows from Operating Activities		
Cash Receipts from Customers	$102,000	
Cash Payments for Salaries Expense	(20,000)	
Net Cash Flow from Operating Activities		$ 82,000
Cash Flows from Investing Activities		
Cash Payment to Purchase CD		(60,000)
Cash Flows from Financing Activities		
Cash Receipt from Common Stock Issue	25,000	
Cash Payment for Dividends	(10,000)	
Net Cash Flow from Financing Activities		15,000
Net Change in Cash		37,000
Plus: Beginning Cash Balance		53,000
Ending Cash Balance		$ 90,000

only $20,000. The net cash inflow from operating activities was therefore $82,000 ($102,000 − $20,000), while net income recognized is $77,000 ($96,000 + $3,000 − $22,000).

Statement of Changes in Stockholders' Equity

The 2004 ending balances in the Common Stock and Retained Earnings accounts become the beginning balances for 2005. Adding the $25,000 received from issuing stock to the $5,000 beginning Common Stock balance produces the $30,000 ending balance. Since Conner distributed $10,000 of the $77,000 net income to the stockholders, Retained Earnings increases by $67,000 ($77,000 net income − $10,000 dividend) from a beginning balance of $66,000 to an ending balance of $133,000. Total stockholders' equity at the end of 2005 is therefore $163,000 ($30,000 common stock + $133,000 retained earnings).

Balance Sheet

Assets are listed in order of liquidity. Note the placement of the Interest Receivable and Certificate of Deposit accounts. Creditor claims (salaries payable) of $8,000, combined with the stockholders' claims of $163,000, produce total claims of $171,000, which equals total assets of $171,000.

Statement of Cash Flows

The $82,000 net cash inflow from operating activities is discussed above in connection with the income statement. Further analysis of the Cash account discloses a $60,000 cash outflow from purchasing the certificate of deposit, a $25,000 cash inflow from issuing common stock, and, finally, a $10,000 cash outflow for dividends paid to stockholders. The net change in cash was a $37,000 increase ($82,000 − $60,000 + $15,000). Comparing the cash balance at the beginning of the period ($53,000) with the Cash balance at the end of the period ($90,000) confirms that cash increased $37,000 in 2005.

Closing the Temporary (Nominal) Accounts

Recall that the temporary accounts (revenue, expense, and dividend) are closed prior to the start of the next accounting cycle. The closing process transfers the amount in each of these accounts to the Retained Earnings account, leaving each temporary account with a zero balance.

LO4 Describe the matching concept, the accounting cycle, and the closing process.

Steps in an Accounting Cycle

A complete accounting cycle, which is represented graphically below, involves several steps. The four steps identified to this point are: (1) recording transactions; (2) adjusting the accounts; (3) preparing financial statements; and (4) closing the temporary accounts. The first step occurs continually throughout the accounting period. Steps 2, 3, and 4 normally occur at the end of the accounting period. Additional steps are described in coming chapters of the text.

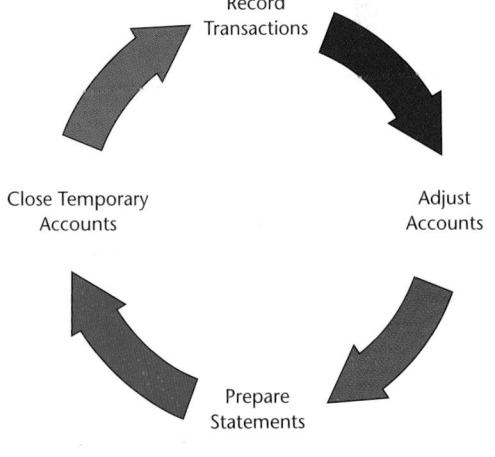

▎Accounting for Notes Payable

How does borrowing money affect a company's financial statements? To illustrate, assume Conner Consultants borrows $90,000 from First City Bank on September 1, 2006. This is an asset source transaction. The transaction acts to increase the asset account Cash and a liability account called **Notes Payable.** The effects of the borrowing event on the financial statements follow.

LO5 Record business events involving interest-bearing receivables and payables in a horizontal financial statements model.

	Assets	=	Liabilities			+	Stockholders' Equity								
Date	Cash	=	Note Pay.	+	Int. Pay.	+	C. Stk.	+	Ret. Ear.	Rev.	−	Exp.	=	Net Inc.	Cash Flow
09/01/06	90,000	=	90,000	+	NA	+	NA	+	NA	NA	−	NA	=	NA	90,000 FA

The liability account Notes Payable derives its name from the fact that banks normally require a borrower to sign a note describing the loan terms. Terms typically specified in a note include the interest rate, the term to maturity, and any collateral pledged to secure the loan. The borrower, who receives money from the bank, is the **issuer** of the note, and the bank is the *creditor* or *lender*. Borrowing funds is reported as a financing activity on the statement of cash flows. The borrowing event does not affect the income statement. The income statement will be affected in the future when interest expense is recognized as a separate event.

Assume the note Conner issued has a 9 percent annual rate of interest and a one-year term. On December 31, 2006, Conner Consultants will make an *adjusting entry* to recognize four months of accrued (incurred but not paid) interest expense from September 1 through December 31. The accrued interest is $2,700 ($90,000 $\times$ 0.09 $\times$ [4/12]). The event is a claims exchange. The liability account Interest Payable increases, and the equity account Retained Earnings decreases. The income statement would reflect interest expense although no cash was paid for interest in 2006. These effects are shown in the following statements model.

	Assets	=	Liabilities			+	Stockholders' Equity							
Date	Cash	=	Note Pay.	+	Int. Pay.	+	C. Stk.	+	Ret. Ear.	Rev.	−	Exp.	=	Net Inc.	Cash Flow
12/31/06	NA	=	NA	+	2,700	+	NA	+	(2,700)	NA	−	2,700	=	(2,700)	NA

Three events are recognized on August 31, 2007 (the maturity date). First, $5,400 of interest expense that accrued in 2007 from January 1 through August 31 ($90,000 $\times$ 0.09 $\times$ [8/12]) is recorded. This entry parallels the adjusting entry made on December 31, 2006. The effects on the financial statements are shown below.

	Assets	=	Liabilities			+	Stockholders' Equity							
Date	Cash	=	Note Pay.	+	Int. Pay.	+	C. Stk.	+	Ret. Ear.	Rev.	−	Exp.	=	Net Inc.	Cash Flow
08/31/07	NA	=	NA	+	5,400	+	NA	+	(5,400)	NA	−	5,400	=	(5,400)	NA

Second, the model shows the cash paid for interest on August 31, 2007. This entry is an asset use transaction that reduces the Cash and Interest Payable accounts. The amount paid is $8,100 ($90,000 $\times$ 0.09 $\times$ [12/12]). This includes the four months' interest accrued in 2006 and the eight months accrued in 2007 ($2,700 + $5,400 = $8,100). There is no effect on the income statement because the interest expense was recognized in two previous events. The statement of cash flows would report an $8,100 cash outflow from operating activities. These effects are shown in the following statements model.

	Assets	=	Liabilities			+	Stockholders' Equity							
Date	Cash	=	Note Pay.	+	Int. Pay.	+	C. Stk.	+	Ret. Ear.	Rev.	−	Exp.	=	Net Inc.	Cash Flow
08/31/07	(8,100)	=	NA	+	(8,100)	+	NA	+	NA	NA	−	NA	=	NA	(8,100) OA

The third entry dated August 31, 2007, reflects repaying the principal. This entry is an asset use transaction. The Cash account and the Notes Payable account decrease by $90,000. There is no income statement effect because repaying a loan is not an expense activity. The statement of cash flows would show a $90,000 cash outflow from financing activities. Recall that *paying interest* is classified as an operating activity while *repaying the principal* is a financing activity. These effects on the financial statements are shown below.

	Assets	=	Liabilities			+	Stockholders' Equity							
Date	Cash	=	Note Pay.	+	Int. Pay.	+	C. Stk.	+	Ret. Ear.	Rev.	−	Exp.	=	Net Inc.	Cash Flow
08/31/07	(90,000)	=	(90,000)	+	NA	+	NA	+	NA	NA	−	NA	=	NA	(90,000) FA

Under accrual accounting, revenue is recognized only after a company completes work. In contrast, investors focus on anticipated income when purchasing stock. This helps explain why the stock of some companies sells for more than the stock of other companies. For example, since the silicon-chip industry has a higher growth potential than the grocery-store industry, Intel's stock will likely sell for a higher earnings multiple than Kroger's stock. Indeed, on August 19, 2003, Intel's stock sold for 50 times earnings, while Kroger's sold for only 11 times earnings.

Significant differences in P/E ratios occur because investors base their stock purchases on a company's potential to earn future profits rather than its past earnings. Does this mean historically based financial statements are not useful in making investment decisions? No! Past earnings provide insight into future earnings. A company with a history of 20 percent per year earnings growth is more likely to experience rapid growth in the future than a company with a 5 percent historical growth rate. Financial statements based on accrual accounting can provide insight into the future even though they are historically based.

Trent, Incorporated, issued a $120,000 note to the National Bank on November 1, 2004. The note had a 12 percent annual interest rate and a one-year term to maturity. Determine the amount of interest expense and the cash flow from operating activities Trent would report on the 2004 and 2005 financial statements.

Answer The amount of interest expense Trent would recognize each year is computed as follows:

	Principal	×	Annual interest rate	×	Time outstanding	=	Interest expense
2004	$120,000	×	0.12	×	(2/12)	=	$ 2,400
2005	$120,000	×	0.12	×	(10/12)	=	$12,000

Because Trent will pay the total amount of interest ($120,000 × 0.12 × 12/12 = $14,400) on the maturity date (October 31, 2005), there is no cash flow from operating activities to report in 2004 and a $14,400 cash outflow from operating activities in 2005.

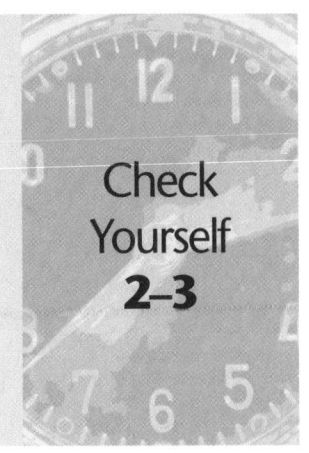

Check Yourself 2–3

Vertical Statements Model

Useful insights can be gained by analyzing financial statements over multiple accounting cycles. A statements model that arranges financial statement information vertically on a single page provides a convenient tool for such analysis. A multicycle vertical statements model is presented in Exhibit 2–6 for Conner Consultants, using 2004 and 2005 accounting data.

Using this model, you can focus on important interrelationships among the financial statements. For each year, notice how the amount of net income is carried forward from the income statement to the statement of changes in stockholders' equity. Next, see how the ending balances of common stock and retained earnings appearing on the statement of changes in stockholders' equity are carried forward to the balance sheet. Also, notice that the amount of cash reported on the balance sheet is consistent with the ending cash balance on the statement of cash flows.

Observe how the ending cash balance on the 2004 balance sheet agrees with the beginning cash balance shown on the 2005 statement of cash flows. Also the ending retained earnings balance shown on the 2004 balance sheet becomes the beginning retained earnings balance on the 2005 statement of stockholders' equity. Finally, confirm that the difference in the amount of cash shown on the 2004 and 2005 balance sheets agrees with the net change in cash reported on the 2005 statement of cash flows.

LO6 Prepare a vertical financial statements model.

LO7 Explain how business events affect financial statements over multiple accounting cycles.

Exhibit 2–6 *Multicycle Vertical Statements Model*

CONNER CONSULTANTS
Financial Statements

For the Years	2004	2005
Income Statements		
Consulting Revenue	$84,000	$ 96,000
Interest Revenue	0	3,000
Salary Expense	(16,000)	(22,000)
Advertising Expense	(2,000)	0
Net Income	$66,000	$ 77,000
Statements of Changes in Stockholders' Equity		
Beginning Common Stock	$ 0	$ 5,000
Plus: Common Stock Issued	5,000	25,000
Ending Common Stock	5,000	30,000
Beginning Retained Earnings	0	66,000
Plus: Net Income	66,000	77,000
Less: Dividends	0	(10,000)
Ending Retained Earnings	66,000	133,000
Total Stockholders' Equity	$71,000	$163,000
Balance Sheets		
Assets		
Cash	$53,000	$ 90,000
Accounts Receivable	24,000	18,000
Interest Receivable	0	3,000
Certificate of Deposit	0	60,000
Total Assets	$77,000	$171,000
Liabilities		
Salaries Payable	$ 6,000	$ 8,000
Stockholders' Equity		
Common Stock	5,000	30,000
Retained Earnings	66,000	133,000
Total Stockholders' Equity	71,000	163,000
Total Liabilities and Stockholders' Equity	$77,000	$171,000
Statements of Cash Flows		
Cash Flows from Operating Activities		
Cash Receipts from Customers	$60,000	$102,000
Cash Payments for Salary Expense	(10,000)	(20,000)
Cash Payments for Advertising Expense	(2,000)	0
Net Cash Flow from Operating Activities	48,000	82,000
Cash Flows from Investing Activities		
Cash Payment to Purchase CD	0	(60,000)
Cash Flows from Financing Activities		
Cash Receipts from Issuing Common Stock	5,000	25,000
Cash Payments for Dividends	0	(10,000)
Net Cash Flow from Financing Activities	5,000	15,000
Net Change in Cash	53,000	37,000
Plus: Beginning Cash Balance	0	53,000
Ending Cash Balance	$53,000	$ 90,000

THE FINANCIAL ANALYST

As previously explained, financial statements are prepared in accordance with certain rules, called *generally accepted accounting principles (GAAP)*. Thus, when General Electric publishes its financial statements, it is saying not only "here are our financial statements," but more specifically, "here are our financial statements prepared according to GAAP." How can a financial analyst know that a company really did follow GAAP? Analysts and other statement users rely on **audits** conducted by **certified public accountants (CPAs).**

LO8 Describe the auditor's role in financial reporting.

The primary roles of an independent auditor (CPA) are summarized below:

1. Conducts a financial audit (a detailed examination of a company's financial statements and underlying accounting records).
2. Assumes both legal and professional responsibilities to the public as well as to the company paying the auditor.
3. Determines if financial statements are **materially** correct rather than **absolutely** correct.
4. Presents conclusions in an audit report that includes an opinion as to whether the statements are prepared in conformity with GAAP. When necessary, the auditor issues a disclaimer.
5. Maintains professional confidentiality of client records. However, this does not exempt the auditor from legal obligations such as testifying in court.

The Financial Audit

What is an audit? There are several different types of audits. The type most relevant to this course is called a **financial audit.** The financial audit is a detailed examination of a company's financial statements and the documents that support those statements. It also tests the reliability of the accounting system used to produce the financial reports. A financial audit is conducted by an **independent auditor** who must be a CPA.

The term *independent auditor* typically refers to a *firm* of certified public accountants. CPAs are licensed by state governments to provide services to the public. They are to be as independent of the companies they audit as is reasonably possible. To help assure independence, CPAs and members of their immediate families may not be employees of the companies they audit. Further, they cannot have investments in the companies they audit. While CPAs are paid by the companies they audit, the audit fee may not be based on the outcome of the audit.

Although the independent auditors are chosen by, paid by, and can be fired by their client companies, the auditors are primarily responsible to *the public*. In fact, auditors have a legal responsibility to those members of the public who have a financial interest in the company being audited. If investors in a company lose money, they sometimes sue the independent auditors in an attempt to recover their losses, especially if the losses were related to financial failure. A lawsuit against auditors will succeed only if the auditors failed in their professional responsibilities when conducting the audit. Auditors are not responsible for the success or failure of a company. Instead, they are responsible for the appropriate reporting of that success or failure. While recent debacles such as Enron produce spectacular headlines, auditors are actually not sued very often, considering the number of audits they perform.

Materiality and Financial Audits

Auditors do not guarantee that financial statements are absolutely correct—only that they are *materially* correct. This is where things get a little fuzzy. What is a **material error?** The concept of materiality is very subjective. If **Wal-Mart** inadvertently overstated its sales by $1 million, would this be material? In 2002, Wal-Mart had approximately $245 billion of sales! A $1 million error in computing sales at Wal-Mart is like a $1 error in computing the pay of a person who makes $245,000 per year—not material at all! An error, or other reporting problem, is *material* if knowing about it would influence the decisions of an *average prudent investor.*

Financial audits are not directed toward the discovery of fraud. Even so, auditors are responsible for providing *reasonable assurance* that statements are free from material misstatements, whether caused by errors or fraud. Also, auditors are responsible for evaluating whether internal control procedures (explained in Chapter 7) are in place to help prevent fraud. If fraud is widespread in a company, normal audit procedures should detect it.

As noted in the text discussion, independent auditors are primarily responsible to the investing public, not to the company that hires and pays them. In 2002 numerous accounting scandals involving some very large public companies caused investors to question whether or not the external auditors really were independent. The public learned that external audit firms were often also serving as consultants to the companies they audited. The fees earned for consulting services were sometimes significantly higher than the fees earned auditing the same company. These arrangements caused many people, including members of Congress, to doubt that auditors would take a tough stance with a company's management over financial reporting issues if doing so might threaten future consulting fees.

No situation demonstrated this concern more than that of Enron. The well-publicized accounting problems that led to Enron's downfall were equally devastating for its auditor, Arthur Andersen. Within six months after Enron's troubles became public knowledge, Arthur Andersen lost over half its public company audit clients and almost two-thirds of its employees. Further, Andersen was convicted of obstruction of justice by a Houston jury and was told by the SEC that it could no longer audit public companies. The partner in charge of the Enron audit was fired and pled guilty to obstruction of justice charges; the previous year, his compensation exceeded $1 million.

In addition to the consequences mentioned above, civil lawsuits were filed against Arthur Andersen, and legal experts believe its partners, even those not involved in the Enron audit, will likely be held personally liable for any damages resulting from inadequate audits. Congress has given CPAs a legal monopoly to provide independent audits for public companies. However, their protected status does not shelter them from the consequences of their actions. As the Enron case demonstrates, when CPAs fail, they are held to a high and costly standard.

Accounting majors take at least one and often two or more courses in auditing to understand how to conduct an audit. An explanation of auditing techniques is beyond the scope of this course, but at least be aware that auditors do not review how the company accounted for every transaction. Along with other methods, auditors use statistics to choose representative samples of transactions to examine.

Types of Audit Opinions

Once an audit is complete, the auditors present their conclusions in a report that includes an *audit opinion.* There are three basic types of audit opinions.

An **unqualified opinion,** despite its negative-sounding name, is the most favorable opinion auditors can express. It means the auditor believes the financial statements are in compliance with GAAP without qualification, reservation, or exception. Most audits result in unqualified opinions because companies correct any reporting deficiencies the auditors find before the financial statements are released.

The most negative report an auditor can issue is an **adverse opinion.** An adverse opinion means that one or more departures from GAAP are so material the financial statements do not present a fair picture of the company's status. The auditor's report explains the unacceptable accounting practice(s) that resulted in the adverse opinion being issued. Adverse opinions are very rare because public companies are required by law to follow GAAP.

A **qualified opinion** falls between an unqualified and an adverse opinion. A qualified opinion means that for the most part, the company's financial statements are in compliance with GAAP, but the auditors have reservations about something in the statements. The auditors' report explains why the opinion is qualified. A qualified opinion usually does not imply a serious accounting problem, but users should read the auditors' report and draw their own conclusions.

If an auditor is unable to perform the audit procedures necessary to determine whether the statements are prepared in accordance with GAAP, the auditor cannot issue an opinion on the financial statements. Instead, the auditor issues a **disclaimer of audit opinion.** A disclaimer is neither negative nor positive. It simply means that the auditor is unable to obtain enough information to confirm compliance with GAAP.

Regardless of the type of report they issue, auditors are only expressing their judgment about whether the financial statements present a fair picture of a company. They do not provide opinions regarding the investment quality of a company.

The ultimate responsibility for financial statements rests with the executives of the reporting company. Just like auditors, managers can be sued by investors who believe they lost money due to improper financial reporting. This is one reason all business persons should understand accounting fundamentals.

Confidentiality

The code of ethics for CPAs prohibits auditors from **voluntarily disclosing** information they have acquired as a result of their accountant-client relationships. However, accountants

focus on INTERNATIONAL ISSUES

Is Historical Cost Used in Other Countries?

Accounting rules in the United States use **historical cost** to record most accounting transactions. If the Coca-Cola Company purchased land in Atlanta for $10,000 in 1920, that land, if still owned, will be reported on the company's 2020 balance sheet at $10,000 even if it is worth $5,000,000 by then. Not everyone in the United States thinks historical cost is the best way to report accounting numbers, but U.S. GAAP requires it.

The accounting rules in most countries around the world also use historical cost as the primary basis for measuring and reporting accounting transactions. There are, however, exceptions, primarily in economies that have experienced high inflation. The 100-year time frame supposed in the hypothetical Coca-Cola example above makes the change in the value of the land look dramatic. Over shorter time spans, land prices in the United States do not change so radically, so historical costs are not actually so dramatically out of date. In some South American countries, prices have risen much faster than those in the United States. For example, while the annual rate of inflation in the United States typically ranges from 2 to 6 percent, in Brazil it has seldom been below 20 percent and in some years has exceeded 1,000 percent. Not surprisingly, the GAAP in Brazil does not use historical cost as the primary basis for reporting financial information.

In some countries, such as the Netherlands, companies use historical costs as the primary reporting measure but may report some assets, such as land and buildings, at the estimated amount it would cost to replace them rather than at their historical costs. Accounting is a discipline created to serve the needs of financial statement users. Accounting rules reflect the unique needs of users in different countries.

may be required to testify in a court of law. In general, federal law does not recognize an accountant-client privilege as it does with attorneys and clergy. Some federal courts have taken exception to this position, especially as it applies to tax cases. State law varies with respect to its treatment of accountant-client privilege. Furthermore, if auditors terminate a client relationship because of ethical or legal disagreements and they are subsequently contacted by a successor auditor, they may be required to inform the successor of the reasons for the termination. In addition, auditors must consider the particular circumstances of a case when assessing the appropriateness of disclosing confidential information. Given the diverse legal positions governing accountant-client confidentiality, auditors should seek legal counsel prior to disclosing any information obtained in an accountant-client relationship.

To illustrate, assume that Joe Smith, CPA, discovers that his client Jane Doe is misrepresenting information reported in her financial statements. Smith tries to convince Doe to correct the misrepresentations, but she refuses to do so. Smith is required by the code of ethics to terminate his relationship with Doe. However, Smith is not permitted to disclose Doe's dishonest reporting practices unless he is called on to testify in a legal hearing or to respond to an inquiry by Doe's successor accountant.

With respect to the discovery of significant fraud, the auditor is required to inform management at least one level above the position of the employee who is engaged in the fraud and to notify the board of directors of the company. Suppose that Joe Smith, CPA, discovers that Jane Doe, employee of Western Company, is embezzling money from Western. Smith is required to inform Doe's supervisor and to notify Western's board of directors. However, Smith is prohibited from publicly disclosing the fraud.

▌Importance of Ethics

LO9 Describe the articles of the AICPA's Code of Professional Conduct and identify the major factors that lead to unethical conduct.

The accountant's role in society requires trust and credibility. An audit opinion is worthless if the auditor is not trustworthy. Similarly, tax and consulting advice is useless if it comes from an incompetent person. The high ethical standards required by the profession state "a certified public accountant assumes an obligation of self-discipline above and beyond requirements of laws and regulations."[1] The **American Institute of Certified Public Accountants** requires its members to comply with the **Code of Professional Conduct.** Section I of the Code includes six articles that are summarized in Exhibit 2–7. The importance of ethical conduct is universally recognized across a broad spectrum of accounting organizations. The Institute of Management Accountants requires its members to follow a set of Standards of Ethical Conduct. The Institute of Internal Auditors also requires its members to subscribe to the organization's Code of Ethics.

Sarbanes-Oxley Act of 2002

Unfortunately, codes of ethics cannot deter all unethical behavior. The massive surprise bankruptcies of Enron in late 2001 and WorldCom several months later suggested major audit failures on the part of the independent auditors. An audit failure means a company's auditor does not detect, or fails to report, that the company's financial reports are not in compliance with GAAP. The audit failures at Enron, WorldCom, and others prompted Congress to pass the Sarbanes-Oxley Act, which became effective on July 30, 2002. The provisions of this legislation are complex, and their full effects will not be known for some time. However, it is clear that the act has tightened the rules governing auditors' independence.

Prior to Sarbanes-Oxley, independent auditors often provided non-audit services, such as installing computer systems, for their audit clients. The fees they earned for these services sometimes greatly exceeded the fees charged for the audit itself. This practice had been questioned prior to the audit failures at Enron and WorldCom. Critics felt the independent audit

---

[1]American Institute of Certified Public Accountants, Inc. (AICPA), *Code of Professional Conduct* (New York: AICPA, 1992).

Exhibit 2–7 *Articles of AICPA Code of Professional Conduct*

Article I Responsibilities
In carrying out their responsibilities as professionals, members should exercise sensitive professional and moral judgments in all their activities.

Article II The Public Interest
Members should accept the obligation to act in a way that will serve the public interest, honor the public trust, and demonstrate commitment to professionalism.

Article III Integrity
To maintain and broaden public confidence, members should perform all professional responsibilities with the highest sense of integrity.

Article IV Objectivity and Independence
A member should maintain objectivity and be free of conflicts of interest in discharging professional responsibilities. A member in public practice should be independent in fact and appearance when providing auditing and other attestation services.

Article V Due Care
A member should observe the profession's technical and ethical standards, strive continually to improve competence and the quality of services, and discharge professional responsibility to the best of the member's ability.

Article VI Scope and Nature of Services
A member in public practice should observe the principles of the Code of Professional Conduct in determining the scope and nature of services to be provided.

---

firm was subject to pressure from the company to conduct a less rigorous audit, or risk losing lucrative nonaudit work. The Sarbanes-Oxley Act prohibits auditors from providing most types of nonaudit services to companies they audit.

Another provision of Sarbanes-Oxley clarifies the legal responsibility that company management has for a company's financial reports. The company's chief executive officer (CEO) and chief financial officer (CFO) must certify in writing that they have reviewed the financial reports being issued, and that the reports present fairly the company's financial status. An executive who falsely certifies the company's financial reports is subject to significant fines and imprisonment.

Additional details of the Sarbanes-Oxley Act are presented in Chapter 4. Further discussion of the problems at WorldCom and Enron are presented in Chapters 7 and 10, respectively.

Common Features of Ethical Misconduct

People who become involved in unethical or criminal behavior usually do so unexpectedly. They start with small indiscretions that evolve gradually into more serious violations of trust. To reduce the incidence of unethical or illegal conduct, business persons must be aware of conditions that lead to trust violations. To increase awareness, Donald Cressey studied hundreds of criminal cases to identify the primary factors behind ethical misconduct. Cressey found three factors common to all cases: (1) the existence of a nonsharable problem, (2) the presence of an opportunity, and (3) the capacity for rationalization.[2]

As the term implies, a *nonsharable problem* is one that must be kept secret. Individuals have different ideas about what they think must be kept to themselves. Consider two responses to the problem of an imminent business failure. One person may feel so ashamed that he or she cannot discuss the problem with anyone. Another person in the same situation may want to talk to anyone, even a stranger, in the hope of getting help. Other nonsharable problems include personal vices such as drug addiction, gambling, and promiscuity. Cressey's findings suggest that the person who is inclined toward secrecy is more likely to accept an unethical or illegal solution. In other words, the perceived need for secrecy increases vulnerability.

Accountants establish policies and procedures designed to reduce *opportunities* for fraud. These policies and procedures are commonly called **internal controls.** Specific internal

---

[2]D. R. Cressey, *Other People's Money* (Montclair, NJ: Paterson Smith, 1973).

control procedures are tailored to meet the individual needs of particular businesses. For example, banks use vaults to protect cash, but universities have little use for this type of equipment. Chapter 7 discusses internal control procedures in more detail. At this point, simply recognize that accountants are very aware of the need to reduce opportunities for unethical and criminal activities.

Few individuals think of themselves as dishonest, so they develop *rationalizations* with which they justify their misconduct. Cressey found a significant number of embezzlers who contended they were only "borrowing the money," even after being convicted and sentenced to jail. Common rationalizations include peer pressure, loyalty to unscrupulous superiors, family needs, revenge, and a sense of entitlement. To avoid involvement in ethical misconduct, accountants must develop a strong sense of personal responsibility. They cannot allow themselves to blame other people or unfair circumstances for their problems. They must learn to hold themselves personally accountable for their actions.

Ethical misconduct is a serious offense in the accounting profession. A single mistake can destroy an accounting career. If you commit a white-collar crime, you normally lose the opportunity to hold a white-collar job. Second chances are rarely granted; it is extremely important that you learn how to recognize and avoid the common features of ethical misconduct. To help you prepare for the real-world situations you are likely to encounter, we include ethical dilemmas in the end-of-chapter materials. When working with these dilemmas, try to identify the (1) secret, (2) opportunity, and (3) rationalization associated with the particular ethical situation described. If you are not an ethical person, accounting is not the career for you.

---

a look back

LO10 Classify accounting events into one of four categories:
a. asset source transactions.
b. asset use transactions.
c. asset exchange transactions.
d. claims exchange transactions.

Chapters 1 and 2 introduced four types of transactions. It is helpful to identify transactions by type. Although businesses engage in an infinite number of different transactions, all transactions fall into one of four types. By learning to identify transactions by type, you can understand how unfamiliar events affect financial statements. The four types of transactions are:

1. *Asset source transactions:* An asset account increases, and a corresponding claims account increases.
2. *Asset use transactions:* An asset account decreases, and a corresponding claims account decreases.
3. *Asset exchange transactions:* One asset account increases, and another asset account decreases.
4. *Claims exchange transactions:* One claims account increases, and another claims account decreases.

Also, the definitions of revenue and expense have been expanded. The complete definitions of these two elements are as follows:

1. **Revenue:** Revenue is the *economic benefit* derived from operating the business. Its recognition is accompanied by an increase in assets or a decrease in liabilities resulting from providing products or services to customers.
2. **Expense:** An expense is an *economic sacrifice* incurred in the process of generating revenue. Its recognition is accompanied by a decrease in assets or an increase in liabilities resulting from consuming assets and services in an effort to produce revenue.

Finally, this chapter introduced the *accrual accounting* concept. Accrual accounting causes the amount of revenues and expenses reported on the income statement to differ significantly from the amount of cash flow from operating activities reported on the statement of cash flows because of timing differences. These differences are readily apparent when relevant events are recorded in a horizontal financial statements model. To review, study the following transactions and the corresponding statements model. Set up a statements model on a piece of paper and try to record the effects of each event before reading the explanation.

Events:

1. Provided $600 of services on account.
2. Collected $400 cash from accounts receivable.

3. Accrued $350 of salary expense.
4. Paid $225 cash in partial settlement of salaries payable.

Event No.	Balance Sheet									Income Statement					Statement of Cash Flows	
	Cash	+	Accts. Rec.	=	Sal. Pay.	+	Ret. Earn.		Rev.	−	Exp.	=	Net Inc.			
1	NA	+	600	=	NA	+	600		600	−	NA	=	600		NA	
2	400	+	(400)	=	NA	+	NA		NA	−	NA	=	NA		400	OA
3	NA	+	NA	=	350	+	(350)		NA	−	350	=	(350)		NA	
4	(225)	+	NA	=	(225)	+	NA		NA	−	NA	=	NA		(225)	OA
Totals	175	+	200	=	125	+	250		600	−	350	=	250		175	NC

Notice the $250 of net income differs from the $175 cash flow from operating activities. The entries in the statements model demonstrate the reasons for the difference. Although $600 of revenue is recognized, only $400 of cash was collected. The remaining $200 will be collected in the future and is currently shown on the balance sheet as Accounts Receivable. Also, although $350 of salary expense is recognized, only $225 was paid in cash. The remaining $125 will be paid in the future. This obligation is shown as Salaries Payable on the balance sheet. Study these relationships carefully to develop a clear understanding of how accrual accounting affects financial reporting.

Chapter 3 explains more features of accrual accounting. In addition to accruals, the accrual system also involves deferrals. *Deferrals* occur when a company receives or pays cash before it recognizes the related revenue or expense. A magazine subscription is an example of a deferral because magazine companies receive the cash before they send magazines to their customers. The cash is collected in advance, but the revenue is not recognized until the magazines are delivered. Chapter 3 reinforces what you have learned about asset source, use, and exchange transactions and claims exchange transactions. You will also expand your understanding of how business events affect financial statements.

a look forward

SELF-STUDY REVIEW PROBLEM

Walberg Company experienced the following accounting events during 2003.

1. Started operations in January 2003 when it acquired $22,000 cash by issuing common stock.
2. During the 2003 period, recognized $246,000 of revenue on account.
3. Collected $222,000 cash from accounts receivable.
4. Paid operating expenses of $205,000 in cash.
5. Paid a $14,000 cash dividend to stockholders.
6. On April 1, 2003, borrowed $18,000 by issuing a note to National Bank.
7. On December 31, 2003, adjusted the accounting records to recognize interest expense incurred on the note it had issued to National bank. The note had a 10 percent annual interest rate and a one-year term to maturity. Interest is due in cash on the maturity date (March 31, 2004).

Walberg Company experienced the following accounting events during 2004.

1. Accrued the remaining interest expense on the note payable through March 31, 2004.
2. Paid cash for the amount of interest payable as of March 31, 2004.
3. Paid cash to repay the principal due on the note payable as of March 31, 2004.
4. Recognized $259,000 of revenue on account.
5. Collected $262,000 cash from accounts receivable.
6. Paid operating expenses of $211,000 in cash.
7. Paid a $24,000 cash dividend to stockholders.

Required
a. Record the events in a financial statements model like the following one. The first event is recorded as an example.

Event No.	Assets		=	Liabilities		+	Stockholders' Equity					Rev. – Exp. = Net Inc.			Cash Flow
	Cash	+ Accts. Rec.	=	Note Pay.	+ Int. Pay.	+	C. Stk.	+	Ret. Ear.						
1	22,000 +	NA	=	NA	+ NA	+	22,000	+	NA			NA – NA = NA			22,000 FA

b. What amount of interest expense would Walberg report on the 2003 and 2004 income statements?

c. What amount of cash outflow for interest would Walberg report in the operating activities sections of the 2003 and 2004 statements of cash flows?

d. What are the 2004 opening balances for the revenue and expense accounts?

e. What amount of total assets would Walberg report on the 2003 balance sheet?

f. What claims on assets would Walberg report on the 2003 balance sheet?

g. Explain what caused the cash balance to change between December 31, 2003, and December 31, 2004.

Solution to Requirement a
The financial statements model follows.

Event No.	Assets		=	Liabilities		+	Stockholders' Equity				Rev.	–	Exp.	= Net Inc.	Cash Flow
	Cash	+ Accts. Rec.	=	Note Pay.	+ Int. Pay.	+	C. Stk.	+	Ret. Ear.						
1	22,000 +	NA	=	NA	+ NA	+	22,000	+	NA		NA –		NA =	NA	22,000 FA
2	NA +	246,000	=	NA	+ NA	+	NA	+	246,000		246,000 –		NA =	246,000	NA
3	222,000 +	(222,000)	=	NA	+ NA	+	NA	+	NA		NA –		NA =	NA	222,000 OA
4	(205,000) +	NA	=	NA	+ NA	+	NA	+	(205,000)		NA –		205,000 =	(205,000)	(205,000) OA
5	(14,000) +	NA	=	NA	+ NA	+	NA	+	(14,000)		NA –		NA =	NA	(14,000) FA
6	18,000 +	NA	=	18,000	+ NA	+	NA	+	NA		NA –		NA =	NA	18,000 FA
7*	NA +	NA	=	NA	+ 1,350	+	NA	+	(1,350)		NA –		1,350 =	(1,350)	NA
Totals	43,000 +	24,000	=	18,000	+ 1,350	+	22,000	+	25,650		246,000 –		206,350 =	39,650	43,000 NC
	Asset, Liability, and Equity Account Balances Carry Forward										Rev. & Exp. Accts. Are Closed				
Bal.	43,000 +	24,000	=	18,000	+ 1,350	+	22,000	+	25,650		NA –		NA =	NA	NA
1†	NA +	NA	=	NA	+ 450	+	NA	+	(450)		NA –		450 =	(450)	NA
2	(1,800) +	NA	=	NA	+ (1,800)	+	NA	+	NA		NA –		NA =	NA	(1,800) OA
3	(18,000) +	NA	=	(18,000)	+ NA	+	NA	+	NA		NA –		NA =	NA	(18,000) FA
4	NA +	259,000	=	NA	+ NA	+	NA	+	259,000		259,000 –		NA =	259,000	NA
5	262,000 +	(262,000)	=	NA	+ NA	+	NA	+	NA		NA –		NA =	NA	262,000 OA
6	(211,000) +	NA	=	NA	+ NA	+	NA	+	(211,000)		NA –		211,000 =	(211,000)	(211,000) OA
7	(24,000) +	NA	=	NA	+ NA	+	NA	+	(24,000)		NA –		NA =	NA	(24,000) FA
Totals	50,200 +	21,000	=	0	+ 0	+	22,000	+	49,200		259,000 –		211,450 =	47,550	7,200 NC

*Accrued interest expense for 2003 = $18,000 × .10 × 9/12 = $1,350.
†Accrued interest expense for 2004 = $18,000 × .10 × 3/12 = $450.

Solution to Requirements b–g

b. Walberg would report interest expense on the 2003 and 2004 income statements of $1,350 and $450, respectively.

c. Walberg made no cash interest payments in 2003. All cash for interest was paid in 2004. Walberg would report zero cash outflow for interest on the 2003 statement of cash flows and $1,800 cash outflow for interest on the 2004 statement.

d. Because all revenue and expense accounts are closed at the end of each accounting period, the beginning balances for revenue and expense accounts are always zero.

e. The total asset balance on the 2003 balance sheet would be $67,000 (Cash $43,000 + Accounts Receivable $24,000).

f. Creditors have a $19,350 (Note Payable $18,000 + Interest Payable $1,350) claim. Owners (investors) have a $47,650 (Common Stock $22,000 + Retained Earnings $25,650) claim on the assets. Total claims of $67,000 ($19,350 + $47,650) are equal to total assets.

g. The net cash inflow from operating activities was $49,200 ($262,000 revenue − $1,800 interest expense − $211,000 operating expense). There were no investing activities. The net cash outflow from financing activities was $42,000 ($18,000 debt payment + $24,000 dividends). The net change in cash was a $7,200 cash inflow ($49,200 from operating activities − $42,000 used by financing activities).

Accounting cycle *61*

Accounts receivable *56*

Accrual *56*

Accrual accounting *55*

Adjusting entry *64*

Adverse opinion *72*

American Institute of Certified Public Accountants *74*

Asset exchange transaction *56*

Asset source transaction *56*

Asset use transaction *57*

Audit *71*

Certified Public Accountant (CPA) *71*

Claims exchange transaction *57*

Closing *61*

Closing the books *61*

Code of Professional Conduct *74*

Disclaimer of audit opinion *73*

Expense *59, 76*

Financial audit *71*

Historical cost *73*

Independent auditor *71*

Internal controls *75*

Investment *63*

Issuer *68*

Matching concept *64*

Material error *71*

Nominal accounts *61*

Notes payable *67*

Period costs *62*

Permanent accounts *61*

Qualified opinion *73*

Realization *55*

Recognition *55*

Revenue *76*

Salaries payable *57*

Temporary accounts *61*

Unqualified opinion *72*

Voluntarily disclosing *73*

1. What does accrual accounting attempt to accomplish?
2. Define *recognition.* How is it independent of collecting or paying cash?
3. What does the term *asset source transaction* mean?
4. What effect does the issue of Common Stock have on the accounting equation?
5. How does the recognition of revenue on account (accounts receivable) affect the income statement compared to its effect on the statement of cash flows?
6. Give an example of an asset source transaction. What is the effect of this transaction on the accounting equation?
7. When is revenue recognized under accrual accounting?
8. Give an example of an asset exchange transaction. What is the effect of this transaction on the accounting equation?
9. What effect does expense recognition have on the accounting equation?
10. What does the term *claims exchange transaction* mean?
11. What type of transaction is a cash payment to creditors? How does this type of transaction affect the accounting equation?
12. When are expenses recognized under accrual accounting?
13. Why may net cash flow from operating activities on the cash flow statement be different from the amount of net income reported on the income statement?
14. What is the relationship between the income statement and changes in assets and liabilities?
15. What does the term *net assets* mean?
16. How does net income affect the stockholders' claims on the business's assets?
17. What does the term *expense* mean?
18. What does the term *revenue* mean?
19. What is the purpose of the statement of changes in stockholders' equity?
20. What is the main purpose of the balance sheet?
21. Why is the balance sheet dated *as of* a specific date when the income statement, statement of changes in stockholders' equity, and statement of cash flows are dated with the phrase *for the period ended?*
22. In what order are assets listed on the balance sheet?
23. What does the statement of cash flows explain?
24. When is interest earned on an investment recognized?
25. What does the term *adjusting entry* mean? Give an example.
26. What type of entry is the entry to record accrued interest revenue? How does it affect the accounting equation?
27. What type of entry is the entry to record accrued interest expense? How does it affect the accounting equation?
28. Is land purchased in 1920 reported on a current balance sheet at its current value? If not, at what value is it shown?
29. What is the historical cost concept of accounting measurement?
30. Do all countries use historical cost for accounting measurement? Why or why not?

31. What types of accounts are closed at the end of the accounting period? Why is it necessary to close these accounts?
32. Give several examples of period costs.
33. Give an example of a cost that can be directly matched with the revenue produced by an accounting firm from preparing a tax return.
34. List and describe the four stages of the accounting cycle discussed in Chapter 2.
35. What is a financial audit? Who is qualified to perform it?
36. What is an independent auditor? Why must auditors be independent?
37. What makes an error in the financial statements material?
38. What three basic types of auditors' opinions can be issued on audited financial statements? Describe each.
39. What are the implications of an unqualified audit opinion?
40. When might an auditor issue a disclaimer on financial statements?
41. In what circumstances can an auditor disclose confidential information about a client without the client's permission?
42. What are the six articles of ethical conduct set out under section I of the AICPA's Code of Professional Conduct?
43. What is the purpose of internal controls in an organization?

EXERCISES—SERIES A

All Exercises in Series A are available with McGraw-Hill's Homework Manager

Where applicable in all exercises, round computations to the nearest dollar.

L.O. 2, 3   **EXERCISE 2–1A** *Effect of Accruals on the Financial Statements*

Hamby, Inc., experienced the following events in 2003, in its first year of operation.

1. Received $15,000 cash from the issue of common stock.
2. Performed services on account for $48,000.
3. Paid the utility expense of $1,250.
4. Collected $36,000 of the accounts receivable.
5. Recorded $8,000 of accrued salaries at the end of the year.
6. Paid a $1,000 cash dividend to the shareholders.

Required
a. Record the events in general ledger accounts under an accounting equation. In the last column of the table, provide appropriate account titles for the Retained Earnings amounts. The first transaction has been recorded as an example.

		HAMBY, INC.						
		General Ledger Accounts						
Event	Assets		=	Liabilities	+	Stockholders' Equity		Acct. Titles for RE
	Cash	Accounts Receivable		Salaries Payable		Common Stock	Retained Earnings	
1.	15,000					15,000		

b. Prepare the income statement, statement of changes in stockholders' equity, balance sheet, and statement of cash flows for the 2003 accounting period.
c. Why is the amount of net income different from the amount of net cash flow from operating activities?

L.O. 2, 3   **EXERCISE 2–2A** *Effect of Collecting Accounts Receivable on the Accounting Equation and Financial Statements*

Pilgram Company earned $6,000 of service revenue on account during 2008. The company collected $5,200 cash from accounts receivable during 2008.

Required

Based on this information alone, determine the following. (*Hint:* Record the events in general ledger accounts under an accounting equation before satisfying the requirements.)

a. The balance of the accounts receivable that Pilgram would report on the December 31, 2008 balance sheet.
b. The amount of net income that Pilgram would report on the 2008 income statement.
c. The amount of net cash flow from operating activities that Pilgram would report on the 2008 statement of cash flows.
d. The amount of retained earnings that Pilgram would report on the 2008 balance sheet.
e. Why are the answers to Requirements *b* and *c* different?

EXERCISE 2–3A *Effect of Earning Revenue on Account on the Financial Statements*   **L.O. 1**

T. Clausen started a computer training center in 2004. The only accounting event in 2004 was the recognition of $9,600 of service revenue earned on account.

Required

Use the following horizontal statements model to show how this event affects the balance sheet, income statement, and statement of cash flows. Indicate whether the event increases (I), decreases (D), or does not affect (NA) each element of the financial statements. Also, in the Cash Flows column, designate the classification of any cash flows using the letters OA for operating activities, IA for investing activities, and FA for financing activities.

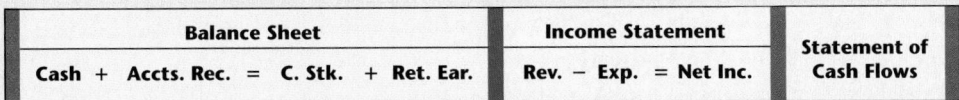

Balance Sheet					Income Statement			Statement of Cash Flows
Cash	+ Accts. Rec.	= C. Stk.	+ Ret. Ear.		Rev.	− Exp.	= Net Inc.	

EXERCISE 2–4A *Effects of Revenue and Expense Recognition on the Income Statement and Statement of Cash Flows*   **L.O. 3**

The following transactions pertain to the operations of Poole & Co., CPAs.

1. Acquired $50,000 cash from the issue of common stock.
2. Performed accounting services and billed clients $60,000.
3. Paid a $5,000 cash dividend to the stockholders.
4. Collected $52,000 cash from accounts receivable.
5. Paid $46,000 cash for other operating expenses.
6. Performed accounting services for $10,000 cash.

Required

a. Identify which of these transactions result in revenue or expense recognition for Poole & Co., CPAs.
b. Based on your response to part *a*, determine the amount of net income Poole will report on its income statement.
c. Identify which of the preceding transactions affect(s) cash flow from operating activities.
d. Based on your response to Requirement *c*, determine the amount of net cash flow from operating activities Poole will report on the statement of cash flows.

EXERCISE 2–5A *Classifying Events on the Statement of Cash Flows*   **L.O. 3**

The following transactions pertain to the operations of Stone Company for 2004:

1. Acquired $24,000 cash from the issue of common stock.
2. Provided $40,000 of services on account.
3. Incurred $25,000 of other operating expenses on account.
4. Collected $32,000 cash from accounts receivable.
5. Paid a $2,000 cash dividend to the stockholders.
6. Paid $18,000 cash on accounts payable.
7. Performed services for $8,000 cash.
8. Paid $1,000 cash for rent expense.

Required

a. Classify the cash flows from these transactions as operating activities (OA), investing activities (IA), or financing activities (FA). Use NA for transactions that do not affect the statement of cash flows.
b. Prepare a statement of cash flows. (There is no beginning cash balance.)

L.O. 1   **EXERCISE 2–6A** *Effect of Accounts Receivable and Accounts Payable Transactions on Financial Statements*

The following events apply to Hill and Hill, a public accounting firm, for the 2004 accounting period.

1. Performed $92,000 of services for clients on account.
2. Performed $65,000 of services for cash.
3. Incurred $45,000 of other operating expenses on account.
4. Paid $26,000 cash to an employee for salary.
5. Collected $73,000 cash from accounts receivable.
6. Paid $38,000 cash on accounts payable.
7. Paid a $8,000 cash dividend to the stockholders.
8. Accrued salaries were $2,500 at the end of 2004.

Required

a. Show the effects of the events on the financial statements using a horizontal statements model like the following one. In the Cash Flow column, use OA to designate operating activity, IA for investment activity, FA for financing activity, and NC for net change in cash. Use NA to indicate the element is not affected by the event. The first event is recorded as an example.

Event No.	Assets		=	Liabilities			+	Equity						
	Cash	+ Accts. Rec.	=	Accts. Pay.	+	Sal. Pay.	+	Ret. Earn.	Rev.	–	Exp.	= Net Inc.	Cash Flow
1	NA	+ 92,000	=	NA	+	NA	+	92,000	92,000	–	NA	= 92,000	NA

b. What is the amount of total assets at the end of 2004?
c. What is the balance of accounts receivable at the end of 2004?
d. What is the balance of accounts payable at the end of 2004?
e. What is the difference between accounts receivable and accounts payable?
f. What is net income for 2004?
g. What is the amount of net cash flow from operating activities for 2004?

L.O. 2, 3   **EXERCISE 2–7A** *Net Income Versus Changes in Cash*

In 2004, Lott Inc., billed its customers $56,000 for services performed. The company collected $42,000 of the amount billed. Lott incurred $38,000 of other operating expenses on account. Lott paid $25,000 of the accounts payable. Lott acquired $30,000 cash from the issue of common stock. The company invested $12,000 cash in the purchase of land.

Required

Use the preceding information to answer the following questions. (*Hint*: Identify the six events described in the paragraph and record them in general ledger accounts under an accounting equation before attempting to answer the questions.)

a. What amount of revenue will Lott report on the 2004 income statement?
b. What amount of cash flow from revenue will Lott report on the statement of cash flows?
c. What is the net income for the period?
d. What is the net cash flow from operating activities for the period?
e. Why is the amount of net income different from the net cash flow from operating activities for the period?
f. What is the amount of net cash flow from investing activities?
g. What is the amount of net cash flow from financing activities?
h. What amounts of total assets, liabilities, and equity will Lott report on the year-end balance sheet?

L.O. 4   **EXERCISE 2–8A** *Closing the Accounts*

The following information was drawn from the accounting records of Pearson Company as of December 31, 2007, before the temporary accounts had been closed. The Cash balance was $3,000, and Notes Payable amounted to $2,500. The company had revenues of $4,000 and expenses of $2,500. The company's Land account had a $5,000 balance. Dividends amounted to $500. There was $1,000 of common stock issued.

Required

a. Identify which accounts would be classified as permanent and which accounts would be classified as nominal (temporary).

b. Assuming that Pearson's beginning balance (as of January 1, 2007) in the Retained Earnings account was $3,500, determine its balance after the nominal accounts were closed at the end of 2007.

c. What amount of net income would Pearson Company report on its 2007 income statement?

d. Explain why the amount of net income differs from the amount of the ending Retained Earnings balance.

e. What are the balances in the revenue, expense, and dividend accounts on January 1, 2008?

EXERCISE 2–9A *Closing Accounts and the Accounting Cycle*   **L.O. 4**

Required

a. Identify which of the following accounts are temporary (will be closed to Retained Earnings at the end of the year) and which are permanent.

   (1) Cash
   (2) Salaries Expense
   (3) Notes Payable
   (4) Utilities Expense
   (5) Service Revenue
   (6) Dividends
   (7) Common Stock
   (8) Land
   (9) Interest Revenue
   (10) Retained Earnings

b. List and explain the three stages of the accounting cycle. Which stage must be first? Which stage is last?

EXERCISE 2–10A *Closing Entries*   **L.O. 4**

Required

Which of the following accounts are closed at the end of the accounting period?

a. Accounts Payable
b. Certificate of Deposit
c. Cash
d. Accounts Receivable
e. Service Revenue
f. Advertising Expense
g. Dividends
h. Retained Earnings
i. Utilities Expense
j. Notes Payable
k. Interest Expense
l. Interest Payable

EXERCISE 2–11A *Matching Concept*   **L.O. 7**

Companies make sacrifices known as *expenses* to obtain benefits called *revenues*. The accurate measurement of net income requires that expenses be matched with revenues. In some circumstances matching a particular expense directly with revenue is difficult or impossible. In these circumstances, the expense is matched with the period in which it is incurred.

Required

a. Identify an expense that could be matched directly with revenue.

b. Identify a period expense that would be difficult to match with revenue. Explain why.

EXERCISE 2–12A *Complete Accounting Cycle*   **L.O. 2, 3**

The following information is available for Zuber Co. for the year 2004:

1. Acquired $40,000 cash from the issue of common stock.
2. Performed $120,000 of services on account.
3. Incurred other operating expenses on account in the amount of $85,000.

4. Purchased land for $20,000 cash.
5. Collected $95,000 cash from accounts receivable.
6. Paid $50,000 cash on accounts payable.
7. Performed services for $26,000 cash.
8. Paid $15,000 cash for salaries expense.
9. Paid a $5,000 cash dividend to the stockholders.
10. Borrowed $10,000 cash from State Bank.

Information for Adjusting Entry

11. Accrued interest expense at the end of the accounting period was $900.

Required

a. Explain how each of the transactions affects the elements of the accounting equation by placing a + for *increase*, − for *decrease*, and NA for *not affected* under each of the elements. Also record the dollar amount of the effect of each event on the accounting equation. In the last column of the table, provide appropriate account titles for Retained Earnings accounts. The first event is recorded as an example.

Event No.	Assets	=	Liabilities	+	Stockholders' Equity Common Stock	+	Retained Earnings	Acct. Title for RE
1	+40,000		NA		+40,000		NA	

b. What is the amount of net income for 2004?
c. What is the amount of total assets at the end of 2004?
d. What is the amount of total liabilities at the end of 2004?

EXERCISE 2–13A *Effects of Recognizing Accrued Interest on Financial Statements*

L.O. 1, 5

Scott Perkins started Perkins Company on January 1, 2005. The company experienced the following events during its first year of operation.

1. Earned $1,500 of cash revenue for performing services.
2. Borrowed $2,400 cash from the bank.
3. Adjusted the accounting records to recognize accrued interest expense on the bank note. The note, issued on August 1, 2005, had a one-year term and a 7 percent annual interest rate.

Required

a. What is the amount of interest expense in 2005?
b. What amount of cash was paid for interest in 2005?
c. Use a horizontal statements model to show how each event affects the balance sheet, income statement, and statement of cash flows. Indicate whether the event increases (I), decreases (D), or does not affect (NA) each element of the financial statements. Also, in the Cash Flows column, designate the cash flows as operating activities (OA), investing activities (IA), or financing activities (FA). The first transaction has been recorded as an example.

Event No.	Balance Sheet Cash	=	Note Pay.	+	Int. Pay.	+	C. Stk.	+	Ret. Earn.	Income Statement Rev.	−	Exp.	=	Net Inc.	Statement of Cash Flows
1	I	=	NA	+	NA	+	NA	+	I	I	−	NA	=	I	I OA

L.O. 2, 5, 7   EXERCISE 2–14A *Recognizing Accrued Interest Revenue*

Hi-Teck Company invested $90,000 in a certificate of deposit on June 1, 2006. The certificate had a 5 percent annual rate of interest and a one-year term to maturity.

Required

a. What amount of interest revenue will Hi-Teck recognize for the year ending December 31, 2006?
b. Show how the December 31, 2006, adjusting entry to recognize the accrued interest revenue affects the accounting equation.

c. What amount of cash will Hi-Teck collect for interest revenue in 2006?
d. What is the amount of interest receivable as of December 31, 2006?
e. What amount of cash will Hi-Teck collect for interest revenue in 2007, assuming it does not renew the CD?
f. What amount of interest revenue will Hi-Teck recognize in 2007, assuming it does not renew the CD?
g. What is the amount of interest receivable as of December 31, 2007, assuming it does not renew the CD?

EXERCISE 2–15A *Recognizing Accrued Interest Expense*

L.O. 3, 5, 7

Classic Corporation borrowed $90,000 from the bank on November 1, 2003. The note had an 8 percent annual rate of interest and matured on April 30, 2004. Interest and principal were paid in cash on the maturity date.

Required
a. What amount of interest expense was paid in cash in 2003?
b. What amount of interest expense was reported on the 2003 income statement?
c. What amount of total liabilities was reported on the December 31, 2003, balance sheet?
d. What total amount of cash was paid to the bank on April 30, 2004, for principal and interest?
e. What amount of interest expense was reported on the 2004 income statement?

EXERCISE 2–16A *Effect of Transactions on the Balance Sheet*

L.O. 2, 3, 5

Star Corp. was formed on January 1, 2006. The business acquired $75,000 cash from the issue of common stock. The business performed $210,000 of services on account and collected $200,000 of the amount due. Other operating expenses incurred on account amounted to $185,000. By the end of 2006, $180,000 of that amount had been paid with cash. The business paid $30,000 cash to purchase land. Star borrowed $30,000 cash from the bank. On December 31, 2006, there was $1,150 of accrued interest expense.

Required
Using the preceding information, answer the following questions. (*Hint:* Identify the eight events described in the preceding paragraph and record them in general ledger accounts under an accounting equation before answering the questions.)

a. What is the cash balance at the end of 2006?
b. What is the balance of accounts receivable at the end of 2006?
c. What is the amount of total assets at the end of 2006?
d. What is the amount of total liabilities at the end of 2006?
e. What is the amount of common stock at the end of 2006?
f. What is the amount of retained earnings at the end of 2006?

EXERCISE 2–17A *Identifying Source, Use, and Exchange Transactions*

L.O. 10

Required
Indicate whether each of the following transactions is an asset source (AS), asset use (AU), asset exchange (AE), or claims exchange (CE) transaction.

a. Acquired cash from the issue of stock.
b. Paid a cash dividend to the stockholders.
c. Paid cash on accounts payable.
d. Incurred other operating expenses on account.
e. Paid cash for rent expense.
f. Performed services for cash.
g. Performed services for clients on account.
h. Collected cash from accounts receivable.
i. Invested cash in a certificate of deposit.
j. Purchased land with cash.

EXERCISE 2–18A *Identifying Asset Source, Use, and Exchange Transactions*

L.O. 10

Required
a. Name an asset use transaction that will *not* affect the income statement.
b. Name an asset exchange transaction that will affect the statement of cash flows.

c. Name an asset source transaction that will *not* affect the income statement.

d. Name an asset source transaction that will *not* affect the statement of cash flows.

e. Name an asset source transaction that will affect the income statement.

L.O. 3   EXERCISE 2–19A *Relation of Elements to Financial Statements*

Required

Identify whether each of the following items would appear on the income statement (IS), statement of changes in stockholders' equity (SE), balance sheet (BS), or statement of cash flows (CF). Some items may appear on more than one statement; if so, identify all applicable statements. If an item would not appear on any financial statement, label it NA.

a. Land
b. Interest Revenue
c. Dividends
d. Salaries Expense
e. Net Income
f. Interest Payable
g. Ending Cash Balance
h. Cash Flow from Investing Activities
i. Note Payable
j. Notes Receivable
k. Accounts Receivable
l. Retained Earnings
m. Interest Receivable
n. Utilities Payable
o. Auditor's Opinion

L.O. 7   EXERCISE 2–20A *Evaluating Cash Management*

The data in the following table apply to DeChow, Incorporated.

	2003	2004
Accounts receivable	$ 24,600,000	$ 27,060,000
Sales	332,700,000	382,606,000
Accounts payable	15,800,000	18,644,000
Operating expenses	257,300,000	285,603,000

Required

a. What is the percentage growth in the Accounts Receivable, Sales, Accounts Payable, and Operating Expenses accounts from 2003 to 2004?

b. Companies must incur interest expense to obtain cash. To minimize interest expense, companies attempt to collect cash from receivables as quickly as possible and to delay the payment of cash to settle payables as long as possible. Based on your answers to Requirement *a,* comment on DeChow's cash management.

L.O. 8   EXERCISE 2–21A *Confidentiality and the Auditor*

West Aston discovered a significant fraud in the accounting records of a high profile client. The story has been broadcast on national airways. Aston was unable to resolve his remaining concerns with the company's management team and ultimately resigned from the audit engagement. Aston knows that he will be asked by several interested parties, including his friends and relatives, the successor auditor, and prosecuting attorneys in a court of law, to tell what he knows. He has asked you for advice.

Required

Write a memo that explains his disclosure responsibilities to each of the interested parties.

L.O. 9   EXERCISE 2–22A *Ethical Conduct*

Required

Name and provide a brief explanation of the six articles of the AICPA Code of Professional Conduct.

All Problems in Series A are available with McGraw-Hill's Homework Manager

PROBLEM 2–23A *Effect of Events on the Accounting Equation*

L.O. 2

Required

Explain how each of the following independent accounting events would affect the accounting equation by writing the letter I for increase, the letter D for decrease, and NA for no effect under the appropriate columns. The effects of the first event are shown for you.

CHECK FIGURES
b. decrease assets, decrease
   Retained Earnings
f. increase assets, increase
   Common Stock

Letter of Event	Assets	=	Liabilities	+	Common Stock	+	Retained Earnings
a	I/D		NA		NA		NA

a. Collected cash from accounts receivable.
b. Paid a cash dividend to the stockholders.
c. Performed services for cash.
d. Paid cash to creditors on account.
e. Bought equipment by issuing a note payable.
f. Acquired cash from the issue of common stock.
g. Paid cash for salary expense.
h. Performed services for clients on account.
i. Incurred operating expenses on account.
j. Repaid note payable and interest expense with cash.
k. Paid monthly rent expense.
l. Accrued interest expense on a note payable.

PROBLEM 2–24A *Classifying Events as Source, Use, or Exchange and Effect of Events on Financial Statements—Horizontal Statements Model*

L.O. 1, 4, 10

The following transactions pertain to A&M Advisory Services for 2006:

CHECK FIGURES
b. Total cash: $7,400
   Net income: $4,100

1. Business started when it acquired $30,000 cash from the issue of common stock.
2. Paid $25,000 cash to purchase land.
3. Paid $4,800 cash for rent expense.
4. Performed services for clients and billed them $14,400. Expected to collect cash at a later date (the revenue was earned on account).
5. Incurred $11,200 of other operating expenses on account (expected to make cash payment at a later date).
6. Received $500 bill for utilities. The amount due was payable within 30 days.
7. Collected $9,400 cash from accounts receivable.
8. Paid $3,800 cash on the account payable.
9. Acquired an additional $5,000 cash from the issue of common stock.
10. Paid $7,600 cash on the balance of the account payable created in Event 5.
11. Performed additional services for $6,200 cash.
12. Paid $2,000 cash dividend to the stockholders.

Required

a. Classify each of A&M's transactions as asset source (AS), asset use (AU), asset exchange (AE), or claims exchange (CE).
b. Show the effects of the events on the financial statements using a horizontal statements model like the following one. In the Cash Flow column, use the initials OA for operating activity, IA for investing activity, FA for financing activity, and NC for net change in cash. Use NA to indicate accounts not affected by the transaction. The first event is recorded as an example.

Event No.	Assets						Stk. Equity								
	Cash	+	Accts. Rec.	+	Land	=	Accts. Pay.	+	C. Stock	+	Ret. Earn.	Rev.	− Exp.	= Net Inc.	Cash Flow
1	30,000	+	NA	+	NA	=	NA	+	30,000	+	NA	NA	− NA	= NA	30,000 FA

c. What is the amount of net income for 2002?
d. What is the amount of net cash flow from operating activities for 2002?
e. Explain how the closing entries affect the retained earnings account.

L.O. 1, 5

www.mhhe.com/edmonds5e

CHECK FIGURES
b. Ending Balance in Retained
   Earnings: $18,690
   Net Income: $18,690

PROBLEM 2–25A *Effect of Events on the Financial Statements*

C&S Auto experienced the following transactions during 2005.

1. Provided services to customers and billed them $18,000.
2. Borrowed $9,000 from the bank on September 1, 2004. The note had a 7 percent annual interest rate and a one-year term to maturity.
3. Paid $2,500 of salary expense.
4. Provided services to customers and collected $12,000 cash.
5. Incurred $8,600 of other operating expenses on account.
6. Collected $15,000 of the accounts receivable.
7. Paid $8,100 of the accounts payable.
8. Recognized the accrued interest on the note payable at December 31, 2004.

Required

a. Show the effects of the transactions on the financial statements using a horizontal statements model like the following one. In the Cash Flows column, use the letters OA for operating activity, IA for investing activity, FA for financing activity, and NC for net change in cash. Use NA to indicate not affected by the transaction. The first one is recorded as an example.

Event No.	Balance Sheet						Income Statement		Statement of Cash Flows
	Assets	=	Liab.			+ Stk. Equity			
	Cash + Accts. Rec.	= Accts. Pay.	Note Pay.	Int. Pay.	+	Ret. Earn.	Rev. − Exp. = Net Inc.		
1.	NA + 18,000	= NA	NA	NA		18,000	18,000− NA = 18,000		NA

b. What is the ending balance of Retained Earnings? What is the amount of net income? Why are these amounts the same in this problem? Is the balance in Retained Earnings likely to be the same as the amount of net income at the end of 2006? Explain your answer.
c. Determine the balances that would appear in the revenue and expense accounts at the beginning of the 2006 accounting period.

L.O. 3

www.mhhe.com/edmonds5e

CHECK FIGURES
2003 Net Income: $48,000
2003 Total Assets: $122,700

PROBLEM 2–26A *Identifying and Arranging Elements on Financial Statements*

The following information was drawn from the records of Winters & Associates at December 31, 2003:

Consulting Revenue	$80,000	Notes Payable	$30,000
Land	48,700	Salaries Payable	5,500
Dividends	10,000	Salary Expense	31,000
Cash Flow from Fin. Activities	20,000	Common Stock Issued	20,000
Interest Revenue	4,000	Beginning Common Stock	15,000
Ending Retained Earnings	50,200	Accounts Receivable	22,000
Cash	52,000	Cash Flow from Inv. Activities	(30,000)
Interest Payable	2,000	Cash Flow from Oper. Activities	22,000
Interest Expense	5,000		

Required
Use the preceding information to construct an income statement, statement of changes in stockholders' equity, balance sheet, and statement of cash flows. (Show only totals for each activity on the statement of cash flows).

L.O. 2, 3, 4, 6, 7

www.mhhe.com/edmonds5e

PROBLEM 2–27A *Two Complete Accounting Cycles*

The following accounting events apply to Tri-State Company, which began operations in 2003.

Accounting Events for 2003
1. Acquired $40,000 cash from the issue of common stock.

2. Recognized $86,000 of revenue on account during the period for services performed.
3. Collected $72,000 cash from accounts receivable.
4. Paid $5,000 cash dividend.
5. Paid $46,000 cash for salaries expense.
6. Paid $11,000 cash for other operating expenses.
7. Invested $30,000 in a certificate of deposit with an 18-month term.

CHECK FIGURES
a. 2003 Ending Retained
   Earnings: $22,200
   2004 Ending Retained
   Earnings: $42,525

Information for Adjusting Entries (Books are closed on December 31)
8. Accrued salaries expense of $2,400.
9. Recorded accrued interest on the certificate of deposit. The certificate was purchased on June 30, 2003, and had a 4 percent annual rate of interest.

Accounting Events for 2004
1. Made cash payment of $2,400 for salaries payable.
2. Borrowed $25,000 from a local bank.
3. Received an additional $10,000 cash from the issue of common stock.
4. Recognized $110,000 of revenue on account during 2004 for services performed.
5. Collected $108,000 of cash on accounts receivable during the period.
6. Purchased land for the company that cost $40,000 cash. A few months later, the land was appraised at $45,000.
7. Paid a $10,000 cash dividend to the stockholders of the company.
8. Received the principal amount plus the interest earned on the certificate of deposit. (See Events 7 and 9 in year 2003 for details regarding the original investment.)
9. Paid cash of $40,000 for salaries expense.
10. Paid $35,000 cash for other operating expenses.

Information for Adjusting Entries
11. Accrued salaries expense was $5,000.
12. Recorded accrued interest expense on the bank note (see Event 2 in 2004). The note was issued to the bank on June 1, 2004. It had a 6 percent annual rate of interest and a two-year term to maturity.

Required
a. Record the effect of each of the events in general ledger accounts under an accounting equation for the 2003 and 2004 fiscal years. In the last column of the table, provide appropriate account titles for Retained Earning accounts.
b. Prepare an income statement, statement of changes in stockholders' equity, balance sheet, and statement of cash flows for the 2003 and 2004 calendar years using the vertical statement format.
c. Determine the balances that would appear in the temporary accounts at the beginning of 2005.

PROBLEM 2–28A *Effect of Accrued Interest on Financial Statements*

Norman Co. borrowed $15,000 from the local bank on April 1, 2008, when the company was started. The note had an 8 percent annual interest rate and a one-year term to maturity. Norman Co. recognized $42,000 of revenue on account in 2008 and $56,000 of revenue on account in 2009. Cash collections from accounts receivable were $38,000 in 2008 and $58,000 in 2009. Norman Co. paid $26,000 of salaries expense in 2008 and $32,000 of salaries expense in 2009. Repaid loan and interest at maturity date.

L.O. 2, 3, 5, 7

CHECK FIGURES
a. $12,000
b. $38,800

Required
Based on the preceding information, answer the following questions. (*Hint:* Record the events in general ledger accounts under an accounting equation before answering the questions.)

a. What amount of net cash flow from operating activities would Norman report on the 2008 cash flow statement?
b. What amount of interest expense would Norman report on the 2008 income statement?
c. What amount of total liabilities would Norman report on the December 31, 2008, balance sheet?
d. What amount of retained earnings would Norman report on the December 31, 2008, balance sheet?
e. What amount of cash flow from financing activities would Norman report on the 2008 statement of cash flows?
f. What amount of interest expense would Norman report on the 2009 income statement?
g. What amount of cash flows from operating activities would Norman report on the 2009 cash flow statement?
h. What amount of total assets would Norman report on the December 31, 2009, balance sheet?

i. What amount of cash flow from investing activities would Norman report on the 2009 cash flow statement?

j. If Norman Co. paid a $700 dividend during 2009, what retained earnings balance would it report on the December 31, 2009, balance sheet?

L.O. 3, 4   PROBLEM 2–29A *Closing the Accounts*

The following accounts and account balances were taken from the records of Green View Company. Except as otherwise indicated, all balances are as of December 31, 2004, before the closing entries had been recorded.

Cash Received from Common Stock Issued during 2004	$ 3,500
Cash	7,800
Revenue	7,400
Salary Expense	2,900
Cash Flow from Operating Activities	2,500
Notes Payable	2,000
Utility Expense	600
Dividends	1,200
Cash Flow from Financing Activities	2,300
Rent Expense	1,400
Land	20,200
Retained Earnings, January 1, 2004	14,700
Common Stock, December 31, 2004	10,000

Required

a. Prepare the income statement Green View would include in its 2004 annual report.

b. Identify the accounts that should be closed to the Retained Earnings account.

c. Determine the Retained Earnings account balance at December 31, 2004. Identify the reasons for the difference between net income and the ending balance in Retained Earnings.

d. What are the balances in the revenue, expense, and dividend accounts on January 1, 2005? Explain.

L.O. 6   PROBLEM 2–30A *Missing Information in Financial Statements*

www.mhhe.com/edmonds5e

Required

Fill in the blank (as indicated by the alphabetic letters in parentheses) in the following financial statements. Assume the company started operations January 1, 2006, and that all transactions involve cash.

	For the Years		
	2006	**2007**	**2008**
Income Statements			
Revenue	$ 700	$ 1,300	$ 2,000
Expense	(a)	(700)	(1,300)
Net Income	$ 200	$ (m)	$ 700
Statement of Changes in Stockholders' Equity			
Beginning Common Stock	$ 0	$ (n)	$ 6,000
Plus: Common Stock Issued	5,000	1,000	2,000
Ending Common Stock	5,000	6,000	(t)
Beginning Retained Earnings	0	100	200
Plus: Net Income	(b)	(o)	700
Less: Dividends	(c)	(500)	(300)
Ending Retained Earnings	100	(p)	600
Total Stockholders' Equity	$ (d)	$ 6,200	$ 8,600

continued

Balance Sheets			
Assets			
Cash	$ (e)	$ (q)	$ (u)
Land	0	(r)	8,000
Total Assets	$ (f)	$11,200	$10,600
Liabilities	$ (g)	$ 5,000	$ 2,000
Stockholders' Equity			
Common Stock	(h)	(s)	8,000
Retained Earnings	(i)	200	600
Total Stockholders' Equity	(j)	6,200	8,600
Total Liabilities and Stockholders' Equity	$8,100	$11,200	$10,600

Statements of Cash Flows			
Cash Flows from Operating Activities			
Cash Receipts from Revenue	$ (k)	$ 1,300	$ (v)
Cash Payments for Expenses	(l)	(700)	(w)
Net Cash Flows from Operating Activities	200	600	700
Cash Flows from Investing Activities			
Cash Payments for Land	0	(8,000)	0
Cash Flows from Financing Activities			
Cash Receipts from Loan	3,000	3,000	0
Cash Payments to Reduce Debt	0	(1,000)	(x)
Cash Receipts from Stock Issue	5,000	1,000	(y)
Cash Payments for Dividends	(100)	(500)	(z)
Net Cash Flows from Financing Activities	7,900	2,500	(1,300)
Net Change in Cash	8,100	(4,900)	(600)
Plus: Beginning Cash Balance	0	8,100	3,200
Ending Cash Balance	$8,100	$ 3,200	$ 2,600

PROBLEM 2–31A *Missing Information in Financial Statements*

L.O. 2, 3, 5

CHECK FIGURES
a. $46,000
b. 2006 Total Assets: $132,000

Shore Properties had the following assets at the beginning of the accounting period (January 1, 2006): Cash—$21,000, Accounts Receivable—$33,000, Certificate of Deposit—$16,000, and Land—$62,000. The beginning balances in the liability accounts were Accounts Payable—$27,000 and Notes Payable—$20,000. A $51,000 balance was in Common Stock at the beginning of the accounting period. During the accounting period, service revenue earned on account was $44,000. The ending balance in the Accounts Receivable account was $31,000. Operating expenses incurred on account amounted to $29,000. There was $33,000 paid on accounts payable. In addition, there was $1,200 of accrued interest revenue and $1,700 of accrued interest expense as of the end of the accounting period (December 31, 2006). Finally, a $2,500 cash dividend was paid to the stockholders. (*Hint:* Record the events in general ledger accounts under an accounting equation before satisfying the requirements.)

Required
a. Determine the amount of cash collected from accounts receivable.
b. Prepare a balance sheet as of January 1, 2006.
c. Prepare an income statement, statement of changes in stockholders' equity, balance sheet, and statement of cash flows for the 2006 accounting period.
d. Determine the interest rate earned on the certificate of deposit.
e. Determine the interest rate paid on the note payable.
f. Determine the balances of the revenue, expense, and dividends accounts on January 1, 2007.

PROBLEM 2–32A *Auditor Responsibilities*

L.O. 8

You have probably heard it said that it is unwise to bite the hand that feeds you. Independent auditors are chosen by, paid by, and can be fired by the companies that they audit. Given this condition, what keeps the auditor independent? In other words, what stops an auditor from blindly following the orders of a client?

Required
Write a memo that explains the reporting responsibilities of an independent auditor.

L.O. 9   PROBLEM 2–33A *Ethics*

Raula Kato discovered a material reporting error in accounting records of Sampoon, Inc. (SI). The error was so significant that it will certainly have an adverse effect on the price of the client's stock which is actively traded on the western stock exchange. After talking to his close friend, and president of SI, Kato agreed to withhold the information until the president had time to sell his SI stock. Kato leaked the information to his parents so that they could sell their shares of stock as well. The reporting matter was a relatively complex issue that involved recently issued reporting standards. Kato told himself that if he were caught he would simply plead ignorance. He would simply say that he did not have time to keep up with the rapidly changing standards and he would be off the hook.

Required
a. Write a memo that identifies specific articles of the AICPA Code of Professional Conduct that were violated by Kato.
b. Would pleading ignorance relieve Kato from his audit responsibilities?

EXERCISES—SERIES B

Where applicable in all exercises, round computations to the nearest dollar.

L.O. 2, 3   EXERCISE 2–1B *Effect of Accruals on the Financial Statements*

Cook, Inc., experienced the following events in 2005, its first year of operations.

1. Received $15,000 cash from the issue of common stock.
2. Performed services on account for $42,000.
3. Paid the utility expense of $800.
4. Collected $32,000 of the accounts receivable.
5. Recorded $5,000 of accrued salaries at the end of the year.
6. Paid a $1,000 cash dividend to the stockholders.

Required
a. Record these events in general ledger accounts under an accounting equation. In the last column of the table, provide appropriate account titles for the Retained Earnings amounts. The first transaction has been recorded as an example.

MARKET, INC. General Ledger Accounts							
Event	Assets		=	Liabilities	+	Stockholders' Equity	Acct. Titles for RE
	Cash	Accounts Receivable		Salaries Payable		Common Stock	Retained Earnings
1.	15,000					15,000	

b. Prepare the income statement, statement of changes in stockholders' equity, balance sheet, and statement of cash flows for the 2005 accounting period.
c. Why is the ending cash balance the same as the net change in cash on the statement of cash flows?

L.O. 2, 3   EXERCISE 2–2B *Effect of Collecting Accounts Receivable on the Accounting Equation and Financial Statements*

Solimon Company earned $13,000 of revenue on account during 2008. The company collected $7,000 cash from accounts receivable during 2008.

Required
Based on this information alone, determine the following. (*Hint:* It may be helpful to record the events in general ledger accounts under an accounting equation before satisfying the requirements.)

a. The balance of accounts receivable that Solimon would report on the December 31, 2008 balance sheet.
b. The amount of net income that Solimon would report on the 2008 income statement.

c. The amount of net cash flow from operating activities that Solimon would report on the 2008 statement of cash flows.
d. The amount of retained earnings that Solimon would report on the December 31, 2008, balance sheet.
e. Why are the answers to Requirements *b* and *c* different?

EXERCISE 2–3B *Effect of Accrued Salaries on the Financial Statements*　　　　　　　L.O. 1

D. Giraud recorded $7,500 of accrued salaries expense at the end of 2006.

Required
Use the following horizontal statements model to show how this event affects the balance sheet, income statement, and statement of cash flows. Indicate whether the event increases (I), decreases (D), or does not affect (NA) each element of the financial statements. Also, in the Cash Flows column, designate the classification of any cash flows using the letters OA for operating activities, IA for investing activities, and FA for financing activities.

Balance Sheet				Income Statement			Statement of Cash Flows
Cash =	Sal. Pay +	C. Stk. +	Ret. Ear.	Rev. −	Exp. =	Net Inc.	

EXERCISE 2–4B *Effects of Revenue and Expense Recognition on the Income Statement and Statement of Cash Flows*　　　　　　　L.O. 3

The following transactions pertain to the operations of Todd & Co., CPAs.

1. Acquired $100,000 cash from the issue of common stock.
2. Performed accounting services and billed clients $130,000.
3. Paid $5,000 cash dividend to the stockholders.
4. Collected $80,000 cash from accounts receivable.
5. Paid $65,000 cash for operating expenses.
6. Performed accounting services for $5,000 cash.

Required
a. Which of these transactions resulted in revenue or expense recognition for Todd & Co., CPAs?
b. Based on your response to Requirement *a*, determine the amount of net income that Todd will report on the income statement.
c. Determine the net cash flow from operating activities for each of the preceding transactions.

EXERCISE 2–5B *Classifying Events on the Statement of Cash Flows*　　　　　　　L.O. 3

The following transactions pertain to the operations of Colton Company for 2006:

1. Acquired $20,000 cash from the issue of common stock.
2. Provided $80,000 of services on account.
3. Paid $20,000 cash on accounts payable.
4. Performed services for $5,000 cash.
5. Collected $65,000 cash from accounts receivable.
6. Incurred $42,000 of operating expenses on account.
7. Paid $1,800 cash for expenses.
8. Paid a $5,000 cash dividend to the stockholders.

Required
a. Classify the cash flows from each of these transactions as operating activities (OA), investing activities (IA), or financing activities (FA). Use NA for transactions that do not affect the statement of cash flows.
b. Prepare a statement of cash flows. (This is the first year of operations.)

EXERCISE 2–6B *Effect of Accounts Receivable and Accounts Payable Transactions on Financial Statements*　　　　　　　L.O. 1

The following events apply to Cain and Vega, a public accounting firm, for the 2005 accounting period.

1. Performed $65,000 of services for clients on account.
2. Performed $40,000 of services for cash.
3. Incurred $35,000 of other operating expenses on account.

4. Paid $10,000 cash to an employee for salary.
5. Collected $47,000 cash from accounts receivable.
6. Paid $12,000 cash on accounts payable.
7. Paid an $8,000 cash dividend to the stockholders.
8. Accrued salaries were $2,000 at the end of 2005.

Required

a. Show the effects of the events on the financial statements using a horizontal statements model like the following one. In the Cash Flow column, use OA to designate operating activity, IA for investment activity, FA for financing activity, and NC for net change in cash. Use NA to indicate the element is not affected by the event. The first event is recorded as an example.

Event No.	Assets		=	Liabilities			+ Stk. Equity					Cash Flow
	Cash	+ Accts. Rec.	=	Accts. Pay.	+	Sal. Pay.	+ Ret. Earn.	Rev.	– Exp.	= Net Inc.		
1	NA	+ 65,000	=	NA	+	NA	+ 65,000	65,000	– NA	= 65,000		NA

b. What is the amount of total assets at the end of 2005?
c. What is the balance of accounts receivable at the end of 2005?
d. What is the balance of accounts payable at the end of 2005?
e. What is the difference between accounts receivable and accounts payable?
f. What is net income for 2005?
g. What is the amount of net cash flow from operating activities for 2005?

L.O. 2, 3   EXERCISE 2–7B *Net Income Versus Changes in Cash*

In 2003, Ace Company billed its customers $100,000 for services performed. The company subsequently collected $73,000 of the amount billed. Ace incurred $69,000 of operating expenses on account. Ace paid $62,000 of that amount. Ace acquired $30,000 cash from the issue of common stock. The company invested $40,000 cash in the purchase of land.

Required

Use the preceding information to answer the following questions. (*Hint:* It may be helpful to identify the six events described in the paragraph and to record them in general ledger accounts under an accounting equation before answering the questions.)

a. What amount of revenue will Ace report on the 2003 income statement?
b. What is the net income for the period?
c. What amount of cash flow from revenue will Ace report on the statement of cash flows?
d. What is the net cash flow from operating activities for the period?
e. Why is the amount of net income different from the net cash flow from operating activities for the period?
f. What is the amount of net cash flow from investing activities?
g. What is the amount of net cash flow from financing activities?
h. What amount of total equity will Ace report on the year-end balance sheet?

L.O. 4   EXERCISE 2–8B *Closing the Accounts*

The following information was drawn from the accounting records of Fulmer Company as of December 31, 2005, before the nominal accounts had been closed. The company's cash balance was $2,500, and its land account had a $6,500 balance. Notes payable amounted to $3,000. The balance in the Common Stock account was $1,500. The company had revenues of $5,500 and expenses of $2,000, and dividends amounted to $900.

Required

a. Identify the accounts that would be closed to Retained Earnings at the end of the accounting period.
b. Assuming that Fulmer's beginning balance (as of January 1, 2005) in the Retained Earnings account was $1,900, determine its balance after the nominal accounts were closed at the end of 2005.
c. What amount of net income would Fulmer Company report on its 2005 income statement?
d. Explain why the amount of net income differs from the amount of the ending Retained Earnings balance.
e. What are the balances in the revenue, expense, and dividend accounts on January 1, 2006?

EXERCISE 2–9B *Closing Accounts and the Accounting Cycle*   **L.O. 4**

Required

a. Identify which of the following accounts are temporary (will be closed to Retained Earnings at the end of the year) and which are permanent.

   (1) Common Stock

   (2) Notes Payable

   (3) Cash

   (4) Service Revenue

   (5) Dividends

   (6) Land

   (7) Salaries Expense

   (8) Retained Earnings

   (9) Utilities Expense

  (10) Interest Revenue

b. Bill bragged that he had five years of accounting experience. Jane disagreed, responding, "No. You have had one year of accounting experience five times." Explain what Jane meant. (*Hint:* Refer to the accounting cycle.)

EXERCISE 2–10B *Closing Entries*   **L.O. 4**

Required

Which of the following accounts are closed at the end of the accounting period?

a. Land

b. Interest Revenue

c. Interest Receivable

d. Rent Expense

e. Notes Payable

f. Interest Payable

g. Retained Earnings

h. Cash

i. Dividends

j. Accounts Receivable

k. Common Stock

l. Advertising Expense

EXERCISE 2–11B *Matching Concept*   **L.O. 7**

Companies make sacrifices known as *expenses* to obtain benefits called *revenues*. The accurate measurement of net income requires that expenses be matched with revenues. In some circumstances matching a particular expense directly with revenue is difficult or impossible. In these circumstances, the expense is matched with the period in which it is incurred.

Required

Distinguish the following items that could be matched directly with revenues from the items that would be classified as period expenses.

a. Sales commissions paid to employees.

b. Advertising expense.

c. Interest expense.

d. The cost of land that has been sold.

EXERCISE 2–12B *Complete Accounting Cycle*   **L.O. 2, 3**

The following information is available for Falcon Co. for the year 2004. The business had the following transactions:

  1. Performed $150,000 of services on account.

  2. Acquired $60,000 cash from the issue of common stock.

  3. Purchased land for $20,000 cash.

  4. Incurred other operating expenses on account in the amount of $80,000.

  5. Performed services for $18,000 cash.

  6. Paid $50,000 cash on accounts payable.

7. Collected $90,000 cash from accounts receivable.
8. Paid $20,000 cash dividend to the stockholders.
9. Paid $9,000 cash for salaries.
10. Borrowed $30,000 cash from State Bank.

Information for Adjusting Entry

11. Accrued interest expense at the end of the accounting period was $1,200.

Required

a. Explain how each of the transactions affects the elements of the accounting equation by placing a +
for *increase,* − for *decrease,* and NA for *not affected* under each of the elements. Also record the dollar amount of the effect of each event on the accounting equation. In the last column of the table, provide appropriate account titles for Retained Earnings amounts. The first event is recorded as an example.

					Stockholders' Equity		
Event No.	Assets	=	Liabilities	+	Common Stock	+ Retained Earnings	Acct. Titles for RE
1	+150,000		NA		NA	+150,000	Service Revenue

b. What is the amount of net income for 2004?
c. What is the amount of total assets at the end of 2004?
d. What is the amount of total liabilities at the end of 2004?

L.O. 1, 5   **EXERCISE 2–13B** *Effects of Recognizing Accrued Interest on Financial Statements*

Bill Parker started Parker Company on January 1, 2007. The company experienced the following events during its first year of operation.

1. Earned $6,200 of cash revenue.
2. Borrowed $4,000 cash from the bank.
3. Adjusted the accounting records to recognize accrued interest expense on the bank note. The note, issued on September 1, 2007, had a one-year term and a 10 percent annual interest rate.

Required

a. What is the amount of interest payable at December 31, 2007?
b. What is the amount of interest expense in 2007?
c. What is the amount of interest paid in 2007?
d. Use a horizontal statements model to show how each event affects the balance sheet, income statement, and statement of cash flows. Indicate whether the event increases (I) decreases (D), or does not affect (NA) each element of the financial statements. Also, in the Cash Flows column, designate the cash flows as operating activities (OA), investing activities (IA), or financing activities (FA). The first transaction has been recorded as an example.

Event No.	Balance Sheet												Income Statement					Statement of Cash Flows
	Cash	=	Note Pay.	+	Int. Pay.	+	C. Stk.	+	Ret. Earn.				Rev.	−	Exp.	=	Net Inc.	
1	I	=	NA	+	NA	+	NA	+	I				I	−	NA	=	I	I OA

L.O. 2, 5, 7   **EXERCISE 2–14B** *Recognizing Accrued Interest Revenue*

Cedar Company invested $80,000 in a certificate of deposit on August 1, 2006. The certificate had a 6 percent annual rate of interest and a one-year term to maturity.

Required

a. What amount of interest revenue will Cedar recognize for the year ending December 31, 2006?
b. Show how the December 31, 2006, adjusting entry to recognize the accrued interest revenue affects the accounting equation.
c. What amount of cash will Cedar collect for interest revenue in 2006?
d. What is the amount of interest receivable as of December 31, 2006?
e. What amount of cash will Cedar collect for interest revenue in 2007, assuming it does not renew the CD?
f. What amount of interest revenue will Cedar recognize in 2007, assuming it does not renew the CD?
g. What is the amount of interest receivable as of December 31, 2007, assuming it does not renew the CD?

EXERCISE 2–15B *Recognizing Accrued Interest Expense*   L.O. 3, 5, 7

Whitewater Corporation borrowed $40,000 from the bank on October 1, 2004. The note had a 9 percent annual rate of interest and matured on March 31, 2005. Interest and principal were paid in cash on the maturity date.

Required
a. What amount of interest expense was paid in cash in 2004?
b. What amount of interest expense was recognized on the 2004 income statement?
c. What amount of total liabilities was reported on the December 31, 2004 balance sheet?
d. What total amount of cash was paid to the bank on March 31, 2005, for principal and interest?
e. What amount of interest expense was reported on the 2005 income statement?

EXERCISE 2–16B *Effect of Transactions on the Balance Sheet*   L.O. 2, 3, 5

Colony Corp. was formed on January 1, 2003. The business acquired $105,000 cash from the issue of common stock. The business performed $300,000 of services on account and collected $250,000 of the amount due. Operating expenses incurred on account amounted to $185,000. By the end of 2003, $120,000 of that amount had been paid with cash. The business paid $20,000 cash to purchase land. The business borrowed $50,000 cash from the bank. On December 31, 2003, there was $750 of accrued interest expense.

Required
Using the preceding information, answer the following questions. (*Hint:* Identify the eight events described in the preceding paragraph and record them in general ledger accounts under an accounting equation before answering the questions.)

a. What is the cash balance at the end of 2003?
b. What is the balance of accounts receivable at the end of 2003?
c. What is the amount of total assets at the end of 2003?
d. What is the amount of total liabilities at the end of 2003?
e. What is the amount of common stock at the end of 2003?
f. What is the amount of net income for 2003?

EXERCISE 2–17B *Identifying Source, Use, and Exchange Transactions*   L.O. 10

Required
Indicate whether each of the following transactions is an asset source (AS), asset use (AU), asset exchange (AE), or claims exchange (CE) transaction.

a. Performed services for clients on account.
b. Paid cash for salary expense.
c. Acquired cash from the issue of common stock.
d. Incurred other operating expenses on account.
e. Performed services for cash.
f. Paid cash on accounts payable.
g. Collected cash from accounts receivable.
h. Paid a cash dividend to the stockholders.
i. Borrowed cash from the bank.
j. Purchased land with cash.

EXERCISE 2–18B *Identifying Asset Source, Use, and Exchange Transactions*   L.O. 10

Required
a. Name an asset use transaction that will affect the income statement.
b. Name an asset use transaction that will *not* affect the income statement.
c. Name an asset exchange transaction that will *not* affect the statement of cash flows.
d. Name an asset exchange transaction that will affect the statement of cash flows.
e. Name an asset source transaction that will *not* affect the income statement.

EXERCISE 2–19B *Relation of Elements to Financial Statements*   L.O. 3

Required
Identify whether each of the following items would appear on the income statement (IS), statement of changes in stockholders' equity (SE), balance sheet (BS), or statement of cash flows (CF). Some items

may appear on more than one statement; if so, identify all applicable statements. If an item would not appear on any financial statement, label it NA.

   a. Accounts Receivable
   b. Accounts Payable
   c. Interest Payable
   d. Dividends
   e. Beginning Cash Balance
   f. Ending Retained Earnings
   g. Interest Expense
   h. Ending Cash Balance
   i. Salaries Expense
   j. Net Income
   k. Utilities Expense
   l. Interest Revenue
   m. Cash Flow from Operating Activities
   n. Service Revenue
   o. Auditor's Opinion

L.O. 7   **EXERCISE 2–20B** *Evaluating Cash Management*

The data in the following table apply to Ducan, Incorporated.

	2005	2006
Accounts receivable	$ 11,605,000	$ 14,736,000
Sales	232,100,000	245,600,000
Accounts payable	5,872,000	4,527,000
Operating expenses	146,800,000	150,900,000

Required

a. The accounts receivable balance is what percent of sales in 2005 and 2006?

b. The accounts payable balance is what percent of operating expenses in 2005 and 2006?

c. Companies must incur interest expense to obtain cash. To minimize interest expense, companies attempt to collect cash from receivables as quickly as possible and to delay the payment of cash to settle payables as long as possible. Based on your answers to Requirements *a* and *b*, comment on Duncan's cash management.

L.O. 8, 9   **EXERCISE 2–21B** *Materiality and the Auditor*

Sharon Waters is an auditor. Her work at two companies disclosed inappropriate recognition of revenue. Both cases involved dollar amounts in the $100,000 range. In one case, Waters considered the item material and required her client to restate earnings. In the other case, Waters dismissed the misstatement as being immaterial.

Required

Write a memo that explains how a $100,000 misstatement of revenue is acceptable for one company but unacceptable for a different company.

L.O. 9   **EXERCISE 2–22B** *Ethical Conduct*

Required

Name and provide a brief explanation of the three common features of ethical misconduct.

PROBLEMS—SERIES B

Where applicable in all problems, round computations to the nearest dollar.

L.O. 2   **PROBLEM 2–23B** *Effect of Events on the Accounting Equation*

Required

Explain how each of the following independent accounting events would affect the accounting equation by writing the letter I for increase, the letter D for decrease, and NA for no effect under the appropriate columns. The effects of the first event are shown for you.

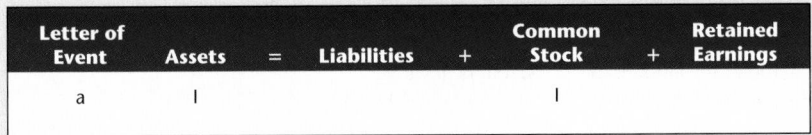

Letter of Event	Assets	=	Liabilities	+	Common Stock	+	Retained Earnings
a	I				I		

a. Received cash from the issue of common stock.
b. Paid cash for interest expense accrued in a previous period.
c. Purchased land with cash.
d. Repaid borrowed funds with cash.
e. Collected cash from accounts receivable.
f. Paid cash for salaries.
g. Recognized service revenue on account.
h. Received utility bill; cash payment will be made in the future.
i. Borrowed cash from creditors.
j. Paid a cash dividend to the stockholders.
k. Accrued interest expense on note payable at the end of the accounting period.

PROBLEM 2–24B *Classifying Events as Source, Use, or Exchange and Effect of Events on Financial Statements—Horizontal Statements Model*   **L.O. 1, 5, 10**

The following transactions pertain to Kramer Financial Services for 2002.

1. Business started when it acquired $10,000 cash from the issue of common stock.
2. Paid $1,200 cash for rent expense.
3. Performed services for clients and billed them $8,000. Expected to collect cash at a later date (the revenue was earned on account).
4. Incurred $1,750 of other operating expenses on account (expected to make cash payment at a later date).
5. Paid $1,400 cash on the account payable created in Event 4.
6. Acquired $1,500 cash from the issue of additional common stock.
7. Paid $350 cash on the balance of the account payable created in Event 4.
8. Performed additional services for $3,500 cash.
9. Paid a $500 cash dividend to the stockholders.
10. Collected $7,250 cash from accounts receivable.

Required
a. Classify each of Kramer's transactions as asset source (AS), asset use (AU), asset exchange (AE), or claims exchange (CE).
b. Show the effects of the events on the financial statements using a horizontal statements model like the following one. In the Cash Flow column, use the initials OA for operating activity, IA for investing activity, FA for financing activity, and NC for net change in cash flow. Use NA to indicate accounts not affected by the transaction. The first one has been recorded as an example.

Event No.	Assets		=	Liab.	+	Stockholders' Equity						
	Cash	+ Accts. Rec.	= Accts. Pay.	+	Common Stock	+ Ret. Earn.	Rev.	– Exp.	= Net Inc.	Cash Flow
1	10,000	+ NA	= NA	+	10,000	+ NA	NA	– NA	= NA	10,000 FA

c. What is the amount of net income for 2002?
d. What is the amount of net cash flow from operating activities for 2002?
e. Explain how the closing entries affect the retained earnings account.

PROBLEM 2–25B *Effect of Events on the Financial Statements*   **L.O. 1, 4**

Auto Services experienced the following transactions during 2003.

1. Provided services to customers and received $5,000 cash.
2. Paid $1,000 cash for other operating expenses.
3. Borrowed $15,000 from the bank on March 1, 2003. The note had an 8 percent annual interest rate and a one-year term to maturity.
4. Provided services to customers and billed them $20,000.

5. Incurred $6,000 of other operating expenses on account.
6. Collected $12,000 of accounts receivable.
7. Paid $3,100 of the amount due on accounts payable.
8. Recognized the accrued interest on the note payable at December 31, 2003.

Required

a. Show the effects of the transactions on the financial statements using a horizontal statements model like the following one. In the Cash Flows column, use the letters OA for operating activity, IA for investing activity, FA for financing activity, and NC for net change in cash. Use NA to indicate accounts not affected by the transaction. The first one is recorded as an example.

Event No.	Balance Sheet								Income Statement			Statement of Cash Flows
	Assets		=	Liab.			+	Stk. Equity				
	Cash	+ Accts. Rec.	= Accts. Pay.	Note Pay.	Int. Pay.	+		Ret. Earn.	Rev.	− Exp.	= Net Inc.	
1.	5,000 +	NA	= NA	NA	NA	+		5,000	5,000 −	NA	= 5,000	5,000 OA

b. What is the ending balance of retained earnings? What is the amount of net income? Why are these amounts the same in this problem? Give an example of a transaction that would cause these amounts to be different.

c. Determine the balances that would appear in the revenue and expense accounts at the beginning of the 2004 accounting period.

L.O. 3   **PROBLEM 2-26B** *Identifying and Arranging Elements on Financial Statements*

The following information was drawn from the records of Vickers & Associates at December 31, 2004:

Land	$97,500	Common Stock Issued	$10,000
Salaries Payable	17,000	Salary Expense	22,500
Interest Expense	1,375	Beginning Common Stock	12,000
Accounts Receivable	20,600	Ending Retained Earnings	60,500
Notes Payable	35,000	Cash Flow from Inv. Activities	(7,700)
Cash Flow from Oper. Activities	30,800	Interest Payable	300
Cash	16,700	Interest Revenue	375
Service Revenue	51,000	Dividends	2,000
Cash Flow from Fin. Activities	(8,400)		

Required

Use the preceding information to construct an income statement, statement of changes in stockholders' equity, balance sheet, and statement of cash flows. (Show only totals for each activity on the statement of cash flows).

L.O. 2, 3, 4, 6, 7   **PROBLEM 2-27B** *Two Complete Accounting Cycles*

The following accounting events apply to Hall Machine Co., which began operation in 1997.

Accounting Events for 2007

1. Acquired $80,000 cash from the issue of common stock.
2. Recognized $190,000 of service revenue on account.
3. Collected $166,000 cash from accounts receivable.
4. Paid the stockholders a $10,000 cash dividend.
5. Paid $92,000 cash for salaries expense.
6. Invested $48,000 cash in a 12–month certificate of deposit.

Information for December 31, 2007, End-of-Year Adjusting Entries

7. Accrued salary expense of $6,000.
8. Recorded accrued interest on the certificate of deposit. The CD was purchased on July 1, 2007, and had a 10 percent annual rate of interest.

Accounting Events for 2008

1. Paid cash for salaries payable of $6,000.
2. Received an additional $60,000 cash from the issue of common stock.
3. Earned service revenue on account of $210,000 for the year.
4. Received cash collections of accounts receivable of $224,000.
5. Paid a $30,000 cash dividend.

6. Paid $70,000 cash for salaries expense.
7. Purchased for $280,000 cash a plot of land on May 31, 2008. The value of the land rose to $300,000 by December 31.
8. Borrowed on June 1, 2008, $84,000 cash on a two-year, 8 percent note issued to State Bank.
9. Received cash for the principal and interest due on the certificate of deposit of $52,800 when it matured on June 30, 2008.

Information for Dec. 31, 2008 Adjusting Entries
10. Accrued salary expenses of $10,000.
11. Recorded accrued interest expense on the bank note (see Event 8 in 2008).

Required
a. Record the effect of each of the events in general ledger accounts under an accounting equation for the 2007 and 2008 fiscal years. In the last column of the table, provide appropriate account titles for Retained Earnings amounts.
b. Prepare an income statement, statement of changes in stockholders' equity, balance sheet, and statement of cash flows for the 2007 and 2008 calendar years.
c. Determine the balance that would appear in the temporary accounts at the beginning of 2005.

PROBLEM 2–28B *Effect of Accrued Interest on Financial Statements*   **L.O. 2, 3, 5, 7**

Magic Enterprises borrowed $18,000 from a local bank on July 1, 2006, when the company was started. The note had a 10 percent annual interest rate and a one-year term to maturity. Magic Enterprises recognized $42,500 of revenue on account in 2006 and $45,000 of revenue on account in 2007. Cash collections of accounts receivable were $36,000 in 2006 and $35,000 in 2007. Magic paid $24,000 of other operating expenses in 2006 and $28,000 of other operating expenses in 2007. Repaid the loan and interest at the maturity date.

Required
Based on this information, answer the following questions. (*Hint:* Record the events in the general ledger accounts under an accounting equation before answering the questions.)

a. What amount of interest expense would Magic report on the 2006 income statement?
b. What amount of net cash flow from operating activities would Magic report on the 2006 statement of cash flows?
c. What amount of total liabilities would Magic report on the December 31, 2006, balance sheet?
d. What amount of retained earnings would Magic report on the December 31, 2006, balance sheet?
e. What amount of net cash flow from financing activities would Magic report on the 2006 statement of cash flows?
f. What amount of interest expense would Magic report on the 2007 income statement?
g. What amount of net cash flow from operating activities would Magic report on the 2007 statement of cash flows?
h. What amount of total assets would Magic report on the December 31, 2007, balance sheet?
i. What amount of net cash flow from investing activities would Magic report on the 2007 statement of cash flows?
j. If Magic Enterprises paid a $1,500 dividend during 2007, what retained earnings balance would it report on the December 31, 2007, balance sheet?

L.O. 3, 4

PROBLEM 2–29B *Closing the Accounts*

The following accounts and account balances were taken from the records of Peaks View Company. Except as otherwise indicated, all balances are as of December 31, 2005, before the closing entries had been recorded.

Consulting Revenue	$14,500
Cash	28,500
Cash Received from Common Stock Issued during 2005	4,500
Travel Expense	1,100
Dividends	3,000
Cash Flow from Investing Activities	3,400
Rent Expense	1,800
Payment to Reduce Debt Principal	8,000
Retained Earnings, January 1, 2005	19,000
Salary Expense	6,900
Cash Flow from Operating Activities	1,500
Common Stock, December 31, 2005	10,000
Other Operating Expenses	2,200

Required

a. Identify the accounts that should be closed to the Retained Earnings account.

b. Prepare the income statement that Peaks View would include in its 2005 annual report.

c. Determine the Retained Earnings account balance at December 31, 2005. Explain how the company could pay cash dividends in excess of the amount of net income earned in 2005.

d. Name the stages of the accounting cycle in the order in which they normally occur.

L.O. 6   PROBLEM 2–30B *Missing Information in Financial Statements*

Required

Fill in the blanks (indicated by the alphabetic letters in parentheses) in the following financial statements. Assume the company started operations January 1, 2005 and all transactions involve cash.

	For the Years		
	2005	**2006**	**2007**
Income Statements			
Revenue	$ 400	$ 500	$ 800
Expense	(250)	(l)	(425)
Net Income	$ (a)	$ 100	$ 375
Statement of Changes in Stockholders' Equity			
Beginning Common Stock	$ 0	$ (m)	$ 9,100
Plus: Common Stock Issued	(b)	1,100	310
Ending Common Stock	8,000	9,100	(s)
Beginning Retained Earnings	0	25	75
Plus: Net Income	(c)	100	375
Less: Dividends	(d)	(50)	(150)
Ending Retained Earnings	25	(n)	300
Total Stockholders' Equity	$ (e)	$ 9,175	$ (t)
Balance Sheets			
Assets			
Cash	$ (f)	$ (o)	$ (u)
Land	0	(p)	2,500
Total Assets	$11,000	$11,650	$10,550
Liabilities	$ (g)	$ (q)	$ 840
Stockholders Equity			
Common Stock	(h)	(r)	9,410
Retained Earnings	(i)	75	300
Total Stockholders' Equity	8,025	9,175	9,710
Total Liabilities and Stockholders' Equity	$11,000	$11,650	$10,550
Statements of Cash Flows			
Cash Flows from Operating Activities			
Cash Receipts from Revenue	$ (j)	$ 500	$ (v)
Cash Payments for Expenses	(k)	(400)	(w)
Net Cash Flows from Operating Activities	150	100	375
Cash Flows from Investing Activities			
Cash Payments for Land	0	(5,000)	0
Cash Receipt from Sale of Land	0	0	2,500
Net Cash Flows from Investing Activities	0	(5,000)	2,500
Cash Flows from Financing Activities			
Cash Receipts from Borrowed Funds	2,975	0	0
Cash Payments to Reduce Debt	0	(500)	(x)
Cash Receipts from Stock Issue	8,000	1,100	(y)
Cash Payments for Dividends	(125)	(50)	(z)
Net Cash Flows from Financing Activities	10,850	550	(1,475)
Net Change in Cash	11,000	(4,350)	1,400
Plus: Beginning Cash Balance	0	11,000	6,650
Ending Cash Balance	$11,000	$ 6,650	$ 8,050

PROBLEM 2–31B *Missing Information in Financial Statements*   **L.O. 2, 3, 5**

Luing Properties had the following assets at the beginning of the accounting period (January 1, 2007): Cash—$1,600, Accounts Receivable—$2,400, Certificate of Deposit—$5,000, and Land—$20,000. The beginning balances in the liability accounts were Accounts Payable—$1,000, and Notes Payable—$8,000. A $5,400 balance was in the Common Stock account at the beginning of the accounting period. During the accounting period, $3,600 of service revenue was earned on account. The ending balance in the Accounts Receivable account was $3,800. Operating expenses incurred on account amounted to $2,100. There was $2,600 paid on accounts payable. In addition, there was $400 of accrued interest revenue and $700 of accrued interest expense as of the end of the accounting period (December 31, 2007). Finally, an $800 cash dividend was paid to the stockholders. (*Hint:* Record the events in general ledger accounts under an accounting equation before satisfying the requirements.)

Required
a. Determine the amount of cash collected from accounts receivable.
b. Prepare a balance sheet as of January 1, 2007.
c. Prepare an income statement, statement of changes in stockholders' equity, balance sheet, and statement of cash flows for December 31, 2007.
d. Determine the interest rate earned on the certificate of deposit.
e. Determine the interest rate charged on the note payable.
f. Determine the balance of the revenues, expenses, and dividends accounts at January 1, 2008.

PROBLEM 2–32B *Types of Audit Reports*   **L.O. 8**

Shay Ding is a partner of a regional accounting firm. Ms. Ding was hired by a potential client to audit the company's books. After extensive work, Ms. Ding determined that she was unable to perform the appropriate audit procedures.

Required
a. Name the type of audit report that Ms. Ding should issue with respect to the work that she did accomplish.
b. If Ms. Ding had been able to perform the necessary audit procedures, there are three types of audit reports that could have been issued depending on the outcome of the audit. Name and describe these three types of audit reports.

PROBLEM 2–33B *Ethics*   **L.O. 9**

Pete Chalance is an accountant with a shady past. Suffice it to say that he owes some very unsavory characters a lot of money. Despite his past, Pete works hard at keeping up a strong professional image. He is a manager at Smith and Associates, a fast-growing CPA firm. Pete is highly regarded around the office because he is a strong producer of client revenue. Indeed, on several occasions he exceeded his authority in establishing prices with clients. This is typically a partner's job but who could criticize Pete, who is most certainly bringing in the business. Indeed, Pete is so good that he is able to pull off the following scheme. He bills clients at inflated rates and then reports the ordinary rate to his accounting firm. Say for example, the normal charge for a job is $2,500. Pete will smooth talk the client, then charge him $3,000. He reports the normal charge of $2,500 to his firm and keeps the extra $500 for himself. He knows it isn't exactly right, but who is getting hurt? His firm gets its regular charges and the client willingly pays for the services rendered. He thinks to himself, as he pockets his ill-gotten gains, who is getting hurt anyway?

Required
The text discusses three common features (conditions) that motivate ethical misconduct. Identify and explain each of the three features as they appear in the above scenario.

ANALYZE, THINK, COMMUNICATE

BUSINESS APPLICATIONS CASE *Understanding Real World Annual Reports*   **ATC 2–1**

Required—Part 1
Use the Topps Company's annual report in Appendix B to answer the following questions.

a. Who are the independent auditors for Topps?
b. What type of opinion did the independent auditors issue on Topps' financial statements?

c. On what date does it appear the independent auditors completed their work related to Topps' 2003 financial statements?

d. Does the auditors' report give any information about how the audit was conducted? If so, what does it suggest was done?

e. Does the auditors' report tell the reader that the audit was concerned with materiality rather than absolute accuracy in the financial statements?

Required—Part 2

Harley-Davidson, Inc.

Use the Harley-Davidson's annual report that came with this book to answer the following questions.

a. Who are the independent auditors for Harley-Davidson?

b. What type of opinion did the independent auditors issue on Harley-Davidson's financial statements?

c. On what date does it appear the independent auditors completed their work related to Harley-Davidson's 2003 financial statements?

d. Does the auditors' report tell the reader that the audit was concerned with materiality rather than absolute accuracy in the financial statements?

e. Read the *Report of Management,* on page 92, and the *Report of the Audit Committee,* on page 93, of Harley's annual report. Based on these reports, and the auditors' report, which you read to answer items 1, 2, 3, and 4 above, who is primarily responsible for the company's financial statements?

Required—Part 3

Why did the auditors for Topps finish their audit work so much later in the year than did the auditors for Harley-Davidson?

ATC 2–2   GROUP ASSIGNMENT *Missing Information*

Verizon Communications, Inc. is one of the world's largest providers of communication services. The following information, taken from the company's annual reports, is available for the years 2003, 2002, and 2001.

	2003	2002	2001
Revenue	$67,752	$67,304	$66,713
Operating Expenses	60,258	52,300	55,240
Interest Expense	2,797	3,130	3,276
All dollar amounts are shown in millions.			

Required

a. Divide the class into groups of four or five students. Organize the groups into three sections. Assign each section of groups the financial data for one of the preceding accounting periods.

Group Tasks

(1) Determine the amount of net income for the year assigned.

(2) How does the result in Requirement *a* affect the retained earnings of the company?

(3) If the average interest rate is 7 percent, what is the average amount of debt for the year?

(4) Have representatives from each section put the income statement for their respective year on the board.

Class Discussion

b. Have the class discuss the trend in revenue and net income.

ATC 2–3   REAL-WORLD CASE *Unusual Types of Liabilities*

In the liabilities section of its 2002 balance sheet, Wachovia Corporation reported "noninterest-bearing deposits" of over $44 billion. Wachovia is a very large banking company. In the liabilities section of its 2002 balance sheet, Newmont Mining Corporation reported "reclamation and remediation liabilities" of more than $302 million. Newmont Mining is involved in gold mining and refining activities. In the accrued liabilities reported on its 2002 balance sheet, Conoco Phillips included $1.7 billion for "accrued dismantlement, removal, and environmental costs."

Required

a. For each of the preceding liabilities, write a brief explanation of what you believe the nature of the liability to be and how the company will pay it off. To develop your answers, think about the nature of the industry in which each of the companies operates.

b. Of the three liabilities described, which do you think poses the most risk for the company? In other words, for which liability are actual costs most likely to exceed the liability reported on the balance sheet? Uncertainty creates risk.

BUSINESS APPLICATIONS CASE *Decisions about Materiality*

ATC 2–4

The accounting firm of Espey & Davis, CPAs, recently completed the audits of three separate companies. During these audits, the following events were discovered, and Espey & Davis is trying to decide if each event is material. If an item is material, the CPA firm will insist that the company modify the financial statements.

1. In 2003, Foxx Company reported service revenues of $1,000,000 and net earnings of $80,000. Because of an accounting error, the company recorded $6,000 as revenue in 2003 for services that will not be performed until early 2004.
2. Guzza Company plans to report a cash balance of $70,000. Because of an accounting error, this amount is $5,000 too high. Guzza also plans to report total assets of $4,000,000 and net earnings of $415,000.
3. Jeter Company's 2003 balance sheet shows a cash balance of $200,000 and total assets of $9,000,000. For 2003, the company had a net income of $750,000. These balances are all correct, but they would have been $5,000 higher if the president of the company had not claimed business travel expenses that were, in fact, the cost of personal vacations for him and his family. He charged the costs of these trips on the company's credit card. The president of Jeter Company owns 25 percent of the business.

Required

Write a memorandum to the partners of Espey & Davis, explaining whether each of these events is material.

BUSINESS APPLICATIONS CASE *Limitations of Audit Opinion*

ATC 2–5

The statement of financial position (balance sheet) of Trident Company reports assets of $4,500,000. Jan Lewis advises you that a major accounting firm has audited the statements and attested that they were prepared in accordance with generally accepted accounting principles. She tells you that she can buy the total owner's interest in the business for only $2,750,000 and is seriously considering the opportunity. She says that the auditor's unqualified opinion validates the $4,500,000 value of the assets. Lewis believes she would be foolish to pass up the opportunity to purchase the assets at a price of only $2,750,000.

Required

a. What part of the accounting equation is Lewis failing to consider?
b. Comment on Lewis's misconceptions regarding the auditor's role in providing information that is useful in making investment decisions.

WRITING ASSIGNMENT *Definition of Elements of Financial Statements*

ATC 2–6

Putting "yum" on people's faces around the world is the mission of YUM Bands, Inc. Yum was spun off from PepsiCo in 1997. A spin-off occurs when a company separates its operations into two or more distinct companies. The company was originally composed of KFC, Pizza Hut, and Taco Bell and was operated as a part of PepsiCo prior to the spin-off. In 2002 YUM acquired A&W All American Foods and Long John Silver's units. The acquisition pushed YUM's debt to $4.8 billion. YUM's net income before interest and taxes in 2002 was $1.03 million.

Required

a. If YUM's debt remains constant at $4.8 billion for 2003, how much interest will YUM incur in 2003, assuming the average interest rate is 7 percent?
b. Does the debt seem excessive compared with the amount of 2002 net income before interest and taxes? Explain.
c. Assume YUM pays tax at the rate of 30 percent, what amount of tax will YUM pay in 2002?
d. Assume that you are the president of the company. Write a memo to the shareholders explaining how YUM is able to meet its obligations and increase stockholders' equity.

ETHICAL DILEMMA *Now It Is Your Turn to Cover for Me*

ATC 2–7

Johnny Travera and Tim Sanders were unusual friends. Travera came from a background of poverty while Sanders had an extremely affluent family. Indeed, the two would have never known each other

except for an unusual set of events. Sanders' parents bought him a new car for his 16th birthday. Not being used to the new vehicle, Sanders misjudged a curve and wrecked the car. Travera happened to see the accident and helped Sanders get out of the vehicle. Sanders was unhurt but extremely distraught. He told Travera that his parents would never trust him again. When the police arrived, Travera told them that he had seen a child run in front of Sanders' car and that Sanders had swerved off the road to save the child's life. Upon hearing the story, Sanders' parents considered him a hero. The insurance company bought a new car, and Sanders made a friend for life.

Sanders went to college and became a CPA in his father's accounting firm. Travera worked for several restaurants and finally managed to start one of his own. The restaurant became successful, and Travera turned the accounting work over to Sanders. Having no formal education, Travera had little knowledge of technical business practices.

At the beginning of 2006, Travera's balance sheet included cash of $10,000, other assets amounting to $380,000, liabilities of $80,000, and common stock of $25,000. Sanders provided Travera with accounting services for several years and was reasonably certain as to the accuracy of these figures. Since Sanders always advised Travera on financial matters, Sanders was aware that during 2006 Travera had paid cash to purchase $50,000 of restaurant equipment. Also, Travera had been able to repay $15,000 cash on a note payable that evidenced the restaurant's liability to a bank. Finally, Travera had received a $20,000 cash dividend from the restaurant. Travera made no contributions to the business during 2006. Even so, the records that Travera provided Sanders for 2006 indicated that the restaurant earned $200,000 in cash revenues and incurred $175,000 in cash expenses. The ending balance in the Cash account was $12,000.

After analyzing the data, Sanders became convinced that Travera was not reporting accurate information to him for the determination of net income. He confronted Travera with the issue, and Travera admitted that he was not reporting all sales information. He said he did not report some of the cash sales because he did not feel the income tax system was fair and he did not want to pay any more taxes than he had to pay. He defended himself by saying, "I'm only doing what everybody else does. Your dad's biggest client, Billy Abbott, has been skimming a million a year off his chain of restaurants. He's been doing it for the last five years. I know; I used to work for him. Even so, you and your dad give him an unqualified audit opinion every year. So why won't you do the same thing for me? I'm supposed to be your friend, and you keep telling me you think this Abbott guy is a real jerk." Indeed, Travera became so indignant that he told Sanders, "Either you sign my tax return, or I find a new accountant and a new friend to boot. I've always stood up for you, and this is the thanks I get."

Required

a. Based on the information provided in the case, determine the amount of Travera's unreported income. (*Hint:* The beginning balances were correct, but the entries for the current year transactions were recorded incorrectly. It may be helpful to use an accounting equation with the beginning balances provided in the case, and record the current period's transactions under the equation. Assume that the ending cash balance is an accurate measure of cash on hand at the end of the accounting period. The amount of unrecorded cash equals the amount of unrecorded income.)

b. Explain how Travera's failure to report cash revenue will affect the elements of financial statements by indicating whether each element will be overstated, understated, or not affected by the reporting omission. The elements to consider are assets, liabilities, common stock, retained earnings, revenue, expenses, net income, and dividends.

c. Explain how Sanders' audit firm could be honest and still have provided an unqualified opinion on Abbott's financial statements. What is the auditor's responsibility for the detection and reporting of fraud?

d. If you were Sanders, would you sign Travera's tax return as Travera presented it to you?

e. Assume that you are Sanders, that you refuse to sign Travera's tax return, and that some other CPA without knowledge of Travera's deceitful reporting practice signs his tax return. Would you report Travera to the Internal Revenue Service?

f. Suppose that you are Sanders and that you investigate Travera's charges regarding Abbott. You find that Abbott is in fact underreporting income to the extent that Travera accused him of so doing. Would you report Abbott to the Internal Revenue Service?

SPREADSHEET ASSIGNMENT *Using Excel*   ATC 2–8

Required

a. Refer to Problem 2–26A. Use an Excel spreadsheet to construct the required financial statements. To complete Requirement *b,* use formulas where normal arithmetic calculations are made within the financial statements (in particular the statement of changes in stockholders' equity).

b. It is interesting to speculate about what would happen if certain operating results change for better or worse. After completing Requirement *a,* change certain account balances for each of the following independent operating adjustments. After each adjustment, notice how the financial statements would differ if the change in operations were to occur. After noting the effect of each adjustment, return the data to the original amounts in Problem 2–26A and then go to the next operating adjustment.

In the following table, note the new amounts on the financial statements for the various operating changes listed.

Original	1	2	3	4	5
Net Income					
Total Assets					
Total Liabilities					
Total Stockholders' Equity					
Total Liabilities & Stockholders' Equity					

Independent Operating Adjustments

1. Revenue and the related Accounts Receivable increased $10,000.

2. Revenue and the related Accounts Receivable decreased $10,000.

3. Salary Expense and the related Salaries Payable decreased $4,000.

4. Salary Expense and the related Salaries Payable increased $4,000.

5. Dividends paid decreased $500 and cash changed accordingly.

SPREADSHEET ASSIGNMENT *Mastering Excel*   ATC 2–9

Refer to Problem 2–24A. Complete Requirements *b, c,* and *d* using an Excel spreadsheet. Refer to Chapter 1 problem ATC 1–8 for ideas on how to structure the spreadsheet.

CHAPTER *three*

ACCOUNTING FOR DEFERRALS

LEARNING *objectives*

After you have mastered the material in this chapter, you will be able to:

1 Provide a more complete explanation of the accrual accounting system.

2 Identify business events that involve deferrals.

3 Record deferral events under an accounting equation.

4 Prepare financial statements that include cash, accrual, and deferral events.

5 Explain how deferral events affect the financial statements.

6 Explain the effects of end-of-period adjustments related to deferrals.

7 Distinguish between a cost that is an asset and a cost that is an expense.

8 Distinguish gains and losses from revenues and expenses.

9 Analyze financial statements and make meaningful comparisons between companies by using a debt to assets ratio, a return on assets ratio, and a return on equity ratio.

10 Record deferral events in a financial statements model.

THE *curious* ACCOUNTANT

If a person wishes to subscribe to *Reader's Digest* for one year (12 issues), the subscriber must pay for the magazines before they are actually published. Suppose Paige Long sends $12 to the Reader's Digest Association in September 2007 for a one-year subscription; she will receive her first issue in October.

How should Reader's Digest account for the receipt of this cash? How would this event be reported on Reader's Digest's December 31, 2007, financial statements? (Answers on page 115.)

CHAPTER *opening*

In Chapter 2, we defined accruals *as the recognition of revenue and expense* before *the receipt or payment of cash. In this chapter, you will learn that accrual accounting involves deferrals and allocations as well as accruals. A **deferral** involves recognizing a revenue or expense at some time after cash has been collected or paid. For example, if a business collects cash in 2001 for services it will perform in 2002, the revenue is recognized in 2002 even though the cash was collected in 2001. When recognition comes before cash is exchanged, the event is an* accrual. *When recognition comes after cash is exchanged, the event is a* deferral.

*Deferred amounts may be recognized over several accounting periods. The process of assigning the total deferral to different accounting periods is called **allocation**. To illustrate, assume an attorney received a retainer fee of $30,000 from a client at the beginning of 2001. In exchange for the cash, the attorney agreed to act as a trustee for the client's children for the years 2001, 2002, and 2003. The recognition of the $30,000 of revenue would be deferred until it was earned. A portion of the revenue would then be allocated to each of the three accounting periods based on the amount earned each year. If the work were spread evenly over the three years, $10,000 would be recognized in each period.*

Topic Tackler

PLUS

3–1

LO1 Provide a more complete explanation of the accrual accounting system.

Accounting for Deferrals Illustrated

Stephen Peck is a brilliant young advertising executive employed by Westberry Corporation. Over a three-year period, he created ad campaigns that doubled Westberry's sales. Peck always wanted to start his own advertising agency. He believed his success with Westberry gave him the credibility necessary to attract a respectable client base. When Peck informed his employer of his plans and resigned, Westberry was stunned. The company's executives urged Peck to reconsider and offered a generous raise. Peck declined the offer. In desperation, Westberry agreed to become Peck's first client, paying Peck's new business $72,000 in advance to develop ad campaigns for Westberry. Peck's company, Marketing Magic, Inc. (MMI), began operations on January 1, 2004. The company experienced the following accounting events during its first year.

Event 1 *MMI acquired $1,000 cash from issuing common stock.*

As discussed in previous chapters, issuing stock is an asset source transaction. If you need help understanding the effects of this event, see Chapters 1 and 2. The impact of the stock issue on the financial statements follows:

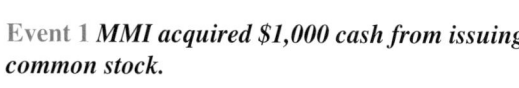

Assets			=	Liab.	+	Stockholders' Equity			Rev. − Exp. = Net Inc.	Cash Flow
Cash + Comp. Equip. − Acc. Dep.			=	Unear. Rev.	+	C. Stk.	+	Ret. Ear.		
1,000 + NA − NA			=	NA	+	1,000	+	NA	NA − NA = NA	1,000 FA

LO2 Identify business events that involve deferrals.

The statements model includes several accounts that have not been discussed previously. These accounts are described as additional accounting events are introduced.

Event 2 *On January 1, 2004, MMI received $72,000 cash in advance from Westberry for services to be performed from March 1, 2004, through February 28, 2005.*

MMI must defer (delay) the revenue recognition until the services are performed (the work is done). The deferred revenue represents a liability to Marketing Magic because the company is *obligated* to perform services in the future. The liability is called **unearned revenue.** The cash receipt is an *asset source* transaction. The asset, Cash, and the liability account, Unearned Revenue, both increase by $72,000. Collecting the cash has no effect on the income statement. The revenue will be reported on the income statement after the service has been rendered. The statement of cash flows reflects a $72,000 cash inflow from operating activities. The effects of this transaction on the financial statements are shown here:

Assets			=	Liab.	+	Stockholders' Equity			Rev. − Exp. = Net Inc.	Cash Flow
Cash + Comp. Equip. − Acc. Dep.			=	Unear. Rev.	+	C. Stk.	+	Ret. Ear.		
72,000 + NA − NA			=	72,000	+	NA	+	NA	NA − NA = NA	72,000 OA

Event 3 *MMI signed contracts to provide $58,000 of marketing services in 2005.*

Even though contracts for $58,000 of services to be performed in 2005 were signed, MMI did not receive any of the cash due from these contracts, nor has it provided any services related to them. There is no historical activity to record in the accounting records. The effect of the contracts will be reported when cash is received or when services are performed. There is no realization or recognition to report in the financial statements merely upon signing the contract agreements.

Assets			=	Liab.	+	Stockholders' Equity			Rev.	−	Exp.	=	Net Inc.	Cash Flow
Cash	+ Comp. Equip.	− Acc. Dep.	=	Unear. Rev.	+	C. Stk.	+	Ret. Ear.						
NA	+ NA	− NA	=	NA	+	NA	+	NA	NA	−	NA	=	NA	NA

Event 4 *MMI paid $12,000 cash to purchase computer equipment.*

Purchasing equipment is an *asset exchange* transaction. The asset, cash, decreases and the asset, computer equipment, increases. Total assets are unchanged. The income statement is not affected. An expense will be recognized later to reflect use of the equipment. The statement of cash flows shows a $12,000 outflow for investing activities. The effects of this transaction on the financial statements are shown here:

Assets			=	Liab.	+	Stockholders' Equity			Rev.	−	Exp.	=	Net Inc.	Cash Flow
Cash	+ Comp. Equip.	− Acc. Dep.	=	Unear. Rev.	+	C. Stk.	+	Ret. Ear.						
(12,000)	+ 12,000	− NA	=	NA	+	NA	+	NA	NA	−	NA	=	NA	(12,000) IA

Event 5 *MMI adjusted its accounts to recognize the revenue earned in 2004.*

LO6 Explain the effects of end-of-period adjustments related to deferrals.

MMI must recognize the revenue earned on the Westberry contract (see Event 2) during the 2004 accounting period. MMI began earning revenue on March 1, 2004. Assuming the work is performed relatively evenly throughout the one-year contract period, the earnings process can be viewed as continual. Recording revenue as it is earned (continually) is impractical, if not impossible. A more reasonable approach is to make a single adjustment to the accounting records at the end of the accounting period to recognize the amount of revenue earned for the entire accounting period. In this case MMI would recognize revenue for 10 months (March 1 through December 31). The amount of the adjustment is computed as follows:

$$\$72,000 \div 12 \text{ months} = \$6,000 \text{ revenue to be recognized per month}$$
$$\$6,000 \times 10 \text{ months} = \$60,000 \text{ revenue to be recognized in 2004}$$

The adjusting entry moves $60,000 from the Unearned Revenue account to the Service Revenue account. This entry is a *claims exchange:* the liability account Unearned Revenue decreases, and equity increases (recognizing that the revenue increases net income and ultimately retained earnings). Total claims remain unchanged. The effect of the revenue recognition on the financial statements follows:

Assets			=	Liab.	+	Stockholders' Equity			Rev.	−	Exp.	=	Net Inc.	Cash Flow
Cash	+ Comp. Equip.	− Acc. Dep.	=	Unear. Rev.	+	C. Stk.	+	Ret. Ear.						
NA	+ NA	− NA	=	(60,000)	+	NA	+	60,000	60,000	−	NA	=	60,000	NA

This effect is consistent with the definition of revenue. Revenue is an economic benefit (an increase in assets or a decrease in liabilities) that results from providing goods and services to customers.

Event 6 *MMI adjusted its accounts to recognize the expense of using the computer equipment during 2004. The equipment was purchased on January 1, 2004. It had an expected useful life of four years and a $2,000 salvage value.*

LO6 Explain the effects of end-of-period adjustments related to deferrals.

To measure the net economic benefit of running the business, MMI must estimate how much of the cost of the computer equipment it used in the process of earning revenue. Since the $2,000 salvage value is expected to be recovered at the end of the equipment's useful life, only $10,000 ($12,000 − $2,000) worth of the equipment is ultimately expected to be used. Assuming the equipment is used evenly over its four-year life, it is logical to allocate an equal amount of the $10,000 to expense each year the equipment is used. The allocation is computed as follows:

$$\text{(Cost − Salvage)} \div \text{Useful life} = \text{Depreciation expense}$$
$$\text{(\$12,000 − \$2,000)} \div \quad 4 \quad = \quad \$2,500$$

This method of allocation is commonly referred to as **straight-line.** The allocated cost of using a long-term tangible asset is commonly called **depreciation expense.** *Long-term* is usually defined as a period longer than one year. Recognizing depreciation expense is an *asset use* transaction. Recall that incurring an expense *decreases* assets or *increases* liabilities. The effects of the expense recognition on the financial statements follow.

Assets			=	Liab.	+	Stockholders' Equity			Rev.	−	Exp.	= Net Inc.	Cash Flow
Cash	+ Comp. Equip.	− Acc. Dep.	=	Unear. Rev.	+	C. Stk.	+	Ret. Ear.					
NA	+ NA	− 2,500	=	NA	+	NA	+	(2,500)	NA	−	2,500	= (2,500)	NA

The asset account, Computer Equipment, is not decreased directly. Instead, the asset reduction is recorded in a **contra asset account** called **Accumulated Depreciation.** This approach is used because it increases the usefulness of the information. The **book value** of the asset is the difference between the balances in the Computer Equipment account and the related Accumulated Depreciation account as follows:

$$\text{Book Value} = \text{Original Cost} − \text{Accumulated Depreciation}$$

Both the historical cost of the asset and the amount of accumulated depreciation are reported in the financial statements. This presentation is shown in the financial statements in Exhibit 3–1.

Event 7 *MMI paid a $50,000 cash dividend to the stockholders.*

As discussed in Chapters 1 and 2, the dividend represents an *asset use* transaction. Its effect on the financial statements is shown here:

Assets			=	Liab.	+	Stockholders' Equity			Rev.	−	Exp.	= Net Inc.	Cash Flow
Cash	+ Comp. Equip.	− Acc. Dep.	=	Unear. Rev.	+	C. Stk.	+	Ret. Ear.					
(50,000) +	NA	− NA	=	NA	+	NA	+	(50,000)	NA	−	NA	= NA	(50,000) FA

Summary of Events and Ledger Accounts

Marketing Magic experienced seven business events during 2004. These events are summarized here.

1. Acquired $1,000 cash from issuing common stock.
2. Obtained $72,000 cash in advance from Westberry for services to be performed from March 1, 2004, through February 28, 2005.
3. Obtained contracts to provide $58,000 of marketing services in 2005.
4. Paid $12,000 cash to purchase computer equipment.
5. Adjusted the accounting records to recognize the revenue earned in 2004.
6. Adjusted the accounting records to recognize the expense for 2004 of using the computer equipment purchased on January 1, 2004. The equipment has an expected useful life of four years and a $2,000 salvage value.
7. Paid a $50,000 cash dividend to the stockholders.

The accounting events have been recorded in the following ledger accounts.

Assets			=	Liabilities	+	Stockholders' Equity		
Cash		**Computer Equipment**		**Unearned Revenue**		**Common Stock**		**Retained Earnings**
(1)	1,000	(4) 12,000		(2) 72,000		(1) 1,000		0
(2)	72,000			(5) (60,000)				**Service Revenue**
(4)	(12,000)	**Accumulated Depreciation**		Bal. 12,000				(5) 60,000
(7)	(50,000)							
Bal.	11,000	(6) (2,500)						**Depreciation Expense**
								(6) (2,500)
								Dividends
								(7) (50,000)

The information in the accounts has been used to prepare the financial statements in Exhibit 3–1.

Exhibit 3–1 *Vertical Statements Model*

MARKETING MAGIC
Financial Statements

Income Statement for the Year Ended December 31, 2004

Service Revenue	$60,000
Depreciation Expense	(2,500)
Net Income	$57,500

Statement of Changes in Stockholders' Equity for the Year Ended December 31, 2004

Beginning Common Stock	$ 0	
Plus: Issue of Stock	1,000	
Ending Common Stock		$ 1,000
Beginning Retained Earnings	0	
Plus: Net income	57,500	
Less: Dividends	(50,000)	
Ending Retained Earnings		7,500
Total Stockholders' Equity		$ 8,500

Balance Sheet as of December 31, 2004

Assets		
Cash		$11,000
Computer Equipment	$12,000	
Less: Accumulated Depreciation	(2,500)	9,500
Total Assets		$20,500
Liabilities		
Unearned Revenue		$12,000
Stockholders' Equity		
Common Stock	$ 1,000	
Retained Earnings	7,500	
Total Stockholders' Equity		8,500
Total Liabilities and Stockholders' Equity		$20,500

Statement of Cash Flows for the Year Ended December 31, 2004

Cash Flows from Operating Activities		
Cash Receipts from Customers		$72,000
Cash Flows from Investing Activities		
Cash Payment for Computer Equipment		(12,000)
Cash Flows from Financing Activities		
Cash Receipt from Issue of Stock	$ 1,000	
Cash Payment for Dividends	(50,000)	
Net Cash Outflow from Financing Activities		(49,000)
Net Increase in Cash		11,000
Plus: Beginning Cash Balance		0
Ending Cash Balance		$11,000

The 2004 Financial Statements

Exhibit 3–1 shows the 2004 financial statements for Marketing Magic. You should be familiar with most of the components of the financial statements by now. It is still important to trace the effects of all the described transactions to the financial statements. Especially observe that deferrals as well as accruals cause the amount of reported net income to differ from the amount of cash flow from operating activities.

The income statement displays revenue of $60,000 and depreciation expense of $2,500, while the operating activities section of the statement of cash flows shows the $72,000 of cash received from the Westberry contract. The $12,000 cash paid for computer equipment is reported in the investing activities section rather than the operating activities section. The cash effects of purchasing or selling any long-term asset are always reported as investing activities.

Observe the statement presentation for the computer equipment that is shown in the balance sheet (Exhibit 3–1). The accumulated depreciation is subtracted from the original cost to determine the carrying value (book value) of the asset ($12,000 − $2,500 = $9,500). The carrying value ($9,500) is added to the other assets to determine total assets on the balance sheet.

Check Yourself 3–1

Sanderson & Associates received a $24,000 cash advance as a retainer to provide legal services to a client. The contract called for Sanderson to render services during a one-year period beginning October 1, 2006. Based on this information alone, determine the cash flow from operating activities Sanderson would report on the 2006 and 2007 statements of cash flows. Also determine the amount of revenue Sanderson would report on the 2006 and 2007 income statements.

Answer Since Sanderson collected all of the cash in 2006, the 2006 statement of cash flows would report a $24,000 cash inflow from operating activities. The 2007 statement of cash flows would report zero cash flow from operating activities. Revenue is recognized in the period in which it is earned. In this case revenue is earned at the rate of $2,000 per month ($24,000 ÷ 12 months = $2,000 per month). Sanderson rendered services for three months in 2006 and nine months in 2007. Sanderson would report $6,000 (3 months × $2,000) of revenue on the 2006 income statement and $18,000 (9 months × $2,000) of revenue on the 2007 income statement.

The Matching Concept

You may have noticed that the recognition of 12 months of computer depreciation expense use does not match with the 10 months of revenue recognition. Certainly, the computer may have been used in ways that do not directly match with the generation of revenue. For example, the computer may be used in the current period to generate advertising ideas that are sold to customers several years in the future. In the real world, perfect matching is virtually impossible. Accountants must settle for the "best fit" rather than the attainment of perfection. The **matching concept** is applied in alternative ways in order to attain the best fit. Three common matching practices include:

1. Costs may be matched directly with the revenues they generate. An example would be matching cost of goods sold with sales revenue.
2. The costs of items with short or undeterminable useful lives are matched with the period in which they are incurred. Examples of period expenses include advertising, rent, and utilities.
3. The costs of long-term assets with identifiable useful lives are systematically allocated over the assets' useful lives. In other words, expenses are spread over the periods in which the assets are used. Depreciation is an example of an expense that is recognized through the **systematic allocation of cost.**

ANSWERS TO THE *curious* ACCOUNTANT

Because the Reader's Digest Association receives cash from customers before actually providing any magazines to them, the company has not earned any revenue when it receives the cash. Thus, Reader's Digest has a liability called *unearned revenue*. If Reader's Digest closed its books on December 31, then $3 of Paige Long's subscription would be recognized as revenue in 2007. The remaining $9 would appear on the balance sheet as a liability.

Reader's Digest actually ends its accounting year on June 30 each year. A copy of the June 30, 2002, balance sheet for Reader's Digest is presented in Exhibit 3–2. The liability for unearned revenue was $561.7 ($426.9 + $134.8) million—which represented about 25 percent of Reader's Digest's total liabilities!

Will Reader's Digest need cash to pay these subscription liabilities? Not exactly. The liabilities will not be paid directly with cash. Instead, they will be satisfied by providing magazines to the subscribers. However, Reader's Digest will need cash to pay for producing and distributing the magazines supplied to the customers. Even so, the amount of cash required to provide magazines will probably differ significantly from the amount of unearned revenues. In most cases, subscription fees do not cover the cost of producing and distributing magazines. By collecting significant amounts of advertising revenue, publishers can provide magazines to customers at prices well below the cost of publication. The amount of unearned revenue is not likely to coincide with the amount of cash needed to cover the cost of satisfying the company's obligation to produce and distribute magazines. Even though the association between unearned revenues and the cost of providing magazines to customers is not direct, a knowledgeable financial analyst can use the information to make estimates of future cash flows and revenue recognition.

Exhibit 3–2 *2002 Balance Sheet for Reader's Digest*

THE READER'S DIGEST ASSOCIATION, INC. AND SUBSIDIARIES
Consolidated Balance Sheets (in millions)

	At June 30,	
	2002	**2001 Restated**
Assets		
Current Assets		
Cash and Cash Equivalents	$ 107.6	$ 35.4
Accounts Receivable, Net	306.0	274.8
Inventories	156.0	167.4
Prepaid and Deferred Promotion Costs	140.9	106.7
Prepaid Expenses and Other Current Assets	153.2	192.1
Total Current Assets	863.7	776.4
Property, Plant, and Equipment, Net	168.1	160.2
Goodwill and Other Intangible Assets, Net	1,244.6	409.8
Other Noncurrent Assets	426.3	334.5
Total Assets	$2,702.7	$1,680.9
Liabilities and Stockholders' Equity		
Current Liabilities		
Loans and Notes Payable	$ 132.7	$ 160.3
Accounts Payable	102.8	86.4
Accrued Expenses	283.2	251.1
Income Taxes Payable	28.4	41.2
Unearned Revenues	426.9	291.6
Other Current Liabilities	6.8	28.9
Total Current Liabilities	980.8	859.5
Postretirement and Postemployment Benefits Other than Pensions	128.1	138.7
Unearned Revenues	134.8	54.1
Long-Term Debt	818.0	9.8
Other Noncurrent Liabilities	169.1	159.0
Total Liabilities	2,230.8	1,221.1
Commitments and Contingencies (Notes 11 and 13)		
Stockholders' Equity		
Capital Stock	25.5	29.6
Paid-In Capital	224.6	226.1
Retained Earnings	1,261.2	1,191.3
Accumulated Other Comprehensive (Loss) Income	(89.7)	(84.6)
Treasury Stock, at Cost	(949.7)	(902.6)
Total Stockholders' Equity	471.9	459.8
Total Liabilities and Stockholders' Equity	$2,702.7	$1,680.9

Accountants may use all three approaches within the same company to attain the best possible matching of revenues with expenses.

Beyond matching inconsistencies, you should be aware that some information in financial reports is based on estimated rather than exact measures. For example, the determination of depreciation expense is based on the asset's salvage value and its expected useful life, both of which are estimated amounts. The book value of the asset and the amounts of depreciation expense, net income, and retained earnings are therefore estimated, not exact, amounts.

Finally, the application of the **concept of materiality** may cause inaccuracies in financial reporting. Recall that generally accepted accounting principles (GAAP) apply only to material items. For example, accountants may expense a pencil sharpener in the period in which it is purchased, even though theoretically it should be capitalized and expensed over its useful life. Recall that an omission or misstatement is considered material if the decision of a reasonable person would be influenced by the omission or misstatement. As a result, the reporting of many insignificant items is determined by practicality rather than theoretical accuracy.

Second Accounting Cycle

LO2 Identify business events that involve deferrals.

Marketing Magic experienced the following transactions during 2005.

1. Acquired an additional $5,000 cash from issuing more common stock.
2. Paid $400 cash for supplies.
3. Paid $1,200 cash for an insurance policy that provided coverage for one year, beginning February 1, 2005.
4. Recognized revenue for $108,000 of services provided on account.
5. Collected $89,000 of the receivables due from customers.
6. Recognized $32,000 of operating expenses purchased on account. These are other operating expenses in addition to supplies and insurance and are classified as other operating expenses.
7. Paid suppliers $28,000 of the amount owed on accounts payable.
8. Paid a $70,000 cash dividend to stockholders.
9. Purchased land for $3,000 cash.

Adjusting Entries

10. Recognized the remainder of the unearned revenue. All services had been provided by February 28, 2005, as specified in the original contract with Westberry.
11. Recognized 2005 depreciation expense.
12. Recognized supplies expense; $150 of supplies was on hand at the close of business on December 31, 2005.
13. Recognized insurance expense for 11 months.

Exhibit 3–3 shows these transactions recorded in accounts that are organized under an accounting equation. The transactions are referenced by the transaction number shown in parentheses to the left of the amount. The beginning balances were carried forward from the 2004 ending balances. The parentheses in the expense and dividend accounts indicate the effect of the account balance on retained earnings. For example, the ($32,000) balance in operating expenses does not imply that expenses were negative. In fact, operating expenses increased during the period which caused net income and ultimately retained earnings to decrease.

LO3 Record deferral events under an accounting equation.

LO5 Explain how deferral events affect the financial statements.

LO6 Explain the effects of end-of-period adjustments related to deferrals.

LO7 Distinguish between a cost that is an asset and a cost that is an expense.

Effect of 2005 Transactions on the Accounting Equation and the Financial Statements

The effects of many of the 2005 transactions have been explained in previous sections of this book. Those transactions that are new are discussed in the following section of the text.

Accounting for Supplies

Transaction 2 is a deferral. To understand this event, it is helpful to distinguish between the terms *cost* and *expense*. A cost can be either an asset or an expense. If a purchased item has

Exhibit 3–3 *Effect of 2005 Transactions on the Accounting Equation*

Assets					=	Liabilities		+	Stockholders' Equity		

Cash

Bal.	11,000
(1)	5,000
(2)	(400)
(3)	(1,200)
(5)	89,000
(7)	(28,000)
(8)	(70,000)
(9)	(3,000)
Bal.	2,400

Accounts Receivable

Bal.	0
(4)	108,000
(5)	(89,000)
Bal.	19,000

Supplies

Bal.	0
(2)	400
(12)	(250)
Bal.	150

Prepaid Insurance

Bal.	0
(3)	1,200
(13)	(1,100)
Bal.	100

Computer Equipment

Bal.	12,000

Accumulated Depreciation

Bal.	(2,500)
(11)	(2,500)
Bal.	(5,000)

Land

Bal.	0
(9)	3,000
Bal.	3,000

Accounts Payable

Bal.	0
(6)	32,000
(7)	(28,000)
Bal.	4,000

Unearned Revenue

Bal.	12,000
(10)	(12,000)
Bal.	0

Common Stock

Bal.	1,000
(1)	5,000
Bal.	6,000

Retained Earnings

Bal.	7,500

Dividends

(8)	(70,000)

Service Revenue

(4)	108,000
(10)	12,000
Bal.	120,000

Other Operating Expenses

(6)	(32,000)

Depreciation Expense

(11)	(2,500)

Supplies Expense

(12)	(250)

Insurance Expense

(13)	(1,100)

Exhibit 3–4 *Relationship between Cost and Expense*

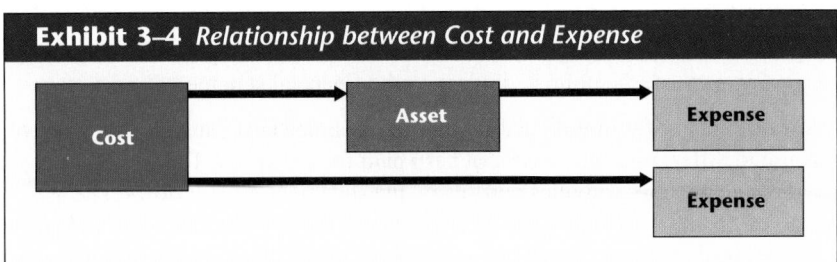

already been used in the process of earning revenue, its cost represents an *expense*. If the item will be used in the future to generate revenue, its cost represents an *asset*. Storing the cost in an asset account enables the accountant to *defer* the recognition of an expense until the future time when the item is used. This explains why assets are sometimes called deferred expenses. Exhibit 3–4 demonstrates the relationship between a cost and an expense. With respect to event 2, the cost of supplies is placed in an asset account. The expense recognition is deferred until the supplies are used to produce revenue.

Impact on Accounting Equation It is impractical to expense supplies as they are being used. For example, it is too tedious to record an expense every time a pencil, a piece of paper, or an envelope is used. Instead, accountants expense the total cost of all supplies used during the entire accounting period in a single year-end adjusting entry. The cost of supplies used is determined by the following formula:

$$\text{Beginning balance} + \text{Purchases} = \text{Supplies available for use} - \text{Ending balance} = \text{Supplies used}$$

In practice, the cost of supplies on hand at the end of the period (ending balance) is determined by physically counting them. We can now determine that Marketing Magic used $250 (zero beginning balance + $400 purchase = $400 available for use − $150 ending balance).

This explains the year-end adjusting entry (transaction 12) that transfers $250 from the Supplies account to the Supplies Expense account. This treatment is consistent with our previous definition of an expense. Recall that an expense is defined as a decrease in assets or increase in liabilities that results from using assets and services to generate revenue. In this case, recognizing the expense decreases the asset, supplies. The $150 of supplies on hand at the end of the accounting period is reported as an asset on the balance sheet.

Impact on Financial Statements Observe how the deferral causes differences between the amount of income reported on the income statement and the amount of cash flow from operating activities shown on the statement of cash flows. Of the $400 cash paid for supplies, only $250 is recognized as expense. The remaining $150 is deferred as an asset. Verify these effects by reviewing the financial statements in Exhibit 3–5.

Accounting for Prepaid Insurance

Event 3 is also a deferral. The cost of the insurance is placed in an asset account called Prepaid Insurance (Transaction 3 in Exhibit 3–3). The expense recognition is deferred until the insurance is used.

Impact on Accounting Equation The amount of the $1,200 cost that represents insurance that was used during the accounting period is transferred from the Prepaid Insurance account to the Insurance Expense account in a single adjusting entry made at the end of the accounting period. In this case the amount of insurance used during the accounting period is computed as follows:

$$\text{Cost of annual policy} \div 12 = \text{Cost per month} \times \text{Months used} = \text{Insurance expense}$$

$$\underset{\text{of policy}}{\$1{,}200 \text{ cost}} \div 12 = \$100 \text{ per month} \times 11 \text{ months} = \$1{,}100 \text{ insurance expense}$$

This explains MMI's $1,100 ($100 × 11) charge to expense for the 2005 accounting period (Event 13 in Exhibit 3–3). The remaining $100 represents an asset, prepaid insurance, that is shown on the balance sheet. Other recording schemes are possible. Some sophisticated computer programs can continually allocate costs between asset and expense accounts. Regardless of the recording method, the ultimate impact on the financial statements is the same.

Impact on Financial Statements Deferring the insurance cost causes the amount of insurance expense to differ from the amount of cash paid for insurance. The $1,200 cash payment is reported as an operating activities outflow on the statement of cash flows. The used portion of the cost is a $1,100 expense on the income statement, and the remaining $100 is deferred as an asset, prepaid insurance, on the balance sheet. Verify these effects by reviewing the financial statements in Exhibit 3–5.

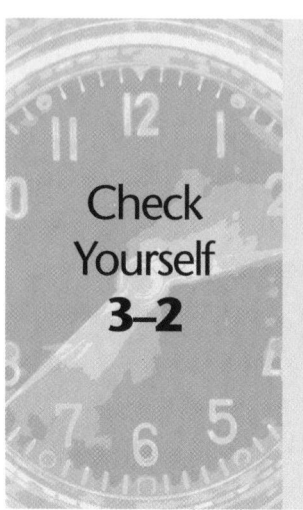

Check Yourself 3–2

Rujoub, Inc., paid $18,000 cash for one year of insurance coverage that began on November 1, 2005. Based on this information alone, determine the cash flow from operating activities that Rujoub would report on the 2005 and 2006 statements of cash flows. Also, determine the amount of insurance expense Rujoub would report on the 2005 income statement and the amount of prepaid insurance (an asset) that Rujoub would report on the December 31, 2005, balance sheet.

Answer Since Rujoub paid all of the cash in 2005, the 2005 statement of cash flows would report an $18,000 cash outflow from operating activities. The 2006 statement of cash flows would report zero cash flow from operating activities. The expense would be recognized in the periods in which the insurance is used. In this case, insurance expense is recognized at the rate of $1,500 per month ($18,000 ÷ 12 months). Rujoub used two months of insurance coverage in 2005 and therefore would report $3,000 (2 months × $1,500) of insurance expense on the 2005 income statement. Rujoub would report a $15,000 (10 months × $1,500) asset, prepaid insurance, on the December 31, 2005, balance sheet. The $15,000 of prepaid insurance would be recognized as insurance expense in 2006 when the insurance coverage is used.

Exhibit 3-5 *Vertical Statements Model*

MARKETING MAGIC
Financial Statements

Income Statement for the Year Ended December 31, 2005

Service Revenue		$120,000
Other Operating Expenses	$32,000	
Depreciation Expense	2,500	
Supplies Expense	250	
Insurance Expense	1,100	
Total Expenses		(35,850)
Net Income		$ 84,150

Statement of Changes in Stockholders Equity for the Year Ended December 31, 2005

Beginning Common Stock	$ 1,000	
Plus: Issue of Stock	5,000	
Ending Common Stock		$ 6,000
Beginning Retained Earnings	7,500	
Plus: Net Income	84,150	
Less: Dividends	(70,000)	
Ending Retained Earnings		21,650
Total Stockholders' Equity		$ 27,650

Balance Sheet as of December 31, 2005

Assets		
Cash		$ 2,400
Accounts Receivable		19,000
Supplies		150
Prepaid Insurance		100
Computer Equipment	$12,000	
Less: Accumulated Depreciation	(5,000)	7,000
Land		3,000
Total Assets		$ 31,650
Liabilities		
Accounts Payable		$ 4,000
Stockholders' Equity		
Common Stock	$ 6,000	
Retained Earnings	21,650	
Total Stockholders' Equity		27,650
Total Liabilities and Stockholders' Equity		$ 31,650

Statement of Cash Flows for the Year Ended December 31, 2005

Cash Flows from Operating Activities		
Cash Receipts from Customers		$ 89,000
Cash Payment for Supplies	$ (400)	
Cash Payment for Insurance	(1,200)	
Cash Payment for Operating Expenses	(28,000)	
Total Cash Outflows from Operating Activities		(29,600)
Net Cash Flow from Operating Activities		59,400
Cash Flows from Investing Activities		
Cash Outflow to Purchase Land		(3,000)
Cash Flows from Financing Activities		
Cash Receipt from Issue of Stock	5,000	
Cash Payment for Dividends	(70,000)	
Net Cash Outflow from Financing Activities		(65,000)
Net Decrease in Cash		(8,600)
Plus: Beginning Cash Balance		11,000
Ending Cash Balance		$ 2,400

Third Accounting Cycle

Marketing Magic experienced the following transactions during 2006.

1. Acquired $1,000 cash from issuing common stock to additional stockholders.
2. Sold the land for $2,500 cash.
3. Paid $400 cash for more supplies.
4. Borrowed $20,000 from a local bank on February 1, 2006. The note issued had a 9 percent interest rate and a one-year term.
5. Paid $1,200 cash to renew the insurance policy for a one-year term beginning February 1, 2006.
6. Recognized revenue for $167,000 of services provided on account.
7. Collected $129,000 of the receivables due from customers.
8. Recognized $62,000 of accrued operating expenses, other than supplies and insurance, charged on account.
9. Paid suppliers $65,000 of the amount owed on accounts payable.
10. Received $18,000 cash in advance from a customer for marketing services to be performed for a one-year period beginning December 1, 2006.
11. Paid an $80,000 cash dividend to stockholders.

Adjusting Entries
12. Recognized one month of the unearned revenue.
13. Recognized 2006 depreciation expense.
14. Recognized supplies expense; $200 of supplies was on hand at the close of business on December 31, 2006.
15. Recognized insurance expense for 12 months.
16. Recognized the accrued interest on the bank note.

The effects of the 2006 accounting events on the accounting equation are shown in Exhibit 3–6.

Effect of 2006 Transactions on the Accounting Equation and the Financial Statements

Again, you should already be familiar with many of these transactions. Those requiring additional commentary are discussed in the following section of the chapter.

Accounting Treatment for Stock Issue

Transaction 1 demonstrates that ownership interests may be shared by two or more individuals. Millions of individuals and institutions hold ownership interests in major corporations such as General Motors, Sears, Roebuck, and International Business Machines (IBM). The effect of the $1,000 cash acquired from issuing more common stock is no different from the effect of the acquisitions shown previously. The acquisition is an *asset source* transaction recorded with increases in the asset account, Cash, and the stockholders' equity account, Common Stock.

Accounting Treatment for Gains and Losses

The asset, land, was recorded in the accounting records at its $3,000 historical cost (book value). Since land carried at $3,000 was sold for $2,500 cash, total assets decreased by $500. This decrease in assets is called a loss. **Losses** are *similar* to expenses in that they coincide with decreases in assets or increases in liabilities. Losses *differ* from expenses in that losses result from **peripheral (incidental) transactions,** rather than ordinary operating activities. Marketing Magic is not in the business of selling land. Because the sale is incidental to normal operating activities, MMI identifies the item as a loss rather than an expense to alert investors and creditors to its nonroutine nature. Identifying the item as a loss rather than an expense signals investors and creditors that this event is not likely to be repeated.

Exhibit 3–6 Effect of 2006 Transactions on the Accounting Equation

Assets		=	Liabilities	+	Stockholders' Equity	

Cash

Bal.	2,400
(1)	1,000
(2)	2,500
(3)	(400)
(4)	20,000
(5)	(1,200)
(7)	129,000
(9)	(65,000)
(10)	18,000
(11)	(80,000)
Bal.	26,300

Accounts Receivable

Bal.	19,000
(6)	167,000
(7)	(129,000)
Bal.	57,000

Supplies

Bal.	150
(3)	400
(14)	(350)
Bal.	200

Prepaid Insurance

Bal.	100
(5)	1,200
(15)	(1,200)
Bal.	100

Computer Equipment

Bal.	12,000

Accumulated Depreciation

Bal.	(5,000)
(13)	(2,500)
Bal.	(7,500)

Land

Bal.	3,000
(2)	(3,000)
Bal.	0

Accounts Payable

Bal.	4,000
(8)	62,000
(9)	(65,000)
Bal.	1,000

Unearned Revenue

Bal.	0
(10)	18,000
(12)	(1,500)
Bal.	16,500

Interest Payable

(16)	1,650

Notes Payable

(4)	20,000

Common Stock

Bal.	6,000
(1)	1,000
Bal.	7,000

Retained Earnings

Bal.	21,650

Dividends

(11)	(80,000)

Service Revenue

(6)	167,000
(12)	1,500
Bal.	168,500

Operating Expenses

(8)	(62,000)

Depreciation Expense

(13)	(2,500)

Supplies Expense

(14)	(350)

Insurance Expense

(15)	(1,200)

Interest Expense

(16)	(1,650)

Loss on Sale of Land

(2)	(500)

Had MMI sold the land for *more* than book value, a *gain* would be recognized. **Gains** are *similar* to revenues in that they coincide with increases in assets or decreases in liabilities. Gains *differ* from revenues in that gains result from peripheral rather than ordinary operating activities. Distinguishing gains from revenues provides insight as to the likelihood of recurrence. Operating revenues are more likely to continue than gains.

The land sale increased the Cash account by $2,500, reduced the Land account by $3,000 (to zero), and reduced retained earnings by $500. These effects are shown as transaction 2 in Exhibit 3–6. The $500 loss is reported separately on the income statement after **operating income,** which is the difference between expenses and revenues. Although the loss *reduces* net income, the sale actually *increases* cash. The $2,500 cash received from selling the land is reported as a source (cash inflow) of cash from investing activities on the statement of cash flows. Cash flow from operating activities is not affected because the sale did not involve an ordinary operating activity. Confirm these effects by reviewing the financial statements in Exhibit 3–7.

Accounting Treatment for Supplies

The amount of supplies expense is determined as in 2005 except that in 2006 there is a beginning balance of $150 in the Supplies account. Specifically, the amount of supplies used is $350 ($150 beginning balance + $400 purchases = $550 supplies available for use − $200 ending balance). The year-end adjusting entry (transaction 14) transfers $350 from the asset account, Supplies, to the Supplies Expense account. Again, the amount of supplies expense differs from

LO6 Explain the effects of end-of-period adjustments related to deferrals.

Exhibit 3–7 *Vertical Statements Model*

MARKETING MAGIC
Financial Statements

Income Statement for the Year Ended December 31, 2006

Service Revenue		$168,500
Other Operating Expenses	$ 62,000	
Depreciation Expense	2,500	
Supplies Expense	350	
Insurance Expense	1,200	
Total Expenses		(66,050)
Operating Income		102,450
Less: Interest Expense*		(1,650)
Less: Loss on Sale of Land		(500)
Net Income		$100,300

Statement of Changes in Stockholders Equity for the Year Ended December 31, 2006

Beginning Common Stock	$ 6,000	
Plus: Issue of Stock	1,000	
Ending Common Stock		$ 7,000
Beginning Retained Earnings	21,650	
Plus: Net Income	100,300	
Less: Dividends	(80,000)	
Ending Retained Earnings		41,950
Total Stockholders' Equity		$ 48,950

Balance Sheet as of December 31, 2006

Assets		
Cash		$ 26,300
Accounts Receivable		57,000
Supplies		200
Prepaid Insurance		100
Computer Equipment	$ 12,000	
Less: Accumulated Depreciation	(7,500)	4,500
Total Assets		$ 88,100
Liabilities		
Accounts Payable	$ 1,000	
Unearned Revenue	16,500	
Interest Payable	1,650	
Notes Payable	20,000	
Total Liabilities		$ 39,150
Stockholders' Equity		
Common Stock	7,000	
Retained Earnings	41,950	
Total Stockholders' Equity		48,950
Total Liabilities and Stockholders' Equity		$ 88,100

Statement of Cash Flows for the Year Ended December 31, 2006

Cash Flows from Operating Activities		
Cash Receipts from Customers	$147,000	
Cash Payment for Supplies	(400)	
Cash Payment for Insurance	(1,200)	
Cash Payment for Operating Expenses	(65,000)	
Net Cash Flow from Operating Activities		$ 80,400
Cash Flows from Investing Activities		
Cash Receipt from Sale of Land		2,500
Cash Flows from Financing Activities		
Cash Receipt from Bank Loan	20,000	
Cash Receipt from Issue of Stock	1,000	
Cash Payment for Dividends	(80,000)	
Net Cash Outflow from Financing Activities		(59,000)
Net Increase in Cash		23,900
Plus: Beginning Cash Balance		2,400
Ending Cash Balance		$ 26,300

*The presentation of interest expense is explained in Chapter 6.

the amount of cash spent. The operating activities section of the statement of cash flows reports the $400 cash outflow to purchase supplies while the income statement shows a $350 expense.

Accounting Treatment for Prepaid Insurance

The $1,200 policy renewal (transaction 5) on February 1, 2006, increased the Prepaid Insurance account. Combined with the $100 beginning balance in the Prepaid Insurance account, MMI had $1,300 of insurance coverage for a 13-month period. Since 12 months of insurance were used in 2006, the year-end adjusting entry transfers $1,200 from the Prepaid Insurance account to the Insurance Expense account (transaction 15).

Accounting Treatment for Bank Loan

The bank loan (transaction 4) requires recognizing interest expense for the 11 months since MMI received the funds. Interest expense is determined by multiplying the principal by the rate and by the length of time the money has been used ($20,000 \times 0.09 \times [11 \div 12] = \$1,650$). Because interest accrues as time passes, MMI has a liability at December 31, 2006, for interest expense incurred but not yet paid. Recording the accrual increases liabilities and interest expense as shown in transaction 16 in Exhibit 3–6.

Accounting Treatment for Unearned Revenue

The cash collection (transaction 10) is a deferral. Upon receiving the cash, MMI recorded a liability, unearned revenue. Assuming work under the contract is performed evenly over the one-year period, the monthly allocation for revenue recognition is $1,500 ($18,000 \div 12$). Since one month of service has been provided by December 31, 2006, the year-end adjusting entry (transaction 12) transfers $1,500 from the liability account to the revenue account. This example shows how revenue recognition may coincide with a decrease in liabilities. Only $1,500 of the $18,000 cash received is recognized as revenue in 2006 ($1,500 is included in the $168,500 of revenue reported on the income statement) but the entire $18,000 is reported in the operating activities section of the statement of cash flows ($18,000 is included in the $147,000 cash receipts from customers). Trace the effects of these transactions to the financial statements.

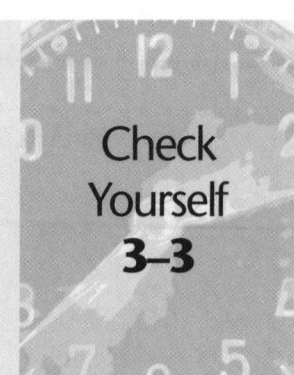

On January 1, 2002, Lambert Company paid $28,000 cash to purchase office furniture. The furniture has a $3,000 salvage value and a five-year useful life. Explain how Lambert would report this asset purchase on the 2002 statement of cash flows. Also, determine the amount of depreciation expense and accumulated depreciation Lambert would report in the *2004* financial statements.

Answer Lambert would report a $28,000 cash outflow in the investing activities section of the 2002 statement of cash flows. During 2004 and every other year of the asset's useful life, Lambert would report $5,000 ([$28,000 − $3,000] ÷ 5) of depreciation expense on the income statement. The accumulated depreciation would increase by $5,000 each year of the asset's useful life. As of December 31, 2004, Lambert would report accumulated depreciation on the balance sheet of $15,000 (3 years × $5,000 per year).

Check Yourself 3–3

THE FINANCIAL ANALYST

Suppose a company earned net income of $1,000,000. Is the company's performance good or poor? If the company is General Motors, the performance is poor. If it is a small shoe store, the performance is outstanding. So, how do financial analysts compare the performance of differing size companies? Financial ratios are very helpful in this regard.

Topic Tackler
PLUS

3–2

Assessing the Effective Use of Assets

LO9 Analyze financial statements and make meaningful comparisons between companies by using a debt to assets ratio, a return on assets ratio, and a return on equity ratio.

Evaluating performance requires considering the size of the investment base used to produce the income. In other words, you expect someone who has a ten million dollar investment base to earn more than someone who has a ten thousand dollar base. The relationship between the level of income and the size of the investment can be expressed as the **return on assets ratio,** as follows:

$$\frac{\text{Net income}[1]}{\text{Total assets}}$$

This ratio permits meaningful comparisons between different-size companies. Compare The Nautilus Group, Inc., the company that makes exercise equipment, with General Motors (GM). In 2002, Nautilus' net income was $98 million and GM's was $1.7 billion, more than 17 times the earnings of Nautilus. However, the return on asset ratios for the two companies reveal that Nautilus produced higher earnings relative to the assets invested. GM's ratio was 0.5 percent while Nautilus' was 35.4 percent. Even though Nautilus earned fewer dollars of net income, the company did a better job than GM of managing its assets.

The preceding example demonstrates the usefulness of the relationship between income and assets. Two more ratios that enhance financial statement analysis are discussed in the following paragraphs.

Assessing Debt Risk

Borrowing money can be a risky business. To illustrate, assume two companies have the following financial structures:

	Assets	=	Liabilities	+	Stockholders' Equity
Eastern Company	100	=	20	+	80
Western Company	100	=	80	+	20

Which company has the greater financial risk? If each company incurred a $30 loss, the financial structures would change as follows:

	Assets	=	Liabilities	+	Stockholders' Equity
Eastern Company	70	=	20	+	50
Western Company	70	=	80	+	(10)

Clearly, Western Company is at greater risk. Eastern Company could survive a $30 loss that reduced assets and stockholders' equity. It would still have a $50 balance in stockholders' equity and more than enough assets ($70) to satisfy the creditors' $20 claim. In contrast, a $30 loss would throw Western Company into bankruptcy. The company would have a $10 deficit (negative) balance in stockholders' equity and the remaining assets ($70) would be less than the creditors' $80 claim on assets.

The level of debt risk can be measured in part by using a **debt to assets ratio,** as follows:

$$\frac{\text{Total debt}}{\text{Total assets}}$$

For example, Eastern Company's debt to assets ratio is 20 percent ($20 ÷ $100) while Western Company's is 80 percent ($80 ÷ $100). Why would the owners of Western Company be willing to accept greater debt risk? Assume that both companies produce $12 of revenue and each must pay 10 percent interest on money owed to creditors. Income statements for the two companies appear as follows:[2]

---

[1] The use of net income in this ratio ignores the effects of debt financing and income taxation. The effect of these variables on the return on assets ratio is explained in Chapter 10.

[2] This illustration ignores the effect of income taxes on debt financing. This subject is discussed in Chapter 10.

	Eastern Company	Western Company
Revenue	$12	$12
Interest Expense	2	8
Net Income	$10	$ 4

At first glance, the owners of Eastern Company appear better off because Eastern produced higher net income. In fact, however, the owners of *Western* Company are better off. The owners of Eastern Company get $10 of income for investing $80 of their own money into the business, a return on their invested funds of 12.5 percent ($10 ÷ $80). In contrast, the owners of Western Company obtain $4 of net income for their $20 investment, a return on invested funds of 20 percent ($4 ÷ $20).

focus on INTERNATIONAL ISSUES

Why Not Have One Global GAAP?

Although no two countries have exactly the same accounting rules, there are many similarities in the various accounting systems used around the world. Furthermore, geographic, political, and social forces tend to promote similar views within selected sets of countries. For example, the GAAP of the United Kingdom is more likely to match the GAAP of New Zealand than the GAAP of Brazil. This has led some to try to group countries based on the similarity of their respective accounting rules.

One accounting research study concluded that the world's accounting systems can be divided into four groups: (1) British Commonwealth model, (2) Latin American model, (3) Continental European model, and (4) U.S. model.*

According to this study, countries with accounting rules similar to (but not exactly the same as) GAAP in the United States include Canada, Japan, Mexico, Panama, and the Philippines.

If there already exist similarities among the GAAP of different countries, why not have only one set of accounting rules for all countries? There are many reasons that one set of rules, and one rule-making body, do not exist for the entire world, but consider two easy examples. First, different countries have different political structures (e.g., democracy versus communism). What are the chances that a country with strong government controls would allow its accounting rules to be established by a nongovernment body such as the Financial Accounting Standards Board? Second, different countries have different economic structures. In the United States, most industries, even those related to national defense, are privately owned. In some countries, major industries are owned by the government while smaller industries are privately owned. In a few countries, almost all resources are owned by the government. It is impossible to have one set of rules that would work well in such diverse settings.

Even though each country establishes its own GAAP, there is an international "rule-suggesting" body for accounting. The

International Accounting Standards Board (IASB) has more than 100 member countries participating in its activities. The IASB tries to improve the uniformity of accounting practices around the world by recommending the appropriate accounting treatment for various business events. However, the IASB has no enforcement power, so its pronouncements are simply recommendations, not requirements.

*R. D. Nair and W. G. Frank, "The Impact of Disclosure and Measurement Practices on International Accounting Classifications," *The Accounting Review,* July 1980.

The relationship between net income and the stockholders' equity used above is the **return on equity ratio,** computed as:

$$\frac{\text{Net income}}{\text{Stockholders' equity}}$$

Using borrowed money to increase the return on stockholders' investment is called **financial leverage.** Financial leverage explains why companies are willing to accept the risk of debt. Companies borrow money to make money. If a company can borrow money at 10 percent and invest it at 12 percent, the owners will be better off by 2 percent of the amount borrowed. A business that does not borrow may be missing an opportunity to increase its return on equity.

Real-World Data

Exhibit 3–8 shows the debt to assets, return on assets, and return on equity ratios for six real-world companies in two different industries. The data are drawn from the companies' 2002 financial reports. Notice Hartford's return on assets ratio was 0.4 percent and Aflac's was 1.8 percent. Neither ratio seems good; banks often pay more than 1.8 percent interest on deposits in savings accounts. The *return on equity* ratios, however, show a different picture; Hartford's was 9.8 percent and Aflac's was 12.8 percent—much better than banks pay depositors.

Exhibit 3–8 also shows that while Hartford's return on assets ratio was lower than Chevron Texaco (0.4 percent versus 1.5 percent), its return on equity ratio was higher than Chevron Texaco's (9.8 percent versus 3.6 percent). How can this happen? Compare the debt to assets ratios. Hartford financed 96 percent of its assets with debt compared to Chevron Texaco's 59 percent. This suggests that financial leverage is a contributing factor to Hartford's higher return on equity. While financial leverage can boost the return on equity, it is not the only factor that effects this ratio. For example, notice that compared to all of the companies shown in Exhibit 3–8, ExxonMobil has the highest return on equity but the lowest debt to assets ratio. Certainly, many factors other than debt management affect profitability. Even so, more financial leverage may have enabled ExxonMobil to increase its return on equity even further.

Since financial leverage offers the opportunity to increase return on equity, why doesn't every company leverage itself to the maximum? There is a down side. When the economy turns down, companies may not be able to produce investment returns that exceed interest rates. A company that has borrowed money at a fixed rate of 8 percent, but can only earn 6 percent on its investments will suffer from financial leverage. In other words, financial leverage is a double-edged sword. It can have a negative as well as a positive impact on a company's return on equity ratio.

Finally, compare the ratios in Exhibit 3–8 for companies in the oil industry to the same ratios for companies in the insurance industry. There are significant differences *between* industries, but there are considerable similarities *within* each industry. The debt to assets ratio is much higher for the insurance industry than for the oil industry. However, within each industry, the ratios are clustered fairly close together. With ExxonMobil being the exception, distinct differences between industries and similarities within industries are common business features. When you compare accounting information for different companies, you must consider the industries in which those companies operate.

Scope of Coverage

Throughout this text, ratios directly related to chapter topics are introduced. Even so, only a few of the many ratios available to users of financial statements are introduced. Introductory finance courses typically include a more extensive study of ratios and other topics related to

Exhibit 3-8 *Three Ratios (in Percentages) for Six Real-World Companies*

Industry	Company	Debt to Assets	Return on Assets	Return on Equity
Insurance	Aflac	86	1.8	12.8
	Hartford	96	0.4	9.8
	John Hancock	94	0.5	8.0
Oil	Chevron Texaco	59	1.5	3.6
	Conoco Phillips	60	0.9	2.4
	ExxonMobil	49	7.2	14.8

financial statement analysis. Many business programs offer an entire course on financial statement analysis. These courses help students learn to judge whether the ratio results signal good or poor performance. Developing such judgment requires understanding how accounting policies and procedures can affect financial ratios. The ratios introduced in this text will enhance your understanding of accounting as a basis for studying more advanced topics in subsequent courses.

This chapter introduced the principle of deferring revenue and expense recognition. *Deferrals* involve recognizing revenue or expense at some time *after* cash has been collected or paid. Deferrals cause significant differences in the amount of revenue and expenses reported on the income statement and the amount of cash flow from operating activities. These differences are readily apparent when deferral events are viewed in a horizontal financial statements model. To illustrate, review the following transactions and the statements model that follows them. To reinforce your understanding, draw a statements model on a piece of paper and try to record the effects of each event before reading the explanation in the text.

a look

back

LO10 Record deferral events in a financial statements model.

List of Events

1. Received an advance payment of $1,200 cash for services to be performed in the future.
2. Provided $800 of the services agreed on in Event 1.
3. Paid $900 in advance for a one-year contract to rent office space.
4. Used eight months (that is, $600) of the office space leased in Event 3.

Event No.	Balance Sheet							Income Statement						Statement of Cash Flows	
	Assets			=	Liab.	+	Stockholders' Equity	Rev.	−	Exp.	=	Net Inc.			
	Cash	+	P. Rent	=	U. Rev.	+	Ret. Earn								
1	1,200	+	NA	=	1,200	+	NA	NA	−	NA	=	NA	1,200	OA	
2	NA	+	NA	=	(800)	+	800	800	−	NA	=	800	NA		
3	(900)	+	900	=	NA	+	NA	NA	−	NA	=	NA	(900)	OA	
4	NA	+	(600)	=	NA	+	(600)	NA	−	600	=	(600)	NA		
Totals	300	+	300	=	400	+	200	800	−	600	=	200	300	NC	

The $200 of net income differs from the $300 of cash flow from operating activities. The entries in the statements model make the reasons for the difference clear. Although $1,200 of cash was collected, only $800 of revenue was recognized. The remaining $400 will be recognized in the future when the rest of the work is done. The $400 obligation to provide future services is currently reported on the balance sheet as unearned revenue. Also, although $900 cash was paid for rent, only $600 of rent expense was recognized. The remaining $300 is shown on the balance sheet as the asset *prepaid rent*. In general, costs are **capitalized** (recorded) in asset accounts when cash is paid. Expense recognition is deferred until the time that the assets (capitalized costs) are used to produce revenue. This principle applies to many costs, including those incurred for supplies, insurance, equipment, and buildings. Study these relationships carefully to develop a clear understanding of how deferrals affect financial reporting.

To this point, we have used plus and minus signs to illustrate the effects of business events on financial statements. In real businesses, so many transactions occur that recording them with simple mathematical notations is impractical. In practice, accountants usually maintain records using a system of rules known as *double-entry bookkeeping*. Chapter 4 introduces the basic components of this bookkeeping system. You will learn how to record business events using a debit/credit format. You will be introduced to ledgers, journals, and trial balances. When you finish Chapter 4, you will have a clear understanding of how accountants maintain records of business activity.

SELF-STUDY REVIEW PROBLEM

Gifford Company experienced the following accounting events during 2005.

1. Started operations on January 1 when it acquired $20,000 cash by issuing common stock.
2. On January 1 paid $15,000 cash to purchase computer equipment.
3. On March 1 collected $36,000 cash as an advance for services to be performed in the future.
4. Paid cash operating expenses of $17,000.
5. Paid a $2,700 cash dividend to the stockholders.
6. On December 31, 2005, adjusted the books to recognize the revenue earned by providing services related to the advance described in Event 3. The contract required Gifford to provide services for a one-year period starting March 1.
7. On December 31, 2005, Gifford adjusted the books to recognize depreciation expense on the computer equipment. The equipment has a three-year useful life and a $3,000 salvage value.

Gifford Company experienced the following accounting events during 2006.

1. Recognized $38,000 of cash revenue.
2. Paid cash operating expenses of $21,000.
3. Paid a $5,000 cash dividend to the stockholders.
4. On December 31, 2006, adjusted the books to recognize the remaining revenue earned by providing services related to the advance described in Event 3 of 2005.
5. On December 31, 2006, Gifford adjusted the books to recognize depreciation expense on the computer equipment purchased in Event 2 of 2005. The equipment has a three-year useful life and a $3,000 salvage value.

Required

a. Record the events in a financial statements model like the following one. The first event is recorded as an example.

Event No.	Assets			=	Liab.	+	Stockholders' Equity		Rev. − Exp. = Net Inc.	Cash Flow
	Cash +	Comp. Equip. −	Acc. Dep. =		Unear. Rev. +		C. Stk. +	Ret. Ear.		
1	20,000 +	NA −	NA =		NA +		20,000 +	NA	NA − NA = NA	20,000 FA

b. What amount of depreciation expense would Gifford report on the 2005 and 2006 income statements?
c. What amount of cash flow for depreciation would Gifford report on the 2006 statement of cash flows?
d. What amount of unearned revenue would Gifford report on the 2005 and 2006 year-end balance sheets?
e. What are the 2006 opening balances for the revenue and expense accounts?
f. What amount of total assets would Gifford report on the December 31, 2005, balance sheet?
g. What claims on the assets would Gifford report on the December 31, 2006, balance sheet?

Solution to Requirement a

The financial statements model follows.

Event No.	Cash	+	Comp. Equip.	−	Acc. Dep.	=	Unear. Rev.	+	C. Stk.	+	Ret. Ear.	Rev.	−	Exp.	=	Net Inc.	Cash Flow	
2005																		
1	20,000	+	NA	−	NA	=	NA	+	20,000	+	NA	NA	−	NA	=	NA	20,000	FA
2	(15,000)	+	15,000	−	NA	=	NA	+	NA	+	NA	NA	−	NA	=	NA	(15,000)	IA
3	36,000	+	NA	−	NA	=	36,000	+	NA	+	NA	NA	−	NA	=	NA	36,000	OA
4	(17,000)	+	NA	−	NA	=	NA	+	NA	+	(17,000)	NA	−	17,000	=	(17,000)	(17,000)	OA
5	(2,700)	+	NA	−	NA	=	NA	+	NA	+	(2,700)	NA	−	NA	=	NA	(2,700)	FA
6*	NA	+	NA	−	NA	=	(30,000)	+	NA	+	30,000	30,000	−	NA	=	30,000	NA	
7†	NA	+	NA	−	4,000	=	NA	+	NA	+	(4,000)	NA	−	4,000	=	(4,000)	NA	
Bal.	21,300	+	15,000	−	4,000	=	6,000	+	20,000	+	6,300	30,000	−	21,000	=	9,000	21,300	NC
	Asset, Liability, and Equity Account Balances Carry Forward											Rev. & Exp. Accts. Are Closed						
2006																		
Bal.	21,300	+	15,000	−	4,000	=	6,000	+	20,000	+	6,300	NA	−	NA	=	NA	NA	
1	38,000	+	NA	−	NA	=	NA	+	NA	+	38,000	38,000	−	NA	=	38,000	38,000	OA
2	(21,000)	+	NA	−	NA	=	NA	+	NA	+	(21,000)	NA	−	21,000	=	(21,000)	(21,000)	OA
3	(5,000)	+	NA	−	NA	=	NA	+	NA	+	(5,000)	NA	−	NA	=	NA	(5,000)	FA
4*	NA	+	NA	−	NA	=	(6,000)	+	NA	+	6,000	6,000	−	NA	=	6,000	NA	
5†	NA	+	NA	−	4,000	=	NA	+	NA	+	(4,000)	NA	−	4,000	=	(4,000)	NA	
Bal.	33,300	+	15,000	−	8,000	=	0	+	20,000	+	20,300	44,000	−	25,000	=	19,000	12,000	NC

*Revenue is earned at the rate of $3,000 ($36,000 ÷ 12 months) per month. Revenue recognized in 2005 is $30,000 ($3,000 × 10 months). Revenue recognized in 2006 is $6,000 ($3,000 × 2 months).

†Depreciation expense is $4,000 ([$15,000 − $3,000] ÷ 3 years) per year.

Solutions to Requirements b–g

b. Gifford would report depreciation expense in 2005 of $4,000 ([$15,000 − $3,000] ÷ 3 years). This same amount would be recognized in 2006 and 2007.

c. There is no cash flow for depreciation in 2006 or any other year. The total cash outflow from purchasing the computer equipment ($15,000) would be reported as a cash outflow from investing activities in the year in which the equipment was purchased.

d. The December 31, 2005, balance sheet will report $6,000 of unearned revenue, which is the amount of the cash advance less the amount of revenue recognized in 2005 ($36,000 − $30,000). The December 31, 2006, balance is zero.

e. Since revenue and expense accounts are closed at the end of each accounting period, the beginning balances in these accounts are always zero.

f. Assets on the December 31, 2005, balance sheet consist of Gifford's cash at year end and the book value (cost − accumulated depreciation) of the computer equipment. Specifically, the amount of total assets is $32,300 ($21,300 + [$15,000 − $4,000]).

g. Since all unearned revenue would be recognized before the financial statements were prepared at the end of 2006, there would be no liabilities on the 2006 balance sheet. Common Stock and Retained Earnings would be the only claims as of December 31, 2006, for a claims total of $40,300 ($20,000 + $20,300).

KEY TERMS

Accumulated depreciation *112*
Allocation *109*
Book value *112*
Capitalized *127*
Concept of materiality *116*
Contra asset account *112*

Debt to assets ratio *124*
Deferral *109*
Depreciation expense *112*
Financial leverage *126*
Gains *121*
Losses *120*

Matching concept *114*
Operating income *121*
Peripheral (incidental) transactions *120*
Return on assets ratio *124*
Return on equity ratio *126*

Straight-line method *112*
Systematic allocation of cost *114*
Unearned revenue *110*

QUESTIONS

1. What role do assets play in business profitability?
2. What does the term *deferral* mean?
3. If cash is collected in advance of performing services, when is the associated revenue recognized?
4. What does the term *salvage value* mean?
5. What is the effect on the claims side of the accounting equation when cash is collected in advance of performing services?
6. What does the term *unearned revenue* mean?
7. How is straight-line depreciation computed?
8. Define the term *depreciation expense*. On what type of asset is depreciation recognized?
9. Define the term *contra asset account*. What is an example?
10. How is the book value of an asset determined?
11. If a piece of equipment originally cost $12,000, has an estimated salvage value of $1,000, and has accumulated depreciation of $10,000, what is the book value of the equipment?
12. What does the term *financial leverage* mean?
13. In which section of the statement of cash flows is cash paid for office equipment reported?
14. What is the difference between a cost and an expense?
15. When does a cost become an expense? Do all costs become expenses?
16. How and when is the cost of the *supplies used* recognized in an accounting period?
17. Give an example of an asset whose cost is systematically allocated over several accounting periods.
18. List the three ways in which expenses are matched with the revenues they produce.
19. Define *losses*. How do losses differ from expenses?
20. Define *gains*. How do gains differ from revenues?
21. How is income from operations computed?
22. What does the term *peripheral activity* mean?
23. Assume that Company A has revenues of $45,000, operating expenses of $36,000, and a gain from the sale of land of $12,500. What is the amount of income from operations? What is the amount of net income?
24. Explain the *concept of materiality*.
25. What are several factors that prevent the establishment of a global GAAP?
26. How is the return on assets ratio computed? How is this measure useful in comparing two companies?
27. How is the debt to assets ratio computed? What does this ratio measure?
28. How can financial leverage increase the return on equity ratio?

EXERCISES—SERIES A

 All Exercises in Series A are available with McGraw-Hill's Homework Manager

L.O. 1   **EXERCISE 3–1A** *Transactions That Affect the Elements of Financial Statements*

Required
Give an example of a transaction that will do the following:
a. Increase an asset and increase equity (asset source event).
b. Decrease an asset and decrease equity (asset use event).
c. Increase an asset and decrease another asset (asset exchange event).
d. Decrease a liability and increase equity (claims exchange event).
e. Increase a liability and decrease equity (claims exchange event).
f. Increase an asset and increase a liability (asset source event).
g. Decrease an asset and decrease a liability (asset use event).

L.O. 2   **EXERCISE 3–2A** *Identifying Deferral and Accrual Events*

Required
Identify each of the following events as an accrual, a deferral, or neither.
a. Paid cash in advance for a one-year insurance policy.
b. Recognized interest income from a certificate of deposit before the cash was received.
c. Collected accounts receivable.

d. Paid cash for current salaries expense.
e. Purchased supplies to be used in the future on account.
f. Provided services on account.
g. Provided services and collected cash.
h. Purchased a delivery van that has a four-year useful life.
i. Recognized accrued salaries at the end of the accounting period.
j. Paid a cash dividend to the stockholders.

EXERCISE 3–3A *Effect of Deferrals on the Accounting Equation* **L.O. 6**

Required

For each of the following independent cases, show the effect on the accounting equation of both the deferral and the related December 31, 2003, adjustment.

a. Ameriship paid $36,000 for a 12-month lease on warehouse space on September 1, 2003.
b. Global Services purchased a new computer system for $26,000 on January 1, 2003. The computer system has an estimated useful life of three years and a $2,000 salvage value.
c. Anthony Park, attorney, accepted $18,000 in advance from his client on September 1, 2003, for services to be performed over the next six months.

EXERCISE 3–4A *Identifying Transaction Type and Effect on the Financial Statements* **L.O. 2, 10**

Required

Identify whether each of the following transactions is an asset source (AS), asset use (AU), asset exchange (AE), or claims exchange (CE). Also show the effects of the events on the financial statements using the horizontal statements model. Indicate whether the event increases (I), decreases (D), or does not affect (NA) each element of the financial statements. In the Cash Flows column, designate the cash flows as operating activities (OA), investing activities (IA), or financing activities (FA). The first two transactions have been recorded as examples.

					Stockholders' Equity						
Event No.	Type of Event	Assets	= Liabilities	+	Common Stock	+	Retained Earnings	Rev.	– Exp.	= Net Inc.	Cash Flows
a	AS	I	NA		NA		I	I	NA	I	I OA
b	AS	I	I		NA		NA	NA	NA	NA	NA

a. Provided services and collected cash.
b. Purchased supplies on account to be used in the future.
c. Paid cash in advance for one year's rent.
d. Purchased office equipment for cash.
e. Paid a cash dividend to the stockholders.
f. Received cash from the issue of common stock.
g. Paid cash on accounts payable.
h. Collected cash from accounts receivable.
i. Received cash advance for services to be provided in the future.
j. Incurred other operating expenses on account.
k. Performed services on account.
l. Adjusted books to reflect the amount of prepaid rent expired during the period.
m. Paid cash for operating expenses.
n. Recorded depreciation expense on office equipment.
o. Recorded accrued salaries.
p. Paid cash for salaries accrued at the end of a prior period.
q. Purchased a building with cash *and* issued a note payable.

EXERCISE 3–5A *Effect of Prepaid Rent on the Accounting Equation and Financial Statements* **L.O. 3, 4, 5, 7**

The following events apply to 2005, the first year of operations of ITS Consulting Services:
1. Acquired $20,000 cash from the issue of common stock.
2. Paid $12,000 cash in advance for one-year rental contract for office space.
3. Provided services for $25,000 cash.
4. Adjusted the records to recognize the use of the office space. The one-year contract started on March 1, 2005. The adjustment was made as of December 31, 2005.

Required

a. Write an accounting equation and record the effects of each accounting event under the appropriate general ledger account headings.

b. Prepare an income statement and statement of cash flows for the 2005 accounting period.

c. Explain the difference between the amount of net income and amount of net cash flow from operating activities.

L.O. 5, 6, 7, 10   **EXERCISE 3–6A** *Effect of Supplies on the Financial Statements*

The Copy Center, Inc., started the 2005 accounting period with $8,000 cash, $6,000 of common stock, and $2,000 of retained earnings. The Copy Center was affected by the following accounting events during 2005:

1. Purchased $11,500 of paper and other supplies on account.
2. Earned and collected $27,000 of cash revenue.
3. Paid $10,000 cash on accounts payable.
4. Adjusted the records to reflect the use of supplies. A physical count indicated that $2,500 of supplies was still on hand on December 31, 2005.

Required

a. Show the effects of the events on the financial statements using a horizontal statements model like the following one. In the Cash Flows column, use OA to designate operating activity, IA for investing activity, FA for financing activity, and NC for net change in cash. Use NA to indicate accounts not affected by the event. The beginning balances are entered in the following example.

Event No.	Assets		=	Liab.	+	Stockholders' Equity			Rev.	–	Exp.	=	Net Inc.	Cash Flows
	Cash	+ Supplies	=	Accts. Pay	+	C. Stock	+	Ret. Earn.						
Beg. Bal.	8,000 +	0	=	0	+	6,000	+	2,000	0	–	0	=	0	0

b. Explain the difference between the amount of net income and amount of net cash flow from operating activities.

L.O. 3, 5, 6, 7   **EXERCISE 3–7A** *Effect of Depreciation on the Accounting Equation and Financial Statements*

The following events apply to The Pizza Factory for the 2008 fiscal year:

1. Started the company when it acquired $18,000 cash from the issue of common stock.
2. Purchased a new pizza oven that cost $15,000 cash.
3. Earned $26,000 in cash revenue.
4. Paid $13,000 cash for salaries expense.
5. Paid $6,000 cash for operating expenses.
6. Adjusted the records to reflect the use of the pizza oven. The oven, purchased on January 1, 2008, has an expected useful life of five years and an estimated salvage value of $3,000. Use straight-line depreciation. The adjusting entry was made as of December 31, 2008.

Required

a. Write an accounting equation and record the effects of each accounting event under the appropriate general ledger account headings.

b. What amount of depreciation expense would The Pizza Factory report on the 2009 income statement?

c. What amount of accumulated depreciation would The Pizza Factory report on the December 31, 2009, balance sheet?

d. Would the cash flow from operating activities be affected by depreciation in 2009?

L.O. 5, 6, 10   **EXERCISE 3–8A** *Effect of Unearned Revenue on Financial Statements*

Meg Sanderfert started a personal financial planning business when she accepted $60,000 cash as advance payment for managing the financial assets of a large estate. Sanderfert agreed to manage the estate for a one-year period, beginning April 1, 2003.

Required

a. Show the effects of the advance payment and revenue recognition on the 2003 financial statements using a horizontal statements model like the following one. In the Cash Flows column, use OA to designate operating activity, IA for investing activity, FA for financing activity, and NC for net change in cash. Use NA if the account is not affected.

Event No.	Assets	=	Liab.	+	Stockholders' Equity	Rev.	−	Exp.	=	Net Inc.	Cash Flows
	Cash	=	Unearn. Rev.	+	Ret. Earn.						

b. How much revenue would Meg recognize on the 2004 income statement?

c. What is the amount of cash flow from operating activities in 2004?

EXERCISE 3–9A *Effect of Gains and Losses on the Accounting Equation and Financial Statements*   **L.O. 8**

On January 1, 2003, Gert Enterprises purchased a parcel of land for $12,000 cash. At the time of purchase, the company planned to use the land for future expansion. In 2004, Gert Enterprises changed its plans and sold the land.

Required

a. Assume that the land was sold for $11,200 in 2004.

  (1) Show the effect of the sale on the accounting equation.

  (2) What amount would Gert report on the income statement related to the sale of the land?

  (3) What amount would Gert report on the statement of cash flows related to the sale of the land?

b. Assume that the land was sold for $13,500 in 2004.

  (1) Show the effect of the sale on the accounting equation.

  (2) What amount would Gert report on the income statement related to the sale of the land?

  (3) What amount would Gert report on the statement of cash flows related to the sale of the land?

EXERCISE 3–10A *Effect of Accounting Events on the Income Statement and Statement of Cash Flows*   **L.O. 5, 6**

Required

Explain how each of the following events and the related adjusting entry will affect the amount of *net income* and the amount of *cash flow from operating activities* reported on the year-end financial statements. Identify the direction of change (increase, decrease, or NA) and the amount of the change. Organize your answers according to the following table. The first event is recorded as an example. If an event does not have a related adjusting entry, record only the effects of the event.

	Net Income		Cash Flows from Operating Activities	
Event No.	Direction of Change	Amount of Change	Direction of Change	Amount of Change
a	NA	NA	NA	NA

a. Acquired $50,000 cash from the issue of common stock.

b. Earned $12,000 of revenue on account. Collected $10,000 cash from accounts receivable.

c. Paid $2,400 cash on October 1 to purchase a one-year insurance policy.

d. Collected $9,600 in advance for services to be performed in the future. The contract called for services to start on August 1 and to continue for one year.

e. Accrued salaries amounting to $4,000.

f. Sold land that cost $15,000 for $17,500 cash.

g. Paid $22,000 cash to purchase equipment. The equipment, purchased on January 1, had an estimated salvage value of $2,000 and an expected useful life of four years.

h. Provided services for $7,500 cash.

i. Purchased $1,200 of supplies on account. Paid $1,000 cash on accounts payable. The ending balance in the Supplies account, after adjustment, was $300.

j. Paid cash for other operating expenses of $1,500.

EXERCISE 3–11A *Effect of Accruals and Deferrals on Financial Statements: the Horizontal Statements Model*   **L.O. 10**

D. Downs, Attorney at Law, experienced the following transactions in 2003, the first year of operations:

1. Purchased $1,200 of office supplies on account.

2. Accepted $18,000 on February 1, 2004, as a retainer for services to be performed evenly over the next 12 months.
3. Performed legal services for cash of $66,000.
4. Paid cash for salaries expense of $20,500.
5. Paid a cash dividend to the stockholders of $5,000.
6. Paid $900 of the amount due on accounts payable.
7. Determined that at the end of the accounting period, $125 of office supplies remained on hand.
8. On December 31, 2003, recognized the revenue that had been earned for services performed in accordance with Transaction 2.

Required

Show the effects of the events on the financial statements using a horizontal statements model like the following one. In the Cash Flow column, use the initials OA to designate operating activity, IA for investing activity, FA for financing activity, and NC for net change in cash. Use NA to indicate accounts not affected by the event. The first event has been recorded as an example.

Event No.	Assets		=	Liabilities			+	Stk. Equity	Rev.	–	Exp.	=	Net Inc.	Cash Flow
	Cash	+ Supp.	=	Accts. Pay.	+	Unearn. Rev.	+	Ret. Earn.						
1	NA	+ 1,200	=	1,200	+	NA	+	NA	NA	–	NA	=	NA	NA

L.O. 7   EXERCISE 3–12A *Distinguishing Between an Expense and a Cost*

Clair Seaton tells you that the accountants where she works are real hair splitters. For example, they make a big issue over the difference between a cost and an expense. She says the two terms mean the same thing to her.

Required

a. Explain to Clair the difference between a cost and an expense from an accountant's perspective.
b. Explain whether each of the following events produces an asset or an expense.
   (1) Purchased a building for cash.
   (2) Purchased equipment on account.
   (3) Used supplies on hand to produce revenue.
   (4) Paid in advance for insurance on the building.
   (5) Recognized accrued salaries.

L.O. 7   EXERCISE 3–13A *Matching Concept*

Required

Place a check mark in the appropriate cell of the following table to indicate whether each of the following costs would be expensed through (1) direct matching, (2) period matching, or (3) systematic allocation.

Cost	Matched Directly with Revenue	Matched with the Period Incurred	Systematically Allocated
Expired insurance			
Delivery van			
Land that has been sold			
Office supplies expense			
Sales commissions			
Building			
Supplies used			

L.O. 5, 6   EXERCISE 3–14A *Effect of an Error on Financial Statements*

On May 1, 2007, Dobler Corporation paid $9,600 to purchase a 24-month insurance policy. Assume that Dobler records the purchase as an asset and that the books are closed on December 31.

Required

a. Show the purchase of the insurance policy and the related adjusting entry to insurance expense in the accounting equation.
b. Assume that Dobler Corporation failed to record the adjusting entry to reflect the expiration of insurance. How would the error affect the company's 2007 income statement and balance sheet?

EXERCISE 3–15A *Revenue and Expense Recognition*

L.O. 1

Required
a. Describe an expense recognition event that results in an increase in liabilities.
b. Describe an expense recognition event that results in a decrease in assets.
c. Describe a revenue recognition event that results in a decrease in liabilities.
d. Describe a revenue recognition event that results in an increase in assets.

EXERCISE 3–16A *Unearned Revenue Defined as a Liability*

L.O. 1, 5

Steve Chang received $500 in advance for tutoring fees when he agreed to help Jon Seng with his introductory accounting course. Upon receiving the cash, Steve mentioned that he would have to record the transaction as a liability on his books. Seng asked, "Why a liability? You don't owe me any money, do you?"

Required
Respond to Seng's question regarding Chang's liability.

PROBLEMS—SERIES A

All Problems in Series A are available with McGraw-Hill's Homework Manager

PROBLEM 3–17A *Recording Events in a Horizontal Statements Model*

L.O. 10

The following events pertain to The Plains Company:

CHECK FIGURES
Net Income: $10,000
Ending Cash Balance: $19,100

1. Acquired $12,000 cash from the issue of common stock.
2. Provided services for $4,000 cash.
3. Provided $12,000 of services on account.
4. Collected $9,000 cash from the account receivable created in Event 3.
5. Paid $900 cash to purchase supplies.
6. Had $100 of supplies on hand at the end of the accounting period.
7. Received $1,800 cash in advance for services to be performed in the future.
8. Performed one-half of the services agreed to in Event 7.
9. Paid $4,600 for salaries expense.
10. Incurred $1,500 of other operating expenses on account.
11. Paid $1,200 cash on the account payable created in Event 10.
12. Paid a $1,000 cash dividend to the stockholders.

Required
Show the effects of the events on the financial statements using a horizontal statements model like the following one. In the Cash Flows column, use the letters OA to designate operating activity, IA for investing activity, FA for financing activity, and NC for net change in cash. Use NA to indicate accounts not affected by the event. The first event is recorded as an example.

Event No.	Assets			=	Liabilities		+	Stockholders' Equity			Rev.	–	Exp.	=	Net Inc.		Cash Flows
	Cash	+ Accts. Rec.	+ Supp.	= Accts. Pay.	+	Unearn. Rev.	+	Com. Stk.	+	Ret. Earn.							
1	12,000	+ NA	+ NA	= NA	+	NA	+	12,000	+	NA	NA	–	NA	=	NA		12,000 FA

PROBLEM 3–18A *Effect of Deferrals on Financial Statements: Three Separate Single-Cycle Examples*

L.O. 3, 4, 5, 6, 10

www.mhhe.com/edmonds5e

Required
a. On February 1, 2005, Business Help, Inc. was formed when it received $60,000 cash from the issue of common stock. On May 1, 2005, the company paid $36,000 cash in advance to rent office space for the coming year. The office space was used as a place to consult with clients. The consulting activity generated $80,000 of cash revenue during 2005. Based on this information alone, record the events and related adjusting entry in the general ledger accounts under the accounting equation. Determine the amount of net income and cash flows from operating activities for 2005.

CHECK FIGURES
a. Net Income: $56,000
b. Net Income: $10,000

b. On January 1, 2003, the accounting firm of Woo & Associates was formed. On August 1, 2003, the company received a retainer fee (was paid in advance) of $24,000 for services to be performed monthly during the coming year. Assuming that this was the only transaction completed in 2003, prepare an income statement, statement of changes in stockholders' equity, balance sheet, and statement of cash flows for 2003.

c. Mae's Flowers was started when it received $40,000 cash from the issue of common stock on January 1, 2003. The cash received by the company was immediately used to purchase a $25,000 asset that had a $5,000 salvage value and an expected useful life of five years. The company earned $11,000 of cash revenue during 2003. Show the effects of these transactions on the financial statements using the horizontal statements model.

L.O. 3, 6   **PROBLEM 3–19A** *Effect of Adjusting Entries on the Accounting Equation*

CHECK FIGURE
b. adjustment amount: $2,250

Required

Each of the following independent events requires a year-end adjusting entry. Show how each event and its related adjusting entry affect the accounting equation. Assume a December 31 closing date. The first event is recorded as an example.

| Event/Adjustment | Total Assets | | | | Stockholders' Equity | |
	Cash	+ Other Assets	= Liabilities	+	Common Stock	+ Retained Earnings
a	−20,000	+20,000	NA		NA	NA
Adj.	NA	+200	NA		NA	+200

a. Invested $20,000 cash in a certificate of deposit that paid 3 percent annual interest. The certificate was acquired on September 1 and had a one-year term to maturity.

b. Paid $3,000 cash in advance on April 1 for a one-year insurance policy.

c. Purchased $1,600 of supplies on account. At year's end, $100 of supplies remained on hand.

d. Paid $6,000 cash in advance on March 1 for a one-year lease on office space.

e. Borrowed $12,000 by issuing a one-year note with 8 percent annual interest to National Bank on May 1.

f. Paid $28,000 cash to purchase a delivery van on January 1. The van was expected to have a three-year life and a $4,000 salvage value. Depreciation is computed on a straight-line basis.

g. Received a $15,000 cash advance for a contract to provide services in the future. The contract required a one-year commitment starting September 1.

L.O. 1, 3, 4   **PROBLEM 3–20A** *Events for Two Complete Accounting Cycles*

www.mhhe.com/edmonds5e

CHECK FIGURES
a Net Income, 2004: $16,400
b. Net Income, 2005: $16,200

Texas Drilling Company was formed on January 1, 2004.

Events Affecting the 2004 Accounting Period
1. Acquired cash of $50,000 from the issue of common stock.
2. Purchased office equipment that cost $27,000 cash.
3. Purchased land that cost $12,000 cash.
4. Paid $800 cash for supplies.
5. Recognized revenue on account of $38,000.
6. Paid $15,000 cash for other operating expenses.
7. Collected $22,000 cash from accounts receivable.

Information for Adjusting Entries
8. Incurred accrued salaries of $1,200 on December 31, 2004.
9. Had $200 of supplies on hand at the end of the accounting period.
10. Used the straight-line method to depreciate the equipment acquired in Event 2. Purchased on January 1, it had an expected useful life of five years and a $3,000 salvage value,

Events Affecting the 2005 Accounting Period
1. Acquired an additional $10,000 cash from the issue of common stock.
2. Paid $1,200 cash to settle the salaries payable obligation.
3. Paid $3,600 cash in advance for a lease on office facilities.
4. Sold the land that cost $12,000 for $11,500 cash.
5. Received $5,400 cash in advance for services to be performed in the future.

6. Purchased $1,000 of supplies on account during the year.
7. Provided services on account of $26,000.
8. Collected $28,000 cash from accounts receivable.
9. Paid a cash dividend of $5,000 to the stockholders.

Information for Adjusting Entries

10. The advance payment for rental of the office facilities (see Event 3) was made on March 1 for a one-year lease term.
11. The cash advance for services to be provided in the future was collected on October 1 (see Event 5). The one-year contract started October 1.
12. Had $150 of supplies on hand at the end of the period.
13. Recorded depreciation on the office equipment for 2005.
14. Incurred accrued salaries of $1,800 at the end of the accounting period.

Required

a. Identify each event affecting the 2004 and 2005 accounting periods as asset source (AS), asset use (AU), asset exchange (AE), or claims exchange (CE). Record the effects of each event under the appropriate general ledger account headings of the accounting equation.
b. Prepare an income statement, statement of changes in stockholders' equity, balance sheet, and statement of cash flows for 2004 and 2005, using the vertical statement model.

PROBLEM 3–21A *Effect of Events on Financial Statements*

L.O. 3, 5

Rios Company had the following balances in its accounting records as of December 31, 2002:

CHECK FIGURES
b. $1,000
h. $(49,000)

Assets		Claims	
Cash	$ 50,000	Accounts Payable	$ 25,000
Accounts Receivable	45,000	Common Stock	80,000
Land	25,000	Retained Earnings	15,000
Totals	$120,000		$120,000

The following accounting events apply to Rios's 2003 fiscal year:

Jan.	1	Acquired an additional $40,000 cash from the issue of common stock.
	1	Purchased a delivery van that cost $26,000 and that had an $8,000 salvage value and a three-year useful life.
Mar.	1	Borrowed $15,000 by issuing a note that had an 8 percent annual interest rate and a one-year term.
April	1	Paid $5,400 cash in advance for a one-year lease for office space.
June	1	Paid a $2,000 cash dividend to the stockholders.
July	1	Purchased land that cost $25,000 cash.
Aug.	1	Made a cash payment on accounts payable of $10,000.
Sept.	1	Received $7,200 cash in advance as a retainer for services to be performed monthly during the next eight months.
Sept.	30	Sold land for $22,000 cash that had originally cost $17,000.
Oct.	1	Purchased $900 of supplies on account.
Nov.	1	Purchased a one-year $20,000 certificate of deposit that paid a 3 percent annual rate of interest.
Dec.	31	Earned $60,000 of service revenue on account during the year.
	31	Received $56,000 cash collections from accounts receivable.
	31	Incurred $12,000 other operating expenses on account during the year.
	31	Incurred accrued salaries expense of $5,000.
	31	Had $150 of supplies on hand at the end of the period.

Required

Based on the preceding information, answer the following questions. All questions pertain to the 2003 financial statements. (*Hint:* Record the events in general ledger accounts under an accounting equation before answering the questions.)

a. What five transactions during the year need adjusting entries at the end of the year?
b. What amount of interest expense would Rios report on the income statement?
c. What amount of net cash flow from operating activities would Rios report on the statement of cash flows?

d. What amount of rent expense would Rios report in the income statement?

e. What amount of total liabilities would Rios report on the balance sheet?

f. What amount of supplies expense would Rios report on the income statement?

g. What amount of unearned revenue would Rios report on the balance sheet?

h. What amount of net cash flow from investing activities would Rios report on the statement of cash flows?

i. What amount of interest payable would Rios report on the balance sheet?

j. What amount of total expenses would Rios report on the income statement?

k. What amount of retained earnings would Rios report on the balance sheet?

l. What total amount of service revenues would Rios report on the income statement?

m. What amount of cash flows from financing activities would Rios report on the statement of cash flows?

n. What is the amount of the gain on sale of land Rios would report on the income statement?

o. What amount of net income would Rios report on the income statement?

L.O. 4 **PROBLEM 3–22A** *Identifying and Arranging Elements on Financial Statements*

www.mhhe.com/edmonds5e

The following accounts and balances were drawn from the records of Warren Company at December 31, 2005:

CHECK FIGURES
Net Income: $34,150
Total Assets: $70,650

Cash	$11,400	Cash Flow from Operating Act.	$ 7,500
Land	20,000	Beginning Retained Earnings	7,500
Insurance Expense	1,100	Beginning Common Stock	1,000
Dividends	5,000	Service Revenue	80,000
Prepaid Insurance	2,500	Cash Flow from Financing Act.	5,500
Notes Payable	29,000	Ending Common Stock	5,000
Supplies	750	Accumulated Depreciation	5,000
Supplies Expense	250	Cash Flow from Investing Act.	(7,000)
Depreciation Expense	2,500	Operating Expenses	42,000
Accounts Receivable	19,000	Office Equipment	22,000

Required

Use the accounts and balances from Warren Company to construct an income statement, statement of changes in stockholders' equity, balance sheet, and statement of cash flows (show only totals for each activity on the statement of cash flows).

L.O. 4 **PROBLEM 3–23A** *Relationship of Accounts to Financial Statements*

Required

Identify whether each of the following items would appear on the income statement (IS), statement of changes in stockholders' equity (SE), balance sheet (BS), or statement of cash flows (CF). Some items may appear on more than one statement; if so, identify all applicable statements. If an item would not appear on any financial statement, label it NA.

a. Interest Receivable

b. Salary Expense

c. Notes Receivable

d. Unearned Revenue

e. Cash Flow from Investing Activities

f. Insurance Expense

g. Ending Retained Earnings

h. Accumulated Depreciation

i. Supplies

j. Beginning Retained Earnings

k. Certificate of Deposit

l. Cash Flow from Financing Activities

m. Accounts Receivable

n. Prepaid Insurance

o. Cash

p. Interest Expense

q. Accounts Payable

r. Beginning Common Stock

s. Dividends

t. Total Assets

u. Consulting Revenue

v. Depreciation Expense

w. Supplies Expense

x. Salaries Payable

y. Notes Payable

z. Ending Common Stock

aa. Interest Payable

bb. Office Equipment

cc. Interest Revenue

dd. Land

ee. Operating Expenses

ff. Total Liabilities

gg. Debt to Equity Ratio

hh. Salaries Expense

ii. Net Income

jj. Service Revenue

kk. Cash Flow from Operating Activities

ll. Return on Assets Ratio

PROBLEM 3–24A *Missing Information in Financial Statements*

L.O. 3, 4

CHECK FIGURES
Net Income: $11,050
Net Cash Flow from Operating
Activities: $36,500

The following data are relevant to the revenue and expense accounts of Tilley Corporation during 2004. The Accounts Receivable balance was $12,000 on January 1, 2004. Consulting services provided to customers on account during the year were $80,000. The receivables balance on December 31, 2004, amounted to $10,500. Tilley received $27,000 in advance payment for training services to be performed over a 24-month period beginning March 1, 2004. Furthermore, Tilley purchased a $40,000 certificate of deposit on September 1, 2004. The certificate paid 6 percent interest, which was payable in cash on August 31 of each year. During 2004, Tilley recorded depreciation expense of $7,000. Salaries paid to employees during 2004 were $32,000. The Salaries Payable account increased by $2,000 during the year. Other operating expenses paid in cash during 2004 amounted to $40,000. No other revenue or expense transactions occurred during 2004. (*Hint:* Compute the amounts that will affect the income statement and statement of cash flows before answering questions.)

Required
a. Prepare an income statement, assuming that Tilley uses the accrual basis of accounting.
b. Determine the net cash flows from operating activities for 2004.

PROBLEM 3–25A *Using Accounting Information*

L.O. 1, 9

Rene Hugh is trying to decide whether to start a small business or put her capital into a savings account. To help her make a decision, two of her friends shared their investing experiences with her. Tom Eubanks had started a small business three years ago. As of the end of the most recent year of operations, Eubanks's business had total assets of $225,000 and net income of $27,000. The second friend, Elaine Parker, had deposited $40,000 in a bank savings account that paid $2,000 in interest during the last year.

Required
a. Assume you are an investment counselor. Show Hugh how the return on assets ratio shows whether Eubanks's or Parker's investment is producing a higher return.
b. Using your personal judgment, identify any other factors that Hugh should consider before she decides whether to start her own business or deposit her money in a savings account. Recommend to Hugh which alternative you think she should accept.

EXERCISE 3–1B *Transactions That Affect the Elements of Financial Statements*

L.O. 1

Required
Give an example of a transaction that will

a. Increase an asset and decrease another asset (asset exchange event).
b. Increase an asset and increase a liability (asset source event).
c. Decrease an asset and decrease a liability (asset use event).
d. Decrease an asset and decrease equity (asset use event).
e. Increase a liability and decrease equity (claims exchange event).
f. Increase an asset and increase equity (asset source event).
g. Decrease a liability and increase equity (claims exchange event).

EXERCISE 3–2B *Identifying Deferral and Accrual Events*

L.O. 2

Required
Identify each of the following events as an accrual, deferral, or neither.

a. Incurred other operating expenses on account.
b. Recorded expense for salaries owed to employees at the end of the accounting period.
c. Paid a cash dividend to the stockholders.
d. Paid cash to purchase supplies to be used over the next several months.
e. Purchased a delivery van with a five-year life.
f. Provided services on account.
g. Recognized interest income on a certificate of deposit before receiving the cash.
h. Paid one year's rent in advance.
i. Paid cash for utilities expense.
j. Collected $2,400 in advance for services to be performed over the next 12 months.

L.O. 6   **EXERCISE 3–3B** *Effect of Deferrals on the Accounting Equation*

Required

For each of the following independent cases, show the effects on the accounting equation of both the deferral and the related December 31, 2001, adjustment.

a. Rob Berry, owner of Berry Business Services, purchased a new computer system for $12,400 on January 1, 2001. The computer system has an estimated useful life of four years and a $1,400 salvage value.

b. King Supply paid $15,000 for a 12-month lease on warehouse space on October 1, 2001.

c. Alan Ritchie, J.D., accepted a $50,000 advance from a client on November 1, 2001. The services are to be performed over the next eight months.

L.O. 2, 10   **EXERCISE 3–4B** *Identifying Transaction Type and Effect on the Financial Statements*

Required

Identify whether each of the following transactions is an asset source (AS), asset use (AU), asset exchange (AE), or claims exchange (CE). Also show the effects of the events on the financial statements using the horizontal statements model. Indicate whether the event increases (I), decreases (D), or does not affect (NA) each element of the financial statements. In the Cash Flows column, designate the cash flows as operating activities (OA), investing activities (IA), or financing activities (FA). The first two transactions have been recorded as examples.

Event No.	Type of Event	Assets	=	Liabilities	+	Common Stock	+	Retained Earnings	Rev.	–	Exp.	=	Net Inc.	Cash Flows	
a	AE	I D		NA		NA		NA	NA		NA		NA	D	IA
b	AS	I		NA		I		NA	NA		NA		NA	I	FA

a. Purchased land for cash.
b. Acquired cash from the issue of common stock.
c. Collected cash from accounts receivable.
d. Paid cash for operating expenses.
e. Recorded accrued salaries.
f. Paid cash to purchase office equipment.
g. Performed services on account.
h. Paid cash advance for rent on office space.
i. Recorded depreciation expense on office equipment.
j. Performed services for cash.
k. Purchased a building with cash *and* issued a note payable.
l. Paid cash for salaries accrued at the end of a prior period.
m. Paid a cash dividend to the stockholders.
n. Adjusted books to reflect the amount of prepaid rent expired during the period.
o. Incurred operating expenses on account.
p. Paid cash on accounts payable.
q. Received cash advance for services to be provided in the future.

L.O. 3, 4, 5, 7   **EXERCISE 3–5B** *Effect of Prepaid Rent on the Accounting Equation and Financial Statements*

The following events apply to 2007, the first year of operations of Shay Services:

1. Acquired $25,000 cash from the issue of common stock.
2. Paid $18,000 cash in advance for one-year rental contract for office space.
3. Provided services for $28,000 cash.
4. Adjusted the records to recognize the use of the office space. The one-year contract started on April 1, 2007. The adjustment was made as of December 31, 2007.

Required

a. Write an accounting equation and record the effects of each accounting event under the appropriate general ledger account headings.
b. Prepare a balance sheet at the end of the 2007 accounting period.
c. What amount of rent expense will Shay report on the 2007 income statement?
d. What amount of net cash flow from operating activities will Shay report on the 2007 statement of cash flows?

EXERCISE 3–6B *Effect of Supplies on the Financial Statements*   **L.O. 5, 6, 7, 10**

Package Express started the 2003 accounting period with $2,000 cash, $1,200 of common stock, and $800 of retained earnings. Package was affected by the following accounting events during 2003:

1. Purchased $2,400 of copier toner and other supplies on account.
2. Earned and collected $10,800 of cash revenue.
3. Paid $1,800 cash on accounts payable.
4. Adjusted the records to reflect the use of supplies. A physical count indicated that $200 of supplies was still on hand on December 31, 2003.

Required

a. Show the effects of the events on the financial statements using a horizontal statements model like the following one. In the Cash Flows column, use OA to designate operating activity, IA for investing activity, FA for financing activity, and NC for net change in cash. Use NA to indicate accounts not affected by the event. The beginning balances are entered in the following example.

| Event No. | Assets | | = | Liab. | + | Stockholders' Equity | | | Rev. | – | Exp. | = | Net Inc. | Cash Flows |
	Cash	+ Supplies	=	Accts. Pay	+	C. Stock	+	Ret. Earn.						
Beg. Bal.	2,000	+ 0	=	0	+	1,200	+	800	0	–	0	=	0	0

b. Explain the difference between the amount of net income and amount of net cash flow from operating activities.

EXERCISE 3–7B *Effect of Depreciation on the Accounting Equation and Financial Statements*   **L.O. 3, 4, 5, 6, 7**

The following events apply to Jim's Deli for the 2006 fiscal year:

1. Started the company when it acquired $30,000 cash by issuing common stock.
2. Purchased a new stove that cost $22,000 cash.
3. Earned $21,000 in cash revenue.
4. Paid $4,000 of cash for salaries expense.
5. Adjusted the records to reflect the use of the stove. Purchased on January 1, 2006, the stove has an expected useful life of four years and an estimated salvage value of $1,000. Use straight-line depreciation. The adjusting entry was made as of December 31, 2006.

Required

a. Write an accounting equation and record the effects of each accounting event under the appropriate general ledger account headings.
b. Prepare a balance sheet and a statement of cash flows for the 2006 accounting period.
c. What is the net income for 2006?
d. What is the amount of depreciation expense Jim's would report on the 2007 income statement?
e. What amount of accumulated depreciation would Jim's report on the December 31, 2007, balance sheet?
f. Would the cash flow from operating activities be affected by depreciation in 2007?

EXERCISE 3–8B *Effect of Unearned Revenue on Financial Statements*   **L.O. 5, 6, 10**

Donald Jones started a personal financial planning business when he accepted $30,000 cash as advance payment for managing the financial assets of a large estate. Donald agreed to manage the estate for a 12-month period, beginning April 1, 2003.

Required

a. Show the effects of the advance payment and revenue recognition on the 2003 financial statements using a horizontal statements model like the following one. In the Cash Flows column, use OA to designate operating activity, IA for investing activity, FA for financing activity, and NC for net change in cash. Use NA if the account is not affected.

| Event No. | Assets | = | Liab. | + | Stockholders' Equity | Rev. | – | Exp. | = | Net Inc. | Cash Flows |
	Cash	=	Unearn. Rev.	+	Ret. Earn.						

b. How much revenue would Jones recognize on the 2004 income statement?
c. What is the amount of cash flow from operating activities in 2004?

L.O. 8   **EXERCISE 3–9B** *Effect of Gains and Losses on the Accounting Equation and Financial Statements*

On January 1, 2002, Arizona Enterprises purchased a parcel of land for $16,000 cash. At the time of purchase, the company planned to use the land for a warehouse site. In 2004, Arizona Enterprises changed its plans and sold the land.

Required

a. Assume that the land was sold for $15,000 in 2004.
   (1) Show the effect of the sale on the accounting equation.
   (2) What amount would Arizona report on the 2004 income statement related to the sale of the land?
   (3) What amount would Arizona report on the 2004 statement of cash flows related to the sale of the land?

b. Assume that the land was sold for $18,000 in 2004.
   (1) Show the effect of the sale on the accounting equation.
   (2) What amount would Arizona report on the 2004 income statement related to the sale of the land?
   (3) What amount would Arizona report on the 2004 statement of cash flows related to the sale of the land?

L.O. 5, 6   **EXERCISE 3–10B** *Effect of Accounting Events on the Income Statement and Statement of Cash Flows*

Required

Explain how each of the following events and any related adjusting entry will affect the amount of *net income* and the amount of *cash flow from operating activities* reported on the year-end financial statements. Identify the direction of change (increase, decrease, or NA) and the amount of the change. Organize your answers according to the following table. The first event is recorded as an example. If an event does not have a related adjusting entry, record only the effects of the event.

	Net Income		Cash Flows from Operating Activities	
Event No.	Direction of Change	Amount of Change	Direction of Change	Amount of Change
a	NA	NA	Decrease	$6,000
Adj	Decrease	$1,000	NA	NA

a. Paid $6,000 cash on November 1 to purchase a one-year insurance policy.
b. Purchased $1,000 of supplies on account. Paid $700 cash on accounts payable. The ending balance in the Supplies account, after adjustment, was $100.
c. Paid $36,000 cash to purchase machinery on January 1. It had an estimated salvage value of $6,000 and an expected useful life of four years.
d. Provided services for $8,000 cash.
e. Collected $1,800 in advance for services to be performed in the future. The contract called for services to start on May 1 and to continue for one year.
f. Accrued salaries amounting to $3,200.
g. Sold land that cost $2,000 for $4,500 cash.
h. Acquired $20,000 cash from the issue of common stock.
i. Earned $8,000 of revenue on account. Collected $5,000 cash from accounts receivable.
j. Paid cash operating expenses of $3,000.

L.O. 10   **EXERCISE 3–11B** *Effect of Accruals and Deferrals on Financial Statements: Horizontal Statements Model*

Grange Attorney at Law experienced the following transactions in 2001, the first year of operations:

1. Accepted $24,000 on April 1, 2001, as a retainer for services to be performed evenly over the next 12 months.
2. Performed legal services for cash of $29,000.
3. Purchased $1,400 of office supplies on account.
4. Paid $1,000 of the amount due on accounts payable.

5. Paid a cash dividend to the stockholders of $5,000.
6. Paid cash for operating expenses of $16,200.
7. Determined that at the end of the accounting period $150 of office supplies remained on hand.
8. On December 31, 2001, recognized the revenue that had been earned for services performed in accordance with Transaction 1.

Required
Show the effects of the events on the financial statements using a horizontal statements model like the following one. In the Cash Flows column, use the initials OA to designate operating activity, IA for investing activity, FA for financing activity, and NC for net change in cash. Use NA to indicate accounts not affected by the event. The first event has been recorded as an example.

Event No.	Assets		=	Liabilities		+	Stk. Equity	Rev.	–	Exp.	=	Net Inc.	Cash Flow
	Cash	+ Supp.	= Accts. Pay.	+ Unearn. Rev.	+ Ret. Earn.								
1	24,000 +	NA	= NA	+ 24,000	+			NA	– NA	=	NA		24,000 OA

EXERCISE 3–12B *Asset Versus Expense*   L.O. 7

A cost can be either an asset or an expense.

Required
a. Distinguish between a cost that is an asset and a cost that is an expense.
b. List three costs that are assets.
c. List three costs that are expenses.

EXERCISE 3–13B *Matching Concept*   L.O. 7

Required
Place a check mark in the appropriate cell of the following table to indicate whether each of the following costs would be expensed through (1) direct matching, (2) period matching, or (3) systematic allocation.

Cost	Matched Directly with Revenue	Matched with the Period Incurred	Systematically Allocated
Delivery van			
Office manager's salary			
Office supplies			
Insurance			
Office building			
Loss on the sale of a warehouse			
Sales commissions			

EXERCISE 3–14B *Effect of an Error on Financial Statements*   L.O. 5, 6

On May 1, 2007, Southern Corporation paid $9,000 cash in advance for a one-year lease on an office building. Assume that Southern records the prepaid rent and that the books are closed on December 31.

Required
a. Show the payment for the one-year lease and the related adjusting entry to rent expense in the accounting equation.
b. Assume that Southern Corporation failed to record the adjusting entry to reflect using the office building. How would the error affect the company's 2007 income statement and balance sheet?

EXERCISE 3–15B *Revenue and Expense Recognition*   L.O. 1

Required
a. Describe a revenue recognition event that results in an increase in assets.
b. Describe a revenue recognition event that results in a decrease in liabilities.
c. Describe an expense recognition event that results in an increase in liabilities.
d. Describe an expense recognition event that results in a decrease in assets.

L.O. 1, 5   **EXERCISE 3–16B** *Unearned Revenue Defined as a Liability*

Lei, an accounting major, and Jim, a marketing major, are watching a *Matlock* rerun on late-night TV. Of course, there is a murder and the suspect wants to hire Matlock as the defense attorney. Matlock will take the case but requires an advance payment of $100,000. Jim remarks that Matlock has earned a cool $100,000 without lifting a finger. Lei tells Jim that Matlock has not earned anything but has a $100,000 liability. Jim asks "How can that be?"

Required

Assume you are Lei. Explain to Jim why Matlock has a liability and when Matlock would actually earn the $100,000.

PROBLEMS—SERIES B

L.O. 10   **PROBLEM 3–17B** *Recording Events in a Horizontal Statements Model*

The following events pertain to Union, Inc.:

1. Acquired $8,000 cash from the issue of common stock.
2. Provided $9,000 of services on account.
3. Provided services for $3,000 cash.
4. Received $2,500 cash in advance for services to be performed in the future.
5. Collected $5,600 cash from the account receivable created in Event 2.
6. Paid $1,100 for cash expenses.
7. Performed $1,400 of the services agreed to in Event 4.
8. Incurred $2,800 of expenses on account.
9. Paid $2,400 cash in advance for one-year contract to rent office space.
10. Paid $2,200 cash on the account payable created in Event 8.
11. Paid a $1,500 cash dividend to the stockholders.
12. Recognized rent expense for nine months' use of office space acquired in Event 9.

Required

Show the effects of the events on the financial statements using a horizontal statements model like the following one. In the Cash Flows column, use the letters OA to designate operating activity, IA for investing activity, FA for financing activity, and NC for net change in cash. Use NA to indicate accounts not affected by the event. The first event is recorded as an example.

Event No.	Assets			=	Liabilities	+	Stockholders' Equity		Rev. − Exp. = Net Inc.	Cash Flows
	Cash +	Accts. Rec. +	Prep. Rent	= Accts. Pay. +	Unearn. Rev.	+	Common Stock +	Ret. Earn.		
1	8,000 +	NA +	NA	= NA +	NA	+	8,000 +	NA	NA − NA = NA	8,000 FA

L.O. 3, 4, 5, 6, 10   **PROBLEM 3–18B** *Effect of Deferrals on Financial Statements: Three Separate Single-Cycle Examples*

Required

a. On February 1, 2006, Elder Company was formed when it acquired $10,000 cash from the issue of common stock. On June 1, 2006, the company paid $2,400 cash in advance to rent office space for the coming year. The office space was used as a place to consult with clients. The consulting activity generated $5,200 of cash revenue during 2006. Based on this information alone, record the events in general ledger accounts under the accounting equation. Determine the amount of net income and cash flows from operating activities for 2006.

b. On August 1, 2005, the consulting firm of Craig & Associates was formed. On September 1, 2005, the company received a $12,000 retainer (was paid in advance) for monthly services to be performed over a one-year period. Assuming that this was the only transaction completed in 2005, prepare an income statement, statement of changes in stockholders' equity, balance sheet, and statement of cash flows for 2005.

c. Bird Company was started when it acquired $10,000 cash from the issue of common stock on January 1, 2004. The company immediately used the cash received to purchase a $10,000 machine that had a $2,000 salvage value and an expected useful life of four years. The machine was used to produce $5,200 of cash revenue during the accounting period. Show the effects of these transactions on the financial statements using the horizontal statements model.

PROBLEM 3–19B *Effect of Adjusting Entries on the Accounting Equation*   **L.O. 3, 6**

Required

Each of the following independent events requires a year-end adjusting entry. Show how each event and its related adjusting entry affects the accounting equation. Assume a December 31 closing date. The first event is recorded as an example.

Event/ Adjustment	Total Assets			=	Liabilities	+	Stockholders' Equity		
	Cash	+	Other Assets	=	Liabilities	+	Common Stock	+	Retained Earnings
a	−3,600		+3,600		NA		NA		NA
Adj.	NA		−900		NA		NA		−900

a. Paid $3,600 cash in advance on October 1 for a one-year insurance policy.

b. Borrowed $20,000 by issuing a one-year note with 9 percent annual interest to National Bank on April 1.

c. Paid $19,000 cash to purchase a delivery van on January 1. The van was expected to have a four-year life and a $4,000 salvage value. Depreciation is computed on a straight-line basis.

d. Received an $1,800 cash advance for a contract to provide services in the future. The contract required a one-year commitment, starting April 1.

e. Purchased $800 of supplies on account. At year's end, $140 of supplies remained on hand.

f. Invested $8,000 cash in a certificate of deposit that paid 6 percent annual interest. The certificate was acquired on May 1 and had a one-year term to maturity.

g. Paid $7,200 cash in advance on August 1 for a one-year lease on office space.

PROBLEM 3–20B *Events for Two Complete Accounting Cycles*   **L.O. 1, 3, 4**

Southwest Plains Company was formed on January 1, 2005.

Events Affecting the 2005 Accounting Period

1. Acquired $25,000 cash from the issue of common stock.
2. Purchased communication equipment that cost $6,000 cash.
3. Purchased land that cost $12,000 cash.
4. Paid $500 cash for supplies.
5. Recognized revenue on account of $9,000.
6. Paid $2,400 cash for other operating expenses.
7. Collected $7,000 cash from accounts receivable.

Information for Adjusting Entries

8. Incurred accrued salaries of $3,200 on December 31, 2005.
9. Had $100 of supplies on hand at the end of the accounting period.
10. Used the straight-line method to depreciate the equipment acquired in Event 2. Purchased on January 1, the equipment had an expected useful life of four years and a $2,000 salvage value,

Events Affecting the 2006 Accounting Period

1. Acquired $12,000 cash from the issue of common stock.
2. Paid $3,200 cash to settle the salaries payable obligation.
3. Paid $6,000 cash in advance for a lease on computer equipment.
4. Sold the land that cost $12,000 for $18,000 cash.
5. Received $8,400 cash in advance for services to be performed in the future.
6. Purchased $2,000 of supplies on account during the year.
7. Provided services on account of $11,000.
8. Collected $9,000 cash from accounts receivable.
9. Paid a cash dividend of $2,000 to the stockholders.

Information for Adjusting Entries

10. The advance payment for rental of the computer equipment (see Event 3) was made on February 1 for a one-year term.

11. The cash advance for services to be provided in the future was collected on October 1 (see Event 5). The one-year contract started on October 1.
12. Had $200 of supplies remaining on hand at the end of the period.
13. Recorded depreciation on the computer equipment for 2006.
14. Incurred accrued salaries of $6,000 at the end of the accounting period.

Required
a. Identify each event affecting the 2005 and 2006 accounting periods as an asset source (AS), asset use (AU), asset exchange (AE), or claims exchange (CE). Record the effects of each event under the appropriate general ledger account headings of the accounting equation.
b. Prepare an income statement, statement of changes in stockholders' equity, balance sheet, and statement of cash flows for 2005 and 2006, using the vertical statements model.

L.O. 3, 5 **PROBLEM 3–21B** *Effect of Events on Financial Statements*

Caban Company had the following balances in its accounting records as of December 31, 2003:

Assets		Claims	
Cash	$23,000	Accounts Payable	$5,000
Accounts Receivable	7,000	Common Stock	24,000
Land	42,000	Retained Earnings	43,000
Total	$72,000	Total	$72,000

The following accounting events apply to Caban Company's 2004 fiscal year:

Jan.	1	Acquired $12,000 cash from the issue of common stock.
	1	Purchased a truck that cost $22,000 and had a $2,000 salvage value and a four-year useful life.
Feb.	1	Borrowed $10,000 by issuing a note that had a 9 percent annual interest rate and a one-year term.
	1	Paid $3,000 cash in advance for a one-year lease for office space.
Mar.	1	Paid a $1,000 cash dividend to the stockholders.
April	1	Purchased land that cost $28,000 cash.
May	1	Made a cash payment on accounts payable of $2,000.
July	1	Received $5,400 cash in advance as a retainer for services to be performed monthly over the coming year.
Sept.	1	Sold land for $60,000 cash that had originally cost $42,000.
Oct.	1	Purchased $3,000 of supplies on account.
Nov.	1	Purchased a one-year $50,000 certificate of deposit that paid a 6 percent annual rate of interest.
Dec.	31	Earned $35,000 of service revenue on account during the year.
	31	Received cash collections from accounts receivable amounting to $40,000.
	31	Incurred other operating expenses on account during the year that amounted to $6,000.
	31	Incurred accrued salaries expense of $4,800.
	31	Had $50 of supplies on hand at the end of the period.

Required
Based on the preceding information, answer the following questions. All questions pertain to the 2004 financial statements. (*Hint:* Enter items in general ledger accounts under the accounting equation before answering the questions.)

a. Based on the preceding transactions, identify five additional adjustments and describe them.
b. What amount of interest expense would Caban report on the income statement?
c. What amount of net cash flow from operating activities would Caban report on the statement of cash flows?
d. What amount of rent expense would Caban report in the income statement?
e. What amount of total liabilities would Caban report on the balance sheet?
f. What amount of supplies expense would Caban report on the income statement?
g. What amount of unearned revenue would Caban report on the balance sheet?
h. What amount of net cash flow from investing activities would Caban report on the statement of cash flows?
i. What amount of interest payable would Caban report on the balance sheet?

j. What amount of total expenses would Caban report on the income statement?

k. What amount of retained earnings would Caban report on the balance sheet?

l. What amount of service revenues would Caban report on the income statement?

m. What amount of cash flows from financing activities would Caban report on the statement of cash flows?

n. What is the amount of the gain on sale of land Caban would report on the income statement?

o. What amount of net income would Caban report on the income statement?

PROBLEM 3–22B *Preparing Financial Statements*   L.O. 4

The following accounts and balances were drawn from the records of Miller Company:

Required

Use the accounts and balances from Miller Company to construct an income statement, statement of changes in stockholders' equity, balance sheet, and statement of cash flows. (Show only totals for each activity on the statement of cash flows.)

Supplies	$ 300	Beginning Retained Earnings	$14,500
Cash Flow from Investing Act.	(7,800)	Cash Flow from Financing Act.	-0-
Prepaid Insurance	600	Depreciation Expense	1,500
Service Revenue	45,450	Dividends	6,000
Operating Expenses	35,000	Cash	9,000
Supplies Expense	750	Accounts Receivable	7,000
Insurance Expense	1,800	Office Equipment	16,000
Beginning Common Stock	24,000	Accumulated Depreciation	8,000
Cash Flow from Operating Act.	10,450	Land	36,000
Common Stock Issued	6,000	Accounts Payable	16,000

PROBLEM 3–23B *Relationship of Accounts to Financial Statements*   L.O. 4

Required

Identify whether each of the following items would appear on the income statement (IS), statement of changes in stockholders' equity (SE), balance sheet (BS), or statement of cash flows (CF). If some items appear on more than one statement, identify all applicable statements. If an item will not appear on any financial statement, label it NA.

a. Depreciation Expense

b. Interest Receivable

c. Certificate of Deposit

d. Unearned Revenue

e. Service Revenue

f. Cash Flow from Investing Activities

g. Consulting Revenue

h. Interest Expense

i. Ending Common Stock

j. Total Liabilities

k. Debt to Assets Ratio

l. Cash Flow from Operating Activities

m. Operating Expenses

n. Supplies Expense

o. Beginning Retained Earnings

p. Beginning Common Stock

q. Prepaid Insurance

r. Salary Expense

s. Accumulated Depreciation

t. Cash

u. Supplies

v. Cash Flow from Financing Activities

w. Interest Revenue

x. Ending Retained Earnings

y. Net Income

z. Dividends

aa. Office Equipment

bb. Debt to Equity Ratio

cc. Land

dd. Interest Payable

ee. Salaries Expense

ff. Notes Receivable

gg. Accounts Payable

hh. Total Assets

ii. Salaries Payable

jj. Insurance Expense

kk. Notes Payable

ll. Accounts Receivable

PROBLEM 3–24B *Missing Information in Financial Statements*   L.O. 3, 4

Sharp Technology started the 2002 accounting period with $6,500 cash, accounts receivable of $8,000, prepaid rent of $4,500, supplies of $150, computers that cost $35,000, accumulated depreciation on computers of $7,000, accounts payable of $10,000, and common stock of $15,000. During 2002, Sharp recognized $93,000 of revenue on account and collected $84,000 of cash from accounts receivable. It paid $5,000 cash for rent in advance and reported $6,000 of rent expense on the income statement. Sharp paid $1,000 cash for supplies, and the income statement reported supplies expense of $1,100. Depreciation expense reported on the income statement amounted to $3,500. It incurred $38,600 of operating expenses on account and paid $34,000 cash toward the settlement of accounts payable. The company acquired capital of $10,000 cash from the issue of common stock. A $700 cash dividend was paid. (*Hint:* Record the events under the general ledger accounts of an accounting equation before satisfying the requirements.)

Required

a. Determine the balance in the Retained Earnings account at the beginning of the accounting period.

b. Prepare an income statement, statement of changes in stockholders' equity, balance sheet, and statement of cash flows as of the end of the accounting period.

L.O. 1   PROBLEM 3–25B *Using Accounting Information*

Jon Richfield told his friend that he was very angry with his father. He had asked his father for a sports car, and his father had replied that he did not have the cash. Richfield said that he knew his father was not telling the truth because he had seen a copy of his father's business records, which included a balance sheet that showed a Retained Earnings account of $650,000. He said that anybody with $650,000 had enough cash to buy his son a car.

Required

Explain why Richfield's assessment of his father's cash position may be invalid. What financial statements and which items on those statements would enable him to make a more accurate assessment of his father's cash position?

ANALYZE, THINK, COMMUNICATE

ATC 3–1   BUSINESS APPLICATIONS CASE *Understanding Real World Annual Reports*

Required—Part 1

Use the Topps Company's annual report in Appendix B to answer the following questions.

a. What was Topps' debt to assets ratio for 2003 and 2002?

b. What was Topps' return on assets ratio for 2003 and 2002?

c. What was Topps' return on equity ratio for 2003 and 2002?

d. Why was Topps' return on equity ratio higher than its return on assets ratio for 2003 and 2002?

Required—Part 2

Use the Harley-Davidson's annual report that came with this book to answer the following questions.

a. What was Harley-Davidson's debt to assets ratio for 2003 and 2002? (Note, total liabilities must be computed.)

b. What was Harley-Davidson's return on assets ratio for 2003 and 2002?

c. What was Harley-Davidson's return on equity ratio for 2003 and 2002?

d. The difference between Harley-Davidson's return on equity ratio and its return on assets ratio for 2003 was greater than in 2002. What explains this?

Required—Part 3

a. Looking only at the debt to assets ratios for Topps and Harley-Davidson, which company appears to have the higher financial risk?

b. Looking only at the return on assets ratios and return on equity ratios for Topps and Harley-Davidson, which company appears to be the more profitable?

ATC 3–2   GROUP ASSIGNMENT *Missing Information*

Little Theater Group is a local performing arts group that sponsors various theater productions. The company sells season tickets for the regular performances. It also sells tickets to individual performances called *door sales.* The season tickets are sold in June, July, and August for the season that runs from September through April of each year. The season tickets package contains tickets to eight performances, one per month. The first year of operations was 2003. All revenue not from season ticket sales is from door sales. The following selected information was taken from the financial records for December 31, 2003, 2004, and 2005, at the company's year end:

	2003	2004	2005
Revenue (per income statement)	$450,000	$575,000	$625,000
Unearned Revenue (per balance sheet)	127,000	249,000	275,000
Operating Expense	231,000	326,000	428,000

Required

a. Divide the class into groups consisting of four or five students. Organize the groups into three sections. Assign the groups in each section the financial data for one of the preceding accounting periods.

Group Tasks

1. Determine the total amount of season ticket sales for the year assigned.
2. Determine the total amount of door sales for the year assigned.
3. Compute the net income for the year assigned.
4. Have a representative of each section put its income statement on the board.

Class Discussion

b. Compare the income statements for 2003, 2004, and 2005. Discuss the revenue trend; that is, are door sales increasing more than season ticket sales? What is the company's growth pattern?

REAL-WORLD CASE *Different Numbers for Different Industries*

ATC 3–3

The following are the debt to assets, return on assets, and return on equity ratios for four companies from two different industries. The approximate interest rate each company was paying on its short-term debt is provided. Each of these public companies is a leader in its particular industry, and the data are for the fiscal years ending in 2000. *All numbers are percentages.*

	Debt to Assets	Return on Assets	Return on Equity	Approximate Average Short-term Interest Rates
Banking Industry				
SunTrust Bank	93	1.1	15.2	1.0
Wells Fargo & Co.	91	1.6	17.9	1.2
Home Construction Industry				
Pulte Corporation	60	6.6	16.4	2.3
Ryland Group	59	11.2	27.3	2.3

Required

a. Based only on the debt to assets ratios, the banking companies appear to have the most financial risk. Generally, lower interest rates are usually charged for companies that have lower financial risk. Given this, explain why the banking companies can borrow money at lower interest rates than the construction companies.

b. Explain why the banks have return on equity ratios that are about equal to those of the construction companies even though the return on assets ratios for the banks are much lower than those of the construction companies.

BUSINESS APPLICATIONS CASE *Using Ratio Analysis to Assess Financial Risk*

ATC 3–4

The following information was drawn from the balance sheets of two companies:

Company	Assets	=	Liabilities	+	Stockholders' Equity
Frozen Treats	416,000		178,500		237,500
Perfect Pastries	164,000		57,500		106,500

Required

a. Compute the debt to assets ratio to measure the level of financial risk of both companies.

b. Compare the two ratios computed in part *a* to determine which company has the higher level of financial risk.

ATC 3–5   BUSINESS APPLICATIONS CASE *Using Ratio Analysis to Make Comparisons between Companies*

At the end of 2007, the following information is available for Fran's Flower Shop and Betty's Bouquets.

Statement Data	Fran's Flowers	Betty's Bouquets
Total Assets	$945,000	$273,000
Total Liabilities	585,000	191,000
Stockholders' Equity	360,000	82,000
Net Income	61,000	17,000

Required

a. For each company, compute the debt to assets ratio and the return on equity ratio.
b. Determine what percentage of each company's assets was financed by the owners.
c. Which company had a higher level of financial risk?
d. Based on profitability alone, which company performed better?
e. Do the preceding ratios support the concept of financial leverage? Explain.

ATC 3–6   WRITING ASSIGNMENT *Effect of Land Sale on Return on Assets*

Toyo Company is holding land that cost $900,000 for future use. However, plans have changed and the company may not need the land in the foreseeable future. The president is concerned about the return on assets. Current net income is $425,000 and total assets are $3,500,000.

Required

a. Write a memo to the company president explaining the effect of disposing of the land, assuming that it has a current value of $1,500,000.
b. Write a memo to the company president explaining the effect of disposing of the land, assuming that it has a current value of $600,000.

ATC 3–7   ETHICAL DILEMMA *What Is a Little Deceit Among Friends?*

Glenn's Cleaning Services Company is experiencing cash flow problems and needs a loan. Glenn has a friend who is willing to lend him the money he needs provided she can be convinced that he will be able to repay the debt. Glenn has assured his friend that his business is viable, but his friend has asked to see the company's financial statements. Glenn's accountant produced the following financial statements:

Income Statement		Balance Sheet	
Service Revenue	$ 38,000	Assets	$85,000
Operating Expenses	(70,000)	Liabilities	$35,000
Net Loss	$(32,000)	Stockholders' Equity	
		Common Stock	82,000
		Retained Earnings	(32,000)
		Total Liabilities and	
		Stockholders' Equity	$85,000

Glenn made the following adjustments to these statements before showing them to his friend. He recorded $82,000 of revenue on account from Barrymore Manufacturing Company for a contract to clean its headquarters office building that was still being negotiated for the next month. Barrymore had scheduled a meeting to sign a contract the following week, so he was sure that he would get the job. Barrymore was a reputable company, and Glenn was confident that he could ultimately collect the $82,000. Also, he subtracted $30,000 of accrued salaries expense and the corresponding liability. He reasoned that since he had not paid the employees, he had not incurred any expense.

Required

a. Reconstruct the income statement and balance sheet as they would appear after Glenn's adjustments. Comment on the accuracy of the adjusted financial statements.
b. Comment on the ethical implications of Glenn's actions. Before you answer, consider the following scenario. Suppose you are Glenn and the $30,000 you owe your employees is due next week. If you are unable to pay them, they will quit and the business will go bankrupt. You are sure you will be able to repay your friend when your employees perform the $82,000 of services for Barrymore and you collect the cash. However, your friend is risk averse and is not likely to make the loan based on the

financial statements your accountant prepared. Would you make the changes that Glenn made to get the loan and thereby save your company? Defend your position with a rational explanation.

SPREADSHEET ASSIGNMENT *Using Excel*

ATC 3–8

Set up the following spreadsheet for Hubbard Company to calculate financial ratios based on given financial information.

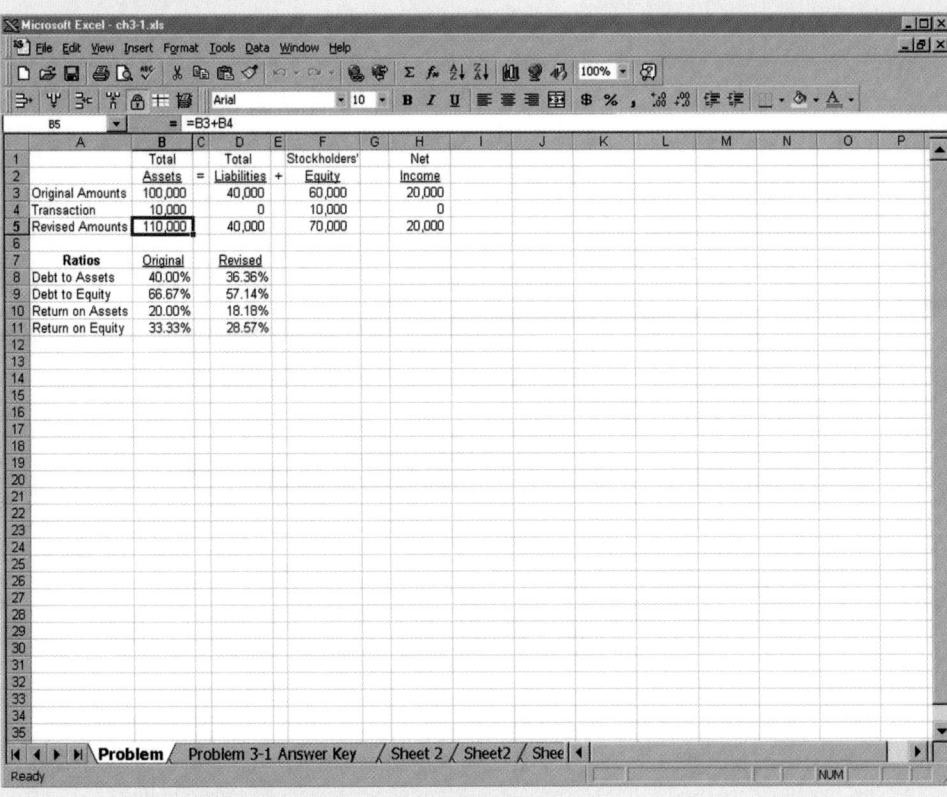

Steps to Prepare Spreadsheet

1. Enter the information in Column A.
2. Enter the headings in rows 1 and 2.
3. In row 3, enter the numbers for the Original Amounts.
4. In Column B, beginning with row 8, formulate the ratios based on the Original Amounts. Format the ratios as percentages.
5. The following independent transactions apply to Hubbard Corporation.
   a. Acquired $10,000 cash from the issue of common stock.
   b. Borrowed $10,000 cash.
   c. Earned $5,000 revenue and received cash.
   d. Accrued $3,000 of expenses.
   e. Incurred and paid $3,000 of expenses.

Required

a. In row 4, enter the effect of Transaction *a* on both the accounting equation and net income.
b. Formulate the revised amounts in row 5 for each heading after considering the effect of Transaction *a* on the original amounts.
c. Design formulas for the ratios in Column D based on the Revised Amounts.
d. Enter the ratios for the Original and Revised Transaction *a* amounts in the following table.

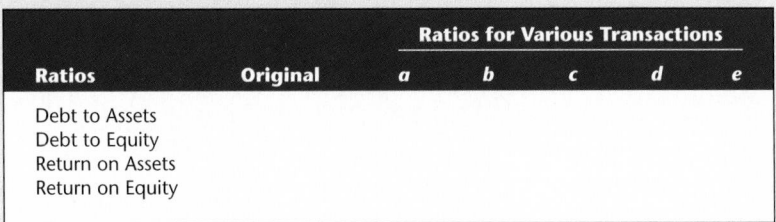

Ratios	Original	Ratios for Various Transactions				
		a	b	c	d	e
Debt to Assets						
Debt to Equity						
Return on Assets						
Return on Equity						

e. Delete the effect of Transaction *a* in row 4. Enter the effect of Transaction *b* in row 4. Notice that Excel automatically recalculates the Revised Amounts and Ratios on your spreadsheet as the result of the changed data.

f. Continue to delete transactions in row 4 as completed and enter the effect of each subsequent transaction *c* through *e* one at a time. Enter the ratios for each independent transaction in the preceding table.

Spreadsheet Tip
Format percentages by choosing Format, Cells, and Percentage.

ATC 3–9   **SPREADSHEET ASSIGNMENT** *Mastering Excel*

a. Refer to Problem 3–22A. Using an Excel spreadsheet, prepare the financial statements as indicated. To complete Requirement *b* here, use formulas where normal arithmetic calculations are made in the financial statements.

b. It is interesting to speculate what would happen if certain operating results change for better or worse. After completing Requirement *a,* change certain account balances for each of the following independent operating adjustments. After each adjustment, note how the financial statements would differ if the change in operations were to occur. After the effect of each adjustment is noted, return the data to the original amounts in Problem 3–22A, and then go to the next operating adjustment.

In the following table, record the new amounts on the financial statements for the various operating changes listed.

	Original	1	2	3	4	5
Net Income						
Total Assets						
Total Liabilities						
Total Stockholders' Equity						
Total Liabilities & Stockholders' Equity						

Independent Operating Adjustments

1. Service Revenue increased $7,500. Assume that all services are provided on account.
2. Insurance Expense decreased $500. The related Prepaid Insurance account changed accordingly.
3. Supplies Expense decreased $100. The related Supplies account changed accordingly.
4. Depreciation Expense increased $300. The related Accumulated Depreciation account changed accordingly.
5. Dividends paid decreased $1,000 and the Cash account changed accordingly.

CHAPTER *four*

THE DOUBLE-ENTRY ACCOUNTING SYSTEM

LEARNING *objectives*

After you have mastered the material in this chapter, you will be able to:

1 Explain the fundamental concepts associated with double-entry accounting systems.

2 Describe business events using debit/credit terminology.

3 Record transactions in T-accounts.

4 Identify the events that need adjusting entries and record them.

5 State the need for and record closing entries.

6 Prepare and interpret a trial balance.

7 Record transactions using the general journal format.

8 Describe the components of an annual report, including the management, discussion, and analysis section and the footnotes to financial statements.

9 Describe the role of the Securities and Exchange Commission in financial reporting.

THE *curious* ACCOUNTANT

As previously indicated, most companies prepare financial statements at least once a year. The year for which accounting records are maintained is called the company's **fiscal year.** This book usually assumes that the fiscal year is the same as a calendar year; that is, it ends on December 31. In practice, many companies have fiscal years that do not end on December 31. For example, Levi Strauss, a company that produces clothing, has a fiscal year that ends the last Sunday in November. The Gap, a company that sells clothing, has a fiscal year that ends on the last Saturday in January or the first Saturday in February.

Why do you think these companies choose these dates to end their fiscal years? (Answers on pages 174–75.)

CHAPTER *opening*

This chapter explains how to record transactions using double-entry accounting. It is insightful to draw a parallel between the requirements of the double-entry system and those of a traffic light. Red could mean "go" rather than "stop." In fact, it makes no difference whether red means go or stop. What is important is that drivers agree on what red means. Similarly, the rules of double-entry accounting could be written differently. In fact, the rules may seem backward to you. You are accustomed to hearing accounting terms like "debit" or "credit" from a customer perspective. You must now reorient yourself to a business perspective. Regardless of how awkward the rules may seem to you, you must accept them as they are. In time, they will become second nature to you. With practice, you can learn to navigate the double-entry accounting system just as effortlessly as you respond to traffic lights.

4–1

LO1 Explain the fundamental concepts associated with double-entry accounting systems.

LO2 Describe business events using debit/credit terminology.

Debit/Credit Terminology

An account form known as a **T-account** is a good starting point for learning double-entry recording procedures. A T-account looks like the letter "T" drawn on a piece of paper. The account title is written across the top of the horizontal bar of the T. The left side of the vertical bar is the **debit** side, and the right side is the **credit** side. An account has been *debited* when an amount is written on the left side and *credited* when an amount is written on the right side. Accountants often abbreviate the term *debit* as "dr." and *credit* as "cr." For any given account, the difference between the total debit and credit amounts is the **account balance.**

The **double-entry accounting** system requires that total debits always equal total credits. This feature is so powerful in promoting accuracy that it has been used for hundreds of years. If debits do not equal credits, accountants know to search for an error. However, an equality of debits and credits does not prove accuracy. For example, an accountant may record the debit and credit of a $500 transaction as $5,000. Total debits and credits will be equal, but the accounting records will be inaccurate. On the other hand, if a debit is recorded as $680 and the corresponding credit as $860, the error will be caught. The system is not flawless, but it is highly effective in reducing errors.

To begin: debits increase asset accounts and credits decrease asset accounts. In T-account form, this rule is expressed as follows:

Asset	
Debit	Credit
+	−

The pluses and minuses are reversed for liability and stockholders' equity accounts. This is algebraically correct because those accounts are on the other side of the equal sign in the accounting equation. In T-account form, these debit and credit rules are as follows:

			Claims			
Assets		=	**Liabilities**	+	**Equity**	
Debit	Credit		Debit	Credit	Debit	Credit
+	−		−	+	−	+

Notice that a debit can represent an increase or a decrease. Likewise, a credit can represent an increase or a decrease. Whether a debit or credit is an increase or a decrease depends on the type of account (asset, liability, or stockholders' equity) in question. The rules of debits and credits are summarized as follows:

1. Debits increase asset accounts; credits decrease asset accounts.
2. Debits decrease liability and stockholders' equity accounts; credits increase liability and stockholders' equity accounts.

Collins Consultants Case

LO3 Record transactions in T-accounts.

We will record the accounting events for a small business, Collins Consultants, to show how the rules for debits and credits work. Each event falls into one of the four transaction types:

1. Asset source transactions
2. Asset exchange transactions
3. Asset use transactions
4. Claims exchange transactions

Asset Source Transactions

A business may obtain assets from three primary sources: (1) from stockholders, (2) from creditors, or (3) through operating activities (earning revenue). An asset source transaction increases an asset account and a corresponding liability or stockholders' equity account. The increase in the asset account is recorded with a debit entry. The increase in a liability or stockholders' equity account is recorded with a credit entry. The following section demonstrates recording procedures for common asset source transactions.

Event 1 Owners Contribute Assets
Collins Consultants was established on January 1, 2003, when it acquired $15,000 cash from Collins.

This accounting event increases both assets and stockholders' equity. The increase in assets (Cash) is recorded with a debit, and the increase in stockholders' equity (Common Stock) with a credit, shown in T-account form as follows:

Assets		=	Liabilities	+	Equity	
Cash					**Common Stock**	
Debit	Credit				Debit	Credit
+						+
(1) 15,000						15,000 (1)

This entry has the following effects on the financial statements:

Assets	=	Liab.	+	Equity	Rev.	−	Exp.	=	Net Inc.	Cash Flow
15,000	=	NA	+	15,000	NA	−	NA	=	NA	15,000 FA

Event 2 Creditor Provides Assets
On February 1, Collins Consultants issued a $10,000 note payable to the National Bank to borrow cash.

The interest rate and maturity date of the note are discussed later. Borrowing the cash increases both assets and liabilities. The increase in assets (Cash) is recorded with a debit, and the increase in liabilities (Notes Payable) is recorded with a credit, as illustrated in the following T-accounts:

Assets		=	Liabilities		+	Equity
Cash			**Notes Payable**			
Debit	Credit		Debit	Credit		
+				+		
(2) 10,000				10,000 (2)		

This illustration shows only the accounts affected by the borrowing event. Throughout the chapter, the effects of each event are labeled with the event number shown in parentheses, in this case (2). Later in the chapter we illustrate the cumulative effect of all the events on each account.

This entry has the following effects on the financial statements:

Assets	=	Liab.	+	Equity	Rev.	−	Exp.	=	Net Inc.	Cash Flow
10,000	=	10,000	+	NA	NA	−	NA	=	NA	10,000 FA

Event 3 Creditor Provides Assets
On February 17, Collins Consultants purchased $850 of office supplies on account (agreed to pay for the supplies at a later date) from Morris Supply Company.

Purchasing supplies on account increases both assets and liabilities. The increase in assets (Supplies) is recorded with a debit, and the increase in liabilities (Accounts Payable) is recorded with a credit, as shown in the following T-accounts:

Assets		=	Liabilities		+	Equity	
Supplies			**Accounts Payable**				
Debit	Credit		Debit	Credit			
+				+			
(3) 850				850 (3)			

This entry has the following effects on the financial statements:

Assets	=	Liab.	+	Equity	Rev.	–	Exp.	=	Net Inc.	Cash Flow
850	=	850	+	NA	NA	–	NA	=	NA	NA

Event 4 Creditor Provides Assets

On February 28, Collins Consultants signed a contract to evaluate the internal control system used by Kendall Food Stores. Kendall paid Collins $5,000 in advance for these future services.

Accepting the $5,000 in advance creates an obligation for Collins Consultants. The obligation is to provide future services to Kendall Food Stores. Collins will recognize a liability called *unearned revenue*. Recording the event increases both assets and liabilities. The increase in assets (Cash) is recorded with a debit, and the increase in liabilities (Unearned Revenue) is recorded with a credit, as shown in the following T-accounts:

Assets		=	Liabilities		+	Equity	
Cash			**Unearned Revenue**				
Debit	Credit		Debit	Credit			
+				+			
(4) 5,000				5,000 (4)			

This entry has the following effects on the financial statements:

Assets	=	Liab.	+	Equity	Rev.	–	Exp.	=	Net Inc.	Cash Flow
5,000	=	5,000	+	NA	NA	–	NA	=	NA	5,000 OA

Event 5 Creditor Provides Assets

On March 1, Collins Consultants received $18,000 from signing a contract to provide professional advice to Harwood Corporation over a one-year period.

The event increases both assets and liabilities. The increase in assets (Cash) is recorded with a debit, and the increase in liabilities (Unearned Revenue) is recorded with a credit, as shown in the following T-accounts:

Assets		=	Liabilities		+	Equity	
Cash			**Unearned Revenue**				
Debit	Credit		Debit	Credit			
+				+			
(5) 18,000				18,000 (5)			

This entry has the following effects on the financial statements:

Assets	=	Liab.	+	Equity	Rev.	–	Exp.	=	Net Inc.	Cash Flow
18,000	=	18,000	+	NA	NA	–	NA	=	NA	18,000 OA

Event 6 Operating Activity Provides Assets

On April 10, Collins Consultants provided $2,000 of services to Rex Company on account (agreed to let the customer pay at a future date).

Recognizing revenue earned on account increases both assets and stockholders' equity. The increase in assets (Accounts Receivable) is recorded with a debit, and the increase in stockholders' equity (Consulting Revenue) is recorded with a credit, as shown in the following T-accounts:

Assets	=	Liabilities	+	Equity
Accounts Receivable				**Consulting Revenue**

Debit	Credit		Debit	Credit
+				+
(6) 2,000				2,000 (6)

This entry has the following effects on the financial statements:

Assets	=	Liab.	+	Equity		Rev.	–	Exp.	=	Net Inc.	Cash Flow
2,000	=	NA	+	2,000		2,000	–	NA	=	2,000	NA

Event 7 Operating Activity Provides Assets
On April 29, Collins performed services and received $8,400 cash.

Recognizing the revenue increases both assets and stockholders' equity. The increase in assets (Cash) is recorded with a debit, and the increase in stockholders' equity (Consulting Revenue) is recorded with a credit, as shown in the following T-accounts:

Assets	=	Liabilities	+	Equity
Cash				**Consulting Revenue**

Debit	Credit		Debit	Credit
+				+
(7) 8,400				8,400 (7)

This entry has the following effects on the financial statements:

Assets	=	Liab.	+	Equity		Rev.	–	Exp.	=	Net Inc.	Cash Flow
8,400	=	NA	+	8,400		8,400	–	NA	=	8,400	8,400 OA

Summary of the Previous Asset Source Transactions

Events 1 through 7 are asset source transactions. In each case, an asset account and a corresponding claims account increased. The increase in the asset account was recorded with a debit and the increase in the liability or stockholders' equity account was recorded with a credit. Any transaction that provides assets to a business is recorded similarly.

What are the three sources of assets? Which accounts are debited and credited when a business acquires an asset?

Answer The three sources of assets are creditors, investors, and earnings. When a company acquires an asset, the asset account is debited and the source account is credited. For example, if a company earns revenue on account, the receivables account is debited and the revenue account is credited.

Check Yourself 4–1

Asset Exchange Transactions

Asset exchange transactions involve trading one asset for another asset. One asset account increases; the other decreases. The total amount of assets remains unchanged. Asset exchange transactions are recorded by debiting the asset account that is increasing and crediting the asset account that is decreasing. In T-account form, asset exchange transactions have the following effects on the accounting equation:

	Assets			=	Claims
Asset 1		**Asset 2**			
Debit	Credit	Debit	Credit		
+			−		

Event 8 Exchange Cash for Note Receivable
On May 1, Collins Consultants loaned Reston Company $6,000. Reston issued a note to Collins.

The terms of the note are discussed later. The note receivable represents an investment to Collins. Recognizing the investment (loan) increases one asset account and decreases another. The increase in assets (Notes Receivable) is recorded with a debit, and the decrease in assets (Cash) is recorded with a credit, as shown in the following T-accounts:

	Assets			=	Claims
Cash		**Notes Receivable**			
Debit	Credit	Debit	Credit		
	−	+			
	6,000 (8)	(8) 6,000			

This entry has the following effects on the financial statements:

Assets		= Liab. + Equity	Rev. − Exp. = Net Inc.	Cash Flow
Cash	**+ Note Rec.**			
(6,000) +	6,000	= NA + NA	NA − NA = NA	(6,000) IA

Event 9 Exchange Cash for Office Equipment
On June 30, Collins purchased office equipment for $42,000 cash.

The increase in assets (Office Equipment) is recorded with a debit, and the decrease in assets (Cash) is recorded with a credit, as shown in the following T-accounts:

	Assets			=	Claims
Cash		**Office Equipment**			
Debit	Credit	Debit	Credit		
	−	+			
	42,000 (9)	(9) 42,000			

This entry has the following effects on the financial statements:

Assets		= Liab. + Equity	Rev. − Exp. = Net Inc.	Cash Flow
Cash	**+ Office Equip.**			
(42,000) +	42,000	= NA + NA	NA − NA = NA	(42,000) IA

Event 10 Exchange Cash for Prepaid Rent
On July 31, Collins paid $3,600 cash in advance for a one-year lease to rent office space beginning August 1.

The increase in assets (Prepaid Rent) is recorded with a debit, and the decrease in assets (Cash) is recorded with a credit, as shown in the following T-accounts:

	Assets			=	Claims
Cash		**Prepaid Rent**			
Debit	Credit	Debit	Credit		
	−	+			
	3,600 (10)	(10) 3,600			

This entry has the following effects on the financial statements:

Assets		= Liab. + Equity		Rev. – Exp. = Net Inc.			Cash Flow
Cash	+ Prep. Rent						
(3,600)	+ 3,600	= NA +	NA	NA – NA =	NA		(3,600) OA

Event 11 **Exchange Receivable for Cash**

On August 8, Collins Consultants collected $1,200 from Rex Company as partial payment of the account receivable (see Event 6).

The increase in assets (Cash) is recorded with a debit, and the decrease in assets (Accounts Receivable) is recorded with a credit, as shown in the following T-accounts:

Assets				=	Claims
Cash		**Accounts Receivable**			
Debit	Credit	Debit	Credit		
+			–		
(11) 1,200			1,200 (11)		

This entry has the following effects on the financial statements:

Assets		= Liab. + Equity		Rev. – Exp. = Net Inc.		Cash Flow
Cash	+ Accts. Rec.					
1,200	+ (1,200)	= NA +	NA	NA – NA =	NA	1,200 OA

Summary of the Previous Asset Exchange Transactions

Events 8 through 11 are all asset exchange transactions. In each case, one asset account increased and another decreased. The asset account that increased was debited, and the asset account that decreased was credited. These asset exchange transactions did not affect the total amounts of either assets or claims.

Asset Use Transactions

There are three primary asset use transactions: (1) expenses may use assets, (2) settling liabilities may use assets, or (3) paying dividends may use assets. An asset use transaction decreases an asset account and also decreases a claims account. The decrease in the asset account is recorded with a credit and the decrease in the claims account is recorded with a debit.

Event 12 **Assets Used to Produce Revenue (Expenses)**

On September 4, Collins Consultants paid employees who worked for the company $2,400 in salaries.

The decrease in assets (Cash) is recorded with a credit, and the decrease in stockholders' equity (Salaries Expense) is recorded with a debit, as shown in the following T-accounts:

Assets		=	Liabilities	+	Equity	
Cash					**Salaries Expense**	
Debit	Credit				Debit	Credit
	–				+ Expense	
	2,400 (12)				– Equity	
					(12) 2,400	

The debit to Salaries Expense represents an *increase* in the salaries expense account which is actually a *decrease* in stockholders' equity (Retained Earnings). Debit entries increase expense accounts. Expenses, however, decrease stockholders' equity (Retained Earnings). Debiting an expense account, therefore, reduces stockholders' equity.

This entry has the following effects on the financial statements:

Assets	=	Liab.	+	Equity	Rev.	−	Exp.	=	Net Inc.	Cash Flow
(2,400)	=	NA	+	(2,400)	NA	−	2,400	=	(2,400)	(2,400) OA

Event 13 Assets Transferred to Owners (Dividends)
On September 20, Collins Consultants paid a $1,500 cash dividend to its owner.

The decrease in assets (Cash) is recorded with a credit, and the decrease in stockholders' equity (Dividends) is recorded with a debit, as shown in the following T-accounts:

Assets	=	Liabilities	+	Equity
Cash				**Dividends**

Debit	Credit			Debit	Credit
	−			+ Div.	
	1,500 (13)			− Equity	
				(13) 1,500	

The debit to Dividends represents both an increase in the dividends account and a decrease in stockholders' equity (Retained Earnings). Since dividends decrease stockholders' equity, an increase in the dividends account reduces stockholders' equity.

This entry has the following effects on the financial statements:

Assets	=	Liab.	+	Equity	Rev.	−	Exp.	=	Net Inc.	Cash Flow
(1,500)	=	NA	+	(1,500)	NA	−	NA	=	NA	(1,500) FA

Event 14 Assets Used to Pay Liabilities
On October 10, Collins Consultants paid Morris Supply Company the $850 owed from purchasing office supplies on account (see Event 3).

The decrease in assets (Cash) is recorded with a credit, and the decrease in liabilities (Accounts Payable) is recorded with a debit, as shown in the following T-accounts:

Assets	=	Liabilities	+	Equity
Cash		**Accounts Payable**		

Debit	Credit	Debit	Credit	
	−	−		
	850 (14)	(14) 850		

This entry has the following effects on the financial statements:

Assets	=	Liab.	+	Equity	Rev.	−	Exp.	=	Net Inc.	Cash Flow
(850)	=	(850)	+	NA	NA	−	NA	=	NA	(850) OA

Summary of Asset Use Transactions

Events 12 through 14 each reduced both an asset account and either a liability or stockholders' equity account. Even though debit entries to expense and dividends accounts represent increases in those accounts, the balances in expense and dividends accounts reduce stockholders' equity. Any asset use transaction is recorded with a debit to a liability or a stockholders' equity account and a credit to an asset account.

Claims Exchange Transactions

Certain transactions involve exchanging one claims account for another claims account. The total amount of claims remains unchanged. Such transactions are recorded by debiting the claims account which is decreasing and crediting the claims account which is increasing.

Event 15 **Recognizing Revenue (Unearned to Earned)**
On November 15, Collins completed its consulting evaluation of the internal control system used by Kendall Food Stores (see Event 4).

Kendall expressed satisfaction with Collins's report. Recall Kendall had paid $5,000 in advance for the consulting services. Upon completing the project, Collins will recognize the revenue earned. Kendall's advance payment had created a liability; recognizing the revenue decreases liabilities and increases stockholders' equity. The decrease in liabilities (Unearned Revenue) is recorded with a debit, and the increase in stockholders' equity (Consulting Revenue) is recorded with a credit, as shown in the following T-accounts:

Assets	=	Liabilities	+	Equity	
		Unearned Revenue		**Consulting Revenue**	
		Debit	Credit	Debit	Credit
		−			+
		(15) 5,000			5,000 (15)

This entry has the following effects on the financial statements:

Assets	=	Liab.	+	Equity	Rev.	−	Exp.	=	Net Inc.	Cash Flow
NA	=	(5,000)	+	5,000	5,000	−	NA	=	5,000	NA

Event 16 **Recognizing Expense**
On December 18, Collins Consultants received a $900 bill from Creative Ads for advertisements which had appeared in regional magazines. Collins plans to pay the bill later.

The event increases liabilities and decreases stockholders' equity. The increase in liabilities (Accounts Payable) is recorded with a credit, and the decrease in stockholders' equity (Advertising Expense) is recorded with a debit, as shown in the following T-accounts:

Assets	=	Liabilities	+	Equity	
		Accounts Payable		**Advertising Expense**	
		Debit	Credit	Debit	Credit
			+	+ Expense	
			900 (16)	− Equity	
				(16) 900	

This entry has the following effects on the financial statements:

Assets	=	Liab.	+	Equity	Rev.	−	Exp.	=	Net Inc.	Cash Flow
NA	=	900	+	(900)	NA	−	900	=	(900)	NA

Summary of Claims Exchange Transactions

Events 15 and 16 reflect exchanges on the claims side of the accounting equation. In each case, one claims account was debited, and another claims account was credited. Claims exchange transactions do not affect the total amounts of either assets or claims.

Adjusting the Accounts

Assume that Collins Consultants' fiscal year ends on December 31, 2003. In order to prepare the financial statements, Collins must first adjust its accounting records to recognize any unrecorded accruals and or deferrals. The appropriate adjustments are discussed in the next section of this chapter. Notice that adjusting entries do not affect the cash account.

LO4 Identify the events that need adjusting entries and record them.

Adjustment 1 Accrual of Interest Revenue
Collins Consultants recognized accrued interest on the $6,000 note receivable from Reston (See Event 8).

The note was issued on May 1, 2003. It had a 9 percent annual rate of interest and a one-year term to maturity. Collins therefore earned $360 ([$6,000 × 0.09] × [8 ÷ 12]) of interest revenue during 2003. The required adjusting entry increases both assets and stockholders' equity. The increase in assets (Interest Receivable) is recorded with a debit, and the increase in stockholders' equity (Interest Revenue) is recorded with a credit, as shown in the following T-accounts:

Assets	=	Liabilities	+	Equity	
Interest Receivable				**Interest Revenue**	
Debit	Credit			Debit	Credit
+					+
(A1) 360					360 (A1)

The label (A1) indicates this is the first adjusting entry. The second adjusting entry is labeled (A2). Subsequent adjusting entries follow this referencing scheme.

This adjustment has the following effects on the financial statements:

Assets	=	Liab.	+	Equity	Rev.	−	Exp.	=	Net Inc.	Cash Flow
360	=	NA	+	360	360	−	NA	=	360	NA

Adjustment 2 Accrual of Interest Expense
Collins Consultants recognized accrued interest expense on the $10,000 note payable it issued to the National Bank (see Event 2).

The note was issued on February 1, 2003. It had a 12 percent annual interest rate and a one-year term to maturity. Interest expense on the note for the 2003 accounting period is $1,100 ([$10,000 × 0.12] × [11 ÷ 12]). The required adjusting entry increases liabilities and decreases stockholders' equity. The increase in liabilities (Interest Payable) is recorded with a credit, and the decrease in stockholders' equity (Interest Expense) is recorded with a debit, as shown in the following T-accounts:

Assets	=	Liabilities	+	Equity	
		Interest Payable		**Interest Expense**	
		Debit	Credit	Debit	Credit
			+	+ Expense	
			1,100 (A2)	− Equity	
				(A2) 1,100	

This adjustment has the following effects on the financial statements:

Assets	=	Liab.	+	Equity	Rev.	−	Exp.	=	Net Inc.	Cash Flow
NA	=	1,100	+	(1,100)	NA	−	1,100	=	(1,100)	NA

Adjustment 3 Accrual of Salary Expense
Collins recognized accrued but unpaid salaries.

Collins Consultants last paid salaries to employees on September 4 (see Event 12). Assume that Collins owes $800 more to employees for work done in 2003 since September 4. Collins will pay these salaries in 2004. The required adjusting entry increases liabilities and decreases stockholders' equity. The increase in liabilities (Salaries Payable) is recorded with a credit, and the decrease in stockholders' equity (Salaries Expense) is recorded with a debit, as shown in the following T-accounts:

Assets	=	Liabilities	+	Equity	
		Salaries Payable		**Salaries Expense**	
Debit		Credit		Debit	Credit
		+		+ Expense	
		800 (A3)		− Equity	
				(A3) 800	

This adjustment has the following effects on the financial statements:

Assets	=	Liab.	+	Equity	Rev.	−	Exp.	=	Net Inc.	Cash Flow
NA	=	800	+	(800)	NA	−	800	=	(800)	NA

Adjustment 4 Equipment Used to Produce Revenue (Depreciation Expense)
Collins recognized depreciation on the office equipment it had purchased on June 30 (see Event 9).

Collins expects the equipment to have a five-year life and a $2,000 salvage value. Since the equipment was purchased at midyear, Collins should recognize a half-year of depreciation expense, which is $4,000 ([$42,000 − $2,000] ÷ 5 = $8,000 ÷ 2 = $4,000). The adjusting entry necessary to record depreciation decreases both assets and stockholders' equity. The decrease in assets (Office Equipment) is recorded with a credit to the contra asset account Accumulated Depreciation and the decrease in stockholders' equity (Depreciation Expense) is recorded with a debit, as shown in the following T-accounts:

Assets	=	Liabilities	+	Equity	
Accumulated Depreciation				**Depreciation Expense**	
Debit	Credit			Debit	Credit
	+ Acc. Depr.			+ Expense	
	− Assets			− Equity	
	4,000 (A4)			(A4) 4,000	

The credit entry to the Accumulated Depreciation account represents an increase in that account. Accumulated Depreciation, however, reduces total assets. The Accumulated Depreciation account is classified as a **contra account** because it normally has a credit balance while most asset accounts have debit balances. Accumulated depreciation increases each time additional amounts of depreciation are recorded.

This adjustment has the following effects on the financial statements:

Assets	=	Liab.	+	Equity	Rev.	−	Exp.	=	Net Inc.	Cash Flow
(4,000)	=	NA	+	(4,000)	NA	−	4,000	=	(4,000)	NA

Adjustment 5 Office Space Used to Produce Revenue (Rent Expense)
Collins recognized rent expense for the portion of prepaid rent used up since entering the lease agreement on July 31 (see Event 10).

Recall that Collins paid $3,600 in advance to lease office space for one year. The monthly rental cost is therefore $300 ($3,600 ÷ 12 months). By December 31, Collins had *used* the office for five months in 2003. Rent expense for those 5 months is therefore $1,500 ($300 × 5). Recognizing the rent expense decreases both assets and stockholders' equity. The decrease in assets (Prepaid Rent) is recorded with a credit, and the decrease in stockholders' equity (Rent Expense) is recorded with a debit, as shown in the following T-accounts:

Assets	=	Liabilities	+	Equity	
Prepaid Rent				**Rent Expense**	
Debit	Credit			Debit	Credit
	−			+ Expense	
	1,500 (A5)			− Equity	
				(A5) 1,500	

FOR Rent expense, prepaid Rent decreases & Rent expense increases [handwritten note]

This adjustment has the following effects on the financial statements:

Assets	=	Liab.	+	Equity		Rev.	−	Exp.	=	Net Inc.		Cash Flow
(1,500)	=	NA	+	(1,500)		NA	−	1,500	=	(1,500)		NA

Adjustment 6 Supplies Used to Produce Revenue (Supplies Expense)
A physical count at the end of the year indicates that $125 worth of the supplies purchased on February 17 is still on hand (see Event 3).

Collins used $725 ($850 − $125) of supplies during the period. Recognizing the supplies expense decreases both assets and stockholders' equity. The decrease in assets (Supplies) is recorded with a credit and the decrease in stockholders' equity (Supplies Expense) is recorded with a debit, as shown in the following T-accounts:

Assets	=	Liabilities	+	Equity

	Supplies			Supplies Expense	
Debit	Credit			Debit	Credit
	−			+ Expense	
	725 (A6)			− Equity	
				(A6) 725	

This adjustment has the following effects on the financial statements:

Assets	=	Liab.	+	Equity		Rev.	−	Exp.	=	Net Inc.		Cash Flow
(725)	=	NA	+	(725)		NA	−	725	=	(725)		NA

Adjustment 7 Recognition of Revenue (Unearned to Earned)
Collins Consultants adjusted its accounting records to reflect revenue earned to date on the contract to provide services to Harwood Corporation for a one-year period beginning March 1 (see Event 5).

Recall that Collins collected $18,000 in advance for this contract. By December 31, 2003, Collins would have provided Harwood professional services for 10 months, earning $15,000 ($18,000 ÷ 12 = $1,500 × 10 = $15,000) of the contract revenue during 2003. This amount must be transferred from the liability account (Unearned Revenue) to an equity account (Consulting Revenue). Recognizing the revenue decreases liabilities and increases stockholders' equity. The decrease in liabilities (Unearned Revenue) is recorded with a debit, and the increase in stockholders' equity (Consulting Revenue) is recorded with a credit, as shown in the following T-accounts:

Assets	=	Liabilities	+	Equity

		Unearned Revenue		Consulting Revenue	
	Debit	Credit		Debit	Credit
	−				+
	(A7) 15,000				15,000 (A7)

This adjustment has the following effects on the financial statements:

Assets	=	Liab.	+	Equity		Rev.	−	Exp.	=	Net Inc.		Cash Flow
NA	=	(15,000)	+	15,000		15,000	−	NA	=	15,000		NA

Check Yourself 4-2

Can an asset exchange transaction be an adjusting entry?

Answer No. Adjusting entries always involve revenue or expense accounts. Since an asset exchange transaction involves only asset accounts, it cannot be an adjusting entry.

Overview of Debit/Credit Relationships

The transactions presented in this chapter illustrate the relationships summarized in Panel A of Exhibit 4–1. Panel B illustrates these relationships in T-account form. Debit/credit terminology is fundamental to understanding and communicating accounting information. Practice using the terminology until it becomes second nature to you.

LO2 Describe business events using debit/credit terminology.

Summary of T-Accounts

Exhibit 4–2 summarizes in T-account form all the activity in the Collins Consultants example. Verify that the accounting equation is in balance. In this case, the total of all asset balances is $48,635, which is equal to the total of all liability and stockholders' equity account balances. The balance in each account, which is the difference between all the debit entries and all the credit entries, is written on the plus (increase) side of that account. Asset, expense, and dividend accounts normally have *debit balances;* liability, stockholders' equity, and revenue accounts normally have *credit balances.*

LO3 Record transactions in T-accounts.

Exhibit 4–1 Debit/Credit Relationships

Panel A

Account	Debits	Credits
Assets	Increase	Decrease
Contra Assets	Decrease	Increase
Liabilities	Decrease	Increase
Equity	Decrease	Increase
Common Stock	Decrease	Increase
Revenue	Decrease	Increase
Expenses	Increase	Decrease
Dividends	Increase	Decrease

Panel B

Assets		=	Liabilities		+	Equity	
Debit	Credit		Debit	Credit		Debit	Credit
+	−		−	+		−	+

Contra Assets					Common Stock	
Debit	Credit				Debit	Credit
+ Assets	− Assets				−	+
− Contra	+ Contra					

					Dividends	
					Debit	Credit
					− Equity	+ Equity
					+ Div.	− Div.

					Revenue	
					Debit	Credit
					−	+

					Expense	
					Debit	Credit
					− Equity	+ Equity
					+ Exp.	− Exp.

LO1 Explain the
fundamental concepts
associated with double-entry
accounting systems.

The Ledger

The collection of all the accounts used by a particular business is called the **ledger**. The ledger for Collins Consultants is displayed in Exhibit 4–2. In a manual system, the ledger could be a book with pages for each account where entries are recorded by hand. In the more sophisticated systems, the ledger is maintained in electronic form. Data is entered into electronic ledgers using computer keyboards or scanners. Companies typically assign each ledger

Exhibit 4–2 *Ledger Accounts*

Assets				=	Liabilities				+	Equity		

Assets

Cash

(1)	15,000	6,000	(8)
(2)	10,000	42,000	(9)
(4)	5,000	3,600	(10)
(5)	18,000	2,400	(12)
(7)	8,400	1,500	(13)
(11)	1,200	850	(14)
Bal.	1,250		

Accounts Receivable

(6)	2,000	1,200	(11)
Bal.	800		

Supplies

(3)	850	725	(A6)
Bal.	125		

Prepaid Rent

(10)	3,600	1,500	(A5)
Bal.	2,100		

Notes Receivable

(8)	6,000	
Bal.	6,000	

Interest Receivable

(A1)	360	
Bal.	360	

Office Equipment

(9)	42,000	
Bal.	42,000	

Accumulated Depreciation

		4,000	(A4)
		4,000	Bal.

Liabilities

Accounts Payable

(14)	850	850	(3)
		900	(16)
		900	Bal.

Unearned Revenue

(15)	5,000	5,000	(4)
(A7)	15,000	18,000	(5)
		3,000	Bal.

Notes Payable

		10,000	(2)
		10,000	Bal.

Interest Payable

		1,100	(A2)
		1,100	Bal.

Salaries Payable

		800	(A3)
		800	Bal.

Equity

Common Stock

		15,000	(1)
		15,000	Bal.

Dividends

(13)	1,500	
Bal.	1,500	

Consulting Revenue

		2,000	(6)
		8,400	(7)
		5,000	(15)
		15,000	(A7)
		30,400	Bal.

Interest Revenue

		360	(A1)
		360	Bal.

Salaries Expense

(12)	2,400	
(A3)	800	
Bal.	3,200	

Advertising Expense

(16)	900	
Bal.	900	

Interest Expense

(A2)	1,100	
Bal.	1,100	

Depreciation Expense

(A4)	4,000	
Bal.	4,000	

Rent Expense

(A5)	1,500	
Bal.	1,500	

Supplies Expense

(A6)	725	
Bal.	725	

Total Assets	=	Total Liabilities	+	Total Equity
		15,800		32,835
		Total Claims		
48,635		48,635		

Do all accounting systems require the use of debits and credits? The answer is a definite no. Indeed, many small businesses use a single-entry system. A checkbook constitutes a sufficient accounting system for many business owners. Deposits represent revenues, and payments constitute expenses. Many excellent automated accounting systems do not require data entry through a debit/credit recording scheme. QuickBooks is a good example of this type of system. Data are entered into the QuickBooks software program through a user-friendly computer interface that does not require knowledge of debit/credit terminology. Even so, the QuickBooks program produces traditional financial reports such as an income statement, balance sheet, and statement of cash flows. How is this possible? Before you become too ingrained in the debit/credit system, recall that throughout the first three chapters of this text, we maintained accounting records without using debits and credits. Financial reports can be produced in many ways without using a double-entry system. Having recognized this point, we also note the fact that the vast majority of medium- to large-size companies use the double-entry system. Indeed, debit/credit terminology is a part of common culture. Most people have an understanding of what is happening when a business tells them that their account is being debited or credited. Accordingly, it is important for you to embrace the double-entry system as well as other financial reporting systems.

account a name and a number. A list of all ledger accounts and their account numbers is called the **chart of accounts**.

The General Journal

It is impractical for most businesses to enter transaction data directly into ledger accounts. Imagine the number of entries involved in a single day's cash transactions for a grocery store. To simplify recordkeeping, a salesclerk may record data on a cash register tape. The tape is a **source document** that the accountant uses to enter the transaction data into the accounting system. Other source documents include invoices, time cards, check stubs, and deposit tickets.

LO7 Record transactions using the general journal format.

1st step: journal

To further simplify the recording process, accountants initially record data from source documents into a **journal.** In other words, *transactions are recorded in journals before they are entered into the ledger accounts.* Journals are therefore called **books of original entry.** A company may use **special journals** to record specific types of repetitive transactions. For example, a company may use a special journal to record cash receipts, another to record cash payments, a third to record purchases on account, and yet another to record sales on account. Transactions that don't fit into any of the special journals are recorded in the **general journal.** Although special journals can be helpful, their use is not required. A business can choose to record all transactions in its general journal. For simplicity, this text uses only the general journal format.

At a minimum, the general journal shows the dates, the account titles, and the amounts of each transaction. The date is recorded in the first column, followed by the title of the account to be debited. The title of the account to be credited is indented and written on the line directly below the account to be debited. The dollar amount of the transaction is recorded in the Debit and Credit columns. For example, providing services for $1,000 cash on August 1 would be recorded in general journal format as follows:

Date	Account Title	Debit	Credit
Aug. 1	Cash	1,000	
	Service Revenue		1,000

Exhibit 4–3 shows the general journal entries for all the Collins Consultants' transactions discussed thus far. After transactions have been recorded in a journal, the dollar amounts of the debits and credits are copied into the ledger accounts. The process of copying information from journals to ledgers is called **posting.**

Exhibit 4–3 *General Journal*

Date		Account Titles	Debit	Credit
Jan.	1	Cash	15,000	
		Common Stock		15,000
Feb.	1	Cash	10,000	
		Notes Payable		10,000
	17	Supplies	850	
		Accounts Payable		850
	28	Cash	5,000	
		Unearned Revenue		5,000
Mar.	1	Cash	18,000	
		Unearned Revenue		18,000
April	10	Accounts Receivable	2,000	
		Consulting Revenue		2,000
	29	Cash	8,400	
		Consulting Revenue		8,400
May	1	Notes Receivable	6,000	
		Cash		6,000
June	30	Office Equipment	42,000	
		Cash		42,000
July	31	Prepaid Rent	3,600	
		Cash		3,600
Aug.	8	Cash	1,200	
		Accounts Receivable		1,200
Sept.	4	Salaries Expense	2,400	
		Cash		2,400
	20	Dividends	1,500	
		Cash		1,500
Oct.	10	Accounts Payable	850	
		Cash		850
Nov.	15	Unearned Revenue	5,000	
		Consulting Revenue		5,000
Dec.	18	Advertising Expense	900	
		Accounts Payable		900
		Adjusting Entries		
Dec.	31	Interest Receivable	360	
		Interest Revenue		360
	31	Interest Expense	1,100	
		Interest Payable		1,100
	31	Salaries Expense	800	
		Salaries Payable		800
	31	Depreciation Expense	4,000	
		Accumulated Depreciation		4,000
	31	Rent Expense	1,500	
		Prepaid Rent		1,500
	31	Supplies Expense	725	
		Supplies		725
	31	Unearned Revenue	15,000	
		Consulting Revenue		15,000

Most companies today use computer technology to record transactions and prepare financial statements. Computers can record and post data pertaining to vast numbers of transactions with incredible speed and unparalleled accuracy. Both manual and computerized accounting systems, however, use the same underlying design. Analyzing a manual accounting system is a useful way to gain insight into how computer-based systems work.

Financial Statements

The general ledger provides the information needed to prepare the financial statements for Collins Consultants. The income statement, statement of changes in stockholders' equity, balance sheet, and statement of cash flows are shown in Exhibits 4–4, 4–5, 4–6, and 4–7.

Exhibit 4–4

COLLINS CONSULTANTS
Income Statement
For the Year Ended December 31, 2003

Revenue		
Consulting Revenue	$30,400	
Interest Revenue	360	
Total Revenue		$30,760
Less Expenses		
Salaries Expense	3,200	
Advertising Expense	900	
Interest Expense	1,100	
Depreciation Expense	4,000	
Rent Expense	1,500	
Supplies Expense	725	
Total Expenses		(11,425)
Net Income		$19,335

Exhibit 4–5

COLLINS CONSULTANTS
Statement of Changes in Stockholders' Equity
For the Year Ended December 31, 2003

Beginning Common Stock	$ 0	
Plus: Stock Issued	15,000	
Ending Common Stock		$15,000
Beginning Retained Earnings	0	
Plus: Net Income	19,335	
Less: Dividends	(1,500)	
Ending Retained Earnings		17,835
Total Stockholders' Equity		$32,835

Exhibit 4–6

COLLINS CONSULTANTS
Balance Sheet
As of December 31, 2003

Assets		
Cash		$ 1,250
Accounts Receivable		800
Supplies		125
Prepaid Rent		2,100
Notes Receivable		6,000
Interest Receivable		360
Office Equipment	$42,000	
Less: Accumulated Depreciation	(4,000)	38,000
Total Assets		$48,635
Liabilities		
Accounts Payable	$ 900	
Unearned Revenue	3,000	
Notes Payable	10,000	
Interest Payable	1,100	
Salaries Payable	800	
Total Liabilities		$15,800
Stockholders' Equity		
Common Stock	15,000	
Retained Earnings	17,835	
Total Stockholders' Equity		32,835
Total Liabilities and Stockholders' Equity		$48,635

Exhibit 4–7

COLLINS CONSULTANTS
Statement of Cash Flows
For the Year Ended December 31, 2003

Cash Flow from Operating Activities		
Inflow from Customers*	$32,600	
Outflow for Rent	(3,600)	
Outflow for Salaries	(2,400)	
Outflow for Supplies	(850)	
Net Cash Inflow from Operating Activities		$25,750
Cash Flow from Investing Activities		
Outflow for Loan	(6,000)	
Outflow to Purchase Equipment	(42,000)	
Net Cash Outflow for Investing Activities		(48,000)
Cash Flow from Financing Activities		
Inflow from Issue of Stock	15,000	
Inflow from Borrowing	10,000	
Outflow for Dividends	(1,500)	
Net Cash Inflow from Financing Activities		23,500
Net Change in Cash		1,250
Plus: Beginning Cash Balance		0
Ending Cash Balance		$ 1,250

*The sum of cash inflows from Events 4, 5, 7, and 11.

Closing Entries

LO5 State the need for and record closing entries.

Exhibit 4–8 shows the **closing entries** for Collins Consultants. These entries move all 2003 data from the Revenue, Expense, and Dividend (temporary) accounts into the Retained Earnings account. For example, the first entry moves the balance in the Consulting Revenue account to the Retained Earnings account. Recall that the Consulting Revenue account has a $30,400 credit balance before it is closed. Debiting the account by that amount brings its after-closing balance to zero. The corresponding $30,400 credit to Retained Earnings increases the balance in that account. Similarly, the second entry (debiting the Interest Revenue account and crediting the Retained Earnings account for $360) moves the balance from the Interest Revenue

Exhibit 4–8 *Closing Entries*

Date		Account Title	Debit	Credit
Dec.	31	Consulting Revenue	30,400	
		Retained Earnings		30,400
	31	Interest Revenue	360	
		Retained Earnings		360
	31	Retained Earnings	3,200	
		Salaries Expense		3,200
	31	Retained Earnings	900	
		Advertising Expense		900
	31	Retained Earnings	1,100	
		Interest Expense		1,100
	31	Retained Earnings	4,000	
		Depreciation Expense		4,000
	31	Retained Earnings	1,500	
		Rent Expense		1,500
	31	Retained Earnings	725	
		Supplies Expense		725
	31	Retained Earnings	1,500	
		Dividends		1,500

account to the Retained Earnings account. The third entry moves the balance in the Salaries Expense account to the Retained Earnings account. Since the Salaries Expense account has a before-closing debit balance, crediting the account for $3,200 leaves it with an after-closing balance of zero. The corresponding $3,200 debit to the Retained Earnings account reduces the balance in that account. The remaining entries close the other expense or dividend accounts by crediting them and debiting the Retained Earnings account.

Notice that the closing entries can be made in a more efficient manner. For example, the two revenue accounts can be closed simultaneously in the following compound journal entry.

Date	Account Title	Debit	Credit
Dec. 31	Consulting Revenue	30,400	
	Interest Revenue	360	
	Retained Earnings		30,760

The expense and dividend accounts could also be closed in a compound journal entry. Other even more efficient recording schemes are possible. For example, revenue, expense, and dividend accounts could all be closed in a single compound journal entry. The exact form of the closing entries is not important. What is important is that the entries move the balances from the revenue, expense, and dividend accounts to the Retained Earnings account. After the closing entries are posted to the ledger accounts, the revenue, expense, and dividend accounts have zero balances. The temporary accounts are then ready to capture revenue, expense, and dividend data for the 2004 fiscal year. For further discussion of the closing process refer back to page 61.

If all companies closed their books on December 31 each year, accountants, printers, lawyers, government agencies, and others would be overburdened by the effort to produce the accounting reports of all companies at the same time. Furthermore, there would be little work to do at other times of the year. In an effort to balance the workload, many companies choose to close their books at the end of the natural business year. A natural business year ends when the operating activities are at their lowest point. For many companies the lowest point in the operating cycle occurs on a date other than December 31. A recent survey found that almost one-half of the companies sampled closed their books in months other than December (see Exhibit 4–9).

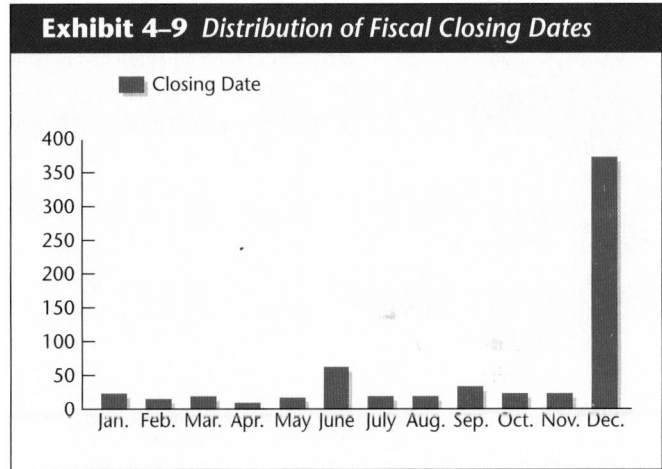

Exhibit 4–9 *Distribution of Fiscal Closing Dates*

Data Source: AICPA Accounting Trends and Techniques

Trial Balance

Companies frequently prepare a **trial balance** to verify the equality of debits and credits in the ledger. A trial balance is a list of all ledger accounts and their balances. The debit and credit balances are listed in separate columns. Each column is totaled, and the two totals are compared for equality. Exhibit 4–10 displays the trial balance for Collins Consultants after the closing entries have been posted to the ledger.

If the debit total does not equal the credit total, the accountant knows to search for an error. However, as previously indicated, equal debit and credit totals does not assure accuracy. For example, the trial balance would not

Exhibit 4–10 *Trial Balance*

Account Titles	Debit	Credit
Cash	$ 1,250	
Accounts Receivable	800	
Supplies	125	
Prepaid Rent	2,100	
Notes Receivable	6,000	
Interest Receivable	360	
Office Equipment	42,000	
Accumulated Depreciation		$4,000
Accounts Payable		900
Unearned Revenue		3,000
Notes Payable		10,000
Interest Payable		1,100
Salaries Payable		800
Common Stock		15,000
Retained Earnings		17,835
Totals	$52,635	$52,635

ANSWERS TO THE *curious* ACCOUNTANT

Part 1

The process of closing the books and going through a year-end audit is time consuming for a business. Also, it is time spent that does not produce revenue. Thus, companies whose business is highly seasonal often choose "slow" periods to end their fiscal year. The Gap does heavy business during the Christmas season, so it might find December 31 an inconvenient time to close its books. Toward the end of January, business activity is slow, and

inventory levels are at their low points. This is a good time to count the inventory and to assess the financial condition of the company. For these reasons, The Gap has chosen to close its books to end its fiscal year around the end of January.

Now that you know why a business like The Gap might choose to end its fiscal year at the end of January, can you think of a reason why Levi Strauss closes its books at the end of November? (See page 175.)

LO6 Prepare and interpret a trial balance.

disclose errors like the following: failure to record transactions; misclassifications, such as debiting the wrong account; or incorrectly recording the amount of a transaction, such as recording a $200 transaction as $2,000. Equal debits and credits in a trial balance should be viewed as evidence rather than proof of accuracy.

How often should a trial balance be prepared? A company can test the equality of debits and credits as often as desired. Some companies prepare a trial balance daily; others may prepare one monthly, quarterly, or annually, depending on the needs of management.

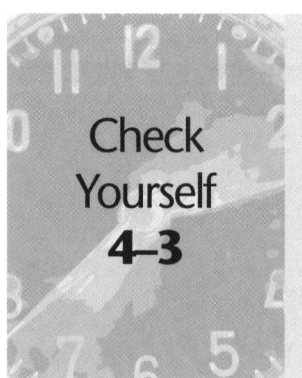

Check Yourself 4–3

Describe an error that would not cause a trial balance to be out of balance.

Answer Many potential errors would not cause a trial balance to be out of balance, such as debiting or crediting the wrong account. For example, if revenue earned on account were recorded with a debit to Cash instead of Accounts Receivable, total assets would be correct and the totals in the trial balance would equal each other even though the balances in the Cash and Accounts Receivable accounts would be incorrect. Recording the same incorrect amount in both the debit and credit part of an entry also would not cause a trial balance to be out of balance. For example, if $20 of revenue earned on account were recorded as a $200 debit to Accounts Receivable and a $200 credit to Consulting Revenue, the totals in the trial balance would equal each other although Accounts Receivable and Consulting Revenue amounts would be incorrect.

THE FINANCIAL ANALYST

LO8 Describe the components of an annual report, including the management, discussion, and analysis section and the footnotes to financial statements.

Companies communicate information to analysts and other users through a document called the *annual report*. These reports are usually printed in color on high quality paper and contain lots of photographs. However, in an effort to reduce cost, some companies issue their annual reports in black and white on low grade paper or in electronic form. A company's annual report contains much more than the financial statements. Annual reports often have 40 or more pages. The financial statements require only four to six pages. What is printed on all those other pages? In general, the annual report of a large company has four major sections: (1) financial statements, (2) footnotes to the financial statements, (3) management's discussion and analysis, and (4) auditors' report. The footnotes and management's discussion and analysis make up the bulk of the report.

Footnotes to the Financial Statements

Accountants frequently have to make estimates when preparing financial statements. Also, GAAP may offer alternative ways of reporting certain transactions. **Footnotes to the financial statements** explain some of the estimates that were made as well as which reporting

Part 2

Levi Strauss does not sell its clothes directly to consumers; rather, it sells most of its clothes through retailers. Levi Strauss must deliver its jeans to retailers before Thanksgiving if the stores are going to have goods available to sell during the

Christmas season. So, Levi's "Christmas season" is probably over by early November, making the end of November a good time to end its fiscal year. Some clothing manufacturers, such as Tommy Hilfiger and Polo Ralph Lauren, close their books around the end of March. By then, goods for both the Christmas and spring seasons have been shipped to retailers.

options were used. Reading the footnotes is critical to understanding the financial statements. The financial statements often include a caveat such as "the accompanying footnotes are an integral part of these financial statements."

Management's Discussion and Analysis

Management's discussion and analysis (MD&A) is usually located at the beginning of the annual report. MD&A is the section of the annual report in which management explains the company's past performance and future plans. For example, MD&A typically compares current year earnings with those of past periods and explains the reasons for significant changes. If the company is planning significant acquisitions of assets or other businesses, this information is usually included in MD&A. Likewise, any plans to discontinue part of the existing business are outlined in MD&A.

Role of the Independent Auditor Revisited

The auditors' role is introduced in Chapter 2. The auditors' responsibilities differ for various parts of the annual report. The auditors' primary responsibility is to express an opinion regarding whether the financial statements conform to GAAP. Since the footnotes are a part of the financial statements, the auditors' opinion extends to the footnotes as well as the statements.

Auditors have less responsibility for information reported in MD&A. Auditors *review* the MD&A section to be sure it does not contain comments that conflict with information in the financial statements. For example, if the current year's net income is down from last year's, management cannot say that "earnings continue to grow." However, MD&A can contain expressions of opinion. If current earnings are down relative to last year's, management could say, "We *believe* the decline to be temporary and expect substantial growth in the coming year." Auditors are not responsible for validating such opinions.

The Securities and Exchange Commission

LO9 Describe the role of the Securities and Exchange Commission in financial reporting.

The annual reports of public companies often differ from those of private companies because public companies are registered with the **Securities and Exchange Commission (SEC).** Public companies, sometimes called SEC companies, have to follow the reporting rules of the SEC as well as GAAP. SEC rules require some additional disclosures not required by GAAP. For example, an MD&A section is required by the SEC, but not by GAAP. As a result, annual reports of non-SEC companies usually do not include MD&A.

The SEC is a government agency authorized to establish and enforce the accounting rules for public companies. Although the SEC can overrule GAAP, it has very seldom done so. Recall that GAAP is established by the Financial Accounting Standards Board, a private professional accounting organization. While SEC rules seldom conflict with GAAP, they frequently require additional disclosures. All companies whose stock trades on public stock exchanges, and some whose do not, are required to register with the SEC. The SEC has no jurisdiction over non-SEC companies.

focus on INTERNATIONAL ISSUES

Is There a Global GAAP Leader?

Chapter 3 discussed some reasons that there is no single set of global GAAP. Nevertheless, one may wonder if there are certain

countries that tend to take the lead in the establishment of GAAP. Although no single country has led in the overall development of accounting rule making, a few countries have led in some specific areas of accounting development.

For example, the double-entry bookkeeping system explained in this chapter began in Italy. This system was first formally publicized in the late 1400s by an Italian monk, Luca Pacioli. Pacioli did not actually develop the double-entry system; he published an explanation of the system as he had observed it in use by Italian merchants of his day. The use of the terms *debit* and *credit* results from the Italian origins of the bookkeeping system. Today, this system is used throughout the world.

As another example, consider that the public accounting profession as we know it in the United States and many other countries originated in the United Kingdom. The idea of an independent auditing professional (the CPA in the United States) came to the United States from the United Kingdom around the turn of the twentieth century. Not all countries have the strong nongovernment accounting profession that exists in the United Kingdom and United States, but those that do can trace their roots back to the United Kingdom.

Imagine you were required to e-mail your family every time something unusual happened in your college studies. Even worse, what if you had to immediately inform your family if there were even a reasonable possibility something negative might happen in the future. For example, if you did not study for an upcoming accounting exam, suppose you had to tell your family before you took the test that your future exam grade might be low because you did not study for it. Essentially, public companies are required to provide just that type of disclosure by filing a Form 8-K with the SEC whenever any significant event occurs.

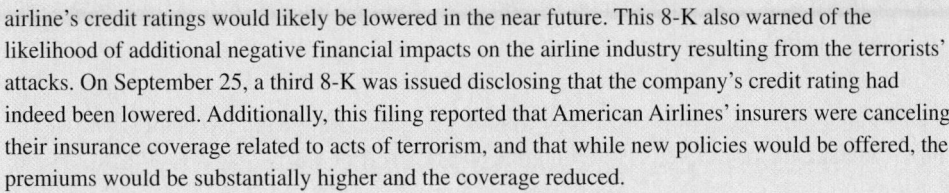

By the middle of the day on September 11, 2001, most of the TVs in the world were probably tuned to the coverage about four airplanes being hijacked and three of them being crashed into the World Trade Center buildings and the Pentagon. Nevertheless, American Airlines, owner of two of the planes, filed an 8-K with the SEC on September 11, acknowledging the loss of its two aircraft and the passengers on board. On September 19, it filed a second 8-K explaining that two credit rating services, Standard & Poor's and Moody's, had warned that the airline's credit ratings would likely be lowered in the near future. This 8-K also warned of the likelihood of additional negative financial impacts on the airline industry resulting from the terrorists' attacks. On September 25, a third 8-K was issued disclosing that the company's credit rating had indeed been lowered. Additionally, this filing reported that American Airlines' insurers were canceling their insurance coverage related to acts of terrorism, and that while new policies would be offered, the premiums would be substantially higher and the coverage reduced.

For more information about these matters, use EDGAR to download the 8-K reports that were filed with the SEC. Appendix A provides instructions for using EDGAR.

SEC companies must file specific information directly with the SEC annually, quarterly, and in-between if required. The most common reports are filed on Form 10-K (annually) and Form 10-Q (quarterly). The *10-Q*s are less detailed than the 10-Ks. While there is significant overlap between the 10Ks (SEC report) and the annual reports that companies issue directly to the public, the 10-Ks usually contain more information but fewer pictures. Most of the reports filed with the SEC are available electronically through the SEC's EDGAR database. EDGAR is an acronym for Electronic Data Gathering, Analysis, and Retrieval system, and it is accessible through the World Wide Web on the Internet. Appendix A provides instructions for using EDGAR.

The SEC regulates audit standards as well as financial reporting. Prior to passage of the Sarbanes-Oxley Act in July 2002, the SEC left much of the regulation and oversight of independent auditors to the American Institute of Certified Public Accountants, a private professional organization. However, a key provision of Sarbanes-Oxley establishes the Public Company Accounting Oversight Board (PCAOB). This board assumes the primary responsibility for establishing and enforcing auditing standards for CPAs who audit SEC companies. The board has five financially astute members, three of whom cannot be CPAs.

This chapter introduced the *double-entry accounting system*. This system was first documented in the 1400s, and is used by most companies today. Key components of the double-entry system are summarized below.

a look back

1. Business events can be classified concisely using debit/credit terminology. *Debits* are used to record increases in asset accounts and decreases in liability and stockholders' equity accounts. *Credits* are used to record decreases in asset accounts and increases in liability and stockholders' equity accounts.

2. *T-accounts* are frequently used to analyze and communicate account activity. The account title is placed at the top of the horizontal bar of the T, and increases and decreases are

placed on either side of the vertical bar. In a T-account, debits are recorded on the left side and credits are recorded on the right side.

3. Accountants initially record transaction data in journals. The *general journal* format is used not only for data entry but also as a shorthand communication tool. Each journal entry includes at least one debit and one credit. An entry is recorded using at least two lines, with the debit recorded on the top line and the credit on the bottom line. The credit is indented to distinguish it from the debit. The general journal format is illustrated here:

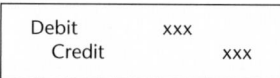

4. Information is posted (copied) from the journals to *ledger* accounts. The ledger accounts provide the information used to prepare the financial statements.

5. *Trial balances* are used to check the mathematical accuracy of the recording process. Ledger accounts with their associated debit and credit balances are listed in the trial balance. The debit and credit amounts are totaled and compared. An equal amount of debits and credits provides evidence that transactions have been recorded correctly, although errors may still exist. If the debits and credits are *not* equal, it is proof that errors exist.

The double-entry system is just a way to organize accounting data. No matter how we organize the data, the objective is to summarize and report it in a way that is useful for making decisions.

a look forward

Chapters 1 through 4 focused on businesses that generate revenue by providing services to their customers. Examples of these types of businesses include consulting, real estate sales, medical services, and legal services. The next chapter introduces accounting practices for businesses that generate revenue by selling goods. Examples of these companies include **Wal-Mart**, **Circuit City**, **Office Depot**, and **Lowes**.

SELF-STUDY REVIEW PROBLEM

The following events apply to the first year of operations for Mestro Financial Services Company:

1. Acquired $28,000 cash by issuing common stock on January 1, 2003.
2. Purchased $1,100 of supplies on account.
3. Paid $12,000 cash in advance for a one-year lease on office space.
4. Earned $23,000 of consulting revenue on account.
5. Incurred $16,000 of general operating expenses on account.
6. Collected $20,000 cash from receivables.
7. Paid $13,000 cash on accounts payable.
8. Paid a $1,000 cash dividend to the stockholders.

Information for Adjusting Entries

9. There was $200 of supplies on hand at the end of the accounting period.
10. The one-year lease on the office space was effective beginning on October 1, 2003.
11. There was $1,200 of accrued salaries at the end of 2003.

Required

a. Record the preceding events in ledger T-accounts.
b. Prepare a trial balance.
c. Prepare an income statement, statement of changes in stockholders' equity, balance sheet, and statement of cash flows.
d. Prepare the appropriate closing entries in general journal format.

Solution to Requirement a

MESTRO FINANCIAL SERVICES COMPANY
T-Accounts, 2003

Assets				=	Liabilities			+	Equity	

Cash

1.	28,000	3.	12,000
6.	20,000	7.	13,000
		8.	1,000
Bal.	22,000		

Accounts Receivable

4.	23,000	6.	20,000
Bal.	3,000		

Supplies

2.	1,100	9.	900
Bal.	200		

Prepaid Rent

3.	12,000	10.	3,000
Bal.	9,000		

Accounts Payable

7.	13,000	2.	1,100
		5.	16,000
		Bal.	4,100

Salaries Payable

		11.	1,200
		Bal.	1,200

Common Stock

		1.	28,000
		Bal.	28,000

Dividends

8.	1,000	

Consulting Revenue

		4.	23,000

General Operating Expenses

5.	16,000	

Salaries Expense

11.	1,200	

Supplies Expense

9.	900	

Rent Expense

10.	3,000	

Solution to Requirement b

MESTRO FINANCIAL SERVICES COMPANY
Trial Balance
December 31, 2003

Account Titles	Debit	Credit
Cash	$22,000	
Accounts Receivable	3,000	
Supplies	200	
Prepaid Rent	9,000	
Accounts Payable		$ 4,100
Salaries Payable		1,200
Common Stock		28,000
Dividends	1,000	
Consulting Revenue		23,000
General Operating Expenses	16,000	
Salaries Expense	1,200	
Supplies Expense	900	
Rent Expense	3,000	
Totals	$56,300	$56,300

Solution to Requirement c

MESTRO FINANCIAL SERVICES COMPANY
Financial Statements
For 2003

Income Statement

Consulting Revenue		$23,000
Expenses		
General Operating Expenses	$16,000	
Salaries Expense	1,200	
Supplies Expense	900	
Rent Expense	3,000	
Total Expenses		(21,100)
Net Income		$ 1,900

Statement of Changes in Stockholders' Equity		
Beginning Common Stock	$ 0	
Plus: Common Stock Issued	28,000	
Ending Common Stock		$28,000
Beginning Retained Earnings	0	
Plus: Net Income	1,900	
Less: Dividends	(1,000)	
Ending Retained Earnings		900
Total Stockholders' Equity		$28,900

Balance Sheet		
Assets		
Cash	$22,000	
Accounts Receivable	3,000	
Supplies	200	
Prepaid Rent	9,000	
Total Assets		$34,200
Liabilities		
Accounts Payable	$4,100	
Salaries Payable	1,200	
Total Liabilities		$ 5,300
Stockholders' Equity		
Common Stock	28,000	
Retained Earnings	900	
Total Stockholders' Equity		28,900
Total Liabilities and Stockholders' Equity		$34,200

Statement of Cash Flows		
Cash Flows from Operating Activities		
Inflow from Customers	$20,000	
Outflow for Expenses	(25,000)	
Net Cash Flow from Operating Activities		$(5,000)
Cash Flows from Investing Activities		0
Cash Flows from Financing Activities		
Inflow from Issue of Common Stock	28,000	
Outflow for Dividends	(1,000)	
Net Cash Flow from Financing Activities		27,000
Net Change in Cash		22,000
Plus: Beginning Cash Balance		0
Ending Cash Balance		$22,000

Solution to Requirement d

Date	Account Titles	Debit	Credit
	Closing Entries		
Dec. 31	Consulting Revenue	23,000	
	Retained Earnings		23,000
Dec. 31	Retained Earnings	21,100	
	General Operating Expenses		16,000
	Salaries Expense		1,200
	Supplies Expense		900
	Rent Expense		3,000
Dec. 31	Retained Earnings	1,000	
	Dividends		1,000

Account balance *156*
Books of original entry *169*
Chart of accounts *169*
Closing entries *172*
Contra account *165*
Credit *156*

Debit *156*
Double-entry accounting *156*
Fiscal year *155*
Footnotes to the financial
    statements *174*
General journal *169*

Journal *169*
Ledger *168*
Management's Discussion and
    Analysis (MD&A) *175*
Posting *170*

Securities and Exchange
    Commission (SEC) *176*
Source document *169*
Special journals *169*
T-account *156*
Trial balance *173*

QUESTIONS

1. What are the two fundamental equality requirements of the double-entry accounting system?
2. Define *debit* and *credit*. How are assets, liabilities, common stock, retained earnings, revenues, expenses, and dividends affected (increased or decreased) by debits and by credits?
3. How is the balance of an account determined?
4. What are the three primary sources of business assets?
5. What are the three primary ways a business may use assets?
6. Why is an adjusting entry necessary to record depreciation expense? What accounts are affected? How are the account balances affected?
7. How does a debit to an expense account ultimately affect retained earnings? Stockholders' equity?
8. What accounts normally have debit balances? What accounts normally have credit balances?
9. What is the primary source of information for preparing the financial statements?
10. What is the purpose of a journal?
11. What is the difference between the *general journal* and special journals?
12. What is a ledger? What is its function in the accounting system?
13. What is the purpose of closing entries?
14. At a minimum, what information is recorded in the general journal?
15. What is the purpose of a trial balance?
16. When should a trial balance be prepared?
17. What does the term *posting* mean?
18. Where did the terms *debit* and *credit* originate?
19. What country is responsible for the accounting profession's having "independent accounting professionals"?
20. What type of information is found in the footnotes to the financial statements?
21. What type of information is found in the MD&A section of the annual report?
22. What is the Securities and Exchange Commission? What are its responsibilities concerning a company's financial statements? What types of companies are under the SEC's jurisdiction?

EXERCISES—SERIES A

All Exercises in Series A are available with McGraw-Hill's Homework Manager

EXERCISE 4–1A *Matching Debit and Credit Terminology with Accounts*   **L.O. 2**

Required
Complete the following table by indicating whether a debit or credit is used to increase or decrease the balance of the following accounts. The appropriate debit/credit terminology has been identified for the first account as an example.

Account Titles	Used to Increase This Account	Used to Decrease This Account
Accounts Receivable	Debit	Credit
Accounts Payable		
Common Stock		
Land		
Interest Expense		
Accumulated Depreciation		
Unearned Revenue		
Service Revenue		
Retained Earnings		
Insurance Expense		

L.O. 1, 2   EXERCISE 4–2A *Debit/Credit Rules*

Matt, Allison, and Sarah, three accounting students, were discussing the rules of debits and credits. Matt says that debits increase account balances and credits decrease account balances. Allison says that Matt is wrong, that credits increase account balances and debits decrease account balances. Sarah interrupts and declares that they are both correct.

Required

Explain what Sarah meant and give examples of transactions where debits increase account balances, credits decrease account balances, credits increase account balances, and debits decrease account balances.

L.O. 2   EXERCISE 4–3A *Matching Debit and Credit Terminology with Account Titles*

Required

Indicate whether each of the following accounts normally has a debit balance or a credit balance.

a. Unearned Revenue   **f.** Cash
b. Service Revenue   **g.** Interest Expense
c. Dividends   **h.** Depreciation Expense
d. Land   **i.** Accumulated Depreciation
e. Accounts Receivable   **j.** Accounts Payable

L.O. 1, 2   EXERCISE 4–4A *Identifying Increases and Decreases in T-Accounts*

Required

For each of the following T-accounts, indicate the side of the account that should be used to record an increase or decrease in the accounting element.

Assets		=	Liabilities		+	Stockholders' Equity	
Debit	Credit		Debit	Credit		Debit	Credit

Contra Assets			Revenue	
Debit	Credit		Debit	Credit

Expense	
Debit	Credit

L.O. 1, 2   EXERCISE 4–5A *Applying Debit/Credit Terminology to Accounting Events*

Required

In parallel columns, list the accounts that would be debited and credited for each of the following unrelated transactions:

a. Provided services for cash.
b. Paid cash for salaries expense.
c. Borrowed cash from a local bank.
d. Acquired cash from the issue of common stock.
e. Provided services on account.
f. Purchased supplies for cash.
g. Purchased equipment for cash.
h. Recorded accrued salaries at the end of the accounting period.

EXERCISE 4–6A *T-Accounts and the Accounting Equation*   **L.O. 2, 3**

Required
Record each of the following Cummings Co. events in T-accounts and then explain how the event affects the accounting equation.

a. Received $20,000 cash by issuing common stock.
b. Purchased supplies for $900 cash.
c. Performed services on account for $7,000.
d. Purchased land for $10,000, paying $2,000 cash and issuing a note payable for the balance.

EXERCISE 4–7A *Recording Transactions in T-Accounts*   **L.O. 3**

The following events apply to Pearson Delivery Co. for 2004, its first year of operation.

1. Received cash of $50,000 from the issue of common stock.
2. Purchased a delivery van for $28,000 cash. The delivery van has a salvage value of $7,000 and a three-year useful life.
3. Performed $90,000 worth of services on account.
4. Paid $64,000 cash for salaries expense.
5. Purchased supplies for $12,000 on account.
6. Collected $78,000 of accounts receivable.
7. Paid $8,500 of the accounts payable.
8. Paid a $5,000 dividend to the stockholders.
9. Recorded depreciation expense for the year on the delivery van.
10. Had $1,500 of supplies on hand at the end of the period.

Required
a. Record these events in the appropriate T-accounts and determine the ending balance in each account.
b. Determine the amount of total assets at the end of 2004.
c. Determine the amount of net income for 2004.

EXERCISE 4–8A *Debit/Credit Terminology*   **L.O. 2**

Required
For each of the following independent events, identify the account that would be debited and the account that would be credited. The accounts for the first event are identified as an example.

Event	Account Debited	Account Credited
a	Cash	Common Stock

a. Received cash by issuing common stock.
b. Received cash for services to be performed in the future.
c. Provided services on account.
d. Paid accounts payable.
e. Purchased office equipment with cash.
f. Recognized accrued interest revenue.
g. Paid cash for operating expenses.
h. Recognized depreciation expense.
i. Paid salaries payable.
j. Purchased supplies on account.
k. Paid cash dividends to the stockholders.
l. Recognized revenue for services completed; collected the cash in Event *b*.
m. Received cash in payment of accounts receivable.
n. Recognized accrued interest expense.
o. Repaid principal balance on note payable.

EXERCISE 4–9A *Identifying Transaction Type, Its Effect on the Accounting Equation, and Whether the Effect Is Recorded with a Debit or Credit*   **L.O. 1, 2**

Required
Identify whether each of the following transactions is an asset source (AS), asset use (AU), asset exchange (AE), or claims exchange (CE). Also explain how each event affects the accounting equation by

placing a + for *increase,* − for *decrease,* and NA for *not affected* under each of the components of the accounting equation. Finally, indicate whether the effect requires a debit or credit entry. The first event is recorded as an example.

						Stockholders' Equity		
Event	Type of Event	Assets	=	Liabilities	+	Common Stock	+	Retained Earnings
a	AS	+ Debit		NA		NA		+ Credit

a. Provided services on account.
b. Received cash in payment of accounts receivable.
c. Borrowed cash by issuing a note.
d. Purchased land by issuing a note.
e. Paid interest payable.
f. Recognized accrued interest revenue.
g. Recognized revenue for services completed; cash collected previously.
h. Paid a cash dividend to the stockholders.
i. Recognized depreciation expense on the equipment.
j. Repaid principal balance on note payable.
k. Paid cash in advance for one-year's rent.
l. Received cash for services to be performed in the future.
m. Recognized accrued interest expense.
n. Incurred other operating expense on account.
o. Paid salaries payable.

L.O. 7   **EXERCISE 4–10A** *Recording Events in the General Journal*

Required
Record each of the following transactions in general journal form.

a. Received $8,000 cash for services to be performed at a later date.
b. Purchased supplies for $1,200 cash.
c. Performed $25,000 worth of services on account.
d. Purchased equipment that cost $42,000 by paying $8,000 cash and issuing a $34,000 note for the balance.
e. Charged $1,200 on account for repairs expense.
f. Sold land that cost $15,000 for $18,000.
g. Collected $19,000 cash on accounts receivable.
h. Paid $900 on accounts payable.
i. Paid $4,800 cash in advance for an insurance policy on the equipment.
j. Recorded accrued interest expense of $1,400.
k. Recorded $5,000 depreciation expense on the equipment.
l. Recorded the adjusting entry to recognize $3,600 of insurance expense.

L.O. 6   **EXERCISE 4–11A** *Preparing a Trial Balance*

Required
On December 31, 2004, Chang Company had the following account balances in its general ledger. Use this information to prepare a trial balance.

Common Stock	$25,000
Salaries Expense	16,000
Office Supplies	1,800
Advertising Expense	2,500
Retained Earnings, 1/1/2004	46,200
Unearned Revenue	18,000
Office Equipment	42,000
Accounts Receivable	6,500
	continued

Accumulated Depreciation	16,000
Cash	60,000
Service Revenue	76,000
Dividends	5,000
Depreciation Expense	6,000
Prepaid Insurance	6,400
Land	22,000
Rent Expense	15,000
Accounts Payable	2,000

EXERCISE 4–12A *Preparing Closing Entries*   L.O. 5, 7

The following financial information was taken from the books of Ritz Salon.

Account Balances as of December 31, 2008	
Accounts Receivable	$28,000
Accounts Payable	7,500
Advertising Expense	2,500
Accumulated Depreciation	12,500
Cash	18,300
Certificate of Deposit	22,000
Common Stock	20,000
Depreciation Expense	8,400
Dividends	5,000
Equipment	30,000
Interest Receivable	400
Interest Revenue	2,800
Notes Payable	10,000
Prepaid Rent	3,200
Rent Expense	7,800
Retained Earnings 1/1/2008	19,400
Salaries Expense	32,000
Salaries Payable	11,800
Service Revenue	76,500
Supplies	400
Supplies Expense	2,500

Required
a. Prepare the necessary closing entries at December 31, 2008, for Ritz Salon.
b. What is the balance in the Retained Earnings account after the closing entries are posted?

EXERCISE 4–13A *Recording Events in T-Accounts and Preparing a Trial Balance*   L.O. 3, 6

The following events apply to Complete Business Service in its first year of operations.

1. Received $30,000 cash from the issue of common stock.
2. Earned $25,000 of service revenue on account.
3. Incurred $10,000 of operating expenses on account.
4. Borrowed $20,000 from First Bank.
5. Paid $8,000 cash to purchase office equipment.
6. Collected $22,000 of cash from accounts receivable.
7. Received a $6,000 cash advance for services to be provided in the future.
8. Purchased $900 of supplies on account.
9. Made an $7,500 payment on accounts payable.
10. Paid a $5,000 cash dividend to the stockholders.
11. Recognized $500 of supplies expense.
12. Recognized $5,000 of revenue for services provided to the customer in Event 7.
13. Recorded accrued interest expense of $900.
14. Recognized $2,000 of depreciation expense.

Required
a. Record the events in T-accounts and determine the ending account balances.
b. Test the equality of the debit and credit balances of the T-accounts by preparing a trial balance.

L.O. 6   **EXERCISE 4–14A** *Determining the Effect of Errors on the Trial Balance*

Required

Explain how each of the following posting errors affects a trial balance. State whether the trial balance will be out of balance because of the posting error, and indicate which side of the trial balance will have a higher amount after each independent entry is posted. If the posting error does not affect the equality of debits and credits shown in the trial balance, state that the error will not cause an inequality and explain why.

a. A $1,000 credit to Notes Payable was not posted.
b. A $2,400 debit to Cash was posted as a $4,200 debit.
c. A $2,000 debit to Prepaid Rent was debited to Rent Expense.
d. The collection of $500 of accounts receivable was posted to Accounts Receivable twice.
e. A $2,000 credit to Accounts Payable was posted as a credit to Cash.

L.O. 3, 5, 7   **EXERCISE 4–15A** *Recording Events in the General Journal, Posting to T-Accounts, and Preparing Closing Entries*

At the beginning of 2005, Mitchell Cleaning Service had the following balances in its accounts:

Account	Balance
Cash	$30,000
Accounts Receivable	19,000
Accounts Payable	12,400
Common Stock	24,000
Retained Earnings	12,600

The following events apply to Mitchell for 2005.

1. Provided $65,000 of services on account.
2. Incurred $3,100 of operating expenses on account.
3. Collected $56,000 of accounts receivable.
4. Paid $36,000 cash for salaries expense.
5. Paid $15,000 cash as a partial payment on accounts payable.
6. Paid an $8,000 cash dividend to the stockholders.

Required

a. Record these events in a general journal.
b. Open T-accounts and post the beginning balances and the preceding transactions to the appropriate accounts. Determine the balance of each account.
c. Record the beginning balances and the events in a horizontal statements model such as the following one:

Assets		=	Liab.	+	Equity		Rev.	–	Exp.	=	Net Inc.	Cash Flow
	Accts.		Accts.		Common	Ret.						
Cash	+ Rec.	=	Pay.	+	Stock	+ Earn.						

d. Record the closing entries in the general journal and post them to the T-accounts. What is the amount of net income for the year?
e. What is the amount of *change* in retained earnings for the year? Is the change in retained earnings different from the amount of net income? If so, why?

L.O. 3, 5   **EXERCISE 4–16A** *Recording Receivables and Identifying Their Effect on Financial Statements*

Wong Company performed services on account for $60,000 in 2006, its first year of operations. Wong collected $48,000 cash from accounts receivable during 2006 and the remaining $12,000 in cash during 2007.

Required

a. Record the 2006 transactions in T-accounts.
b. Record the 2006 transactions in a horizontal statements model like the following one:

Assets	= Liab. +	Equity	Rev. − Exp. = Net Inc.	Cash Flow
Cash + Accts. Rec.	= NA +	Ret. Earn.		

c. Determine the amount of revenue Wong would report on the 2006 income statement.

d. Determine the amount of cash flow from operating activities Wong would report on the 2006 statement of cash flows.

e. Open a T-account for Retained Earnings, and close the 2006 Service Revenue account to the Retained Earnings account.

f. Record the 2007 cash collection in the appropriate T-accounts.

g. Record the 2007 transaction in a horizontal statements model like the one shown in Requirement *b*.

h. Assuming no other transactions occur in 2007, determine the amount of net income and the net cash flow from operating activities for 2007.

EXERCISE 4–17A *Recording Supplies and Identifying Their Effect on Financial Statements*   L.O. 3–6

Kim Perz started and operated a small family consulting firm in 2005. The firm was affected by two events: (1) Perz provided $18,000 of services on account, and (2) she purchased $5,000 of supplies on account. There were $900 of supplies on hand as of December 31, 2005.

Required

a. Open T-accounts and record the two transactions in the accounts.

b. Record the required year-end adjusting entry to reflect the use of supplies.

c. Record the above transactions in a horizontal statements model like the following one.

Assets		= Liab. +	Equity	Rev. − Exp. = Net Inc.	Cash Flow
Accts. Rec.	+ Supp.	= Accts. Pay. +	Ret. Earn.		

d. Explain why the amount of net income and the net cash flow from operating activities differ.

e. Record and post the required closing entries, and prepare an after-closing trial balance.

EXERCISE 4–18A *Recording Prepaids and Identifying Their Effect on Financial Statements*   L.O. 4, 7

California Mining began operations by issuing common stock for $100,000. The company paid $90,000 cash in advance for a one-year contract to lease machinery for the business. The lease agreement was signed on March 1, 2005, and was effective immediately. California Mining earned $115,000 of cash revenue in 2005.

Required

a. Record the March 1 cash payment in general journal format.

b. Record in general journal format the adjustment required as of December 31, 2005.

c. Record all 2005 events in a horizontal statements model like the following one:

Assets	= Liab. +	Equity	Rev. − Exp. = Net Inc.	Cash Flow
Cash + PrPd. Rent		Ret. Earn.		

d. What amount of net income would California Mining report on the 2005 income statement? What is the amount of net cash flow from operating activities for 2005?

e. Determine the amount of prepaid rent California Mining would report on the December 31, 2005, balance sheet.

EXERCISE 4–19A *Recording Accrued Salaries and Identifying Their Effect on Financial Statements*   L.O. 4, 7

On December 31, 2008, Red River Company had accrued salaries of $9,500.

Required

a. Record in general journal format the adjustment required as of December 31, 2008.

b. Determine the amount of net income Red River would report on the 2008 income statement, assuming that Red River earns $25,000 of cash revenue. What is the amount of net cash flow from operating activities for 2008?

c. What amount of Salaries Payable would Red River report on the December 31, 2008, balance sheet?

L.O. 3, 4   **EXERCISE 4–20A** *Recording Depreciation and Identifying Its Effect on Financial Statements*

On January 1, 2007, Lopez bought a computer system for $35,000 cash. The computer had a useful life of four years and a salvage value of $3,000.

Required

a. Record in T-accounts Lopez's purchase of the computer system.
b. Record in T-accounts the adjustment required on December 31, 2007.
c. Determine the book value of the computer Lopez would report on the December 31, 2007, balance sheet.
d. Determine the amount of net income Lopez would report on the 2007 income statement, assuming that Lopez earned $12,000 of cash revenue in 2007.
e. What is the amount of net cash flow from operating activities for 2007?
f. What amount of depreciation expense would Lopez report on the 2008 income statement?
g. Determine the book value of the computer Lopez would report on the December 31, 2008, balance sheet.

L.O. 3, 4   **EXERCISE 4–21A** *Recording a Note Payable and Identifying Its Effect on Financial Statements*

On May 1, 2003, Nail Company borrowed $60,000 from First Bank. The note had a 8 percent annual interest rate and a one-year term to maturity.

Required

a. Identify the transaction type (asset source, use, or exchange or claims exchange), and record in T-accounts the entry for the financing event on May 1, 2003.
b. Identify the transaction type, and record in T-accounts the adjustment as of December 31, 2003.
c. Determine the amount of net income on the 2003 income statement, assuming Nail Company earned $25,000 of cash revenue.
d. What is the amount of net cash flow from operating activities for 2003?
e. Determine the total liabilities on the December 31, 2003, balance sheet.
f. Record (1) the 2004 accrual of interest and (2) the cash payment of principal and interest on May 1, 2004.
g. Are the May 1, 2004, transactions asset source, asset use, asset exchange, or claims exchange transactions?

L.O. 3, 4   **EXERCISE 4–22A** *Recording Unearned Revenue and Identifying Its Effect on Financial Statements*

Zhen received a $60,000 cash advance on March 1, 2005, for legal services to be performed in the future. Services were to be provided for a one-year term beginning March 1, 2005.

Required

a. Record the March 1 cash receipt in T-accounts.
b. Record in T-accounts the adjustment required as of December 31, 2005.
c. Record the preceding transaction and related adjustment in a horizontal statements model like the following one:

Assets	=	Liab.	+	Equity	Rev.	–	Exp.	=	Net Inc.	Cash Flow

d. Determine the amount of net income on the 2005 income statement. What is the amount of net cash flow from operating activities for 2005?
e. What amount of Unearned Revenue would Zhen report on the December 31, 2005, balance sheet?

L.O. 3   **EXERCISE 4–23A** *Using a T-Account to Determine Cash Flow From Operating Activities*

Koch, Inc., began the accounting period with a $75,000 debit balance in its Accounts Receivable account. During the accounting period, Koch earned revenue on account of $320,000. The ending Accounts Receivable balance was $62,000.

Required

Based on this information alone, determine the amount of cash inflow from operating activities during the accounting period. (*Hint:* Use a T-account for Accounts Receivable. Enter the debits and credits for the given events, and solve for the missing amount.)

EXERCISE 4–24A *Using a T-Account to Determine Cash Flow From Operating Activities*

L.O. 3

Cole Company began the accounting period with an $18,000 credit balance in its Accounts Payable account. During the accounting period, Cole incurred expenses on account of $54,000. The ending Accounts Payable balance was $24,000.

Required

Based on this information, determine the amount of cash outflow for expenses during the accounting period. (*Hint:* Use a T-account for Accounts Payable. Enter the debits and credits for the given events, and solve for the missing amount.)

PROBLEMS—SERIES A

All Problems in Series A are available with McGraw-Hill's Homework Manager

PROBLEM 4–25A *Identifying Debit and Credit Balances*

L.O. 2

Required

Indicate whether each of the following accounts normally has a debit or credit balance.

CHECK FIGURES
a. Interest Receivable: Debit
v. Accounts Payable: Credit

a. Interest Receivable
b. Land
c. Notes Payable
d. Salaries Expense
e. Certificate of Deposit
f. Interest Revenue
g. Rent Expense
h. Common Stock
i. Cash
j. Salaries Payable
k. Accounts Receivable
l. Insurance Expense
m. Prepaid Insurance
n. Retained Earnings

o. Supplies Expense
p. Prepaid Rent
q. Accumulated Depreciation
r. Equipment
s. Interest Payable
t. Service Revenue
u. Supplies
v. Accounts Payable
w. Depreciation Expense
x. Unearned Revenue
y. Loss on Sale of Equipment
z. Gain on Sale of Land
aa. Truck
bb. Operating Expense
cc. Dividends

PROBLEM 4–26A *Transaction Type and Debit/Credit Terminology*

L.O. 1, 2

The following events apply to Box Enterprises.

1. Acquired $30,000 cash from the issue of common stock.
2. Paid salaries to employees, $8,000 cash.
3. Collected $9,000 cash for services to be performed in the future.
4. Paid cash for utilities, expense $1,200.
5. Recognized $28,000 of service revenue on account.
6. Purchased equipment costing $90,000 by paying cash of $30,000 and borrowing the balance from Third National Bank by issuing a four-year note.
7. Paid a $5,000 cash dividend to the stockholders.
8. Purchased $2,000 of supplies on account.
9. Received $18,000 cash for services rendered.
10. Paid cash to rent office space for the next 12 months, $7,800.
11. Made a $5,000 principal payment on the bank note.
12. Paid cash of $9,200 for operating expenses.
13. Paid on accounts payable, $1,200.
14. Paid cash to purchase office furniture, $3,600.
15. Recognized $18,000 of depreciation expense.
16. Recognized $3,250 of rent expense that had been paid in cash in a prior transaction (see Event 10).

17. Recognized $6,000 of revenue for services performed for which cash had been previously collected (see Event 3).
18. Recognized $4,800 of accrued interest expense.

Required
Identify each event as asset source (AS), asset use (AU), asset exchange (AE), or claims exchange (CE). Also identify the account to be debited and the account to be credited when the transaction is recorded. The first event is recorded as an example.

Event No.	Type of Event	Account Debited	Account Credited
1	AS	Cash	Common Stock

L.O. 4, 7

PROBLEM 4–27A *Recording Adjusting Entries in General Journal Format*

Required
Each of the following independent events requires a year-end adjusting entry. Record each event and the related adjusting entry in general journal format. The first event is recorded as an example. Assume a December 31 closing date.

Date	Account Titles	Debit	Credit
Oct. 1	Prepaid Rent	9,600	
	Cash		9,600
Dec. 31	Rent Expense (9,600 × 3/12)	2,400	
	Prepaid Rent		2,400

a. Paid $9,600 cash in advance on October 1 for a one-year lease on office space.
b. Borrowed $80,000 cash by issuing a note to Third National Bank on May 1. The note had a one-year term and a 6 percent annual rate of interest.
c. Paid $46,000 cash to purchase equipment on October 1. The equipment was expected to have a five-year useful life and a $6,000 salvage value. Depreciation is computed on a straight-line basis.
d. Invested $15,000 cash in a certificate of deposit that paid 4 percent annual interest. The certificate was acquired on April 1 and had a one-year term to maturity.
e. Purchased $3,200 of supplies on account on June 15. At year end, $300 of supplies remained on hand.
f. Received a $9,600 cash advance on September 1 for a contract to provide services for one year.
g. Paid $3,600 cash in advance on May 1 for a one-year insurance policy.

L.O. 3–7

PROBLEM 4–28A *One Complete Accounting Cycle*

The following events apply to Paradise Vacations' first year of operations:

1. Acquired $20,000 cash from the issue of common stock on January 1, 2005.
2. Purchased $800 of supplies on account.
3. Paid $4,200 cash in advance for a one-year lease on office space.
4. Earned $28,000 of revenue on account.
5. Incurred $12,500 of other operating expenses on account.
6. Collected $24,000 cash from accounts receivable.
7. Paid $9,000 cash on accounts payable.
8. Paid a $3,000 cash dividend to the stockholders.

Information for Adjusting Entries
9. There was $150 of supplies on hand at the end of the accounting period.
10. The lease on the office space covered a one-year period beginning November 1.
11. There was $3,600 of accrued salaries at the end of the period.

Required
a. Record these transactions in general journal form.
b. Post the transaction data from the journal to ledger T-accounts.
c. Prepare a trial balance.
d. Prepare an income statement, statement of changes in stockholders' equity, a balance sheet, and a statement of cash flows.
e. Record the entries to close the temporary accounts (Revenue, Expense, and Dividends) to Retained Earnings in general journal form.
f. Post the closing entries to the T-accounts, and prepare an after-closing trial balance.

PROBLEM 4–29A *Two Complete Accounting Cycles*

L.O. 3–7

www.mhhe.com/edmonds5e

Pacific Machining experienced the following events during 2004.

1. Started operations by acquiring $50,000 of cash from the issue of common stock.
2. Paid $6,000 cash in advance for rent during the period from February 1, 2004, to February 1, 2005.
3. Received $4,800 cash in advance for services to be performed evenly over the period from September 1, 2004, to September 1, 2005.
4. Performed services for customers on account for $65,200.
5. Incurred operating expenses on account of $31,500.
6. Collected $56,900 cash from accounts receivable.
7. Paid $22,000 cash for salaries expense.
8. Paid $28,000 cash as a partial payment on accounts payable.

CHECK FIGURES
b. Ending Cash Balance, 2004: $55,700
g. Net Income, 2005: $28,650

Adjusting Entries

9. Made the adjusting entry for the expired rent. (See Event 2.)
10. Recognized revenue for services performed in accordance with Event 3.
11. Recorded $2,100 of accrued salaries at the end of 2004.

Events for 2005

1. Paid $2,100 cash for the salaries accrued at the end of the previous year.
2. Performed services for cash, $40,500.
3. Borrowed $20,000 cash from the local bank by issuing a note.
4. Paid $25,000 cash to purchase land.
5. Paid $5,400 cash in advance for rent during the period from February 1, 2005, to February 1, 2006.
6. Performed services for customers on account for $82,000.
7. Incurred operating expenses on account of $49,100.
8. Collected $76,300 cash from accounts receivable.
9. Paid $48,000 cash as a partial payment on accounts payable.
10. Paid $41,000 cash for salaries expense.
11. Paid a $5,000 cash dividend to the stockholders.

Adjusting Entries

12. Recognized revenue for services performed in accordance with Event 3 in 2004.
13. Made the adjusting entry for the expired rent. (*Hint:* Part of the rent was paid in 2004.)
14. Recorded accrued interest. The note was issued on March 1, 2005, for a one-year term and had an interest rate of 9 percent (see Event 3).

Required

a. Record the events and adjusting entries for 2004 in general journal form.
b. Post the events for 2004 to T accounts.
c. Prepare a trial balance for 2004.
d. Prepare an income statement, statement of changes in stockholders' equity, balance sheet, and statement of cash flows for 2004.
e. Record the entries to close the 2004 temporary accounts to Retained Earnings in the general journal and post to the T-accounts.
f. Prepare an after-closing trial balance for December 31, 2004.
g. Repeat Requirements *a* through *f* for 2005.

PROBLEM 4–30A *Identifying Accounting Events From Journal Entries*

L.O. 2, 7

Required

The following information is from the records of Swan Design. Write a brief description of the accounting event represented in each of the general journal entries.

Date	Account Titles	Debit	Credit
Jan. 1	Cash	12,500	
	Common Stock		12,500
Feb. 10	Supplies	1,550	
	Accounts Payable		1,550
Mar. 1	Cash	13,000	
	Unearned Revenue		13,000

continued

Date	Account Titles	Debit	Credit
Apr. 1	Prepaid Rent	10,200	
	Cash		10,200
20	Accounts Receivable	18,400	
	Service Revenue		18,400
May 1	Office Equipment	17,000	
	Cash		4,000
	Note Payable		13,000
June 15	Salaries Expense	6,100	
	Cash		6,100
30	Property Tax Expense	3,000	
	Cash		3,000
July 28	Cash	9,300	
	Service Revenue		9,300
Aug. 30	Dividends	3,000	
	Cash		3,000
Sept. 19	Cash	16,000	
	Accounts Receivable		16,000
Dec. 31	Depreciation Expense	2,700	
	Accumulated Depreciation		2,700
31	Supplies Expense	2,025	
	Supplies		2,025
31	Rent Expense	6,400	
	Prepaid Rent		6,400
31	Unearned Revenue	8,500	
	Service Revenue		8,500

L.O. 3, 4, 6   **PROBLEM 4–31A** *Recording Events in Statements Model and T-Accounts and Preparing a Trial Balance*

The following accounting events apply to Parks Co. for the year 2004:

Asset Source Transactions

1. Began operations when the business acquired $20,000 cash from the issue of common stock.
2. Purchased $6,500 of equipment on account.
3. Performed services and collected cash of $1,000.
4. Collected $4,500 of cash in advance for services to be provided over the next 12 months.
5. Provided $12,000 of services on account.
6. Purchased supplies of $420 on account.

Asset Exchange Transactions

7. Purchased $4,000 of equipment for cash.
8. Collected $8,500 of cash from accounts receivable.
9. Loaned $1,000 to Ted Marples, who issued a 12-month, 9 percent note.
10. Purchased $500 of supplies with cash.
11. Purchased a $3,600 certificate of deposit that had a six-month term and paid 4 percent annual interest.

Asset Use Transactions

12. Paid $3,000 cash for salaries of employees.
13. Paid a cash dividend of $2,000 to the stockholders.
14. Paid for the equipment that had been purchased on account (see Event 2).
15. Paid $420 for supplies that had been purchased on account.

Claims Exchange Transactions

16. Placed an advertisement in the local newspaper for $150 and agreed to pay for the ad later.
17. Incurred utilities expense of $125 on account.

Adjusting Entries

18. Recognized $3,000 of revenue for performing services. The collection of cash for these services occurred in a prior transaction. (See Event 4.)
19. Recorded $45 of interest revenue that had accrued on the note receivable from Marples (see Event 9).
20. Recorded $72 of interest revenue that had accrued on the certificate of deposit (see Event 11).
21. Recorded $900 of accrued salary expense at the end of 2004.
22. Recognized $1,200 of depreciation on the equipment (see Events 2 and 7).
23. Recorded supplies expense. Had $120 of supplies on hand at the end of the accounting period.

Required

a. Use a horizontal statements model to show how each event affects the balance sheet, income state-ment, and statement of cash flows. Indicate whether the event increases (+), decreases (−), or does not affect (NA) each element of the financial statements. Also, in the Cash Flow column, use the let-ters OA to designate operating activity, IA for investing activity, and FA for financing activity. The first event is recorded as an example.

Assets	=	Liab.	+	Equity	Rev.	−	Exp.	=	Net Inc.	Cash Flow
+		NA		+	NA		NA		NA	+ FA

b. Record each of the preceding transactions in T-accounts and determine the balance of each account.
c. Prepare a before-closing trial balance.

PROBLEM 4–32A *Effect of Journal Entries on Financial Statements*   L.O. 1, 7

Entry No.	Account Titles	Debit	Credit
1	Cash	xxx	
	Common Stock		xxx
2	Cash	xxx	
	Unearned Revenue		xxx
3	Supplies	xxx	
	Accounts Payable		xxx
4	Office Equipment	xxx	
	Cash		xxx
	Note Payable		xxx
5	Accounts Receivable	xxx	
	Service Revenue		xxx
6	Cash	xxx	
	Accounts Receivable		xxx
7	Cash	xxx	
	Service Revenue		xxx
8	Salaries Expense	xxx	
	Cash		xxx
9	Dividends	xxx	
	Cash		xxx
10	Prepaid Rent	xxx	
	Cash		xxx
11	Property Tax Expense	xxx	
	Cash		xxx
12	Depreciation Expense	xxx	
	Accumulated Depreciation		xxx
13	Supplies Expense	xxx	
	Supplies		xxx
14	Rent Expense	xxx	
	Prepaid Rent		xxx
15	Unearned Revenue	xxx	
	Service Revenue		xxx

Required

The preceding 15 different accounting events are presented in general journal format. Use a horizontal statements model to show how each event affects the balance sheet, income statement, and statement of cash flows. Indicate whether the event increases (+), decreases (−), or does not affect (NA) each element of the financial statements. Also, in the Cash Flow column, use the letters OA to designate operating ac-tivity, IA for investing activity, and FA for financing activity. The first event is recorded as an example.

Assets	=	Liab.	+	Equity	Rev.	−	Exp.	=	Net Inc.	Cash Flow
+		NA		+	NA		NA		NA	+ FA

PROBLEM 4–33A *Effect of Errors on the Trial Balance*   L.O. 6

Required

Consider each of the following errors independently (assume that each is the only error that has oc-curred). Complete the following table. The first error is recorded as an example.

CHECK FIGURE
Error (e): Not out of balance

Error	Is the Trial Balance Out of Balance?	By What Amount?	Which Is Larger, Total Debits or Credits?
a	yes	90	credit

a. A credit of $780 to Accounts Payable was recorded as $870.
b. A credit of $500 to Accounts Receivable was not recorded.
c. A debit of $900 to Rent Expense was recorded as a debit of $700 to Salaries Expense.
d. An entry requiring a debit of $450 to Cash and a credit of $450 to Accounts Receivable was not posted to the ledger accounts.
e. A credit of $1,500 to Prepaid Insurance was recorded as a debit of $1,500 to Prepaid Insurance.
f. A debit of $500 to Cash was recorded as a credit of $500 to Cash.

L.O. 6

PROBLEM 4–34A *Effect of Errors on the Trial Balance*

CHECK FIGURE
Corrected cash balance: $2,100

The following trial balance was prepared from the ledger accounts of Cook, Inc.:

COOK, INC.
Trial Balance
May 31, 2006

Account Title	Debit	Credit
Cash	$ 1,100	
Accounts Receivable	1,770	
Supplies	420	
Prepaid Insurance	2,400	
Office Equipment	10,000	
Accounts Payable		$ 1,500
Notes Payable		1,000
Common Stock		1,800
Retained Earnings		7,390
Dividends	400	
Service Revenue		19,600
Rent Expense	3,600	
Salaries Expense	9,000	
Operating Expenses	2,500	
Totals	$31,190	$31,290

The accountant for Cook, Inc., made the following errors during May 2006.
1. The cash purchase of a $2,100 typewriter was recorded as a $2,000 debit to Office Equipment and a $2,100 credit to Cash.
2. An $800 purchase of supplies on account was properly recorded as a debit to the Supplies account but was incorrectly recorded as a credit to the Cash account.
3. The company provided services valued at $8,600 to a customer. The accountant recorded the transaction in the proper accounts but in the incorrect amount of $6,800.
4. A $600 cash receipt for a payment on an account receivable was not recorded.
5. A $400 cash payment of an account payable was not recorded.
6. The May utility bill, which amounted to $550 on account, was not recorded.

Required
a. Identify the errors that would cause a difference in the total amounts of debits and credits that would appear in a trial balance. Indicate whether the Debit or Credit column would be larger as a result of the error.
b. Indicate whether each of the preceding errors would overstate, understate, or have no effect on the amount of total assets, liabilities, and equity. Your answer should take the following form:

Event No.	Assets	=	Liabilities	+	Stockholders' Equity
1	Understate		No effect		No effect

c. Prepare a corrected trial balance.

PROBLEM 4–35A *Comprehensive Problem: Single Cycle*

L.O. 3–7

www.mhhe.com/edmonds5e

The following transactions pertain to Abbott Corporation for 2005.

Jan. 1 Began operations when the business acquired $50,000 cash from the issue of common stock.

Mar. 1 Paid rent for office space for two years, $16,800 cash.

Apr. 1 Borrowed $40,000 cash from First National Bank. The note issued had an 8 percent annual rate of interest and matured in one year.

  14 Purchased $800 of supplies on account.

June 1 Paid $27,000 cash for a computer system. The computer system had a five-year useful life and no salvage value.

  30 Received $24,000 cash in advance for services to be provided over the next year.

July 5 Paid $600 of the accounts payable from April 14.

Aug. 1 Billed a customer $9,600 for services provided during July.

  8 Completed a job and received $3,200 cash for services rendered.

Sept. 1 Paid employee salaries of $36,000 cash.

  9 Received $8,500 cash from accounts receivable.

Oct. 5 Billed customers $34,000 for services rendered on account.

Nov. 2 Paid a $1,000 cash dividend to the stockholders.

Dec. 31 Adjusted records to recognize the services provided on the contract of June 30.

  31 Recorded the accrued interest on the note to First National Bank. (See April 1.)

  31 Recorded depreciation on the computer system used in the business. (See June 1.)

  31 Recorded $2,200 of accrued salaries as of December 31.

  31 Recorded the rent expense for the year. (See March 1.)

  31 Physically counted supplies; $100 was on hand at the end of the period.

Required

a. Record the preceding transactions in the general journal.

b. Post the transactions to T-accounts and calculate the account balances.

c. Prepare a trial balance.

d. Prepare the income statement, statement of changes in stockholders' equity, balance sheet, and statement of cash flows.

e. Prepare the closing entries at December 31.

f. Prepare a trial balance after the closing entries are posted.

CHECK FIGURES
d. Net Income: $7,350
  Total Assets: $113,150

PROBLEM 4–36A *Comprehensive Problem: Two Cycles*

L.O. 3–7

www.mhhe.com/edmonds5e

This is a two-cycle problem. The second cycle is in Problem 4–36B. The first cycle *can* be completed without referring to the second cycle.

John and Larry organized a rental shop that began operations on April 1, 2007. Turner Rentals consummated the following transactions during the first month of operation.

April 1 Acquired $40,000 to establish the company, $20,000 from the issue of common stock and $20,000 from issuing a bank note. The note had a five-year term and a 9 percent annual interest rate. Interest is payable in cash on March 31 of each year.

  1 Paid $3,600 in advance rent for a one-year lease on office space.

  1 Paid $30,000 to purchase rental tools. The tools were expected to have a useful life of five years and a salvage value of $3,000.

  6 Purchased supplies for $220 cash.

  9 Received $500 cash as an advance payment from Don Orr to reserve tools to be used in May.

  10 Recorded rentals to customers. Cash receipts were $850, and invoices for rentals on account were $1,200.

  15 Paid $960 cash for employee salaries.

  16 Collected $450 from accounts receivable.

  23 Received monthly utility bills amounting to $233. The bills will be paid during May.

  25 Paid advertising expense for advertisements run during April, $240.

  30 Recorded rentals to customers. Cash sales were $1,150 and invoices for rentals on account were $1,600.

  30 Paid $960 cash for employee salaries.

Information for April 30 Adjusting Entries

1. Counted the supplies inventory. Had $80 of supplies on hand.

2. Make adjustments for interest expense, rent expense, and depreciation expense.

CHECK FIGURES
Cash, April 30, 2007: $6,970
Net Income: $1,367

Required

a. Record the transactions for April in general journal format.
b. Open a general ledger, using T-accounts, and post the general journal entries to the ledger.
c. Prepare a trial balance.
d. Record and post the appropriate adjusting entries.
e. Prepare a before-closing trial balance.
f. Prepare an income statement, statement of changes in stockholders' equity, balance sheet, and statement of cash flows.
g. Record and post the closing entries.
h. Prepare an after-closing trial balance.

EXERCISES—SERIES B

L.O. 2   EXERCISE 4–1B *Matching Debit and Credit Terminology with Accounting Elements*

Required

Complete the following table by indicating whether a debit or credit is used to increase or decrease the balance of accounts belonging to each category of accounting elements. The appropriate debit/credit terminology has been identified for the first category (assets) as an example.

Category of Elements	Used to Increase This Element	Used to Decrease This Element
Assets	Debit	Credit
Contra Asset		
Liabilities		
Common Stock		
Retained Earnings		
Revenue		
Expense		
Dividends		

L.O. 1, 2   EXERCISE 4–2B *Debit/Credit Terminology*

Two introductory accounting students were arguing about how to record a transaction involving an exchange of cash for land. Trisha stated that the transaction should have a debit to Land and a credit to Cash; Tony argued that the reverse (debit to Cash and credit to Land) represented the appropriate treatment.

Required

Which student was correct? Defend your position.

L.O. 1, 2   EXERCISE 4–3B *Matching Debit and Credit Terminology with Account Titles*

Required

Indicate whether each of the following accounts normally has a debit balance or a credit balance.

a. Land   f. Salaries Expense
b. Dividends   g. Accumulated Depreciation
c. Accounts Payable   h. Cash
d. Unearned Revenue   i. Prepaid Insurance
e. Consulting Revenue   j. Common Stock

L.O. 1, 2   EXERCISE 4–4B *Identifying Increases and Decreases in T-Accounts*

Required

For each of the following T-accounts, indicate the side of the account that should be used to record an increase or decrease in the account balance.

Cash		Accounts Payable		Common Stock	
Debit	Credit	Debit	Credit	Debit	Credit

Accounts Receivable		Notes Payable		Dividends	
Debit	Credit	Debit	Credit	Debit	Credit

Accumulated Depreciation				Service Revenue	
Debit	Credit			Debit	Credit

				Other Operating Expense	
				Debit	Credit

EXERCISE 4–5B *Applying Debit/Credit Terminology to Accounting Events*   L.O. 2

Required

In parallel columns, list the accounts that would be debited and credited for each of the following unrelated transactions:

a. Provided services on account.
b. Paid cash for operating expense.
c. Acquired cash from the issue of common stock.
d. Purchased supplies on account.
e. Purchased equipment for cash.
f. Paid a cash dividend to the stockholders.
g. Provided services for cash.
h. Recognized accrued salaries at the end of the period.

EXERCISE 4–6B *T-Accounts and the Accounting Equation*   L.O. 2, 3

Required

Record each of the following Lang Co. events in T-accounts, and then explain how the event affects the accounting equation.

a. Borrowed $5,000 cash by issuing a note to a bank.
b. Purchased supplies for $250 cash.
c. Purchased land for $10,000. The company paid $3,000 cash and issued a note for the balance.
d. Performed services for $800 cash.

EXERCISE 4–7B *Recording Transactions in T-Accounts*   L.O. 3

The following events apply to Godwin Company for 2005, its first year of operation.

1. Received cash of $48,000 from the issue of common stock.
2. Purchased for $25,000 cash a delivery van that has a salvage value of $5,000 and a four-year useful life.
3. Performed $85,000 of services on account.
4. Incurred $8,000 of other operating expenses on account.
5. Paid $34,000 cash for salaries expense.
6. Collected $65,000 of accounts receivable.
7. Paid a $5,000 dividend to the stockholders.
8. Performed $9,200 of services for cash.
9. Paid $4,400 of the accounts payable.
10. Recorded depreciation expense for the year on the delivery van.

Required

a. Record the preceding transactions in the appropriate T-accounts and determine the ending balance in each account.
b. Determine the amount of total assets at the end of 2005.
c. Determine the amount of net income for 2005.

EXERCISE 4–8B *Debit/Credit Terminology*   L.O. 2

Required

For each of the following independent events, identify the account that would be debited and the account that would be credited. The accounts for the first event are identified as an example.

Event	Account Debited	Account Credited
a	Cash	Notes Payable

a. Borrowed cash by issuing a note.
b. Received cash for services to be performed in the future.
c. Recognized depreciation expense.
d. Paid salaries payable.
e. Provided services on account.
f. Repaid principal balance on note payable.
g. Paid cash for operating expenses.
h. Purchased supplies on account.
i. Recognized accrued interest expense.
j. Recognized revenue for services completed. Cash had been collected in Event *b*.
k. Paid accounts payable.
l. Purchased office equipment with cash.
m. Received cash in payment of accounts receivable.
n. Recognized accrued interest revenue.
o. Paid a cash dividend to the stockholders.

L.O. 1, 2   **EXERCISE 4–9B** *Identification of the Type of Transaction, Its Effect on the Accounting Equation, and Whether the Effect Is Recorded with a Debit or Credit*

Required
Identify whether each of the following transactions is an asset source (AS), asset use (AU), asset exchange (AE), or claims exchange (CE). Also explain how each event affects the accounting equation by placing a + for *increase,* − for *decrease,* and NA for *not affected* under each of the components of the accounting equation. Finally, indicate whether the effect requires a debit or credit entry. The first event is recorded as an example.

						Stockholders' Equity		
Event	Type of Event	Assets	=	Liabilities	+	Common Stock	+	Retained Earnings
a	AE	+ Debit − Credit		NA		NA		NA

a. Purchased office equipment with cash.
b. Provided services for cash.
c. Repaid principal balance on note payable.
d. Purchased supplies on account.
e. Paid accounts payable.
f. Acquired cash from the issue of common stock.
g. Received cash in payment of accounts receivable.
h. Paid cash in advance for one year of rent.
i. Paid salaries payable.
j. Received cash for services to be performed in the future.
k. Recognized accrued interest expense.
l. Paid a cash dividend to the stockholders.
m. Recognized revenue for services completed for which cash had been collected previously.
n. Recognized depreciation expense on the equipment.
o. Recognized accrued interest revenue.

L.O. 7   **EXERCISE 4–10B** *Recording Events in the General Journal*

Required
Record each of the following transactions in general journal form.
a. Performed $19,000 of services on account.
b. Purchased equipment that cost $24,000 by paying $4,000 cash and issuing a $20,000 note for the balance.

c. Purchased supplies for $530 cash.

d. Received $3,000 cash for services to be performed at a later date.

e. Collected $8,400 cash on accounts receivable.

f. Had repairs made on equipment; the $1,700 for repairs expense was charged on account.

g. Sold land that cost $10,000 for $13,400.

h. Paid $2,300 cash in advance for an insurance policy on the equipment.

i. Paid $1,200 on accounts payable.

j. Recorded the adjusting entry to recognize $800 of insurance expense.

k. Recorded $6,200 depreciation expense on the equipment.

l. Recorded accrued interest expense of $800.

EXERCISE 4–11B *Preparing a Trial Balance*   **L.O. 6**

Required

On December 31, 2006, Grey Company had the following account balances in its general ledger. Use this information to prepare a trial balance.

Land	$ 80,000
Unearned Revenue	52,000
Dividends	20,000
Depreciation Expense	6,000
Prepaid Rent	19,200
Cash	28,800
Salaries Expense	50,000
Accounts Payable	12,000
Common Stock	80,000
Operating Expense	50,000
Office Supplies	10,000
Advertising Expense	4,000
Retained Earnings, 1/1/2006	18,000
Service Revenue	184,000
Office Equipment	64,000
Accounts Receivable	26,000
Accumulated Depreciation	12,000

EXERCISE 4–12B *Preparing Closing Entries*   **L.O. 5, 7**

The following financial information was taken from the books of Better Shape Health Club, a small spa and health club.

Account Balances as of December 31, 2008	
Accounts Receivable	$ 6,150
Accounts Payable	5,500
Accrued Salaries Payable	2,150
Accumulated Depreciation	7,800
Cash	20,725
Certificate of Deposit	5,650
Depreciation Expense	3,150
Dividends	1,750
Equipment	12,500
Interest Expense	1,150
Interest Payable	250
Operating Expense	31,550
Prepaid Rent	600
Rent Expense	4,200
Retained Earnings 1/1/2008	32,650
Salaries Expense	11,200
Service Revenue	48,400
Supplies	400
Supplies Expense	4,240
Common Stock	6,515

Required

a. Prepare the necessary closing entries at December 31, 2008, for Better Shape Health Club.

b. What is the balance in the Retained Earnings account after the closing entries are posted?

L.O. 3, 6   EXERCISE 4–13B *Recording Events in T-Accounts and Preparing a Trial Balance*

The following events apply to Electronics Services, Inc., in its first year of operation.

1. Acquired $80,000 cash from the issue of common stock.
2. Borrowed $64,000 from State Bank.
3. Earned $56,000 of service revenue on account.
4. Incurred $30,400 of operating expenses on account.
5. Collected $52,800 cash from accounts receivable.
6. Made a $27,200 payment on accounts payable.
7. Paid a $4,000 cash dividend to the stockholders.
8. Paid $16,000 cash to purchase office equipment.
9. Received a $14,200 cash advance for services to be provided in the future.
10. Purchased $3,200 of supplies on account.
11. Recorded accrued interest expense of $4,160.
12. Recognized $3,200 of depreciation expense.
13. Recognized $4,800 of revenue for services provided to the customer in Event 9.
14. Recognized $2,400 of supplies expense.

Required
a. Record the events in T-accounts and determine the ending account balances.
b. Test the equality of the debit and credit balances of the T-accounts by preparing a trial balance.

L.O. 6   EXERCISE 4–14B *Determining the Effect of Errors on the Trial Balance*

Required
Explain how each of the following posting errors affects a trial balance. State whether the trial balance will be out of balance because of the posting error, and indicate which side of the trial balance will have a higher amount after each independent entry is posted. If the posting error does not affect the equality of debits and credits shown in the trial balance, state that the error will not cause an inequality and explain why.

a. A $400 debit to Rent Expense was posted twice.
b. A $1,200 credit to Accounts Payable was not posted.
c. A $400 credit to Notes Payable was credited to Revenue.
d. A $200 debit to Cash was posted as a $2,000 debit.
e. A $520 debit to Office Supplies was debited to Office Equipment.

L.O. 3, 5, 7   EXERCISE 4–15B *Recording Events in the General Journal, Posting to T-Accounts, and Preparing Closing Entries*

At the beginning of 2006, Tim's Consulting had the following balances in its accounts:

Account	Balance
Cash	$13,000
Accounts Receivable	9,500
Accounts Payable	3,600
Common Stock	9,900
Retained Earnings	9,000

The following events apply to Tim's Consulting for 2006.

1. Provided $118,000 of services on account.
2. Incurred $11,980 of operating expenses on account.
3. Collected $124,000 of accounts receivable.
4. Paid $71,000 cash for salaries expense.
5. Paid $13,600 cash as a partial payment on accounts payable.
6. Paid an $11,000 cash dividend to the stockholders.

Required
a. Record these transactions in a general journal.
b. Open T-accounts, and post the beginning balances and the preceding transactions to the appropriate accounts.

c. Record the beginning balances and the transactions in a horizontal statements model such as the following one:

Assets		= Liab. +	Equity		Rev. − Exp. = Net Inc.	Cash Flow
Cash +	Accts. Rec. =	Accts. Pay. +	Common Stock +	Ret. Earn.		

d. Record the closing entries in the general journal and post them to the T-accounts. What is the amount of net income for the year?
e. What is the amount of *change* in retained earnings for the year? Is the change in retained earnings different from the amount of net income? If so, why?

EXERCISE 4–16B *Recording Receivables and Identifying Their Effect on Financial Statements*   L.O. 3, 5

Boone Company performed services on account for $40,000 in 2006. Boone collected $25,000 cash from accounts receivable during 2006, and the remaining $15,000 was collected in cash during 2007.

Required
a. Record the 2006 transactions in T-accounts.
b. Record the 2006 transactions in a horizontal statements model like the following one:

Assets		= Liab. +	Equity	Rev. − Exp. = Net Inc.	Cash Flow
Cash + Accts. Rec.		= NA +	Ret. Earn.		

c. Determine the amount of revenue Boone would report on the 2006 income statement.
d. Determine the amount of cash flow from operating activities Boone would report on the 2006 statement of cash flows.
e. Open a T-account for Retained Earnings, and close the 2006 Revenue account to the Retained Earnings account.
f. Record the 2007 cash collection in the appropriate T-accounts.
g. Record the 2007 transaction in a horizontal statements model like the one shown in Requirement *b.*
h. Assuming no other transactions occur in 2007, determine the amount of net income and the net cash flow from operating activities for 2007.

EXERCISE 4–17B *Recording Supplies and Identifying Their Effect on Financial Statements*   L.O. 3–6

Wayne Dunn started and operated a small family architectural firm in 2007. The firm was affected by two events: (1) Dunn provided $25,000 of services on account, and (2) he purchased $6,000 of supplies on account. There were $500 of supplies on hand as of December 31, 2007.

Required
a. Open T-accounts and record the two transactions in the accounts.
b. Record the required year-end adjusting entry to reflect the use of supplies.
c. Record the preceding transactions in a horizontal statements model like the following one:

Assets		= Liab. +	Equity	Rev. − Exp. = Net Inc.	Cash Flow
Accts. Rec.	Supp. =	Accts. Pay. +	Ret. Earn.		

d. Explain why the amount of net income and the net cash flow from operating activities differ.
e. Record and post the required closing entries, and prepare an after-closing trial balance.

EXERCISE 4–18B *Recording Prepaids and Identifying Their Effect on Financial Statements*   L.O. 4, 7

The Far East Company began operations when it issued common stock for $50,000 cash. It paid $48,000 cash in advance for a one-year contract to lease delivery equipment for the business. It signed the lease agreement on March 1, 2007, which was effective immediately. Far East earned $60,000 of cash revenue in 2007.

Required

a. Record the March 1 cash payment in general journal format.

b. Record in general journal format the adjustment required as of December 31, 2007.

c. Record all events in a horizontal statements model like the following one:

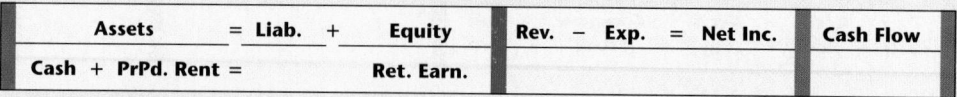

Assets	= Liab.	+	Equity	Rev.	−	Exp.	=	Net Inc.	Cash Flow
Cash + PrPd. Rent =			Ret. Earn.						

d. What amount of net income will Far East report on the 2007 income statement? What is the amount of net cash flow from operating activities for 2007?

e. Determine the amount of prepaid rent Far East would report on the December 31, 2007, balance sheet.

L.O. 4, 7   EXERCISE 4–19B *Recording Accrued Salaries and Identifying Their Effect on Financial Statements*

On December 31, 2008, IBC Company had accrued salaries of $9,600.

Required

a. Record in general journal format the adjustment required as of December 31, 2008.

b. Determine the amount of net income IBC would report on the 2008 income statement, assuming that IBC earns $12,000 of cash revenue. What is the amount of net cash flow from operating activities for 2008?

c. What amount of Salaries Payable would IBC report on the December 31, 2008, balance sheet?

L.O. 3, 4   EXERCISE 4–20B *Recording Depreciation and Identifying Its Effect on Financial Statements*

On January 1, 2007, Carco bought a computer for $40,000 cash. The computer had a useful life of three years and a salvage value of $7,000.

Required

a. Record in T-accounts Carco's purchase of the computer.

b. Record in T-accounts the adjustment required on December 31, 2007.

c. Determine the book value of the computer Carco would report on the December 31, 2007, balance sheet.

d. Determine the amount of net income Carco would report on the 2007 income statement, assuming that Carco earned $14,000 of cash revenue in 2007.

e. What is the amount of net cash flow from operating activities for 2007?

f. What amount of depreciation expense would Carco report on the 2008 income statement?

g. Determine the book value of the computer Carco would report on the December 31, 2008, balance sheet.

L.O. 3, 4   EXERCISE 4–21B *Recording a Note Payable and Identifying Its Effect on Financial Statements*

On April 1, 2007, Max Co. borrowed $60,000 from First Boston Bank. The note had a 10 percent annual interest rate and a one-year term to maturity.

Required

a. Identify the transaction type (asset source, use, or exchange or claims exchange), and record in T-accounts the entry for the financing event on April 1, 2007.

b. Identify the transaction type, and record in T-accounts the adjustment as of December 31, 2007.

c. Determine the amount of net income on the 2007 income statement, assuming Max Co. earned $10,000 of cash revenue.

d. What is the amount of net cash flow from operating activities for 2007?

e. Determine the total liabilities on the December 31, 2007, balance sheet.

f. Record in T-accounts (1) the 2008 accrual of interest and (2) the cash payment of principal and interest on April 1, 2008.

g. Are the April 1, 2008, transactions asset source, asset use, asset exchange, or claims exchange transactions?

EXERCISE 4–22B *Recording Unearned Revenue and Identifying Its Effect on Financial Statements*   **L.O. 3, 4**

Margarete received a $60,000 cash advance payment on June 1, 2005, for consulting services to be performed in the future. Services were to be provided for a one-year term beginning June 1, 2005.

Required

a. Record the June 1 cash receipt in T-accounts.
b. Record in T-accounts the adjustment required as of December 31, 2005.
c. Record the preceding transaction and related adjustment in a horizontal statements model like the following one:

Assets	=	Liab.	+	Equity	Rev.	–	Exp.	=	Net Inc.	Cash Flow

d. Determine the amount of net income on the 2005 income statement. What is the amount of net cash flow from operating activities for 2005?
e. What amount of liabilities would Margarete report on the 2005 balance sheet?

EXERCISE 4–23B *Using a T-Account to Determine Cash Flow From Operating Activities*   **L.O. 3**

ABC began the accounting period with a $58,000 debit balance in its Accounts Receivable account. During the accounting period, ABC earned revenue on account of $126,000. The ending accounts receivable balance was $54,000.

Required

Based on this information alone, determine the amount of cash inflow from operating activities during the accounting period. (*Hint:* Use a T-account for Accounts Receivable. Enter the debits and credits for the given events, and solve for the missing amount.)

EXERCISE 4–24B *Using a T-Account to Determine Cash Flow From Operating Activities*   **L.O. 3**

The Dive Company began the accounting period with a $40,000 credit balance in its Accounts Payable account. During the accounting period, The Dive incurred expenses on account of $95,000. The ending Accounts Payable balance was $28,000.

Required

Based on this information, determine the amount of cash outflow for expenses during the accounting period. (*Hint:* Use a T-account for Accounts Payable. Enter the debits and credits for the given events, and solve for the missing amount.)

PROBLEMS—SERIES B

PROBLEM 4–25B *Identifying Debit and Credit Balances*   **L.O. 2**

Required

Indicate whether each of the following accounts normally has a debit or credit balance.

a. Common Stock
b. Retained Earnings
c. Certificate of Deposit
d. Interest Expense
e. Accounts Receivable
f. Interest Revenue
g. Insurance Expense
h. Interest Payable
i. Cash
j. Dividends
k. Unearned Revenue
l. Operating Expense
m. Accumulated Depreciation
n. Accounts Payable
o. Office Equipment
p. Depreciation Expense
q. Service Revenue
r. Notes Payable
s. Notes Receivable
t. Supplies
u. Utilities Payable
v. Consulting Revenue
w. Interest Receivable
x. Supplies Expense
y. Salaries Expense
z. Equipment
aa. Salaries Payable
bb. Land
cc. Prepaid Insurance

L.O. 1, 2   PROBLEM 4–26B *Transaction Type and Debit/Credit Terminology*

The following events apply to Mask Enterprises.

1. Acquired $25,000 cash from the issue of common stock.
2. Paid salaries to employees, $1,750 cash.
3. Collected $8,100 cash for services to be performed in the future.
4. Paid cash for utilities expense, $402.
5. Recognized $22,500 of service revenue on account.
6. Purchased equipment costing $15,000 by paying cash of $3,000 and borrowing the balance from First National Bank by issuing a four-year note.
7. Paid a $1,250 cash dividend to the stockholders.
8. Purchased $1,600 of supplies on account.
9. Received $6,250 cash for services rendered.
10. Paid cash to rent office space for the next 12 months, $6,000.
11. Made a $3,750 principal payment on the bank note.
12. Paid cash of $8,750 for other operating expenses.
13. Paid on account payable, $876.
14. Paid cash to purchase office furniture, $5,000.
15. Recognized $3,750 of depreciation expense.
16. Recognized $1,500 of rent expense. Cash had been paid in a prior transaction (see Event 10).
17. Recognized $2,500 of revenue for services performed. Cash had been previously collected (see Event 3).
18. Recognized $376 of accrued interest expense.

Required

Identify each event as asset source (AS), asset use (AU), asset exchange (AE), or claims exchange (CE). Also identify the account that is to be debited and the account that is to be credited when the transaction is recorded. The first event is recorded as an example.

Event No.	Type of Event	Account Debited	Account Credited
1	AS	Cash	Common Stock

L.O. 4, 7   PROBLEM 4–27B *Recording Adjusting Entries in General Journal Format*

Required

Each of the following independent events requires a year-end adjusting entry. Record each event and the related adjusting entry in general journal format. The first event is recorded as an example. Assume a December 31 closing date.

Event No.	Date	Account Titles	Debit	Credit
a	Sept. 1	Prepaid Rent	15,000	
		Cash		15,000
a	Dec. 31	Rent Expense (15,000 × 4/12)	5,000	
		Prepaid Rent		5,000

a. Paid $15,000 cash in advance on September 1 for a one-year lease on office space.
b. Borrowed $22,500 cash by issuing a note to Bay City National Bank on October 1. The note had a one-year term and an 8 percent annual rate of interest.
c. Paid $9,700 cash to purchase equipment on September 1. The equipment was expected to have a five-year useful life and a $2,500 salvage value. Depreciation is computed on a straight-line basis.
d. Invested $11,000 cash in a certificate of deposit that paid 6 percent annual interest rate. The certificate was acquired on June 1 and had a one-year term to maturity.
e. Purchased $2,000 of supplies on account on April 15. At year-end, $300 of supplies remained on hand.
f. Received a $3,600 cash advance on July 1 for a contract to provide services for one year.
g. Paid $5,100 cash in advance on February 1 for a one-year insurance policy.

PROBLEM 4–28B *One Complete Accounting Cycle*   L.O. 3–7

The following events apply to Jeater Company's first year of operations:

1. Acquired $20,000 cash from issuing common stock on January 1, 2006.
2. Purchased $600 of supplies on account.
3. Paid $12,000 cash in advance for a one-year lease on office space.
4. Earned $11,500 of revenue on account.
5. Incurred $8,970 of operating expenses on account.
6. Collected $5,900 cash from accounts receivable.
7. Paid $6,500 cash on accounts payable.

Information for Adjusting Entries
8. There was $100 of supplies on hand at the end of the accounting period.
9. The lease on the office space covered a one-year period beginning September 1, 2006.
10. There was $2,200 of accrued salaries at the end of the period.

Required
a. Record these transactions in general journal form.
b. Post the transaction data from the journal to ledger T-accounts.
c. Prepare a trial balance.
d. Prepare an income statement, statement of changes in stockholders' equity, a balance sheet, and a statement of cash flows.
e. Close the temporary accounts (Revenue, Expense, and Dividends) to Retained Earnings.
f. Post the closing entries to the T-accounts, and prepare an after-closing trial balance.

PROBLEM 4–29B *Two Complete Accounting Cycles*   L.O. 3–7

Cummings Enterprises experienced the following events for 2006, the first year of operation.

1. Acquired $13,000 cash from the issue of common stock.
2. Paid $4,000 cash in advance for rent. The payment was for the period April 1, 2006, to March 31, 2007.
3. Performed services for customers on account for $27,000.
4. Incurred operating expenses on account of $13,500.
5. Collected $25,150 cash from accounts receivable.
6. Paid $8,500 cash for salary expense.
7. Paid $11,500 cash as a partial payment on accounts payable.

Adjusting Entries
8. Made the adjusting entry for the expired rent. (See Event 2.)
9. Recorded $900 of accrued salaries at the end of 2006.

Events for 2007
1. Paid $900 cash for the salaries accrued at the end of the prior accounting period.
2. Performed services for cash of $8,500.
3. Borrowed $6,000 from the local bank by issuing a note.
4. Paid $4,500 cash in advance for rent. The payment was for one year beginning April 1, 2007.
5. Performed services for customers on account for $42,000.
6. Incurred operating expense on account of $19,250.
7. Collected $40,500 cash from accounts receivable.
8. Paid $20,000 cash as a partial payment on accounts payable.
9. Paid $14,000 cash for salary expense.
10. Paid a $6,000 cash dividend to the owners.

Adjusting Entries
11. Made the adjusting entry for the expired rent. (*Hint:* Part of the rent was paid in 2006.)
12. Recorded accrued interest. The note was issued on September 1, 2007, for a one-year term and had an interest rate of 9 percent. (See Event 3.)

Required
a. Record the events and adjusting entries for 2006 in general journal form.
b. Post the 2006 events to T-accounts.
c. Prepare a trial balance for 2006.

d. Prepare an income statement, statement of changes in stockholders' equity, balance sheet, and statement of cash flows for 2006.

e. Record the entries to close the 2006 temporary accounts to Retained Earnings in the general journal and post to the T-accounts.

f. Prepare an after-closing trial balance for December 31, 2006.

g. Repeat requirements *a* through *f* for 2007.

L.O. 2, 7   **PROBLEM 4–30B** *Identifying Accounting Events from Journal Entries*

Required

The following information is from the records of attorney Steve Ray. Write a brief description of the accounting event represented in each of the general journal entries.

Date	Account Titles	Debit	Credit
Jan. 1	Cash	20,000	
	Common Stock		20,000
Feb. 10	Cash	4,000	
	Unearned Revenue		4,000
Mar. 5	Supplies	2,000	
	Cash		2,000
Apr. 10	Office Equipment	12,000	
	Cash		2,000
	Note Payable		10,000
Apr. 30	Prepaid Rent	800	
	Cash		800
May 1	Accounts Receivable	24,000	
	Service Revenue		24,000
June 1	Salaries Expense	2,000	
	Cash		2,000
Aug. 5	Accounts Receivable	12,000	
	Service Revenue		12,000
10	Dividends	1,000	
	Cash		1,000
Sept. 10	Cash	4,400	
	Accounts Receivable		4,400
Oct. 1	Property Tax Expense	3,000	
	Cash		3,000
Dec. 31	Depreciation Expense	1,000	
	Accumulated Depreciation		1,000
31	Supplies Expense	800	
	Supplies		800
31	Rent Expense	4,400	
	Prepaid Rent		4,400
31	Unearned Revenue	6,240	
	Service Revenue		6,240

L.O. 3, 4, 6   **PROBLEM 4–31B** *Recording Events in Statements Model and T-Accounts and Preparing a Trial Balance*

The following accounting events apply to Ginger's Designs for the year 2007.

Asset Source Transactions

1. Began operations by acquiring $40,000 of cash from the issue of common stock.
2. Purchased $14,000 of equipment on account.
3. Performed services and collected cash of $2,000.
4. Collected $12,000 of cash in advance for services to be provided over the next 12 months.
5. Provided $24,000 of services on account.
6. Purchased supplies of $3,000 on account.

Asset Exchange Transactions

7. Purchased $8,000 of equipment for cash.
8. Collected $14,000 of cash from accounts receivable.
9. Loaned $4,800 to Jose, who issued a 12-month, 7 percent note.
10. Purchased $1,260 of supplies with cash.
11. Purchased a $9,600 certificate of deposit. The CD had a six-month term and paid 4 percent annual interest.

Asset Use Transactions

12. Paid $8,000 cash for salaries of employees.
13. Paid a cash dividend of $4,000 to the stockholders.
14. Paid for the equipment that had been purchased on account (see Event 2).
15. Paid off $1,260 of the accounts payable with cash.

Claims Exchange Transactions

16. Placed an advertisement in the local newspaper for $1,600 on account.
17. Incurred utility expense of $1,200 on account.

Adjusting Entries

18. Recognized $8,800 of revenue for performing services. The collection of cash for these services occurred in a prior transaction. (See Event 4.)
19. Recorded $200 of interest revenue that had accrued on the note receivable from Jose. (See Event 9.)
20. Recorded $336 of interest revenue that had accrued on the certificate of deposit. (See Event 11.)
21. Recorded $3,000 of accrued salary expense at the end of 2007.
22. Recognized $2,800 of depreciation on the equipment. (See Events 2 and 7.)
23. Recorded supplies expense. Had $1,200 of supplies on hand at the end of the accounting period.

Required

a. Use a horizontal statements model to show how each event affects the balance sheet, income statement, and statement of cash flows. Indicate whether the event increases (+), decreases (−), or does not affect (NA) each element of the financial statements. Also, in the Cash Flow column, use the letters OA to designate operating activity, IA for investing activity, and FA for financing activity. The first event is recorded as an example.

Assets	=	Liab.	+	Equity	Rev.	−	Exp.	=	Net Inc.	Cash Flow
+		NA		+	NA		NA		NA	+ FA

b. Record each of the preceding events in T-accounts.
c. Prepare a before-closing trial balance.

PROBLEM 4–32B *Effect of Journal Entries on Financial Statements*

L.O. 1, 7

Entry No.	Account Titles	Debit	Credit
1	Cash	xxx	
	Common Stock		xxx
2	Office Equipment	xxx	
	Cash		xxx
	Note Payable		xxx
3	Prepaid Rent	xxx	
	Cash		xxx
4	Dividends	xxx	
	Cash		xxx
5	Utility Expense	xxx	
	Cash		xxx
6	Accounts Receivable	xxx	
	Service Revenue		xxx
7	Salaries Expense	xxx	
	Cash		xxx
8	Cash	xxx	
	Service Revenue		xxx
9	Cash	xxx	
	Unearned Revenue		xxx
10	Supplies	xxx	
	Accounts Payable		xxx
11	Depreciation Expense	xxx	
	Accumulated Depreciation		xxx
12	Cash	xxx	
	Accounts Receivable		xxx
13	Rent Expense	xxx	
	Prepaid Rent		xxx
14	Supplies Expense	xxx	
	Supplies		xxx
15	Unearned Revenue	xxx	
	Service Revenue		xxx

Required

The preceding 15 different accounting events are presented in general journal format. Use a horizontal statements model to show how each event affects the balance sheet, income statement, and statement of cash flows. Indicate whether the event increases (+), decreases (−), or does not affect (NA) each element of the financial statements. Also, in the Cash Flow column, use the letters OA to designate operating activity, IA for investing activity, and FA for financing activity. The first event is recorded as an example.

Assets	=	Liab.	+	Equity	Rev.	−	Exp.	=	Net Inc.	Cash Flow
+		NA		+	NA		NA		NA	+ FA

L.O. 6   PROBLEM 4–33B *Effect of Errors on the Trial Balance*

Required

Consider each of the following errors independently (assume that each is the only error that has occurred). Complete the following table. The first error is recorded as an example.

Error	Is the Trial Balance Out of Balance?	By What Amount?	Which Is Larger, Total Debits or Credits?
a	no	NA	NA

a. A debit of $800 to Supplies Expense was recorded as a debit of $800 to Rent Expense.
b. A credit of $500 to Consulting Revenue was not recorded.
c. A credit of $360 to Accounts Payable was recorded as $680.
d. A debit of $3,000 to Cash was recorded as a credit of $3,000 to Cash.
e. An entry requiring a debit to Cash of $850 and a credit to Accounts Receivable of $850 was not posted to the ledger accounts.
f. A debit of $4,200 to Prepaid Rent was recorded as a credit of $4,200 to Prepaid Rent.

L.O. 6   PROBLEM 4–34B *Effect of Errors on the Trial Balance*

The following trial balance was prepared from the ledger accounts of Kona Company.

KONA COMPANY
Trial Balance
April 30, 2006

Account Title	Debit	Credit
Cash	$ 7,150	
Accounts Receivable	40,000	
Supplies	2,400	
Prepaid Insurance	3,200	
Equipment	56,800	
Accounts Payable		$ 8,950
Notes Payable		32,000
Common Stock		96,000
Retained Earnings		56,720
Dividends	6,000	
Service Revenue		40,000
Rent Expense	7,200	
Salaries Expense	26,400	
Operating Expense	65,240	
Totals	$214,390	$233,670

When the trial balance failed to balance, the accountant reviewed the records and discovered the following errors:

1. The company received $470 as payment for services rendered. The credit to Service Revenue was recorded correctly, but the debit to Cash was recorded as $740.
2. A $430 receipt of cash that was received as a payment on accounts receivable was not recorded.
3. A $450 purchase of supplies on account was properly recorded as a debit to the Supplies account. However, the credit to Accounts Payable was not recorded.
4. Equipment valued at $10,000 was contributed to the business in exchange for common stock. The entry to record the transaction was recorded as a $10,000 credit to both the Equipment account and the Common Stock account.

5. A $200 rent payment was properly recorded as a credit to Cash. However, the Salaries Expense account was incorrectly debited for $200.

Required
Based on this information, prepare a corrected trial balance for Kona Company.

PROBLEM 4–35B *Comprehensive Problem: Single Cycle*

L.O. 3–7

The following transactions pertain to Sky Training Company for 2008.

Jan.	30	Established the business when it acquired $75,000 cash from the issue of common stock.
Feb.	1	Paid rent for office space for two years, $24,000 cash.
Mar.	1	Borrowed $20,000 cash from National Bank. The note issued had a 9 percent annual rate of interest and matured in one year.
Apr.	10	Purchased $5,300 of supplies on account.
June	1	Paid $27,000 cash for a computer system which had a three-year useful life and no salvage value.
July	1	Received $50,000 cash in advance for services to be provided over the next year.
	20	Paid $1,800 of the accounts payable from April 10.
Aug.	15	Billed a customer $32,000 for services provided during August.
Sept.	15	Completed a job and received $19,000 cash for services rendered.
Oct.	1	Paid employee salaries of $20,000 cash.
	15	Received $25,000 cash from accounts receivable.
Nov.	16	Billed customers $37,000 for services rendered on account.
Dec.	1	Paid a dividend of $6,000 cash to the stockholders.
	31	Adjusted records to recognize the services provided on contract of July 1.
	31	Recorded the accrued interest on the note to National Bank. (See March 1.)
	31	Recorded depreciation on the computer system used in the business. (See June 1.)
	31	Recorded $4,500 of accrued salaries as of December 31.
	31	Recorded the rent expense for the year. (See February 1.)
	31	Physically counted supplies; $480 was on hand at the end of the period.

Required
a. Record the preceding transactions in the general journal.
b. Post the transactions to T-accounts and calculate the account balances.
c. Prepare a trial balance.
d. Prepare the income statement, statement of changes in stockholders' equity, balance sheet, and statement of cash flows.
e. Prepare the closing entries at December 31.
f. Prepare a trial balance after the closing entries are posted.

PROBLEM 4–36B *Comprehensive Problem: Two Cycles*

L.O. 3–7

This problem extends Problem 4–36A involving Turner Rentals and *should not* be attempted until that problem has been completed. The transactions consummated by Turner Rentals during May 2007 (the company's second month of operation) consisted of the following:

May	1	Recorded rentals of tools to customers. Cash receipts were $420, and invoices for rentals on account were $1,200.
	2	Purchased supplies on account that cost $300.
	7	Collected $2,500 cash from customer accounts receivable.
	8	Don Orr rented the tools that had been paid for in advance (see April 9 in Problem 4–36A).
	10	Paid the utility company for the monthly utility bills that had been received in the previous month, $233.
	15	Paid $2,100 cash for employee salaries.
	15	Purchased a one-year insurance policy that cost $1,200 with coverage beginning immediately.
	16	Paid $300 on the account payable that was established when supplies were purchased on May 2.
	20	Paid a $300 cash dividend to the stockholders.
	27	Received monthly utility bills amounting to $310. The bills would be paid during the month of June.
	31	Recorded rentals of tools to customers. Cash sales were $625, and invoices for rentals on account were $4,100.
	31	Paid $2,100 cash for employee salaries.
	31	Counted the supplies inventory. Had $40 of supplies on hand.

Required

a. Open a general ledger with T-accounts, using the ending account balances computed in Problem 4–36A.

b. Record the preceding transactions directly into the T-accounts.

c. Record the adjusting entries directly into the T-accounts. (*Note:* Refer to Problem 4–36A to obtain all the information needed to prepare the adjusting entries.)

d. Prepare an income statement, statement of changes in stockholders' equity, balance sheet, and statement of cash flows.

e. Record the closing entries directly into the T-accounts.

f. Answer the following questions.

   (1) Why is the amount in the May 31, 2007 Retained Earnings account not equal to the amount of net income or loss for the month of May?

   (2) Why is the amount of Accumulated Depreciation on the May 31, 2007 balance sheet not equal to the amount of depreciation expense for the month of May?

ANALYZE, THINK, COMMUNICATE

ATC 4–1   BUSINESS APPLICATIONS CASE *Understanding Real World Annual Reports*

Required

The Topps Company, Inc.

a. Use the Topps Company's annual report in Appendix B to answer the following questions.

   (1) On March 1, 2003 Topps had a balance of $262,877,000 in Retained Earnings. On March 2, 2002 the balance in Retained Earnings was $245,941,000. Why did Retained Earnings change during 2003?

   (2) Why did Topps' Net Sales and Net Income decrease so much in 2003 compared to 2002?

   (3) Could requirement 2 be answered by examining only Topps' income statement, balance sheet, and cash statement? If not, where did you find the information?

   (4) Does the Treasury Stock account in the Stockholders' Equity section of the 2003 balance sheet have a debit or credit balance?

Harley-Davidson, Inc.

b. Use the Harley-Davidson's annual report that came with this book to answer the following questions.

   (1) On December 31, 2003 Harley-Davidson had a balance of $3,074 million in Retained Earnings. On December 31, 2002 the balance in Retained Earnings was $2,372 million. Why did Retained Earnings change during 2003?

   (2) Harley-Davidson's Net Revenue increased during 2003 compared to 2002. The MD&A section of its annual report explains the reasons this occurred. What are these reasons?

   (3) Does the Accumulated and Other Comprehensive Income (Loss) account in the Shareholders' Equity section of the 2002 balance sheet have a debit or credit balance?

ATC 4–2   GROUP ASSIGNMENT *Financial Statement Analysis*

The account balances for Mabry Company were as follows:

	January 1		
	2002	**2003**	**2004**
Cash	$12,000	$ 5,800	$29,400
Accounts Receivable	6,000	10,000	6,000
Equipment	25,000	25,000	25,000
Accumulated Depreciation	(12,000)	(13,200)	(14,400)
Prepaid Rent	0	1,000	1,400
Accounts Payable	4,000	3,000	7,000
Notes Payable	12,000*	0	0
Interest Payable	300	0	0
Salaries Payable	0	0	2,100
Common Stock	10,000	10,000	10,000
Retained Earnings	4,700	15,600	28,300

*Funds were originally borrowed on October 1, 2001, with an interest rate of 10 percent.

Mabry Company experienced the following events for the accounting periods 2002, 2003, and 2004.

2002

1. Performed services for $36,000 on account.
2. Paid rent of $6,000 for the period March 1, 2002, to March 1, 2003.
3. Incurred operating expense of $18,000 on account.
4. Collected $32,000 of accounts receivable.
5. Paid $19,000 of accounts payable.
6. Paid note and interest due on October 1.
7. Recorded expired rent.
8. Recorded depreciation expense of $1,200.

2003

1. Performed services on account of $48,000.
2. Paid rent of $8,400 for the period March 1, 2003, to March 1, 2004, and recorded the expired rent for the period January 1, 2003, to March 1, 2003.
3. Incurred operating expenses of $24,000 on account.
4. Collected $52,000 of accounts receivable.
5. Paid $20,000 of accounts payable.
6. Recorded expired rent.
7. Recorded accrued salaries of $2,100.
8. Recorded depreciation expense of $1,200.

2004

1. Paid accrued salaries.
2. Performed services on account of $56,000.
3. Paid rent of $9,000 for the period March 1, 2004, to March 1, 2005, and recorded the expired rent for the period January 1, 2004, to March 1, 2004.
4. Incurred operating expenses of $32,000 on account.
5. Collected $55,000 of accounts receivable.
6. Paid $33,000 of accounts payable.
7. Sold equipment for $2,000; the equipment had a cost of $5,000 and accumulated depreciation of $4,000.
8. Recorded expired rent.
9. Recorded depreciation expense of $1,000.

Required

a. Divide the class into groups of four or five students. Organize the groups into three sections. Assign each section of groups the financial data for one of the preceding accounting periods.

Group Task

Prepare an income statement, balance sheet, and statement of cash flows. It may be helpful to open T-accounts and post transactions to these accounts before attempting to prepare the statements.

Class Discussion

b. Review the cash flows associated with the collection of receivables and the payment of payables. Comment on the company's collection and payment strategy.
c. Explain why depreciation decreased in 2004.
d. Did net income increase or decrease between 2002 and 2003? What were the primary causes?
e. Did net income increase or decrease between 2003 and 2004? What were the primary causes?

REAL-WORLD CASE *Choice of Fiscal Year*

ATC 4–3

Consider the following brief descriptions of four companies from different industries. Toll Brothers, Inc., is one of the largest homebuilders in the nation, with operations in 22 states. Toys R Us, Inc., is the well-known, international retailer of toys. Six Flags, Inc., claims to be the world's largest operator of regional theme parks. It operates 39 parks worldwide, including 15 of the largest 50 parks in the United States. Vail Resorts, Inc., operates several ski resorts in Colorado, including Vail Mountain, the largest in the United States, and Breckenridge Mountain Resort.

The chapter explained that companies often choose to close their books when business is slow. Each of these companies ends its fiscal year on a different date. The closing dates, listed chronologically, are:

January 31
July 31
October 31
December 31

Required

a. Try to determine which fiscal year-end matches which company. Write a brief explanation of the reason for your decisions.

b. Because many companies deliberately choose to prepare their financial statements at a slow time of year, try to identify problems this may present for someone trying to analyze the balance sheet for Toys R Us. Write a brief explanation of the issues you identify.

ATC 4–4 BUSINESS APPLICATIONS CASE *Components of Financial Statements*

A stockbroker handed Dr. Nguyen a set of financial statements for a company the broker described as a "sure bet" for a major increase in stock price. The broker assured Nguyen that the company was a legitimate business. As proof, she stated that the company was listed with the Securities and Exchange Commission. After looking over the financial statements, Nguyen wanted additional information. He has an Internet connection and can access SEC files. Assume that Nguyen obtains a 10-K annual report through the EDGAR database.

Required

Identify three major sections of information that are likely to be contained in the 10-K annual report. Describe the content of each section, and explain the independent auditor's role as it relates to each section.

ATC 4–5 BUSINESS APPLICATIONS CASE *Components of Financial Statements*

Beth Hughes just finished reading the annual report of Muncy Company. Hughes is enthusiastic about the possibility of investing in the company. In the management's discussion and analysis section of the report, Muncy's new president, Bill Karn, stated that he was committed to an annual growth rate of 25 percent over the next five years. Hughes tells you that the company's financial statements received an unqualified audit opinion from a respected firm of CPAs. Based on the audit report, Hughes concluded that the auditors agree with Karn's forecast of a five-year, 25 percent growth rate. She tells you, "These accountants are usually very conservative. If they forecast 25 percent growth, actual growth is likely to be close to 35 percent. I'm not going to miss an opportunity like this. I am buying the stock."

Required

Comment on Hughes' understanding of the relationship between the auditor's report and management's discussion and analysis in a company's annual report.

ATC 4–6 WRITING ASSIGNMENT *Fiscal Closing Date*

Assume you are the auditor for Metro Auto Sales. Metro currently has a December 31 year end as of which you perform the audit. You would like for Metro to change the year end to another time (almost any time except December 31).

Required

Write a memo to the owners of Metro Auto Sales and propose a new year end. In the memo explain why it would be reasonable or better to have a different year end and specify what the year end would be. Also give reasons that the change would be beneficial from your perspective.

ATC 4–7 ETHICAL DILEMMA *Choice of Brothers: Ethics, Risk, and Accounting Numbers in a Medieval Setting*

In the late 1400s, a wealthy land owner named Caster was trying to decide which of his twin sons, Rogan or Argon, to designate as the first heir to the family fortune. He decided to set up each son with a small farm consisting of 300 sheep and 20 acres of land. Each twin would be allowed to manage his property as he deemed appropriate. After a designated period, Caster would call his sons before him to account for their actions. The heir to the family fortune would be chosen on the basis of which son had produced a larger increase in wealth during the test period.

On the appointed day of reckoning, Argon boasted that he had 714 sheep under his control while Rogan had only 330. Furthermore, Argon stated that he had increased his land holdings to 27 acres. The seven-acre increase resulted from two transactions: first, on the day the contest started, Argon used 20 sheep to buy 10 additional acres; and second, he sold three of these acres for a total of 9 sheep on the day of reckoning. Also, Argon's flock had produced 75 newborn sheep during the period of accounting. He had been able to give his friends 50 sheep in return for the help that they had given him in building a fence, thereby increasing not only his own wealth but the wealth of his neighbors as well. Argon boasted that the fence was strong and would keep his herd safe from predatory creatures for five years (assume the fence had been used for one year during the contest period). Rogan countered that Argon was holding 400 sheep that belonged to another herder. Argon had borrowed these sheep on the day that the contest had started. Furthermore, Argon had agreed to return 424 sheep to the herder. The 24 additional sheep represented consideration for the use of the herder's flock. Argon had agreed to return the sheep immediately after the day of reckoning.

During the test period, Rogan's flock had produced 37 newborn sheep, but 2 sheep had gotten sick and died during the accounting period. Rogan had also lost 5 sheep to predatory creatures. He had no fence, and some of his sheep strayed from the herd, thereby exposing themselves to danger. Knowing that he was falling behind, Rogan had taken a wife in order to boost his productivity. His wife owned 170 sheep on the day they were married; her sheep had produced 16 newborn sheep since the date of her marriage to Rogan. Argon had not included the wife's sheep in his count of Rogan's herd. If his wife's sheep had been counted, Rogan's herd would contain 516 instead of 330 sheep suggested by Argon's count.

Argon charged that seven of Rogan's sheep were sick with symptoms similar to those exhibited by the two sheep that were now dead. Rogan interjected that he should not be held accountable for acts of nature such as illness. Furthermore, he contended that by isolating the sick sheep from the remainder of the herd, he had demonstrated prudent management practices that supported his case to be designated first heir.

Required

a. Prepare an income statement, balance sheet, statement of sheep flow (cash flow) for each twin, using contemporary (2004) accounting standards. Note that you have to decide whether to include the sheep owned by Rogan's wife when making his financial statements (what is the accounting entity?). (*Hint:* Use the number of sheep rather than the number of dollars as the common unit of measure.)
b. Refer to the statements you prepared in Requirement *a* to answer the following questions:
   (1) Which twin has more owner's equity at the end of the accounting period?
   (2) Which twin produced the higher net income during the accounting period?
   (3) Which son should be designated heir based on conventional accounting and reporting standards?
c. What is the difference in the value of the land of the twins if the land is valued at market value (that is, three sheep per acre) rather than historical cost (that is, two sheep per acre)?
d. Did Argon's decision to borrow sheep increase his profitability? Support your answer with appropriate financial data.
e. Was Argon's decision to build a fence financially prudent? Support your answer with appropriate financial data.
f. Assuming that the loan resulted in a financial benefit to Argon, identify some reasons that the shepherd who owned the sheep may have been willing to loan them to Argon.
g. Which twin is likely to take risks to improve profitability? What would be the financial condition of each twin if one-half of the sheep in both flocks died as a result of illness? How should such risk factors be reported in financial statements?
h. Should Rogan's decision to "marry for sheep" be considered from an ethical perspective, or should the decision be made solely on the basis of the bottom-line net income figure?
i. Prepare a report that recommends which twin should be designated heir to the family business. Include a set of financial statements that supports your recommendation. Since this is a managerial report that will not be distributed to the public, you are not bound by generally accepted accounting principles.

EDGAR DATABASE *Investigating Nike's 10-K report*

ATC 4–8

As explained in this chapter, many companies must file financial reports with the SEC. Many of these reports are available electronically through the EDGAR database. EDGAR is an acronym for Electronic Data Gathering, Analysis, and Retrieval system, and it is accessible through the World Wide Web on the Internet. Instructions for using EDGAR are in Appendix A.

Using the most current 10-K available on EDGAR, answer the following questions about Nike Company.

a. In what year did Nike begin operations?
b. Other than athletic shoes and clothing, what business does Nike operate?
c. How many employees does Nike have?
d. Describe, in dollar amounts, Nike's accounting equation at the end of the most recent year.
e. Has Nike's performance been improving or deteriorating over the past three years? Explain your answer.

ATC 4–9   SPREADSHEET ASSIGNMENT *Use of Excel*

Adams Company started operations on January 1, 2002. Six months later on June 30, 2002, the company decided to prepare financial statements. The company's accountant decided to problem solve for the adjusting journal entries and the final adjusted account balances by using an electronic spreadsheet. Once the spreadsheet is complete, she will record the adjusting entries in the general journal and post to the ledger. The accountant has started the following spreadsheet but wants you to finish it for her.

Required

a. On a blank spreadsheet, enter the following trial balance in Columns A through C. Also enter the headings for Columns E through I.

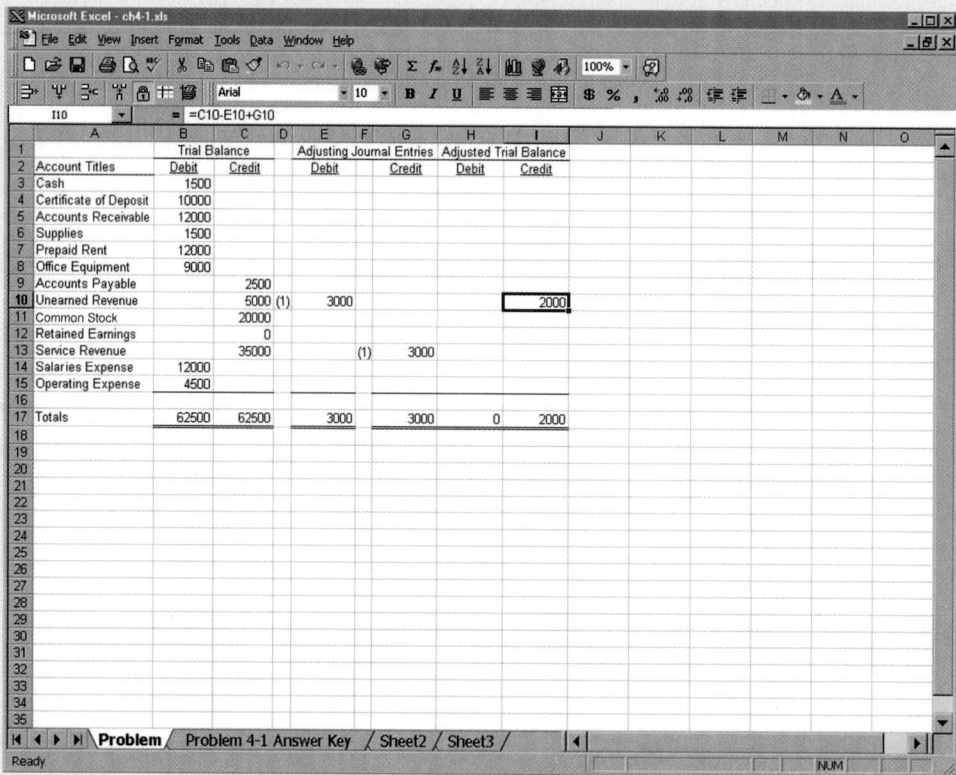

b. Each of the following events requires an adjusting journal entry. Instead of recording entries in general journal format, record the adjusting entries in the Debit and Credit columns under the heading Adjusting Journal Entries. Entry (1) has already been recorded as an example. Be sure to number your adjusting entries on the spreadsheet. It will be necessary to insert new accounts for the adjustments. Recall that the accounting period is for six months.

   (1) Received a $5,000 cash advance on April 1 for a contract to provide five months of service.
   (2) Had accrued salaries on June 30 amounting to $1,500.
   (3) On January 1 invested in a one-year, $10,000 certificate of deposit that had a 5 percent interest rate.
   (4) On January 1 paid $12,000 in advance for a one-year lease on office space.
   (5) Received in the mail a utility bill dated June 30 for $150.
   (6) Purchased $1,500 of supplies on January 1. As of June 30, $700 of supplies remained on hand.
   (7) Paid $9,000 for office equipment on January 1. The equipment was expected to have a four-year useful life and a $1,000 salvage value. Depreciation is computed on a straight-line basis.

c. Develop formulas to sum both the Debit and Credit columns under the Adjusting Journal Entries heading.

d. Develop formulas to derive the adjusted balances for the adjusted trial balance. For example, the formula for the ending balance of Unearned Revenue is =C10−E10+G10. In other words, a credit balance minus debit entries plus credit entries equals the ending balance. Once an ending balance is formulated for one credit account, that formula can be copied to all other credit accounts; the same is true for debit accounts. Once an ending balance is formulated for a debit account, that formula can be copied to all other debit accounts.

e. Develop formulas to sum both the Debit and Credit columns under the Adjusted Trial Balance heading.

Spreadsheet Tips

1. Rows and columns can be inserted by positioning the mouse on the immediate row or column after the desired position. Click on the *right* mouse button. With the *left* mouse button, choose Insert and then either Entire Column or Entire Row. Use the same method to delete columns or rows.
2. Enter the sequential numbering of the adjusting entries as labels rather than values by positioning an apostrophe in front of each entry. The first adjusting entry should be labeled '(1).

SPREADSHEET ASSIGNMENT *Mastery of Excel*

ATC 4–10

At the end of the accounting period, Adams Company's general ledger contained the following adjusted balances.

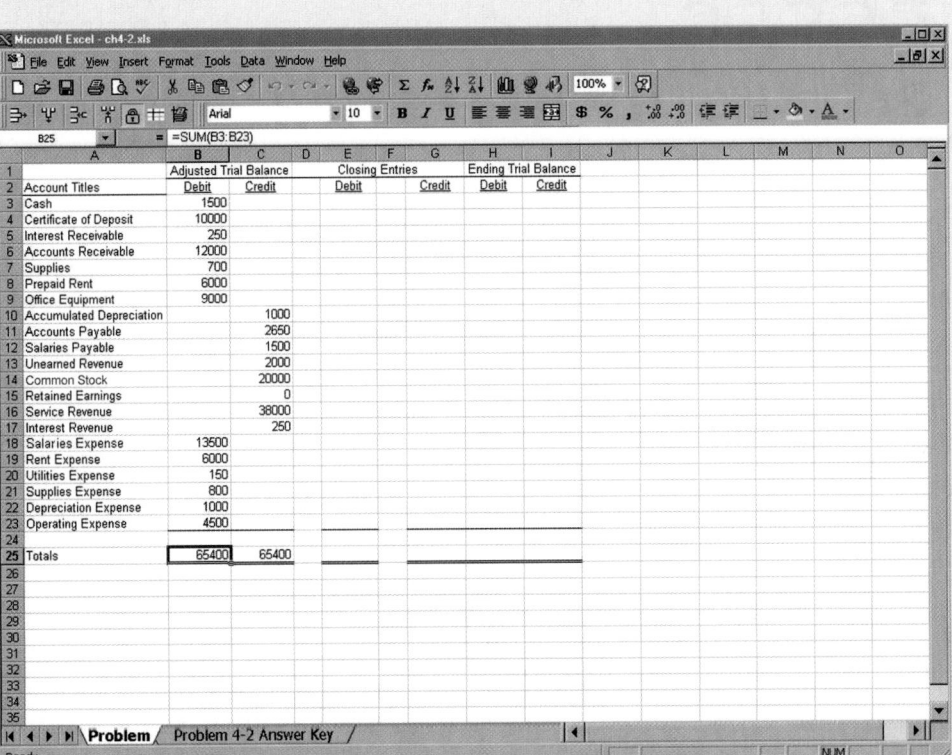

	Adjusted Trial Balance		Closing Entries		Ending Trial Balance	
Account Titles	Debit	Credit	Debit	Credit	Debit	Credit
Cash	1500					
Certificate of Deposit	10000					
Interest Receivable	250					
Accounts Receivable	12000					
Supplies	700					
Prepaid Rent	6000					
Office Equipment	9000					
Accumulated Depreciation		1000				
Accounts Payable		2650				
Salaries Payable		1500				
Unearned Revenue		2000				
Common Stock		20000				
Retained Earnings		0				
Service Revenue		38000				
Interest Revenue		250				
Salaries Expense	13500					
Rent Expense	6000					
Utilities Expense	150					
Supplies Expense	800					
Depreciation Expense	1000					
Operating Expense	4500					
Totals	65400	65400				

Required

a. Set up the preceding spreadsheet format. (The spreadsheet tips for ATC 4–9 also apply for this problem.)
b. Record the closing entries in the Closing Entries column of the spreadsheet.
c. Compute the Ending Trial Balance amounts.

CHAPTER five

ACCOUNTING FOR MERCHANDISING BUSINESSES

LEARNING *objectives*

After you have mastered the material in this chapter you will be able to:

1 Distinguish between service and merchandising businesses.

2 Identify and explain the primary features of the perpetual inventory system.

3 Explain the meaning of terms used to describe transportation costs, cash discounts, returns or allowances, and financing costs.

4 Compare and contrast single and multistep income statements.

5 Show the effect of lost, damaged, or stolen inventory on financial statements.

6 Use common size financial statements to evaluate managerial performance.

7 Use ratio analysis to evaluate managerial performance.

8 Identify the primary features of the periodic inventory system. (Appendix)

THE *curious* ACCOUNTANT

Leila recently purchased a book for $25 from her local **Borders** bookstore. The next day she learned that Rachael had bought the same book from **Amazon.com** for only $20. Leila questioned how Amazon.com could sell the book for so much less than Borders, given the low markup that retail booksellers enjoy. Rachael suggested that although both booksellers purchase their books from the same publishers at about the same price, Amazon.com can charge lower prices because it does not have to operate expensive bricks-and-mortar stores, thus lowering its operating costs. Leila disagrees. She thinks the cost of operating huge distribution centers and Internet server centers would offset any cost savings Amazon.com enjoys from not owning retail bookstores.

Exhibit 5–1 presents the income statements for Amazon.com and Borders. Based on these income statements, do you think Leila or Rachael is correct? (Answer on page 220.)

CHAPTER *opening*

Previous chapters have discussed accounting for service businesses. These businesses obtain revenue by providing some kind of service such as medical or legal advice to their customers. Other examples of service companies include dry cleaning companies, maid service companies, and car washes. This chapter introduces accounting practices for merchandising businesses. **Merchandising businesses** *generate revenue by selling goods. They buy the merchandise they sell from companies called suppliers. The goods purchased for resale are called* **merchandise inventory.** *Merchandising businesses include* **retail companies** *(companies that sell goods to the final consumer) and* **wholesale** *companies (companies that sell to other businesses). Sears Roebuck and Co., JC Penney, Target, and Sam's Clubs are real-world merchandising businesses.*

Product Costs Versus Selling and Administrative Costs

LO1 Distinguish between service and merchandising businesses.

Inventory costs are shown on the balance sheet in an asset account named Merchandise Inventory. All costs incurred to acquire merchandise and ready it for sale are included in the inventory account. Examples of inventory costs include the price of goods purchased, shipping and handling costs, transit insurance, and storage costs. Since inventory items are referred to as products, inventory costs are frequently called **product costs.**

Costs that are not included in inventory are usually called **selling and administrative costs.** Examples of selling and administrative costs include advertising, administrative salaries, sales commissions, insurance, and interest. Since selling and administrative costs are usually recognized as expenses *in the period* in which they are incurred, they are sometimes called **period costs.** In contrast, product costs are expensed when inventory is sold regardless of when it was purchased. In other words, product costs are matched directly with sales revenue, while selling and administrative costs are matched with the period in which they are incurred.

S&AC expensed when incurred
product cost expensed later

Allocation of Inventory Cost Between Asset and Expense Accounts

The amount of inventory that is available for sale during a specific accounting period is determined as follows:

$$\begin{matrix} \text{Beginning} & & \text{Inventory Purchased} & & \text{Cost of Goods} \\ \text{Inventory} & + & \text{During the} & = & \text{Available} \\ \text{Balance} & & \text{Period} & & \text{for Sale} \end{matrix}$$

The **cost of goods available for sale** is allocated between the asset account Merchandise Inventory and an expense account called **Cost of Goods Sold.** The cost of inventory items that have not been sold (Merchandise Inventory) is reported as an asset on the balance sheet, and the cost of the items sold (Cost of Goods Sold) is expensed on the income statement. This allocation is depicted graphically as follows.

Cost of Goods Available for Sale
→ Merchandise Inventory (Balance Sheet)
→ Cost of Goods Sold (Income Statement)

The difference between the sales revenue and the cost of goods sold is called **gross margin** or **gross profit**. The selling and administrative expenses (period costs) are subtracted from gross margin to obtain the net income.

Exhibit 5–1 displays income statements from the annual reports of **Amazon.com, Inc.,** and **Borders Group, Inc.** For each company, review the most current income statement and determine the amount of gross margin. You should find a gross profit of $992,618 (in thousands) for Amazon.com and a gross margin of $960.9 (in millions) for Borders.

Exhibit 5–1 *Comparative Income Statements*

AMAZON.COM, INC.
Consolidated Statements of Operations
(dollars in thousands)

	Years Ended December 31,		
	2002	2001	2000
Net Sales	$3,932,936	$3,122,433	$ 2,761,983
Cost of Sales	2,940,318	2,323,875	2,106,206
Gross Profit	992,618	798,558	655,777
Operating Expenses:			
Fulfillment	392,467	374,250	414,509
Marketing	125,383	138,283	179,980
Technology and Content	215,617	241,165	269,326
General and Administrative	79,049	89,862	108,962
Stock-Based Compensation	68,927	4,637	24,797
Amortization of Goodwill and Other Intangibles	5,478	181,033	321,772
Restructuring-Related and Other	41,573	181,585	200,311
Total Operating Expenses	928,494	1,210,815	1,519,657
Income (Loss) from Operations	64,124	(412,257)	(863,880)
Interest Income	23,687	29,103	40,821
Interest Expense	(142,925)	(139,232)	(130,921)
Other Income (Expense), Net	5,623	(1,900)	(10,058)
Other Gains (Losses), Net	(96,273)	(2,141)	(142,639)
Total Nonoperating Expenses, Net	(209,888)	(114,170)	(242,797)
Loss before Equity in Losses of Equity-Method Investees	(145,764)	(526,427)	(1,106,677)
Equity in Losses of Equity-Method Investees	(4,169)	(30,327)	(304,596)
Net Loss before Change in Accounting Principle	(149,933)	(556,754)	(1,411,273)
Cumulative Effect of Change in Accounting Principle	801	(10,523)	—
Net Loss	$ (149,132)	$ (567,277)	$(1,411,273)

BORDERS GROUP, INC.
Consolidated Statements of Operations
(dollars in millions)

	Fiscal Year Ended		
	January 26, 2003	January 27, 2002	January 28, 2001
Sales	$ 3,486.1	$ 3,387.9	$ 3,271.2
Other Revenue	26.9	25.3	25.9
Total Revenue	3,513.0	3,413.2	3,297.1
Cost of Merchandise Sold (Includes Occupancy)	2,550.3	2,464.5	2,380.4
Fulfillment Center and Other Inventory Writedowns	1.8	10.1	—
Gross Margin	960.9	938.6	916.7
Selling, General, and Administrative Expenses	745.2	744.8	736.2
Legal Settlement Expense	—	2.4	—
Preopening Expense	6.9	6.3	6.4
Asset Impairments and Other Writedowns	14.9	25.4	36.2
Goodwill Amortization	—	2.7	2.8
Operating Income	193.9	157.0	135.1
Interest Expense	12.6	14.4	13.1
Income from Continuing Operations before Income Tax	181.3	142.6	122.0
Income Tax Provision	69.6	55.2	48.2
Income from Continuing Operations	111.7	87.4	73.8
Discontinued Operations (Note 3)			
Loss from Operations of All Wound Up, Net of Income Tax Credits of $7.0 and $2.4	—	—	10.8
Loss on Disposition of All Wound Up, Net of Deferred Income Tax Credit of $8.9	—	—	19.4
Net Income	$ 111.7	$ 87.4	$ 43.6

The income statement data show that Amazon.com had higher operating expenses than Borders although it does not have to operate traditional stores. As explained later in this chapter, the *gross margin percentage* indicates to some degree how much a company is charging in relation to what it pays to purchase the goods it is selling (its cost of goods sold). The *return on sales ratio* reveals how much profit, as a percentage of sales, a company is making after *all* of its expenses have been taken into account. For the calendar year 2002, the gross margin percentage for Borders was 27.4 percent and for Amazon.com was 25.2 percent, indicating that, on average, Amazon.com really does charge less for its books. The return on sales for Borders was 3.2 percent and for Amazon.com was −3.8 percent, suggesting that Borders is the one with the lower operating costs. In fact, Amazon.com's expenses were higher than those of Borders. Excluding cost of goods sold, the expenses at Borders were 24.4 percent of sales and at Amazon.com were 29.7 percent.

Topic Tackler

PLUS

5–1

LO2 Identify and explain the primary features of the perpetual inventory system.

Perpetual Inventory System

Most modern companies maintain their inventory records using the **perpetual inventory system.** This inventory system derives its name from the fact that the inventory account is adjusted perpetually (continually) throughout the accounting period. Each time merchandise is purchased, the inventory account is increased; each time it is sold, the inventory account is decreased. The following illustration demonstrates the basic features of the perpetual inventory system.

June Gardener loved plants and grew them with such remarkable success that she decided to open a small retail plant store. She started June's Plant Shop (JPS) on January 1, 2001. The following business events occurred during the first year the company operated.

1. Acquired $15,000 cash by issuing common stock.
2. Purchased merchandise inventory (plants) for $14,000 cash.
3. Sold inventory for $12,000 cash. This inventory had cost $8,000.
4. Paid $1,000 cash for selling expenses.

The effects of each of these events are explained and illustrated in the following discussion.

Effects of 2001 Events on Financial Statements

Event 1 *JPS acquired $15,000 cash by issuing common stock.*

This event is an asset source transaction. It increases both assets (cash) and stockholders' equity (common stock). The income statement is not affected. The statement of cash flows reflects an inflow from financing activities. These effects are shown here:

Cash	+ Inventory	= C. Stk.	+ Ret. Earn.	Rev.	− Exp.	= Net Inc.	Cash Flow
15,000 +	NA	= 15,000 +	NA	NA	− NA	= NA	15,000 FA

Event 2 *JPS purchased merchandise inventory for $14,000 cash.*

This event is an asset exchange transaction. One asset, cash, decreases and another asset, merchandise inventory, increases; total assets remains unchanged. Because product costs are expensed when inventory is sold, not when it is purchased, the event does not affect the income statement. The cash outflow, however, is reported in the operating activities section of the statement of cash flows. These effects are illustrated below:

Cash	+ Inventory	= C. Stk.	+ Ret. Earn.	Rev.	− Exp.	= Net Inc.	Cash Flow
(14,000) +	14,000	= NA	+ NA	NA	− NA	= NA	(14,000) OA

Event 3a *JPS recognized sales revenue from selling inventory for $12,000 cash.*

The revenue recognition is the first part of a two-part transaction. The *sales part* represents a source of assets (cash increases from earning sales revenue). Both assets (cash) and stockholders' equity (retained earnings) increase. Sales revenue on the income statement increases. The $12,000 cash inflow is reported in the operating activities section of the statement of cash flows. These effects are shown in the following financial statements model:

Cash	+ Inventory	= C. Stk.	+ Ret. Earn.	Rev.	−	Exp.	= Net Inc.	Cash Flow
12,000 +	NA	= NA	+ 12,000	12,000 −		NA	= 12,000	12,000 OA

Event 3b *JPS recognized $8,000 of cost of goods sold.*

The expense recognition is the second part of the two-part transaction. The *expense part* represents a use of assets. Both assets (merchandise inventory) and stockholders' equity (retained earnings) decrease. An expense account, Cost of Goods Sold, is reported on the income statement. This part of the transaction does not affect the statement of cash flows. A cash outflow occurred when the goods were bought, not when they were sold. These effects are shown here:

Cash	+ Inventory	= C. Stk.	+ Ret. Earn.	Rev.	−	Exp.	= Net Inc.	Cash Flow
NA	+ (8,000)	= NA	+ (8,000)	NA	−	8,000	= (8,000)	NA

Event 4 *JPS paid $1,000 cash for selling expenses.*

This event is an asset use transaction. The payment decreases both assets (cash) and stockholders' equity (retained earnings). The increase in selling expenses decreases net income. The $1,000 cash payment is reported in the operating activities section of the statement of cash flows. These effects are illustrated below:

Cash	+ Inventory	= C. Stk.	+ Ret. Earn.	Rev.	−	Exp.	= Net Inc.	Cash Flow
(1,000) +	NA	= NA	+ (1,000)	NA	−	1,000	= (1,000)	(1,000) OA

Ledger T-Accounts

Exhibit 5–2 shows the 2001 accounting transactions experienced by June's Plant Shop in ledger T-accounts. The entries in the T-accounts are referenced to the transactions using numbers in parentheses. The closing entry, referenced *cl,* transfers the balances in the revenue and

---

Exhibit 5–2 *General Ledger*

Assets			=	Liabilities		+	Equity		
Cash				**Accounts Payable**			**Common Stock**		
(1) 15,000	14,000	(2)			0 Bal.			15,000	(1)
(3a) 12,000	1,000	(4)						15,000	Bal.
Bal. 12,000									
							Retained Earnings		
Merchandise Inventory								3,000	(cl.)
(2) 14,000	8,000	(3b)						3,000	Bal.
Bal. 6,000									
							Sales Revenue		
							(cl.) 12,000	12,000	(3a)
								0	Bal.
							Cost of Goods Sold		
							(3b) 8,000	8,000	(cl.)
							Bal. 0		
							Selling Expenses		
							(4) 1,000	1,000	(cl.)
							Bal. 0		

Exhibit 5–3 *Financial Statements*

2001 Income Statement		12/31/01 Balance Sheet			2001 Statement of Cash Flows	
Sales Revenue	$12,000	Assets			Operating Activities	
Cost of Goods		Cash	$12,000		Inflow from Customers	$12,000
Sold	(8,000)	Merchandise Inventory	6,000		Outflow for Inventory	(14,000)
Gross Margin	4,000	Total Assets		$18,000	Outflow for Selling	
Less: Operating Exp.					& Admin.	(1,000)
Selling and		Liabilities		$ 0		
Admin. Exp.	(1,000)	Stockholders' Equity			Net Cash Outflow for	
Net Income	$ 3,000	Common Stock	$15,000		Operating Activities	$ (3,000)
		Retained Earnings	3,000		Investing Activities	0
		Total Stockholders' Equity		18,000	Financing Activities	
					Inflow from Stock Issue	15,000
		Total Liab. and Stk. Equity		$18,000	Net Change in Cash	12,000
					Plus Beginning Cash Balance	0
					Ending Cash Balance	$12,000

expense accounts to the Retained Earnings account. Closing entries are claims exchange transactions. They increase some equity accounts and decrease others. The amount of total equity is not affected by the closing entry.

The information in the ledger accounts is used to prepare the financial statements displayed in Exhibit 5–3. Before reading further, trace the ledger account balances to the financial statements.

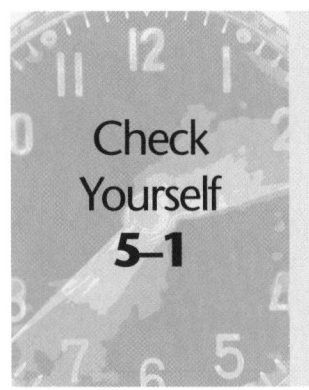

Check Yourself 5–1

Phambroom Company began 2006 with $35,600 in its Inventory account. During the year, it purchased inventory costing $356,800 and sold inventory that had cost $360,000 for $520,000. Based on this information alone, determine (1) the inventory balance as of December 31, 2006, and (2) the amount of gross margin Phambroom would report on its 2006 income statement.

Answer

1. Beginning inventory + Purchases = Goods available − Ending inventory = Cost of goods sold
   $35,600 + $356,800 = $392,400 − Ending inventory = $360,000
   Ending inventory = $32,400
2. Sales revenue − Cost of goods sold = Gross margin
   $520,000 − $360,000 = $160,000

Topic Tackler

PLUS

5–2

LO3 Explain the meaning of terms used to describe transportation costs, cash discounts, returns or allowances, and financing costs.

Transportation Cost, Purchase Returns and Allowances, and Cash Discounts Related to Inventory Purchases

Purchasing inventory often involves: (1) incurring transportation costs, (2) returning inventory or receiving purchase allowances (cost reductions), and (3) taking cash discounts (also cost reductions). During its second accounting cycle, JPS encountered these kinds of events. The final account balances at the end of the 2001 fiscal year become the beginning balances for 2002: Cash, $12,000; Merchandise Inventory, $6,000; Common Stock, $15,000; and Retained Earnings, $3,000.

Effects of 2002 Events on Financial Statements

JPS experienced the following events during its 2002 accounting period. The effects of each of these events are explained and illustrated in the following discussion.

Event 1 *JPS purchased merchandise inventory on account with a list price of $8,000. The payment terms were 2/10 n/30.*

The expression **2/10 n/30** (two-ten net thirty) means the seller will allow a 2 percent discount if the purchaser pays cash for the merchandise within 10 days from the date of purchase. If the purchaser pays later than 10 days from the purchase date, the full amount is due within 30 days. Based on these terms, the net (cash) cost of the inventory is $7,840 [$8,000 × (100% − 2%)]. While alternative recording practices exist, this textbook uses the **net method,** recording inventory purchases at the net price (the list price minus the purchase discount). A **cash discount** represents a price reduction offered by a seller to a buyer to encourage prompt payment. Since JPS is the buyer, this cash discount is a **purchase discount.**

The inventory purchase increases both assets (merchandise inventory) and liabilities (accounts payable) on the balance sheet. The income statement is not affected until later, when inventory is sold. Since the inventory was purchased on account, there was no cash outflow. These effects are shown here:

Record inventory at discounted price

Cash	+	Accts. Rec.	+	Inventory	=	Accts. Pay.	+	C. Stk.	+	Retained Earnings		Rev.	−	Exp.	=	Net Inc.		Cash Flow
NA	+	NA	+	7,840	=	7,840	+	NA	+	NA		NA	−	NA	=	NA		NA

Event 2 *JPS returned some of the inventory purchased in Event 1. The list price of the returned merchandise was $1,000.*

To promote customer satisfaction, many businesses allow customers to return goods for reasons such as wrong size, wrong color, wrong design, or even simply because the purchaser changed his mind. The effect of a purchase return is the *opposite* of the original purchase. For JPS the purchase return decreases both assets (merchandise inventory) and liabilities (accounts payable). There is no effect on either the income statement or the statement of cash flows. Since the inventory purchase was originally recorded at the net price (list price less purchase discount), the return is also recorded at the net price, $980 ($1,000 × .98). These effects are shown below:

Cash	+	Accts. Rec.	+	Inventory	=	Accts. Pay.	+	C. Stk.	+	Retained Earnings		Rev.	−	Exp.	=	Net Inc.		Cash Flow
NA	+	NA	+	(980)	=	(980)	+	NA	+	NA		NA	−	NA	=	NA		NA

Sometimes dissatisfied buyers will agree to keep goods instead of returning them if the seller offers to reduce the price. Such reductions are called **allowances.** Purchase allowances affect the financial statements the same way purchase returns do.

Event 3 *JPS paid cash to settle the account payable due on the inventory purchased in Event 1. The payment was made after the end of the discount period.*

By delaying the payment, JPS is holding on to money that belongs to the supplier. In other words, delaying payment is equivalent to borrowing money. JPS is required to pay the full list price rather than the net price for the privilege of delaying the payment (borrowing money). Indeed, the *difference between the list price and the net price is classified as interest expense.*

The amount due is $7,000 ($8,000 original list price minus $1,000 return). Recall that JPS had recorded the net price, $6,860 ($7,000 × .98) in its Accounts Payable account. The amount of the interest expense is $140 ($7,000 list price − $6,860 net price *or* $7,000 list price × .02 discount). The $7,000 cash payment results in a compound entry that reduces the asset account, Cash, reduces the liability account, Accounts Payable, and recognizes interest expense. The interest expense reduces net income. Since paying the account payable and paying interest expense are both operating activities, the statement of cash flows reflects a single outflow of $7,000. These effects are illustrated in the following financial statements model:

Cash	+	Accts. Rec.	+	Inventory	=	Accts. Pay.	+	C. Stk.	+	Retained Earnings		Rev.	−	Exp.	=	Net Inc.		Cash Flow
(7,000)	+	NA	+	NA	=	(6,860)	+	NA	+	(140)		NA	−	140	=	(140)		(7,000) OA

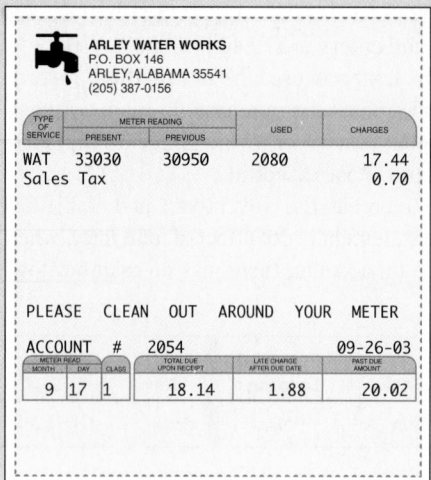

Many real-world companies have found it more effective to impose a penalty for late payment than to use a cash discount to encourage early payment. The invoice from Arley Water Works is an example of the penalty strategy. Notice that the amount due, if paid by the due date, is $18.14. A $1.88 late charge is imposed if the bill is paid after the due date. The $1.88 late charge is in fact interest. If Arley Water Works collects the payment after the due date, the utility will receive cash of $20.02. The collection will increase cash ($20.02), reduce accounts receivable ($18.14), and increase interest revenue ($1.88).

Event 4 *The shipping terms for the inventory purchased in Event 1 were FOB shipping point. JPS paid the freight company $300 cash for delivering the merchandise.*

The terms **FOB shipping point** and **FOB destination** identify whether the buyer or the seller is responsible for transportation costs. If goods are delivered FOB shipping point, the buyer is responsible for the freight cost. If goods are delivered FOB destination, the seller is responsible. When the buyer is responsible, the freight cost is called **transportation-in.** When the seller is responsible, the cost is called **transportation-out.** The following table summarizes freight cost terms.

Responsible Party	Buyer	Seller
Freight Terms	FOB shipping point	FOB destination
Cost Title	Transportation-in	Transportation-out

Event 4 indicates the inventory was delivered FOB shipping point, so JPS (the buyer) is responsible for the $300 freight cost. Since incurring transportation-in costs is necessary to obtain inventory, these costs are added to the inventory account. The freight cost increases one asset account (Merchandise Inventory) and decreases another asset account (Cash). The income statement is not affected by this transaction because transportation-in costs are not expensed when they are incurred. Instead they are expensed as part of *cost of goods sold* when the inventory is sold. However, the cash paid for freight when inventory is delivered to customers is reported as an outflow in the operating activities section of the statement of cash flows. The effects of *transportation-in costs* are shown here:

Cash	+	Accts. Rec.	+	Inventory	=	Accts. Pay.	+	C. Stk.	+	Retained Earnings		Rev.	−	Exp.	=	Net Inc.		Cash Flow
(300)	+	NA	+	300	=	NA	+	NA	+	NA		NA	−	NA	=	NA		(300) OA

Event 5a *JPS recognized $24,750 of revenue on the cash sale of merchandise that cost $11,500.*

The sale increases assets (cash) and stockholders' equity (retained earnings). The revenue recognition increases net income. The $24,750 cash inflow from the sale is reported in the operating activities section of the statement of cash flows. These effects are shown below:

Cash	+	Accts. Rec.	+	Inventory	=	Accts. Pay.	+	C. Stk.	+	Retained Earnings		Rev.	–	Exp.	=	Net Inc.		Cash Flow
24,750	+	NA	+	NA	=	NA	+	NA	+	24,750		24,750	–	NA	=	24,750		24,750 OA

Event 5b *JPS recognized $11,500 of cost of goods sold.*

When goods are sold, the product cost—*including a proportionate share of transportation-in and adjustments for purchase returns and allowances*—is transferred from the Merchandise Inventory account to the expense account, Cost of Goods Sold. Recognizing cost of goods sold decreases both assets (merchandise inventory) and stockholders' equity (retained earnings). The expense recognition for cost of goods sold decreases net income. Cash flow is not affected. These effects are shown here:

Cash	+	Accts. Rec.	+	Inventory	=	Accts. Pay.	+	C. Stk.	+	Retained Earnings		Rev.	–	Exp.	=	Net Inc.		Cash Flow
NA	+	NA	+	(11,500)	=	NA	+	NA	+	(11,500)		NA	–	11,500	=	(11,500)		NA

Event 6 *JPS incurred $450 of freight costs on inventory delivered to customers.*

Assume the merchandise sold in Event 5 was shipped FOB destination. Also assume JPS paid the freight cost in cash. FOB destination means the seller is responsible for the freight cost, which is called transportation-out. Transportation-out is reported on the income statement as an operating expense in the section below gross margin. The cost of freight on goods shipped to customers is incurred *after* the goods are sold. It is not part of the costs to obtain goods or ready them for sale. Recognizing the expense of transportation-out reduces assets (cash) and stockholders' equity (retained earnings). Operating expenses increase and net income decreases. The cash outflow is reported in the operating activities section of the statement of cash flows. These effects are shown below:

Cash	+	Accts. Rec.	+	Inventory	=	Accts. Pay.	+	C. Stk.	+	Retained Earnings		Rev.	–	Exp.	=	Net Inc.		Cash Flow
(450)	+	NA	+	NA	=	NA	+	NA	+	(450)		NA	–	450	=	(450)		(450) OA

Event 7 *JPS purchased $14,000 of merchandise inventory on account with credit terms of 1/10 n/30. The inventory was delivered FOB destination. The freight costs were $400.*

Merchandise inventory and accounts payable both increase by the net price of the merchandise, $13,860 ($14,000 × .99). Net income and cash flow are not affected. *The freight costs do not affect JPS since the freight terms are FOB destination and the seller is responsible for them.* These effects are shown here:

Cash	+	Accts. Rec.	+	Inventory	=	Accts. Pay.	+	C. Stk.	+	Retained Earnings		Rev.	–	Exp.	=	Net Inc.		Cash Flow
NA	+	NA	+	13,860	=	13,860	+	NA	+	NA		NA	–	NA	=	NA		NA

Event 8a *JPS recognized $16,800 of revenue from the sale on account of merchandise that cost $8,660. The freight terms were FOB shipping point. The party responsible paid freight costs of $275 in cash. JPS does not offer a cash discount to customers.*

The effect on the balance sheet of recognizing revenue is an increase in both assets (accounts receivable) and stockholders' equity (retained earnings). The event increases revenue and net income. Since JPS sold the inventory on account, cash flow is not currently affected. These effects are illustrated here:

Cash	+	Accts. Rec.	+	Inventory	=	Accts. Pay.	+	C. Stk.	+	Retained Earnings		Rev.	–	Exp.	=	Net Inc.		Cash Flow
NA	+	16,800	+	NA	=	NA	+	NA	+	16,800		16,800	–	NA	=	16,800		NA

Event 8b *JPS recognized $8,660 of cost of goods sold.*

As discussed previously, when inventory is sold, the product cost is transferred from the Merchandise Inventory account to the expense account, Cost of Goods Sold. Recognizing cost of goods sold decreases both assets (merchandise inventory) and stockholders' equity (retained earnings) by $8,660. The expense recognition for cost of goods sold decreases net income. Cash flow is not affected. *The freight costs do not affect JPS since the freight terms are FOB shipping point and the buyer is responsible for them.* These effects are shown here:

Cash	+	Accts. Rec.	+	Inventory	=	Accts. Pay.	+	C. Stk.	+	Retained Earnings		Rev.	–	Exp.	=	Net Inc.		Cash Flow
NA	+	NA	+	(8,660)	=	NA	+	NA	+	(8,660)		NA	–	8,660	=	(8,660)		NA

Event 9 *JPS paid $9,900 cash in partial settlement of the account payable that arose from purchasing inventory on account in Event 7. The partial payment was made within the discount period for merchandise with a list price of $10,000.*

Assume that JPS was not able to pay the entire account payable of $13,860 (recorded at the net amount) in time to receive the 1% purchase discount offered by the supplier, but JPS was able to pay part of the liability within the discount period. The effect of the event on the balance sheet is to decrease both assets (cash) and liabilities (accounts payable) by $9,900 (10,000 × .99). The $9,900 cash outflow is included in the operating activities section of the statement of cash flows. These effects are shown below.

Cash	+	Accts. Rec.	+	Inventory	=	Accts. Pay.	+	C. Stk.	+	Retained Earnings		Rev.	–	Exp.	=	Net Inc.		Cash Flow
(9,900)	+	NA	+	NA	=	(9,900)	+	NA	+	NA		NA	–	NA	=	NA		(9,900) OA

Event 10 *JPS paid $8,000 cash for selling and administrative expenses.*

The effect on the balance sheet is to decrease both assets (cash) and stockholders' equity (retained earnings). Recognizing the selling and administrative expenses decreases net income. The $8,000 cash outflow is reported in the operating activities section of the statement of cash flows. These effects are shown below.

Cash	+	Accts. Rec.	+	Inventory	=	Accts. Pay.	+	C. Stk.	+	Retained Earnings		Rev.	–	Exp.	=	Net Inc.		Cash Flow
(8,000)	+	NA	+	NA	=	NA	+	NA	+	(8,000)		NA	–	8,000	=	(8,000)		(8,000) OA

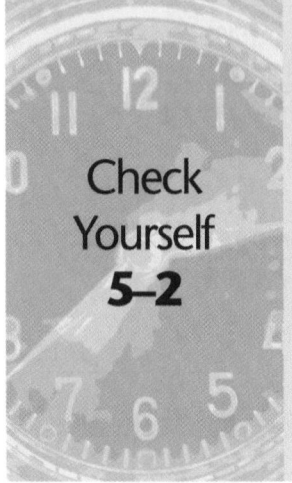

Check Yourself 5–2

Choi Company purchased $24,000 of inventory on account with payment terms of 2/10, n/30 and freight terms FOB shipping point. Freight costs were $1,200. Choi paid $18,000 of the accounts payable within the 10-day discount period and the remaining $6,000 after the discount period had expired. Choi sold all of the inventory for $32,000. Based on this information, determine the amount of gross margin and interest expense Choi would report on the income statement.

Answer The cost of the inventory is determined as follows:

Net price (24,000 × .98)	$23,520
Plus Transportation-in	1,200
Total cost	$24,720

The gross margin is $7,280, the sales price less cost of goods sold ($32,000 − $24,720). The amount of interest expense is $120 (6,000 × .02).

General Ledger Accounts

Exhibit 5–4 summarizes in T-account form the 2002 accounting events just described. A summary of these events follows here for your convenience. Before reading further, trace the effects of each event to the ledger accounts. Then trace the information in the ledger accounts to the 2002 financial statements displayed in Exhibit 5–5.

Event 1   JPS purchased on account merchandise inventory with a list price of $8,000, payment terms 2/10 n/ 30.

Event 2   JPS returned some of the inventory purchased in Event 1. The list price of the returned merchandise was $1,000.

Event 3   JPS paid cash to settle the account payable due on the inventory purchased in Event 1. The payment was made after the end of the discount period.

Event 4   The inventory purchased in Event 1 was delivered FOB shipping point. JPS paid the freight company $300 cash for delivering the merchandise.

Event 5a   JPS recognized $24,750 of revenue on the cash sale of merchandise that cost $11,500.

Event 5b   JPS recognized $11,500 of cost of goods sold.

Event 6   JPS incurred $450 of freight costs on inventory delivered to customers.

Exhibit 5–4 Ledger Accounts, 2002

Assets				=	Liabilities			+	Equity		

Cash   **Accounts Payable**   **Common Stock**

Cash					Accounts Payable					Common Stock	
Bal.	12,000	7,000	(3)	(2)	980	7,840	(1)			15,000	Bal.
(5a)	24,750	300	(4)	(3)	6,860	13,860	(7)				
		450	(6)	(9)	9,900						
		9,900	(9)			3,960	Bal.				
		8,000	(10)								
Bal.	11,100										

Retained Earnings

				Retained Earnings	
				3,000	Bal.
				12,800	(cl.)
				15,800	Bal.

Accounts Receivable

Accounts Receivable				Sales Revenue	
(8a)	16,800				24,750	(5a)
Bal.	16,800		(cl.)	41,550	16,800	(8a)
					-0-	Bal.

Merchandise Inventory

Merchandise Inventory				Cost of Goods Sold	
Bal.	6,000	980	(2)			
(1)	7,840	11,500	(5b)	(5b)	11,500	
(4)	300	8,660	(8b)	(8b)	8,660	20,160	(cl.)
(7)	13,860			Bal.	-0-	
Bal.	6,860					

Transportation-out

Transportation-out	
(6)	450	450	(cl.)
Bal.	-0-	

Selling and Admin. Expenses

Selling and Admin. Expenses	
(10)	8,000	8,000	(cl.)
Bal.	-0-	

Interest Expense

Interest Expense	
(3)	140	140	(cl.)
Bal.	-0-	

Total Assets	=	Total Liabilities	+	Total Equity
$34,760		**$3,960**		**$30,800**

Exhibit 5–5 Financial Statements

2002 Income Statement	
Net Sales	$41,550
Cost of Goods Sold	(20,160)
Gross Margin	21,390
Less: Operating Expenses	
Selling and Admin. Exp.	(8,000)
Transportation-out	(450)
Operating Income	12,940
Nonoperating Items	
Interest Expense	(140)
Net Income	$12,800

12/31/02 Balance Sheet		
Assets		
Cash	$11,100	
Accounts Receivable	16,800	
Merchandise Inventory	6,860	
Total Assets		$34,760
Liabilities		
Accounts Payable		$ 3,960
Stockholders' Equity		
Common Stock	$15,000	
Retained Earnings	15,800	
Total Stockholders' Equity		30,800
Total Liab. and Stk. Equity		$34,760

2002 Statement of Cash Flows		
Operating Activities		
Inflow from		
Customers	$24,750	
Outflow for		
Inventory	(17,060)	
Outflow for		
Transportation-out	(450)	
Outflow for Selling		
and Admin. Exp.	(8,000)	
Outflow for Interest	(140)	
Net Cash Outflow for		
Operating Activities		$ (900)
Investing Activities		-0-
Financing Activities		-0-
Net Change in Cash		(900)
Plus Beginning Cash Balance		12,000
Ending Cash Balance		$11,100

Event 7   JPS purchased $14,000 of merchandise inventory on account with credit terms of 1/10 n/30. The inventory was delivered FOB destination. The freight costs were $400.

Event 8a   JPS recognized $16,800 of revenue from the sale on account of merchandise that cost $8,660. The freight terms were FOB shipping point. The party responsible paid freight costs of $275 in cash.

Event 8b   JPS recognized $8,660 of cost of goods sold.

Event 9   JPS paid $9,900 cash in partial settlement of the account payable that arose from purchasing inventory on account in Event 7.

Event 10   JPS paid $8,000 cash for selling and administrative expenses.

Financial Statements

LO4 Compare and contrast single and multistep income statements.

The income statement displayed in Exhibit 5–5 is more informative than one which simply subtracts expenses from revenues. By reporting gross margin, it shows the relationship between the cost of goods sold and the sales revenue earned from those particular goods. This income statement also separates routine operating results from nonoperating results, which enables analysts to distinguish between recurring revenues and expenses and those related to peripheral transactions, such as gains and losses, interest revenue, and interest expense. Income statements that show these additional relationships are called **multistep income statements.** Income statements that display a single comparison of total revenues and total expenses are called **single-step income statements.** Exhibit 5–6 shows the percentage of companies that use the multistep versus the single-step format.

On a multistep income statement, interest revenue and interest expense are classified as nonoperating items. In contrast, cash receipts of interest revenue and cash payments of interest expense are reported as operating activities on the statement of cash flows. When developing the statement of cash flows, the Financial Accounting Standards Board (FASB) faced two alternatives regarding how to classify interest, each of which had legitimate theoretical support. Even though interest is reported as a nonoperating item on the income statement, the FASB voted to require that interest be reported as an operating activity on the statement of cash flows. Awareness of this inconsistency is helpful in avoiding confusion when reading financial statements.

Exhibit 5–6 Income Statement Format Used by U.S. Companies

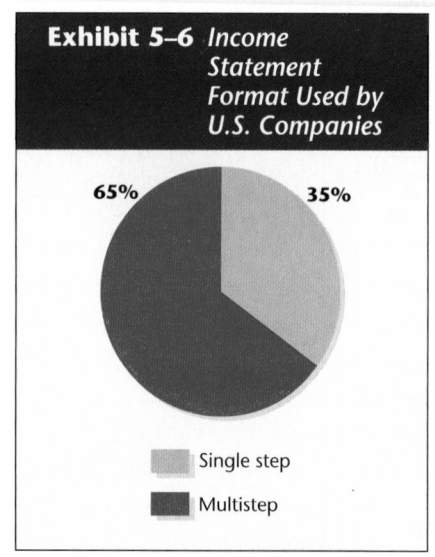

65%   35%

- Single step
- Multistep

Data Source: AICPA, Accounting Trends and Techniques, 2002.

Whether using the single-step or multistep income statement format, companies are required to report revenues or expenses from discontinued operations or extraordinary items on separate lines just above net income.

Events Affecting Sales

To this point we assumed JPS did not offer cash discounts to its customers. However, sales of inventory can also be affected by returns, allowances, and discounts. To illustrate, assume JPS engaged in the following selected events during January 2003.

Event 1a *JPS sold on account merchandise with a list price of $8,500. Payment terms were 1/10 n/30. The merchandise had cost JPS $5,100.*

The sale is recorded at the net price of $8,415 ($8,500 × .99). It increases both assets (accounts receivable) and shareholders' equity (retained earnings). Recognizing revenue increases net income. The statement of cash flows is not affected. These effects are illustrated in the following financial statements model:

Event No.	Cash	+	Accts. Rec.	+	Inventory	=	Accts. Pay.	+	C. Stk.	+	Retained Earnings	Rev.	−	Exp.	=	Net Inc.	Cash Flow
1a	NA	+	8,415	+	NA	=	NA	+	NA	+	8,415	8,415	−	NA	=	8,415	NA

Event 1b *JPS recognized $5,100 of cost of goods sold.*

Recognizing the expense decreases assets (merchandise inventory) and stockholders' equity (retained earnings). Cost of goods sold increases and net income decreases. Cash flow is not affected. These effects are shown below:

Event No.	Cash	+	Accts. Rec.	+	Inventory	=	Accts. Pay.	+	C. Stk.	+	Retained Earnings	Rev.	−	Exp.	=	Net Inc.	Cash Flow
1b	NA	+	NA	+	(5,100)	=	NA	+	NA	+	(5,100)	NA	−	5,100	=	(5,100)	NA

Event 2a *The customer from Event 1a returned inventory with a $1,000 list price that JPS had sold with 1/10 n/30 payment terms. The merchandise had cost JPS $600.*

Since JPS originally recorded the sales revenue at the net price, it must also record the sales return at the net price, $990 ($1,000 × .99). The return decreases both assets (accounts receivable) and stockholders' equity (retained earnings) on the balance sheet. Sales and net income decrease. Cash flow is not affected. These effects follow:

Event No.	Cash	+	Accts. Rec.	+	Inventory	=	Accts. Pay.	+	C. Stk.	+	Retained Earnings	Rev.	−	Exp.	=	Net Inc.	Cash Flow
2a	NA	+	(990)	+	NA	=	NA	+	NA	+	(990)	(990)	−	NA	=	(990)	NA

Event 2b *The cost of the goods ($600) is returned to the inventory account.*

Since JPS got the inventory back, the sales return increases both assets (merchandise inventory) and stockholders' equity (retained earnings). The expense (cost of goods sold) decreases and net income increases. Cash flow is not affected. These effects are illustrated here:

Event No.	Cash	+	Accts. Rec.	+	Inventory	=	Accts. Pay.	+	C. Stk.	+	Retained Earnings	Rev.	−	Exp.	=	Net Inc.	Cash Flow
2b	NA	+	NA	+	600	=	NA	+	NA	+	600	NA	−	(600)	=	600	NA

Event 3 *JPS collected the balance of the account receivable from the customer that purchased the goods in Event 1a.*

If the customer paid within the discount period, JPS would receive the net amount, which equals the balance in the Accounts Receivable account. The cash collection would represent an asset exchange, with cash increasing and accounts receivable decreasing for the net amount of $7,425 ($7,500 × .99). The statement of cash flows would report an inflow of $7,425 from operating activities. These effects are shown here:

Event No.	Cash	+	Accts. Rec.	+	Inventory	=	Accts. Pay.	+	C. Stk.	+	Retained Earnings	Rev.	−	Exp.	=	Net Inc.	Cash Flow
3	7,425	+	(7,425)	+	NA	=	NA	+	NA	+	NA	NA	−	NA	=	NA	7,425 OA

Alternatively, if the customer paid after the discount period expired, JPS would receive the list price of $7,500. The $75 ($7,500 − $7,425) difference between the list price and the net price is interest revenue. The asset cash would increase, the asset accounts receivable would decrease, and revenue would increase. The statement of cash flows would report an inflow of $7,500 from operating activities. These effects are illustrated here:

Event No.	Cash	+	Accts. Rec.	+	Inventory	=	Accts. Pay.	+	C. Stk.	+	Retained Earnings	Rev.	−	Exp.	=	Net Inc.	Cash Flow
3	7,500	+	(7,425)	+	NA	=	NA	+	NA	+	75	75	−	NA	=	75	7,500 OA

Lost, Damaged, or Stolen Inventory

LO5 Show the effect of lost, damaged, or stolen inventory on financial statements.

Most merchandising companies experience some level of inventory **shrinkage,** a term that reflects decreases in inventory for reasons other than sales to customers. Inventory may be stolen by shoplifters, damaged by customers or employees, or even simply lost or misplaced. Since the *perpetual* inventory system is designed to record purchases and sales of inventory as they occur, the balance in the merchandise inventory account represents the amount of inventory that *should* be on hand at any given time. By taking a physical count of the merchandise inventory at the end of the accounting period and comparing that amount with the book balance in the Merchandise Inventory account, managers can determine the amount of any inventory shrinkage. If goods have been lost, damaged, or stolen, the book balance will be higher than the actual amount of inventory on hand and an adjusting entry is required to reduce assets and equity. The Merchandise Inventory account is reduced, and an expense for the amount of the lost, damaged, or stolen inventory is recognized.

Adjustment for Lost, Damaged, or Stolen Inventory

To illustrate, assume that Midwest Merchandising Company maintains perpetual inventory records. Midwest determined, through a physical count, that it had $23,500 of merchandise inventory on hand at the end of the accounting period. The balance in the Inventory account was $24,000. Midwest must make an adjusting entry to write down the Inventory account so the amount reported on the financial statements agrees with the amount actually on hand at the end of the period. The write-down decreases both assets (inventory) and stockholders' equity (retained earnings). The write-down increases expenses and decreases net income. Cash flow is not affected. The effects on the statements are as follows:

Assets	=	Liab.	+	Equity	Rev.	−	Exp.	=	Net Inc.	Cash Flow
(500)	=	NA	+	(500)	NA	−	500	=	(500)	NA

"Closed for Inventory Count" is a sign you frequently see on retail stores sometime during the month of January. Even if companies use a perpetual inventory system, the amount of inventory on hand may be unknown because of lost, damaged, or stolen goods. The only way to determine the amount of inventory on hand is to count it. Why count it in January? Christmas shoppers and many after-Christmas sales shoppers are satiated by mid-January, leaving the stores low on both merchandise and customers. Accordingly, stores have less merchandise to count and "lost sales" are minimized during January. Companies that do not depend on seasonal sales (e.g., plumbing supplies wholesale business) may choose to count inventory at some other time during the year. Counting inventory is not a revenue-generating activity. It is a necessary evil that should be conducted when it least disrupts operations.

In general journal form, the entry is as follows:

Account Title	Debit	Credit
Inventory Loss (Cost of Goods Sold)	500	
Inventory		500

Theoretically, inventory losses are operating expenses. Because such losses are normally immaterial in amount, however, they are usually added to cost of goods sold for external reporting purposes.

THE FINANCIAL ANALYST

Merchandising is a highly competitive business. In order to succeed, merchandisers develop different strategies to distinguish themselves in the marketplace. For example, some companies like **Wal-Mart**, **Kmart**, and **Target** focus on price competition while others such as **Neiman Marcus** and **Saks Fifth Avenue** sell high price goods that offer high quality, style, and strong guaranties. Financial analysts have developed specific tools that are useful in scrutinizing the success or failure of a company's sales strategy. The first step in the analytical process is to develop common size statements so that comparisons can be made between companies.

LO6 Use common size financial statements to evaluate managerial performance.

Common Size Financial Statements

As previously discussed, raw accounting numbers can be difficult to interpret. Suppose that Smith Company earns a 10 percent return on its assets while Jones Company earns only 8 percent on its assets. If Smith Company's total assets are $1,000,000 and Jones Company's are $2,000,000, Smith Company would report less income ($1,000,000 × 0.10 = $100,000) than Jones Company ($2,000,000 × 0.08 = $160,000) even though Smith Company was doing a better job of investing its assets.

Exhibit 5-7

JUNE'S PLANT SHOP
Common Size Income Statement*
For the Year Ended 2002

Net Sales	$41,550	100.00%
Cost of Goods Sold	(20,160)	(48.52)
Gross Margin	21,390	51.48
Less: Operating Expenses		
Selling and Administrative Expenses	(8,000)	(19.25)
Transportation-out	(450)	(1.08)
Operating Income	12,940	31.14
Nonoperating Items		
Interest Expense	(140)	(.34)
Net Income	$12,800	30.81%

*Percentages do not add exactly because they have been rounded.

Similar difficulties arise when comparing a single company's current period financial statements to those of prior periods. How good is a $1,000,000 increase in net income? The increase is certainly not as good if the company is IBM rather than a small computer store. To more easily compare between accounting periods or between companies, analysts prepare **common size financial statements** by converting absolute dollar amounts to percentages.

With respect to the income statement, we begin by defining net sales as the base figure, or 100%. Recall that **net sales** is total sales minus sales returns, sales allowances, and sales discounts. The other amounts on the statement are then shown as a percentage of net sales. For example, the cost of goods sold percentage is the dollar amount of cost of goods sold divided by the dollar amount of net sales, and so on for the other items on the statement. Exhibit 5–7 displays a common size income statement derived from JPS's 2002 income statement shown in Exhibit 5–5.

Comparisons between Companies

Gross Margin Percentage

LO7 Use ratio analysis to evaluate managerial performance.

Does **Wal-Mart** sell merchandise at a higher or lower price than **Target**? The gross margin percentage is useful in answering questions such as this. Specifically, the **gross margin percentage** is defined as:

$$\frac{\text{Gross margin}}{\text{Net sales}}$$

When comparing two retail companies, all other things being equal, the company with the higher gross margin percentage is pricing its products higher.

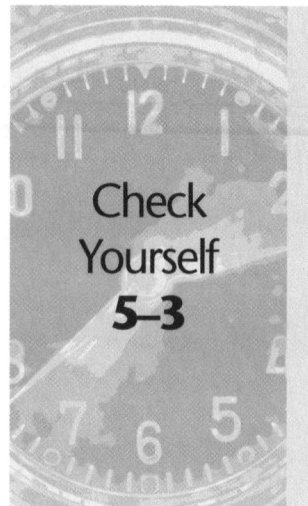

Check Yourself 5-3

The following sales data are from the records of two retail sales companies. All amounts are in thousands.

	Company A	Company B
Sales	$21,234	$43,465
Cost of goods sold	14,864	34,772
Gross margin	$ 6,370	$ 8,693

One company is an upscale department store, and the other is a discount sales store. Which company is the upscale department store?

Answer The gross margin percentage for Company A is approximately 30 percent ($6,370 ÷ $21,234). The gross margin percentage for Company B is 20 percent ($8,693 ÷ $43,465). These percentages suggest that Company A is selling goods with a higher markup than Company B, which implies that Company A is the upscale department store.

Net Income Percentage

Another commonly used ratio is the net income percentage. The **net income percentage** (sometimes called **return on sales**) is determined as follows:

$$\frac{\text{Net income}}{\text{Net sales}}$$

Exhibit 5–8

JUNE'S PLANT SHOP
Common Size Income Statements*

	2002		2003	
Net Sales	$41,550	100%	$49,860	100%
Cost of Goods Sold	(20,160)	49	(19,944)	(40)
Gross Margin	21,390	51	29,916	60
Less: Operating Expenses				
Selling and Administrative Expenses	(8,000)	(19)	(12,465)	(25)
Transportation-out	(450)	(1)	(500)	(1)
Operating Income	12,940	31	16,951	34
Nonoperating Items				
Interest Expense	(140)	0	(400)	(1)
Net Income	$12,800	31%	$16,551	33%

Net income expressed as a percentage of sales provides insight as to how much of each sales dollar is left as net income after *all* expenses are paid. When comparing two companies, all other things being equal, the company with the higher return on sales ratio is doing a better job of controlling expenses.

Comparisons within a Particular Company

The previous discussion focused on using common size income data to make comparisons among different companies. Analysts also find it useful to compare a particular company's performance over different periods. To illustrate, assume that June's Plant Shop relocated its store to an upscale shopping mall with a wealthier customer base. June has to pay more for rent but believes she will more than offset the higher rent cost by selling her merchandise at higher prices. June changed locations on January 1, 2003. Exhibit 5–8 contains JPS's 2002 and 2003 income statements. Use the data in this exhibit to determine whether June's strategy was successful.

Analyzing the common size statements suggests that June's strategy did increase the profitability of her business. The increase in the gross margin percentage (51% to 60%) confirms the fact that JPS raised its prices. The increase in the return on sales ratio (31% to 33%) shows that the increase in sales revenue was larger than the increase in total expenses.

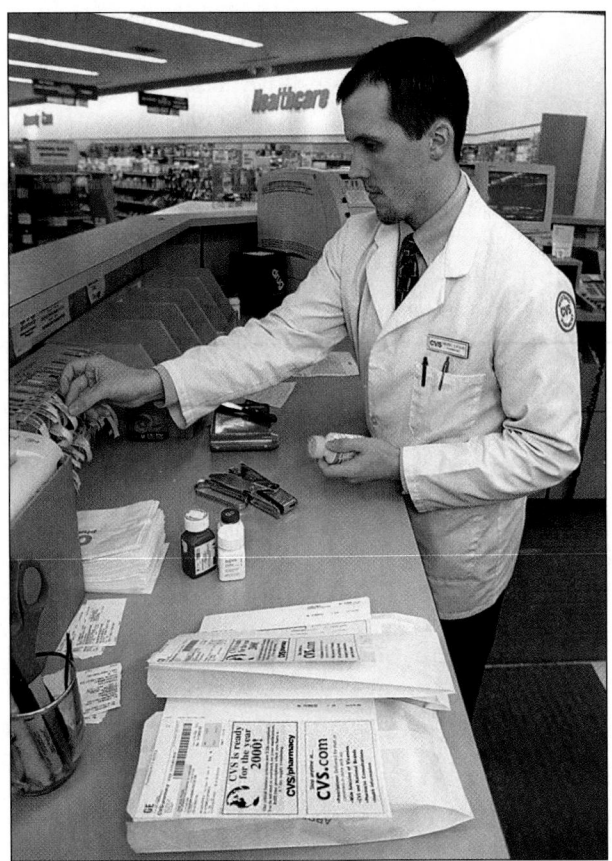

▌Real-World Data

Exhibit 5–9 shows the gross margin percentages and return on sales ratios for 10 companies. Three of the companies are manufacturers that produce pharmaceutical products, and the remaining seven companies sell various products at the retail level. These data are for the companies' fiscal years that ended in late 2002 or early 2003.

A review of the data confirms our earlier finding that ratios for companies in the same industry are often more similar than are ratios for companies from different industries. For example, note that the manufacturers have much higher margins, both for gross profit and for net earnings, than do the retailers. Manufacturers are often able to charge higher prices than are

Exhibit 5–9

Industry/Company	Gross Margin %	Return on Sales
Pharmaceutical manufacturers		
Bristol Meyers-Squibb	64.7%	11.4%
Johnson & Johnson	71.2	18.2
Pfizer	87.5	28.2
Retail pharmacies		
CVS	25.1	3.0
Rite Aid	23.4	(0.7)
Walgreens	26.5	3.6
Department stores		
Neiman Marcus	32.2	3.4
Wal-Mart	21.5	3.3
Office supplies		
Office Depot	29.6	2.7
Staples	25.4	3.8

retailers because they obtain patents which give them a legal monopoly on the products they create. When a company such as **Pfizer** develops a new drug, no one else can produce that drug until the patent expires, giving it lots of control over its price at the wholesale level. Conversely, when **Walgreens** sells Pfizer's drug at the retail level, it faces price competition from **CVS**, a company that is trying to sell the same drug to the same consumers. One way CVS can try to get customers to shop at its store is to charge lower prices than its competitors, but this reduces its profit margins, since it must pay the same price to get Pfizer's drug as did Walgreens. As the data in Exhibit 5–9 show, in 2002 CVS had a lower gross margin percentage than did Walgreens, indicating it is charging slightly lower prices for similar goods.

In the examples presented in Exhibit 5–9, the companies with higher gross margin percentages usually had higher return on sales ratios than their competitors, but this was not always the case. In the office supplies business, **Office Depot's** gross margin percentage was significantly higher that that of its rival, **Staples**, but its return on sales ratio was considerably lower. Also, while **Neiman Marcus** had a gross margin percentage that was 50 percent greater than **Wal-Mart's** ([32.2 − 21.5] ÷ 21.5) their return on sales ratios were almost equal. This is not surprising when you consider how much more luxurious, and costly, the interior of a Neiman Marcus store is compared to a Wal-Mart.

Financing Merchandise Inventory

Suppose a store purchases inventory in October to sell during the Christmas season. If the store sells the inventory on account, much of the cash from the sales won't be collected until January or February of the next year. With cash collections from customers lagging three or four months behind when the goods were purchased, how will the store pay for the inventory? One way is to borrow the money. The company could pay for the merchandise in October with money borrowed from a bank. When the cash from fall sales is collected in January and February, the company could repay the bank.

An obvious drawback to obtaining a loan to pay for inventory is the interest expense incurred on the borrowed funds. However, other alternatives for financing inventory purchases are also expensive. If the owner's money is used, it cannot be invested elsewhere, such as in an interest-earning savings account. This failure to earn interest revenue is called an **opportunity cost;** it is effectively a financing cost that is just as real as actual payment of interest expense. Net income falls regardless of whether a business incurs expenses or loses revenue.

A third alternative is to purchase the inventory on account. However, when purchases are made on account, the seller usually charges the buyer an interest fee. This charge may be hidden in the form of higher prices. So while interest costs are lower, the cost of goods sold is higher. As indicated earlier in this chapter, many companies recognize financing costs by offering buyers the opportunity to receive cash discounts by paying for purchases within a short time after the sale. From any perspective, merchandisers incur significant inventory-financing costs.

Accounting information can help companies minimize the cost of financing inventory. As much as possible, businesses should limit how long goods stay in inventory before they are sold. Ratios to help manage inventory turnover are explained in Chapter 6. Companies should also take steps to collect cash as quickly as possible from customers for the goods they purchase. Managing accounts receivable turnover is explained in Chapter 8. The preceding discussion explains the need for such management techniques.

Merchandising companies earn profits by selling inventory at prices that are higher than the cost paid for the goods. Merchandising companies include *retail companies* (companies that sell goods to the final consumer) and *wholesale companies* (companies that sell to other merchandising companies). The products sold by merchandising companies are called *inventory.* The costs to purchase inventory, to receive it, and to ready it for sale are *product costs,* which are first accumulated in an inventory account (balance sheet asset account) and then recognized as cost of goods sold (income statement expense account) in the period in which goods are sold. Purchases and sales of inventory can be recorded continually as goods are bought and sold (perpetual system) or at the end of the accounting period (periodic system).

Accounting for inventory includes the treatment of cash discounts, transportation costs, and returns and allowances. The cost of inventory is the list price less any *cash discount* offered by the seller. The cost of freight paid to acquire inventory (*transportation-in*) is considered a product cost. The cost of freight paid to deliver inventory to customers (*transportation-out*) is a selling expense. *Sales returns and allowances* and *sales discounts* are subtracted from sales revenue to determine the amount of *net sales* reported on the income statement. Purchase returns and allowances reduce product cost. Theoretically, the cost of lost, damaged, or stolen inventory is an operating expense. However, because these costs are usually immaterial in amount they are typically included as part of cost of goods sold on the income statement.

Some companies use a *multistep income statement* which reports product costs separately from selling and administrative costs. Cost of goods sold is subtracted from sales revenue to determine *gross margin.* Selling and administrative expenses are subtracted from gross margin to determine income from operations. Other companies report income using a *single-step format* in which the cost of goods sold is listed along with selling and administrative items in a single expense category that is subtracted in total from revenue to determine income from operations.

Managers of merchandising businesses operate in a highly competitive environment. They must manage company operations carefully to remain profitable. *Common size financial statements* (statements presented on a percentage basis) and ratio analysis are useful monitoring tools. Common size financial statements permit ready comparisons among different-size companies. Although a $1 million increase in sales may be good for a small company and bad for a large company, a 10 percent increase can apply to any size company. The two most common ratios used by merchandising companies are the *gross margin percentage* (gross margin ÷ net sales) and the *net income percentage* (net income ÷ net sales). Interpreting these ratios requires an understanding of industry characteristics. For example, a discount store such as Wal-Mart would be expected to have a much lower gross margin percentage than an upscale store such as Neiman Marcus.

Managers should be aware of the financing cost of carrying inventory. By investing funds in inventory, a firm loses the opportunity to invest them in interest-bearing assets. The cost of financing inventory is an *opportunity cost.* To minimize financing costs, a company should minimize the amount of inventory it carries, the length of time it holds the inventory, and the time it requires to collect accounts receivable after the inventory is sold.

a look
back

To this point, the text has explained the basic accounting cycle for service and merchandising businesses. Future chapters more closely address specific accounting issues. For example, in Chapter 6 you will learn how to deal with inventory items that are purchased at differing prices. You will also learn how to handle inventory that has been damaged or stolen. Other chapters will discuss a variety of specific practices that are widely used by real world companies.

APPENDIX

Periodic Inventory System

Under certain conditions, it is impractical to record inventory sales transactions as they occur. Consider the operations of a fast-food restaurant. To maintain perpetual inventory records, the restaurant would have to transfer from the Inventory account to the Cost of Goods Sold account the *cost* of each hamburger, order of fries, soft drink, or other food items as they were sold. Obviously, recording the cost of each item at the point of sale would be impractical without using highly sophisticated computer equipment (recording the selling price the customer pays is captured by cash registers; the difficulty lies in capturing inventory cost).

The **periodic inventory system** offers a practical solution for recording inventory transactions in a low-technology, high-volume environment. Inventory costs are recorded in a Purchases account at the time of purchase. Purchase returns and allowances and transportation-in are recorded in separate accounts. No entries for the cost of merchandise purchases or sales are recorded in the Inventory account during the period. The cost of goods sold is determined at the end of the period as shown in Exhibit 5–11.

The perpetual and periodic inventory systems represent alternative procedures for recording the same information. The amounts of cost of goods sold and ending inventory reported in the financial statements will be the same regardless of the method used. Exhibit 5–10 presents the general journal entries JPS would make if it used the periodic inventory method for the 2002 transactions. Cost of goods sold is recorded in an adjusting entry at the end of the accounting period.

The **schedule of cost of goods sold** presented in Exhibit 5–11 is used for internal reporting purposes. It is normally not shown in published financial statements. The amount of cost of goods sold is reported as a single line item on the income statement. The financial statements in Exhibit 5–5 will be the same whether JPS maintains perpetual or periodic inventory records.

Advantages and Disadvantages of the Periodic System versus the Perpetual System

The chief advantage of the periodic method is recording efficiency. Recording inventory transactions occasionally (periodically) requires less effort than recording them continually (perpetually). Historically,

Exhibit 5–10 General Journal Entries

Event No.	Account Title	Debit	Credit
1	Purchases	7,840	
	Accounts Payable		7,840
2	Accounts Payable	980	
	Purchase Returns and Allowances		980
3	Accounts Payable	6,860	
	Interest Expense	140	
	Cash		7,000
4	Transportation-in	300	
	Cash		300
5	Cash	24,750	
	Sales Revenue		24,750
6	Transportation-out	450	
	Cash		450
7	Purchases	13,860	
	Accounts Payable		13,860
8	Accounts Receivable	16,800	
	Sales Revenue		16,800
9	Accounts Payable	9,900	
	Cash		9,900
10	Selling and Administrative Expenses	8,000	
	Cash		8,000
ADJ	Cost of Goods Sold	20,160	
	Inventory	860	
	Purchases Returns and Allowances	980	
	Purchases		21,700
	Transportation-in		300
CL	Sales Revenue	41,550	
	Cost of Goods Sold		20,160
	Transportation-out		450
	Selling and Administrative Expenses		8,000
	Interest Expense		140
	Retained Earnings		12,800

practical limitations offered businesses like fast-food restaurants or grocery stores no alternative to using the periodic system. The sheer volume of transactions made recording individual decreases to the Inventory account balance as each item was sold impossible. Imagine the number of transactions a grocery store would have to record every business day to maintain perpetual records.

Although the periodic system provides a recordkeeping advantage over the perpetual system, perpetual inventory records provide significant control advantages over periodic records. With perpetual records, the book balance in the Inventory account should agree with the amount of inventory in stock at any given time. By comparing that book balance with the results of a physical inventory count, management can determine the amount of lost, damaged, destroyed, or stolen inventory. Perpetual records also permit more timely and accurate reorder decisions and profitability assessments.

When a company uses the *periodic* inventory system, lost, damaged, or stolen merchandise is automatically included in cost of goods sold. Because such goods are not included in the year-end physical count, they are treated as sold regardless of the reason for their absence. Since the periodic system does not separate the cost of lost, damaged, or stolen merchandise from the cost of goods sold, the amount of any inventory shrinkage is unknown. This feature is a major disadvantage of the periodic system. Without knowing the amount of inventory losses, management cannot weigh the costs of various security systems against the potential benefits.

Advances in such technology as electronic bar code scanning and increased computing power have eliminated most of the practical constraints that once prevented merchandisers with high-volume, low dollar-value inventories from recording inventory transactions on a continual basis. As a result, use of the perpetual inventory system has expanded rapidly in recent years and continued growth can be expected. This text, therefore, concentrates on the perpetual inventory system.

Exhibit 5–11 *Schedule of Cost of Goods Sold*

Beginning Inventory	$ 6,000
Purchases	21,700
Purchase Returns and Allowances	(980)
Transportation-in	300
Cost of Goods Available for Sale	27,020
Ending Inventory	(6,860)
Cost of Goods Sold	$20,160

Academy Sales Company (ASC) started the 2004 accounting period with the balances given in the following financial statements model. During 2004 ASC experienced the following business events.

1. Purchased $16,000 of merchandise inventory on account, terms 2/10, n/30.
2. The goods that were purchased in Event 1 were delivered FOB shipping point. Freight costs of $600 were paid in cash by the responsible party.
3. Returned $500 of goods purchased in Event 1.
4. Paid the balance due on the account payable. The payment was made after the discount period had expired.
5a. Recognized $21,000 of cash revenue from the sale of merchandise.
5b. Recognized $15,000 of cost of goods sold.
6. The merchandise in Event 5a was sold to customers FOB destination. Freight costs of $950 were paid in cash by the responsible party.
7. Paid cash of $4,000 for selling and administrative expenses.

Required

a. Record these transactions in a financial statements model like the following one.

Event No.	Cash	+	Inv.	=	Accts. Pay.	+	C. Stk.	+	Ret. Earn.		Rev.	−	Exp.	=	Net Inc.		Cash Flow
Bal.	25,000	+	3,000	=	0	+	18,000	+	10,000		NA	−	NA	=	NA		NA

b. Calculate the gross margin percentage. Based on ASC's gross margin percentage and the information shown in Exhibit 5–9, classify ASC as an upscale department store, a retail discount store, or an office supplies store.

Solution to Requirement a

Event No.	Cash	+	Inv.	=	Accts. Pay.	+	C. Stk.	+	Ret. Earn.	Rev.	−	Exp.	=	Net Inc.	Cash Flow
Bal.	25,000	+	3,000	=	0	+	18,000	+	10,000	NA	−	NA	=	NA	NA
1		+	15,680	=	15,680	+		+			−		=		
2	(600)	+	600	=		+		+			−		=		(600) OA
3		+	(490)	=	(490)	+		+			−		=		
4	(15,500)	+		=	(15,190)	+		+	(310)		−	310	=	(310)	(15,500) OA
5a	21,000	+		=		+		+	21,000	21,000	−		=	21,000	21,000 OA
5b		+	(15,000)	=		+		+	(15,000)		−	15,000	=	(15,000)	
6	(950)	+		=		+		+	(950)		−	950	=	(950)	(950) OA
7	(4,000)	+		=		+		+	(4,000)		−	4,000	=	(4,000)	(4,000) OA
Bal.	24,950	+	3,790	=	0	+	18,000	+	10,740	21,000	−	20,260	=	740	(50) NC

Solution to Requirement b

Gross margin equals sales minus cost of goods sold. In this case, the gross margin is $6,000 ($21,000 − $15,000). The gross margin percentage is computed by dividing gross margin by sales. In this case, the gross margin percentage is 28.6 percent ($6,000 ÷ $21,000). Since this percentage is closest to the percentage shown for Office Depot, the data suggest ASC may be an office supplies store.

KEY TERMS

Allowance *223*

Cash discount *223*

Common size financial statements *232*

Cost of goods available for sale *218*

Cost of goods sold *218*

FOB (free on board) destination *224*

FOB (free on board) shipping point *224*

Gross margin *218*

Gross margin percentage *232*

Gross profit *218*

Merchandise inventory *217*

Merchandising businesses *217*

Multistep income statement *228*

Net income percentage *232*

Net method *223*

Net sales *232*

Opportunity cost *234*

Period costs *218*

Periodic inventory system *236*

Perpetual inventory system *220*

Product cost *218*

Purchase discount *223*

Retail companies *217*

Return on sales *232*

Schedule of cost of goods sold *236*

Selling and administrative costs *218*

Shrinkage *230*

Single-step income statement *228*

Transportation-in (freight-in) *224*

Transportation-out (freight-out) *224*

2/10, n/30 *223*

Wholesale companies *217*

QUESTIONS

1. Define *merchandise inventory*. What types of costs are included in the Merchandise Inventory account?
2. What is the difference between a product cost and a selling and administrative cost?
3. How is the cost of goods available for sale determined?
4. What portion of cost of goods available for sale is shown on the balance sheet? What portion is shown on the income statement?
5. When are period costs expensed? When are product costs expensed?
6. If PetCo had net sales of $600,000, goods available for sale of $450,000, and cost of goods sold of $375,000, what is its gross margin? What amount of inventory will be shown on its balance sheet?
7. Describe how the perpetual inventory system works. What are some advantages of using the perpetual inventory system? Is it necessary to take a physical inventory when using the perpetual inventory system?
8. What are the effects of the following types of transactions on the accounting equation? Also identify the financial statements that are affected. (Assume that the perpetual inventory system is used.)
   a. Acquisition of cash from the issue of common stock.

    b. Contribution of inventory by an owner of a company.

    c. Purchase of inventory with cash by a company.

    d. Sale of inventory for cash.

9. Northern Merchandising Company sold inventory that cost $12,000 for $20,000 cash. How does this event affect the accounting equation? What financial statements and accounts are affected? (Assume that the perpetual inventory system is used.)

10. If goods are shipped FOB shipping point, which party (buyer or seller) is responsible for the shipping costs?

11. Define *transportation-in.* Is it a product or a period cost?

12. Quality Cellular Co. paid $80 for freight on merchandise that it had purchased for resale to customers (transportation-in) and paid $135 for freight on merchandise delivered to customers (transportation-out). What account is debited for the $80 payment? What account is debited for the $135 payment?

13. Why would a seller grant an allowance to a buyer of the seller's merchandise?

14. Dyer Department Store purchased goods with the terms 2/10 n/30. What do these terms mean?

15. Eastern Discount Stores incurred a $5,000 cash cost. How does the accounting treatment of this cost differ if the cash were paid for inventory versus commissions to sales personnel?

16. What is the purpose of giving a cash discount to charge customers?

17. Define *transportation-out.* Is it a product cost or a period cost for the seller?

18. Explain the difference between purchase returns and sales returns. How do purchase returns affect the financial statements of both buyer and seller? How do sales returns affect the financial statements of both buyer and seller?

19. How is net sales determined?

20. What is the difference between a multistep income statement and a single-step income statement?

21. What is the advantage of using common size income statements to present financial information for several accounting periods?

22. What information is provided by the return on sales ratio?

23. What is the purpose of preparing a schedule of cost of goods sold?

24. Explain how the periodic inventory system works. What are some advantages of using the periodic inventory system? What are some disadvantages of using the periodic inventory system? Is it necessary to take a physical inventory when using the periodic inventory system?

25. Why does the periodic inventory system impose a major disadvantage for management in accounting for lost, stolen, or damaged goods?

EXERCISES—SERIES A

All Exercises in Series A are available with McGraw-Hill's Homework Manager

When the instructions for *any* exercise or problem call for the preparation of an income statement, use the *multistep format* unless otherwise indicated.

EXERCISE 5–1A *Comparing a Merchandising Company with a Service Company*   L.O. 1, 2

The following information is available for two different types of businesses for the 2007 accounting period. Markin Consulting is a service business that provides consulting services to small businesses. College Book Mart is a merchandising business that sells books to college students.

Data for Markin Consulting

1. Borrowed $20,000 from the bank to start the business.
2. Performed services for customers and collected $15,000 cash.
3. Paid salary expense of $9,600.

Data for College Book Mart

1. Borrowed $20,000 from the bank to start the business.
2. Purchased $9,500 of inventory for cash.
3. Inventory costing $8,400 was sold for $15,000 cash.
4. Paid $1,200 cash for operating expenses.

Required

a. Prepare an income statement, balance sheet, and statement of cash flows for each of the companies.

b. What is different about the income statements of the two businesses?

c. What is different about the balance sheets of the two businesses?

d. How are the statements of cash flow different for the two businesses?

L.O. 2   **EXERCISE 5–2A** *Effect of Inventory Transactions on Journals, Ledgers, and Financial Statements: Perpetual System*

Justin Harris started a small merchandising business in 2006. The business experienced the following events during its first year of operation. Assume that Harris uses the perpetual inventory system.

1. Acquired $30,000 cash from the issue of common stock.
2. Purchased inventory for $25,000 cash.
3. Sold inventory costing $18,000 for $28,000 cash.

Required
a. Record the events in general journal format.
b. Post the entries to T-accounts.
c. Prepare an income statement for 2006 (use the multistep format).
d. What is the amount of total assets at the end of the period?

L.O. 2   **EXERCISE 5–3A** *Effect of Inventory Transactions on the Income Statement and Statement of Cash Flows: Perpetual System*

During 2007, Etc. Merchandising Company purchased $40,000 of inventory on account. The company sold inventory on account that cost $30,000 for $45,000. Cash payments on accounts payable were $25,000. There was $40,000 cash collected from accounts receivable. Etc. also paid $8,000 cash for operating expenses. Assume that Etc. started the accounting period with $36,000 in both cash and common stock.

Required
a. Identify the events described in the preceding paragraph and record them in a horizontal statements model like the following one:

Assets			=	Liab.	+	Equity			Rev.	−	Exp.	=	Net Inc.	Cash Flow
Cash	+ Accts. Rec.	+ Inv.	= Accts. Pay.		+ C. Stk.	+ Ret. Earn.								
36,000 +	NA	+ NA =	NA		+ 36,000 +	NA			NA	− NA	=	NA		NA

b. What is the balance of accounts receivable at the end of 2007?
c. What is the balance of accounts payable at the end of 2007?
d. What are the amounts of gross margin and net income for 2007?
e. Determine the amount of net cash flow from operating activities.
f. Explain any differences between net income and net cash flow from operating activities.

L.O. 2   **EXERCISE 5–4A** *Recording Inventory Transactions in the General Journal and Posting Entries to T-Accounts: Perpetual System*

Tom's Paint Supply experienced the following events during 2006, its first year of operation:
1. Acquired $15,000 cash from the issue of common stock.
2. Purchased inventory for $12,000 cash.
3. Sold inventory costing $6,500 for $11,000 cash.
4. Paid $800 for advertising expense.

Required
a. Record the general journal entries for the preceding transactions.
b. Post each of the entries to T-accounts.
c. Prepare a trial balance to prove the equality of debits and credits.

L.O. 3   **EXERCISE 5–5A** *Determining Which Party Is Responsible for Freight Cost*

Required
Determine which party, buyer or seller, is responsible for freight charges in each of the following situations:

a. Sold merchandise, freight terms, FOB destination.
b. Sold merchandise, freight terms, FOB shipping point.
c. Purchased merchandise, freight terms, FOB destination.
d. Purchased merchandise, freight terms, FOB shipping point.

EXERCISE 5–6A *Effect of Purchase Returns and Allowances and Freight Costs on the Journal,*   **L.O. 2, 3**
Ledger, and Financial Statements: Perpetual System

The trial balance for The Copy Shop as of January 1, 2006 was as follows:

Account Titles	Debit	Credit
Cash	$12,000	
Inventory	6,000	
Common Stock		$15,000
Retained Earnings		3,000
Total	$18,000	$18,000

The following events affected the company during the 2006 accounting period:

1. Purchased merchandise on account that cost $8,200.
2. Purchased goods FOB shipping point with freight cost of $300 cash.
3. Returned $1,000 of damaged merchandise for credit on account.
4. Agreed to keep other damaged merchandise for which the company received a $500 allowance.
5. Sold merchandise that cost $5,500 for $9,500 cash.
6. Delivered merchandise to customers under terms FOB destination with freight costs amounting to $200 cash.
7. Paid $6,000 on the merchandise purchased in Event 1.

Required

a. Record the transactions in general journal format.
b. Open general ledger T-accounts with the appropriate beginning balances, and post the journal entries to the T-accounts.
c. Prepare an income statement and statement of cash flows for 2006.
d. Explain why a difference does or does not exist between net income and net cash flow from operating activities.

EXERCISE 5–7A *Accounting for Product Costs: Perpetual Inventory System*   **L.O. 2, 3**

Which of the following would be debited to the Inventory account for a merchandising business using the perpetual inventory system?

Required
a. Transportation-out.
b. Purchase discount.
c. Transportation-in.
d. Purchase of a new computer to be used by the business.
e. Purchase of inventory.
f. Allowance received for damaged inventory.

EXERCISE 5–8A *Effect of Product Cost and Period Cost: Horizontal Statements Model*   **L.O. 1, 2, 3**

Brislin Co. experienced the following events for the 2007 accounting period:

1. Acquired $5,000 cash from the issue of common stock.
2. Purchased $18,000 of inventory on account.
3. Received goods purchased in Event 2 FOB shipping point. Freight cost of $500 paid in cash.
4. Returned $2,000 of goods purchased in Event 2 because of poor quality.
5. Sold inventory on account that cost $14,300 for $22,000.
6. Freight cost on the goods sold in Event 5 was $200. The goods were shipped FOB destination. Cash was paid for the freight cost.
7. Collected $16,500 cash from accounts receivable.
8. Paid $12,000 cash on accounts payable.
9. Paid $1,100 for advertising expense.
10. Paid $2,200 cash for insurance expense.

Required
a. Which of these transactions result in period (selling and administrative) costs? Which result in product costs? If neither, label the transaction NA.

b. Record each event in a horizontal statements model like the following one. The first event is recorded as an example.

Assets				=	Liab.	+	Equity				Rev.	−	Exp.	=	Net Inc.	Cash Flow
Cash	+	Accts. Rec.	+ Inv.	=	Accts. Pay.	+	C. Stk.	+	Ret. Earn.							
5,000	+	NA	+ NA	=	NA	+	5,000	+	NA		NA	−	NA	=	NA	5,000 FA

L.O. 3   **EXERCISE 5–9A** *Cash Discounts and Purchase Returns (Net Method)*

On March 6, 2006, Lie's Imports purchased merchandise from The Glass Exchange with a list price of $15,500, terms 2/10 n/45. On March 10, Lie's returned merchandise to The Glass Exchange for credit. The list price of the returned merchandise was $3,200. Lie's paid cash to settle the accounts payable on March 15, 2006.

Required
a. What is the amount of the check that Lie's must write to The Glass Exchange on March 15?
b. Record the events in a horizontal statements model like the following one.

Assets			=	Liab.	+	Equity				Rev.	−	Exp.	=	Net Inc.	Cash Flow
Cash	+	Inv.	=	Accts. Pay.	+	C. Stk.	+	Ret. Earn.							

c. How much would Lie's pay for the merchandise purchased if the payment is not made until March 20, 2006?
d. Record the payment of the merchandise in Event *c* in a horizontal statements model like the one shown above.
e. Why would The Glass Exchange sell merchandise with the terms 2/10 n/45?

L.O. 2, 3   **EXERCISE 5–10A** *Effect of Sales Returns and Allowances and Freight Costs on the Journal, Ledger, and Financial Statements: Perpetual System*

Cain Company began the 2006 accounting period with $18,000 cash, $50,000 inventory, $40,000 common stock, and $28,000 retained earnings. During the 2006 accounting period, Cain experienced the following events:

1. Sold merchandise costing $38,200 for $66,500 on account to Jones' General Store.
2. Delivered the goods to Jones under terms FOB destination. Freight costs were $600 cash.
3. Received returned damaged goods from Jones. The goods cost Cain $4,000 and were sold to Jones for $7,600.
4. Granted Jones a $2,000 allowance for other damaged goods that Jones agreed to keep.
5. Collected partial payment of $52,000 cash from accounts receivable.

Required
a. Record the transactions in general journal format.
b. Open general ledger T-accounts with the appropriate beginning balances and post the journal entries to the T-accounts.
c. Prepare an income statement, balance sheet, and statement of cash flows.
d. Why would Cain grant the $2,000 allowance to Jones? Who benefits more?

L.O. 2, 3   **EXERCISE 5–11A** *Effect of Cash Discounts on the Journal, Ledger, and Financial Statements: Perpetual System (Net Method)*

Lane Sales was started in 2006. The company experienced the following accounting events during its first year of operation:

1. Started business when it acquired $40,000 cash from the issue of common stock.
2. Purchased merchandise with a list price of $42,000 on account, terms 2/10, n/30.
3. Paid off $21,000 of the account payable within the discount period.
4. Sold merchandise on account that had a list price of $25,000. Credit terms were 1/20, n/30. The merchandise had cost Lane $18,000.
5. Collected cash from the account receivable within the discount period.
6. Paid $2,600 cash for operating expenses.
7. Paid the balance due on accounts payable. The payment was not made within the discount period.

Required

a. Record the transactions in general journal format.
b. Open general ledger T-accounts, and post the journal entries to the T-accounts.
c. Record the events in a horizontal statements model like the following one.

Assets			=	Liab.	+	Equity		Rev.	–	Exp.	=	Net Inc.	Cash Flow
Cash	+ Accts. Rec.	+ Inv.	= Accts. Pay.	+ C. Stk.	+ Ret. Earn.								

d. What is the amount of gross margin for the period? What is the net income for the period?
e. Why would Lane sell merchandise with the terms 1/20 n/30?
f. What do the terms 2/10 n/30 in event 2 mean to Lane?

EXERCISE 5–12A *Effect of Inventory Transactions on the Financial Statements:*   **L.O. 2, 3**
Comprehensive Exercise with Sales and Purchase Returns and Discounts

Boone Sales Company had the following balances in its accounts on January 1, 2005:

Cash	$30,000
Merchandise Inventory	20,000
Common Stock	40,000
Retained Earnings	10,000

Boone experienced the following events during 2005:

1. Purchased merchandise inventory on account with a list price of $30,000, terms 1/10 n/30.
2. Paid freight of $600 on the merchandise purchased.
3. Sold merchandise inventory with a list price of $30,000 on account, terms 2/10 n/45. The inventory had cost Boone $19,000.
4. Returned damaged merchandise purchased in Event 1. The list price of the returned merchandise was $1,000.
5. Agreed to keep other merchandise that was slightly damaged and was granted an allowance of $200.
6. The customer in Event 3 returned for credit inventory with a list price of $5,000. The inventory had cost Boone $3,200.
7. Collected the balance of accounts receivable within the discount period.
8. Paid for one-half of the accounts payable within the discount period.
9. Paid $3,200 cash for selling and administrative expenses.
10. Paid the balance of accounts payable (not within the discount period).

Required

a. Record each of these events in general journal format.
b. Open general ledger T-accounts. Post the beginning balances and the events to the accounts.
c. Prepare a trial balance.
d. Prepare an income statement, balance sheet (assume closing entries have been made), and a statement of cash flows.

EXERCISE 5–13A *Effect of Inventory Losses: Perpetual System*   **L.O. 2, 5**

Mia Sales experienced the following events during 2005, its first year of operation:
1. Started the business when it acquired $50,000 cash from the issue of common stock.
2. Paid $42,000 cash to purchase inventory.
3. Sold inventory costing $25,000 for $53,000 cash.
4. Physically counted inventory showing $15,800 inventory was on hand at the end of the accounting period.

Required

a. Open appropriate ledger T-accounts, and record the events in the accounts.
b. Prepare an income statement and balance sheet for 2005.
c. Explain how differences between the book balance and the physical count of inventory could arise. Why is being able to determine whether differences exist useful to management?

L.O. 2   EXERCISE 5–14A *Determining the Effect of Inventory Transactions on the Horizontal Statements Model: Perpetual System*

Lopez Sales Company experienced the following events:

1. Purchased merchandise inventory for cash.
2. Purchased merchandise inventory on account.
3. Sold merchandise inventory for cash. Label the revenue recognition 3a and the expense recognition 3b.
4. Sold merchandise inventory on account. Label the revenue recognition 4a and the expense recognition 4b.
5. Returned merchandise purchased on account.
6. Paid cash for selling and administrative expenses.
7. Paid cash on accounts payable not within the discount period.
8. Paid cash for transportation-in.
9. Collected cash from accounts receivable.
10. Paid cash for transportation-out.

Required

Identify each event as asset source (AS), asset use (AU), asset exchange (AE), or claims exchange (CE). Also explain how each event affects the financial statements by placing a + for increase, − for decrease, or NA for not affected under each of the components in the following statements model. Assume the use of the perpetual inventory system. The first event is recorded as an example.

Event No.	Event Type	Assets	=	Liab.	+	Equity	Rev.	−	Exp.	=	Net Inc.	Cash Flow
1	AE	+ −	=	NA	+	NA	NA	−	NA	=	NA	− OA

L.O. 4   EXERCISE 5–15A *Single-Step and Multistep Income Statements*

The following information was taken from the accounts of Good Foods Store, a delicatessen. The accounts are listed in alphabetical order, and each has a normal balance.

Accounts Payable	$300
Accounts Receivable	200
Accumulated Depreciation	50
Advertising Expense	100
Cash	205
Common Stock	100
Cost of Goods Sold	300
Interest Expense	35
Merchandise Inventory	225
Prepaid Rent	20
Retained Earnings	255
Sales Revenue	500
Salaries Expense	65
Supplies Expense	55

Required

First, prepare an income statement using the single-step approach. Then prepare another income statement using the multistep approach.

L.O. 2   EXERCISE 5–16A *Determining the Cost of Financing Inventory*

On January 1, 2008, Mel Stark started a small sailboat merchandising business that he named Mel's Sails. The company experienced the following events during the first year of operation:

1. Started the business when Stark borrowed $20,000 from his parents. He issued them a one-year note dated January 1, 2008. The note had a 6 percent annual rate of interest.
2. Paid $14,000 cash to purchase inventory.
3. Sold a sailboat that cost $9,000 for $16,000 on account.
4. Collected $10,000 cash from accounts receivable.
5. Paid $2,500 for operating expenses.
6. Recognized accrued interest on the note payable on December 31.

Required

a. Record the events in general journal format, using the perpetual system.

b. Open general ledger T-accounts, and post the journal entries to the T-accounts.

c. Prepare an income statement, balance sheet, and statement of cash flows. (Assume that year-end closing entries have been made.)

d. "Since Mel sold inventory for $16,000, he will be able to repay more than half of the $20,000 loan from his parents when it comes due on January 1, 2009." Do you agree with this statement? Why or why not?

EXERCISE 5–17A *Financing Inventory and Cash Discounts*   L.O. 3

May Haynes came to you for advice. She has just purchased a large amount of inventory with the terms 2/10 n/60. The amount of the invoice is $260,000. She is currently short on cash but has good credit. She can borrow the money at the appropriate time to take advantage of the discount. The annual interest rate is 7% if she decides to borrow the money. Haynes is sure she will have the necessary cash by the due date of the invoice (but not by the discount date).

Required

a. For how long would Haynes need to borrow the money to take advantage of the discount?

b. How much money would Haynes need to borrow?

c. Write a memo to Haynes outlining the most cost-effective strategy for her to follow. Include in your memo the amount of savings from the alternative you suggest.

EXERCISE 5–18A *Effect of Inventory Transactions on the Income Statement and Balance Sheet: Periodic System (Appendix)*   L.O. 8

Don Moon is the owner of The Clothes Shop. At the beginning of the year, Moon had $1,200 in inventory. During the year, Moon purchased inventory that cost $6,500. At the end of the year, inventory on hand amounted to $1,800.

Required

Calculate the following:

a. Cost of goods available for sale during the year.

b. Cost of goods sold for the year.

c. Inventory amount The Clothes Shop would report on its year-end balance sheet.

EXERCISE 5–19A *Determining Cost of Goods Sold: Periodic System (Appendix)*   L.O. 8

Sunset Retailers uses the periodic inventory system to account for its inventory transactions. The following account titles and balances were drawn from Sunset's records for the year 2007: beginning balance in inventory, $24,900; purchases, $306,400; purchase returns and allowances, $9,600; sales, $680,000; sales returns and allowances, $6,370; freight-in, $2,160; and operating expenses, $51,400. A physical count indicated that $29,300 of merchandise was on hand at the end of the accounting period.

Required

a. Prepare a schedule of cost of goods sold.

b. Prepare a multistep income statement.

EXERCISE 5–20A *Basic Transactions: Periodic System, Single Cycle (Appendix)*   L.O. 8

The following events apply to Tops Gift Shop for 2007, its first year of operation:

1. Acquired $33,500 cash from the issue of common stock.
2. Issued common stock to Kayla Taylor, one of the owners, in exchange for gift merchandise worth $2,500 Taylor had acquired prior to opening the shop.
3. Purchased $43,500 of inventory on account.
4. Paid $2,750 for advertising expense.
5. Sold inventory for $77,500.
6. Paid $8,000 in salary to a part-time salesperson.
7. Paid $35,000 on accounts payable (see Event 3).
8. Physically counted inventory, which indicated that $7,000 of inventory was on hand at the end of the accounting period.

Required

a. Record each of these events in general journal form. Tops Gift Shop uses the periodic system.

b. Post each of the events to ledger T-accounts.

c. Prepare an income statement, statement of changes in stockholders' equity, balance sheet, and statement of cash flows for 2007.

d. Prepare the necessary closing entries at the end of 2007, and post them to the appropriate T-accounts.

e. Prepare an after-closing trial balance.

f. Discuss an advantage of using the periodic system instead of the perpetual system.

g. Why is the common stock issued on the statement of changes in stockholders' equity different from the common stock issued in the cash flow from financing activities section of the cash flow statement?

PROBLEMS—SERIES A

 All Problems in Series A are available with McGraw-Hill's Homework Manager

L.O. 2   **PROBLEM 5–21A** *Basic Transactions for Three Accounting Cycles: Perpetual System*

CHECK FIGURES
2007 Net Income: $5,300
2009 Total Assets: $45,300

Ramsey Company was started in 2007 when it acquired $30,000 from the issue of common stock. The following data summarize the company's first three years' operating activities. Assume that all transactions were cash transactions.

	2007	2008	2009
Purchases of Inventory	$24,000	$12,000	$18,500
Sales	26,000	32,000	36,000
Cost of Goods Sold	15,200	18,500	20,000
Selling and Administrative Expenses	5,500	9,400	10,100

Required

Prepare an income statement (use the multistep format) and balance sheet for each fiscal year. (*Hint:* Record the transaction data for each accounting period in T-accounts before preparing the statements for that year.)

L.O. 1   **PROBLEM 5–22A** *Identifying Product and Period Costs*

Required

Indicate whether each of the following costs is a product cost or a period cost:

a. Depreciation on office equipment.

b. Insurance on vans used to deliver goods to customers.

c. Salaries of sales supervisors.

d. Monthly maintenance expense for a copier.

e. Goods purchased for resale.

f. Cleaning supplies for the office.

g. Freight on goods purchased for resale.

h. Salary of the marketing director.

i. Freight on goods sold to customer with terms FOB destination.

j. Utilities expense incurred for office building.

L.O. 3   **PROBLEM 5–23A** *Identifying Freight Cost*

CHECK FIGURE
Event (b): Freight Costs Paid: $150

Required

For each of the following events, determine the amount of freight paid by Tom's Parts House. Also indicate whether the freight is classified as a product or period cost.

a. Purchased inventory with freight costs of $700, FOB destination.

b. Shipped merchandise to customers with freight costs of $150, FOB destination.

c. Purchased additional merchandise with costs of $250, FOB shipping point.

d. Sold merchandise to a customer. Freight costs were $400, FOB shipping point.

PROBLEM 5–24A *Effect of Purchase Returns and Allowances and Purchase Discounts on the Financial Statements: Perpetual System (Net Method)*

L.O. 2, 3

The following events were completed by Chris Toy Shop in September 2009:

Sept.	1	Acquired $30,000 cash from the issue of common stock.
	1	Purchased $22,000 of merchandise on account with terms 2/10 n/30.
	5	Paid $500 cash for freight to obtain merchandise purchased on September 1.
	8	Sold merchandise that cost $5,000 to customers for $9,500 on account, with terms 1/10 n/30.
	8	Returned $800 of defective merchandise from the September 1 purchase to the supplier.
	10	Paid cash for one-half of the balance due on the merchandise purchased on September 1.
	20	Received cash from customers of September 8 sale in settlement of the account balances, but not within the discount period.
	30	Paid the balance due on the merchandise purchased on September 1.
	30	Paid $1,950 cash for selling expenses.

CHECK FIGURES
a. Ending Cash: $16,062
d. Net Income: $2,338

Required

a. Record each event in a statements model like the following one. The first event is recorded as an example.

Assets			=	Liab.	+	Equity			Rev.	–	Exp.	=	Net Inc.	Cash Flow
Cash	+ Accts. Rec.	+ Inv.	= Accts. Pay.		+ C. Stk.	+ Ret. Earn.								
30,000 +	NA	+ NA =	NA		+ 30,000 +	NA			NA	– NA	=	NA		30,000 FA

b. Record each of these transactions in general journal form.
c. Post each of the transactions to general ledger T-accounts.
d. Prepare an income statement for the month ending September 30.
e. Prepare a statement of cash flows for the month ending September 30.
f. Explain why there is a difference between net income and cash flow from operating activities.

PROBLEM 5–25A *Comprehensive Cycle Problem: Perpetual System*

L.O. 2, 3, 5

e**X**cel
www.mhhe.com/edmonds5e

At the beginning of 2005, the C. Eaton Company had the following balances in its accounts:

Cash	$ 6,500
Inventory	9,000
Common Stock	10,000
Retained Earnings	5,500

CHECK FIGURES
d. Retained Earnings Ending
    Balance: $7,220
    Net Income: $1,720

During 2005, the company experienced the following events.

1. Purchased inventory with a list price of $3,000 on account from Blue Company under terms 1/10 n/30. The merchandise was delivered FOB shipping point. Freight costs of $150 were paid in cash.
2. Returned $300 of the inventory that it had purchased because the inventory was damaged in transit. The freight company agreed to pay the return freight cost.
3. Paid the amount due on its account payable to Blue Company but not within the cash discount period.
4. Sold inventory with a list price of $6,000 and a cost of $3,500 on account, under terms 2/10 n/45.
5. Received returned merchandise from a customer. The merchandise originally cost $400 and was sold to the customer for $650 cash. The customer was paid $650 cash for the returned merchandise.
6. Delivered goods in Event 4 FOB destination. Freight costs of $80 were paid in cash.
7. Collected the amount due on the account receivable but not within the discount period.
8. Took a physical count indicating that $8,300 of inventory was on hand at the end of the accounting period.

Required

a. Identify each of these events as asset source (AS), asset use (AU), asset exchange (AE), or claims exchange (CE). Also explain how each event would affect the financial statements by placing a + for increase, − for decrease, or NA for not affected under each of the components in the following statements model. Assume that the perpetual inventory method is used. When an event has more than one part, use letters to distinguish the effects of each part. The first event is recorded as an example.

Event No.	Event Type	Assets	=	Liab.	+	Equity	Rev.	–	Exp.	=	Net Inc.	Cash Flow
1a	AS	+	=	+	+	NA	NA	–	NA	=	NA	NA
1b	AE	+ –	=	NA	+	NA	NA	–	NA	=	NA	– OA

b. Record the events in general journal format.
c. Open ledger T-accounts, and post the beginning balances and the events to the accounts.
d. Prepare an income statement, a statement of changes in stockholders' equity, a balance sheet, and a statement of cash flows.
e. Record and post the closing entries, and prepare an after-closing trial balance.

L.O. 6   **PROBLEM 5–26A** *Using Common Size Income Statements to Make Comparisons*

The following income statements were drawn from the annual reports of Hall Company:

	2005*	2006*
Net Sales	$302,900	$370,500
Cost of Goods Sold	(217,400)	(264,700)
Gross Margin	85,500	105,800
Less: Operating Expense		
Selling and Administrative Expenses	(40,800)	(58,210)
Net Income	$ 44,700	$ 47,590

*All dollar amounts are reported in thousands.

The president's message in the company's annual report stated that the company had implemented a strategy to increase market share by spending more on advertising. The president indicated that prices held steady and sales grew as expected. Write a memo indicating whether you agree with the president's statements. How has the strategy affected profitability? Support your answer by measuring growth in sales and selling expenses. Also prepare common size income statements and make appropriate references to the differences between 2005 and 2006.

L.O. 4, 8   **PROBLEM 5–27A** *Preparing a Schedule of Cost of Goods Sold and Multistep and Single-Step Income Statements: Periodic System (Appendix)*

www.mhhe.com/edmonds5e

CHECK FIGURES
a. Cost of Goods Available for Sale: $150,800
b. Net Income: $27,700

The following account titles and balances were taken from the adjusted trial balance of Scoggins Sales Co. at December 31, 2004. The company uses the periodic inventory method.

Account Title	Balance
Advertising Expense	$ 12,800
Depreciation Expense	3,000
Income Taxes	10,700
Interest Expense	5,000
Merchandise Inventory, January 1	18,000
Merchandise Inventory, December 31	20,100
Miscellaneous Expense	800
Purchases	130,000
Purchase Returns and Allowances	2,700
Rent Expense	14,000
Salaries Expense	53,000
Sales	290,000
Sales Returns and Allowances	8,000
Transportation-in	5,500
Transportation-out	10,800

Required
a. Prepare a schedule to determine the amount of cost of goods sold.
b. Prepare a multistep income statement.
c. Prepare a single-step income statement.

PROBLEM 5–28A *Comprehensive Cycle Problem: Periodic System (Appendix)*

The following trial balance pertains to Reeves Hardware as of January 1, 2005:

Account Title	Debit	Credit
Cash	$14,000	
Accounts Receivable	9,000	
Merchandise Inventory	60,000	
Accounts Payable		$ 5,000
Common Stock		70,000
Retained Earnings		8,000
Total	$83,000	$83,000

The following events occurred in 2005. Assume that Reeves Hardware uses the periodic inventory system.

1. Purchased land for $8,000 cash and a building for $45,000 by paying $5,000 cash and issuing a 20-year note with an annual interest rate of 8 percent. The building has a 40-year estimated life with no salvage value.
2. Purchased merchandise on account for $23,000, terms 2/10 n/30.
3. The merchandise purchased was shipped FOB shipping point for $230 cash.
4. Returned $2,000 of defective merchandise purchased in Event 2.
5. Sold merchandise for $27,000 cash.
6. Sold merchandise on account for $50,000, terms 1/20 n/30.
7. Paid cash within the discount period on accounts payable due on merchandise purchased in Event 2.
8. Paid $1,200 cash for selling expenses.
9. Collected part of the balance due from accounts receivable in Event 6. Collections were made after the discount period on $12,000 of the receivables. Collections were made during the discount period on $35,000 of the receivables.
10. Paid cash to the bank for one full year's interest on the note issued in Event 1.
11. Paid $2,000 on the principal of the note issued in Event 1.
12. Recorded one full year's depreciation on the building purchased in Event 1.
13. Performed a physical count indicating that $30,000 of inventory was on hand at the end of the accounting period.

Required
a. Record these transactions in a general journal.
b. Post the transactions to ledger T-accounts.
c. Prepare a schedule of cost of goods sold, an income statement, a statement of changes in stockholders' equity, a balance sheet, and a statement of cash flows for 2005.

EXERCISES—SERIES B

When the instructions for *any* exercise or problem call for the preparation of an income statement, use the *multistep format* unless otherwise indicated.

EXERCISE 5–1B *Comparing a Merchandising Company with a Service Company*

L.O. 1, 2

The following information is available for two different types of businesses for the 2006 accounting period. Moore CPAs is a service business that provides accounting services to small businesses. Campus Sports Shop is a merchandising business that sells diving gear to college students.

Data for Moore CPAs
1. Borrowed $20,000 from the bank to start the business.
2. Provided $15,000 of services to customers and collected $15,000 cash.
3. Paid salary expense of $10,000.

Data for Campus Sports Shop
1. Borrowed $20,000 from the bank to start the business.
2. Purchased $12,500 inventory for cash.
3. Inventory costing $8,200 was sold for $15,000 cash.
4. Paid $1,800 cash for operating expenses.

Required

a. Prepare an income statement, balance sheet, and statement of cash flows for each of the companies.

b. Which of the two businesses would have product costs? Why?

c. Why does Moore CPAs not compute gross margin on its income statement?

d. Compare the assets of both companies. What assets do they have in common? What assets are different? Why?

L.O. 2 **EXERCISE 5–2B** *Effect of Inventory Transactions on Journals, Ledgers, and Financial Statements: Perpetual System*

Troy Lane started a small merchandising business in 2005. The business experienced the following events during its first year of operation. Assume that Lane uses the perpetual inventory system.

1. Acquired $20,000 cash from the issue of common stock.
2. Purchased inventory for $15,000 cash.
3. Sold inventory costing $10,000 for $16,000 cash.

Required

a. Record the events in general journal format.

b. Post the entries to T-accounts.

c. Prepare an income statement for 2005 (use the multistep format).

d. What is the amount of net cash flow from operating activities for 2005?

L.O. 2 **EXERCISE 5–3B** *Effect of Inventory Transactions on the Income Statement and Statement of Cash Flows: Perpetual System*

During 2005, Bond Merchandising Company purchased $30,000 of inventory on account. Bond sold inventory on account that cost $25,000 for $35,000. Cash payments on accounts payable were $20,000. There was $22,000 cash collected from accounts receivable. Bond also paid $7,000 cash for operating expenses. Assume that Bond started the accounting period with $28,000 in both cash and common stock.

Required

a. Identify the events described in the preceding paragraph and record them in a horizontal statements model like the following one:

Assets			=	Liab.	+	Equity			Rev.	−	Exp.	=	Net Inc.	Cash Flow
Cash	+ Accts. Rec.	+ Inv.	= Accts. Pay.		+ C. Stk.	+ Ret. Earn.								
28,000 +	NA	+ NA =	NA		+ 28,000 +	NA			NA	− NA	=	NA		NA

b. What is the balance of accounts receivable at the end of 2005?

c. What is the balance of accounts payable at the end of 2005?

d. What are the amounts of gross margin and net income for 2005?

e. Determine the amount of net cash flow from operating activities.

f. Explain why net income and retained earnings are the same for Bond. Normally would these amounts be the same? Why or why not?

L.O. 2 **EXERCISE 5–4B** *Recording Inventory Transactions in the General Journal and Posting Entries to T-Accounts: Perpetual System*

Toro Clothing experienced the following events during 2006, its first year of operation:

1. Acquired $7,000 cash from the issue of common stock.
2. Purchased inventory for $4,000 cash.
3. Sold inventory costing $3,000 for $4,500 cash.
4. Paid $400 for advertising expense.

Required

a. Record the general journal entries for the preceding transactions.

b. Post each of the entries to T-accounts.

c. Prepare a trial balance to prove the equality of debits and credits.

EXERCISE 5–5B *Understanding the Freight Terms FOB Shipping Point and FOB Destination* **L.O. 3**

Required

For each of the following events, indicate whether the freight terms are FOB Destination or FOB Shipping Point.

a. Sold merchandise and paid the freight costs.
b. Purchased merchandise and paid the freight costs.
c. Sold merchandise and the buyer paid the freight costs.
d. Purchased merchandise and the seller paid the freight costs.

EXERCISE 5–6B *Effect of Purchase Returns and Allowances and Freight Costs on the Journal,* **L.O. 2, 3**
Ledger, and Financial Statements: Perpetual System

The trial balance for The Garden Shop as of January 1, 2005 follows:

Account Titles	Debit	Credit
Cash	$32,000	
Inventory	12,000	
Common Stock		$40,000
Retained Earnings		4,000
Total	$44,000	$44,000

The following events affected the company during the 2005 accounting period:

1. Purchased merchandise on account that cost $22,000.
2. Purchased goods in Event 1 FOB shipping point with freight cost of $1,000 cash.
3. Returned $3,200 of damaged merchandise for credit on account.
4. Agreed to keep other damaged merchandise for which the company received a $1,400 allowance.
5. Sold merchandise that cost $16,000 for $31,000 cash.
6. Delivered merchandise to customers in Event 5 under terms FOB destination with freight costs amounting to $800 cash.
7. Paid $15,000 on the merchandise purchased in Event 1.

Required

a. Record the events in general journal format.
b. Open general ledger T-accounts with the appropriate beginning balances, and post the journal entries to the T-accounts.
c. Prepare an income statement, balance sheet, and statement of cash flows. (Assume that closing entries have been made.)
d. Explain why a difference does or does not exist between net income and net cash flow from operating activities.

EXERCISE 5–7B *Accounting for Product Costs: Perpetual Inventory System* **L.O. 2, 3**

Which of the following would be debited to the Inventory account for a merchandising business using the perpetual inventory system?

Required

a. Purchase of inventory.
b. Allowance received for damaged inventory.
c. Transportation-in.
d. Cash discount given on goods sold.
e. Transportation-out.
f. Purchase of office supplies.

EXERCISE 5–8B *Effect of Product Cost and Period Cost: Horizontal Statements Model* **L.O. 1, 2, 3**

The Health Food Store experienced the following events for the 2006 accounting period:

1. Acquired $10,000 cash from the issue of common stock.
2. Purchased $56,000 of inventory on account.
3. Received goods purchased in Event 2 FOB shipping point; freight cost of $600 paid in cash.
4. Sold inventory on account that cost $33,000 for $57,400.

5. Freight cost on the goods sold in Event 4 was $420. The goods were shipped FOB destination. Cash was paid for the freight cost.
6. Customer in Event 4 returned $2,000 worth of goods that had a cost of $1,400.
7. Collected $47,000 cash from accounts receivable.
8. Paid $40,000 cash on accounts payable.
9. Paid $1,100 for advertising expense.
10. Paid $2,000 cash for insurance expense.

Required

a. Which of these events result in period (selling and administrative) costs? Which result in product costs? If neither, label the transaction NA.
b. Record each event in a horizontal statements model like the following one. The first event is recorded as an example.

Assets			=	Liab.	+	Equity			Rev.	−	Exp.	=	Net Inc.	Cash Flow
Cash	+ Accts. Rec.	+ Inv.	= Accts. Pay.		+ C. Stk.	+ Ret. Earn.								
10,000 +	NA	+ NA	= NA		+ 10,000	+ NA			NA	− NA	=	NA		10,000 FA

L.O. 3   EXERCISE 5–9B *Cash Discounts and Purchase Returns*

On April 6, 2003, Ming Furnishings purchased $6,200 of merchandise from Exchange Emporium, terms 2/10 n/45. On April 5, Ming returned $600 of the merchandise to the Exchange Emporium for credit. Wang paid cash for the merchandise on April 15, 2003.

Required

a. What is the amount that Ming must pay the Exchange Emporium on April 15?
b. Record the events in a horizontal statements model like the following one.

Assets		=	Liab.	+	Equity			Rev.	−	Exp.	=	Net Inc.	Cash Flow
Cash	+ Inv.	= Accts. Pay.		+ C. Stock.		+ Ret. Earn.							

c. How much must Ming pay for the merchandise purchased if the payment is not made until April 20, 2003?
d. Record the payment in event (c) in a horizontal statements model like the one above.
e. Why would Ming want to pay for the merchandise by April 15?

L.O. 2, 3   EXERCISE 5–10B *Effect of Sales Returns and Allowances and Freight Costs on the Journal, Ledger, and Financial Statements: Perpetual System*

Rainey Company began the 2004 accounting period with $7,000 cash, $38,000 inventory, $25,000 common stock, and $20,000 retained earnings. During 2004, Rainey experienced the following events:

1. Sold merchandise costing $32,000 for $50,000 on account to Mitchell's Furniture Store.
2. Delivered the goods to Mitchell under terms FOB destination. Freight costs were $500 cash.
3. Received returned damaged goods from Mitchell. The goods cost Rainey $3,000 and were sold to Mitchell for $4,000.
4. Granted Mitchell a $2,000 allowance for other damaged goods that Mitchell agreed to keep.
5. Collected partial payment of $30,000 cash from accounts receivable.

Required

a. Record the events in general journal format.
b. Open general ledger T-accounts with the appropriate beginning balances and post the journal entries to the T-accounts.
c. Prepare an income statement, balance sheet, and statement of cash flows.
d. Why would Mitchell agree to keep the damaged goods? Who benefits more?

L.O. 2, 3   EXERCISE 5–11B *Effect of Cash Discounts on the Journal, Ledger, and Financial Statements: Perpetual System*

Batte Supply, Inc. was started in 2006 and experienced the following accounting events during its first year of operation:

1. Started business when it acquired $15,000 cash from the issue of common stock.
2. Purchased merchandise with a list price of $9,000 on account, terms 2/10 n/30.

3. Paid off the account payable but not within the discount period.
4. Sold inventory on account with a list price of $7,500 that had a cost of $5,000. Credit terms were 1/20 n/30.
5. Collected cash from the account receivable but not within the discount period.
6. Paid $1,900 cash for operating expenses.

Required

a. Record the transactions in general journal format.
b. Open general ledger T-accounts, and post the journal entries to the T-accounts.
c. Record the events in a horizontal statements model like the following one.

Assets			=	Liab.	+	Equity		Rev.	–	Exp.	=	Net Inc.	Cash Flow
Cash	+ Accts. Rec.	+ Inv.	= Accts. Pay.		+ C. Stk.	+ Ret. Earn.							

d. What is the amount of gross margin for the period? What is the net income for the period?
e. Why would Batte sell merchandise with the terms 1/20 n/30?
f. What do the terms 2/10 n/30 mean to Batte?

EXERCISE 5–12B *Effect of Inventory Transactions on the Financial Statements:* **L.O. 2, 3**
Comprehensive Exercise with Sales and Purchase Returns and Discounts

Fuller Merchandise Company had the following balances in its accounts on January 1, 2006:

Cash	$20,000
Merchandise Inventory	15,000
Common Stock	25,000
Retained Earnings	10,000

Fuller experienced the following events during 2006:

1. Purchased merchandise inventory on account for $45,000, terms 2/10 n/30.
2. Paid freight of $600 on the merchandise purchased.
3. Sold merchandise inventory that cost $23,000 for a list price of $42,000 on account, terms 1/10 n/45.
4. Returned $1,500 of damaged merchandise purchased in Event 1.
5. Agreed to keep other merchandise that was slightly damaged and was granted an allowance of $500.
6. The customer in Event 3 returned merchandise that had a list price of $6,000 and a cost of $3,400.
7. Collected the balance of accounts receivable within the discount period.
8. Paid for one-half of the accounts payable within the discount period.
9. Paid $4,300 cash for selling and administrative expenses.
10. Paid the balance of accounts payable (not within the discount period).

Required

a. Record each of these events in general journal format.
b. Open general ledger T-accounts. Post the beginning balances and the events to the accounts.
c. Prepare a trial balance.
d. Prepare an income statement, balance sheet (assume closing entries have been made), and a statement of cash flows.

EXERCISE 5–13B *Effect of Inventory Losses: Perpetual System* **L.O. 2, 5**

Dodd Traders experienced the following events during 2005, its first year of operation:

1. Started the business when it acquired $20,000 cash from the issue of common stock.
2. Paid $14,000 cash to purchase inventory.
3. Sold inventory costing $10,750 for $17,100 cash.
4. Physically counted inventory; had inventory of $2,900 on hand at the end of the accounting period.

Required

a. Open appropriate ledger T-accounts, and record the events in the accounts.
b. Prepare an income statement and balance sheet.
c. If all purchases and sales of merchandise are reflected as increases or decreases to the merchandise inventory account, why is it necessary for management to even bother to take a physical count of goods on hand (ending inventory) at the end of the year?

L.O. 2 **EXERCISE 5–14B** *Determining the Effect of Inventory Transactions on the Accounting Equation: Perpetual System*

Marshall Company experienced the following events:

1. Purchased merchandise inventory on account.
2. Purchased merchandise inventory for cash.
3. Sold merchandise inventory on account. Label the revenue recognition 3a and the expense recognition 3b.
4. Returned merchandise purchased on account.
5. Sold merchandise inventory for cash. Label the revenue recognition 5a and the expense recognition 5b.
6. Paid cash on accounts payable within the discount period.
7. Paid cash for selling and administrative expenses.
8. Collected cash from accounts receivable not within the discount period.
9. Paid cash for transportation-out.
10. Paid cash for transportation-in.

Required

Identify each event as asset source (AS), asset use (AU), asset exchange (AE), or claims exchange (CE). Also explain how each event affects the financial statements by placing a + for increase, − for decrease, or NA for not affected under each of the components in the following statements model. Assume the company uses the perpetual inventory system. The first event is recorded as an example.

Event No.	Event Type	Assets	=	Liab.	+	Equity	Rev.	−	Exp.	=	Net Inc.	Cash Flow
1	AS	+	=	+	+	NA	NA	−	NA	=	NA	NA

L.O. 4 **EXERCISE 5–15B** *Single-Step and Multistep Income Statements*

The following information was taken from the accounts of North Street Market, a small grocery store. The accounts are listed in alphabetical order, and all have normal balances.

Accounts Payable	$ 600
Accounts Receivable	700
Accumulated Depreciation	200
Advertising Expense	400
Cash	820
Common Stock	400
Cost of Goods Sold	900
Interest Expense	140
Merchandise Inventory	300
Prepaid Rent	80
Retained Earnings	910
Sales Revenue	1,600
Salaries Expense	260
Supplies Expense	110

Required

First, prepare an income statement using the single-step approach. Then prepare another income statement using the multistep approach.

L.O. 2 **EXERCISE 5–16B** *Determining the Cost of Financing Inventory*

On January 1, 2006, Jay Xie started a small home appliance merchandising business that he named J's Appliances. J's uses the perpetual system. The company experienced the following events during the first year of operation:

1. Started the business when Xie borrowed $100,000 by issuing a one-year note dated January 1, 2006. The note had a 7 percent annual rate of interest.
2. Paid $80,000 cash to purchase inventory.
3. Sold appliances that cost $36,000 for $68,000 on account.
4. Collected $28,000 cash from accounts receivable.
5. Paid $10,000 for operating expenses.
6. Recognized accrued interest on the note payable on December 31.

Required

a. Record the transactions in general journal format.

b. Open general ledger T-accounts, and post the journal entries to the T-accounts.

c. Prepare an income statement, balance sheet, and statement of cash flows. (Assume that year-end closing entries have been made.)

EXERCISE 5–17B *Financing Inventory and Cash Discounts*   **L.O. 3**

Tarius Henry came to you for advice. He has just purchased a large amount of inventory with the terms 1/10, n/45. The amount of the invoice is $65,000. He is currently short on cash but has good credit and so can borrow the money at the appropriate time to take advantage of the discount. The annual interest rate is 7 percent if he decides to borrow the money. Henry is sure he will have the necessary cash by the due date of the invoice (but not by the discount date).

Required

a. For how long would Henry need to borrow the money to take advantage of the discount?

b. How much money would Henry need to borrow?

c. What action would you recommend Henry take? Explain.

EXERCISE 5–18B *Effect of Inventory Transactions on the Income Statement and Balance*   **L.O. 8**
Sheet: Periodic System (Appendix)

Nat Briscoe owns Nat's Sporting Goods. At the beginning of the year, Nat's had $4,200 in inventory. During the year, Nat's purchased inventory that cost $21,000. At the end of the year, inventory on hand amounted to $8,800.

Required

Calculate the following:

a. Cost of goods available for sale during the year.

b. Cost of goods sold for the year.

c. Amount of inventory Nat's would report on the year-end balance sheet.

EXERCISE 5–19B *Determining Cost of Goods Sold: Periodic System (Appendix)*   **L.O. 8**

Hill Antiques uses the periodic inventory system to account for its inventory transactions. The following account titles and balances were drawn from Hill's records: beginning balance in inventory, $12,000; purchases, $150,000; purchase returns and allowances, $5,000; sales, $400,000; sales returns and allowances, $3,000; freight-in, $1,000; and operating expenses, $26,000. A physical count indicated that $15,000 of merchandise was on hand at the end of the accounting period.

Required

a. Prepare a schedule of cost of goods sold.

b. Prepare a multistep income statement.

EXERCISE 5–20B *Basic Transactions: Periodic System, Single Cycle (Appendix)*   **L.O. 8**

The following transactions apply to Kay's Specialties Shop for 2005, its first year of operations:

1. Acquired $70,000 cash from the issue of common stock.
2. Acquired $8,000 of gift merchandise from Kay Pierce, the owner, who had acquired the merchandise prior to opening the shop. Issued common stock to Kay in exchange for the merchandise.
3. Purchased $90,000 of inventory on account.
4. Paid $6,000 for radio ads.
5. Sold inventory for $160,000 cash.
6. Paid $20,000 in salary to a part-time salesperson.
7. Paid $75,000 on accounts payable (see Event 3).
8. Physically counted inventory, which indicated that $20,000 of inventory was on hand at the end of the accounting period.

Required

a. Record each of these transactions in general journal form using the periodic method.

b. Post each of the transactions to ledger T-accounts.

c. Prepare an income statement, statement of changes in stockholders' equity, balance sheet, and statement of cash flows for 2005.

d. Prepare the necessary closing entries at the end of 2005, and post them to the appropriate T-accounts.

e. Prepare an after-closing trial balance.

f. Give an example of a business that may want to use the periodic system. Give an example of a business that may use the perpetual system.

g. Give some examples of assets other than cash that are commonly contributed to a business in exchange for stock.

PROBLEMS—SERIES B

L.O. 2   **PROBLEM 5–21B** *Basic Transactions for Three Accounting Cycles: Perpetual System*

Carol's Flower Company was started in 2005 when it acquired $80,000 cash from the issue of common stock. The following data summarize the company's first three years' operating activities. Assume that all transactions were cash transactions.

	2005	2006	2007
Purchases of Inventory	$ 60,000	$ 90,000	$130,000
Sales	102,000	146,000	220,000
Cost of Goods Sold	54,000	78,000	140,000
Selling and Administrative Expenses	40,000	52,000	72,000

Required

Prepare an income statement (use multistep format) and balance sheet for each fiscal year. (*Hint:* Record the transaction data for each accounting period in T-accounts before preparing the statements for that year.)

L.O. 1   **PROBLEM 5–22B** *Identifying Product and Period Costs*

Required

Indicate whether each of the following costs is a product cost or a period (selling and administrative) cost.

a. Transportation-in.

b. Insurance on the office building.

c. Office supplies.

d. Costs incurred to improve the quality of goods available for sale.

e. Goods purchased for resale.

f. Salaries of salespersons.

g. Advertising costs.

h. Transportation-out.

i. Interest on a note payable.

j. Salary of the company president.

L.O. 3   **PROBLEM 5–23B** *Identifying Freight Costs*

Required

For each of the following events, determine the amount of freight paid by The Book Shop. Also indicate whether the freight cost would be classified as a product or period (selling and administrative) cost.

a. Purchased additional merchandise with freight costs of $300. The merchandise was shipped FOB shipping point.

b. Shipped merchandise to customers, freight terms FOB shipping point. The freight costs were $100.

c. Purchased inventory with freight costs of $1,000. The goods were shipped FOB destination.

d. Sold merchandise to a customer. Freight costs were $500. The goods were shipped FOB destination.

L.O. 2, 3   **PROBLEM 5–24B** *Effect of Purchase Returns and Allowances and Purchase Discounts on the Financial Statements: Perpetual System*

The following transactions were completed by The Jewel Shop in May 2008.

May 1   Acquired $100,000 cash from the issue of common stock.

  1   Purchased $60,000 of merchandise on account with terms 2/10 n/30.

  2   Paid $1,200 cash for freight to obtain merchandise purchased on May 1.

  4   Sold merchandise that cost $44,000 for $74,000 to customers on account.

4   Returned $5,000 of defective merchandise from the May 1 purchase for credit on account.
10   Paid cash for one-half of the balance due on the merchandise purchased on May 1.
13   Received cash from customers of May 4 sale in settlement of the account balance.
31   Paid the balance due on the merchandise purchased on May 1.
31   Paid selling expenses of $7,800.

Required

a. Record each event in a horizontal statements model like the following one. The first event is recorded as an example.

Assets			=	Liab.	+	Equity			Rev.	–	Exp.	=	Net Inc.	Cash Flow
Cash	+ Accts. Rec.	+ Inv.	= Accts. Pay.		+ C. Stk.	+ Ret. Earn.								
100,000 +	NA	+ NA =	NA		+ 100,000 +	NA			NA	– NA	=	NA		100,000 FA

b. Record each of the transactions in general journal form.
c. Post each of the transactions to general ledger T-accounts.
d. Prepare an income statement for the month ending May 31.
e. Prepare a statement of cash flows for the month ending May 31.
f. Explain why there is a difference between net income and cash flow from operating activities.

PROBLEM 5–25B *Comprehensive Cycle Problem: Perpetual System*   L.O. 2, 3, 5

At the beginning of 2006, M & M Enterprises had the following balances in its accounts:

Cash	$8,400
Inventory	2,000
Common Stock	8,000
Retained Earnings	2,400

During 2006, M & M Enterprises experienced the following events:

1. Purchased inventory with a list price of $5,600 on account from Smoot Company under terms 2/10 n/30. The merchandise was delivered FOB shipping point. Freight costs of $500 were paid in cash.
2. Returned inventory with a list price of $400 because the inventory had been damaged in transit. The freight company agreed to pay the return freight cost.
3. Paid the amount due on its account payable to Smoot Company but not within the cash discount period.
4. Sold inventory that had cost $6,000 for a list price of $9,000. The sale was on account under terms 2/10 n/45.
5. Received returned merchandise from a customer. The merchandise had originally cost $520 and had been sold to the customer for $840 cash. The customer was paid $840 cash for the returned merchandise.
6. Delivered goods in Event 4 FOB destination. Freight costs of $600 were paid in cash.
7. Collected the amount due on accounts receivable but not within the discount period.
8. Took a physical count indicating that $1,800 of inventory was on hand at the end of the accounting period.

Required

a. Identify each of these events as asset source (AS), asset use (AU), asset exchange (AE), or claims exchange (CE). Also explain how each event affects the financial statements by placing a + for increase, – for decrease, or NA for not affected under each of the components in the following statements model. Assume that the perpetual inventory method is used. When an event has more than one part, use letters to distinguish the effects of each part. The first event is recorded as an example.

Event No.	Event Type	Assets	= Liab.	+	Equity	Rev.	–	Exp.	=	Net Inc.	Cash Flow
1a	AS	+	= +	+	NA	NA	–	NA	=	NA	NA
1b	AE	+ –	= NA	+	NA	NA	–	NA	=	NA	– OA

b. Record the events in general journal format.
c. Open ledger T-accounts and post the beginning balances and the events to the accounts.
d. Prepare an income statement, statement of changes in stockholders' equity, balance sheet, and statement of cash flows.
e. Record and post the closing entries, and prepare an after-closing trial balance.

L.O. 6   PROBLEM 5–26B *Using Common Size Income Statements to Make Comparisons*

The following income statements were drawn from the annual reports of Madison Company:

	2006*	2007*
Net Sales	$74,507	$80,000
Cost of Goods Sold	(28,317)	(34,400)
Gross Margin	46,190	45,600
Less: Operating Expenses		
Selling and Administrative Expenses	(43,210)	(40,800)
Net Income	$ 2,980	$ 4,800

*All figures are reported in thousands of dollars.

Required

The president's message in the company's annual report stated that the company increased profitability by decreasing prices and controlling operating expenses. Write a memorandum indicating whether you agree with the president's statement. Support your answer by preparing common size income statements and making appropriate references to the differences between 2006 and 2007.

L.O. 4, 8   PROBLEM 5–27B *Preparing Schedule of Cost of Goods Sold and Multistep and Single-Step Income Statements: Periodic System (Appendix)*

The following account titles and balances were taken from the adjusted trial balance of Huggins Farm Co. for 2006. The company uses the periodic inventory system.

Account Title	Balance
Sales Returns and Allowances	$ 2,250
Income Taxes	3,700
Miscellaneous Expense	400
Transportation-out	600
Sales	69,750
Advertising Expense	2,750
Salaries Expense	7,900
Transportation-in	1,725
Purchases	40,000
Interest Expense	360
Merchandise Inventory, January 1	5,075
Rent Expense	5,000
Merchandise Inventory, December 31	4,050
Purchase Returns and Allowances	1,450
Depreciation Expense	710

Required

a. Prepare a schedule to determine the amount of cost of goods sold.
b. Prepare a multistep income statement.
c. Prepare a single-step income statement.

L.O. 8   PROBLEM 5–28B *Comprehensive Cycle Problem: Periodic System (Appendix)*

The following trial balance pertains to John's Jungle as of January 1, 2008:

Account Title	Debit	Credit
Cash	$26,000	
Accounts Receivable	4,000	
Merchandise Inventory	50,000	
Accounts Payable		$ 4,000
Common Stock		43,000
Retained Earnings		33,000
Totals	$80,000	$80,000

The following events occurred in 2008. Assume that John's uses the periodic inventory method.

1. Purchased land for $20,000 cash and a building for $90,000 by paying $10,000 cash and issuing a 20-year note with an annual interest rate of 8 percent. The building has a 40-year estimated life with no residual value.
2. Purchased merchandise on account for $126,000, terms 1/10 n/45.
3. Paid freight of $1,000 cash on merchandise purchased FOB shipping point.
4. Returned $3,600 of defective merchandise purchased in Event 2.
5. Sold merchandise for $86,000 cash.
6. Sold merchandise on account for $120,000, terms 2/10 n/30.
7. Paid cash within the discount period on accounts payable due on merchandise purchased in Event 2.
8. Paid $11,600 cash for selling expenses.
9. Collected part of the balance due from accounts receivable in Event 6. Collections were made after the discount period on $60,000 of the receivables. Collections were made during the discount period on $50,000 of the receivables.
10. Paid cash to the bank for one full year's interest on the note issued in Event 1.
11. Paid $10,000 on the principal of the note issued in Event 1.
12. Recorded one full year's depreciation on the building purchased in Event 1.
13. A physical count indicated that $27,600 of inventory was on hand at the end of the accounting period.

Required
a. Record these transactions in a general journal.
b. Post the transactions to ledger T-accounts.
c. Prepare a schedule of costs of goods sold, an income statement, statement of changes in stockholders' equity, balance sheet, and statement of cash flows for 2008.

ANALYZE, THINK, COMMUNICATE

BUSINESS APPLICATIONS CASE *Understanding Real World Annual Reports*

ATC 5–1

Required
a. Use the Topps Company's annual report in Appendix B to answer the following questions.

(1) What was Topps' gross margin percentage for 2003 and 2002?
(2) What was Topps' return on sales percentage for 2003 and 2002?
(3) Topps' Gross Profit on Sales was about $12 million lower in 2003 than in 2002 and this caused its Net Income to be lower as well. However, its gross margin percentage also decreased in 2003. Ignoring taxes, how much higher would its 2003 net income have been if the gross margin percentage in 2003 had been the same as for 2002?

b. Use the Harley-Davidson's annual report that came with this book to answer the following questions.

(1) What was Harley-Davidson's gross margin percentage for 2003 and 2002?
(2) What was Harley-Davidson's return on sales percentage for 2003 and 2002?
(3) Harley-Davidson's gross margin percentage increased during 2003 compared to 2002. The MD&A section of its annual report explains the reasons this occurred. What are these reasons?

GROUP EXERCISE *Multistep Income Statement*

ATC 5–2

The following quarterly information is given for Raybon for the year ended 2002 (amounts shown are in millions).

	First Quarter	Second Quarter	Third Quarter	Fourth Quarter
Net Sales	$736.0	$717.4	$815.2	$620.1
Gross Margin	461.9	440.3	525.3	252.3
Net Income	37.1	24.6	38.6	31.4

Required
a. Divide the class into groups and organize the groups into four sections. Assign each section financial information for one of the quarters.
(1) Each group should compute the cost of goods sold and operating expenses for the specific quarter assigned to its section and prepare a multistep income statement for the quarter.
(2) Each group should compute the gross margin percentage and cost of goods sold percentage for its specific quarter.

(3) Have a representative of each group put that quarter's sales, cost of goods sold percentage, and gross margin percentage on the board.

Class Discussion

b. Have the class discuss the change in each of these items from quarter to quarter and explain why the change might have occurred. Which was the best quarter and why?

ATC 5–3   REAL-WORLD CASE *Identifying Companies Based on Financial Statement Information*

Presented here is selected information from the 2002 fiscal-year 10-K reports of four companies. The four companies, in alphabetical order, are Caterpillar, Inc., a manufacturer of heavy machinery; Oracle Corporation, a company that develops software; Peet's Coffee & Tea, a company that sells coffee products; and Tiffany & Company, a company that operates high-end jewelry and department stores. The data for the companies, presented in the order of the amount of their sales in millions of dollars, follow:

	A	B	C	D
Sales	$18,648	$ 9,673	$1,706.6	$104.1
Cost of goods sold	14,709	2,406	695.2	48.1
Net earnings	798	2,224	189.9	4.7
Inventory	2,763	0	732.1	11.0
Accounts receivable	2,838	2,036	113.1	2.2
Total assets	32,851	10,800	1,923.6	95.1

Required

Based on these financial data and your knowledge and assumptions about the nature of the businesses that the companies operate, determine which data relate to which companies. Write a memorandum explaining your decisions. Include a discussion of which ratios you used in your analysis, and show the computations of these ratios in your memorandum.

ATC 5–4   BUSINESS APPLICATIONS CASE *Using Ratios to Make Comparisons*

The following income statements were drawn from the annual reports of Asphalt Company and Concrete Company.

	Asphalt	Concrete
Net Sales	$95,700	$52,300
Cost of Goods Sold	68,900	31,400
Gross Margin	26,800	20,900
Less: Selling and Admin. Expenses	22,000	18,800
Net Income	$ 4,800	$ 2,100

*All figures are reported in thousands of dollars

Required

a. One of the companies is a high-end retailer that operates in exclusive shopping malls. The other operates discount stores located in low-cost stand-alone buildings. Identify the high-end retailer and the discounter. Support your answer with appropriate ratios.

b. If Asphalt and Concrete have equity of $40,000 and $21,000, respectively, which company is the more profitable?

ATC 5–5   BUSINESS APPLICATIONS CASE *Using Common Size Statements and Ratios to Make Comparisons*

At the end of 2006, the following information is available for Kinlaw and Parker companies:

	Kinlaw	Parker
Sales	$2,000	$2,000,000
Cost of Goods Sold	1,400	1,200,000
Selling and Administrative Expenses	520	640,000
Total Assets	2,500	2,500,000
Stockholders' Equity	750	730,000

Required

a. Prepare common size income statements for each company.

b. Compute the return on assets and return on equity for each company.

c. Which company is more profitable from the stockholders' perspective?

d. One company is a high-end retailer, and the other operates a discount store. Which is the discounter? Support your selection by referring to appropriate ratios.

WRITTEN ASSIGNMENT, CRITICAL THINKING *Effect of Sales Returns on Financial Statements*

ATC 5–6

Bell Farm and Garden Equipment reported the following information for 2005:

Net sales of equipment	$2,450,567
Other income	6,786
Cost of goods sold	1,425,990
Selling, general, and administrative expense	325,965
Depreciation and amortization	3,987
Net operating income	$ 701,411

Selected information from the balance sheet as of December 31, 2005 follows:

Cash and Marketable Securities	$113,545
Inventory	248,600
Accounts Receivable	82,462
Property, Plant, and Equipment—net	335,890
Other Assets	5,410
Total Assets	$785,907

Assume that a major customer returned a large order to Bell on December 31, 2005. The amount of the sale had been $146,800 with a cost of sales of $94,623. The return was recorded in the books on January 1, 2006. The company president does not want to correct the books. He argues that it makes no difference as to whether the return is recorded in 2005 or 2006. Either way, the return has been duly recognized.

Required

a. Assume that you are the CFO for Bell Farm and Garden Equipment Co. Write a memo to the president explaining how omitting the entry on December 31, 2005, could cause the financial statements to be misleading to investors and creditors. Explain how omitting the return from the customer would affect net income and the balance sheet.

b. Why might the president want to record the return on January 1, 2006, instead of December 31, 2005?

c. Would the failure to record the customer return violate the AICPA Code of Professional Conduct? (See Exhibit 2–7 in Chapter 2.)

d. If the president of the company refuses to correct the financial statements, what action should you take?

ETHICAL DILEMMA *Wait Until I Get Mine*

ATC 5–7

Ada Fontanez is the president of a large company that owns a chain of athletic shoe stores. The company was in dire financial condition when she was hired three years ago. In an effort to motivate Fontanez, the board of directors included a bonus plan as part of her compensation package. According to her employment contract, on January 15 of each year, Fontanez is paid a cash bonus equal to 5 percent of the amount of net income reported on the preceding December 31 income statement. Fontanez was sufficiently motivated. Through her leadership, the company prospered. Her efforts were recognized throughout the industry, and she received numerous lucrative offers to leave the company. One offer was so enticing that she decided to change jobs. Her decision was made in late December 2005. However, she decided to resign effective February 1, 2006, to ensure the receipt of her January bonus. On December 31, 2005, the chief accountant, Walter Smith, advised Fontanez that the company had a sizable quantity of damaged inventory. A warehouse fire had resulted in smoke and water damage to approximately $600,000 of inventory. The warehouse was not insured, and the accountant recommended that the loss be recognized immediately. After examining the inventory, Fontanez argued that it could be sold as *damaged goods* to customers at reduced prices. Accordingly, she refused to allow the write-off the accountant recommended.

She stated that so long as she is president, the inventory stays on the books at cost. She told the accountant that he could take up the matter with the new president in February.

Required

a. How would an immediate write-off of the damaged inventory affect the December 31, 2005, income statement, balance sheet, and statement of cash flows?

b. How would the write-off affect Fontanez's bonus?

c. If the new president is given the same bonus plan, how will Fontanez's refusal to recognize the loss affect his or her bonus?

d. Assuming that the damaged inventory is truly worthless, comment on the ethical implications of Fontanez's refusal to recognize the loss in the 2005 accounting period.

e. Assume that the damaged inventory is truly worthless and that you are Smith. How would you react to Fontanez's refusal to recognize the loss?

ATC 5–8 EDGAR DATABASE *Analyzing Alcoa's Profit Margins*

Instructions for using EDGAR are in Appendix A. Using the most current 10-K annual report available on EDGAR, answer the following questions about Alcoa, Inc.

Required

a. What was Alcoa's gross margin percentage for the most current year?

b. What was Alcoa's gross margin percentage for the previous year? Has it changed significantly?

c. What was Alcoa's return on sales percentage for the most current year?

d. What percentage of Alcoa's total sales for the most current year was from operations in the United States?

e. Comment on the appropriateness of comparing Alcoa's gross margin with that of Ford Motor Company. If Ford has a higher/lower margin, does that mean that Ford is a better managed company?

ATC 5–9 SPREADSHEET ANALYSIS *Using Excel*

The following accounts, balances, and other financial information are drawn from the records of Vong Company for the year 2004:

Net Sales Revenue	$18,800	Beginning Common Stock	$ 9,000
Unearned Revenue	2,600	Land	8,000
Accounts Receivable	6,000	Certificate of Deposit	10,000
Cost of Goods Sold	6,000	Interest Revenue	100
Inventory	5,000	Interest Receivable	100
Accounts Payable	5,800	Dividends	1,500
Notes Payable	6,000	Beginning Retained Earnings	8,500
Interest Expense	550	Cash from Stock Issued	3,000
Accrued Interest Payable	550	Cash	7,200
Supplies	50	Gain on Sale of Land	1,050
Supplies Expense	750	Loss on Sale of Property	50
Office Equipment	3,500	Salaries Expense	1,400
Depreciation Expense	500	Accrued Salaries Payable	400
Accumulated Depreciation	1,000	Rent Expense	1,100
Transportation-out Expense	500	Prepaid Rent	100
Miscellaneous Operating Expense	4,500		

The Cash account revealed the following cash flows:

Received cash from advances from customers	$ 2,600
Purchased office equipment	(3,500)
Received cash from issuing stock	3,000
Collected cash from accounts receivable	3,800
Purchased land	(8,000)
Received cash from borrowing funds	6,000
Paid cash for rent	(1,200)
Sold land	10,000
Paid cash for dividends	(1,500)
Paid cash for operating expenses	(1,000)
Purchased certificate of deposit	(10,000)

Required

Build an Excel spreadsheet to construct a multistep income statement, statement of changes in stockholders' equity, balance sheet, and statement of cash flows for the year 2004.

SPREADSHEET ANALYSIS *Mastering Excel*

At the end of 2004, the following information is available for Short and Wise Companies:

ATC 5–10

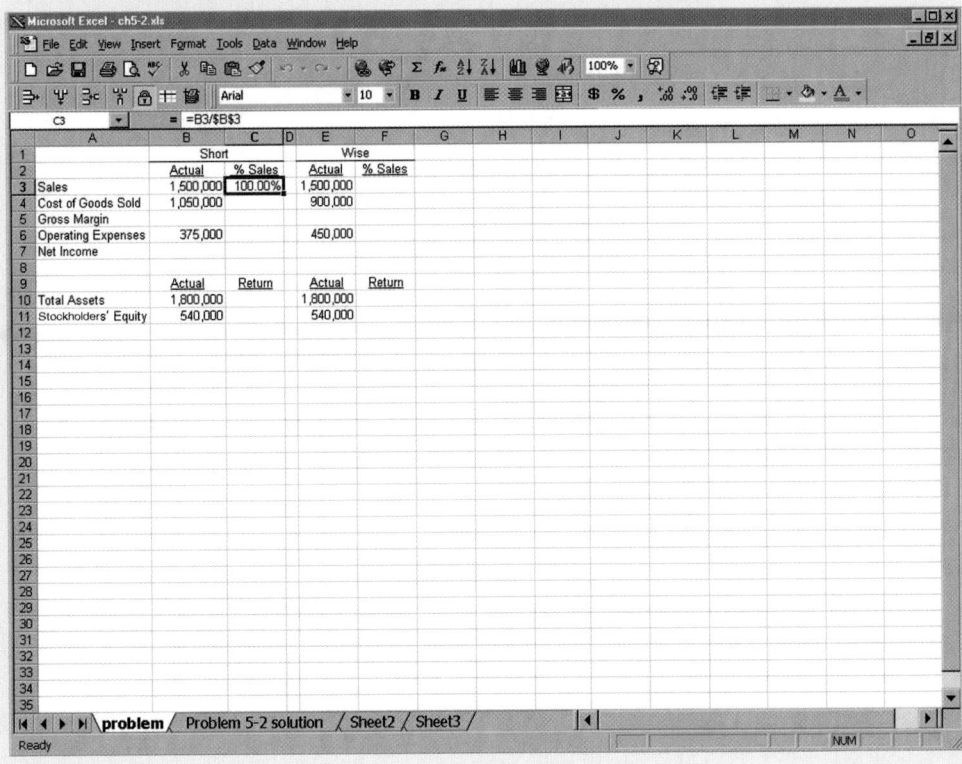

Required

a. Set up the spreadsheet shown here. Complete the income statements by using Excel formulas.
b. Prepare a common size income statement for each company by completing the % Sales columns.
c. One company is a high-end retailer, and the other operates a discount store. Which is the discounter? Support your selection by referring to the common size statements.
d. Compute the return on assets and return on equity for each company.
e. Which company is more profitable from the stockholders' perspective?
f. Assume that a shortage of goods from suppliers is causing cost of goods sold to increase 10 percent for each company. Change the respective cost of goods sold balances in the Actual income statement column for each company. Note the new calculated amounts on the income statement and in the ratios. Which company's profits and returns are more sensitive to inventory price hikes?

COMPREHENSIVE PROBLEM

The following information is available for Pacilio Security Systems Sales and Service for 2005, its first year of operations. Pacilio sells security systems and provides 24-hour alarm monitoring service. Pacilio sells two types of alarm systems, standard and deluxe. The following summary transactions occurred during 2005. (Round calculations to the nearest whole dollar.)

1. Acquired $50,000 cash from the issue of common stock.
2. Rented a building for a period of 12 months. On March 2, 2005, paid $6,000 for one year's rent in advance.
3. Purchased $800 of supplies with cash to be used over the next several months by the business.
4. Purchased 50 standard alarm systems for resale at a list price of $12,245 and 20 deluxe alarm systems at a list price of $10,204. The alarm systems were purchased on account with the terms 2/10 n/30.

5. Returned one of the standard alarms that had a list price of $245.
6. Installed 40 alarm systems during the year for a total sales amount of $23,000. The cost of these systems amounted to $12,200 (the standard alarms cost $7,200 and the delux alarms cost $5,000). $15,000 of the sales were on account and $8,000 were cash sales.
7. Paid the installers a total of $7,500 in salaries.
8. Sold $36,000 of monitoring services for the year. The services are billed to the customer each month.
9. Paid cash to settle accounts payable. The payment was made **before** the discount period expired. At the time of purchase, the inventory had a list price of $9,000 and a net price of $8,820.
10. Paid cash to settle additional accounts payable. The payment was made **after** the discount period expired. At the time of purchase, the inventory had a list price of $9,000 and a net price of $8,820.
11. Collected $43,000 of accounts receivable during the year.
12. Paid advertising cost of $1,400 for the year.
13. Paid $1,100 for utilities expense for the year.
14. Paid a cash dividend of $2,000 to the shareholders.

Adjustments
15. There was $150 of supplies on hand at the end of the year.
16. Recognized the expired rent for the year.

Required
a. Record the above transactions in general journal form.
b. Post the transactions to T-accounts.
c. Prepare a trial balance.
d. Prepare an income statement, statement of changes in stockholders' equity, balance sheet, and statement of cash flows.
e. Close the temporary accounts to retained earnings.
f. Post the closing entries to T-accounts and prepare an after-closing trial balance.

CHAPTER *six*

ACCOUNTING FOR MERCHANDISING BUSINESSES— ADVANCED TOPICS

LEARNING *objectives*

After you have mastered the material in this chapter, you will be able to:

1 Explain how different inventory cost flow methods (specific identification, FIFO, LIFO, and weighted average) affect financial statements.

2 Demonstrate the computational procedures for FIFO, LIFO, and weighted average.

3 Apply the lower-of-cost-or-market rule to inventory valuation.

4 Explain how fraud can be avoided through inventory control.

5 Use the gross margin method to estimate ending inventory.

6 Explain the importance of inventory turnover to a company's profitability.

7 Explain how accounting for investment securities differs when the securities are classified as held to maturity, trading, or available for sale. (Appendix)

THE *curious* ACCOUNTANT

Kroger is one of the largest food store chains in the United States, operating about 2,500 stores. As of February 1, 2003, the company had approximately $4.2 billion of inventory reported on its balance sheet. In the footnotes to its financial statements, Kroger reported that it uses an inventory method that assumes its newest goods are sold first and its oldest goods are kept in inventory.

Can you think of any reason why a company selling perishable goods such as milk and vegetables uses an inventory method that assumes older goods are kept while newer goods are sold? (Answer on page 281.)

CHAPTER *opening*

*Assume Baker Company purchased two identical inventory items. The first item cost $100; the second was purchased sometime later for $110. Suppose Baker loses track of which item was purchased first. If Baker sells one of the inventory items, should it record $100 or $110 as cost of goods sold? Several **inventory cost flow methods** offer solutions to this problem. These cost flow methods are discussed in the following section of this chapter.*

LO1 Explain how different inventory cost flow methods (specific identification, FIFO, LIFO, and weighted average) affect financial statements.

Inventory Cost Flow Methods

The four common inventory cost flow methods are (1) specific identification; (2) first-in, first-out (FIFO); (3) last-in, first-out (LIFO); and (4) weighted average. Recall that when goods are sold, product costs *flow* (are transferred) from the Inventory account to the Cost of Goods Sold account. Companies choose one of the four cost flow methods to identify which costs to transfer. These cost flow methods are explained in the following discussion.

Specific Identification

Suppose Baker Company tags inventory items so that it can identify which one is sold at the time of sale. Baker could then charge the actual cost of the specific item sold to cost of goods sold. Recall that the first inventory item Baker purchased cost $100 and the second item cost $110. Using specific identification, cost of goods sold would be $100 if the first item purchased were sold or $110 if the second item purchased were sold.

When a company's inventory consists of many low-priced, high-turnover goods the record keeping necessary to use **specific identification** isn't practical. Imagine the difficulty of recording the cost of each specific food item in a grocery store. Another disadvantage of the specific identification method is the opportunity for managers to manipulate the income statement. For example, Baker can report a lower cost of goods sold by selling the first instead of the second item. Specific identification is, however, frequently used for high-priced, low-turnover inventory items such as automobiles. For big ticket items like cars, customer demands for specific products limit management's ability to select the merchandise being sold and volume is low enough to manage the record keeping.

First-In, First-Out (FIFO)

The **first-in, first-out (FIFO) cost flow method** requires that the cost of the items purchased *first* be assigned to cost of goods sold. Using FIFO, Baker Company's cost of goods sold is $100.

Last-In, First-Out (LIFO)

The **last-in, first-out (LIFO) cost flow method** requires that the cost of the items purchased *last* be charged to cost of goods sold. Using LIFO, Baker Company's cost of goods sold is $110.

Weighted Average

To use the **weighted-average cost flow method,** you first calculate the average cost per unit by dividing the *total cost* of the inventory available by the *total number* of units available. In the case of Baker Company, the average cost per unit of the inventory is $105 ([$100 + $110] ÷ 2). Cost of goods sold is then calculated by multiplying the average cost per unit by the number of units sold. Using weighted average, Baker Company's cost of goods sold is $105 ($105 × 1).

Physical Flow

The preceding discussion pertains to the flow of *costs* through the accounting records, *not* the actual **physical flow of goods.** Goods usually move physically on a FIFO basis, which means that the first items of merchandise acquired by a company (first-in) are the first items sold to its customers (first-out). The last items in (the most recently acquired goods) are the items of inventory that are left over at the end of the accounting period. If this were not the case, inventories would include dated, less marketable merchandise. However, *cost flow* can be done on a different basis than *physical flow*. For example, LIFO or weighted average could be used for cost flow even when FIFO is being used for physical flow.

Effect of Cost Flow on Financial Statements

Effect on Income Statement

The cost flow method a company uses can significantly affect the gross margin reported in the income statement. To demonstrate, assume that Baker Company sold the inventory item discussed previously for $120. The amounts of gross margin using the FIFO, LIFO, and weighted-average cost flow assumptions are shown in the following table:

	FIFO	LIFO	Weighted Average
Sales	$120	$120	$120
Cost of Goods Sold	100	110	105
Gross Margin	$ 20	$ 10	$ 15

Notice that even though the physical flow is assumed to be identical for each method, the gross margin reported under FIFO is double the amount reported under LIFO. Companies experiencing identical economic events (same units of inventory purchased and sold) can report significantly different results in their financial statements. This explains why financial analysis requires an understanding of financial reporting practices.

Effect on Balance Sheet

Since total product costs are allocated between costs of goods sold and ending inventory, the cost flow method a company uses affects its balance sheet as well as its income statement. Since FIFO transfers the first cost to the income statement, it leaves the last cost on the balance sheet. Similarly, by transferring the last cost to the income statement, LIFO leaves the first cost in ending inventory. The weighted-average method bases both cost of goods sold and ending inventory on the average cost per unit. To illustrate, the ending inventory Baker Company would report on the balance sheet using each of the three cost flow methods is shown in the following table:

	FIFO	LIFO	Weighted Average
Ending Inventory	$110	$100	$105

The FIFO, LIFO, and weighted-average methods are all used extensively in business practice. The same company may even use one cost flow method for some of its products and different cost flow methods for other products. Exhibit 6–1 illustrates the relative use of the different cost flow methods among U.S. companies.

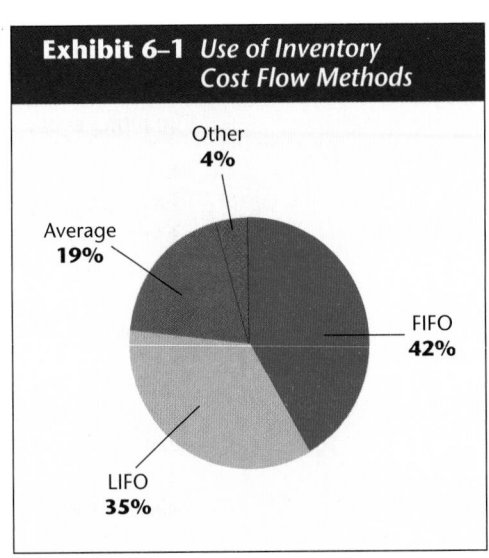

Exhibit 6–1 *Use of Inventory Cost Flow Methods*

Other 4%
Average 19%
FIFO 42%
LIFO 35%

Data source: AICPA, *Accounting Trends and Techniques*, 2000.

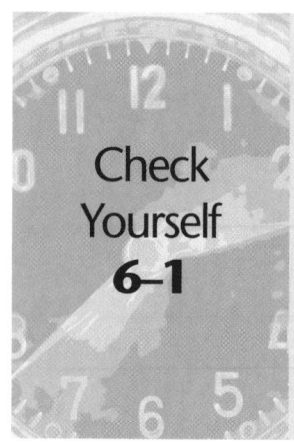

Nash Office Supply (NOS) purchased two Model 303 copiers at different times. The first copier purchased cost $400 and the second copier purchased cost $450. NOS sold one of the copiers for $600. Determine the gross margin on the sale and the ending inventory balance assuming NOS accounts for inventory using (1) FIFO, (2) LIFO, and (3) weighted average.

Answer

	FIFO	LIFO	Weighted Average
Sales	$600	$600	$600
Cost of Goods Sold	(400)	(450)	(425)
Gross Margin	$200	$150	$175
Ending Inventory	$450	$400	$425

Inventory Cost Flow Under a Perpetual System

Multiple Layers With Multiple Quantities

LO2 Demonstrate the computational procedures for FIFO, LIFO, and weighted average.

The Baker Company example illustrates different inventory cost flow methods using only two cost layers ($100 and $110) with only one unit of inventory in each layer. Actual business inventories are considerably more complex. Most real-world inventories are composed of multiple cost layers with different quantities of inventory in each layer. The underlying allocation concepts, however, remain unchanged. The following illustration demonstrates this condition.

The accounting records of The Mountain Bike Company (TMBC) reflect the following account balances as of January 1, 2006: Cash, $12,000; Inventory, $2,000; Common Stock, $6,000; and Retained Earnings, $8,000. During 2006, TMBC made two cash purchases of inventory. The following table provides details about the beginning inventory balance and the two purchases:

Jan. 1	Beginning inventory	10 units @ $200	=	$ 2,000
Mar. 18	First purchase	20 units @ $220	=	4,400
Aug. 21	Second purchase	25 units @ $250	=	6,250
	Total cost of the 55 bikes available for sale			$12,650

Including the inventory purchases shown above, TMBC experienced the following five accounting events during 2006:

Event 1   Paid cash to purchase 20 units of inventory that cost $220 per unit.
Event 2   Paid cash to purchase 25 units of inventory that cost $250 per unit.
Event 3(a) Recognized revenue on sales of 43 bikes at a price of $350 cash per bike.
Event 3(b) Recognized cost of goods sold for the 43 bikes sold.
Event 4   Paid $2,600 cash for operating expenses.
Event 5   Paid cash for income tax. Assume a tax rate of 30% of earnings before tax.

Exhibit 6–2 shows the effects of each event on the financial statements under three different inventory cost flow assumptions: FIFO, LIFO, and weighted average. The exhibit assumes that TMBC uses a *perpetual inventory* system.

Events 1 and 2 **Purchase of Inventory**

As shown in Exhibit 6–2, the effects of inventory *purchases* are the same regardless of the cost flow assumption used. In each case, purchasing inventory for cash represents an asset exchange. The asset Inventory increases and the asset Cash decreases. Total assets remains

Exhibit 6–2 Effect of Events on Financial Statements

Panel 1: FIFO Cost Flow

Event No.	Balance Sheet						Income Statement						Statement of Cash Flows	
	Assets			=	Stockholders' Equity									
	Cash	+	Inventory	=	C. Stk.	+	Ret. Earn.	Rev.	–	Exp.	=	Net Inc.		
Bal.	12,000	+	2,000	=	6,000	+	8,000	0	–	0	=	0	0	
1	(4,400)	+	4,400	=	NA	+	NA	NA	–	NA	=	NA	(4,400)	OA
2	(6,250)	+	6,250	=	NA	+	NA	NA	–	NA	=	NA	(6,250)	OA
3(a)	15,050	+	NA	=	NA	+	15,050	15,050	–	NA	=	15,050	15,050	OA
3(b)	NA	+	(9,650)	=	NA	+	(9,650)	NA	–	9,650	=	(9,650)	NA	
4	(2,600)	+	NA	=	NA	+	(2,600)	NA	–	2,600	=	(2,600)	(2,600)	OA
5	(840)	+	NA	=	NA	+	(840)	NA	–	840	=	(840)	(840)	OA
Bal.	12,960	+	3,000	=	6,000	+	9,960	15,050	–	13,090	=	1,960	960	NC

Panel 2: LIFO Cost Flow

Event No.	Balance Sheet						Income Statement						Statement of Cash Flows	
	Assets			=	Stockholders' Equity									
	Cash	+	Inventory	=	C. Stk.	+	Ret. Earn.	Rev.	–	Exp.	=	Net Inc.		
Bal.	12,000	+	2,000	=	6,000	+	8,000	0	–	0	=	0	0	
1	(4,400)	+	4,400	=	NA	+	NA	NA	–	NA	=	NA	(4,400)	OA
2	(6,250)	+	6,250	=	NA	+	NA	NA	–	NA	=	NA	(6,250)	OA
3(a)	15,050	+	NA	=	NA	+	15,050	15,050	–	NA	=	15,050	15,050	OA
3(b)	NA	+	(10,210)	=	NA	+	(10,210)	NA	–	10,210	=	(10,210)	NA	
4	(2,600)	+	NA	=	NA	+	(2,600)	NA	–	2,600	=	(2,600)	(2,600)	OA
5	(672)	+	NA	=	NA	+	(672)	NA	–	672	=	(672)	(672)	OA
Bal.	13,128	+	2,440	=	6,000	+	9,568	15,050	–	13,482	=	1,568	1,128	NC

Panel 3: Weighted-Average Cost Flow

Event No.	Balance Sheet						Income Statement						Statement of Cash Flows	
	Assets			=	Stockholders' Equity									
	Cash	+	Inventory	=	C. Stk.	+	Ret. Earn.	Rev.	–	Exp.	=	Net Inc.		
Bal.	12,000	+	2,000	=	6,000	+	8,000	0	–	0	=	0	0	
1	(4,400)	+	4,400	=	NA	+	NA	NA	–	NA	=	NA	(4,400)	OA
2	(6,250)	+	6,250	=	NA	+	NA	NA	–	NA	=	NA	(6,250)	OA
3(a)	15,050	+	NA	=	NA	+	15,050	15,050	–	NA	=	15,050	15,050	OA
3(b)	NA	+	(9,890)	=	NA	+	(9,890)	NA	–	9,890	=	(9,890)	NA	
4	(2,600)	+	NA	=	NA	+	(2,600)	NA	–	2,600	=	(2,600)	(2,600)	OA
5	(768)	+	NA	=	NA	+	(768)	NA	–	768	=	(768)	(768)	OA
Bal.	13,032	+	2,760	=	6,000	+	9,792	15,050	–	13,258	=	1,792	1,032	NC

unchanged. The income statement is not affected. The cash outflow is reported in the operating activities section of the statement of cash flows.

Event 3a Sale of Inventory

The effects of earning sales revenue are also the same under all three cost flow methods. Sales amounted to $15,050 (43 bikes × $350 per bike). The cash sales represent sources of assets. Recognizing the sales revenue increases both assets (Cash) and stockholders' equity (retained earnings). The sales revenue increases net income. The cash inflow from the sales is reported in the operating activities section of the statement of cash flows.

Event 3b **Cost of Sale**

When goods are sold, the cost of those goods is transferred from the Inventory account to the Cost of Goods Sold account. Both assets (inventory) and stockholders' equity (retained earnings) decrease. The *amount* transferred from inventory to cost of goods sold depends on the cost flow method used.

FIFO Inventory Cost Flow

The FIFO method transfers to the Cost of Goods Sold account the *cost of the first 43 bikes* TMBC had available to sell, regardless of which bikes were actually sold. Remember, the actual physical flow of inventory items and cost flow methods used for accounting records are independent of each other. The first 43 bikes acquired by TMBC were the 10 bikes in the beginning inventory (these were purchased in the prior period) plus the 20 bikes purchased in March and 13 of the bikes purchased in August. The expense recognized for the cost of these bikes ($9,650) is computed as follows:

Jan. 1	Beginning inventory	10 units @ $200	=	$2,000
Mar. 18	First purchase	20 units @ $220	=	4,400
Aug. 21	Second purchase	13 units @ $250	=	3,250
	Total cost of the 43 bikes sold			$9,650

As shown in Exhibit 6–2, Panel 1, Event 3(b), the cost of goods sold expense recognition decreases net income. There is no cash flow effect; the cash outflow occurred when the inventory was purchased.

LIFO Inventory Cost Flow

As shown in Exhibit 6–2, Panel 2, Event 3(b), the cost transferred from inventory to cost of goods sold under LIFO is $10,210, determined by computing the *cost of the last 43 bikes* acquired by TMBC as follows:

Aug. 21	Second purchase	25 units @ $250	=	$ 6,250
Mar. 18	First purchase	18 units @ $220	=	3,960
	Total cost of the 43 bikes sold			$10,210

Weighted-Average Cost Flow

The weighted-average cost per unit is determined by dividing the *total cost of goods available for sale* by the *total number of units* available for sale. For TMBC, the weighted-average cost per unit is $230 ($12,650 ÷ 55). The weighted-average cost of goods sold is determined by multiplying the average cost per unit by the number of units sold ($230 × 43 = $9,890). Exhibit 6–2, Panel 3, Event 3(b) shows the cost of goods sold expense recognition.

Event 4 **Paid Operating Expenses**

The inventory cost flow method used has no effect on paying operating expenses. In all cases, paying for $2,600 of operating expenses reduces both assets (cash) and stockholders' equity (retained earnings). The expense recognition decreases net income. The cash outflow is reported in the operating activities section of the statement of cash flows.

Event 5 **Paid Income Taxes**

Since the inventory cost flow method affects the amount of cost of goods sold, it also affects the amount of income before taxes and, therefore, the *amount* of income tax expense (earnings before tax times the tax rate). As shown in Exhibit 6–2, Event 5, the *effect* of the tax expense on the financial statements is the same under all three methods. In each case, the tax expense reduces both assets (cash) and stockholders' equity (retained earnings). The expense recognition decreases net income. The cash outflow is reported in the operating activities section of the statement of cash flows.

Effect of Cost Flow on Financial Statements

Exhibit 6–3 displays income statements, balance sheets, and statements of cash flows for each of the three cost flow assumptions. Based on these financial statements, which cost flow method would you recommend TMBC use? Most people initially suggest FIFO because FIFO reports the highest net income, the largest balance in ending inventory, and the highest total assets.

LO1 Explain how different inventory cost flow methods (specific identification, FIFO, LIFO, and weighted average) affect financial statements.

Exhibit 6–3

TMBC COMPANY
Comparative Financial Statements

Income Statements

	FIFO	LIFO	Weighted Average
Sales	$15,050	$15,050	$15,050
Cost of Goods Sold	(9,650)	(10,210)	(9,890)
Gross Margin	5,400	4,840	5,160
Operating Expenses	(2,600)	(2,600)	(2,600)
Income before Taxes (IBT)	2,800	2,240	2,560
Income Tax Expense (IBT × 0.30)	(840)	(672)	(768)
Net Income	$ 1,960	$ 1,568	$ 1,792

Balance Sheets

	FIFO	LIFO	Weighted Average
Assets			
Cash	$12,960	$13,128	$13,032
Inventory	3,000	2,440	2,760
Total Assets	$15,960	$15,568	$15,792
Stockholders' Equity			
Common Stock	$ 6,000	$ 6,000	$ 6,000
Retained Earnings	9,960	9,568	9,792
Total Stockholders' Equity	$15,960	$15,568	$15,792

Statements of Cash Flows

	FIFO	LIFO	Weighted Average
Operating Activities			
Cash Inflow from Customers	$15,050	$15,050	$15,050
Cash Outflow for Inventory	(10,650)	(10,650)	(10,650)
Cash Outflow for Operating Expenses	(2,600)	(2,600)	(2,600)
Cash Outflow for Tax Expense	(840)	(672)	(768)
Net Cash Inflow from Operating Activities	960	1,128	1,032
Investing Activities	0	0	0
Financing Activities	0	0	0
Net Increase in Cash	960	1,128	1,032
Beginning Cash Balance	12,000	12,000	12,000
Ending Cash Balance	$12,960	$13,128	$13,032

As reported on the statements of cash flows, however, FIFO requires the largest cash payment for income taxes, while taxes paid under LIFO are the lowest. Will investors favor a company with more assets and higher net income or one with lower tax expense? Research suggests that investors are astute. They make investment decisions based on economic substance regardless of how financial information is reported. As a result, investors would likely be more attracted to TMBC if it used LIFO because the lower tax payments allow the company to keep more value in the business.

In some instances companies may use one accounting method for financial reporting and a different method to compute income taxes (the tax return must explain any differences). With respect to LIFO, however, the Internal Revenue Service requires that companies using LIFO for income tax purposes must also use LIFO for financial reporting. A company could not, therefore, get both the lower tax benefit provided by LIFO and the financial reporting advantage offered under FIFO.

Our illustration assumes an inflationary environment (rising inventory prices). In a deflationary environment, the impact of using LIFO versus FIFO is reversed. LIFO produces tax advantages in an inflationary environment, while FIFO produces tax advantages in a deflationary environment. Companies operating in the computer industry where prices are falling would obtain a tax advantage by using FIFO. In contrast, companies that sell medical supplies in an inflationary environment would obtain a tax advantage by using LIFO.

Check Yourself 6–2

The following information was drawn from the inventory records of Fields, Inc.

Beginning inventory	200 units @ $20
First purchase	400 units @ $22
Second purchase	600 units @ $24

Assume that Fields sold 900 units of inventory.

1. Determine the amount of cost of goods sold using FIFO.
2. Would using LIFO produce a higher or lower amount of cost of goods sold? Why?

Answer

1. Cost of goods sold using FIFO

Beginning inventory	200 units @ $20	=	$ 4,000
First purchase	400 units @ $22	=	8,800
Second purchase	300 units @ $24	=	7,200
Total cost of goods sold			$20,000

2. The inventory records reflect an inflationary environment of steadily rising prices. Since LIFO charges the latest costs (in this case the highest costs) to the income statement, using LIFO would produce a higher amount of cost of goods sold than would using FIFO.

Inventory Cost Flow When Sales and Purchases Occur Intermittently

LO2 Demonstrate the computational procedures for FIFO, LIFO, and weighted average.

In the previous illustrations, all purchases were made before any goods were sold. This section addresses more realistic conditions, when sales transactions occur intermittently with purchases. Assume the following table describes the beginning inventory, purchases, and sales transactions for Sharon Sales Company (SSC) during 2008:

Date	Transaction	Description
Jan. 1	Beginning inventory	100 units @ $20.00
Feb. 14	Purchased	200 units @ $21.50
Apr. 5	Sold	220 units @ $30.00
June 21	Purchased	160 units @ $22.50
Aug. 18	Sold	100 units @ $30.00
Sept. 2	Purchased	280 units @ $23.50
Nov. 10	Sold	330 units @ $30.00

FIFO Cost Flow

Exhibit 6–4 displays the computations for cost of goods sold and inventory if SSC uses the FIFO cost flow method. The inventory records are maintained in layers. Each time a sales transaction occurs, the unit cost in the first layer of inventory is assigned to the items sold. If the number of items sold exceeds the number of items in the first layer, the unit cost of the next layer is assigned to the remaining number of units sold, and so on. For example, the cost assigned to the 220 units of inventory sold on April 5 is determined as follows:

100 units of inventory in the first layer × $20.00 per unit	= $2,000
+ 120 units of inventory in the second layer × $21.50 per unit	= 2,580
220 units for total cost of goods sold for the April 5 sale	= $4,580

The cost of goods sold for subsequent sales transactions is similarly computed.

focus on INTERNATIONAL ISSUES

The Influence of Tax Accounting on GAAP

As noted earlier in this chapter, a U.S. company can use LIFO for income tax purposes *only* if it also uses LIFO for GAAP purposes. This is an unusual situation because tax accounting in the United States is separate and distinct from financial reporting under GAAP, which means that the Internal Revenue Service has no formal power to control GAAP. In the case of LIFO, however, the IRS has an indirect influence on the inventory method that a company chooses for financial reporting. The tax accounting rules of most other countries do not allow the use of the LIFO cost flow method, even if the country's GAAP does allow its use. If U.S. tax rules did not allow the use of LIFO under any circumstances, how many companies would use it for financial reporting? Very few!

The separation between tax accounting and GAAP accounting that exists in the United States does not exist in many other countries. In some countries, a company cannot deduct a cost for tax purposes unless the same cost is shown as an expense on the company's GAAP–based income statement. In other words, the unusual situation that exists in the United States only for the use of LIFO is the general rule in many countries. Countries whose tax laws greatly influence GAAP reporting include France, Germany, and Japan.

Exhibit 6–4 *Inventory Balance and Cost of Goods Sold using FIFO Cost Flow*

Date	Description	Units		Cost		Total	Cost of Goods Sold
				Inventory			
Jan. 1	Beginning Balance	100	@	$20.00	=	$2,000	
Feb. 14	Purchase	200	@	21.50	=	4,300	
Apr. 5	Sale of 220 Units	(100)	@	20.00	=	(2,000)	
		(120)	@	21.50	=	(2,580)	$ 4,580
	Inventory Balance after Sale	80	@	21.50	=	1,720	
June 21	Purchase	160	@	22.50	=	3,600	
Aug. 18	Sale of 100 Units	(80)	@	21.50	=	(1,720)	
		(20)	@	22.50	=	(450)	2,170
	Inventory Balance after Sale	140	@	22.50	=	3,150	
Sept. 2	Purchase	280	@	23.50	=	6,580	
Nov. 10	Sale of 330 Units	(140)	@	22.50	=	(3,150)	
		(190)	@	23.50	=	(4,465)	7,615
	Ending Inventory Balance	90	@	23.50	=	$2,115	
	Total Cost of Goods Sold						$14,365

Using FIFO, and assuming a selling price of $30 per unit, gross margin for 2008 is computed as follows:

Sales (650 units @ $30 each)	$19,500
Cost of Goods Sold	14,365
Gross Margin	$ 5,135

Weighted-Average and LIFO Cost Flows

When maintaining perpetual inventory records, using the weighted-average or LIFO cost flow methods leads to timing difficulties. For example, under LIFO, the cost of the *last* items purchased *during an accounting period* is the first amount transferred to cost of goods sold. When sales and purchases occur intermittently, the cost of the last items purchased isn't known at the time earlier sales occur. Suppose Stanley Office Supply sells merchandise in January 2005 and purchases replacement inventory in December 2005. The January cost of goods sold cannot be recorded in January because the cost of the inventory sold will not be known until December.

Accountants can solve cost flow timing problems by keeping perpetual records of the quantities (number of units) of items purchased and sold separately from the related costs. Keeping records of quantities moving in and out of inventory, even though cost information is unavailable, provides many of the benefits of a perpetual inventory system. For example, management can determine the quantity of lost, damaged, or stolen goods and the point at which they need to reorder merchandise. At the end of the accounting period, when the cost of all inventory purchases is available, costs are assigned to the quantity data that have been maintained perpetually. Although further discussion of the weighted-average and LIFO cost flow methods is beyond the scope of this text, recognize that timing problems associated with intermittent sales are manageable.

Lower-of-Cost-or-Market Rule

LO3 Apply the lower-of-cost-or-market rule to inventory valuation.

Regardless of whether a company uses FIFO, LIFO, weighted average, or specific identification, once the cost of ending inventory has been determined, generally accepted accounting

To avoid spoilage, most companies use a first-in, first-out (FIFO) approach for the flow of physical goods. The older goods (i.e., first units purchased) are sold before the newer goods are sold. For example, Kroger and other food stores stack older merchandise at the front of the shelf where customers are more likely to pick it up first. As a result, merchandise is sold before it becomes spoiled. However, when spoilage is not an issue, convenience may dictate the use of the last-in, first-out (LIFO) method. Examples of products that frequently move on a LIFO basis include rock, gravel, dirt, or other nonwasting assets. Indeed, rock, gravel, and dirt are normally stored in piles that are unprotected from weather. New inventory is simply piled on top of the old. Inventory that is sold is taken from the top of the pile because it is convenient to do so. Accordingly, the last inventory purchased is the first inventory sold. Regardless of whether the flow of physical goods is accomplished on a LIFO or FIFO basis, costs can flow differently. The flow of inventory through the physical facility is a separate issue from the flow of costs through the accounting system.

principles require that the cost be compared with the end of period market value and that the inventory be reported at *lower of cost or market. Market* is defined as the amount the company would have to pay to *replace* the merchandise. If the replacement cost is less than the actual cost, regardless of whether the decline in market value is due to physical damage, deterioration, obsolescence, or a general price-level decline, the loss must be recognized in the current period.

The **lower-of-cost-or-market rule** can be applied to (1) each individual inventory item, (2) major classes or categories of inventory, or (3) the entire stock of inventory in the aggregate. The most common practice is the individualized application. To illustrate applying the rule to individual inventory items, assume that Wilson Office Supply Company has in ending inventory 100 calculators it purchased at a cost of $14 each. If the year-end replacement cost of the calculators is above $14, Wilson will report the ending inventory at cost (100 × $14 = $1,400). However, if a technological advance permits the manufacturer to reduce the unit price of the calculators to $11, then Wilson's replacement cost falls below the historical cost, and the inventory must be written down to $1,100 (100 × $11).

Exhibit 6–5 illustrates computing the ending inventory value on an item-by-item basis for a company that has four different inventory items. The company must write down the $30,020 historical cost of its ending inventory to $28,410. This $1,610 write-down reduces the company's gross margin for the period. If the company keeps perpetual inventory records, the effect of the write-down and the journal entry to record it are as follows:

Assets	=	Liab.	+	Equity	Rev.	−	Exp.	=	Net Inc.	Cash Flow
(1,610)	=	NA	+	(1,610)	NA	−	1,610	=	(1,610)	NA

Exhibit 6–5 *Determination of Ending Inventory at Lower of Cost or Market*

Item	Quantity (a)	Unit Cost (b)	Unit Market (c)	Total Cost (a × b)	Total Market (a × c)	Lower of Cost or Market
A	320	$21.50	$22.00	$ 6,880	$ 7,040	$ 6,880
B	460	18.00	16.00	8,280	7,360	7,360
C	690	15.00	14.00	10,350	9,660	9,660
D	220	20.50	23.00	4,510	5,060	4,510
				$30,020	$29,120	$28,410

Account Title	Debit	Credit
Cost of Goods Sold (Inventory Loss)	1,610	
Inventory		1,610

Conceptually, the loss should be reported as an operating expense on the income statement. However, if the amount is immaterial, it can be included in cost of goods sold.

Topic Tackler
PLUS
6–2

LO4 Explain how fraud can be avoided through inventory control.

Fraud Avoidance in Merchandising Businesses

For merchandising businesses, inventory is often the largest single asset reported on the balance sheet and cost of goods sold is normally the largest single expense reported on the income statement. For example, the 2002 income statement for Publix (a large grocery store chain) reported $16.0 billion of sales and approximately $11.6 billion of cost of goods sold, which means cost of goods sold for Publix was about 72% of revenue. In contrast, the next largest expense (operating and administrative expense) was approximately $3.4 billion, or 21% of revenue. While cost of goods sold represents only one expense account, the operating and administrative expense category actually combines many, perhaps hundreds, of individual expense accounts, such as depreciation, salaries, utilities, and so on. Because the inventory and cost of goods sold accounts are so significant, they are attractive targets for concealing fraud. For example, suppose a manager attempts to perpetuate a fraud by deliberately understating expenses. The understatement is less likely to be detected if it is hidden in the $11.6 billion dollar Cost of Goods Sold account than if it is recorded in one of the smaller operating expense accounts.

Because the inventory and cost of goods sold accounts are susceptible to abuse, auditors and financial analysts carefully examine them for signs of fraud. Using tools to detect possible inventory misstatements requires understanding how overstatement or understatement of inventory affects the financial statements. To illustrate, assume that McCrary Merchandising overstates its year-end inventory balance by $1,000. This inventory overstatement results in a $1,000 understatement of cost of goods sold, as shown in the following schedule:

	Ending Inventory Is Accurate	Ending Inventory Is Overstated	
Beginning Inventory	$ 4,000	$ 4,000	
Purchases	6,000	6,000	
Cost of Goods Available for Sale	10,000	10,000	
Ending Inventory	(3,000)	(4,000)	$1,000 Overstated
Cost of Goods Sold	$ 7,000	$ 6,000	$1,000 Understated

The understatement of cost of goods sold results in the overstatement of gross margin, which leads to an overstatement of net earnings, as indicated in the following income statement:

	Ending Inventory Is Accurate	Ending Inventory Is Overstated	Effect on Cost of Goods Sold
Sales	$11,000	$11,000	
Cost of Goods Sold	(7,000)	(6,000)	$1,000 Understated
Gross Margin	$ 4,000	$ 5,000	$1,000 Overstated

On the balance sheet, assets (inventory) and stockholders' equity (retained earnings) are overstated as follows:

	Ending Inventory Is Accurate	Ending Inventory Is Overstated	
Assets			
Cash	$1,000	$ 1,000	
Inventory	3,000	4,000	$1,000 Overstated
Other Assets	5,000	5,000	
Total Assets	$9,000	$10,000	
Stockholders' Equity			
Common Stock	$5,000	$ 5,000	
Retained Earnings	4,000	5,000	$1,000 Overstated
Total Stockholders' Equity	$9,000	$10,000	

Managers may be tempted to overstate the physical count of the ending inventory in order to report higher amounts of gross margin on the income statement and larger amounts of assets on the balance sheet. How can companies discourage managers from deliberately overstating the physical count of the ending inventory? The first line of defense is to assign the task of recording inventory transactions to different employees from those responsible for counting inventory.

Recall that under the perpetual system, increases and decreases in inventory are recorded at the time inventory is purchased and sold. If the records are maintained accurately, the balance in the inventory account should agree with the amount of physical inventory on hand. If a manager were to attempt to manipulate the financial statements by overstating the physical count of inventory, there would be a discrepancy between the accounting records and the physical count. In other words, a successful fraud requires controlling both the physical count and the recording process. If the counting and recording duties are performed by different individuals, fraud requires collusion, which reduces the likelihood of its occurrence. The separation of duties is an internal control procedure discussed further in the next chapter.

Because motives for fraud persist, even the most carefully managed companies cannot guarantee that no fraud will ever occur. As a result, auditors and financial analysts have developed tools to test for financial statement manipulation. The gross margin method of estimating the ending inventory balance is such a tool.

Estimating the Ending Inventory Balance

The **gross margin method** assumes that the percentage of gross margin to sales remains relatively stable over time. To the extent that this assumption is accurate, the gross margin ratio from prior periods can be used to accurately estimate the current period's ending inventory. To illustrate, first review the information in Exhibit 6–6 which pertains to the T-Shirt Company.

LO5 Use the gross margin method to estimate ending inventory.

Exhibit 6–6

THE T-SHIRT COMPANY
Schedule for Estimating the Ending Inventory Balance
For the Six Months Ending June 30, 2006

Beginning Inventory	$ 5,100	
Purchases	18,500	
Goods Available for Sale		$23,600
Sales through June 30, 2006	22,000	
Less: Estimated Gross Margin*	?	
Estimated Cost of Goods Sold		?
Estimated Ending Inventory		$?

*Historically, gross margin has amounted to approximately 25 percent of sales.

The estimated cost of ending inventory can be computed as follows:

1. Calculate the expected gross margin ratio using financial statement data from prior periods. Accuracy may be improved by averaging gross margin and sales data over several accounting periods. For the T-Shirt Company, assume the average gross margin for the prior five years ÷ the average sales for the same five-year period = 25% expected gross margin ratio.
2. Multiply the expected gross margin ratio by the current period's sales ($22,000 × 0.25 = $5,500) to estimate the amount of gross margin.
3. Subtract the estimated gross margin from sales ($22,000 − $5,500 = $16,500) to estimate the amount of cost of goods sold.
4. Subtract the estimated cost of goods sold from the amount of goods available for sale ($23,600 − $16,500 = $7,100) to estimate the amount of ending inventory.

The estimated amount of ending inventory ($7,100) can be compared to the book balance and the physical count of inventory. If the book balance or the physical count is significantly higher than the estimated inventory balance, the analysis suggests the possibility of financial statement manipulation.

Other analytical comparisons are also useful. For example, the current year's gross margin ratio can be compared to last year's ratio. If cost of goods sold has been understated (ending inventory overstated), the gross margin ratio will be inflated. If this year's ratio is significantly higher than last year's, further analysis is required.

Although it may seem common because of the intense publicity generated when it occurs, fraud is the exception rather than the norm. In fact, growth in the inventory account balance usually results from natural business conditions. For example, a company that is adding new stores is expected to report growth in its inventory balance. Nevertheless, significant growth in inventory that is not explained by accompanying sales growth signals the need to analyze further for evidence of manipulation.

Since one year's ending inventory balance becomes the next year's beginning inventory balance, inaccuracies carry forward from one accounting period to the next. Persistent inventory overstatements result in an inventory account balance that spirals higher and higher. A fraudulently increasing inventory balance is likely to be discovered eventually.

To avoid detection, a manager who has previously overstated inventory will need to write the inventory back down in a subsequent accounting period. Therefore significant decreases, as well as increases, in the inventory balance or the gross margin ratio should be investigated. A manager may try to justify inventory write-downs by claiming that the inventory was lost, damaged, stolen, or had declined in value below historical cost. While there are valid reasons for writing down inventory, the possibility of fraud should be investigated.

ANSWERS TO THE *curious* ACCOUNTANT

Even though Kroger uses the last-in, first-out cost flow *assumption* for financial reporting purposes, it, like most other companies, actually sells its oldest inventory first. As explained in the text material, GAAP allows a company to assume its goods are sold in an order that is different from the actual

physical flow of its goods. The primary reason some companies use the LIFO assumption is to reduce income taxes. Over the years, Kroger has saved approximately $100 million in taxes by using the LIFO versus the FIFO cost flow assumption when computing its taxable income.

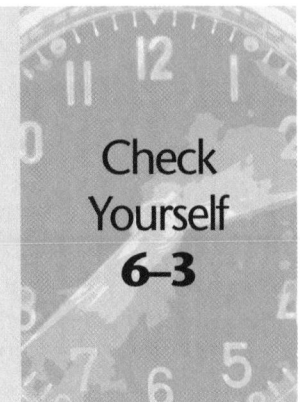

Check Yourself 6–3

A physical count of Cantrell, Inc.'s inventory revealed an ending balance of $6,020. The company's auditor decided to use the gross margin method to test the accuracy of the physical count. The accounting records indicate that the beginning inventory balance had been $20,000. During the period Cantrell had purchased $70,000 of inventory and had recognized $140,000 of sales revenue. Cantrell's gross margin percentage is normally 40 percent of sales. Develop an estimate of the amount of ending inventory and comment on the accuracy of the physical count.

Answer Goods available for sale is $90,000 ($20,000 beginning inventory + $70,000 purchases). Estimated cost of goods sold is $84,000 ($140,000 sales − [$140,000 × 0.40] gross margin). Estimated ending inventory is $6,000 ($90,000 goods available for sale − $84,000 cost of goods sold). The difference between the physical count and the estimated balance ($6,020 − $6,000 = $20) is immaterial. Therefore the gross margin estimate is consistent with the physical count.

THE FINANCIAL ANALYST

Assume a grocery store sells two brands of kitchen cleansers, Zjax and Cosmos. Zjax costs $1 and sells for $1.25, resulting in a gross margin of $0.25 ($1.25 − $1.00). Cosmos costs $1.20 and sells for $1.60, resulting in a gross margin of $0.40 ($1.60 − $1.20). Is it more profitable to stock Cosmos than Zjax? Not if the store can sell significantly more cans of Zjax.

LO6 Explain the importance of inventory turnover to a company's profitability.

Suppose the lower price results in higher customer demand for Zjax. If the store can sell 7,000 units of Zjax but only 3,000 units of Cosmos, Zjax will provide a total gross profit of $1,750 (7,000 units × $0.25 per unit), while Cosmos will provide only $1,200 (3,000 units × $0.40 per unit). How fast inventory sells is as important as the spread between cost and selling price. To determine how fast inventory is selling, financial analysts calculate a ratio that measures the *average number of days it takes to sell inventory.*

Average Number of Days to Sell Inventory

The first step in calculating the average number of days it takes to sell inventory is to compute the **inventory turnover,** as follows:

$$\frac{\text{Cost of goods sold}}{\text{Inventory}}$$

The result of this computation is the number of times the balance in the Inventory account is turned over (sold) each year. To more easily interpret the inventory turnover ratio, analysts often take a further step and determine the **average number of days to sell inventory** (also called the **average days in inventory ratio**), computed as

$$\frac{365}{\text{Inventory turnover}}$$

Is It a Marketing or an Accounting Decision?

As suggested, overall profitability depends upon two elements: gross margin and inventory turnover. The most profitable combination would be to carry high margin inventory that turns over rapidly. To be competitive, however, companies must often concentrate on one or the other of the elements. For example, *discount merchandisers* such as Wal-Mart offer lower prices to stimulate rapid sales. In contrast, fashionable stores such as Saks Fifth Avenue charge higher prices to compensate for their slower inventory turnover. These upscale stores justify their higher prices by offering superior style, quality, convenience, service, etc. While decisions about pricing, advertising, service, and so on are often viewed as marketing decisions, effective choices require understanding the interaction between the gross margin percentage and inventory turnover.

Real-World Data

LO6 Explain the importance of inventory turnover to a company's profitability.

Exhibit 6–7 shows the *average number of days to sell inventory* for eight real-world companies in three different industries. The numbers pertain to fiscal years that ended in late 2002 or early 2003. The data raise several questions.

First, why do Chalone and Mondavi take so long to sell their inventories compared to the other companies? Both of these companies produce and sell wine. Quality wine is aged before it is sold; time spent in inventory is actually a part of the production process. In the wine world, wines produced by Chalone are, on average, considered to be of higher quality than those produced by Mondavi. This higher quality results, in part, from the longer time Chalone's wines spend aging prior to sale.

Why does Starbucks hold its inventory so much longer than the other two fast-food businesses? Starbucks' inventory is mostly coffee. It is more difficult for Starbucks to obtain coffee than it is for McDonald's to obtain beef or Domino's to obtain flour, cheese, and fresh vegetables. Very little coffee is grown in the United States (Hawaii is the only state that produces coffee). Since purchasing coffee requires substantial delivery time, Starbucks cannot order its inventory at the last minute. This problem is further complicated by the fact that coffee harvests are seasonal. Cattle, on the other hand, can be processed into hamburgers year-round. As a result, Starbucks must hold inventory longer than McDonald's or Domino's.

Finally, why do companies in the office supply business take longer to sell inventory than those in the fast-food business? Part of the answer is that food is perishable and stationery is not. But there is also the fact that office supply stores carry many more inventory items than do fast-food restaurants. It is much easier to anticipate customer demand if a company sells only 20 different items than if the company sells 20,000 different items. The problem of anticipating customer demand is solved by holding larger quantities of inventory.

Exhibit 6–7

Industry	Company	Average Number of Days to Sell Inventory
Fast Food	Domino's	9
	McDonald's	10
	Starbucks	65
Office Supplies	Office Depot	58
	OfficeMax	92
	Staples	64
Wine	Chalone	642
	Mondavi	548

Effects of Cost Flow on Ratio Analysis

Since the amounts of ending inventory and cost of goods sold are affected by the cost flow method (FIFO, LIFO, etc.) a company uses, the gross margin and inventory turnover ratios are also affected by the cost flow method used. Further, since cost of goods sold affects the amount of net income and retained earnings, a wide range of other ratios are also affected by the inventory cost flow method that a company uses. Financial analysts must consider that the ratios they use can be significantly influenced by which accounting methods a company chooses.

a look
back

This chapter discussed the inventory cost flow methods of first-in, first-out (FIFO), last-in, first-out (LIFO), weighted average, and specific identification. Under *FIFO,* the cost of the items purchased first is reported on the income statement, and the cost of the items purchased last is reported on the balance sheet. Under *LIFO,* the cost of the items purchased last is reported on the income statement, and the cost of the items purchased first is reported on the balance sheet. Under the *weighted-average method,* the average cost of inventory is reported on both the income statement and the balance sheet. Finally, under specific identification the actual cost of the goods is reported on the income statement and the balance sheet.

Generally accepted accounting principles often allow companies to account for the same types of events in different ways. The different cost flow methods presented in this chapter—FIFO, LIFO, weighted average, and specific identification—are examples of alternative accounting procedures allowed by GAAP. Financial analysts must be aware that financial statement amounts are affected by the accounting methods that a company uses as well as the economic activity it experiences.

This chapter also explains how to calculate the time it takes a company to sell its inventory. The measure of how fast inventory sells is called *inventory turnover;* it is computed by dividing cost of goods sold by inventory. The result of this computation is the number of times the balance in the inventory account is turned over each year. The *average number of days in inventory ratio* can be determined by dividing the number of days in a year (365) by the inventory turnover ratio.

Accounting for investment securities is discussed in the appendix to this chapter.

a look
forward

Chapter 7 examines accounting for cash and the system of internal controls. Internal controls are the accounting practices and procedures that companies use to protect assets and to ensure that transactions are recorded accurately. You will learn that companies account for small disbursements of cash, called *petty cash disbursements,* differently than they do for large disbursements. You will also learn how to prepare a formal bank reconciliation. Finally, in Chapter 7 we will begin to classify assets and liabilities as being either short or long term in nature.

APPENDIX

Types of Investment Securities

LO7 Explain how accounting for investment securities differs when the securities are classified as held to maturity, trading, or available for sale.

A financial investment occurs when one entity provides assets or services to another entity in exchange for a certificate known as a *security.* The entity that provides the assets and receives the security certificate is called the **investor.** The entity that receives the assets or services and gives the security certificate is called the **investee.** This appendix discusses accounting practices that apply to securities held by investors.

There are two primary types of investment securities: debt securities and equity securities. An investor receives a **debt security** when assets *are loaned* to the investee. In general, a debt security describes the investee's obligation to return the assets and to pay interest for the use of the assets. Common types of debt securities include bonds, notes, certificates of deposit, and commercial paper.

An **equity security** is obtained when an investor acquires an *ownership interest* in the investee. An equity security usually describes the rights of ownership, including the right to influence the operations of the investee and to share in profits or losses that accrue from those operations. The most common types of equity securities are common stock and preferred stock. In summary, **investment securities** are certificates that describe the rights and privileges that investors receive when they loan or give assets or services to investees.

Transactions between the investor and the investee constitute the **primary securities market.** There is a **secondary securities market** in which investors exchange (buy and sell) investment securities with other investors. Securities that regularly trade in established secondary markets are called **marketable securities.** Investee companies are affected by secondary-market transactions only to the extent that their obligations are transferred to a different party. For example, assume that Tom Williams (investor) loans assets to American Can Company (investee). Williams receives a bond (investment security) from American Can that describes American Can's obligation to return assets and pay interest to Williams. This exchange represents a primary securities market transaction. Now assume that in a secondary-market transaction Williams sells his investment security (bond) to Tina Tucker. American Can Company is affected by this transaction only to the extent that the company's obligation transfers from Williams to Tucker. In other words, American Can's obligation to repay principal and interest does not change. The only thing that changes is the party to whom American Can makes payments. *An investee's financial statements are not affected when the securities it has issued to an investor are traded in the secondary market.*

The **fair value,** also called **market value,** of an investor's securities is established by the prices at which they sell in the secondary markets. For financial reporting purposes, fair value is established as the closing (last) price paid for an identical security on the investor's fiscal closing date. Whether securities are reported at fair value or historical cost depends on whether the investor intends to sell or hold the securities. Generally accepted accounting principles require companies to classify their financial investments into one of three categories: (1) held-to-maturity securities, (2) trading securities, and (3) available-for-sale securities.

Held-to-Maturity Securities

Since equity securities representing ownership interests have no maturity date, the held-to-maturity classification applies only to debt securities. Debt securities should be classified as held-to-maturity securities if the investor has a *positive intent* and the *ability* to hold the securities until the maturity date. **Held-to-maturity securities** are reported on the balance sheet at *amortized historical cost.*[1]

Trading Securities

Both debt and equity securities can be classified as *trading securities.* **Trading securities** are bought and sold for the purpose of generating profits on the short-term appreciation of stock or bond prices. They are usually traded within three months of when they are acquired. Trading securities are reported on the investor's balance sheet at their fair value on the investor's fiscal closing date.

Available-for-Sale Securities

All marketable securities that are not classified as held-to-maturity or trading securities must be classified as **available-for-sale securities.** These securities are also reported on the investor's balance sheet at fair value as of the investor's fiscal closing date.

Two of the three classifications, therefore, must be reported at fair value, which is a clear exception to the historical cost concept. Other exceptions to the use of historical cost measures for asset valuation are discussed in later sections of this appendix.

Reporting Events that Affect Investment Securities

The effects on the investor's financial statements of four distinct accounting events involving marketable investment securities are illustrated in the following section. The illustration assumes that the investor, Arapaho Company, started the accounting period with cash of $10,000 and common stock of $10,000.

Event 1 **Investment Purchase**
Arapaho paid $9,000 cash to purchase marketable investment securities.

This event is an asset exchange. One asset (cash) decreases, and another asset (investment securities) increases. The income statement is not affected. The $9,000 cash outflow is reported as either an operating activity or an investing activity, depending on how the securities are classified. Since *trading securities* are short-term assets that are regularly traded for the purpose of producing income, cash flows

---

[1]Debt securities are frequently purchased for amounts that are more or less than their face value (the amount of principal due at the maturity date). If the purchase price is above the face value, the difference between the face value and the purchase price is called a *premium.* If the purchase price is below the face value, the difference is called a *discount.* Premiums and discounts increase or decrease the amount of interest revenue earned and affect the carrying value of the bond investment reported on the balance sheet. The presentation in this section of the text makes the simplifying assumption that the bonds are purchased at a price that is equal to their face value. The treatment of discounts and premiums is discussed in Chapter 10.

from the purchase or sale of trading securities are reported in the operating activities section of the statement of cash flows. In contrast, cash flows involving the purchase or sale of securities classified as *held-to-maturity* or *available-for-sale* are reported in the investing activities section of the statement of cash flows. The only difference among the three alternatives lies in the classification of the cash outflow reported on the statement of cash flows, as shown in the following statements model:

Event No.	Type	Assets			=	Liab.	+	Equity	Rev.	–	Exp.	=	Net Inc.	Cash Flow	
		Cash	+	Inv. Sec.											
1	Held	(9,000)	+	9,000	=	NA	+	NA	NA	–	NA	=	NA	(9,000)	IA
1	Trading	(9,000)	+	9,000	=	NA	+	NA	NA	–	NA	=	NA	(9,000)	OA
1	Available	(9,000)	+	9,000	=	NA	+	NA	NA	–	NA	=	NA	(9,000)	IA

Event 2 Recognition of Investment Revenue
Arapaho earned $1,600 of cash investment revenue.

Investment revenue is reported the same way regardless of whether the investment securities are classified as held to maturity, trading, or available for sale. Investment revenue comes in two forms. Earnings from equity investments are called **dividends.** Revenue from debt securities is called **interest.** Both forms have the same impact on the financial statements. Recognizing the investment revenue increases both assets and stockholders' equity. Revenue and net income increase. The cash inflow from investment revenue is reported in the operating activities section of the statement of cash flows regardless of how the investment securities are classified.

Event No.	Assets	=	Liab.	+	Equity	Rev.	–	Exp.	=	Net Inc.	Cash Flow	
2	1,600	=	NA	+	1,600	1,600	–	NA	=	1,600	1,600	OA

Event 3 Sale of Investment Securities
Arapaho sold securities that cost $2,000 for $2,600 cash.

This event results in recognizing a $600 realized gain that increases both total assets and stockholders' equity. Specifically, the asset cash increases by $2,600 and the asset investment securities decreases by $2,000, resulting in a $600 increase in total assets. The $600 realized gain is reported on the income statement, increasing net income and retained earnings. The $600 gain does not appear on the statement of cash flows. Instead, the entire $2,600 cash inflow is reported in one section of the statement of cash flows. Cash inflows from the sale of held-to-maturity and available-for-sale securities are reported as investing activities. Cash flows involving trading securities are reported as operating activities. These effects are shown below.

Event No.	Type	Assets			=	Liab.	+	Equity	Rev. or Gain	–	Exp. or Loss	=	Net Inc.	Cash Flow	
		Cash	+	Inv. Sec.											
3	Held	2,600	+	(2,000)	=	NA	+	600	600	–	NA	=	600	2,600	IA
3	Trading	2,600	+	(2,000)	=	NA	+	600	600	–	NA	=	600	2,600	OA
3	Available	2,600	+	(2,000)	=	NA	+	600	600	–	NA	=	600	2,600	IA

Event 4 Market Value Adjustment
Arapaho recognized a $700 unrealized gain.

After Event 3, the historical cost of Arapaho's portfolio of remaining investment securities is $7,000 ($9,000 purchased less $2,000 sold). Assume that at Arapaho's fiscal closing date, these securities have a fair value of $7,700, giving Arapaho a $700 unrealized gain on its investment. This type of gain (sometimes called a *paper profit*) is classified as *unrealized* because the securities have not been sold. The treatment of **unrealized gains or losses** in the financial statements depends on whether the securities are classified as held to maturity, trading, or available for sale. Unrealized gains or losses on securities classified as *held to maturity* are not recognized in the financial statements; they have no effect on the balance sheet, income statement, and statement of cash flows. Even so, many companies choose to disclose the market value of the securities as part of the narrative description or in the footnotes that accompany the statements. Whether or not the market value is disclosed, held-to-maturity securities are reported on the balance sheet at amortized cost.

Investments classified as trading securities are reported in the financial statements at fair value. Unrealized gains or losses on *trading securities* are recognized in net income even though the securities have not been sold. In Arapaho's case, the $700 gain increases the carrying value of the investment securities. The gain increases net income, which in turn increases retained earnings. Unrealized gains and losses have no effect on cash flows.

Investments classified as available-for-sale securities are also reported in the financial statements at fair value. However, an important distinction exists with respect to how the unrealized gains and losses affect the financial statements. Even though unrealized gains or losses on available-for-sale securities are included in the assets on the balance sheet, they *are not* recognized in determining net income.[2] On Arapaho's balance sheet, the $700 gain increases the carrying value of the investment securities. A corresponding increase is reported in a separate equity account called Unrealized Gain or Loss on Available-for-Sale Securities. The statement of cash flows is not affected by recognizing unrealized gains and losses on available-for-sale securities.

The effects of these alternative treatments of unrealized gains and losses on Arapaho's financial statements are shown here:

Event No.	Type	Assets	=	Liab.	+	Equity				Rev. or Gain	−	Exp. or Loss	=	Net Inc.	Cash Flow
		Inv. Sec.				Ret. Earn.	+	Unreal. Gain							
4	Held	NA	=	NA	+	NA	+	NA		NA	−	NA	=	NA	NA
4	Trading	700	=	NA	+	700	+	NA		700	−	NA	=	700	NA
4	Available	700	=	NA	+	NA	+	700		NA	−	NA	=	NA	NA

Financial Statements

As the preceding discussion implies, the financial statements of Arapaho Company are affected by not only the business events relating to its security transactions but also the accounting treatment used to report those events. In other words, the same economic events are reflected differently in the financial statements depending on whether the securities are classified as held to maturity, trading, or available for sale. Exhibit 6–8 displays the financial statements for Arapaho under each investment classification alternative.

The net income reported under the trading securities alternative is $700 higher than that reported under the held-to-maturity and available-for-sale alternatives because unrealized gains and losses on trading securities are recognized on the income statement. Similarly, total assets and total stockholders' equity are $700 higher under the trading and available-for-sale alternatives than they are under the held-to-maturity category because the $700 unrealized gain is recognized on the balance sheet for those two classifications. The gain is not reported on the income statement for available-for-sale securities; it is reported on the balance sheet in a special equity account called Unrealized Gain on Investment Securities. The statements of cash flows report purchases and sales of trading securities as operating activities while purchases and sales of available-for-sale and held-to-maturity securities are investing activities. Exhibit 6–9 summarizes the reporting differences among the three classifications of investment securities.

Alternative Reporting Practices for Equity Securities

If an investor owns 20 percent or more of an investee's equity securities, the investor is presumed able, unless there is evidence to the contrary, to exercise *significant influence* over the investee company. Investors owning more than 50 percent of the stock of an investee company are assumed to have control over the investee. The previous discussion of accounting rules for equity securities assumed the investor

---

[2]*Statement of Financial Accounting Standards No. 130* permits companies to report unrealized gains and losses on available-for-sale securities as additions to or subtractions from net income with the result being titled *comprehensive income.* Alternatively, the unrealized gains and losses can be reported on a separate statement or as part of the statement of changes in stockholders' equity.

Exhibit 6–8

ARAPAHO COMPANY
Comparative Financial Statements

Income Statements

Investment Securities Classified as	Held	Trading	Available
Investment Revenue	$ 1,600	$ 1,600	$ 1,600
Realized Gain	600	600	600
Unrealized Gain		700	
Net Income	$ 2,200	$ 2,900	$ 2,200

Balance Sheets

	Held	Trading	Available
Assets			
Cash	$ 5,200	$ 5,200	$ 5,200
Investment Securities, at Cost			
(Market Value $7,700)	7,000		
Securities, at Market (Cost $7,000)		7,700	7,700
Total Assets	$12,200	$12,900	$12,900
Stockholders' Equity			
Common Stock	$10,000	$10,000	$10,000
Retained Earnings	2,200	2,900	2,200
Unrealized Gain on Investment Securities			700
Total Stockholders' Equity	$12,200	$12,900	$12,900

Statements of Cash Flows

	Held	Trading	Available
Operating Activities			
Cash Inflow from Investment Revenue	$ 1,600	$ 1,600	$ 1,600
Outflow to Purchase Securities		(9,000)	
Inflow from Sale of Securities		2,600	
Investing Activities			
Outflow to Purchase Securities	(9,000)		(9,000)
Inflow from Sale Securities	2,600		2,600
Financing Activities*	0	0	0
Net Decrease in Cash	(4,800)	(4,800)	(4,800)
Beginning Cash Balance	10,000	10,000	10,000
Ending Cash Balance	$ 5,200	$ 5,200	$ 5,200

*The $10,000 capital acquisition is assumed to have occurred prior to the start of the accounting period.

Exhibit 6–9

Investment Category	Types of Securities	Types of Revenue Recognized	Reported on Balance Sheet at	Recognition of Unrealized Gains and Losses on the Income Statement	Cash Flow From Purchase or Sale of Securities Classified As
Held to maturity	Debt	Interest	Amortized cost	No	Investing activity
Trading	Debt and equity	Interest and dividends	Market value	Yes	Operating activity
Available for sale	Debt and equity	Interest and dividends	Market value	No	Investing activity

did not significantly influence or control the investee. Alternative accounting rules apply to securities owned by investors who exercise significant influence or control over an investee company. Accounting for equity investment securities differs depending on the level of the investor's ability to influence or control the operating, investing, and financing activities of the investee.

As previously demonstrated, investors who do not have significant influence (they own less than 20 of the stock of the investee) account for their investments in equity securities at fair value. Investors exercising significant influence (they own 20 to 50 percent of the investee's stock) must account for their investments using the **equity method.** A detailed discussion of the equity method is beyond the scope of this text. However, *be aware that investments reported using the equity method represent a measure of the book value of the investee rather than the cost or fair value of the equity securities owned.*

Investors who have a controlling interest (they own more than 50 percent of the investee's stock) in an investee company are required to issue **consolidated financial statements.** The company that holds the controlling interest is referred to as the **parent company,** and the company that is controlled is called the **subsidiary company.** Usually, the parent and subsidiary companies maintain separate accounting records. However, a parent company is also required to report to the public its accounting data along with that of its subsidiaries in a single set of combined financial statements. These consolidated statements represent a separate accounting entity composed of the parent and its subsidiaries. A parent company that owns one subsidiary will produce three sets of financial statements: statements for the parent company, statements for the subsidiary company, and statements for the consolidated entity.

SELF-STUDY REVIEW PROBLEM

Erie Jewelers sells gold earrings. Its beginning inventory of Model 407 gold earrings consisted of 100 pairs of earrings at $50 per pair. Erie purchased two batches of Model 407 earrings during the year. The first batch purchased consisted of 150 pairs at $53 per pair; the second batch consisted of 200 pairs at $56 per pair. During the year, Erie sold 375 pairs of Model 407 earrings.

Required

Determine the amount of product cost Erie would allocate to cost of goods sold and ending inventory assuming that Erie uses (a) FIFO, (b) LIFO, and (c) weighted average.

Solution to Requirements a–c

Goods Available for Sale

Beginning inventory	100	@	$50 =	$ 5,000
First purchase	150	@	53 =	7,950
Second purchase	200	@	56 =	11,200
Goods available for sale	450			$24,150

a. FIFO

Cost of Goods Sold	Pairs		Cost per Pair	Cost of Goods Sold
From beginning inventory	100	@	$50 =	$ 5,000
From first purchase	150	@	53 =	7,950
From second purchase	125	@	56 =	7,000
Total pairs sold	375			$19,950

Ending inventory = Goods available for sale − Cost of goods sold
Ending inventory = $24,150 − $19,950 = $4,200

b. LIFO

Cost of Goods Sold	Pairs		Cost per Pair	Cost of Goods Sold
From second purchase	200	@	$56 =	$11,200
From first purchase	150	@	53 =	7,950
From beginning inventory	25	@	50 =	1,250
Total pairs sold	375			$20,400

Ending inventory = Goods available for sale − Cost of goods sold
Ending inventory = $24,150 − $20,400 = $3,750

c. Weighted average

$$\text{Goods available for sale} \div \text{Total pairs} = \text{Cost per pair}$$
$$\$24,150 \qquad \div \qquad 450 \quad = \quad \$53.6667$$

$$\text{Cost of goods sold} \quad 375 \text{ units @ } \$53.6667 = \$20,125$$
$$\text{Ending inventory} \qquad 75 \text{ units @ } \$53.6667 = \$\ \ 4,025$$

KEY TERMS

Available-for-sale securities *284*

Average days in inventory ratio (sometimes called average number of days to sell inventory ratio) *281*

Consolidated financial statements *288*

Debt security *283*

Dividends *285*

Equity method *288*

Equity security *283*

Fair value *284*

First-in, first-out (FIFO) cost flow method *268*

Gross margin method *279*

Held-to-maturity securities *284*

Interest *285*

Inventory cost flow methods *267*

Inventory turnover *281*

Investee *283*

Investment securities *283*

Investor *283*

Last-in, first-out (LIFO) cost flow method *268*

Lower-of-cost-or-market rule *277*

Market value *284*

Marketable securities *284*

Parent company *288*

Physical flow of goods *268*

Primary securities market *284*

Secondary securities market *284*

Specific identification *268*

Subsidiary company *288*

Trading securities *284*

Unrealized gain or loss *285*

Weighted-average cost flow method *268*

QUESTIONS

1. Name and discuss the four cost flow methods discussed in this chapter.
2. What are some advantages and disadvantages of the specific identification method of accounting for inventory?
3. What are some advantages and disadvantages of using the FIFO method of inventory valuation?
4. What are some advantages and disadvantages of using the LIFO method of inventory valuation?
5. In an inflationary period, which inventory cost flow method will produce the highest net income? Explain.
6. In an inflationary period, which inventory cost flow method will produce the largest amount of total assets on the balance sheet? Explain.
7. What is the difference between the flow of costs and the physical flow of goods?
8. Does the choice of cost flow method (FIFO, LIFO, or weighted average) affect the statement of cash flows? Explain.
9. Assume that Key Co. purchased 1,000 units of merchandise in its first year of operations for $25 per unit. The company sold 850 units for $40. What is the amount of cost of goods sold using FIFO? LIFO? Weighted average?
10. Assume that Key Co. purchased 1,500 units of merchandise in its second year of operation for $27 per unit. Its beginning inventory was determined in Question 9. Assuming that 1,500 units are sold, what is the amount of cost of goods sold using FIFO? LIFO? Weighted average?
11. Refer to Questions 9 and 10. Which method might be preferable for financial statements? For income tax reporting? Explain.
12. In an inflationary period, which cost flow method, FIFO or LIFO, produces the larger cash flow? Explain.
13. Which inventory cost flow method produces the highest net income in a deflationary period?
14. How does the phrase *lower-of-cost-or-market* apply to inventory valuation?
15. If some merchandise declined in value because of damage or obsolescence, what effect will the lower-of-cost-or-market rule have on the income statement? Explain.
16. What is a situation in which estimates of the amount of inventory may be useful or even necessary?
17. How can management manipulate net income using inventory fraud?
18. If the amount of goods available for sale is $123,000, the amount of sales is $130,000, and the gross margin is 25 percent of sales, what is the amount of ending inventory?

19. Assume that inventory is overstated by $1,500 at the end of 2001 but is corrected in 2002. What effect will this have on the 2001 income statement? The 2001 balance sheet? The 2002 income statement? The 2002 balance sheet?

20. What information does inventory turnover provide?

21. What is an example of a business that would have a high inventory turnover? A low inventory turnover?

22. Why are historical costs generally used in financial statements?

23. What are some instances in which the Financial Accounting Standards Board requires using market values for financial reporting?

24. What is an example of an asset easily valued at fair market value? What is an example of an asset that is difficult to value at fair market value?

25. What are the two primary types of investment securities?

26. What is a debt security? Give an example.

27. What is an equity security? Give an example.

28. What is the difference between the primary securities market and the secondary securities market?

29. What are marketable securities?

30. Generally accepted accounting principles require companies to classify investment securities into three categories. Name and describe them.

31. When must the equity method of accounting for investments be used for financial statement reporting?

EXERCISES—SERIES A

 All Exercises in Series A are available with McGraw-Hill's Homework Manager

L.O. 1   **EXERCISE 6–1A** *Effect of Inventory Cost Flow Assumption on Financial Statements*

Required
For each of the following situations, indicate whether FIFO, LIFO, or weighted average applies.

a. In a period of rising prices, net income would be highest.
b. In a period of rising prices, cost of goods sold would be highest.
c. In a period of rising prices, ending inventory would be highest.
d. In a period of falling prices, net income would be highest.
e. In a period of falling prices, the unit cost of goods would be the same for ending inventory and cost of goods sold.

L.O. 1, 2   **EXERCISE 6–2A** *Allocating Product Cost Between Cost of Goods Sold and Ending Inventory*

Mix Co. started the year with no inventory. During the year, it purchased two identical inventory items. The inventory was purchased at different times. The first purchase cost $1,200 and the other, $1,500. One of the items was sold during the year.

Required
Based on this information, how much product cost would be allocated to cost of goods sold and ending inventory on the year-end financial statements, assuming use of

a. FIFO?
b. LIFO?
c. Weighted average?

L.O. 1, 2   **EXERCISE 6–3A** *Allocating Product Cost Between Cost of Goods Sold and Ending Inventory: Multiple Purchases*

Laird Company sells coffee makers used in business offices. Its beginning inventory of coffee makers was 200 units at $45 per unit. During the year, Laird made two batch purchases of coffee makers. The first was a 300-unit purchase at $50 per unit; the second was a 350-unit purchase at $52 per unit. During the period, Laird sold 800 coffee makers.

Required

Determine the amount of product costs that would be allocated to cost of goods sold and ending inventory, assuming that Laird uses

a. FIFO.
b. LIFO.
c. Weighted average.

EXERCISE 6–4A *Effect of Inventory Cost Flow (FIFO, LIFO, and Weighted Average) on Gross Margin*

L.O. 1, 2

The following information pertains to Porter Company for 2005.

Beginning inventory	70 units @ $13
Units purchased	280 units @ $18

Ending inventory consisted of 30 units. Porter sold 320 units at $30 each. All purchases and sales were made with cash.

Required

a. Compute the gross margin for Porter Company using the following cost flow assumptions: (1) FIFO, (2) LIFO, and (3) weighted average.
b. What is the dollar amount of difference in net income between using FIFO versus LIFO? (Ignore income tax considerations.)
c. Determine the cash flow from operating activities, using each of the three cost flow assumptions listed in Requirement *a.* Ignore the effect of income taxes. Explain why these cash flows have no differences.

EXERCISE 6–5A *Effect of Inventory Cost Flow on Ending Inventory Balance and Gross Margin*   L.O. 1, 2

Bristol Sales had the following transactions for DVDs in 2004, its first year of operations.

Jan. 20	Purchased 75 units @ $17	=	$1,275
Apr. 21	Purchased 450 units @ $19	=	8,550
July 25	Purchased 200 units @ $23	=	4,600
Sept. 19	Purchased 100 units @ $29	=	2,900

During the year, Bristol Sales sold 775 DVDs for $60 each.

Required

a. Compute the amount of ending inventory Bristol would report on the balance sheet, assuming the following cost flow assumptions: (1) FIFO, (2) LIFO, and (3) weighted average.
b. Compute the difference in gross margin between the FIFO and LIFO cost flow assumptions.

EXERCISE 6–6A *Income Tax Effect of Shifting From FIFO to LIFO*   L.O. 1, 2

The following information pertains to the inventory of the La Bonne Company:

Jan. 1	Beginning Inventory	500 units @ $20
Apr. 1	Purchased	2,500 units @ $25
Oct. 1	Purchased	800 units @ $26

During the year, La Bonne sold 3,400 units of inventory at $40 per unit and incurred $17,000 of operating expenses. La Bonne currently uses the FIFO method but is considering a change to LIFO. All transactions are cash transactions. Assume a 30 percent income tax rate.

Required

a. Prepare income statements using FIFO and LIFO.
b. Determine the amount of income taxes La Bonne would save if it changed cost flow methods.
c. Determine the cash flow from operating activities under FIFO and LIFO.
d. Explain why cash flow from operating activities is lower under FIFO when that cost flow method produced the higher gross margin.

L.O. 1, 2   EXERCISE 6–7A *Effect of FIFO Versus LIFO on Income Tax Expense*

Holly Hocks, Inc. had sales of $225,000 for 2006, its first year of operation. On April 2, the company purchased 200 units of inventory at $190 per unit. On September 1, an additional 150 units were purchased for $210 per unit. The company had 50 units on hand at the end of the year. The company's income tax rate is 40 percent. All transactions are cash transactions.

Required

a. The preceding paragraph describes five accounting events: (1) a sales transaction, (2) the first purchase of inventory, (3) a second purchase of inventory, (4) the recognition of cost of goods sold expense, and (5) the payment of income tax expense. Record the amounts of each event in horizontal statements models like the following ones, assuming first a FIFO and then a LIFO cost flow.

Effect of Events on Financial Statements										
Panel 1: FIFO Cost Flow										
Event No.	Balance Sheet					Income Statement				Statement of Cash Flows
	Cash	+ Inventory	=	C. Stk.	+ Ret. Earn.	Rev.	– Exp.	= Net Inc.		
Panel 2: LIFO Cost Flow										
Event No.	Balance Sheet					Income Statement				Statement of Cash Flows
	Cash	+ Inventory	=	C. Stk.	+ Ret. Earn.	Rev.	– Exp.	= Net Inc.		

b. Compute net income using FIFO.

c. Compute net income using LIFO.

d. Explain the difference, if any, in the amount of income tax expense incurred using the two cost flow assumptions.

e. How does the use of the FIFO versus the LIFO cost flow assumptions affect the statement of cash flows?

L.O. 2   EXERCISE 6–8A *Recording Inventory Transactions Using the Perpetual System: Intermittent Sales and Purchases*

The following inventory transactions apply to TNT Company for 2004.

Jan. 1	Purchased	250 units @ $10
Apr. 1	Sold	125 units @ $18
Aug. 1	Purchased	400 units @ $11
Dec. 1	Sold	500 units @ $19

The beginning inventory consisted of 175 units at $11 per unit. All transactions are cash transactions.

Required

a. Record these transactions, in general journal format, assuming that TNT uses the FIFO cost flow assumption and keeps perpetual records.

b. Compute the ending balance in the Inventory account.

L.O. 2   EXERCISE 6–9A *Effect of Cost Flow on Ending Inventory: Intermittent Sales and Purchases*

Solar Heating, Inc., had the following series of transactions for 2007:

Date	Transaction	Description
Jan. 1	Beginning inventory	50 units @ $20
Mar. 15	Purchased	200 units @ $24
May 30	Sold	170 units @ $40
Aug. 10	Purchased	275 units @ $25
Nov. 20	Sold	340 units @ $40

Required

a. Determine the quantity and dollar amount of inventory at the end of the year, assuming Solar Heating, Inc. uses the FIFO cost flow assumption and keeps perpetual records.

b. Write a memo explaining why Solar Heating, Inc., would have difficulty applying the LIFO method on a perpetual basis. Include a discussion of how to overcome these difficulties.

EXERCISE 6–10A *Lower-of-Cost-or-Market Rule: Perpetual System*   **L.O. 3**

The following information pertains to Royal Auto Parts's ending inventory for the current year.

Item	Quantity	Unit Cost	Unit Market Value
P	100	$6	$7
D	50	8	6
S	20	7	8
J	15	9	7

Required

a. Determine the value of the ending inventory using the lower-of-cost-or-market rule applied to (1) each individual inventory item and (2) the inventory in aggregate.

b. Prepare any necessary journal entries, assuming the decline in value is immaterial, using the (1) individual method and (2) aggregate method. Royal Auto Parts uses the perpetual inventory system.

EXERCISE 6–11A *Lower-of-Cost-or-Market Rule*   **L.O. 3**

Guzman Company carries three inventory items. The following information pertains to the ending inventory:

Item	Quantity	Unit Cost	Unit Market Value
O	200	$10	$ 9
J	250	15	14
R	175	5	8

Required

a. Determine the ending inventory that will be reported on the balance sheet, assuming that Guzman applies the lower-of-cost-or-market rule to individual inventory items.

b. Explain how the write-down would be recorded under the perpetual inventory system.

EXERCISE 6–12A *Estimating Ending Inventory Using the Gross Margin Method*   **L.O. 4, 5**

Rich French, the owner of Rich's Fishing Supplies, is surprised at the amount of actual inventory at the end of the year. He thought there should be more inventory on hand based on the amount of sales for the year. The following information is taken from the books of Rich's Fishing Supplies:

Beginning Inventory	$200,000
Purchases for the year	400,000
Sales for the year	600,000
Inventory at the end of the year (based on actual count and the balance in the inventory account)	100,000

Historically, Rich has made a 20 percent gross margin on his sales. Rich thinks there may be some problem with the inventory. Evaluate the situation based on the historical gross profit percentage.

Required

Estimate the following:

a. Gross margin in dollars.

b. Cost of goods sold in dollars.

c. Estimated ending inventory.

d. Inventory shortage.

e. Give an explanation for the shortage.

EXERCISE 6–13A *Estimating Ending Inventory: Perpetual System*   **L.O. 4, 5**

Carol Lapaz owned a small company that sold boating equipment. The equipment was expensive, and a perpetual system was maintained for control purposes. Even so, lost, damaged, and stolen merchandise normally amounted to 5 percent of the inventory balance. On June 14, Carol's warehouse was destroyed by fire. Just prior to the fire, the accounting records contained a $150,000 balance in the Inventory account. However, inventory costing $15,000 had been sold and delivered to customers the day of the fire but had not been recorded in the books at the time of the fire. The fire did not affect the showroom, which contained inventory that cost $40,000.

Required
Estimate the amount of inventory destroyed by fire.

L.O. 4, 5   EXERCISE 6–14A *Effect of Inventory Error on Financial Statements: Perpetual System*

Marshall Company failed to count $12,000 of inventory in its 2007 year-end physical count.

Required
Explain how this error will affect Marshall's 2007 financial statements, assuming that Marshall uses the perpetual inventory system.

L.O. 4, 5   EXERCISE 6–15A *Effect of Inventory Misstatement on Elements of Financial Statements*

The ending inventory for Tokro Co. was erroneously written down causing an understatement of $5,200 at the end of 2005.

Required
Was each of the following amounts overstated, understated, or not affected by the error?

Item No.	Year	Amount
1	2005	Beginning inventory
2	2005	Purchases
3	2005	Goods available for sale
4	2005	Cost of goods sold
5	2005	Gross margin
6	2005	Net income
7	2006	Beginning inventory
8	2006	Purchases
9	2006	Goods available for sale
10	2006	Cost of goods sold
11	2006	Gross margin
12	2006	Net income

L.O. 7   EXERCISE 6–16A *Identifying Asset Values for Financial Statements (Appendix)*

Required
Indicate whether each of the following assets should be valued at fair market value (FMV), lower of cost or market (LCM), or historical cost (HC) on the balance sheet. For certain assets, historical cost may be called amortized cost (AC.)

Asset	FMV	LCM	HC/AC
Supplies			
Land			
Trading Securities			
Cash			
Held-to-Maturity Securities			
Buildings			
Available-for-Sale Securities			
Office Equipment			
Inventory			

L.O. 7   EXERCISE 6–17A *Accounting for Investment Securities (Appendix)*

Brooks Bros. purchased $18,000 of marketable securities on March 1, 2004. On the company's fiscal year closing date, December 31, 2004, the securities had a market value of $13,500. During 2004, Brooks recognized $5,000 of revenue and $1,000 of expenses.

Required
a. Record a +, −, or NA in a horizontal statements model to show how the purchase of the securities affects the financial statements, assuming that the securities are classified as (1) held to maturity,

(2) trading, or (3) available for sale. In the Cash Flow column, indicate whether the event is an operating activity (OA), investing activity (IA), or financing activity (FA). Record only the effects of the purchase event.

Event No.	Type	Cash	+	Inv. Sec.	=	Liab.	+	Equity	Rev.	–	Exp.	=	Net Inc.	Cash Flow
1	Held													
2	Trading													
3	Available													

b. Determine the amount of net income that would be reported on the 2004 income statement, assuming that the marketable securities are classified as (1) held to maturity, (2) trading, or (3) available for sale.

EXERCISE 6–18A *Effect of Investment Securities Transactions on Financial Statements (Appendix)*   **L.O. 7**

The following information pertains to Regan Supply Co. for 2006.

1. Purchased $100,000 of marketable investment securities.
2. Earned $5,000 of cash investment revenue.
3. Sold for $30,000 securities that cost $28,000.
4. The fair value of the remaining securities at December 31, 2006, was $92,000.

Required

a. Record the four events in a statements model like the following one. Use a separate model for each classification: (1) held to maturity, (2) trading, and (3) available for sale. The first event for the first classification is shown as an example.

Held to Maturity

Event No.	Cash	+	Inv. Sec.	=	Liab.	+	Ret. Earn.	+	Unreal. Gain.	Rev. or Gains	–	Exp. or Loss	=	Net Inc.	Cash Flow
1	(100,000)	+	100,000	=	NA	+	NA	+	NA	NA	–	NA	=	NA	(100,000) IA

b. What is the amount of net income under each of the three classifications?
c. What is the change in cash from operating activities under each of the three classifications?
d. Are the answers to Requirements *b* and *c* different for each of the classifications? Why or why not?

EXERCISE 6–19A *Preparing Financial Statements for Investment Securities (Appendix)*   **L.O. 7**

Barnett, Inc., began 2007 with $50,000 in both cash and common stock. The company engaged in the following investment transactions during 2007:

1. Purchased $20,000 of marketable investment securities.
2. Earned $800 cash from investment revenue.
3. Sold investment securities for $14,000 that cost $12,000.
4. Purchased $9,000 of additional marketable investment securities.
5. Determined that the investment securities had a fair value of $22,000 at the end of 2007.

Required

Use a vertical statements model to prepare income statements, balance sheets, and statements of cash flow for Barnett, Inc., assuming the securities were (*a*) held to maturity, (*b*) trading, and (*c*) available for sale.

EXERCISE 6–20A *Differences Among Marketable Investment Securities Classifications (Appendix)*   **L.O. 7**

Complete the following table for the three categories of marketable investment securities:

Investment Category	Types of Securities	Types of Revenue Recognized	Value Reported on Balance Sheet	Recognition of Unrealized Gains and Losses on the Income Statement	Cash Flow from Purchase or Sale of Securities Is Classified as
Held to maturity	Debt	Interest	Amortized Cost	No	Investing Activity
Trading					
Available for sale					

PROBLEMS—SERIES A

All Problems in Series A are available with McGraw-Hill's Homework Manager

L.O. 1, 2

www.mhhe.com/edmonds5e

CHECK FIGURES
a. Cost of Goods Sold—FIFO: $27,540
b. Net Income—LIFO: $6,780

PROBLEM 6–21A *Effect of Different Inventory Cost Flow Methods on Financial Statements*

The accounting records of Clear Photography, Inc., reflected the following balances as of January 1, 2007:

Cash	$18,000
Beginning Inventory	13,500 (150 units @ $90)
Common Stock	15,000
Retained Earnings	16,500

The following five transactions occurred in 2007:

1. First purchase (cash)   120 units @ $92
2. Second purchase (cash)   200 units @ $100
3. Sales (all cash)   300 units @ $185
4. Paid $15,000 cash for operating expenses.
5. Paid cash for income tax at the rate of 40 percent of income before taxes.

Required

a. Compute the cost of goods sold and ending inventory, assuming (1) FIFO cost flow, (2) LIFO cost flow, and (3) weighted-average cost flow.
b. Use a vertical model to prepare the 2007 income statement, balance sheet, and statement of cash flows under FIFO, LIFO, and weighted average. (*Hint:* Record the events under an accounting equation before preparing the statements.)

L.O. 2

www.mhhe.com/edmonds5e

CHECK FIGURES
b. Cost of Goods Sold: $22,850
c. Ending Inventory: $4,550

PROBLEM 6–22A *Allocating Product Costs Between Cost of Goods Sold and Ending Inventory: Intermittent Purchases and Sales of Merchandise*

Lacey, Inc., had the following sales and purchase transactions during 2006. Beginning inventory consisted of 80 items at $120 each. Lacey uses the FIFO cost flow assumption and keeps perpetual inventory records.

Date	Transaction	Description
Mar. 5	Purchased	80 items @ $125
Apr. 10	Sold	60 items @ $245
June 19	Sold	70 items @ $245
Sept. 16	Purchased	60 items @ $130
Nov. 28	Sold	55 items @ $255

Required

a. Record the inventory transactions in general journal format.
b. Calculate the gross margin Lacey would report on the 2006 income statement.
c. Determine the ending inventory balance Lacey would report on the December 31, 2006, balance sheet.

L.O. 3

www.mhhe.com/edmonds5e

CHECK FIGURES
a. $5,980
c. $6,640

PROBLEM 6–23A *Inventory Valuation Based on the Lower-of-Cost-or-Market Rule*

At the end of the year, Upton Computer Repair had the following items in inventory:

Item	Quantity	Unit Cost	Unit Market Value
D1	60	$20	$26
D2	30	50	48
D3	44	35	42
D4	40	60	45

Required

a. Determine the amount of ending inventory using the lower-of-cost-or-market rule applied to each individual inventory item.
b. Provide the general journal entry necessary to write down the inventory based on Requirement *a.* Assume that Upton Computer Repair uses the perpetual inventory system.

   c. Determine the amount of ending inventory, assuming that the lower-of-cost-or-market rule is applied to the inventory in aggregate.

   d. Provide the general journal entry necessary to write down the inventory based on Requirement *c.* Assume that Upton Computer Repair uses the perpetual inventory system.

PROBLEM 6–24A *Estimating Ending Inventory: Gross Margin Method*

Metal Supplies had its inventory destroyed by a hurricane on September 21 of the current year. Although some of the accounting information was destroyed, the following information was discovered for the period of January 1 through September 21:

Beginning inventory, January 1	$ 70,000
Purchases through September 21	360,000
Sales through September 21	500,000

The gross margin for Metal Supplies has traditionally been 25 percent of sales.

Required

   a. For the period ending September 21, compute the following:

     (1) Estimated gross margin.

     (2) Estimated cost of goods sold.

     (3) Estimated inventory at September 21.

   b. Assume that $10,000 of the inventory was not damaged. What is the amount of the loss from the hurricane?

   c. Metal Supplies uses the perpetual inventory system. If some of the accounting records had not been destroyed, how would Metal determine the amount of the inventory loss?

PROBLEM 6–25A *Estimating Ending Inventory: Gross Margin Method*

Don Green, owner of Plains Company, is reviewing the quarterly financial statements and thinks the cost of goods sold is out of line with past years. The following historical data is available for 2004 and 2005:

	2004	2005
Net sales	$160,000	$200,000
Cost of goods sold	70,000	90,000

At the end of the first quarter of 2006, Plains Company's ledger had the following account balances:

Sales	$240,000
Purchases	160,000
Beginning Inventory, January 1, 2006	60,000

Required

Using the information provided, estimate the following for the first quarter of 2006:

   a. Cost of goods sold. (Use average cost of goods sold percentage.)

   b. Ending inventory at March 31 based on historical cost of goods sold percentage.

   c. Inventory shortage if inventory balance as of March 31 is $100,000.

PROBLEM 6–26A *Effect of Inventory Errors on Financial Statements*

The following income statement was prepared for Bell Company for the year 2006:

BELL COMPANY Income Statement For the Year Ended December 31, 2006	
Sales	$69,000
Cost of Goods Sold	(38,640)
Gross Margin	30,360
Operating Expenses	(9,100)
Net Income	$21,260

L.O. 5

CHECK FIGURES
a. Gross Margin: $125,000
b. Total Inventory Loss: $45,000

L.O. 5

CHECK FIGURE
b. Estimated Ending Inventory: $114,400

L.O. 4

During the year-end audit, the following errors were discovered.

1. A $1,400 payment for repairs was erroneously charged to the Cost of Goods Sold account. (Assume that the perpetual inventory system is used.)
2. Sales to customers for $2,400 at December 31, 2006, were not recorded in the books for 2006. Also, the $1,344 cost of goods sold was not recorded. The error was not discovered in the physical count because the goods had not been delivered to the customer.
3. A mathematical error was made in determining ending inventory. Ending inventory was understated by $1,200. (The Inventory account was written down in error to the Cost of Goods Sold account.)

Required

Determine the effect, if any, of each of the errors on the following items. Give the dollar amount of the effect and whether it would overstate (+), understate (−), or not affect (NA) the account. The effect on sales is recorded as an example.

Error No. 1	Amount of Error	Effect
Sales, 2006	NA	NA
Ending inventory, December 31, 2006		
Gross margin, 2006		
Beginning inventory, January 1, 2007		
Cost of goods sold, 2006		
Net income, 2006		
Retained earnings, December 31, 2006		
Total assets, December 31, 2006		

Error No. 2	Amount of Error	Effect
Sales, 2006	$2,400	−
Ending inventory, December 31, 2006		
Gross margin, 2006		
Beginning inventory, January 1, 2007		
Cost of goods sold, 2006		
Net income, 2006		
Retained earnings, December 31, 2006		
Total assets, December 31, 2006		

Error No. 3	Amount of Error	Effect
Sales, 2006	NA	NA
Ending inventory, December 31, 2006		
Gross margin, 2006		
Beginning inventory, January 1, 2007		
Cost of goods sold, 2006		
Net income, 2006		
Retained earnings, December 31, 2006		
Total assets, December 31, 2006		

L.O. 7   **PROBLEM 6–27A** *Effect of Marketable Investment Securities Transactions on Financial Statements (Appendix)*

The following transactions pertain to Quality Answering Service for 2007:

1. Started business by acquiring $30,000 cash from the issue of common stock.
2. Provided $70,000 of services for cash.
3. Invested $35,000 in marketable investment securities.
4. Paid $24,000 of operating expense.
5. Received $500 of investment income from the securities.
6. Invested an additional $12,000 in marketable investment securities.
7. Paid a $2,000 cash dividend to the stockholders.
8. Sold investment securities that cost $8,000 for $11,000.
9. Received another $1,000 in investment income.
10. Determined the market value of the investment securities at the end of the year was $36,000.

Required

Use a vertical model to prepare a 2007 income statement, balance sheet, and statement of cash flows, assuming that the marketable investment securities were classified as (a) held to maturity, (b) trading, and (c) available for sale. (*Hint:* Record the events in T-accounts prior to preparing the financial statements.)

PROBLEM 6–28A *Comprehensive Horizontal Statements Model (Appendix)* L.O. 1, 3, 7

Woody's Catering experienced the following independent events.

1. Acquired cash from issuing common stock.
2. Purchased inventory on account.
3. Paid cash to purchase marketable securities classified as trading securities.
4. Recorded unrealized loss on marketable securities that were classified as trading securities.
5. Recorded unrealized loss on marketable securities that were classified as available-for-sale securities.
6. Recorded unrealized loss on marketable securities that were classified as held-to-maturity securities.
7. Wrote down inventory to comply with lower-of-cost-or-market rule. (Assume that the company uses the perpetual inventory system.)
8. Recognized cost of goods sold under FIFO.
9. Recognized cost of goods sold under the weighted-average method.

Required

a. Show the effect of each event on the elements of the financial statements using a horizontal statements model like the following one. Use + for increase, − for decrease, and NA for not affected. In the Cash Flow column, indicate whether the item is an operating activity (OA), investing activity (IA), or financing activity (FA). The first transaction is entered as an example.

Event No.	Assets	=	Liab.	+	Equity	Rev. or Gain	−	Exp. or Loss	=	Net Inc.	Cash Flow
1	+		NA		+	NA		NA		NA	+ FA

b. Explain why there is or is not a difference in the way Events 8 and 9 affect the financial statements model.

EXERCISE 6–1B *Effect of Inventory Cost Flow Assumption on Financial Statements* L.O. 1

Required
For each of the following situations, fill in the blank with *FIFO, LIFO,* or *weighted average.*

a. _____ would produce the highest amount of net income in an inflationary environment.
b. _____ would produce the highest amount of assets in an inflationary environment.
c. _____ would produce the lowest amount of net income in a deflationary environment.
d. _____ would produce the same unit cost for assets and cost of goods sold in an inflationary environment.
e. _____ would produce the lowest amount of net income in an inflationary environment.
f. _____ would produce an asset value that was the same regardless of whether the environment was inflationary or deflationary.
g. _____ would produce the lowest amount of assets in an inflationary environment.
h. _____ would produce the highest amount of assets in a deflationary environment.

EXERCISE 6–2B *Allocating Product Cost Between Cost of Goods Sold and Ending Inventory* L.O. 1, 2

Berryhill Co. started the year with no inventory. During the year, it purchased two identical inventory items at different times. The first purchase cost $750 and the other, $1,000. Berryhill sold one of the items during the year.

Required
Based on this information, how much product cost would be allocated to cost of goods sold and ending inventory on the year-end financial statements, assuming use of

a. FIFO?
b. LIFO?
c. Weighted average?

L.O. 1, 2   EXERCISE 6–3B *Allocating Product Cost Between Cost of Goods Sold and Ending Inventory: Multiple Purchases*

Alfonza Company sells chairs that are used at computer stations. Its beginning inventory of chairs was 100 units at $40 per unit. During the year, Alfonza made two batch purchases of this chair. The first was a 150-unit purchase at $50 per unit; the second was a 200-unit purchase at $60 per unit. During the period, it sold 260 chairs.

Required

Determine the amount of product costs that would be allocated to cost of goods sold and ending inventory, assuming that Alfonza uses

a. FIFO.
b. LIFO.
c. Weighted average.

L.O. 1, 2   EXERCISE 6–4B *Effect of Inventory Cost Flow (FIFO, LIFO, and Weighted Average) on Gross Margin*

The following information pertains to Ping Company for 2006.

Beginning inventory	40 units @ $20
Units purchased	200 units @ $25

Ending inventory consisted of 30 units. Ping sold 210 units at $50 each. All purchases and sales were made with cash.

Required

a. Compute the gross margin for Ping Company using the following cost flow assumptions: (1) FIFO, (2) LIFO, and (3) weighted average.
b. What is the amount of net income using FIFO, LIFO, and weighted average? (Ignore income tax considerations.)
c. Compute the amount of ending inventory using (1) FIFO, (2) LIFO, and (3) weighted average.

L.O. 1, 2   EXERCISE 6–5B *Effect of Inventory Cost Flow on Ending Inventory Balance and Gross Margin*

University Sales had the following transactions for T-shirts for 2006, its first year of operations.

Jan. 20	Purchased 450 units @ $5	=	$2,250
Apr. 21	Purchased 200 units @ $6	=	1,200
July 25	Purchased 100 units @ $10	=	1,000
Sept. 19	Purchased 75 units @ $8	=	600

During the year, University Sales sold 725 T-shirts for $20 each.

Required

a. Compute the amount of ending inventory University would report on the balance sheet, assuming the following cost flow assumptions: (1) FIFO, (2) LIFO, and (3) weighted average.
b. Compute the difference in gross margin between the FIFO and LIFO cost flow assumptions.

L.O. 1, 2   EXERCISE 6–6B *Income Tax Effect of Shifting From FIFO to LIFO*

The following information pertains to the inventory of the Starr Company:

Jan. 1	Beginning Inventory	500 units @ $20
Apr. 1	Purchased	2,500 units @ $22
Oct. 1	Purchased	800 units @ $28

During the year, Starr sold 3,400 units of inventory at $40 per unit and incurred $34,000 of operating expenses. Starr currently uses the FIFO method but is considering a change to LIFO. All transactions are cash transactions. Assume a 30 percent income tax rate.

Required

a. Prepare income statements using FIFO and LIFO.
b. Determine the amount of income taxes that Starr would pay using each cost flow method.

c. Determine the cash flow from operating activities under FIFO and LIFO.

d. Why is the cash flow from operating activities different under FIFO and LIFO?

EXERCISE 6–7B Effect of FIFO Versus LIFO on Income Tax Expense

L.O. 1, 2

The Keys Company had sales of $250,000 for 2005, its first year of operation. On April 2, the company purchased 200 units of inventory at $350 per unit. On September 1, an additional 150 units were purchased for $375 per unit. The company had 100 units on hand at the end of the year. The company's income tax rate is 40 percent. All transactions are cash transactions.

Required

a. The preceding paragraph describes five accounting events: (1) a sales transaction, (2) the first purchase of inventory, (3) a second purchase of inventory, (4) the recognition of cost of goods sold expense, and (5) the payment of income tax expense. Record the amounts of each event in horizontal statements models like the following ones, assuming first a FIFO and then a LIFO cost flow.

Effect of Events on Financial Statements											
Panel 1: FIFO Cost Flow											
Event No.	Balance Sheet					Income Statement					Statement of Cash Flows
	Cash	+	Inventory	=	Ret. Earn.	Rev.	–	Exp.	=	Net Inc.	
Panel 2: LIFO Cost Flow											
Event No.	Balance Sheet					Income Statement					Statement of Cash Flows
	Cash	+	Inventory	=	Ret. Earn.	Rev.	–	Exp.	=	Net Inc.	

b. Compute net income using FIFO.

c. Compute net income using LIFO.

d. Explain the difference, if any, in the amount of income tax expense incurred using the two cost flow assumptions.

e. Which method, FIFO or LIFO, produced the larger amount of assets on the balance sheet?

EXERCISE 6–8B Recording Inventory Transactions Using the Perpetual Method: Intermittent Sales and Purchases

L.O. 2

The following inventory transactions apply to Willow Company for 2006.

Jan. 1	Purchased	250 units @ $40
Apr. 1	Sold	125 units @ $70
Aug. 1	Purchased	400 units @ $44
Dec. 1	Sold	500 units @ $76

The beginning inventory consisted of 175 units at $34 per unit. All transactions are cash transactions.

Required

a. Record these transactions, in general journal format, assuming that Willow uses the FIFO cost flow assumption and keeps perpetual records.

b. Compute cost of goods sold for 2006.

EXERCISE 6–9B Effect of Cost Flow on Ending Inventory: Intermittent Sales and Purchases

L.O. 2

Sand Hill, Inc., had the following series of transactions for 2008:

Date	Transaction	Description
Jan. 1	Beginning inventory	50 units @ $30
Mar. 15	Purchased	200 units @ $35
May 30	Sold	170 units @ $70
Aug. 10	Purchased	275 units @ $40
Nov. 20	Sold	340 units @ $75

Required

a. Determine the quantity and dollar amount of inventory at the end of the year, assuming Sand Hill uses the FIFO cost flow assumption and keeps perpetual records.

b. Write a memo explaining why Sand Hill, Inc., would have difficulty applying the weighted-average method on a perpetual basis.

L.O. 3   EXERCISE 6–10B *Lower-of-Cost-or-Market Rule: Perpetual System*

The following information pertains to Superior Woodwork Co.'s ending inventory for the current year.

Item	Quantity	Unit Cost	Unit Market Value
P	100	$16	$12
D	50	18	16
S	20	24	26
J	15	20	22

Required

a. Determine the value of the ending inventory using the lower-of-cost-or-market rule applied to (1) each individual inventory item and (2) the inventory in aggregate.

b. Prepare any necessary journal entries, assuming the decline in value is immaterial. Superior Woodwork Co. uses the perpetual inventory system. (Make entries for both methods.)

L.O. 3   EXERCISE 6–11B *Lower-of-Cost-or-Market Rule*

Wygal Company carries three inventory items. The following information pertains to the ending inventory:

Item	Quantity	Unit Cost	Unit Market Value
B	100	$40	$36
C	150	60	56
D	90	20	30

Required

a. Determine the ending inventory that Wygal will report on the balance sheet, assuming that it applies the lower-of-cost-or-market rule to individual inventory items.

b. Explain how adjustments to ending inventory would be recorded.

L.O. 4, 5   EXERCISE 6–12B *Estimating Ending Inventory*

A substantial portion of inventory owned by Prairie Hunting Goods was recently destroyed when the roof collapsed during a rainstorm. It also lost some of its accounting records. Prairie must estimate the loss from the storm for insurance reporting and financial statement purposes. Prairie uses the periodic inventory system. The following accounting information was recovered from the damaged records.

Beginning inventory	$ 25,000
Purchases to date of storm	100,000
Sales to date of storm	137,500

The value of undamaged inventory counted was $2,000. Historically Prairie's gross margin percentage has been approximately 25 percent of sales.

Required

Estimate the following:

a. Gross margin in dollars.

b. Cost of goods sold.

c. Ending inventory.

d. Amount of lost inventory.

EXERCISE 6–13B *Estimating Ending Inventory: Perpetual System*   **L.O. 4, 5**

Ralph Kaye owned a small company that sold garden equipment. The equipment was expensive, and a perpetual system was maintained for control purposes. Even so, lost, damaged, and stolen merchandise normally amounted to 5 percent of the inventory balance. On June 14, Kaye's warehouse was destroyed by fire. Just prior to the fire, the accounting records contained a $338,000 balance in the Inventory account. However, inventory costing $42,000 had been sold and delivered to customers but had not been recorded in the books at the time of the fire. The fire did not affect the showroom, which contained inventory that cost $75,000.

Required
Estimate the amount of inventory destroyed by fire.

EXERCISE 6–14B *Effect of Inventory Error on Financial Statements: Perpetual System*   **L.O. 4, 5**

Sharp Company failed to count $50,000 of inventory in its 2005 year-end physical count.

Required
Write a memo explaining how Sharp Company's balance sheet will be affected in 2005. Assume Sharp uses the perpetual inventory system.

EXERCISE 6–15B *Effect of Inventory Error on Elements of Financial Statements*   **L.O. 4, 5**

The ending inventory for Elm Co. was incorrectly adjusted, which caused it to be understated by $12,500 for 2006.

Required
Was each of the following amounts overstated, understated, or not affected by the error?

Item No.	Year	Amount
1	2006	Beginning inventory
2	2006	Purchases
3	2006	Goods available for sale
4	2006	Cost of goods sold
5	2006	Gross margin
6	2006	Net income
7	2007	Beginning inventory
8	2007	Purchases
9	2007	Goods available for sale
10	2007	Cost of goods sold
11	2007	Gross margin
12	2007	Net income

EXERCISE 6–16B *Identifying Asset Values for Financial Statements (Appendix)*   **L.O. 7**

Required
Indicate whether each of the following assets should be valued at fair market value (FMV), lower-of-cost-or-market (LCM), or historical cost (HC) on the balance sheet. For certain assets, historical cost may be called amortized cost (AC.)

Asset	FMV	LCM	HC/AC
Inventory			
Prepaid Rent			
Cash			
Held-to-Maturity Securities			
Machinery			
Available-for-Sale Securities			
Certificate of Deposit			
Trading Securities			

EXERCISE 6–17B *Accounting for Investment Securities (Appendix)*   **L.O. 7**

Jones Bros. purchased $20,000 of marketable securities on March 1, 2005. On the company's fiscal closing date, December 31, 2005, the securities had a market value of $27,000. During 2005, Jones recognized $10,000 of revenue and $4,000 of expenses.

Required

a. Record a +, −, or NA in a horizontal statements model to show how the purchase of the securities affects the financial statements, assuming that the securities are classified as (1) held to maturity, (2) trading, or (3) available for sale. In the Cash Flow column, indicate whether the event is an operating activity (OA), investing activity (IA), or financing activity (FA). Record only the effects of the purchase event.

Event No.	Type	Cash	+	Inv. Sec.	=	Liab.	+	Equity	Rev.	−	Exp.	=	Net Inc.	Cash Flow
1	Held													
2	Trading													
3	Available													

b. Determine the amount of net income that would be reported on the 2005 income statement, assuming that the marketable securities are classified as (1) held to maturity, (2) trading, or (3) available for sale.

L.O. 7   **EXERCISE 6–18B** *Effect of Investment Securities Transactions on Financial Statements (Appendix)*

The following information pertains to City Electronics for 2003.

1. Purchased $75,000 of marketable investment securities.
2. Earned $4,500 of cash investment revenue.
3. Sold for $15,000 securities that cost $12,500.
4. The fair market value of the remaining securities at December 31, 2003, was $50,000.

Required

a. Record the four events in a statements model like the following one. Use a separate model for each classification: (1) held to maturity, (2) trading, and (3) available for sale. The first event for the first classification is shown as an example.

Held to Maturity

Event No.	Cash	+	Inv. Sec.	=	Liab.	+	Ret. Earn.	+	Unreal. Gain.	Rev. or Gains	−	Exp. or Loss	=	Net Inc.	Cash Flow
1	(75,000)	+	75,000	=	NA	+	NA	+	NA	NA	−	NA	=	NA	(75,000) IA

b. What is the amount of net income under each of the three classifications?
c. What is the change in cash from operating activities under each of the three assumptions?
d. What is the ending amount of Investment Securities under each of the three assumptions?

L.O. 7   **EXERCISE 6–19B** *Preparing Financial Statements for Investment Securities (Appendix)*

Coopers, Inc., began 2006 with $60,000 in both cash and common stock. The company engaged in the following investment transactions during 2006:

1. Purchased $30,000 of marketable investment securities.
2. Earned $800 cash from investment revenue.
3. Sold investment securities for $10,000 that cost $7,000.
4. Purchased $10,000 of additional marketable investment securities.
5. Determined that the investment securities had a fair value of $34,000 at the end of 2006.

Required

Use a vertical statements model to prepare income statements, balance sheets, and statements of cash flow for Coopers, Inc., assuming the securities were (*a*) held to maturity, (*b*) trading, and (*c*) available for sale.

L.O. 7   **EXERCISE 6–20B** *Differences Among Classifications of Marketable Investment Securities (Appendix)*

Required

List the three classifications of investment securities and give an example of each.

PROBLEM 6–21B *Effect of Different Inventory Cost Flow Methods on Financial Statements*   **L.O. 1, 2**

The accounting records of Helen's Clock Shop reflected the following balances as of January 1, 2007.

Cash	$50,800
Beginning Inventory	56,000 (200 units @ $280)
Common Stock	43,000
Retained Earnings	63,800

The following five transactions occurred in 2007:

1. First purchase (cash)   120 units @ $300
2. Second purchase (cash)   140 units @ $330
3. Sales (all cash)   400 units @ $450
4. Paid $30,000 cash for salaries expense.
5. Paid cash for income tax at the rate of 25 percent of income before taxes.

Required

a. Compute the cost of goods sold and ending inventory, assuming (1) FIFO cost flow, (2) LIFO cost flow, and (3) weighted-average cost flow.

b. Use a vertical model to prepare the 2007 income statement, balance sheet, and statement of cash flows under FIFO, LIFO, and weighted average. (*Hint:* Record the events under an accounting equation before preparing the statements.)

PROBLEM 6–22B *Allocating Product Costs Between Cost of Goods Sold and Ending   **L.O. 2**
Inventory: Intermittent Purchases and Sales of Merchandise*

The Fireplace Shop had the following sales and purchase transactions during 2008. Beginning inventory consisted of 60 items at $350 each. The company uses the FIFO cost flow assumption and keeps perpetual inventory records.

Date	Transaction	Description
Mar. 5	Purchased	50 items @ $370
Apr. 10	Sold	40 items @ $450
June 19	Sold	50 items @ $450
Sept. 16	Purchased	50 items @ $390
Nov. 28	Sold	35 items @ $470

Required

a. Record the inventory transactions in general journal format.
b. Calculate the gross margin The Fireplace Shop would report on the 2008 income statement.
c. Determine the ending inventory balance The Fireplace Shop would report on the December 31, 2008, balance sheet.

PROBLEM 6–23B *Inventory Valuation Based on the Lower-of-Cost-or-Market Rule*   **L.O. 3**

At the end of the year, Ralph's Repair Service had the following items in inventory:

Item	Quantity	Unit Cost	Unit Market Value
P1	80	$ 80	$ 90
P2	60	60	66
P3	100	140	130
P4	50	130	140

Required

a. Determine the amount of ending inventory using the lower-of-cost-or-market rule applied to each individual inventory item.
b. Provide the general journal entry necessary to write down the inventory based on Requirement *a.* Assume that Ralph's Repair Service uses the perpetual inventory system.
c. Determine the amount of ending inventory, assuming that the lower-of-cost-or-market rule is applied to the total inventory in aggregate.

d. Provide the general journal entry necessary to write down the inventory based on Requirement *c.* Assume that Ralph's Repair Service uses the perpetual inventory system.

e. Explain how the inventory loss would be reported when the periodic inventory system is used.

L.O. 5 **PROBLEM 6–24B** *Estimating Ending Inventory: Gross Margin Method*

Second Chance Grocery had its inventory destroyed by a tornado on October 6 of the current year. Fortunately, some of the accounting records were at the home of one of the owners and were not damaged. The following information was available for the period of January 1 through October 6:

Beginning inventory, January 1	$ 162,000
Purchases through October 6	680,000
Sales through October 6	1,140,000

Gross margin for Second Chance has traditionally been 30 percent of sales.

Required

a. For the period ending October 6, compute the following:
   (1) Estimated gross margin.
   (2) Estimated cost of goods sold.
   (3) Estimated inventory at October 6.
b. Assume that $20,000 of the inventory was not damaged. What is the amount of the loss from the tornado?
c. If Second Chance Grocery had used the perpetual inventory system, how would it have determined the amount of the inventory loss?

L.O. 5 **PROBLEM 6–25B** *Estimating Ending Inventory: Gross Margin Method*

Mae's Market Place wishes to produce quarterly financial statements, but it takes a physical count of inventory only at year end. The following historical data were taken from the 2006 and 2007 accounting records:

	2006	2007
Net sales	$60,000	$70,000
Cost of goods sold	31,000	36,500

At the end of the first quarter of 2008, Mae's ledger had the following account balances:

Sales	$56,500
Purchases	41,000
Beginning Inventory 1/1/2008	12,500
Ending Inventory 3/31/2008	15,000

Mae thinks her inventory is low based on purchases and sales.

Required

Using the information provided, estimate the following for the first quarter of 2008:

a. Cost of goods sold. (Use average cost of goods sold percentage.)
b. Ending inventory at March 31.
c. What could explain the difference in actual and estimated inventory?

L.O. 4 **PROBLEM 6–26B** *Effect of Inventory Errors on Financial Statements*

The following income statement was prepared for Hot Fireworks for the year 2006:

HOT FIREWORKS Income Statement For the Year Ended December 31, 2006	
Sales	$140,000
Cost of Goods Sold	(77,200)
Gross Margin	62,800
Operating Expenses	(40,900)
Net Income	$ 21,900

During the year-end audit, the following errors were discovered:

1. A $2,000 payment for repairs was erroneously charged to the Cost of Goods Sold account. (Assume that the perpetual inventory system is used.)
2. Sales to customers for $500 at December 31, 2006, were not recorded in the books for 2006. Also, the $300 cost of goods sold was not recorded. The error was not discovered in the physical count because the goods had not been delivered to the customers.
3. A mathematical error was made in determining ending inventory. Ending inventory was understated by $1,800. (The Inventory account was written down in error to the cost of goods sold account.)

Required

Determine the effect, if any, of each of the errors on the following items. Give the dollar amount of the effect and whether it would overstate (+), understate (−), or not affect (NA) the account. The first item for each error is recorded as an example.

Error No. 1	Amount of Error	Effect
Sales, 2006	NA	NA
Ending inventory, December 31, 2006		
Gross margin, 2006		
Beginning inventory, January 1, 2007		
Cost of goods sold, 2006		
Net income, 2006		
Retained earnings, December 31, 2006		
Total assets, December 31, 2006		

Error No. 2	Amount of Error	Effect
Sales, 2006	$500	−
Ending inventory, December 31, 2006		
Gross margin, 2006		
Beginning inventory, January 1, 2007		
Cost of goods sold, 2006		
Net income, 2006		
Retained earnings, December 31, 2006		
Total assets, December 31, 2006		

Error No. 3	Amount of Error	Effect
Sales, 2006	NA	NA
Ending inventory, December 31, 2006		
Gross margin, 2006		
Beginning inventory, January 1, 2007		
Cost of goods sold, 2006		
Net income, 2006		
Retained earnings, December 31, 2006		
Total assets, December 31, 2006		

PROBLEM 6–27B *Effect of Marketable Inventory Securities of Financial Statements (Appendix)*   L.O. 7

The following transactions pertain to Five State Trucking Co. for 2007.

1. Started business when it acquired $15,000 cash from stock issue, Heather Brogan.
2. Provided $50,000 of services for cash.
3. Invested $12,000 in marketable investment securities.
4. Paid $17,000 of operating expense.
5. Received $400 investment income from the securities.
6. Invested an additional $16,000 in marketable investment securities.
7. Paid a $1,000 cash dividend to the owner.
8. Sold investment securities that cost $6,000 for $6,400.
9. Received $900 in investment income.
10. Determined the value of the investment securities at the end of the year to be $20,000.

Required

Use a vertical model to prepare an income statement, balance sheet, and statement of cash flows, assuming that the marketable investment securities were classified as (a) held to maturity, (b) trading, and (c) available for sale. (*Hint:* It may be helpful to record the events in T-accounts prior to preparing the financial statements.)

L.O. 1, 3, 7   PROBLEM 6–28B *Comprehensive Horizontal Statements Model (Appendix)*

Beach Front Sales Co. experienced the following independent events.

1. Acquired cash from the issue of common stock.
2. Paid cash to purchase marketable securities classified as available for sale.
3. Paid cash to purchase inventory.
4. Recorded unrealized gain on marketable securities that were classified as trading securities.
5. Recorded unrealized gain on marketable securities that were classified as available-for-sale securities.
6. Recorded unrealized gain on marketable securities that were classified as held-to-maturity securities.
7. Wrote down inventory to comply with the lower-of-cost-or-market rule. (Assume that the company uses the perpetual inventory system.)
8. Recognized cost of goods sold under FIFO.
9. Recognized cost of goods sold under LIFO.

Required

a. Show the effect of each event on the elements of the financial statements using a horizontal statements model like the following one. Use + for increase, − for decrease, and NA for not affected. In the Cash Flow column, indicate whether the item is an operating activity (OA), investing activity (IA) or financing activity (FA). The first transaction is entered as an example.

Event No.	Assets	=	Liab.	+	Equity	Rev. or Gain	−	Exp. or Loss	=	Net Inc.	Cash Flow
1	+		NA		+	NA		NA		NA	+ FA

b. Explain why there is or is not a difference in the way Events 8 and 9 affect the financial statements model.

ANALYZE, THINK, COMMUNICATE

ATC 6–1   BUSINESS APPLICATIONS CASE *Understanding Real World Annual Reports*

Required—Part 1

Use the Topps Company's annual report in Appendix B to answer the following questions.

a. What was Topps' inventory turnover ratio and average days to sell inventory for the years ended March 1, 2003 and March 2, 2002?
b. Is the company's management of inventory getting better or worse?
c. What cost flow method(s) did Topps use to account for inventory?

Required—Part 2

Use the Harley-Davidson's annual report that came with this book to answer the following questions.

a. What was Harley-Davidson's inventory turnover ratio and average days to sell inventory for the year ended December 31, 2003?
b. What cost flow method(s) did Harley-Davidson use to account for inventory?
c. How much different, lower or higher, would Harley-Davidson's ending inventory have been if it had used the FIFO cost flow method for all of its inventory (see Note 2)?

Required—Part 3

Speculate as to why Harley-Davidson sells its inventory more quickly than Topps.

ATC 6–2   GROUP ASSIGNMENT *Inventory Cost Flow*

The accounting records of Blue Bird Co. showed the following balances at January 1, 2008:

Cash	$30,000
Beginning inventory (100 units @ $50, 70 units @ $55)	8,850
Common stock	20,000
Retained earnings	18,850

Transactions for 2008 were as follows:

> Purchased 100 units @ $54 per unit.
> Sold 220 units @ $80 per unit.
> Purchased 250 units @ $58 per unit.
> Sold 200 units @ $90 per unit.
> Paid operating expenses of $3,200.
> Paid income tax expense. The income tax rate is 30%.

Required

a. Organize the class into three sections, and divide each section into groups of three to five students. Assign each section one of the cost flow methods, FIFO, LIFO, or weighted average.

Group Tasks

Determine the amount of ending inventory, cost of goods sold, gross margin, and net income after income tax for the cost flow method assigned to your section. Also prepare an income statement using that cost flow assumption.

Class Discussion

b. Have a representative of each section put its income statement on the board. Discuss the effect that each cost flow method has on assets (ending inventory), net income, and cash flows. Which method is preferred for tax reporting? For financial reporting? What restrictions are placed on the use of LIFO for tax reporting?

REAL-WORLD CASE *Evaluating the Cost Savings from Managing Inventory More Efficiently*   ATC 6–3

After a decade of almost continually good economic news, the U.S. economy began to slow during 2000. Automobile manufacturers are among the first industries to feel the effects of a slowing economy, as Ford Motor Company did in 2000. Although Ford sold more vehicles in 2000 as a whole than it did in 1999, its sales were down in the fourth quarter of that year. Ford sold 1,919,000 automobiles in the fourth quarter of 1999 but only 1,849,000 in the same quarter of 2000, a reduction of just under 4 percent.

Companies often find themselves with more inventory than desired when sales begin to slow. This increase in inventory has two negative consequences. First, as explained in the chapter, the longer it takes a company to sell inventory, the higher the costs incurred to finance that inventory. Second, companies may have to reduce their selling prices to reduce inventory levels, which results in lower profit margins. Automobile manufacturers commonly use rebates to effectively reduce the selling prices of their cars. Both of these situations occurred at Ford during 2000.

The following information for Ford Motor Company is in pretax dollars and relates *only to the automotive operations* at Ford. (In 1999 and 2000, Ford generated about 70 percent of its pretax earnings from automotive operations and about 30 percent from financial services.) The dollar amounts are in millions.

	2000	1999
Sales	$141,230	$135,073
Income before taxes	5,267	7,275
Ending inventory	7,514	5,684
Gross margin %	10.7%	11.9%
Average days to sell inventory	22 days	17 days
Estimated weighted-average interest rate	7.5%	

Required

a. How much higher would Ford's pretax earnings from automotive operations in 2000 have been if its gross margin percentage in 2000 had been the same as it was in 1999?

b. What percentage of the $2,008 reduction in pretax earnings at Ford's automotive operations from 1999 to 2000 can be explained by the inventory-related issues addressed in Requirement *a?*

ATC 6-4   **BUSINESS APPLICATIONS CASE** *Using the Average Days to Sell Inventory Ratio to Make a Lending Decision*

Edna Valley Fruits has applied for a loan and has agreed to use its inventory to collateralize the loan. The company currently has an inventory balance of $206,000. The cost of goods sold for the past year was $5,781,000. The average shelf life for the fruit that Edna Valley sells is 10 days, after which time it begins to spoil and must be sold at drastically reduced prices to dispose of it rapidly. The company had maintained steady sales over the past three years and expects to continue at current levels for the foreseeable future.

Required

Based on your knowledge of inventory turnover, write a memo that describes the quality of the inventory as collateral for the loan.

ATC 6-5   **BUSINESS APPLICATIONS CASE** *Using Ratios to Make Comparisons*

The following accounting information pertains to Java Joint and Coffee Corner at the end of 2008. The only difference between the two companies is that Java uses FIFO while Coffee uses LIFO.

	Java Joint	Coffee Corner
Cash	$ 60,000	$ 60,000
Accounts Receivable	240,000	240,000
Merchandise Inventory	180,000	140,000
Accounts Payable	160,000	160,000
Cost of Goods Sold	900,000	940,000
Building	300,000	300,000
Sales	1,500,000	1,500,000

Required

a. Compute the gross margin percentage for each company, and identify the company that *appears* to be charging the higher prices in relation to its costs.
b. For each company, compute the inventory turnover ratio and the average number of days to sell inventory. Identify the company that *appears* to be incurring the higher inventory financing cost.
c. Explain why the company with the lower gross margin percentage has the higher inventory turnover ratio.

ATC 6-6   **WRITING ASSIGNMENT** *Marketable Securities in Financial Statements*

The following information is taken from the annual report of The Maximum Companies at December 31, 2005, for investment securities (amounts given in millions):

	Amortized Cost	Gross Unrealized Gains	Gross Unrealized Losses	Estimated Fair Value
Investments				
Available for sale	$19,107.1	$951.3	$79.9	$19,978.5
Held to maturity	143.0	21.7	.4	164.3
Trading securities	16,521.9	13.8	0.0	16,535.7

Required

a. Using the preceding information, what amounts would Maximum report on the balance sheet at December 31, 2005?
b. Write a memo to the shareholders explaining why some investments are reported at cost and others are reported at market value. Explain how the values of these investments are reported at market value. Also explain how gains and losses on the various types of securities are reported in the financial statements.

ETHICAL DILEMMA *Show Them Only What You Want Them to See*

ATC 6–7

Clair Coolage is the chief accountant for a sales company called Far Eastern Imports. The company has been highly successful and is trying to increase its capital base by attracting new investors. The company operates in an inflationary environment and has been using the LIFO inventory cost flow method to minimize its net earnings and thereby reduce its income taxes. Katie Bailey, the vice president of finance, asked Coolage to estimate the change in net earnings that would occur if the company switched to FIFO. After reviewing the company's books, Coolage estimated that pretax income would increase by $1,200,000 if the company adopted the FIFO cost flow method. However, the switch would result in approximately $400,000 of additional taxes. The overall effect would result in an increase of $800,000 in net earnings. Bailey told Coolage to avoid the additional taxes by preparing the tax return on a LIFO basis but to prepare a set of statements on a FIFO basis to be distributed to potential investors.

Required
a. Comment on the legal and ethical implications of Bailey's decision.
b. How will the switch to FIFO affect Far Eastern's balance sheet?
c. If Bailey reconsiders and makes a decision to switch to FIFO for tax purposes as well as financial reporting purposes, net income will increase by $800,000. Comment on the wisdom of paying $400,000 in income taxes to obtain an additional $800,000 of net income.

EDGAR DATABASE *Analyzing Inventory at Gap Company*

ATC 6–8

Required
Using the most current 10-K available on EDGAR, answer the following questions about Gap Company. Instructions for using EDGAR are in Appendix A.
a. What was the average amount of inventory per store? Use *all* stores operated by Gap, not just those called *The Gap*. (*Hint:* The answer to this question must be computed. The number of stores in operation at the end of the most recent year can be found in the MD&A of the 10-K.)
b. How many *new* stores did Gap open during the year?
c. Using the quarterly financial information contained in the 10-K, complete the following chart.

Quarter	Sales During Each Quarter
1	$
2	
3	
4	

d. Referring to the chart in Requirement *c*, explain why Gap's sales vary so widely throughout its fiscal year. Do you believe that Gap's inventory level varies throughout the year in relation to sales?

SPREADSHEET ANALYSIS *Using Excel*

ATC 6–9

At January 1, 2005, the accounting records of Bronco Boutique had the following balances:

Cash	$1,000
Inventory	2,250 (150 units @ $15)
Common Stock	2,000
Retained Earnings	1,250

During January, Bronco Boutique entered into five cash transactions:

1. Purchased 120 units of inventory @ $16 each.
2. Purchased 160 units of inventory @ $17 each.
3. Sold 330 units of inventory @ $30 each.
4. Incurred $1,700 of operating expenses.
5. Paid income tax at the rate of 30 percent of income before taxes.

Required
a. Set up rows 1 through 10 of the following spreadsheet to compute cost of goods sold and ending inventory, assuming (1) FIFO, (2) LIFO, and (3) weighted-average cost flows. Notice that the FIFO cost flow has already been completed for you. Use columns O through W to complete the LIFO and weighted-average cost flow computations. Be sure to use formulas for all calculations.

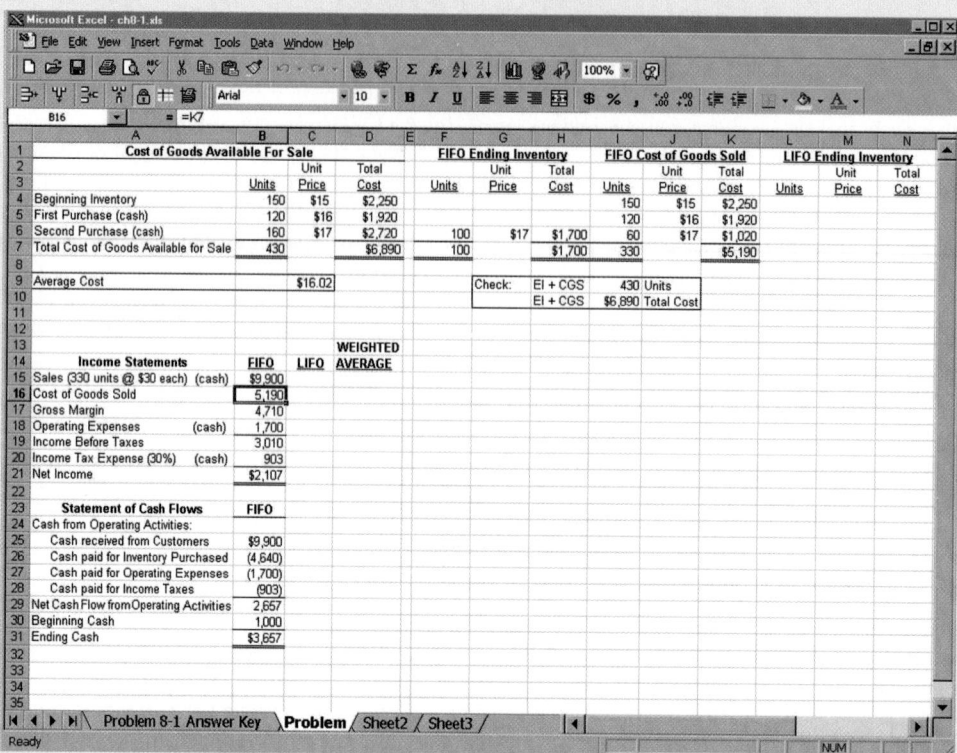

b. In rows 13 through 31, compute the amount of net income and net cash flow from operations under FIFO, LIFO, and weighted average. The FIFO column has been provided as an example.

ATC 6–10   SPREADSHEET ASSIGNMENT *Mastering Excel*

Required

Complete ATC 6–5 using an Excel spreadsheet. Use Excel problem ATC 6–9 as a resource for structuring the spreadsheet.

COMPREHENSIVE PROBLEM

The trial balance of Pacilio Security System Sales and Service as on January 1, 2006, was as follows:

Cash	$64,380
Accounts Receivable	8,000
Supplies	150
Prepaid Rent	1,000
Merchandise Inventory–Std. Alarms 19 @ $240	4,560
Merchandise Inventory–Deluxe Alarms 10 @ $500	5,000
Accounts Payable	4,120
Common Stock	50,000
Retained Earnings	28,970

During 2006, Pacilio Security System Sales and Service experienced the following transactions:

1. On January 1, 2006, purchased a company van for $9,200 cash. The van had an estimated life of three years and estimated salvage value of $2,000.
2. On January 15, purchased 20 standard alarm systems for cash at a cost of $250 each.
3. On February 1, paid $4,120 on accounts payable, but not within the discount period. Total cash paid was $4,204.
4. Paid $7,200 on March 2, 2006, for one year's rent in advance.

5. Purchased $500 of office supplies for cash.
6. Purchased 10 deluxe alarm systems for cash on April 1 at a cost of $550 each.
7. Purchased another 25 standard alarm systems on August 1 for resale at a cost of $260 each.
8. On September 5, purchased on account 30 standard alarm systems at a cost of $265 each and 20 deluxe alarm systems at a cost of $575 each.
9. Installed 60 standard alarm systems for $33,000 and 30 deluxe alarm systems for $27,000. $45,000 of the sales were on account and $15,000 were cash sales. (Note: Be sure to record cost of goods sold using FIFO method.)
10. Made a full refund to a dissatisfied customer who returned her deluxe system. The sale had been a cash sale for $900 with a cost of $575.
11. Paid installers a total of $16,200 cash for salaries.
12. Sold $68,000 of monitoring services during the year on account. The services are billed to the customers each month.
13. Collected $98,000 of accounts receivable during the year.
14. Paid $10,880 on accounts payable during the year.
15. Paid $3,500 of advertising expense during the year.
16. Paid $2,300 of utilities expense for the year.

Adjustments
17. $200 of supplies were on hand at the end of the year.
18. Recognized the expired rent for the year.
19. Recognized depreciation expense for 2006.

Required
a. Record the above transactions in general journal form. Pacilio uses FIFO cost flow assumption.
b. Post the transactions to the T-accounts.
c. Prepare a trial balance.
d. Prepare an income statement, statement of changes in stockholders' equity, balance sheet, and statement of cash flows.
e. Close the temporary accounts to retained earnings.
f. Post the closing entries to the T-accounts and prepare a after-closing trial balance.

CHAPTER seven

INTERNAL CONTROL AND ACCOUNTING FOR CASH

LEARNING *objectives*

After you have mastered the material in this chapter, you will be able to:

1 Identify the key elements of a strong system of internal control.

2 Identify special internal controls for cash.

3 Prepare a bank reconciliation.

4 Explain the use of a petty cash fund.

5 Prepare a classified balance sheet.

6 Use the current ratio to assess the level of liquidity.

THE *curious* ACCOUNTANT . . .

On June 25, 2002, WorldCom, the second largest long-distance telecommunications company in the United States, announced that its expenses had been incorrectly understated by approximately $3.6 billion. This understatement occurred because certain costs that should have been recorded as expenses were, instead, recorded as assets. On June 26, the company, which was experiencing difficulties before the revelation of its accounting problems, announced it would lay off 17,000 of its 80,000 employees, and the NASDAQ stopped trading of its stock. The company predicted its accounting misstatements would total over $11 billion by August 2003.

The restatement of WorldCom's earnings resulting from this discovery was the largest in corporate history, replacing the previous record set by Waste Management in 1998. Obviously, this is not a record a company wants to hold. As a result of these accounting irregularities, some members of management were fired or asked to resign.

How do you think such a large understatement of expenses goes undetected? Try to *speculate as to how it was ultimately discovered.* (Answer on page 319.)

CHAPTER *opening*

To operate successfully, businesses must employ systems of control. How can Wal-Mart's upper-level managers ensure that every store will open on time? How can the president of General Motors be confident that the company's financial reports fairly reflect the company's operations? How can the owner of a restaurant prevent a waiter from serving food to his friends and relatives without charging them for it? The answer: by exercising effective control over the enterprise. The policies and procedures used to provide reasonable assurance that the objectives of an enterprise will be accomplished are called **internal controls.**[1]

　　Internal controls can be divided into two categories: (1) **accounting controls** *are designed to safeguard company assets and ensure reliable accounting records; and (2)* **administrative controls** *are concerned with evaluating performance and assessing the degree of compliance with company policies and public laws.*

Topic Tackler
PLUS
7–1

LO1 Identify the key elements of a strong system of internal control.

Key Features of Internal Control Systems

Internal control systems vary from company to company. However, most systems include certain basic policies and procedures that have proven effective over time. A discussion of the more common features of a strong system of internal control follows.

Separation of Duties

The likelihood of fraud or theft is reduced if collusion is required to accomplish the act. As a result, a clear **separation of duties** is frequently used as a deterrent to corruption. When duties are separated, the work of one employee can act as a check on the work of another employee. For example, a person selling seats to a movie may be tempted to steal money received from customers who enter the theater. This temptation is reduced if the person staffing the box office is required to issue tickets that a second employee collects as people enter the theater. If ticket stubs collected by the second employee are compared with the cash receipts from ticket sales, any cash shortages would become apparent. Furthermore, friends and relatives of the ticket agent could not easily enter the theater without paying. Theft or unauthorized entry would require collusion between the ticket agent and the usher who collects the tickets. Both individuals would have to be dishonest enough to steal, yet trustworthy enough to convince each other they would keep the embezzlement secret. Whenever possible, the functions of *authorization, recording,* and *custody* should be performed by separate individuals.

Quality of Employees

A business is only as good as the people who run it. Cheap labor is not a bargain if the employees are incompetent. Employees should be properly trained. In fact, they should be trained to perform a variety of tasks. The ability of employees to substitute for one another prevents disruptions when co-workers are absent because of illnesses, vacations, or other commitments. The capacity to rotate jobs also relieves boredom and increases respect for the contributions of other employees. Every business should strive to maximize the productivity of each and every employee. Ongoing training programs are essential to a strong system of internal control.

Bonded Employees

The best way to ensure employee honesty is to hire individuals with *high levels of personal integrity.* Employers should screen job applicants using interviews, background checks, and recommendations from prior employers or educators. Even so, screening programs may fail to identify character weaknesses. Further, unusual circumstances may cause honest employees to go astray. Therefore, employees in positions of trust should be bonded. A **fidelity bond** provides insurance that protects a company from loss caused by employee dishonesty.

Required Absences

Employees should be required to take regular vacations and their duties should be rotated periodically. Employees may be able to cover up fraudulent activities if they are always

---

[1]*AICPA Professional Standards,* vol. 1, sec. 320, par. 6 (June 1, 1989).

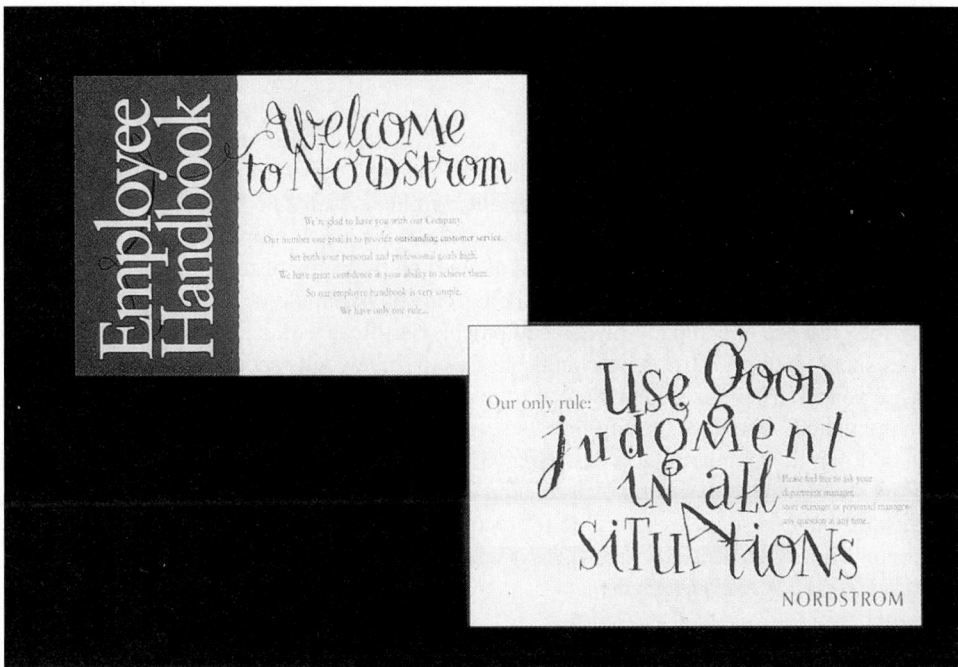

present at work. Consider the case of a parking meter collection agent who covered the same route for several years with no vacation. When the agent became sick, a substitute collected more money each day than the regular reader usually reported. Management checked past records and found that the ill meter reader had been understating the cash receipts and pocketing the difference. If management had required vacations or rotated the routes, the embezzlement would have been discovered much earlier.

Procedures Manual

Appropriate accounting procedures should be documented in a **procedures manual.** The manual should be routinely updated. Periodic reviews should be conducted to ensure that employees are following the procedures outlined in the manual.

Authority and Responsibility

Employees are motivated by clear lines of authority and responsibility. They work harder when they have the authority to use their own judgment and they exercise reasonable caution when they are held responsible for their actions. Businesses should prepare an **authority manual** that establishes a definitive *chain of command*. The authority manual should guide both specific and general authorizations. **Specific authorizations** apply to specific positions within the organization. For example, investment decisions are authorized at the division level while hiring decisions are authorized at the departmental level. In contrast, **general authority** applies across different levels of management. For example, employees at all levels may be required to fly coach or to make purchases from specific vendors.

Prenumbered Documents

How would you know if a check were stolen from your check book? If you keep a record of your check numbers, the missing number would tip you off immediately. Businesses also use prenumbered checks to avoid the unauthorized use of their bank accounts. In fact, prenumbered forms are used for all important documents such as purchase orders, receiving reports, invoices, and checks. To reduce errors, prenumbered forms should be as simple and as easy to use as possible. Also, the documents should allow for authorized signatures. For example, credit sales slips should be signed by the customer to clearly establish who made the purchase. Thus, the likelihood of unauthorized transactions is reduced.

Physical Control

Employees walk away with billions of dollars of business assets each year. To limit losses, companies should establish adequate physical control over valuable assets. For example, inventory should be kept in a storeroom and not released without proper authorization. Serial numbers on equipment should be recorded along with the name of the individual who is responsible for the equipment. Unannounced physical counts should be conducted randomly to verify the presence of company-owned equipment. Certificates of deposit and marketable securities should be kept in fireproof vaults. Access to these vaults should be limited to authorized personnel. These procedures protect the documents from fire and limit access to only those individuals who have the appropriate security clearance to handle the documents.

In addition to safeguarding assets, there should be physical control over the accounting records. The accounting journals, ledgers, and supporting documents should be kept in a fireproof safe. Only personnel responsible for recording transactions in the journals should have access to them. With limited access, there is less chance that someone will change the records to conceal fraud or embezzlement.

Performance Evaluations

Because few people can evaluate their own performance objectively, internal controls should include independent verification of employee performance. For example, someone other than the person who has control over inventory should take a physical count of inventory. Internal and external audits serve as independent verification of performance. Auditors should evaluate the effectiveness of the internal control system as well as verify the accuracy of the accounting records. In addition, the external auditors attest to the company's use of generally accepted accounting principles in the financial statements.

Limitations

A system of internal controls is designed to prevent or detect errors and fraud. However, no control system is foolproof. Internal controls can be circumvented by collusion among employees. Two or more employees working together can hide embezzlement by covering for each other. For example, if an embezzler goes on vacation, fraud will not be reported by a replacement who is in collusion with the embezzler. No system can prevent all fraud. However, a good system of internal controls minimizes illegal or unethical activities by reducing temptation and increasing the likelihood of early detection.

Check Yourself 7–1

What are nine features of an internal control system?

Answer
The nine features follow.

1. Separating duties so that fraud or theft requires collusion.
2. Hiring and training competent employees.
3. Bonding employees to recover losses through insurance.
4. Requiring employees to be absent from their jobs so that their replacements can discover errors or fraudulent activity that might have occurred.
5. Establishing proper procedures for processing transactions.
6. Establishing clear lines of authority and responsibility.
7. Using prenumbered documents.
8. Implementing physical controls such as locking cash in a safe.
9. Conducting performance evaluations through independent internal and external audits.

Bernie Ebbers, founder of WorldCom, is quoted as once having ordered Cynthia Cooper, WorldCom's vice president of internal audit, never to use the phrase *internal control*. Ebbers said he didn't understand it. Apparently, he was right. It was Mrs. Cooper and her team of internal auditors who ultimately uncovered the vast fraud. Perhaps a different attitude at the top about internal control could have avoided this fiasco.

As noted earlier, WorldCom had been experiencing difficulties prior to June 2002. In April 2002 its longtime CEO was ousted, and its board of directors launched an internal investigation of the company's operations. Mrs. Cooper found and reported the questionable accounting procedures to the company's audit committee. The chief financial officer at WorldCom was fired upon discovery of the accounting fraud. He and a few other key executives were ultimately indicted on criminal charges. After others had pled guilty to the fraud

charges, the chief financial officer reportedly continued to claim the company was within the rules to record the costs in question as assets and depreciate them in future periods, rather than recognize them immediately as expenses. The company's external auditor and board of directors did not agree with him.

Another question to consider is why no one asked to see the $3.6 billion of assets the company was supposed to be purchasing. The answer to this is not as obvious as one might expect. In the telecommunications business, many legitimate assets do not have any physical existence; they are said to be intangible assets, so it is not surprising that no one noticed they did not exist. Intangible assets are discussed in Chapter 9. WorldCom has since changed its name to MCI, but all of the legal issues surrounding the accounting fraud at the company have not yet been settled.

Accounting for Cash

For financial reporting purposes, **cash** generally includes currency and other items that are payable *on demand,* such as checks, money orders, bank drafts, and certain savings accounts. Savings accounts that impose substantial penalties for early withdrawal should be classified as *investments* rather than cash. Postdated checks or IOUs represent *receivables* and should not be included in cash. As illustrated in Exhibit 7–1, most companies combine currency and other payable on demand items in a single balance sheet account with varying titles.

LO2 Identify special internal controls for cash.

Companies must maintain a sufficient amount of cash to pay employees, suppliers, and other creditors. When a company fails to pay its legal obligations, the creditors can force the company into bankruptcy. Even so, management should avoid accumulating more cash than is needed. The failure to invest excess cash in earning assets reduces profitability. Cash inflows and outflows must be managed to prevent a shortage or surplus of cash.

Controlling Cash

Controlling cash, more than any other asset, requires strict adherence to internal control procedures. Cash has universal appeal. A relatively small suitcase filled with high-denomination currency can represent significant value. Furthermore, the rightful owner of currency is difficult to prove. In most cases, possession constitutes ownership. As a result, cash is highly susceptible to theft and must be carefully protected. Cash is most susceptible to embezzlement when it is received or disbursed. The following controls should be employed to reduce the likelihood of theft.

Cash Receipts

A record of all cash collections should be prepared immediately upon receipt. The amount of cash on hand should be counted regularly. Missing amounts of money can be detected by comparing the actual cash on hand with the book balance. Employees who receive cash should give customers a copy of a written receipt. Customers usually review their receipts to ensure they have gotten credit for the amount paid and call any errors to the receipts clerk's attention. This not only

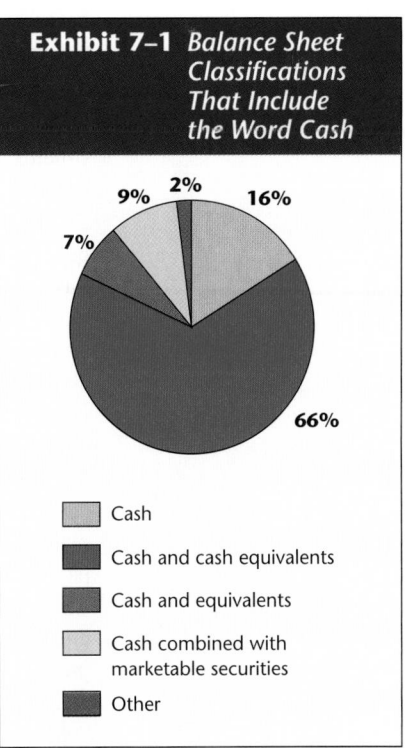

Exhibit 7–1 *Balance Sheet Classifications That Include the Word Cash*

- Cash
- Cash and cash equivalents
- Cash and equivalents
- Cash combined with marketable securities
- Other

Data Source: AICPA, *Accounting Trends and Techniques,* 2002.

The Cost of Protecting Cash

Could you afford to buy a safe like the one shown here? The vault is only one of many expensive security devices used by banks to safeguard cash. By using checking accounts, companies are able to avoid many of the costs associated with keeping cash safe. In addition to providing physical control, checking accounts enable companies to maintain a written audit trail regarding cash receipts and payments. Indeed, checking accounts represent the most widely used internal control device in modern society. It is difficult to imagine a business operating without the use of checking accounts.

reduces errors but also provides a control on the clerk's honesty. Cash receipts should be deposited in a bank on a timely basis. Cash collected late in the day should be deposited in a night depository. Every effort should be made to minimize the amount of cash on hand. Keeping large amounts of cash on hand not only increases the risk of loss from theft but also places employees in danger of being harmed by criminals who may be tempted to rob the company.

Cash Payments

To effectively control cash, a company should make all disbursements using checks, thereby providing a record of cash payments. All checks should be prenumbered, and unused checks should be locked up. Using prenumbered checks allows companies to easily identify lost or stolen checks by comparing the numbers on unused and canceled checks with the numbers used for legitimate disbursements.

The duties of approving disbursements, signing checks, and recording transactions should be separated. If one person is authorized to approve, sign, and record checks, he or she could falsify supporting documents, write an unauthorized check, and record a cover-up transaction in the accounting records. By separating these duties, the check signer reviews the documentation provided by the approving individual before signing the check. Likewise, the recording clerk reviews the work of both the approving person and the check signer when the disbursement is recorded in the accounting records. Thus writing unauthorized checks requires trilevel collusion.

Supporting documents with authorized approval signatures should be required when checks are presented to the check signer. For example, a warehouse receiving order should be matched with a purchase order before a check is approved to pay a bill from a supplier. Before payments are approved, invoice amounts should be checked and payees verified as valid vendors. Matching supporting documents with proper authorization discourages employees from creating phony documents for a disbursement to a friend or fictitious business. Also, the approval process serves as a check on the accuracy of the work of all employees involved.

Supporting documents should be marked *Paid* when the check is signed. If the documents are not indelibly marked, they could be retrieved from the files and resubmitted for a duplicate, unauthorized payment. A payables clerk could collude with the payee to split extra cash paid out by submitting the same supporting documents for a second payment.

All spoiled and voided checks should be defaced and retained. If defaced checks are not retained, an employee could steal a check and then claim that it was written incorrectly and thrown away. The clerk could then use the stolen check to make an unauthorized payment.

Checking Account Documents

The previous section explained the need for businesses to use checking accounts. A description of four main types of forms associated with a bank checking account follows:

Signature Card

A bank **signature card** shows the bank account number and the signatures of the people authorized to sign checks. The card is retained in the bank's files. If a bank employee is unfamiliar with the signature on a check, he or she can refer to the signature card to verify the signature before cashing the check.

Deposit Ticket

Each deposit of cash or checks is accompanied by a **deposit ticket,** which normally identifies the account number and the name of the account. The depositor lists the individual amounts of currency, coins, and checks, as well as the total deposited, on the deposit ticket.

Bank Check

A written check affects three parties: (1) the person or business writing the check (the *payer*); (2) the bank on which the check is drawn; and (3) the person or business to whom the check is payable (the *payee*). Companies often write **checks** using multicopy, prenumbered forms, with the name of the issuing business preprinted on the face of each check. A remittance notice is usually attached to the check forms. This portion of the form provides the issuer space to record what the check is for (e.g., what invoices are being paid), the amount being disbursed, and the date of payment. When signed by the person whose signature is on the signature card, the check authorizes the bank to transfer the face amount of the check from the payer's account to the payee.

Bank Statement

Periodically, the bank sends the depositor a **bank statement.** The bank statement is presented from the bank's point of view. Checking accounts are liabilities to a bank because the bank is obligated to pay back the money that customers have deposited in their accounts. Therefore, in the bank's accounting records a customer's checking account has a *credit* balance. As a result, **bank statement debit memos** describe transactions that reduce the customer's account balance (the bank's liability). **Bank statement credit memos** describe activities that increase the customer's account balance (the bank's liability). Since a checking account is an asset (cash) to the depositor, a *bank statement debit memo* requires a *credit entry* to the cash account on the depositor's books. Likewise, when a bank tells you that it has credited your account, you will debit your cash account in response.

Bank statements normally report (a) the balance of the account at the beginning of the period; (b) additions for customer deposits made during the period; (c) other additions described in credit memos (e.g., for interest earned); (d) subtractions for the payment of checks drawn on the account during the period; (e) other subtractions described in debit memos (e.g., for service charges); (f) a running balance of the account; and (g) the balance of the account at the end of the period. The sample bank statement in Exhibit 7–2 illustrates these items with references to the preceding letters in parentheses. Normally, the canceled checks or copies of them are enclosed with the bank statement.

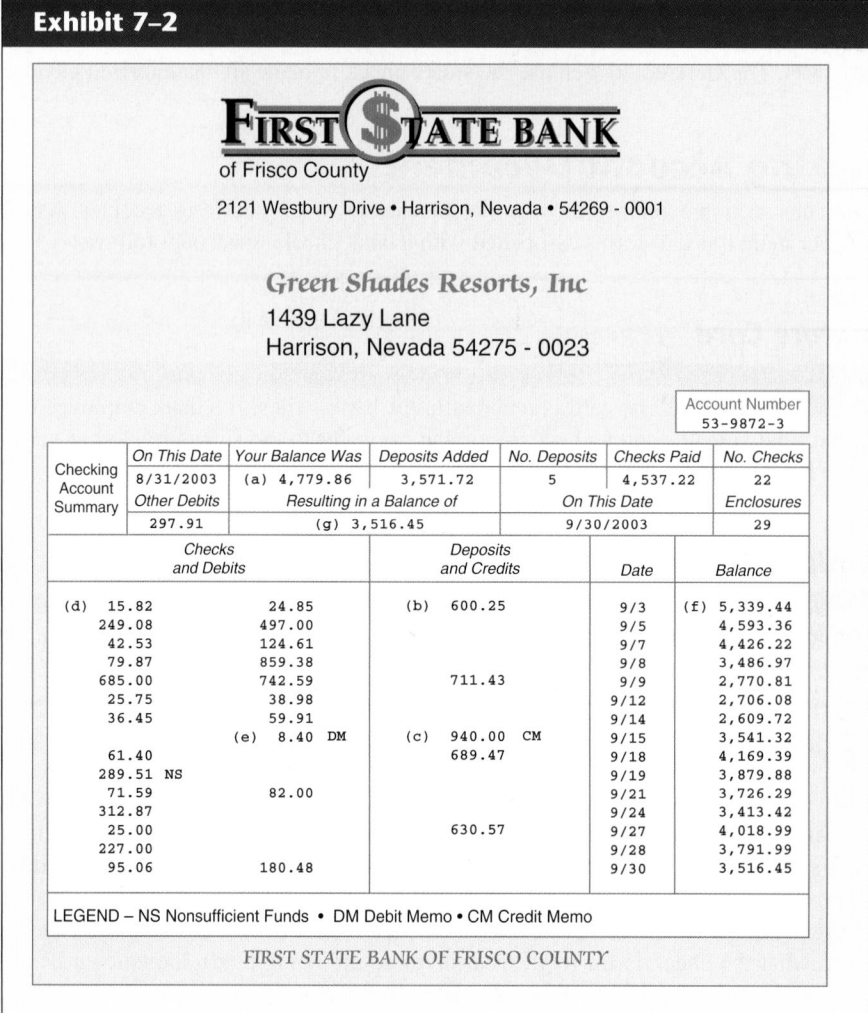

Exhibit 7–2

FIRST STATE BANK
of Frisco County

2121 Westbury Drive • Harrison, Nevada • 54269 - 0001

Green Shades Resorts, Inc
1439 Lazy Lane
Harrison, Nevada 54275 - 0023

Account Number
53-9872-3

Checking Account Summary	On This Date	Your Balance Was	Deposits Added	No. Deposits	Checks Paid	No. Checks
	8/31/2003	(a) 4,779.86	3,571.72	5	4,537.22	22
	Other Debits	Resulting in a Balance of			On This Date	Enclosures
	297.91	(g) 3,516.45			9/30/2003	29

Checks and Debits			Deposits and Credits		Date	Balance
(d) 15.82	24.85		(b) 600.25		9/3	(f) 5,339.44
249.08	497.00				9/5	4,593.36
42.53	124.61				9/7	4,426.22
79.87	859.38				9/8	3,486.97
685.00	742.59		711.43		9/9	2,770.81
25.75	38.98				9/12	2,706.08
36.45	59.91				9/14	2,609.72
	(e) 8.40 DM		(c) 940.00 CM		9/15	3,541.32
61.40			689.47		9/18	4,169.39
289.51 NS					9/19	3,879.88
71.59	82.00				9/21	3,726.29
312.87					9/24	3,413.42
25.00			630.57		9/27	4,018.99
227.00					9/28	3,791.99
95.06	180.48				9/30	3,516.45

LEGEND – NS Nonsufficient Funds • DM Debit Memo • CM Credit Memo

FIRST STATE BANK OF FRISCO COUNTY

Topic Tackler

PLUS

7–2

LO3 Prepare a bank reconciliation.

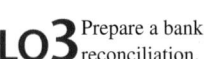

Reconciling the Bank Statement

Usually the ending balance reported on the bank statement differs from the balance in the depositor's cash account as of the same date. The discrepancy is normally attributable to timing differences. For example, a depositor deducts the amount of a check from its cash account at the same time the check is written. However, the bank does not deduct the amount of the check from the depositor's account until the payee presents it for payment, which may be days, weeks, or even months after the check is written. As a result, the balance on the depositor's books is lower than the balance on the bank's books. Companies prepare a **bank reconciliation** to explain the differences between the cash balance reported on the bank statement and the cash balance recorded in the depositor's accounting records.

Determining True Cash Balance

A bank reconciliation normally begins with the cash balance reported by the bank which is called the **unadjusted bank balance.** The adjustments necessary to determine the amount of cash that the depositor actually owns as of the date of the bank statement are then added to and subtracted from the unadjusted bank balance. The final total is the **true cash balance.** The true cash balance is independently reached a second time by making adjustments to the **unadjusted book balance.** The bank account is reconciled when the true cash balance determined from the perspective of the unadjusted *bank* balance agrees with the true cash balance determined from the perspective of the unadjusted *book* balance. The procedures a company uses to determine the *true cash balance* from the two different perspectives are outlined here.

Adjustments to the Bank Balance

A typical format for determining the true cash balance beginning with the unadjusted bank balance is

```
Unadjusted bank balance
+ Deposits in transit
− Outstanding checks
─────────────────────
= True cash balance
```

Deposits in transit. Companies frequently leave deposits in the bank's night depository or make them on the day following the receipt of cash. Since these deposits have been recorded in the depositor's accounting records but have not yet been added to the depositor's account by the bank, they must be added to the unadjusted bank balance.

Outstanding checks. These are disbursements that have been properly recorded as cash deductions on the depositor's books. However, the bank has not deducted the amounts from the depositor's bank account because the checks have not yet been presented by the payee to the bank for payment; that is, the checks have not "cleared" the bank. Outstanding checks must be subtracted from the unadjusted bank balance to determine the true cash balance.

Adjustments to the Book Balance

A typical format for determining the true cash balance beginning with the unadjusted book balance is as follows:

```
Unadjusted book balance
+ Accounts receivable collections
+ Interest earned
− Bank service charges
− Non-sufficient-funds (NSF) checks
─────────────────────────────────
= True cash balance
```

Accounts receivable collections. To collect cash as quickly as possible, many companies have their customers send payments directly to the bank. The bank adds the collection directly to the depositor's account and notifies the depositor about the collection through a credit memo that is included on the bank statement. The depositor adds the amount of the cash collections to the unadjusted book balance in the process of determining the true cash balance.

Interest earned. Banks pay interest on certain checking accounts. The amount of the interest is added directly to the depositor's bank account. The bank notifies the depositor about the interest through a credit memo that is included on the bank statement. The depositor adds the amount of the interest revenue to the unadjusted book balance in the process of determining the true cash balance.

Service charges. Banks frequently charge depositors fees for services performed. They may also charge a penalty if the depositor fails to maintain a specified minimum cash balance throughout the period. Banks deduct such fees and penalties directly from the depositor's account and advise the depositor of the deduction through a debit memo that is included on the bank statement. The depositor deducts such **service charges** from the unadjusted book balance to determine the true cash balance.

Non-sufficient-funds (NSF) checks. **NSF checks** are checks that a company obtains from its customers. The checks are then deposited in the company's checking account. However, when the checks are submitted to the customers' banks for payment, the banks refuse payment because there is insufficient money in the customers' accounts. When such checks are returned, the amounts of the checks are deducted from the company's bank account balance. The company is advised of NSF checks through debit memos that appear on the bank statement. The depositor deducts the amounts of the NSF checks from the unadjusted book balance in the process of determining the true cash balance.

Correction of Errors

In the course of reconciling the bank statement with the cash account, the depositor may discover errors in the bank's records, the depositor's records, or both. If an error is found on the bank statement, an adjustment for it is made to the unadjusted bank balance to determine the true cash balance, and the bank should be notified immediately to correct its records. Errors made by the depositor require adjustments to the book balance to arrive at the true cash balance.

Certified Checks

A **certified check** is guaranteed for payment by a bank. Whereas a regular check is deducted from the customer's account when it is presented for payment, a certified check is deducted from the customer's account when the bank certifies that the check is good. Certified checks, therefore, *have* been deducted by the bank in determining the unadjusted bank balance, whether they have cleared the bank or remain outstanding as of the date of the bank statement. Since certified checks are deducted both from bank and depositor records immediately, they do not cause differences between the depositor and bank balances. As a result, certified checks are not included in a bank reconciliation.

Illustrating a Bank Reconciliation

The following example illustrates preparing the bank reconciliation for Green Shades Resorts, Inc. (GSRI). The bank statement for GSRI is displayed in Exhibit 7–2. Exhibit 7–3 illustrates the completed bank reconciliation. The items on the reconciliation are described below.

Exhibit 7–3

GREEN SHADES RESORTS, INC.
Bank Reconciliation
September 30, 2003

Unadjusted Bank Balance, September 30, 2003	$3,516.45
Add: Deposits in Transit	724.11
Bank Error: Check drawn on Green Valley Resorts Charged to GSRI	25.00
Less: Outstanding Checks	

Check No.	Date	Amount
639	Sept. 18	$ 13.75
646	Sept. 20	29.00
672	Sept. 27	192.50

Total	(235.25)
True Cash Balance, September 30, 2003	$4,030.31
Unadjusted Book Balance, September 30, 2003	$3,361.22
Add: Receivable Collected by Bank	940.00
Error Made by Accountant (Check no. 633 recorded as $63.45 instead of $36.45)	27.00
Less: Bank Service Charges	(8.40)
NSF Check	(289.51)
True Cash Balance, September 30, 2003	$4,030.31

Adjustments to the Bank Balance

As of September 30, 2003, the bank statement showed an unadjusted balance of $3,516.45. A review of the bank statement disclosed three adjustments that had to be made to the unadjusted bank balance to determine GSRI's true cash balance.

1. Comparing the deposits on the bank statement with deposits recorded in GSRI's accounting records indicated there was $724.11 of deposits in transit.
2. An examination of the returned checks disclosed that the bank had erroneously deducted a $25 check written by Green Valley Resorts from GSRI's bank account. This amount must be added back to the unadjusted bank balance to determine the true cash balance.
3. The checks returned with the bank statement were sorted and compared to the cash records. Three checks with amounts totaling $235.25 were outstanding.

After these adjustment are made GSRI's true cash balance is determined to be $4,030.31.

Adjustments to the Book Balance

As indicated in Exhibit 7–3, GSRI's unadjusted book balance as of September 30, 2003, was $3,361.22. This balance differs from GSRI's true cash balance because of four unrecorded accounting events:

1. The bank collected a $940 account receivable for GSRI.
2. GSRI's accountant made a $27 recording error.
3. The bank charged GSRI an $8.40 service fee.
4. GSRI had deposited a $289.51 check from a customer who did not have sufficient funds to cover the check.

Two of these four adjustments increase the unadjusted cash balance. The other two decrease the unadjusted cash balance. After the adjustments have been recorded, the cash account reflects the true cash balance of $4,030.31 ($3,361.22 unadjusted cash balance + $940.00 receivable collection + $27.00 recording error − $8.40 service charge − $289.51 NSF check). Since the true balance determined from the perspective of the bank statement agrees with the true balance determined from the perspective of GSRI's books, the bank statement has been successfully reconciled with the accounting records.

Updating GSRI's Accounting Records

Each of the adjustments to the book balance must be recorded in GSRI's financial records. The effects of each adjustment on the financial statements are as follows.

Adjustment 1 *Recording the $940 receivable collection increases cash and reduces accounts receivable.*

The event is an asset exchange transaction. The effect of the collection on GSRI's financial statements is:

Assets		= Liab. + Equity	Rev. − Exp. = Net Inc.	Cash Flow
Cash	+ Accts. Rec.			
940	+ (940)	= NA + NA	NA − NA = NA	940 OA

Adjustment 2 *Assume the $27 recording error occurred because GSRI's accountant accidentally transposed two numbers when recording check no. 633 for utilities expense.*

The check was written to pay utilities expense of $36.45 but was recorded as a $63.45 disbursement. Since cash payments are overstated by $27.00 ($63.45 − $36.45), this amount must be added back to GSRI's cash balance and deducted from the utilities expense account, which increases net income. The effects on the financial statements are:

Assets	=	Liab.	+	Equity	Rev.	−	Exp.	=	Net Inc.	Cash Flow
27	=	NA	+	27	NA	−	(27)	=	27	27 OA

Adjustment 3 *The $8.40 service charge is an expense that reduces assets, stockholders' equity, net income, and cash.*

The effects are:

Assets	=	Liab.	+	Equity	Rev.	−	Exp.	=	Net Inc.	Cash Flow
(8.40)	=	NA	+	(8.40)	NA	−	8.40	=	(8.40)	(8.40) OA

Adjustment 4 *The $289.51 NSF check reduces GSRI's cash balance.*

When it originally accepted the customer's check, GSRI increased its cash account. Since there is not enough money in the customer's bank account to pay the check, GSRI didn't actually receive cash so GSRI must reduce its cash account. GSRI will still try to collect the money from the customer. In the meantime, it will show the amount of the NSF check as an account receivable. The adjusting entry to record the NSF check is an asset exchange transaction. Cash decreases and accounts receivable increases. The effect on GSRI's financial statements is:

Assets			=	Liab.	+	Equity	Rev.	−	Exp.	=	Net Inc.	Cash Flow
Cash	+	Accts. Rec.										
(289.51)	+	289.51	=	NA	+	NA	NA	−	NA	=	NA	(289.51) OA

Journal Entries

The journal entries for the four adjustments described above are as follows:

Account Title	Debit	Credit
Cash	940.00	
Accounts Receivable		940.00
To record the account receivable collected by the bank		
Cash	27.00	
Utilities Expense		27.00
To correct error on recording check no. 633		
Bank Service Charge Expense	8.40	
Cash		8.40
To record service charge expense		
Accounts Receivable	289.51	
Cash		289.51
To establish receivable due from customer who wrote the bad check		

Cash Short and Over

Sometimes employees make mistakes when collecting cash from or making change for customers. When such errors occur, the amount of money in the cash register will not agree with the amount of cash receipts recorded on the cash register tape. For example, suppose that when a customer paid for $17.95 of merchandise with a $20 bill, the sales clerk returned $3.05 in change instead of $2.05. If, at the end of the day, the cash register tape shows total receipts of $487.50, the cash drawer would contain only $486.50. The actual cash balance is less than the expected cash balance by $1. Any shortage of cash or excess of cash is recorded in a special account called **Cash Short and Over.** In this example, the shortage is recorded with the following journal entry:

Account Title	Debit	Credit
Cash	486.50	
Cash Short and Over	1.00	
Sales		487.50

A cash shortage is an expense. It is recorded by debiting the Cash Short and Over account. An overage of cash represents revenue and is recorded by crediting the Cash Short and Over account. As with other expense and revenue items, the balance of the Cash Short and Over account is closed to the Retained Earnings account at the end of the accounting period.

The following information was drawn from Reliance Company's October bank statement. The unadjusted bank balance on October 31 was $2,300. The statement showed that the bank had collected a $200 account receivable for Reliance. The statement also included $20 of bank service charges for October and a $100 check payable to Reliance that was returned NSF. A comparison of the bank statement with company accounting records indicates that there was a $500 deposit in transit and $1,800 of checks outstanding at the end of the month. Based on this information, determine the true cash balance on October 31.

Answer Since the unadjusted book balance is not given, start with the unadjusted bank balance to determine the true cash balance. The collection of the receivable, the bank service charges, and the NSF check are already recognized in the unadjusted bank balance, so these items are not used to determine the true cash balance. Determine the true cash balance by adding the deposit in transit to and subtracting the outstanding checks from the unadjusted bank balance. The true cash balance is $1,000 ($2,300 unadjusted bank balance + $500 deposit in transit − $1,800 outstanding checks).

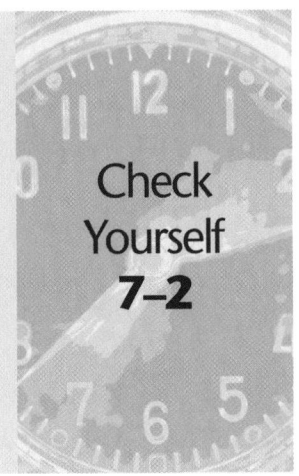

Check Yourself 7–2

Using Petty Cash Funds

While checks are used for most disbursements, payments for small items such as postage, delivery charges, taxi fares, employees' supper money, and so on are frequently made with currency. Companies frequently establish a **petty cash fund** to maintain effective control over these small cash disbursements. The fund is established for a specified dollar amount, such as $300, and is controlled by one employee, called the *petty cash custodian*.

LO4 Explain the use of a petty cash fund.

Petty cash funds are usually maintained on an **imprest basis,** which means that the money disbursed is replenished on a periodic basis. The fund is created by drawing a check on the regular checking account, cashing it, and giving the currency to the petty cash custodian. The custodian normally keeps the currency under lock and key. The amount of the petty cash fund depends on what it is used for, how often it is used, and how often it is replenished. It should be large enough to handle disbursements for a reasonable time period, such as several weeks or a month.

Establishing a petty cash fund merely transfers cash from a bank account to a safety box inside the company offices. The establishment is an asset exchange event. The cash account decreases, and an account called Petty Cash increases. The effects on the financial statements of establishing a $300 petty cash fund and the related journal entry are shown here:

Assets		=	Liab.	+	Equity	Rev.	−	Exp.	=	Net Inc.	Cash Flow
Cash	+ Petty Cash										
(300)	+ 300	=	NA	+	NA	NA	−	NA	=	NA	NA

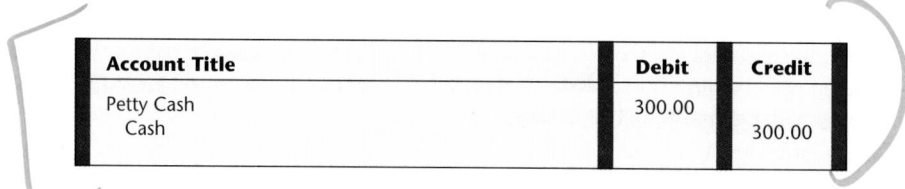

Account Title	Debit	Credit
Petty Cash	300.00	
Cash		300.00

When money is disbursed from the petty cash fund, the custodian should complete a **petty cash voucher,** such as the one in Exhibit 7–4. Any supporting documents, such as an invoice, restaurant bill, or parking fee receipt, should be attached to the petty cash voucher. The person who receives the cash should sign the voucher as evidence of receiving the money. The total of the amounts recorded on the petty cash vouchers plus the remaining coins and currency should equal the balance of the petty cash ledger account. *No journal entry is made in the accounting records when petty cash funds are disbursed.* The effects on the financial statements are recorded at the time when the petty cash fund is replenished (when additional currency is put into the petty cash safety box).

When the amount of currency in the petty cash fund is relatively low, the fund is replenished. The petty cash vouchers are totaled, the amount of any cash short or over is determined, and a check is issued to the bank to obtain the currency needed to return the fund to its imprest balance. For example, suppose the $300 petty cash fund is replenished when the total of the petty cash vouchers is $216. The vouchers can be classified according to different types of expenses or listed in total as miscellaneous expense. Assuming the company classifies petty cash expenditures as miscellaneous expense, the journal entries to record replenishing the fund are as follows:

Account Title	Debit	Credit
Miscellaneous Expense	216.00	
Petty Cash		216.00
To record expenses paid from the petty cash fund		
Petty Cash	216.00	
Cash		216.00
To replenish the petty cash fund		

If desired, the effect of the entries could be recorded more efficiently. Since the credit to the Petty Cash account is offset by a debit to the same account, a single entry debiting miscellaneous expense and crediting cash would have the same effect on the accounts. The entry more frequently used in practice to record replenishing petty cash is:

Account Title	Debit	Credit
Miscellaneous Expense	216.00	
Cash		216.00

Exhibit 7–4

Petty cash voucher no. _____

To: _____ Date _____ , 20 _____

Explanation: Account No. _____ Amount _____

Approved by _____   Received by _____

The replenishment affects the financial statements in the same manner as any other cash expense. It reduces assets, stockholders' equity, net income, and cash flow, as follows:

Assets	=	Liab.	+	Equity	Rev.	–	Exp.	=	Net Inc.	Cash Flow
(216)	=	NA	+	(216)	NA	–	216	=	(216)	(216) OA

If management desires more detailed information about petty cash expenditures, the vouchers can be sorted into postage, $66; delivery charges, $78.40; taxi fares, $28; and supper money, $43.60, in which case the journal entry to replenish the fund could be recorded as follows:

Account Title	Debit	Credit
Postage Expense	66.00	
Delivery Expense	78.40	
Taxi Fares Expense	28.00	
Employee Meal Expense	43.60	
Cash		216.00

Once the vouchers are checked, the fund replenished, and the journal entry recorded, the vouchers should be indelibly marked *Paid* so they cannot be reused.

Sometimes, cash shortages and overages are discovered when the money in the petty cash fund is physically counted. Suppose that a physical count discloses $212.30 in petty cash vouchers and only $87 in currency and coins. Assuming an imprest petty cash balance of $300, the journal entries necessary to replenish the fund are as follows:

Account Title	Debit	Credit
Miscellaneous Expense	212.30	
Cash Short and Over	.70	
Cash		213.00
To replenish the petty cash fund		

If cash shortages or overages do not occur frequently and are of insignificant amounts, companies are likely to include them in miscellaneous expense or miscellaneous revenue.

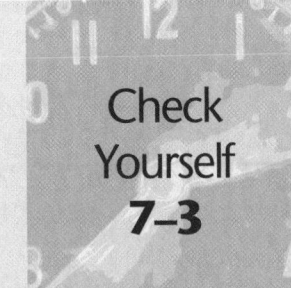

Check Yourself 7-3

Cornerstone Corporation established a $400 petty cash fund that was replenished when it contained $30 of currency and coins and $378 of receipts for miscellaneous expenses. Based on this information, determine the amount of cash short or over to be recognized. Explain how the shortage or overage would be reported in the financial statements. Also determine the amount of petty cash expenses that were recognized when the fund was replenished.

Answer The fund contained $408 of currency and receipts ($30 currency + $378 of receipts), resulting in a cash overage of $8 ($408 − $400). The overage would be reported as miscellaneous revenue on the income statement. The amount of petty cash expenses recognized would equal the amount of the expense receipts, which is $378.

THE FINANCIAL ANALYST

Current Versus Noncurrent

Having enough money to pay bills is critical to business survival. To assess the ability of a business to pay its bills, financial analysts frequently classify assets and liabilities according

LO5 Prepare a classified balance sheet.

to their liquidity. The more quickly an asset is converted to cash, the more *liquid* it is. To assist analysts in assessing a company's liquidity, assets are usually divided into two major classifications: *current* and *noncurrent*. Current items are also referred to as *short term* and noncurrent items as *long term*.

A **current (short-term) asset** is expected to be converted to cash or consumed within one year or an operating cycle, whichever is longer. An **operating cycle** is defined as the average time it takes a business to convert cash to inventory, inventory to accounts receivable, and accounts receivable back to cash. The financial tools used to measure the length of an operating cycle for particular businesses are discussed in Chapter 8. For most businesses, the operating cycle is less than one year. As a result, the one-year rule normally prevails with respect to classifying assets as current. The current assets section of a balance sheet typically includes the following items:

```
Current Assets
    Cash
    Marketable Securities
    Accounts Receivable
    Short-Term Notes Receivable
    Interest Receivable
    Inventory
    Supplies
    Prepaids
```

Given the definition of current assets, it seems reasonable to assume that **current (short-term) liabilities** would be those due within one year or an operating cycle, whichever is longer. This assumption is usually correct. However, an exception is made for long-term renewable debt. For example, consider a liability that was issued with a 20-year term to maturity. After 19 years, the liability becomes due within one year and is, therefore, a current liability. Even so, the liability will be classified as long term if the company plans to issue new long-term debt and to use the proceeds from that debt to repay the maturing liability. This situation is described as *refinancing short-term debt on a long-term basis*. In general, if a business does not plan to use any of its current assets to repay a debt, that debt is listed as long term even if it is due within one year. The current liabilities section of a balance sheet typically includes the following items:

```
Current Liabilities
    Accounts Payable
    Short-Term Notes Payable
    Wages Payable
    Taxes Payable
    Interest Payable
```

Balance sheets that distinguish between current and noncurrent items are called **classified balance sheets.** To enhance the usefulness of accounting information, most real-world balance sheets are classified. Exhibit 7–5 displays an example of a classified balance sheet.

Liquidity Versus Solvency

Liquidity describes the ability to generate sufficient short-term cash flows to pay obligations as they come due. **Solvency** is the ability to repay liabilities in the long run. Liquidity and solvency are both important to the survival of a business. Financial analysts rely on several ratios to help them evaluate a company's liquidity and solvency. The *debt to assets* ratio introduced in Chapter 3 is one tool used to measure solvency. The primary ratio used to evaluate liquidity is the current ratio.

Exhibit 7–5

LIMBAUGH COMPANY
Classified Balance Sheet
As of December 31, 2006

Assets

Current Assets

Cash	$ 20,000	
Accounts Receivable	35,000	
Inventory	230,000	
Prepaid Rent	3,600	
Total Current Assets		$288,600

Property, Plant, and Equipment

Office Equipment	$ 80,000		
Less: Accumulated Depreciation	(25,000)	55,000	
Building	340,000		
Less: Accumulated Depreciation	(40,000)	300,000	
Land		120,000	
Total Property, Plant, and Equipment			475,000
Total Assets			$763,600

Liabilities and Stockholders' Equity

Current Liabilities

Accounts Payable	$ 32,000	
Notes Payable	120,000	
Salaries Payable	32,000	
Unearned Revenue	9,800	
Total Current Liabilities		$193,800

Long-Term Liabilities

Note Payable		100,000
Total Liabilities		293,800

Stockholders' Equity

Common Stock	200,000	
Retained Earnings	269,800	469,800
Total Liabilities and Stockholders' Equity		$763,600

Current Ratio

The **current ratio** is defined as:

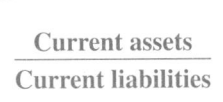

$$\frac{\text{Current assets}}{\text{Current liabilities}}$$

LO6 Use the current ratio to assess the level of liquidity.

Since current assets normally exceed current liabilities, this ratio is usually greater than 100 percent. For example, if a company has $250 in current assets and $100 in current liabilities, current assets are 250 percent of current liabilities. The current ratio is traditionally expressed as a decimal rather than as a percentage, however; most analysts would describe this example as a current ratio of 2.5 to 1 ($250 ÷ $100 = $2.50 in current assets for every $1 in current liabilities). This book uses the traditional format when referring to the current ratio.

The current ratio is among the most widely used ratios in analyzing financial statements. Current ratios can be too high as well as too low. A low ratio suggests that the company may have difficulty paying its short-term obligations. A high ratio suggests that a company is not maximizing its earnings potential because investments in liquid assets usually do not earn as much money as investments in other assets. Companies must try to maintain an effective balance between liquid assets (so they can pay bills on time) and nonliquid assets (so they can earn a good return).

Exhibit 7–6

Industry	Company	Current Ratio	Debt to Assets Ratio
Electric utilities	Duke Energy	0.99	0.72
	Dominion Resources	0.81	0.72
Grocery stores	Albertsons	1.24	0.66
	Safeway	1.08	0.77
Building supplies	Home Depot	1.48	0.34
	Lowe's	1.56	0.48

▌Real-World Data

Exhibit 7–6 presents the 2002 current ratios and debt to assets ratios for six companies in three different industries.

   Which of these companies has the highest level of financial risk? Perhaps Safeway because it has the highest debt to assets ratio. The electric utilities have higher debt to assets ratios and lower current ratios than those of the companies in the building supplies business. Does this mean that electric utilities are riskier investments? Not necessarily; since the companies are in different industries, the ratios may not be comparable. Utility companies have a more stable revenue base than building companies. If the economy turns downward, people are likely to continue to use utilities. However, they are less likely to buy a new home or to add on to their existing home. Because utility companies have a stable source of revenue, creditors are likely to feel comfortable with higher levels of debt for them than they would for building companies. As previously stated, the industry must be considered when interpreting ratios.

focus on INTERNATIONAL ISSUES

Why Are These Balance Sheets Backward?

Many of the differences in accounting rules used around the world would be difficult to detect by merely comparing financial statements from companies in different countries. For example, if a balance sheet for a U.S. company and one for a U.K. company both report an asset called *land,* it might not be clear whether the reported amounts were computed by using the same measurement rules or different measurement rules. Did both companies use historical cost as a basis for measurement? Perhaps not, but this would be difficult to determine by merely comparing balance sheets from two countries.

   However, one difference between financial reporting in the United Kingdom and the United States that is very obvious is the arrangement of assets on the balance sheet. In this chapter, we explain that U.S. GAAP requires current assets to be shown first and noncurrent assets second; the same is true of liabilities. In the United Kingdom, noncurrent assets appear first, followed by current assets; however, liabilities are shown in the same order as in the United States. In other countries (e.g., France), both assets and liabilities are shown with noncurrent items first. The accounting rules of some countries require that equity be shown before liabilities; this is the opposite of U.S. GAAP. Therefore, to someone who learned accounting in the United States, the balance sheets of companies from some countries may appear "backward" or "upside down."

   No matter in what order the assets, liabilities, and equity accounts are arranged on a company's balance sheet, one accounting concept is true throughout the free world:

$$\text{Assets} = \text{Liabilities} + \text{Equity}$$

Finally, note that the debt to assets ratios, with the exception of the grocery stores, tend to be grouped by industry. Current ratios do vary somewhat among different industries, but they probably do not vary as much as the debt to assets ratios. Why? Because all companies, regardless of how they finance their total assets, must keep sufficient current assets on hand to repay current liabilities.

a look
back

The policies and procedures used to provide reasonable assurance that the objectives of an enterprise will be accomplished are called *internal controls,* which can be subdivided into two categories: accounting controls and administrative controls. *Accounting controls* are composed of procedures designed to safeguard the assets and ensure that the accounting records contain reliable information. *Administrative controls* are designed to evaluate performance and the degree of compliance with company policies and public laws. While the mechanics of internal control systems vary from company to company, the more prevalent features include the following:

1. *Separation of duties.* Whenever possible, the functions of authorization, recording, and custody should be exercised by different individuals.
2. *Quality of employees.* Employees should be qualified to competently perform the duties that are assigned to them. Companies must establish hiring practices to screen out unqualified candidates. Furthermore, procedures should be established to ensure that employees receive appropriate training to maintain their competence.
3. *Bonded employees.* Employees in sensitive positions should be covered by a fidelity bond that provides insurance to reimburse losses due to illegal actions committed by employees.
4. *Required absences.* Employees should be required to take extended absences from their jobs so that they are not always present to hide unscrupulous or illegal activities.
5. *Procedures manual.* To promote compliance, the procedures for processing transactions should be clearly described in a manual.
6. *Authority and responsibility.* To motivate employees and promote effective control, clear lines of authority and responsibility should be established.
7. *Prenumbered documents.* Prenumbered documents minimize the likelihood of missing or duplicate documents. Prenumbered forms should be used for all important documents such as purchase orders, receiving reports, invoices, and checks.
8. *Physical control.* Locks, fences, security personnel, and other physical devices should be employed to safeguard assets.
9. *Performance evaluations.* Because few people can evaluate their own performance objectively, independent performance evaluations should be performed. Substandard performance will likely persist unless employees are encouraged to take corrective action.

Because cash is such an important business asset and because it is tempting to steal, much of the discussion of internal controls in this chapter focused on cash controls. Special procedures should be employed to control the receipts and payments of cash. One of the most common control policies is to use *checking accounts* for all except petty cash disbursements.

A *bank reconciliation* should be prepared each month to explain differences between the bank statement and a company's internal accounting records. A common reconciliation format determines the true cash balance based on both bank and book records. Items that typically appear on a bank reconciliation include the following:

Unadjusted Bank Balance	xxx	Unadjusted Book Balance	xxx
Add		Add	
Deposits in Transit	xxx	Interest Revenue	xxx
		Collection of Receivables	xxx
Subtract		Subtract	
Outstanding Checks	xxx	Bank Service Charges	xxx
		NSF Checks	xxx
True Cash Balance	xxx	True Cash Balance	xxx

Agreement of the two true cash balances provides evidence that accounting for cash transactions has been accurate.

Another common internal control policy for protecting cash is using a *petty cash fund*. Normally, an employee who is designated as the petty cash custodian is entrusted with a small amount of cash. The custodian reimburses employees for small expenditures made on behalf of the company in exchange for authorized receipts from the employees at the time they are reimbursed. The total of these receipts plus the remaining currency in the fund should always equal the amount of funds entrusted to the custodian. Journal entries to recognize the expenses incurred are made at the time the fund is replenished.

Finally, the chapter discussed assessing organizational *liquidity*. The *current ratio* is determined by dividing current assets by current liabilities. The higher the ratio, the more liquid the company's assets.

Accounting for receivables and payables was introduced in Chapter 2 using relatively simple illustrations. For example, we assumed that customers who purchased services on account always paid their bills. In real business practice, some customers do not pay their bills. Among other topics, Chapter 8 examines how companies account for bad debts.

SELF-STUDY REVIEW PROBLEM

The following information pertains to Terry's Pest Control Company (TPCC) for July:

1. The unadjusted bank balance at July 31 was $870.
2. The bank statement included the following items:
   (a) A $60 credit memo for interest earned by TPCC.
   (b) A $200 NSF check made payable to TPCC.
   (c) A $110 debit memo for bank service charges.
3. The unadjusted book balance at July 31 was $1,400.
4. A comparison of the bank statement with company accounting records disclosed the following:
   (a) A $400 deposit in transit at July 31.
   (b) Outstanding checks totaling $120 at the end of the month.

Required

a. Prepare a bank reconciliation.
b. Prepare in general journal format the entries necessary to adjust TPCC's cash account to its true balance.

Solution to Requirement *a*

TERRY'S PEST CONTROL COMPANY
Bank Reconciliation
July 31

Unadjusted bank balance	$ 870
Add: Deposits in transit	400
Less: Outstanding checks	(120)
True cash balance	$1,150
Unadjusted book balance	$1,400
Add: Interest revenue	60
Less: NSF check	(200)
Less: Bank service charges	(110)
True cash balance	$1,150

Solution to Requirement *b*

Ref.	Account Title	Debit	Credit
1.	Cash	60	
	Interest Revenue		60
2.	Accounts Receivable	200	
	Cash		200
3.	Service Charge Expense	110	
	Cash		110

KEY TERMS

Accounting controls *316*

Administrative controls *316*

Authority manual *317*

Bank reconciliation *322*

Bank statement *321*

Bank statement credit memo *321*

Bank statement debit memo *321*

Cash *319*

Cash short and over *327*

Certified check *324*

Checks *321*

Classified balance sheet *330*

Current (short-term) asset *330*

Current (short-term) liability *330*

Current ratio *331*

Deposit ticket *321*

Deposits in transit *323*

Fidelity bond *316*

General authority *317*

Imprest basis *327*

Internal controls *316*

Liquidity *330*

Non-sufficient-funds (NSF) check *323*

Operating cycle *330*

Outstanding checks *323*

Petty cash fund *327*

Petty cash voucher *328*

Procedures manual *317*

Separation of duties *316*

Service charges *323*

Signature card *321*

Solvency *330*

Specific authorizations *317*

True cash balance *322*

Unadjusted bank balance *322*

Unadjusted book balance *322*

QUESTIONS

1. What are the policies and procedures called that are used to provide reasonable assurance that the objectives of an enterprise will be accomplished?
2. What is the difference between accounting controls and administrative controls?
3. What are several features of a strong internal control system?
4. What is meant by *separation of duties*? Give an illustration.
5. What are the attributes of a high-quality employee?
6. What is a fidelity bond? Explain its purpose.
7. Why is it important that every employee periodically take a leave of absence or vacation?
8. What are the purpose and importance of a procedures manual?
9. What is the difference between specific and general authorizations?
10. Why should documents (checks, invoices, receipts) be prenumbered?
11. What procedures are important in the physical control of assets and accounting records?
12. What is the purpose of independent verification of performance?
13. What items are considered cash?
14. Why is cash more susceptible to theft or embezzlement than other assets?
15. Giving written copies of receipts to customers can help prevent what type of illegal acts?
16. What procedures can help to protect cash receipts?
17. What procedures can help protect cash disbursements?
18. What effect does a debit memo in a bank statement have on the Cash account? What effect does a credit memo in a bank statement have on the Cash account?
19. What information is normally included in a bank statement?
20. Why might a bank statement reflect a balance that is larger than the balance recorded in the depositor's books? What could cause the bank balance to be smaller than the book balance?
21. What is the purpose of a bank reconciliation?
22. What is an outstanding check?
23. What is a deposit in transit?
24. What is a certified check?
25. How is an NSF check accounted for in the accounting records?
26. What is the purpose of the Cash Short and Over account?
27. What is the purpose of a petty cash fund?
28. What types of expenditures are usually made from a petty cash fund?

29. What is the difference between a current asset and a noncurrent asset?
30. What are some common current assets?
31. What does the term *operating cycle* mean?
32. What are some common current liabilities?
33. What is a classified balance sheet?
34. What is the difference between the liquidity and the solvency of a business?
35. How does the arrangement of assets and liabilities on financial statements differ for the United States, the United Kingdom, and France?
36. The higher the current ratio, the better the company's financial condition. Do you agree or disagree with this statement? Explain.
37. Does a high (80 to 95 percent) debt to assets ratio mean that a business is in financial difficulty? What types of businesses traditionally operate with high debt to assets ratios?

EXERCISES—SERIES A

 All Exercises in Series A are available with McGraw-Hill's Homework Manager

L.O. 1   **EXERCISE 7–1A** *Features of a Strong Internal Control System*

Required
List and describe nine features of a strong internal control system described in this chapter.

L.O. 1, 2   **EXERCISE 7–2A** *Internal Controls for Small Businesses*

Required
Assume that you are the owner of a small business that has only two employees.

a. Which of the internal control procedures are most important to you?
b. How can you help overcome the limited separation-of-duties control procedure?

L.O. 2   **EXERCISE 7–3A** *Internal Control for Cash*

Required
a. Why are special controls needed for cash?
b. What is included in the definition of *cash*?

L.O. 1   **EXERCISE 7–4A** *Internal Control Procedures to Prevent Embezzlement*

Bell Gates was in charge of the returns department at The Software Company. She was responsible for evaluating returned merchandise. She sent merchandise that was reusable back to the warehouse, where it was restocked in the supply of inventory. Gates was also responsible for taking the merchandise that she determined to be defective to the city dump for disposal. She had agreed to buy a friend a tax planning program at a discount through her contacts at work. That is when the idea came to her. She could simply classify one of the reusable returns as defective and bring it home instead of taking it to the dump. She did so and made a quick $150. She was happy, and her friend was ecstatic; he was able to buy a $400 software package for only $150. He told his friends about the deal, and soon Gates had a regular set of customers. She was caught when a retail store owner complained to the marketing manager that his pricing strategy was being undercut by The Software Company's direct sales to the public. The marketing manager was suspicious because The Software Company had no direct marketing program. When the outside sales were ultimately traced back to Gates, the company discovered that it had lost over $10,000 in sales revenue because of her criminal activity.

Required
Identify an internal control procedure that could have prevented the company's losses. Explain how the procedure would have stopped the embezzlement.

L.O. 1   **EXERCISE 7–5A** *Internal Control Procedures to Prevent Deception*

Emergency Care Medical Centers (ECMC) hired a new physician, Ken Major, who was an immediate success. Everyone loved his bedside manner; he could charm the most cantankerous patient. Indeed, he was a master salesman as well as an expert physician. Unfortunately, Major misdiagnosed a case that resulted in serious consequences to the patient. The patient filed suit against ECMC. In preparation for the defense, ECMC's attorneys discovered that Major was indeed an exceptional salesman. He had worked for several years as district marketing manager for a pharmaceutical company. In fact, he was not a physician at all! He had changed professions without going to medical school. He had lied on his application form. His knowledge of medical terminology had enabled him to fool everyone. ECMC was found negligent and lost a $3 million lawsuit.

Required

Identify the relevant internal control procedures that could have prevented the company's losses. Explain how these procedures would have prevented Major's deception.

EXERCISE 7–6A *Treatment of NSF Check*   L.O. 3

The bank statement of Zone Supplies included a $200 NSF check that one of Zone's customers had written to pay for services that were provided by Zone.

Required

a. Show the effects of recognizing the NSF check on the financial statements by recording the appropriate amounts in a horizontal statements model like the following one.

Assets		= Liab. + Equity	Rev. – Exp. = Net Inc.	Cash Flow
Cash	+ Accts. Rec.			

b. Is the recognition of the NSF check on Zone's books an asset source, use, or exchange transaction?
c. Suppose the customer redeems the check by giving Zone $225 cash in exchange for the bad check. The additional $25 paid a service fee charged by Zone. Show the effects on the financial statements in the horizontal statements model in Requirement *a*.
d. Is the receipt of cash referred to in Requirement *c* an asset source, use, or exchange transaction?

EXERCISE 7–7A *Adjustments to the Balance per Books*   L.O. 3

Required

Identify which of the following items are added to or subtracted from the unadjusted *book balance* to arrive at the true cash balance. Distinguish the additions from the subtractions by placing a + beside the items that are added to the unadjusted book balance and a − beside those that are subtracted from it. The first item is recorded as an example.

Reconciling Items	Book Balance Adjusted?	Added or Subtracted?
Outstanding checks	No	N/A
Interest revenue earned on the account		
Deposits in transit		
Service charge		
Automatic debit for utility bill		
Charge for checks		
NSF check from customer		
ATM fee		

EXERCISE 7–8A *Adjustments to the Balance per Bank*   L.O. 3

Required

Identify which of the following items are added to or subtracted from the unadjusted *bank balance* to arrive at the true cash balance. Distinguish the additions from the subtractions by placing a + beside the items that are added to the unadjusted bank balance and a − beside those that are subtracted from it. The first item is recorded as an example.

Reconciling Items	Bank Balance Adjusted?	Added or Subtracted?
Bank service charge	No	N/A
Outstanding checks		
Deposits in transit		
Debit memo		
Credit memo		
ATM fee		
Petty cash voucher		
NSF check from customer		
Interest revenue		

L.O. 3   **EXERCISE 7–9A** *Adjusting the Cash Account*

As of May 31, 2004, the bank statement showed an ending balance of $17,250. The unadjusted Cash account balance was $16,450. The following information is available:

1. Deposit in transit, $2,630.
2. Credit memo in bank statement for interest earned in May, $12.
3. Outstanding check, $3,428.
4. Debit memo for service charge, $10.

Required

a. Determine the true cash balance by preparing a bank reconciliation as of May 31, 2004, using the preceding information.
b. Record in general journal format the adjusting entries necessary to correct the unadjusted book balance.

L.O. 3   **EXERCISE 7–10A** *Determining the True Cash Balance, Starting with the Unadjusted Bank Balance*

The following information is available for Stone Company for the month of August:

1. The unadjusted balance per the bank statement on August 31 was $56,300.
2. Deposits in transit on August 31 were $2,600.
3. A debit memo was included with the bank statement for a service charge of $20.
4. A $4,925 check written in August had not been paid by the bank.
5. The bank statement included a $1,000 credit memo for the collection of a note. The principal of the note was $950, and the interest collected was $50.

Required

Determine the true cash balance as of August 31. (*Hint:* It is not necessary to use all of the preceding items to determine the true balance.)

L.O. 3   **EXERCISE 7–11A** *Determining the True Cash Balance, Starting with the Unadjusted Book Balance*

Lee Company had an unadjusted cash balance of $7,850 as of April 30. The company's bank statement, also dated April 30, included a $75 NSF check written by one of Lee's customers. There were $920 in outstanding checks and $250 in deposits in transit as of April 30. According to the bank statement, service charges were $50, and the bank collected a $900 note receivable for Lee. The bank statement also showed $12 of interest revenue earned by Lee.

Required

Determine the true cash balance as of April 30. (*Hint:* It is not necessary to use all of the preceding items to determine the true balance.)

L.O. 4   **EXERCISE 7–12A** *Effect of Establishing a Petty Cash Account*

Macon Timber Company established a $150 petty cash fund on January 1, 2003.

Required

a. Is the establishment of the petty cash fund an asset source, use, or exchange transaction?
b. Record the establishment of the petty cash fund in a horizontal statements model like the following one:

Assets		= Liab. + Equity	Rev. − Exp. = Net Inc.	Cash Flow
Cash	+ Petty Cash			

c. Record the establishment of the fund in general journal format.

L.O. 4   **EXERCISE 7–13A** *Effect of Petty Cash Events on the Financial Statements*

Toro, Inc., established a petty cash fund of $200 on January 2. On January 31, the fund contained cash of $15.30 and vouchers for the following cash payments:

Postage	$25.00
Office supplies	48.50
Printing expense	30.00
Entertainment expense	79.20

The three distinct accounting events affecting the petty cash fund for the period were (1) establishment of the fund, (2) reimbursements made to employees, and (3) recognition of expenses and replenishment of the fund.

Required

a. Record each of the three events in a horizontal statements model like the following one. In the Cash Flow column, indicate whether the item is an operating activity (OA), investing activity (IA), or a financing activity (FA). Use NA to indicate that an account was not affected by the event.

Assets		= Liab. + Equity	Rev. – Exp. = Net Inc.	Cash Flow
Cash	+ Petty Cash			

b. Record the events in general journal format.

EXERCISE 7–14A *Determining the Amount of Petty Cash Expense*

L.O. 4

Consider the following events:

1. A petty cash fund of $100 was established on April 1, 2006.
2. Employees were reimbursed when they presented petty cash vouchers to the petty cash custodian.
3. On April 30, 2006, the petty cash fund contained vouchers totaling $87.30 plus $13.50 of currency.

Required
Answer the following questions:

a. How did the establishment of the petty cash fund affect (increase, decrease, or have no effect on) total assets?
b. What is the amount of total petty cash expenses to be recognized during April?
c. When are petty cash expenses recognized (at the time of establishment, reimbursement, or replenishment)?

EXERCISE 7–15A *Preparing a Classified Balance Sheet*

L.O. 5

Required
Use the following information to prepare a classified balance sheet for Steller Co. at the end of 2008.

Accounts Receivable	$42,500
Accounts Payable	8,000
Cash	15,260
Common Stock	42,000
Long-Term Notes Payable	23,000
Merchandise Inventory	29,000
Office Equipment	28,500
Retained Earnings	45,460
Prepaid Insurance	3,200

EXERCISE 7–16A *Operating Cycle*

L.O. 6

New England Co. sells gifts and novelty items mostly on account. It takes an average of 100 days to sell its inventory and an average of 40 days to collect the accounts receivable.

Required

a. Draw a diagram of the operating cycle for New England Co.
b. Compute the length of the operating cycle based on the information given.

PROBLEMS—SERIES A

All Problems in Series A are available with McGraw-Hill's Homework Manager

PROBLEM 7–17A *Using Internal Control to Restrict Illegal or Unethical Behavior*

L.O. 1, 2

Required
For each of the following fraudulent acts, describe one or more internal control procedures that could have prevented (or helped prevent) the problems.

a. Everyone in the office has noticed what a dedicated employee Jennifer Reidel is. She never misses work, not even for a vacation. Reidel is in charge of the petty cash fund. She transfers funds from the company's bank account to the petty cash account on an as-needed basis. During a surprise audit, the petty cash fund was found to contain fictitious receipts. Over a three-year period, Reidel had used more than $4,000 of petty cash to pay for personal expenses.

  b. Bill Bruton was hired as the vice president of the manufacturing division of a corporation. His impressive resume listed a master's degree in business administration from a large state university and numerous collegiate awards and activities, when in fact Bruton had only a high school diploma. In a short time, the company was in poor financial condition because of his inadequate knowledge and bad decisions.

  c. Havolene Manufacturing has good internal control over its manufacturing materials inventory. However, office supplies are kept on open shelves in the employee break room. The office supervisor has noticed that he is having to order paper, tape, staplers, and pens on an increasingly frequent basis.

L.O. 3 **PROBLEM 7–18A** *Preparing a Bank Reconciliation*

CHECK FIGURE
a. True Cash Balance, October 31, 2006: $9,350

Jim Guidry owns a construction business, Guidry Supply Co. The following cash information is available for the month of October 2006.

As of October 31, the bank statement shows a balance of $12,300. The October 31 unadjusted balance in the Cash account of Guidry Supply Co. is $11,200. A review of the bank statement revealed the following information:

  1. A deposit of $1,500 on October 31, 2006, does not appear on the October 31 bank statement.
  2. A debit memo for $50 was included in the bank statement for the purchase of a new supply of checks.
  3. When checks written during the month were compared with those paid by the bank, three checks amounting to $4,450 were found to be outstanding.
  4. It was discovered that a check to pay for repairs was correctly written and paid by the bank for $3,100 but was recorded on the books as $1,300.

Required
  a. Prepare a bank reconciliation at the end of October showing the true cash balance.
  b. Prepare any necessary journal entries to adjust the books to the true cash balance.

L.O. 3 **PROBLEM 7–19A** *Missing Information in a Bank Reconciliation*

www.mhhe.com/edmonds5e

CHECK FIGURE
True Cash Balance, April 30, 2007: $12,850

The following data apply to Smoot Sports, Inc. for April 2007:

  1. Balance per the bank on April 30, $12,250.
  2. Deposits in transit not recorded by the bank, $2,100.
  3. Bank error; check written by Smoot on his personal checking account was drawn on Smoot Sports, Inc.'s account, $800.
  4. The following checks written and recorded by Smoot Sports, Inc. were not included in the bank statement:

1901	$ 220
1920	580
1921	1,500

  5. Credit memo for note collected by the bank, $700.
  6. Service charge for collection of note, $10.
  7. The bookkeeper recorded a check written for $560 to pay for April's office supplies as $650 in the cash disbursements journal.
  8. Bank service charge in addition to the note collection fee, $30.
  9. NSF checks returned by the bank, $150.

Required
Determine the amount of the unadjusted cash balance per Smoot Sports, Inc.'s books.

L.O. 3 **PROBLEM 7–20A** *Adjustments to the Cash Account Based on the Bank Reconciliation*

www.mhhe.com/edmonds5e

CHECK FIGURE
h. Theft Loss: $800

Required
Determine whether the following items in National Imports' bank reconciliation require adjusting or correcting entries on National Imports' books. When an entry is required, record it in general journal format.

  a. The bank collected $5,000 of National Imports' accounts receivable. National Imports had instructed its customers to send their payments directly to the bank.
  b. The bank mistakenly gave Imports, Inc., credit for a $500 deposit made by National Imports.

c. Deposits in transit were $5,600.

d. National Imports' bank statement contained a $525 NSF check. National Imports had received the check from a customer and had included it in one of its bank deposits.

e. The bank statement indicated that National Imports earned $80 of interest revenue.

f. National Imports' accountant mistakenly recorded a $230 check that was written to purchase supplies as $320.

g. Bank service charges for the month were $50.

h. The bank reconciliation disclosed the fact that $800 had been stolen from National Imports' business.

i. Outstanding checks amounted to $1,700.

PROBLEM 7-21A *Bank Reconciliation and Adjustments to the Cash Account*

The following information is available for Mountain Top Hotel for July 2005:

L.O. 3

CHECK FIGURE
a. True Cash Balance, July 31, 2005: $16,234

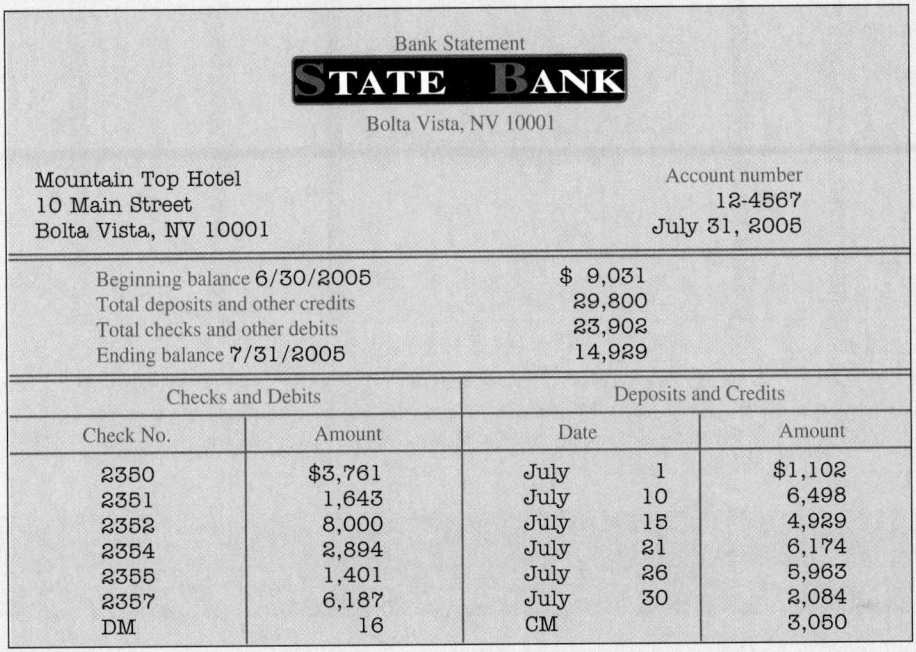

Bank Statement
STATE BANK
Bolta Vista, NV 10001

Mountain Top Hotel
10 Main Street
Bolta Vista, NV 10001

Account number
12-4567
July 31, 2005

Beginning balance 6/30/2005	$ 9,031
Total deposits and other credits	29,800
Total checks and other debits	23,902
Ending balance 7/31/2005	14,929

Checks and Debits		Deposits and Credits		
Check No.	Amount	Date		Amount
2350	$3,761	July	1	$1,102
2351	1,643	July	10	6,498
2352	8,000	July	15	4,929
2354	2,894	July	21	6,174
2355	1,401	July	26	5,963
2357	6,187	July	30	2,084
DM	16	CM		3,050

The following is a list of checks and deposits recorded on the books of the Mountain Top Hotel for July 2005:

Date		Check No.	Amount of Check	Date		Amount of Deposit
July	2	2351	$1,643	July	8	$6,498
July	4	2352	8,000	July	14	4,929
July	10	2353	1,500	July	21	6,174
July	10	2354	2,894	July	26	5,963
July	15	2355	1,401	July	29	2,084
July	20	2356	745	July	30	3,550
July	22	2357	6,187			

Other Information

1. Check no. 2350 was outstanding from June.

2. Credit memo was for collection of notes receivable.

3. All checks were paid at the correct amount.

4. Debit memo was for printed checks.

5. The June 30 bank reconciliation showed a deposit in transit of $1,102.

6. The unadjusted Cash account balance at July 31 was $13,200.

Required

a. Prepare the bank reconciliation for Mountain Top Hotel at the end of July.

b. Record in general journal form any necessary entries to the Cash account to adjust it to the true cash balance.

L.O. 3   PROBLEM 7–22A *Effect of Adjustments to Cash on the Accounting Equation*

After reconciling its bank account, Hull Equipment Company made the following adjusting entries:

Entry No.	Account Titles	Debit	Credit
1	Cash	40	
	Interest Revenue		40
	To record interest revenue		
2	Accounts Receivable	250	
	Cash		250
	To record NSF check from Wilson		
3	Rent Expense	35	
	Cash		35
	To correct understatement of expense		
4	Service Charge Expense	15	
	Cash		15
	To record bank service charge		
5	Cash	175	
	Accounts Receivable		175
	To record bank collection		

Required

Identify the event depicted in each journal entry as asset source (AS), asset use (AU), asset exchange (AE), or claims exchange (CE). Also explain how each entry affects the accounting equation by placing a + for increase, − for decrease, or NA for not affected under the following components of the accounting equation. The first event is recorded as an example.

Event No.	Type of Event	Assets	=	Liabilities	+	Stockholders' Equity Common Stock	+	Retained Earnings
1	AS	+		NA		NA		+

L.O. 1, 2, 3   PROBLEM 7–23A *Bank Reconciliation and Internal Control*

CHECK FIGURE
a. True Cash Balance, May 31, 2006: $22,550

Following is a bank reconciliation for Holt's Sandwich Shop for May 31, 2006:

	Cash Account	Bank Statement
Balance as of 5/31/06	$25,000	$22,000
Deposit in transit		4,250
Outstanding checks		(465)
Note collected by bank	1,815	
Bank service charge	(30)	
Automatic payment on loan	(1,000)	
Adjusted cash balance as of 5/31/06	$25,785	$25,785

Because of limited funds, Holt's employed only one accountant who was responsible for receiving cash, recording receipts and disbursements, preparing deposits, and preparing the bank reconciliation. The accountant left the company on June 8, 2006, after preparing the preceding statement. His replacement compared the checks returned with the bank statement to the cash disbursements journal and found the total of outstanding checks to be $3,700.

Required

a. Prepare a corrected bank reconciliation.

b. What is the total amount of cash missing, and how was the difference between the "true cash" per the bank and the "true cash" per the books hidden on the reconciliation prepared by the former employee?

c. What could Holt's do to avoid cash theft in the future?

PROBLEM 7–24A *Petty Cash Fund*

L.O. 4

CHECK FIGURE
a. Cash Over: $3

The following data pertain to the petty cash fund of Zelda Company:

1. The petty cash fund was created on an imprest basis at $150 on March 1.
2. On March 31, a physical count of the fund disclosed $18 in currency and coins, vouchers authorizing meal allowances totaling $75, vouchers authorizing purchase of postage stamps of $19, and vouchers for payment of delivery charges of $35.

Required

a. Prepare all general journal entries necessary to (1) establish the fund, (2) reimburse employees, and (3) recognize the expenses and replenish the fund as of March 31. (*Hint:* Journal entries may not be required for all three events.)

b. Explain how the Cash Short and Over account required in this case affects the income statement.

c. Identify the event depicted in each journal entry recorded in Requirement *a* as asset source (AS), asset use (AU), asset exchange (AE), or claims exchange (CE).

d. Record the effects on the financial statements of the events in Requirement *a* using a horizontal statements model like the following one. In the Cash Flow column, indicate whether the item is an operating activity (OA), investing activity (IA), or financing activity (FA). Use NA to indicate that an account was not affected by the event.

Assets		= Liab. + Equity	Rev. – Exp. = Net Inc.	Cash Flow
Cash	+ Petty Cash			

PROBLEM 7–25A *Multistep Income Statement and Classified Balance Sheet*

L.O. 5

e**X**cel
www.mhhe.com/edmonds5e

CHECK FIGURES
Total Current Assets: $29,940
Operating Income: $18,000

Required

Use the following information to prepare a multistep income statement and a classified balance sheet for Nixon Enterprises for the year end of December 31, 2005.

Accounts Receivable	$ 6,000
Common Stock	47,000
Salaries Expense	118,000
Interest Expense	12,200
Cash	3,600
Accounts Payable	5,000
Retained Earnings, Jan. 1, 2005	20,380
Accumulated Depreciation	6,800
Unearned Revenue	9,600
Land	50,000
Salaries Payable	1,800
Cost of Goods Sold	185,000
Supplies	500
Note Receivable (long term)	6,000
Inventory	9,000
Office Equipment	58,000
Gain on Sale of Equipment	6,400
Interest Receivable (short term)	1,240
Operating Expenses	19,000
Sales Revenue	340,000
Prepaid Rent	9,600
Interest Payable (short term)	740
Interest Revenue	420
Notes Payable (long term)	40,000

EXERCISE 7–1B *Internal Control Procedures*

L.O. 1

Required

a. Name and describe the two categories of internal controls.

b. What is the purpose of internal controls?

L.O. 1   EXERCISE 7–2B *Internal Controls for Equipment*

Required

List the internal control procedures that pertain to the protection of business equipment.

L.O. 2   EXERCISE 7–3B *Features of Internal Control Procedures for Cash*

Required

List and discuss effective internal control procedures that apply to cash.

L.O. 1   EXERCISE 7–4B *Internal Control Procedures*

Dick Haney is opening a new business that will sell sporting goods. It will initially be a small operation, and he is concerned about the security of his assets. He will not be able to be at the business all of the time and will have to rely on his employees and internal control procedures to ensure that transactions are properly accounted for and assets are safeguarded. He will have a store manager and two other employees who will be sales personnel and stock personnel and who will also perform any other duties necessary. Dick will be in the business on a regular basis. He has come to you for advice.

Required

Write a memo to Dick outlining the procedures that he should implement to ensure that his store assets are protected and that the financial transactions are properly recorded.

L.O. 1   EXERCISE 7–5B *Internal Controls to Prevent Theft*

Rhonda Cox worked as the parts manager for State Line Automobiles, a local automobile dealership. Rhonda was very dedicated and never missed a day of work. Since State Line was a small operation, she was the only employee in the parts department. Her duties consisted of ordering parts for stock and as needed for repairs, receiving the parts and checking them in, distributing them as needed to the shop or to customers for purchase, and keeping track of and taking the year-end inventory of parts. State Line decided to expand and needed to secure additional financing. The local bank agreed to a loan contingent on an audit of the dealership. One requirement of the audit was to oversee the inventory count of both automobiles and parts on hand. Rhonda was clearly nervous, explaining that she had just inventoried all parts in the parts department and supplied the auditors with a detailed list. The inventory showed parts on hand worth $225,000. This seemed a little excessive, and the accountants decided they needed to verify at least a substantial part of the inventory. When the auditors began their counts, a pattern began to develop. Each type of part seemed to be one or two items short when the actual count was taken. This raised more concern. Although Rhonda assured the auditors the parts were just misplaced, the auditors continued the count. After completing the count of parts on hand, the auditors could document only $155,000 of actual parts. Suddenly, Rhonda quit her job and moved to another state.

Required

a. What do you suppose caused the discrepancy between the actual count and the count that Rhonda had supplied?

b. What procedures could be put into place to prevent this type of problem?

L.O. 3   EXERCISE 7–6B *Treatment of NSF Check*

Rankin Stationery's bank statement contained a $250 NSF check that one of its customers had written to pay for supplies purchased.

Required

a. Show the effects of recognizing the NSF check on the financial statements by recording the appropriate amounts in a horizontal statements model like the following one:

Assets		= Liab. + Equity	Rev. – Exp. = Net Inc.	Cash Flow
Cash	+ Accts. Rec.			

b. Is the recognition of the NSF check on Rankin's books an asset source, use, or exchange transaction?

c. Suppose the customer redeems the check by giving Rankin $270 cash in exchange for the bad check. The additional $20 paid a service fee charged by Rankin. Show the effects on the financial statements in the horizontal statements model in Requirement *a*.

d. Is the receipt of cash referenced in Requirement *c* an asset source, use, or exchange transaction?

EXERCISE 7–7B *Adjustments to the Balance per Books*   **L.O. 3**

Required

Identify which of the following items are added to or subtracted from the unadjusted *book balance* to arrive at the true cash balance. Distinguish the additions from the subtractions by placing a + beside the items that are added to the unadjusted book balance and a − beside those that are subtracted from it. The first item is recorded as an example.

Reconciling Items	Book Balance Adjusted?	Added or Subtracted?
Interest revenue	Yes	+
Deposits in transit		
Debit memo		
Service charge		
Charge for checks		
NSF check from customer		
Note receivable collected by the bank		
Outstanding checks		
Credit memo		

EXERCISE 7–8B *Adjustments to the Balance per Bank*   **L.O. 3**

Required

Identify which of the following items are added to or subtracted from the unadjusted *bank balance* to arrive at the true cash balance. Distinguish the additions from the subtractions by placing a + beside the items that are added to the unadjusted bank balance and a − beside those that are subtracted from it. The first item is recorded as an example.

Reconciling Items	Bank Balance Adjusted?	Added or Subtracted?
Deposits in transit	Yes	+
Debit memo		
Credit memo		
Certified checks		
Petty cash voucher		
NSF check from customer		
Interest revenue		
Bank service charge		
Outstanding checks		

EXERCISE 7–9B *Adjusting the Cash Account*   **L.O. 3**

As of June 30, 2006, the bank statement showed an ending balance of $13,879.85. The unadjusted Cash account balance was $13,483.75. The following information is available:

1. Deposit in transit, $1,476.30.
2. Credit memo in bank statement for interest earned in June, $35.
3. Outstanding check, $1,843.74.
4. Debit memo for service charge, $6.34.

Required

a. Determine the true cash balance by preparing a bank reconciliation as of June 30, 2006, using the preceding information.
b. Record in general journal format the adjusting entries necessary to correct the unadjusted book balance.

EXERCISE 7–10B *Determining the True Cash Balance, Starting with the Unadjusted Bank*   **L.O. 3**
                  Balance

The following information is available for Hamby Company for the month of June:

1. The unadjusted balance per the bank statement on June 30 was $68,714.35.
2. Deposits in transit on June 30 were $1,464.95.
3. A debit memo was included with the bank statement for a service charge of $25.38.

4. A $4,745.66 check written in June had not been paid by the bank.
5. The bank statement included a $944 credit memo for the collection of a note. The principal of the note was $859, and the interest collected amounted to $85.

Required

Determine the true cash balance as of June 30. (*Hint:* It is not necessary to use all of the preceding items to determine the true balance.)

L.O. 3   **EXERCISE 7–11B** *Determining the True Cash Balance, Starting with the Unadjusted Book Balance*

Crumbley Company had an unadjusted cash balance of $6,450 as of May 31. The company's bank statement, also dated May 31, included a $38 NSF check written by one of Crumbley's customers. There were $548.60 in outstanding checks and $143.74 in deposits in transit as of May 31. According to the bank statement, service charges were $30, and the bank collected a $450 note receivable for Crumbley. The bank statement also showed $18 of interest revenue earned by Crumbley.

Required

Determine the true cash balance as of May 31. (*Hint:* It is not necessary to use all of the preceding items to determine the true balance.)

L.O. 4   **EXERCISE 7–12B** *Effect of Establishing a Petty Cash Account*

Manu Company established a $300 petty cash fund on January 1, 2003.

Required

a. Is the establishment of the petty cash fund an asset source, use, or exchange transaction?
b. Record the establishment of the petty cash fund in a horizontal statements model like the following one:

Assets		= Liab.	+ Equity	Rev.	− Exp.	= Net Inc.	Cash Flow
Cash	+ Petty Cash						

c. Record the establishment of the fund in general journal format.

L.O. 4   **EXERCISE 7–13B** *Effect of Petty Cash Events on the Financial Statements*

Family Medical Center established a petty cash fund of $100 on January 2. On January 31, the fund contained cash of $16.75 and vouchers for the following cash payments:

Postage	$34.68
Office supplies	18.43
Printing expense	7.40
Transportation expense	23.92

The three distinct accounting events affecting the petty cash fund for the period were (1) establishment of the fund, (2) reimbursements made to employees, and (3) recognition of expenses and replenishment of the fund.

Required

a. Record each of the three events in a horizontal statements model like the following one. In the Cash Flow column, indicate whether the item is an operating activity (OA), investing activity (IA), or a financing activity (FA). Use NA to indicate that an account was not affected by the event.

Assets		= Liab.	+ Equity	Rev.	− Exp.	= Net Inc.	Cash Flow
Cash	+ Petty Cash						

b. Record the events in general journal format.

L.O. 4   **EXERCISE 7–14B** *Determining the Amount of Petty Cash Expense*

Consider the following events:

1. A petty cash fund of $220 was established on April 1, 2008.

2. Employees were reimbursed when they presented petty cash vouchers to the petty cash custodian.

3. On April 30, 2008, the petty cash fund contained vouchers totaling $184.93 plus $28.84 of currency.

Required

Answer the following questions:

a. How did the establishment of the petty cash fund affect (increase, decrease, or have no effect on) total assets?

b. What is the amount of total petty cash expenses to be recognized during April?

c. When are petty cash expenses recognized (at the time of establishment, reimbursement, or replenishment)?

EXERCISE 7–15B *Preparing a Classified Balance Sheet*

L.O. 5

Required

Use the following information to prepare a classified balance sheet for Chapley Co. at the end of 2007.

Accounts Receivable	$12,150
Accounts Payable	5,500
Cash	10,992
Common Stock	12,000
Land	12,500
Long-Term Notes Payable	11,500
Merchandise Inventory	16,000
Retained Earnings	22,642

EXERCISE 7–16B *Operating Cycle*

L.O. 6

O'Conner Co. sells fine silk articles mostly on account. O'Conner Co. takes an average of 80 days to sell its inventory and an average of 42 days to collect the accounts receivable.

Required

a. Draw a diagram of the operating cycle for O'Conner Co.

b. Compute the length of the operating cycle based on the information given.

PROBLEM 7–17B *Using Internal Control to Restrict Illegal or Unethical Behavior*

L.O. 1, 2

Required

For each of the following fraudulent acts, describe one or more internal control procedures that could have prevented (or helped prevent) the problems.

a. Paula Wissel, the administrative assistant in charge of payroll, created a fictional employee, wrote weekly checks to the fictional employee, and then personally cashed the checks for her own benefit.

b. Larry Kent, the receiving manager of Southern Lumber, created a fictitious supplier named F&M Building Supply. F&M regularly billed Southern Lumber for supplies purchased. Kent had printed shipping slips and billing invoices with the name of the fictitious company and opened a post office box as the mailing address. Kent simply prepared a receiving report and submitted it for payment to the accounts payable department. The accounts payable clerk then paid the invoice when it was received because Kent acknowledged receipt of the supplies.

c. Holly Baker works at a local hobby shop and usually operates the cash register. She has developed a way to give discounts to her friends. When they come by, she rings a lower price or does not charge the friend for some of the material purchased. At first, Baker thought she would get caught, but no one seemed to notice. Indeed, she has become so sure that there is no way for the owner to find out that she has started taking home some supplies for her own personal use.

L.O. 3   PROBLEM 7–18B *Preparing a Bank Reconciliation*

Bob Carson owns a card shop, Card Talk. The following cash information is available for the month of August, 2006.

As of August 31, the bank statement shows a balance of $17,000. The August 31 unadjusted balance in the Cash account of Card Talk is $16,000. A review of the bank statement revealed the following information:

1. A deposit of $2,260 on August 31, 2006, does not appear on the August bank statement.
2. It was discovered that a check to pay for baseball cards was correctly written and paid by the bank for $4,040 but was recorded on the books as $4,400.
3. When checks written during the month were compared with those paid by the bank, three checks amounting to $3,000 were found to be outstanding.
4. A debit memo for $100 was included in the bank statement for the purchase of a new supply of checks.

Required

a. Prepare a bank reconciliation at the end of August showing the true cash balance.
b. Prepare any necessary journal entries to adjust the books to the true cash balance.

L.O. 3   PROBLEM 7–19B *Missing Information in a Bank Reconciliation*

The following data apply to Superior Auto Supply, Inc., for May 2007.

1. Balance per the bank on May 31, $8,000.
2. Deposits in transit not recorded by the bank, $975.
3. Bank error; check written by Allen Auto Supply was drawn on Superior Auto Supply's account, $650.
4. The following checks written and recorded by Superior Auto Supply were not included in the bank statement:

3013	$ 385
3054	735
3056	1,900

5. Note collected by the bank, $500.
6. Service charge for collection of note, $10.
7. The bookkeeper recorded a check written for $188 to pay for the May utilities expense as $888 in the cash disbursements journal.
8. Bank service charge in addition to the note collection fee, $25.
9. Customer checks returned by the bank as NSF, $125.

Required

Determine the amount of the unadjusted cash balance per Superior Auto Supply's books.

L.O. 3   PROBLEM 7–20B *Adjustments to the Cash Account Based on the Bank Reconciliation*

Required

Determine whether the following items included in Yang Company's bank reconciliation will require adjusting or correcting entries on Yang's books. When an entry is required, record it in general journal format.

a. An $877 deposit was recorded by the bank as $778.
b. Four checks totaling $450 written during the month of January were not included with the January bank statement.
c. A $54 check written to Office Max for office supplies was recorded in the general journal as $45.
d. The bank statement indicated that the bank had collected a $330 note for Yang.
e. Yang recorded $500 of receipts on January 31, 2006, which was deposited in the night depository of the bank. These deposits were not included in the bank statement.
f. Service charges of $22 for the month of January were listed on the bank statement.
g. The bank charged a $297 check drawn on Cave Restaurant to Yang's account. The check was included in Yang's bank statement.

h. A check of $31 was returned to the bank because of insufficient funds and was noted on the bank statement. Yang received the check from a customer and thought that it was good when it was deposited into the account.

PROBLEM 7–21B *Bank Reconciliation and Adjustments to the Cash Account*   **L.O. 3**

The following information is available for Cooters Garage for March 2002:

BANK STATEMENT
HAZARD STATE BANK
215 MAIN STREET
HAZARD, GA 30321

Cooters Garage   Account number
629 Main Street   62-00062
Hazard, GA 30321   March 31, 2002

Beginning balance 3/1/2002	$15,000.00
Total deposits and other credits	7,000.00
Total checks and other debits	6,000.00
Ending balance 3/31/2002	16,000.00

Checks and Debits		Deposits and Credits	
Check No.	Amount	Date	Amount
1462	$ 1,163.00	March 1	$ 1,000.00
1463	62.00	March 2	1,340.00
1464	1,235.00	March 6	210.00
1465	750.00	March 12	1,940.00
1466	1,111.00	March 17	855.00
1467	964.00	March 22	1,480.00
DM	15.00	CM	175.00
1468	700.00		

The following is a list of checks and deposits recorded on the books of Cooters Garage for March 2002:

Date	Check No.	Amount of Check	Date	Amount of Deposit
March 1	1463	$ 62.00	March 1	$1,340.00
March 5	1464	1,235.00	March 5	210.00
March 6	1465	750.00		
March 9	1466	1,111.00	March 10	1,940.00
March 10	1467	964.00		
March 14	1468	70.00	March 16	855.00
March 19	1469	1,500.00	March 19	1,480.00
March 28	1470	102.00	March 29	2,000.00

Other Information
1. Check no. 1462 was outstanding from February.
2. A credit memo for collection of accounts receivable was included in the bank statement.
3. All checks were paid at the correct amount.
4. The bank statement included a debit memo for service charges.
5. The February 28 bank reconciliation showed a deposit in transit of $1,000.
6. Check no. 1468 was for the purchase of equipment.
7. The unadjusted Cash account balance at March 31 was $16,868.

Required
a. Prepare the bank reconciliation for Cooters Garage at the end of March.
b. Record in general journal form any necessary entries to the Cash account to adjust it to the true cash balance.

L.O. 3   **PROBLEM 7–22B** *Effect of Adjustments to Cash on the Accounting Equation*

After reconciling its bank account, Obian Company made the following adjusting entries:

Entry No.	Account Titles	Debit	Credit
1	Cash	845	
	Accounts Receivable		845
	To record bank collection		
2	Cash	44	
	Interest Revenue		44
	To record interest revenue		
3	Service Charge Expense	35	
	Cash		35
	To record bank service charge		
4	Accounts Receivable	174	
	Cash		174
	To record NSF check from Beat		
5	Cash	20	
	Supplies Expense		20
	To correct overstatement of expense		

Required

Identify the event depicted in each journal entry as asset source (AS), asset use (AU), asset exchange (AE), or claims exchange (CE). Also explain how each entry affects the accounting equation by placing a + for increase, − for decrease, or NA for not affected under the following components of the accounting equation. The first event is recorded as an example.

Event No.	Type of Event	Assets	=	Liabilities	+	Stockholders' Equity Common Stock	+	Stockholders' Equity Retained Earnings
1	AE	+ −		NA		NA		NA

L.O. 1, 2, 3   **PROBLEM 7–23B** *Bank Reconciliation and Internal Control*

Following is a bank reconciliation for Surf Shop for June 30, 2005:

	Cash Account	Bank Statement
Balance as of 6/30/05	$1,618	$3,000
Deposit in transit		600
Outstanding checks		(1,507)
Note collected by bank	2,000	
Bank service charge	(25)	
NSF check	(1,500)	
Adjusted cash balance as of 6/30/05	$2,093	$2,093

When reviewing the bank reconciliation, Surf's auditor was unable to locate any reference to the NSF check on the bank statement. Furthermore, the clerk who reconciles the bank account and records the adjusting entries could not find the actual NSF check that should have been included in the bank statement. Finally, there was no specific reference in the accounts receivables supporting records identifying a party who had written a bad check.

Required

a. Prepare the adjusting entry that the clerk would have made to record the NSF check.

b. Assume that the clerk who prepares the bank reconciliation and records the adjusting entries also makes bank deposits. Explain how the clerk could use a fictitious NSF check to hide the theft of cash.

c. How could Surf avoid the theft of cash that is concealed by the use of fictitious NSF checks?

PROBLEM 7–24B *Petty Cash Fund*

L.O. 4

Martinez Co. established a petty cash fund by issuing a check for $250 and appointing Bob Potts as petty cash custodian. Potts had vouchers for the following petty cash payments during the month:

Stamps	$14.00
Miscellaneous items	25.00
Employee supper money	75.00
Taxi fare	80.00
Window-washing service	22.00

There was $32 of currency in the petty cash box at the time it was replenished.

Required

a. Prepare all general journal entries necessary to (1) establish the fund, (2) reimburse employees, (3) recognize expenses, and replenish the fund. (*Hint:* Journal entries may not be required for all the events.)

b. Explain how the Cash Short and Over account required in this case will affect the income statement.

c. Identify the event depicted in each journal entry recorded in Requirement *a* as asset source (AS), asset use (AU), asset exchange (AE), or claims exchange (CE).

d. Record the effects of the events in Requirement *a* on the financial statements using a horizontal statements model like the following one. In the Cash Flow column, indicate whether the item is an operating activity (OA), investing activity (IA), or financing activity (FA). Use NA to indicate that an account was not affected by the event.

Assets		= Liab.	+ Equity	Rev.	− Exp.	= Net Inc.	Cash Flow
Cash	+ Petty Cash						

PROBLEM 7–25B *Multistep Income Statement and Classified Balance Sheet*

L.O. 5

Required

Use the following information to prepare a multistep income statement as of December 31, 2004, and a classified balance sheet for the year ending December 31, 2004.

Accounts Receivable	$ 6,000
Common Stock	68,000
Salaries Expense	154,000
Interest Expense	5,000
Cash	20,000
Accounts Payable	1,800
Retained Earnings 12/31	76,000
Accumulated Depreciation	10,000
Unearned Revenue	16,000
Land	90,000
Salaries Payable	3,400
Cost of Goods Sold	175,000
Supplies	900
Note Receivable (long term)	10,000
Inventory	16,000
Office Equipment	52,000
Gain on Sale of Equipment	10,000
Interest Receivable (short term)	400
Operating Expenses	34,000
Sales Revenue	400,000
Prepaid Rent	8,000
Interest Payable (short term)	1,200
Notes Payable (long term)	26,900
Interest Revenue	800

ANALYZE, THINK, COMMUNICATE

ATC 7–1   BUSINESS APPLICATIONS CASE *Understanding Real World Annual Reports*

Required—Part 1

The Topps Company, Inc.

Use the Topps Company's annual report in Appendix B to answer the following questions.

a. What was Topps' current ratio as of March 1, 2003?
b. Which of Topps' current assets had the largest balance at March 1, 2003?
c. What percentage of Topps' total assets consisted of current assets?
d. Instead of "Cash," Topps' balance sheet shows an account named "Cash and cash equivalents." What do cash equivalents include? (See the footnotes.)
e. Does Topps' have any restrictions placed on it by its creditors? (*Hint*: See Note 9.)

Required—Part 2

Harley-Davidson, Inc.

Use the Harley-Davidson's annual report that came with this book to answer the following questions.

a. What was Harley-Davidson's current ratio as of December 31, 2003 and December 31, 2002?
b. Did its current ratio get stronger or weaker from 2002 to 2003?
c. Which of Harley-Davidson's current assets had the largest balance at December 31, 2003?
d. What percentage of Harley-Davidson's total assets consisted of current assets?

Required—Part 3

Why are Harley-Davidson's receivables, as a percentage of total assets, so much higher than Topps?

ATC 7–2   GROUP ASSIGNMENT *Analyzing Financial Statements*

The following selected information was taken from the annual reports of three companies: Southwest Airlines, Pier 1 Imports, and Wendy's. Amounts are given in thousands of dollars.

	Company 1	Company 2	Company 3
Accounts Receivable	$ 76,530	$ 4,128	$ 66,755
Accounts Payable	160,891	105,541	107,157
Other Current Liabilities	707,622	4,845	105,457
Allowance for Depreciation	1,375,631	138,179	537,910
Cash	623,343	32,280	234,262
Property, Plant, and Equipment	4,811,324	355,015	1,803,410
Inventories	0	220,013	35,633
Retained Earnings	1,632,115	118,721	839,215
Common Stock	376,903	204,327	345,019
Other Current Assets	108,543	29,057	44,904
Other Long-Term Assets	4,051	67,954	294,626
Long-Term Liabilities	1,370,629	136,834	544,832

Required

a. Organize the class into three sections and divide each section into three groups of three to five students. Assign Company 1 to groups in section 1, Company 2 to groups in section 2, and Company 3 to groups in section 3.

Group Tasks

1. Identify the company that is represented by the financial data assigned to your group.
2. Prepare a classified balance sheet for the company assigned to your group.
3. Select a representative from a group in each section and put the balance sheet on the board.

Class Discussion

b. Discuss the balance sheets of each company and the rationale for matching the financial information with the company.

ATC 7–3   REAL-WORLD CASE *Whose Numbers Are They Anyway?*

The following excerpt, sometimes referred to as *management's statement of responsibility,* was taken from JC Penney's 10-K report for its 2003 fiscal year. The authors have italicized and numbered selected portions of the excerpt.

Company Statement on Financial Information (partial)

[1] *The Company is responsible for the information presented in this Annual Report.* The consolidated financial statements have been prepared in accordance with accounting principles generally accepted in the United States of America and present fairly, in all material respects, the Company's results of operations, financial position and cash flows. The Company's CEO and CFO have signed certification statements as required by Sections 302 and 906 of the Sarbanes-Oxley Act of 2002. These signed certifications have been filed with the Securities and Exchange Commission as part of the Company's 2002 Form 10-K. Certain amounts included in the consolidated financial statements are estimated based on currently available information and judgment as to the outcome of future conditions and circumstances. . . .

The Company's system of internal controls is supported by written policies and procedures and supplemented by a staff of internal auditors. [2] *This system is designed to provide reasonable assurance, at suitable costs,* that assets are safeguarded and that transactions are executed in accordance with appropriate authorization and are recorded and reported properly. The system is continually reviewed, evaluated and where appropriate, modified to accommodate current conditions. Emphasis is placed on the careful [3] *selection,* [4] *training and development of professional finance and internal audit managers.*

An organizational alignment that is premised upon appropriate [5] *delegation of authority* and [6] *division of responsibility* is fundamental to this system. [7] *Communication programs are aimed at assuring that established policies and procedures are disseminated and understood throughout the Company.*

The consolidated financial statements have been audited by independent auditors whose report appears below. Their audit was conducted in accordance with auditing standards generally accepted in the United States of America, which include the consideration of the Company's internal controls to the extent necessary to form an independent opinion on the consolidated financial statements prepared by management.

The Audit Committee of the Board of Directors is composed solely of directors who are not officers or employees of the Company . . .

Required

Assume that a colleague, who has never taken an accounting course, asks you to explain JC Penney's "company statement on financial information." Write a memorandum that explains each of the numbered portions of the material. When appropriate, include examples to explain these concepts of internal control to your colleague.

BUSINESS APPLICATIONS CASE *Using the Current Ratio*   ATC 7–4

	Hamburger House	Hot Dog Heaven
Current assets	$90,000	$60,000
Current liabilities	65,000	33,000

Required

a. Compute the current ratio for each company.
b. Which company has the greater likelihood of being able to pay its bills?
c. Assuming that both companies have the same amount of total assets, speculate as to which company would produce the higher return on assets ratio.

BUSINESS APPLICATIONS CASE *Using Current Ratios to Make Comparisons*   ATC 7–5

The following accounting information pertains to Eckert and Ragland companies at the end of 2006:

Account Title	Eckert	Ragland
Cash	$ 22,000	$ 30,000
Wages Payable	30,000	30,000
Merchandise Inventory	45,000	66,000
Building	120,000	95,000
Accounts Receivable	53,000	37,000
Long-term Notes Payable	115,000	145,000
Land	68,000	60,000
Accounts Payable	60,000	54,000
Sales Revenue	330,000	325,000
Expenses	285,000	295,000

Required

a. Identify the current assets and current liabilities, and compute the current ratio for each company.

b. Assuming that all assets and liabilities are listed here, compute the debt to assets ratio for each company.

c. Determine which company has the greater financial risk in both the short term and the long term.

ATC 7–6   WRITING ASSIGNMENT *Internal Control Procedures*

Alison Marsh was a trusted employee of Small City State Bank. She was involved in everything. She worked as a teller, she accounted for the cash at the other teller windows, and she recorded many of the transactions in the accounting records. She was so loyal that she never would take a day off, even when she was really too sick to work. She routinely worked late to see that all the day's work was posted into the accounting records. She would never take even a day's vacation because they might need her at the bank. Tick and Tack, CPAs were hired to perform an audit, the first complete audit that had been done in several years. Marsh seemed somewhat upset by the upcoming audit. She said that everything had been properly accounted for and that the audit was a needless expense. When Tick and Tack examined some of the bank's internal control procedures, it discovered problems. In fact, as the audit progressed, it became apparent that a large amount of cash was missing. Numerous adjustments had been made to customer accounts with credit memorandums, and many of the transactions had been posted several days late. In addition, there were numerous cash payments for "office expenses." When the audit was complete, it was determined that more than $200,000 of funds was missing or improperly accounted for. All fingers pointed to Marsh. The bank's president, who was a close friend of Marsh, was bewildered. How could this type of thing happen at this bank?

Required

Prepare a written memo to the bank president, outlining the procedures that should be followed to prevent this type of problem in the future.

ATC 7–7   ETHICAL DILEMMA *See No Evil, Hear No Evil, Report No Evil*

Cindy Putman recently started her first job as an accounting clerk with the Wheeler Company. When reconciling Wheeler's bank statement, Putman discovered that the bank had given the company a $42,245 credit for a deposit made in the amount of $24,245. As a result, the bank account was overstated by $18,000. Putman brought the error to the attention of Ed Wheeler, who told her to reconcile the two accounts by subtracting the amount of the error from the unadjusted bank balance. Wheeler told Putman, "Don't bother informing the bank. They'll find the mistake soon enough." Three months later, Putman was still having to include the bank error in the bank reconciliation. She was convinced that the bank would not find the mistake and asked Wheeler what to do. He told Putman that it was not her job to correct bank mistakes. He told her to adjust the company books by making a debit to Cash and a credit to Retained Earnings. He said "We can always reverse the entry if the bank discovers the mistake." Putman was uneasy about this solution. Wheeler told her that his years of business experience had taught him to *go with the flow.* He said, "Sometimes you win, sometimes you lose. I'm sure that we have made mistakes that were to our disadvantage, and no one ever told us about them. We just got a good break. Keep quiet and share in the good fortune." At the end of the month, Putman discovered a $500 cash bonus included in her paycheck. She had been working hard, and she rationalized that she deserved the bonus. She told herself that it had nothing to do with the treatment of the bank error. Anyway, she thought that Wheeler was probably right. The bank would eventually find the mistake, she could reverse the adjusting entry, and everything would be set straight.

Two years later, a tax auditor for the Internal Revenue Service (IRS) discovered the adjusting entry that debited Cash and credited Retained Earnings for $18,000. The IRS agent charged Wheeler Company with income tax evasion. Being unable to identify the source of the increase in cash, the agent concluded that the company was attempting to hide revenue by making direct credits to Retained Earnings. Wheeler denied any knowledge of the entry. He told the agent that Putman rarely brought anything to his attention. He said that Putman was the independent sort who had probably made an honest mistake. He pointed out that at the time the entry was made, Putman had little experience.

Later in a private conversation, Wheeler told Putman to plead ignorance and that they both would get off the hook. He said that if she did not keep quiet, they would go down together. He reminded her of the $500 bonus. Wheeler told Putman that accepting payment to defraud the IRS constituted a crime that would land her in jail. Putman was shocked that Wheeler would not tell the truth. She had expected some loyalty from him, and it was clear that she was not going to get it.

Required

Answer the following questions:

a. Explain how the direct credit to retained earnings understated net income.
b. What course of action would you advise Putman to take?
c. Why was Putman foolish to expect loyalty from Wheeler?
d. Suppose Putman had credited Miscellaneous Revenue instead of Retained Earnings and the company had paid income taxes on the $18,000. Under these circumstances, the bank error would never have been discovered. Is it OK to hide the error from the bank if it is reported on the tax return?

EDGAR DATABASE *Analyzing Pep Boys' Liquidity*

ATC 7–8

Required

Using the most current 10-K available on EDGAR, answer the following questions about Pep Boys, Manny, Moe & Jack, for the most recent year reported. Type in *Pep Boys* as the company name when you search EDGAR. Instructions for using EDGAR are in Appendix A.

a. What is Pep Boys' current ratio?
b. Which of Pep Boys' current assets had the largest balance?
c. What percentage of Pep Boys' total assets consisted of current assets?
d. Did Pep Boys have any "currently maturing" long-term debt included in current liabilities on its balance sheet?
e. If Pep Boys were a company that manufactured auto parts rather than a retailer of auto parts, how do you think its balance sheet would be different?

SPREADSHEET ASSIGNMENT *Using Excel*

ATC 7–9

At the end of 2005, the following accounting information is available for Bainbridge and Crist Companies.

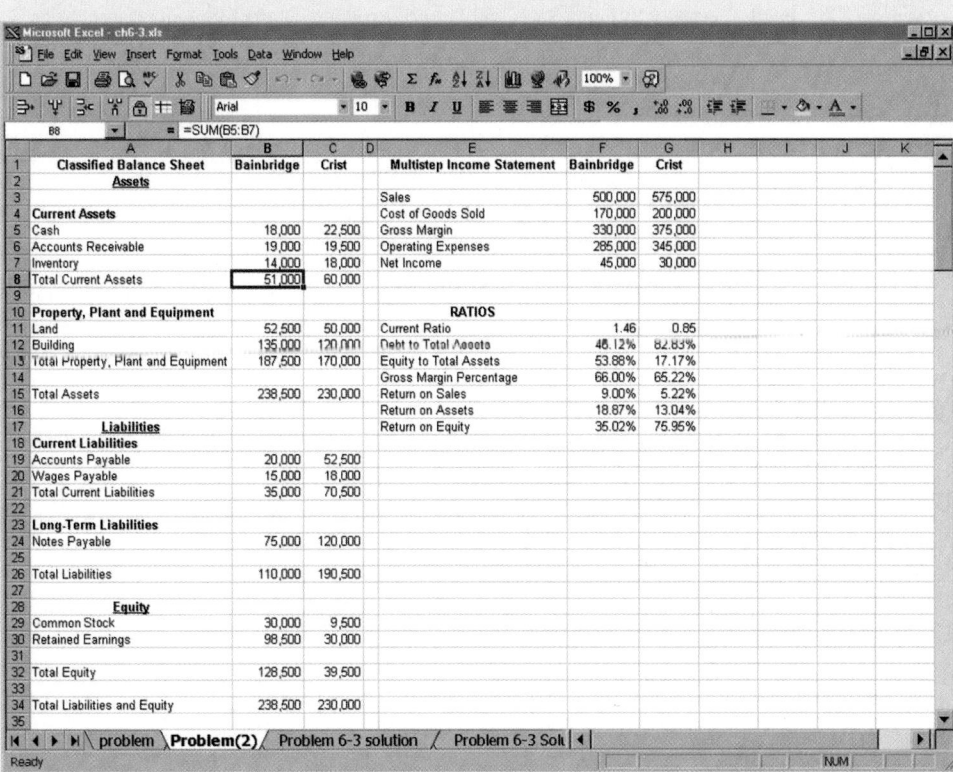

Required

a. Set up the preceding spreadsheet. Complete the balance sheet and income statement. Use Excel formulas for rows that "total" on the balance sheet and for gross margin and net income on the income statement.
b. Calculate the designated ratios using Excel formulas.
c. Which company is more likely to be able to pay its current liabilities?

d. Which company carries a greater financial risk?
e. Which company is more profitable from the stockholders' perspective?
f. Based on profitability alone, which company performed better?
g. Assume that sales increased 10 percent and that the additional sales were made on account. Adjust the balance sheet and income statement for the effects. Notice that Retained Earnings will also need to be adjusted to keep the balance sheet in balance. What is the resultant effect on the ratios?

COMPREHENSIVE PROBLEM

The trial balance of Pacilio Security System Sales and Service as of January 1, 2007, was as follows:

Cash	$105,496
Supplies	200
Accounts Receivable	23,000
Merchandise Inventory–Std. Alarms 4 @ $260; 30 @ $265	8,990
Merchandise Inventory–Deluxe Alarms 11 @ $575	6,325
Prepaid Rent	1,200
Van	9,200
Accumulated Depreciation	2,400
Accounts Payable	8,570
Common Stock	50,000
Retained Earnings	93,441

During 2007, Pacilio Security Systems Sales and Service experienced the following transactions:

1. On March 1, 2007, Pacilio created a petty cash fund for $100 to handle small expenditures.
2. Paid $7,200 on March 2, 2007, for one year's rent in advance.
3. Purchased $400 of supplies on account.
4. Purchased 80 standard alarm systems for $22,400 and 50 deluxe alarm systems for $28,500 during the year for cash.
5. Sold 82 standard alarm systems for $45,920 and 28 deluxe systems for $25,480. All sales were on account. (Be sure to compute cost of goods sold using the FIFO cost flow method.)
6. Paid $6,000 on accounts payable for the year.
7. Replenished the petty cash fund on August 1. At this time, the petty cash fund had only $7 of cash left. It contained the following receipts: office supplies $23, cutting grass $55, and miscellaneous expense $14.
8. Billed $75,000 of monitoring services for the year.
9. Paid installer salaries of $25,000 for the year.
10. Collected $122,300 of accounts receivable for the year.
11. Paid $3,600 of advertising expense for the year.
12. Paid $2,500 of utilities expense for the year.

Adjustments
13. There were $160 of supplies on hand at the end of the year.
14. Recognized expired rent for the year.
15. Recognized depreciation expense for the year.

Requirements shown on following page.

Required

a. Record the above transactions in general journal form.

b. Post the transactions to the T-accounts.

c. Prepare a bank reconciliation at the end of the year. The following information is available for the bank reconciliation:

    (1) Checks written but not paid by the bank, $8,350.

    (2) A deposit of $6,500 made on December 31, 2007, had been recorded but was not shown on the bank statement.

    (3) A debit memo for $55 for new supply of checks.

    (4) A credit memo for $20 for interest earned on the checking account.

    (5) An NSF check for $120.

    (6) The balance shown on the bank statement was $134,098.

d. Record and post any adjustments necessary from the bank reconciliation.

e. Prepare a trial balance

f. Prepare an income statement, statement of changes in stockholders' equity, balance sheet, and statement of cash flows.

g. Close the temporary accounts to retained earnings.

h. Post the closing entries to the T-accounts and prepare an after-closing trial balance.

CHAPTER *eight*

ACCOUNTING FOR ACCRUALS—ADVANCED TOPICS: RECEIVABLES AND PAYABLES

LEARNING *objectives*

After you have mastered the material in this chapter, you will be able to:

1 Explain the importance of offering credit terms to customers.

2 Explain how the allowance method of accounting for bad debts affects financial statements.

3 Show how the direct write-off method of accounting for bad debts affects financial statements.

4 Explain how accounting for credit card sales affects financial statements.

5 Explain how accounting for warranty obligations affects financial statements.

6 Explain the effects of the cost of financing credit sales.

7 Show how discount notes and related interest charges affect financial statements. (Appendix)

THE *curious* ACCOUNTANT

Suppose **Costco** orders goods from **Procter & Gamble**. Assume that Costco offers to pay for the goods on the day it receives them from Procter & Gamble (a cash purchase) or 30 days later (a purchase on account).

Assume that Procter & Gamble is absolutely sure Costco will pay its account when due. Do you think Procter & Gamble should care whether Costco pays for the goods upon delivery or 30 days later? Why? (Answers on page 361.)

CHAPTER *opening*

Many people buy on impulse. If they must wait, the desire to buy wanes. To take advantage of impulse buyers, most merchandising companies offer customers credit because it increases their sales. A disadvantage of this strategy occurs when some customers are unable or unwilling to pay their bills. Nevertheless, the widespread availability of credit suggests that the advantages of increased sales outweigh the disadvantages of some uncollectible accounts.

*When a company allows a customer to "buy now and pay later," the company's right to collect cash in the future is called an **account receivable.** Typically, amounts due from individual accounts receivable are relatively small and the terms to maturity are short. Most accounts receivable are collected within 30 days. When a longer credit term is needed or when a receivable is large, the seller usually requires the buyer to issue a note reflecting a credit agreement between the parties. The note specifies the maturity date, interest rate, and other credit terms. Receivables evidenced by such notes are called **notes receivable.** Accounts and notes receivable are reported as assets on the balance sheet. For every receivable on one company's books, there is a corresponding **payable** on another company's books. If one company* *expects to collect, another company must be obligated to pay. Accounts payable and notes payable[1] are reported as liabilities on the balance sheet.*

LO1 Explain the importance of offering credit terms to customers.

Most companies will not collect cash for the full face value of their receivables because some of their customers will be unable or unwilling to pay. To avoid overstating assets, companies report receivables at **net realizable value**, which is face value less an allowance for doubtful accounts (accounts estimated to be uncollectible). Only the amount actually expected to be collected is included in total assets. Payables, in contrast, are normally reported on the balance sheet at face value because of the **going concern assumption**. Specifically, companies operate under the assumption that they will continue to exist (they are going concerns). Under this assumption, companies expect to pay their obligations in full.

Reporting the net realizable value of receivables in the financial statements is commonly called the **allowance method of accounting for bad debts.** The following section illustrates using the allowance method for Allen's Tutoring Services.

Accounting Events Affecting the 2004 Period

LO2 Explain how the allowance method of accounting for bad debts affects financial statements.

Allen's Tutoring Services is a small company that provides tutoring services to college students. Allen's started operations on January 1, 2004. During 2004, Allen's experienced three types of accounting events. These events are discussed below.

Event 1 Revenue Recognition
Allen's Tutoring Services recognized $14,000 of service revenue earned on account during 2004.

This is an asset source transaction. Allen's Tutoring Services obtained assets (accounts receivable) by providing services to customers. Both assets and stockholders' equity (retained earnings) increase. The event increases revenue and net income. Cash flow is not affected. These effects follow:

Event No.	Assets	=	Liab.	+	Equity	Rev.	−	Exp.	=	Net Inc.	Cash Flow
1	14,000	=	NA	+	14,000	14,000	−	NA	=	14,000	NA

Event 2 Collection of Receivables
Allen's Tutoring Services collected $12,500 cash from accounts receivable in 2004.

This event is an asset exchange transaction. The asset cash increases; the asset accounts receivable decreases. Total assets remains unchanged. Net income is not affected because the revenue was recognized in the previous transaction. The cash inflow is reported in the operating activities section of the statement of cash flows.

Event No.	Assets			=	Liab.	+	Equity	Rev.	−	Exp.	=	Net Inc.	Cash Flow
	Cash	+	Accts. Rec.										
2	12,500	+	(12,500)	=	NA	+	NA	NA	−	NA	=	NA	12,500 OA

---

[1]Notes payable and other liabilities may be classified as short term or long term, depending on the time to maturity. Short-term liabilities mature within one year or the operating cycle, whichever is longer. Liabilities with longer maturities are classified as long term. This chapter focuses on accounting for short-term liabilities; accounting for long-term liabilities is discussed in Chapter 10.

Procter & Gamble would definitely prefer to make the sale to Costco in cash rather than on account. Even though it may be certain to collect its accounts receivable from Costco, the sooner Procter & Gamble gets its cash, the sooner the cash can be reinvested.

The interest cost related to a small account receivable of $50 that takes 30 days to collect may seem immaterial; at 4 percent, the lost interest amounts to less than $.20. However, when one considers that Procter & Gamble had approximately $3.4 billion

of accounts receivable on June 30, 2002, the cost of financing receivables for a real-world company becomes apparent. At 4 percent, the cost of waiting 30 days to collect $3.4 billion of cash is $11.2 million ($3.4 billion $\times$ 0.04 $\times$ [30 $\div$ 365]). For one full year, the cost to Procter & Gamble would be more than $136 million ($3.4 billion $\times$ 0.04). In 2002 it took Procter & Gamble approximately 31 days to collect its accounts receivable, and the weighted-average interest rate on its debt was approximately 3.7 percent.

Event 3 **Recognizing Bad Debts Expense[2]**
Allen's Tutoring Services recognized bad debts expense for accounts expected to be uncollectible in the future.

The year-end balance in the accounts receivable account is $1,500 ($14,000 of revenue on account −$12,500 of collections). Although Allen's Tutoring Services has the legal right to receive this $1,500 in 2005, the company is not likely to collect the entire amount because some of its customers may not pay the amounts due. Allen's will not know the actual amount of uncollectible accounts until some future time when the customers default (fail to pay). However, the company can *estimate* the amount of receivables that will be uncollectible.

Suppose Allen's Tutoring Services estimates that $75 of the receivables is uncollectible. To improve financial reporting, the company can recognize the estimated expense in 2004. In this way, bad debts expense and the matching revenue will be recognized in the same accounting period (2004). Recognizing an estimated expense is better than recognizing no expense. The *matching* of revenues and expenses is improved and the statements are, therefore, more accurate.

The estimated amount of **bad debts expense** is recognized in a year-end adjusting entry. The adjusting entry reduces the book value of total assets, reduces stockholders' equity (retained earnings), and reduces the amount of reported net income. The statement of cash flows is not affected. The effects of recognizing bad debts expense are shown here:

Event No.	Assets	=	Liab.	+	Equity	Rev.	−	Exp.	=	Net Inc.	Cash Flow
3	(75)	=	NA	+	(75)	NA	−	75	=	(75)	NA

The amount of receivables expected to be uncollectible ($75) is recorded in a contra asset account called **Allowance for Doubtful Accounts.** The difference between the amount in accounts receivable and the contra account is the *net realizable value* of accounts receivable. In this case, the net realizable value of receivables is:

Accounts Receivable	$1,500
Less: Allowance for Doubtful Accounts	(75)
Net Realizable Value of Receivables	$1,425

The **net realizable value** of receivables represents the amount of cash the company estimates it will actually collect. Generally accepted accounting principles require disclosure of both the net realizable value of receivables and the amount of the allowance account. Most companies disclose these amounts in their balance sheets. However, a significant number of

---

[2]The term *bad debts* may be misleading. It is some *receivables* that are "bad" rather than some company debt. Businesses, however, commonly refer to bad receivables as bad debts. We believe it is important to use real-world terminology, but be aware of the misleading nature of the term *bad debts expense.*

companies report only the net amount on the balance sheet and report the allowance amount in the footnotes. Typical alternative balance sheet captions that Allen's Tutoring Services could use to report accounts receivable follow:

Alternative 1	
Accounts Receivable	$1,500
Less Allowance for Doubtful Accounts	(75)
Net Realizable Value	$1,425
Alternative 2	
Trade Accounts Receivable, Less Allowance of $75	$1,425
Alternative 3	
Receivables, Less Allowance for Losses of $75	$1,425
Alternative 4	
Accounts and Notes Receivable, net	$1,425
Alternative 5	
Accounts Receivable	$1,425

As the different captions indicate, companies report the amount of receivables on their balance sheets in a variety of ways. Exhibit 8–1 identifies the most frequently used captions.

General Ledger T-Accounts

Exhibit 8–2 displays in T-account form the general ledger for the three business events experienced by Allen's Tutoring Services. The transactions data are referenced by the event number shown in parentheses. The entries to close the revenue and expense accounts at the end of the 2004 accounting period are also included. The closing entries are referenced with the letters *cl*. The ledger accounts provide the information to prepare the financial statements in Exhibit 8–3. The accounting events are summarized here:

1. Earned $14,000 of revenue on account.
2. Collected $12,500 cash from accounts receivable.
3. Adjusted the accounts to reflect management's estimate that bad debts expense would be $75.
4. Closed the revenue and expense accounts. (Referenced with letters *cl*.)

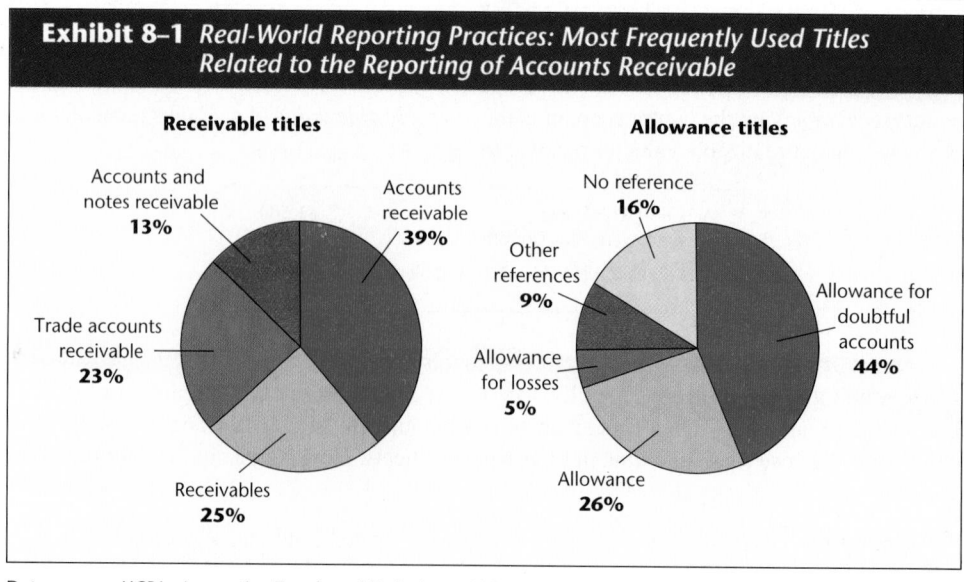

Exhibit 8–1 *Real-World Reporting Practices: Most Frequently Used Titles Related to the Reporting of Accounts Receivable*

Receivable titles

Accounts and notes receivable **13%**
Accounts receivable **39%**
Trade accounts receivable **23%**
Receivables **25%**

Allowance titles

No reference **16%**
Other references **9%**
Allowance for losses **5%**
Allowance **26%**
Allowance for doubtful accounts **44%**

Data source: AICPA, *Accounting Trends and Techniques,* 2002.

Exhibit 8–2 General Ledger

Assets		=	Liabilities		+	Equity	
Cash			**Liabilities**			**Retained Earnings**	
(2) 12,500				0 Bal.			13,925 (cl.)
Bal. 12,500							13,925 Bal.
Accounts Receivable						**Service Revenue**	
(1) 14,000	12,500 (2)					(cl.) 14,000	14,000 (1)
Bal. 1,500							0 Bal.
Allowance for						**Bad Debts Expense**	
Doubtful Accounts						(3) 75	75 (cl.)
	75 (3)					Bal. 0	
	75 Bal.						

Exhibit 8–3 Financial Statements for 2004

Income Statement		Balance Sheet			Statement of Cash Flows	
Service Revenue	$14,000	Assets			**Operating Activities**	
Bad Debts Exp.	(75)	Cash		$12,500	Inflow from Customers	$12,500
Net Income	$13,925	Accounts Receivable	$1,500		**Investing Activities**	0
		Less: Allowance	(75)		**Financing Activities**	0
		Net Realizable Value		1,425	Net Change in Cash	12,500
		Total Assets		$13,925	Plus: Beginning Cash Balance	0
		Stockholders' Equity			Ending Cash Balance	$12,500
		Retained Earnings		$13,925		

Financial Statements

As previously indicated, estimating bad debts improves the usefulness of the 2004 financial statements in two ways. First, the balance sheet reports the amount of cash ($1,500 − $75 = $1,425) the company actually expects to collect (net realizable value of accounts receivable). Second, the income statement provides a clearer picture of managerial performance because it better *matches* the bad debts expense with the revenue it helped produce. The statements in Exhibit 8–3 show that the cash flow from operating activities ($12,500) differs from net income ($13,925). The statement of cash flows reports only cash collections, whereas the income statement reports revenues earned on account less the estimated amount of bad debts expense.

Pamlico, Inc., began operations on January 1, 2006. During 2006, it earned $400,000 of revenue on account. The company collected $370,000 of accounts receivable. At the end of the year, Pamlico estimates bad debts expense will be 1 percent of sales. Based on this information alone, what is the net realizable value of accounts receivable as of December 31, 2006?

Answer Accounts receivable at year end are $30,000 ($400,000 sales on account − $370,000 collection of receivables). The amount in the allowance for doubtful accounts would be $4,000 ($400,000 credit sales × 0.01). The net realizable value of accounts receivable is therefore $26,000 ($30,000 − $4,000).

Check Yourself 8–1

Estimating Bad Debts Expense

In the Allen's Tutoring Services example, the estimated amount of bad debts expense was simply given. How do practicing accountants make such estimates? They normally base the

Topic Tackler

PLUS

8–1

estimate on the company's actual collection history. For example, assume that in the previous accounting period, Tannon Company was unable to collect $10,000 of $1,000,000 of sales on account. Expressed as a percentage, Tannon's bad debts expense is 1 percent of its credit sales ($10,000 ÷ $1,000,000). Estimates of future bad debts can be made by multiplying the historical percentage by current sales. If sales for the current period are $1,200,000, the estimated bad debts expense would be $12,000 ($1,200,000 × .01).

It may be necessary to adjust the historical percentage for anticipated future circumstances. For example, the percentage would be reduced if a company adopts more rigorous approval standards for new credit applicants. Alternatively, the percentage may be increased if economic forecasts signal an economic downturn that would make future defaults more likely.

Determining the estimated bad debts percentage of credit sales may be difficult when a company is in its first year of operation because it has no credit history. In such cases, accountants can consult with trade associations or business associates (other people in the same industry who do have experience) to develop a reasonable estimate of expected losses.

Accounting Events Affecting the 2005 Period

LO2 Explain how the allowance method of accounting for bad debts affects financial statements.

To further illustrate accounting for bad debts, we discuss eight accounting events affecting Allen's Tutoring Services during 2005.

Event 1 Write-Off of an Uncollectible Account Receivable
Allen's Tutoring Services wrote off an uncollectible account receivable with a $70 balance.

This is an asset exchange transaction. The amount of the uncollectible account is removed from the Accounts Receivable account and from the Allowance for Bad Debts account. Since the balances in both the Accounts Receivable and the Allowance accounts decrease, the net realizable value of receivables—and therefore total assets—remains unchanged. The write-off does not affect the income statement. Since the bad debts expense was recognized in the previous year, the expense would be double counted if it were recognized again at the time the uncollectible account is written off. Finally, the statement of cash flows is not affected by the write-off. These effects are shown in the following statements model:

Event No.	Assets			=	Liab.	+	Equity	Rev.	−	Exp.	=	Net Inc.	Cash Flow
	Accts. Rec.	−	Allow.										
1	(70)	−	(70)	=	NA	+	NA	NA	−	NA	=	NA	NA

The computation of the *net realizable value,* before and after the write-off, is shown below.

	Before Write-Off	After Write-Off
Accounts Receivable	$1,500	$1,430
Allowance for Doubtful Accounts	(75)	(5)
Net Realizable Value	$1,425	$1,425

Event 2 Investment in Note Receivable
Allen's Tutoring Services invested in a note receivable.

Mr. Allen realized that he could improve his company's profitability by investing some of the idle cash in his company's growing cash account. On May 1, 2005, Allen's Tutoring Service loaned $12,000 cash to another business. The borrower issued a 9 percent interest-bearing note to Allen's. The note had a one-year term. For Allen's Tutoring Services, the loan represents an investment. The asset account, Cash, decreases; the asset account, Notes Receivable, increases. Total assets are unchanged. The income statement is unaffected. The cash outflow is reported in the investing activities section of the statement of cash flows. These effects are shown here:

Event No.	Assets			=	Liab.	+	Equity	Rev.	–	Exp.	=	Net Inc.	Cash Flow
	Cash	+	Note Rec.										
2	(12,000)	+	12,000	=	NA	+	NA	NA	–	NA	=	NA	(12,000) IA

Event 3 Revenue Recognition
Allen's Tutoring Services provided $10,000 of tutoring services on account during 2005.

Assets (accounts receivable) and stockholders' equity (retained earnings) increase. Recognizing revenue increases net income. Cash flow is not affected. These effects are illustrated below:

Event No.	Assets	=	Liab.	+	Equity	Rev.	–	Exp.	=	Net Inc.	Cash Flow
3	10,000	=	NA	+	10,000	10,000	–	NA	=	10,000	NA

Event 4 Collection of Accounts Receivable
Allen's Tutoring Services collected $8,430 cash from accounts receivable.

The balance in the cash account increases, and the balance in the Accounts Receivable account decreases. Total assets are unaffected. Net income is not affected because revenue was recognized previously. The cash inflow is reported in the operating activities section of the statement of cash flows.

Event No.	Assets			=	Liab.	+	Equity	Rev.	–	Exp.	=	Net Inc.	Cash Flow
	Cash	+	Accts. Rec.										
4	8,430	+	(8,430)	=	NA	+	NA	NA	–	NA	=	NA	8,430 OA

Event 5 Recovery of Bad Debt: Reinstate Receivable
Allen's Tutoring Services recovered a bad debt that was previously written off.

Occasionally, a company receives payment from a customer whose account was previously written off. In such cases, the customer's account should be reinstated and the cash received should be recorded the same way as any other collection on account. The account receivable is reinstated because a complete record of the customer's payment history may be useful if the customer requests credit again at some future date. To illustrate, assume that Allen's Tutoring Services received a $10 cash payment from a customer whose account had previously been written off. The first step is to reinstate the account receivable by reversing the previous write-off. The balances in the Accounts Receivable and the Allowance accounts increase. Since the Allowance is a contra asset account, the increase in it offsets the increase in the Accounts Receivable account, and total assets are unchanged. Net income and cash flow are unaffected. These effects are shown here:

Event No.	Assets			=	Liab.	+	Equity	Rev.	–	Exp.	=	Net Inc.	Cash Flow
	Accts. Rec.	–	Allow.										
5	10	–	10	=	NA	+	NA	NA	–	NA	=	NA	NA

Event 6 Recovery of Bad Debt: Collection of Receivable
Allen's Tutoring Services recorded collection of the reinstated receivable.

The collection of $10 is recorded like any other collection of a receivable account. Cash increases, and accounts receivables account decreases.

Event No.	Assets			=	Liab.	+	Equity	Rev.	−	Exp.	=	Net Inc.	Cash Flow
	Cash	+	Accts. Rec.										
6	10	+	(10)	=	NA	+	NA	NA	−	NA	=	NA	10 OA

Year-End Adjusting Entries

The next two transactions are required to adjust Allen's accounts to make them ready for the preparation of the 2005 financial statements. The adjusting entries are made as of December 31, 2005.

Event 7 Adjustment for Recognition of Bad Debts Expense
Allen's Tutoring Services recognized bad debts expense for 2005.

Assume Allen's estimated 2005 bad debts expense to be 1.35 percent of 2005 credit sales. The amount of bad debts expense would be $135 ($10,000 × 0.0135). Recognizing the $135 bad debts expense decreases both assets (net realizable value of receivables) and stockholders' equity (retained earnings). The expense recognition decreases net income. The statement of cash flows is not affected. The financial statements are affected as shown here:

Event No.	Assets			=	Liab.	+	Equity	Rev.	−	Exp.	=	Net Inc.	Cash Flow
	Accts. Rec.	−	Allow.										
7	NA	−	135	=	NA	+	(135)	NA	−	135	=	(135)	NA

Event 8 Recognition of Interest Revenue
Allen's Tutoring Services recognized interest revenue on the note receivable.

Recall that on May 1, 2005, Allen's Tutoring Services invested $12,000 in a note receivable with a one-year term and a 9 percent annual interest rate. By December 31, 2005, the note had earned $720 ($12,000 × 0.09 × [8 ÷ 12]). Recognizing the earned interest increases assets (interest receivable) and stockholders' equity (retained earnings). The revenue recognition increases net income. Cash flow is not affected. These effects are illustrated below:

Event No.	Assets	=	Liab.	+	Equity	Rev.	−	Exp.	=	Net Inc.	Cash Flow
8	720	=	NA	+	720	720	−	NA	=	720	NA

General Ledger T-Accounts

Exhibit 8–4 displays in T-account form the ledger accounts for the 2005 business events experienced by Allen's Tutoring Services. The entry to close the revenue and expense accounts at the end of the 2005 accounting period is included. The ledger accounts provide the information to prepare the financial statements in Exhibit 8–5. The accounting events are summarized here:

1. Wrote off a $70 uncollectible account receivable.
2. Invested $12,000 in a note receivable.
3. Earned $10,000 of tutoring service revenue on account.
4. Collected $8,430 cash from accounts receivable.

Exhibit 8–4 *General Ledger*

Assets		=	Liabilities		+	Equity	

Cash

Bal.	12,500	12,000	(2)
(4)	8,430		
(6)	10		
Bal.	8,940		

Accounts Receivable

Bal.	1,500	70	(1)
(3)	10,000	8,430	(4)
(5)	10	10	(6)
Bal.	3,000		

Allowance for Doubtful Accounts

(1)	70	75	Bal.
		10	(5)
		135	(7)
		150	Bal.

Notes Receivable

(2)	12,000	
Bal.	12,000	

Interest Receivable

(8)	720	
Bal.	720	

Liabilities

	0	Bal.

Retained Earnings

		13,925	Bal.
		10,585	(cl.)
		24,510	Bal.

Service Revenue

(cl.)	10,000	10,000	(3)
		0	Bal.

Interest Revenue

(cl.)	720	720	(8)
		0	Bal.

Bad Debts Expense

(7)	135	135	(cl.)
Bal.	0		

5. Reinstated a $10 account receivable that had previously been written off.
6. Recorded collection of $10 from the reinstated receivable.
7. Adjusted accounts to recognize $135 of estimated bad debts expense.
8. Adjusted accounts to recognize $720 of accrued interest revenue.
9. Closed the revenue and expense accounts.

The transaction data in the T-accounts for events 1 through 8 are referenced by event number shown in parentheses. Event 9 is referenced with the letters *cl* indicating that journal entry is for closing the accounts.

Analysis of Financial Statements

Exhibit 8–5 displays the 2005 financial statements. Observe that the amount of bad debts expense ($135) differs from the ending balance of the Allowance account ($150). The balance in the Allowance account was $15 before the 2005 adjusting entry for bad debts expense was recorded. At the end of 2004, Allen's Tutoring Services estimated there would be $75 of uncollectible accounts as a result of 2004 credit sales. Actual write-offs, however, amounted to $70 and $10 of that amount was recovered, indicating the actual bad debts expense for 2004 was only $60. Hindsight shows the expense for 2004 was overstated by $15. However, if no estimate had been made, the amount of bad debts expense would have been understated by $60. In some accounting periods estimated bad debts expense will likely be overstated; in others it may be understated. The allowance method cannot produce perfect results, but it does improve the accuracy of the financial statements.

Since no dividends were paid, retained earnings at the end of 2005 equals 2004's retained earnings plus 2005's net income (that is, $13,925 + $10,585 = $24,510). Again, the cash flow from operating activities ($8,440) differs from net income ($10,585) because the statement of cash flows does not include the effects of revenues earned on account or the recognition of bad debts expense.

Exhibit 8–5 *Financial Statements for 2005*

Income Statement		Balance Sheet			Statement of Cash Flows	
Service Revenue	$10,000	Assets			**Operating Activities**	
Bad Debts Exp.	(135)	Cash		$ 8,940	Inflow from Customers	$ 8,440
		Accounts Receivable	$3,000		**Investing Activities**	
Operating Income	9,865	Less: Allowance	(150)		Outflow for the Note Rec.	(12,000)
Interest Revenue	720				**Financing Activities**	0
		Net Realizable Value		2,850		
Net Income	$10,585	Note Receivable		12,000	Net Change in Cash	(3,560)
		Interest Receivable		720	Plus: Beginning Cash Balance	12,500
		Total Assets		$24,510	Ending Cash Balance	$ 8,940
		Stockholders' Equity				
		Retained Earnings		$24,510		

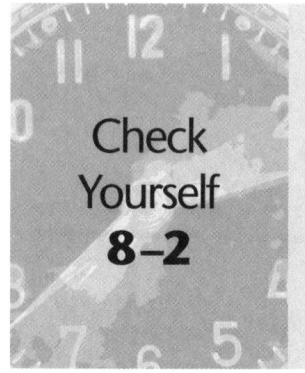

Check Yourself 8–2

Maher Company had beginning balances in Accounts Receivable and Allowance for Doubtful Accounts of $24,200 and $2,000, respectively. During the accounting period Maher earned $230,000 of revenue on account and collected $232,500 of cash from receivables. The company also wrote off $1,950 of uncollectible accounts during the period. Maher estimates bad debts expense will be 1 percent of credit sales. Based on this information, what is the net realizable value of receivables at the end of the period?

Answer The balance in the Accounts Receivable account is $19,750 ($24,200 + $230,000 − $232,500 − $1,950). The amount of bad debts expense for the period is $2,300 ($230,000 × 0.01). The balance in the Allowance for Doubtful Accounts is $2,350 ($2,000 − $1,950 + $2,300). The net realizable value of receivables is therefore $17,400 ($19,750 − $2,350).

Recognition of Bad Debts Expense Using the Direct Write-Off Method

LO3 Show how the direct write-off method of accounting for bad debts affects financial statements.

If the amount of uncollectible accounts is immaterial, generally accepted accounting principles allow companies to use the **direct write-off method** of accounting for bad debts, under which bad debts expense is not recognized until accounts are determined to be uncollectible. The direct write-off method fails to match revenues with expenses and it overstates the net realizable value of receivables. However, if the amount of uncollectible accounts is immaterial, the reporting inaccuracies are accepted as a reasonable trade-off for the recording convenience offered by the direct write-off method.

The direct write-off method does not use estimates, an allowance account, or adjusting entries. Instead, bad debts expense is recorded when uncollectible accounts are identified. Sales or services on account are, as always, recognized in the period in which goods are sold or services are provided. Bad debts expense, however, is recognized in a later period when an account is determined to be uncollectible. To illustrate, assume that the following events apply to Dr. Price's optical services business.

Event 1 Recognition of Revenue Earned on Account
During 2004, the company provided $50,000 of services on account.

The effects of this event are:

Event No.	Assets	=	Liab.	+	Equity	Rev.	−	Exp.	=	Net Inc.	Cash Flow
1	50,000	=	NA	+	50,000	50,000	−	NA	=	50,000	NA

The general journal entry to record the transaction is:

Account Title	Debit	Credit
Accounts Receivable	50,000	
Service Revenue		50,000

There is no year-end adjusting entry made for estimated bad debts expense. Instead, bad debts expense will be recognized when an account is determined to be uncollectible.

Event 2 Recognition of Bad Debts Expense
Assume that Price determines in 2005 that a customer who owes $200 for services delivered in 2004 is unable to pay the amount due.

Writing off the account using the direct write-off method results in recognizing bad debts expense in 2005, even though the associated revenue was recognized in 2004. Financial reporting accuracy is compromised because expenses *are not matched* with related revenues. Such inaccuracies are acceptable only to the extent they are deemed immaterial. The effects of the write-off of the uncollectible account on the financial statements are:

Event No.	Assets	=	Liab.	+	Equity	Rev.	–	Exp.	=	Net Inc.	Cash Flow
2	(200)	=	NA	+	(200)	NA	–	200	=	(200)	NA

In general journal form, the entry to recognize bad debts expense in 2005 is recorded as follows:

Account Title	Debit	Credit
Bad Debts Expense	200	
Accounts Receivable		200

LO4 Explain how accounting for credit card sales affects financial statements.

Accounting for Credit Card Sales

Maintaining accounts receivable is expensive. In addition to bad debts expense, companies extending credit to their customers incur considerable costs for such clerical tasks as running background checks and maintaining customer records. Many businesses find it more efficient to accept third-party credit cards instead of offering credit directly to their customers. Credit card companies service the merchant's credit sales for a fee that typically ranges between 2 and 8 percent of gross sales.

The credit card company provides customers with plastic cards that permit cardholders to charge purchases at various retail outlets. When a sale takes place, the seller records the transaction on a receipt the customer signs. The receipt is forwarded to the credit card company, which immediately pays the merchant.

The credit card company deducts its service fee from the gross amount of the sale, and pays the merchant the net balance (gross amount of sale less credit card fee) in cash. The credit card company collects the gross sale amount directly from the customer. The merchant avoids the risk of bad debts as well as the cost of maintaining customer credit records. To illustrate, assume that the following events apply to Joan Wilson's consulting practice.

Event 1 Recognition of Revenue and Expense on Credit Card Sales
Wilson accepts a credit card payment for $1,000 of services rendered to one of her customers.

Assume the credit card company charges a 5 percent fee for handling the transaction ($1,000 × 0.05 = $50). Wilson's income increases by the amount of revenue ($1,000) and decreases by the amount of the credit card expense ($50). Net income increases by $950. The event increases an asset, accounts receivable, due from the credit card company, and stockholders' equity (retained earnings) by $950 ($1,000 revenue − $50 credit card expense). Cash flow is not affected. These effects are shown here:

Event No.	Assets	=	Liab.	+	Equity	Rev.	−	Exp.	=	Net Inc.	Cash Flow
1	950	=	NA	+	950	1,000	−	50	=	950	NA

In general journal form, the entry to record the transaction is as follows:

Account Title	Debit	Credit
Accounts Receivable—Credit Card Company	950	
Credit Card Expense	50	
Service Revenue		1,000

Event 2 Collection of Credit Card Receivable
The collection of the receivable due from the credit card company is recorded like any other receivable collection.

When Wilson collects the net amount of $950 ($1,000 − $50) from the credit card company, one asset account (Cash) increases and another asset account (Accounts Receivable) decreases. Total assets are not affected. The income statement is not affected. A $950 cash inflow is reported in the operating activities section of the statement of cash flows. These effects are illustrated below:

Event No.	Assets			=	Liab.	+	Equity	Rev.	−	Exp.	=	Net Inc.	Cash Flow
	Cash	+	Accts. Rec.										
2	950	+	(950)	=	NA	+	NA	NA	−	NA	=	NA	950 OA

The following entry records the transaction in the general journal.

Account Title	Debit	Credit
Cash	950	
Accounts Receivable—Credit Card Company		950

Warranty Obligations

LO5 Explain how accounting for warranty obligations affects financial statements.

To attract customers, many companies guarantee their products or services. Such guarantees are called **warranties.** Warranties take many forms. Usually, they extend for a specified period of time. Within this period, the seller promises to replace or repair defective products without charge. While the amount and timing of warranty obligations are uncertain, warranties usually represent legal liabilities that must be reported in the financial statements.

To illustrate accounting for warranty obligations, assume Perfect Picture Frame (PPF) Company had cash of $2,000, inventory of $6,000, common stock of $5,000, and retained earnings of $3,000 on January 1, 2005. The 2005 accounting period is affected by three accounting events: (1) sale of merchandise under warranty; (2) recognition of warranty obligations to customers who purchased the merchandise; and (3) settlement of a customer's warranty claim.

Event 1 Sale of Merchandise
PPF sold for $7,000 cash merchandise that had cost $4,000.

In the statements model displayed here, revenue from the sale is referenced as 1a and the cost of the sale as 1b. The effects of the sales transaction on the financial statements are shown below:

Event No.	Assets			=	Liab.	+	Equity	Rev.	−	Exp.	=	Net Inc.	Cash Flow
	Cash	+	Inventory										
1a	7,000	+	NA	=	NA	+	7,000	7,000	−	NA	=	7,000	7,000 OA
1b	NA	+	(4,000)	=	NA	+	(4,000)	NA	−	4,000	=	(4,000)	NA

Event 2 Recognition of Warranty Expense
PPF guaranteed the merchandise sold in event 1 to be free from defects for one year following the date of sale.

Although the exact amount of future warranty claims is unknown, PPF must inform financial statement users of the company's obligation. PPF must estimate the amount of the warranty liability and report the estimate in the 2005 financial statements. Assume the warranty obligation is estimated to be $100. Recognizing this obligation increases liabilities (warranties payable) and reduces stockholders' equity (retained earnings). Recognizing the warranty expense reduces net income. The statement of cash flows is not affected when the obligation and the corresponding expense are recognized. These effects follow:

Event No.	Assets	=	Liab.	+	Equity	Rev.	−	Exp.	=	Net Inc.	Cash Flow
2	NA	=	100	+	(100)	NA	−	100	=	(100)	NA

Event 3 Settlement of Warranty Obligation
PPF paid $40 cash to repair defective merchandise returned by a customer.

The cash payment for the repair is not an expense. Warranty expense was recognized in the period in which the sale was made (when the Warranties Payable account was created). The payment reduces an asset (cash) and a liability (warranties payable). The income statement is not affected by the repairs payment. However, there is a $40 cash outflow reported in the operating activities section of the statement of cash flows.

Event No.	Assets	=	Liab.	+	Equity	Rev.	−	Exp.	=	Net Inc.	Cash Flow
3	(40)	=	(40)	+	NA	NA	−	NA	=	NA	(40) OA

General Ledger T-Accounts and Financial Statements

Exhibit 8–6 presents in T-account form the ledger accounts for the business events experienced by PPF. The entry to close the revenue and expense accounts at the end of the 2005 accounting period is included. The ledger accounts provide the information to prepare the financial statements in Exhibit 8–7. The accounting events are summarized here:

Transactions for 2005

1. Sold merchandise that cost $4,000 for $7,000 cash.
2. Recognized a $100 warranty obligation and the corresponding expense.

Exhibit 8–6 *General Ledger*

Assets				=	Liabilities				+	Equity	

Cash

Bal.	2,000	40	(3)
(1a)	7,000		
Bal.	8,960		

Inventory

Bal.	6,000	4,000	(1b)
Bal.	2,000		

Warranties Payable

(3)	40	100	(2)
		60	Bal.

Common Stock

	5,000	Bal.

Retained Earnings

	3,000	Bal.
	2,900	(cl.)
	5,900	Bal.

Sales Revenue

(cl.)	7,000	7,000	(1a)
		0	Bal.

Cost of Goods Sold

(1b)	4,000	4,000	(cl.)
Bal.	0		

Warranty Expense

(2)	100	100	(cl.)
Bal.	0		

Exhibit 8–7 *Financial Statements for 2005*

Income Statement		Balance Sheet		Statement of Cash Flows	
Sales Revenue	$7,000	Assets		**Operating Activities**	
Cost of Goods Sold	(4,000)	Cash	$ 8,960	Inflow from Customers	$7,000
		Inventory	2,000	Outflow for Warranty	(40)
Gross Margin	3,000				
Warranty Exp.	(100)	Total Assets	$10,960	Net Inflow from	
				Operating Activities	6,960
Net Income	$2,900	Liabilities		**Investing Activities**	0
		Warranties Payable	$ 60	**Financing Activities**	0
		Stockholders' Equity			
		Common Stock	5,000	Net Change in Cash	6,960
		Retained Earnings	5,900	Plus: Beginning Cash Balance	2,000
		Total Liab. and Stockholders' Equity	$10,960	Ending Cash Balance	$8,960

3. Paid $40 to satisfy a warranty claim.
4. Closed the revenue and expense accounts.

The transaction data in the T-accounts for events 1 through 3 are referenced by event number shown in parentheses. Event 4 is referenced with the letters *cl* indicating that journal entry is for closing the accounts.

THE FINANCIAL ANALYST

Topic Tackler

PLUS

8–2

Costs of Credit Sales

As mentioned earlier, two costs of extending credit to customers are bad debts expense and record-keeping costs. These costs can be significant. Large companies spend literally millions of dollars to buy the equipment and pay the staff necessary to operate entire departments devoted to managing accounts receivable. Further, there is an implicit interest charge associated

Most electrical appliances come with a manufacturer's warranty that obligates the manufacturer to pay for defects that occur during some designated period of time after the point of sale. Why would Circuit City issue warranties that obligate it to pay for defects that occur after the manufacturer's warranty has expired? Warranties are in fact insurance policies that generate profits. Indeed, the Circuit City Group reported that the gross dollar sales from extended warranty programs were 3.6 percent of its total sales in fiscal year 2003. Even more important, Circuit City notes that gross profit margins on products sold with extended warranties are higher than the gross profit margins on products sold without extended warranties. It should be noted that warranties produce revenues for manufacturers as well as retailers. The only difference is that the revenues generated from manufacturer's warranties are embedded in the sales price. Indeed, products with longer, more comprehensive warranties usually sell at higher prices than products with shorter, less extensive warranties.

with extending credit. When a customer is permitted to delay payment, the creditor foregoes the opportunity to invest the amount the customer owes.

LO6 Explain the effects of the cost of financing credit sales.

Exhibit 8–8 presents part of a footnote from the 2002 annual report of PepsiCo, Inc. This excerpt provides insight into the credit costs real companies incur. First, observe that PepsiCo was owed $2.65 billion of accounts receivable. These receivables represent money that could be in the bank earning interest if all sales had been made in cash. If PepsiCo could have earned interest at 5 percent on that money, the opportunity cost of this lost interest is approximately $132.5 million ($2.65 billion $\times$ .05) a year. Next, observe that PepsiCo expects to have uncollectible accounts amounting to $116 million (balance in the allowance account). These are indeed significant costs.

Average Number of Days to Collect Accounts Receivable

The longer it takes to collect accounts receivable, the greater the opportunity cost of lost income. Also, business experience indicates that the older an account receivable becomes, the less likely it is to be collected. Finally, taking longer to collect an account typically costs more for salaries, equipment, and supplies used in the process of trying to collect it. Businesses are therefore concerned about how long it takes to collect their receivables.

Two ratios help management, or other users, measure a company's collection period. One is the **accounts receivable turnover ratio**, computed as:[3]

$$\frac{\text{Sales}}{\text{Accounts receivable}}$$

Exhibit 8–8

PepsiCo Dec. 28, 2002
PARTIAL FOOTNOTE regarding Allowance for Doubtful Accounts (amounts are shown in millions)

Note 14 Supplemental Financial Information

	2002	2001
Accounts receivable:		
Trade receivables	$1,924	$1,663
Other receivables	723	600
	2,647	2,263
Allowance, beginning of year	121	126
Charged to expense	38	41
Other additions (a)	3	2
Deductions (b)	(46)	(48)
Allowance, end of year	116	121
Net receivables	$2,531	$2,142

---

[3]To be more precise, the ratio could be computed using only credit sales and average accounts receivable. Usually, however, companies do not report credit sales separately from cash sales in published financial statements. Average accounts receivable, if desired, is computed as ([beginning receivables + ending receivables] ÷ 2). For this course, use the simpler computation shown here (sales ÷ accounts receivable).

Dividing a company's sales by its accounts receivable tells how many times the accounts receivable balance is "turned over" (converted into cash) each year. The higher the turnover, the shorter the collection period. To simplify its interpretation, the accounts receivable turnover ratio is often taken one step further to determine the **average number of days to collect accounts receivable,** sometimes called the *average collection period.* This is computed as:

$$\frac{365}{\text{Accounts receivable turnover ratio}}$$

This ratio measures how many days, on average, it takes a company to collect its accounts receivable. Since longer collection periods increase costs, shorter periods are obviously more desirable. To illustrate computing the *average number of days to collect accounts receivable* ratio for Allen's Tutoring Services, refer to the 2005 financial statements in Exhibit 8–5. On average, the company takes 104 days to collect its receivables, computed in two steps:

1. The accounts receivable turnover is 3.509 ($10,000 ÷ $2,850) times.
2. The average number of days to collect receivables is 104 (365 ÷ 3.509) days.

In the preceding computations, the net realizable value of accounts receivable was used because that is the amount typically reported in published financial statements. The results would not have been materially different had total accounts receivable been used.

Real-World Data

What is the collection period for real companies? The time required to collect receivables varies among industries and among companies within industries. Column 4 in Exhibit 8–9 displays the average number of days to collect receivables for eight companies in three different industries. These numbers are for the 2002 calendar year.

Since fast-food restaurants require customers to pay cash when they purchase hamburgers or coffee, why do these companies have accounts receivable? The accounts receivable for **Domino's**, **McDonald's**, and **Starbucks** arise because these companies sell goods to restaurants that are independent franchisees. So, for example, Domino's accounts receivable represents future collections from restaurant owners, not customers who purchase pepperoni pizzas.

Are the collection periods for **Mondavi** and **Chalone Wine Group** too long? The answer depends on their credit policies. If they are selling goods to customers on net 30-day terms, there may be reason for concern, but if they allow customers 90 days to pay and the cost of this policy has been built into their pricing structure, the collection periods may not be unreasonable.

Some companies allow their customers extended time to pay their bills because the customers would otherwise have difficulty coming up with the money. For example, Mondavi

Exhibit 8–9

Industry	Company	Average Days to Sell Inventory	Average Days to Collect Receivables	Length of Operating Cycle
Fast Food	Domino's	9	16	25
	McDonald's	10	21	31
	Starbucks	65	10	75
Office Supplies	Office Depot	58	25	83
	OfficeMax	92	7	99
	Staples	64	11	75
Wine	Chalone	642	74	716
	Mondavi	548	82	630

may sell to a wine retailer that does not have the cash available to pay immediately. If Mondavi allows the retailer sufficient time, the retailer can sell the wine to customers and obtain the cash it needs to pay Mondavi. Many small companies do not have cash available to pay up front. Buying on credit is the only way they can obtain the inventory they need. If a manufacturer or wholesaler wants to sell to such companies, credit sales represent the only option available.

The **operating cycle** is defined as the average time it takes a business to convert inventory to accounts receivable plus the time it takes to convert accounts receivable into cash. The average number of days to collect receivables ratio is one component of the operating cycle for a particular company. The other component is the average number of days to sell inventory ratio that was explained in Chapter 6. The length of the operating cycles for the real-world companies discussed herein is shown in the last column of Exhibit 8–9.

What is the significance of the different operating cycle lengths in Exhibit 8–9? As previously explained, the longer the operating cycle takes, the more it costs the company. Exhibit 8–9 shows it takes **OfficeMax** an average of 24 days longer than Staples to complete an operating cycle. All other things being equal, approximately how much did this longer time reduce OfficeMax's earnings? Assume OfficeMax could invest excess cash at 8 percent (or alternatively, assume it pays 8 percent to finance its inventory and accounts receivable). Using the accounting information reported in OfficeMax's January 25, 2003, financial statements, we can answer the question as follows:

OfficeMax's investment in inventory	×	Interest rate	×	Time	=	Cost
$906,253,000	×	8%	×	24/365		$4,767,139

With 3.69 operating cycles per year (365 ÷ 99), the extended operating cycle costs OfficeMax $17.6 million annually. Based on the assumptions used here, OfficeMax would increase its after-tax net earnings by approximately 15 percent if it could reduce its operating cycle by 24 days. Although this illustration is a rough estimate, it demonstrates that it is important for businesses to minimize the length of their operating cycles.

focus on INTERNATIONAL ISSUES

A Rose by Any Other Name . . .

If a person who studied U.S. GAAP wanted to look at the financial statements of a non-U.S. company, choosing statements of a company from another English-speaking country might seem logical. Presumably, this would eliminate language differences, and only the differences in GAAP would remain. Unfortunately, this is not true.

When an accountant in the United States uses the term *turnover,* she or he is usually thinking of a financial ratio, such as the accounts receivable turnover ratio. However, in the United Kingdom, the term *turnover* refers to what U.S. accountants call *sales.* U.K. balance sheets do not usually show an account named *Inventory;* rather, they use the term *Stocks.* In the United States, accountants typically use the term *stocks* to refer to certificates representing ownership in a corporation. Finally, if an accountant or banker from the United Kingdom should ever ask you about your *gearing ratio,* he or she probably is not interested in your bicycle but in your debt to assets ratio.

Randolph Corporation had sales for the year of $535,333 and an Accounts Receivable balance at year end of $22,000. Determine Randolph's average number of days to collect accounts receivable.

Answer The accounts receivable turnover is 24.33 ($535,333 ÷ $22,000) times per year. The average number of days to collect accounts receivable is 15 (365 ÷ 24.33).

a look back

Accounting for receivables and payables was first introduced in Chapter 2. This chapter presented additional complexities related to short-term receivables and payables, such as the *allowance method of accounting for bad debts.* The allowance method improves matching of expenses with revenues. This chapter illustrated the percent of sales method of estimating bad debts expense. Under this method bad debts expense is estimated to be a certain percentage of credit sales. For example, if credit sales were $500,000 and bad debts were estimated to be 1 percent of credit sales, then bad debts expense would be $5,000 ($500,000 × .01). This is an estimate of the uncollectible accounts that will occur in the future. The estimated amount of bad debts expense is recognized in the same period in which the associated revenue is recognized, thereby matching bad debts expense with the revenue. Bad debts expense decreases stockholders' equity, net income, and the net realizable value of receivables (accounts receivable − allowance for doubtful accounts).

The allowance method of accounting for bad debts is contrasted with the *direct write-off method,* which recognizes bad debts expense when an account is determined to be uncollectible. The method is conceptually inferior because it overstates the value of accounts receivable reported on the balance sheet and it fails to match expenses with related revenues. However, the direct write-off method is easier to apply and may be used when the amount of bad debts is insignificant. When bad debts are immaterial, the benefits of recording convenience outweigh a need for conceptual accuracy.

This chapter also discussed accounting for *warranty obligations.* The amount of warranty expense is recognized in the period in which warranteed sales are made or services provided. Warranty obligations are reported as liabilities on the balance sheet until the future period when they are settled.

Finally, the chapter discussed the costs of making credit sales. In addition to bad debts, interest is a major cost of financing receivables. Determining the length of the collection period provides a measure of the quality of receivables. Short collection periods usually indicate low amounts of uncollectible accounts and interest cost. Long collection periods imply higher costs. The collection period can be measured in two steps. First, determine the *accounts receivable turnover ratio* by dividing sales by the accounts receivable balance. Next, determine the *average number of days to collect accounts receivable* by dividing the number of days in the year (365) by the accounts receivable turnover ratio.

a look forward

Chapter 9 discusses accounting for long-term assets such as buildings and equipment. As with inventory cost flow, discussed in Chapter 6, GAAP allows companies to use different accounting methods to report on similar types of business events. Life would be easier for accounting students if all companies used the same accounting methods. However, the business world is a complicated place. For the foreseeable future, people are likely to continue to have diverse views as to the best way to account for a variety of business transactions. To function effectively in today's business environment, it is important for you to be able to recognize differences in reporting practices.

APPENDIX

LO7 Show how discount notes and related interest charges affect financial statements.

Accounting for Discount Notes

All notes payable discussed previously have been "add-on" **interest-bearing notes.** At maturity, the amount due is the *face value* of the note *plus accrued interest.* In contrast, interest on a **discount note** is included in the face value of the note. A $5,000 face value discount note is repaid with $5,000 cash at maturity. This payment includes both principal and accrued interest. To illustrate, assume the following four events apply to Beacon Management Services.

Event 1 Borrowing by Issuing a Discount Note
Beacon Management Services was started when it issued a $10,000 face value discount note to State Bank on March 1, 2001.

The note had a 9 percent *discount rate* and a one-year term to maturity. As with interest-bearing notes, the **issuer of the note** exchanges the promissory note for cash. The first step in accounting for the discount note is to divide the face amount between the discount and the principal (amount borrowed). The discount is computed by multiplying the face value of the note by the interest rate by the time period. In this case, the discount is $900 ($10,000 × 0.09 × 1). The amount borrowed is determined by subtracting the discount from the face value of the note ($10,000 − $900 = $9,100). In this case the **principal** (the amount of cash borrowed) is $9,100, and the **discount** (the amount of interest to be incurred over the term of the loan) is $900.

On the issue date, assets and liabilities increase by the amount borrowed (the $9,100 principal). The income statement is not affected by the borrowing transaction on the issue date. The $9,100 cash inflow is reported in the financing activities section of the statement of cash flows. These effects follow:

Event No.	Assets	=	Liab.	+	Equity	Rev.	−	Exp.	=	Net Inc.	Cash Flow
1	9,100	=	9,100	+	NA	NA	−	NA	=	NA	9,100 FA

For internal record-keeping purposes, the amount of the discount is normally recorded in a **contra liability account** titled **Discount on Notes Payable**. The *carrying value* of the liability is the difference between the notes payable account and the discount account. Carrying value, also known as *book value,* is so called because it is the amount at which the liability is shown (carried) on the books. In this case, the Notes Payable account in Beacon's ledger has a $10,000 credit balance and the Discount on Notes Payable account has a $900 debit balance. The carrying value on the issue date is computed as follows:

Notes Payable	$10,000
Discount on Notes Payable	(900)
Carrying value of liability	$ 9,100

Event 2 Recognition of Operating Expenses
Beacon incurred $8,000 of cash operating expenses.

Paying these expenses reduces assets and stockholders' equity. The effect on the income statement is to increase expenses and decrease net income. The cash outflow is reported in the operating activities section of the statement of cash flows. These effects are shown below:

Event No.	Assets	=	Liab.	+	Equity	Rev.	−	Exp.	=	Net Inc.	Cash Flow
2	(8,000)	=	NA	+	(8,000)	NA	−	8,000	=	(8,000)	(8,000) OA

Event 3 Recognition of Revenue
Beacon recognized $12,000 of cash revenue.

Recognizing the revenue increases assets and stockholders' equity. Net income increases. The cash inflow is reported in the operating activities section of the statement of cash flows. These effects follow.

Event No.	Assets	=	Liab.	+	Equity	Rev.	−	Exp.	=	Net Inc.	Cash Flow
3	12,000	=	NA	+	12,000	12,000	−	NA	=	12,000	12,000 OA

Event 4 Adjustment for Accrued Interest
Beacon recognized accrued interest expense.

On December 31, 2001, Beacon must adjust its accounting records to recognize 10 months of interest expense incurred in the 2001 accounting period. For this note, interest expense accrues at $75 per month ($900 discount ÷ 12). As of December 31, $750 ($75 × 10) of interest expense has accrued. Since no cash payment is due until the note matures in 2002, the reduction in equity from recognizing the interest expense is accompanied by an increase in liabilities.

The increase in liabilities is recorded by *reducing the contra liability account,* Discount on Notes Payable. Recall that the carrying value of the liability was $9,100 on the day the note was issued. The adjusting entry to record the accrued interest expense removes $750 from the discount account, leaving a discount balance of $150 ($900 − $750) after the adjusting entry is posted.

The bookkeeping technique of converting the discount to interest expense over the term of the loan is described as **amortizing** the discount. After amortizing 10 months' interest expense, the carrying value of the liability reported on the December 31, 2001, balance sheet in Exhibit 8–11 is $9,850 ($10,000 face value − $150 discount). The effect of the interest recognition on the income statement is to increase expenses and decrease net income by $750. The statement of cash flows is not affected by the accrual. Cash is paid for the interest at the maturity date. The effects of the adjusting entry for accrued interest expense follow.

Event No.	Assets	=	Liab.	+	Equity	Rev.	−	Exp.	=	Net Inc.	Cash Flow
4	NA	=	750	+	(750)	NA	−	750	=	(750)	NA

General Ledger T-Accounts and Financial Statements

Exhibit 8–10 displays in T-account form the ledger accounts for the business events experienced by Beacon Management Services. The entry to close the revenue and expense accounts at the end of the 2001 accounting period is included. The ledger accounts provide the information to prepare the financial statements in Exhibit 8–11. The accounting events are summarized here:

1. Issued a $10,000 face value, 1-year, discount note with a 9 percent discount rate.
2. Paid $8,000 cash for operating expenses.
3. Earned $12,000 cash revenue.
4. Recognized $750 of accrued interest expense.
5. Closed the revenue and expense accounts. The letters *cl* are the posting reference for the closing entries.

Exhibit 8–10 *General Ledger*

	Assets		=	Liabilities		+	Equity	
	Cash			**Notes Payable**			**Retained Earnings**	
(1)	9,100	8,000 (2)			10,000 (1)			3,250 (cl.)
(3)	12,000				10,000 Bal.			3,250 Bal.
Bal.	13,100							

	Discount on Notes Payable			**Service Revenue**	
(1)	900	750 (4)	(cl.)	12,000	12,000 (3)
Bal.	150				0 Bal.

	Operating Expenses	
(2)	8,000	8,000 (cl.)
Bal.	0	

	Interest Expense	
(4)	750	750 (cl.)
Bal.	0	

Exhibit 8–11 *Financial Statements for 2001*

Income Statement		Balance Sheet			Statement of Cash Flows	
Service Revenue	$12,000	Assets			**Operating Activities**	
Operating Exp.	(8,000)	Cash		$13,100	Inflow from Customers	$12,000
					Outflow for Expenses	(8,000)
Operating Income	4,000	Liabilities				
Interest Exp.	(750)	Notes Payable	$10,000		Net Inflow from	
		Less: Disc. on Notes Pay.	(150)		Operating Activities	4,000
Net Income	$ 3,250					
		Total Liabilities		$ 9,850	**Investing Activities**	0
		Stockholders' Equity			**Financing Activities**	
		Retained Earnings		3,250	Inflow from Creditors	9,100
		Total Liab. and Stockholders' Equity		$13,100	Net Change in Cash	13,100
					Plus: Beginning Cash Balance	0
					Ending Cash Balance	$13,100

Accounting Events Affecting the 2002 Period

This section illustrates four accounting events that apply to Beacon's 2002 accounting cycle.

LO7 Show how discount notes and related interest charges affect financial statements.

Event 1 Accrual of Interest for 2002
Beacon recognized 2 months of accrued interest.

Since the note had a one-year term, interest for two months remains to be accrued at the maturity date on March 1, 2002. Since interest expense accrues at $75 per month ($900 discount ÷ 12), there is $150 ($75 × 2) of interest expense to recognize in 2002. Recognizing the interest increases liabilities (the discount account is reduced to zero) and decreases stockholders' equity. The effect of the interest recognition on the income statement is to increase expenses and decrease net income by $150. The statement of cash flows is not affected by the interest recognition. These effects follow:

Event No.	Assets	=	Liab.	+	Equity	Rev.	–	Exp.	=	Net Inc.	Cash Flow
1	NA	=	150	+	(150)	NA	–	150	=	(150)	NA

Event 2 Payment of Face Value
Beacon repaid the face value of the discount note.

The face value ($10,000) of the note is due on the maturity date. The repayment of the note is an asset use transaction that decreases both assets and liabilities. The income statement is not affected by the repayment. The $10,000 cash payment includes $900 for interest and $9,100 for principal. On the statement of cash flows a $900 outflow for interest is reported in the operating activities section and a $9,100 outflow for repaying the loan is reported in the financing activities section. These effects follow:

Event No.	Assets	=	Liab.	+	Equity	Rev.	–	Exp.	=	Net Inc.	Cash Flow
2	(10,000)	=	(10,000)	+	NA	NA	–	NA	=	NA	(900) OA (9,100) FA

Event 3 Revenue Recognition
Beacon recognized $13,000 of cash revenue.

Recognizing the revenue increases assets and stockholders' equity. Net income also increases. The cash inflow is reported in the operating activities section of the statement of cash flows. These effects follow:

Event No.	Assets	=	Liab.	+	Equity	Rev.	–	Exp.	=	Net Inc.	Cash Flow
3	13,000	=	NA	+	13,000	13,000	–	NA	=	13,000	13,000 OA

Event 4 Recognition of Operating Expenses
Beacon incurred $8,500 of cash operating expenses.

This event decreases assets and stockholders' equity. Net income also decreases. The cash outflow is reported in the operating activities section of the statement of cash flows. These effects follow:

Event No.	Assets	=	Liab.	+	Equity	Rev.	−	Exp.	=	Net Inc.	Cash Flow
4	(8,500)	=	NA	+	(8,500)	NA	−	8,500	=	(8,500)	(8,500) OA

General Ledger T-Accounts and Financial Statements
Exhibits 8–12 and 8–13 present the relevant ledger T-accounts and financial statements, respectively. Notice in Exhibit 8–13 that no liabilities are reported because both interest and principal have been paid, leaving Beacon with no obligations as of the 2002 fiscal closing date. Since no dividends were paid to owners during 2001 or 2002, retained earnings includes the total of net income for 2001 and 2002.

Exhibit 8–12 *General Ledger*

Assets				=	Liabilities				+	Equity			
Cash					**Notes Payable**					**Retained Earnings**			
Bal.	13,100	10,000	(2)		(2)	10,000	10,000	Bal.				3,250	Bal.
(3)	13,000	8,500	(4)				0	Bal.				4,350	(cl.)
Bal.	7,600											7,600	Bal.

				Discount on Notes Payable					**Service Revenue**			
				Bal.	150	150	(1)	(cl.)	13,000	13,000	(3)
				Bal.	0					0	Bal.

							Operating Expense			
						(4)	8,500	8,500	(cl.)
						Bal.	0		

							Interest Expense			
						(1)	150	150	(cl.)
						Bal.	0		

Exhibit 8–13 *Financial Statements for 2002*

Income Statement			Balance Sheet			Statement of Cash Flows		
Service Revenue	$13,000		Assets			**Operating Activities**		
Operating Expenses	(8,500)		Cash		$7,600	Inflow from Customers		$13,000
						Outflow for Expenses		(8,500)
Operating Income	4,500		Liabilities		$ 0	Outflow for Interest		(900)
Interest Exp.	(150)							
			Stockholders' Equity			Net Inflow from		
Net Income	$ 4,350		Retained Earnings		7,600	Operating Activities		3,600
			Total Liab. and Stockholders' Equity		$7,600	**Investing Activities**		0
						Financing Activities		
						Outflow to Creditors		(9,100)
						Net Change in Cash		(5,500)
						Plus: Beginning Cash Balance		13,100
						Ending Cash Balance		$ 7,600

SELF-STUDY REVIEW PROBLEM

During 2007 Calico Company experienced the following accounting events:

1. Provided $120,000 of services on account.
2. Collected $85,000 cash from accounts receivable.

3. Wrote off $1,800 of accounts receivable that were uncollectible.
4. Paid $90,500 cash for operating expenses.
5. Estimated that bad debts expense would be 2 percent of credit sales. Recorded the adjusting entry.
6. Estimated warranty expense would be $900. Recorded the adjusting entry.

The following ledger accounts present the balances in Calico Company's records on January 1, 2007.

Event No.	Assets				=	Liabilities	+	Equity		
	Cash	+	Accts. Rec.	− Allow.	=	War. Pay.	+	C. Stk.	+	Ret. Ear.
Bal.	12,000	+	18,000	− 2,200	=	NA	+	20,000	+	7,800

Required

a. Record the 2007 accounting events in the ledger accounts.
b. Determine net income for 2007.
c. Determine net cash flow from operating activities for 2007.
d. Determine the net realizable value of accounts receivable at December 31, 2007.

Solution to Requirement *a*.

Event No.	Assets				=	Liabilities	+	Equity		
	Cash	+	Accts. Rec.	− Allow.	=	War. Pay.	+	C. Stk.	+	Ret. Ear.
Bal.	12,000	+	18,000	− 2,200	=	NA	+	20,000	+	7,800
1	NA	+	120,000	− NA	=	NA	+	NA	+	120,000
2	85,000	+	(85,000)	− NA	=	NA	+	NA	+	NA
3	NA	+	(1,800)	− (1,800)	=	NA	+	NA	+	NA
4	(90,500)	+	NA	− NA	=	NA	+	NA	+	(90,500)
5	NA	+	NA	− 2,400	=	NA	+	NA	+	(2,400)
6	NA	+	NA	− NA	=	900	+	NA	+	(900)
Totals	6,500	+	51,200	− 2,800	=	900	+	20,000	+	34,000

Solution to Requirements *b–d*.
b. Net income is $26,200 ($120,000 − $90,500 − $2,400 − $900).
c. Net cash flow from operating activities is an outflow of $5,500 ($85,000 − $90,500).
d. The net realizable value of accounts receivable is $48,400 ($51,200 − $2,800).

KEY TERMS

Accounts receivable *359*
Accounts receivable turnover ratio *373*
Allowance for Doubtful Accounts *361*
Allowance method of accounting for bad debts *360*

Amortization *378*
Average number of days to collect accounts receivable *374*
Bad debts expense *361*
Contra liability account *377*
Direct write-off method *368*

Discount *377*
Discount notes *376*
Discount on Notes Payable *377*
Going concern assumption *360*
Interest-bearing notes *376*
Issuer of the note *377*

Net realizable value *360, 361*
Notes receivable *359*
Operating cycle *375*
Payables *359*
Principal *377*
Warranty *370*

QUESTIONS

1. What is the difference between accounts receivable and notes receivable?
2. What is the *net realizable value* of receivables?
3. Explain the *going concern* assumption. How does it affect the way accounts receivable versus accounts payable are reported in financial statements?
4. What is the difference between the allowance method and the direct write-off method of accounting for bad debts?
5. What is the most common format for reporting accounts receivable on the balance sheet? What information does this method provide beyond showing only the net amount?

6. What are two ways in which estimating bad debts improves the accuracy of the financial statements?
7. Why is it necessary to make an entry to reinstate a previously written off account receivable before the collection is recorded?
8. What are some factors considered in estimating the amount of uncollectible accounts receivable?
9. What is the effect on the accounting equation of recognizing bad debts expense?
10. What is the effect on the accounting equation of writing off an uncollectible account receivable when the allowance method is used? When the direct write-off method is used?
11. How does the recovery of a bad debt affect the income statement when the allowance method is used? How does the recovery of a bad debt affect the statement of cash flows when the allowance method is used?
12. What is the advantage of using the allowance method of accounting for bad debts? What is the advantage of using the direct write-off method?
13. When is it acceptable to use the direct write-off method of accounting for bad debts?
14. Why is it generally beneficial for a business to accept major credit cards as payment for goods and services even when the fee charged by the credit card company is substantial?
15. What types of costs do businesses avoid when they accept major credit cards as compared with handling credit sales themselves?
16. What does the term *warranty* mean?
17. What effect does recognizing warranty expense have on the balance sheet? On the income statement?
18. When is warranty cost reported on the statement of cash flows?
19. How is the accounts receivable turnover ratio computed? What information does the ratio provide?
20. How is the average number of days to collect accounts receivable computed? What information does the ratio provide?
21. Is accounting terminology standard in all countries? What term is used in the United Kingdom to refer to *sales?* What term is used to refer to *inventory?* What is a *gearing ratio?* Is it important to know about these differences?
22. What is the difference between an interest-bearing note and a discount note?
23. How is the carrying value of a discount note computed?
24. Will the effective rate of interest be the same on a $10,000 face value, 12 percent interest-bearing note and a $10,000 face value, 12 percent discount note? Is the amount of cash received upon making these two loans the same? Why or why not?
25. How does the *amortization* of a discount affect the income statement, balance sheet, and statement of cash flows?
26. What is the effect on the accounting equation of borrowing $8,000 by issuing a discount note that has a 10 percent discount rate and a one-year term to maturity? What is the effect on the accounting equation of the periodic amortization of the discount? What is the effect on the accounting equation of the payment of the face value of the note at maturity?
27. What type of account is Discount on Notes Payable?

EXERCISES—SERIES A

 All Exercises in Series A are available with McGraw-Hill's Homework Manager

L.O. 2   EXERCISE 8–1A *Effect of Recognizing Bad Debts Expense on Financial Statements: Allowance Method*

Big A's Auto Service was started on January 1, 2005. The company experienced the following events during its first year of operation.

Events affecting 2005
1. Provided $30,000 of repair services on account.
2. Collected $25,000 cash from accounts receivable.
3. Adjusted the accounting records to reflect the estimate that bad debt expense would be 1 percent of the service revenue on account.

Events affecting 2006
1. Wrote off a $280 account receivable that was determined to be uncollectible.
2. Provided $35,000 of repair services on account.
3. Collected $31,000 cash from accounts receivable.
4. Adjusted the accounting records to reflect the estimate that bad debt expense would be 1 percent of the service revenue on account.

Required
a. Record the events for 2005 in T-accounts.
b. Determine the following amounts:
   (1) Net income for 2005.
   (2) Net cash flow from operating activities for 2005.
   (3) Balance of accounts receivable at the end of 2005.
   (4) Net realizable value of accounts receivable at the end of 2005.
c. Repeat Requirements *a* and *b* for the 2006 accounting period.

EXERCISE 8–2A *Analyzing Financial Statement Effects of Accounting for Bad Debts Using   **L.O. 2**
                    the Allowance Method*

Gray Bros. uses the allowance method to account for bad debts expense. Gray experienced the following four events in 2005:

1. Recognition of $48,000 of revenue on account.
2. Collection of $42,000 cash from accounts receivable.
3. Determination that $300 of its accounts were not collectible and wrote off these receivables.
4. Recognition of bad debts expense for the year. Gray estimates that bad debts expense will be 2 percent of its sales.

Required
Show the effect of each of these event on the elements of the financial statements, using a horizontal statements model like the following one. Use + for increase, − for decrease, and NA for not affected. In the cash flow column, indicate whether the item is an operating activity (OA), investing activity (IA), or financing activity (FA).

Event No.	Assets			=	Liab.	+	Equity						
	Cash	+ A. Rec.	− Allow.	=			Ret. Earn.	Rev.	−	Exp.	=	Net Inc.	Cash Flow

EXERCISE 8–3A *Analyzing Account Balances for a Company Using the Allowance Method of   **L.O. 2**
                    Accounting for Bad Debts*

The following account balances come from the records of Teton Company.

	Beginning Balance	Ending Balance
Accounts Receivable	$3,000	$3,500
Allowance for Doubtful Accounts	120	200

During the accounting period, Teton recorded $12,000 of service revenue on account. The company also wrote off a $150 account receivable.

Required
a. Determine the amount of cash collected from receivables.
b. Determine the amount of bad debts expense recognized during the period.

EXERCISE 8–4A *Effect of Recovering a Receivable Previously Written Off*   **L.O. 2**

The accounts receivable balance for City Shoes at December 31, 2006, was $84,000. Also on that date, the balance in Allowance for Doubtful Accounts was $2,400. During 2007, $2,100 of accounts receivable were written off as uncollectible. In addition, City Shoes unexpectedly collected $150 of receivables that had been written off in a previous accounting period. Sales on account during 2007 were $218,000, and cash collections from receivables were $220,000. Bad debts expense was estimated to be 1 percent of the sales on account for the period.

Required
(*Hint:* Post the transactions to T-accounts under the accounting equation before completing the requirements.)

a. Based on the preceding information, compute (after year-end adjustment):
   (1) Balance of Allowance for Doubtful Accounts at December 31, 2007.
   (2) Balance of Accounts Receivable at December 31, 2007.

(3) Net realizable value of Accounts Receivable at December 31, 2007.

b. What amount of bad debts expense will City Shoes report for 2007?

c. Explain how the $150 recovery of receivables affected the accounting equation.

L.O. 2, 3   **EXERCISE 8–5A** *Accounting for Bad Debts: Allowance Versus Direct Write-Off Method*

Classic Auto Parts sells new and used auto parts. Although a majority of its sales are cash sales, it makes a significant amount of credit sales. During 2008, its first year of operations, Classic Auto Parts experienced the following:

Sales on account	$280,000
Cash sales	650,000
Collections of accounts receivable	265,000
Uncollectible accounts charged off during the year	1,200

Required

a. Assume that Classic Auto Parts uses the allowance method of accounting for bad debts and estimates that 1 percent of its sales on account will not be collected. Answer the following questions:

    (1) What is the Accounts Receivable balance at December 31, 2008?

    (2) What is the ending balance of Allowance for Doubtful Accounts at December 31, 2008, after all entries and adjusting entries are posted?

    (3) What is the amount of bad debts expense for 2008?

    (4) What is the net realizable value of accounts receivable at December 31, 2008?

b. Assume that Classic Auto Parts uses the direct write-off method of accounting for bad debts. Answer the following questions:

    (1) What is the Accounts Receivable balance at December 31, 2008?

    (2) What is the amount of bad debts expense for 2008?

    (3) What is the net realizable value of accounts receivable at December 31, 2008?

L.O. 3   **EXERCISE 8–6A** *Accounting for Bad Debts: Direct Write-Off Method*

Hogan Business Systems has mostly a cash business but does have a small number of sales on account. Consequently, it uses the direct write-off method to account for bad debts. During 2006 Hogan Business Systems earned $32,000 of cash revenue and $8,000 of revenue on account. Cash operating expenses were $26,500. After numerous attempts to collect a $250 account receivable from Sam Smart, the account was determined to be uncollectible in 2007.

Required

a. Record the effects of (1) cash revenue, (2) revenue on account, (3) cash expenses, and (4) write-off of the uncollectible account on the financial statements using a horizontal statements model like the one shown here. In the Cash Flow column, indicate whether the item is an operating activity (OA), investing activity (IA), or financing activity (FA). Use NA to indicate that an element is not affected by the event.

Assets	= Liab. +	Equity	Rev. −	Exp.	= Net Inc.	Cash Flow
Cash + Accts. Rec.						

b. What amount of net income did Hogan Business Systems report on the 2006 income statement?

c. Prepare the general journal entries for the four accounting events listed in Requirement *a*.

L.O. 4   **EXERCISE 8–7A** *Effect of Credit Card Sales on Financial Statements*

Royal Carpet Cleaning provided $90,000 of services during 2006. All customers paid for the services with major credit cards. Royal turned the credit card receipts over to the credit card company immediately. The credit card company paid Royal cash in the amount of face value less a 3 percent service charge.

Required

a. Record the credit card sales and the subsequent collection of accounts receivable in a horizontal statements model like the one shown here. In the Cash Flow column, indicate whether the item is an operating activity (OA), investing activity (IA), or financing activity (FA). Use NA to indicate that an element is not affected by the event.

Assets	= Liab. +	Equity	Rev.	− Exp.	= Net Inc.	Cash Flow
Cash + Accts. Rec.						

b. Answer the following questions:
  (1) What is the amount of total assets at the end of the accounting period?
  (2) What is the amount of revenue reported on the income statement?
  (3) What is the amount of cash flow from operating activities reported on the statement of cash flows?
  (4) Why would Royal Carpet Cleaning accept credit cards instead of providing credit directly to its customers? In other words, why would Royal be willing to pay 3 percent of sales to have the credit card company handle its sales on account?

EXERCISE 8–8A *Recording Credit Card Sales*   L.O. 4

Baucom Company accepted credit cards in payment for $6,850 of merchandise sold during March 2006. The credit card company charged Baucom a 4 percent service fee. The credit card company paid Baucom as soon as it received the invoices.

Required
a. Prepare the general journal entry to record the merchandise sale.
b. Prepare the general journal entry for the collection of the receivable from the credit card company.
c. Based on this information alone, what is the amount of net income earned during the month of March?

EXERCISE 8–9A *Effect of Warranties on Income and Cash Flow*   L.O. 5

To support herself while attending school, Ellen Abba sold computers to other students. During her first year of operation, she sold computers that had cost her $120,000 cash for $260,000 cash. She provided her customers with a one-year warranty against defects in parts and labor. Based on industry standards, she estimated that warranty claims would amount to 5 percent of sales. During the year she paid $920 cash to replace a defective hard drive.

Required
a. Prepare the journal entries to record the:
  (1) Purchase of inventory.
  (2) Sale of computers.
  (3) Warranty expense.
  (4) Payment for repairs.
b. Post the above transactions to the T-accounts.
c. Prepare an income statement and statement of cash flows for Abba's first year of operation.
d. Explain the difference between net income and the amount of cash flow from operating activities.

EXERCISE 8–10A *Effect of Warranty Obligations and Payments on Financial Statements*   L.O. 5

The Ja-San Appliance Co. provides a 120-day parts-and-labor warranty on all merchandise it sells. Ja-San estimates the warranty expense for the current period to be $1,250. During the period a customer returned a product that cost $920 to repair.

Required
a. Show the effects of these transactions on the financial statements using a horizontal statements model like the example shown here. Use a + to indicate increase, a − for decrease, and NA for not affected. Also in the Cash Flow column, indicate whether the item is an operating activity (OA), investing activity (IA), or financing activity (FA).

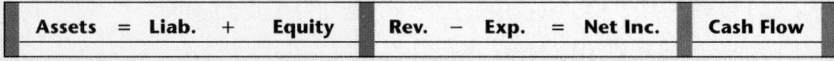

Assets	= Liab. +	Equity	Rev.	− Exp.	= Net Inc.	Cash Flow

b. Prepare the journal entry to record the warranty expense for the period.
c. Prepare the journal entry to record payment for the actual repair costs.
d. Discuss the advantage of estimating the amount of warranty expense.

EXERCISE 8–11A *Comprehensive Single-Cycle Problem*   L.O. 2, 5

The following after-closing trial balance was drawn from the accounts of Spruce Timber Co. as of December 31, 2006.

	Debit	Credit
Cash	$ 6,000	
Accounts Receivable	18,000	
Allowance for Doubtful Accounts		$ 2,000
Inventory	24,000	
Accounts Payable		9,200
Common Stock		20,000
Retained Earnings		16,800
Totals	$48,000	$48,000

Transactions for 2007

1. Acquired an additional $10,000 cash from the issue of common stock.
2. Purchased $60,000 of inventory on account.
3. Sold inventory that cost $62,000 for $95,000. Sales were made on account.
4. The products sold in Event 3 were warranted, and Spruce estimated future warranty costs would amount to 3 percent of sales.
5. The company wrote off $1,100 of uncollectible accounts.
6. On September 1, Spruce issued a $9,000 short-term interest-bearing note with a 7 percent stated rate of interest. The note had a one-year term.
7. Paid $875 cash to satisfy warranty claims.
8. Paid $15,800 cash for salaries expense.
9. The company collected $80,000 cash from accounts receivable.
10. A cash payment of $52,000 was paid on accounts payable.
11. The company paid a $5,000 cash dividend to the stockholders.
12. Bad debts are estimated to be 1 percent of sales on account.
13. Recorded the accrued interest at December 31, 2006.

Required

a. Open T-accounts and record the beginning balances and the effects of the 2007 accounting events.
b. Prepare an income statement, statement of changes in stockholders' equity, balance sheet, and statement of cash flows for 2007.

L.O. 7   EXERCISE 8–12A *Effect of a Discount Note on Financial Statements (Appendix)*

Pat Waverly started a moving company on January 1, 2006. On March 1, 2006, Waverly borrowed cash from a local bank by issuing a one-year $50,000 face value note with annual interest based on a 12 percent discount. During 2006, Waverly provided services for $36,800 cash.

Required

Answer the following questions. Record the events in T-accounts prior to answering the questions.
a. What is the amount of total liabilities on the December 31, 2006 balance sheet?
b. What is the amount of net income on the 2006 income statement?
c. What is the amount of cash flow from operating activities on the 2006 statement of cash flows?
d. Provide the general journal entries necessary to record issuing the note on March 1, 2006; recognizing accrued interest on December 31, 2006; and repaying the loan on February 28, 2007.

L.O. 7   EXERCISE 8–13A *Comparing Effective Interest Rates on Discount Versus Interest-Bearing Notes (Appendix)*

Glen Pounds borrowed money by issuing two notes on January 1, 2006. The financing transactions are described here.

1. Borrowed funds by issuing a $30,000 face value discount note to State Bank. The note had an 8 percent discount rate, a one-year term to maturity, and was paid off on December 31, 2006.
2. Borrowed funds by issuing a $30,000 face value, interest-bearing note to Community Bank. The note had an 8 percent stated rate of interest, a one-year term to maturity, and was paid off on December 31, 2006.

Required

a. Show the effects of issuing the two notes on the financial statements using separate horizontal financial statement models like the ones here. Record the transaction amounts under the appropriate categories.

Also in the Cash Flow column, indicate whether the item is an operating activity (OA), investing activity (IA), or financing activity (FA). Record only the events occurring on the date of issue. Do not record accrued interest or the repayment at maturity.

Discount Note

Assets	=	Liabilities			+	Equity	Rev.	−	Exp.	=	Net Inc.	Cash Flow
Cash	=	Notes Pay.	−	Disc. on Notes Pay.	+	Ret. Ear.						

Interest-Bearing Note

Assets	=	Liabilities	+	Equity	Rev.	−	Exp.	=	Net Inc.	Cash Flow
Cash	=	Notes Pay.	+	Ret. Ear.						

b. What is the total amount of interest to be paid on each note?

c. What amount of cash was received from each note?

d. Which note has the higher effective interest rate? Support your answer with appropriate computations.

EXERCISE 8–14A *Recording Accounting Events for a Discount Note (Appendix)*   **L.O. 7**

Cross Co issued a $50,000 face value discount note to First Bank on June 1, 2006. The note had a 6 percent discount rate and a one-year term to maturity.

Required
Prepare general journal entries for the following transactions:

a. The issuance of the note on June 1, 2006.

b. The adjustment for accrued interest at the end of the year, December 31, 2006.

c. Recording interest expense for 2007 and repaying the principal on May 31, 2007.

PROBLEMS—SERIES A

All Problems in Series A are available with McGraw-Hill's Homework Manager

PROBLEM 8–15A *Accounting for Bad Debts—Two Cycles Using the Allowance Method*   **L.O. 2**

The following transactions apply to Sharp Consulting for 2006, the first year of operation:

CHECK FIGURES
d. Ending Accounts Receivable, 2006: $7,000
d. Net Income, 2007: $23,275

1. Recognized $65,000 of service revenue earned on account.
2. Collected $58,000 from accounts receivable.
3. Adjusted accounts to recognize bad debts expense. Sharp uses the allowance method of accounting for bad debts and estimates that bad debts expense will be 2 percent of sales on account.

The following transactions apply to Sharp Consulting for 2007:

1. Recognized $72,500 of service revenue on account.
2. Collected $66,000 from accounts receivable.
3. Determined that $900 of the accounts receivable were uncollectible and wrote them off.
4. Collected $100 of an account that had been written off previously.
5. Paid $48,500 cash for operating expenses.
6. Adjusted accounts to recognize bad debts expense for 2007. Sharp estimates that bad debts expense will be 1 percent of sales on account.

Required
Complete all the following requirements for 2006 and 2007. Complete all requirements for 2006 prior to beginning the requirements for 2007.

a. Identify the type of each transaction (asset source, asset use, asset exchange, or claims exchange).

b. Show the effect of each transaction on the elements of the financial statements, using a horizontal statements model like the one shown here. Use + for increase, − for decrease, and NA for not affected. Also, in the Cash Flow column, indicate whether the item is an operating activity (OA), investing activity (IA), or financing activity (FA). The first transaction is entered as an example. (*Hint:* Closing entries do not affect the statements model.)

Event No.	Assets	=	Liab.	+	Equity		Rev.	−	Exp.	=	Net Inc.	Cash Flow
1	+		NA		+		+		NA		+	NA

c. Record the transactions in general journal form, and post them to T-accounts (begin 2007 with the ending T-account balances from 2006).

d. Prepare the income statement, statement of changes in stockholders' equity, balance sheet, and statement of cash flows.

e. Prepare closing entries and post these closing entries to the T-accounts. Prepare an after-closing trial balance.

L.O. 2   PROBLEM 8–16A *Determining Account Balances and Preparing Journal Entries: Allowance Method of Accounting for Bad Debts*

The following information pertains to Bay Cabinet Company's sales on account and accounts receivable:

Accounts Receivable Balance, January 1, 2007	$125,400
Allowance for Doubtful Accounts, January 1, 2007	3,250
Sales on Account, 2007	875,000
Cost of Goods Sold, 2007	620,000
Collections of Accounts Receivable, 2007	910,000

After several collection attempts, Bay Cabinet Company wrote off $2,800 of accounts that could not be collected. Bay estimates that bad debts expense will be 0.5 percent of sales on account.

Required

a. Prepare the general journal entries to:
   (1) Record sales on account for 2007.
   (2) Record cash collections from accounts receivable for 2007.
   (3) Write off the accounts that are not collectible.
   (4) Record the estimated bad debts expense for 2007.

b. Compute the following amounts:
   (1) Using the allowance method, the amount of bad debts expense for 2007.
   (2) Net realizable value of receivables at the end of 2007.

c. Explain why the bad debts expense amount is different from the amount that was written off as uncollectible.

L.O. 3–5   PROBLEM 8–17A *Accounting for Credit Card Sales, Warranties, and Bad Debts: Direct Write-Off Method*

www.mhhe.com/edmonds5e

Bishop Supply Company had the following transactions in 2006:

1. Acquired $60,000 cash from the issue of common stock.
2. Purchased $180,000 of merchandise for cash in 2006.
3. Sold merchandise that cost $110,000 for $200,000 during the year under the following terms:

$ 50,000	Cash Sales
140,000	Credit Card Sales (The credit card company charges a 3 percent service fee.)
10,000	Sales on Account

4. Collected all the amount receivable from the credit card company.
5. Collected $9,200 of accounts receivable.
6. Used the direct write-off method to account for bad debts expense and wrote off $150 of accounts receivable that were uncollectible.
7. Bishop gives a one-year warranty on equipment it sells. It estimated that warranty expense for 2006 would be $520.
8. Paid selling and administrative expenses of $46,000.

Required

a. Show the effects of each of the transactions on the elements of the financial statements, using a horizontal statements model like the one shown here. Use + for increase, − for decrease, and NA for not affected. The first transaction is entered as an example. (*Hint:* Closing entries do not affect the statements model.)

Event No.	Assets	=	Liab.	+	Equity	Rev.	–	Exp.	=	Net Inc.	Cash Flow
1	+		NA		+	NA		NA		NA	+ FA

b. Prepare general journal entries for each of the transactions, and post them to T-accounts.

c. Prepare an income statement, statement of changes in stockholders' equity, balance sheet, and statement of cash flows for 2006.

PROBLEM 8–18A *Effect of Transactions on the Elements of Financial Statements*   L.O. 3–5

Required

Identify each of the following independent transactions as asset source (AS), asset use (AU), asset exchange (AE), or claims exchange (CE). Also explain how each event affects assets, liabilities, stockholders' equity, net income, and cash flow by placing a + for increase, – for decrease, or NA for not affected under each of the categories. The first event is recorded as an example.

Event	Type of Event	Assets	Liabilities	Common Stock	Retained Earnings	Net Income	Cash Flow
a	AE	+/–	NA	NA	NA	NA	+

a. Collected cash from customers paying their accounts.

b. Recovered a bad debt that was previously written off (assume direct write-off method was used).

c. Paid cash for equipment.

d. Recognized warranty expense.

e. Sold merchandise at a price above cost. Accepted payment by credit card. The credit card company charges a service fee. The receipts have not yet been forwarded to the credit card company for collection.

f. Realized a gain when equipment was sold for cash.

g. Paid cash to satisfy warranty obligations.

h. Submitted receipts to the credit card company in Requirement *e* above and collected cash.

i. Issued a short-term note to First National Bank.

j. Paid cash to creditors on accounts payable.

k. Accrued three months' interest on the short-term note payable.

l. Provided services for cash.

m. Paid cash for salaries expense.

n. Provided services on account.

o. Wrote off an uncollectible account (use direct write-off method).

PROBLEM 8–19A *Multistep Income Statement and Classified Balance Sheet*   L.O. 2, 5

www.mhhe.com/edmonds5e

Required

Use the following information to prepare a multistep income statement and a classified balance sheet for Daniels Company for 2004. (*Hint:* Some of the items will *not* appear on either statement, and ending retained earnings must be calculated.)

CHECK FIGURES
Total Current Assets: $317,800
Total Current Liabilities: $135,000

Operating Expenses	$ 90,000	Cash	$ 23,000
Land	50,000	Interest Receivable (short term)	800
Accumulated Depreciation	38,000	Cash Flow from Investing Activities	102,000
Accounts Payable	60,000	Allowance for Doubtful Accounts	7,000
Unearned Revenue	58,000	Interest Payable (short term)	3,000
Warranties Payable (short term)	2,000	Sales Revenue	500,000
Equipment	77,000	Bad Debts Expense	14,000
Notes Payable (long term)	129,000	Interest Expense	32,000
Salvage Value of Equipment	7,000	Accounts Receivable	113,000
Dividends	12,000	Salaries Payable	12,000
Warranty Expense	5,000	Supplies	3,000
Beginning Retained Earnings	28,800	Prepaid Rent	14,000
Interest Revenue	6,000	Common Stock	52,000
Gain on Sale of Equipment	10,000	Cost of Goods Sold	179,000
Inventory	154,000	Salaries Expense	122,000
Notes Receivable (short term)	17,000		

L.O. 2, 5 **PROBLEM 8–20A** *Missing Information*

The following information comes from the accounts of Kemper Company:

Account Title	Beginning Balance	Ending Balance
Accounts Receivable	$30,000	$36,000
Allowance for Doubtful Accounts	1,800	2,400
Warranties Payable	3,000	3,600
Notes Payable	50,000	50,000
Interest Payable	1,000	5,000

Required

a. There were $180,000 in sales on account during the accounting period. Write-offs of uncollectible accounts were $2,100. What was the amount of cash collected from accounts receivable? What amount of bad debts expense was reported on the income statement? What was the net realizable value of receivables at the end of the accounting period?

b. Warranty expense for the period was $2,100. How much cash was paid to settle warranty claims?

c. What amount of interest expense was recognized during the period? How much cash was paid for interest? The note has an 8 percent interest rate and 24 months to maturity.

L.O. 3–5 **PROBLEM 8–21A** *Comprehensive Accounting Cycle Problem (Uses Direct Write-Off Method)*

The following trial balance was prepared for Lakeview Sales and Service on December 31, 2006, after the closing entries were posted.

Account Title	Debit	Credit
Cash	$ 87,100	
Accounts Receivable	17,800	
Inventory	94,600	
Accounts Payable		$ 44,000
Common Stock		90,000
Retained Earnings		65,500
Totals	$199,500	$199,500

Lakeview had the following transactions in 2007:

1. Purchased merchandise on account for $270,000.
2. Sold merchandise that cost $215,000 on account for $350,000.
3. Performed $80,000 of services for cash.
4. Sold merchandise for $76,000 to credit card customers. The merchandise cost $47,500. The credit card company charges a 5 percent fee.
5. Collected $360,000 cash from accounts receivable.
6. Paid $274,000 cash on accounts payable.
7. Paid $126,000 cash for selling and administrative expenses.
8. Collected cash for the full amount due from the credit card company.
9. Issued a $60,000 face value short-term note with an 8 percent interest rate and a one-year term to maturity.
10. Wrote off $650 of accounts as uncollectible (use the direct write-off method).
11. Made the following adjusting entries:
    (a) Recorded three months' interest on the short-term note at December 31, 2007.
    (b) Estimated warranty expense to be $2,600.

Required

Prepare general journal entries for these transactions; post the entries to T-accounts; and prepare an income statement, a statement of changes in stockholders' equity, a balance sheet, and a statement of cash flows for 2007.

L.O. 7 **PROBLEM 8–22A** *Accounting for a Discount Note—Two Accounting Cycles (Appendix)*

Una Corp. was started in 2006. The following summarizes transactions that occurred during 2006:

1. Issued a $20,000 face value discount note to Golden Savings Bank on April 1, 2006. The note had a 6 percent discount rate and a one-year term to maturity.

2. Recognized revenue from services performed for cash, $125,000.
3. Incurred and paid $95,000 cash for selling and administrative expenses.
4. Amortized the discount on the note at the end of the year, December 31, 2006.
5. Prepared the necessary closing entries at December 31, 2006.

CHECK FIGURES
c. Net Income, 2006: $29,100
Total Assets, 2007: $77,800

The following summarizes transactions that occurred in 2007:

1. Recognized $195,000 of service revenue in cash.
2. Incurred and paid $146,000 for selling and administrative expenses.
3. Amortized the remainder of the discount for 2007 and paid the face value of the note.
4. Prepared the necessary closing entries at December 31, 2007.

Required

a. Show the effects of each of the transactions on the elements of the financial statements, using a horizontal statements model like the one shown here. Use + for increase, − for decrease, and NA for not affected. The first transaction is entered as an example. (*Hint:* Closing entries do not affect the statements model.)

Event No.	Assets	=	Liab.	+	Equity	Rev.	−	Exp.	=	Net Inc.	Cash Flow
1	+		+		NA	NA		NA		NA	+ FA

b. Prepare the entries in general journal form for the transactions for 2006 and 2007, and post them to T-accounts.
c. Prepare an income statement, statement of changes in stockholders' equity, balance sheet, and statement of cash flows for 2006 and 2007.

EXERCISES—SERIES B

EXERCISE 8–1B *Effect of Recognizing Bad Debts Expense on Financial Statements: Allowance Method*

L.O. 2

Hughes Dry Cleaning was started on January 1, 2003. It experienced the following events during its first year of operation.

Events affecting 2003
1. Provided $10,000 of cleaning services on account.
2. Collected $8,000 cash from accounts receivable.
3. Adjusted the accounting records to reflect the estimate that bad debt expense would be 1 percent of the service revenue on account.

Events affecting 2004
1. Wrote off an $80 account receivable that was determined to be uncollectible.
2. Provided $12,000 of cleaning services on account.
3. Collected $10,000 cash from accounts receivable.
4. Adjusted the accounting records to reflect the estimate that bad debt expense would be 1 percent of the service revenue on account.

Required
a. Record the events for 2003 in T-accounts.
b. Determine the following amounts:
   (1) Net income for 2003.
   (2) Net cash flow from operating activities for 2003.
   (3) Balance of accounts receivable at the end of 2003.
   (4) Net realizable value of accounts receivable at the end of 2003.
c. Repeat Requirements *a* and *b* for the 2004 accounting period.

EXERCISE 8–2B *Analyzing Financial Statement Effects of Accounting for Bad Debts Using the Allowance Method*

L.O. 2

Businesses using the allowance method to account for bad debts expense routinely experience four accounting events:

1. Recognition of revenue on account.

2. Collection of cash from accounts receivable.
3. Recognition of bad debts expense through a year-end adjusting entry.
4. Write-off of uncollectible accounts.

Required

Show the effect of each event on the elements of the financial statements, using a horizontal statements model like the one shown here. Use + for increase, − for decrease, and NA for not affected. In the cash flow column, indicate whether the item is an operating activity (OA), investing activity (IA), or financing activity (FA). The first transaction is entered as an example.

Event No.	Assets	=	Liab.	+	Equity		Rev.	−	Exp.	=	Net Inc.	Cash Flow
1	+		NA		+		+		NA		+	NA

L.O. 2   EXERCISE 8–3B *Analyzing Account Balances for a Company Using the Allowance Method of Accounting for Bad Debts*

The following account balances come from the records of Fiesta Company.

	Beginning Balance	Ending Balance
Accounts Receivable	$1,500	$2,000
Allowance for Doubtful Accounts	150	175

During the accounting period, Fiesta recorded $7,000 of sales revenue on account. The company also wrote off an $80 account receivable.

Required

a. Determine the amount of cash collected from receivables.
b. Determine the amount of bad debts expense recognized during the period.

L.O. 2   EXERCISE 8–4B *Effect of Recovering a Receivable Previously Written Off*

The accounts receivable balance for Get-N-Shape Spa at December 31, 2007, was $80,000. Also on that date, the balance in Allowance for Doubtful Accounts was $3,000. During 2008, $3,500 of accounts receivable were written off as uncollectible. In addition, Get-N-Shape unexpectedly collected $900 of receivables that had been written off in a previous accounting period. Sales on account during 2008 were $200,000, and cash collections from receivables were $190,000. Bad debts expense was estimated to be 2 percent of the sales on account for the period.

Required

(*Hint:* Post the transactions to T-accounts before you complete the requirements.)

a. Based on the preceding information, compute (after year-end adjustment):
  (1) Balance of Allowance for Doubtful Accounts at December 31, 2008.
  (2) Balance of Accounts Receivable at December 31, 2008.
  (3) Net realizable value of Accounts Receivable at December 31, 2008.
b. What amount of bad debts expense will Get-N-Shape report for 2008?
c. Explain how the $900 recovery of receivables affects the income statement.

L.O. 2, 3   EXERCISE 8–5B *Accounting for Bad Debts: Allowance Versus Direct Write-Off Method*

Ted's Bike Shop sells new and used bicycle parts. Although a majority of its sales are cash sales, it makes a significant amount of credit sales. During 2004, its first year of operations, Ted's Bike Shop experienced the following:

Sales on account	$300,000
Cash sales	555,000
Collections of Accounts Receivable	260,000
Uncollectible accounts charged off during the year	250

Required

a. Assume that Ted's Bike Shop uses the allowance method of accounting for bad debts and estimates that 1 percent of its sales on account will not be collected. Answer the following questions:

(1) What is the Accounts Receivable balance at December 31, 2004?

(2) What is the ending balance of the Allowance for Doubtful Accounts at December 31, 2004, after all entries and adjusting entries are posted?

(3) What is the amount of bad debts expense for 2004?

(4) What is the net realizable value of accounts receivable at December 31, 2004?

b. Assume that Ted's Bike Shop uses the direct write-off method of accounting for bad debts. Answer the following questions:

(1) What is the Accounts Receivable balance at December 31, 2004?

(2) What is the amount of bad debts expense for 2004?

(3) What is the net realizable value of accounts receivable at December 31, 2004?

EXERCISE 8–6B *Accounting for Bad Debts: Direct Write-Off Method*   L.O. 3

Hunan Service Co. does mostly a cash business but does make a few sales on account. Consequently, it uses the direct write-off method to account for bad debts. During 2005 Hunan Service Co. earned $10,000 of cash revenue and $2,000 of revenue on account. Cash operating expenses were $8,000. After numerous attempts to collect a $70 account receivable from Bill Smith, the account was determined to be uncollectible in 2005.

Required

a. Record the effects of (1) cash revenue, (2) revenue on account, (3) cash expenses, and (4) write-off of the uncollectible account on the financial statements using a horizontal statements model like the one shown here. In the Cash Flow column, indicate whether the item is an operating activity (OA), investing activity (IA), or financing activity (FA). Use NA to indicate that an element is not affected by the event.

Assets		= Liab. +	Equity	Rev. −	Exp.	= Net Inc.	Cash Flow
Cash +	Accts. Rec.						

b. What amount of net income did Hunan Service Co. report on the 2005 income statement?

c. Prepare the general journal entries for the four accounting events listed in Requirement *a*.

EXERCISE 8–7B *Effect of Credit Card Sales on Financial Statements*   L.O. 4

Super Day Spa provided $120,000 of services during 2004. All customers paid for the services with credit cards. Super turned the credit card receipts over to the credit card company immediately. The credit card company paid Super cash in the amount of face value less a 5 percent service charge.

Required

a. Record the credit card sales and the subsequent collection of accounts receivable in a horizontal statements model like the one shown here. In the Cash Flow column, indicate whether the item is an operating activity (OA), investing activity (IA), or financing activity (FA). Use NA to indicate that an element is not affected by the event.

Assets		= Liab. +	Equity	Rev. −	Exp.	= Net Inc.	Cash Flow
Cash +	Accts. Rec.						

b. Answer the following questions:

(1) What is the amount of total assets at the end of the accounting period?

(2) What is the amount of revenue reported on the income statement?

(3) What is the amount of cash flow from operating activities reported on the statement of cash flows?

(4) What costs would a business incur if it maintained its own accounts receivable? What cost does a business incur by accepting credit cards?

EXERCISE 8–8B *Recording Credit Card Sales*   L.O. 4

Elk Company accepted credit cards in payment for $3,000 of merchandise sold during July 2004. The credit card company charged Elk a 4 percent service fee; it paid Elk as soon as it received the invoices.

Required

a. Prepare the general journal entry to record the merchandise sale.

b. Prepare the general journal entry for the collection of the receivable from the credit card company.

c. Based on this information alone, what is the amount of net income earned during the month of July?

L.O. 5   **EXERCISE 8–9B** *Effect of Warranties on Income and Cash Flow*

To support herself while attending school, Kim Lee sold stereo systems to other students. During her first year of operation, she sold systems that had cost her $95,000 cash for $140,000 cash. She provided her customers with a one-year warranty against defects in parts and labor. Based on industry standards, she estimated that warranty claims would amount to 6 percent of sales. During the year she paid $200 cash to replace a defective tuner.

Required

Prepare an income statement and statement of cash flows for Lee's first year of operation. Based on the information given, what is Lee's total warranties liability at the end of the accounting period?

L.O. 5   **EXERCISE 8–10B** *Effect of Warranty Obligations and Payments on Financial Statements*

The Cycle Company provides a 120-day parts-and-labor warranty on all merchandise it sells. Cycle estimates the warranty expense for the current period to be $1,400. During the period a customer returned a product that cost $596 to repair.

Required

a. Show the effects of these transactions on the financial statements using a horizontal statements model like the example shown here. Use a + to indicate increase, a − for decrease, and NA for not affected. Also in the Cash Flow column, indicate whether the item is an operating activity (OA), investing activity (IA), or financing activity (FA).

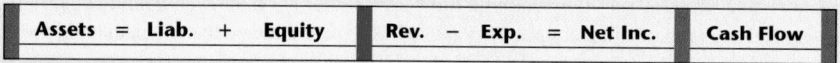

Assets	=	Liab.	+	Equity		Rev.	−	Exp.	=	Net Inc.		Cash Flow

b. Prepare the journal entry to record the warranty expense for the period.
c. Prepare the journal entry to record payment for the actual repair costs.
d. Why do companies estimate warranty expense and record the expense before the repairs are actually made?

L.O. 2, 5   **EXERCISE 8–11B** *Comprehensive Single-Cycle Problem*

The following after-closing trial balance was drawn from the accounts of Millers Metal Co. (MMC) as of December 31, 2004.

	Debit	Credit
Cash	$ 4,000	
Accounts Receivable	20,000	
Allowance for Doubtful Accounts		$ 1,000
Inventory	40,000	
Accounts Payable		10,000
Common Stock		20,000
Retained Earnings		33,000
Totals	$64,000	$64,000

Transactions for 2005

1. MMC acquired an additional $4,000 cash from the issue of common stock.
2. MMC purchased $80,000 of inventory on account.
3. MMC sold inventory that cost $76,000 for $128,000. Sales were made on account.
4. The products sold in Event 3 were warrantied, and MMC estimated future warranty costs would amount to 5 percent of sales.
5. The company wrote off $800 of uncollectible accounts.
6. On September 1, MMC issued a $10,000 face value, 9 percent interest bearing note. The note had a one-year term.
7. MMC paid $2,000 cash to satisfy warranty claims.
8. MMC paid $16,000 cash for operating expenses.
9. The company collected $133,200 cash from accounts receivable.
10. A cash payment of $68,000 was paid on accounts payable.
11. The company paid a $2,000 cash dividend to the stockholders.
12. Bad debts are estimated to be 1 percent of sales on account.
13. Recorded the accrued interest at December 31, 2005.

Required
a. Open T-accounts and record the beginning balances and the effects of the 2005 accounting events.
b. Prepare an income statement, statement of changes in stockholders' equity, balance sheet, and statement of cash flows for 2005.

EXERCISE 8–12B *Effect of a Discount Note on Financial Statements (Appendix)*   **L.O. 7**

Ken Kersey started a design company on January 1, 2004. On April 1, 2004, Kersey borrowed cash from a local bank by issuing a one-year $200,000 face value note with annual interest based on a 10 percent discount. During 2004, Kersey provided services for $55,000 cash.

Required
Answer the following questions. (*Hint:* Record the events in T-accounts prior to answering the questions.)

a. What is the amount of total liabilities on the December 31, 2004 balance sheet?
b. What is the amount of net income on the 2004 income statement?
c. What is the amount of cash flow from operating activities on the 2004 statement of cash flows?
d. Provide the general journal entries necessary to record issuing the note on April 1, 2004; recognizing accrued interest on December 31, 2004; and repaying the loan on March 31, 2005.

EXERCISE 8–13B *Comparing Effective Interest Rates on Discount Versus Interest-Bearing Notes (Appendix)*   **L.O. 7**

Cheyenne Ross borrowed money by issuing two notes on March 1, 2005. The financing transactions are described here.

1. Borrowed funds by issuing a $30,000 face value discount note to Farmers Bank. The note had a 10 percent discount rate, a one-year term to maturity, and was paid off on March 1, 2006.
2. Borrowed funds by issuing a $30,000 face value, interest-bearing note to Valley Bank. The note had a 10 percent stated rate of interest, a one-year term to maturity, and was paid off on March 1, 2006.

Required
a. Show the effects of issuing the two notes on the financial statements using separate horizontal financial statement models like the ones here. Record the transaction amounts under the appropriate categories. Also in the Cash Flow column, indicate whether the item is an operating activity (OA), investing activity (IA), or financing activity (FA). Record only the events occurring on the date of issue. Do not record accrued interest or the repayment at maturity.

Discount Note

Assets	=		Liabilities		+	Equity	Rev.	−	Exp.	=	Net Inc.	Cash Flow
Cash	=	Notes Pay.	−	Disc. on Notes Pay.	+	Ret. Ear.						

Interest-Bearing Note

Assets	=	Liabilities	+	Equity	Rev.	−	Exp.	=	Net Inc.	Cash Flow
Cash	=	Notes Pay.	+	Ret. Ear.						

b. What is the total amount of interest to be paid on each note?
c. What amount of cash was received from each note?
d. Which note has the higher effective interest rate? Support your answer with appropriate computations.

EXERCISE 8–14B *Recording Accounting Events for a Discount Note (Appendix)*   **L.O. 7**

Hopkins Co. issued a $40,000 face value discount note to National Bank on July 1, 2005. The note had a 12 percent discount rate and a one-year term to maturity.

Required
Prepare general journal entries for the following:

a. The issuance of the note on July 1, 2005.
b. The adjustment for accrued interest at the end of the year, December 31, 2005.
c. Recording interest expense for 2006 and repaying the principal on June 30, 2006.

PROBLEMS—SERIES B

L.O. 2 PROBLEM 8–15B *Accounting for Bad Debts: Two Cycles Using the Allowance Method*

The following transactions apply to KC Company for 2005, the first year of operation:

1. Recognized $255,000 of service revenue earned on account.
2. Collected $159,000 from accounts receivable.
3. Paid $150,000 cash for operating expenses.
4. Adjusted the accounts to recognize bad debts expense. KC uses the allowance method of accounting for bad debts and estimates that bad debts expense will be 1 percent of sales on account.

The following transactions apply to KC for 2006:

1. Recognized $408,000 of service revenue on account.
2. Collected $411,000 from accounts receivable.
3. Determined that $1,800 of the accounts receivable were uncollectible and wrote them off.
4. Collected $600 of an account that had previously been written off.
5. Paid $126,000 cash for operating expenses.
6. Adjusted the accounts to recognize bad debts expense for 2006. KC estimates bad debts expense will be 0.5 percent of sales on account.

Required

Complete the following requirements for 2005 and 2006. Complete all requirements for 2005 prior to beginning the requirements for 2006.

a. Identify the type of each transaction (asset source, asset use, asset exchange, or claims exchange).
b. Show the effect of each transaction on the elements of the financial statements, using a horizontal statements model like the one shown here. Use + for increase, − for decrease, and NA for not affected. Also, in the Cash Flow column, indicate whether the item is an operating activity (OA), investing activity (IA), or financing activity (FA). The first transaction is entered as an example. (*Hint:* Closing entries do not affect the statements model.)

Event No.	Assets	=	Liab.	+	Equity	Rev.	−	Exp.	=	Net Inc.	Cash Flow
1	+		NA		+	+		NA		+	NA

c. Record the transactions in general journal form, and post them to T-accounts (begin 2006 with the ending T-account balances from 2005).
d. Prepare the income statement, statement of changes in stockholders' equity, balance sheet, and statement of cash flows.
e. Prepare closing entries and post these closing entries to the T-accounts. Prepare the after-closing trail balance.

L.O. 2 PROBLEM 8–16B *Determining Account Balances and Preparing Journal Entries: Allowance Method of Accounting for Bad Debts*

During the first year of operation, 2006, Wells Appliance Co. recognized $300,000 of service revenue on account. At the end of 2006, the accounts receivable balance was $58,000. For this first year in business, the owner believes bad debts expense will be about 1 percent of sales on account.

Required

a. What amount of cash did Wells collect from accounts receivable during 2006?
b. Assuming Wells uses the allowance method to account for bad debts, what amount should Wells record as bad debts expense for 2006?
c. Prepare the journal entries to:
   (1) Record service revenue on account.
   (2) Record collections from accounts receivable.
   (3) Record the entry to recognize bad debts expense.
d. What is the net realizable value of receivables at the end of 2006?
e. Show the effects of the transactions in Requirement *c* on the financial statements by recording the appropriate amounts in a horizontal statements model like the one shown here. In the Cash Flow column, indicate whether the item is an operating activity (OA), investing activity (IA), or financing activity (FA). Use NA for not affected.

Assets			=	Liab.	+	Equity	Rev.	−	Exp.	=	Net Inc.	Cash Flow
Cash	+	Accts. Rec.	−	Allow.								

PROBLEM 8–17B Accounting for Credit Card Sales, Warranties, and Bad Debts: Direct Write-Off Method

L.O. 3, 4, 5

Northeast Sales had the following transactions in 2005:

1. The business was started when it acquired $500,000 cash from the issue of common stock.
2. Northeast purchased $1,200,000 of merchandise for cash in 2005.
3. During the year, the company sold merchandise for $1,600,000. The merchandise cost $900,000. Sales were made under the following terms:

> a. $600,000 Cash sales
> b. 500,000 Credit card sales (The credit card company charges a 4 percent service fee.)
> c. 500,000 Sales on account

4. The company collected all the amount receivable from the credit card company.
5. The company collected $400,000 of accounts receivable.
6. Northeast used the direct write-off method to account for bad debts expense and wrote off $5,000 of accounts receivable that were uncollectible.
7. Northeast gives a one-year warranty on equipment it sells. It estimated that warranty expense for 2005 would be $4,500.
8. The company paid $100,000 cash for selling and administrative expenses.

Required

a. Show the effects of each of the transactions on the elements of the financial statements, using a horizontal statements model like the one shown here. Use + for increase, − for decrease, and NA for not affected. The first transaction is entered as an example. (*Hint:* Closing entries do not affect the statements model.)

Event No.	Assets	=	Liab.	+	Equity	Rev.	−	Exp.	=	Net Inc.	Cash Flow
1	+		NA		+	NA		NA		NA	+ FA

b. Prepare general journal entries for each of the transactions, and post them to T-accounts.
c. Prepare an income statement, statement of changes in stockholders' equity, balance sheet, and statement of cash flows for 2005.

PROBLEM 8–18B Effect of Transactions on the Elements of Financial Statements

L.O. 3–5

Required

Identify each of the following independent transactions as asset source (AS), asset use (AU), asset exchange (AE), or claims exchange (CE). Also explain how each event affects assets, liabilities, stockholders' equity, net income, and cash flow by placing a + for increase, − for decrease, or NA for not affected under each of the categories. The first event is recorded as an example.

Event	Type of Event	Assets	Liabilities	Common Stock	Retained Earnings	Net Income	Cash Flow
a	AE	+−	NA	NA	NA	NA	−

a. Paid cash for equipment.
b. Sold merchandise at a price above cost. Accepted payment by credit card. The credit card company charges a service fee. The receipts have not yet been forwarded to the credit card company for collection.
c. Submitted receipts to the credit card company and collected cash.
d. Realized a gain when equipment was sold for cash.

e. Provided services for cash.

f. Paid cash to satisfy warranty obligations.

g. Paid cash for salaries expense.

h. Recovered a bad debt that had been previously written off (assume the direct write-off method is used to account for bad debts).

i. Paid cash to creditors on accounts payable.

j. Issued a short-term note to State Bank.

k. Provided services on account.

l. Wrote off an uncollectible account (use the direct write-off method).

m. Recorded three months of accrued interest on the note payable.

n. Collected cash from customers paying their accounts.

o. Recognized warranty expense.

L.O. 2, 5   **PROBLEM 8–19B** *Multistep Income Statement and Classified Balance Sheet*

Required

Use the following information to prepare a multistep income statement and a classified balance sheet for Belmont Equipment Co. for 2003. (*Hint:* Some of the items will *not* appear on either statement, and ending retained earnings must be calculated.)

Salaries Expense	$ 96,000	Interest Receivable (short term)	$ 500
Common Stock	40,000	Beginning Retained Earnings	10,400
Notes Receivable (short term)	12,000	Warranties Payable (short term)	1,300
Allowance for Doubtful Accounts	4,000	Gain on Sale of Equipment	6,400
Accumulated Depreciation	30,000	Operating Expenses	70,000
Notes Payable (long term)	103,600	Cash Flow from Investing Activities	80,000
Salvage Value of Building	4,000	Prepaid Rent	9,600
Interest Payable (short term)	1,800	Land	36,000
Bad Debts Expense	10,800	Cash	17,800
Supplies	1,600	Inventory	122,800
Equipment	60,000	Accounts Payable	46,000
Interest Revenue	4,200	Interest Expense	24,000
Sales Revenue	396,000	Salaries Payable	9,200
Dividends	8,000	Unearned Revenue	52,600
Warranty Expense	3,400	Cost of Goods Sold	143,000
		Accounts Receivable	90,000

L.O. 2, 5, 6   **PROBLEM 8–20B** *Missing Information*

The following information comes from the accounts of Jersey Company:

Account Title	Beginning Balance	Ending Balance
Accounts Receivable	$30,000	$34,000
Allowance for Doubtful Accounts	1,800	1,700
Warranties Payable	4,000	3,000
Notes Payable	40,000	40,000
Interest Payable	1,200	3,600

Required

a. There were $170,000 of sales on account during the accounting period. Write-offs of uncollectible accounts were $1,400. What was the amount of cash collected from accounts receivable? What amount of bad debts expense was reported on the income statement? What was the net realizable value of receivables at the end of the accounting period?

b. Warranty expense for the period was $3,600. How much cash was paid to settle warranty claims?

c. What amount of interest expense was recognized during the period? How much cash was paid for interest? The note payable has a two-year term with a 6 percent interest rate.

L.O. 2, 3, 4, 5, 6   **PROBLEM 8–21B** *Comprehensive Accounting Cycle Problem (Uses Allowance Method)*

The following trial balance was prepared for Candles, Etc., Inc. on December 31, 2006, after the closing entries were posted.

Account Title	Debit	Credit
Cash	$118,000	
Accounts Receivable	172,000	
Allowance for Doubtful Accounts		$ 10,000
Inventory	690,000	
Accounts Payable		142,000
Common Stock		720,000
Retained Earnings		108,000
Totals	$980,000	$980,000

Candles, Etc. had the following transactions in 2007:

1. Purchased merchandise on account for $420,000.
2. Sold merchandise that cost $288,000 for $480,000 on account.
3. Sold for $240,000 cash merchandise that had cost $144,000.
4. Sold merchandise for $180,000 to credit card customers. The merchandise had cost $108,000. The credit card company charges a 4 percent fee.
5. Collected $526,000 cash from accounts receivable.
6. Paid $540,000 cash on accounts payable.
7. Paid $134,000 cash for selling and administrative expenses.
8. Collected cash for the full amount due from the credit card company.
9. Issued a $48,000 face value interest-bearing note with a 10 percent interest rate and a one-year term to maturity.
10. Wrote off $7,200 of accounts as uncollectible.
11. Made the following adjusting entries:
    (a) Recorded bad debts expense estimated at 1 percent of sales on account.
    (b) Recorded seven months of accrued interest on the note at December 31, 2007.
    (c) Estimated warranty expense to be $1,800.

Required

a. Prepare general journal entries for these transactions; post the entries to T-accounts; and prepare an income statement, a statement of changes in stockholders' equity, a balance sheet, and a statement of cash flows for 2007.
b. Compute the net realizable value of accounts receivable at December 31, 2007.
c. If Candles, Etc. used the direct write-off method, what amount of bad debts expense would it report on the income statement?

PROBLEM 8-22B *Accounting for a Discount Note across Two Accounting Cycles (Appendix)*   **L.O. 7**

Laura White opened White & Company, an accounting practice, in 2006. The following summarizes transactions that occurred during 2006:

1. Issued a $200,000 face value discount note to First National Bank on July 1, 2006. The note had a 10 percent discount rate and a one-year term to maturity.
2. Recognized cash revenue of $336,000.
3. Incurred and paid $132,000 of operating expenses.
4. Adjusted the books to recognize interest expense at December 31, 2006.
5. Prepared the necessary closing entries at December 31, 2006.

The following summarizes transactions that occurred in 2007:

1. Recognized $984,000 of cash revenue.
2. Incurred and paid $416,000 of operating expenses.
3. Recognized the interest expense for 2007 and paid the face value of the note.
4. Prepared the necessary closing entries at December 31, 2007.

Required

a. Show the effects of each of the transactions on the elements of the financial statements, using a horizontal statements model like the one shown here. Use + for increase, − for decrease, and NA for not affected. The first transaction is entered as an example. (*Hint:* Closing entries do not affect the statements model.)

Event No.	Assets	=	Liab.	+	Equity	Rev.	−	Exp.	=	Net Inc.	Cash Flow
1	+		+		NA	NA		NA		NA	+ FA

b. Prepare entries in general journal form for the transactions for 2006 and 2007, and post them to T-accounts.

c. Prepare an income statement, statement of changes in stockholders' equity, balance sheet, and statement of cash flows for 2006 and 2007.

ANALYZE, THINK, COMMUNICATE

ATC 8–1   BUSINESS APPLICATIONS CASE   *Understanding Real World Annual Reports*

Required—Part 1

Use the Topps Company's annual report in Appendix B to answer the following questions.

a. How long did it take Topps to collect accounts receivable during the year ended March 1, 2003?

b. Approximately what percentage of accounts receivable, as of March 1, 2003, does the company think will not be collected (see Note 3)? Caution, "Reserve for returns," also shown in Note 3, is not related to uncollectible accounts receivable.

c. What do you think the balance in the Reserve for Returns account represents?

Required—Part 2

Use the Harley-Davidson's annual report that came with this book to answer the following questions.

a. How long did it take Harley-Davidson to collect receivables during the year ended December 31, 2003? Note: For the purposes of this computation, use all three receivables accounts shown on Harley-Davidson's balance sheet.

b. Why does Harley-Davidson take so long to collect its receivables? Does this indicate the company has a problem with its receivables?

c. Approximately what percentage of accounts receivable, as of December 31, 2003, does the company think will not be collected (see Note 2)?

d. How much warranty liability did Harley-Davidson have as of December 31, 2003 (see Note 1)?

ATC 8–2   GROUP ASSIGNMENT   *Missing Information*

The following selected financial information is available for three companies:

	Bell	Card	Zore
Total sales	$125,000	$210,000	?
Cash sales	?	26,000	$120,000
Sales on account	40,000	?	75,000
Accounts receivable, January 1, 2008	6,200	42,000	?
Accounts receivable, December 31, 2008	5,600	48,000	7,500
Allowance for doubtful accounts, January 1, 2008	?	?	405
Allowance for doubtful accounts, December 31, 2008	224	1,680	?
Bad debt expense, 2008	242	1,200	395
Uncollectible accounts written off	204	1,360	365
Collections of accounts receivable, 2008	?	?	75,235

Required

a. Divide the class into three sections and divide each section into groups of three to five students. Assign one of the companies to each of the sections.

Group Tasks

(1) Determine the missing amounts for your company.

(2) Determine the percentage of accounts receivable estimated to be uncollectible at the end of 2007 and 2008 for your company.

(3) Determine the percentage of total sales that are sales on account for your company.

(4) Determine the accounts receivable turnover for your company.

Class Discussion

b. Have a representative of each section put the missing information on the board and explain how it was determined.

c. Which company has the highest percentage of sales that are on account?
d. Which company is doing the best job of collecting its accounts receivable? What procedures and policies can a company use to better collect its accounts receivable?

REAL-WORLD CASE *Time Needed to Collect Accounts Receivable*

ATC 8–3

Presented here are the average days to collect accounts receivable ratios for four companies in different industries. The data are for 2002.

Company	Average Days to Collect Accounts Receivable
Boeing (aircraft manufacturer)	34
Ford (automobile manufacturer)	6
Haverty's (furniture retailer)	81
Colgate Palmolive (consumer products manufacturer)	45

Required

Write a brief memorandum that provides possible answers to each of the following questions:

a. Why would a company that manufactures cars (**Ford**) collect its accounts receivable faster than a company that sells furniture (**Haverty's**)? (*Hint:* Ford sells cars to dealerships, not to individual customers.)
b. Why would a company that manufactures and sells large airplanes (**Boeing**) collect its accounts receivable faster than a company that sells toothpaste and soap (**Colgate Palmolive**)?

BUSINESS APPLICATIONS CASE *Using Average Number of Days to Collect Accounts Receivable to Make Comparisons*

ATC 8–4

The following information was drawn from the accounting records of Oakville and Monteray.

Account Title	Oakville	Monteray
Accounts Receivable (year end)	$ 60,000	$ 90,000
Sales on account	610,000	1,200,000

Required

a. Determine the average number of days to collect accounts receivable for each company.
b. Which company is likely to incur more costs associated with extending credit?
c. Identify and discuss some of the costs associated with extending credit.
d. Explain why a company would be willing to accept the costs of extending credit to its customers.

BUSINESS APPLICATIONS CASE *Using Ratios to Make Comparisons*

ATC 8–5

The following accounting information exists for Blackjack and Roulette companies at the end of 2007.

	Blackjack	Roulette
Cash	$ 50,000	$ 60,000
Accounts receivable	190,000	200,000
Allowance for doubtful accounts	5,000	10,000
Merchandise inventory	175,000	165,000
Accounts payable	185,000	175,000
Cost of goods sold	1,125,000	700,000
Building	250,000	200,000
Sales	1,500,000	1,000,000

Required

a. For each company, compute the gross margin percentage and the average number of days to collect accounts receivable (use the net realizable value of receivables to compute the average days to collect accounts receivable).

b. In relation to cost, which company is charging more for its merchandise?

c. Which company is likely to incur higher financial costs associated with the granting of credit to customers? Explain.

d. Which company appears to have more restrictive credit standards when authorizing credit to its customers? (*Hint:* There is no specific answer to this question. Use your judgment and general knowledge of ratios to answer.)

ATC 8–6   WRITING ASSIGNMENT *Elements of Financial Statements*

Paul South is opening a men's clothing store in University City. He has some of the necessary funds to lease the building and purchase the inventory but will need to borrow between $45,000 and $50,000. He has talked with two financial institutions that have offered the money according to the following terms:

1. South can borrow the money from Bank 1 by issuing a $50,000, one-year note with an interest rate of 10 percent.

2. South can borrow the money from Bank 2 by issuing a $50,000 face value discount note. The note will have a 9.5 percent discount rate and a one-year term to maturity.

Required

Write a memo to South explaining the difference in the two types of notes. Also advise him regarding the best alternative and why. Include in your explanation the true cost of each of the loans.

ATC 8–7   ETHICAL DILEMMA *What They Don't Know Won't Hurt Them, Right?*

Alonzo Saunders owns a small training services company that is experiencing growing pains. The company has grown rapidly by offering liberal credit terms to its customers. While his competitors require payment for services provided within 30 days, Saunders permits his customers to delay payment for up to 90 days. This extended delay allows his customers time to fully evaluate the training that employees receive before being required to pay for that training. Saunders guarantees satisfaction. If the customer is unhappy, the customer does not have to pay. Saunders works with reputable companies, provides top quality training, and rarely encounters dissatisfied customers. However, the long collection period has left Saunders with a cash flow problem. He has a large accounts receivable balance, but needs cash to pay the current bills. He has recently negotiated a loan agreement with National Bank of Brighton County that should solve his cash flow problems. A condition of the loan is that the accounts receivable be pledged as collateral for the loan. The bank agreed to loan Saunders 70 percent of the value of his receivables balance. The current balance in the receivables account is approximately $100,000, thereby giving him access to $70,000 cash. Saunders feels very comfortable with this arrangement because he estimates that he needs approximately $60,000, which is well within the range permitted by the bank. Unfortunately, on the day Saunders was scheduled to execute the loan agreement, he heard a rumor that his largest customer was experiencing financial problems and was considering the declaration of bankruptcy. The customer owed Saunders $45,000. Saunders immediately called the company's chief accountant and was told "off the record" that the rumor was true. The accountant advised Saunders that the company had a substantial negative net worth and that most of the valuable assets were collateralized against bank loans. He said that, in his opinion, Saunders was unlikely to be able to collect the balance due. Saunders' immediate concern was the impact that the situation would have on his loan agreement with the bank. Removing the receivable from the collateral pool would leave only $55,000 in the pool and thereby reduce his available credit to $38,500 ($55,000 × 0.70). Even worse, the recognition of the bad debts expense would so adversely affect his income statement that the bank might decide to reduce the available credit by lowering the percentage of receivables allowed under the current loan agreement. As Saunders heads for the bank, he wonders how he will make ends meet. If he cannot obtain the cash he needs, he will soon be declaring bankruptcy himself. He wonders whether he should even tell the bank about the bad debt or just let the bank discover the situation after the fact. He knows that he will have to sign an agreement attesting to the quality of the receivables at the date of the loan. However, he reasons that the information he received is off the record and that therefore he *may not* be legally bound to advise the bank of the condition of the receivables balance. He wishes that he had gone to the bank before he called to confirm the rumor.

Required

a. Assuming that Saunders uses the direct write-off method of accounting for bad debts, explain how the $45,000 write-off of the uncollectible account affects his financial statements.

b. Should Saunders advise the bank of the condition of the receivables? What are the ethical implications associated with telling or not telling the bank about the uncollectible account?

EDGAR DATABASE *Analyzing Maytag's Accounts Receivable*

ATC 8–8

Required

Using the most current 10-K available on EDGAR, answer the following questions about Maytag Company for the most recent year reported. Instructions for using EDGAR are in Appendix A.

a. What was Maytag's average days to collect accounts receivable?

b. What percentage of accounts receivable did Maytag estimate would not be collected?

c. Did Maytag provide any information about warranties that it provides to customers? If so, what information was provided? (*Hint:* Look in the warranty reserve footnote.)

d. Maytag Company manufactures products under brand names other than *Maytag*. What are these brand names?

e. Does it appear that Maytag's warranty costs have been decreasing or increasing? Explain why this may have occurred.

SPREADSHEET ANALYSIS *Using Excel*

ATC 8–9

Set up the following spreadsheet comparing Vong and Crist Companies.

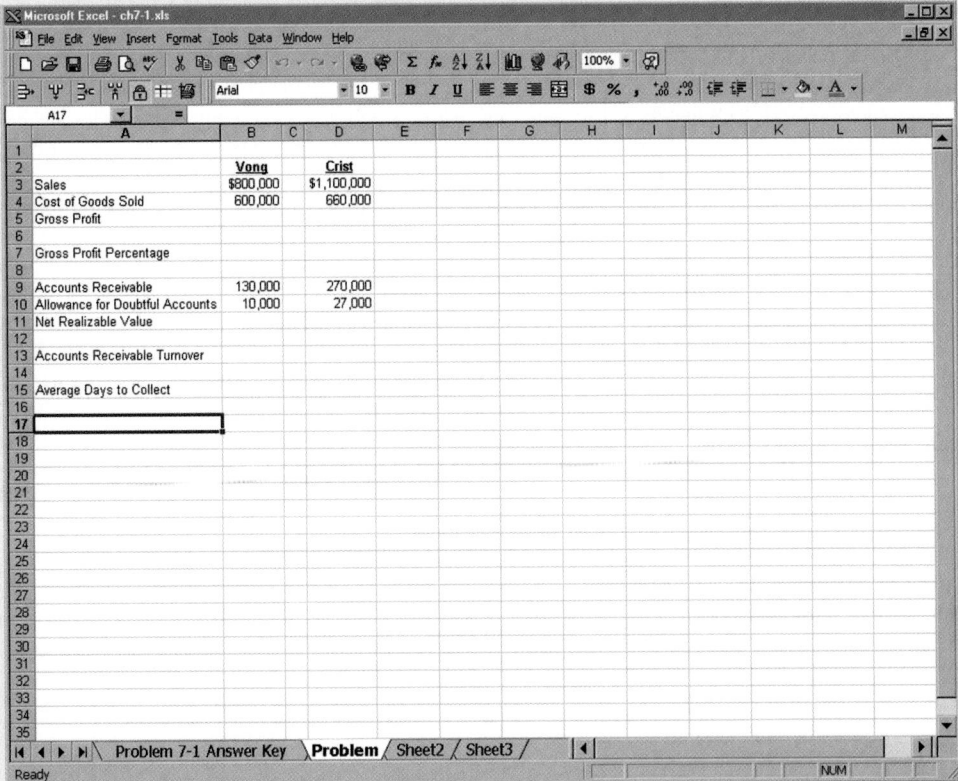

Required

a. For each company, compute gross profit, gross profit percentage, net realizable value, accounts receivable turnover, and average days to collect.

b. In relation to cost, which company is charging more for its merchandise?

c. Which company is likely to incur higher financial costs associated with granting credit to customers? Explain the reasons for your answer.

d. Which company appears to have more restrictive credit standards when authorizing credit to customers? How do you know?

COMPREHENSIVE PROBLEM

The trial balance of Pacilio Security Systems Sales and Service as of January 1, 2008, was:

Cash	$132,248
Petty Cash	100
Accounts Receivable	47,220
Supplies	160
Inventory—Standard Alarm (32 @ $280)	8,960
Inventory—Deluxe Alarm (33 @ $570)	18,810
Prepaid Rent	1,200
Van	9,200
Accumulated Depreciation	4,800
Accounts Payable	2,970
Common Stock	50,000
Retained Earnings	160,128

During 2008 Pacilio Security Systems Sales and Service experienced the following transactions:

1. Paid $8,400 on March 2, 2008, for one year's rent in advance.
2. Purchased $550 of supplies for cash.
3. Purchased 45 standard alarm systems on March 30 at a cost of $265 each, and 30 deluxe alarm systems at a cost of $580 each. Cash was paid for the purchase. Purchased 30 more standard alarm systems on November 3, at a cost of $275 each. Paid cash for the purchase.
4. Paid the balance of the accounts payable.
5. Pacilio has noticed that its accounts receivable are rising more than desired and some collection problems exist. It feels that its bad accounts are approximately 2 percent of total credit sales. Pacilio has decided that this year it will use the allowance method of accounting for bad debts. The estimate will be made at the end of the year.
6. Pacilio has tried to collect several of its delinquent accounts and has learned that these customers have either taken bankruptcy or have moved and left no forwarding address. These accounts amount to $1,900.
7. Installed 100 standard alarm systems for a total of $58,000 and 34 deluxe alarm systems for a total of $32,300. All sales were on account. Cost of goods sold was $27,210 for the standard alarms and $19,390 for the deluxe alarms.
8. Pacilio decided to accept credit cards for some of its monitoring service sales. Total monitoring services for the year were $82,000, of which Pacilio accepted credit cards for $24,000 of this amount. The credit card company charges a fee of 4 percent. The balance of $58,000 was sales on accounts.
9. July 1, 2008, Pacilio replenished the petty cash fund. The fund had $21 cash and receipts of $50 for yard mowing, $22 for office supplies, and $9 for miscellaneous expense.
10. Collected the amount due from the credit card company.
11. Collected $146,000 of accounts receivable for the year.
12. Paid installers $32,000 for salaries.
13. Paid $4,500 for advertising expense.
14. Paid $3,100 for utilities expense for the year.

Adjustments

15. Supplies of $250 were on hand at the end of the year.
16. Recognized expired rent for the year.
17. Recognized depreciation expense for the year.
18. Recognized bad debt expense for the year using the allowance method.
19. Pacilio has decided to provide a one-year warranty on its Deluxe alarm systems. It estimates that its warranty expense will be 5 percent of its Deluxe alarm sales.

Required

a. Record the above transactions in general journal form. Pacilio uses FIFO cost flow assumption.
b. Post the transactions to the T-accounts.
c. Prepare a trial balance.
d. Prepare an income statement, statement of changes in stockholders' equity, balance sheet, and statement of cash flows.
e. Close the temporary accounts to retained earnings.
f. Post the closing entries to the T-accounts and prepare an after-closing trial balance.

CHAPTER *nine*

ACCOUNTING FOR LONG-TERM OPERATIONAL ASSETS

LEARNING *objectives*

After you have mastered the material in this chapter, you will be able to:

1 Identify different types of long-term operational assets.

2 Determine the cost of long-term operational assets.

3 Explain how different depreciation methods affect financial statements.

4 Determine how gains and losses on disposals of long-term operational assets affect financial statements.

5 Identify some of the tax issues which affect long-term operational assets.

6 Show how revising estimates affects financial statements.

7 Explain how continuing expenditures for operational assets affect financial statements.

8 Explain how expense recognition for natural resources (depletion) affects financial statements.

9 Explain how expense recognition for intangible assets (amortization) affects financial statements.

10 Understand how expense recognition choices and industry characteristics affect financial performance measures.

THE *curious* ACCOUNTANT

In the normal course of operations, most companies acquire long-term assets each year. The way in which a company hopes to make money with these assets varies according to the type of business and the asset acquired. During 2002, Weyerhaeuser Company made cash acquisitions of property and equipment of $930 million and cash acquisitions of timber and timberlands of $89 million.

In chapter 3 you learned the basics of accounting for equipment, such as trucks. Can you think of how Weyerhaeuser's use of trees to produce revenue differs from its use of trucks? Do you think the procedures used to account for timber should be similar to or different from those used to account for trucks, and if so, how? (Answers on page 411.)

CHAPTER *opening*

*Companies use assets to produce revenue. Some assets, like inventory or office supplies, are called **current assets** because they are used relatively quickly (within a single accounting period). Other assets, like equipment or buildings, are used for extended periods of time (two or more accounting periods). These assets are called **long-term operational assets.** Accounting for long-term assets raises several interesting questions. For example, what is the cost of the asset? Is it the list price only or should the cost of transportation, transit insurance, set up, and so on be added to the list price? Should the cost of a long-term asset be recognized as expense in the period the asset is purchased or should the cost be expensed over the useful life of the asset? What happens to the accounting records when a long-term asset is retired from use? This chapter answers these questions. It explains the accounting treatment for long-term operational assets from the date of purchase through the date of disposal.*

▌Tangible Versus Intangible Assets

Long-term assets may be tangible or intangible. **Tangible assets** have a physical presence; they can be seen and touched. Tangible assets include equipment, machinery, natural resources, and land. In contrast, intangible assets have no physical form. While they may be represented by physical documents, **intangible assets** are, in fact, rights or privileges. They cannot be seen or touched. For example, a **patent** represents an exclusive legal *privilege* to produce and sell a particular product. It protects inventors by making it illegal for others to profit by copying their inventions. While a patent may be represented by legal documents, the privilege is the actual asset. Since the privilege cannot be seen or touched, the patent is an intangible asset.

Tangible Long-Term Assets

Tangible long-term assets are classified as (1) property, plant, and equipment; (2) natural resources, or (3) land.

Property, Plant, and Equipment

Property, plant, and equipment is sometimes called *plant assets* or *fixed assets*. Examples of property, plant, and equipment include furniture, cash registers, machinery, delivery trucks, computers, mechanical robots, and buildings. The level of detail used to account for these assets varies. One company may include all office equipment in one account, whereas another company might divide office equipment into computers, desks, chairs, and so on. The term used to recognize expense for property, plant, and equipment is **depreciation.**

Natural Resources

Mineral deposits, oil and gas reserves, timber stands, coal mines, and stone quarries are examples of **natural resources.** Conceptually, natural resources are inventories. When sold, the cost of these assets is frequently expensed as *cost of goods sold.* While inventories are usually classified as short-term assets, natural resources are normally classified as long term because the resource deposits generally have long lives. For example, it may take decades to extract all of the diamonds from a diamond mine. The term used to recognize expense for natural resources is **depletion.**

Land

Land is classified separately from other property because land is not subject to depreciation or depletion. Land has an infinite life. In other words, land is not worn out or consumed as it is used. When buildings or natural resources are purchased simultaneously with land, the amount paid must be divided between the land and the other assets because of the nondepreciable nature of the land.

Intangible Assets

Intangible assets fall into two categories, those with *identifiable useful lives* and those with *indefinite useful lives.*

Intangible Assets with Identifiable Useful Lives

Intangible assets with identifiable useful lives include patents and copyrights. These assets may become obsolete (a patent may become worthless if new technology provides a superior product) or may reach the end of their legal lives. The term used when recognizing expense for intangible assets with identifiable useful lives is called **amortization.**

Intangible Assets with Indefinite Useful Lives

The benefits of some intangible assets may extend so far into the future that their useful lives cannot be estimated. For how many years will the Coca-Cola trademark attract customers? When will the value of a McDonald's franchise end? There are no answers to these questions. Intangible assets such as renewable franchises, trademarks, and goodwill have indefinite useful lives. The costs of such assets are not expensed unless the value of the assets becomes impaired.

Determining the Cost of Long-Term Assets

The **historical cost concept** requires that an asset be recorded at the amount paid for it. This amount includes the purchase price plus any costs necessary to get the asset in the location and condition for its intended use. Common examples are:

LO2 Determine the cost of long-term operational assets.

Buildings: (1) purchase price, (2) sales taxes, (3) title search and transfer document costs, (4) realtor's and attorney's fees, and (5) remodeling costs.

Land: (1) purchase price, (2) sales taxes, (3) title search and transfer document costs, (4) realtor's and attorney's fees, (5) costs for removal of old buildings, and (6) grading costs.

Equipment: (1) purchase price (less discounts), (2) sales taxes, (3) delivery costs, (4) installation costs, and (5) costs to adapt for intended use.

The cost of an asset does not include payments for fines, damages, and so on that could have been avoided.

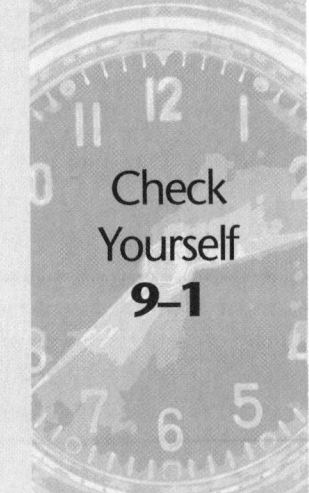

Check Yourself 9–1

Sheridan Construction Company purchased a new bulldozer that had a $260,000 list price. The seller agreed to allow a 4 percent cash discount in exchange for immediate payment. The bulldozer was delivered FOB shipping point at a cost of $1,200. Sheridan hired a new employee to operate the dozer for an annual salary of $36,000. The employee was trained to operate the dozer for a one-time training fee of $800. The cost of the company's theft insurance policy increased by $300 per year as a result of adding the dozer to the policy. The dozer had a five-year useful life and an expected salvage value of $26,000. Determine the asset's cost.

Answer

List price	$260,000
Less: Cash discount ($260,000 × 0.04)	(10,400)
Shipping cost	1,200
Training cost	800
Total asset cost (amount capitalized)	$251,600

Basket Purchase Allocation

Acquiring a group of assets in a single transaction is known as a **basket purchase.** The total price of a basket purchase must be allocated among the assets acquired. Accountants commonly allocate the purchase price using the **relative fair market value method.** To illustrate, assume that Beatty Company purchased land and a building for $240,000 cash. A real estate appraiser determined the fair market value of each asset to be:

Building	$270,000
Land	90,000
Total	$360,000

The appraisal indicates that the land is worth 25 percent ($90,000 ÷ $360,000) of the total value and the building is worth 75 percent ($270,000 ÷ $360,000). Using these percentages, the actual purchase price is allocated as follows:

Building	0.75 × $240,000 =	$180,000
Land	0.25 × $240,000 =	60,000
Total		$240,000

Topic Tackler

PLUS

9–1

LO3 Explain how different depreciation methods affect financial statements.

▌Life Cycle of Operational Assets

The life cycle of an operational asset involves (1) acquiring the funds to buy the asset, (2) purchasing the asset, (3) using the asset, and finally, (4) retiring (disposing of) the asset. The revenue generated from using the asset plus the funds acquired from its disposal, should be sufficient to replace the asset and to provide a reasonable profit. Exhibit 9–1 depicts the life cycle of an operational asset.

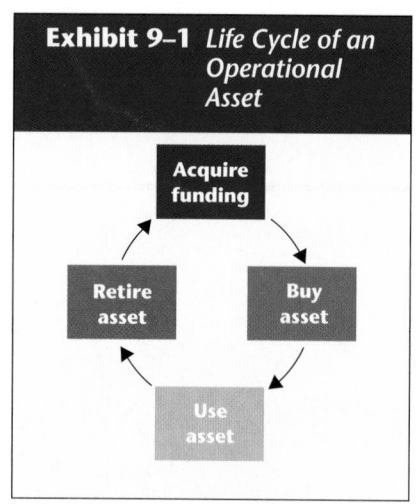

Exhibit 9–1 *Life Cycle of an Operational Asset*

▌Methods of Recognizing Depreciation Expense

The method used to recognize depreciation expense should match the asset's usage pattern. More expense should be recognized in periods when the asset is used more and less in periods when the asset is used less. Since assets are used to produce revenue, matching expense recognition with asset usage also matches expense recognition with revenue recognition. Three alternative methods for recognizing depreciation expense are (1) straight-line, (2) double-declining-balance, and (3) units-of-production.

The **straight-line** method produces the same amount of depreciation each accounting period. **Double-declining-balance,** an accelerated method, produces more depreciation expense in the early years of an asset's life, with a declining amount of expense in later years. **Units-of-production** produces varying amounts of depreciation in different accounting periods (more in some accounting periods and less in others). Exhibit 9–2 contrasts the different depreciation methods that U.S. companies use.

To illustrate the different depreciation methods, consider the accounting treatment for a van purchased by Dryden Enterprises. Dryden plans to use the van as rental property. The van had a list price of $23,500. Dryden obtained a 10 percent cash discount from the dealer. The van was delivered FOB shipping point, and Dryden paid an additional $250 for transportation costs. Dryden also paid $2,600 for a custom accessory package to increase the van's appeal as a rental vehicle. The cost of the van is computed as follows:

List price	$23,500	
Less: Cash discount	(2,350)	$23,500 × 0.10
Plus: Transportation costs	250	
Plus: Cost of customization	2,600	
Total	$24,000	

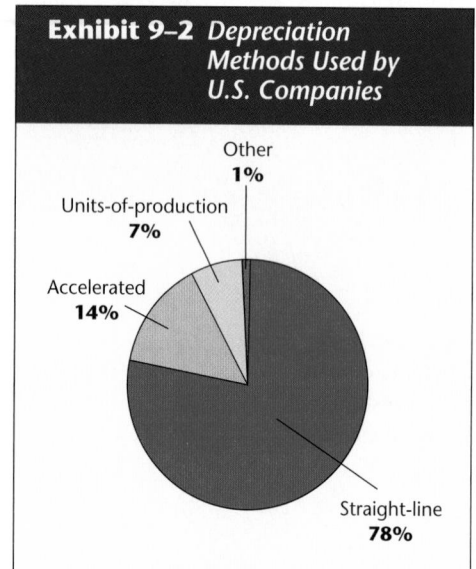

Exhibit 9–2 *Depreciation Methods Used by U.S. Companies*

Other
1%

Units-of-production
7%

Accelerated
14%

Straight-line
78%

Data source: AICPA Accounting Trends and Techniques, 2002.

The van has an estimated **salvage value** of $4,000 and an **estimated useful life** of four years. The following section examines three different patterns of expense recognition for this van.

Equipment is a long-term asset used for the purpose of producing revenue. The portion of the equipment used each accounting period is recognized as depreciation expense. Accordingly, the expense recognition for the cost of equipment is spread over the useful life of the asset. Timber, however, is not used until the trees are grown. Conceptually, the cost of the trees should be treated as inventories and expensed as cost of goods sold at the time the products made from trees are sold. Even so, some timber companies recognize a periodic charge called *depletion* in a manner similar to that used for depreciation.

Accounting for unusual long-term assets such as timber requires an understanding of specialized "industry practice" accounting rules that are beyond the scope of this course. Be aware that many industries have unique accounting problems, and business managers in such industries must make the effort to understand specialized accounting rules that relate to their companies.

Straight-Line Depreciation

The first scenario assumes the van was used evenly over its four-year life. Specifically, the revenue from renting the van is assumed to be $8,000 per year. The matching concept calls for the expense recognition pattern to match the revenue stream. Since the same amount of revenue is recognized in each accounting period, Dryden should use straight-line depreciation because it recognizes equal amounts of depreciation expense each year.

Life Cycle Phase 1

The first phase of the asset life cycle is to acquire funds to purchase the asset. Assume Dryden acquired $25,000 cash on January 1, 2001, by issuing common stock. The effect of this stock issue on the financial statements follows:

Assets				=	Equity			Rev.	−	Exp.	=	Net Inc.	Cash Flow
Cash	+	Van	− Acc. Dep.	=	Com. Stk.	+	Ret. Earn.						
25,000	+	NA	− NA	=	25,000	+	NA	NA	−	NA	=	NA	25,000 FA

Exhibit 9–3 displays financial statements for the life of the asset. The $25,000 cash inflow from the stock issue appears in the financing activities section of the 2001 statement of cash flows. Also, the balance sheet shows a $25,000 balance in Common Stock. The Cash account does not have a $25,000 balance because it is affected by other events in addition to the stock issue. For example, Dryden used cash to buy the asset and Dryden collected cash from rent revenue.

Life Cycle Phase 2

The second phase of the life cycle is to purchase the van. The cost of the van, previously computed, was $24,000 cash. The effect of the investment on the financial statements follows:

Assets				=	Equity			Rev.	−	Exp.	=	Net Inc.	Cash Flow
Cash	+	Van	− Acc. Dep.	=	Com. Stk.	+	Ret. Earn.						
(24,000)	+	24,000	− NA	=	NA	+	NA	NA	−	NA	=	NA	(24,000) IA

Trace the effects of this event to the financial statements in Exhibit 9–3. The cash outflow occurs only in 2001 (see the investing activities section of the statement of cash flows). However, the $24,000 cost of the asset is reported on the balance sheet throughout the van's entire life cycle (2001–2004). The historical cost is removed from the asset account when the van is retired in 2005.

Exhibit 9–3 *Financial Statements under Straight-Line Depreciation*

DRYDEN ENTERPRISES
Financial Statements

	2001	2002	2003	2004	2005
Income Statements					
Rent Revenue	$ 8,000	$ 8,000	$ 8,000	$ 8,000	$ 0
Depreciation Expense	(5,000)	(5,000)	(5,000)	(5,000)	0
Operating Income	3,000	3,000	3,000	3,000	0
Gain on Sale of Van	0	0	0	0	500
Net Income	$ 3,000	$ 3,000	$ 3,000	$ 3,000	$ 500
Balance Sheets					
Assets					
Cash	$ 9,000	$17,000	$25,000	$33,000	$37,500
Van	24,000	24,000	24,000	24,000	0
Accumulated Depreciation	(5,000)	(10,000)	(15,000)	(20,000)	0
Total Assets	$28,000	$31,000	$34,000	$37,000	$37,500
Stockholders' Equity					
Common Stock	$25,000	$25,000	$25,000	$25,000	$25,000
Retained Earnings	3,000	6,000	9,000	12,000	12,500
Total Stockholders' Equity	$28,000	$31,000	$34,000	$37,000	$37,500
Statements of Cash Flows					
Operating Activities					
Inflow from Customers	$ 8,000	$ 8,000	$ 8,000	$ 8,000	$ 0
Investing Activities					
Outflow to Purchase Van	(24,000)				
Inflow from Sale of Van					4,500
Financing Activities					
Inflow from Stock Issue	25,000				
Net Change in Cash	9,000	8,000	8,000	8,000	4,500
Beginning Cash Balance	0	9,000	17,000	25,000	33,000
Ending Cash Balance	$ 9,000	$17,000	$25,000	$33,000	$37,500

Life Cycle Phase 3

Using the asset generates $8,000 revenue per year. Depreciation expense calculated on a straight-line basis is determined as follows:

$$\text{(Asset cost} - \text{Salvage value)} \div \text{Useful life} = \text{Depreciation expense}$$
$$(\$24,000 - \$4,000) \div 4 \text{ years} = \$5,000 \text{ per year.}$$

Recognizing the depreciation expense is an asset use transaction that reduces assets and equity. The reduction in assets is reported using a **contra asset account** called **Accumulated Depreciation.** These effects are shown in the following statements model. Although illustrated only once, these effects actually would occur four times—once for each year the asset is in use.

Assets					Equity			Rev.	–	Exp.	=	Net Inc.	Cash Flow
Cash	+	Van	–	Acc. Dep.	=	Com. Stk.	+	Ret. Earn.					
8,000	+	NA	–	NA	=	NA	+	8,000	8,000 – NA = 8,000				8,000 OA
NA	+	NA	–	5,000	=	NA	+	(5,000)	NA – 5,000 = (5,000)				NA

As shown in Exhibit 9–3, the same amount of depreciation expense ($5,000) is recognized on the income statement each year throughout the life cycle (2001–2004). The accumulated depreciation is reported on the balance sheet, increasing from $5,000 to $10,000 to $15,000 and finally to $20,000 between 2001 and 2004. Trace these effects to the financial statements.

Recognizing depreciation expense does not affect cash flow. The entire cash outflow for this asset occurred in 2001 when it was purchased. Depreciation reflects using plant assets rather spending cash to purchase them.

Life Cycle Phase 4

The final stage in the life cycle of an operational asset is its retirement and removal from the company's records. Dryden retired the van from service on January 1, 2005, selling it for $4,500 cash. The van's book value when it was sold was $4,000 ($24,000 cost − $20,000 accumulated depreciation), so Dryden recognized a $500 gain ($4,500 − $4,000) on the sale. The effects of the retirement on the financial statements are shown here:

LO4 Determine how gains and losses on disposals of long-term operational assets affect financial statements.

Assets					=	Equity			Rev. or Gain	−	Exp. or Loss	=	Net Inc.	Cash Flow
Cash	+	Van	−	Acc. Dep.	=	C. Stk.	+	Ret. Earn.						
4,500	+	(24,000)	−	(20,000)	=	NA	+	500	500	−	NA	=	500	4,500 IA

Although the gain reported on the 2005 income statement is $500, the cash inflow from selling the van is $4,500. Gains and losses are not reported separately on the statement of cash flows. Instead they are included in the total amount of cash collected from the sale of the asset. In this case, the entire $4,500 is shown in the cash flow from investing activities section of the 2005 statement of cash flows.

Tracing the effects of these events to the financial statements in Exhibit 9–3 illustrates how businesses recover their invested funds. The total cash inflow from using and retiring the van is $36,500 ([$8,000 revenue × 4 years] + $4,500 actual salvage value). Dryden not only recovered the cost of the asset ($24,000) but also generated a $12,500 ($36,500 − $24,000) return on its investment. This is consistent with the total amount of net income that was earned over the life cycle ([$3,000 × 4 years] + $500 gain). The difference between net income and cash flow is a matter of timing.

Finally, note that the amount of retained earnings shown on the 2005 balance sheet is also $12,500. Since the amount of retained earnings equals the sum of the amounts of net income reported on the 2001 through 2005 income statements, we conclude that Dryden paid no dividends to its stockholders.

Recording Procedures

Exhibit 9–4 displays the general journal entries to record the transactions over the life cycle of the van.

Double-Declining-Balance Depreciation

For the second scenario, assume demand for the van is strong when it is new, but fewer people rent the van as it ages. As a result, the van produces smaller amounts of revenue as time goes by. To match expenses with revenues, it is reasonable to recognize more depreciation expense in the van's early years and less as it ages.

LO3 Explain how different depreciation methods affect financial statements.

Double-declining-balance depreciation produces a large amount of depreciation in the first year of an asset's life and progressively smaller levels of expense in each succeeding year. Since the double-declining-balance method recognizes depreciation expense more rapidly than the straight-line method does, it is called an **accelerated depreciation method.** Depreciation expense recognized using double-declining-balance is computed in three steps.

1. *Determine the straight-line rate.* Divide one by the asset's useful life. Since the estimated useful life of Dryden's van is four years, the straight-line rate is 25 percent (1 ÷ 4) per year.
2. *Determine the double-declining-balance rate.* Multiply the straight-line rate by 2 (*double* the rate). The double-declining-balance rate for the van is 50 percent (25 percent × 2).

Exhibit 9–4 *General Journal Entries*

Account Title	Debit	Credit
Cash	25,000	
Common Stock		25,000
Entry on January 1, 2001, to record capital acquisition		
Van	24,000	
Cash		24,000
Entry on January 1, 2001, to record investment in van		
Cash	8,000	
Rent Revenue		8,000
Revenue recognition entries on December 31, 2001–2004		
Depreciation Expense	5,000	
Accumulated Depreciation		5,000
Expense recognition entries on December 31, 2001–2004		
Cash	4,500	
Accumulated Depreciation	20,000	
Van		24,000
Gain on Sale of Van		500
Entry on January 1, 2005, to record asset disposal		

3. *Determine the depreciation expense.* Multiply the double-declining-balance rate by the book value of the asset *at the beginning of the period* (recall that **book value** is historical cost minus *accumulated depreciation*). The following table shows the amount of depreciation expense Dryden will recognize over the van's useful life (2001–2004).

Year	Book Value at Beginning of Period	×	Double the Straight-Line Rate	=	Annual Depreciation Expense	
2001	($24,000 − $ 0)	×	0.50	=	$12,000	
2002	(24,000 − 12,000)	×	0.50	=	6,000	
2003	(24,000 − 18,000)	×	0.50	=	~~3,000~~	2,000
2004	(24,000 − 20,000)	×	0.50	=	~~2,000~~	0

Regardless of the depreciation method used, *an asset cannot be depreciated below its salvage value.* This restriction affects depreciation computations for the third and fourth years. Because the van had a cost of $24,000 and a salvage value of $4,000, the total amount of **depreciable cost** (historical cost − salvage value) is $20,000 ($24,000 − $4,000). Since $18,000 ($12,000 + $6,000) of the depreciable cost is recognized in the first two years, only $2,000 ($20,000 − $18,000) remains to be recognized after the second year. Depreciation expense recognized in the third year is therefore $2,000 even though double-declining-balance computations suggest that $3,000 should be recognized. Similarly, zero depreciation expense is recognized in the fourth year even though the computations indicate a $2,000 charge.

Effects on the Financial Statements

Exhibit 9–5 displays financial statements for the life of the asset assuming Dryden uses double-declining-balance depreciation. The illustration assumes a cash revenue stream of $15,000, $9,000, $5,000, and $3,000 for the years 2001, 2002, 2003, and 2004, respectively. Trace the depreciation expense from the table above to the income statements. Reported depreciation expense is greater in the earlier years and smaller in the later years of the asset's life.

The double-declining-balance method smoothes the amount of net income reported over the asset's useful life. In the early years, when heavy asset use produces higher revenue, depreciation expense is also higher. Similarly, in the later years, lower levels of revenue are matched with lower levels of depreciation expense. Net income is constant at $3,000 per year.

Exhibit 9–5 *Financial Statements under Double-Declining-Balance Depreciation*

DRYDEN ENTERPRISES
Financial Statements

	2001	2002	2003	2004	2005
Income Statements					
Rent Revenue	$15,000	$ 9,000	$ 5,000	$ 3,000	$ 0
Depreciation Expense	(12,000)	(6,000)	(2,000)	0	0
Operating Income	3,000	3,000	3,000	3,000	0
Gain on Sale of Van	0	0	0	0	500
Net Income	$ 3,000	$ 3,000	$ 3,000	$ 3,000	$ 500
Balance Sheets					
Assets					
Cash	$16,000	$25,000	$30,000	$33,000	$37,500
Van	24,000	24,000	24,000	24,000	0
Accumulated Depreciation	(12,000)	(18,000)	(20,000)	(20,000)	0
Total Assets	$28,000	$31,000	$34,000	$37,000	$37,500
Stockholders' Equity					
Common Stock	$25,000	$25,000	$25,000	$25,000	$25,000
Retained Earnings	3,000	6,000	9,000	12,000	12,500
Total Stockholders' Equity	$28,000	$31,000	$34,000	$37,000	$37,500
Statements of Cash Flows					
Operating Activities					
Inflow from Customers	$15,000	$ 9,000	$ 5,000	$ 3,000	$ 0
Investing Activities					
Outflow to Purchase Van	(24,000)				
Inflow from Sale of Van					4,500
Financing Activities					
Inflow from Stock Issue	25,000				
Net Change in Cash	16,000	9,000	5,000	3,000	4,500
Beginning Cash Balance	0	16,000	25,000	30,000	33,000
Ending Cash Balance	$16,000	$25,000	$30,000	$33,000	$37,500

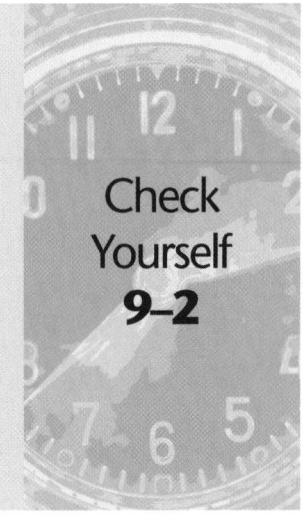

Olds Company purchased an asset that cost $36,000 on January 1, 2001. The asset had an expected useful life of five years and an estimated salvage value of $5,000. Assuming Olds uses the double-declining-balance method, determine the amount of depreciation expense and the amount of accumulated depreciation Olds would report on the 2003 financial statements.

Answer

Year	Book Value at the Beginning of the Period	×	Double the Straight-Line Rate*	=	Annual Depreciation Expense
2001	($36,000 − $ 0)	×	0.40	=	$14,400
2002	(36,000 − 14,400)	×	0.40	=	8,640
2003	(36,000 − 23,040)	×	0.40	=	5,184
Total accumulated depreciation at December 31, 2003					$28,224

*Double-declining-balance rate = 2 × Straight-line rate = 2 × (1 ÷ 5 years) = 0.40

Check Yourself 9–2

The depreciation method a company uses *does not* affect how it acquires the financing, invests the funds, and retires the asset. For Dryden's van, the accounting effects of these life cycle phases are the same as under the straight-line approach. Similarly, the *recording procedures* are not affected by the depreciation method. Different depreciation methods affect only the amounts of depreciation expense recorded each year, not which accounts are used. The general journal entries are therefore not illustrated for the double-declining-balance or the units-of-production depreciation methods.

Units-of-Production Depreciation

LO3 Explain how different depreciation methods affect financial statements.

Suppose rental demand for Dryden's van depends on general economic conditions. In a robust economy, travel increases, and demand for renting vans is high. In a stagnant economy, demand for van rentals declines. In such circumstances, revenues fluctuate from year to year. To accomplish the matching objective, depreciation should also fluctuate from year to year. A method of depreciation known as **units-of-production** accomplishes this goal by basing depreciation expense on actual asset usage.

Computing depreciation expense using units-of-production begins with identifying a measure of the asset's productive capacity. For example, the number of miles Dryden expects its van to be driven may be a reasonable measure of its productive capacity. If the depreciable asset were a saw, an appropriate measure of productive capacity could be the number of board feet the saw was expected to cut during its useful life. In other words, the basis for measuring production depends on the nature of the depreciable asset.

To illustrate computing depreciation using the units-of-production depreciation method, assume that Dryden measures productive capacity based on the total number of miles the van will be driven over its useful life. Assume Dryden estimates this productive capacity to be 100,000 miles. The first step in determining depreciation expense is to compute the cost per unit of production. For Dryden's van, this amount is total depreciable cost (historical cost − salvage value) divided by total units of expected productive capacity (100,000 miles). The depreciation cost per mile is therefore $0.20 ([$24,000 cost − $4,000 salvage] ÷ 100,000 miles). Annual depreciation expense is computed by multiplying the cost per mile by the number of miles driven. Odometer readings indicate the van was driven 40,000 miles, 20,000 miles, 30,000 miles, and 15,000 miles in 2001, 2002, 2003, and 2004, respectively. Dryden developed the following schedule of depreciation charges.

Year	Cost per Mile (a)	Miles Driven (b)	Depreciation Expense (a × b)
2001	$.20	40,000	$8,000
2002	.20	20,000	4,000
2003	.20	30,000	6,000
2004	.20	15,000	~~3,000~~ 2,000

As pointed out in the discussion of the double-declining-balance method, an asset cannot be depreciated below its salvage value. Since $18,000 of the $20,000 ($24,000 cost − $4,000 salvage) depreciable cost is recognized in the first three years of using the van, only $2,000 ($20,000 − $18,000) remains to be charged to depreciation in the fourth year, even though the depreciation computations suggest the charge should be $3,000. As the preceding table indicates, the general formula for computing units-of-production depreciation is:

$$\frac{\text{Cost} - \text{Salvage value}}{\text{Total estimated units of production}} \times \begin{matrix}\text{Units of production}\\\text{in current}\\\text{accounting period}\end{matrix} = \begin{matrix}\text{Annual}\\\text{depreciation}\\\text{expense}\end{matrix}$$

Exhibit 9–6 displays financial statements that assume Dryden uses units-of-production depreciation. The exhibit assumes a cash revenue stream of $11,000, $7,000, $9,000, and $5,000 for 2001, 2002, 2003, and 2004, respectively. Trace the depreciation expense from the schedule above to the income statements. Depreciation expense is greater in years the van is driven more and smaller in years the van is driven less, providing a reasonable matching of depreciation expense with revenue produced. Net income is again constant at $3,000 per year.

Comparing the Depreciation Methods

LO3 Explain how different depreciation methods affect financial statements.

The total amount of depreciation expense Dryden recognized using each of the three methods was $20,000 ($24,000 cost − $4,000 salvage value). The different methods affect the *timing,*

Exhibit 9–6 Financial Statements under Units-of-Production Depreciation

DRYDEN ENTERPRISES
Financial Statements

	2001	2002	2003	2004	2005
Income Statements					
Rent Revenue	$11,000	$ 7,000	$ 9,000	$ 5,000	$ 0
Depreciation Expense	(8,000)	(4,000)	(6,000)	(2,000)	0
Operating Income	3,000	3,000	3,000	3,000	0
Gain on Sale of Van	0	0	0	0	500
Net Income	$ 3,000	$ 3,000	$ 3,000	$ 3,000	$ 500
Balance Sheets					
Assets					
Cash	$12,000	$19,000	$28,000	$33,000	$37,500
Van	24,000	24,000	24,000	24,000	0
Accumulated Depreciation	(8,000)	(12,000)	(18,000)	(20,000)	0
Total Assets	$28,000	$31,000	$34,000	$37,000	$37,500
Stockholders' Equity					
Common Stock	$25,000	$25,000	$25,000	$25,000	$25,000
Retained Earnings	3,000	6,000	9,000	12,000	12,500
Total Stockholders' Equity	$28,000	$31,000	$34,000	$37,000	$37,500
Statements of Cash Flows					
Operating Activities					
Inflow from Customers	$11,000	$ 7,000	$ 9,000	$ 5,000	$ 0
Investing Activities					
Outflow to Purchase Van	(24,000)				
Inflow from Sale of Van					4,500
Financing Activities					
Inflow from Stock Issue	25,000				
Net Change in Cash	12,000	7,000	9,000	5,000	4,500
Beginning Cash Balance	0	12,000	19,000	28,000	33,000
Ending Cash Balance	$12,000	$19,000	$28,000	$33,000	$37,500

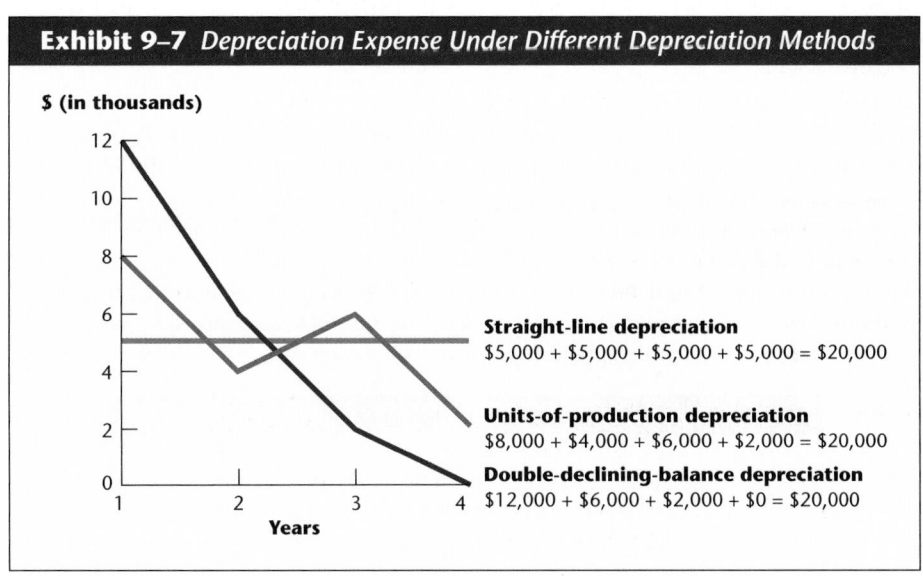

Exhibit 9–7 Depreciation Expense Under Different Depreciation Methods

Straight-line depreciation
$5,000 + $5,000 + $5,000 + $5,000 = $20,000

Units-of-production depreciation
$8,000 + $4,000 + $6,000 + $2,000 = $20,000

Double-declining-balance depreciation
$12,000 + $6,000 + $2,000 + $0 = $20,000

but not the *total amount*, of expense recognized. The different methods simply assign the $20,000 to different accounting periods. Exhibit 9–7 presents graphically the differences among the three depreciation methods discussed above. A company should use the method that most closely matches expenses with revenues.

Income Tax Considerations

The matching principle is not relevant to income tax reporting. The objective of tax reporting is to minimize tax expense. For tax purposes the most desirable depreciation method is the one that produces the highest amount of depreciation expense. Higher expenses mean lower taxes.

The maximum depreciation currently allowed by tax law is computed using an accelerated depreciation method known as the **modified accelerated cost recovery system (MACRS).** MACRS specifies the useful life for designated categories of assets. For example, under the law, companies must base depreciation computations for automobiles, light trucks, technological equipment, and other similar asset types on a 5-year useful life. In contrast, a 7-year life must be used for office furniture, fixtures, and many types of conventional machinery. The law classifies depreciable property, excluding real estate, into one of six categories: 3-year property, 5-year property, 7-year property, 10-year property, 15-year property, and 20-year property. Tables have been established for each category that specify the percentage of cost that can be expensed (deducted) in determining the amount of taxable income. A tax table for 5- and 7-year property is shown here as an example.

Year	5-Year Property, %	7-Year Property, %
1	20.00	14.29
2	32.00	24.49
3	19.20	17.49
4	11.52	12.49
5	11.52	8.93
6	5.76	8.92
7		8.93
8		4.46

The amount of depreciation a company can deduct each year for tax purposes is determined by multiplying the cost of a depreciable asset by the percentage shown in the table. For example, the depreciation expense for year 1 of a 7-year property asset is the cost of the property multiplied by 14.29 percent. Depreciation for year 2 is the cost multiplied by 24.49 percent.

The tables present some apparent inconsistencies. For example, if MACRS is an accelerated depreciation method, why is less depreciation permitted in year 1 than in years 2 and 3? Also, why is depreciation computed in year 6 for property with a 5-year life and in year 8 for property with a 7-year life? In fact, these conditions are the consequence of using the **half-year convention.**

The half-year convention is designed to simplify computing taxable income. Instead of requiring taxpayers to calculate depreciation from the exact date of purchase to the exact date of disposal, the tax code requires one-half year's depreciation to be charged in the year in which an asset is acquired and one-half year's depreciation in the year of disposal. As a result, the percentages shown in the table for the first and last years represent depreciation for one-half year instead of the actual time of usage.

To illustrate computing depreciation using MACRS, assume that Wilson Company purchased furniture (7-year property) for $10,000 cash on July 21. Tax depreciation charges over the useful life of the asset are computed as shown:

Year	Table Factor, %	×	Cost	=	Depreciation Amount
1	14.29		$10,000		$ 1,429
2	24.49		10,000		2,449
3	17.49		10,000		1,749
4	12.49		10,000		1,249
5	8.93		10,000		893
6	8.92		10,000		892
7	8.93		10,000		893
8	4.46		10,000		446
Total over useful life					$10,000

As an alternative to MACRS, the tax code permits using straight-line depreciation. For certain types of assets such as real property (buildings), the tax code requires using straight-line depreciation.

There is no requirement that depreciation methods used for financial reporting be consistent with those used in preparing the income tax return. For example, a company may use straight-line depreciation in its financial statements and MACRS for the tax return. A company making this choice would reduce taxes in the early years of an asset's life because it would report higher depreciation charges on the tax return than in the financial statements. In later years, however, taxes will be higher because under MACRS, the amount of depreciation declines as the asset becomes older. Taxes are delayed but not avoided. The amount of taxes delayed for future payment represent a **deferred tax liability.** Delaying tax payments is advantageous. During the delay period, the money that would have been used to pay taxes can be used instead to make revenue-generating investments.

Revision of Estimates

In order to report useful financial information on a timely basis, accountants must make many estimates of future results, such as the salvage value and useful life of depreciable assets, bad debts expense, and warranty obligations. Estimates are frequently revised when new information surfaces. Because revisions of estimates are common, generally accepted accounting principles call for incorporating the revised information into present and future calculations. Prior reports are not corrected.

LO6 Show how revising estimates affects financial statements.

To illustrate, assume that McGraw Company purchased a machine on January 1, 2003, for $50,000. McGraw estimated the machine would have a useful life of eight years and a salvage value of $3,000. Using the straight-line method, McGraw determined the annual depreciation charge as follows:

$$(\$50,000 - \$3,000) \div 8 \text{ years} = \$5,875 \text{ per year}$$

At the beginning of the fifth year, accumulated depreciation on the machine is $23,500 ($5,875 × 4). The machine's book value is $26,500 ($50,000 − $23,500). At this point, what happens if McGraw changes its estimates of useful life or the salvage value? Consider the following revision examples independently of each other.

Revision of Life

Assume McGraw revises the expected life to 14, rather than 8, years. The machine's *remaining* life would then be 10 more years instead of 4 more years. Assume salvage value remains $3,000. Depreciation for each remaining year is:

$$(\$26,500 \text{ book value} - \$3,000 \text{ salvage}) \div 10\text{-year remaining life} = \$2,350$$

Revision of Salvage

Alternatively, assume the original expected life remained eight years, but McGraw revised its estimate of salvage value to $6,000. Depreciation for each of the remaining four years would be

$$(\$26,500 \text{ book value} - \$6,000 \text{ salvage}) \div 4\text{-year remaining life} = \$5,125$$

Note that the revised amounts are determined for the full year, regardless of when McGraw revised its estimates. For example, if McGraw decides to change the estimated useful life on October 1, 2008, the change would be effective as of January 1, 2008. The year-end adjusting entry for depreciation would include a full year's depreciation calculated on the basis of the new estimated useful life.

Continuing Expenditures for Plant Assets

Most plant assets require additional expenditures for maintenance or improvement during their useful lives. Accountants must determine if these expenditures should be expensed or capitalized.

Costs that Are Expensed

The cost of routine maintenance and minor repairs that are incurred to *keep* an asset in good working order are expensed in the period in which they are incurred. With respect to the previous example, assume McGraw spent $500 for routine lubrication and to replace minor parts. The effect of the expenditure on the financial statements and the journal entry necessary to record it follow:

Assets	=	Equity			Rev.	−	Exp.	=	Net Inc.	Cash Flow
Cash	=	C. Stk.	+	Ret. Earn.						
(500)	=	NA	+	(500)	NA	−	500	=	(500)	(500) OA

Account Title	Debit	Credit
Repairs Expense	500	
Cash		500

Costs that Are Capitalized

Substantial amounts spent to improve the quality or extend the life of an asset are described as **capital expenditures.** Capital expenditures are accounted for in one of two ways, depending on whether the cost incurred *improves the quality* or *extends the life* of the asset.

Improving Quality

If the expenditure improves the quality of the asset, the amount is added to the historical cost of the asset. The additional cost is then expensed through higher depreciation charges over the asset's remaining useful life.

To demonstrate, return to the McGraw Company example. Recall that the machine originally cost $50,000, had an estimated salvage of $3,000, and had a predicted life of eight years. Recall further that accumulated depreciation at the beginning of the fifth year is $23,500 ($5,875 × 4) so the book value is $26,500 ($50,000 − $23,500). Assume McGraw makes a major expenditure of $4,000 in the machine's fifth year to improve its productive capacity. The effect of the $4,000 expenditure on the financial statements and the journal entry necessary to record it follow:

Assets				=	Equity			Rev.	−	Exp.	=	Net Inc.	Cash Flow
Cash	+	Mach.	−	Acc. Dep.	=	C. Stk.	+	Ret. Earn.					
(4,000)	+	4,000	−	NA	=	NA	+	NA	NA	−	NA	=	NA	(4,000) IA

Account Title	Debit	Credit
Machine	4,000	
Cash		4,000

After recording the expenditure, the machine account balance is $54,000 and the asset's book value is $30,500 ($54,000 − $23,500). The depreciation charges for the remaining four years are:

($30,500 book value − $3,000 salvage) ÷ 4-year remaining life = $6,875

Extending Life

When a company makes a capital expenditure that extends the life of an asset but not its quality, accountants view the expenditure as canceling some of the depreciation previously charged to expense. The event is still an asset exchange; cash decreases, and the book value of the machine increases. However, the increase in the book value of the machine results from reducing the balance in the contra asset account, Accumulated Depreciation.

To illustrate, assume that instead of increasing productive capacity, McGraw's $4,000 expenditure had extended the useful life of the machine by two years. The effect of the expenditure on the financial statements and the journal entry necessary to record it follow:

Assets				=	Equity			Rev.	−	Exp.	=	Net Inc.	Cash Flow
Cash	+	Mach.	− Acc. Dep.	=	C. Stk.	+	Ret. Earn.						
(4,000)	+	NA	− (4,000)	=	NA	+	NA	NA	−	NA	=	NA	(4,000) IA

Account Title	Debit	Credit
Accumulated Depreciation—Machine	4,000	
Cash		4,000

After the expenditure is recorded, the book value is the same as if the $4,000 had been added to the Machine account ($50,000 cost − $19,500 adjusted balance in Accumulated Depreciation = $30,500). Depreciation expense for each of the remaining six years follows:

($30,500 book value − $3,000 salvage) ÷ 6-year remaining life = $4,583

On January 1, 2003, Dager, Inc., purchased an asset that cost $18,000. It had a five-year useful life and a $3,000 salvage value. Dager uses straight-line depreciation. On January 1, 2005, it incurred a $1,200 cost related to the asset. With respect to this asset, determine the amount of expense and accumulated depreciation Dager would report in the 2005 financial statements under each of the following assumptions.

1. The $1,200 cost was incurred to repair damage resulting from an accident.
2. The $1,200 cost improved the operating capacity of the equipment. The total useful life and salvage value remained unchanged.
3. The $1,200 cost extended the useful life of the asset by one year. The salvage value remained unchanged.

Check Yourself 9-3

Answer
1. Dager would report the $1,200 repair cost as an expense. Dager would also report depreciation expense of $3,000 ([$18,000 − $3,000] ÷ 5). Total expenses related to this asset in 2005 would be $4,200 ($1,200 repair expense + $3,000 depreciation expense). Accumulated depreciation at the end of 2005 would be $9,000 ($3,000 depreciation expense × 3 years).
2. The $1,200 cost would be capitalized in the asset account, increasing both the book value of the asset and the annual depreciation expense.

continued

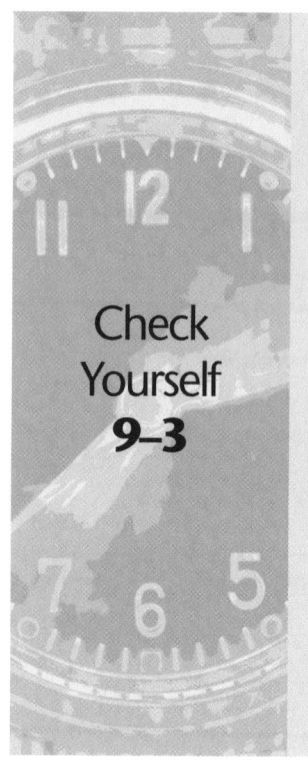

Check Yourself 9–3

	After Effects of Capital Improvement
Amount in asset account ($18,000 + $1,200)	$19,200
Less: Salvage value	(3,000)
Accumulated depreciation on January 1, 2005	(6,000)
Remaining depreciable cost before recording 2005 depreciation	$10,200
Depreciation for 2005 ($10,200 ÷ 3 years)	$ 3,400
Accumulated depreciation at December 31, 2005 ($6,000 + $3,400)	$ 9,400

3. The $1,200 cost would be subtracted from the Accumulated Depreciation account, increasing the book value of the asset. The remaining useful life would increase to four years, which would decrease the depreciation expense.

	After Effects of Capital Improvement
Amount in asset account	$18,000
Less: Salvage value	(3,000)
Accumulated depreciation on January 1, 2005 ($6,000 − $1,200)	(4,800)
Remaining depreciable cost before recording 2005 depreciation	$10,200
Depreciation for 2005 ($10,200 ÷ 4 years)	$ 2,550
Accumulated depreciation at December 31, 2005 ($4,800 + $2,550)	$ 7,350

▌Natural Resources

LO8 Explain how expense recognition for natural resources (depletion) affects financial statements.

The cost of natural resources includes not only the purchase price but also related items such as the cost of exploration, geographic surveys, and estimates. The process of expensing natural resources is commonly called depletion.[1] The most common method used to calculate depletion is units-of-production.

To illustrate, assume Apex Coal Mining paid $4,000,000 cash to purchase a mine with an estimated 16,000,000 tons of coal. The unit depletion charge is:

$$\$4,000,000 \div 16,000,000 \text{ tons} = \$0.25 \text{ per ton}$$

If Apex mines 360,000 tons of coal in the first year, the depletion charge is:

$$360,000 \text{ tons} \times \$0.25 \text{ per ton} = \$90,000$$

The depletion of a natural resource has the same effect on the accounting equation as other expense recognition events. Assets (in this case, a *coal mine*) and stockholders' equity decrease. The depletion expense reduces net income. The effect on the financial statements and the journal entries necessary to record the acquisition and depletion of the coal mine follow:

Assets			=	Equity			Rev.	−	Exp.	=	Net Inc.	Cash Flow	
Cash	+	Coal Mine	=	C. Stk.	+	Ret. Earn.							
(4,000,000)	+	4,000,000	=	NA	+	NA	NA	−	NA	=	NA	(4,000,000)	IA
NA	+	(90,000)	=	NA	+	(90,000)	NA	−	90,000	=	(90,000)	NA	

---

[1]In practice, the depletion charge is considered a product cost and allocated between inventory and cost of goods sold. This text uses the simplifying assumption that all resources are sold in the same accounting period in which they are extracted. The full depletion charge is therefore expensed in the period in which the resources are extracted.

Account Title	Debit	Credit
Coal Mine	4,000,000	
Cash		4,000,000
Depletion Expense	90,000	
Coal Mine		90,000

Intangible Assets

Intangible assets provide rights, privileges, and special opportunities to businesses. Common intangible assets include trademarks, patents, copyrights, franchises, and goodwill. Some of the unique characteristics of these intangible assets are described in the following sections.

LO9 Explain how expense recognition for intangible assets (amortization) affects financial statements.

Trademarks

A **trademark** is a name or symbol that identifies a company or a product. Familiar trademarks include the Polo emblem, the name *Coca-Cola*, and the Nike slogan, "Just do it." Trademarks are registered with the federal government and have an indefinite legal lifetime.

The costs incurred to design, purchase or defend a trademark are capitalized in an asset account called Trademarks. Companies want their trademarks to become familiar but also face the risk of a trademark being used as the generic name for a product. To protect a trademark, companies in this predicament spend large sums on legal fees and extensive advertising programs to educate consumers. Well-known trademarks that have been subject to this problem include Coke, Xerox, Kleenex, and Vaseline.

Patents

A **patent** grants its owner an exclusive legal right to produce and sell a product that has one or more unique features. Patents issued by the U.S. Patent Office have a legal life of 17 years. Companies may obtain patents through purchase, lease, or internal development. The costs capitalized in the Patent account are usually limited to the purchase price and legal fees to obtain and defend the patent. The research and development costs that are incurred to develop patentable products are usually expensed in the period in which they are incurred.

Copyrights

A **copyright** protects writings, musical compositions, works of art, and other intellectual property for the exclusive benefit of the creator or persons assigned the right by the creator. The cost of a copyright includes the purchase price and any legal costs associated with obtaining and defending the copyright. Copyrights granted by the federal government extend for the life of the creator plus 50 years. A radio commercial could legally use a Bach composition as background music; it could not, however, use the theme song from the movie, The Matrix, without obtaining permission from the copyright owner. The cost of a copyright is often expensed early because future royalties may be uncertain.

Franchises

Franchises grant exclusive rights to sell products or perform services in certain geographic areas. Franchises may be granted by governments or private businesses. Franchises granted by governments include federal broadcasting licenses. Private business franchises include fast-food restaurant chains and brand labels such as Healthy Choice. The legal and useful lives of a franchise are frequently difficult to determine. Judgment is often crucial to establishing the estimated useful life for franchises.

Goodwill

Goodwill is the value attributable to favorable factors such as reputation, location, and superior products. Consider the most popular restaurant in your town. If the owner sold the restaurant, do you think the purchase price would be simply the total value of the chairs, tables, kitchen equipment, and building? Certainly not, because much of the restaurant's value lies in its popularity; in other words, its ability to generate a high return is based on the goodwill (reputation) of the business.

focus on INTERNATIONAL ISSUES

U.S. GAAP: A Competitive Disadvantage?

The accounting rules of various countries have many differences, but, over the years, perhaps none caused as much concern to companies involved in global competition as the rules related to accounting for goodwill and research and development (R&D).

Suppose that Company A paid $300,000 to purchase Company B's assets. Furthermore, suppose Company B's assets have a market value of only $200,000. In the United States, the $100,000 difference is classified as *goodwill.* Before July 2001, this goodwill would have been amortized (expensed) over its useful life. In the United Kingdom, the treatment is very different. A U.K. company is allowed

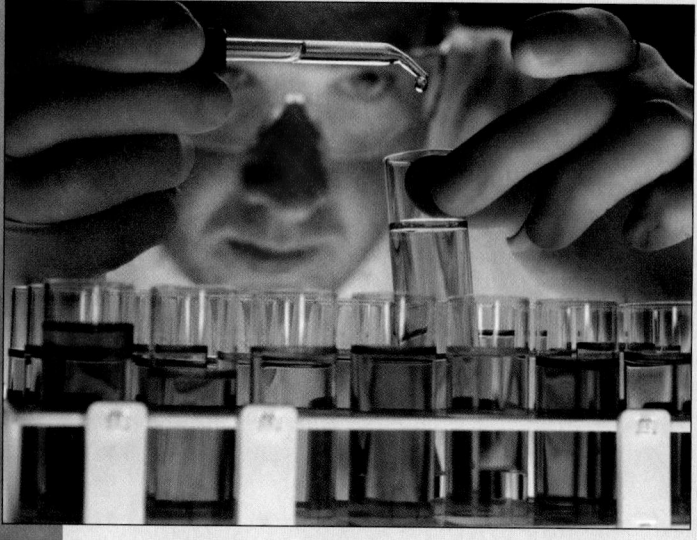

to charge the entire $100,000 *directly against equity* in the year of the purchase. Normally, a cost is placed in an asset account and then expensed. When the expense is recognized, net income decreases and retained earnings decreases. Under the U.K. approach, you simply skip the income statement by making a charge directly to Retained Earnings.

In July 2001, the FASB voted to change radically the U.S. GAAP related to accounting for business combinations, which includes accounting for goodwill. Now goodwill is placed on the balance sheet as an asset, but it never has to be written off as an expense, so long as the value of the goodwill does not decrease. The rules governing accounting for business combinations in the United States are now more like those of other industrialized nations.

Suppose Company X is a pharmaceutical company that spends $10 million on the R&D of a new drug. Under U.S. GAAP, the company is required to expense the $10 million immediately. In Japan, the company is allowed to capitalize the cost in an asset account and then to expense it gradually over the useful life of the asset. Accordingly, in the year in which R&D costs are incurred, a U.S. company reports more expense and less income than its Japanese counterpart.

Some businesspeople believe that U.S. GAAP can put U.S. companies at a competitive disadvantage in the search for capital. Certainly, the rules pertaining to goodwill and R&D demonstrate how U.S. companies may be forced to report lower earnings. Foreign companies that report higher earnings may be able to attract international investors who would otherwise invest in U.S. companies. Keep in mind that well-informed business professionals know how different accounting rules affect a company's financial statements. If they believe that U.S. GAAP cause a company's earnings to be understated, they take this into consideration when making investment decisions.

In September 2001, Hewlett-Packard Company (HP) agreed to pay approximately $24 billion to acquire Compaq Computer Corporation. At the time, Compaq's balance sheet showed net assets (assets minus liabilities) of approximately $11.7 billion. Why would HP pay the owners of Compaq twice the value of the assets reported on the company's balance sheet?

HP was likely willing to pay twice the book value of the assets for three reasons. First, the value of the assets on Compaq's balance sheet represented the historical cost of the assets. The current market value of these assets was probably higher than their historical cost, especially for assets such as the Compaq trademark. Second, HP believed that the two companies combined could operate at a lower cost than the two could as separate companies, thus increasing the total income they could generate. Finally, HP probably believed that Compaq had *goodwill,* which enables a company to generate above average earnings from using its assets. In other words, HP was paying for a hidden asset not reported on Compaq's balance sheet.

Calculating goodwill can be very complex; here we present a simple example to illustrate how it is determined. Suppose the accounting records of a restaurant named Bendigo's show:

$$\text{Assets} = \text{Liabilities} + \text{Stockholders' Equity}$$
$$\$200,000 = \$50,000 + \$150,000$$

Assume a buyer agrees to purchase the restaurant by paying the owner $300,000 cash and assuming the existing liabilities. In other words, the restaurant is purchased at a price of $350,000 ($300,000 cash + $50,000 assumed liabilities). Now assume that the assets of the business (tables, chairs, kitchen equipment, etc.) have a fair market value of only $280,000. Why would the buyer pay $350,000 to purchase assets with a market value of $280,000? Obviously, the buyer is purchasing more than just the assets. Indeed, the buyer is purchasing the business's goodwill. The amount of the goodwill is the difference between the purchase price and the fair market value of the assets. In this case, the goodwill is $70,000 ($350,000 − $280,000). The effects of the purchase on the financial statements of the buyer follow:

Assets					=	Liab.	+	Equity	Rev.	−	Exp.	=	Net Inc.	Cash Flow
Cash	+	Rest. Assets	+	Goodwill										
(300,000)	+	280,000	+	70,000	=	50,000	+	NA	NA	−	NA	=	NA	(300,000) IA

The journal entry to record the purchase of the restaurant is:

Account Title	Debit	Credit
Restaurant Assets	280,000	
Goodwill	70,000	
Cash		300,000
Liabilities		50,000

The fair market value of the restaurant assets represents the historical cost to the new owner. It becomes the basis for future depreciation charges.

Expense Recognition for Intangible Assets

As mentioned earlier, intangible assets fall into two categories, those with *identifiable useful lives* and those with *indefinite useful lives*. Expense recognition for intangible assets depends on which classification applies.

Expensing Intangible Assets with Identifiable Useful Lives

The costs of intangible assets with identifiable useful lives are normally expensed on a straight-line basis using a process called *amortization*. An intangible asset should be amortized over the shorter of two possible time periods: (1) its legal life or (2) its useful life.

To illustrate, assume that Flowers Industries purchased a newly granted patent for $44,000 cash. Although the patent has a legal life of 17 years, Flowers estimates that it will be useful for only 11 years. The annual amortization charge is therefore $4,000 ($44,000 ÷ 11 years). The effect on the financial statements of the patent purchase and first year amortization and the journal entries to record these events follow:

Assets			=	Equity			Rev.	−	Exp.	=	Net Inc.	Cash Flow
Cash	+	Patent	=	C. Stk.	+	Ret. Earn.						
(44,000)	+	44,000	=	NA	+	NA	NA	−	NA	=	NA	(44,000) IA
NA	+	(4,000)	=	NA	+	(4,000)	NA	−	4,000	=	(4,000)	NA

Account Title	Debit	Credit
Patent	44,000	
Cash		44,000
Amortization Expense, Patent	4,000	
Patent		4,000

Impairment Losses for Intangible Assets with Indefinite Useful Lives

Intangible assets with indefinite useful lives must be tested for impairment annually. The impairment test consists of comparing the fair value of the intangible asset to its carrying value (book value). If the fair value is less than the book value, an impairment loss must be recognized.

To illustrate, return to the example of the Bendigo's restaurant purchase. Recall that the buyer of Bendigo's paid $70,000 for goodwill. Assume the restaurant experiences a significant decline in revenue because many of its former regular customers are dissatisfied with the food prepared by the new chef. Suppose the decline in revenue is so substantial that the new owner believes the Bendigo's name is permanently impaired. The owner decides to hire a different chef and change the name of the restaurant. In this case, the business has suffered a permanent decline in value of goodwill. The company must recognize an impairment loss.

The restaurant's name has lost its value, but the owner believes the location continues to provide the opportunity to produce above-average earnings. Some, but not all, of the goodwill has been lost. Assume the fair value of the remaining goodwill is determined to be $40,000.

The impairment loss to recognize is $30,000 ($70,000 − $40,000). The loss reduces the intangible asset (goodwill), stockholder's equity (retained earnings), and net income. The statement of cash flows would not be affected. These effects on the financial statements follow:

Assets	=	Liab.	+	Equity		Rev.	−	Exp./Loss	=	Net Inc.		Cash Flow
Goodwill	=			Ret. Earn.								
(30,000)	=	NA	+	(30,000)		NA	−	30,000	=	(30,000)		NA

The journal entry to recognize the impairment loss is:

Account Title	Debit	Credit
Impairment Loss	30,000	
Goodwill		30,000

Balance Sheet Presentation

This chapter explained accounting for the acquisition, expense recognition, and disposal of a wide range of long-term assets. Exhibit 9–8 illustrates typical balance sheet presentation of many of the assets discussed.

Exhibit 9–8 *Balance Sheet Presentation of Operational Assets*

Balance Sheet

Long-Term Assets			
Plant and Equipment			
Buildings	$4,000,000		
Less: Accumulated Depreciation	(2,500,000)	$1,500,000	
Equipment	1,750,000		
Less: Accumulated Depreciation	(1,200,000)	550,000	
Total Plant and Equipment			$2,050,000
Land			850,000
Natural Resources			
Mineral Deposits (Less: Depletion)		2,100,000	
Oil Reserves (Less: Depletion)		890,000	
Total Natural Resources			2,990,000
Intangibles			
Patents (Less: Amortization)		38,000	
Goodwill		175,000	
Total Intangible Assets			213,000
Total Long-Term Assets			$6,103,000

THE FINANCIAL ANALYST

Managers may have differing opinions about which allocation method (straight-line, accelerated, or units-of-production) best matches expenses with revenues. As a result, one company may use straight-line depreciation while another company in similar circumstances uses double-declining balance. Since the allocation method a company uses affects the amount of expense it recognizes, analysts reviewing financial statements must consider the accounting procedures companies use in preparing the statements.

LO10 Understand how expense recognition choices and industry characteristics affect financial performance measures.

Effect of Judgment and Estimation

Assume that two companies, Alpha and Zeta, experience identical economic events in 2005 and 2006. Both generate revenue of $50,000 and incur cost of goods sold of $30,000 during each year. In 2005, each company pays $20,000 for an asset with an expected useful life of five years and no salvage value. How will the companies' financial statements differ if one uses straight-line depreciation and the other uses the double-declining-balance method? To answer this question, first compute the depreciation expense for both companies for 2005 and 2006.

If Alpha Company uses the straight-line method, depreciation for 2005 and 2006 is:

$$(\text{Cost} - \text{Salvage}) \div \text{Useful life} = \text{Depreciation expense per year}$$
$$(\$20,000 - \$0) \div 5 \text{ years} = \$4,000$$

In contrast, if Zeta Company uses the double-declining-balance method, Zeta recognizes the following amounts of depreciation expense for 2005 and 2006:

	(Cost − Accumulated Depreciation)	× 2 ×	(Straight-Line Rate)	=	Depreciation Expense
2005	($20,000 − $0)	×	(2 × [1 ÷ 5])	=	$8,000
2006	($20,000 − $8,000)	×	(2 × [1 ÷ 5])	=	$4,800

Based on these computations, the income statements for the two companies are:

Income Statements

	2005 Alpha Co.	2005 Zeta Co.	2006 Alpha Co.	2006 Zeta Co.
Sales	$50,000	$50,000	$50,000	$50,000
Cost of Goods Sold	(30,000)	(30,000)	(30,000)	(30,000)
Gross Margin	20,000	20,000	20,000	20,000
Depreciation Expense	(4,000)	(8,000)	(4,000)	(4,800)
Net Income	$16,000	$12,000	$16,000	$15,200

The relevant sections of the balance sheets are:

Plant Assets

	2005 Alpha Co.	2005 Zeta Co.	2006 Alpha Co.	2006 Zeta Co.
Asset	$20,000	$20,000	$20,000	$20,000
Accumulated Depreciation	(4,000)	(8,000)	(8,000)	(12,800)
Book Value	$16,000	$12,000	$12,000	$ 7,200

The depreciation method is not the only aspect of expense recognition that can vary between companies. Companies may also make different assumptions about the useful lives and salvage values of long-term operational assets. Thus, even if the same depreciation method is used, depreciation expense may still differ.

Since the depreciation method and the underlying assumptions regarding useful life and salvage value affect the determination of depreciation expense, they also affect the amounts of net income, retained earnings, and total assets. Financial statement analysis is affected if it is based on ratios that include these items. Previously defined ratios that are affected include the (1) debt to assets ratio, (2) return on assets ratio, (3) return on equity ratio, and (4) return on sales ratio.

To promote meaningful analysis, public companies are required to disclose all significant accounting policies used to prepare their financial statements. This disclosure is usually provided in the footnotes that accompany the financial statements.

Effect of Industry Characteristics

As indicated in previous chapters, industry characteristics affect financial performance measures. For example, companies in manufacturing industries invest heavily in machinery while insurance companies rely more on human capital. Manufacturing companies therefore have relatively higher depreciation charges than insurance companies. To illustrate how the type of industry affects financial reporting, examine Exhibit 9–9. This exhibit compares the ratio of sales to property, plant, and equipment for two companies in each of three different industries. These data are for 2002.

The table indicates that for every $1.00 invested in property, plant, and equipment, **Manpower, Inc.** produced $56.20 of sales. In contrast, **Comcast Corp.** and **Delta Airlines** produced only $0.66 and $.80, respectively for each $1.00 they invested in operational assets. Does this mean the management of Manpower, Inc. is doing a better job than the management of Comcast or Delta? Not necessarily. It means that these companies operate in different economic environments. In other words, it takes significantly more equipment to operate a cable company or an airline than it takes to operate an employment agency.

Effective financial analysis requires careful consideration of industry characteristics, accounting policies, and the reasonableness of assumptions such as useful life and salvage value.

Exhibit 9–9 *Industry Data Reflecting the Use of Operational Assets*

Industry	Company	Sales ÷ Property, Plant, and Equipment
Cable Companies	Comcast Corp.	0.66
	Cox Communication	0.65
Airlines	Delta	0.80
	United	0.85
Employment Agencies	Kelly Services	21.37
	Manpower, Inc.	56.20

a look
back

Chapter 3 explained that the primary objective of recognizing depreciation is to match the cost of a long-term operational asset with the revenues the asset is expected to generate. This chapter extended applications of the matching concept to natural resources (depletion) and intangible assets (amortization). This chapter also explained how alternative methods can be used to account for the same event (e.g., straight-line versus double-declining-balance depreciation). Companies experiencing exactly the same business events could produce different financial statements. The alternative accounting methods for depreciating, depleting, or amortizing assets include the (1) straight-line, (2) double-declining-balance, and (3) units-of-production methods.

The *straight-line method* recognizes equal amounts of expense in each accounting period. The amount of the expense recognized is determined using the formula [(cost − salvage) ÷ number of years of useful life]. The *double-declining-balance method* recognizes proportionately larger amounts of expense in the early years of an asset's useful life and increasingly smaller amounts of expense in the later years of the asset's useful life. The formula for calculating double-declining-balance depreciation is [book value at beginning of period × (2 × the straight-line rate)]. The *units-of-production method* recognizes expense in direct proportion to the number of units produced during an accounting period. The formula for the amount of expense recognized each period is [(cost − salvage) ÷ total estimated units of production = allocation rate x units of production in current accounting period].

The chapter also discussed *MACRS depreciation,* an accelerated tax reporting method. MACRS is not acceptable under GAAP for public reporting. A company may use MACRS depreciation for tax purposes and straight-line or one of the other methods for public reporting. As a result, differences may exist between the amount of tax expense and the amount of tax liability. Such differences are reported as *deferred income taxes.*

This chapter showed how to account for *changes in estimates* such as the useful life or the salvage value of a depreciable asset. Changes in estimates do not affect the amount of depreciation recognized previously. Instead, the remaining book value of the asset is expensed over its remaining useful life.

After an asset has been placed into service, companies typically incur further costs for maintenance, quality improvement, and extensions of useful life. *Maintenance costs* are expensed in the period in which they are incurred. *Costs that improve the quality* of an asset are added to the cost of the asset, increasing the book value and the amount of future depreciation charges. *Costs that extend the useful life* of an asset are subtracted from the asset's Accumulated Depreciation account, increasing the book value and the amount of future depreciation charges.

a look forward

In Chapter 10 we move from the assets section of the balance sheet to issues in accounting for long-term liabilities. You will also learn how income tax regulations influence the consequences of borrowing money.

SELF-STUDY REVIEW PROBLEM

The following information pertains to a machine purchased by Bakersfield Company on January 1, 2005.

Purchase price	$ 63,000
Delivery cost	$ 2,000
Installation charge	$ 3,000
Estimated useful life	8 years
Estimated units the machine will produce	130,000
Estimated salvage value	$ 3,000

The machine produced 14,400 units during 2005 and 17,000 units during 2006.

Required

Determine the depreciation expense Bakersfield would report for 2005 and 2006 using each of the following methods.

a. Straight-line.
b. Double-declining-balance.
c. Units-of-production.
d. MACRS assuming that the machine is classified as seven-year property.

Solution to Requirements a–d.
a. Straight-line

Purchase price	$63,000
Delivery cost	2,000
Installation charge	3,000
Total cost of machine	68,000
Less: Salvage value	(3,000)
	$65,000 ÷ 8 = $8,125 Depreciation per year
2005	$ 8,125
2006	$ 8,125

b. Double-declining-balance

Year	Cost	–	Accumulated Depreciation at Beginning of Year	×	2 × S-L Rate	=	Annual Depreciation
2005	$68,000	–	$ 0	×	(2 × 0.125)	=	$17,000
2006	68,000	–	17,000	×	(2 × 0.125)	=	12,750

c. Units-of-production

(1) (Cost − Salvage value) ÷ Estimated units of production = Depreciation cost per unit produced

$$\frac{\$68,000 - \$3,000}{130,000} = \$0.50 \text{ per unit}$$

(2) Cost per unit × Annual units produced = Annual depreciation expense

2005 $0.50 × 14,400 = $7,200
2006   0.50 × 17,000 = 8,500

d. MACRS

Cost × MACRS percentage = Annual depreciation
2005 $68,000 × 0.1429 = $ 9,717
2006   68,000 × 0.2449 = 16,653

KEY TERMS

Accelerated depreciation method *413*

Accumulated depreciation *412*

Amortization *408*

Basket purchase *409*

Book value *414*

Capital expenditures *420*

Contra asset account *412*

Copyright *423*

Current assets *407*

Deferred tax liability *419*

Depletion *408*

Depreciable cost *414*

Depreciation *408*

Double-declining-balance depreciation *410*

Estimated useful life *410*

Franchise *423*

Goodwill *424*

Half-year convention *418*

Historical cost concept *409*

Intangible assets *408*

Long-term operational assets *407*

Modified accelerated cost recovery system (MACRS) *418*

Natural resources *408*

Patent *408, 423*

Property, plant, and equipment *408*

Relative fair market value method *409*

Salvage value *410*

Straight-line depreciation *410*

Tangible assets *408*

Trademark *423*

Units-of-production depreciation *410, 416*

QUESTIONS

1. What is the difference in the functions of long-term operational assets and investments?
2. What is the difference between tangible and intangible assets? Give an example of each.
3. What is the difference between goodwill and specifically identifiable intangible assets?
4. Define *depreciation*. What kind of asset is depreciated?
5. Why are natural resources called *wasting assets?*
6. Is land a depreciable asset? Why or why not?
7. Define *amortization*. What kind of assets are amortized?
8. Explain the historical cost concept as it applies to long-term operational assets. Why is the book value of an asset likely to be different from the current market value of the asset?
9. What different kinds of expenditures might be included in the recorded cost of a building?
10. What is a basket purchase of assets? When a basket purchase is made, how is cost assigned to individual assets?
11. What is the life cycle of a long-term operational asset?
12. Explain straight-line, units-of-production, and double-declining-balance depreciation. When is it appropriate to use each of these depreciation methods?
13. What effect does the recognition of depreciation expense have on total assets? On total equity?
14. Does the recognition of depreciation expense affect cash flows? Why or why not?
15. MalMax purchased a depreciable asset. What would be the difference in total assets at the end of the first year if MalMax chooses straight-line depreciation versus double-declining-balance?

16. John Smith mistakenly expensed the cost of a long-term tangible fixed asset. Specifically, he charged the cost of a truck to a delivery expense account. How will this error affect the income statement and the balance sheet in the year in which the mistake is made?

17. What is *salvage value?*

18. What type of account (classification) is accumulated depreciation?

19. Why is depreciation that has been recognized over the life of an asset shown in a contra account? Why not just reduce the asset account?

20. Assume that a piece of equipment cost $5,000 and had accumulated depreciation recorded of $3,000. What is the book value of the equipment? Is the book value equal to the fair market value of the equipment? Explain.

21. Why would a company choose to depreciate one piece of equipment using the double-declining-balance method and another piece of equipment using straight-line depreciation?

22. Explain MACRS depreciation. When is its use appropriate?

23. Does the method of depreciation required to be used for tax purposes reflect the use of a piece of equipment? Can you use double-declining-balance depreciation for tax purposes?

24. Define *deferred taxes.* Where does the account *Deferred Taxes* appear in the financial statements?

25. Why may it be necessary to revise the estimated life of a plant asset? When the estimated life is revised, does it affect the amount of depreciation per year? Why or why not?

26. How are capital expenditures made to improve the quality of a capital asset accounted for? Would the answer change if the expenditure extended the life of the asset but did not improve quality? Explain.

27. When a long-term operational asset is sold at a gain, how is the balance sheet affected? Is the statement of cash flows affected? If so, how?

28. Define *depletion.* What is the most commonly used method of computing depletion?

29. List several of the most common intangible assets. How is the life determined that is to be used to compute amortization?

30. List some differences between U.S. GAAP and GAAP of other countries.

31. How do differences in expense recognition and industry characteristics affect financial performance measures?

EXERCISES—SERIES A

 All Exercises in Series A are available with McGraw-Hill's Homework Manager

Unless specifically included, income tax considerations should be ignored in all exercises and problems.

L.O. 1 **EXERCISE 9–1A** *Long-Term Operational Assets Used in a Business*

Required
Give some examples of long-term operational assets that each of the following companies is likely to own: *(a)* AT&T, *(b)* Caterpillar, *(c)* Amtrak, and *(d)* The Walt Disney Co.

L.O. 1 **EXERCISE 9–2A** *Identifying Long-Term Operational Assets*

Required
Which of the following items should be classified as long-term operational assets?

a. Cash	**g.** Inventory
b. Buildings	**h.** Patent
c. Production machinery	**i.** Tract of timber
d. Accounts receivable	**j.** Land
e. Certificate of deposit (6 months)	**k.** Computer
f. Franchise	**l.** Goodwill

L.O. 1 **EXERCISE 9–3A** *Classifying Tangible and Intangible Assets*

Required
Identify each of the following long-term operational assets as either tangible (T) or intangible (I).

a. Retail store building	**g.** 18-wheel truck
b. Shelving for inventory	**h.** Timber
c. Trademark	**i.** Log loader
d. Gas well	**j.** Dental chair
e. Drilling rig	**k.** Goodwill
f. FCC license for TV station	**l.** Business Web page

EXERCISE 9–4A *Determining the Cost of an Asset*

Northeast Logging Co. purchased an electronic saw to cut various types and sizes of logs. The saw had a list price of $120,000. The seller agreed to allow a 5 percent discount because Northeast paid cash. Delivery terms were FOB shipping point. Freight cost amounted to $2,500. Northeast had to hire an individual to operate the saw. Northeast had to build a special platform to mount the saw. The cost of the platform was $1,000. The saw operator was paid an annual salary of $40,000. The cost of the company's theft insurance policy increased by $2,000 per year as a result of the acquisition of the saw. The saw had a four-year useful life and an expected salvage value of $10,000.

Required
Determine the amount to be capitalized in an asset account for the purchase of the saw.

EXERCISE 9–5A *Allocating Costs on the Basis of Relative Market Values*

Midwest Company purchased a building and the land on which the building is situated for a total cost of $900,000 cash. The land was appraised at $200,000 and the building at $800,000.

Required
a. What is the accounting term for this type of acquisition?
b. Determine the amount of the purchase cost to allocate to the land and the amount to allocate to the building.
c. Would the company recognize a gain on the purchase? Why or why not?
d. Record the purchase in a statements model like the following one.

Assets			=	Liab.	+	Equity	Rev.	–	Exp.	=	Net Inc.	Cash Flow
Cash	+ Land	+ Building										

EXERCISE 9–6A *Allocating Costs for a Basket Purchase*

Jourdan Company purchased a restaurant building, land, and equipment for $700,000. Jourdan paid $100,000 in cash and issued a 20-year, 8 percent note to First Bank for the balance. The appraised value of the assets was as follows:

Land	$160,000
Building	400,000
Equipment	240,000
Total	$800,000

Required
a. Compute the amount to be recorded on the books for each of the assets.
b. Record the purchase in a horizontal statements model like the following one.

Assets				=	Liab.	+	Equity	Rev.	–	Exp.	=	Net Inc.	Cash Flow
Cash	+ Land	+ Building	+ Equip.										

c. Prepare the general journal entry to record the purchase.

EXERCISE 9–7A *Effect of Double-Declining-Balance Depreciation on Financial Statements*

Smith Company started operations by acquiring $100,000 cash from the issue of common stock. The company purchased equipment that cost $100,000 cash on January 1, 2005. The equipment had an expected useful life of five years and an estimated salvage value of $20,000. Smith Company earned $92,000 and $65,000 of cash revenue during 2005 and 2006, respectively. Smith Company uses double-declining-balance depreciation.

Required
Prepare income statements, balance sheets, and statements of cash flows for 2005 and 2006. Use a vertical statements format. (*Hint:* Record the events in T-accounts prior to preparing the statements.)

L.O. 3, 4   EXERCISE 9–8A *Events Related to the Acquisition, Use, and Disposal of a Tangible Plant Asset: Straight-Line Depreciation*

CJ's Pizza purchased a delivery van on January 1, 2005, for $25,000. In addition, CJ's paid sales tax and title fees of $1,000 for the van. The van is expected to have a four-year life and a salvage value of $6,000.

Required

a. Using the straight-line method, compute the depreciation expense for 2005 and 2006.
b. Prepare the general journal entry to record the 2005 depreciation.
c. Assume the van was sold on January 1, 2008, for $12,000. Prepare the journal entry for the sale of the van in 2008.

L.O. 3   EXERCISE 9–9A *Computing and Recording Straight-Line Versus Double-Declining-Balance Depreciation*

At the beginning of 2006, Precision Manufacturing purchased a new computerized drill press for $50,000. It is expected to have a five-year life and a $5,000 salvage value.

Required

a. Compute the depreciation for each of the five years, assuming that the company uses
   (1) Straight-line depreciation.
   (2) Double-declining-balance depreciation.
b. Record the purchase of the drill press and the depreciation expense for the first year under the straight-line and double-declining-balance methods in a financial statements model like the following one:

Assets				=	Equity		Rev.	–	Exp.	=	Net Inc.	Cash Flow
Cash	+	Drill Press	– Acc. Dep.	=	Ret. Earn.							

c. Prepare the journal entries to recognize depreciation for each of the five years, assuming that the company uses
   (1) Straight-line depreciation.
   (2) Double-declining-balance depreciation.

L.O. 4   EXERCISE 9–10A *Effect of the Disposal of Plant Assets on the Financial Statements*

A plant asset with a cost of $40,000 and accumulated depreciation of $36,000 is sold for $6,000.

Required

a. What is the book value of the asset at the time of sale?
b. What is the amount of gain or loss on the disposal?
c. How would the sale affect net income (increase, decrease, no effect) and by how much?
d. How would the sale affect the amount of total assets shown on the balance sheet (increase, decrease, no effect) and by how much?
e. How would the event affect the statement of cash flows (inflow, outflow, no effect) and in what section?

L.O. 3, 4   EXERCISE 9–11A *Double-Declining-Balance and Units-of-Production Depreciation: Gain or Loss on Disposal*

Print Service Co. purchased a new color copier at the beginning of 2005 for $35,000. The copier is expected to have a five-year useful life and a $5,000 salvage value. The expected copy production was estimated at 2,000,000 copies. Actual copy production for the five years was as follows:

2005	550,000
2006	480,000
2007	380,000
2008	390,000
2009	240,000
Total	2,040,000

The copier was sold at the end of 2009 for $5,200.

Required

a. Compute the depreciation expense for each of the five years, using double-declining-balance depreciation.

b. Compute the depreciation expense for each of the five years, using units-of-production depreciation. (Round cost per unit to three decimal places.)

c. Calculate the amount of gain or loss from the sale of the asset under each of the depreciation methods.

EXERCISE 9–12A *Computing Depreciation for Tax Purposes*   **L.O. 5**

Quality Lumber Company purchased $120,000 of equipment on September 1, 2006.

Required

a. Compute the amount of depreciation expense that is deductible under MACRS for 2006 and 2007, assuming that the equipment is classified as seven-year property.

b. Compute the amount of depreciation expense that is deductible under MACRS for 2006 and 2007, assuming that the equipment is classified as five-year property.

EXERCISE 9–13A *Revision of Estimated Useful Life*   **L.O. 6**

On January 1, 2006, Harris Machining Co. purchased a compressor and related installation equipment for $64,000. The equipment had a three-year estimated life with a $4,000 salvage value. Straight-line depreciation was used. At the beginning of 2008, Harris revised the expected life of the asset to four years rather than three years. The salvage value was revised to $3,000.

Required

Compute the depreciation expense for each of the four years.

EXERCISE 9–14A *Distinguishing Between Maintenance Costs and Capital Expenditures*   **L.O. 7**

Zell's Shredding Service has just completed a minor repair on a shredding machine. The repair cost was $900, and the book value prior to the repair was $5,000. In addition, the company spent $8,000 to replace the roof on a building. The new roof extended the life of the building by five years. Prior to the roof replacement, the general ledger reflected the Building account at $90,000 and related Accumulated Depreciation account at $40,000.

Required

After the work was completed, what book value should Zell's report on the balance sheet for the shredding machine and the building?

EXERCISE 9–15A *Effect of Maintenance Costs Versus Capital Expenditures on Financial Statements*   **L.O. 7**

Sequoia Construction Company purchased a forklift for $110,000 cash. It had an estimated useful life of four years and a $10,000 salvage value. At the beginning of the third year of use, the company spent an additional $8,000 that was related to the forklift. The company's financial condition just prior to this expenditure is shown in the following statements model.

Assets				=	Equity			Rev.	–	Exp.	=	Net Inc.	Cash Flow
Cash	+	Forklift	– Acc. Dep.	=	C. Stk.	+	Ret. Earn.						
12,000	+	110,000	– 50,000	=	24,000	+	48,000	NA	–	NA	=	NA	NA

Required

Record the $8,000 expenditure in the statements model under each of the following *independent* assumptions:

a. The expenditure was for routine maintenance.

b. The expenditure extended the forklift's life.

c. The expenditure improved the forklift's operating capacity.

L.O. 7   **EXERCISE 9–16A** *Effect of Maintenance Costs Versus Capital Expenditures on Financial Statements*

On January 1, 2005, Valley Power Company overhauled four turbine engines that generate power for customers. The overhaul resulted in a slight increase in the capacity of the engines to produce power. Such overhauls occur regularly at two-year intervals and have been treated as maintenance expense in the past. Management is considering whether to capitalize this year's $25,000 cash cost in the engine asset account or to expense it as a maintenance expense. Assume that the engines have a remaining useful life of two years and no expected salvage value. Assume straight-line depreciation.

Required
a. Determine the amount of additional depreciation expense Valley would recognize in 2005 and 2006 if the cost were capitalized in the engine account.
b. Determine the amount of expense Valley would recognize in 2005 and 2006 if the cost were recognized as maintenance expense.
c. Determine the effect of the overhaul on cash flow from operating activities for 2005 and 2006 if the cost were capitalized and expensed through depreciation charges.
d. Determine the effect of the overhaul on cash flow from operating activities for 2005 and 2006 if the cost were recognized as maintenance expense.

L.O. 8   **EXERCISE 9–17A** *Computing and Recording Depletion Expense*

Ecru Sand and Gravel paid $600,000 to acquire 800,000 cubic yards of sand reserves. The following statements model reflects Ecru's financial condition just prior to purchasing the sand reserves. The company extracted 420,000 cubic yards of sand in year 1 and 360,000 cubic yards in year 2.

Assets			=	Equity			Rev.	–	Exp.	=	Net Inc.	Cash Flow
Cash	+	Sand Res.	=	C. Stk.	+	Ret. Earn.						
700,000	+	NA	=	700,000	+	NA	NA	–	NA	=	NA	NA

Required
a. Compute the depletion charge per unit.
b. Record the acquisition of the sand reserves and the depletion expense for years 1 and 2 in a financial statements model like the preceding one.
c. Prepare the general journal entries to record the depletion expense for years 1 and 2.

L.O. 9   **EXERCISE 9–18A** *Computing and Recording the Amortization of Intangibles*

Texas Manufacturing paid cash to purchase the assets of an existing company. Among the assets purchased were the following items:

Patent with 5 remaining years of legal life	$36,000
Goodwill	40,000

Texas's financial condition just prior to the purchase of these assets is shown in the following statements model:

Assets					=	Liab.	+	Equity	Rev.	–	Exp.	=	Net Inc.	Cash Flow
Cash	+	Patent	+	Goodwill										
94,000	+	NA	+	NA	=	NA	+	94,000	NA	–	NA	+	NA	NA

Required
a. Compute the annual amortization expense for these items if applicable.
b. Record the purchase of the intangible assets and the related amortization expense for year 1 in a horizontal statements model like the preceding one.
c. Prepare the journal entries to record the purchase of the intangible assets and the related amortization for year 1.

EXERCISE 9–19A *Computing and Recording Goodwill*   L.O. 9

Mike Wallace purchased the business Magnum Supply Co. for $275,000 cash and assumed all liabilities at the date of purchase. Magnum's books showed assets of $280,000, liabilities of $40,000, and equity of $240,000. An appraiser assessed the fair market value of the tangible assets at $270,000 at the date of purchase. Wallace's financial condition just prior to the purchase is shown in the following statements model:

Assets			=	Liab.	+	Equity	Rev.	–	Exp.	=	Net Inc.	Cash Flow
Cash	+	Assets	+	Goodwill								
325,000	+	NA	+	NA	=	NA	+	325,000	NA	–	NA	=	NA	NA

Required
a. Compute the amount of goodwill purchased.
b. Record the purchase in a financial statements model like the preceding one.

All Problems in Series A are available with McGraw-Hill's Homework Manager

PROBLEM 9–20A *Accounting for Acquisition of Assets Including a Basket Purchase*   L.O. 2

Khan Company made several purchases of long-term assets in 2009. The details of each purchase are presented here.

CHECK FIGURES
Total cost of equipment: $40,900
Cost allocated to copier: $7,500

New Office Equipment
1. List price: $40,000; terms: 1/10 n/30; paid within the discount period.
2. Transportation-in: $800.
3. Installation: $500.
4. Cost to repair damage during unloading: $500.
5. Routine maintenance cost after eight months: $120.

Basket Purchase of Office Furniture, Copier, Computers, and Laser Printers for $50,000 With Fair Market Values
1. Office furniture, $24,000.
2. Copier, $9,000.
3. Computers and printers, $27,000.

Land for New Headquarters With Old Barn Torn Down
1. Purchase price, $80,000.
2. Demolition of barn, $5,000.
3. Lumber sold from old barn, $2,000.
4. Grading in preparation for new building, $8,000.
5. Construction of new building, $250,000.

Required
In each of these cases, determine the amount of cost to be capitalized in the asset account.

PROBLEM 9–21A *Accounting for Depreciation Over Multiple Accounting Cycles*   L.O. 3, 4

www.mhhe.com/edmonds5e

KC Company began operations when it acquired $30,000 cash from the issue of common stock on January 1, 2005. The cash acquired was immediately used to purchase equipment for $30,000 that had a $5,000 salvage value and an expected useful life of four years. The equipment was used to produce the following revenue stream (assume all revenue transactions are for cash). At the beginning of the fifth year, the equipment was sold for $4,500 cash. KC uses straight-line depreciation.

CHECK FIGURES
Net Income, 2005: $1,250
Total Assets, 2009: $35,200

	2005	2006	2007	2008	2009
Revenue	$7,500	$8,000	$8,200	$7,000	$0

Required

Prepare income statements, statements of changes in stockholders' equity, balance sheets, and statements of cash flows for each of the five years.

PROBLEM 9–22A *Purchase and Use of Tangible Asset: Three Accounting Cycles, Double-Declining-Balance Depreciation*

The following transactions pertain to Optimal Solutions Inc. Assume the transactions for the purchase of the computer and any capital improvements occur on January 1 each year.

2007

1. Acquired $60,000 cash from the issue of common stock.
2. Purchased a computer system for $25,000. It has an estimated useful life of five years and a $3,000 salvage value.
3. Paid $1,500 sales tax on the computer system.
4. Collected $35,000 in data entry fees from clients.
5. Paid $1,200 in fees to service the computers.
6. Recorded double-declining-balance depreciation on the computer system for 2007.
7. Closed the revenue and expense accounts to Retained Earnings at the end of 2007.

2008

1. Paid $800 for repairs to the computer system.
2. Bought a case of toner cartridges for the printers that are part of the computer system, $1,200.
3. Collected $38,000 in data entry fees from clients.
4. Paid $900 in fees to service the computers.
5. Recorded double-declining-balance depreciation for 2008.
6. Closed the revenue and expense accounts to Retained Earnings at the end of 2008.

2009

1. Paid $3,000 to upgrade the computer system, which extended the total life of the system to six years.
2. Paid $900 in fees to service the computers.
3. Collected $35,000 in data entry fees from clients.
4. Recorded double-declining-balance depreciation for 2009.
5. Closed the revenue and expense accounts at the end of 2009.

Required

a. Use a horizontal statements model like the following one to show the effect of these transactions on the elements of financial statements. Use + for increase, − for decrease, and NA for not affected. The first event is recorded as an example.

2007 Event No.	Assets	=	Liabilities	+	Equity	Net Inc.	Cash Flow
1	+		NA		+	NA	+ FA

b. Use a vertical model to present financial statements for 2007, 2008, and 2009. (Record the transactions in T-accounts before attempting to prepare the financial statements.)

PROBLEM 9–23A *Calculating Depreciation Expense Using Four Different Methods*

O'Brian Service Company purchased a copier on January 1, 2008, for $17,000 and paid an additional $200 for delivery charges. The copier was estimated to have a life of four years or 800,000 copies. Salvage was estimated at $1,200. The copier produced 230,000 copies in 2008 and 250,000 copies in 2009.

Required

Compute the amount of depreciation expense for the copier for calendar years 2008 and 2009, using these methods:

a. Straight-line.
b. Units-of-production.
c. Double-declining-balance.
d. MACRS, assuming that the copier is classified as five-year property.

www.mhhe.com/edmonds5e

PROBLEM 9–24A *Effect of Straight-Line Versus Double-Declining-Balance Depreciation on the Recognition of Expense and Gains or Losses*

L.O. 3, 4

Same Day Laundry Services purchased a new steam press machine on January 1, for $35,000. It is expected to have a five-year useful life and a $3,000 salvage value. Same Day expects to use the equipment more extensively in the early years.

Required

a. Calculate the depreciation expense for each of the five years, assuming the use of straight-line depreciation.

b. Calculate the depreciation expense for each of the five years, assuming the use of double-declining-balance depreciation.

c. Would the choice of one depreciation method over another produce a different amount of annual cash flow for any year? Why or why not?

d. Assume that Same Day Laundry Services sold the steam press machine at the end of the third year for $20,000. Compute the amount of gain or loss using each depreciation method.

PROBLEM 9–25A *Computing and Recording Units-of-Production Depreciation*

L.O. 3, 4

McNabb Corporation purchased a delivery van for $25,500 in 2007. The firm's financial condition immediately prior to the purchase is shown in the following horizontal statements model:

Assets				=	Equity			Rev.	−	Exp.	=	Net Inc.	Cash Flow
Cash	+	Van	−	Acc. Dep.	=	C. Stk.	+	Ret. Earn.					
50,000	+	NA	−	NA	=	50,000	+	NA	NA	−	NA	=	NA	NA

The van was expected to have a useful life of 150,000 miles and a salvage value of $3,000. Actual mileage was as follows:

2007	50,000
2008	70,000
2009	58,000

Required

a. Compute the depreciation for each of the three years, assuming the use of units-of-production depreciation.

b. Assume that McNabb earns $21,000 of cash revenue during 2007. Record the purchase of the van and the recognition of the revenue and the depreciation expense for the first year in a financial statements model like the preceding one.

c. Assume that McNabb sold the van at the end of the third year for $4,000. Record the general journal entry for the sale.

PROBLEM 9–26A *Determining the Effect of Depreciation Expense on Financial Statements*

L.O. 3

Three different companies each purchased a machine on January 1, 2005, for $54,000. Each machine was expected to last five years or 200,000 hours. Salvage value was estimated to be $4,000. All three machines were operated for 50,000 hours in 2005, 55,000 hours in 2006, 40,000 hours in 2007, 44,000 hours in 2008, and 31,000 hours in 2009. Each of the three companies earned $30,000 of cash revenue during each of the five years. Company A uses straight-line depreciation, company B uses double-declining-balance depreciation, and company C uses units-of-production depreciation.

Required

Answer each of the following questions. Ignore the effects of income taxes.

a. Which company will report the highest amount of net income for 2005?

b. Which company will report the lowest amount of net income for 2007?

c. Which company will report the highest book value on the December 31, 2007, balance sheet?

d. Which company will report the highest amount of retained earnings on the December 31, 2008, balance sheet?

e. Which company will report the lowest amount of cash flow from operating activities on the 2007 statement of cash flows?

PROBLEM 9–27A Accounting for Depletion

Favre Exploration Corporation engages in the exploration and development of many types of natural resources. In the last two years, the company has engaged in the following activities:

Jan. 1, 2007	Purchased a coal mine estimated to contain 200,000 tons of coal for $800,000.
July 1, 2007	Purchased for $1,950,000 a tract of timber estimated to yield 3,000,000 board feet of lumber and to have a residual land value of $150,000.
Feb. 1, 2008	Purchased a silver mine estimated to contain 30,000 tons of silver for $750,000.
Aug. 1, 2008	Purchased for $736,000 oil reserves estimated to contain 250,000 barrels of oil, of which 20,000 would be unprofitable to pump.

Required

a. Prepare the journal entries to account for the following:
   (1) The 2007 purchases.
   (2) Depletion on the 2007 purchases, assuming that 70,000 tons of coal were mined and 1,000,000 board feet of lumber were cut.
   (3) The 2008 purchases.
   (4) Depletion on the four reserves, assuming that 62,000 tons of coal, 1,200,000 board feet of lumber, 9,000 tons of silver, and 80,000 barrels of oil were extracted.
b. Prepare the portion of the December 31, 2008, balance sheet that reports natural resources.
c. Assume that in 2009 the estimates changed to reflect only 50,000 tons of coal remaining. Prepare the depletion journal entry for 2009 to account for the extraction of 35,000 tons of coal.

PROBLEM 9–28A Recording Continuing Expenditures for Plant Assets

Big Sky, Inc., recorded the following transactions over the life of a piece of equipment purchased in 2005:

Jan. 1, 2005	Purchased the equipment for $36,000 cash. The equipment is estimated to have a five-year life and $6,000 salvage value and was to be depreciated using the straight-line method.
Dec. 31, 2005	Recorded depreciation expense for 2005.
May 5, 2006	Undertook routine repairs costing $750.
Dec. 31, 2006	Recorded depreciation expense for 2006.
Jan. 1, 2007	Made an adjustment costing $3,000 to the equipment. It improved the quality of the output but did not affect the life estimate.
Dec. 31, 2007	Recorded depreciation expense for 2007.
Mar. 1, 2008	Incurred $320 cost to oil and clean the equipment.
Dec. 31, 2008	Recorded depreciation expense for 2008.
Jan. 1, 2009	Had the equipment completely overhauled at a cost of $7,500. The overhaul was estimated to extend the total life to seven years and revised the salvage value to $4,000.
Dec. 31, 2009	Recorded depreciation expense for 2009.
July 1, 2010	Sold the equipment for $9,000 cash.

Required

a. Use a horizontal statements model like the following one to show the effects of these transactions on the elements of the financial statements. Use + for increase, − for decrease, and NA for not affected. The first event is recorded as an example.

Date	Assets	=	Liabilities	+	Equity	Net Inc.	Cash Flow
Jan. 1, 2005	+ −		NA		NA	NA	− IA

b. Determine amount of depreciation expense Big Sky will report on the income statements for the years 2005 through 2009.
c. Determine the book value (cost − accumulated depreciation) Big Sky will report on the balance sheets at the end of the years 2005 through 2009.
d. Determine the amount of the gain or loss Big Sky will report on the disposal of the equipment on July 1, 2010.

PROBLEM 9–29A Accounting for Continuing Expenditures

Vernon Manufacturing paid $58,000 to purchase a computerized assembly machine on January 1, 2002. The machine had an estimated life of eight years and a $2,000 salvage value. Vernon's financial condition as of January 1, 2005, is shown in the following financial statements model. Vernon uses the straight-line method for depreciation.

Assets				=	Equity			Rev.	−	Exp.	=	Net Inc.	Cash Flow
Cash	+	Mach.	−	Acc. Dep.	=	C. Stk.	+	Ret. Earn.					
15,000	+	58,000	−	21,000	=	8,000	+	44,000	NA	−	NA	=	NA	NA

CHECK FIGURE
b. Depreciation Expense: $8,000

Vernon Manufacturing made the following expenditures on the computerized assembly machine in 2005.

Jan. 2   Added an overdrive mechanism for $6,000 that would improve the overall quality of the performance of the machine but would not extend its life. The salvage value was revised to $3,000.

Aug. 1   Performed routine maintenance, $1,150.

Oct. 2   Replaced some computer chips (considered routine), $950.

Dec. 31   Recognized 2005 depreciation expense.

Required

a. Record the 2005 transactions in a statements model like the preceding one.

b. Prepare journal entries for the 2005 transactions.

PROBLEM 9–30A *Accounting for Intangible Assets*

L.O. 9

Mia-Tora Company purchased a fast-food restaurant for $1,400,000. The fair market values of the assets purchased were as follows. No liabilities were assumed.

CHECK FIGURE
a. Goodwill Purchased: $130,000

Equipment	$320,000
Land	200,000
Building	650,000
Franchise (5-year life)	100,000

Required

a. Calculate the amount of goodwill purchased.

b. Prepare the journal entry to record the amortization of the franchise fee at the end of year 1.

PROBLEM 9–31A *Accounting for Goodwill*

L.O. 9

Springhill Co. purchased the assets of Canyon Co. for $1,000,000 in 2005. The estimated fair market value of the assets at the purchase date was $920,000. Goodwill of $80,000 was recorded at purchase. In 2007, because of negative publicity, one-half of the goodwill purchased from Canyon Co. was judged to be permanently impaired.

CHECK FIGURE
b. Impairment Loss: $40,000

Required

a. How will Springhill account for the impairment of the goodwill?

b. Prepare the journal entry to record the permanent impairment of goodwill.

EXERCISES—SERIES B

Unless specifically included, income tax considerations should be ignored in all exercises and problems.

EXERCISE 9–1B *Using Long-Term Operational Assets Used in a Business*

L.O. 1

Required

Give some examples of long-term operational assets that each of the following companies is likely to own: *(a)* Lansing Farms, *(b)* American Airlines, *(c)* IBM, and *(d)* Northwest Mutual Insurance Co.

L.O. 1 **EXERCISE 9–2B** *Identifying Long-Term Operational Assets*

Required
Which of the following items should be classified as long-term operational assets?

a. Prepaid insurance
b. Coal mine
c. Office equipment
d. Notes receivable (short-term)
e. Supplies
f. Copyright

g. Delivery van
h. Land held for investment
i. 10-year treasury note
j. Cash
k. Filing cabinet
l. Tax library of accounting firm

L.O. 1 **EXERCISE 9–3B** *Classifying Tangible and Intangible Assets*

Required
Identify each of the following long-term operational assets as either tangible (T) or intangible (I).

a. Pizza oven
b. Land
c. Franchise
d. Filing cabinet
e. Copyright
f. Silver mine

g. Office building
h. Drill press
i. Patent
j. Oil well
k. Desk
l. Goodwill

L.O. 2 **EXERCISE 9–4B** *Determining the Cost of an Asset*

Xpert Milling Co. purchased a front-end loader to move stacks of lumber. The loader had a list price of $100,000. The seller agreed to allow a 4 percent discount because Xpert Milling paid cash. Delivery terms were FOB shipping point. Freight cost amounted to $500. Xpert Milling had to hire a consultant to train an employee to operate the loader. The training fee was $1,000. The loader operator is paid an annual salary of $30,000. The cost of the company's theft insurance policy increased by $800 per year as a result of the acquisition of the loader. The loader had a four-year useful life and an expected salvage value of $6,500.

Required
Determine the amount to be capitalized in an asset account for the purchase of the loader.

L.O. 2 **EXERCISE 9–5B** *Allocating Costs on the Basis of Relative Market Values*

Diaz, Inc., purchased a building and the land on which the building is situated for a total cost of $800,000 cash. The land was appraised at $270,000 and the building at $630,000.

Required
a. Determine the amount of the purchase cost to allocate to the land and the amount to allocate to the building.
b. Would the company recognize a gain on the purchase? Why or why not?
c. Record the purchase in a statements model like the following one.

Assets			=	Liab.	+	Equity	Rev.	–	Exp.	=	Net Inc.	Cash Flow
Cash	+	Land	+	Building								

L.O. 2 **EXERCISE 9–6B** *Allocating Costs for a Basket Purchase*

Marker Co. purchased an office building, land, and furniture for $300,000. It paid $50,000 in cash and issued a 20-year, 6 percent note to First Bank for the balance. The appraised value of the assets was as follows:

Land	$105,000
Building	210,000
Furniture	35,000
Total	$350,000

Required
a. Compute the amount to be recorded on the books for each asset.

b. Record the purchase in a horizontal statements model like the following one.

Assets				=	Liab.	+	Equity	Rev.	–	Exp.	=	Net Inc.	Cash Flow
Cash	+ Land	+ Building	+ Furn.										

c. Prepare the general journal entry to record the purchase.

EXERCISE 9–7B *Effect of Double-Declining-Balance Depreciation on Financial Statements* **L.O. 3**

Ram Manufacturing Company started operations by acquiring $120,000 cash from the issue of common stock. The company purchased equipment that cost $120,000 cash on January 1, 2006, that had an expected useful life of six years and an estimated salvage value of $6,000. Ram Manufacturing earned $76,000 and $85,200 of cash revenue during 2006 and 2007, respectively. Ram Manufacturing uses double-declining-balance depreciation.

Required

Prepare income statements, balance sheets, and statements of cash flows for 2006 and 2007. Use a vertical statements format. (*Hint:* Record the events in T-accounts prior to preparing the statements.)

EXERCISE 9–8B *Events Related to the Acquisition, Use, and Disposal of a Tangible Plant Asset: Straight-Line Depreciation* **L.O. 3, 4**

Fast Taxi Service purchased a new auto to use as a taxi on January 1, 2002, for $27,000. In addition, Fast paid sales tax and title fees of $500 for the van. The taxi is expected to have a five-year life and a salvage value of $2,500.

Required

a. Using the straight-line method, compute the depreciation expense for 2002 and 2003.
b. Prepare the general journal entry to record the 2002 depreciation.
c. Assume that the taxi was sold on January 1, 2004, for $15,000. Prepare the journal entry for the sale of the taxi in 2004.

EXERCISE 9–9B *Computing and Recording Straight-Line Versus Double-Declining-Balance Depreciation* **L.O. 3**

At the beginning of 2005, Macon Drugstore purchased a new computer system for $48,000. It is expected to have a five-year life and a $3,000 salvage value.

Required

a. Compute the depreciation for each of the five years, assuming that the company uses
  (1) Straight-line depreciation.
  (2) Double-declining-balance depreciation.
b. Record the purchase of the computer system and the depreciation expense for the first year under straight-line and double-declining-balance methods in a financial statements model like the following one:

Assets				=	Equity	Rev.	–	Exp.	=	Net Inc.	Cash Flow
Cash	+ Comp. Sys.	– Acc. Dep.		=	Ret. Earn.						

c. Prepare the journal entries to recognize depreciation for each of the five years, assuming that the company uses
  (1) Straight-line depreciation.
  (2) Double-declining-balance depreciation.

EXERCISE 9–10B *Effect of the Disposal of Plant Assets on the Financial Statements* **L.O. 4**

Mertz Company sold office equipment with a cost of $27,000 and accumulated depreciation of $13,000 for $14,000.

Required

a. What is the book value of the asset at the time of sale?
b. What is the amount of gain or loss on the disposal?

c. How would the sale affect net income (increase, decrease, no effect) and by how much?

d. How would the sale affect the amount of total assets shown on the balance sheet (increase, decrease, no effect) and by how much?

e. How would the event affect the statement of cash flows (inflow, outflow, no effect) and in what section?

L.O. 3, 4   **EXERCISE 9–11B** *Double-Declining-Balance and Units-of-Production Depreciation: Gain or Loss on Disposal*

Kate's Photo Service purchased a new color printer at the beginning of 2006 for $28,000. It is expected to have a four-year useful life and a $2,000 salvage value. The expected print production is estimated at 1,300,000 pages. Actual print production for the four years was as follows:

2006	350,000
2007	370,000
2008	280,000
2009	320,000
Total	1,320,000

The printer was sold at the end of 2009 for $1,500.

Required

a. Compute the depreciation expense for each of the four years, using double-declining-balance depreciation.

b. Compute the depreciation expense for each of the four years, using units-of-production depreciation. (Round cost per unit to three decimal places.)

c. Calculate the amount of gain or loss from the sale of the asset under each of the depreciation methods.

L.O. 5   **EXERCISE 9–12B** *Computing Depreciation for Tax Purposes*

Vision Eye Care Company purchased $40,000 of equipment on March 1, 2001.

Required

a. Compute the amount of depreciation expense that is deductible under MACRS for 2001 and 2002, assuming that the equipment is classified as seven-year property.

b. Compute the amount of depreciation expense that is deductible under MACRS for 2001 and 2002, assuming that the equipment is classified as five-year property.

L.O. 6   **EXERCISE 9–13B** *Revision of Estimated Useful Life*

On January 1, 2001, Maxie Storage Company purchased a freezer and related installation equipment for $36,000. The equipment had a three-year estimated life with a $6,000 salvage value. Straight-line depreciation was used. At the beginning of 2003, Maxie revised the expected life of the asset to four years rather than three years. The salvage value was revised to $4,000.

Required

Compute the depreciation expense for each of the four years.

L.O. 7   **EXERCISE 9–14B** *Distinguishing Between Maintenance Costs and Capital Expenditures*

Reliable Wrecker Service has just completed a minor repair on a tow truck. The repair cost was $620, and the book value prior to the repair was $5,600. In addition, the company spent $4,000 to replace the roof on a building. The new roof extended the life of the building by five years. Prior to the roof replacement, the general ledger reflected the Building account at $90,000 and related Accumulated Depreciation account at $26,500.

Required

After the work was completed, what book value should appear on the balance sheet for the tow truck and the building?

L.O. 7   **EXERCISE 9–15B** *Effect of Maintenance Costs Versus Capital Expenditures on Financial Statements*

Kauai Construction Company purchased a compressor for $42,000 cash. It had an estimated useful life of four years and a $4,000 salvage value. At the beginning of the third year of use, the company spent an additional $3,000 related to the equipment. The company's financial condition just prior to this expenditure is shown in the following statements model.

Assets				=	Equity			Rev.	–	Exp.	=	Net Inc.	Cash Flow
Cash	+	Compressor	– Acc. Dep. =		C. Stk.	+	Ret. Earn.						
37,000	+	42,000	– 19,000 =		40,000	+	20,000	NA	–	NA	=	NA	NA

Required

Record the $3,000 expenditure in the statements model under each of the following *independent* assumptions:

a. The expenditure was for routine maintenance.
b. The expenditure extended the compressor's life.
c. The expenditure improved the compressor's operating capacity.

EXERCISE 9–16B *Effect of Maintenance Costs Versus Capital Expenditures on Financial Statements*   **L.O. 7**

On January 1, 2001, Grayson Construction Company overhauled four cranes resulting in a slight increase in the life of the cranes. Such overhauls occur regularly at two-year intervals and have been treated as maintenance expense in the past. Management is considering whether to capitalize this year's $26,000 cash cost in the Cranes asset account or to expense it as a maintenance expense. Assume that the cranes have a remaining useful life of two years and no expected salvage value. Assume straight-line depreciation.

Required
a. Determine the amount of additional depreciation expense Grayson would recognize in 2001 and 2002 if the cost were capitalized in the Cranes account.
b. Determine the amount of expense Grayson would recognize in 2001 and 2002 if the cost were recognized as maintenance expense.
c. Determine the effect of the overhaul on cash flow from operating activities for 2001 and 2002 if the cost were capitalized and expensed through depreciation charges.
d. Determine the effect of the overhaul on cash flow from operating activities for 2001 and 2002 if the cost were recognized as maintenance expense.

EXERCISE 9–17B *Computing and Recording Depletion Expense*   **L.O. 8**

Mountain Coal paid $450,000 to acquire a mine with 22,500 tons of coal reserves. The following statements model reflects Mountain's financial condition just prior to purchasing the coal reserves. The company extracted 10,000 tons of coal in year 1 and 8,000 tons in year 2.

Assets			=	Equity			Rev.	–	Exp.	=	Net Inc.	Cash Flow
Cash	+	Coal Res.	=	C. Stk.	+	Ret. Earn.						
600,000	+	NA	=	600,000	+	NA	NA	–	NA	=	NA	NA

Required
a. Compute the depletion charge per unit.
b. Record the acquisition of the coal reserves and the depletion expense for years 1 and 2 in a financial statements model like the preceding one.
c. Prepare the general journal entries to record the depletion expense for years 1 and 2.

EXERCISE 9–18B *Computing and Recording the Amortization of Intangibles*   **L.O. 9**

Hi-Tech Manufacturing paid cash to purchase the assets of an existing company. Among the assets purchased were the following items:

Patent with 2 remaining years of legal life	$24,000
Goodwill	20,000

Hi-Tech's financial condition just prior to the purchase of these assets is shown in the following statements model:

Assets			=	Liab.	+	Equity		Rev.	–	Exp.	=	Net Inc.	Cash Flow
Cash	+	Patent	+	Goodwill									
90,000	+	NA	+	NA	=	NA	+	90,000	NA	–	NA	=	NA	NA

Required

a. Compute the annual amortization expense for these items.

b. Record the purchase of the intangible assets and the related amortization expense for year 1 in a horizontal statements model like the preceding one.

c. Prepare the journal entries to record the purchase of the intangible assets and the related amortization for year 1.

L.O. 9   EXERCISE 9–19B *Computing and Recording Goodwill*

Sea Corp purchased the business Beta Resources for $200,000 cash and assumed all liabilities at the date of purchase. Beta's books showed assets of $150,000, liabilities of $40,000, and stockholders' equity of $110,000. An appraiser assessed the fair market value of the tangible assets at $185,000 at the date of purchase. Sea Corp's financial condition just prior to the purchase is shown in the following statements model:

Assets			=	Liab.	+	Equity		Rev.	–	Exp.	=	Net Inc.	Cash Flow
Cash	+	Assets	+	Goodwill									
300,000	+	NA	+	NA	=	NA	+	300,000	NA	–	NA	=	NA	NA

Required

a. Compute the amount of goodwill purchased.

b. Record the purchase in a financial statements model like the preceding one.

c. When will the goodwill be written off under the impairment rules?

PROBLEMS—SERIES B

L.O. 2   PROBLEM 9–20B *Accounting for Acquisition of Assets Including a Basket Purchase*

Moon Co., Inc., made several purchases of long-term assets in 2009. The details of each purchase are presented here.

New Office Equipment
1. List price: $60,000; terms: 2/10 n/30; paid within discount period.
2. Transportation-in: $1,600.
3. Installation: $2,200.
4. Cost to repair damage during unloading: $1,000.
5. Routine maintenance cost after six months: $300.

Basket Purchase of Copier, Computer, and Scanner for $15,000 with Fair Market Values
1. Copier, $10,000.
2. Computer, $6,000.
3. Scanner, $4,000.

Land for New Warehouse With an Old Building Torn Down
1. Purchase price, $200,000.
2. Demolition of building, $10,000.
3. Lumber sold from old building, $7,000.
4. Grading in preparation for new building, $14,000.
5. Construction of new building, $500,000.

Required

In each of these cases, determine the amount of cost to be capitalized in the asset account.

PROBLEM 9–21B *Accounting for Depreciation Over Multiple Accounting Cycles: Straight-Line Depreciation*

L.O. 3, 4

Altoids Company started business by acquiring $60,000 cash from the issue of common stock on January 1, 2001. The cash acquired was immediately used to purchase equipment for $60,000 that had a $12,000 salvage value and an expected useful life of four years. The equipment was used to produce the following revenue stream (assume that all revenue transactions are for cash). At the beginning of the fifth year, the equipment was sold for $6,800 cash. Altoids uses straight-line depreciation.

	2001	2002	2003	2004	2005
Revenue	$15,200	$14,400	$13,000	$12,000	$0

Required

Prepare income statements, statements of changes in stockholders' equity, balance sheets, and statements of cash flows for each of the five years. Present the statements in the form of a vertical statements model.

PROBLEM 9–22B *Purchase and Use of Tangible Asset: Three Accounting Cycles, Straight-Line Depreciation*

L.O. 3, 6, 7

The following transactions relate to Jim's Towing Service. Assume the transactions for the purchase of the wrecker and any capital improvements occur on January 1 of each year.

2007
1. Acquired $40,000 cash from the issue of common stock.
2. Purchased a used wrecker for $26,000. It has an estimated useful life of three years and a $2,000 salvage value.
3. Paid sales tax on the wrecker of $1,800.
4. Collected $17,600 in towing fees.
5. Paid $3,000 for gasoline and oil.
6. Recorded straight-line depreciation on the wrecker for 2007.
7. Closed the revenue and expense accounts to Retained Earnings at the end of 2007.

2008
1. Paid for a tune-up for the wrecker's engine, $400.
2. Bought four new tires, $600.
3. Collected $18,000 in towing fees.
4. Paid $4,200 for gasoline and oil.
5. Recorded straight-line depreciation for 2008.
6. Closed the revenue and expense accounts to Retained Earnings at the end of 2008.

2009
1. Paid to overhaul the wrecker's engine, $1,400, which extended the life of the wrecker to a total of four years.
2. Paid for gasoline and oil, $3,600.
3. Collected $30,000 in towing fees.
4. Recorded straight-line depreciation for 2009.
5. Closed the revenue and expense accounts at the end of 2009.

Required

a. Use a horizontal statements model like the following one to show the effect of these transactions on the elements of financial statements. Use + for increase, − for decrease, and NA for not affected. The first event is recorded as an example.

2007 Event No.	Assets	=	Liabilities	+	Equity	Net Inc.	Cash Flow
1	+		NA		+	NA	+ FA

b. Use a vertical model to present financial statements for 2007, 2008, and 2009. (*Hint:* Record the transactions in T-accounts before attempting to prepare the financial statements.)

L.O. 3   PROBLEM 9–23B *Calculating Depreciation Expense Using Four Different Methods*

Action, Inc., manufactures sporting goods. The following information applies to a machine purchased on January 1, 2001:

Purchase price	$ 70,000
Delivery cost	$ 2,000
Installation charge	$ 1,000
Estimated life	5 years
Estimated units	140,000
Salvage estimate	$ 3,000

During 2001, the machine produced 26,000 units and during 2002, it produced 21,000 units.

Required

Determine the amount of depreciation expense for 2001 and 2002 using each of the following methods:

a. Straight line.
b. Double-declining-balance.
c. Units of production.
d. MACRS, assuming that the machine is classified as seven-year property.

L.O. 3, 4   PROBLEM 9–24B *Effect of Straight-Line Versus Double-Declining-Balance Depreciation on the Recognition of Expense and Gains or Losses*

Graves Office Service purchased a new computer system in 2008 for $60,000. It is expected to have a five-year useful life and a $5,000 salvage value. The company expects to use the equipment more extensively in the early years.

Required

a. Calculate the depreciation expense for each of the five years, assuming the use of straight-line depreciation.
b. Calculate the depreciation expense for each of the five years, assuming the use of double-declining-balance depreciation.
c. Would the choice of one depreciation method over another produce a different amount of cash flow for any year? Why or why not?
d. Assume that Graves Office Service sold the computer system at the end of the fourth year for $15,000. Compute the amount of gain or loss using each depreciation method.
e. Explain any differences in gain or loss due to using the different methods.

L.O. 3, 4   PROBLEM 9–25B *Computing and Recording Units-of-Production Depreciation*

Marvel purchased assembly equipment for $700,000 on January 1, 2001. Marvel's financial condition immediately prior to the purchase is shown in the following horizontal statements model:

Assets				=	Equity			Rev.	−	Exp.	=	Net Inc.	Cash Flow
Cash	+	Equip.	−	Acc. Dep.	=	C. Stk.	+	Ret. Earn.					
800,000	+	NA	−	NA	=	800,000	+	NA	NA	−	NA	=	NA	NA

The equipment is expected to have a useful life of 100,000 machine hours and a salvage value of $20,000. Actual machine-hour use was as follows:

2001	32,000
2002	33,000
2003	35,000
2004	28,000
2005	12,000

Required

a. Compute the depreciation for each of the five years, assuming the use of units-of-production depreciation.

b. Assume that Marvel earns $320,000 of cash revenue during 2001. Record the purchase of the equipment and the recognition of the revenue and the depreciation expense for the first year in a financial statements model like the preceding one.

c. Assume that Marvel sold the equipment at the end of the fifth year for $18,000. Record the general journal entry for the sale.

PROBLEM 9–26B *Determining the Effect of Depreciation Expense on Financial Statements*   **L.O. 3**

Three different companies each purchased trucks on January 1, 2001, for $40,000. Each truck was expected to last four years or 200,000 miles. Salvage value was estimated to be $5,000. All three trucks were driven 66,000 miles in 2001, 42,000 miles in 2002, 40,000 miles in 2003, and 60,000 miles in 2004. Each of the three companies earned $30,000 of cash revenue during each of the four years. Company A uses straight-line depreciation, company B uses double-declining-balance depreciation, and company C uses units-of-production depreciation.

Required
Answer each of the following questions. Ignore the effects of income taxes.

a. Which company will report the highest amount of net income for 2001?

b. Which company will report the lowest amount of net income for 2004?

c. Which company will report the highest book value on the December 31, 2003, balance sheet?

d. Which company will report the highest amount of retained earnings on the December 31, 2004, balance sheet?

e. Which company will report the lowest amount of cash flow from operating activities on the 2003 statement of cash flows?

PROBLEM 9–27B *Accounting for Depletion*   **L.O. 6, 8**

Sanchez Company engages in the exploration and development of many types of natural resources. In the last two years, the company has engaged in the following activities:

Jan. 1, 2001   Purchased for $1,600,000 a silver mine estimated to contain 100,000 tons of silver ore.

July 1, 2001   Purchased for $1,500,000 a tract of timber estimated to yield 1,000,000 board feet of lumber and the residual value of the land was estimated at $100,000.

Feb. 1, 2002   Purchased for $1,800,000 a gold mine estimated to yield 30,000 tons of gold-veined ore.

Sept. 1, 2002   Purchased oil reserves for $1,360,000. The reserves were estimated to contain 282,000 barrels of oil, of which 10,000 would be unprofitable to pump.

Required
a. Prepare the journal entries to account for the following:
   (1) The 2001 purchases.
   (2) Depletion on the 2001 purchases, assuming that 12,000 tons of silver were mined and 500,000 board feet of lumber were cut.
   (3) The 2002 purchases.
   (4) Depletion on the four natural resource assets, assuming that 20,000 tons of silver ore, 300,000 board feet of lumber, 4,000 tons of gold ore, and 50,000 barrels of oil were extracted.
b. Prepare the portion of the December 31, 2002, balance sheet that reports natural resources.
c. Assume that in 2003 the estimates changed to reflect only 20,000 tons of gold ore remaining. Prepare the depletion journal entry in 2003 to account for the extraction of 6,000 tons of gold ore.

PROBLEM 9–28B *Recording Continuing Expenditures for Plant Assets*   **L.O. 3, 4, 6, 7**

Harris, Inc., recorded the following transactions over the life of a piece of equipment purchased in 2001:

Jan. 1, 2001   Purchased equipment for $80,000 cash. The equipment was estimated to have a five-year life and $5,000 salvage value and was to be depreciated using the straight-line method.

Dec. 31, 2001   Recorded depreciation expense for 2001.

Sept. 30, 2002   Undertook routine repairs costing $750.

Dec. 31, 2002   Recorded depreciation expense for 2002.

Jan. 1, 2003   Made an adjustment costing $3,000 to the equipment. It improved the quality of the output but did not affect the life estimate.

Dec. 31, 2003   Recorded depreciation expense for 2003.

June 1, 2004	Incurred $620 cost to oil and clean the equipment.
Dec. 31, 2004	Recorded depreciation expense for 2004.
Jan. 1, 2005	Had the equipment completely overhauled at a cost of $8,000. The overhaul was estimated to extend the total life to seven years.
Dec. 31, 2005	Recorded depreciation expense for 2005.
Oct. 1, 2006	Received and accepted an offer of $18,000 for the equipment.

Required

a. Use a horizontal statements model like the following one to show the effects of these transactions on the elements of the financial statements. Use + for increase, − for decrease, and NA for not affected. The first event is recorded as an example.

Date	Assets	=	Liabilities	+	Equity	Net Inc.	Cash Flow
Jan. 1, 2001	+ −		NA		NA	NA	− IA

b. Determine the amount of depreciation expense to be reported on the income statements for the years 2001 through 2005.

c. Determine the book value (cost − accumulated depreciation) Harris will report on the balance sheets at the end of the years 2001 through 2005.

d. Determine the amount of the gain or loss Harris will report on the disposal of the equipment on October 1, 2006.

L.O. 6, 7 **PROBLEM 9–29B** *Continuing Expenditures With Statements Model*

Venus Company owned a service truck that was purchased at the beginning of 2007 for $20,000. It had an estimated life of three years and an estimated salvage value of $2,000. Venus uses straight-line depreciation. Its financial condition as of January 1, 2009, is shown in the following financial statements model:

Assets				=	Equity			Rev.	−	Exp.	=	Net Inc.	Cash Flow
Cash	+	Truck	− Acc. Dep.	=	C. Stk.	+	Ret. Earn.						
14,000	+	20,000	− 12,000	=	4,000	+	18,000	NA	−	NA	=	NA	NA

In 2009, Venus spent the following amounts on the truck:

Jan. 4	Overhauled the engine for $4,000. The estimated life was extended one additional year, and the salvage value was revised to $3,000.
July 6	Obtained oil change and transmission service, $160.
Aug. 7	Replaced the fan belt and battery, $360.
Dec. 31	Purchased gasoline for the year, $5,000.
31	Recognized 2009 depreciation expense.

Required

a. Record the 2009 transactions in a statements model like the preceding one.

b. Prepare journal entries for the 2009 transactions.

L.O. 9 **PROBLEM 9–30B** *Accounting for Intangible Assets*

Xie Company purchased Atlantic Transportations Co. for $1,200,000. The fair market values of the assets purchased were as follows. No liabilities were assumed.

Equipment	$400,000
Land	100,000
Building	400,000
Franchise (10-year life)	20,000

Required

a. Calculate the amount of goodwill purchased.

b. Prepare the journal entry to record the amortization of the franchise fee at the end of year 1.

PROBLEM 9–31B *Accounting for Goodwill*   **L.O. 9**

Sulley Equipment Manufacturing Co. purchased the assets of Malcom Inc., a competitor, in 2001. It recorded goodwill of $50,000 at purchase. Because of defective machinery Malcom had produced prior to the purchase, it has been determined that all of the purchased goodwill has been permanently impaired.

Required

Prepare the journal entry to record the permanent impairment of the goodwill.

ANALYZE, THINK, COMMUNICATE

BUSINESS APPLICATIONS CASE *Understanding Real World Annual Reports*   **ATC 9–1**

Required—Part 1

Use the Topps Company's annual report in Appendix B to answer the following questions.

The Topps Company, Inc.

a. What method of depreciation does Topps use?
b. What types of intangible assets does Topps have?
c. What are the estimated lives that Topps uses for the various types of long-term assets?
d. As of March 1, 2003, what is the original cost of Topps': Land; Buildings and improvements; and Machinery, equipment and software (see the footnotes)?
e. What was Topps' depreciation expense and amortization expense for 2003 (see the footnotes)?

Required—Part 2

Use the Harley-Davidson's annual report that came with this book to answer the following questions.

Harley-Davidson, Inc.

a. What method of depreciation does Harley-Davidson use?
b. What types of intangible assets, if any, does Harley-Davidson have?
c. What are the estimated lives that Harley-Davidson uses for of the various types of long-term assets?
d. What dollar amount of Harley-Davidson's "identifiable assets" is associated with its Motorcycles Segment and what amount is associated with its Financial Services segment (see Note 11)?
e. What dollar amount of Harley-Davidson's "long-lived assets" is located in the United States and what amount is located in other countries (see Note 11)?

GROUP ASSIGNMENT *Different Depreciation Methods*   **ATC 9–2**

Sweet's Bakery makes cakes, pies, and other pastries that it sells to local grocery stores. The company experienced the following transactions during 2008.

1. Started business by acquiring $60,000 cash from the issue of common stock.
2. Purchased bakery equipment for $46,000.
3. Had sales in 2008 amounting to $42,000.
4. Paid $8,200 of cash for supplies expense used to make baked goods.
5. Incurred other operating expenses of $12,000 for 2008.
6. Recorded depreciation assuming the equipment had a four-year life and a $6,000 salvage value. The MACRS recovery period is five years.
7. Paid income tax. The rate is 30 percent.

Required

a. Organize the class into three sections and divide each section into groups of three to five students. Assign each section a depreciation method: straight-line, double-declining-balance, or MACRS.

Group Task

Prepare an income statement and balance sheet using the preceding information and the depreciation method assigned to your group.

Class Discussion

b. Have a representative of each section put its income statement on the board. Are there differences in net income? In the amount of income tax paid? How will these differences in the amount of depreciation expense change over the life of the equipment?

ATC 9–3   REAL-WORLD CASE   *Different Numbers for Different Industries*

The following ratios are for four companies in different industries. Some of these ratios have been discussed in the textbook, others have not, but their names explain how the ratio was computed. The four sets of ratios, presented randomly are:

Ratio	Company 1	Company 2	Company 3	Company 4
Current assets ÷ total assets	24%	20%	11%	6%
Operating cycle	39 days	11 days	27 days	234 days
Return-on-assets	24%	11%	14%	2%
Gross margin	54%	39%	40%	27%
Sales ÷ property, plant and equipment	64.8 times	2.6 times	1.6 times	2.9 times
Sales ÷ number of full-time employees	$21,000	$40,000	$585,000	$284,000

The four companies to which these ratios relate, listed in alphabetical order, are:

Anheuser Busch Companies, Inc. is a company that produces beer and related products. Its fiscal year-end was December 31, 2002.

Caterpillar, Inc. is a company that manufactures heavy construction equipment. Its fiscal year-end was December 31, 2002.

Outback Steakhouse, Inc. operates over 800 restaurants worldwide, most of them under the name Outback Steakhouse. Its fiscal year-end was December 31, 2002.

Weight Watchers International, Inc. is a company that provides weight loss services and products. Its fiscal year-end was December 28, 2002, during which 64 percent of its revenues came from meeting fees, and 29 percent came from product sales.

Required

Determine which company should be matched with each set of ratios. Write a memorandum explaining the rational for your decisions.

ATC 9–4   BUSINESS APPLICATIONS CASE   *Effect of Depreciation on the Return on Assets Ratio*

Organic Bagel Bakery (OBB) was started on January 1, 2005, when it acquired $100,000 cash from the issue of common stock. The company immediately purchased an oven that cost $100,000 cash. The over had an estimated salvage value of $10,000 and an expected useful life of eight years. OBB used the over during 2005 to produce $30,000 of cash revenue. Assume that these were the only events affecting OBB during 2005.

Required

(*Hint:* Prepare an income statement and a balance sheet prior to completing the following requirements.)

a. Compute the return on assets ratio as of December 31, 2005, assuming OBB uses the straight-line depreciation method.

b. Recompute the ratio assuming OBB uses the double-declining-balance method.

c. Which depreciation method makes it *appear* that OBB is utilizing its assets more effectively?

ATC 9–5   BUSINESS APPLICATIONS CASE   *Effect of Depreciation on Financial Statement Analysis: Straight-Line versus Double-Declining-Balance*

Qin Company and Roche Company experienced the exact same set of economic events during 2001. Both companies purchased machines on January 1, 2001. Except for the effects of this purchase, the accounting records of both companies had the following accounts and balances.

As of January 1, 2001	
Total Assets	$200,000
Total Liabilities	80,000
Total Stockholders' Equity	120,000
During 2001	
Total Sales Revenue	100,000
Total Expenses (not including depreciation)	60,000
Liabilities were not affected by transactions in 2001.	

The machines purchased by the companies each cost $40,000 cash. The machines had expected useful lives of five years and estimated salvage values of $4,000. Qin uses straight-line depreciation. Roche uses double-declining-balance depreciation.

Required

a. For both companies, calculate the balances in the preceding accounts on December 31, 2001, after the effects of the purchase and depreciation of the machines have been applied. (*Hint:* The purchases of the machines are asset exchange transactions that do not affect total assets. However, the effect of depreciating the machines changes the amounts in total assets, expense, and equity [retained earnings]).

b. Based on the revised account balances determined in Requirement *a,* calculate the following ratios for both companies:

　(**1**) Debt to assets ratio.

　(**2**) Return on assets ratio.

　(**3**) Return on equity ratio.

c. Disregarding the effects of income taxes, which company produced the higher increase in real economic wealth during 2001?

WRITING ASSIGNMENT *Impact of Historical Cost on Asset Presentation on the Balance Sheet*

ATC 9–6

Assume that you are examining the balance sheets of two companies and note the following information:

	Company A	Company B
Equipment	$1,130,000	$900,000
Accumulated Depreciation	(730,000)	(500,000)
Book Value	$ 400,000	$400,000

Maxie Smith, a student who has had no accounting courses, remarks that Company A and Company B have the same amount of equipment.

Required

In a short paragraph, explain to Maxie that the two companies do not have equal amounts of equipment. You may want to include in your discussion comments regarding the possible age of each company's equipment, the impact of the historical cost concept on balance sheet information, and the impact of different depreciation methods on book value.

ETHICAL DILEMMA *Good Standards/Bad People or Just Plain Bad Standards?*

ATC 9–7

Eleanor Posey has been reading the financial statements of her fiercest competitor, Barron Bailey, who like herself owns a regionally based heating and cooling services company. The statements were given to her by a potential investor, Jim Featherson, who told her that the statements convinced him to put his investment money in Bailey's business instead of Posey's. Bailey's statements show a net income figure 10 percent higher than that reported by Posey's company. When analyzing the footnotes to the financial statements, Posey noticed that Bailey depreciates all property, plant, and equipment on a straight-line basis. In contrast, she depreciates only her building on a straight-line basis. All her equipment is depreciated by the double-declining-balance method, which she believes matches the pattern of use of equipment in the heating and cooling services business.

Posey arranges a meeting with Featherson in which she attempts to inform him of the effects of depreciation on financial statements. She explains that Bailey's reporting practices are deceptive. While Bailey's income figure is higher now, the situation will reverse in the near future because her depreciation charges will decline whereas Bailey's will stay constant. She explains that Bailey may even have to report losses because declines in the use of equipment also translate to lower revenues. Featherson tells Posey that Bailey's financial statements were audited by a very respectable CPA and that the company received an unqualified opinion. He tells her that nobody can predict the future and that he makes his decisions on the basis of current facts.

After Featherson leaves, Posey becomes somewhat resentful of the rules of accounting. Reporting depreciation in the way that she and her accountant believe to be consistent with actual use has caused her to lose an investor with a significant base of capital. She writes a letter to the chairperson of the Financial Accounting Standards Board in which she suggests that the Board establish a single depreciation method that is required to be used by all companies. She argues that this approach would be better for investors who know little about accounting alternatives. If all companies were required to use the same accounting rules, comparability would be significantly improved.

Required

Answer the following questions under the assumption that actual use is, in fact, greater in the earlier part of the life of equipment in the heating and cooling services business.

a. Are Posey's predictions regarding Bailey's future profitability accurate? Explain.
b. Comment on the ethical implications associated with Bailey's decision to depreciate his equipment using the straight-line method.
c. Comment on Posey's recommendation that the FASB eliminate alternative depreciation methods to improve comparability.
d. Comment on Featherson's use of accounting information.

ATC 9–8   EDGAR DATABASE *Comparing Microsoft and Intel*

Required

a. Using the EDGAR database, fill in the missing data in the following table, drawing on the most current 10-K reports available for Microsoft Corporation and Intel Corporation. The percentages must be computed; they are not included in the companies' 10-Ks. See Appendix A for instructions on using EDGAR. (*Note:* The percentages for current assets and property, plant, and equipment will not sum to 100.)

	Current Assets	Property, Plant, and Equipment	Total Assets
Microsoft			
Dollar Amount	$	$	$
% of Total Assets	%	%	100%
Intel			
Dollar Amount	$	$	$
% of Total Assets	%	%	100%

b. Briefly explain why these two companies have different percentages of their assets in current assets versus property, plant, and equipment.

ATC 9–9   SPREADSHEET ASSIGNMENT *Reporting to the IRS Versus Financial Statement Reporting*

Crist Company operates a lawn mowing service. Crist has chosen to depreciate its equipment for financial statement purposes using the straight-line method. However, to save cash in the short run, Crist has elected to use the MACRS method for income tax reporting purposes.

Required

a. Set up the following spreadsheet to reflect the two different methods of reporting. Notice that the first two years of revenues and operating expenses are provided.
b. Enter in the effects of the following items for 2001.
  (1) At the beginning of 2001, Crist purchased for $10,000 cash a lawn mower it expects to use for five years. Salvage value is estimated to be $2,000. As stated, Crist uses the straight-line method of depreciation for financial statement purposes and the MACRS method for income tax purposes. Use formulas to calculate depreciation expense for each method.
  (2) No equipment was sold during 2001; therefore, no gain or loss would be reported this year.
  (3) The income tax rate is 30 percent. For simplicity, assume that the income tax payable was paid in 2001.
  (4) Complete the schedules for income reporting, reporting of equipment, and reporting of cash flows for 2001. Use formulas for all calculations.
c. Enter in the effects of the following items for 2002.
  (1) Crist used the mower for the entire 2002 year. Enter 2002 depreciation expense amounts for the income reporting section of your spreadsheet.
  (2) At December 31, Crist sold the lawn mower for $7,000. Calculate the gain or loss on the sale for the income reporting section. Use formulas to make the calculations.
  (3) The income tax rate is 30 percent. For simplicity, assume that the income tax payable was paid in 2002.
  (4) Complete the schedules for income reporting and reporting of cash flows for 2002.
d. Calculate the Total columns for the income reporting and reporting of cash flows sections.
e. Respond to the following.
  (1) In 2001, by adopting the MACRS method of depreciation for tax purposes instead of the straight-line method, what is the difference in the amount of cash paid for income taxes?
  (2) In the long term, after equipment has been disposed of, is there any difference in total income under the two methods?

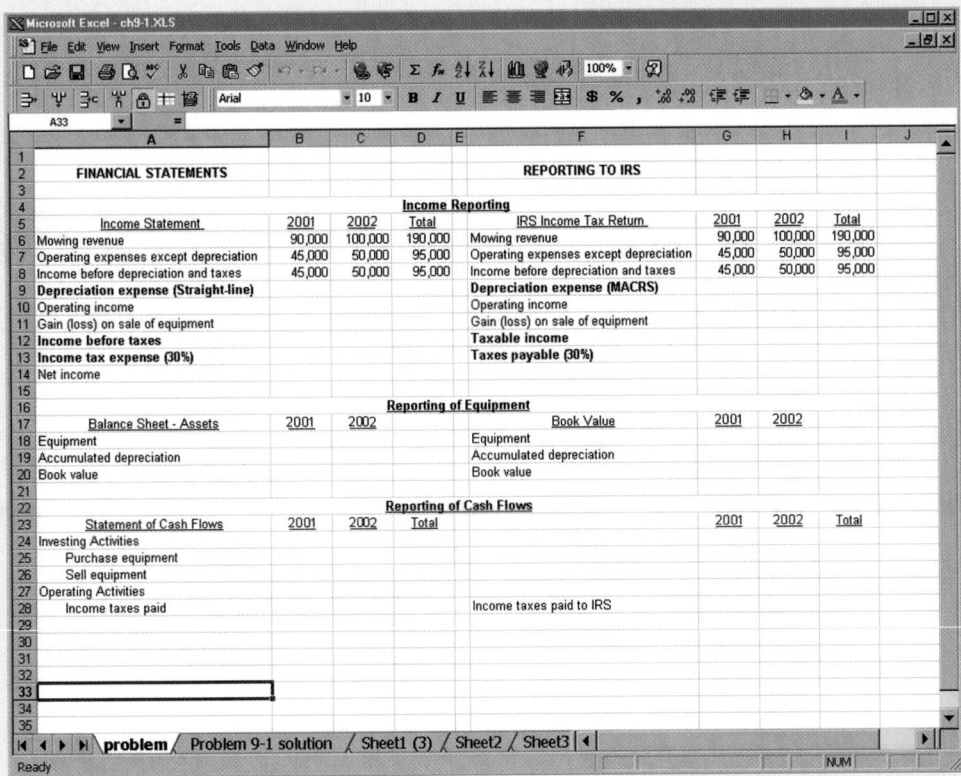

(3) In the long term, after equipment has been disposed of, is there any difference between total income tax expense and total income tax paid?

(4) Explain why Crist Company would use two different depreciation methods, particularly the straight-line method for the financial statements and an accelerated method (MACRS) for reporting to the IRS.

SPREADSHEET ASSIGNMENT *Alternative Methods of Depreciation*

ATC 9–10

Short Company purchased a computer on January 1, 2001, for $5,000. An additional $100 was paid for delivery charges. The computer was estimated to have a life of five years or 10,000 hours. Salvage value was estimated at $300. During the five years, the computer was used as follows:

2001	2,500 hours
2002	2,400 hours
2003	2,000 hours
2004	1,700 hours
2005	1,400 hours

Required

a. Prepare a five-year depreciation schedule for the computer using the straight-line depreciation method. Be sure to use formulas for all computations including depreciation expense. Set up the following headings for your schedule:

		Beginning				Ending	
Year	Cost	Accumulated Depreciation	Book Value	Depreciation Expense	Cost	Accumulated Depreciation	Book Value

b. Prepare another five-year depreciation schedule for the computer using the units-of-production method. Use (copy) the headings used in Requirement *a*.

c. Prepare another five-year depreciation schedule for the computer using the double-declining-balance method. Use (copy) the headings used in Requirement *a*.

d. Prepare another five-year depreciation schedule for the computer using the MACRS method. Use (copy) the headings used in Requirement *a*.

Spreadsheet Tip

After the year 2001, enter subsequent dates automatically. Position the mouse in the lower right-hand corner of the highlighted cell "2001" until a thin cross appears. Click and drag down four additional rows.

COMPREHENSIVE PROBLEM

The trial balance of Pacilio Security Systems Sales and Service as of January 1, 2009, was:

Cash	$212,114
Petty Cash	100
Accounts Receivable	47,620
Allowance for Doubtful Accounts	1,066
Supplies	250
Prepaid Rent	1,400
Inventory—Standard Alarms (7 @ $275)	1,925
Inventory—Deluxe Alarms (29 @ $580)	16,820
Van	9,200
Accumulated Depreciation	7,200
Warranties Payable	1,615
Common Stock	50,000
Retained Earnings	229,548

During 2009, Pacilio Security Systems Sales and Service experienced the following transactions:

1. Purchased a building, land, and office equipment on January 2, 2009, for a total cost of $120,000. The equipment was appraised at $14,000, the building was appraised at $84,000 and the land was appraised at $42,000. Pacilio paid a cash down payment of $80,000 and issued a mortgage for the balance. The mortgage is a 20-year loan with a 6 percent interest rate. Interest is payable annually on December 31 along with a $2,000 payment on principal.
2. Purchased $300 of supplies for cash.
3. Purchased for cash 100 standard alarm systems at a cost of $280 each and 40 deluxe alarms systems at a cost of $590 each.
4. Replenished the petty cash fund on June 30. At this time petty cash had $12 cash and receipts for $28 office supplies, $45 for cutting grass, and $11 for miscellaneous expense.
5. Sold 95 standard alarm systems for $580 each on account and 55 deluxe alarm systems for $960 each on account. (Be sure to record cost of goods sold.)
6. Billed $96,000 in monitoring services for the year. Credit card sales amounted to $36,000, and the credit-card company charged a 4 percent fee. The remaining $60,000 were sales on account.
7. Collected amount due from the credit card company.
8. Paid $900 to repair deluxe alarm systems that were still under warranty.
9. After numerous attempts to collect from customers, wrote off $2,350 of accounts receivable.
10. Collected $162,000 of accounts receivable for the year.
11. Paid installers $35,000 for salaries for the year.
12. Paid $4,200 in advertising expense for the year.
13. Paid $4,800 of utilities expense for the year.
14. On December 31, 2009, paid the interest and principal due on the note payable.

Adjustments

15. Office supplies of $180 were on hand at the end of the year.
16. Recognized expired rent for the year.
17. Recognized warranty expense for the year at 4 percent of the deluxe alarm sales.
18. Recognized bad debt expense for the year. Pacilio uses the allowance method and estimates that 2 percent of sales on account will not be collected.
19. Recognized depreciation expense on the building and equipment. The equipment has a 5-year life and a $2,000 salvage value. The building has a 30-year life with a $12,000 salvage value. The company uses double-declining-balance depreciation for the equipment and straight-line depreciation for the building.

Required

a. Record the above transactions in general journal form. Pacilio uses FIFO cost flow assumption.
b. Post the transactions to the T-accounts.
c. Prepare a trial balance.
d. Prepare an income statement, statement of changes in stockholders' equity, balance sheet, and statement of cash flows.
e. Close the nominal accounts to retained earnings.
f. Post the closing entries to the T-accounts and prepare an after-closing trial balance.

CHAPTER *ten*

ACCOUNTING FOR LONG-TERM DEBT

LEARNING *objectives*

After you have mastered the material in this chapter, you will be able to:

1 Show how the amortization of long-term notes affects financial statements.

2 Show how a line of credit affects financial statements.

3 Describe the different types of bonds that companies issue.

4 Explain why bonds are issued at face value, a discount, or a premium.

5 Show how bond liabilities and their related interest costs affect financial statements.

6 Explain how to account for bonds and their related interest costs.

7 Explain the advantages and disadvantages of debt financing.

8 Explain the time value of money. (Appendix)

THE *curious* ACCOUNTANT

For its 2002 fiscal year, AOL Time Warner (now called Time Warner) reported a net loss of $98.7 billion. That same year, the company had $1.8 billion of interest expense.

　　With such a huge loss on its income statement, do you think Time Warner was able to make the interest payments on its debt? If so, how? (Answers on page 462.)

CHAPTER *opening*

*Like individuals, most businesses borrow money to accomplish their goals and objectives. Like individuals, businesses are concerned about interest charges and methods of repayment. Depending on the loan agreement between the borrower and the lender, interest payments on borrowed funds may be due on an annual, a semiannual, a monthly, or some other basis, including payment at maturity along with the principal balance of the debt. **Fixed interest rates** remain constant over the life of a loan, while **variable interest rates** fluctuate.*

　　*The amount borrowed (the principal) is sometimes repaid in one lump sum at the maturity date of the debt. Alternatively, the principal is sometimes repaid in systematic installments over the life of the loan, a repayment arrangement commonly called **amortization**.[1] Some debt instruments combine these options by amortizing a portion of the principal over the loan term with the remainder due in full at maturity. This type of payment schedule is an*

---

[1]In Chapter 9 the term amortization described the expense recognized when the *cost of an intangible asset* is systematically allocated to expense over the useful life of the asset. This chapter shows that the term amortization refers more broadly to a variety of allocation processes. Here it means the systematic process of allocating the *principal repayment* over the life of a loan.

10–1

LO1 Show how the amortization of long-term notes affects financial statements.

amortization with a ***balloon payment***. *This chapter explains the major forms of debt financing and effects of different principal and interest payment options on the financial statements.*

Long-Term Notes Payable

Long-term notes payable usually have terms from two to five years. Payments on these notes frequently include both interest and principal. For example, when you make a payment on your car loan, you are paying interest as well as repaying some of the principal.

To illustrate the accounting treatment for long-term notes payable, assume that Blair Company was started when it issued a $100,000 face value long-term note to National Bank on January 1, 2005. Issuing the note payable increases both assets (cash) and liabilities (notes payable). There is no effect on the income statement when the note is issued. The cash inflow is reported in the financing activities section of the statement of cash flows. The effects on the financial statements are shown below:

Assets	=	Liab.	+	Equity	Rev.	−	Exp.	=	Net Inc.	Cash Flow	
100,000	=	100,000	+	NA	NA	−	NA	=	NA	100,000	FA

The note had a 9 percent annual interest rate and a five-year term. The loan agreement called for five equal payments of $25,709[2] to be made on December 31 of each year from 2005 through 2009. Each payment includes both principal and interest, allocated[3] as shown in Exhibit 10–1. When the final payment is made, both the principal and interest will be paid in full.

The amount of interest paid each year (Column 4) is determined by multiplying the outstanding principal balance of the loan (Column 2) by the 9 percent interest rate. The portion of the payment not allocated to interest reduces the principal balance of the loan. For example, $9,000 ($100,000 × 0.09) of the first $25,709 payment (made on December 31, 2005) is allocated to interest and $16,709 ($25,709 − $9,000) to principal repayment. After the first payment, the principal balance drops to $83,291 ($100,000 − $16,709). Since the annual principal repayment reduces the outstanding loan balance, the amount of each payment applied to interest each period declines. The amount allocated to principal increases. Of the second $25,709 payment (made on December 31, 2006), $7,496 ($83,291 × .09) is interest and $18,213 ($25,709 − $7,496) is principal repayment. Allocations for the remaining three payments are similarly computed.

Although the amounts allocated to principal and interest differ each year, the effects of the annual payment on the financial statements are the same. On the balance sheet, assets (cash)

Exhibit 10–1 *Amortization Schedule for Note Issued by Blair Company*

Accounting Period	Principal Balance on Jan. 1	Cash Payment Dec. 31	Applied to Interest	Applied to Principal
2005	$100,000	$25,709	$9,000	$16,709
2006	83,291	25,709	7,496	18,213
2007	65,078	25,709	5,857	19,852
2008	45,226	25,709	4,070	21,639
2009	23,587	25,710	2,123	23,587

---

[2]The amount of the annual payment is determined using the present value concepts presented in the appendix to this chapter. Usually the lender (bank or other financial institution) calculates the amount of the payment for the customer.
[3]All computations are rounded to the nearest dollar. To fully liquidate the liability, the final payment is one dollar more than the others because of rounding differences.

decrease by the total amount of the payment; liabilities (note payable) decrease by the amount allocated to principal repayment; and stockholders' equity (retained earnings) decreases by the amount applied to interest expense. Net income decreases from recognizing interest expense. On the statement of cash flows, the portion of the cash payment applied to interest is reported in the operating activities section and the portion applied to principal is reported in the financing activities section. The effects on the 2005 financial statements follow:

Assets	=	Liab.	+	Equity	Rev.	−	Exp.	=	Net Inc.	Cash Flow
(25,709)	=	(16,709)	+	(9,000)	NA	−	9,000	=	(9,000)	(9,000) OA
										(16,709) FA

Exhibit 10–2 displays income statements, balance sheets, and statements of cash flows for Blair Company for the accounting periods 2005 through 2009. The illustration assumes that Blair earned $12,000 of rent revenue each year. Since some of the principal is repaid each year, the note payable amount reported on the balance sheet and the amount of the interest expense on the income statement both decline each year.

Security for Bank Loan Agreements

To reduce the risk that they won't get paid, lenders frequently require debtors to pledge designated assets as **collateral for loans.** For example, when a bank makes a car loan, it usually retains legal title to the car until the loan is fully repaid. If the debtor is unable to make the monthly payments, the bank repossesses the car, sells it to someone else, and uses the proceeds from the sale to pay the original owner's debt balance.

Exhibit 10–2

BLAIR COMPANY
Financial Statements

	2005	2006	2007	2008	2009
Income Statements					
Rent Revenue	$12,000	$12,000	$12,000	$12,000	$12,000
Interest Expense	(9,000)	(7,496)	(5,857)	(4,070)	(2,123)
Net Income	$ 3,000	$ 4,504	$ 6,143	$ 7,930	$ 9,877
Balance Sheets					
Assets					
Cash	$86,291	$72,582	$58,873	$45,164	$31,454
Liabilities					
Note Payable	$83,291	$65,078	$45,226	$23,587	$ 0
Stockholders' Equity					
Retained Earnings	3,000	7,504	13,647	21,577	31,454
Total Liabilities and Stk. Equity	$86,291	$72,582	$58,873	$45,164	$31,454
Statements of Cash Flows					
Operating Activities					
Inflow from Customers	$12,000	$12,000	$12,000	$12,000	$12,000
Outflow for Interest	(9,000)	(7,496)	(5,857)	(4,070)	(2,123)
Investing Activities	0	0	0	0	0
Financing Activities					
Inflow from Note Issue	100,000	0	0	0	0
Outflow to Repay Note	(16,709)	(18,213)	(19,852)	(21,639)	(23,587)
Net Change in Cash	86,291	(13,709)	(13,709)	(13,709)	(13,710)
Plus: Beginning Cash Balance	0	86,291	72,582	58,873	45,164
Ending Cash Balance	$86,291	$72,582	$58,873	$45,164	$31,454

In addition to requiring collateral, bankers often obtain additional protection by including **restrictive covenants** in loan agreements. Such covenants may restrict additional borrowing, limit dividend payments, or restrict salary increases. If the loan restrictions are violated, the borrower is in default and the loan balance is due immediately.

Finally, banks often ask key personnel to provide copies of their personal tax returns and financial statements. The financial condition of key executives is important because they may be asked to pledge personal property as collateral for business loans.

Check Yourself 10–1

On January 1, 2004, Krueger Company issued a $50,000 note to State Bank. The note had a 10-year term and an 8 percent interest rate. Krueger agreed to repay the principal and interest in 10 annual payments of $7,451.47 at the end of each year. Determine the amount of principal and interest Krueger paid during the first and second year that the note was outstanding.

Answer

Accounting Period	Principal Balance January 1 A	Cash Payment December 31 B	Applied to Interest C = A × 0.08	Applied to Principal B − C
2004	$50,000.00	$7,451.47	$4,000.00	$3,451.47
2005	46,548.53	7,451.47	3,723.88	3,727.59

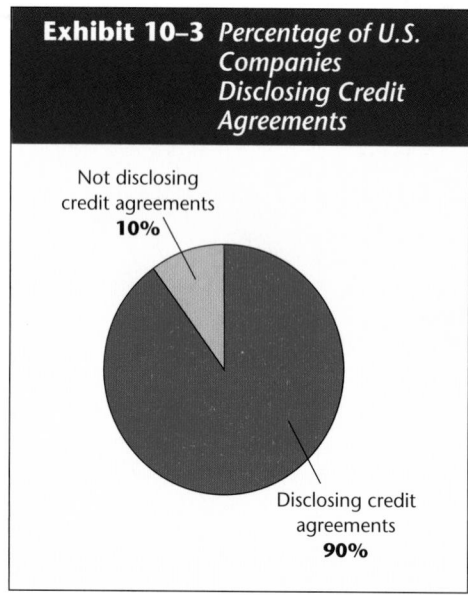

Exhibit 10–3 *Percentage of U.S. Companies Disclosing Credit Agreements*

Not disclosing credit agreements **10%**

Disclosing credit agreements **90%**

Data source: AICPA, *Accounting Trends and Techniques,* 2002.

Line of Credit

A **line of credit** represents a common, highly flexible form of short- and intermediate-term financing. Lines of credit enable companies to borrow or repay funds as needed up to the maximum borrowing limit set by the creditor. Interest rates on lines of credit usually fluctuate in proportion to some standard such as the bank prime rate or the rate paid on U.S. Treasury bills. The typical term of a line of credit is one year. Although they are classified on the balance sheet as short-term liabilities, lines of credit are frequently extended, year after year, by simply renewing the credit agreement. As a result, lines of credit represent relatively permanent forms of financing. As indicated in Exhibit 10–3, credit agreements are used widely in business.

To illustrate, assume Terry Parker owns a wholesale jet-ski distributorship. In the spring, Parker needs to build up inventory levels to be ready for warm-weather demand. He pays for the increased inventory by using a line of credit to borrow money. He repays the money in the summer months using cash generated from jet-ski sales. He pays interest at the end of each month on any outstanding borrowings. Parker's line of credit has a variable interest rate. Parker's borrowing, repayments, and interest charges during the current year follow:

Date	Amount Borrowed (Repaid)	Loan Balance at End of Month	Effective Interest Rate per Month (%)	Interest Expense (rounded to nearest $1)
Mar. 1	$20,000	$ 20,000	0.09 ÷ 12	$150
Apr. 1	30,000	50,000	0.09 ÷ 12	375
May 1	50,000	100,000	0.105 ÷ 12	875
June 1	(10,000)	90,000	0.10 ÷ 12	750
July 1	(40,000)	50,000	0.09 ÷ 12	375
Aug. 1	(50,000)	0	0.09 ÷ 12	0

LO2 Show how a line of credit affects financial statements.

Each borrowing event (March 1, April 1, and May 1) is an asset source transaction. Both the asset cash and the line-of-credit liability increase. Each repayment (June 1, July 1, and August 1) is an asset use transaction, decreasing assets and liabilities. The interest expense recognized and paid each month is an asset use transaction. Assets (cash) and stockholders' equity (retained earnings) decrease, as does net income. The effects of borrowing, repayment, and interest recognition on the financial statements follow:

Date	Assets	=	Liabilities	+	Equity	Rev.	−	Exp.	=	Net Inc.	Cash Flow	
Mar. 1	20,000	=	20,000	+	NA	NA	−	NA	=	NA	20,000	FA
31	(150)	=	NA	+	(150)	NA	−	150	=	(150)	(150)	OA
Apr. 1	30,000	=	30,000	+	NA	NA	−	NA	=	NA	30,000	FA
30	(375)	=	NA	+	(375)	NA	−	375	=	(375)	(375)	OA
May 1	50,000	=	50,000	+	NA	NA	−	NA	=	NA	50,000	FA
31	(875)	=	NA	+	(875)	NA	−	875	=	(875)	(875)	OA
June 1	(10,000)	=	(10,000)	+	NA	NA	−	NA	=	NA	(10,000)	FA
30	(750)	=	NA	+	(750)	NA	−	750	=	(750)	(750)	OA
July 1	(40,000)	=	(40,000)	+	NA	NA	−	NA	=	NA	(40,000)	FA
31	(375)	=	NA	+	(375)	NA	−	375	=	(375)	(375)	OA
Aug. 1	(50,000)	=	(50,000)	+	NA	NA	−	NA	=	NA	(50,000)	FA
31	NA	=	NA	+	NA	NA	−	NA	=	NA	NA	

▌Bond Liabilities

Many companies meet their long-term financing needs by issuing bonds. A bond certificate represents an agreement that describes a company's obligation to pay interest while the bonds are outstanding and repay the principal when the bonds mature. Bond agreements usually include restrictive covenants designed to protect the creditors (bondholders). Most bonds are issued in individual increments of $1,000. If a company wishes to borrow $10 million by issuing bonds, it will therefore typically issue 10,000 individual bonds, each with a principal (maturity) amount of $1,000. A typical bond certificate is illustrated below.

Topic Tackler
PLUS

10–2

LO3 Describe the different types of bonds that companies issue.

Bond financing offers several advantages to companies. First, bonds usually have longer terms than notes payable issued to banks. The typical bond term is 20 years; term loans from banks normally mature in 5 or fewer years. Second, bond interest rates may be lower than interest rates banks charge. Banks earn profits by charging a higher rate of interest on money they lend than they pay for money customers deposit. For example, a bank may charge 9 percent interest on a commercial loan but only pay 2 percent interest on a certificate of deposit. If a company could borrow directly from the depositor, it could avoid paying the 7 percent spread (9 percent − 2 percent) charged by the bank. Companies using bonds reduce interest costs by eliminating the middleman (banks and other financial institutions).

Since bonds are not insured by the federal government, they are riskier investments than bank certificates of deposit, which are insured. To compensate the public for the higher risk, bonds usually pay higher interest than bank deposits. Even so, interest on bonds is usually less than the interest charged by banks on commercial loans. This condition is possible because savings from eliminating the bank's spread is normally divided between the bond issuers and the bondholders. As a result, bond issuers pay less interest and bondholders receive higher interest than they would if they used banks or other financial institutions.

Characteristics of Bonds

From the issuer's point of view, a **bond** represents an obligation to pay a sum of money to the bondholder on the bond's maturity date. The amount to be paid at maturity is the **face value** of the bond. Most bonds also require the issuer to make interest payments based on a **stated interest rate** at regular intervals over the life of the bond.

Security of Bonds

Bonds may be either secured or unsecured.

1. **Secured bonds** grant their holders a priority legal claim on specified identifiable assets should the issuer default. A common type of secured bond is a **mortgage bond,** which conditionally transfers the title of designated property to the bondholder until the bond is paid.
2. **Unsecured bonds,** also called **debentures,** are issued based on the general strength of the borrower's credit. Bond certificates often specify the priority of debenture holders' claims relative to other creditors. Holders of **subordinated debentures** have lower priority claims than other creditors, whereas holders of **unsubordinated debentures** have equal claims.

Timing of Maturity

The maturity dates of bonds can be specified in various ways. Even bonds sold as separate components of a single issue may have different maturity dates.

1. **Term bonds** mature on a specified date in the future.
2. **Serial bonds** mature at specified intervals throughout the life of the total issue. For example, bonds with a total face value of $1,000,000 may mature in increments of $100,000 every year for 10 years.

To ensure there is enough cash available at maturity to pay off the debt, the bond certificate may require the issuer to make regular payments into a **sinking fund.** Money deposited in the sinking fund is usually managed by an independent trustee who invests the funds until the bonds mature. At maturity, the funds and the proceeds from the investments are used to repay the bond debt.

Special Features

Some bonds feature one or both of the following characteristics.

On November 8, 2001, Enron Corporation announced that it would have to reduce its stockholders' equity by approximately $1.2 billion. On December 2, 2001, the company filed for Chapter 11 bankruptcy protection.

When covering this story, most of the media's attention focused on the overstatement of earnings that resulted from Enron's improper use of a form of partnerships called "special purpose entities." However, these entities were also used to improperly keep as much as $1 billion of debt off of Enron's balance sheet. Why did this matter to Enron? Enron was a very rapidly growing company and it used lots of debt to finance this growth. From 1999 to 2000 its assets grew from $33.4 billion to $65.5 billion, but its debt grew from $23.8 billion to $54.0 billion. This caused its debt to assets ratio to rise from 71.3 percent to 82.4 percent. The higher debt burden put Enron at risk of having to pay higher interest rates, a very unattractive option for a company with this much debt.

1. **Convertible bonds** are liabilities that can be exchanged at the option of the bondholder for common stock or some other specified ownership interest. The issuing company benefits because bondholders (investors) are willing to accept a lower interest rate in exchange for the conversion feature. Bondholders benefit because they obtain the option to share in potential rewards of ownership. If the market value of the company's stock increases, bondholders can convert their bonds to stock. If the stock price does not increase bondholders are still guaranteed interest payments and priority claims in bankruptcy settlements.

2. **Callable bonds** allow the issuing company to redeem (pay off) the bond debt before the maturity date. If interest rates decline, this feature benefits the issuing company because it could borrow additional money at a lower rate and use the proceeds to pay off its higher rate bonds. Since an early redemption would eliminate their higher interest bond investments, bondholders consider call features undesirable. To encourage investors to buy callable bonds, the **call price** normally exceeds the *face value* of the bonds. For example, the issuing company may agree to pay the holder of a $1,000 face value bond a call price of $1,050 if the bond is redeemed before its maturity date. The difference between the call price and the face value ($50 [$1,050 − $1,000] in this case) is commonly called a **call premium.**

Bond Ratings

Various financial services, such as Moody's, analyze the risk of default for corporate bond issues and publish ratings of the risk as guides to bond investors. The highest rating (lowest risk) a company can achieve is AAA, the next highest AA, and so forth. Bond issuers try to maintain high credit ratings because lower ratings force them to pay higher interest rates.

▎Bonds Issued at Face Value

Fixed-Rate, Fixed-Term, Annual Interest Bonds

LO5 Show how bond liabilities and their related interest costs affect financial statements.

Assume Marsha Mason needs cash in order to seize a business opportunity. Mason knows of a company seeking a plot of land on which to store its inventory of crushed stone. Mason also knows of a suitable tract of land she could purchase for $100,000. The company has agreed to lease the land it needs from Mason for $12,000 per year. Mason's only problem is that she lacks the funds to buy the land.

Some of Mason's friends recently complained about the low interest banks were paying on certificates of deposit. Mason suggested that her friends invest in bonds instead of CDs. She offered to sell them bonds with a 9 percent stated interest rate. The terms specified in the bond certificate Mason drafted included making interest payments in cash on December 31 of each year, a five-year term to maturity, and pledging the land as collateral for the bonds.[4] Her friends were favorably impressed, and Mason issued the bonds to them in exchange for cash on January 1, 2001.

Mason used the bond proceeds to purchase the land and immediately contracted to lease it for five years. On December 31, 2005, the maturity date of the bonds, Mason sold the land for its $100,000 book value and used the proceeds from the sale to repay the bond liability.

Effect of Events on Financial Statements

Mason's business venture involves six distinct accounting events:

1. Received $100,000 cash from issuing five-year bonds at face value.
2. Invested proceeds from the bond issue to purchase land for $100,000 cash.
3. Earned $12,000 cash revenue annually from leasing the land.
4. Paid $9,000 annual interest on December 31 of each year.
5. Sold the land for $100,000 cash.
6. Repaid the bond principal to bondholders.

Explanations of the effects of these events on Mason's financial statements follow.

Event 1 Issue Bonds for Cash
Issuing bonds is an asset source transaction.

Assets (cash) and liabilities (bonds payable) increase. Net income is not affected. The $100,000 cash inflow is reported in the financing activities section of the statement of cash flows. These effects are shown here:

Assets	=	Liab.	+	Equity	Rev.	−	Exp.	=	Net Inc.	Cash Flow	
100,000	=	100,000	+	NA	NA	−	NA	=	NA	100,000	FA

Event 2 Investment in Land
Paying $100,000 cash to purchase land is an asset exchange transaction.

The asset cash decreases and the asset land increases. The income statement is not affected. The cash outflow is reported in the investing activities section of the statement of cash flows. These effects are illustrated below:

Assets			= Liab.	+	Equity	Rev.	−	Exp.	=	Net Inc.	Cash Flow	
Cash	+	Land	=									
(100,000)	+	100,000	= NA	+	NA	NA	−	NA	=	NA	(100,000)	IA

Event 3 Revenue Recognition
Recognizing $12,000 cash revenue from renting the property is an asset source transaction.

---

[4]In practice, bonds are usually issued for much larger sums of money, often hundreds of millions of dollars. Also, terms to maturity are normally long, with 20 years being common. Using such large amounts for such long terms is unnecessarily cumbersome for instructional purposes. The effects of bond issues can be illustrated efficiently by using smaller amounts of debt with shorter maturities, as assumed in the case of Marsha Mason.

This event is repeated each year from 2001 through 2005. The event increases assets and stockholders' equity. Recognizing revenue increases net income. The cash inflow is reported in the operating activities section of the statement of cash flows. These effects follow:

Assets	=	Liab.	+	Equity	Rev.	−	Exp.	=	Net Inc.	Cash Flow
12,000	=	NA	+	12,000	12,000	−	NA	=	12,000	12,000 OA

Event 4 Expense Recognition
Mason's $9,000 ($100,000 × 0.09) cash payment represents interest expense.

This event is also repeated each year from 2001 through 2005. The interest payment is an asset use transaction. Cash and stockholders' equity (retained earnings) decrease. The expense recognition decreases net income. The cash outflow is reported in the operating activities section of the statement of cash flows. These effects follow:

Assets	=	Liab.	+	Equity	Rev.	−	Exp.	=	Net Inc.	Cash Flow
(9,000)	=	NA	+	(9,000)	NA	−	9,000	=	(9,000)	(9,000) OA

Event 5 Sale of Investment in Land
Selling the land for cash equal to its $100,000 book value is an asset exchange transaction.

Cash increases and land decreases. Since there was no gain or loss on the sale, the income statement is not affected. The cash inflow is reported in the investing activities section of the statement of cash flows. These effects follow:

Assets			= Liab.	+	Equity	Rev.	−	Exp.	=	Net Inc.	Cash Flow
Cash	+	Land	=								
100,000	+	(100,000) =	NA	+	NA	NA	−	NA	=	NA	100,000 IA

Event 6 Payoff of Bond Liability
Repaying the face value of the bond liability is an asset use transaction.

Cash and bonds payable decrease. The income statement is not affected. The cash outflow is reported in the financing activities section of the statement of cash flows:

Assets	=	Liab.	+	Equity	Rev.	−	Exp.	=	Net Inc.	Cash Flow
(100,000)	=	(100,000)	+	NA	NA	−	NA	=	NA	(100,000) FA

Financial Statements

Exhibit 10–4 displays Mason Company's financial statements. For simplicity, the income statement does not distinguish between operating and nonoperating items. Rent revenue and interest expense are constant across all accounting periods, so Mason recognizes $3,000 of net income in each accounting period. On the balance sheet, cash increases by $3,000 each year because cash revenue exceeds cash paid for interest. Land remains constant each year at its $100,000 historical cost until it is sold in 2005. Similarly, the bonds payable liability is reported at $100,000 from the date the bonds were issued in 2001 until they are paid off on December 31, 2005.

Compare the income statements for Blair Company presented in Exhibit 10–2 with those of Mason Company in Exhibit 10–4. Both companies borrowed $100,000 cash at a stated interest rate of 9 percent. Both companies paid off the liability at the end of five years. Both companies also earned $12,000 revenue per year, yet Blair produced a total net income of

LO5 Show how bond liabilities and their related interest costs affect financial statements.

Exhibit 10–4 *Financial Statements Mason Company*

Bonds Issued at Face Value

	2001	2002	2003	2004	2005
Income Statements					
Rent Revenue	$ 12,000	$ 12,000	$ 12,000	$ 12,000	$ 12,000
Interest Expense	(9,000)	(9,000)	(9,000)	(9,000)	(9,000)
Net Income	$ 3,000	$ 3,000	$ 3,000	$ 3,000	$ 3,000
Balance Sheets					
Assets					
Cash	$ 3,000	$ 6,000	$ 9,000	$ 12,000	$ 15,000
Land	100,000	100,000	100,000	100,000	0
Total Assets	$103,000	$106,000	$109,000	$112,000	$ 15,000
Liabilities					
Bonds Payable	$100,000	$100,000	$100,000	$100,000	$ 0
Stockholders' Equity					
Retained Earnings	3,000	6,000	9,000	12,000	15,000
Total Liabilities and Stockholders' Equity	$103,000	$106,000	$109,000	$112,000	$ 15,000
Statements of Cash Flows					
Operating Activities					
Inflow from Customers	$ 12,000	$ 12,000	$ 12,000	$ 12,000	$ 12,000
Outflow for Interest	(9,000)	(9,000)	(9,000)	(9,000)	(9,000)
Investing Activities					
Outflow to Purchase Land	(100,000)				
Inflow from Sale of Land					100,000
Financing Activities					
Inflow from Bond Issue	100,000				
Outflow to Repay Bond Liab.					(100,000)
Net Change in Cash	3,000	3,000	3,000	3,000	3,000
Beginning Cash Balance	0	3,000	6,000	9,000	12,000
Ending Cash Balance	$ 3,000	$ 6,000	$ 9,000	$ 12,000	$ 15,000

$31,454 while Mason's net earnings for the same five-year period were only $15,000. The difference is attributable solely to the additional interest Mason paid because no principal was repaid until the maturity date. By repaying part of the loan each year, Blair reduced its liabilities and thereby the amount of interest expense in each succeeding year.

Recording Procedures

LO6 Explain how to account for bonds and their related interest costs.

Exhibit 10–5 presents the general journal entries to record the six events that Mason Company experienced.

▌Bonds Issued at a Discount

LO4 Explain why bonds are issued at face value, a discount, or a premium.

Return to the Mason Company illustration with one change. Assume Mason's bond certificates have been prepared with a 9 percent stated rate of interest printed on them. Suppose Mason's friends find they can buy bonds from another entrepreneur willing to pay a higher rate of interest. They explain to Mason that business decisions cannot be made on the basis of friendship. Mason provides a counteroffer. There is no time to change the bond certificates, so Mason offers to accept $95,000 for the bonds today and still repay the full face value of $100,000 at the maturity date. The $5,000 differential is called a **bond discount.** Mason's friends agree to buy the bonds for $95,000.

Exhibit 10–5

Event No.	Account Title	Debit	Credit
1	Cash	100,000	
	Bonds Payable		100,000
	Entry on January 1, 2001, to record bond issue		
2	Land	100,000	
	Cash		100,000
	Entry on January 1, 2001, to record investment in land		
3	Cash	12,000	
	Rent Revenue		12,000
	Revenue recognition entries on December 31, 2001–2005		
4	Interest Expense	9,000	
	Cash		9,000
	Expense recognition entries on December 31, 2001–2005		
5	Cash	100,000	
	Land		100,000
	Entry on December 31, 2005, to record sale of land		
6	Bonds Payable	100,000	
	Cash		100,000
	Entry on December 31, 2005, to record bond payment		

Effective Interest Rate

The bond discount increases the interest Mason must pay in two ways. First, Mason must still make the annual cash payments described in the bond certificate. In other words, Mason must pay cash of $9,000 (.09 × $100,000) annually even though she actually borrowed only $95,000. Second, Mason will have to pay back $5,000 more than she received ($100,000 − $95,000). The extra $5,000 (bond discount) is also additional interest. Although the $5,000 of additional interest is not paid until maturity, when spread over the life of the bond it amounts to $1,000 of additional interest expense per year.

The actual rate of interest that Mason must pay is called the **effective interest rate.** A rough estimate of the effective interest rate for the discounted Mason bonds is 10.5 percent [($9,000 annual stated interest + $1,000 annual amortization of the discount) ÷ $95,000 amount borrowed]. Selling the bonds at a $5,000 discount permits Mason to raise the 9 percent stated rate of interest to an effective rate of roughly 10.5 percent. Deeper discounts would raise the effective rate even higher. More shallow discounts would reduce the effective rate of interest. Mason can set the effective rate of interest to any level desired by adjusting the amount of the discount.

Bond Prices

It is common business practice to use discounts to raise the effective rate of interest above the stated rate. Bonds frequently sell for less than face value. Bond prices are normally expressed *as a percentage of the face value.* For example, Mason's discounted bonds sold for 95, meaning the bonds sold at 95 percent of face value ($100,000 × .95 = $95,000). Amounts of less than 1 percentage point are usually expressed as a fraction. Therefore, a bond priced at 98 ¾ sells for 98.75 percent of face value.

Mason Company Revisited

To illustrate accounting for bonds issued at a discount, return to the Mason Company example using the assumption the bonds are issued for 95 instead of face value. The same six events are examined using this revised assumption. This revision changes some amounts reported on the financial statements. For example, Event 1 in year 2001 reflects receiving only $95,000 cash from the bond issue. Since Mason had only $95,000 available to invest in land, the illustration assumes that a less desirable piece of property was acquired and it therefore generated only $11,400 of rent revenue per year.

LO6 Explain how to account for bonds and their related interest costs.

Event 1 Issue Bonds for Cash
Bonds with a face value of $100,000 are issued at 95.

Because Mason must pay the face value at maturity, the $100,000 face value of the bonds is recorded in the Bonds Payable account. The $5,000 discount is recorded in a separate contra account called **Discount on Bonds Payable.** As shown below, the contra account is subtracted from the face value to determine the **carrying value** (book value) of the bond liability.

Bonds Payable	$100,000
Less: Discount on Bonds Payable	(5,000)
Carrying Value	$ 95,000

The bond issue is an asset source transaction. Both assets and total liabilities increase by $95,000. Net income is not affected. The cash inflow is reported in the financing activities section of the statement of cash flows. The effect of the bond issue on the financial statements and the journal entry required to record it follow:

Assets =	Liabilities		+ Equity	Rev.	−	Exp.	=	Net Inc.	Cash Flow
Cash =	Bonds Pay.	− Discount	+ Equity						
95,000 =	100,000	− 5,000	+ NA	NA	−	NA	=	NA	95,000 FA

Account Title	Debit	Credit
Cash	95,000	
Discount on Bonds Payable	5,000	
Bonds Payable		100,000

Event 2 Investment in Land
Paying $95,000 cash to purchase land is an asset exchange transaction.

The asset cash decreases and the asset land increases. The income statement is not affected. The cash outflow is reported in the investing activities section of the statement of cash flows. These effects follow:

Assets			= Liab.	+ Equity	Rev.	−	Exp.	=	Net Inc.	Cash Flow
Cash	+	Land =								
(95,000)	+	95,000 =	NA	+ NA	NA	−	NA	=	NA	(95,000) IA

Event 3 Revenue Recognition
Recognizing $11,400 cash revenue from renting the property is an asset source transaction.

This event is repeated each year from 2001 through 2005. The event is an asset source transaction that increases assets and stockholders' equity. Recognizing revenue increases net income. The cash inflow is reported in the operating activities section of the statement of cash flows. These effects follow:

Assets	=	Liab.	+	Equity	Rev.	−	Exp.	=	Net Inc.	Cash Flow
11,400	=	NA	+	11,400	11,400	−	NA	=	11,400	11,400 OA

Event 4 Expense Recognition

The interest cost of borrowing has two components: the $9,000 paid in cash each year and the $5,000 discount paid at maturity.

Using **straight-line amortization,** the amount of the discount recognized as expense in each accounting period is $1,000 ($5,000 discount ÷ 5 years). Mason will therefore recognize $10,000 of interest expense each year ($9,000 at the stated interest rate plus $1,000 amortization of the bond discount). On the balance sheet, the asset cash decreases by $9,000, the carrying value of the bond liability increases by $1,000 (through a decrease in the bond discount), and retained earnings (interest expense) decreases by $10,000. The effect on the financial statements of recognizing the interest expense and the journal entry to record it for each accounting period are shown here:

Assets =	Liabilities	+ Equity	Rev. −	Exp. =	Net Inc.	Cash Flow
Cash =	Bonds Pay. − Discount					
(9,000) =	NA − (1,000)	+ (10,000)	NA −	10,000 =	(10,000)	(9,000) OA

Account Title	Debit	Credit
Interest Expense	10,000	
Cash		9,000
Discount on Bonds Payable		1,000

Event 5 Sale of Investment in Land

Selling the land for cash equal to its $95,000 book value is an asset exchange transaction.

Cash increases and land decreases. Since there was no gain or loss on the sale, the income statement is not affected. The cash inflow is reported in the investing activities section of the statement of cash flows. These effects follow:

Assets	= Liab. + Equity	Rev. −	Exp. =	Net Inc.	Cash Flow
Cash + Land =					
95,000 + (95,000) −	NA + NA	NA	NA =	NA	95,000 IA

Event 6 Payoff of Bond Liability

Repaying the face value of the bond liability is an asset use transaction.

Cash and bonds payable decrease. The income statement is not affected. For reporting purposes, the cash outflow is separated into two parts on the statement of cash flows: $95,000 of the cash outflow is reported in the financing activities section because it represents repaying the principal amount borrowed; the remaining $5,000 cash outflow is reported in the operating activities section because it represents the interest arising from issuing the bonds at a discount. In practice, the amount of the discount is frequently immaterial and is combined in the financing activities section with the principal repayment.

Assets =	Liab. +	Equity	Rev. −	Exp. =	Net Inc.	Cash Flow
(100,000) =	(100,000) +	NA	NA −	NA =	NA	(95,000) FA
						(5,000) OA

Effect on Financial Statements

Exhibit 10–6 displays Mason Company's financial statements assuming the bonds were issued at a discount. Contrast the net income reported in Exhibit 10–6 (bonds issued at a discount) with

LO5 Show how bond liabilities and their related interest costs affect financial statements.

Exhibit 10–6 *Financial Statements Mason Company*

Bonds Issued at a Discount

	2001	2002	2003	2004	2005
Income Statements					
Rent Revenue	$ 11,400	$ 11,400	$ 11,400	$ 11,400	$11,400
Interest Expense	(10,000)	(10,000)	(10,000)	(10,000)	(10,000)
Net Income	$ 1,400	$ 1,400	$ 1,400	$ 1,400	$ 1,400
Balance Sheets					
Assets					
Cash	$ 2,400	$ 4,800	$ 7,200	$ 9,600	$ 7,000
Land	95,000	95,000	95,000	95,000	0
Total Assets	$ 97,400	$ 99,800	$102,200	$104,600	$ 7,000
Liabilities					
Bonds Payable	$100,000	$100,000	$100,000	$100,000	$ 0
Discount on Bonds Payable	(4,000)	(3,000)	(2,000)	(1,000)	0
Carrying Value of Bond Liab.	96,000	97,000	98,000	99,000	0
Stockholders' Equity					
Retained Earnings	1,400	2,800	4,200	5,600	7,000
Total Liabilities and					
Stockholders' Equity	$ 97,400	$ 99,800	$102,200	$104,600	$ 7,000
Statements of Cash Flows					
Operating Activities					
Inflow from Customers	$ 11,400	$ 11,400	$ 11,400	$ 11,400	$ 11,400
Outflow for Interest	(9,000)	(9,000)	(9,000)	(9,000)	(14,000)
Investing Activities					
Outflow to Purchase Land	(95,000)				
Inflow from Sale of Land					95,000
Financing Activities					
Inflow from Bond Issue	95,000				
Outflow to Repay Bond Liab.					(95,000)
Net Change in Cash	2,400	2,400	2,400	2,400	(2,600)
Beginning Cash Balance	0	2,400	4,800	7,200	9,600
Ending Cash Balance	$ 2,400	$ 4,800	$ 7,200	$ 9,600	$ 7,000

the net income reported in Exhibit 10–4 (bonds sold at face value). Two factors cause the net income in Exhibit 10–6 to be lower. First, since the bonds were sold at a discount, Mason had less money to spend on its land investment. It bought less desirable land which generated less revenue. Second, the effective interest rate was higher than the stated rate, resulting in higher interest expense. Lower revenues coupled with higher expenses result in less profitability.

On the balance sheet, the carrying value of the bond liability increases each year until the maturity date, December 31, 2005, when it is equal to the $100,000 face value of the bonds (the amount Mason is obligated to pay). Because Mason did not pay any dividends, retained earnings ($7,000) on December 31, 2005, is equal to the total amount of net income reported over the five-year period ($1,400 × 5). All earnings were retained in the business.

Several factors account for the differences between net income and cash flow. First, although $10,000 of interest expense is reported on each income statement, only $9,000 of cash was paid for interest each year until 2005, when $14,000 was paid for interest ($9,000 based on the stated rate + $5,000 for discount). The $1,000 difference between interest expense and cash paid for interest in 2001, 2002, 2003, and 2004 results from amortizing the bond discount. The cash outflow for the interest related to the discount is included in the $100,000 payment made at maturity on December 31, 2005. Even though $14,000 of cash is paid for interest in 2005, only $10,000 is recognized as interest expense on the income statement that year. Although the total increase in cash over the five-year life of the business ($7,000) is equal to the total net income reported for the same period, there are significant timing differences between when the interest expense is recognized and when the cash out-flows occur to pay for it.

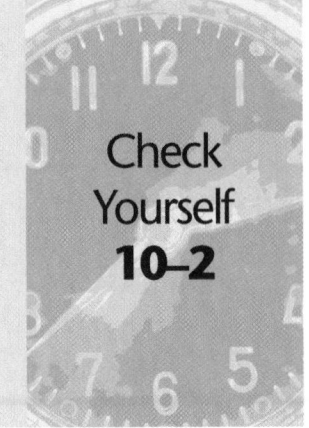

On January 1, 2004, Moffett Company issued bonds with a $600,000 face value at 98. The bonds had a 9 percent annual interest rate and a 10-year term. Interest is payable in cash on December 31 of each year. What amount of interest expense will Moffett report on the 2006 income statement? What carrying value for bonds payable will Moffett report on the December 31, 2006, balance sheet?

Answer The bonds were issued at a $12,000 ($600,000 × 0.02) discount. The discount will be amortized over the 10-year life at the rate of $1,200 ($12,000 ÷ 10 years) per year. The amount of interest expense for 2006 is $55,200 ([$600,000 × .09] = $54,000 annual cash interest + $1,200 discount amortization).

The carrying value of the bond liability is equal to the face value less the unamortized discount. By the end of 2006, $3,600 of the discount will have been amortized ($1,200 × 3 years = $3,600). The unamortized discount as of December 31, 2006, will be $8,400 ($12,000 − $3,600). The carrying value of the bond liability as of December 31, 2006, will be $591,600 ($600,000 − $8,400).

Check Yourself 10–2

Effect of Semiannual Interest Payments

The previous examples assumed that interest payments were made annually. In practice, most bond certificates call for interest to be paid semiannually, which means that interest is paid in cash twice each year. If Marsha Mason's bond certificate had stipulated semiannual interest payments, her company would have paid $4,500 ($100,000 × 0.09 = $9,000 ÷ 2 = $4,500) cash to bond-holders for interest on June 30 and December 31 of each year. The journal entries to record semi-annual interest payments each year (for the bonds issued at a discount) are as follows:

LO6 Explain how to account for bonds and their related interest costs.

Date	Account Title	Debit	Credit
June 30	Interest Expense	5,000	
	Discount on Bonds Payable		500
	Cash		4,500
Dec. 31	Interest Expense	5,000	
	Discount on Bonds Payable		500
	Cash		4,500

Bonds Issued at a Premium

When bonds are sold for more than their face value, the difference between the amount received and the face value is called a **bond premium.** Bond premiums reduce the effective interest rate. For example, assume Mason Company issued its 9% bonds at 105, receiving $105,000 cash on the issue date. The company is still only required to repay the $100,000 face value of the bonds at the maturity date. The $5,000 difference between the amount received and the amount repaid at maturity reduces the total amount of interest expense. The premium is recorded in a separate liability account called Premium on Bonds Payable. This account is reported on the balance sheet as an addition to Bonds Payable, increasing the carrying value of the bond liability. On the issue date, the bond liability would be reported on the balance sheet as follows:

LO4 Explain why bonds are issued at face value, a discount, or a premium.

Bonds Payable	$100,000
Plus: Premium on Bonds Payable	5,000
Carrying Value	$105,000

The effect on the financial statements of issuing the bonds at a premium follows:

Assets	=	Liabilities			+	Equity	Rev.	–	Exp.	=	Net Inc.	Cash Flow
Cash	=	Bonds Pay.	+	Premium								
105,000	=	100,000	+	5,000	+	NA	NA	–	NA	=	NA	105,000 FA

The entire $105,000 cash inflow is reported in the financing activities section of the statement of cash flows even though the $5,000 premium is conceptually an operating activities cash flow because it pertains to interest. In practice, premiums are usually so small they are immaterial and the entire cash inflow is normally classified as a financing activity.

The journal entries to record issuing the bonds at a premium and the first interest payment are as follows (assume annual interest payments):

Date	Account Title	Debit	Credit
Jan. 1	Cash	105,000	
	Bonds Payable		100,000
	Premium on Bonds Payable		5,000
Dec. 31	Interest Expense	8,000	
	Premium on Bonds Payable	1,000	
	Cash		9,000

The Market Rate of Interest

LO4 Explain why bonds are issued at face value, a discount, or a premium.

When a bond is issued, the effective interest rate is determined by current market conditions. Market conditions are influenced by many factors such as the state of the economy, government policy, and the law of supply and demand. These conditions are collectively reflected in the **market interest rate.** The *effective rate of interest* investors are willing to accept *for a particular bond* equals the *market rate of interest* for other investments with similar levels of risk at the time the bond is issued. When the market rate of interest is higher than the stated rate of interest, bonds will sell at a discount so as to increase the effective rate of interest to the market rate. When the market rate is lower than the stated rate, bonds will sell at a premium so as to reduce the effective rate to the market rate.

▌ Bond Redemptions

LO6 Explain how to account for bonds and their related interest costs.

In the previous illustration, Mason Company's five-year, 9 percent bonds were redeemed (paid off) on the maturity date. After Mason Company paid the bondholders the face value of the bonds, the balance in the bonds payable account was zero. The balance in the fully amortized discount account was also zero.

Companies may redeem bonds with a *call provision* prior to the maturity date. If a company calls bonds prior to maturity, it must pay the bondholders the call price. As explained previously, the call price is normally above face value. For example, suppose Mason Company's bond certificate allows it to call the bonds at 103. Assume Marsha Mason's client breaks the land rental contract two years early, at the end of 2003. Mason is forced to sell the land and pay off the bonds. Assuming the bonds were originally issued at a $5,000 discount, Exhibit 10–6 shows there is a $2,000 balance in the Discount on Bonds Payable account at the end of 2003.

To redeem the bonds on January 1, 2004, Mason must pay the bondholders $103,000 ($100,000 face value × 1.03 call price). Since the book value of the bond liability is $98,000 ($100,000 face value − $2,000 remaining discount), Mason recognizes a $5,000 loss ($103,000 redemption price − $98,000 book value) when the bonds are called. The early redemption decreases cash, the carrying value of the bond liability, and stockholders' equity. The effect of the redemption on the financial statements follows:

Assets	=	Liabilities		+ Equity	Rev.	– Exp.	= Net Inc.	Cash Flow
Cash	=	Bond Pay.	– Discount					
(103,000)	=	(100,000)	– (2,000)	+ (5,000)	NA	– 5,000	= (5,000)	(103,000) FA

The entire $103,000 cash outflow is reported in the financing activities section of the statement of cash flows. Conceptually, some of this outflow is attributable to activities other than financing. In practice, the amounts paid in an early redemption which are not attributable to financing activities are usually immaterial and the entire cash outflow is therefore classified as a financing activity.

The general journal entry to record the bond redemption follows:

Account Title	Debit	Credit
Loss on Bond Redemption	5,000	
Bonds Payable	100,000	
Discount on Bonds Payable		2,000
Cash		103,000

THE FINANCIAL ANALYST

Bond financing has advantages and disadvantages for the stockholders of a business. Assessing a company's investment potential requires understanding both the potential rewards and the potential risks of debt financing.

LO7 Explain the advantages and disadvantages of debt financing.

Financial Leverage and Tax Advantage of Debt Financing

As with other forms of credit, bonds may provide companies increased earnings through **financial leverage** (previously discussed in Chapter 3). If a company can borrow money at 7 percent through a bond issue and invest the proceeds at 12 percent, the company's earnings benefit from the 5 percent (12 percent − 7 percent) **spread.**

Also, bond interest expense, like other forms of interest expense, is tax deductible, making the effective cost of borrowing less than the interest expense because the interest expense reduces the tax expense. Because dividend payments are not tax deductible, equity financing (e.g., issuing common stock) does not offer this advantage.

To illustrate, assume its organizers obtain $100,000 to start Maduro Company. During its first year of operation, Maduro earns $60,000 of revenue and incurs $40,000 of expenses other than interest expense. Consider two different forms of financing. First, assume the initial $100,000 is obtained by issuing common stock (equity financing) and Maduro pays an 8 percent dividend ($100,000 × .08 = $8,000 dividend). Second, assume Maduro issues $100,000 of bonds that pay 8 percent annual interest ($100,000 × .08 = $8,000). Assuming a 30 percent tax rate, which form of financing produces the larger increase in retained earnings? Refer to the following computations:

Computation of Addition to Retained Earnings	Equity Financing	Debt Financing
Revenue	$60,000	$60,000
Expense (excluding interest)	(40,000)	(40,000)
Earnings before Interest and Taxes	20,000	20,000
Interest (100,000 × 8%)	0	(8,000)
Pretax Income	20,000	12,000
Income Tax (30%)	(6,000)	(3,600)
Net Income	14,000	8,400
Dividend	(8,000)	0
Addition to Retained Earnings	$ 6,000	$ 8,400

Debt financing produces $2,400 more retained earnings than equity financing. If equity financing is obtained, the company pays $6,000 in income taxes; debt financing requires only $3,600 of income taxes. Maduro's cost of financing, whether paid in dividends to investors or interest to creditors, is $8,000. With debt financing, however, the Internal Revenue Service receives $2,400 less.

The after-tax interest cost of debt can be computed as:

$$\text{Total interest expense} \times (1.0 - \text{Tax rate})$$
$$\$8{,}000 \times (1.0 - 0.30) = \$5{,}600$$

The after-tax interest rate that Maduro is paying can be computed using the same logic:

$$\text{Debt interest rate} \times (1.0 - \text{Tax rate})$$
$$8\% \times (1.0 - 0.30) = 5.6\%$$

Unlike interest expense, there is no difference in the before-tax and after-tax effects of a dividend. For Maduro, $1 of dividends costs the company a full $1 of retained earnings, while $1 of interest has an after-tax cost of only $0.70 (assuming a 30 percent tax rate). This tax benefit only applies to profitable businesses. There are no tax savings if a company has no income because businesses that produce consistent losses pay no taxes.

EBIT and Ratio Analysis

The tax consequences of debt financing can influence ratio analysis. For example, consider the *return on assets* (ROA) ratio discussed in Chapter 3. In that chapter ROA was defined as:

$$\text{Net income} \div \text{Total assets}$$

Recall that the ROA ratio is used to measure the effectiveness of asset management. In general, higher ROAs suggest better performance. However, the Maduro example demonstrates that a higher ROA can be obtained by using equity financing rather than debt financing without regard to how assets are managed. Recall that Maduro obtained $100,000 of assets whether through equity or debt financing. The assets were used exactly the same way regardless of the financing method used. With equity financing, Maduro's ROA is 14 percent ($14,000 ÷ $100,000) and with debt financing it is 8.4 percent ($8,400 ÷ $100,000). The difference in the ROA results from the financing approach rather than asset management.

The effects of the financing strategy can be avoided in ROA calculations by using *earnings before interest and taxes* (EBIT) rather than net income when computing the ratio. For example, if Maduro uses EBIT to compute ROA, the result is 20 percent ($20,000 ÷ $100,000) regardless of whether debt or equity financing is used. Using EBIT to compute ROA provides a less biased measure of asset utilization. For simplicity, however, this text uses net income to determine ROA unless otherwise indicated.

Times Interest Earned Ratio

Financing with bonds also has disadvantages. The issuer is legally obligated to make interest payments on time and to repay the principal at maturity. If a company fails to make scheduled payments, the creditors (bondholders) can force the company into bankruptcy. The claims on a company's assets held by bondholders and other creditors have priority over the claims of the owners. If a company in bankruptcy is forced to liquidate its assets, creditor claims must be fully paid before any owner claims can be paid. Bond issues therefore increase the owners' risk.

Financial analysts use several ratios to help assess the risk of bankruptcy. One is the *debt to assets ratio*, explained in Chapter 3. Another is the **times interest earned ratio,** defined as:

EBIT ÷ Interest expense

This ratio measures *how many times* a company would be able to pay its interest using its earnings. The *times interest earned ratio* is based on EBIT rather than net income because it is the amount of earnings before interest and taxes that is available to pay interest. The higher the ratio, the less likely a company will be unable to make its interest payments. Higher times interest earned ratios suggest lower levels of risk. Examples of times interest earned ratios and debt to assets ratios for six real-world companies follow. These numbers are based on financial data for the year 2002.

Industry	Company	Times Interest Earned	Debt to Assets
Breakfast Cereal	Kellogg's	3.93 times	0.91
	General Mills	2.60	0.77
Tools	Black & Decker	6.32	0.85
	Stanley Works	10.56	0.59
Hotel	Hilton Hotels	1.82	0.75
	Marriott	6.48	0.57

Since bills are paid with cash, not income, a company may be able to make interest payments even if it has a negative times interest earned ratio. A company with no EBIT may yet have cash. Meaningful financial statement analysis cannot rely on any single ratio or any set of ratios. Making sound business decisions requires considering other information in addition to the insights provided from analyzing ratios. A company with inferior ratios and a patent on a newly discovered drug that cures cancer may be a far better investment than a company with great ratios and a patent on a chemotherapy product that will soon be out of date. Ratio computations are based on historical data. They are useful only to the extent that history is likely to repeat itself.

Selected financial data pertaining to Shaver and Goode Companies follow (amounts are in thousands):

	Shaver Company	Goode Company
Earnings before interest and taxes	$750,720	$2,970,680
Interest expense	234,600	645,800

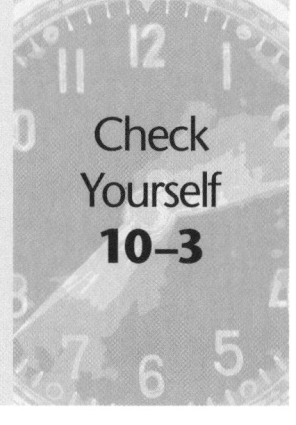

Check Yourself 10–3

Based on this information, which company is more likely to be able to make its interest payments?

Answer The times interest earned ratio for Shaver Company is 3.2 ($750,720 ÷ $234,600) times. The times interest earned ratio for Goode Company is 4.6 ($2,970,680 ÷ $645,800) times. Based on this data, Goode Company is more likely to be able to make its interest payments.

This chapter explained basic accounting for long-term debt. *Long-term notes payable* mature in two to five years and usually require payments that include a return of principal plus interest. *Lines of credit* enable companies to borrow limited amounts on an as-needed basis. Although lines of credit normally have one-year terms, companies frequently renew them, extending the effective maturity date to the intermediate range of five or more years. Interest on a line of credit is normally paid monthly.

Long-term debt financing for more than 10 years usually requires issuing *bonds*. Bond agreements normally commit a company to pay *semiannual interest* at a fixed percentage of the bond face value. The amount of interest required by the bond agreement is based on the *stated interest rate.* If bonds are issued when the *market interest rate* is different from the stated interest rate, companies will receive more or less than the face value in order for the effective rate of interest to be consistent with market conditions. Selling bonds at a *discount* (below face value) increases the effective interest rate above the stated rate. Selling bonds at a *premium* decreases the effective rate of interest.

This chapter explained the tax advantages of using debt versus equity financing. Interest is a *tax-deductible expense* subtracted prior to determining taxable income. In contrast, dividends paid to owners are not deductible in determining taxable income.

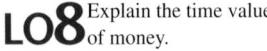

A company seeking long-term financing might choose to use debt, such as the types of bonds or term loans that were discussed in this chapter. Owners' equity is another source of long-term financing. Several equity alternatives are available, depending on the type of business organization the owners choose to establish. For example, a company could be organized as a sole proprietorship, partnership, or corporation. Chapter 11 presents accounting issues related to equity transactions for each of these types of business structures.

APPENDIX

LO8 Explain the time value of money.

Time Value of Money

Future Value

Suppose that you recently won a $10,000 cash prize in a local lottery. You decide to save the money to have funds available to obtain a masters of business administration (MBA) degree. You plan to enter the program three years from today. Assuming that you invest the money in an account that earns 8 percent annual interest, how much money will you have available in three years? The answer depends on whether your investment will earn *simple* or *compound* interest.

To determine the amount of funds available assuming that you earn 8 percent **simple interest,** multiply the principal balance by the interest rate to determine the amount of interest earned per year ($10,000 × 0.08 = $800). Next, multiply the amount of annual interest by the number of years for which the funds will be invested ($800 × 3 = $2,400). Finally, add the interest earned to the principal balance to determine the total amount of funds available at the end of the three-year term ($10,000 principal + $2,400 interest = $12,400 cash available at the end of three years).

Most investors can increase their returns by reinvesting the income earned from their investments. For example, at the beginning of the second year, you will have available for investment not only the original $10,000 principal balance but also $800 of interest earned during the first year. In other words, you will be able to earn interest on the interest that you previously earned. The practice of earning interest on interest is called **compounding.** Assuming that you are able to earn 8 percent compound interest, the amount of funds available to you at the end of three years can be computed, as shown in Exhibit 10–7.

Obviously, you earn more with compound interest ($2,597.12 compound versus $2,400 simple). The number of computations required for **compound interest** can become cumbersome when the investment term is long. Fortunately, there are mathematical formulas, interest tables, and computer programs that reduce the computational burden. For example, a compound interest factor can be developed from the formula

$$(1 + i)^n$$

where i = interest
  n = number of periods

Exhibit 10–7

Year	Amount Invested	×	Interest Rate	=	Interest Earned	+	Amount Invested	=	New Balance
1	$10,000.00	×	0.08	=	$ 800.00	+	$10,000.00	=	$10,800.00
2	10,800.00	×	0.08	=	864.00	+	10,800.00	=	11,664.00
3	11,664.00	×	0.08	=	933.12	+	11,664.00	=	12,597.12
	Total interest earned			=	$2,597.12				

The value of the investment is determined by multiplying the compound interest factor by the principal balance. The compound interest factor for a three-year term and an 8 percent interest rate is 1.259712 (1.08 × 1.08 × 1.08 = 1.259712). Assuming a $10,000 original investment, the value of the investment at the end of three years is $12,597.12 ($10,000 × 1.259712). This is, of course, the same amount that was computed in the previous illustration (see final figure in the New Balance column of Exhibit 10–7).

The mathematical formulas have been used to develop tables containing interest factors that can be used to determine the **future value** of an investment under a variety of interest rates and time periods. For example, Table I on page 483 contains the interest factor for an investment with a three-year term earning 8 percent compound interest. To confirm this point, move down the column marked n to the third period. Next move across to the column marked 8%, where you will find the value 1.259712. This is identical to the amount computed by using the mathematical formula in the preceding paragraph. Here also, the value of the investment at the end of three years can be determined by multiplying the principal balance by the compound interest factor ($10,000 × 1.259712 = $12,597.12). These same factors and amounts can be determined through the use of computer programs contained in calculators and spreadsheet software.

Clearly, a variety of ways can be used to determine the future value of an investment, given a principal balance, interest rate, and term to maturity. In our case, we showed that your original investment of $10,000 would be worth $12,597 in three years, assuming an 8 percent compound interest rate. Suppose that you determine that this amount is insufficient to get you through the MBA program you want to complete. Indeed, assume that you believe you will need $18,000 three years from today to sustain yourself while you finish the degree. Suppose your parents agree to cover the shortfall. They ask how much money you need today in order to have $18,000 three years from now.

Present Value

The mathematical formula required to convert the future value of a dollar to its **present value** equivalent is

$$\frac{1}{(1 + i)^n}$$

where i = interest
       n = number of periods

For easy conversion, the formula has been used to develop Table II, titled Present Value of $1. At an 8 percent annual compound interest rate, the present value equivalent of $18,000 to be received three years from today is computed as follows: Move down the far-left column to the spot where $n = 3$. Next, move right to the column marked 8%. At this point, you should see the interest factor 0.793832. Multiplying this factor by the desired future value of $18,000 yields the present value result of $14,288.98 ($18,000 × 0.793832). This means that if you invest $14,288.98 (present value) today at an annual compound interest rate of 8 percent, you will have the $18,000 (future value) you need to enter the MBA program three years from now.

If you currently have $10,000, you will need an additional $4,288.98 from your parents to make the required $14,288.98 investment that will yield the future value of $18,000 you need to enter the MBA program. In other words, having $14,288.98 today is the same thing as having $18,000 three years from today, assuming you can earn 8 percent compound interest. To validate this conclusion, use Table I to determine the future value of $14,288.98, given a three-year term and 8 percent annual compound interest. As previously indicated, the future-value conversion factor under these conditions is 1.259712. Multiplying this factor by the $14,288.98 present value produces the expected future value of $18,000 ($14,288.98 × 1.259712 = $18,000). Accordingly, the factors in Table I can be used to convert present values to future values, and the corresponding factors in Table II are used to convert future values to present values.

Future Value Annuities

The previous examples described present and future values associated with a single lump-sum payment. Many financial transactions involve a series of payments. To illustrate, we return to the example in which you want to have $18,000 available three years from today. We continue the assumption that you can earn 8 percent compound interest. However, now we assume that you do not have $14,288.98 to invest today. Instead, you decide to save part of the money during each of the next three years. How much money must you save each year to have $18,000 at the end of three years? *The series of equal payments made over a number of periods in order to acquire a future value is called an* **annuity.** The factors contained in Table III, Future Value of an Annuity of $1, can be used to determine the amount of the annuity needed to produce the desired $18,000 future value. The table is constructed so that future values can be determined by multiplying the conversion factor by the amount of the annuity. These relationships can be expressed algebraically as follows:

$$\text{Amount of annuity payment} \times \text{Table conversion factor} = \text{Future value}$$

To determine the amount of the required annuity payment in our example, first locate the future value conversion factor. In Table III, move down the first column on the left-hand side until you locate period 3. Next move to the right until you locate the 8% column. At this location you will see a conversion factor of 3.2464. This factor can be used to determine the amount of the annuity payment as indicated here:

$$\text{Amount of annuity payment} \times \text{Table conversion factor} = \text{Future value}$$
$$\text{Amount of annuity payment} = \text{Future value} \div \text{Table conversion factor}$$
$$\text{Amount of annuity payment} = \$18,000.00 \div 3.2464$$
$$\text{Amount of annuity payment} = \$5,544.60$$

If you deposit $5,544.60 in an investment account at the end of each of the next three years,[6] the investment account balance will be $18,000, assuming your investment earns 8 percent interest compounded annually. This conclusion is validated by the following schedule.

End of Year	Beg. Acct. Bal.	+	Interest Computation	+	Payment	=	End. Acct. Bal.
1	NA	+	NA	+	$5,544.60	=	$ 5,544.60
2	$ 5,544.60	+	$ 5,544.60 × 0.08 = $443.57	+	5,544.60	=	11,532.77
3	11,532.77	+	11,532.77 × 0.08 = 922.62	+	5,544.60	=	18,000.00*

*Total does not add exactly due to rounding.

Present Value Annuities

We previously demonstrated that a future value of $18,000 is equivalent to a present value of $14,288.98, given annual compound interest of 8 percent for a three-year period. Accordingly, if the future value of a $5,544.60 annuity for three years is equivalent to $18,000, that same annuity should have a present value of $14,288.98. We can test this conclusion by using the conversion factors shown in Table IV, Present Value of an Annuity of $1. The present value annuity table is constructed so that present values can be determined by multiplying the conversion factor by the amount of the annuity. These relationships can be expressed algebraically as follows:

$$\text{Amount of annuity payment} \times \text{Table conversion factor} = \text{Present value}$$

To determine the present value of the annuity payment in our example, first locate the present value conversion factor. In Table IV, move down the first column on the left-hand side until you locate period 3. Next move to the right until you locate the column for the 8 percent interest rate. At this location you will see a conversion factor of 2.577097. This factor can be used to determine the amount of the present value of the annuity payment, as indicated:

$$\begin{array}{ccccc} \text{Amount of annuity payment} & \times & \text{Table conversion factor} & = & \text{Present value} \\ \$5,544.60 & \times & 2.577097 & = & \$14,288.97* \end{array}$$

*The 1 cent difference between this value and the expected value of $14,288.98 is due to rounding.

In summary, Tables III and IV can be used to convert annuities to future or present values for a variety of different assumptions regarding interest rates and time periods.

---

[6]A payment made at the end of a period is known as an *ordinary annuity.* A payment made at the beginning of a period is called an *annuity due.* Tables are generally set up to assume ordinary annuities. Minor adjustments must be made when dealing with an annuity due. For the purposes of this text, we consider all annuities to be ordinary.

Business Applications

Long-Term Notes Payable

In the early part of this chapter, we considered a case in which Blair Company borrowed $100,000 from National Bank. We indicated that Blair agreed to repay the bank through a series of annual payments (an *annuity*) in the amount of $25,709 each. How was this amount determined? Recall that Blair agreed to pay the bank 9 percent interest over a five-year term. Under these circumstances, we are trying to find the annuity equivalent to the $100,000 present value that the bank is loaning Blair. The first step in determining the annuity (annual payment) is to locate the appropriate present value conversion factor from Table IV. At the fifth row under the 9% column, you will find the value 3.889651. This factor can be used to determine the amount of the annuity payment as indicated here:

Amount of annuity payment × Table conversion factor = Present value
Amount of annuity payment = Present value ÷ Table conversion factor
Amount of annuity payment = $100,000 ÷ 3.889651
Amount of annuity payment = $25,709

There are many applications in which debt repayment is accomplished through annuities. Common examples with which you are probably familiar include auto loans and home mortgages. Payment schedules for such loans may be determined from the interest tables, as demonstrated here. However, most real-world businesses have further refined the computational process through the use of sophisticated computer programs. The software program prompts the user to provide the relevant information regarding the present value of the amount borrowed, number of payments, and interest rate. Given this information and a few simple keystrokes, the computer program produces the amount of the amortization payment along with an amortization schedule showing the amounts of principal and interest payments over the life of the loan. Similar results can be accomplished with spreadsheet software applications such as Excel and Lotus. Even many handheld calculators have present and future value functions that enable users to quickly compute annuity payments for an infinite number of interest rate and time period assumptions.

Bond Liabilities: Determine Price

We discussed the use of discounts and premiums as means of producing an effective rate of interest that is higher or lower than the stated rate of interest. For example, if the stated rate of interest is lower than the market rate of interest at the time the bonds are issued, the issuer can increase the effective interest rate by selling the bonds for a price lower than their face value. At maturity, the issuer will settle the obligation by paying the face value of the bond. The difference between the discounted bond price and the face value of the bond is additional interest. To illustrate, assume that Tower Company issues $100,000 face value bonds with a 20-year term and a 9 percent stated rate of annual interest. At the time the bonds are issued, the market rate of interest for bonds of comparable risk is 10 percent annual interest. For what amount would Tower Company be required to sell the bonds in order to move its 9 percent stated rate of interest to an effective rate of 10 percent?

Information from present value Tables II and IV is required to determine the amount of the discount required to produce a 10 percent effective rate of interest. First, we define the future cash flows that will be generated by the bonds. Based on the stated interest rate, the bonds will pay $9,000 ($100,000 face value × 0.09 interest) interest per year. This constitutes a 20-year annuity that should be discounted back to its present value equivalent. Also, at the end of 20 years, the bonds will require a single $100,000 lump-sum payment to settle the principal obligation. This amount must also be discounted back to its present value in order to determine the bond price. The computations required to determine the discounted bond price are shown here:

Present value of principal	$100,000 × 0.148644	=	$14,864.40
	(Table II, $n = 20$, $i = 10\%$)		
Present value of interest	$9,000 × 8.513564	=	76,622.08
	(Table IV, $n = 20$, $i = 10\%$)		
Bond price			$91,486.48

Tower Company bonds sell at an $8,513.52 discount ($100,000 − $91,486.48) to produce a 10 percent effective interest rate. Note carefully that in these computations, the stated rate of interest was used to determine the amount of cash flow, and the effective rate of interest was used to determine the table conversion factor.

Bond Liabilities: Effective Interest Method of Amortization

To this point, the straight-line method has been used to amortize bond discounts or premiums. This method is commonly used in practice because it is simple to apply and easy to understand. However, the method is theoretically deficient because it results in the recognition of a constant amount of interest expense while the carrying value of the bond liability fluctuates. Consider the discount on Tower Company bonds just discussed as an example. In this case, the amount of interest expense recognized each period is computed as follows:

Stated rate of interest	$100,000.00 × 0.09	=	$9,000.00
Amortization of discount	8,513.52 ÷ 20	=	425.68
Interest expense recognized each accounting period		=	$9,425.68

As previously demonstrated, the amortization of the bond discount increases the carrying value of the bond liability. Accordingly, under the straight-line method, the bond liability increases while the amount of interest expense recognized remains constant. Logically, the amount of interest expense should increase as the amount of liability increases. This rational relationship can be accomplished by applying the **effective interest rate method** to the amortization of bond discounts and premiums. The effective interest rate method is required when the result of its application will cause a material effect on the financial statements.

Under the effective interest rate method, the amount of interest expense recognized in the financial statements is determined by multiplying the effective rate of interest by the carrying value of the bond liability. The amount of the discount to be amortized is determined by the difference between the interest expense and the cash outflow, as defined by the stated rate of interest. The following schedule demonstrates the application of the effective interest rate method for the recognition of interest expense during the first three years that Tower Company bonds were outstanding.

End of Year	Cash Payment	Interest Expense	Discount Amortization	Carrying Value
1	$9,000*	$9,148.65†	$148.65‡	$91,635.13§
2	9,000	9,163.51	163.51	91,798.64
3	9,000	9,179.86	179.86	91,978.50

*Cash outflow based on the stated rate of interest ($100,000 × 0.09).

†Effective interest rate times the carrying value (.10 × $91,486.48).

‡Interest expense minus cash outflow ($9,148.65 − $9,000.00).

§Previous carrying value plus portion of discount amortized ($91,486.48 + $148.65).

Notice that the effective interest rate method results in increasingly larger amounts of expense recognition as the carrying value of the bond liability increases. The effect of the expense recognition on the financial statements and the journal entry necessary to record it for the first accounting period are as follows:

Cash	=	Bond Liab.	+	Equity	Rev.	−	Exp.	=	Net Inc.	Cash Flow
(9,000)	=	148.65*	+	(9,148.65)	NA	−	9,148.65	=	(9,148.65)	(9,000) OA

*The decrease in the amount of the discount increases the bond liability.

Account Title	Debit	Credit
Interest Expense	9,148.65	
Cash		9,000.00
Discount on Bonds Payable		148.65

Table I *Future Value of $1*

n	4%	5%	6%	7%	8%	9%	10%	12%	14%	16%	20%
1	1.040000	1.050000	1.060000	1.070000	1.080000	1.090000	1.100000	1.120000	1.140000	1.160000	1.200000
2	1.081600	1.102500	1.123600	1.144900	1.166400	1.188100	1.210000	1.254400	1.299600	1.345600	1.440000
3	1.124864	1.157625	1.191016	1.225043	1.259712	1.295029	1.331000	1.404928	1.481544	1.560896	1.728000
4	1.169859	1.215506	1.262477	1.310796	1.360489	1.411582	1.464100	1.573519	1.688960	1.810639	2.073600
5	1.216653	1.276282	1.338226	1.402552	1.469328	1.538624	1.610510	1.762342	1.925415	2.100342	2.488320
6	1.265319	1.340096	1.418519	1.500730	1.586874	1.677100	1.771561	1.973823	2.194973	2.436396	2.985984
7	1.315932	1.407100	1.503630	1.605781	1.713824	1.828039	1.948717	2.210681	2.502269	2.826220	3.583181
8	1.368569	1.477455	1.593848	1.718186	1.850930	1.992563	2.143589	2.475963	2.852586	3.278415	4.299817
9	1.423312	1.551328	1.689479	1.838459	1.999005	2.171893	2.357948	2.773079	3.251949	3.802961	5.159780
10	1.480244	1.628895	1.790848	1.967151	2.158925	2.367364	2.593742	3.105848	3.707221	4.411435	6.191736
11	1.539454	1.710339	1.898299	2.104852	2.331639	2.580426	2.853117	3.478550	4.226232	5.117265	7.430084
12	1.601032	1.795856	2.012196	2.252192	2.518170	2.812665	3.138428	3.895976	4.817905	5.936027	8.916100
13	1.665074	1.885649	2.132928	2.409845	2.719624	3.065805	3.452271	4.363493	5.492411	6.885791	10.699321
14	1.731676	1.979932	2.260904	2.578534	2.937194	3.341727	3.797498	4.887112	6.261349	7.987518	12.839185
15	1.800944	2.078928	2.396558	2.759032	3.172169	3.642482	4.177248	5.473566	7.137938	9.265521	15.407022
16	1.872981	2.182875	2.540352	2.952164	3.425943	3.970306	4.594973	6.130394	8.137249	10.748004	18.488426
17	1.947900	2.292018	2.692773	3.158815	3.700018	4.327633	5.054470	6.866041	9.276464	12.467685	22.186111
18	2.025817	2.406619	2.854339	3.379932	3.996019	4.717120	5.559917	7.689966	10.575169	14.462514	26.623333
19	2.106849	2.526950	3.025600	3.616528	4.315701	5.141661	6.115909	8.612762	12.055693	16.776517	31.948000
20	2.191123	2.653298	3.207135	3.869684	4.660957	5.604411	6.727500	9.646293	13.743490	19.460759	38.337600

483

Table II *Present Value of $1*

n	4%	5%	6%	7%	8%	9%	10%	12%	14%	16%	20%
1	0.961538	0.952381	0.943396	0.934579	0.925926	0.917431	0.909091	0.892857	0.877193	0.862069	0.833333
2	0.924556	0.907029	0.889996	0.873439	0.857339	0.841680	0.826446	0.797194	0.769468	0.743163	0.694444
3	0.888996	0.863838	0.839619	0.816298	0.793832	0.772183	0.751315	0.711780	0.674972	0.640658	0.578704
4	0.854804	0.822702	0.792094	0.762895	0.735030	0.708425	0.683013	0.635518	0.592080	0.552291	0.482253
5	0.821927	0.783526	0.747258	0.712986	0.680583	0.649931	0.620921	0.567427	0.519369	0.476113	0.401878
6	0.790315	0.746215	0.704961	0.666342	0.630170	0.596267	0.564474	0.506631	0.455587	0.410442	0.334898
7	0.759918	0.710681	0.665057	0.622750	0.583490	0.547034	0.513158	0.452349	0.39637	0.353830	0.279082
8	0.730690	0.676839	0.627412	0.582009	0.540269	0.501866	0.466507	0.403883	0.350559	0.305025	0.232568
9	0.702587	0.644609	0.591898	0.543934	0.500249	0.460428	0.424098	0.360610	0.307508	0.262953	0.193807
10	0.675564	0.613913	0.558395	0.508349	0.463193	0.422411	0.385543	0.321973	0.269744	0.226684	0.161506
11	0.649581	0.584679	0.526788	0.475093	0.428883	0.387533	0.350494	0.287476	0.236617	0.195417	0.134588
12	0.624597	0.556837	0.496969	0.444012	0.397114	0.355535	0.318631	0.256675	0.207559	0.168463	0.112157
13	0.600574	0.530321	0.468839	0.414964	0.367698	0.326179	0.289664	0.229174	0.182069	0.145227	0.093464
14	0.577475	0.505068	0.442301	0.387817	0.340461	0.299246	0.263331	0.204620	0.159710	0.125195	0.077887
15	0.555265	0.481017	0.417265	0.362446	0.315242	0.274538	0.239392	0.182696	0.140096	0.107927	0.064905
16	0.533908	0.458112	0.393646	0.338735	0.291890	0.251870	0.217629	0.163122	0.122892	0.093041	0.054088
17	0.513373	0.436297	0.371364	0.316574	0.270269	0.231073	0.197845	0.145644	0.107800	0.080207	0.045073
18	0.493628	0.415521	0.350344	0.295864	0.250249	0.211994	0.179859	0.130040	0.094561	0.069144	0.037561
19	0.474642	0.395734	0.330513	0.276508	0.231712	0.194490	0.163508	0.116107	0.082948	0.059607	0.031301
20	0.456387	0.376889	0.311805	0.258419	0.214548	0.178431	0.148644	0.103667	0.072762	0.051385	0.026084

484

Table III *Future Value of an Annuity of $1*

n	4%	5%	6%	7%	8%	9%	10%	12%	14%	16%	20%
1	1.000000	1.000000	1.000000	1.000000	1.000000	1.000000	1.000000	1.000000	1.000000	1.000000	1.000000
2	2.040000	2.050000	2.060000	2.070000	2.080000	2.090000	2.100000	2.120000	2.140000	2.160000	2.200000
3	3.121600	3.152500	3.183600	3.214900	3.246400	3.278100	3.310000	3.374400	3.439600	3.505600	3.640000
4	4.246464	4.310125	4.374616	4.439943	4.506112	4.573129	4.641000	4.779328	4.921144	5.066496	5.368000
5	5.416323	5.525631	5.637093	5.750739	5.866601	5.984711	6.105100	6.352847	6.610104	6.877135	7.441600
6	6.632975	6.801913	6.975319	7.153291	7.335929	7.523335	7.715610	8.115189	8.535519	8.977477	9.929920
7	7.898294	8.142008	8.393838	8.654021	8.922803	9.200435	9.487171	10.089012	10.730491	11.413873	12.915904
8	9.214226	9.549109	9.897468	10.259803	10.636628	11.028474	11.435888	12.299693	13.232760	14.240093	16.499085
9	10.582795	11.026564	11.491316	11.977989	12.487558	13.021036	13.579477	14.775656	16.085347	17.518508	20.798902
10	12.006107	12.577893	13.180795	13.816448	14.486562	15.192930	15.937425	17.548735	19.337295	21.321469	25.958682
11	13.486351	14.206787	14.971643	15.783599	16.645487	17.560293	18.531167	20.654583	23.044516	25.732904	32.150419
12	15.025805	15.917127	16.869941	17.888451	18.977126	20.140720	21.384284	24.133133	27.270749	30.850169	39.580502
13	16.626838	17.712983	18.882138	20.140643	21.495297	22.953385	24.522712	28.029109	32.088654	36.786196	48.496603
14	18.291911	19.598632	21.015066	22.550488	24.214920	26.019189	27.974983	32.392602	37.581065	43.671987	59.195923
15	20.023588	21.578564	23.275970	25.129022	27.152114	29.360916	31.772482	37.279715	43.842414	51.659505	72.035108
16	21.824531	23.657492	25.672528	27.888054	30.324283	33.003399	35.949730	42.753280	50.980352	60.925026	87.442129
17	23.697512	25.840366	28.212880	30.840217	33.750226	36.973705	40.544703	48.883674	59.117601	71.673030	105.930555
18	25.645413	28.132385	30.905653	33.999033	37.450244	41.301338	45.599173	55.749715	68.394066	84.140715	128.116666
19	27.671229	30.539004	33.759992	37.378965	41.446263	46.018458	51.159090	63.439681	78.969235	98.603230	154.740000
20	29.778079	33.065954	36.785591	40.995492	45.761964	51.160120	57.274999	72.052442	91.024928	115.379747	186.688000

Table IV *Present Value of an Annuity of $1*

n	4%	5%	6%	7%	8%	9%	10%	12%	14%	16%	20%
1	0.961538	0.952381	0.943396	0.934579	0.925926	0.917431	0.909091	0.892857	0.877193	0.862069	0.833333
2	1.886095	1.859410	1.833393	1.808018	1.783265	1.759111	1.735537	1.690051	1.646661	1.605232	1.527778
3	2.775091	2.723248	2.673012	2.624316	2.577097	2.531295	2.486852	2.401831	2.321632	2.245890	2.106481
4	3.629895	3.545951	3.465106	3.387211	3.312127	3.239720	3.169865	3.037349	2.913712	2.798181	2.588735
5	4.451822	4.329477	4.212364	4.100197	3.992710	3.889651	3.790787	3.604776	3.433081	3.274294	2.990612
6	5.242137	5.075692	4.917324	4.766540	4.622880	4.485919	4.355261	4.111407	3.888668	3.684736	3.325510
7	6.002055	5.786373	5.582381	5.389289	5.206370	5.032953	4.868419	4.563757	4.288305	4.038565	3.604592
8	6.732745	6.463213	6.209794	5.971299	5.746639	5.534819	5.334926	4.967640	4.638864	4.343591	3.837160
9	7.435332	7.107822	6.801692	6.515232	6.246888	5.995247	5.759024	5.328250	4.946372	4.606544	4.030967
10	8.110896	7.721735	7.360087	7.023582	6.710081	6.417658	6.144567	5.650223	5.216116	4.833227	4.192472
11	8.760477	8.306414	7.886875	7.498674	7.138964	6.805191	6.495061	5.937699	5.452733	5.028644	4.327060
12	9.385074	8.863252	8.383844	7.942686	7.536078	7.160725	6.813692	6.194374	5.660292	5.197107	4.439217
13	9.985648	9.393573	8.852683	8.357651	7.903776	7.486904	7.103356	6.423548	5.842362	5.342334	4.532681
14	10.563123	9.898641	9.294984	8.745468	8.244237	7.786150	7.366687	6.628168	6.002072	5.467529	4.610567
15	11.118387	10.379658	9.712249	9.107914	8.559479	8.060688	7.606080	6.810864	6.142168	5.575456	4.675473
16	11.652296	10.837770	10.105895	9.446649	8.851369	8.312558	7.823709	6.973986	6.265060	5.668497	4.729561
17	12.165669	11.274066	10.477260	9.763223	9.121638	8.543631	8.021553	7.119630	6.372859	5.748704	4.774634
18	12.659297	11.689587	10.827603	10.059087	9.371887	8.755625	8.201412	7.249670	6.467420	5.817848	4.812195
19	13.133939	12.085321	11.158116	10.335595	9.603599	8.905115	8.364920	7.365777	6.550369	5.877455	4.843496
20	13.590326	12.462210	11.469921	10.594014	9.818147	9.128546	8.513564	7.469444	6.623131	5.928841	4.869580

During 2004 and 2005, Herring Corp. completed the following selected transactions relating to its bond issue. The corporation's fiscal year ends on December 31.

2004

Jan. 1   Sold $400,000 of 10–year, 9 percent bonds at 97. Interest is payable in cash on December 31 each year.

Dec. 31   Paid the bond interest and recorded the amortization of the discount using the straight-line method.

2005

Dec. 31   Paid the bond interest and recorded the amortization of the discount using the straight-line method.

Required

a. Show how these events would affect Herring's financial statements by recording them in a financial statements model like the following one.

	Assets	=	Liabilities			+	Equity	Rev.	–	Exp.	=	Net Inc.	Cash Flow
	Cash	=	Bond Pay.	–	Discount	+	Ret. Ear.						
1/1/04													
12/31/04													
12/31/05													

b. Determine the carrying value of the bond liability as of December 31, 2005.

c. Assuming Herring had earnings before interest and taxes of $198,360 in 2005, calculate the times interest earned ratio.

Solution to Requirements a–c

a.

	Assets	=	Liabilities			+	Equity	Rev.	–	Exp.	=	Net Inc.	Cash Flow	
	Cash	=	Bond Pay.	–	Discount	+	Ret. Ear.							
1/1/04	388,000	=	400,000	–	12,000	+	NA	NA	–	NA	=	NA	388,000	FA
12/31/04	(36,000)	=	NA	–	(1,200)	+	(37,200)	NA	–	37,200	=	(37,200)	(36,000)	OA
12/31/05	(36,000)	=	NA	–	(1,200)	+	(37,200)	NA	–	37,200	=	(37,200)	(36,000)	OA

b. The unamortized discount as of December 31, 2005, is $9,600 ($12,000 − $1,200 − $1,200). The carrying value of the bond liability is $390,400 ($400,000 − $9,600).

c. The times interest earned ratio is 5.3 times ($198,360 ÷ $37,200).

Amortization of loan *459*

Annuity *480*

Balloon payment *460*

Bond *464*

Bond discount *468*

Bond premium *473*

Call premium *465*

Call price *465*

Callable bonds *465*

Carrying value *470*

Collateral for loans *461*

Compound interest *478*

Compounding *478*

Convertible bonds *465*

Debenture *464*

Discount on Bonds Payable *470*

Effective interest rate *469*

Effective interest rate method *482*

Face value *464*

Financial leverage *475*

Fixed interest rate *459*

Future value *479*

Line of credit *462*

Market interest rate *474*

Mortgage bonds *464*

Present value *479*

Restrictive covenants *462*

Secured bonds *464*

Serial bonds *464*

Simple interest *478*

Sinking fund *464*

Spread *475*

Stated interest rate *464*

Straight-line amortization *471*

Subordinated debentures *464*

Term bonds *464*

Times interest earned ratio *477*

Time value of money *478*

Unsecured bonds *464*

Unsubordinated debentures *464*

Variable interest rate *459*

QUESTIONS

1. What is the difference between classification of a note as short term or long term?
2. At the beginning of year 1, B Co. has a note payable of $72,000 that calls for an annual payment of $16,246, which includes both principal and interest. If the interest rate is 8 percent, what is the amount of interest expense in year 1 and in year 2? What is the balance of the note at the end of year 2?
3. What is the purpose of a line of credit for a business? Why would a company choose to obtain a line of credit instead of issuing bonds?
4. What are the primary sources of debt financing for most large companies?
5. What are some advantages of issuing bonds versus borrowing from a bank?
6. What are some disadvantages of issuing bonds?
7. Why can a company usually issue bonds at a lower interest rate than the company would pay if the funds were borrowed from a bank?
8. What effect does income tax have on the cost of borrowing funds for a business?
9. What is the concept of financial leverage?
10. Which type of bond, secured or unsecured, is likely to have a lower interest rate? Explain.
11. What is the function of restrictive covenants attached to bond issues?
12. What is the difference between term bonds and serial bonds?
13. What is the purpose of establishing a sinking fund?
14. What is the call price of a bond? Is it usually higher or lower than the face amount of the bond? Explain.
15. If Roc Co. issued $100,000 of 5 percent, 10-year bonds at the face amount, what is the effect of the issuance of the bonds on the financial statements? What amount of interest expense will Roc Co. recognize each year?
16. What mechanism is used to adjust the stated interest rate to the market rate of interest?
17. When the effective interest rate is higher than the stated interest rate on a bond issue, will the bond sell at a discount or premium? Why?
18. What type of transaction is the issuance of bonds by a company?
19. What factors may cause the effective interest rate and the stated interest rate to be different?
20. If a bond is selling at 97 ½, how much cash will the company receive from the sale of a $1,000 bond?
21. How is the carrying value of a bond computed?
22. Gay Co. has a balance in the Bonds Payable account of $25,000 and a balance in the Discount on Bonds Payable account of $5,200. What is the carrying value of the bonds? What is the total amount of the liability?
23. When the effective interest rate is higher than the stated interest rate, will interest expense be higher or lower than the amount of interest paid?
24. Assuming that the selling price of the bond and the face value are the same, would the issuer of a bond rather make annual or semiannual interest payments? Why?
25. Rato Co. called some bonds and had a loss on the redemption of the bonds of $2,850. How is this amount reported on the income statement?
26. Which method of financing, debt or equity, is generally more advantageous from a tax standpoint? Why?
27. If a company has a tax rate of 30 percent and interest expense was $10,000, what is the after-tax cost of the debt?
28. Which type of financing, debt or equity, increases the risk factor of a business? Why?
29. What information does the times interest earned ratio provide?
30. What is the difference between simple and compound interest?
31. What is meant by the future value of an investment? How is it determined?
32. If you have $10,000 to invest at the beginning of year 1 at an interest rate of 8 percent, what is the future value of the investment at the end of year 4?
33. What is meant by the present value of an investment? How is it determined?
34. Assume that your favorite aunt gave you $25,000, but you will not receive the gift until you are 25 years old. You are presently 22 years old. What is the current value of the gift, assuming an interest rate of 8 percent?
35. What is the present value of four payments of $4,000 each to be received at the end of each of the next four years, assuming an interest rate of 8 percent?
36. How does the effective interest rate method of amortization differ from the straight-line method of amortization? Which method is conceptually more correct?

All Exercises in Series A are available with McGraw-Hill's Homework Manager

EXERCISE 10–1A *How Credit Terms Affect Financial Statements*

L.O. 1

Marshall Co. is planning to finance an expansion of its operations by borrowing $50,000. City Bank has agreed to loan Marshall the funds. Marshall has two repayment options: (1) to issue a note with the principal due in 10 years and with interest payable annually or (2) to issue a note to repay $5,000 of the principal each year along with the annual interest based on the unpaid principal balance. Assume the interest rate is 9 percent for each option.

Required
a. What amount of interest will Marshall pay in year 1
 (1) Under option 1?
 (2) Under option 2?
b. What amount of interest will Marshall pay in year 2
 (1) Under option 1?
 (2) Under option 2?
c. Explain the advantage of each option.

EXERCISE 10–2A *Accounting for a Long-Term Note Payable With Annual Payments That Include Interest and Principal*

L.O. 1

On January 1, 2004, Mooney Co. borrowed $60,000 cash from First Bank by issuing a four-year, 6 percent note. The principal and interest are to be paid by making annual payments in the amount of $17,315. Payments are to be made December 31 of each year, beginning December 31, 2004.

Required
Prepare an amortization schedule for the interest and principal payments for the four-year period.

EXERCISE 10–3A *Long-Term Installment Note Payable*

L.O. 1

Jim Felix started a business by issuing a $80,000 face value note to State National Bank on January 1, 2004. The note had a 7 percent annual rate of interest and a 10-year term. Payments of $11,390 are to be made each December 31 for 10 years.

Required
a. What portion of the December 31, 2004, payment is applied to
 (1) Interest expense?
 (2) Principal?
b. What is the principal balance on January 1, 2005?
c. What portion of the December 31, 2005, payment is applied to
 (1) Interest expense?
 (2) Principal?

EXERCISE 10–4A *Amortization of a Long-Term Loan*

L.O. 1

A partial amortization schedule for a five-year note payable that Chacon Co. issued on January 1, 2004, is shown here:

Accounting Period	Principal Balance January 1	Cash Payment	Applied to Interest	Applied to Principal
2004	$120,000	$30,851	$10,800	$20,051
2005	99,949	30,851	8,995	21,856

Required
a. What rate of interest is Chacon Co. paying on the note?
b. Using a financial statements model like the one shown on the following page, record the appropriate amounts for the following two events:
 (1) January 1, 2004, issue of the note payable.
 (2) December 31, 2005, payment on the note payable.

Event No.	Assets	=	Liab.	+	Equity	Rev.	−	Exp.	=	Net Inc.	Cash Flow
1											

    c. If the company earned $90,000 cash revenue and paid $50,000 in cash expenses in addition to the interest in 2004, what is the amount of each of the following?

       (1) Net income for 2004.

       (2) Cash flow from operating activities for 2004.

       (3) Cash flow from financing activities for 2004.

    d. What is the amount of interest expense on this loan for 2006?

L.O. 2   **EXERCISE 10–5A** *Accounting for a Line of Credit*

Casper Company has a line of credit with Federal Bank. Casper can borrow up to $400,000 at any time over the course of the 2004 calendar year. The following table shows the prime rate expressed as an annual percentage along with the amounts borrowed and repaid during the first four months of 2004. Casper agreed to pay interest at an annual rate equal to 2 percent above the bank's prime rate. Funds are borrowed or repaid on the first day of each month. Interest is payable in cash on the last day of the month. The interest rate is applied to the outstanding monthly balance. For example, Casper pays 6 percent (4 percent + 2 percent) annual interest on $80,000 for the month of January.

Month	Amount Borrowed or (Repaid)	Prime Rate for the Month, %
January	$80,000	4
February	40,000	3
March	(20,000)	3.5
April	30,000	4

Required

Provide all journal entries pertaining to Casper's line of credit for the first four months of 2004.

L.O. 6   **EXERCISE 10–6A** *Annual Versus Semiannual Interest Payments*

Gardner Co. issued bonds with a face value of $100,000 on January 1, 2004. The bonds had a 6 percent stated rate of interest and a five-year term. The bonds were issued at face value.

Required

    a. What total amount of interest will Gardner pay in 2004 if bond interest is paid annually each December 31?

    b. What total amount of interest will Gardner pay in 2004 if bond interest is paid semiannually each June 30 and December 31?

    c. Write a memo explaining which option Gardner would prefer.

L.O. 4, 6   **EXERCISE 10–7A** *Determining Cash Receipts From Bond Issues*

Required

Compute the cash proceeds from bond issues under the following terms. For each case, indicate whether the bonds sold at a premium or discount.

    a. May, Inc., issued $200,000 of 8-year, 7 percent bonds at 101.

    b. Tom Co. issued $100,000 of 4-year, 6 percent bonds at 98.

    c. Hill Co. issued $150,000 of 10-year, 7 percent bonds at 102 ¼.

    d. Day, Inc., issued $50,000 of 5-year, 6 percent bonds at 97 ½.

L.O. 4   **EXERCISE 10–8A** *Identifying the Relationship Between the Stated Rate of Interest and the Market Rate of Interest*

Required

Indicate whether a bond will sell at a premium (P), discount (D), or face value (F) for each of the following conditions:

    a. _____ The market rate of interest is less than the stated rate.

    b. _____ The market rate of interest is equal to the stated rate.

c. _____ The stated rate of interest is higher than the market rate.

d. _____ The market rate of interest is higher than the stated rate.

e. _____ The stated rate of interest is less than the market rate.

EXERCISE 10–9A *Identifying Bond Premiums and Discounts*   L.O. 4

Required

In each of the following situations, state whether the bonds will sell at a premium or discount.

a. Jaco issued $100,000 of bonds with a stated interest rate of 6.5 percent. At the time of issue, the market rate of interest for similar investments was 6 percent.

b. Webnet issued $150,000 of bonds with a stated interest rate of 5.5 percent. At the time of issue, the market rate of interest for similar investments was 6 percent.

c. Pearl Inc. issued callable bonds with a stated interest rate of 6 percent. The bonds were callable at 102. At the date of issue, the market rate of interest was 6.5 percent for similar investments.

EXERCISE 10–10A *Determining the Amount of Bond Premiums and Discounts*   L.O. 4

Required

For each of the following situations, calculate the amount of bond discount or premium, if any.

a. Lind Co. issued $60,000 of 7 percent bonds at 101 ¼.

b. Schwarz, Inc., issued $90,000 of 10-year, 6 percent bonds at 95 ½.

c. Zoe, Inc., issued $200,000 of 20-year, 6 percent bonds at 102.

d. Uddin Co. issued $150,000 of 15-year, 7 percent bonds at 98.

EXERCISE 10–11A *Effect of a Bond Discount on Financial Statements: Annual Interest*   L.O. 5, 6

Keeley Company issued $100,000 face value of bonds on January 1, 2005. The bonds had a 7 percent stated rate of interest and a 10-year term. Interest is paid in cash annually, beginning December 31, 2005. The bonds were issued at 98.

Required

a. Use a financial statements model like the one shown below to demonstrate how (1) the January 1, 2005 bond issue and (2) the December 31, 2005 recognition of interest expense, including the amortization of the discount and the cash payment, affects the company's financial statements. Use + for increase, − for decrease, and NA for not affected.

Event No.	Assets	=	Liab.	+	Equity	Rev.	−	Exp.	=	Net Inc.	Cash Flow
1											

b. Determine the amount of interest expense reported on the 2005 income statement.

c. Determine the carrying value (face value less discount or plus premium) of the bond liability as of December 31, 2005.

d. Determine the amount of interest expense reported on the 2006 income statement.

e. Determine the carrying value (face value less discount or plus premium) of the bond liability as of December 31, 2006.

EXERCISE 10–12A *Effect of a Bond Premium on Financial Statements: Annual Interest*   L.O. 5, 6

Ball Company issued $200,000 face value of bonds on January 1, 2004. The bonds had a 6 percent stated rate of interest and a 10-year term. Interest is paid in cash annually, beginning December 31, 2004. The bonds were issued at 102.

Required

a. Use a financial statements model like the one shown below to demonstrate how (1) the January 1, 2004 bond issue and (2) the December 31, 2004 recognition of interest expense, including the amortization of the premium and the cash payment, affects the company's financial statements. Use + for increase, − for decrease, and NA for not affected.

Event No.	Assets	=	Liab.	+	Equity	Rev.	−	Exp.	=	Net Inc.	Cash Flow
1											

b. Determine the carrying value (face value less discount or plus premium) of the bond liability as of December 31, 2004.

c. Determine the amount of interest expense reported on the 2004 income statement.

d. Determine the carrying value of the bond liability as of December 31, 2005.

e. Determine the amount of interest expense reported on the 2005 income statement.

L.O. 5, 6   **EXERCISE 10–13A** *Effect of Bonds Issued at a Discount on Financial Statements: Semiannual Interest*

Farm Supplies, Inc., issued $150,000 of 10-year, 6 percent bonds on July 1, 2005, at 95. Interest is payable in cash semiannually on June 30 and December 31.

Required

a. Prepare the journal entries to record issuing the bonds and any necessary journal entries for 2005 and 2006. Post the journal entries to T-accounts.

b. Prepare the liabilities section of the balance sheet at the end of 2005 and 2006.

c. What amount of interest expense will Farm Supplies report on the financial statements for 2005 and 2006?

d. What amount of cash will Farm Supplies pay for interest in 2005 and 2006?

L.O. 6   **EXERCISE 10–14A** *Recording Bonds Issued at Face Value and Associated Interest for Two Accounting Cycles: Annual Interest*

On January 1, 2006, Demski Corp. issued $300,000 of 10-year, 5 percent bonds at their face amount. Interest is payable on December 31 of each year with the first payment due December 31, 2006.

Required

Prepare all the general journal entries related to these bonds for 2006 and 2007.

L.O. 6   **EXERCISE 10–15A** *Recording Bonds Issued at a Discount: Annual Interest*

On January 1, 2005, Marva Co. issued $200,000 of five-year, 6 percent bonds at 96. Interest is payable annually on December 31. The discount is amortized using the straight-line method.

Required

Prepare the journal entries to record the bond transactions for 2005 and 2006.

L.O. 6   **EXERCISE 10–16A** *Recording Bonds Issued at a Premium: Annual Interest*

On January 1, 2006, Stone Company issued $200,000 of five-year, 6 percent bonds at 102. Interest is payable annually on December 31. The premium is amortized using the straight-line method.

Required

Prepare the journal entries to record the bond transactions for 2006 and 2007.

L.O. 5, 6   **EXERCISE 10–17A** *Two Complete Accounting Cycles: Bonds Issued at Face Value With Annual Interest*

Wyatt Company issued $400,000 of 20-year, 6 percent bonds on January 1, 2005. The bonds were issued at face value. Interest is payable in cash on December 31 of each year. Wyatt immediately invested the proceeds from the bond issue in land. The land was leased for an annual $60,000 of cash revenue, which was collected on December 31 of each year, beginning December 31, 2005.

Required

a. Prepare the journal entries for these events, and post them to T-accounts for 2005 and 2006.

b. Prepare the income statement, balance sheet, and statement of cash flows for 2005 and 2006.

L.O. 6   **EXERCISE 10–18A** *Recording Callable Bonds*

Ball Co. issued $200,000 of 6 percent, 10-year, callable bonds on January 1, 2004, for their face value. The call premium was 2 percent (bonds are callable at 102). Interest was payable annually on December 31. The bonds were called on December 31, 2007.

Required

Prepare the journal entries to record the bond issue on January 1, 2004, and the bond redemption on December 31, 2007. Assume that all entries to accrue and pay interest were recorded correctly.

EXERCISE 10–19A *Determining the After-Tax Cost of Debt* **L.O. 7**

The following 2004 information is available for three companies:

	Crow Co.	Dahl Co.	Snow Co.
Face value of bonds payable	$300,000	$600,000	$500,000
Interest rate	8%	7%	6%
Income tax rate	35%	20%	25%

Required
a. Determine the annual before-tax interest cost for each company *in dollars.*
b. Determine the annual after-tax interest cost for each company *in dollars.*
c. Determine the annual after-tax interest cost for each company as *a percentage* of the face value of the bonds.

EXERCISE 10–20A *Future Value and Present Value (Appendix)* **L.O. 8**

Required
Using Tables I, II, III, or IV in the appendix, calculate the following:

a. The future value of $20,000 invested at 6 percent for 10 years.
b. The future value of eight annual payments of $1,200 at 7 percent interest.
c. The amount that must be deposited today (present value) at 6 percent to accumulate $50,000 in five years.
d. The annual payment on a 10-year, 6 percent, $40,000 note payable.

EXERCISE 10–21A *Computing the Payment Amount (Appendix)* **L.O. 8**

Nancy Swift is a business major at State U. She will be graduating this year and is planning to start a consulting business. She will need to purchase computer equipment that costs $22,000. She can borrow the money from the local bank but will have to make annual payments of principal and interest.

Required
a. Compute the annual payment Nancy will be required to make on a $22,000, four-year, 7 percent loan.
b. If Nancy can afford to make annual payments of $8,000, how much can she borrow?

EXERCISE 10–22A *Saving for a Future Value (Appendix)* **L.O. 8**

Billy Joe and Betty Ann were recently married and want to start saving for their dream home. They expect the house they want will cost approximately $250,000. They hope to be able to purchase the house for cash in 10 years.

Required
a. How much will Billy Joe and Betty Ann have to invest each year to purchase their dream home at the end of 10 years? Assume an interest rate of 8 percent.
b. Billy Joe's parents want to give the couple a substantial wedding gift for the purchase of their future home. How much must Billy Joe's parents give them now if they are to have the desired amount of $250,000 in 12 years? Assume an interest rate of 8 percent?

EXERCISE 10–23A *Sale of Bonds at a Discount Using Present Value (Appendix)* **L.O. 6, 8**

Jones Corporation issued $60,000 of 6 percent, 10-year bonds on January 1, 2003, for a price that reflected a 7 percent market rate of interest. Interest is payable annually on December 31.

Required
a. What was the selling price of the bonds?
b. Prepare the journal entry to record issuing the bonds.
c. Prepare the journal entry for the first interest payment on December 31, 2003, using the effective interest rate method.

EXERCISE 10–24A *Comparing the Effective Interest Rate Method With the Straight-Line Method (Appendix)* **L.O. 6, 8**

Required
Write a short memo explaining why the effective interest rate method produces a different amount of interest expense from the straight-line method in any given year.

All Problems in Series A are available with McGraw-Hill's Homework Manager

L.O. 1

CHECK FIGURES
a. Year 1 Ending Principal Balance:
   $41,337
b. 2007 Net Income: $28,505

PROBLEM 10–25A   *Effect of a Term Loan on Financial Statements*

On January 1, 2005, Miller Co. borrowed cash from First City Bank by issuing a $60,000 face value, three-year term note that had a 7 percent annual interest rate. The note is to be repaid by making annual payments of $22,863 that include both interest and principal on December 31. Jones invested the proceeds from the loan in land that generated lease revenues of $30,000 cash per year.

Required
a. Prepare an amortization schedule for the three-year period.
b. Prepare an income statement, balance sheet, and statement of cash flows for each of the three years. (*Hint:* Record the transactions for each year in T-accounts before preparing the financial statements.)
c. Does cash outflow from operating activities remain constant or change each year? Explain.

L.O. 2

www.mhhe.com/edmonds5e

CHECK FIGURES
a. Interest Expense: $4,817
   Total Assets: $53,183

PROBLEM 10–26A   *Effect of a Line of Credit on Financial Statements*

Shim Company has a line of credit with Bay Bank. Shim can borrow up to $200,000 at any time over the course of the 2006 calendar year. The following table shows the prime rate expressed as an annual percentage along with the amounts borrowed and repaid during 2006. Shim agreed to pay interest at an annual rate equal to 1 percent above the bank's prime rate. Funds are borrowed or repaid on the first day of each month. Interest is payable in cash on the last day of the month. The interest rate is applied to the outstanding monthly balance. For example, Shim pays 5 percent (4 percent + 1 percent) annual interest on $70,000 for the month of January.

Month	Amount Borrowed or (Repaid)	Prime Rate for the Month, %
January	$70,000	4
February	40,000	4
March	(20,000)	5
April through October	No change	No change
November	(30,000)	5
December	(20,000)	4

Shim earned $18,000 of cash revenue during 2006.

Required
a. Prepare an income statement, balance sheet, and statement of cash flows for 2006.
b. Write a memo discussing the advantages of arranging a line of credit to a business.

L.O. 5, 6

www.mhhe.com/edmonds5e

CHECK FIGURES
2004 Operating Income: $4,667
2007 Total Assets: $11,000

PROBLEM 10–27A   *Accounting for a Bond Premium Over Multiple Accounting Cycles*

Tyrone Company was started when it issued bonds with $200,000 face value on January 1, 2004. The bonds were issued for cash at 105. They had a 15-year term to maturity and an 8 percent annual interest rate. Interest was payable annually. Tyrone immediately purchased land with the proceeds (cash received) from the bond issue. Tyrone leased the land for $20,000 cash per year. On January 1, 2007, the company sold the land for $211,000 cash. Immediately after the sale, Tyrone repurchased its bonds (repaid the bond liability) at 106. Assume that no other accounting events occurred in 2007.

Required
Prepare an income statement, statement of changes in equity, balance sheet and statement of cash flows for each of the 2004, 2005, 2006, and 2007 accounting periods. Assume that the company closes its books on December 31 of each year. Prepare the statements using a vertical statements format. (*Hint:* Record each year's transactions in T-accounts prior to preparing the financial statements.)

L.O. 4–6

PROBLEM 10–28A   *Recording and Reporting a Bond Discount over Two Cycles: Semiannual Interest*

During 2005 and 2006, Martin Co. completed the following transactions relating to its bond issue. The company's fiscal year ends on December 31.

2005

Mar. 1 Issued $60,000 of eight-year, 7 percent bonds for $57,000. The semiannual cash payment for interest is due on March 1 and September 1, beginning September 2005.

Sept. 1 Recognized interest expense including the amortization of the discount and made the semi-annual cash payment for interest.

Dec. 31 Recognized accrued interest expense including the amortization of the discount.

Dec. 31 Closed the interest expense account.

2006

Mar. 1 Recognized interest expense including the amortization of the discount and made the semi-annual cash payment for interest.

Sept. 1 Recognized interest expense including the amortization of the discount and made the semi-annual cash payment for interest.

Dec. 31 Recognized accrued interest expense including the amortization of the discount.

Dec. 31 Closed the interest expense account.

Required

a. When the bonds were issued, was the market rate of interest more or less than the stated rate of interest? If the bonds had sold at face value, what amount of cash would Martin Co. have received?

b. Prepare the general journal entries for these transactions.

c. Prepare the liabilities section of the balance sheet at December 31, 2005 and 2006.

d. Determine the amount of interest expense Martin would report on the income statements for 2005 and 2006.

e. Determine the amount of interest Martin would pay to the bondholders in 2005 and 2006.

PROBLEM 10-29A *Effect of a Bond Premium on the Elements of Financial Statements*   **L.O. 5, 6**

Valley Land Co. was formed when it acquired cash from the issue of common stock. The company then issued bonds at a premium on January 1, 2006. Interest is payable annually on December 31 of each year, beginning December 31, 2006. On January 2, 2006, Valley Land Co. purchased a piece of land and leased it for an annual rental fee. The rent is received annually on December 31, beginning December 31, 2006. At the end of the eight-year period (December 31, 2013), the land was sold at a gain, and the bonds were paid off. A summary of the transactions for each year follows:

2006

1. Acquired cash from the issue of common stock.
2. Issued eight-year bonds.
3. Purchased land.
4. Received land-lease income.
5. Recognized interest expense including the amortization of the premium and made the cash payment for interest on December 31.
6. Prepared the December 31 entry to close Rent Revenue.
7. Prepared the December 31 entry to close Interest Expense.

2007-2012

8. Received land-lease income.
9. Recognized interest expense including the amortization of the premium and made the cash payment for interest on December 31.
10. Prepared the December 31 entry to close Rent Revenue.
11. Prepared the December 31 entry to close Interest Expense.

2013

12. Sold land at a gain.
13. Retired bonds at face value.

Required

Identify each of these 13 transactions as asset source (AS), asset use (AU), asset exchange (AE), or claims exchange (CE). Explain how each event affects assets, liabilities, equity, net income, and cash flow by placing a + for increase, − for decrease, or NA for not affected under each category. In the Cash Flow column, indicate whether the item is an operating activity (OA), investing activity (IA), or financing activity (FA). The first event is recorded as an example.

Event No.	Type of Event	Assets	=	Liabilities	+	Common Stock	+	Retained Earnings	Net Income	Cash Flow
1	AS	+		NA		+		NA	NA	+ FA

L.O. 5, 6 **PROBLEM 10–30A** *Recording Transactions for Callable Bonds*

CHECK FIGURES
b. Interest Expense: $9,600
b. Loss on Bond Redemption
   $1,800

Franklin Co. issued $120,000 of 10-year, 8 percent, callable bonds on January 1, 2006, with interest payable annually on December 31. The bonds were issued at their face amount. The bonds are callable at 101 ½. The fiscal year of the corporation is the calendar year.

Required

a. Show the effect of the following events on the financial statements by recording the appropriate amounts in a horizontal statements model like the following one. In the Cash Flow column, indicate whether the item is an operating activity (OA), investing activity (IA), or financing activity (FA). Use NA if an element was not affected by the event.

   (1) Issued the bonds on January 1, 2006.
   (2) Paid interest due to bondholders on December 31, 2006.
   (3) On January 1, 2010, Franklin Co. called the bonds. Assume that all interim entries were correctly recorded.

Event No.	Assets	=	Liab.	+	Equity	Rev.	–	Exp.	=	Net Inc.	Cash Flow
1											

b. Prepare journal entries for the three events listed in Requirement *a*.

L.O. 1, 2, 5 **PROBLEM 10–31A** *Effect of Debt Transactions on Financial Statements*

Required

Show the effect of each of the following independent accounting events on the financial statements using a horizontal statements model like the following one. Use + for increase, – for decrease, and NA for not affected. The first event is recorded as an example.

Event No.	Assets	=	Liab.	+	Equity	Rev.	–	Exp.	=	Net Inc.	Cash Flow
1	+		+		NA	NA		NA		NA	+ FA

a. Issued a bond at a premium.
b. Made an interest payment on a bond that had been issued at a premium and amortized the premium.
c. Borrowed funds using a line of credit.
d. Made an interest payment for funds that had been borrowed against a line of credit.
e. Made a cash payment on a note payable for both interest and principal.
f. Issued a bond at face value.
g. Made an interest payment on a bond that had been issued at face value.
h. Issued a bond at a discount.
i. Made an interest payment on a bond that had been issued at a discount and amortized the discount.

L.O. 6, 8 **PROBLEM 10–32A** *Sale of Bonds at a Premium and Amortization Using the Effective Interest Rate Method (Appendix)*

CHECK FIGURES
a. Selling price of bond: $321,071
c. 2007 Interest Expense: $22,475

On January 1, 2007, Keel Corp. sold $300,000 of its own 8 percent, 10-year bonds. Interest is payable annually on December 31. The bonds were sold to yield an effective interest rate of 7 percent. Keel Corp. uses the effective interest rate method.

Required

a. Using the information in the appendix, calculate the selling price of the bonds.
b. Prepare the journal entry for the issuance of the bonds.
c. Prepare the journal entry for the amortization of the bond premium and the payment of the interest on December 31, 2009.
d. Calculate the amount of interest expense for 2010.

EXERCISES—SERIES B

L.O. 1 **EXERCISE 10–1B** *How Credit Terms Affect Financial Statements*

Marco Co. borrowed $40,000 from the National Bank by issuing a note with a five-year term. Marco has two options with respect to the payment of interest and principal. Option 1 requires the payment of interest only on an annual basis with the full amount of the principal due at maturity. Option 2 calls for an annual payment that includes interest due plus a partial repayment of the principal balance. The effective annual interest rate on both notes is identical.

Required

Write a memo explaining how the two alternatives will affect *(a)* the carrying value of liabilities, *(b)* the amount of annual interest expense, *(c)* the total amount of interest that will be paid over the life of the note, and *(d)* the cash flow consequences.

EXERCISE 10–2B *Accounting for a Long-Term Note Payable With Annual Payments That Include Interest and Principal*   L.O. 1

On January 1, 2006, Baco Co. borrowed $120,000 cash from Central Bank by issuing a five-year, 8 percent note. The principal and interest are to be paid by making annual payments in the amount of $30,055. Payments are to be made December 31 of each year, beginning December 31, 2006.

Required

Prepare an amortization schedule for the interest and principal payments for the five-year period.

EXERCISE 10–3B *Long-Term Installment Note Payable*   L.O. 1

Terek Amer started a business by issuing an $80,000 face value note to First State Bank on January 1, 2004. The note had a 10 percent annual rate of interest and a five-year term. Payments of $21,104 are to be made each December 31 for five years.

Required

a. What portion of the December 31, 2004, payment is applied to
   (1) Interest expense?
   (2) Principal?
b. What is the principal balance on January 1, 2005?
c. What portion of the December 31, 2005, payment is applied to
   (1) Interest expense?
   (2) Principal?

EXERCISE 10–4B *Amortization of a Long-Term Loan*   L.O. 1

A partial amortization schedule for a 10-year note payable issued on January 1, 2006, is shown below:

Accounting Period	Principal Balance January 1	Cash Payment	Applied to Interest	Applied to Principal
2006	$200,000	$32,549	$20,000	$12,549
2007	187,451	32,549	18,745	13,804
2008	173,647	32,549	17,365	15,184

Required

a. Using a financial statements model like the one shown here, record the appropriate amounts for the following two events:
   (1) January 1, 2006, issue of the note payable.
   (2) December 31, 2006, payment on the note payable.

Event No.	Assets	=	Liab.	+	Equity	Rev.	−	Exp.	=	Net Inc.	Cash Flow
1											

b. If the company earned $100,000 cash revenue and paid $50,000 in cash expenses in addition to the interest in 2006, what is the amount of each of the following?
   (1) Net income for 2006.
   (2) Cash flow from operating activities for 2006.
   (3) Cash flow from financing activities for 2006.
c. What is the amount of interest expense on this loan for 2009?

EXERCISE 10–5B *Accounting for a Line of Credit*   L.O. 2

Vanheis Company has a line of credit with United Bank. Vanheis can borrow up to $200,000 at any time over the course of the 2007 calendar year. The following table shows the prime rate expressed as an annual percentage along with the amounts borrowed and repaid during the first three months of 2007. Vanheis agreed to pay interest at an annual rate equal to 2 percent above the bank's prime rate. Funds are borrowed or repaid on the first day of each month. Interest is payable in cash on the last day of the month. The interest rate is applied to the outstanding monthly balance. For example, Vanheis pays 6 percent (4 percent + 2 percent) annual interest on $80,000 for the month of February.

Month	Amount Borrowed or (Repaid)	Prime Rate for the Month, %
January	$50,000	3.0
February	30,000	4.0
March	(40,000)	4.5

Required
Provide all journal entries pertaining to Vanheis's line of credit for the first three months of 2007.

L.O. 6   EXERCISE 10–6B *Annual Versus Semiannual Interest Payments*

Colgan Company issued bonds with a face value of $10,000 on January 1, 2005. The bonds had an 8 percent stated rate of interest and a six-year term. The bonds were issued at face value. Interest is payable on an annual basis.

Required
Write a memo explaining whether the total cash outflow for interest would be more, less, or the same if the bonds pay semiannual versus annual interest.

L.O. 4, 6   EXERCISE 10–7B *Determining Cash Receipts From Bond Issues*

Required
Compute the cash proceeds from bond issues under the following terms. For each case, indicate whether the bonds sold at a premium or discount.

a. Petal, Inc., issued $200,000 of 10-year, 8 percent bonds at 103.
b. Stem Inc. issued $80,000 of five-year, 12 percent bonds at 95 ½.
c. Rose Co. issued $100,000 of five-year, 6 percent bonds at 101 ¾.
d. Tulip, Inc., issued $50,000 of four-year, 8 percent bonds at 98.

L.O. 4   EXERCISE 10–8B *Identifying the Relationship Between the Stated Rate of Interest and the Market Rate of Interest*

Required
Indicate whether a bond will sell at a premium (P), discount (D), or face value (F) for each of the following conditions:

a. _____ The market rate of interest is equal to the stated rate.
b. _____ The market rate of interest is less than the stated rate.
c. _____ The market rate of interest is higher than the stated rate.
d. _____ The stated rate of interest is higher than the market rate.
e. _____ The stated rate of interest is less than the market rate.

L.O. 4   EXERCISE 10–9B *Identifying Bond Premiums and Discounts*

Required
In each of the following situations, state whether the bonds will sell at a premium or discount.

a. Stokes issued $200,000 of bonds with a stated interest rate of 8 percent. At the time of issue, the market rate of interest for similar investments was 7 percent.
b. Shaw issued $100,000 of bonds with a stated interest rate of 8 percent. At the time of issue, the market rate of interest for similar investments was 9 percent.
c. Link Inc. issued callable bonds with a stated interest rate of 8 percent. The bonds were callable at 104. At the date of issue, the market rate of interest was 9 percent for similar investments.

L.O. 4   EXERCISE 10–10B *Determining the Amount of Bond Premiums and Discounts*

Required
For each of the following situations, calculate the amount of bond discount or premium, if any.

a. Ball Co. issued $80,000 of 6 percent bonds at 102.

b. Link, Inc., issued $50,000 of 10-year, 8 percent bonds at 98.

c. Hall, Inc., issued $100,000 of 15-year, 9 percent bonds at 102 ¼.

d. Mink Co. issued $500,000 of 20-year, 8 percent bonds at 98 ¾.

EXERCISE 10–11B *Effect of a Bond Discount on Financial Statements: Annual Interest*   **L.O. 5, 6**

Landry Company issued $100,000 face value of bonds on January 1, 2004. The bonds had an 8 percent stated rate of interest and a five-year term. Interest is paid in cash annually, beginning December 31, 2004. The bonds were issued at 96.

Required

a. Use a financial statements model like the one shown below to demonstrate how (1) the January 1, 2004 bond issue and (2) the December 31, 2004 recognition of interest expense, including the amortization of the discount and the cash payment, affects the company's financial statements. Use + for increase, − for decrease, and NA for not affected.

Event No.	Assets	=	Liab.	+	Equity	Rev.	−	Exp.	=	Net Inc.	Cash Flow
1											

b. Determine the carrying value (face value less discount or plus premium) of the bond liability as of December 31, 2004.

c. Determine the amount of interest expense reported on the 2004 income statement.

d. Determine the carrying value (face value less discount or plus premium) of the bond liability as of December 31, 2005.

e. Determine the amount of interest expense reported on the 2005 income statement.

EXERCISE 10–12B *Effect of a Bond Premium on Financial Statements: Annual Interest*   **L.O. 5, 6**

Switzer Company issued $100,000 face value of bonds on January 1, 2004. The bonds had an 8 percent stated rate of interest and a five-year term. Interest is paid in cash annually, beginning December 31, 2004. The bonds were issued at 102.

Required

a. Use a financial statements model like the one shown below to demonstrate how (1) the January 1, 2004 bond issue and (2) the December 31, 2004 recognition of interest expense, including the amortization of the premium and the cash payment, affects the company's financial statements. Use + for increase, − for decrease, and NA for not affected

Event No.	Assets	=	Liab.	+	Equity	Rev.	−	Exp.	=	Net Inc.	Cash Flow
1											

b. Determine the carrying value (face value less discount or plus premium) of the bond liability as of December 31, 2004.

c. Determine the amount of interest expense reported on the 2004 income statement.

d. Determine the carrying value of the bond liability as of December 31, 2005.

e. Determine the amount of interest expense reported on the 2005 income statement.

EXERCISE 10–13B *Effect of Bonds Issued at a Premium on Financial Statements: Semiannual*   **L.O. 5, 6**
Interest

Garden Supplies, Inc., issued $200,000 of 10-year, 6 percent bonds on July 1, 2006, at 104. Interest is payable in cash semiannually on June 30 and December 31.

Required

a. Prepare the journal entries to record issuing the bonds and any necessary journal entries for 2006 and 2007. Post the journal entries to T-accounts.

b. Prepare the liabilities section of the balance sheet at the end of 2006 and 2007.

c. What amount of interest expense will Garden report on the financial statements for 2006 and 2007?

d. What amount of cash will Garden pay for interest in 2006 and 2007?

EXERCISE 10–14B *Recording Bonds Issued at Face Value and Associated Interest for Two*   **L.O. 6**
Accounting Cycles: Annual Interest

On January 1, 2006, Miller Corp. issued $100,000 of 10-year, 9 percent bonds at their face amount. Interest is payable on December 31 of each year with the first payment due December 31, 2006.

Required

Prepare all the general journal entries related to these bonds for 2006 and 2007.

L.O. 6   EXERCISE 10–15B *Recording Bonds Issued at a Discount: Annual Interest*

On January 1, 2005, Creason Co. issued $100,000 of five-year, 8 percent bonds at 97 ½. Interest is payable annually on December 31. The discount is amortized using the straight-line method.

Required

Prepare the journal entries to record the bond transactions for 2005 and 2006.

L.O. 6   EXERCISE 10–16B *Recording Bonds Issued at a Premium: Semiannual Interest*

On January 1, 2006, Vickers Company issued $200,000 of five-year, 12 percent bonds at 103. Interest is payable semiannually on June 30 and December 31. The premium is amortized using the straight-line method.

Required

Prepare the journal entries to record the bond transactions for 2006 and 2007.

L.O. 5, 6   EXERCISE 10–17B *Two Complete Accounting Cycles: Bonds Issued at Face Value With Annual Interest*

Upton Company issued $1,000,000 of 10-year, 10 percent bonds on January 1, 2004. The bonds were issued at face value. Interest is payable in cash on December 31 of each year. Upton immediately invested the proceeds from the bond issue in land. The land was leased for an annual $140,000 of cash revenue, which was collected on December 31 of each year, beginning December 31, 2004.

Required

a. Prepare the journal entries for these events, and post them to T-accounts for 2004 and 2005.
b. Prepare the income statement, balance sheet, and statement of cash flows for 2004 and 2005.

L.O. 6   EXERCISE 10–18B *Recording Callable Bonds*

Han Co. issued $500,000 of 8 percent, 10-year, callable bonds on January 1, 2005, for their face value. The call premium was 4 percent (bonds are callable at 104). Interest was payable annually on December 31. The bonds were called on December 31, 2009.

Required

Prepare the journal entries to record the bond issue on January 1, 2005, and the bond redemption on December 31, 2009. Assume that all entries for accrual and payment of interest were recorded correctly.

L.O. 7   EXERCISE 10–19B *Determining the After-Tax Cost of Debt*

The following 2006 information is available for three companies:

	Pace Co.	Pile Co.	Park Co.
Face value of bonds payable	$300,000	$600,000	$500,000
Interest rate	10%	9%	8%
Income tax rate	40%	30%	35%

Required

a. Determine the annual before-tax interest cost for each company *in dollars.*
b. Determine the annual after-tax interest cost for each company *in dollars.*
c. Determine the annual after-tax interest cost for each company as *a percentage* of the face value of the bonds.

L.O. 8   EXERCISE 10–20B *Future Value and Present Value (Appendix)*

Required

Using Tables I, II, III, or IV in the appendix, calculate the following:

a. The future value of $10,000 invested at 6 percent for four years.
b. The future value of five annual payments of $2,000 at 10 percent interest.
c. The amount that must be deposited today (present value) at 9 percent to accumulate $200,000 in 10 years.
d. The annual payment on a five-year, 8 percent, $100,000 note payable.

EXERCISE 10–21B *Computing the Amount of Payment (Appendix)*   **L.O. 8**

Required
a. Donna Kirk has just graduated from Ivory Tower University with a degree in theater. She wants to buy a new car but does not know if she can afford the payments. Since Kirk knows that you have had an accounting course, she asks you to compute the annual payment on a $30,000, 10 percent, five-year note. What would Kirk's annual payment be?
b. If Kirk can afford an annual payment of only $4,000, what price vehicle should she look for, assuming an interest rate of 10 percent and a five-year term?

EXERCISE 10–22B *Saving for a Future Value (Appendix)*   **L.O. 8**

Mary and Mark Yuppy are celebrating the birth of their son, Marcus Andrew Yuppy IV. They want to send Little Andy to the best university and know they must begin saving for his education right away. They project that Little Andy's education will cost $500,000.

Required
a. How much must the Yuppys set aside annually to accumulate the necessary $500,000 in 18 years? Assume an 8 percent interest rate.
b. If the Yuppys wish to make a one-time investment currently for Little Andy's education, how much must they deposit today, assuming an 8 percent interest rate?

EXERCISE 10–23B *Sale of Bonds at a Discount Using Present Value (Appendix)*   **L.O. 6, 8**

Thompson Corporation issued $100,000 of 10 percent, 10-year bonds on January 1, 2006, for a price that reflected a 9 percent market rate of interest. Interest is payable annually on December 31.

Required
a. What was the selling price of the bonds?
b. Prepare the journal entry to record issuing the bonds.
c. Prepare the journal entry for the first interest payment on December 31, 2006, using the effective interest rate method.

EXERCISE 10–24B *Effect of Semiannual Interest on Investment Returns (Appendix)*   **L.O. 6, 8**

Required
Write a short memo explaining why an investor would find a bond that pays semiannual interest more attractive than one that pays annual interest.

PROBLEMS—SERIES B

PROBLEM 10–25B *Effect of a Long-Term Note Payable on Financial Statements*   **L.O. 1**

On January 1, 2007, Mixon Co. borrowed cash from Best Bank by issuing a $100,000 face value, four-year term note that had a 10 percent annual interest rate. The note is to be repaid by making annual cash payments of $31,547 that include both interest and principal on December 31 of each year. Mixon used the proceeds from the loan to purchase land that generated rental revenues of $40,000 cash per year.

Required
a. Prepare an amortization schedule for the four-year period.
b. Prepare an income statement, balance sheet, and statement of cash flows for each of the four years. (*Hint:* Record the transactions for each year in T-accounts before preparing the financial statements.)
c. Given that revenue is the same for each period, explain why net income increases each year.

PROBLEM 10–26B *Effect of a Line of Credit on Financial Statements*   **L.O. 2**

Libby Company has a line of credit with State Bank. Libby can borrow up to $200,000 at any time over the course of the 2006 calendar year. The following table shows the prime rate expressed as an annual percentage along with the amounts borrowed and repaid during 2006. Libby agreed to pay interest at an annual rate equal to 2 percent above the bank's prime rate. Funds are borrowed or repaid on the first day of each month. Interest is payable in cash on the last day of the month. The interest rate is applied to the outstanding monthly balance. For example, Libby pays 7 percent (5 percent + 2 percent) annual interest on $100,000 for the month of January.

Month	Amount Borrowed or (Repaid)	Prime Rate for the Month, %
January	$100,000	5
February	50,000	6
March	(40,000)	7
April through October	No change	No change
November	(80,000)	6
December	(20,000)	5

Libby earned $30,000 of cash revenue during 2006.

Required

a. Prepare an income statement, balance sheet, and statement of cash flows for 2006. (*Note:* Round computations to the nearest dollar.)

b. Write a memo to explain how the business was able to generate retained earnings when the owner contributed no assets to the business.

L.O. 5, 6   PROBLEM 10–27B *Accounting for a Bond Discount Over Multiple Accounting Cycles*

Box Company was started when it issued bonds with a $400,000 face value on January 1, 2005. The bonds were issued for cash at 96. They had a 20-year term to maturity and an 8 percent annual interest rate. Interest was payable on December 31 of each year. Box Company immediately purchased land with the proceeds (cash received) from the bond issue. Box leased the land for $50,000 cash per year. On January 1, 2008, the company sold the land for $400,000 cash. Immediately after the sale of the land, Box redeemed the bonds at 98. Assume that no other accounting events occurred during 2008.

Required

Prepare an income statement, statement of changes in equity, balance sheet, and statement of cash flows for the 2005, 2006, 2007, and 2008 accounting periods. Assume that the company closes its books on December 31 of each year. Prepare the statements using a vertical statements format. (*Hint:* Record each year's transactions in T-accounts prior to preparing the financial statements.)

L.O. 4, 5, 6   PROBLEM 10–28B *Recording and Reporting Bond Discount Over Two Cycles*

During 2006 and 2007, Joy Corp. completed the following transactions relating to its bond issue. The corporation's fiscal year is the calendar year.

2006

Jan. 1   Issued $100,000 of ten-year, 10 percent bonds for $96,000. The annual cash payment for interest is due on December 31.

Dec. 31   Recognized interest expense, including the amortization of the discount, and made the cash payment for interest.

Dec. 31   Closed the interest expense account.

2007

Dec. 31   Recognized interest expense, including the amortization of the discount, and made the cash payment for interest.

Dec. 31   Closed the interest expense account.

Required

a. When the bonds were issued, was the market rate of interest more or less than the stated rate of interest? If Joy had sold the bonds at their face amount, what amount of cash would Joy have received?

b. Prepare the general journal entries for these transactions.

c. Prepare the liabilities section of the balance sheet at December 31, 2006 and 2007.

d. Determine the amount of interest expense that will be reported on the income statements for 2006 and 2007.

e. Determine the amount of interest that will be paid in cash to the bondholders in 2006 and 2007.

PROBLEM 10–29B *Effect of a Bond Discount on the Elements of Financial Statements*

L.O. 5, 6

Stafford Co. was formed when it acquired cash from the issue of common stock. The company then issued bonds at a discount on January 1, 2003. Interest is payable on December 31 with the first payment made December 31, 2003. On January 2, 2003, Stafford Co. purchased a piece of land that produced rent revenue annually. The rent is collected on December 31 of each year, beginning December 31, 2003. At the end of the six-year period (January 1, 2009), the land was sold at a gain, and the bonds were paid off at face value. A summary of the transactions for each year follows:

2003
1. Acquired cash from the issue of common stock.
2. Issued six-year bonds.
3. Purchased land.
4. Received land-lease income.
5. Recognized interest expense, including the amortization of the discount, and made the cash payment for interest on December 31.
6. Prepared December 31 entry to close Rent Revenue.
7. Prepared December 31 entry to close Interest Expense.

2004–2008
8. Received land-lease income.
9. Recognized interest expense, including the amortization of the discount, and made the cash payment for interest December 31.
10. Prepared December 31 entry to close Rent Revenue.
11. Prepared December 31 entry to close Interest Expense.

2009
12. Sold the land at a gain.
13. Retired the bonds at face value.

Required
Identify each of these 13 transactions as asset source (AS), asset use (AU), asset exchange (AE), or claims exchange (CE). Explain how each event affects assets, liabilities, equity, net income, and cash flow by placing a + for increase, − for decrease, or NA for not affected under each of the categories. In the Cash Flow column, indicate whether the item is an operating activity (OA), investing activity (IA), or financing activity (FA). The first event is recorded as an example.

Event No.	Type of Event	Assets	=	Liabilities	+	Common Stock	+	Retained Earnings	Net Income	Cash Flow
1	AS	+		NA		+		NA	NA	+ FA

PROBLEM 10–30B *Recording Transactions for Callable Bonds*

L.O. 5, 6

IHL Corp. issued $300,000 of 20-year, 10 percent, callable bonds on January 1, 2004, with interest payable annually on December 31. The bonds were issued at their face amount. The bonds are callable at 105. The fiscal year of the corporation ends December 31.

Required
a. Show the effect of the following events on the financial statements by recording the appropriate amounts in a horizontal statements model like the following one. In the Cash Flow column, indicate whether the item is an operating activity (OA), investing activity (IA), or financing activity (FA). Use NA if an element was not affected by the event.
   (1) Issued the bonds on January 1, 2004.
   (2) Paid interest due to bondholders on December 31, 2004.
   (3) On January 1, 2009, IHL Corp. called the bonds. Assume that all interim entries were correctly recorded.

Event No.	Assets	=	Liab.	+	Equity	Rev.	−	Exp.	=	Net Inc.	Cash Flow
1											

b. Prepare journal entries for the three events listed in Requirement *a*.

L.O. 5, 6   PROBLEM 10–31B *Effect of Debt Transactions on Financial Statements*

The three typical accounting events associated with borrowing money through a bond issue are:

1. Exchanging the bonds for cash on the day of issue.
2. Making cash payments for interest expense and recording amortization when applicable.
3. Repaying the principal at maturity.

Required

a. Assuming the bonds are issued at face value, show the effect of each of the three events on the financial statements, using a horizontal statements model like the following one. Use + for increase, − for decrease, and NA for not affected.

Event No.	Assets	=	Liab.	+	Equity	Rev.	−	Exp.	=	Net Inc.	Cash Flow
1											

b. Repeat the requirements in Requirement *a,* but assume instead that the bonds are issued at a discount.
c. Repeat the requirements in Requirement *a,* but assume instead that the bonds are issued at a premium.

L.O. 6, 8   PROBLEM 10–32B *Sale of Bonds at a Discount and Amortization Using the Effective Interest Method (Appendix)*

On January 1, 2004, Pond Corp. sold $500,000 of its own 8 percent, 10-year bonds. Interest is payable annually on December 31. The bonds were sold to yield an effective interest rate of 9 percent. Pond uses the effective interest rate method.

Required

a. Using the information in the appendix, calculate the selling price of the bonds.
b. Prepare the journal entry for the issuance of the bonds.
c. Prepare the journal entry for the amortization of the bond discount and the payment of the interest at December 31, 2004.
d. Calculate the amount of interest expense for 2005.

ANALYZE, THINK, COMMUNICATE

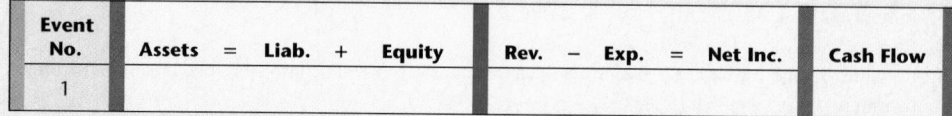

ATC 10–1   BUSINESS APPLICATIONS CASE *Understanding Real World Annual Reports*

Required—Part 1

Use the Topps Company's annual report in Appendix B to answer the following questions.

a. On its balance sheet Topps shows "Other liabilities" of $22,601,000. Does the company explain what these are? If so, what are they?
b. In the footnotes, Topps reveals that it entered into a credit agreement with two banks in 2000. What amount of credit is available to Topps under this agreement, and when does it expire?
c. What restrictions does the credit agreement place on Topps? Be specific.

Required—Part 2

Use the Harley-Davidson's annual report that came with this book to answer the following questions.

a. As of December 31, 2003, Harley-Davidson has $994,305,000 of "finance debt." How much of this is current debt and how much is long-term debt (see the footnotes)?
b. Specifically, what types of borrowings are included in this $994,305,000 of finance debt?
c. What is the range of interest rates that Harley-Davidson has to pay on its finance debt?

ATC 10–2   GROUP ASSIGNMENT *Missing Information*

The following three companies issued the following bonds:

1. Lot, Inc., issued $100,000 of 8 percent, five-year bonds at 102 ¼ on January 1, 2006. Interest is payable annually on December 31.
2. Max, Inc., issued $100,000 of 8 percent, five-year bonds at 98 on January 1, 2006. Interest is payable annually on December 31.

3. Par, Inc., issued $100,000 of 8 percent, five-year bonds at 104 on January 1, 2006. Interest is payable annually on December 31.

Required

a. Organize the class into three sections and divide each section into groups of three to five students. Assign each of the sections one of the companies.

Group Tasks

(1) Compute the following amounts for your company:
  (a) Cash proceeds from the bond issue.
  (b) Interest paid in 2006.
  (c) Interest expense for 2006.

(2) Prepare the liabilities section of the balance sheet as of December 31, 2006.

Class Discussion

b. Have a representative of each section put the liabilities section for its company on the board.

c. Is the amount of interest expense different for the three companies? Why or why not?

d. Is the amount of interest paid different for each of the companies? Why or why not?

e. Is the amount of total liabilities different for each of the companies? Why or why not?

REAL-WORLD CASE *Using Accounting Numbers to Assess Creditworthiness*

ATC 10–3

Standard & Poor's (S&P) and Moody's are two credit-rating services that evaluate the creditworthiness of various companies. Their "grading" systems are similar, but not exactly the same. S&P's grading scheme works as follows: AAA is the highest rating, followed by AA, then A, then BBB, and so on. For each grade, a "+" or "−" may also be used.

The following are selected financial data for four companies whose overall, long-term creditworthiness was rated by S&P. The companies, listed alphabetically, are:

Alliance Imaging, Inc. provides mobile imaging services to hospitals and other healthcare providers.
American Airlines, Inc. is one of the largest scheduled airlines in the United States.
3M Company develops, manufactures, and markets a wide variety of products for uses ranging from healthcare, to communications, to consumer products.
7-Eleven, Inc. operates, franchises or licenses over 24 000 convenience stores worldwide.

Dollar amounts are in thousands.

	Net Income	Cash Flow from Operations	Current Ratio	Debt-to-Assets Ratio	Times Interest Earned	Return-on-Assets Ratio
Alliance Imaging						
2002	$ 35,939	$ 138,960	1.78	1.06	2.3	5%
2001	10,530	96,364	1.42	1.12	1.3	2%
American Airlines						
2002	(3,495,000)	(1,379,000)	0.68	.97	(7.3)	(13%)
2001	(1,562,000)	380,000	0.90	.82	(9.0)	(5%)
3M						
2002	1,974,000	2,992,000	1.36	.61	38.6	13%
2001	1,430,000	3,078,000	1.40	.58	18.6	10%
7-Eleven						
2002	12,777	496,747	0.81	.95	2.4	0%
2001	83,720	278,235	0.80	.95	3.6	3%

Each company received a different credit rating by S&P. The grades awarded, as of June 9, 2003, in descending order, were AA, BBB, B+, and CCC.

Required

Determine which grade was assigned to each company. Write a memorandum explaining the rationale for your decisions.

BUSINESS APPLICATIONS CASE *Using Ratios to Make Comparisons*

ATC 10–4

The following accounting information pertains to On-Time Cleaners and Drive-Thru Laundry, Inc., at the end of 2001.

	On-Time Cleaners	Drive-Thru Laundry
Current assets	$ 30,000	$ 30,000
Total assets	530,000	530,000
Current liabilities	38,000	52,000
Total liabilities	330,000	450,000
Stockholders' equity	200,000	80,000
Interest expense	30,000	41,000
Income tax expense	50,500	46,000
Net income	76,500	70,000

Required

a. Compute the following ratios for each company: debt to assets, current, and times interest earned (EBIT must be computed). Identify the company with the greater financial risk.

b. For each company, compute the return on equity and return on assets ratios. Use EBIT instead of net income to compute the return on assets ratio. Identify the company that is managing its assets more effectively. Identify the company that is producing the higher return from the stockholders' perspective. Explain how one company was able to produce a higher return on equity than the other.

ATC 10–5   BUSINESS APPLICATIONS CASE *Determining the Effects of Financing Alternatives on Ratios*

Fenn Research Associates has the following account balances:

Current Assets	$200,000	Current Liabilities	$125,000
Noncurrent Assets	500,000	Noncurrent Liabilities	300,000
		Stockholders' Equity	275,000

The company wishes to raise $100,000 in cash and is considering two financing options. Either it can sell $100,000 of bonds payable, or it can issue additional common stock for $100,000. To help in the decision process, Fenn's management wants to determine the effects of each alternative on its current ratio and debt to assets ratio.

Required

a. Help the company's management by completing the following chart:

Ratio	Currently	If Bonds Are Issued	If Stock Is Issued
Current ratio			
Debt to assets ratio			

b. Assume that after the funds are invested, EBIT amounts to $50,000. Also assume that the company pays $10,000 in dividends or $10,000 in interest, depending on which source of financing is used. Based on a 30 percent tax rate, determine the amount of the increase in retained earnings under each financing option.

ATC 10–6   WRITING ASSIGNMENT *Debt Versus Equity Financing*

Mack Company plans to invest $50,000 in land that will produce annual rent revenue equal to 15 percent of the investment starting on January 1, 2003. The revenue will be collected in cash at the end of each year, starting December 31, 2003. Mack can obtain the cash necessary to purchase the land from two sources. Funds can be obtained by issuing $50,000 of 10 percent, five-year bonds at their face amount. Interest due on the bonds is payable on December 31 of each year with the first payment due on December 31, 2003. Alternatively, the $50,000 needed to invest in land can be obtained from equity financing. In this case, the stockholders (holders of the equity) will be paid a $5,000 annual distribution. Mack Company is in a 30 percent income tax bracket.

Required

a. Prepare an income statement and statement of cash flows for 2003 under the two alternative financing proposals.

b. Write a short memorandum explaining why one financing alternative provides more net income but less cash flow than the other.

ETHICAL DILEMMA *I Don't Want to Pay Taxes*

ATC 10–7

Dana Harbert recently started a very successful small business. Indeed, the business had grown so rapidly that she was no longer able to finance its operations by investing her own resources in the business. She needed additional capital but had no more of her own money to put into the business. A friend, Gene Watson, was willing to invest $100,000 in the business. Harbert estimated that with Watson's investment, the company would be able to increase revenue by $40,000. Furthermore, she believed that operating expenses would increase by only 10 percent. Harbert and Watson agree that Watson's investment should entitle him to receive a cash dividend equal to 20 percent of net income. A set of forecasted statements with and without Watson's investment is presented here. (Assume that all transactions involving revenue, expense, and dividends are cash transactions.)

Financial Statements		
	Forecast 1 Without Watson's Investment	**Forecast 2 With Watson's Investment**
Income Statement		
Revenue	$120,000	$160,000
Operating Expenses	(70,000)	(77,000)
Income before Interest and Taxes	50,000	83,000
Income Tax Expense (effective tax rate is 30%)	(15,000)	(24,900)
Net Income	$ 35,000	$ 58,100
Statement of Changes in Stockholders' Equity		
Beginning Retained Earnings	$ 15,000	$ 15,000
Plus: Net Income	35,000	58,100
Less: Dividend to Watson (20% of $58,100)	0	(11,620)
Ending Retained Earnings	$ 50,000	$ 61,480
Balance Sheets		
Assets (computations explained in following paragraph)	$400,000	$511,480
Liabilities	$ 0	$ 0
Equity		
Common Stock	350,000	450,000
Retained Earnings	50,000	61,480
Total Liabilities and Equity	$400,000	$511,480

The balance for assets in forecast 1 is computed as the beginning balance of $365,000 plus net income of $35,000. The balance for assets in forecast 2 is computed as the beginning balance of $365,000, plus the $100,000 cash investment, plus net income of $58,100, less the $11,620 dividend. Alternatively, total assets can be computed by determining the amount of total claims (total assets = total claims).

Harbert tells Watson that there would be a $3,486 tax advantage associated with debt financing. She says that if Watson is willing to become a creditor instead of an owner, she could pay him an additional $697.20 (that is, 20 percent of the tax advantage). Watson tells Harbert that he has no interest in participating in the management of the business, but Watson wants an ownership interest to guarantee that he will always receive 20 percent of the profits of the business. Harbert suggests that they execute a formal agreement in which Watson is paid 11.62 percent interest on his $100,000 loan to the business. This agreement will be used for income tax reporting. In addition, Harbert says that she is willing to establish a private agreement to write Watson a personal check for any additional amount necessary to make Watson's total return equal to 20 percent of all profits plus a $697.20 bonus for his part of the tax advantage. She tells Watson, "It's just like ownership. The only difference is that we call it debt for the Internal Revenue Service. If they want to have some silly rule that says if you call it debt, you get a tax break, then we are foolish if we don't call it debt. I will call it anything they want, just as long as I don't have to pay taxes on it."

Required

a. Construct a third set of forecasted financial statements (forecast 3) at 11.62 percent annual interest, assuming that Watson is treated as creditor (he loans the business $100,000).

b. Verify the tax advantage of debt financing by comparing the balances of the Retained Earnings account in forecast 2 and forecast 3.

c. If you were Watson, would you permit Harbert to classify the equity transaction as debt to provide a higher return to the business and to you?

d. Comment on the ethical implications of misnaming a financing activity for the sole purpose of reducing income taxes.

ATC 10–8  **EDGAR DATABASE** *Analyzing Long-Term Debt at Delta Air Lines*

Many companies have a form of debt called *capital leases.* A capital lease is created when a company agrees to rent an asset, such as equipment or a building, for such a long time that GAAP treats this lease as if the asset were purchased by using borrowed funds. Thus, a capital lease creates a liability for the company that acquired the leased asset because the company has promised to make payments to another company for several years in the future. If a company has any capital leases, it must disclose them in the footnotes to the financial statements and sometimes disclose them on a separate line in the liabilities section of the balance sheet.

Required

Using the most current 10-K available on EDGAR, answer the following questions about Delta Air Lines, Inc. Instructions for using EDGAR are in Appendix A.

a. What was Delta's debt to assets ratio?

b. How much interest expense did Delta incur?

c. What amount of liabilities did Delta have as a result of capital leases?

d. What percentage of Delta's long-term liabilities was the result of capital leases?

e. Many companies try to structure (design) leasing agreements so that their leases will *not* be classified as capital leases. Explain why a company such as Delta might want to avoid having capital leases.

ATC 10–9 **SPREADSHEET ASSIGNMENT** *Using Excel*

On January 1, 2001, Bainbridge Company borrowed $100,000 cash from a bank by issuing a 10-year, 9 percent note. The principal and interest are to be paid by making annual payments in the amount of $15,582. Payments are to be made December 31 of each year beginning December 31, 2001.

Required

a. Set up the spreadsheet as shown on the following page. Notice that Excel can be set up to calculate the loan payment. If you're unfamiliar with this, see the following Spreadsheet Tips section. The Beginning Principal Balance (B12) and Cash Payment (C12) can be referenced from the Loan Information section. The interest rate used to calculate Interest Expense (D12) can also be referenced from the Loan Information section.

b. Complete the spreadsheet for the 10 periods.

c. In Row 23, calculate totals for cash payments, interest expense, and applied to principal.

d. Consider how the amounts would differ if Bainbridge were to borrow the $100,000 at different interest rates and time periods. The results of the original data (option 1) have been entered in the following schedule. In the spreadsheet, delete 9 percent and 10 from cells B4 and B5, respectively. Enter the data for the second option (8 percent and 10 years) in cells B4 and B5. Enter the recomputed payment and total interest in the schedule for the second option. Continue the same process for options 3 through 9 by deleting the prior rate and number of periods in the spreadsheet and entering in the next option's data. The number of years scheduled (rows 12 through 21) will have to be shortened for the 7-year options and lengthened for the 13-year options.

	Option								
	1	**2**	**3**	**4**	**5**	**6**	**7**	**8**	**9**
Rate	9%	8%	10%	9%	8%	10%	9%	8%	10%
Years	10	10	10	7	7	7	13	13	13
Payment	15,582								
Total interest	55,820								

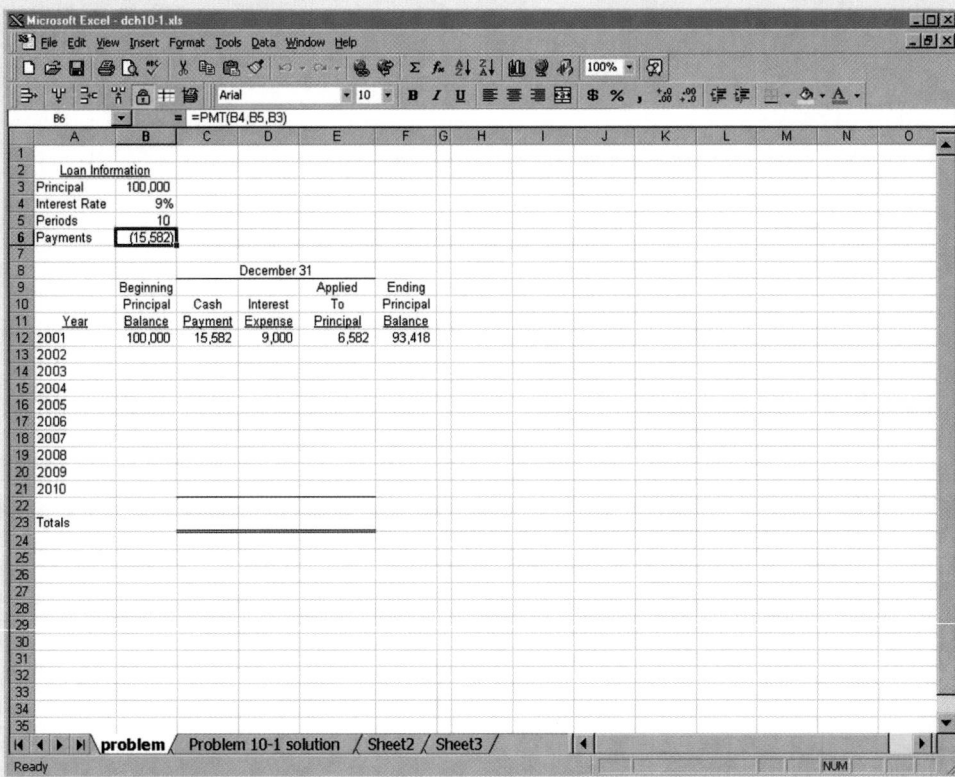

Spreadsheet Tips

1. Excel will calculate an installment loan payment. The interest rate (%), number of periods (nper), and amount borrowed or otherwise known as present value (PV) must be entered in the payment formula. The formula for the payment is =PMT(rate,nper,pv). The rate, number of periods, and amount borrowed (present value) may be entered as actual amounts or referenced to other cells. In the preceding spreadsheet, the payment formula can be either =PMT(9%,10,100000) or =PMT(B4,B5,B3). In our case, the latter is preferred so that variables can be altered in the spreadsheet without also having to rewrite the payment formula. Notice that the payment is a negative number.

2. Using positive numbers is preferred in the amortization schedule. The loan payment (cell B6) in the loan information section shows up as a negative number. Any reference to it in the amortization schedule should be preceded by a minus sign to convert it to a positive number. For example, the formula in cell C12 for the cash payment is =−B6.

3. Recall that to copy a fixed number, a $ sign must be positioned before the column letter and row number. The complete formula then for cell C12 is =−B6.

SPREADSHEET ANALYSIS *Mastering Excel*

ATC 10–10

Wise Company was started on January 1, 2001, when it issued 20-year, 10 percent, $200,000 face value bonds at a price of 90. Interest is payable annually at December 31 of each year. Wise immediately purchased land with the proceeds (cash received) from the bond issue. Wise leased the land for $27,000 cash per year. The lease revenue payments are due every December 31.

Required
Set up the following horizontal statements model on a blank spreadsheet. The SCF Activity column is for the classifications operating, financing, or investing.

a. Enter the effects of the 2001 transactions. Assume that both the interest and lease payments occurred on December 31. Notice that the entry for the lease has already been entered as an example. Calculate the ending balances.

b. Enter the effects of the 2002 transactions. Assume that both the interest and lease payments occurred on December 31. Calculate the ending balances.

c. Enter the effects of the 2003 transactions. Assume that both the interest and lease payments occurred on December 31. Calculate the ending balances.

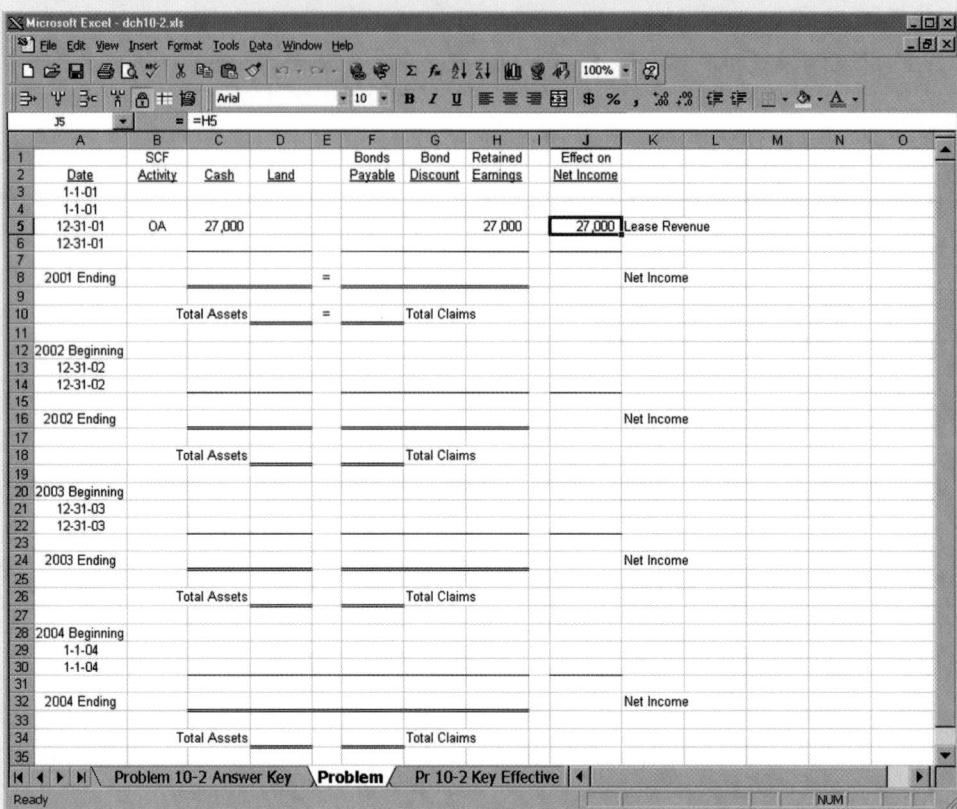

d. On January 1, 2004, Wise Company sold the land for $190,000 cash. Immediately after the sale of the land, Wise repurchased its bond at a price of 93. Assume that no other accounting events occurred during 2004. Enter the effects of the 2004 transactions. Calculate the ending balances.

COMPREHENSIVE PROBLEM

The account balances of Pacilio Security Systems Sales and Service as of January 1, 2010, was:

Cash	$227,386
Petty Cash	100
Accounts Receivable	51,170
Allowance for Doubtful Accounts	2,074
Supplies	180
Inventory—Standard Alarms (12 @ $280)	3,360
Inventory—Deluxe Alarms (14 @ $590)	8,260
Van	9,200
Equipment	12,000
Building	72,000
Land	36,000
Accumulated Depreciation	14,000
Warranties Payable	2,827
Notes Payable	38,000
Common Stock	50,000
Retained Earnings	312,755

During 2010, Pacilio Security Systems Sales and Service experienced the following transactions:

1. On January 2, Pacilio refinanced its loan on the building by issuing a new 10-year amortized loan at 5 percent. The amount refinanced was the $38,000 balance of the old notes payable. Pacilio will make annual payments of $4,921 each year.

2. Also on January 2, 2010, Pacilio issued bonds for $80,000 of 4 percent 10-year bonds. The bonds were issued at 98. Interest is payable annually on December 31.
3. On February 1, Pacilio purchased the assets of Safety Alarm System for $110,000 cash. The assets obtained were:

Accounts Receivable	$33,500
Inventory (130 standard alarm systems)	35,750
Goodwill	40,750

   Pacilio received 320 Safety Alarm monitoring accounts.
4. Purchased $425 of supplies for cash.
5. On May 1, 2010, Pacilio replenished its petty cash fund. The fund had $18 cash and receipts for $26 office supplies and $56 for cutting the grass.
6. Paid cash to purchase 80 standard alarm systems for $285 each and 40 deluxe alarm systems at $600 each.
7. Sold on account 200 standard alarm systems for $120,000 and 45 deluxe alarm systems for $45,000 during the year. (Be sure to record cost of goods sold using the FIFO cost flow method.)
8. Billed $154,000 for monitoring services for the year. Of this amount, $40,000 was credit card sales. The credit card company charges a 4 percent service fee.
9. Collected the amount due from the credit card company.
10. Paid $1,050 to repair deluxe alarm systems that were still under warranty.
11. After numerous attempts to collect from customers, wrote off $1,875 of bad accounts.
12. Collected $305,000 of accounts receivable for the year.
13. Paid $9,000 advertising expense for the year.
14. Paid $6,000 utilities expense during the year.
15. Paid installers $95,000 for salaries for the year.
16. Paid officers $90,000 for salaries for the year.
17. Paid bond interest expense and amortized discount.
18. Paid annual installment on amortized note.

Adjustments
19. There were $210 of office supplies on hand at the end of the year.
20. Recognized warranty expense for the year. Pacilio estimates warranty expense at about 2 percent of its deluxe model alarm sales.
21. Recognized bad debt expense for the year. Bad debt expense is estimated to be 1 percent of sales on account.
22. Recognized depreciation expense for the year. (See chapter 9 problem)

Required
a. Record the above transactions in general journal form. Pacilio uses FIFO cost flow assumption.
b. Post the transactions to the T-accounts.
c. Prepare a trial balance.
d. Prepare an income statement, statement of changes in stockholders' equity, balance sheet, and statement of cash flows.
e. Close the temporary accounts to retained earnings.
f. Post the closing entries to the T-accounts and prepare an after-closing trial balance.

CHAPTER eleven

ACCOUNTING FOR EQUITY TRANSACTIONS

LEARNING *objectives*

After you have mastered the material in this chapter, you will be able to:

1 Identify the primary characteristics of sole proprietorships, partnerships, and corporations.

2 Analyze financial statements to identify the different types of business organizations.

3 Explain the characteristics of major types of stock issued by corporations.

4 Explain how to account for different types of stock issued by corporations.

5 Show how treasury stock transactions affect a company's financial statements.

6 Explain the effects of declaring and paying cash dividends on a company's financial statements.

7 Explain the effects of stock dividends and stock splits on a company's financial statements.

8 Show how the appropriation of retained earnings affects financial statements.

9 Explain some uses of accounting information in making stock investment decisions.

10 Explain accounting for not-for-profit entities and governmental organizations. (Appendix)

THE *curious* ACCOUNTANT

Imagine your rich uncle rewarded you for doing well in your first accounting course by giving you $15,000 to invest in the stock of one company. After reviewing many recent annual reports, you narrowed your choice to two companies with the following characteristics:

Mystery Company A: This company's stock has only been trading publicly since May 2003. In the three years prior to going public, it had net losses totaling about $16 million. This stock is selling for about $22 per share, so you can buy about 680 shares. A friend told you it was a "sure winner," especially at its current price, since it is just starting out and has a lot of growth potential.

Mystery Company B: This company has existed since 1923 and been profitable most years. In the most recent five years, its net earnings totaled over $5 *billion*, and it paid dividends of over $1.7 *billion*. This stock is selling for about $21 per share, so you can buy 715 shares of it. Your friend said "you would have to be goofy to buy this stock."

The names of the real-world companies described above will be disclosed later. Based on the information provided, which company's stock would you buy? (Answer on page 516.)

CHAPTER *opening*

You want to start a business. How should you structure it? Should it be a sole proprietorship, partnership, or corporation? Each form of business structure presents advantages and disadvantages. For example, a sole proprietorship allows maximum independence and control while partnerships and corporations allow individuals to pool resources and talents with other people. This chapter discusses these and other features of the three primary forms of business structure.

Topic Tackler
PLUS

11–1

LO1 Identify the primary characteristics of sole proprietorships, partnerships, and corporations.

Formation of Business Organizations
Ownership Agreements

Sole proprietorships are owned by a single individual who is responsible for making business and profit distribution decisions. If you want to be the absolute master of your destiny, you should organize your business as a proprietorship. Establishing a sole proprietorship is usually as simple as obtaining a business license from local government authorities. Usually no legal ownership agreement is required.

Partnerships allow persons to share their talents, capital, and the risks and rewards of business ownership. Since two or more individuals share ownership, partnerships require clear agreements about how authority, risks, and profits will be shared. Prudent partners minimize misunderstandings by hiring attorneys to prepare a **partnership agreement** which defines the responsibilities of each partner and describes how income or losses will be divided. Since the measurement of income affects the distribution of profits, partnerships frequently hire accountants to ensure that records are maintained in accordance with generally accepted accounting principles (GAAP). Partnerships (and sole proprietorships) also may need professional advice to deal with tax issues.

A **corporation** is a separate legal entity created by the authority of a state government. The paperwork to start a corporation is complex. For most laypersons, engaging professional attorneys and accountants to assist with the paperwork is usually well worth the fees charged.

Each state has separate laws governing establishing corporations. Many states follow the standard provisions of the Model Business Corporation Act. All states require the initial application to include **articles of incorporation** which normally include the following information: (1) the corporation's name and proposed date of incorporation; (2) the purpose of the corporation; (3) the location of the business and its expected life (which can be *perpetuity,* meaning *endless*); (4) provisions for capital stock; and (5) the names and addresses of the members of the first board of directors, the individuals with the ultimate authority for operating the business. If the articles are in order, the state establishes the legal existence of the corporation by issuing a charter of incorporation. The charter and the articles are public documents.

Advantages and Disadvantages of Different Forms of Business Organization

LO1 Identify the primary characteristics of sole proprietorships, partnerships, and corporations.

Each form of business organization presents a different combination of advantages and disadvantages. Persons wanting to start a business or invest in one should consider the characteristics of each type of business structure.

Regulation

Few laws specifically affect the operations of proprietorships and partnerships. Corporations, however, are usually heavily regulated. The extent of government regulation depends on the size and distribution of a company's ownership interests. Ownership interests in corporations are normally evidenced by **stock certificates.**

Edward Nusbaum, CEO of Grant Thornton, a Chicago accounting firm, believes that "Sarbanes-Oxley is most likely creating the desired effect in making businesses realize that very strong responsibilities come with being a public company." However, a recent study conducted by Grant Thornton indicates that the cost of regulatory compliance is so significant that many smaller companies are taking their firms' stock off the exchanges. More specifically, the study found that the number of public companies making the switch to private ownership is up 30 percent since the Sarbanes-Oxley Act went into effect July 30, 2002. A different study by Thomson Financial found similar results. The Thomson study found 60 public companies went private in the first nine months of 2003, up from 49 during the same period in 2002 and nearly double the 32 firms that went private in 2001. Clearly, the expense of regulatory compliance is a distinct disadvantage of the corporate form of business. In contrast, ease of formation and light regulation are clear advantages of proprietorships and, to a lesser extent, partnerships.

Ownership of corporations can be transferred from one individual to another through exchanging stock certificates. As long as the exchanges (buying and selling of shares of stock, often called *trading*) are limited to transactions between individuals, a company is defined as a **closely held corporation.** However, once a corporation reaches a certain size, it may list its stock on a stock exchange such as the New York Stock Exchange or the American Stock Exchange. Trading on a stock exchange is limited to the stockbrokers who are members of the exchange. These brokers represent buyers and sellers who are willing to pay the brokers commissions for exchanging stock certificates on their behalf. Although closely held corporations are relatively free from government regulation, companies whose stock is publicly traded on the exchanges by brokers are subject to extensive regulation.

The extensive regulation of trading on stock exchanges began in the 1930s. The stock market crash of 1929 and the subsequent Great Depression led Congress to the pass the **Securities Act of 1933** and the **Securities Exchange Act of 1934** to regulate issuing stock and to govern the exchanges. The 1934 act also created the Securities and Exchange Commission (SEC) to enforce the securities laws. Congress gave the SEC legal authority to establish accounting principles for corporations that are registered on the exchanges. However, the SEC has generally deferred its rule-making authority to private sector accounting bodies such as the Financial Accounting Standards Board (FASB), effectively allowing the accounting profession to regulate itself.

A number of high-profile business failures around the turn of the century raised questions about the effectiveness of self-regulation and the usefulness of audits to protect the public. The **Sarbanes-Oxley Act of 2002** was adopted to address these concerns. The act creates a five-member Public Company Accounting Oversight Board (PCAOB) with the authority to set and enforce auditing, attestation, quality control, and ethics standards for auditors of public companies. The PCAOB is empowered to impose disciplinary and remedial sanctions for violations of its rules, securities laws, and professional auditing and accounting standards. Public corporations operate in a complex regulatory environment that requires the services of attorneys and professional accountants.

Double Taxation

Corporations pay income taxes on their earnings and then owners pay income taxes on distributions (dividends) received from corporations. As a result, distributed corporate profits are taxed twice—first when income is reported on the corporation's income tax return and a second time when distributions are reported on individual owners' tax returns. This phenomenon is commonly called **double taxation** and is a significant disadvantage of the corporate form of business organization.

To illustrate, assume Glide Corporation earns pretax income of $100,000. Glide is in a 30 percent tax bracket. The corporation itself will pay income tax of $30,000 ($100,000 × 0.30). If the corporation distributes the after-tax income of $70,000 ($100,000 − $30,000) to individual stockholders in 15 percent tax brackets,[1] the $70,000 dividend will be reported on the individual tax returns, requiring tax payments of $10,500 ($70,000 × .15). Total income tax of $40,500 ($30,000 + $10,500) is due on $100,000 of earned income. In contrast, consider a proprietorship that is owned by an individual in a 30 percent tax bracket. If the proprietorship earns and distributes $100,000 profit, the total tax would be only $30,000 ($100,000 × .30).

Double taxation can be a burden for small companies. To reduce that burden, tax laws permit small closely held corporations to elect "S Corporation" status. S Corporations are taxed as proprietorships or partnerships. Also, many states have recently enacted laws permitting the formation of **limited liability companies (LLCs)** which offer many of the benefits of corporate ownership yet are in general taxed as partnerships. Since proprietorships and partnerships are not separate legal entities, company earnings are taxable to the owners rather than the company itself.

Limited Liability

Given the disadvantages of increased regulation and double taxation, why would anyone choose the corporate form of business structure over a partnership or proprietorship? A major reason is that the corporate form limits an investor's potential liability as an owner of a business venture. Because a corporation is legally separate from its owners, creditors cannot claim owners' personal assets as payment for the company's debts. Also, plaintiffs must sue the corporation, not its owners. The most that owners of a corporation can lose is the amount they have invested in the company (the value of the company's stock).

Unlike corporate stockholders, the owners of proprietorships and partnerships are *personally liable* for actions they take in the name of their companies. In fact, partners are responsible not only for their own actions but also for those taken by any other partner on behalf of the partnership. The benefit of **limited liability** is one of the most significant reasons the corporate form of business organization is so popular.

---

[1]As a result of the Jobs and Growth Tax Relief Reconciliation Act (JGTRRA) of 2003, dividends received in tax years after 2002 are taxed at a maximum rate of 15 percent for most taxpayers. Lower income individuals pay a 5 percent tax on dividends received on December 31, 2007, or earlier. This rate falls to zero in 2008. The provisions of JGTRRA are set to expire on December 31, 2008.

Continuity

Unlike partnerships or proprietorships, which terminate with the departure of their owners, a corporation's life continues when a shareholder dies or sells his or her stock. Because of **continuity** of existence, many corporations formed in the 1800s still thrive today.

Transferability of Ownership

The **transferability** of corporate ownership is easy. An investor simply buys or sells stock to acquire or give up an ownership interest in a corporation. Hundreds of millions of shares of stock are bought and sold on the major stock exchanges each day.

Transferring the ownership of proprietorships is much more difficult. To sell an ownership interest in a proprietorship, the proprietor must find someone willing to purchase the entire business. Since most proprietors also run their businesses, transferring ownership also requires transferring management responsibilities. Consider the difference in selling $1 million of Exxon stock versus selling a locally owned gas station. The stock could be sold on the New York Stock Exchange within minutes. In contrast, it could take years to find a buyer who is financially capable of and interested in owning and operating a gas station.

Transferring ownership in partnerships can also be difficult. As with proprietorships, ownership transfers may require a new partner to make a significant investment and accept management responsibilities in the business. Further, a new partner must accept and be accepted by the other partners. Personality conflicts and differences in management style can cause problems in transferring ownership interests in partnerships.

Management Structure

Partnerships and proprietorships are usually managed by their owners. Corporations, in contrast, have three tiers of management authority. The *owners* (**stockholders**) represent the highest level of organizational authority. The stockholders *elect* a **board of directors** to oversee company operations. The directors then *hire* professional executives to manage the company on a daily basis. Since large corporations can offer high salaries and challenging career opportunities, they can often attract superior managerial talent.

While the management structure used by corporations is generally effective, it sometimes complicates dismissing incompetent managers. The chief executive officer (CEO) is usually a member of the board of directors and is frequently influential in choosing other board members. The CEO is also in a position to reward loyal board members. As a result, board members may be reluctant to fire the CEO or other top executives even if the individuals are performing poorly. Corporations operating under such conditions are said to be experiencing **entrenched management.**

Ability to Raise Capital

Because corporations can have millions of owners (shareholders), they have the opportunity to raise huge amounts of capital. Few individuals have the financial means to build and operate a telecommunications network such as AT&T or a marketing distribution system such as Wal-Mart. However, by pooling the resources of millions of owners through public stock and bond offerings, corporations generate the billions of dollars of capital needed for such massive investments. In contrast, the capital resources of proprietorships and partnerships are limited to a relatively small number of private owners. Although proprietorships and partnerships can also obtain resources by borrowing, the amount creditors are willing to lend them is usually limited by the size of the owners' net worth.

Appearance of Capital Structure in Financial Statements

LO2 Analyze financial statements to identify the different types of business organizations.

The ownership interest (equity) in a business is composed of two elements: (1) owner/investor contributions and (2) retained earnings. The way these two elements are reported in the financial statements differs for each type of business structure (proprietorship, partnership, or corporation).

Presentation of Equity in Proprietorships

Owner contributions and retained earnings are combined in a single Capital account on the balance sheets of proprietorships. To illustrate, assume that Worthington Sole Proprietorship was started on January 1, 2005, when it acquired a $5,000 capital contribution from its owner, Phil Worthington. During the first year of operation, the company generated $4,000 of cash revenues, incurred $2,500 of cash expenses, and distributed $1,000 cash to the owner. Exhibit 11–1 displays 2005 financial statements for Worthington's company. Note on the *capital statement* that distributions are called **withdrawals.** Verify that the $5,500 balance in the Capital account on the balance sheet includes the $5,000 owner contribution and the retained earnings of $500 ($1,500 net income − $1,000 withdrawal).

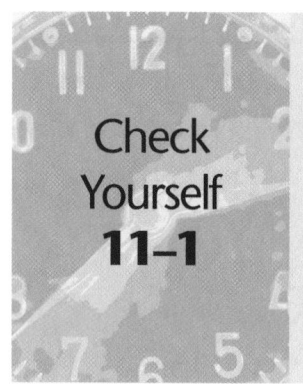

Check Yourself 11-1

Weiss Company was started on January 1, 2004, when it acquired $50,000 cash from its owners. During 2004 the company earned $72,000 of net income. Explain how the equity section of Weiss's December 31, 2004, balance sheet would differ if the company were a proprietorship versus a corporation.

Answer *Proprietorship* records combine capital acquisitions from the owner and earnings from operating the business in a single capital account. In contrast, *corporation* records separate capital acquisitions from the owners and earnings from operating the business. If Weiss were a proprietorship, the equity section of the year-end balance sheet would report a single capital component of $122,000. If Weiss were a corporation, the equity section would report two separate equity components, most likely common stock of $50,000 and retained earnings of $72,000.

Presentation of Equity in Partnerships

The financial statement format for reporting partnership equity is similar to that used for proprietorships. Contributed capital and retained earnings are combined. However, a separate capital account is maintained for each partner in the business to reflect each partner's ownership interest.

To illustrate, assume that Sara Slater and Jill Johnson formed a partnership on January 1, 2006. The partnership acquired $2,000 of capital from Slater and $4,000 from Johnson. The

---

Exhibit 11–1

WORTHINGTON SOLE PROPRIETORSHIP
Financial Statements
As of December 31, 2005

Income Statement		Capital Statement		Balance Sheet	
Revenue	$4,000	Beginning Capital Balance	$ 0	Assets	
Expenses	2,500	Plus: Investment by Owner	5,000	Cash	$5,500
Net Income	$1,500	Plus: Net Income	1,500		
		Less: Withdrawal by Owner	(1,000)	Equity	
				Worthington, Capital	$5,500
		Ending Capital Balance	$5,500		

Exhibit 11–2

SLATER AND JOHNSON PARTNERSHIP
Financial Statements
As of December 31, 2006

Income Statement		Capital Statement		Balance Sheet	
Revenue	$5,000	Beginning Capital Balance	$ 0	Assets	
Expenses	3,000	Plus: Investment by Owners	6,000	Cash	$7,400
Net Income	$2,000	Plus: Net Income	2,000	Equity	
		Less: Withdrawal by Owners	(600)	Slater, Capital	$2,700
				Johnson, Capital	4,700
		Ending Capital Balance	$7,400	Total Capital	$7,400

partnership agreement called for each partner to receive an annual distribution equal to 10 percent of her capital contribution. Any further earnings were to be retained in the business and divided equally between the partners. During 2006, the company earned $5,000 of cash revenue and incurred $3,000 of cash expenses, for net income of $2,000 ($5,000 − $3,000). As specified by the partnership agreement, Slater received a $200 ($2,000 × 0.10) cash withdrawal and Johnson received $400 ($4,000 × 0.10). The remaining $1,400 ($2,000 − $200 − $400) of income was retained in the business and divided equally, adding $700 to each partner's capital account.

Exhibit 11–2 displays financial statements for the Slater and Johnson partnership. Again, note that distributions are called *withdrawals.* Also find on the balance sheet a *separate capital account* for each partner. Each capital account includes the amount of the partner's contributed capital plus her proportionate share of the retained earnings.

Presentation of Equity in Corporations

Corporations have more complex capital structures than proprietorships and partnerships. Explanations of some of the more common features of corporate capital structures and transactions follow.

Characteristics of Capital Stock

Stock issued by corporations may have a variety of different characteristics. For example, a company may issue different classes of stock that grant owners different rights and privileges. Also, the number of shares a corporation can legally issue may differ from the number it actually has issued. Further, a corporation can even buy back its stock. Finally, a corporation may assign different values to the stock it issues. The accounting treatment for corporate equity transactions is discussed in the next section of the text.

Par Value

Many states require assigning a **par value** to stock. Historically, par value represented the maximum liability of the investors. Par value multiplied by the number of shares of stock issued represents the minimum amount of assets that must be retained in the company as protection for creditors. This amount is known as **legal capital.** To ensure that the amount of legal capital is maintained in a corporation, many states require that purchasers pay at least the par value for a share of stock initially purchased from a corporation. To minimize the amount of assets that owners must maintain in the business, many corporations issue stock with very low par values, often $1 or less. Therefore, *legal capital* as defined by par value has come to have very little relevance to investors or creditors. As a result, many states allow corporations to issue no-par stock.

Topic Tackler
PLUS
11–2

LO3 Explain the characteristics of major types of stock issued by corporations.

Stated Value

No-par stock may have a stated value. Like par value, **stated value** is an arbitrary amount assigned by the board of directors to the stock. It also has little relevance to investors and creditors. Stock with a par value and stock with a stated value are accounted for exactly the same way. When stock has no par or stated value, accounting for it is slightly different. These accounting differences are illustrated later in this chapter.

Other Valuation Terminology

The price an investor must pay to purchase a share of stock is the **market value.** The sales price of a share of stock may be more or less than the par value. Another term analysts frequently associate with stock is *book value.* **Book value per share** is calculated by dividing total stockholders' equity (assets − liabilities) by the number of shares of stock owned by investors. Book value per share differs from market value per share because equity is measured in historical dollars and market value reflects investors' estimates of a company's current value.

Stock: Authorized, Issued, and Outstanding

As part of the regulatory function, states approve the maximum number of shares of stock corporations are legally permitted to issue. This maximum number is called **authorized stock.** Authorized stock that has been sold to the public is called **issued stock.** When a corporation buys back some of its issued stock from the public, the repurchased stock is called **treasury stock.** Treasury stock is still considered to be issued stock, but it is no longer outstanding.

focus on INTERNATIONAL ISSUES

Who Provides the Financing?

The accounting rules in a country are affected by who provides financing to businesses in that country. Equity (versus debt) financing is a large source of financing for most businesses in the United States. The stock (equity ownership) of most large U.S. companies is said to be *widely held.* This means that many different institutional investors (e.g., pension funds) and individuals own stock. At the other extreme is a country in which the government owns most industries. In between might be a country in which large banks provide a major portion of business financing, such as Japan or Germany.

It is well beyond the scope of this course to explain specifically how a country's GAAP are affected by who provides the financing of the country's major industries. Nevertheless, a businessperson should be aware that the source of a company's financing affects the financial reporting that it must do. Do not assume that business practices or accounting rules in other countries are like those in the United States.

Outstanding stock (total issued stock minus treasury stock) is stock owned by investors outside the corporation. For example, assume a company that is authorized to issue 150 shares of stock issues 100 shares to investors, and then buys back 20 shares of treasury stock. There are 150 shares authorized, 100 shares issued, and 80 shares outstanding.

Classes of Stock

The corporate charter defines the number of shares of stock authorized, the par value or stated value (if any), and the classes of stock that a corporation can issue. Most stock issued is either *common* or *preferred.*

Common Stock

All corporations issue **common stock.** Common stockholders bear the highest risk of losing their investment if a company is forced to liquidate. On the other hand, they reap the greatest rewards when a corporation prospers. Common stockholders generally enjoy several rights, including these: (1) the right to buy and sell stock, (2) the right to share in the distribution of profits, (3) the right to share in the distribution of corporate assets in the case of liquidation, (4) the right to vote on significant matters that affect the corporate charter, and (5) the right to participate in the election of directors.

Preferred Stock

Many corporations issue **preferred stock** in addition to common stock. Holders of preferred stock receive certain privileges relative to holders of common stock. In exchange for special privileges in some areas, preferred stockholders give up rights in other areas. Preferred stockholders usually have no voting rights and the amount of their dividends is usually limited. Preferences granted to preferred stockholders include the following:

1. *Preference as to assets.* Preferred stock often has a liquidation value. In case of bankruptcy, preferred stockholders must be paid the liquidation value before any assets are distributed to common stockholders. However, preferred stockholder claims still fall behind creditor claims.
2. *Preference as to dividends.* Preferred shareholders are frequently guaranteed the right to receive dividends before common stockholders. The amount of the preferred dividend is normally stated on the stock certificate. It may be stated as a dollar value (say, $5) per share or as a percentage of the par value. Most preferred stock has **cumulative dividends,** meaning that if a corporation is unable to pay the preferred dividend in any year, the dividend is not lost but begins to accumulate. Cumulative dividends that have not been paid are called **dividends in arrears.** When a company pays dividends, any preferred stock arrearages must be paid before any other dividends are paid. Noncumulative preferred stock is not often issued because preferred stock is much less attractive if missed dividends do not accumulate.

To illustrate the effects of preferred dividends, consider Dillion, Incorporated, which has the following shares of stock outstanding:

```
Preferred stock, 4%, $10 par, 10,000 shares
Common stock, $10 par, 20,000 shares
```

Assume the preferred stock dividend has not been paid for two years. If Dillion pays $22,000 in dividends, how much will each class of stock receive? It depends on whether the preferred stock is cumulative.

Allocation of Distribution for Cumulative Preferred Stock		
	To Preferred	**To Common**
Dividends in arrears	$ 8,000	$ 0
Current year's dividends	4,000	10,000
Total distribution	$12,000	$10,000

Allocation of Distribution for Noncumulative Preferred Stock		
	To Preferred	**To Common**
Dividends in arrears	$ 0	$ 0
Current year's dividends	4,000	18,000
Total distribution	$ 4,000	$18,000

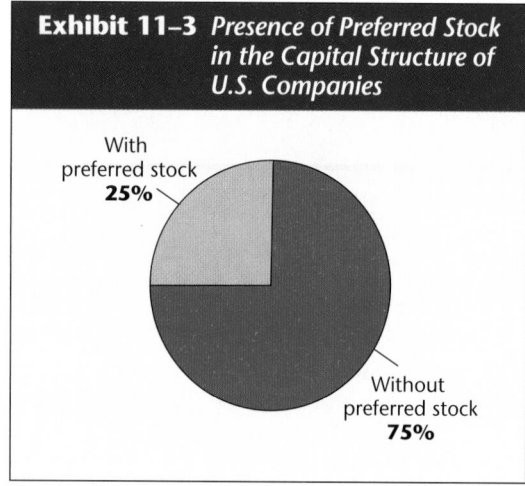

Exhibit 11–3 *Presence of Preferred Stock in the Capital Structure of U.S. Companies*

With preferred stock **25%**

Without preferred stock **75%**

Data source: AICPA, *Accounting Trends and Techniques,* 2002.

The total annual dividend on the preferred stock is $4,000 (0.04 × $10 par × 10,000 shares). If the preferred stock is cumulative, the $8,000 in arrears must be paid first. Then $4,000 for the current year's dividend is paid next. The remaining $10,000 goes to common stockholders. If the preferred stock is noncumulative, the $8,000 of dividends from past periods is ignored. This year's $4,000 preferred dividend is paid first, with the remaining $18,000 going to common.

Other features of preferred stock may include the right to participate in distributions beyond the established amount of the preferred dividend, the right to convert preferred stock to common stock or to bonds, and the potential for having the preferred stock called (repurchased) by the corporation. Detailed discussion of these topics is left to more advanced courses. Exhibit 11–3 indicates that roughly 25 percent of U.S. companies have preferred shares outstanding.

Accounting for Stock Transactions on the Day of Issue

LO4 Explain how to account for different types of stock issued by corporations.

The issue of stock with a par or stated value is treated differently than no-par stock. For stock with either a par or stated value, the total amount acquired from the owners is divided between two separate equity accounts. The amount of the par or stated value is recorded in the stock account. Any amount received above the par or stated value is recorded in an account called **Paid-in Capital in Excess of Par** (or **Stated**) **Value.**

Issuing Par Value Stock

To illustrate the issue of common stock with a par value, assume that Nelson, Incorporated is authorized to issue 250 shares of common stock. During 2005, Nelson issued 100 shares of $10 par common stock for $22 per share. The event increases assets and stockholders' equity by $2,200 ($22 × 100 shares). The increase in stockholders' equity is divided into two parts, $1,000 of par value ($10 per share × 100 shares) and $1,200 ($2,200 − $1,000) received in excess of par value. The income statement is not affected. The $2,200 cash inflow is reported in the financing activities section of the statement of cash flows. The effects on the financial statements and the journal entry to record the event follow:

Assets	=	Liab.	+		Equity			Rev.	−	Exp.	=	Net Inc.	Cash Flow
Cash	=	Liab.	+	C. Stk.	+	Paid-in-Excess							
2,200	=	NA	+	1,000	+	1,200		NA	−	NA	=	NA	2,200 FA

Account Title	Debit	Credit
Cash	2,200	
Common Stock, $10 Par Value		1,000
Paid-in Capital in Excess of Par Value—Common		1,200

The *legal capital* of the corporation is $1,000, the total par value of the issued common stock. The number of shares issued can be easily verified by dividing the total amount in the common stock account by the par value ($1,000 ÷ $10 = 100 shares).

Stock Classification

Assume Nelson, Incorporated obtains authorization to issue 400 shares of Class B, $20 par value common stock. The company issues 150 shares of this stock at $25 per share. The event increases assets and stockholders' equity by $3,750 ($25 × 150 shares). The increase in stockholders' equity is divided into two parts, $3,000 of par value ($20 per share × 150 shares) and $750 ($3,750 − $3,000) received in excess of par value. The income statement is not affected. The $3,750 cash inflow is reported in the financing activities section of the statement of cash flows. The effects on the financial statements and the journal entry to record the event follow:

Assets	=	Liab.	+		Equity			Rev.	−	Exp.	=	Net Inc.	Cash Flow
Cash	=	Liab.	+	C. Stk.	+	Paid-in-Excess							
3,750	=	NA	+	3,000	+	750		NA	−	NA	=	NA	3,750 FA

Account Title	Debit	Credit
Cash	3,750	
Common Stock, Class B, $20 Par Value		3,000
Paid-in Capital in Excess of Par Value—Class B Common		750

As the preceding event suggests, companies can issue numerous classes of common stock. The specific rights and privileges for each class are described in the individual stock certificates.

Stock Issued at Stated Value

Assume Nelson is authorized to issue 300 shares of a third class of stock, 7 percent cumulative preferred stock with a stated value of $10 per share. Nelson issued 100 shares of the preferred stock at a price of $22 per share. The effect on the financial statements is identical to that described for the issue of the $10 par value common stock. The journal entry differs only to reflect the name of the different class of stock.

Assets	=	Liab.	+		Equity			Rev.	−	Exp.	=	Net Inc.	Cash Flow
Cash	=	Liab.	+	P. Stk.	+	Paid-in-Excess							
2,200	=	NA	+	1,000	+	1,200		NA	−	NA	=	NA	2,200 FA

Account Title	Debit	Credit
Cash	2,200	
Preferred Stock, $10 Stated Value, 7% cumulative		1,000
Paid-in Capital in Excess of Stated Value—Preferred		1,200

Stock Issued with No Par Value

Assume that Nelson, Incorporated is authorized to issue 150 shares of a fourth class of stock. This stock is no-par common stock. Nelson issues 100 shares of this no-par stock at $22 per share. The entire amount received ($22 × 100 = $2,200) is recorded in the stock account. The effects on the financial statements and the journal entry to record the event follow:

Assets	=	Liab.	+		Equity		Rev.	−	Exp.	=	Net Inc.	Cash Flow
Cash	=	Liab.	+	C. Stk.	+	Paid-in-Excess						
2,200	=	NA	+	2,200	+	NA	NA	−	NA	=	NA	2,200 FA

Account Title	Debit	Credit
Cash	2,200	
Common Stock, No Par		2,200

Financial Statement Presentation

Exhibit 11–4 displays Nelson, Incorporated's balance sheet after the four stock issuances described above. The exhibit assumes that Nelson earned and retained $5,000 of cash income during 2005. The stock accounts are presented first, followed by the paid-in capital in excess accounts. A wide variety of reporting formats is used in practice. For example, another popular format is to group accounts by stock class, with the paid-in capital in excess accounts listed with their associated stock accounts. Alternatively, many companies combine the different classes of stock into a single amount and provide the detailed information in footnotes to the financial statements.

Exhibit 11–4

NELSON, INCORPORATED
Balance Sheet
As of December 31, 2005

Assets	
Cash	$15,350
Stockholders' Equity	
Preferred Stock, $10 Stated Value, 7% cumulative,	
300 shares authorized, 100 issued and outstanding	$ 1,000
Common Stock, $10 Par Value, 250 shares authorized,	
100 issued and outstanding	1,000
Common Stock, Class B, $20 Par Value, 400 shares	
authorized, 150 issued and outstanding	3,000
Common Stock, No Par, 150 shares authorized,	
100 issued and outstanding	2,200
Paid-in Capital in Excess of Stated Value—Preferred	1,200
Paid-in Capital in Excess of Par—Common	1,200
Paid-in Capital in Excess of Par—Class B Common	750
Total Paid-in Capital	10,350
Retained Earnings	5,000
Total Stockholders' Equity	$15,350

Stockholders' Equity Transactions after the Day of Issue

LO5 Show how treasury stock transactions affect a company's financial statements.

Treasury Stock

When a company buys its own stock, the stock purchased is called *treasury stock*. Why would a company buy its own stock? Common reasons include (1) to have stock available to give employees pursuant to stock option plans, (2) to accumulate stock in preparation for a merger or business combination, (3) to reduce the number of shares outstanding in order to increase earnings per share, (4) to keep the price of the stock high when it appears to be falling, and (5) to avoid a hostile takeover (removing shares from the open market reduces the opportunity for outsiders to obtain enough voting shares to gain control of the company).

Conceptually, purchasing treasury stock is the reverse of issuing stock. When a business issues stock, the assets and equity of the business increase. When a business buys treasury stock, the assets and equity of the business decrease. To illustrate, return to the Nelson, Incorporated example. Assume that in 2006 Nelson paid $20 per share to buy back 50 shares of the $10 par value common stock that it originally issued at $22 per share. The purchase of treasury stock is an asset use transaction. Assets and stockholders' equity decrease by the cost of the purchase ($20 × 50 shares = $1,000). The income statement is not affected. The cash outflow is reported in the financing activities section of the statement of cash flows. The effects on the financial statements and the journal entry to record the event follow:

Assets	=	Liab.	+	Equity			Rev.	−	Exp.	=	Net Inc.	Cash Flow
Cash	=	Liab.	+	Other Equity Accts.	−	Treasury Stk.						
(1,000)	=	NA	+	NA	−	1,000	NA	−	NA	=	NA	(1,000) FA

Account Title	Debit	Credit
Treasury Stock	1,000	
Cash		1,000

The Treasury Stock account is a contra equity account. It is deducted from the other equity accounts in determining total stockholders' equity. In this example, the treasury stock account is debited for the full amount paid ($1,000). The original issue price and the par value of the stock have no effect on the entry. Recording the full amount paid in the treasury stock account is called the **cost method of accounting for treasury stock** transactions. Although other methods could be used, the cost method is the most common.

Assume Nelson reissues 30 shares of treasury stock at a price of $25 per share. As with any other stock issue, the sale of treasury stock is an asset source transaction. In this case, assets and stockholders' equity increase by $750 ($25 × 30 shares). The income statement is not affected. The cash inflow is reported in the financing activities section of the statement of cash flows. The effect of this event on the financial statements and the journal entry to record it follow:

Assets	=	Liab.	+	Equity					Rev.	−	Exp.	=	Net Inc.	Cash Flow
Cash	=	Liab.	+	Other Equity Accounts	−	Treasury Stock	+	Paid in from Treasury Stk.						
750	=	NA	+	NA	−	(600)	+	150	NA	−	NA	=	NA	750 FA

Account Title	Debit	Credit
Cash	750	
Treasury Stock		600
Paid-in Capital in Excess of Cost of Treasury Stock		150

The decrease in the Treasury Stock account increases stockholders' equity. The $150 difference between the cost of the treasury stock ($20 per share × 30 shares = $600) and the sales price ($750) is *not* reported as a gain. The sale of treasury stock is a capital acquisition, not a revenue transaction. The $150 is additional paid-in capital. *Corporations do not recognize gains or losses on the sale of treasury stock.*

After selling 30 shares of treasury stock, 20 shares remain in Nelson's possession. These shares cost $20 each, so the balance in the Treasury Stock account is now $400 ($20 × 20 shares). Treasury stock is reported on the balance sheet directly below retained earnings.

Although this placement suggests that treasury stock reduces retained earnings, the reduction actually applies to the entire stockholders' equity section. Exhibit 11–5 shows the presentation of treasury stock in the balance sheet.

Check Yourself 11–2

On January 1, 2006, Janell Company's Common Stock account balance was $20,000. On April 1, 2006, Janell paid $12,000 cash to purchase some of its own stock. Janell resold this stock on October 1, 2006, for $14,500. What is the effect on the company's cash and stockholders' equity from both the April 1 purchase and the October 1 resale of the stock?

Answer The April 1 purchase would reduce both cash and stockholders' equity by $12,000. The treasury stock transaction represents a return of invested capital to those owners who sold stock back to the company.

The sale of the treasury stock on October 1 would increase both cash and stockholders' equity by $14,500. The difference between the sales price of the treasury stock and its cost ($14,500 − $12,000) represents additional paid-in capital from treasury stock transactions. The stockholders' equity section of the balance sheet would include Common Stock, $20,000, and Additional Paid-in Capital from Treasury Stock Transactions, $2,500.

Cash Dividend

LO6 Explain the effects of declaring and paying cash dividends on a company's financial statements.

Cash dividends are affected by three significant dates: *the declaration date, the date of record,* and *the payment date.* Assume that on October 15, 2006, the board of Nelson, Incorporated declared the cash dividend on the 100 outstanding shares of its $10 stated value preferred stock. The dividend will be paid to stockholders of record as of November 15, 2006. The cash payment will be made on December 15, 2006.

Declaration Date

Although corporations are not required to declare dividends, they are legally obligated to pay dividends once they have been declared. They must recognize a liability on the **declaration date** (in this case, October 15, 2006). The increase in liabilities is accompanied by a decrease in retained earnings. The income statement and statement of cash flows are not affected. The effect on the financial statements of *declaring* the $70 ($0.07 \times \$10 \times 100$ shares) dividend and the journal entry to record the declaration follow:

Assets	=	Liab.	+		Equity			Rev.	−	Exp.	=	Net Inc.	Cash Flow
Cash	=	Div. Pay.	+	C. Stk.	+	Ret. Earn.							
NA	=	70	+	NA	+	(70)		NA	−	NA	=	NA	NA

Account Title	Debit	Credit
Dividends	70	
Dividends Payable		70

Date of Record

Cash dividends are paid to investors who owned the preferred stock on the **date of record** (in this case November 15, 2006). Any stock sold after the date of record but before the payment date (in this case December 15, 2006) is traded **ex-dividend,** meaning the buyer will not receive the upcoming dividend. The date of record is merely a cutoff date. It does not affect the financial statements.

Payment Date

Nelson actually paid the cash dividend on the **payment date.** This event has the same effect as paying any other liability. Assets (cash) and liabilities (dividends payable) both decrease.

The income statement is not affected. The cash outflow is reported in the financing activities section of the statement of cash flows. The effect of the cash payment on the financial statements and the journal entry to record it follow:

Assets	=	Liab.	+		Equity			Rev.	−	Exp.	=	Net Inc.		Cash Flow	
Cash	=	Div. Pay.	+	C. Stk.	+	Ret. Earn.									
(70)	=	(70)	+	NA	+	NA		NA	−	NA	=	NA		(70)	FA

Account Title	Debit	Credit
Dividends Payable	70	
Cash		70

Stock Dividend

LO7 Explain the effects of stock dividends and stock splits on a company's financial statements.

Dividends are not always paid in cash. Companies sometimes choose to issue **stock dividends,** wherein they distribute additional shares of stock to the stockholders. To illustrate, assume that Nelson, Incorporated decided to issue a 10 percent stock dividend on its class B, $20 par value common stock. Since dividends apply to outstanding shares only, Nelson will issue 15 (150 outstanding shares × 0.10) additional shares of class B stock.

Assume the new shares are distributed when the market value of the stock is $30 per share. As a result of the stock dividend, Nelson will transfer $450 ($30 × 15 new shares) from retained earnings to paid-in capital.[2] The stock dividend is an equity exchange transaction. The income statement and statement of cash flows are not affected. The effect of the stock dividend on the financial statements and the journal entry to record it follow:

Assets	=	Liab.	+			Equity				Rev.	−	Exp.	=	Net Inc.	Cash Flow
	=		+	C. Stk.	+	Paid-in Excess	+	Ret. Earn.							
NA	=	NA	+	300	+	150	+	(450)		NA	−	NA	=	NA	NA

Account Title	Debit	Credit
Retained Earnings	450	
Common Stock, Class B, $20 Par Value		300
Paid-in Capital in Excess of Par Value—Class B Common		150

Stock dividends have no effect on assets. They merely increase the number of shares of stock outstanding. Since a greater number of shares represents the same ownership interest in the same amount of assets, the market value per share of a company's stock normally declines when a stock dividend is distributed. A lower market price makes the stock more affordable and may increase demand for the stock, which benefits both the company and its stockholders.

Stock Split

A corporation may also reduce the market price of its stock through a **stock split.** A stock split replaces existing shares with a greater number of new shares. Any par or stated value of the stock is proportionately reduced to reflect the new number of shares outstanding. For example, assume Nelson, Incorporated declared a 2-for-1 stock split on the 165 outstanding shares (150 originally issued + 15 shares distributed in a stock dividend) of its $20 par value, class B common stock. Nelson notes in the accounting records that the 165 old $20 par shares are

---

[2]The accounting here applies to small stock dividends. Accounting for large stock dividends is explained in a more advanced course.

replaced with 330 new $10 par shares. Investors who owned the 165 shares of old common stock would now own 330 shares of the new common stock.

Stock splits have no effect on the dollar amounts of assets, liabilities, and stockholders' equity. They only affect the number of shares of stock outstanding. In Nelson's case, the ownership interest that was previously represented by 165 shares of stock is now represented by 330 shares. Since twice as many shares now represent the same ownership interest, the market value per share should be one-half as much as it was prior to the split. However, as with a stock dividend, the lower market price will probably stimulate demand for the stock. As a result, doubling the number of shares will likely reduce the market price to slightly more than one-half of the pre-split value. For example, if the stock were selling for $30 per share before the 2-for-1 split, it might sell for $15.50 after the split.

Appropriation of Retained Earnings

LO8 Show how the appropriation of retained earnings affects financial statements.

The board of directors may restrict the amount of retained earnings available to distribute as dividends. The restriction may be required by credit agreements, or it may be completely discretionary. A retained earnings restriction, often called an *appropriation,* is an equity exchange event. It transfers a portion of existing retained earnings to **Appropriated Retained Earnings.** Total retained earnings remains unchanged. To illustrate, assume that Nelson appropriates $1,000 of retained earnings for future expansion. The income statement and the statement of cash flows are not affected. The effect on the financial statements of appropriating $1,000 of retained earnings and the journal entry to record it follow:

Assets	=	Liab.	+			Equity				Rev.	−	Exp.	=	Net Inc.	Cash Flow
	=		+	C. Stk.	+	Ret. Earn.	+	App. Ret. Earn.							
NA	=	NA	+	NA	+	(1,000)	+	1,000		NA	−	NA	=	NA	NA

Account Title	Debit	Credit
Retained Earnings	1,000	
Appropriated Retained Earnings		1,000

Financial Statement Presentation

The 2005 and 2006 events for Nelson Incorporated are summarized below. Events 1 through 8 are cash transactions. The results of the 2005 transactions (Nos. 1–5) are reflected in Exhibit 11–4. The results of the 2006 transactions (Nos. 6–9) are shown in Exhibit 11–5.

1. Issued 100 shares of $10 par value common stock at a market price of $22 per share.
2. Issued 150 shares of class B, $20 par value common stock at a market price of $25 per share.
3. Issued 100 shares of $10 stated value, 7 percent cumulative preferred stock at a market price of $22 per share.
4. Issued 100 shares of no-par common stock at a market price of $22 per share.
5. Earned and retained $5,000 cash from operations.
6. Purchased 50 shares of $10 par value common stock as treasury stock at a market price of $20 per share.
7. Sold 30 shares of treasury stock at a market price of $25 per share.
8. Declared and paid a $70 cash dividend on the preferred stock.
9. Issued a 10 percent stock dividend on the 150 shares of outstanding class B, $20 par value common stock (15 additional shares). The additional shares were issued when the market price of the stock was $30 per share. There are 165 (150 + 15) class B common shares outstanding after the stock dividend.

Exhibit 11-5

NELSON, INCORPORATED
Balance Sheet
As of December 31, 2006

Assets
Cash $21,030

Stockholders' Equity
Preferred Stock, $10 Stated Value, 7% cumulative,
   300 shares authorized, 100 issued and outstanding $1,000
Common Stock, $10 Par Value, 250 shares authorized,
   100 issued, and 80 outstanding   1,000
Common Stock, Class B, $10 Par, 800 shares authorized,
   330 issued and outstanding   3,300
Common Stock, No Par, 150 shares authorized,
   100 issued and outstanding   2,200
Paid-in Capital in Excess of Par—Preferred   1,200
Paid-in Capital in Excess of Par—Common   1,200
Paid-in Capital in Excess of Par—Class B Common   900
Paid-in Capital in Excess of Cost of Treasury Stock   150

   Total Paid-in Capital $10,950
Retained Earnings
   Appropriated   1,000
   Unappropriated   9,480

   Total Retained Earnings   10,480
Less: Treasury Stock, 20 shares @ $20 per share   (400)

Total Stockholders' Equity $21,030

10. Issued a 2-for-1 stock split on the 165 shares of class B, $20 par value common stock. After this transaction, there are 330 shares outstanding of the class B common stock with a $10 par value.
11. Appropriated $1,000 of retained earnings.

The illustration assumes that Nelson earned net income of $6,000 in 2006. The ending retained earnings balance is determined as follows: Beginning Balance $5,000 − $70 Cash Dividend − $450 Stock Dividend + $6,000 Net Income = $10,480.

THE FINANCIAL ANALYST

Stockholders may benefit in two ways when a company generates earnings. The company may distribute the earnings directly to the stockholders in the form of dividends. Alternatively, the company may retain some or all of the earnings to finance growth and increase its potential for future earnings. If the company retains earnings, the market value of its stock should increase to reflect its greater earnings prospects. How can analysts use financial reporting to help assess the potential for dividend payments or growth in market value?

LO9 Explain some uses of accounting information in making stock investment decisions.

Receiving Dividends

Is a company likely to pay dividends in the future? The financial statements can help answer this question. They show if dividends were paid in the past. Companies with a history of paying dividends usually continue to pay dividends. Also, to pay dividends in the future, a company must have sufficient cash and retained earnings. These amounts are reported on the balance sheet and the statement of cash flows.

Increasing the Price of Stock

Is the market value (price) of a company's stock likely to increase? Increases in a company's stock price occur when investors believe the company's earnings will grow. Financial statements provide information that is useful in predicting the prospects for earnings growth. Here also, a company's earnings history is an indicator of its growth potential. However, because published financial statements report historical information, investors must recognize their limitations. Investors want to know about the future. Stock prices are therefore influenced more by forecasts than by history.

For example:

- On May 6, 2003, Cisco Systems, Inc. announced that its profits for the third quarter of the 2003 fiscal year were 35 percent higher than profits in the same quarter of 2002. In reaction to this news, the price of Cisco's stock *fell* 2.6 percent. Why? Because on the same day, Cisco announced that it believed revenue for the fourth quarter of 2003 would be flat compared to the third quarter, and analysts who follow the company were expecting revenues to grow slightly.
- On May 8, 2003, Comcast Corporation announced a first quarter *loss* of $297 million. This loss was over three times greater than its loss had been for the first quarter of the 2002 fiscal year. Yet the stock market's reaction to the news was to *increase* the price of Comcast's stock by 3 percent. In that same announcement the company reported strong revenue growth, which made investors more optimistic about Comcast's future.

In each case, investors reacted to the potential for earnings growth rather than the historical earnings reports. Because investors find forecasted statements more relevant to decision making than historical financial statements, most companies provide forecasts in addition to historical financial statements.

The value of a company's stock is also influenced by nonfinancial information that financial statements cannot provide. For example, suppose ExxonMobil announced in the middle of its fiscal year that it had just discovered substantial oil reserves on property to which it held drilling rights. Consider the following questions:

- What would happen to the price of ExxonMobil's stock on the day of the announcement?
- What would happen to ExxonMobil's financial statements on that day?

The price of ExxonMobil's stock would almost certainly increase as soon as the discovery was made public. However, nothing would happen to its financial statements on that day. There would probably be very little effect on its financial statements for that year. Only after the company began to develop the oil field and sell the oil would its financial statements reflect the discovery. Changes in financial statements tend to lag behind the announcements companies make regarding their earnings potential.

Stock prices are also affected by general economic conditions and consumer confidence as well as the performance measures reported in financial statements. For example, the stock prices of virtually all companies declined sharply immediately after the September 11, 2001, terrorist attacks on the World Trade Center and the Pentagon. Historical based financial statements are of little benefit in predicting general economic conditions or changes in consumer confidence.

Price Earnings Ratio

The most commonly reported measure of a company's value is the price-earnings ratio, frequently called the P/E ratio. The P/E ratio is a company's market price per share of stock divided by the company's annual earnings per share (EPS). In general, high P/E ratios indicate that

investors are optimistic about a company's earnings growth potential. For a more a detailed discussion of this important ratio refer back to the coverage in Chapter 1.

Exercising Control through Stock Ownership

The more influence an investor has over the operations of a company, the more the investor can benefit from owning stock in the company. For example, consider a power company that needs coal to produce electricity. The power company may purchase some common stock in a coal mining company to ensure a stable supply of coal. What percentage of the mining company's stock must the power company acquire to exercise significant influence over the mining company? The answer depends on how many investors own stock in the mining company and how the number of shares is distributed among the stockholders.

The greater its number of stockholders, the more *widely held* a company is. If stock ownership is concentrated in the hands of a few persons, a company is *closely held.* Widely held companies can generally be controlled with smaller percentages of ownership than closely held companies. Consider a company in which no existing investor owns more one than 1 percent of the voting stock. A new investor who acquires a 5 percent interest would immediately become, by far, the largest shareholder and would likely be able to significantly influence board decisions. In contrast, consider a closely held company in which one current shareholder owns 51 percent of the company's stock. Even if another investor acquired the remaining 49 percent of the company, that investor could not control the company.

Financial statements contain some, but not all, of the information needed to help an investor determine ownership levels necessary to permit control. For example, the financial statements disclose the total number of shares of stock outstanding, but they normally contain little information about the number of shareholders and even less information about any relationships between shareholders. Relationships between shareholders are critically important because related shareholders, whether bound by family or business interests, might exercise control by voting as a block. For publicly traded companies, information about the number of shareholders and the identity of some large shareholders is disclosed in reports filed with the Securities and Exchange Commission.

Starting a business requires obtaining financing; it takes money to make money. Although some money may be borrowed, lenders are unlikely to make loans to businesses that lack some degree of owner financing. Equity financing is therefore critical to virtually all profit-oriented businesses. This chapter has examined some of the issues related to accounting for equity transactions.

a look
back

The idea that a business must obtain financing from its owners was one of the very first events presented in this textbook. This chapter discussed the advantages and disadvantages of organizing a business as a sole proprietorship versus a partnership versus a corporation. These advantages and disadvantages include the following:

1. *Double taxation*—Income of corporations is subject to double taxation, but that of proprietorships and partnerships is not.
2. *Regulation*—Corporations are subject to more regulation than are proprietorships and partnerships.
3. *Limited liability*—An investor's personal assets are not at risk as a result of owning corporate securities. The investor's liability is limited to the amount of the investment. In general proprietorships and partnerships do not offer limited liability. However, laws in some states permit the formation of limited liability companies which operate like proprietorships and partnerships yet place some limits on the personal liability of their owners.
4. *Continuity*—Proprietorships and partnerships dissolve when one of the owners leaves the business. Corporations are separate legal entities that continue to exist regardless of changes in ownership.
5. *Transferability*—Ownership interests in corporations are easier to transfer than those of proprietorships or partnerships.

6. *Management structure*—Corporations are more likely to have independent professional managers than are proprietorships or partnerships.

7. *Ability to raise capital*—Because they can be owned by millions of investors, corporations have the opportunity to raise more capital than proprietorships or partnerships.

Corporations issue different classes of common stock and preferred stock as evidence of ownership interests. In general, *common stock* provides the widest range of privileges including the right to vote and participate in earnings. *Preferred stockholders* usually give up the right to vote in exchange for preferences such as the right to receive dividends or assets upon liquidation before common stockholders. Stock may have a *par value* or *stated value,* which relates to legal requirements governing the amount of capital that must be maintained in the corporation. Corporations may also issue *no-par stock*, avoiding some of the legal requirements that pertain to par or stated value stock.

Stock that a company issues and then repurchases is called *treasury stock.* Purchasing treasury stock reduces total assets and stockholders' equity. Reselling treasury stock represents a capital acquisition. The difference between the reissue price and the cost of the treasury stock is recorded directly in the equity accounts. Treasury stock transactions do not result in gains or losses on the income statement.

Companies may issue *stock splits* or *stock dividends.* These transactions increase the number of shares of stock without changing the net assets of a company. The per share market value usually drops when a company issues stock splits or dividends.

a look **forward**

Chapter 12 examines the statement of cash flows in more detail than past chapters have. It introduces a more practical way to prepare the statement than analyzing every single entry in the cash account, and presents the more formal format for the statement of cash flows used by most real-world companies.

APPENDIX

Accounting for Not-for-Profit (NFP) Organizations

LO10 Explain accounting for not-for-profit entities and governmental organizations.

To this point, our primary focus has been on profit-oriented business organizations. We turn now to a group of organizations classified as *not-for-profit (NFP) entities.* These NFP organizations are distinguished from profit-oriented businesses by three characteristics: (1) the receipt of significant resources from contributors not expecting repayment or economic returns, (2) the operation for purposes other than profit, and (3) the absence of defined ownership interests. Types of organizations that clearly fall within the scope of the NFP classification include museums, churches, clubs, professional associations, and foundations. Organizations that clearly fall outside the scope of the NFP classification include investor-owned enterprises and mutual organizations that provide dividends, lower costs, or other economic benefits directly and proportionately to their owners, members, or participants. The line of demarcation between business and NFP organizations can be vague. Consider a nonprofit school that finances the majority of its capital needs from the proceeds of debt and operating activities. Should this organization be classified as a business or an NFP organization? The ultimate decision is left to the judgment of the interested parties.

Fortunately, much of the information about accounting for business organizations that you have learned is applicable to NFP organizations as well. For example, the financial statements of both profit and NFP organizations contain assets, liabilities, revenues, expenses, gains, and losses. However, investments by owners and distributions to them are not appropriate for NFP entities. Also, the composition of net assets for business and NFP organizations differs. Business organizations subdivide net assets into owner contributions and retained earnings. In contrast, NFP entities subdivide net assets into three classes based on the degree of donor-imposed restrictions: (1) permanently restricted, (2) temporarily restricted, or (3) unrestricted. The double-entry recording system, including debits and credits, journal entries, ledgers, T-accounts, trial balances, and so on, applies to organizations operating in an NFP context. Also, like business organizations, NFP entities are governed by a set of generally accepted accounting principles (GAAP) established by the Financial Accounting Standards Board (FASB).

The NFP organizations issue three general-purpose external financial statements designed to help external users assess (1) the services an NFP organization provides, (2) the organization's ability to continue providing those services, and (3) the performance of the organization's management. The complete set of financial statements and accompanying notes includes a:

1. Statement of financial position as of the end of the period.
2. Statement of activities for the period.
3. Statement of cash flows for the period.

The **statement of financial position** reports on the organization's assets, liabilities, and net assets. This statement contains many common account titles, including Cash, Cash Equivalents, Accounts and Notes Receivable and Payable, Inventories, Marketable Securities, Long-Term Assets and Liabilities, Buildings, and Land. However, as indicated, the equity section of the statement of financial position is subdivided into three categories: *permanently restricted net assets, temporarily restricted net assets,* and *unrestricted net assets.*

The **statement of activities** reports on revenues, expenses, gains, and losses that increase or decrease net assets. Revenues and gains are increases in assets or decreases in liabilities generated by the organization's operating activities. Donor contributions are classified as revenues. Expenses and losses are decreases in assets or increases in liabilities incurred through operating activities. The statement is arranged in three sections: (1) changes in unrestricted net assets, (2) changes in temporarily restricted net assets, and (3) changes in permanently restricted net assets. The bottom-line figure is computed by adding the net change in net assets to the beginning balance in net assets to arrive at the ending net asset balance.

The **statement of cash flows** reports the cash consequences of the organization's operating, investing, and financing activities. Unrestricted and temporarily restricted donor contributions are included in the operating activities section of the statement of cash flows. Permanently restricted donor contributions are considered financing activities. Other items are treated in a manner similar to the treatment used by profit-oriented businesses.

To illustrate financial reporting for NFP entities, assume that a private nonprofit school, Palmer Primary School of Excellence, is established when it receives a $10 million cash contribution from Dana Palmer, a wealthy benefactor who wants to promote excellence in early childhood education for minority students. A total of $1 million was designated as unrestricted funds; $2 million was temporarily restricted for the purchase of land and construction of buildings. The remaining $7 million was permanently restricted for an endowed investment fund that will produce investment income to be used to supplement school operations. Parents are required to pay the school for educational services on a scale based on their level of income. During 2001, the first year of operation, $1,200,000 cash was spent to acquire land and buildings. The $7 million of cash was invested in the endowed fund. The endowment generated investment income amounting to $700,000 cash. Operating revenues amounted to $100,000 cash. Cash operating expenses amounted to $950,000, not including $50,000 of depreciation expense. The results of these events are reported in the set of financial statements in Exhibit 11–6. Study these statements carefully, noting the following differentiating features:

1. That which is classified as equity in business statements is called *net assets* in the NFP statement. The net assets are subdivided into three components, depending on the nature of the donor restrictions originally placed on the use of the resources.
2. The statement of activities is divided into three categories, including activities that affect unrestricted, temporarily restricted, and permanently restricted assets. Notice that unrestricted contributions are treated in a manner similar to the way revenue is treated in profit-oriented businesses. Finally, observe the reconciliation between the beginning and ending balances in net assets shown at the bottom of the statement.
3. With respect to the statement of cash flows, unrestricted and temporarily restricted donor contributions are classified as operating activities. Only permanently restricted donor contributions are classified as financing activities. In contrast, all contributed capital of profit-oriented businesses is classified as a financing activity.

Governmental Accounting

Governmental entities have characteristics that require a unique accounting system in order to satisfy the needs of information users. These characteristics include (1) involuntary contributors of resources known as *taxpayers;* (2) monopoly supplier of goods and services; (3) resources heavily invested in nonrevenue-producing assets such as buildings, bridges, highways, schools, and military and police forces; and (4) management by elected representation. The primary users of governmental financial reports include citizens, researchers, media agents, special-interest groups, legislative and oversight bodies, and investors and creditors. The information contained in the financial reports is used to (1) compare actual results with budgeted estimates, (2) assess the entities' financial condition and operating results, (3) determine compliance with the laws and regulations, and (4) evaluate the effectiveness and efficiency of management.

The GAAP for governmental accounting is set forth by the Governmental Accounting Standards Board (GASB), a sister organization of the FASB. The presence of two separate standards-setting

LO10 Explain accounting for not-for-profit entities and governmental organizations.

Exhibit 11–6

PALMER PRIMARY SCHOOL OF EXCELLENCE
Financial Statements
As of December 31, 2001

Statement of Activities

Changes in Unrestricted Net Assets	
Donor Contributions	$1,000,000
Released from Temp. Building Restriction	1,200,000
Investment Revenue	700,000
Tuition	100,000
Expenses for Educational Programs	(950,000)
Depreciation Expense	(50,000)
Net Change in Unrestricted Net Assets	2,000,000
Changes in Temporarily Restricted Net Assets	
Temp. Restricted Contributions for Buildings	2,000,000
Released from Temp. Building Restriction	(1,200,000)
Changes in Permanently Restricted Net Assets	
Donor Contributions	7,000,000
Increase in Net Assets	9,800,000
Net Assets at Beginning of Period	0
Net Assets at End of Year	$9,800,000

Statement of Financial Position

Assets	
Cash	$1,650,000
Endowed Investment Fund	7,000,000
Buildings and Land	1,200,000
Less: Accumulated Depreciation	(50,000)
Total Assets	$9,800,000
Net Assets	
Permanently Restricted	$7,000,000
Temporarily Restricted	800,000
Unrestricted	2,000,000
Total Net Assets	$9,800,000

Statement of Cash Flows

Operating Activities	
Temp. Restricted Donor Contributions	$2,000,000
Unrestricted Donor Contributions	1,000,000
Investment Revenue	700,000
Tuition	100,000
Operating Expenses	(950,000)
Net Inflow from Operating Activities	2,850,000
Investing Activities	
Endowed Investment Fund	(7,000,000)
Purchase Building and Land	(1,200,000)
Financing Activities	
Perm. Restricted Donor Contributions	7,000,000
Net Change in Cash	$1,650,000

authorities can lead to confusion regarding which authoritative body has jurisdiction over certain types of organizations. For example, a hospital can be operated as a profit-oriented business enterprise, a private nonprofit entity, or a branch of a governmental entity. Often a single hospital possesses some mixture of the characteristics of the two or three forms of organization. Accordingly, the lines of distinction can be vague, and judgment may be required as to which GAAP applies.

The GASB has concluded that *the diversity of governmental activities and the need for legal compliance preclude the use of a single accounting entity approach* for governmental bodies. Instead, financial reporting is accomplished through distinct fiscal entities called *funds* or *account groups.* Accordingly, governmental accounting is frequently called **fund accounting.** A **fund** is an independent accounting entity with a self-balancing set of accounts segregated for the purpose of carrying on specific activities. For example, a local governmental municipality may maintain separate funds for schools, police, and parks and recreation. **Account groups** are self-balancing entities that account for the governmental unit's general fixed assets and the outstanding principal of its general long-term liabilities.

Because governmental entities are not subject to the constraints imposed by competition in the free markets, the GASB has taken a budgetary approach to accounting. Governmental entities frequently are required by law to establish budgets. When a governmental entity adopts a budget, GASB principles require that the budget be incorporated into the accounts, including the adoption of a report form that provides comparisons between budget and actual data in the financial statements. A formal budget is a critical component of accounting for government entities because it (1) provides an expression of public policy, (2) represents a statement of financial intent with regard to how funds raised through taxation will be spent, (3) acts as a legally enforceable instrument that limits spending by requiring financial managers to attain formally approved budgetary amendments prior to making expenditures that exceed the budgetary limits, (4) provides a standard to which actual results can be compared, thereby enabling the evaluation of performance, and (5) facilitates the planning process for the future needs of the governmental entity.

Governmental entities are required to issue a **comprehensive annual financial report (CAFR)** that covers all funds and account groups under their jurisdictions. The CAFR includes (1) the report of the independent auditor, (2) general-purpose financial statements, (3) combined statements organized by fund type when the primary entity has more than one fund of a given type, (4) individual fund statements when the primary governmental entity has only one fund of a given type, (5) schedules that provide detail sufficient to demonstrate compliance with specific regulations, and (6) appropriate statistical tables. Governmental reports are characterized by multiple columns that provide information on individual funds and account groups. No single summation is provided for the entity as a whole. Clearly, the appearance of financial statements prepared by governmental entities will differ significantly from that of those prepared by profit-oriented businesses.

The coverage of the details of accounting for governmental entities is beyond the scope of this book, but the preceding discussion should improve your understanding of the need for flexibility in financial reporting. Always remember that accounting should provide information that is useful to current and potential resource providers, consumers, and monitors of a variety of organizational entities. To preserve its relevance, accounting must maintain an appropriate level of versatility in reporting practices so as to meet the needs of its users.

SELF-STUDY REVIEW PROBLEM

Edwards, Inc., experienced the following events:

1. Issued common stock for cash.
2. Declared a cash dividend.
3. Issued noncumulative preferred stock for cash.
4. Appropriated retained earnings.
5. Distributed a stock dividend.
6. Paid cash to purchase treasury stock.
7. Distributed a 2-for-1 stock split.
8. Issued cumulative preferred stock for cash.
9. Paid a cash dividend that had previously been declared.
10. Sold treasury stock for cash at a higher amount than the cost of the treasury stock.

Required

Show the effect of each event on the elements of the financial statements using a horizontal statements model like the one shown here. Use + for increase, − for decrease, and NA for not affected. In the Cash

Flow column, indicate whether the item is an operating activity (OA), investing activity (IA), or a financing activity (FA). The first transaction is entered as an example.

Event	Assets	=	Liab.	+	Equity	Rev.	−	Exp.	=	Net Inc.	Cash Flow
1	+		NA		+	NA		NA		NA	+ FA

Solution to Self-Study Review Problem

Event	Assets	=	Liab.	+	Equity	Rev.	−	Exp.	=	Net Inc.	Cash Flow
1	+		NA		+	NA		NA		NA	+ FA
2	NA		+		−	NA		NA		NA	NA
3	+		NA		+	NA		NA		NA	+ FA
4	NA		NA		− +	NA		NA		NA	NA
5	NA		NA		− +	NA		NA		NA	NA
6	−		NA		−	NA		NA		NA	− FA
7	NA		NA		NA	NA		NA		NA	NA
8	+		NA		+	NA		NA		NA	+ FA
9	−		−		NA	NA		NA		NA	− FA
10	+		NA		+	NA		NA		NA	+ FA

KEY TERMS

Account groups *535*

Appropriated Retained Earnings account *528*

Articles of incorporation *514*

Authorized stock *520*

Board of directors *517*

Book value per share *520*

Closely held corporation *515*

Common stock *521*

Comprehensive annual financial report (CAFR) *535*

Continuity *517*

Corporation *514*

Cost method of accounting for treasury stock *525*

Cumulative dividends *521*

Date of record *526*

Declaration date *526*

Dividends in arrears *521*

Double taxation *516*

Entrenched management *517*

Ex-dividend *526*

Fund *535*

Fund accounting *535*

Issued stock *520*

Legal capital *519*

Limited liability *516*

Limited liability company (LLC) *516*

Market value *520*

Outstanding Stock *521*

Paid-in Capital in Excess of Par Value *522*

Par value *519*

Partnership *514*

Partnership agreement *514*

Payment date *526*

Preferred stock *521*

Sarbanes-Oxley Act of 2002 *515*

Securities Act of 1933 and Securities Exchange Act of 1934 *515*

Sole proprietorship *514*

Stated value *520*

Statement of activities *533*

Statement of cash flows *533*

Statement of financial position *533*

Stock certificate *514*

Stock dividend *527*

Stock split *527*

Stockholders *517*

Transferability *517*

Treasury stock *520*

Withdrawals *518*

QUESTIONS

1. What are the three major forms of business organizations? Describe each.
2. How are sole proprietorships formed?
3. Discuss the purpose of a partnership agreement. Is such an agreement necessary for partnership formation?
4. What is meant by the phrase *separate legal entity*? To which type of business organization does it apply?
5. What is the purpose of the articles of incorporation? What information do they provide?
6. What is the function of the stock certificate?
7. What prompted Congress to pass the Securities Act of 1933 and the Securities Exchange Act of 1934? What is the purpose of these laws?
8. What are the advantages and disadvantages of the corporate form of business organization?
9. What is a limited liability company? Discuss its advantages and disadvantages.
10. How does the term *double taxation* apply to corporations? Give an example of double taxation.
11. What is the difference between contributed capital and retained earnings for a corporation?

12. What are the similarities and differences in the equity structure of a sole proprietorship, a partnership, and a corporation?
13. Why is it easier for a corporation to raise large amounts of capital than it is for a partnership?
14. What is the meaning of each of the following terms with respect to the corporate form of organization?
    (a) Legal capital
    (b) Par value of stock
    (c) Stated value of stock
    (d) Market value of stock
    (e) Book value of stock
    (f) Authorized shares of stock
    (g) Issued stock
    (h) Outstanding stock
    (i) Treasury stock
    (j) Common stock
    (k) Preferred stock
    (l) Dividends
15. What is the difference between cumulative preferred stock and noncumulative preferred stock?
16. What is no-par stock? How is it recorded in the accounting records?
17. Assume that Best Co. has issued and outstanding 1,000 shares of $100 par value, 10 percent, cumulative preferred stock. What is the dividend per share? If the preferred dividend is two years in arrears, what total amount of dividends must be paid before the common shareholders can receive any dividends?
18. If Best Co. issued 10,000 shares of $20 par value common stock for $30 per share, what amount is credited to the Common Stock account? What amount of cash is received?
19. What is the difference between par value stock and stated value stock?
20. Why might a company repurchase its own stock?
21. What effect does the purchase of treasury stock have on the equity of a company?
22. Assume that Day Company repurchased 1,000 of its own shares for $30 per share and sold the shares two weeks later for $35 per share. What is the amount of gain on the sale? How is it reported on the balance sheet? What type of account is treasury stock?
23. What is the importance of the declaration date, record date, and payment date in conjunction with corporate dividends?
24. What is the difference between a stock dividend and a stock split?
25. Why would a company choose to distribute a stock dividend instead of a cash dividend?
26. What is the primary reason that a company would declare a stock split?
27. If Best Co. had 10,000 shares of $20 par value common stock outstanding and declared a 5-for-1 stock split, how many shares would then be outstanding and what would be their par value after the split?
28. When a company appropriates retained earnings, does the company set aside cash for a specific use? Explain.
29. What is the largest source of financing for most U.S. businesses?
30. What is meant by *equity financing*? What is meant by *debt financing*?
31. What is a widely held corporation? What is a closely held corporation?
32. What are some reasons that a corporation might not pay dividends?

EXERCISES—SERIES A

All Exercises in Series A are available with McGraw-Hill's Homework Manager

EXERCISE 11–1A *Effect of Accounting Events on the Financial Statements of a Sole Proprietorship*

L.O. 1, 2

A sole proprietorship was started on January 1, 2005, when it received $60,000 cash from Mark Pruitt, the owner. During 2005, the company earned $40,000 in cash revenues and paid $19,300 in cash expenses. Pruitt withdrew $5,000 cash from the business during 2005.

Required
Prepare an income statement, capital statement (statement of changes in equity), balance sheet, and statement of cash flows for Pruitt's 2005 fiscal year.

L.O. 1, 2   EXERCISE 11–2A *Effect of Accounting Events on the Financial Statements of a Partnership*

Justin Harris and Paul Berryhill started the HB partnership on January 1, 2006. The business acquired $56,000 cash from Harris and $84,000 from Berryhill. During 2006, the partnership earned $65,000 in cash revenues and paid $32,000 for cash expenses. Harris withdrew $2,000 cash from the business, and Berryhill withdrew $3,000 cash. The net income was allocated to the capital accounts of the two partners in proportion to the amounts of their original investments in the business.

Required

Prepare an income statement, capital statement, balance sheet, and statement of cash flows for the HB partnership for the 2006 fiscal year.

L.O. 1, 2   EXERCISE 11–3A *Effect of Accounting Events on the Financial Statements of a Corporation*

Morris Corporation was started with the issue of 5,000 shares of $10 par common stock for cash on January 1, 2007. The stock was issued at a market price of $18 per share. During 2007, the company earned $63,000 in cash revenues and paid $41,000 for cash expenses. Also a $4,000 cash dividend was paid to the stockholders.

Required

Prepare an income statement, statement of changes in stockholders' equity, balance sheet, and statement of cash flows for Morris Corporation's 2007 fiscal year.

L.O. 4   EXERCISE 11–4A *Effect of Issuing Common Stock on the Balance Sheet*

Newly formed Home Medical Corporation has 100,000 shares of $5 par common stock authorized. On March 1, 2006, Home Medical issued 10,000 shares of the stock for $12 per share. On May 2 the company issued an additional 20,000 shares for $20 per share. Home Medical was not affected by other events during 2006.

Required

a. Record the transactions in a horizontal statements model like the following one. In the Cash Flow column, indicate whether the item is an operating activity (OA), investing activity (IA), or financing activity (FA). Use NA to indicate that an element was not affected by the event.

Assets	=	Liab.	+		Equity		Rev.	–	Exp.	=	Net Inc.	Cash Flow
Cash	=		+	C. Stk.	+	Paid-in Excess						

b. Determine the amount Home Medical would report for common stock on the December 31, 2006, balance sheet.
c. Determine the amount Home Medical would report for paid-in capital in excess of par.
d. What is the total amount of capital contributed by the owners?
e. What amount of total assets would Home Medical report on the December 31, 2006, balance sheet?
f. Prepare journal entries to record the March 1 and May 2 transactions.

L.O. 4   EXERCISE 11–5A *Recording and Reporting Common and Preferred Stock Transactions*

Rainey, Inc., was organized on June 5, 2007. It was authorized to issue 400,000 shares of $10 par common stock and 50,000 shares of 4 percent cumulative class A preferred stock. The class A stock had a stated value of $25 per share. The following stock transactions pertain to Rainey, Inc.:

1. Issued 20,000 shares of common stock for $15 per share.
2. Issued 10,000 shares of the class A preferred stock for $30 per share.
3. Issued 50,000 shares of common stock for $18 per share.

Required

a. Prepare general journal entries for these transactions.
b. Prepare the stockholders' equity section of the balance sheet immediately after these transactions.

L.O. 4   EXERCISE 11–6A *Effect of No-Par Common and Par Preferred Stock on the Horizontal Statements Model*

Eaton Corporation issued 5,000 shares of no-par common stock for $20 per share. Eaton also issued 2,000 shares of $50 par, 6 percent noncumulative preferred stock at $60 per share.

Required

a. Record these events in a horizontal statements model like the following one. In the cash flow column, indicate whether the item is an operating activity (OA), investing activity (IA), or financing activity (FA). Use NA to indicate that an element was not affected by the event.

Assets =			Equity		Rev. – Exp. = Net Inc.	Cash Flow
Cash	= P. Stk. +	C. Stk. +	Paid-in Excess			

b. Prepare journal entries to record these transactions.

EXERCISE 11–7A *Issuing Stock for Assets Other Than Cash*   L.O. 4

Kaylee Corporation was formed when it issued shares of common stock to two of its shareholders. Kaylee issued 5,000 shares of $10 par common stock to K. Breslin in exchange for $60,000 cash (the issue price was $12 per share). Kaylee also issued 2,500 shares of stock to T. Lindsay in exchange for a one-year-old delivery van on the same day. Lindsay had originally paid $35,000 for the van.

Required

a. What was the market value of the delivery van on the date of the stock issue?
b. Show the effect of the two stock issues on Kaylee's books in a horizontal statements model like the following one. In the Cash Flow column, indicate whether the item is an operating activity (OA), investing activity (IA), or financing activity (FA). Use NA to indicate that an element was not affected by the event.

Assets		=	Equity		Rev. – Exp. = Net Inc.	Cash Flow
Cash +	Van	= C. Stk. +	Paid-in Excess			

EXERCISE 11–8A *Treasury Stock Transactions*   L.O. 5

Graves Corporation repurchased 2,000 shares of its own stock for $40 per share. The stock has a par of $10 per share. A month later Graves resold 1,200 shares of the treasury stock for $48 per share.

Required

a. Record the two events in general journal format.
b. What is the balance of the treasury stock account after these transactions?

EXERCISE 11–9A *Recording and Reporting Treasury Stock Transactions*   L.O. 5

The following information pertains to Smoot Corp. at January 1, 2006.

Common stock, $10 par, 10,000 shares authorized,	
2,000 shares issued and outstanding	$20,000
Paid-in capital in excess of par, common stock	15,000
Retained earnings	65,000

Smoot Corp. completed the following transactions during 2006:

1. Issued 1,000 shares of $10 par common stock for $28 per share.
2. Repurchased 200 shares of its own common stock for $25 per share.
3. Resold 50 shares of treasury stock for $26 per share.

Required

a. How many shares of common stock were outstanding at the end of the period?
b. How many shares of common stock had been issued at the end of the period?
c. Prepare journal entries for these transactions.
d. Prepare the stockholders' equity section of the balance sheet reflecting these transactions. Include the number of shares authorized, issued, and outstanding in the description of the common stock.

EXERCISE 11–10A *Effect of Cash Dividends on Financial Statements*   L.O. 6

On October 1, 2005, Smart Corporation declared a $60,000 cash dividend to be paid on December 30 to shareholders of record on November 20.

Required

a. Record the events occurring on October 1, November 20, and December 30 in a horizontal statements model like the following one. In the Cash Flow column, indicate whether the item is an operating activity (OA), investing activity (IA), or financing activity (FA).

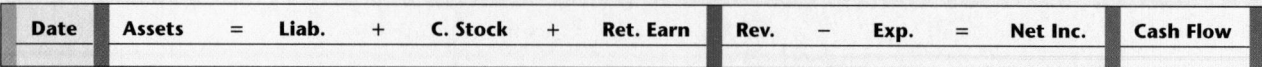

Date	Assets	=	Liab.	+	C. Stock	+	Ret. Earn	Rev.	−	Exp.	=	Net Inc.	Cash Flow

b. Prepare journal entries for all events associated with the dividend.

L.O. 6   EXERCISE 11–11A *Accounting for Cumulative Preferred Dividends*

When Polledo Corporation was organized in January 2007, it immediately issued 5,000 shares of $50 par, 5 percent, cumulative preferred stock and 10,000 shares of $10 par common stock. The company's earnings history is as follows: 2007, net loss of $15,000; 2008, net income of $60,000; 2009, net income of $95,000. The corporation did not pay a dividend in 2007.

Required

a. How much is the dividend arrearage as of January 1, 2008?
b. Assume that the board of directors declares a $40,000 cash dividend at the end of 2008 (remember that the 2007 and 2008 preferred dividends are due). How will the dividend be divided between the preferred and common stockholders?

L.O. 6   EXERCISE 11–12A *Cash Dividends for Preferred and Common Shareholders*

B&S Corporation had the following stock issued and outstanding at January 1, 2007:

1. 100,000 shares of $5 par common stock.
2. 5,000 shares of $100 par, 5 percent, noncumulative preferred stock.

On May 10, B&S Corporation declared the annual cash dividend on its 5,000 shares of preferred stock and a $1 per share dividend for the common shareholders. The dividends will be paid on June 15 to the shareholders of record on May 30.

Required

a. Determine the total amount of dividends to be paid to the preferred shareholders and common shareholders.
b. Prepare general journal entries to record the declaration and payment of the cash dividends (be sure to date your entries).

L.O. 6   EXERCISE 11–13A *Cash Dividends: Common and Preferred Stock*

Wu Corp., had the following stock issued and outstanding at January 1, 2006:

1. 50,000 shares of no-par common stock.
2. 10,000 shares of $100 par, 4 percent, cumulative preferred stock. (Dividends are in arrears for one year, 2005.)

On February 1, 2006, Wu declared a $100,000 cash dividend to be paid March 31 to shareholders of record on March 10.

Required

a. What amount of dividends will be paid to the preferred shareholders versus the common shareholders?
b. Prepare the journal entries required for these transactions. (Be sure to include the dates of the entries.)

L.O. 7   EXERCISE 11–14A *Accounting for Stock Dividends*

Merino Corporation issued a 4 percent stock dividend on 30,000 shares of its $10 par common stock. At the time of the dividend, the market value of the stock was $25 per share.

Required

a. Compute the amount of the stock dividend.
b. Show the effects of the stock dividend on the financial statements using a horizontal statements model like the following one.

Assets	=	Liab.	+	C. Stk.	+	Paid-in Excess	+	Ret. Earn	Rev.	−	Exp.	=	Net Inc.	Cash Flow

c. Prepare the journal entry to record the stock dividend.

EXERCISE 11–15A *Determining the Effects of Stock Splits on the Accounting Records*

L.O. 7

The market value of Coe Corporation's common stock had become excessively high. The stock was currently selling for $180 per share. To reduce the market price of the common stock, Coe declared a 2-for-1 stock split for the 300,000 outstanding shares of its $10 par common stock.

Required
a. How will Coe Corporation's books be affected by the stock split?
b. Determine the number of common shares outstanding and the par value after the split.
c. Explain how the market value of the stock will be affected by the stock split.

EXERCISE 11–16A *Corporate Announcements*

L.O. 9

Mighty Drugs (one of the three largest drug makers) just reported that its 2004 third quarter profits are essentially the same as the 2003 third quarter profits. In addition to this announcement, the same day, Mighty Drugs also announced that the Food and Drug Administration has just approved a new drug used to treat high blood pressure that Mighty Drugs developed. This new drug has been shown to be extremely effective and has few or no side effects. It will also be less expensive than the other drugs currently on the market.

Required
Using the above information, answer the following questions:

a. What do you think will happen to the stock price of Mighty Drugs on the day these two announcements are made? Explain your answer.
b. How will the balance sheet be affected on that day by the above announcements?
c. How will the income statement be affected on that day by the above announcements?
d. How will the statement of cash flows be affected on that day by the above announcements?

EXERCISE 11–17A *Not for Profit (Appendix)*

L.O. 10

Kelly Curtis, an enterprising accounting student, agreed to prepare financial statements for Salem City Arts Theater. She prepared the financial statements using the format for profit institutions (income statement, balance sheet, and statement of cash flows). She has asked you to review the statements.

Required
Write a memo that describes the financial statements that are required for not-for-profit entities. In the memo explain the differences in the financial statements required for profit businesses and those required for not-for-profit entities.

PROBLEMS—SERIES A

All Problems in Series A are available with McGraw-Hill's Homework Manager

PROBLEM 11–18A *Effect of Business Structure on Financial Statements*

L.O. 1, 2

www.mhhe.com/edmonds5e

Ja-San Company was started on January 1, 2007, when the owners invested $160,000 cash in the business. During 2007, the company earned cash revenues of $90,000 and incurred cash expenses of $65,000. The company also paid cash distributions of $10,000.

Required
Prepare a 2007 income statement, capital statement (statement of changes in equity), balance sheet, and statement of cash flows using each of the following assumptions. (Consider each assumption separately.)

a. Ja-San is a sole proprietorship owned by J. Sanford.
b. Ja-San is a partnership with two partners, Kim James and Mary Sanders. James invested $100,000 and Sanders invested $60,000 of the $160,000 cash that was used to start the business. Sanders was expected to assume the vast majority of the responsibility for operating the business. The partnership agreement called for Sanders to receive 60 percent of the profits and James the remaining 40 percent.

CHECK FIGURES
a. Net Income: $25,000
b. James Capital: $103,000

With regard to the $10,000 distribution, Sanders withdrew $3,000 from the business and James withdrew $7,000.

c. Ja-San is a corporation. The owners were issued 10,000 shares of $10 par common stock when they invested the $160,000 cash in the business.

L.O. 4–6

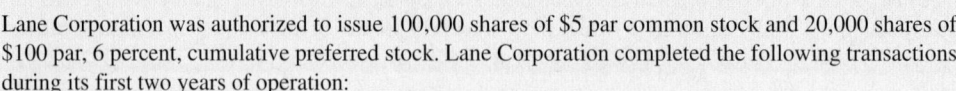

www.mhhe.com/edmonds5e

CHECK FIGURES
b. Preferred Stock, 2006: $200,000
c. Common Shares Outstanding, 2007: 34,500

PROBLEM 11–19A *Recording and Reporting Stock Transactions and Cash Dividends Across Two Accounting Cycles*

Lane Corporation was authorized to issue 100,000 shares of $5 par common stock and 20,000 shares of $100 par, 6 percent, cumulative preferred stock. Lane Corporation completed the following transactions during its first two years of operation:

2006

Jan. 2   Issued 15,000 shares of $5 par common stock for $7 per share.
     15   Issued 2,000 shares of $100 par preferred stock for $110 per share.
Feb. 14   Issued 20,000 shares of $5 par common stock for $9 per share.
Dec. 31   During the year, earned $310,000 of cash revenues and paid $240,000 of cash operating expenses.
     31   Declared the cash dividend on outstanding shares of preferred stock for 2006. The dividend will be paid on January 31 to stockholders of record on January 15, 2007.
     31   Closed revenue, expense, and dividend accounts to the retained earnings account.

2007

Jan. 31   Paid the cash dividend declared on December 31, 2006.
Mar. 1   Issued 3,000 shares of $100 par preferred stock for $120 per share.
June 1   Purchased 500 shares of common stock as treasury stock at $10 per share.
Dec. 31   During the year, earned $250,000 of cash revenues and paid $175,000 of cash operating expenses.
     31   Declared the dividend on the preferred stock and a $0.50 per share dividend on the common stock.
     31   Closed revenue, expense, and dividend accounts to the retained earnings account.

Required

a. Prepare journal entries for these transactions for 2006 and 2007.
b. Prepare the stockholders' equity section of the balance sheet at December 31, 2006.
c. Prepare the balance sheet at December 31, 2007.

L.O. 5, 6, 8

www.mhhe.com/edmonds5e

CHECK FIGURE
b. Total Paid-In Capital: $264,900

PROBLEM 11–20A *Recording and Reporting Treasury Stock Transactions*

Midwest Corp. completed the following transactions in 2007, the first year of operation:

1. Issued 20,000 shares of $10 par common stock at par.
2. Issued 2,000 shares of $30 stated value preferred stock at $32 per share.
3. Purchased 500 shares of common stock as treasury stock for $15 per share.
4. Declared a 5 percent dividend on preferred stock.
5. Sold 300 shares of treasury stock for $18 per share.
6. Paid the cash dividend on preferred stock that was declared in Event 4.
7. Earned revenue of $75,000 and incurred operating expenses of $42,000.
8. Closed revenue, expense, and dividend accounts to the retained earnings account.
9. Appropriated $6,000 of retained earnings.

Required

a. Prepare journal entries to record these transactions.
b. Prepare the stockholders' equity section of the balance sheet as of December 31, 2007.

L.O. 5

CHECK FIGURES
b. Total Paid-In Capital: $451,200
b. Total Stockholders' Equity: $570,000

PROBLEM 11–21A *Recording and Reporting Treasury Stock Transactions*

Boley Corporation reports the following information in its January 1, 2006, balance sheet:

Stockholders' Equity	
Common Stock, $10 Par Value,	
50,000 shares authorized, 30,000 shares issued and outstanding	$300,000
Paid-in Capital in Excess of Par Value	150,000
Retained Earnings	100,000
Total Stockholders' Equity	$550,000

During 2006, Boley was affected by the following accounting events:

1. Purchased 1,000 shares of treasury stock at $18 per share.
2. Reissued 600 shares of treasury stock at $20 per share.
3. Earned $64,000 of cash revenues.
4. Paid $38,000 of cash operating expenses.

Required
a. Provide journal entries to record these events in the accounting records.
b. Prepare the stockholders' equity section of the year-end balance sheet.

PROBLEM 11–22A *Recording and Reporting Stock Dividends*

Chen Corp. completed the following transactions in 2007, the first year of operation:

1. Issued 20,000 shares of $20 par common stock for $30 per share.
2. Issued 5,000 shares of $50 par, 5 percent, preferred stock at $51 per share.
3. Paid the annual cash dividend to preferred shareholders.
4. Issued a 5 percent stock dividend on the common stock. The market value at the dividend declaration date was $40 per share.
5. Later that year, issued a 2-for-1 split on the 21,000 shares of outstanding common stock.
6. Earned $210,000 of cash revenues and paid $140,000 of cash operating expenses.

Required
a. Record each of these events in a horizontal statements model like the following one. In the Cash Flow column, indicate whether the item is an operating activity (OA), investing activity (IA), or financing activity (FA). Use NA to indicate that an element is not affected by the event.

Assets = Liab. +	Equity					Rev. – Exp. = Net Inc.	Cash Flow
	Paid-in			Paid-in			
	P. Stk. +	Excess PS +	C. Stk. +	Excess CS +	Ret. Earn.		

b. Record the 2007 transactions in general journal form.
c. Prepare the stockholders' equity section of the balance sheet at the end of 2007.

PROBLEM 11–23A *Analyzing the Stockholders' Equity Section of the Balance Sheet*

The stockholders' equity section of the balance sheet for Atkins Company at December 31, 2007, is as follows:

Stockholders' Equity		
Paid-in Capital		
Preferred Stock, ? Par Value, 6% cumulative,		
50,000 shares authorized,		
30,000 shares issued and outstanding	$300,000	
Common Stock, $10 Stated Value,		
150,000 shares authorized,		
50,000 shares issued and ? outstanding	500,000	
Paid-in Capital in Excess of Par—Preferred	30,000	
Paid-in Capital in Excess of Par—Common	200,000	
Total Paid-in Capital		$1,030,000
Retained Earnings		250,000
Treasury Stock, 1,000 shares		(100,000)
Total Stockholders' Equity		$1,180,000

Note: The market value per share of the common stock is $25, and the market value per share of the preferred stock is $12.

Required
a. What is the par value per share of the preferred stock?
b. What is the dividend per share on the preferred stock?
c. What is the number of common stock shares outstanding?
d. What was the average issue price per share (price for which the stock was issued) of the common stock?

L.O. 4, 6, 7

CHECK FIGURES
c. Total Paid-In Capital: $895,000
c. Retained Earnings: $17,500

L.O. 4, 7

CHECK FIGURES
a. Par value per share: $10
b. Dividend per share: $.60

e. Explain the difference between the average issue price and the market price of the common stock.
f. If Atkins declared a 2-for-1 stock split on the common stock, how many shares would be outstanding after the split? What amount would be transferred from the retained earnings account because of the stock split? Theoretically, what would be the market price of the common stock immediately after the stock split?

L.O. 1   **PROBLEM 11–24A** *Different Forms of Business Organization*

Shawn Bates was working to establish a business enterprise with four of his wealthy friends. Each of the five individuals would receive a 20 percent ownership interest in the company. A primary goal of establishing the enterprise was to minimize the amount of income taxes paid. Assume that the five investors are in a 35 percent personal tax bracket and that the corporate tax rate is 25 percent. Also assume that the new company is expected to earn $200,000 of cash income before taxes during its first year of operation. All earnings are expected to be immediately distributed to the owners.

Required
Calculate the amount of after-tax cash flow available to each investor if the business is established as a partnership versus a corporation. Write a memo explaining the advantages and disadvantages of these two forms of business organization. Explain why a limited liability company may be a better choice than either a partnership or a corporation.

L.O. 4–8   **PROBLEM 11–25A** *Effects of Equity Transactions on Financial Statements*

The following events were experienced by Abbot, Inc.:

1. Issued cumulative preferred stock for cash.
2. Issued common stock for cash.
3. Distributed a 2-for-1 stock split on the common stock.
4. Issued noncumulative preferred stock for cash.
5. Appropriated retained earnings.
6. Sold treasury stock for an amount of cash that was more than the cost of the treasury stock.
7. Distributed a stock dividend.
8. Paid cash to purchase treasury stock.
9. Declared a cash dividend.
10. Paid the cash dividend declared in Event 9.

Required
Show the effect of each event on the elements of the financial statements using a horizontal statements model like the following one. Use + for increase, − for decrease, and NA for not affected. In the Cash Flow column, indicate whether the item is an operating activity (OA), investing activity (IA), or financing activity (FA). The first transaction is entered as an example.

Event No.	Assets	=	Liab.	+	Equity	Rev.	−	Exp.	=	Net Inc.	Cash Flow
1	+		NA		+	NA		NA		NA	+ FA

L.O. 10   **PROBLEM 11–26A** *Not for Profit (Appendix)*

The City Theater is an NFP organization established to encourage the performing arts in Monroe, Louisiana. The City Theater experienced the following accounting events during 2006. Assume that all transactions are cash transactions unless otherwise stated.

1. Acquired cash contributions from donors, including $500,000 of permanently restricted, $300,000 of temporarily restricted, and $200,000 of unrestricted contributions.
2. The $500,000 of permanently restricted funds was invested in an endowed fund designed to provide investment income that will be made available for operating expenses.
3. The endowed investment fund produced $40,000 of cash revenue.
4. The $300,000 of temporarily restricted funds was used in accordance with donor restrictions to purchase a theater in which plays will be presented. The theater had an expected useful life of 40 years and an anticipated salvage value of $50,000.
5. Of the unrestricted assets, $70,000 was spent to purchase theatrical equipment. The equipment was expected to have a five-year useful life and zero salvage value.
6. Tickets sales produced $140,000 of revenue during the accounting period.

7. The company incurred and paid $110,000 of operating expenses.

8. Recognized depreciation on the theater and theatrical equipment.

Required

Prepare a statement of activities, statement of financial position, and statement of cash flows.

EXERCISE 11–1B *Effect of Accounting Events on the Financial Statements of a Sole Proprietorship*   L.O. 1, 2

A sole proprietorship was started on January 1, 2009, when it received $20,000 cash from Dan Jones, the owner. During 2009, the company earned $14,500 in cash revenues and paid $9,300 in cash expenses. Jones withdrew $500 cash from the business during 2009.

Required

Prepare an income statement, capital statement (statement of changes in equity), balance sheet, and statement of cash flows for Jones' 2009 fiscal year.

EXERCISE 11–2B *Effect of Accounting Events on the Financial Statements of a Partnership*   L.O. 1, 2

Claire Mills and Polly Price started the M&P partnership on January 1, 2009. The business acquired $24,500 cash from Mills and $45,500 from Price. During 2009, the partnership earned $15,000 in cash revenues and paid $6,300 for cash expenses. Mills withdrew $600 cash from the business, and Price withdrew $1,400 cash. The net income was allocated to the capital accounts of the two partners in proportion to the amounts of their original investments in the business.

Required

Prepare an income statement, capital statement, balance sheet, and statement of cash flows for M&P's 2009 fiscal year.

EXERCISE 11–3B *Effect of Accounting Events on the Financial Statements of a Corporation*   L.O. 1, 2

Stone Corporation was started with the issue of 1,000 shares of $5 par stock for cash on January 1, 2009. The stock was issued at a market price of $18 per share. During 2009, the company earned $23,000 in cash revenues and paid $17,000 for cash expenses. Also a $1,200 cash dividend was paid to the stockholders.

Required

Prepare an income statement, statement of changes in stockholders' equity, balance sheet, and statement of cash flows for Stone Corporation's 2009 fiscal year.

EXERCISE 11–4B *Effect of Issuing Common Stock on the Balance Sheet*   L.O. 4

Newly formed Super Max Corporation has 30,000 shares of $10 par common stock authorized. On March 1, 2009, Super Max issued 5,000 shares of the stock for $20 per share. On May 2 the company issued an additional 6,000 shares for $24 per share. Super Max was not affected by other events during 2009.

Required

a. Record the transactions in a horizontal statements model like the following one. In the Cash Flow column, indicate whether the item is an operating activity (OA), investing activity (IA), or financing activity (FA). Use NA to indicate that an element was not affected by the event.

Assets = Liab. +		Equity		Rev. – Exp. = Net Inc.	Cash Flow
Cash =	+ C. Stk.	+ Paid-in Excess			

b. Determine the amount Super Max would report for common stock on the December 31, 2009, balance sheet.

c. Determine the amount Super Max would report for paid-in capital in excess of par.

d. What is the total amount of capital contributed by the owners?

e. What amount of total assets would Super Max report on the December 31, 2009, balance sheet?

f. Prepare journal entries to record the March 1 and May 2 transactions.

L.O. 4   EXERCISE 11–5B *Recording and Reporting Common and Preferred Stock Transactions*

E.Com, Inc., was organized on June 5, 2009. It was authorized to issue 200,000 shares of $5 par common stock and 20,000 shares of 5 percent cumulative class A preferred stock. The class A stock had a stated value of $50 per share. The following stock transactions pertain to E.Com, Inc.:

1. Issued 10,000 shares of common stock for $8 per share.
2. Issued 3,000 shares of the class A preferred stock for $80 per share.
3. Issued 80,000 shares of common stock for $10 per share.

Required
a. Prepare general journal entries for these transactions.
b. Prepare the stockholders' equity section of the balance sheet immediately after these transactions.

L.O. 4   EXERCISE 11–6B *Effect of No-Par Common and Par Preferred Stock on the Horizontal Statements Model*

Master Corporation issued 4,000 shares of no-par common stock for $30 per share. Master also issued 1,000 shares of $50 par, 6 percent noncumulative preferred stock at $80 per share.

Required
a. Record these events in a horizontal statements model like the following one. In the Cash Flow column, indicate whether the item is an operating activity (OA), investing activity (IA), or financing activity (FA). Use NA to indicate that an element was not affected by the event.

Assets =	Equity			Rev. − Exp. = Net Inc.	Cash Flow
Cash = P. Stk. +	C. Stk. +	Paid-in Excess			

b. Prepare journal entries to record these transactions.

L.O. 4   EXERCISE 11–7B *Issuing Stock for Assets other than Cash*

James Lee, a wealthy investor, exchanged a plot of land that originally cost him $30,000 for 1,000 shares of $10 par common stock issued to him by Bay Corp. On the same date, Bay Corp. issued an additional 400 shares of stock to Lee for $31 per share.

Required
a. What was the value of the land at the date of the stock issue?
b. Show the effect of the two stock issues on Bay's books in a horizontal statements model like the following one. In the Cash Flow column, indicate whether the item is an operating activity (OA), investing activity (IA), or financing activity (FA). Use NA to indicate that an element was not affected by the event.

Assets	=	Equity		Rev. − Exp. = Net Inc.	Cash Flow
Cash + Land =		C. Stk. + Paid-in Excess			

L.O. 5   EXERCISE 11–8B *Treasury Stock Transactions*

Hawk Corporation repurchased 1,000 shares of its own stock for $38 per share. The stock has a par of $10 per share. A month later Hawk resold 500 shares of the treasury stock for $55 per share.

Required
a. Record the two events in general journal format.
b. What is the balance of the treasury stock account after these transactions?

L.O. 5   EXERCISE 11–9B *Recording and Reporting Treasury Stock Transactions*

The following information pertains to Sneed Corp. at January 1, 2006.

Common stock, $10 par, 10,000 shares authorized, 800 shares issued and outstanding	$ 8,000
Paid-in capital in excess of par, common stock	12,000
Retained earnings	75,000

Sneed Corp. completed the following transactions during 2006:

1. Issued 2,000 shares of $10 par common stock for $43 per share.
2. Repurchased 300 shares of its own common stock for $38 per share.
3. Resold 100 shares of treasury stock for $40 per share.

Required
a. How many shares of common stock were outstanding at the end of the period?
b. How many shares of common stock had been issued at the end of the period?
c. Prepare journal entries for these transactions.
d. Prepare the stockholders' equity section of the balance sheet reflecting these transactions. Include the number of shares authorized, issued, and outstanding in the description of the common stock.

EXERCISE 11–10B *Effect of Cash Dividends on Financial Statements*   **L.O. 6**

On May 1, 2005, Lott Corporation declared a $120,000 cash dividend to be paid on May 31 to shareholders of record on May 15.

Required
a. Record the events occurring on May 1, May 15, and May 31 in a horizontal statements model like the following one. In the Cash Flow column, indicate whether the item is an operating activity (OA), investing activity (IA), or financing activity (FA).

Date	Assets	=	Liab.	+	C. Stock	+	Ret. Earn	Rev.	–	Exp.	=	Net Inc.	Cash Flow

b. Prepare journal entries for all events associated with the dividend.

EXERCISE 11–11B *Accounting for Cumulative Preferred Dividends*   **L.O. 6**

When Express Corporation was organized in January 2007, it immediately issued 2,000 shares of $50 par, 7 percent, cumulative preferred stock and 30,000 shares of $20 par common stock. Its earnings history is as follows: 2007, net loss of $25,000; 2008, net income of $120,000; 2009, net income of $250,000. The corporation did not pay a dividend in 2007.

Required
a. How much is the dividend arrearage as of January 1, 2008?
b. Assume that the board of directors declares a $30,000 cash dividend at the end of 2008 (remember that the 2007 and 2008 preferred dividends are due). How will the dividend be divided between the preferred and common stockholders?

EXERCISE 11–12B *Cash Dividends for Preferred and Common Shareholders*   **L.O. 6**

Iuka Corporation had the following stock issued and outstanding at January 1, 2005:

1. 100,000 shares of $1 par common stock.
2. 10,000 shares of $100 par, 8 percent, noncumulative preferred stock.

On June 10, Iuka Corporation declared the annual cash dividend on its 10,000 shares of preferred stock and a $1 per share dividend for the common shareholders. The dividends will be paid on July 1 to the shareholders of record on June 20.

Required
a. Determine the total amount of dividends to be paid to the preferred shareholders and common shareholders.
b. Prepare general journal entries to record the declaration and payment of the cash dividends (be sure to date your entries).

EXERCISE 11–13B *Cash Dividends: Common and Preferred Stock*   **L.O. 6**

Varsity, Inc., had the following stock issued and outstanding at January 1, 2004:

1. 200,000 shares of no-par common stock.
2. 10,000 shares of $100 par, 8 percent, cumulative preferred stock. (Dividends are in arrears for one year, 2003.)

On March 8, 2004, Varsity declared a $200,000 cash dividend to be paid March 31 to shareholders of record on March 20.

Required

a. What amount of dividends will be paid to the preferred shareholders versus the common shareholders?

b. Prepare the journal entries required for these transactions. (Be sure to include the dates of the entries.)

L.O. 7   EXERCISE 11–14B *Accounting for Stock Dividends*

Rollins Corporation issued a 5 percent stock dividend on 10,000 shares of its $10 par common stock. At the time of the dividend, the market value of the stock was $14 per share.

Required

a. Compute the amount of the stock dividend.

b. Show the effects of the stock dividend on the financial statements using a horizontal statements model like the following one.

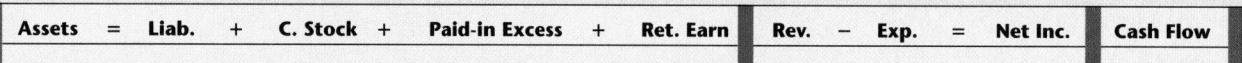

Assets	=	Liab.	+	C. Stock	+	Paid-in Excess	+	Ret. Earn	Rev.	–	Exp.	=	Net Inc.	Cash Flow

c. Prepare the journal entry to record the stock dividend.

L.O. 7   EXERCISE 11–15B *Determining the Effects of Stock Splits on the Accounting Records*

The market value of West Corporation's common stock had become excessively high. The stock was currently selling for $240 per share. To reduce the market price of the common stock, West declared a 4-for-1 stock split for the 100,000 outstanding shares of its $20 par value common stock.

Required

a. What entry will be made on the books of West Corporation for the stock split?

b. Determine the number of common shares outstanding and the par value after the split.

c. Explain how the market value of the stock will be affected by the stock split.

L.O. 9   EXERCISE 11–16B *Accounting Information*

The Cutting Edge (TCE) is one of the world's largest lawn mower distributors. TCE is concerned about maintaining an adequate supply of the economy-line mowers that it sells in its stores. TCE currently obtains its economy-line mowers from two suppliers. To ensure a steady supply of mowers, the management of TCE is considering the purchase of an ownership interest in one of the companies that supply its mowers. More specifically, TCE wants to own enough stock of one of the suppliers to enable it to exercise significant influence over the management of the company. The following is a description of the two suppliers.

The first supplier, Dobbs, Incorporated, is a closely held company. Large blocks of the Dobbs stock are held by individual members of the Dobbs family. TCE's investment advisor has discovered that one of the members of the Dobbs family is interested in selling her 5 percent share of the company's stock.

The second supplier, National Mowers, Inc., has a widely disbursed ownership with no one single stockholder owning more than 1 percent of the stock. TCE's investment advisor believes that 5 percent of this company's stock could be acquired gradually over an extended period of time without having a significant effect on the company's stock price.

Required

Provide a recommendation to TCE's management as to whether they should pursue the purchase of 5 percent of Dobbs, Incorporated, or 5 percent of National Mowers, Inc. Your answer should be supported by an appropriate logical explanation of your recommendation.

L.O. 10   EXERCISE 11–17B *Not for Profit (Appendix)*

Mark Hayes was arguing with his friend Sewon Ow regarding contributions of financial resources that are acquired by an organization. Ow contends that such events constitute revenue that should be reported in the operating activities section of the income statement and statement of cash flows. Hayes disagrees. He believes that acquisitions of capital should not be shown on the income statement and should be shown as a financing activity in the statement of cash flows.

Required

Write a brief memo explaining how both of the apparently contradictory arguments could be correct.

PROBLEM 11–18B *Effect of Business Structure on Financial Statements*   L.O. 1, 2

Calloway Company was started on January 1, 2009, when it acquired $40,000 cash from the owners. During 2009, the company earned cash revenues of $18,000 and incurred cash expenses of $12,500. The company also paid cash distributions of $3,000.

Required

Prepare a 2009 income statement, capital statement (statement of changes in equity), balance sheet, and statement of cash flows under each of the following assumptions. (Consider each assumption separately.)

a. Calloway is a sole proprietorship owned by Macy Calloway.
b. Calloway is a partnership with two partners, Macy Calloway and Artie Calloway. Macy Calloway invested $25,000 and Artie Calloway invested $15,000 of the $40,000 cash that was used to start the business. A. Calloway was expected to assume the vast majority of the responsibility for operating the business. The partnership agreement called for A. Calloway to receive 60 percent of the profits and M. Calloway to get the remaining 40 percent. With regard to the $3,000 distribution, A. Calloway withdrew $1,200 from the business and M. Calloway withdrew $1,800.
c. Calloway is a corporation. It issued 5,000 shares of $5 par common stock for $40,000 cash to start the business.

PROBLEM 11–19B *Recording and Reporting Stock Transactions and Cash Dividends Across*   L.O. 4–6
                   Two Accounting Cycles

Hamby Corporation received a charter that authorized the issuance of 100,000 shares of $10 par common stock and 50,000 shares of $50 par, 6 percent cumulative preferred stock. Hamby Corporation completed the following transactions during its first two years of operation.

2008

Jan.   5   Sold 10,000 shares of the $10 par common stock for $28 per share.
      12   Sold 1,000 shares of the 6 percent preferred stock for $70 per share.
Apr.   5   Sold 40,000 shares of the $10 par common stock for $40 per share.
Dec. 31   During the year, earned $170,000 in cash revenue and paid $110,000 for cash operating expenses.
      31   Declared the cash dividend on the outstanding shares of preferred stock for 2008. The dividend will be paid on February 15 to stockholders of record on January 10, 2009.
      31   Closed the revenue, expense, and dividend accounts to the retained earnings account.

2009

Feb. 15   Paid the cash dividend declared on December 31, 2008.
Mar. 3   Sold 10,000 shares of the $50 par preferred stock for $78 per share.
May   5   Purchased 500 shares of the common stock as treasury stock at $43 per share.
Dec. 31   During the year, earned $210,000 in cash revenues and paid $140,000 for cash operating expenses.
      31   Declared the annual dividend on the preferred stock and a $0.60 per share dividend on the common stock.
      31   Closed revenue, expense, and dividend accounts to the retained earnings account.

Required

a. Prepare journal entries for these transactions for 2008 and 2009.
b. Prepare the balance sheets at December 31, 2008 and 2009.
c. What is the number of common shares *outstanding* at the end of 2008? At the end of 2009? How many common shares had been *issued* at the end of 2008? At the end of 2009? Explain any differences between issued and outstanding common shares for 2008 and for 2009.

PROBLEM 11–20B *Recording and Reporting Treasury Stock Transactions*   L.O. 4, 5, 8

One Co. completed the following transactions in 2009, the first year of operation:

1. Issued 20,000 shares of $5 par common stock for $5 per share.
2. Issued 1,000 shares of $20 stated value preferred stock for $20 per share.
3. Purchased 1,000 shares of common stock as treasury stock for $7 per share.
4. Declared a $1,500 dividend on preferred stock.
5. Sold 500 shares of treasury stock for $10 per share.
6. Paid $1,500 cash for the preferred dividend declared in Event 4.
7. Earned cash revenues of $54,000 and incurred cash expenses of $32,000.

8. Closed revenue, expense, and dividend accounts to the retained earnings account.
9. Appropriated $5,000 of retained earnings.

Required

a. Prepare journal entries to record these transactions.
b. Prepare a balance sheet as of December 31, 2009.

L.O. 4, 5   PROBLEM 11-21B *Analyzing Journal Entries for Treasury Stock Transactions*

The following correctly prepared entries without explanations pertain to Triangle Corporation.

	Account Title	Debit	Credit
1.	Cash	2,100,000	
	Common Stock		1,000,000
	Paid-in Capital in Excess of Par Value		1,100,000
2.	Treasury Stock	22,500	
	Cash		22,500
3.	Cash	13,600	
	Treasury Stock		12,000
	Paid-in Capital in Excess of Cost of Treasury Stock		1,600

The original sale (Entry 1) was for 200,000 shares, and the treasury stock was acquired for $15 per share (Entry 2).

Required

a. What was the sales price per share of the original stock issue?
b. How many shares of stock did the corporation acquire in Event 2?
c. How many shares were reissued in Event 3?
d. How many shares are outstanding immediately following Events 2 and 3, respectively?

L.O. 4, 6, 7   PROBLEM 11-22B *Recording and Reporting Stock Dividends*

Deaton Co. completed the following transactions in 2006, the first year of operation:

1. Issued 20,000 shares of no-par common stock for $10 per share.
2. Issued 5,000 shares of $20 par, 6 percent, preferred stock for $20 per share.
3. Paid a cash dividend of $6,000 to preferred shareholders.
4. Issued a 10 percent stock dividend on no-par common stock. The market value at the dividend declaration date was $15 per share.
5. Later that year, issued a 2-for-1 split on the shares of outstanding common stock. The market price of the stock at that time was $35 per share.
6. Produced $145,000 of cash revenues and incurred $97,000 of cash operating expenses.

Required

a. Record each of the six events in a horizontal statements model like the following one. In the Cash Flow column, indicate whether the item is an operating activity (OA), investing activity (IA), or financing activity (FA). Use NA to indicate that an element is not affected by the event.

Assets	=		Equity		Rev.	−	Exp.	=	Net Inc.	Cash Flow
		P. Stk.	+ C. Stk. +	Ret. Earn.						

b. Record the 2006 transactions in general journal form.
c. Prepare the stockholders' equity section of the balance sheet at the end of 2006. (Include all necessary information.)
d. Theoretically, what is the market value of the common stock after the stock split?

L.O. 4, 7   PROBLEM 11-23B *Analyzing the Stockholders' Equity Section of the Balance Sheet*

The stockholders' equity section of the balance sheet for Cross Electric Co. at December 31, 2007, is as follows:

Stockholders' Equity		
Paid-in Capital		
Preferred Stock, ? Par Value, 8% cumulative,		
100,000 shares authorized,		
5,000 shares issued and outstanding	$ 250,000	
Common Stock, $20 Stated Value,		
200,000 shares authorized,		
100,000 shares issued and outstanding	2,000,000	
Paid-in Capital in Excess of Par—Preferred	100,000	
Paid-in Capital in Excess of Stated Value—Common	500,000	
Total Paid-in Capital		$2,850,000
Retained Earnings		500,000
Total Stockholders' Equity		$3,350,000

Note: The market value per share of the common stock is $36, and the market value per share of the preferred stock is $75.

Required

a. What is the par value per share of the preferred stock?

b. What is the dividend per share on the preferred stock?

c. What was the average issue price per share (price for which the stock was issued) of the common stock?

d. Explain the difference between the par value and the market price of the preferred stock.

e. If Cross declares a 3-for-1 stock split on the common stock, how many shares will be outstanding after the split? What amount will be transferred from the retained earnings account because of the stock split? Theoretically, what will be the market price of the common stock immediately after the stock split?

PROBLEM 11–24B *Different Forms of Business Organization*

L.O. 1

Paul Salvy established a partnership with Lisa Witlow. The new company, S&W Fuels, purchased coal directly from mining companies and contracted to ship the coal via waterways to a seaport where it was delivered to ships that were owned and operated by international utilities companies. Salvy was primarily responsible for running the day-to-day operations of the business. Witlow negotiated the buy-and-sell agreements. She recently signed a deal to purchase and deliver $2,000,000 of coal to Solar Utilities. S&W Fuels purchased the coal on account from Miller Mining Company. After accepting title to the coal, S&W Fuels agreed to deliver the coal under terms FOB destination, Port of Long Beach. Unfortunately, Witlow failed to inform Salvy of the deal in time for Salvy to insure the shipment. While in transit, the vessel carrying the coal suffered storm damage that rendered the coal virtually worthless by the time it reached its destination. S&W Fuels immediately declared bankruptcy. The company not only was responsible for the $2,000,000 due to Miller Mining Company but also was sued by Solar for breach of contract. Witlow had a personal net worth of virtually zero, but Salvy was a wealthy individual with a net worth approaching $2,500,000. Accordingly, Miller Mining and Solar filed suit against Salvy's personal assets. Salvy claimed that he was not responsible for the problem because Witlow had failed to inform him of the contracts in time to obtain insurance coverage. Witlow admitted that she was personally responsible for the disaster.

Required

Write a memo describing Salvy's risk associated with his participation in the partnership. Comment on how other forms of ownership would have affected his level of risk.

PROBLEM 11–25B *Effects of Equity Transactions on Financial Statements*

L.O. 4–8

The following events were experienced by Baskin, Inc.

1. Issued common stock for cash.
2. Paid cash to purchase treasury stock.
3. Declared a cash dividend.
4. Issued cumulative preferred stock.
5. Issued noncumulative preferred stock.
6. Appropriated retained earnings.
7. Sold treasury stock for an amount of cash that was more than the cost of the treasury stock.

8. Distributed a stock dividend.
9. Declared a 2-for-1 stock split on the common stock.
10. Paid a cash dividend that was previously declared.

Required

Show the effect of each event on the elements of the financial statements using a horizontal statements model like the following one. Use + for increase, − for decrease, and NA for not affected. In the Cash Flow column indicate whether the item is an operating activity (OA), investing activity (IA), or financing activity (FA). The first transaction is entered as an example.

Event No.	Assets	=	Liab.	+	Equity	Rev.	−	Exp.	=	Net Inc.	Cash Flow
1	+		NA		+	NA		NA		NA	+ FA

L.O. 10   **PROBLEM 11–26B** *Not for Profit (Appendix)*

Marshall County Public Library (MCPL) experienced the following accounting events during 2009. Assume that all transactions are cash transactions unless otherwise stated.

1. Acquired $500,000 in contributions.
2. Paid $450,000 for facilities and equipment.
3. Earned $120,000 of revenue.
4. Incurred $80,000 in operating expenses.
5. Recognized $25,000 of depreciation expense.

Required

a. Assume that MCPL is a profit-oriented corporation and that the first event results from the issue of no-par common stock. Prepare an income statement, balance sheet, and statement of cash flows.
b. Assume that MCPL is a not-for-profit organization and that the first event represents an unrestricted donor contribution. Prepare a statement of activities, statement of financial position, and statement of cash flows.

ANALYZE, THINK, COMMUNICATE

ATC 11–1   **BUSINESS APPLICATIONS CASE** *Understanding Real World Annual Reports*

Required—Part 1

The Topps Company, Inc.

Use the Topps Company's annual report in Appendix B to answer the following questions.

a. Does Topps' common stock have a par value, and if so how much is it?
b. How many shares of Topps' common stock were *outstanding* as of March 1, 2003? Do not forget to consider treasury stock.
c. The dollar-value balance in Topps' Treasury Stock account is larger than the balance in its Common Stock and Additional Paid-In-Capital accounts. How can this be?
d. How many members of Topps' Board of Directors are also officers (employees) of the company as of March 1, 2003?
e. What was the highest and lowest price per share that Topps' common stock sold for during the fiscal year ending on March 1, 2003?

Required—Part 2

Harley-Davidson, Inc.

Use the Harley-Davidson's annual report that came with this book to answer the following questions.

a. Does Harley-Davidson's common stock have a par value, and if so how much is it?
b. How many shares of Harley-Davidson's common stock were outstanding as of December 31, 2003?
c. Did Harley-Davidson pay cash dividends in 2003, and if so, how much?
d. What was the highest and lowest price per share that Harley-Davidson's common stock sold for during the fiscal year ending on December 31, 2003?

GROUP ASSIGNMENT *Missing Information*

Listed here are the stockholders' equity sections of three public companies for years ending 2003 and 2002:

	2003	2002
Wendy's (dollar amounts are presented in thousands)		
Stockholders' Equity		
Common stock, ?? Stated Value per share, authorized:		
200,000,000; 116,760,000 in 2003 and 114,692,000 in		
2002 shares issued, respectively	$ 11,676	$ 10,895
Capital in Excess of Stated Value	54,310	–0–
Retained Earnings	1,703,488	1,498,607
Acc. Other Comp. Income (Exp.)	46,124	(60,897)
Treasury Stock, at cost: 2,063,000 in 2003	(56,992)	–0–
Coca-Cola (dollar amounts are presented in millions)		
Stockholders' Equity		
Common Stock, ?? Par Value per share, authorized:		
5,600,000,000; issued: 3,494,799,258 shares in 2003		
and 3,490,818,627 shares in 2002	874	873
Capital Surplus	4,395	3,857
Reinvested Earnings	26,687	24,506
Acc. Other Comp. Inc. (loss)	(1,995)	(3,047)
Treasury Stock, at cost: (1,053,267,474 shares in 2003;		
1,019,839,490 shares in 2002)	(15,871)	(14,389)
Harley-Davidson (dollar amounts are presented in thousands)		
Stockholders' Equity		
Common stock, ?? Par Value per share, authorized:		
800,000,000, issued: 326,489,291 in 2003 and		
325,298,404 shares in 2002	3,266	3,254
Additional Paid-in Capital	419,455	386,284
Retained Earnings	3,074,037	2,372,095
Acc. Other Comp. Inc. (loss)	47,174	(46,266)
Treasury Stock, at cost: 24,978,798 for 2003 and		
22,636,295 for 2002	(586,240)	(482,360)
Unearned Compensation	–0–	(92)

Required

a. Divide the class in three sections and divide each section into groups of three to five students. Assign each section one of the companies.

Group Tasks

Based on the company assigned to your group, answer the following questions.

b. What is the per share par or stated value of the common stock in 2003?
c. What was the average issue price of the common stock for each year?
d. How many shares of stock are outstanding at the end of each year?
e. What is the average cost per share of the treasury stock for 2003?
f. Do the data suggest that your company was profitable in 2003?
g. Can you determine the amount of net income from the information given? What is missing?
h. What is the total stockholders' equity of your company for each year?

Class Discussion

i. Have each group select a representative to present the information about its company. Compare the share issue price and the par or stated value of the companies.
j. Compare the average issue price to the current market price for each of the companies. Speculate about what might cause the difference.

REAL-WORLD CASE *Computing P/E Ratios for Four Companies*

Many companies grant certain members of management stock options that allow them to purchase designated amounts of stock for less than its market price. These arrangements are referred to as *stock compensation plans* and are intended to help the company retain high-quality management and to encourage management to increase the market value of the company's stock.

Deciding on the appropriate way to account for these plans is complex and controversial. Therefore, companies are allowed to *exclude* the estimated costs of the options they grant their management from net earnings provided that they disclose the estimated costs in the footnotes to the financial statements.

Listed here are data from four different companies that grant stock options to members of their management. The data are based on information provided in the companies' 10-K reports.

Costco Wholesale Corporation

Basic EPS as reported on the fiscal year 2002 income statement	$ 1.48
Basic EPS if stock compensation is deducted	1.32
Selling price of the company's stock on July 1, 2003	36.51

Target Corporation

Basic EPS as reported on the fiscal year 2003 income statement	$ 1.82
Basic EPS if stock compensation is deducted	1.79
Selling price of the company's stock on July 1, 2003	37.62

Cisco Systems, Inc.

Basic EPS as reported on the fiscal year 2002 income statement	$ 0.26
Basic EPS if stock compensation is deducted	0.05
Selling price of the company's stock on July 1, 2003	17.24

Oracle Corporation

Basic EPS as reported on the fiscal year 2003 income statement	$ 0.44
Basic EPS if stock compensation is deducted	0.37
Selling price of the company's stock on July 1, 2003	12.33

Required

a. Compute each company's P/E ratio on July 1, 2003, based on (1) EPS as reported and (2) EPS with stock compensation deducted. You will have eight P/E ratios.

b. Assuming these companies are representative of their respective industries (department stores and software companies), what conclusions can you draw from the data provided and from your P/E computations? Write a brief report presenting your conclusions and the reasons for them.

ATC 11–4   BUSINESS APPLICATIONS CASE *Finding Stock Market Information*

This problem requires stock price quotations for the New York Stock Exchange, the American Stock Exchange, and NASDAQ. These are available in *The Wall Street Journal* and in the business sections of many daily newspapers as well as various websites. Stock prices are also available on electronic data services such as CompuServe.

Required

For each company listed here, provide the requested information as of Thursday of last week. (*Hint:* Information about Thursday's stock market is in Friday's newspaper.)

Name of Company	Stock Exchange Where Listed	Closing Price	P/E Ratio
Berkshire Hathaway A			
Devron Energy Corp.			
Intel			
Yahoo			
Xerox			

ATC 11–5   BUSINESS APPLICATIONS CASE *Using the P/E Ratio*

During 2007, Musicland Corporation and Jazztown Corporation reported net incomes of $62,000 and $54,000, respectively. Each company had 10,000 shares of common stock issued and outstanding. The market price per share of Musicland's stock was $80, while Jazztown's stock sold for $88 per share.

Required

a. Determine the P/E ratio for each company.

b. Based on the P/E ratios computed in Requirement *a*, which company do investors believe has more potential for growth in income?

WRITING ASSIGNMENT *Comparison of Organizational Forms*

Jim Baku and Scott Hanson are thinking about opening a new restaurant. Baku has extensive marketing experience but does not know that much about food preparation. However, Hanson is an excellent chef. Both will work in the business, but Baku will provide most of the funds necessary to start the business. At this time, they cannot decide whether to operate the business as a partnership or a corporation.

Required

Prepare a written memo to Baku and Hanson describing the advantages and disadvantages of each organizational form. Also, from the limited information provided, recommend the organizational form you think they should use.

ETHICAL DILEMMA *Bad News Versus Very Bad News*

Louise Stinson, the chief financial officer of Bostonian Corporation, was on her way to the president's office. She was carrying the latest round of bad news. There would be no executive bonuses this year. Corporate profits were down. Indeed, if the latest projections held true, the company would report a small loss on the year-end income statement. Executive bonuses were tied to corporate profits. The executive compensation plan provided for 10 percent of net earnings to be set aside for bonuses. No profits meant no bonuses. While things looked bleak, Stinson had a plan that might help soften the blow.

After informing the company president of the earnings forecast, Stinson made the following suggestion: Since the company was going to report a loss anyway, why not report a big loss? She reasoned that the directors and stockholders would not be much more angry if the company reported a large loss than if it reported a small one. There were several questionable assets that could be written down in the current year. This would increase the current year's loss but would reduce expenses in subsequent accounting periods. For example, the company was carrying damaged inventory that was estimated to have a value of $2,500,000. If this estimate were revised to $500,000, the company would have to recognize a $2,000,000 loss in the current year. However, next year when the goods were sold, the expense for cost of goods sold would be $2,000,000 less and profits would be higher by that amount. Although the directors would be angry this year, they would certainly be happy next year. The strategy would also have the benefit of adding $200,000 to next year's executive bonus pool ($2,000,000 × 0.10). Furthermore, it could not hurt this year's bonus pool because there would be no pool this year since the company is going to report a loss.

Some of the other items that Stinson is considering include (1) converting from straight-line to accelerated depreciation, (2) increasing the percentage of receivables estimated to be uncollectible in the current year and lowering the percentage in the following year, and (3) raising the percentage of estimated warranty claims in the current period and lowering it in the following period. Finally, Stinson notes that two of the company's department stores have been experiencing losses. The company could sell these stores this year and thereby improve earnings next year. Stinson admits that the sale would result in significant losses this year, but she smiles as she thinks of next year's bonus check.

Required

a. Explain how each of the three numbered strategies for increasing the amount of the current year's loss would affect the stockholders' equity section of the balance sheet in the current year. How would the other elements of the balance sheet be affected?

b. If Stinson's strategy were effectively implemented, how would it affect the stockholders' equity in subsequent accounting periods?

c. Comment on the ethical implications of running the company for the sake of management (maximization of bonuses) versus the maximization of return to stockholders.

d. Formulate a bonus plan that will motivate managers to maximize the value of the firm instead of motivating them to manipulate the reporting process.

e. How would Stinson's strategy of overstating the amount of the reported loss in the current year affect the company's current P/E ratio?

EDGAR DATABASE *Analyzing PepsiCo's Equity Structure*

Required

Using the most current 10-K available on EDGAR, answer the following questions about **PepsiCo** for the most recent year reported. (PepsiCo is the company that produces Pepsi soft drinks, among other things.) Instructions for using EDGAR are in Appendix A.

a. What is the *book value* of PepsiCo's stockholders' equity that is shown on the company's balance sheet?

b. What is the par value of PepsiCo's common stock?

c. Does PepsiCo have any treasury stock? If so, how many shares of treasury stock does the company hold?

d. Why does the stock of a company such as PepsiCo have a market value that is higher than its book value?

ATC 11–9   **SPREADSHEET ANALYSIS** *Using Excel*

Annette's Accessories had the following stock issued and outstanding at January 1, 2005.

> 150,000 Shares of $1 Par Common Stock
> 10,000 Shares of $50 Par, 8%, Cumulative Preferred Stock

On March 5, 2005, Annette's declared a $100,000 cash dividend to be paid March 31 to shareholders of record on March 21.

Required

Set up a spreadsheet to calculate the total amount of dividends to be paid to preferred and common shareholders under the following alternative situations:

a. No dividends are in arrears for preferred shareholders.

b. One year's worth of dividends is in arrears for preferred shareholders.

c. Two years' worth of dividends is in arrears for preferred shareholders.

d. Instead of a $100,000 dividend, Annette's paid a $70,000 dividend and one year of dividends was in arrears.

Spreadsheet Tips

The following spreadsheet provides one method of setting up formulas for all possible alternatives. The spreadsheet also reflects the results of Requirement *a*.

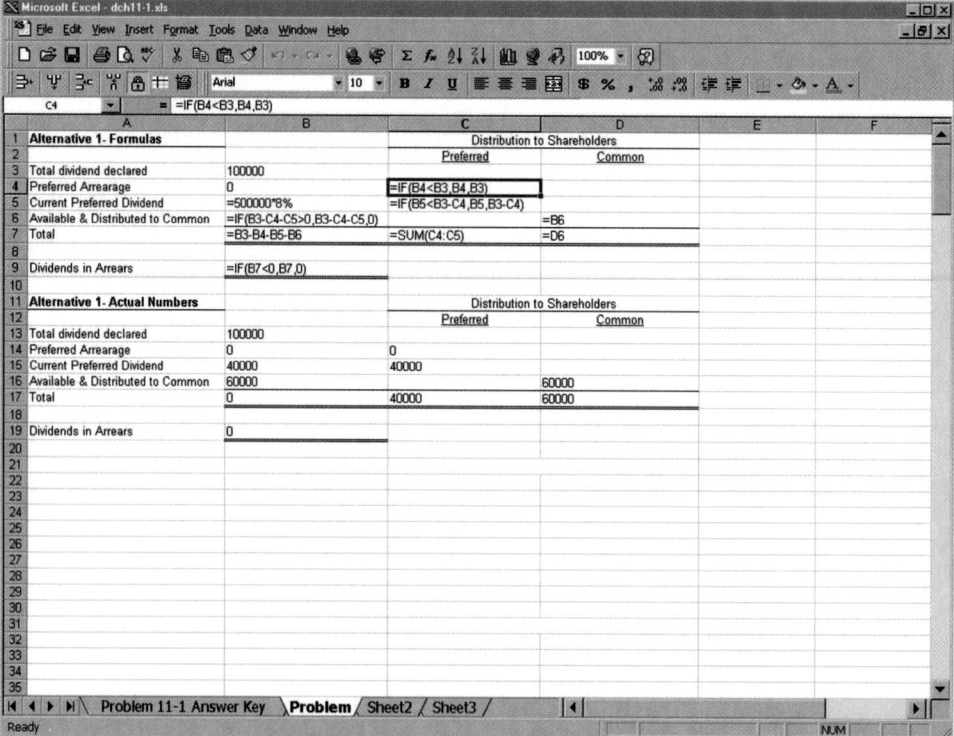

Notice the use of the IF function. The IF function looks like =IF(condition, true, false). To use the IF function, first describe a certain condition to Excel. Next indicate the desired result if that condition is found to be true. Finally, indicate the desired result if that condition is found to be false. Notice in cell C4 of the spreadsheet (dividends in arrears distributed to preferred shareholders) that the condition provided is B4<B3, which is asking whether the dividends in arrears are less than the total dividend. If this

condition is true, the formula indicates to display B4, which is the amount of the dividends in arrears. If the condition is false, the formula indicates that B3 should be displayed, which is the total amount of the dividend.

The IF function can also be used to determine the amount of the current dividend distributed to preferred shareholders, the amount available for common shareholders, and the dividends in arrears after the dividend.

SPREADSHEET ASSIGNMENT *Mastering Excel*   **ATC 11–10**

Required
Complete Requirement *a* of Problem 11–22B using an Excel spreadsheet.

COMPREHENSIVE PROBLEM

The account balances of Pacilio Security Systems Sales and Service as of January 1, 2011, was:

Cash	$282,708
Petty Cash	100
Accounts Receivable	56,795
Allowance for Doubtful Accounts	2,989
Supplies	210
Inventory—Standard Alarms (22 @ $285)	6,270
Inventory—Deluxe Alarms (9 @ $600)	5,400
Van	9,200
Equipment	12,000
Building	72,000
Land	36,000
Accumulated Depreciation	18,880
Goodwill	40,750
Warranties Payable	2,677
Notes Payable	34,979
Bonds Payable	80,000
Discount of Bonds Payable	1,440
Common Stock (10,000 shares of $5 par value, common stock)	50,000
Retained Earnings	333,348

During 2011, Pacilio Security Systems Sales and Service experienced the following transactions:

1. Pacilio issued 5,000 additional shares of common stock for $8 per share and 1,000 shares of $50 stated value, 5 percent cumulative preferred stock for $52 per share.
2. Purchased $500 of supplies for cash.
3. April 2, 2011, replenished the petty cash fund. The fund had $13 of cash and receipts for $32 office supplies, $40 for cutting the grass, and $12 miscellaneous expense.
4. Purchased 190 standard alarm systems for $290 each and 50 deluxe alarm systems for $605 each.
5. Sold on account 195 standard alarm systems for $130,000 and 52 deluxe alarm systems for $49,000 during the year. (Be sure to record cost of goods sold using the FIFO cost flow method)
6. Billed $160,000 for monitoring services for the year. Of this amount, $46,000 was credit card sales. The credit card company charges a 4 percent service fee.
7. Collected the amount due from the credit card company.
8. Paid $875 to repair deluxe alarm systems that were still under warranty.
9. After numerous attempts to collect from customers, wrote off $2,465 of bad accounts.
10. On September 30, declared a dividend on the preferred stock and a $3 per share dividend on the common stock to be paid to shareholders of record on October 15, payable on October 31, 2011.
11. Collected $302,000 of accounts receivable for the year.
12. On October 31, paid the dividend that had previously been declared.
13. Paid $12,000 of advertising expense for the year.
14. Paid installers $94,000 for salaries for the year.
15. Paid officers $95,000 for salaries for the year.
16. Paid $6,500 utilities expenses for the year.
17. Paid bond interest and amortized the discount. (See chapter 10)
18. Paid annual installment on the amortized note.

Adjustments

19. There were $195 of office supplies on hand at the end of the year.
20. Recognized warranty expense for the year. Pacilio estimates warranty expense at 2 percent of deluxe model sales.
21. Recognized bad debt expense for the year. Pacilio uses the allowance method and estimates bad debts at 1 percent of sales on account.
22. Recognized depreciation expense for the year. (See chapter 9)

Required

a. Record the above transactions in general journal form. Pacilio uses FIFO cost flow assumption.
b. Post the transactions to the T-accounts.
c. Prepare a trial balance.
d. Prepare an income statement, balance sheet, and statement of cash flows.
e. Close the temporary accounts to retained earnings.
f. Post the closing entries to the T-accounts and prepare an after-closing trial balance.

STATEMENT OF CASH FLOWS

LEARNING *objectives*

After you have mastered the material in this chapter, you will be able to:

1 Identify the types of business events that are reported in the three sections of the statement of cash flows.

2 Convert account balances from accrual to cash.

3 Use the T-account method to prepare a statement of cash flows.

4 Explain how the indirect method differs from the direct method in reporting cash flow from operating activities.

5 Explain how the statement of cash flows could mislead decision makers if not interpreted with care.

THE *curious* ACCOUNTANT

Priceline.com began operations in April 1998 and first sold its stock to the public on March 30, 1999. By the end of 2002, the company had cumulative net losses of more than $1.5 billion. Even though its sales grew from $35 million in 1998 to more than $1 billion in 2002, it did not make a profit in any of those years.

How could Priceline.com lose so much money and still be able to pay its bills? (Answer on page 565.)

CHAPTER *opening*

*To make informed investment and credit decisions, financial statement users need information to help them assess the amounts, timing, and uncertainty of a company's prospective cash flows. This chapter explains more about the items reported on the statement of cash flows and describes a more practical way to prepare the statement than analyzing every entry in the cash account. As previously shown, the statement of cash flows reports how a company obtained and spent cash during an accounting period. Sources of cash are **cash inflows,** and uses are **cash outflows.** Cash receipts (inflows) and payments (outflows) are reported as either operating activities, investing activities, or financing activities.*

LO1 Identify the types of business events that are reported in the three sections of the statement of cash flows.

Operating Activities

Cash inflows and outflows resulting from running (operating) a business are classified as **operating activities.** Items reported as operating activities include:

1. Cash receipts from sales, commissions, fees, and receipts from interest and dividends.
2. Cash payments for inventories, salaries, operating expenses, interest, and taxes.

Gains and *losses* from disposals of long-term operational assets are not shown on the statement of cash flows. The total amount of cash collected from selling long-term assets (including cash associated with gains and losses) is reported in the investing activities section of the statement of cash flows.

Investing Activities

Investing activities always involve assets. Items reported as investing activities include:

1. Cash receipts (inflows) from selling property, plant, equipment, or marketable securities as well as collecting loans.
2. Cash payments (outflows) for purchasing property, plant, equipment, or marketable securities as well as lending to others.

Financing Activities

Financing activities always involve liabilities or equity. Items reported as financing activities include:

1. Cash receipts (inflows) from issuing stock and borrowing money.
2. Cash payments (outflows) to purchase treasury stock, repay debt, and pay dividends.

It is helpful to note that the classification of cash flows is based on the type of activity rather than the type of account. For example, cash flows involving common stock represent investing activities if the company is purchasing or selling its investment in another company's common stock. In contrast, common stock transactions represent financing activities if the company is issuing or buying back its own stock (treasury stock). Similarly, receiving dividends is an operating activity, but paying dividends is a financing activity. Furthermore, lending cash is an investing activity while borrowing cash is a financing activity.

Noncash Investing and Financing Activities

Occasionally, companies engage in significant **noncash investing and financing activities.** For example, a company could issue common stock in exchange for land or acquire a building by accepting a mortgage obligation. Since these types of transactions do not involve exchanging cash, they cannot be reported in the main body of the statement of cash flows. However, the Financial Accounting Standards Board (FASB) has concluded that full and fair reporting requires disclosing all material investing and financing activities whether or not they involve exchanging cash. Companies must therefore include with the statement of cash flows a separate schedule that reports noncash investing and financing activities.

Reporting Format for the Statement of Cash Flows

Cash flows are shown on the statement of cash flows in the following order, (1) operating activities, (2) investing activities, and (3) financing activities. At the end of each category, the difference between the inflows and outflows is presented as a net cash inflow or outflow for the category. These net amounts are combined to determine the net change (increase or

Exhibit 12–1

WESTERN COMPANY
Statement of Cash Flows
For the Year Ended December 31, 2001

Cash Flows from Operating Activities

Plus: List of Individual Inflows	$XXX	
Less: List of Individual Outflows	(XXX)	
Net Increase (Decrease) from Operating Activities		$XXX

Cash Flows from Investing Activities

Plus: List of Individual Inflows	XXX	
Less: List of Individual Outflows	(XXX)	
Net Increase (Decrease) from Investing Activities		XXX

Cash Flows from Financing Activities

Plus: List of Individual Inflows	XXX	
Less: List of Individual Outflows	(XXX)	
Net Increase (Decrease) from Financing Activities		XXX

Net Increase (Decrease) in Cash	XXX
Plus: Beginning Cash Balance	XXX
Ending Cash Balance	$XXX

Schedule of Noncash Investing and Financing Activities

List of Noncash Transactions	$XXX

decrease) in the company's cash for the period. The net change in cash is combined with the beginning cash balance to determine the ending cash balance. The ending cash balance on the statement of cash flows is the same as the cash balance shown on the balance sheet. The schedule of noncash investing and financing activities is typically presented at the bottom of the statement of cash flows. Exhibit 12–1 outlines this format.

As indicated in Exhibit 12–2, most companies present the statement of cash flows as the last of the four primary financial statements. However, a sizable number of companies present it after the income statement and balance sheet but before the statement of changes in stockholders' equity. Some companies place the statement of cash flows first, before the other three statements.

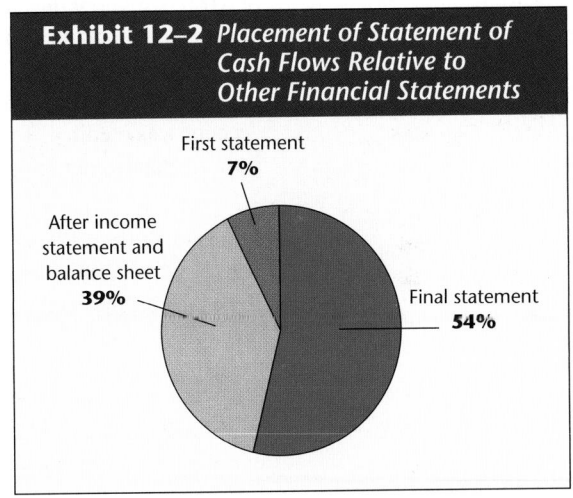

Exhibit 12–2 *Placement of Statement of Cash Flows Relative to Other Financial Statements*

First statement **7%**

After income statement and balance sheet **39%**

Final statement **54%**

Data source: AICPA, *Accounting Trends and Techniques*, 2002.

Converting from Accrual to Cash-Basis Accounting

The operating activities section of the statement of cash flows is essentially a cash-basis income statement. Since accounting records are normally maintained on an accrual basis, determining the cash flow from operating activities requires converting the accrual based records to cash equivalents.

LO2 Convert account balances from accrual to cash.

Operating Activities
Converting Accruals to Cash

The adjustments to convert **accrual transactions** to cash are explained in the following sections.

Revenue Transactions. The amount of revenue a company recognizes in a given accounting period normally differs from the amount of cash the company collects from customers. The amount of revenue recognized on the income statement can be converted to the amount of cash collected from customers by analyzing the change in the Accounts Receivable balance. For example, assume a company reported on its income statement $500 of sales revenue for the period. Also assume the company's Accounts Receivable balance at the beginning of the period was $100 and at the end of the period was $160 for an increase in receivables of $60 ($160 − $100). These circumstances indicate that $60 of the $500 in sales has not yet been collected from customers. Therefore, the amount of cash collected must have been $440 ($500 revenue − $60 increase in accounts receivable).

LO3 Use the T-account method to prepare a statement of cash flows.

The conclusion that $440 of cash was collected from the revenue transactions can be confirmed using the **T-account method.** This method uses a T-account to analyze the changes in Accounts Receivable for the period. The beginning and ending Accounts Receivable balances are entered in the T-account, in this case, the beginning balance of $100, and the ending balance of $160. Next a $500 debit is posted to the account to reflect the sales on account recognized during the period. The T-account then appears as follows:

	Accounts Receivable	
Beginning Balance	100	
Debit to Record Sales	500	?
Ending Balance	160	

Since adding $500 to the beginning balance of $100 does not produce the ending balance of $160, we know that Accounts Receivable must have been credited for some amount. We can use algebra to determine the amount of the credit in the receivables account ($100 + $500 − x = $160; x = $440). Since credits to Accounts Receivable are normally the result of cash collections from customers, the Cash account would have been debited when the receivables account was credited. T-account analysis, therefore, suggests that $440 of cash was collected from revenue generating activities.

Expense Transactions. Accrual accounting requires recognizing expenses when they are incurred, which is frequently before the accounting period when cash is paid for the expenses. Expenses on the income statement that include accrued amounts must be analyzed in conjunction with related balance sheet liabilities in order to determine the amount of cash paid for the expenses during the period. For example, assume a company reports $200 of utilities expense on its income statement. Furthermore, assume the beginning and ending balances of Utilities Payable are $70 and $40, respectively. The company therefore paid not only for the current period's utilities but also paid an additional $30 ($70 − $40) to reduce utility obligations from prior periods. The cash outflow for utility use must have been $230 ($200 expense incurred + $30 reduction in liability).

The T-account method confirms that $230 cash was paid. Enter the beginning and ending balances of Utilities Payable into a T-account. Post a credit of $200 to the account to reflect recognizing the current period's utility expense. The T-account then appears as follows:

Utilities Payable		
	70	Beginning Balance
?	200	Credit to Record Expense
	40	Ending Balance

Algebra dictates that the account must have been debited $230 to produce the $40 ending balance ($70 + $200 − x = $40; x = $230). Since debits to payable accounts are normally the result of cash payments, the Cash account would have been credited when Utilities Payable was debited, indicating that cash outflows for utility expenses were $230.

ANSWERS TO THE *curious* ACCOUNTANT

First, it should be remembered that GAAP requires that earnings and losses be computed on an accrual basis. A company can have negative earnings and still have positive cash flows from operating activities. This was not the case at Priceline.com, however. From 1998 through 2001, the company's cash flows from operating activities totaled a negative $94.8 million. Although this is much less than the $1.5 billion cumulative losses the company incurred during the same period, it still does not pay the bills.

Priceline.com, like many new companies, was able to stay in business because of the cash it raised through financing activities. These cash flows were a positive $376.9 million for 1998 through 2001. The company also had some significant noncash transactions. Exhibit 12–3 presents Priceline.com's statement of cash flows from the first four years (1998–2001) of its life.

Exhibit 12–3

PRICELINE.COM INCORPORATED
Statements of Cash Flows
(dollars in thousands)

	Year Ended December 31			
	2001	**2000**	**1999**	**1998**
Operating Activities				
Net loss	$ (7,303)	$(315,145)	$(1,055,090)	$(112,243)
Adjustments to reconcile net loss to net cash used in operating activities:				
Depreciation and amortization	16,578	17,385	5,348	1,860
Provision for uncollectible accounts	18,548	7,354	3,127	581
Warrant costs	—	8,595	1,189,111	67,866
Webhouse warrant	—	189,000	(189,000)	—
Net loss on disposal of fixed assets	17	12,398	—	—
Net loss on sale of equity investments	946	2,558	—	—
Impairment of Myprice loan	—	4,886	—	—
Equity in net income of pricelinemortgage	(551)	—	—	—
Noncash severance	3,076	—	—	—
Enhanced withholding on restricted shares	3,136	—	—	—
Compensation expense arising from deferred stock awards	13,395	1,711	—	—
Changes in assets and liabilities:				
Accounts receivable	(19,768)	7,401	(29,617)	(4,757)
Prepaid expenses and other current assets	699	1,194	(12,043)	(1,922)
Related party receivables	—	(3,484)	—	—
Accounts payable and accrued expenses	(1,501)	45,155	28,470	8,300
Other	824	1,276	(3,331)	112
Net cash used in operating activities	28,096	(19,716)	(63,025)	(40,203)
Investing Activities				
Additions to property and equipment	(9,415)	(37,320)	(27,416)	(6,607)
Proceeds from sales of fixed assets	170	—	—	—
Purchase of convertible notes and warrants of licencees	—	(25,676)	(2,000)	—
Proceeds from sales/maturities of investments	770	31,101	—	—
Funding of restricted cash and bank certificate of deposits	2,646	(4,779)	(8,789)	(680)
Investment in priceline.com europe Ltd.	(14,248)	—	—	—
Cash acquired from acquisition of priceline europe Ltd.	2,779	—	—	—
Investment in marketable securities	(38,878)	(5,000)	(38,771)	—
Net cash used in investing activities	(56,176)	(41,674)	(76,976)	(7,287)
Financing Activities				
Related party payable	—	—	—	(1,072)
Issuance of long-term debt	—	—	—	1,000
Payment of long-term debt	—	—	(1,000)	—
Principal payments under capital lease obligations	—	—	(25)	(22)
Shares reacquired for withholding taxes	(8,716)	—	—	—
Proceeds from sale of common stock, net	49,459	—	208,417	26,495
Proceeds from exercise of stock options and warrants	10,256	14,031	3,399	—
Payment received on stockholder note	—	—	—	250
Issuance of Series A convertible preferred stock	—	—	—	20,000
Issuance of Series B convertible preferred stock	—	—	—	54,415
Net cash provided by financing activities	50,999	14,031	210,791	101,066
Net increase (decrease) in cash and cash equivalents	22,919	(47,359)	70,790	53,576
Cash and cash equivalents, beginning of period	77,024	124,383	53,593	17
Cash and cash equivalents, end of period	$99,943	$ 77,024	$ 124,383	$ 53,593
Supplemental Cash Flow Information				
Cash paid during the period for interest	$ —	$ 4	$ 37	$ 61
Acquisition of priceline.com europe Ltd. —net liabilities assumed	$ 7,896	$ —	$ —	$ —

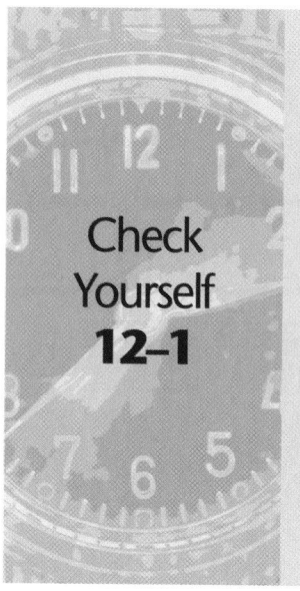

Check
Yourself
12–1

Hammer, Inc., had a beginning balance of $22,400 in its Accounts Receivable account. During the accounting period, Hammer earned $234,700 of revenue on account. The ending balance in the Accounts Receivable account was $18,200. Based on this information alone, determine the amount of cash received from revenue transactions. In what section of the statement of cash flows would this cash flow appear?

Answer

Beginning accounts receivable balance	$ 22,400
Plus: Revenue earned on account during the period	234,700
Receivables available for collection	257,100
Less: Ending accounts receivable balance	(18,200)
Cash collected from receivables (revenue)	$238,900

A $238,900 credit to accounts receivable is required to balance the account. This credit would be offset by a corresponding debit to cash. Cash received from revenue transactions appears in the operating activities section of the statement of cash flows.

Converting Deferrals to Cash

With **deferral transactions,** cash receipts or payments occur before the related revenue or expense is recognized. The following section explains how to convert deferred income and expense items to their cash equivalents.

Revenue Transactions. When a company collects cash from customers before it delivers goods or services, it incurs an obligation (liability) to provide the goods or services at some future date. If the goods or services are provided in a different accounting period from the cash collection, the amount of revenue reported on the income statement will differ from the amount of cash collected. Converting deferred revenue to its cash equivalent requires analyzing the revenue reported on the income statement in conjunction with the liability unearned revenue.

To illustrate, assume revenue of $400 was recognized and Unearned Revenue increased from a beginning balance of $80 to an ending balance of $110. The increase in the liability means that the company received more cash than the amount of revenue it recognized. Not only did the company earn the $400 of revenue reported on the income statement but also it received $30 ($110 − $80) for goods and services to be provided in a future period. Cash receipts from customers was $430 ($400 earned revenue + $30 unearned revenue).

Analyzing the T-account for Unearned Revenue confirms that $430 cash was received. Enter the beginning and ending balances into the Unearned Revenue account. Post a debit of $400 to reflect the revenue earned. The account then appears as follows:

Unearned Revenue

		80	Beginning Balance
Debit to Recognize Revenue	400	?	
		110	Ending Balance

Use algebra to determine that $430 must have been credited to the account ($80 + x − $400 = $110; x = $430). Since credit entries to the Unearned Revenue account are normally the result of cash collections, the T-account analysis indicates that $430 of cash receipts was generated by revenue activities.

Expense Transactions. Companies often pay cash for goods or services before using them. The costs of such goods or services are normally recorded first in asset accounts. The assets are then recognized as expenses in later periods when the goods or services are used. The amount of cash paid for expenses therefore normally differs from the amount of expense recognized in a given period.

Expenses recognized on the income statement can be converted to cash flows by analyzing the changes in relevant asset accounts in conjunction with their corresponding expenses. For example, assume the beginning and ending balances of Prepaid Rent are $60 and $80, respectively, and reported rent expense is $800. These circumstances indicate the company not only paid enough cash for the $800 of recognized expense but also paid an additional $20 ($80 − $60) to increase the Prepaid Rent account. Therefore, the cash outflow for rent was $820 ($800 recognized expense + $20 prepaid rent).

Analyzing the T-account for Prepaid Rent confirms that $820 was paid for rent. Enter the beginning and ending balances, then post an $800 credit to reflect the rent expense. The account then appears as follows:

Prepaid Rent

Beginning Balance	60		
	?	800	Credit to Recognize Expense
Ending Balance	80		

Use algebra to determine that the account must have been debited for $820 ($60 + x − $800 = $80; x = $820). Since debit entries to the Prepaid Rent account are normally the result of cash payments, the analysis confirms that the cash outflow for rent was $820.

Investing Activities

Determining cash flow from investing activities also requires analyzing changes in various account balances along with related income statement amounts. For example, assume the beginning and ending balances in the Land account were $900 and $300, respectively. Furthermore, assume the income statement recognized a $200 gain on the sale of land. The $600 ($900 − $300) decrease in book value means land was sold. The gain on the income statement means the land was sold for $200 more than its book value. This suggests that land was sold for $800 cash ($600 decrease in Land account + $200 Gain). The cash flow amount is different from the gain amount reported on the income statement. The full $800 cash inflow is reported in the investing activities section of the statement of cash flows. The gain has no effect on the operating activities section of the statement of cash flows.

The $800 cash inflow from selling land can be confirmed using the T account method. Analyzing the beginning and ending Land balances indicates that land costing $600 ($900 beginning balance − $300 ending balance) was sold. Because of the $200 gain (which is closed to Retained Earnings), $800 cash must have been collected from the sale. The relevant T-accounts appear as follows:

Cash		**Land**		**Retained Earnings**	
?		900	600		200
		300			

Financing Activities

Cash flow from financing activities can frequently be determined by simply analyzing the changes in liability and stockholders' equity accounts. For example, an increase in bond liabilities from $500 to $800 implies that a company issued new bonds for $300 cash. The T-account method supports this conclusion. Enter the beginning and ending balances in Bonds Payable as shown:

Bonds Payable

	500	Beginning Balance
	?	
	800	Ending Balance

To have an ending balance of $800, the T-account must have been credited for $300. Since increases in bond liabilities are normally the result of borrowing cash, the analysis suggests $300 of cash inflow must have been derived from issuing bonds.

Other explanations are possible. Some of the company's stockholders may have exchanged their equity securities for debt securities or the company may have incurred the obligation in exchange for some asset (property, plant, or equipment) other than cash. Such transactions would be reported in the schedule of noncash investing and financing activities.

Comprehensive Example Using the T-Account Approach

LO3 Use the T-account method to prepare a statement of cash flows.

The preceding discussion suggests that a statement of cash flows can be prepared by analyzing other financial statements. Beginning and ending asset, liability, and equity account balances can be obtained from two successive balance sheets. Revenues, expenses, gains, and losses can be found on the intervening income statement. Notes to the financial statements may contain information about noncash transactions. Exhibits 12–4 and 12–5 display the balance sheets, income statement, and additional information needed to prepare a statement of cash flows.

Exhibit 12–4

THE NEW SOUTH CORPORATION
Comparative Balance Sheets
As of December 31

	2004	2005
Current Assets		
Cash	$ 400	$ 900
Accounts Receivable	1,200	1,000
Interest Receivable	300	400
Inventory	8,200	8,900
Prepaid Insurance	1,400	1,100
Total Current Assets	11,500	12,300
Long-Term Assets		
Marketable Securities	3,500	5,100
Equipment	4,600	5,400
Less: Accumulated Depreciation	(1,200)	(900)
Land	6,000	8,500
Total Long-Term Assets	12,900	18,100
Total Assets	$24,400	$30,400
Current Liabilities		
Accounts Payable—Inventory Purchases	$ 1,100	$ 800
Salaries Payable	900	1,000
Other Operating Expenses Payable	1,300	1,500
Interest Payable	500	300
Unearned Rent Revenue	1,600	600
Total Current Liabilities	5,400	4,200
Long-Term Liabilities		
Mortgage Payable	0	2,500
Bonds Payable	4,000	1,000
Total Long-Term Liabilities	4,000	3,500
Stockholders' Equity		
Common Stock	8,000	10,000
Retained Earnings	7,000	12,700
Total Stockholders' Equity	15,000	22,700
Total Liabilities and Stockholders' Equity	$24,400	$30,400

Exhibit 12–5

THE NEW SOUTH CORPORATION
Income Statement
For the Year Ended December 31, 2005

Sales		$20,600
Cost of Goods Sold		(10,500)
Gross Margin		10,100
Operating Expenses		
Depreciation Expense	$ 800	
Salaries Expense	2,700	
Insurance Expense	600	
Other Operating Expenses	1,400	
Total Operating Expenses		(5,500)
		4,600
Other Income—Rent Revenue		2,400
Total Operating Income		7,000
Nonoperating Revenue and Expenses		
Interest Revenue	700	
Interest Expense	(400)	
Loss on Sale of Equipment	(100)	
Total Nonoperating Items		200
Net Income		$ 7,200

Additional information
1. The corporation sold equipment for $300 cash. This equipment had an original cost of $1,500 and accumulated depreciation of $1,100 at the time of the sale.
2. The corporation issued a $2,500 mortgage note in exchange for land.
3. There was a $1,500 cash dividend paid during the accounting period.

Preparing a Statement of Cash Flows

Analyzing the financial statements begins by setting up T-accounts for each balance sheet item, entering beginning balances from the 2004 balance sheet (see Exhibit 12–4) and ending balances from the 2005 balance sheet. Enough room is left in the Cash account to separately record cash flows as operating, investing, and financing activities. For convenience, the T-account analysis uses only balance sheet accounts; any entries to revenue, expense, or dividend accounts is posted directly to retained earnings. Exhibit 12–6 displays the full set of T-accounts after all transactions have been analyzed. Each transaction is labeled with a lower-case letter and a number to clarify the details of the analysis. The following section explains each transaction. Trace every transaction from its explanation to Exhibit 12–6.

Cash Flows from Operating Activities

Determining cash flows from operating activities essentially requires converting the accrual-based revenues and expenses reported on the income statement to their cash equivalents. Each income statement amount should be analyzed separately to assess its cash flow consequences.

Cash Receipts from Sales

The first item reported on the income statement is $20,600 of sales revenue. Assuming all sales were on account, the entry to record sales would have debited Accounts Receivable and credited Sales Revenue. Since sales revenue increases retained earnings, the entry posted to the T-accounts is a debit to Accounts Receivable and a credit to Retained Earnings. This entry is labeled (a1) in Exhibit 12–6.

After recording the sales revenue transaction, the cash inflow from sales can be determined by analyzing the Accounts Receivable T-account. Use algebra to determine that $20,800 ($1,200 + $20,600 − x = $1,000; x = $20,800) of receivables must have been collected. The

Exhibit 12–6 Balance Sheet T-Accounts

	Assets		=	Liabilities	+	Equity

Cash

Bal.	400	

Operating Activities

(a2)	20,800	11,500	(b3)
(g2)	1,400	2,600	(d2)
(h2)	600	300	(e2)
		1,200	(f2)
		600	(i2)

Investing Activities

(k1)	300	1,600	(j1)
		2,300	(l1)

Financing Activities

(o1)	2,000	3,000	(n1)
		1,500	(p1)
Bal.	900		

Accounts Receivable

Bal.	1,200	20,800	(a2)
(a1)	20,600		
Bal.	1,000		

Interest Receivable

Bal.	300	600	(h2)
(h1)	700		
Bal.	400		

Inventory

Bal.	8,200	10,500	(b1)
(b2)	11,200		
Bal.	8,900		

Prepaid Insurance

Bal.	1,400	600	(e1)
(e2)	300		
Bal.	1,100		

Marketable Securities

Bal.	3,500	
(j1)	1,600	
Bal.	5,100	

Equipment

Bal.	4,600	1,500	(k1)
(l1)	2,300		
Bal.	5,400		

Accumulated Depreciation

(k1)	1,100	1,200	Bal.
		800	(c1)
		900	Bal.

Land

Bal.	6,000	
(m1)	2,500	
Bal.	8,500	

Accounts Payable—Inventory

(b3)	11,500	1,100	Bal.
		11,200	(b2)
		800	Bal.

Salaries Payable

(d2)	2,600	900	Bal.
		2,700	(d1)
		1,000	Bal.

Other Operating Exp. Payable

(f2)	1,200	1,300	Bal.
		1,400	(f1)
		1,500	Bal.

Interest Payable

(i2)	600	500	Bal.
		400	(i1)
		300	Bal.

Unearned Rent Revenue

(g1)	2,400	1,600	Bal.
		1,400	(g2)
		600	Bal.

Mortgage Payable

		0	Bal.
		2,500	(m1)
		2,500	Bal.

Bonds Payable

(n1)	3,000	4,000	Bal.
		1,000	Bal.

Common Stock

		8,000	Bal.
		2,000	(o1)
		10,000	Bal.

Retained Earnings

(b1)	10,500	7,000	Bal.
(c1)	800	20,600	(a1)
(d1)	2,700	2,400	(g1)
(e1)	600	700	(h1)
(f1)	1,400		
(i1)	400		
(k1)	100		
(p1)	1,500		
		12,700	Bal.

cash inflow is recorded with a debit to the Cash account in the operating activities section and a credit to the Accounts Receivable account. This entry is labeled (a2) in Exhibit 12–6.

The analysis is complete when the difference between the beginning and ending balances in an account has been fully explained. In this case, the analysis of Accounts Receivable is complete. However, the analysis of retained earning will not be complete until all revenue, expense, and dividend events have been recorded.

Cash Payments Associated with Cost of Goods Sold (Inventory Purchases)

The next item on the income statement is cost of goods sold.

When analyzing the inventory account, it is helpful to make two simplifying assumptions. First, assume the company maintains perpetual inventory records; second, assume all inventory purchases are made on account. The following analysis uses these two assumptions.

Recording the $10,500 cost of goods sold (reported on the income statement in Exhibit 12–5) would have required crediting Inventory and debiting Cost of Goods Sold. Since cost of good sold reduces retained earnings, the entry is posted as a debit to Retained Earnings and a credit to Inventory. This entry is labeled (b1) in Exhibit 12–6. Further review of the Inventory account indicates that some inventory must have been purchased. Use algebra to determine that $11,200 ($8,200 + x − $10,500 = $8,900; x = $11,200) of inventory must have been purchased. The entry to record the inventory purchase, labeled (b2), involves a debit to Inventory and a credit to Accounts Payable. This entry completes the analysis of the Inventory account.

The Accounts Payable analysis is still incomplete. Use algebra and entry (b2) to determine that Accounts Payable decreased by $11,500 ($1,100 + $11,200 − x = $800; x = $11,500), reflecting cash payments that must have been made to reduce the liability. The entry to record this cash outflow, labeled (b3), involves a debit to Accounts Payable and a credit in the operating activities section of the Cash account. The analysis of the Accounts Payable account is now complete.

Noncash Effects of Depreciation

The next item on the income statement is depreciation expense, a noncash charge against revenues. No cash is paid when depreciation expense is recorded. The entry to record depreciation expense (c1) involves a debit to Retained Earnings (depreciation expense) and a credit to Accumulated Depreciation. This entry only partly explains the change in accumulated depreciation. Since cash flow consequences related to long-term assets and their respective contra accounts affect the investing activities section of the statement of cash flows, the analysis of Accumulated Depreciation will be completed in the discussion of investing activities after the analysis of cash flows from operating activities is completed.

Cash Payments for Salaries

The entry to record $2,700 of salary expense (d1) involves a debit to Retained Earnings (salary expense) and a credit to Salaries Payable. This entry partly explains the change in the Salaries Payable account. Use algebra to determine that Salaries Payable decreased $2,600 ($900 + $2,700 − x = $1,000; x = $2,600), reflecting cash paid for salaries. The entry to record the cash outflows for salaries (d2) involves a debit to the Salaries Payable account and a credit to the operating activities section of the Cash account.

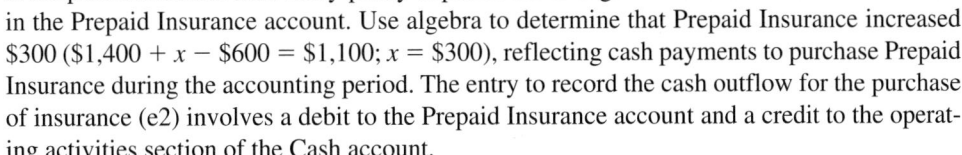

Cash Payments for Insurance

The entry to record $600 of insurance expense (e1) requires a debit to Retained Earnings (insurance expense) and a credit to Prepaid Insurance. This entry partly explains the change in the Prepaid Insurance account. Use algebra to determine that Prepaid Insurance increased $300 ($1,400 + x − $600 = $1,100; x = $300), reflecting cash payments to purchase Prepaid Insurance during the accounting period. The entry to record the cash outflow for the purchase of insurance (e2) involves a debit to the Prepaid Insurance account and a credit to the operating activities section of the Cash account.

Cash Payments for Other Operating Expenses

The $1,400 of other operating expenses reported on the income statement is recorded in the T-accounts with a debit to Retained Earnings and a credit to the Other Operating Expenses Payable account. This entry (f1) partly explains the change in the Other Operating Expenses

Payable account. Use algebra to determine that the liability decreased by $1,200 ($1,300 + $1,400 − x = $1,500; x = $1,200), reflecting cash payments for other operating expenses. The entry to record the cash outflow (f2) involves a debit to the Other Operating Expenses Payable account and a credit to the operating activities section of the Cash account.

Cash Receipts for Rent

The entry to record $2,400 of rent revenue (g1) involves a debit to the Unearned Rent Revenue account and a credit to the Retained Earnings account. This entry partly explains the change in the Unearned Rent Revenue account. Use algebra to determine that the account must have been credited for $1,400 ($1,600 + x − $2,400 = $600; x = $1,400), reflecting cash received in advance for rent revenue. The entry to record the cash inflow involves a credit to the Unearned Rent Revenue account and a debit to the operating activities section of the Cash account, (g2) in Exhibit 12–6.

Cash Receipts of Interest Revenue

The entry to record $700 of interest revenue (h1) involves a debit to the Interest Receivable account and a credit to Retained Earnings (interest revenue). This entry partly explains the change in the Interest Receivable account. Use algebra to determine that interest receivable must have decreased by $600 ($300 + $700 − x = $400; x = $600), reflecting cash collection of interest revenue. The entry to record this cash inflow (h2) involves a credit to Interest Receivable and a debit to the operating activities section of the Cash account.

Cash Payments for Interest Expense

The entry to record $400 of interest expense (i1) involves a debit to Retained Earnings (interest expense) and a credit to Interest Payable. The entry partly explains the change in the Interest Payable account. Use algebra to determine that interest payable decreased by $600 ($500 + $400 − x = $300; x = $600), reflecting cash payments of interest obligations. The entry to recognize the cash outflow for interest payments (i2) involves a debit to the Interest Payable account and a credit to the operating activities section of the Cash account.

Noncash Effects of Loss

The loss on sale of equipment does not represent a cash flow. The cash flow represented by the proceeds of the sale is explained shortly in the investing activities discussion. Cash flow from operating activities is not affected by gains or losses on the disposal of long-term assets.

Completion of Analysis of Operating Activities

Since all income statement items have now been analyzed, the conversion of revenues and expenses from accrual to cash for operating activities is complete. The example now moves to cash flows from investing activities.

Check Yourself 12–2

Q Magazine, Inc., reported $234,800 of revenue for the month. At the beginning of the month, its Unearned Revenue account had a balance of $78,000. At the end of the month, the account had a balance of $67,000. Based on this information alone, determine the amount of cash received from revenue.

Answer The Unearned Revenue account decreased by $11,000 ($78,000 − $67,000). This decrease in unearned revenue would have coincided with an increase in revenue that did not involve receiving cash. As a result, $11,000 of the revenue earned had no effect on cash flow during this month. To determine the cash received from revenue, subtract the noncash increase from reported revenue. Cash received from revenue is $223,800 ($234,800 − $11,000).

Cash Flows from Investing Activities

Since investing activities generally involve the acquisition (purchase) or disposal (sale) of long-term assets, determining cash flows from investing activities centers on analyzing balance sheet changes in these asset accounts.

Cash Payments to Purchase Marketable Securities

The first long-term asset reported on the balance sheets, Marketable Securities, increased from $3,500 at the beginning of the year to $5,100 at the end of the year. The increase most likely resulted from purchasing additional securities for $1,600 ($5,100 − $3,500). In the absence of evidence to the contrary, it is assumed securities were purchased with cash. The entry to record the purchase (j1) involves a debit to the Marketable Securities account and a credit to the investing activities section of the Cash account. Trace this entry into Exhibit 12–6.

Cash Receipts from Sale of Equipment

The next asset on the balance sheets is Equipment. Previous review of the income statement disclosed a loss on sale of equipment, indicating some equipment was sold during the period. The additional information below the income statement discloses that equipment costing $1,500 with accumulated depreciation of $1,100 was sold for $300. The difference between the $400 ($1,500 − $1,100) book value and the $300 sales price explains the $100 loss on the income statement. The cash inflow from the sale, $300, is unaffected by the original cost, accumulated depreciation, or the amount of the loss. The entry to recognize the cash receipt (k1) involves a debit to the investing activities section of the Cash account, a debit to Retained Earnings (loss), a debit to the Accumulated Depreciation account, and a credit to the Equipment account. Trace this entry into Exhibit 12–6.

Cash Payments to Purchase Equipment

The sale of equipment partly explains the change in the Equipment account. However, further analysis indicates some equipment must have been purchased. Use algebra and entry (k1) to determine that the Equipment account must have increased by $2,300 ($4,600 + x − $1,500 = $5,400; x = $2,300), reflecting the purchase of additional equipment. The entry to record the equipment purchase (l1) involves a debit to the Equipment account and a credit to the investing activities section of the Cash account.

Noncash Transaction for Land Acquisition

Land increased from $6,000 to $8,500, indicating that land costing $2,500 ($8,500 − $6,000) was acquired during the accounting period. The additional information below the income statement discloses that the corporation issued a mortgage to acquire this land. The entry to record the transaction (m1), a noncash exchange, involves a debit to Land and a credit to Mortgage Payable in Exhibit 12–6. Since the transaction does not affect cash, it is reported in the separate schedule for noncash investing and financing activities included with the statement of cash flows.

Since the changes in all long-term asset accounts have now been explained, the analysis of cash flows from investing activities is complete. The example continues with determining cash flows from financing activities.

Cash Flows from Financing Activities

Since financing activities involve borrowing and repayment transactions and transactions with owners, determining cash flows from financing activities requires analyzing the long-term liability and stockholders' equity sections of the balance sheets. The first long-term liability on the balance sheet is Mortgage Payable. The change in this account was explained previously

How did Florida Power and Light (FPL) acquire $501 million of property and equipment without spending any cash? Oddly enough, the answer can be found in the company's statement of cash flows. The supplemental schedule of noncash investing and financing activities section of FPL's cash statement shows that it acquired $81 million of equipment by accepting lease obligations and that it acquired $420 million of property by assuming debt. In other words, FPL acquired $501 million ($81 million + $420 million) in property and equipment by agreeing to pay for it later.

in conjunction with analyzing the land account. The financing activity of issuing the mortgage payable is reported along with the investing activity of acquiring land in the separate schedule for noncash transactions.

Cash Repayment for Bond Principal

The Bonds Payable balance decreased from $4,000 to $1,000. In the absence of evidence to the contrary, it is likely that $3,000 ($4,000 − $1,000) cash was paid to reduce bond liabilities. The entry to record the cash outflow (n1) involves a debit to the Bonds Payable account and a credit to the financing activities section of the Cash account.

Cash Receipt from Stock Issue

The Common Stock balance increased from $8,000 to $10,000. It is reasonable to assume the company issued common stock for $2,000 ($10,000 − $8,000) cash. The entry to record this cash inflow (o1) involves a credit to Common Stock and a debit to the financing activities section of the Cash account.

Cash Payments for Dividends

Finally, additional information below the income statement discloses a cash dividend of $1,500. The transaction to record this cash outflow (p1) involves a debit to the Retained Earnings account and a credit to the financing activities section of the Cash account.

Now all income statement items have been accounted for, all changes in balance sheet accounts have been analyzed, and all additional information has been considered. Review the analysis by tracing each entry into the T-accounts in Exhibit 12–6.

Exhibit 12–7

THE NEW SOUTH CORPORATION
Statement of Cash Flows
For the Year Ended December 31, 2005

Cash Flows from Operating Activities

Cash Receipts from

Sales	$20,800		
Rent	1,400		
Interest	600		
Total Cash Inflows		$22,800	
Cash Payments for Inventory Purchases	11,500		
Salaries	2,600		
Insurance	300		
Other Operating Expenses	1,200		
Interest	600		
Total Cash Outflows		(16,200)	
Net Cash Flow from Operating Activities			$6,600

Cash Flows from Investing Activities

Inflow from Sale of Equipment		300	
Outflow to Purchase Marketable Securities		(1,600)	
Outflow to Purchase Equipment		(2,300)	
Net Cash Flow for Investing Activities			(3,600)

Cash Flows from Financing Activities

Inflow from Stock Issue		2,000	
Outflow to Repay Debt		(3,000)	
Outflow for Dividends		(1,500)	
Net Cash Flow for Financing Activities			(2,500)

Net Increase in Cash			500
Plus: Beginning Cash Balance			400
Ending Cash Balance			$ 900

Schedule of Noncash Investing and Financing Activities

Issue of Mortgage for Land			$ 2,500

Presenting Information in the Statement of Cash Flows

To prepare the formal statement of cash flows, the inflows and outflows summarized in the Cash T-account must be appropriately organized and labeled. Cash flows from operating activities are presented first, followed by cash flows from investing activities, and finally, cash flows from financing activities. Noncash investing and financing activities are reported in a separate schedule or in the footnotes. Exhibit 12–7 displays the statement of cash flows and a separate schedule for noncash activities.

Statement of Cash Flows Presented under the Indirect Method

Topic Tackler

PLUS

12–2

LO4 Explain how the indirect method differs from the direct method in reporting cash flow from operating activities.

In all previous examples this textbook has illustrated the operating activities section of the statement of cash flows using the **direct method.** Although the direct method is easier to understand and is preferred by the Financial Accounting Standards Board, most companies use an alternative format called the **indirect method.** The amount of net cash flow from operating activities is the same using either method, but the presentation of the operating activities section differs. The indirect method starts with net income as reported on the income statement followed by the adjustments necessary to convert the accrual-based net income figure to a cash-basis equivalent. The conversion process uses three basic rules.

Rule 1: Increases in current assets are deducted from net income, and decreases in current assets are added to net income. For example, an increase in accounts receivable suggests that not all sales were collected in cash. The amount of sales revenue reported on the income statement exceeds the amount of cash collections. The increase in receivables must therefore be subtracted from the amount of net income to convert the net income figure to its cash equivalent. Similarly, a decrease in receivables must be added to the net income figure. Comparable logic holds for all current assets.

Rule 2: Increases in current liabilities are added to net income, and decreases in current liabilities are deducted from net income. The rule for current liabilities is the opposite of the rule for current assets. For example, an increase in accounts payable suggests that not all expenses were paid in cash. A greater amount of expenses was subtracted in determining net income than the amount of cash payments for those expenses. The increase in payables must be added to the amount of net income to convert the net income figure to its cash equivalent. Conversely, decreases in payable accounts are deducted from net income. This logic applies to all current liabilities that are affected by operating activities.

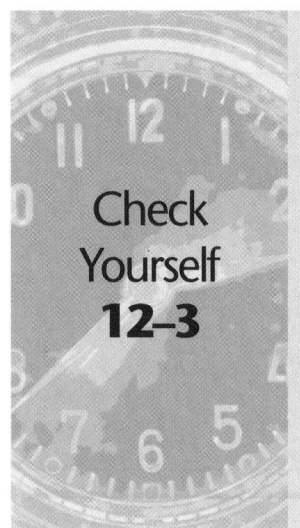

Check Yourself 12–3

The following account balances were drawn from the accounting records of Loeb, Inc.

Account Title	Beginning Balance	Ending Balance
Prepaid Rent	$4,200	$3,000
Interest Payable	2,900	2,650

Loeb reported $7,400 of net income during the accounting period. Based on this information alone, determine the amount of cash flow from operating activities.

Answer Based on Rule 1, the $1,200 decrease ($3,000 − $4,200) in Prepaid Rent (current asset) must be added to net income to determine the amount of cash flow from operating activities. Rule 2 requires that the $250 decrease ($2,650 − $2,900) in Interest Payable (current liability) must be deducted from net income. Accordingly, the cash flow from operating activities is $8,350 ($7,400 + $1,200 − $250). Note that paying interest is defined as an operating activity and should not be confused with dividend payments, which are classified as financing activities.

Rule 3: All noncash expenses and losses are added to net income, and all noncash revenue and gains are subtracted from net income. Some expense and revenue transactions do not have cash consequences. For example, although depreciation is an expense subtracted in determining net income, it does not require a cash payment. The amount of depreciation expense must therefore be added to net income to convert net income to its cash equivalent. Similarly, losses and gains reported on the income statement do not have cash consequences. Net income must be adjusted to remove the effects of losses and gains to convert it to cash flow.

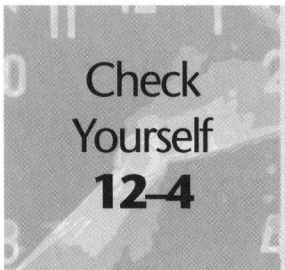

Check Yourself 12–4

Arley Company's income statement reported net income (in millions) of $326 for the year. The income statement included depreciation expense of $45 and a net loss on the sale of disposable assets of $22. Based on this information alone, determine the net cash flow from operating activities.

Answer Based on Rule 3, both the depreciation expense and the loss would have to be added to net income to determine cash flow from operating activities. Net cash flow from operating activities would be $393 ($326 + $45 + $22).

Exhibit 12–8

THE NEW SOUTH CORPORATION
Statement of Cash Flows (Indirect Method)
For the Year Ended December 31, 2005

Cash Flows from Operating Activities

Net Income	$7,200	
Plus: Decreases in Current Assets and Increases in Current Liabilities		
Decrease in Accounts Receivable	200	
Decrease in Prepaid Insurance	300	
Increase in Salaries Payable	100	
Increase in Other Operating Expenses Payable	200	
Less: Increases in Current Assets and Decreases in Current Liabilities		
Increase in Interest Receivable	(100)	
Increase in Inventory	(700)	
Decrease in Accounts Payable	(300)	
Decrease in Interest Payable	(200)	
Decrease in Unearned Rent Revenue	(1,000)	
Plus: Noncash Charges		
Depreciation Expense	800	
Loss on Sale of Equipment	100	
Net Cash Flow from Operating Activities		$6,600
Cash Flows from Investing Activities		
Inflow from Sale of Equipment	300	
Outflow to Purchase Marketable Securities	(1,600)	
Outflow to Purchase Equipment	(2,300)	
Net Cash Flow for Investing Activities		(3,600)
Cash Flows from Financing Activities		
Inflow from Stock Issue	2,000	
Outflow to Repay Debt	(3,000)	
Outflow for Dividends	(1,500)	
Net Cash Flow for Financing Activities		(2,500)
Net Increase in Cash		500
Plus: Beginning Cash Balance		400
Ending Cash Balance		$ 900
Schedule of Noncash Investing and Financing Activities		
Issue of Mortgage for Land		$2,500

Exhibit 12–8 displays the statement of cash flows with operating activities presented using the indirect method. The statement was constructed by applying the three basic conversion rules to The New South Corporation data from Exhibits 12–4 and 12–5. The only difference between the indirect method (Exhibit 12–8) and the direct method (Exhibit 12–7) is in the presentation of the cash flows from operating activities section. Cash flows from investing and financing activities and the schedule of noncash investing and financing activities are the same for both reporting formats.

THE FINANCIAL ANALYST

Why are financial analysts interested in the statement of cash flows? Understanding the cash flows of a business is essential because cash is used to pay the bills. A company, especially one experiencing rapid growth, can be short of cash in spite of earning substantial net income. To illustrate, assume you start a computer sales business. You borrow $2,000 and spend the money to purchase two computers for $1,000 each. You sell one of the computers on account for $1,500. If your loan required a payment at this time, you could not make it. Even though you have net income of $500 ($1,500 sales − $1,000 cost of goods sold), you have no cash until you collect the $1,500 account receivable. A business cannot survive without managing cash flow carefully. It is little wonder that financial analysts are keenly interested in cash flow.

LO5 Explain how the statement of cash flows could mislead decision makers if not interpreted with care.

Real-World Data

The statement of cash flows frequently provides a picture of business activity that would otherwise be lost in the complexities of accrual accounting. For example, **IBM Corporation**'s combined operating losses (before taxes) for 1991, 1992, and 1993 were more than $17.9 *billion*. During this same period, IBM reported "restructuring charges" of more than $24 billion. Restructuring costs relate to reorganizing a company. They may include the costs of closing facilities and losses on asset disposals. Without the restructuring charges, IBM would have reported operating *profits* of about $6 billion (before taxes). Do restructuring charges signal positive or negative changes? Different financial analysts have different opinions about this issue. However, one aspect of IBM's performance during these years is easily understood. The company produced over $21 billion in positive cash flow from operating activities. It had no trouble paying its bills.

Investors consider cash flow information so important that they are willing to pay for it, even when the FASB discourages its use. The FASB *prohibits* companies from disclosing *cash flow per share* in audited financial statements. However, one prominent stock analysis service, *Value Line Investment Survey*, sells this information to a significant customer base. Clearly, Value Line's customers value information about cash flows.

Exhibit 12–9 compares income from operations and cash flow from operating activities for six real-world companies from five different industries for the 2000, 2001, and 2002 fiscal years.

Several things are apparent from Exhibit 12–9. The cash flow from operating activities exceeds income from operations for all of the companies except **Toll Brothers**. Many real-world companies report such a result because depreciation, a noncash expense, is usually significant. The most dramatic example is for **Sprint** in 2001. Even though Sprint reported a *net loss* from operations of approximately $2.3 billion, it generated *positive* cash flow from operating activities of more than $4.5 *billion*. This difference between cash flow from operating activities and operating income helps explain how some companies can have significant losses over a few years and continue to stay in business and pay their bills.

The exhibit shows that cash flow from operating activities can be more stable than operating income. Results for Sprint also demonstrate this clearly. Although the company's earnings were negative in 2000, more negative in 2001, and positive in 2002, its cash flows from operating activities were always positive. Stability is one of the reasons many financial analysts prefer cash flow over earnings as a predictor of future performance.

Exhibit 12–9 *Operating Income versus Cash flow From Operating Activities (Amounts in $000)*

Company		2002	2001	2000
Alaska Airlines	Oper. Income	$ (57,000)	$ (11,800)	$ (14,800)
	Cash Flow Oper. Activities	119,600	202,000	282,900
Southwest Airlines	Oper. Income	240,969	511,147	625,224
	Cash Flow Oper. Activities	520,209	1,484,608	1,298,286
Boeing	Oper. Income	2,319,000	2,826,000	2,128,000
	Cash Flow Oper. Activities	4,375,000	3,894,000	6,226,000
Mattel	Oper. Income	455,042	310,920	170,177
	Cash Flow Oper. Activities	1,156,084	756,793	555,090
Sprint	Oper. Income	468,000	(2,274,000)	(963,000)
	Cash Flow Oper. Activities	6,206,000	4,563,000	4,096,000
Toll Brothers	Oper. Income	219,887	213,673	145,943
	Cash Flow Oper. Activities	(94,105)	(148,379)	(16,863)

Finally, what could explain why Toll Brothers has *less* cash flow from operating activities than operating income? Does the company have a problem? Not necessarily. Toll Brothers is experiencing the kind of growth described earlier for your computer sales business. Its cash is supporting growth in inventory levels. Toll Brothers is one of the nation's largest new-home construction companies. Its growth rates, based on revenue from sales of new homes, for the 2002, 2001, and 2000 fiscal years were 5 percent, 24 percent, and 23 percent, respectively. When Toll Brothers begins to build new homes, it needs more inventory. Increases in inventory *do* affect cash flow from operating activities. Remember, increases in current assets decrease cash flow from operating activities. This condition alone might explain why the company has less cash flow from operating activities than operating income. Is this situation unfavorable? Chapter 6 made the point that, *other things being equal*, it is better to have less inventory. At Toll Brothers, however, other things are not equal. The company has been growing rapidly.

The Toll Brothers situation highlights a potential weakness in the format of the statement of cash flows. Some accountants consider it misleading to classify all increases in long-term assets as *investing activities* and all changes in inventory as affecting cash flow from operating activities. They argue that the increase in inventory at Toll Brothers that results from building more houses should be classified as an investing activity, just as the cost of a new building is. Although inventory is classified as a current asset and buildings are classified as long-term assets, in reality there is a certain level of inventory a company must permanently maintain to stay in business. The GAAP format of the statement of cash flows penalizes cash flow from operating activities for increases in inventory that are really a permanent investment in assets.

Conversely, the same critics might argue that some purchases of long-term assets are not actually *investments* but merely replacements of old, existing property, plant, and equipment. In other words, the *investing activities* section of the statement of cash flows makes no distinction between expenditures that expand the business and those that simply replace old equipment (sometimes called *capital maintenance* expenditures).

Users of the statement of cash flows must exercise the same care interpreting it as when they use the balance sheet or the income statement. Numbers alone are insufficient. Users must evaluate numbers based on knowledge of the particular business and industry they are analyzing.

Accounting information alone cannot guide a businessperson to a sound decision. Making good business decisions requires an understanding of the business in question, the environmental and economic factors affecting the operation of that business, and the accounting concepts on which the financial statements of that business are based.

---

a look
back

Thus far in this text, you have considered many different accounting events that businesses experience. You have been asked to consider the effects these events have on a company's balance sheet, income statement, and statement of cash flows. By now, you should recognize that each financial statement shows a different, but equally important, view of a company's financial situation.

This chapter examined in detail only one financial statement, the statement of cash flows. The chapter provided a more comprehensive discussion of how accrual accounting relates to cash-based accounting. Effective use of financial statements requires understanding not only accrual and cash-based accounting systems but also how they relate to each other. That relationship is why a statement of cash flows can begin with a reconciliation of net income, an accrual measurement, to net cash flow from operating activities, a cash measurement. Finally, this chapter explained how the conventions for classifying cash flows as operating, investing, or financing activities require analysis and understanding to make informed decisions with the financial information.

This chapter probably completes your first course in accounting. We sincerely hope that this text has provided you a meaningful learning experience that will serve you well as you progress through your academic training and ultimately, your career. Good luck and best wishes!

The following financial statements pertain to Schlemmer Company.

Balance Sheets As of December 31		
	2003	2004
Cash	$ 2,800	$48,400
Accounts Receivable	1,200	2,200
Inventory	6,000	5,600
Equipment	22,000	18,000
Accumulated Depreciation—Equip.	(17,400)	(13,650)
Land	10,400	17,200
Total Assets	$25,000	$77,750
Accounts Payable	$ 4,200	$ 5,200
Long-Term Debt	6,400	5,600
Common Stock	10,000	19,400
Retained Earnings	4,400	47,550
Total Liabilities and Equity	$25,000	$77,750

Income Statement For the Year Ended December 31, 2004	
Sales Revenue	$67,300
Cost of Goods Sold	(24,100)
Gross Margin	43,200
Depreciation Expense	(1,250)
Operating Income	41,950
Gain on Sale of Equipment	2,900
Loss on Disposal of Land	(100)
Net Income	$44,750

Additional Data

1. During 2004 the company sold equipment for $8,900 that had originally cost $11,000. Accumulated depreciation on this equipment was $5,000 at the time of sale. Also, the company purchased equipment for $7,000.
2. The company sold for $2,500 land that had cost $2,600, resulting in the recognition of a $100 loss. Also, common stock was issued in exchange for land valued at $9,400 at the time of the exchange.
3. The company declared and paid dividends of $1,600.

Required

a. Use T-accounts to analyze the preceding data.
b. Using the direct method, prepare in good form a statement of cash flows for the year ended December 31, 2004.

Solution to Requirement a
Transactions Legend

a1. Revenue, $67,300.
a2. Collection of accounts receivable, $66,300 ($1,200 + $67,300 − $2,200).
b1. Cost of goods sold, $24,100.
b2. Inventory purchases, $23,700 ($5,600 + $24,100 − $6,000).
b3. Payments for inventory purchases, $22,700 ($4,200 + $23,700 − $5,200).
c1. Depreciation expense, $1,250 (noncash).
d1. Sale of equipment, $8,900; cost of equipment sold, $11,000; accumulated depreciation on equipment sold, $5,000.
d2. Purchase of equipment, $7,000.
e1. Sale of land, $2,500; cost of land sold, $2,600.
f1. Issue of stock in exchange for land, $9,400.
g1. Paid dividends, $1,600.
h1. Paid off portion of long-term debt, $800.

SCHLEMMER COMPANY
T-Accounts

Assets			=	Liabilities			+	Equity		

Cash

Bal.	2,800		
(a2)	66,300	(b3)	22,700
(d1)	8,900	(d2)	7,000
(e1)	2,500	(g1)	1,600
		(h1)	800
Bal.	48,400		

Accounts Payable

		Bal.	4,200
(b3)	22,700	(b2)	23,700
		Bal.	5,200

Common Stock

		Bal.	10,000
		(f1)	9,400
		Bal.	19,400

Accounts Receivable

Bal.	1,200		
(a1)	67,300	(a2)	66,300
Bal.	2,200		

Long-Term Debt

		Bal.	6,400
(h1)	800		
		Bal.	5,600

Retained Earnings

		Bal.	4,400
(b1)	24,100	(a1)	67,300
(c1)	1,250	(d1)	2,900
(e1)	100		
(g1)	1,600		
		Bal.	47,550

Inventory

Bal.	6,000		
(b2)	23,700	(b1)	24,100
Bal.	5,600		

Equipment

Bal.	22,000		
(d2)	7,000	(d1)	11,000
Bal.	18,000		

Accumulated Depreciation

		Bal.	17,400
(d1)	5,000	(c1)	1,250
		Bal.	13,650

Land

Bal.	10,400		
(f1)	9,400	(e1)	2,600
Bal.	17,200		

Solution to Requirement b

SCHLEMMER COMPANY
Statement of Cash Flows
For the Year Ended December 31, 2004

Cash Flows from Operating Activities		
Cash Receipts from Customers	$66,300	
Cash Payments for Inventory Purchases	(22,700)	
Net Cash Flow Provided by Operating Activities		$43,600
Cash Flows from Investing Activities		
Inflow from Sale of Equipment	8,900	
Inflow from Sale of Land	2,500	
Outflow to Purchase Equipment	(7,000)	
Net Cash Flow Provided by Investing Activities		4,400
Cash Flows from Financing Activities		
Outflow for Dividends	(1,600)	
Outflow for Repayment of Debt	(800)	
Net Cash Flow Used by Financing Activities		(2,400)
Net Increase in Cash		45,600
Plus: Beginning Cash Balance		2,800
Ending Cash Balance		$48,400
Schedule of Noncash Investing and Financing Activities		
Issued Common Stock for Land		$ 9,400

KEY TERMS

Accrual transactions *563*

Cash inflows *561*

Cash outflows *561*

Deferral transactions *566*

Direct method *575*

Expense transactions *564*

Financing activities *562*

Indirect method *575*

Investing activities *562*

Noncash investing and
   financing activities *562*

Operating activities *562*

Revenue transactions *564*

T-account method *564*

QUESTIONS

1. What is the purpose of the statement of cash flows?
2. What are the three categories of cash flows reported on the cash flow statement? Discuss each and give an example of an inflow and an outflow for each category.
3. What are noncash investing and financing activities? Provide an example. How are such transactions shown on the statement of cash flows?
4. Best Company had beginning accounts receivable of $12,000 and ending accounts receivable of $14,000. If total sales were $110,000, what amount of cash was collected?
5. Best Company's Utilities Payable account had a beginning balance of $3,300 and an ending balance of $5,200. Utilities expense reported on the income statement was $87,000. What was the amount of cash paid for utilities for the period?
6. Best Company had a balance in the Unearned Revenue account of $4,300 at the beginning of the period and an ending balance of $5,700. If the portion of unearned revenue Best recognized as earned during the period was $15,600, what amount of cash did Best collect?
7. Which of the following activities are financing activities?
    (a) Payment of accounts payable.
    (b) Payment of interest on bonds payable.
    (c) Sale of common stock.
    (d) Sale of preferred stock at a premium.
    (e) Payment of a cash dividend.
8. Does depreciation expense affect net cash flow? Explain.
9. If Best Company sold land that cost $4,200 at a $500 gain, how much cash did it collect from the sale of land?
10. If Best Company sold office equipment that originally cost $7,500 and had $7,200 of accumulated depreciation at a $100 loss, what was the selling price for the office equipment?
11. In which section of the statement of cash flows would the following transactions be reported?
    (a) Cash receipt of interest income.
    (b) Cash purchase of marketable securities.
    (c) Cash purchase of equipment.
    (d) Cash sale of merchandise.
    (e) Cash sale of common stock.
    (f) Payment of interest expense.
    (g) Cash proceeds from loan.
    (h) Cash payment on bonds payable.
    (i) Cash receipt from sale of old equipment.
    (j) Cash payment for operating expenses.
12. What is the difference between preparing the statement of cash flows using the direct method and using the indirect method?
13. Which method (direct or indirect) of presenting the statement of cash flows is more intuitively logical? Why?
14. What is the major advantage of using the indirect method to present the statement of cash flows?
15. What is the advantage of using the direct method to present the statement of cash flows?
16. How would Best Company report the following transactions on the statement of cash flows?
    (a) Purchased new equipment for $46,000 cash.
    (b) Sold old equipment for $8,700 cash. The equipment had a book value of $4,900.
17. Can a company report negative net cash flows from operating activities for the year on the statement of cash flows but still have positive net income on the income statement? Explain.
18. Why does the FASB prohibit disclosing cash flow per share in audited financial statements?

All Exercises in Series A are available with McGraw-Hill's Homework Manager

EXERCISE 12–1A *Classifying Cash Flows into Categories—Direct Method*   L.O. 1

Required

Classify each of the following as operating activities, investing activities, financing activities, or noncash transactions. (Assume the use of the direct method.)

a. Paid cash to settle note payable.
b. Sold land for cash.
c. Paid cash to purchase a computer.
d. Paid cash for employee compensation.
e. Received cash interest from a bond investment.
f. Recognized depreciation expense.
g. Acquired cash from issue of common stock.
h. Provided services for cash.
i. Acquired cash by issuing a note payable.
j. Paid cash for interest.
k. Paid cash dividends.

EXERCISE 12–2A *Cash Outflows from Operating Activities—Direct Method*   L.O. 1

Required

Which of the following transactions produce cash outflows from operating activities (assume the use of the direct method)?

a. Cash receipt from collecting accounts receivable.
b. Cash receipt from sale of land.
c. Cash payment for dividends.
d. Cash payment to settle an account payable.
e. Cash payment to purchase inventory.
f. Cash payment for equipment.

EXERCISE 12–3A *Using Account Balances to Determine Cash Flows from Operating*   L.O. 2
                              Activities—Direct Method

The following account balances are available for Max Company for 2007.

Account Title	Beginning of Year	End of Year
Accounts Receivable	$42,000	$46,000
Interest Receivable	6,000	5,000
Accounts Payable	22,000	26,000
Salaries Payable	12,000	15,000

Other Information for 2007

Sales on Account	$680,000
Interest Revenue	24,000
Operating Expenses	270,000
Salaries Expense for the Year	172,000

Required

(*Hint:* It may be helpful to assume that all revenues and expenses are on account.)

a. Compute the amount of cash *inflow* from operating activities.
b. Compute the amount of cash *outflow* from operating activities.

L.O. 2   EXERCISE 12–4A *Using Account Balances to Determine Cash Flow from Operating Activities—Direct Method*

The following account balances were available for Theri Enterprises for 2007.

Account Title	Beginning of Year	End of Year
Unearned Revenue	$5,000	$6,500
Prepaid Rent	2,400	1,800

During the year, $68,000 of unearned revenue was recognized as having been earned. Rent expense for the period was $15,000. Theri Enterprises maintains its books on the accrual basis.

Required

Using T-accounts and the preceding information, determine the amount of cash inflow from revenue and cash outflow for rent.

L.O. 2, 3   EXERCISE 12–5A *Using Account Balances to Determine Cash Flow from Investing Activities*

The following account information pertains to Guidry Company for 2005.

	Land			Marketable Securities	
Bal.	46,000	56,000	Bal.	82,000	46,000
	128,000			120,000	
Bal.	118,000		Bal.	156,000	

The income statement reported a $3,000 loss on the sale of land and a $2,500 gain on the sale of marketable securities.

Required

Prepare the investing activities section of the 2005 statement of cash flows.

L.O. 2, 3   EXERCISE 12–6A *Using Account Balances to Determine Cash Flow from Financing Activities*

The following account balances pertain to Olack, Inc., for 2006.

	Bonds Payable			Common Stock		Paid-in Capital in Excess of Par Value		
		Bal. 220,000			Bal. 280,000		Bal.	90,000
90,000					180,000			50,000
		Bal. 130,000			Bal. 460,000		Bal.	140,000

Required

Prepare the financing activities section of the 2006 statement of cash flows.

L.O. 2   EXERCISE 12–7A *Using Account Balances to Determine Cash Outflow for Inventory Purchases*

The following account information pertains to Maze Company, which uses the perpetual inventory method and purchases all inventory on account.

	Inventory			Accounts Payable	
Bal.	52,000				Bal. 44,000
	?	352,000		?	?
Bal.	61,000				Bal. 41,000

Required

Compute the amount of cash paid for the purchase of inventory.

EXERCISE 12–8A *Using Account Balances to Determine Cash Flow from Operating Activities—Indirect Method*   **L.O. 2, 4**

Kwon Company presents its statement of cash flows using the indirect method. The following accounts and corresponding balances were drawn from Kwon's accounting records for the period.

Account Titles	Beginning Balances	Ending Balances
Accounts Receivable	$32,000	$28,000
Prepaid Rent	1,500	1,800
Interest Receivable	500	700
Accounts Payable	9,800	8,500
Salaries Payable	3,200	3,600
Unearned Revenue	6,000	4,000

Net income for the period was $52,000.

Required
Using the preceding information, compute the net cash flow from operating activities using the indirect method.

EXERCISE 12–9A *Using Account Balances to Determine Cash Flow from Operating Activities—Direct and Indirect Methods*   **L.O. 2, 3, 4**

The following account balances are from Marlin Company's accounting records. Assume Marlin had no investing or financing transactions during 2007.

December 31	2006	2007
Cash	$65,000	$107,000
Accounts Receivable	75,000	78,000
Prepaid Rent	900	800
Accounts Payable	33,000	34,000
Utilities Payable	1,200	1,500
Sales Revenue		$272,000
Operating Expenses		(168,000)
Utilities Expense		(36,400)
Rent Expense		(24,000)
Net Income		$ 43,600

Required
a. Prepare the operating activities section of the 2007 statement of cash flows using the direct method.
b. Prepare the operating activities section of the 2007 statement of cash flows using the indirect method.

EXERCISE 12–10A *Interpreting Statement of Cash Flows Information*   **L.O. 3, 5**

The following selected transactions pertain to Johnston Corporation for 2007.

1. Paid $35,200 cash to purchase delivery equipment.
2. Sold delivery equipment for $3,500. The equipment had originally cost $18,000 and had accumulated depreciation of $12,000.
3. Borrowed $50,000 cash by issuing bonds at face value.
4. Purchased a building that cost $220,000. Paid $50,000 cash and issued a mortgage for the remaining $170,000.
5. Exchanged no-par common stock for machinery valued at $38,700.

Required
a. Prepare the appropriate sections of the 2007 statement of cash flows.
b. Explain how a company could spend more cash on investing activities than it collected from financing activities during the same accounting period.

PROBLEMS—SERIES A

 All Problems in Series A are available with McGraw-Hill's Homework Manager

L.O. 1 **PROBLEM 12–11A** *Classifying Cash Flows*

Required

Classify each of the following as an operating activity (OA), an investing activity (IA), or a financing activity (FA) cash flow, or a noncash transaction (NT).

  a. Provided services for cash.
  b. Purchased marketable securities with cash.
  c. Paid cash for rent.
  d. Received interest on note receivable.
  e. Paid cash for salaries.
  f. Received advance payment for services.
  g. Paid a cash dividend.
  h. Provided services on account.
  i. Purchased office supplies on account.
  j. Bought land with cash.
  k. Collected cash from accounts receivable.
  l. Issued common stock for cash.
  m. Repaid principal and interest on a note payable.
  n. Declared a stock split.
  o. Purchased inventory with cash.
  p. Recorded amortization of goodwill.
  q. Paid insurance with cash.
  r. Issued a note payable in exchange for equipment.
  s. Recorded depreciation expense.

L.O. 2, 3 **PROBLEM 12–12A** *Using Transaction Data to Prepare a Statement of Cash Flows*

CHECK FIGURE
Net Cash Flow from Operating
Activities: $(110,775)

Store Company engaged in the following transactions during the 2007 accounting period. The beginning cash balance was $28,600.

  1. Sales on account were $250,000. The beginning receivables balance was $87,000 and the ending balance was $83,000.
  2. Salaries expense for the period was $56,000. The beginning salaries payable balance was $3,500 and the ending balance was $2,000.
  3. Other operating expenses for the period were $125,000. The beginning operating expense payable balance was $4,500 and the ending balance was $8,500.
  4. Recorded $19,500 of depreciation expense. The beginning and ending balances in the Accumulated Depreciation account were $14,000 and $33,500, respectively.
  5. The Equipment account had beginning and ending balances of $210,000 and $240,000, respectively. The increase was caused by the cash purchase of equipment.
  6. The beginning and ending balances in the Notes Payable account were $50,000 and $150,000, respectively. The increase was caused by additional cash borrowing.
  7. There was $6,000 of interest expense reported on the income statement. The beginning and ending balances in the Interest Payable account were $1,500 and $1,000, respectively.
  8. The beginning and ending Merchandise Inventory account balances were $90,000 and $108,000, respectively. The company sold merchandise with a cost of $156,000 (cost of goods sold for the period was $156,000). The beginning and ending balances of Accounts Payable were $9,500 and $11,500, respectively.
  9. The beginning and ending balances of Notes Receivable were $5,000 and $10,000, respectively. The increase resulted from a cash loan to one of the company's employees.
  10. The beginning and ending balances of the Common Stock account were $100,000 and $120,000, respectively. The increase was caused by the issue of common stock for cash.
  11. Land had beginning and ending balances of $50,000 and $41,000, respectively. Land that cost $9,000 was sold for $12,200, resulting in a gain of $3,200.
  12. The tax expense for the period was $7,700. The Taxes Payable account had a $950 beginning balance and an $875 ending balance.

13. The Investments account had beginning and ending balances of $25,000 and $29,000, respectively. The company purchased investments for $18,000 cash during the period, and investments that cost $14,000 were sold for $9,000, resulting in a $5,000 loss.

Required
Convert the preceding information to cash-equivalent data and prepare a statement of cash flows.

PROBLEM 12–13A *Using Financial Statement Data to Determine Cash Flow from Operating Activities*

The following account information is available for Park Company for 2004:

Account Title	Beginning of Year	End of Year
Accounts Receivable	$26,000	$24,000
Merchandise Inventory	52,000	56,000
Prepaid Insurance	24,000	20,000
Accounts Payable (Inventory)	20,000	23,000
Salaries Payable	4,200	4,600

Other Information
1. Sales for the period were $180,000.
2. Purchases of merchandise for the period were $90,000.
3. Insurance expense for the period was $42,000.
4. Other operating expenses (all cash) were $30,000.
5. Salary expense was $35,000.

Required
a. Compute the net cash flow from operating activities.
b. Prepare the cash flow from the operating activities section of the statement of cash flows.

PROBLEM 12–14A *Using Financial Statement Data to Determine Cash Flow from Investing Activities*

The following information pertaining to investing activities is available for Leach Company for 2005:

Account Title	Beginning of Year	End of Year
Machinery and Equipment	$425,000	$520,000
Marketable Securities	112,000	102,000
Land	90,000	140,000

Other Information for 2005
1. Marketable securities were sold at book value. No gain or loss was recognized.
2. Machinery was purchased for $120,000. Old machinery with a book value of $5,000 (cost of $25,000, accumulated depreciation of $20,000) was sold for $8,000.
3. No land was sold during the year.

Required
a. Compute the net cash flow from investing activities.
b. Prepare the cash flow from investing activities section of the statement of cash flows.

PROBLEM 12–15A *Using Financial Statement Data to Determine Cash Flow from Financing Activities*

The following information pertaining to financing activities is available for Rebel Company for 2007:

Account Title	Beginning of Year	End of Year
Bonds Payable	$300,000	$210,000
Common Stock	200,000	260,000
Paid-in Capital in Excess of Par	75,000	110,000

Other Information

1. Dividends paid during the period amounted to $30,000.
2. No new funds were borrowed during the period.

Required

a. Compute the net cash flow from financing activities for 2007.
b. Prepare the cash flow from the financing activities section of the statement of cash flows.

L.O. 2, 3   **PROBLEM 12–16A** *Using Financial Statements to Prepare a Statement of Cash Flows—*
                 Direct Method

The following financial statements were drawn from the records of Pacific Company.

Balance Sheets As of December 31		
	2006	**2007**
Assets		
Cash	$ 2,800	$24,200
Accounts Receivable	1,200	2,000
Inventory	6,000	6,400
Equipment	42,000	19,000
Accumulated Depreciation—Equipment	(17,400)	(9,000)
Land	10,400	18,400
Total Assets	$45,000	$61,000
Liabilities and Equity		
Accounts Payable	$ 4,200	$ 2,600
Long-Term Debt	6,400	2,800
Common Stock	10,000	22,000
Retained Earnings	24,400	33,600
Total Liabilities and Equity	$45,000	$61,000

Income Statement For the Year Ended December 31, 2007	
Sales Revenue	$35,700
Cost of Goods Sold	(14,150)
Gross Margin	21,550
Depreciation Expense	(3,600)
Operating Income	17,950
Gain on Sale of Equipment	500
Loss on Disposal of Land	(50)
Net Income	$18,400

Additional Data

1. During 2007, the company sold equipment for $18,500; it had originally cost $30,000. Accumulated depreciation on this equipment was $12,000 at the time of the sale. Also, the company purchased equipment for $7,000 cash.
2. The company sold land that had cost $4,000. This land was sold for $3,950, resulting in the recognition of a $50 loss. Also, common stock was issued in exchange for title to land that was valued at $12,000 at the time of exchange.
3. Paid dividends of $9,200.

Required

Use the T-account method to analyze the data and prepare a statement of cash flows using the direct method.

PROBLEM 12–17A *Using Financial Statements to Prepare a Statement of Cash Flows—Direct Method*

L.O. 2, 3

The following financial statements were drawn from the records of Raceway Sports:

CHECK FIGURES
Net Cash Flow from Operating Activities: $86,800
Net Increase in Cash: $95,400

Balance Sheets As of December 31		
	2006	**2007**
Assets		
Cash	$ 28,200	$123,600
Accounts Receivable	66,000	57,000
Inventory	114,000	126,000
Notes Receivable	30,000	0
Equipment	255,000	147,000
Accumulated Depreciation—Equipment	(141,000)	(74,740)
Land	52,500	82,500
Total Assets	$404,700	$461,360
Liabilities and Equity		
Accounts Payable	$ 48,600	$ 42,000
Salaries Payable	24,000	30,000
Utilities Payable	1,200	600
Interest Payable	1,800	0
Note Payable	60,000	0
Common Stock	240,000	300,000
Retained Earnings	29,100	88,760
Total Liabilities and Equity	$404,700	$461,360

Income Statement For the Year Ended December 31, 2007	
Sales Revenue	$580,000
Cost of Goods Sold	(288,000)
Gross Margin	292,000
Operating Expenses	
Salary Expense	(184,000)
Depreciation Expense	(17,740)
Utilities Expense	(12,200)
Operating Income	78,060
Nonoperating Items	
Interest Expense	(3,000)
Gain or (Loss)	(1,800)
Net Income	$ 73,260

Additional Information

1. Sold equipment costing $108,000 with accumulated depreciation of $84,000 for $22,200 cash.
2. Paid a $13,600 cash dividend to owners.

Required

Use the T-account method to analyze the data and prepare a statement of cash flows using the direct method.

eXcel
www.mhhe.com/edmonds5e

L.O. 2, 4   PROBLEM 12–18A *Using Financial Statements to Prepare a Statement of Cash Flows—Indirect Method*

The comparative balance sheets for Redwood Corporation for 2006 and 2007 follow:

CHECK FIGURES
Net Cash Flow from Operating
Activities: $170,200
Net Increase in Cash: $28,200

Balance Sheets As of December 31		
	2006	**2007**
Assets		
Cash	$ 40,600	$ 68,800
Accounts Receivable	22,000	30,000
Merchandise Inventory	176,000	160,000
Prepaid Rent	4,800	2,400
Equipment	288,000	256,000
Accumulated Depreciation	(236,000)	(146,800)
Land	80,000	192,000
Total Assets	$375,400	$562,400
Liabilities		
Accounts Payable (Inventory)	$ 76,000	$ 67,000
Salaries Payable	24,000	28,000
Stockholders' Equity		
Common Stock, $25 Par Value	200,000	250,000
Retained Earnings	75,400	217,400
Total Liabilities and Equity	$375,400	$562,400

Income Statement For the Year Ended December 31, 2007	
Sales	$1,500,000
Cost of Goods Sold	(797,200)
Gross Profit	702,800
Operating Expenses	
Depreciation Expense	(22,800)
Rent Expense	(24,000)
Salaries Expense	(256,000)
Other Operating Expenses	(258,000)
Net Income	$ 142,000

Other Information
1. Purchased land for $112,000.
2. Purchased new equipment for $100,000.
3. Sold old equipment that cost $132,000 with accumulated depreciation of $112,000 for $20,000 cash.
4. Issued common stock for $50,000.

Required
Prepare the statement of cash flows for 2007 using the indirect method.

EXERCISES—SERIES B

L.O. 1   EXERCISE 12–1B *Classifying Cash Flows into Categories—Direct Method*

Required
Identify whether the cash flows in the following list should be classified as operating activities, investing activities, or financing activities on the statement of cash flows (assume the use of the direct method).

a. Sold merchandise on account.
b. Paid employee salary.
c. Received cash proceeds from bank loan.
d. Paid dividends.
e. Sold used equipment for cash.

f. Received interest income on a certificate of deposit.

g. Issued stock for cash.

h. Repaid bank loan.

i. Purchased equipment for cash.

j. Paid interest on loan.

EXERCISE 12–2B *Cash Inflows from Operating Activities—Direct Method*   **L.O. 1**

Required

Which of the following transactions produce cash inflows from operating activities (assume the use of the direct method)?

a. Cash payment for utilities expense.

b. Cash payment for equipment.

c. Cash receipt from interest.

d. Cash payment for dividends.

e. Collection of cash from accounts receivable.

f. Provide services for cash.

EXERCISE 12–3B *Using Account Balances to Determine Cash Flow from Operating*   **L.O. 2**
Activities—Direct Method

The following account balances are available for Norstom Company for 2002.

Account Title	Beginning of Year	End of Year
Accounts Receivable	$40,000	$46,000
Interest Receivable	5,000	3,000
Accounts Payable	30,000	33,000
Salaries Payable	12,000	10,500

Other Information for 2002

Sales on Account	$275,000
Interest Revenue	25,000
Operating Expenses	196,000
Salaries Expense for the Year	75,000

Required

(*Hint:* It may be helpful to assume that all revenues and expenses are on account.)

a. Compute the amount of cash *inflow* from operating activities.

b. Compute the amount of cash *outflow* from operating activities.

EXERCISE 12–4B *Using Account Balances to Determine Cash Flow from Operating*   **L.O. 2**
Activities—Direct Method

The following account balances were available for Earles Candy Company for 2001:

Account Title	Beginning of Year	End of Year
Unearned Revenue	$18,000	$8,000
Prepaid Rent	2,000	900

During the year, $41,000 of unearned revenue was recognized as having been earned. Rent expense for the period was $8,000. Earles Candy Company maintains its books on the accrual basis.

Required

Using T-accounts and the preceding information, determine the amount of cash inflow from revenue and cash outflow for rent.

L.O. 2, 3   EXERCISE 12–5B *Using Account Balances to Determine Cash Flow from Investing Activities*

The following account information is available for McClung, Inc., for 2005:

Land		
Bal.	20,000	50,000
	100,000	
Bal.	70,000	

Marketable Securities		
Bal.	75,000	30,000
	40,000	
Bal.	85,000	

The income statement reported a $9,000 gain on the sale of land and a $1,200 loss on the sale of marketable securities.

Required

Prepare the investing activities section of the statement of cash flows for 2005.

L.O. 2, 3   EXERCISE 12–6B *Using Account Balances to Determine Cash Flow from Financing Activities*

The following account balances were available for Golden Company for 2007:

Mortgage Payable			Capital Stock			Paid-in Capital in Excess of Par		
		148,000 Bal.			200,000 Bal.			65,000 Bal.
62,000					50,000			30,000
		86,000 Bal.			250,000 Bal.			95,000 Bal.

Required

Prepare the financing activities section of the statement of cash flows for 2007.

L.O. 2   EXERCISE 12–7B *Using Account Balances to Determine Cash Outflow for Inventory Purchases*

The following account information is available for Sherman Company. The company uses the perpetual inventory method and makes all inventory purchases on account.

Inventory		
Bal.	41,000	
	?	120,000
Bal.	65,000	

Accounts Payable		
		42,000 Bal.
?		?
		52,000 Bal.

Required

Compute the amount of cash paid for the purchase of inventory.

L.O. 2, 4   EXERCISE 12–8B *Using Account Balances to Determine Cash Flow from Operating Activities—Indirect Method*

Maple Company presents its statement of cash flows using the indirect method. The following accounts and corresponding balances were drawn from Maple's accounting records.

Account Titles	Beginning Balances	Ending Balances
Accounts Receivable	$30,000	$35,000
Prepaid Rent	2,000	1,200
Interest Receivable	800	400
Accounts Payable	9,000	9,500
Salaries Payable	2,500	2,100
Unearned Revenue	1,200	2,200

Net income for the period was $45,000.

Required

Using the preceding information, compute the net cash flow from operating activities using the indirect method.

EXERCISE 12–9B *Using Account Balances to Determine Cash Flow from Operating*   **L.O. 2–4**
                           Activities—Direct and Indirect Methods

The following information is from the accounting records of Mong Company:

	2000	2001
Cash	$ 42,000	$ 88,800
Accounts Receivable	158,000	159,800
Prepaid Rent	3,000	5,600
Accounts Payable	120,000	125,000
Utilities Payable	12,000	8,400
Sales Revenue		$212,000
Operating Expenses		(135,000)
Utilities Expense		(17,200)
Rent Expense		(10,000)
Net Income		$ 49,800

Required

a. Prepare the operating activities section of the 2001 statement of cash flows using the direct method.

b. Prepare the operating activities section of the 2001 statement of cash flows using the indirect method.

EXERCISE 12–10B *Interpreting Statement of Cash Flows Information*   **L.O. 3, 5**

The following selected transactions pertain to Johnston Company for 2003.

1. Purchased new office equipment for $9,800 cash.
2. Sold old office equipment for $2,000 that originally cost $12,000 and had accumulated depreciation of $11,000.
3. Borrowed $20,000 cash from the bank for six months.
4. Purchased land for $125,000 by paying $50,000 in cash and issuing a note for the balance.
5. Exchanged no-par common stock for an automobile valued at $26,500.

Required

a. Prepare the appropriate sections of the statement of cash flows for 2003.

b. What information does the noncash investing and financing activities section of the statement provide? If this information were omitted, could it affect a decision to invest in a company?

PROBLEM 12–11B *Classifying Cash Flows*   **L.O. 1**

Required

Classify each of the following as an operating activity (OA), an investing activity (IA), or a financing activity (FA) cash flow, or a noncash transaction (NT).

a. Paid cash for operating expenses.
b. Wrote off an uncollectible account receivable using the allowance method.
c. Wrote off an uncollectible account receivable using the direct write-off method.
d. Issued common stock for cash.
e. Declared a stock split.
f. Issued a mortgage to purchase a building.
g. Purchased equipment with cash.
h. Repaid the principal balance on a note payable.
i. Made a cash payment for the balance due in the Dividends Payable account.
j. Received a cash dividend from investment in marketable securities.

k. Purchased supplies on account.
l. Collected cash from accounts receivable.
m. Accrued warranty expense.
n. Borrowed cash by issuing a bond.
o. Loaned cash to a business associate.
p. Paid cash for interest expense.
q. Incurred a loss on the sale of equipment.
r. Wrote down inventory because the year-end physical count was less than the balance in the Inventory account.
s. Paid cash to purchase inventory.

L.O. 2, 3   PROBLEM 12–12B *Using Transaction Data to Prepare a Statement of Cash Flows*

Greenstein Company engaged in the following transactions during 2003. The beginning cash balance was $86,000.

1. Sales on account were $548,000. The beginning receivables balance was $128,000 and the ending balance was $90,000.
2. Salaries expense was $232,000. The beginning salaries payable balance was $16,000 and the ending balance was $8,000.
3. Other operating expenses were $236,000. The beginning Operating Expense Payable balance was $16,000 and the ending balance was $10,000.
4. Recorded $30,000 of depreciation expense. The beginning and ending balances in the Accumulated Depreciation account were $12,000 and $42,000, respectively.
5. The Equipment account had beginning and ending balances of $44,000 and $56,000, respectively. The increase was caused by the cash purchase of equipment.
6. The beginning and ending balances in the Notes Payable account were $44,000 and $36,000, respectively. The decrease was caused by the cash repayment of debt.
7. There was $4,600 of interest expense reported on the income statement. The beginning and ending balances in the Interest Payable account were $8,400 and $7,500, respectively.
8. The beginning and ending Merchandise Inventory account balances were $22,000 and $29,400, respectively. The company sold merchandise with a cost of $83,600. The beginning and ending balances of Accounts Payable were $8,000 and $6,400, respectively.
9. The beginning and ending balances of Notes Receivable were $100,000 and $60,000, respectively. The decline resulted from the cash collection of a portion of the receivable.
10. The beginning and ending balances of the Common Stock account were $120,000 and $160,000, respectively. The increase was caused by the issue of common stock for cash.
11. Land had beginning and ending balances of $24,000 and $14,000, respectively. Land that cost $10,000 was sold for $6,000, resulting in a loss of $4,000.
12. The tax expense for 2003 was $6,600. The Tax Payable account had a $2,400 beginning balance and a $2,200 ending balance.
13. The Investments account had beginning and ending balances of $20,000 and $60,000, respectively. The company purchased investments for $50,000 cash during 2003, and investments that cost $10,000 were sold for $22,000, resulting in a $12,000 gain.

Required
Convert the preceding information to cash-equivalent data and prepare a statement of cash flows.

L.O. 2, 3   PROBLEM 12–13B *Using Financial Statement Data to Determine Cash Flow from Operating Activities*

The following account information is available for Gables Auto Supplies for 2003:

Account Title	Beginning of Year	End of Year
Accounts Receivable	$ 17,800	$ 21,000
Merchandise Inventory	136,000	142,800
Prepaid Insurance	1,600	1,200
Accounts Payable (Inventory)	18,800	19,600
Salaries Payable	6,400	5,800

Other Information
1. Sales for the period were $248,000.
2. Purchases of merchandise for the period were $186,000.
3. Insurance expense for the period was $8,000.
4. Other operating expenses (all cash) were $27,400.
5. Salary expense was $42,600.

Required
a. Compute the net cash flow from operating activities.
b. Prepare the cash flow from the operating activities section of the statement of cash flows.

PROBLEM 12–14B *Using Financial Statement Data to Determine Cash Flow from Investing Activities*   **L.O. 2, 3**

The following information pertaining to investing activities is available for Tony's Flea Markets, Inc., for 2001.

Account Title	Beginning of Year	End of Year
Trucks and Equipment	$162,000	$170,000
Marketable Securities	66,000	51,200
Land	42,000	34,000

Other Information for 2001
1. Tony's sold marketable securities at book value. No gain or loss was recognized.
2. Trucks were purchased for $40,000. Old trucks with a cost of $32,000 and accumulated depreciation of $24,000 were sold for $11,000.
3. Land that cost $8,000 was sold for $10,000.

Required
a. Compute the net cash flow from investing activities.
b. Prepare the cash flow from the investing activities section of the statement of cash flows.

PROBLEM 12–15B *Using Financial Statement Data to Determine Cash Flow from Financing Activities*   **L.O. 2, 3**

The following information pertaining to financing activities is available for Engineered Components Company for 2002.

Account Title	Beginning of Year	End of Year
Bonds Payable	$170,000	$180,000
Common Stock	210,000	280,000
Paid-in Capital in Excess of Par	84,000	116,000

Other Information
1. Dividends paid during the period amounted to $28,000.
2. Additional funds of $40,000 were borrowed during the period by issuing bonds.

Required
a. Compute the net cash flow from financing activities for 2002.
b. Prepare the cash flow from the financing activities section of the statement of cash flows.

PROBLEM 12–16B *Using Financial Statements to Prepare a Statement of Cash Flows—Direct Method*   **L.O. 2, 3**

The following financial statements were drawn from the records of Healthy Products Co.

Balance Sheets As of December 31		
	2002	**2003**
Assets		
Cash	$ 1,940	$16,120
Accounts Receivable	2,000	2,400
Inventory	2,600	2,000
Equipment	17,100	13,700
Accumulated Depreciation—Equipment	(12,950)	(11,300)
Land	8,000	13,000
Total Assets	$18,690	$35,920
Liabilities and Equity		
Accounts Payable	$ 2,400	$ 3,600
Long-Term Debt	4,000	3,200
Common Stock	10,000	17,000
Retained Earnings	2,290	12,120
Total Liabilities and Stockholders' Equity	$18,690	$35,920

Income Statement For the Year Ended December 31, 2003	
Sales Revenue	$17,480
Cost of Goods Sold	(6,200)
Gross Margin	11,280
Depreciation Expense	(1,750)
Operating Income	9,530
Gain on Sale of Equipment	1,800
Loss on Disposal of Land	(600)
Net Income	$10,730

Additional Data

1. During 2003, the company sold equipment for $6,800; it had originally cost $8,400. Accumulated depreciation on this equipment was $3,400 at the time of the sale. Also, the company purchased equipment for $5,000 cash.
2. The company sold land that had cost $2,000. This land was sold for $1,400, resulting in the recognition of a $600 loss. Also, common stock was issued in exchange for title to land that was valued at $7,000 at the time of exchange.
3. Paid dividends of $900.

Required

Use the T-account method to analyze the data and prepare a statement of cash flows using the direct method.

L.O. 2, 3   **PROBLEM 12–17B** *Using Financial Statements to Prepare a Statement of Cash Flows—Direct Method*

The following financial statements were drawn from the records of Norton Materials, Inc.

Balance Sheets As of December 31		
	2000	**2001**
Assets		
Cash	$ 14,100	$ 94,300
Accounts Receivable	40,000	36,000
Inventory	64,000	72,000
Notes Receivable	16,000	0
Equipment	170,000	98,000
Accumulated Depreciation—Equipment	(94,000)	(47,800)
Land	30,000	46,000
Total Assets	$240,100	$298,500

continued

	2000	2001
Liabilities and Equity		
Accounts Payable	$ 26,400	$ 24,000
Salaries Payable	10,000	15,000
Utilities Payable	1,400	800
Interest Payable	1,000	0
Note Payable	24,000	0
Common Stock	110,000	150,000
Retained Earnings	67,300	108,700
Total Liabilities and Equity	$240,100	$298,500

Income Statement For the Year Ended December 31, 2001	
Sales Revenue	$300,000
Cost of Goods Sold	(144,000)
Gross Margin	156,000
Operating Expenses	
Salary Expense	(88,000)
Depreciation Expense	(9,800)
Utilities Expense	(6,400)
Operating Income	51,800
Nonoperating Items	
Interest Expense	(2,400)
Loss	(800)
Net Income	$ 48,600

Additional Information

1. Sold equipment costing $72,000 with accumulated depreciation of $56,000 for $15,200 cash.
2. Paid a $7,200 cash dividend to owners.

Required

Use the T-account method to analyze the data and prepare a statement of cash flows using the direct method.

PROBLEM 12–18B *Using Financial Statements to Prepare a Statement of Cash Flows—Indirect Method*   L.O. 2, 4

The comparative balance sheets for Lind Beauty Products, Inc., for 2002 and 2003 follow:

Balance Sheets As of December 31		
	2002	2003
Assets		
Cash	$ 48,400	$ 6,300
Accounts Receivable	7,260	10,200
Merchandise Inventory	56,000	45,200
Prepaid Rent	2,140	700
Equipment	144,000	140,000
Accumulated Depreciation	(118,000)	(73,400)
Land	50,000	116,000
Total Assets	$189,800	$245,000
Liabilities and Equity		
Accounts Payable (Inventory)	$ 40,000	$ 37,200
Salaries Payable	10,600	12,200
Stockholders' Equity		
Common Stock, $50 Par Value	120,000	150,000
Retained Earnings	19,200	45,600
Total Liabilities and Equity	$189,800	$245,000

Income Statement For the Year Ended December 31, 2003	
Sales	$480,000
Cost of Goods Sold	(264,000)
Gross Profit	216,000
Operating Expenses	
Depreciation Expense	(11,400)
Rent Expense	(7,000)
Salaries Expense	(95,200)
Other Operating Expenses	(76,000)
Net Income	$ 26,400

Other Information
1. Purchased land for $66,000.
2. Purchased new equipment for $62,000.
3. Sold old equipment that cost $66,000 with accumulated depreciation of $56,000 for $10,000 cash.
4. Issued common stock for $30,000.

Required
Prepare the statement of cash flows for 2003 using the indirect method.

ANALYZE, THINK, COMMUNICATE

ATC 12–1   BUSINESS APPLICATIONS CASE *Understanding Real World Annual Reports*

Required—Part 1

The Topps Company, Inc.

Use the Topps Company's annual report in Appendix B to answer the following questions.

a. For the 2003 fiscal year, which was larger, Topps' *net income* or its *cash flow from operating activities?* By what amount did they differ?
b. What two items are most responsible for the difference between Topps' *net income* and its *cash flow from operating activities* in 2003?
c. In 2003 Topps generated approximately $6.2 million of cash from operating activities, and its cash balance decreased by about $6.8 million. How did the company use this $13 million of cash?

Required—Part 2

Harley-Davidson, Inc.

Use the Harley-Davidson's annual report that came with this book to answer the following questions.

a. For the 2003 fiscal year, which was larger, Harley-Davidson's *net income* or its *cash flow from operating activities?* By what amount did they differ?
b. What item is most responsible for the difference between Harley-Davidson's *net income* and its *cash flow from operating activities* in 2003?
c. In 2003 Harley-Davidson generated approximately $936 million of cash from operating activities. What did the company do with this cash?

ATC 12–2   REAL-WORLD CASE *Following the Cash*

Panera Bread Company (Panera) was formerly known as **Au Bon Pain Company** (ABP). In May 1999, the ABP division of the company was sold to private investors for $72 million, and assumed the new name.

Panera operates retail bakery-cafes under the names Panera Bread and Saint Louis Bread Company. The following table shows the number of these cafes in operation for each of the past five years.

Year	Company Owned	Franchise Owned	Total
2000	90	172	262
1999	81	100	181
1998	70	45	115
1997	57	19	76
1996	52	10	62

Most of Panera's baked goods are distributed to the stores in the form of frozen dough. In March 1998, the company sold its frozen dough production facility to the Bunge Food Corporation for $13 million. Panera agreed to purchase its frozen dough from Bunge for at least the next five years.

Panera's statements of cash flows for 1998, 1999, and 2000 follow.

PANERA BREAD COMPANY
Consolidated Statements of Cash Flows
(Dollars in thousands)

	For the Fiscal Years Ended		
	December 30, 2000	December 25, 1999	December 26, 1998
Cash flows from operations			
Net income (loss)	$ 6,853	$ (629)	$(20,494)
Adjustments to reconcile net income (loss) to net cash provided by operating activities:			
Depreciation and amortization	8,412	6,379	12,667
Amortization of deferred financing costs	88	406	683
Provision for losses on accounts receivable	(111)	93	56
Minority interest	—	(25)	(127)
Tax benefit from exercise of stock options	4,001	—	75
Deferred income taxes	664	42	(6,664)
Loss on early extinguishment of debt	—	382	—
Nonrecurring charge	494	5,545	26,236
Loss on disposal of assets	—	—	735
Changes in operating assets and liabilities:			
Accounts receivable	(308)	(1,596)	15
Inventories	(562)	(65)	212
Prepaid expenses	(543)	(3,560)	(535)
Refundable income taxes	(376)	—	480
Accounts payable	1,861	(3,037)	4,069
Accrued expenses	(645)	769	3,104
Deferred revenue	234	2,011	—
Net cash provided by operating activities	20,062	6,715	20,512
Cash flows from investing activities			
Additions to property and equipment	(20,089)	(15,306)	(21,706)
Proceeds from sale of assets	—	72,163	12,694
Change in cash included in net current liabilities held for sale	—	(466)	(1,305)
Payments received on notes receivable	35	114	240
Increase in intangible assets	—	(50)	(139)
Increase (decrease) in deposits and other	(771)	855	(956)
Increase in notes receivable	—	(30)	(45)
Net cash (used in) provided by investing activities	(20,825)	57,280	(11,217)
Cash flows from financing activities			
Exercise of employee stock options	8,206	96	1,203
Proceeds from long-term debt issuance	765	41,837	75,418
Principal payments on long-term debt	(391)	(106,073)	(84,253)
Purchase of treasury stock	(900)	—	—
Proceeds from issuance of common stock	182	148	268
Common stock issued for employee stock bonus	—	304	—
Increase in deferred financing costs	(24)	(110)	(506)
Decrease in minority interest	—	(121)	(418)
Net cash provided by (used in) financing activities	7,838	(63,919)	(8,288)
Net increase in cash and cash equivalents	7,075	76	1,007
Cash and cash equivalents at beginning of year	1,936	1,860	853
Cash and cash equivalents at end of year	$ 9,011	$ 1,936	$ 1,860
Supplemental cash flow information:			
Cash paid during the year for:			
Interest	$ 85	$ 4,250	$ 5,544
Income taxes	512	241	268

Required

Using the information provided, including a careful analysis of Panera's statements of cash flows, answer the following questions. Be sure to explain the rationale for your answers and present any computations necessary to support them.

a. Was the sale of the frozen dough production facility for $13 million a cash sale? If so, what did Panera do with the cash it received?

b. Was the sale of the ABP division for $72 million a cash sale? If so, what did Panera do with the cash it received?

c. As shown in the preceding table, Panera has expanded its operations in each of the past five years. Approximately how much cash was spent on expansion in 1998, 1999, and 2000, and what were the sources of this cash for each year?

ATC 12–3   GROUP ASSIGNMENT *Preparing a Statement of Cash Flows*

The following financial statements and information are available for Blythe Industries, Inc.

Balance Sheets As of December 31		
	2004	**2005**
Assets		
Cash	$120,600	$ 160,200
Accounts Receivable	85,000	103,200
Inventory	171,800	186,400
Marketable Securities (Available for Sale)	220,000	284,000
Equipment	490,000	650,000
Accumulated Depreciation	(240,000)	(310,000)
Land	120,000	80,000
Total Assets	$967,400	$1,153,800
Liabilities and Equity		
Liabilities		
Accounts Payable (Inventory)	$ 66,200	$ 36,400
Notes Payable—Long-Term	250,000	230,000
Bonds Payable	100,000	200,000
Total Liabilities	416,200	466,400
Stockholders' Equity		
Common Stock, No Par	200,000	240,000
Preferred Stock, $50 Par	100,000	110,000
Paid-in Capital in Excess of Par—Preferred Stock	26,800	34,400
Total Paid-In Capital	326,800	384,400
Retained Earnings	264,400	333,000
Less: Treasury Stock	(40,000)	(30,000)
Total Stockholders' Equity	551,200	687,400
Total Liabilities and Stockholders' Equity	$967,400	$1,153,800

Income Statement For the Year Ended December 31, 2005		
Sales Revenue		$1,050,000
Cost of Goods Sold		(766,500)
Gross Profit		283,500
Operating Expenses		
Supplies Expense	$20,400	
Salaries Expense	92,000	
Depreciation Expense	90,000	
Total Operating Expenses		(202,400)
Operating Income		81,100
Nonoperating Items		
Interest Expense		(16,000)
Gain from the Sale of Marketable Securities		30,000
Gain from the Sale of Land and Equipment		12,000
Net Income		$ 107,100

Additional Information

1. Sold land that cost $40,000 for $44,000.
2. Sold equipment that cost $30,000 and had accumulated depreciation of $20,000 for $18,000.

3. Purchased new equipment for $190,000.
4. Sold marketable securities, classified as available-for-sale, that cost $40,000 for $70,000.
5. Purchased new marketable securities, classified as available-for-sale, for $104,000.
6. Paid $20,000 on the principal of the long-term note.
7. Paid off a $100,000 bond issue and issued new bonds for $200,000.
8. Sold 100 shares of treasury stock at its cost.
9. Issued some new common stock.
10. Issued some new $50 par preferred stock.
11. Paid dividends. (*Note:* The only transactions to affect retained earnings were net income and dividends.)

Required

Organize the class into three sections, and divide each section into groups of three to five students. Assign each section of groups an activity section of the statement of cash flows (operating activities, investing activities, or financing activities).

Group Task

Prepare your assigned portion of the statement of cash flows. Have a representative of your section put your activity section of the statement of cash flows on the board. As each adds its information on the board, the full statement of cash flows will be presented.

Class Discussion

Have the class finish the statement of cash flows by computing the net change in cash. Also have the class answer the following questions:

a. What is the cost per share of the treasury stock?
b. What was the issue price per share of the preferred stock?
c. What was the book value of the equipment sold?

BUSINESS APPLICATIONS CASE *Identifying Different Presentation Formats*

ATC 12–4

In *Statement of Financial Accounting Standards No. 95,* the Financial Accounting Standards Board (FASB) recommended but did not require that companies use the direct method. In Appendix B, Paragraphs 106–121, the FASB discussed its reasons for this recommendation.

Required
Obtain a copy of *Standard No. 95* and read Appendix B Paragraphs 106–21. Write a brief response summarizing the issues that the FASB considered and its specific reaction to those issues. Your response should draw heavily on paragraphs 119–121.

WRITING ASSIGNMENT *Explaining Discrepancies between Cash Flow and Operating Income*

ATC 12–5

The following selected information was drawn from the records of Fleming Company:

Assets	2005	2006
Accounts Receivable	$ 400,000	$ 840,200
Merchandise Inventory	720,000	1,480,000
Equipment	1,484,000	1,861,200
Accumulated Depreciation	(312,000)	(402,400)

Fleming is experiencing cash flow problems. Despite the fact that it reported significant increases in operating income, operating activities produced a net cash outflow. Recent financial forecasts predict that Fleming will have insufficient cash to pay its current liabilities within three months.

Required
Write a response explaining Fleming's cash shortage. Include a recommendation to remedy the problem.

ETHICAL DILEMMA *Would I Lie to You, Baby?*

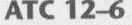

ATC 12–6

Andy and Jean Crocket are involved in divorce proceedings. When discussing a property settlement, Andy told Jean that he should take over their investment in an apartment complex because she would be unable to absorb the loss that the apartments are generating. Jean was somewhat distrustful and asked Andy to support his contention. He produced the following income statement, which was supported by a CPA's unqualified opinion that the statement was prepared in accordance with generally accepted accounting principles.

CROCKET APARTMENTS		
Income Statement		
For the Year Ended December 31, 2003		
Rent Revenue		$ 580,000
Less: Expenses		
Depreciation Expense	$280,000	
Interest Expense	184,000	
Operating Expense	88,000	
Management Fees	56,000	
Total Expenses		(608,000)
Net Loss		$ (28,000)

All revenue is earned on account. Interest and operating expenses are incurred on account. Management fees are paid in cash. The following accounts and balances were drawn from the 2002 and 2003 year-end balance sheets.

Account Title	2002	2003
Rent Receivable	$40,000	$44,000
Interest Payable	12,000	18,000
Accounts Payable (Oper. Exp.)	6,000	4,000

Jean is reluctant to give up the apartments but feels that she must because her present salary is only $40,000 per year. She says that if she takes the apartments, the $28,000 loss would absorb a significant portion of her salary, leaving her only $12,000 with which to support herself. She tells you that while the figures seem to support her husband's arguments, she believes that she is failing to see something. She knows that she and her husband collected a $20,000 distribution from the business on December 1, 2003. Also, $150,000 cash was paid in 2003 to reduce the principal balance on a mortgage that was taken out to finance the purchase of the apartments two years ago. Finally, $24,000 cash was paid during 2003 to purchase a computer system used in the business. She wonders, "If the apartments are losing money, where is my husband getting all the cash to make these payments?"

Required

a. Prepare a statement of cash flows for the 2003 accounting period.
b. Compare the cash flow statement prepared in Requirement *a* with the income statement and provide Jean Crocket with recommendations.
c. Comment on the value of an unqualified audit opinion when using financial statements for decision-making purposes.

ATC 12–7 **SPREADSHEET ANALYSIS** *Preparing a Statement of Cash Flows Using the Direct Method*

Refer to the information in Problem 12–18A. Solve for the statement of cash flows using the direct method. Instead of using the T-account method, set up the following spreadsheet to work through the analysis. The Debit/Credit entries are very similar to the T-account method except that they are entered onto a spreadsheet. Two distinct differences are as follows:

1. Instead of making entries on row 2 for Cash, cash entries are made beginning on row 24 under the heading Cash Transactions.
2. Entries for Retained Earnings are made on rows 15 through 20 since there are numerous revenue and expense entries to that account.

Required

a. Enter information in Column A.
b. Enter the beginning balance sheet amounts in Column B and ending balances in Column G. Total the debits and credits for each column.
c. To prevent erroneous entries to Cash in row 2, darken the area in Columns C through F.

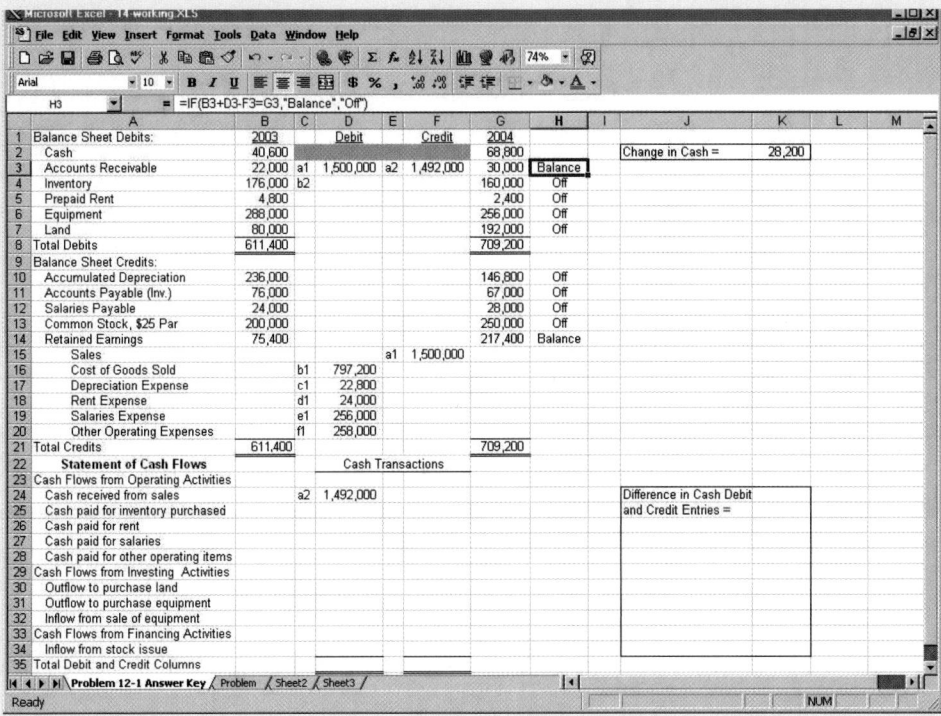

d. In Columns C through F, record entries for the revenue and expenses and then the related conversions to cash flow. The first entry (a1) and (a2) converting Sales to Cash Received from Sales has been provided for you. So has the labeling for the expense entries (b1 through f1).

e. Record the four entries from the Other Information provided in Problem 12–18A. These are investing and financing activities.

f. In Column H, set up the IF function to determine whether the balance sheet accounts are in balance or not ("off"). Cell H3 for Accounts Receivable is provided for you. Cell H3 can be copied to all the balance sheet debit accounts. The balance sheet credit account formulas will differ given the different debit/credit rules for those accounts. The formula for Retained Earnings will need to include rows 14 through 20. *When the word "Balance" is reflected in every balance sheet cell in column H, the spreadsheet analysis is complete.*

g. Total the Debit and Credit columns to ensure that the two columns are equal.

h. As a final check, beginning in cell J2, compute the change in the Cash account by subtracting the beginning balance from the ending balance. The difference will equal $28,200. Also beginning in cell J24, compute the difference in the debit and credit cash entries in rows 24 through 34. The difference should also equal $28,200.

Spreadsheet Tip

Darken cells by highlighting the cells to be darkened. Select Format and then Cells. Click on the tab titled Patterns and choose a color.

SPREADSHEET ANALYSIS *Preparing a Statement of Cash Flows Using the Indirect Method*   ATC 12–8

(*Note:* If you completed ATC 12–7, that spreadsheet can be modified to complete this problem.)

Refer to the information in Problem 12–18A. Solve for the statement of cash flows using the indirect method. Instead of using the T-account method, set up the following spreadsheet to work through the analysis. The Debit/Credit entries are very similar to the T-account method except that they are entered onto a spreadsheet. Instead of making entries on row 2 for Cash, Cash Flow entries are made beginning on row 18.

Required

a. Enter information in Column A.

b. Enter the beginning balance sheet amounts in Column B and ending balances in Column G. Total the debits and credits for each column.

c. To prevent erroneous entries to Cash in row 2, darken the area in Columns C through F.

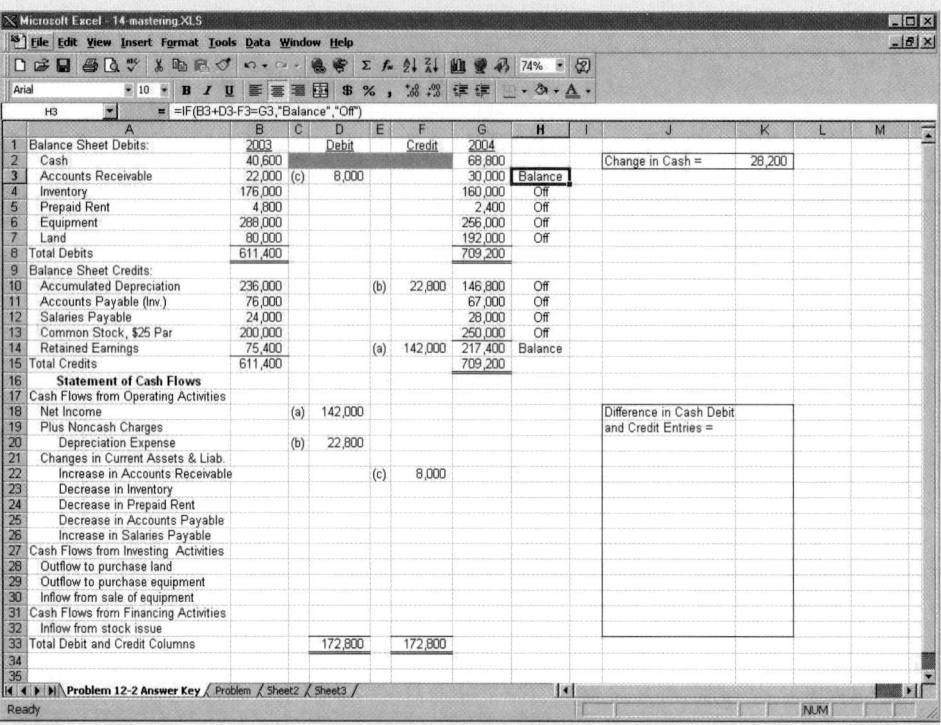

d. Record the entry for Net Income. This is entry (a) provided.

e. Record the entry for Depreciation expense. This is entry (b) provided.

f. Record the entries for the changes in current assets and liabilities. The entry for the change in Accounts Receivable has been provided and is referenced as entry (c).

g. Record the four entries from the Other Information provided in Problem 12–18A. These are the investing and financing activities.

h. In Column H set up the IF function to determine whether the balance sheet accounts are in balance or not ("off"). Cell H3 for Accounts Receivable is provided for you. Cell H3 can be copied to all the balance sheet debit accounts. The balance sheet credit account formulas will differ given the different debit/credit rules for those accounts. *When the word "Balance" is reflected in every balance sheet cell in column H, the spreadsheet analysis is complete.*

i. Total the Debit and Credit columns to ensure that the two columns are equal.

j. As a final check, beginning in cell J2, compute the change in the Cash account by subtracting the beginning balance from the ending balance. The difference will equal $28,200. Also beginning in cell J18, compute the difference in the debit and credit cash entries in rows 18 through 32. The difference should also equal $28,200.

Accessing the EDGAR Database Through the Internet

Successful business managers need many different skills, including communication, interpersonal, computer, and analytical. Most business students become very aware of the data analysis skills used in accounting, but they may not be as aware of the importance of "data-finding" skills. There are many sources of accounting and financial data. The more sources you are able to use, the better.

One very important source of accounting information is the EDGAR database. Others are probably available at your school through the library or business school network. Your accounting instructor will be able to identify these for you and make suggestions regarding their use. By making the effort to learn to use electronic databases, you will enhance your abilities as a future manager and your marketability as a business graduate.

These instructions assume that you know how to access and use an Internet navigator, such as Netscape. After you activate the Navigator program on your computer, follow the instructions to retrieve data from the Securities and Exchange Commission's EDGAR database. Be aware that the SEC may have changed its interface since this appendix was written. Accordingly, be prepared for slight differences between the following instructions and what appears on your computer screen. Take comfort in the fact that changes are normally designed to simplify user access. If you encounter a conflict between the following instructions and the instructions provided in the SEC interface, remember that the SEC interface is more current and should take precedence over the following instructions.

1. To connect to EDGAR, type in the following address: **http://www.sec.gov/**.
2. After the SEC home page appears, under the heading **Filings & Forms (EDGAR),** click on **Search for Company Filings.**
3. From the screen that appears, click on **Companies & Other Filers.**
4. On the screen that appears, enter the name of the company whose file you wish to retrieve and click on the **Find Companies** button.
5. The following screen will present a list of companies that have the same, or similar, names to the one you entered. Identify the company you want and click on the CIK number beside it.
6. Enter the SEC form number that you want to retrieve in the window titled **Form Type** that appears in the upper right portion of the screen that appears. For example, if you want Form 10-K, which will usually be the case, enter **10-K,** and click on the **Retrieve Filings** button.
7. A list of the forms you requested will be presented, along with the date they were filed with the SEC. You may be given a choice of **[text]** or **[html]** file format. The **[text]** format will present one large file for the form you requested. The **[html]** format will probably present several separate files from which you must choose. These will be named Document 1 . . ., Document 2 . . ., etc. Usually, you should choose the file whose name ends in **10k.txt.** Form 10-K/A is an amended Form 10-K and it sometimes contains more timely information, but usually, the most recent Form 10-K will contain the information you need.
8. Once the 10-K has been retrieved, you can search it online or save it on your hard drive or diskette. If you want to save it, do so by using the **Save As** command from the pulldown menu at the top of the screen named **File.**
9. The financial statements are seldom located near the beginning of a company's 10-K, so it is necessary to scroll down the file until you find them. Typically, they are located about one-half to three-fourths of the way through the report.

Topps Annual Report 2003

Stockholders' Letter

Dear Stockholders:

Fiscal 2003, ended March 1, 2003, marked the beginning of a Company-wide program devoted to building for future growth. In last year's Annual Report, we characterized the upcoming year as one of strategic investment. It was all of that and more as the Company made meaningful progress against targeted initiatives, in a difficult business environment.

Overall, we aimed to strengthen Topps position as a global marketer of branded confectionery and entertainment products. In fact, we recently announced that we will be reporting the sports and entertainment segments as one business—Entertainment — due to their similarities and the way we are now organized to manage them.

Here is a sampling of Topps strategies that guided our activities last year along with some specific achievements against them to date. For financial details see Management's Discussion beginning on page 7.

Confectionery

In fiscal 2003, we set out to grow the core brand franchises of Ring Pop, Push Pop and Baby Bottle Pop, as measured by heightened consumer awareness, greater retail distribution, and increased sales.

Ring Pop and Push Pop brands both delivered strong performances with impressive sales gains in the United States. The impetus for progress was execution against our three-pronged strategy—providing children with compelling high quality products, expanding product availability (distribution and in-store location) and advertising on kids' television programs. Overseas, we also aimed to secure confectionery listings in several key retailers and were on the mark in virtually every instance.

Baby Bottle Pop presented a particular challenge, coming off a year-long special retail promotion at Wal-Mart, as well as our expectation of lower sales in Japan after the product's rollout there last year. Still, we had reason to envision that much, if not all, of that lost ground could be made up by a highly anticipated brand extension. "Baby Bottle Pop with Candy Juice," was originally scheduled to reach market early enough in the fiscal year to impact financial results. Technical

1

difficulties, however, delayed its introduction until this past January when first shipments were made, at last.

Fast-forwarding to today, we are very encouraged by early reports of consumer response to the new entry as well as solid trade acceptance. "Candy Juice" may well turn out to have been worth the wait. Further, a new brand, "Juicy Drop Pop," is making its initial appearance overseas as we speak.

Another goal for us in fiscal 2003 was to begin branching out into other kids' confectionery segments by creating one or more brands outside the lollipop category, for marketing in fiscal 2004. We analyzed the candy universe to identify areas of opportunity based on a variety of factors such as segment size and growth, price points, trade channel development and competitive framework. Qualitative and quantitative research was conducted to gain consumer insights about targeted segments. That data was used to guide internal and external new product development activities.

At present, there are several candidates in development, at least one of which is expected to see light of day this fiscal year. Work on these and other new confectionery products continues apace.

Entertainment

In fiscal 2003, the principal focus was on leveraging our strengths (brands and know-how) against current products and new formats. As mentioned earlier, this segment is now comprised of sports and non-sports products, including trading cards, stickers, albums, internet, and other entertainment offerings.

Our traditional sports card products performed relatively well during the period, winning an enviable number of industry awards and, as best one can tell, gaining market share.

Nonetheless, the consumer base for traditional cards declined yet again and there is little protection for sales and margins in such a lengthy down cycle. Simply too many competitors vie for bits of too small a pie. Accordingly, in the fourth quarter, we significantly modified our expectations regarding next year's traditional card sales and took the steps necessary to bring staffing, costs and marketing plans more in line with reality.

That said, we are as resolved as ever to advance the market leadership position Topps has held for decades, by continuing to create innovative products with purpose and appeal. After all, the Topps brand itself is and can continue to be a powerful sponsor for traditional and non-traditional offerings alike. Take "etopps" for instance, a relatively new brand of cards we sell exclusively on the internet via Initial Player Offerings (IPOs). Last year the number of registered etopps users and buyers expanded and we will continue to invest in its future. If you haven't already done so, we invite you to go to the site (www.etopps.com) and see for yourself what etopps is all about.

Another major strategy in fiscal 2003 was to improve the performance of our European football sticker album products. Results were outstanding, even excluding World Cup sales which occur only once every four years. We offered consumers compelling product innovations, utilized considerably more in-store merchandising than before and increased album sampling which appears to have brought more sticker buyers into the fold.

By way of example, Topps Italy successfully introduced a brand new concept marketed through our confectionery distribution system – Bubble Gum with Mini Stickers – featuring Calcio football players. This product was a significant success, making the case that combining creativity with brand equity is more than a good idea. It is an imperative going forward. Additional efforts along this line can be anticipated.

Last but not least, other Entertainment opportunities continue to dot our radar screen such as Simpsons Sticker Gum, released late last year. Presently scheduled for marketing this year are Yu-Gi-Oh! Stickers and Albums, The Incredible Hulk cards and punch-out cards featuring Beyblade, a popular Japanese animation property. We remain highly selective as to which licenses are pursued.

3

Conclusion

We hope the foregoing is helpful in providing perspective on last year's performance. No doubt, attention to strategic goals will continue to play a key role in shaping the Company's future.

We would like to express our appreciation to the entire Topps family of employees, both here and abroad, for their tireless efforts. These are the people in every discipline of the business that make the trains go on time, so to speak, and not bump into one another. And Happy Anniversary Bazooka Joe—50 years young is worth celebrating!

On behalf of the Organization, we also thank our fans, collectors, customers, licensors, stockholders and suppliers for their valued support.

Chairman, Chief Executive Officer and President

OFFICERS OF THE TOPPS COMPANY, INC.

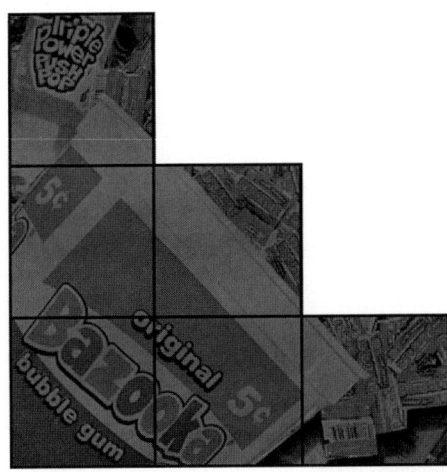

financial highlights

	Year Ended		
	March 1, 2003	March 2, 2002	March 3, 2001
	(In thousands of dollars, except share data)		
Net sales	$ **290,079**	$ 300,180	$ 437,440
Income from operations	**20,782**	36,564	121,917
Net income	**16,936**	28,462	88,489
Cash provided by operations	**6,200**	1,619	104,120
Working capital	**141,484**	136,389	140,487
Stockholders' equity	**196,768**	194,054	196,542
Net income per share - basic	$ **0.41**	$ 0.66	$ 1.97
- diluted	$ **0.40**	$ 0.64	$ 1.91
Weighted average shares outstanding - basic	**41,353,000**	43,073,000	45,011,000
- diluted	**42,065,000**	44,276,000	46,366,000

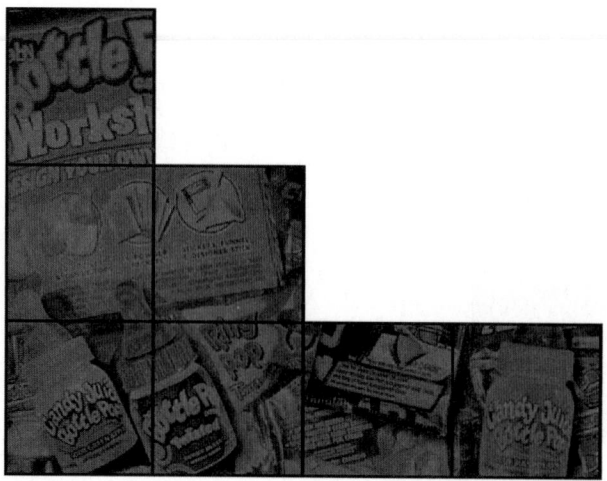

The Company has two reportable business segments: Confectionery and Entertainment. Consistent with Topps organizational structure and product line similarities, Entertainment now combines the former Sports and Entertainment segments into one.

The following table sets forth, for the periods indicated, net sales by key business segment:

	Year Ended		
	March 1, 2003	March 2, 2002	March 3, 2001
	(In thousands of dollars)		
Confectionery	**$146,865**	$152,127	$170,700
Entertainment	**143,214**	148,053	266,740
Total	**$290,079**	$300,180	$437,440

Fiscal 2003 Versus 2002*

In fiscal 2003, the Company's consolidated net sales decreased 3.4% to $290.1 million from $300.2 million in fiscal 2002. This decrease was primarily a function of a reduction in the popularity of products featuring Pokémon, which generated $6.0 million in sales in fiscal 2003 versus $24.1 million in fiscal 2002. Stronger European currencies served to increase fiscal 2003 sales by $3.9 million.

Net sales of the Confectionery segment, which includes Ring Pop, Push Pop, Baby Bottle Pop and Bazooka brand bubble gum, decreased 3.5% in 2003 to $146.9 million from $152.1 million in 2002. Excluding sales of Pokémon products, confectionery sales decreased 0.7%. Sales results reflect growth in the U.S. of Ring Pop and Push Pop, the successful roll out of Pro Flip Pop in Japan and the introduction of Yu-Gi-Oh! sticker pops in the U.S. and Canada. These gains were offset by lower sales of Baby Bottle Pop. Confectionery products accounted for 51% of the Company's consolidated net sales in both 2003 and 2002.

Net sales of the Entertainment segment, which includes cards, sticker albums and Internet activities, decreased 3.3% in fiscal 2003 to $143.2 million. Excluding sales of Pokémon products which decreased to $4.5 million in fiscal 2003 from $18.2 million, Entertainment sales increased 6.9%. Sales of European sports sticker albums increased significantly, driven by the World Cup soccer tour which occurs once every four

Unless otherwise indicated, all date references to 2003, 2002 and 2001 refer to the fiscal years ended March 1, 2003, March 2, 2002 and March 3, 2001, respectively.

years, substantial increases in sales of U.K. Premier League soccer products and the successful introduction of a new concept — bubble gum with mini stickers — in Italy. Internet activities, which include etopps (cards sold online via an IPO format) and thePit.com (an online sports card exchange), generated $11.9 million in sales and $0.7 million in contributed margin losses (before overhead) in 2003 versus $5.8 million in sales and $1.4 million in contributed margin losses in the prior year. Sales of traditional U.S. sports cards were lower in fiscal 2003, reflecting continued industry declines. In February 2003, the Company restructured its U.S. sports operations, reducing headcount and the number of products it expects to release going forward. In fiscal 2003, the Company also marketed products featuring the Star Wars, Spider-Man, Yu-Gi-Oh! and Hamtaro properties, among others. Entertainment products represented 49% of the Company's consolidated net sales in both 2003 and 2002.

Consolidated gross profit as a percentage of net sales decreased to 35.1% in 2003 from 37.9% in 2002. Margins this year were negatively impacted by the reduction in sales of high-margin Pokémon products, an increase in sales of lower margin products and the absence of rebates received last year from a foreign distributor.

Other income (expense) was $184,000 this year versus an expense of $215,000 last year, in part the result of government cash incentives to maintain our New York office location received in 2003, versus non-cash foreign exchange losses in 2002 on dollar-denominated cash balances held in Europe.

Selling, general & administrative expenses ("SG&A") increased as a percentage of net sales to 28.0% in 2003 from 25.7% a year ago. SG&A dollar spending increased to $81.1 million from $77.1 million due to the absence of a $2.4 million favorable Internet-related legal settlement received in 2002, a $1.6 million unfavorable legal settlement recorded in 2003 and an increase in marketing costs primarily related to etopps. Partially offsetting these increases was the elimination of goodwill amortization in 2003 in accordance with FAS 142, which totaled $1.6 million, and lower costs associated with the employee incentive compensation program.

Net interest income decreased to $2.5 million in fiscal 2003 from $4.9 million in fiscal 2002

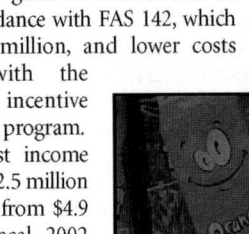

7

reflecting less favorable interest rates and a lower average cash balance.

The effective tax rate in 2003 of 27.3% reflects provisions for federal, state and local income taxes in accordance with statutory income tax rates. The decrease versus the 2002 rate of 31.3% was a function of certain one-time R&D and foreign tax benefits received this year.

Net income in fiscal 2003 was $16.9 million, or $0.40 per diluted share, versus $28.5 million, or $0.64 per diluted share in 2002.

Fiscal 2002 Versus 2001

In fiscal 2002, the Company's consolidated net sales decreased $137.2 million or 31.4% to $300.2 million from $437.4 million in fiscal 2001. This decrease was primarily a function of a $155.5 million decline in Pokémon sales to $24.1 million in fiscal 2002 from $179.6 million in fiscal 2001.

Net sales of the Confectionery segment decreased $18.6 million or 10.9% in 2002 to $152.1 million from $170.7 million in 2001. Sales of Pokémon confectionery products decreased $33.0 million to $5.9 million in 2002 from $38.9 million in 2001. Topps branded (non-Pokémon) confectionery sales increased 10.9%, reflecting strong domestic growth of Ring Pop and Push Pop, worldwide growth of Baby Bottle Pop and the introduction of seasonal candy products. Confectionery products accounted for 51% of the Company's consolidated net sales in 2002, compared with 39% in 2001.

Net sales of the Entertainment segment decreased $118.7 million or 44.5% in fiscal 2002 to $148.1 million, reflecting a $122.4 million decrease in sales of Pokémon products to $18.2 million. Sales of traditional sports products decreased 8.4% due to lower sales of football and basketball products, partially offset by higher sales of baseball and European soccer products. Internet activities, which include etopps and thePit.com, generated $5.8 million in sales and $1.4 million in contributed margin losses (before overhead) in the year versus $0.1 million in sales and $0.5 million in contributed margin losses in the prior year. Non-sports card and sticker album releases in 2002 included Lord of the Rings, Monsters, Inc., Planet of the Apes and Enduring Freedom. Entertainment products represented 49% of the Company's consolidated net sales in 2002, compared with 61% in 2001.

Consolidated gross profit as a percentage of net sales decreased to 37.9% in 2002 from 45.7% in 2001. Margins in 2002 were impacted by the reduction in sales of high-margin Pokémon products as well as an increase in sports autograph and relic costs and lower gross profit margins at thePit.com.

Other income (expense) was an expense of $215,000 in 2002 versus income of $3.0 million in 2001 primarily as a result of non-cash foreign exchange losses in 2002 on dollar-denominated cash balances held in Europe, as well as lower levels of prompt payment discounts on European inventory purchases.

Selling, general & administrative expenses increased as a percentage of net sales to 25.7% in 2002 from 18.5% in 2001 as a result of lower sales. SG&A dollar spending decreased to $77.1 million from $81.0 million due to a $2.4 million favorable Internet-related legal settlement, a reduction in etopps overhead expenses and lower marketing expenditures overseas.

Net interest income decreased to $4.9 million in fiscal 2002 from $5.7 million in fiscal 2001 reflecting lower interest rates and a lower average cash balance than in 2001.

The effective tax rate in 2002 of 31.3% reflects provisions for federal, state and local income taxes in accordance with statutory income tax rates. The increase versus the 2001 rate of 30.7% was a function of the lower mix of international earnings and the lower effective rates on those earnings as well as the absence of certain one-time tax benefits present in 2001.

Net income in fiscal 2002 was $28.5 million, or $0.64 per diluted share, versus $88.5 million, or $1.91 per diluted share in 2001.

Quarterly Comparisons

Management believes that quarter-to-quarter comparisons of sales and operating results are affected by a number of factors, including but not limited to new product introductions, the scheduling of product releases, seasonal products and the timing of various expenses such as advertising. Thus, quarterly results vary. See Note 17 of Notes to Consolidated Financial Statements.

Inflation

In the opinion of management, inflation has not had a material effect on the operations of the Company.

Liquidity and Capital Resources

Management believes that the Company has adequate means to meet its liquidity and capital resource needs over the foreseeable future as a result of the combination of cash on hand, anticipated cash from operations and credit line availability.

As of March 1, 2003, the Company had $114.3 million in cash and cash equivalents.

On June 26, 2000, the Company entered into a credit agreement with Chase Manhattan Bank and LaSalle Bank National Association. The agreement provides for a $35.0 million unsecured facility to cover revolver and letter of credit needs and expires on June 26, 2004. Interest rates are variable and a function of the Company's EBITDA. The credit agreement contains restrictions and prohibitions of a nature generally found in loan agreements of this type and requires the Company, among other things, to comply with certain financial covenants, limits the Company's ability to repurchase its shares, sell or acquire assets or borrow additional money and prohibits the payment of dividends. The credit agreement may be terminated by the Company at any point over the four-year term (provided the Company repays all outstanding amounts thereunder) without penalty. The full $35.0 million credit line was available as of March 1, 2003.

In October 1999, the Board of Directors authorized the Company to purchase up to 5 million shares of the Company's common stock. In October 2001, purchases against this authorization were completed, and the Board of Directors authorized the purchase of up to an additional 5 million shares of stock. As of March 2003, the Company had purchased 2.6 million shares against this new authorization. During fiscal 2003, the Company purchased a total of 1.6 million shares at an average price per share of $9.01.

During 2003, the Company's net decrease in cash and cash equivalents was $6.8 million versus a decrease of $37.7 million in 2002. Cash flow from operating activities in 2003 was $6.2 million versus $1.6 million last year, primarily as a result of European tax payments in 2002 on the prior year's Pokémon product sales, partially offset by lower net income in 2003. Cash flow from investing

activities this year reflects $3.8 million in capital expenditures, principally on computer software and systems and Ring Pop production equipment, versus the $5.7 million acquisition of thePit.com and $5.1 million in capital expenditures last year. Cash flow from financing activities was driven by treasury stock purchases net of cash received from options exercised of $12.9 million this year versus $24.3 million last year.

Stockholders' equity of $196.8 million in fiscal 2003 was $2.7 million above fiscal 2002 levels, as net income of $16.9 million was partially offset by $12.9 million in net treasury stock purchases.

Future minimum payments under non-cancelable leases which extend into the year 2014 are $1,531,000 (2004), $1,531,000 (2005), $1,531,000 (2006), $1,454,000 (2007), $1,400,000 (2008) and $2,980,000 thereafter.

Future minimum payments required under the Company's existing sports and entertainment contracts, with various expiration dates extending into the year 2004, are estimated to be $12,162,000.

Critical Accounting Policies

The preparation of financial statements in conformity with accounting principles generally accepted in the United States of America requires Topps management to make estimates and assumptions that affect the reported amounts of revenue, expenses, assets, liabilities and the disclosure of contingent assets and liabilities.

On an on-going basis, Topps management evaluates its estimates and judgments, including those related to revenue recognition, intangible assets and reserves, based on historical experience and on various other factors that are believed to be reasonable under the circumstances. Actual results may differ from these estimates. Note 1 to the Company's consolidated financial statements, "Summary of Significant Accounting Policies," summarizes each of its significant accounting policies. Additionally, Topps management believes the following critical accounting policies, among others, affect its more significant judgments and estimates used in the preparation of its consolidated financial statements.

Revenue Recognition: Revenue related to sales of the Company's products is generally recognized when products are shipped, the title and risk of loss has passed to the customer, the sales price is fixed or determinable and collectibility is reasonably assured. Sales made on a returnable basis are recorded net of a provision for estimated returns. These estimates are revised, as necessary, to reflect actual experience and market conditions.

Intangible Assets: Intangible assets include trademarks and the value of sports, entertainment and proprietary product rights. Amortization is by the straight-line method over estimated lives of up to twenty years. Management evaluates the recoverability of intangible assets under the provisions of SFAS 144, based on undiscounted projections of future cash flows attributable to the individual assets.

Estimates: The preparation of financial statements in conformity with generally accepted accounting principles requires management to make estimates and assumptions which affect the reporting of assets and liabilities as of the dates of the financial statements and revenues and expenses during the reporting period. These estimates primarily relate to the provision for sales returns, allowance for doubtful accounts, inventory obsolescence and asset valuations. Actual results could differ from these estimates.

Disclosures About Market Risk

The Company's exposure to market risk associated with activities in derivative financial instruments (e.g., hedging or currency swap agreements), other financial instruments and derivative commodity instruments is confined to the impact of mark-to-market changes in foreign currency rates on the Company's forward contracts and options. The Company has no long-term debt and does not engage in any commodity-related derivative transactions. As of March 1, 2003, the Company had $27.3 million in forward contracts which were entered into for the purpose of hedging foreign exchange risk associated with forecasted receipts and disbursements.

New Accounting Pronouncements

In June 2001, the FASB issued SFAS 141 "Business Combinations." SFAS 141 applies prospectively to all business combinations initiated after June 30, 2001 and to all business combinations accounted for using the purchase method for which the date of acquisition is July 1, 2001, or later. The Company adopted SFAS 141 during fiscal 2002. The adoption of this standard did not have a material impact on the Company's financial condition or results of operations.

In June 2001, the FASB issued SFAS 142 "Goodwill and Other Intangible Assets." SFAS 142 addresses financial accounting and reporting for acquired goodwill and other intangible assets. Under SFAS 142, goodwill and some intangible assets are no longer amortized, but rather are reviewed for impairment on a periodic basis. In addition, the standard includes provisions for the reclassification of certain intangibles as goodwill, reassessment of the useful lives of intangibles and the identification of reporting units for purposes of assessing potential future impairment of goodwill. The standard also required the Company to complete a transitional impairment test within six months of the date of adoption. The Company adopted the provisions of this Statement effective March 3, 2002. Amortization of existing goodwill, which was $1.6 million for each of the years ended March 2, 2002, March 3, 2001 and February 26, 2000, respectively, ceased upon adoption. The Company completed an impairment test of goodwill on August 31, 2002 and concluded that no impairment exists.

In August 2001, the FASB issued SFAS 143 "Accounting for Asset Retirement Obligations." SFAS 143 addresses financial accounting and reporting for obligations associated with the retirement of tangible long-lived assets and the associated retirement costs. The adoption of SFAS 143 was effective March 3, 2002. The adoption of this standard did not have a material impact on the Company's financial condition or results of operations.

In October 2001, the FASB issued SFAS 144 "Accounting for the Impairment or Disposal of Long-Lived Assets." SFAS 144 superseded previous guidance for financial accounting and reporting for the impairment or disposal of long-lived assets and for segments of a business to be disposed of. The Company adopted SFAS 144 during fiscal 2002. The adoption of this standard did not have a material impact on the Company's financial condition or results of operations.

In April 2002, the FASB issued SFAS 145 "Rescission of FASB Statements No. 4, 44, and 64, Amendment of FASB Statement No. 13, and Technical Corrections." Among other changes, SFAS 145 rescinded SFAS 4 "Reporting Gains and Losses from Extinguishment of Debt," which required all gains and losses from the extinguishment of debt to be aggregated and, if material, to be classified as an extraordinary item, net of related income tax effects. The rescission of SFAS 4 is effective for fiscal years beginning after May 15, 2002. The primary impact of SFAS 145 on the Company is that future gains and losses from the extinguishment of debt will be subject to the criteria of APB Opinion 30 "Reporting the Results of Operations – Reporting the Effects of Disposal of a Segment of a Business, and Extraordinary Unusual and Infrequently Occurring Events and Transactions." Therefore, debt extinguishments in future periods may not be classified as an extraordinary item, net of related income tax effects, but instead as a component of income from continuing operations. The adoption of this standard did not have a material impact on the Company's financial condition or results of operations.

In June 2002, the FASB issued SFAS 146 "Accounting for Costs Associated with Exit or Disposal Activities" which is effective for exit or disposal activities initiated after

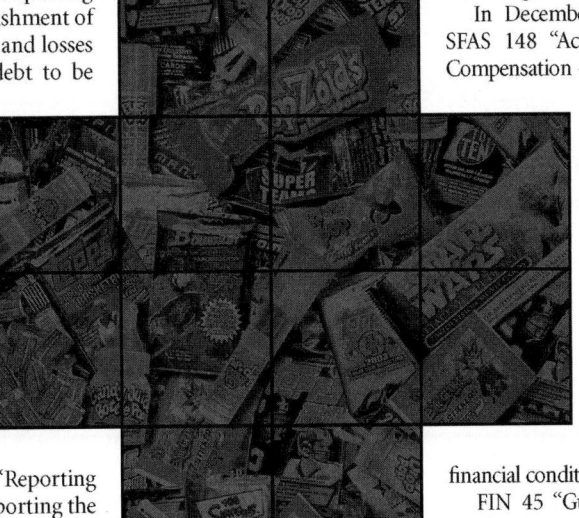

December 31, 2002. SFAS 146 addresses financial accounting and reporting for costs incurred in connection with exit or disposal activities, including restructurings, and supersedes Emerging Issues Task Force (EITF) Issue No. 94-3 "Liability Recognition for Certain Employee Termination Benefits and Other Costs to Exit an Activity (including Certain Costs Incurred in a Restructuring)." Under SFAS 146, a liability related to an exit or disposal activity is not recognized until such liability has actually been incurred, as opposed to a liability being recognized at the time of a commitment to an exit plan, which was the standard for liability recognition under EITF Issue 94-3. As a result of adopting SFAS 146, the Company did not record $570,000 in restructuring expenses in fiscal 2003 and will recognize them in fiscal 2004.

In December 2002, the FASB issued SFAS 148 "Accounting for Stock-Based Compensation - Transition and Disclosure" which is effective for fiscal years ending after December 15, 2002. SFAS 148 provides alternative methods of transition for any entity that voluntarily changes to the fair value based method of accounting for stock-based employee compensation. The Company does not expect the adoption of SFAS 148 to have a material effect on its financial condition or results of operations.

FIN 45 "Guarantor's Accounting and Disclosure Requirements for Guarantees, Including Indirect Guarantees of Indebtedness of Others" was issued in November 2002. FIN 45 elaborates on certain disclosure requirements and clarifies certain recognition criteria related to guarantees. The disclosure requirements of FIN 45 are effective for periods ending after December 15, 2002, and the recognition criteria of FIN 45 are effective on a prospective basis for guarantees issued or modified after December 31, 2002. The impact of FIN 45 on the Company's financial condition or results of operations is not determinable since FIN 45 primarily impacts guarantees issued or modified in future periods.

consolidated statements of operations

The Topps Company, Inc. and Subsidiaries
(In thousands of dollars, except share data)

		Year Ended		
	March 1, 2003		March 2, 2002	March 3, 2001
Net sales	$ 290,079	$	300,180	$ 437,440
Cost of sales	188,345		186,339	237,529
Gross profit on sales	101,734		113,841	199,911
Other income (expense)	184		(215)	2,964
Selling, general and administrative expenses	81,136		77,062	80,958
Income from operations	20,782		36,564	121,917
Interest income, net	2,516		4,894	5,717
Income before provision for income taxes	23,298		41,458	127,634
Provision for income taxes	6,362		12,996	39,145
Net income	$ 16,936	$	28,462	$ 88,489
Net income per share - basic	$ 0.41	$	0.66	$ 1.97
- diluted	$ 0.40	$	0.64	$ 1.91
Weighted average shares outstanding - basic	41,353,000		43,073,000	45,011,000
- diluted	42,065,000		44,276,000	46,366,000

See Notes to Consolidated Financial Statements.

consolidated balance sheets

The Topps Company, Inc. and Subsidiaries
(In thousands of dollars, except share data)

	March 1, 2003	March 2, 2002
ASSETS		
Current assets:		
Cash and cash equivalents	$ 114,259	$ 121,057
Accounts receivable, net	25,205	20,039
Inventories	28,681	23,096
Income tax receivable	2,029	3,230
Deferred tax assets	3,267	4,343
Prepaid expenses and other current assets	10,302	11,807
Total current assets	183,743	183,572
Property, plant and equipment, net	14,606	14,606
Goodwill	48,839	46,773
Intangible assets, net	6,041	7,251
Other assets	8,399	5,748
Total assets	$ 261,628	$ 257,950
LIABILITIES AND STOCKHOLDERS' EQUITY		
Current liabilities:		
Accounts payable	$ 9,074	$ 10,966
Accrued expenses and other liabilities	29,243	30,274
Income taxes payable	3,942	5,943
Total current liabilities	42,259	47,183
Deferred income taxes	-	-
Other liabilities	22,601	16,713
Total liabilities	64,860	63,896
Commitments and contingencies	-	-
Stockholders' equity:		
Preferred stock, *par value $.01 per share, authorized 10,000,000 shares, none issued*	-	-
Common stock, *par value $.01 per share, authorized 100,000,000 shares, issued 49,244,000 in 2003 and 49,189,000 in 2002*	492	492
Additional paid-in capital	27,344	26,824
Treasury stock, *8,564,000 shares in 2003 and 7,143,000 shares in 2002*	(80,791)	(67,415)
Retained earnings	262,877	245,941
Accumulated other comprehensive loss	(13,154)	(11,788)
Total stockholders' equity	196,768	194,054
Total liabilities and stockholders' equity	$ 261,628	$ 257,950

See Notes to Consolidated Financial Statements.

13

consolidated statements of cash flows

The Topps Company, Inc. and Subsidiaries
(In thousands of dollars, except share data)

	Year Ended		
	March 1, 2003	March 2, 2002	March 3, 2001
Operating Activities			
Net income	$ 16,936	$ 28,462	$ 88,489
Add (subtract) non-cash items included in net income:			
Depreciation and amortization	5,038	5,525	4,345
Deferred taxes on income	1,076	(3,242)	2,007
Net effect of changes in:			
Receivables	(5,166)	(9,176)	14,960
Inventories	(5,585)	789	(2,188)
Income tax receivable	1,201	8,339	(11,317)
Prepaid expenses and other current assets	1,505	(7,446)	1,029
Payables and other current liabilities	(4,924)	(26,439)	7,752
Other	(3,881)	4,807	(957)
Cash provided by operating activities	6,200	1,619	104,120
Investing Activities			
Purchase of subsidiary	-	(5,680)	-
Net additions to property, plant and equipment	(3,807)	(5,108)	(3,360)
Cash used in investing activities	(3,807)	(10,788)	(3,360)
Financing Activities			
Exercise of employee stock options	1,449	5,074	3,266
Purchase of treasury stock	(14,305)	(29,364)	(21,374)
Cash used in financing activities	(12,856)	(24,290)	(18,108)
Effect of exchange rate changes on cash and cash equivalents	3,665	(4,225)	236
Net (decrease) increase in cash and cash equivalents	(6,798)	(37,684)	82,888
Cash and cash equivalents at beginning of year	121,057	158,741	75,853
Cash and cash equivalents at end of year	$ 114,259	$ 121,057	$ 158,741
Supplemental disclosure of cash flow information:			
Interest paid	$ 91	$ 83	$ 119
Income taxes paid	$ 12,578	$ 24,024	$ 30,854

See Notes to Consolidated Financial Statements.

14

consolidated statements of stockholders' equity and comprehensive income

The Topps Company, Inc. and Subsidiaries
(In thousands of dollars)

	Total	Common Stock	Additional Paid-in Capital	Treasury Stock	Retained Earnings	Other Comprehensive Income (Loss)
Stockholders' equity as of 2/26/2000	$ 129,175	$ 478	$ 18,498	$ (16,677)	$ 128,990	$ (2,114)
Net income	88,489	-	-	-	88,489	-
Translation adjustment	(1,430)	-	-	-	-	(1,430)
Minimum pension liability	(1,584)	-	-	-	-	(1,584)
Total comprehensive income	85,475	-	-	-	88,489	(3,014)
Purchase of treasury stock	(21,374)	-	-	(21,374)	-	-
Exercise of employee stock options	3,266	6	3,260	-	-	-
Stockholders' equity as of 3/3/2001	$ 196,542	$ 484	$ 21,758	$ (38,051)	$ 217,479	$ (5,128)
Net income	28,462	-	-	-	28,462	-
Translation adjustment	(3,304)	-	-	-	-	(3,304)
Minimum pension liability	(3,356)	-	-	-	-	(3,356)
Total comprehensive income	21,802	-	-	-	28,462	(6,660)
Purchase of treasury stock	(29,364)	-	-	(29,364)	-	-
Exercise of employee stock options	5,074	8	5,066	-	-	-
Stockholders' equity as of 3/2/2002	$ 194,054	$ 492	$ 26,824	$ (67,415)	$ 245,941	$ (11,788)
Net income	16,936	-	-	-	16,936	-
Translation adjustment	3,399	-	-	-	-	3,399
Minimum pension liability	(4,765)	-	-	-	-	(4,765)
Total comprehensive income	15,570	-	-	-	16,936	(1,366)
Purchase of treasury stock	(14,305)	-	-	(14,305)	-	-
Exercise of employee stock options	1,449	-	520	929	-	-
Stockholders' equity as of 3/1/2003	**$ 196,768**	**$ 492**	**$ 27,344**	**$ (80,791)**	**$ 262,877**	**$ (13,154)**

See Notes to Consolidated Financial Statements.

notes to consolidated financial statements

NOTE 1

Summary of Significant Accounting Policies

Principles of Consolidation: The consolidated financial statements include the accounts of The Topps Company, Inc. and its subsidiaries ("the Company"). All intercompany items and transactions have been eliminated in consolidation.

The Company and its subsidiaries operate and report financial results on a fiscal year of 52 or 53 weeks which ends on the Saturday closest to the end of February. Fiscal 2001 was comprised of 53 weeks versus 52 weeks in both fiscal 2002 and fiscal 2003.

Foreign Currency Translation: The financial statements of subsidiaries outside the United States, except those subsidiaries located in highly inflationary economies or where costs are primarily U.S. dollar-based, are generally measured using the local currency as the functional currency. Assets and liabilities of these subsidiaries are translated at the rates of exchange as of the balance sheet date. The resultant translation adjustments are included in accumulated other comprehensive income. Income and expense items are translated at the average exchange rate for the month. Gains and losses from foreign currency transactions of these subsidiaries are included in net income. For subsidiaries operating in highly inflationary economies or where inventory costs are U.S. dollar-based, the financial statements are measured using the U.S. dollar as the functional currency. Gains and losses from balance sheet translation adjustments are also included in net income.

Derivative Financial Instruments: Derivative financial instruments are used for hedging purposes by the Company in the management of its foreign currency exposures. The Company does not hold or issue derivative financial instruments for trading purposes.

Gains or losses arising from the derivative financial instruments are recorded in earnings. On March 4, 2001, the Company adopted the provisions of SFAS 133 "Accounting for Derivative Instruments and Hedging Activities" and related standards, as amended. SFAS 133 provides a comprehensive standard for the recognition and measurement of derivatives and hedging activities.

Cash Equivalents: The Company considers investments in highly liquid debt instruments with a maturity of three months or less to be cash equivalents.

Inventories: Inventories are stated at lower of cost or market. Cost is determined on the first-in, first-out basis.

Property, Plant and Equipment ("PP&E"): PP&E is stated at cost. Depreciation is computed using the straight-line method. Estimated useful lives used in computing depreciation are twenty-five years for buildings, three to twelve years for machinery, equipment and software and the remaining lease period for leasehold improvements. In accordance with SFAS 144, the Company periodically evaluates the carrying value of its PP&E for circumstances which may indicate impairment.

Intangible Assets: Intangible assets include trademarks and the value of sports, entertainment and proprietary product rights. Amortization is by the straight-line method over estimated lives of up to twenty years. Management evaluates the recoverability of intangible assets under the provisions of SFAS 144, based on undiscounted projections of future cash flows attributable to the individual assets.

Revenue Recognition: Revenue related to sales of the Company's products is generally recognized when products are shipped, the title and risk of loss has passed to the customer, the sales price is fixed or determinable and collectibility is reasonably assured. Sales made on a returnable basis are recorded net of a provision for estimated returns. These estimates are revised, as necessary, to reflect actual experience and market conditions.

Estimates: The preparation of financial statements in conformity with generally accepted accounting principles requires management to make estimates and assumptions which affect the reporting of assets and liabilities as of the dates of the financial statements and revenues and expenses during the reporting period. These estimates primarily relate to the provision for sales returns, allowance for doubtful accounts, inventory obsolescence and asset valuations. Actual results could differ from these estimates.

Reclassifications: Certain items in the prior years' financial statements have been reclassified to conform with the current year's presentation. Beginning in the first quarter of fiscal 2002, prepress, autograph and relic costs related to future period releases, which previously had been included in prepaid expenses and other current assets, were reclassified to inventory. Autograph, relic and freight costs related to merchandise sold in the period, which previously were included in selling, general and administrative expenses, were reclassified to cost of goods sold.

The Company has adopted the EITF Issue 01-9 accounting standards that require certain trade promotion expenses, such as slotting fees, to be reported as a reduction of net sales rather than as marketing expense. This presentation has been reflected on the Consolidated Statements of Operations for the fiscal years ended March 1, 2003, March 2, 2002 and March 3, 2001.

Income Taxes: The Company provides for deferred income

taxes resulting from temporary differences between the valuation of assets and liabilities in the financial statements and the carrying amounts for tax purposes. Such differences are measured using the enacted tax rates and laws that will be in effect when the differences are expected to reverse.

Employee Stock Options: The Company accounts for stock-based employee compensation based on the intrinsic value of stock options granted in accordance with the provisions of APB 25 "Accounting for Stock Issued to Employees." Information relating to stock-based employee compensation, including the pro forma effects had the Company accounted for stock-based employee compensation based on the fair value of stock options granted in accordance with SFAS 123 "Accounting for Stock-Based Compensation," is as follows:

	2003		2002		2001	
	As reported	Pro forma	As reported	Pro forma	As reported	Pro forma
Net income	$ 16,936	$ 15,586	$ 28,462	$ 26,721	$ 88,489	$ 87,279
Earnings per share	$ 0.40	$ 0.37	$ 0.64	$ 0.60	$ 1.91	$ 1.88

(In thousands of dollars, except share data)

In determining the preceding pro forma amounts under SFAS 123, the fair value of each option grant is estimated as of the date of grant using the Black-Scholes option-pricing model with the following assumptions: no dividend yield in any year; risk free interest rate, estimated volatility and expected life, as follows: fiscal 2003 - 4.5%, 35% and 6.5 years respectively; fiscal 2002 - 5.7%, 59% and 6.7 years respectively; and fiscal 2001 - 6.5%, 56% and 6.6 years respectively

NOTE 2

Earnings Per Share

Earnings per share is computed in accordance with SFAS 128. Basic EPS is computed using weighted average shares outstanding, while diluted EPS is computed using weighted average shares outstanding plus shares representing stock distributable under stock-based plans computed using the treasury stock method.

The following table represents the computation of weighted average shares outstanding - diluted:

	Year Ended		
	March 1, 2003	March 2, 2002	March 3, 2001
Weighted average shares outstanding:			
Basic	41,353,000	43,073,000	45,011,000
Effect of dilutive stock options	712,000	1,203,000	1,355,000
Diluted	42,065,000	44,276,000	46,366,000

In the above calculation, the following shares were not included in the effect of dilutive stock options because they had an anti-dilutive effect: 1,532,000 (2003), 469,000 (2002) and 918,000 (2001).

NOTE 3

Accounts Receivable

	March 1, 2003	March 2, 2002
	(In thousands of dollars)	
Gross receivables	$ 43,250	$ 37,565
Reserve for returns	(16,443)	(15,877)
Allowance for discounts and doubtful accounts	(1,602)	(1,649)
Net	$ 25,205	$ 20,039

NOTE 4

Inventories

	March 1, 2003	March 2, 2002
	(In thousands of dollars)	
Raw materials	$ 6,162	$ 6,395
Work in process	2,229	1,274
Finished products	20,290	15,427
Total	$ 28,681	$ 23,096

NOTE 5

Property, Plant and Equipment, Net

	March 1, 2003	March 2, 2002
	(In thousands of dollars)	
Land	$ 42	$ 42
Buildings and improvements	2,278	2,291
Machinery, equipment and software	26,621	22,801
Total PP&E	$ 28,941	$ 25,134
Accumulated depreciation and amortization	(14,335)	(10,528)
Net	$ 14,606	$ 14,606

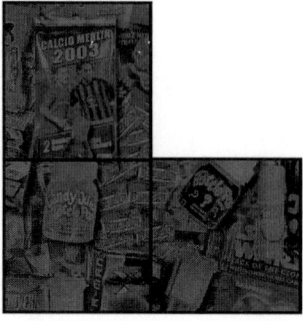

NOTE 6

Intangible Assets

On March 3, 2002, the Company adopted SFAS 141 "Business Combinations" and SFAS 142 "Goodwill and Other Intangible Assets" which require the Company to prospectively cease amortization of goodwill and instead conduct periodic tests of goodwill for impairment. The table below compares reported earnings and earnings per share for the year ended March 1, 2003, with earnings and earnings per share assuming pro forma application of the new accounting standards for the year ended March 2, 2002.

	March 1, 2003	March 2, 2002
	(In thousands of dollars)	
Net income	$ 16,936	$ 28,462
Add back: Goodwill amortization	-	1,568
Adjusted net income	$ 16,936	$ 30,030
Adjusted basic net income per share	$ 0.41	$ 0.70
Adjusted diluted net income per share	$ 0.40	$ 0.68

The Company has evaluated its goodwill and intangible assets acquired prior to June 30, 2002 using the criteria of SFAS 141, and has determined that no intangible assets should be reclassified to goodwill. The Company has also evaluated its intangible assets and determined that all such assets have determinable lives. Furthermore, the Company has reassessed the useful lives and residual values of all intangible assets to review for any necessary amortization period adjustments. Based on that assessment, no adjustments were made to the amortization period or residual values of the intangible assets. In order to conform with the definitions contained in SFAS 142, the Company reclassified $1.5 million in deferred financing fees from intangible assets to other assets and $0.8 million in software development costs from intangible assets to property, plant and equipment. Additionally, $1.9 million of deferred tax assets related to thePit.com acquisition were reclassified to goodwill.

SFAS 142 prescribes a two-phase process for impairment testing of goodwill. The first phase, completed on August 31, 2002, screens for impairment; while the second phase (if necessary), required to be completed by March 1, 2003, measures the impairment. The Company has completed the first phase and has concluded that no impairment of goodwill exists. Therefore, completion of phase two of the transitional impairment test was not necessary.

For the year ended March 1, 2003, no goodwill or other intangibles were acquired, impaired or disposed. Intangible assets consisted of the following as of March 1, 2003 and March 2, 2002:

March 1, 2003

	Gross Carrying Value	Accumulated Amortization	Net
	(In thousands of dollars)		
Licenses & contracts	$ 21,879	$ (16,594)	$ 5,285
Intellectual property	12,584	(12,473)	111
Software & other	2,953	(2,602)	351
FAS 132 pension	294	-	294
Total intangibles	$ 37,710	$ (31,669)	$ 6,041

March 2, 2002

	Gross Carrying Value	Accumulated Amortization	Net
	(In thousands of dollars)		
Licenses & contracts	$ 21,879	$ (15,717)	$ 6,162
Intellectual property	12,584	(12,315)	269
Software & other	2,953	(2,477)	476
FAS 132 pension	344	-	344
Total intangibles	$ 37,760	$ (30,509)	$ 7,251

Over the next five years the Company expects the annual amortization of the intangible assets detailed above to be as follows:

Fiscal Year	Amount (in thousands)
2004	$ 1,060
2005	$ 826
2006	$ 826
2007	$ 748
2008	$ 670

NOTE 7

Accrued Expenses and Other Liabilities

	March 1, 2003	March 2, 2002
	(In thousands of dollars)	
Royalties	$ 6,407	$ 9,009
Employee compensation	5,563	7,136
Payments received in advance	3,700	1,391
Advertising and marketing expenses	2,271	2,908
Legal settlement	1,612	-
Other	9,690	9,830
Total	$ 29,243	$ 30,274

NOTE 8

Depreciation and Amortization

	Year Ended		
	March 1, 2003	March 2, 2002	March 3, 2001
	(In thousands of dollars)		
Depreciation expense	$ 3,756	$ 2,601	$ 1,685
Amortization of intangible assets	1,160	1,237	1,004
Amortization of goodwill	-	1,568	1,568
Amortization of deferred financing fees	122	119	88
Total	$ 5,038	$ 5,525	$ 4,345

NOTE 9

Long-Term Debt

On June 26, 2000, the Company entered into a credit agreement with Chase Manhattan Bank and LaSalle Bank National Association. The agreement provides for a $35.0 million unsecured facility to cover revolver and letter of credit needs and expires on June 26, 2004. Interest rates are variable and a function of the Company's EBITDA. The credit agreement contains restrictions and prohibitions of a nature generally found in loan agreements of this type and requires the Company, among other things, to comply with certain financial covenants, limits the Company's ability to repurchase its shares, sell or acquire assets or borrow additional money and prohibits the payment of dividends. The credit agreement may be terminated by the Company at any point over the four-year term (provided the Company repays all outstanding amounts thereunder) without penalty. The full $35.0 million credit line was available as of March 1, 2003.

NOTE 10

Income Taxes

The Company provides for deferred income taxes resulting from temporary differences between the valuation of assets and liabilities in the financial statements and the carrying amounts for tax purposes. Such differences are measured using the enacted tax rates and laws that will be in effect when the differences are expected to reverse.

U.S. and foreign operations contributed to income before provision for income taxes as follows:

| | Year Ended | | |
	March 1, 2003	March 2, 2002	March 3, 2001
	(In thousands of dollars)		
United States	$ 14,157	$ 25,275	$ 36,359
Europe	7,861	15,744	89,201
Canada	992	739	1,762
Latin America	288	(300)	312
Total income before provision for income taxes	$ 23,298	$ 41,458	$ 127,634

Provision for income taxes consists of:

| | Year Ended | | |
	March 1, 2003	March 2, 2002	March 3, 2001
	(In thousands of dollars)		
Current income taxes:			
Federal	$ 3,899	$ 8,609	$ 6,467
Foreign	3,301	3,889	27,323
State and local	146	614	2,459
Total current	$ 7,346	$ 13,112	$ 36,249
Deferred income taxes (benefit):			
Federal	$ (434)	$ (719)	$ 1,554
Foreign	(330)	262	1,020
State and local	(220)	341	322
Total deferred	$ (984)	$ (116)	$ 2,896
Total provision for income taxes	$ 6,362	$ 12,996	$ 39,145

The reasons for the difference between the provision for income taxes and the amount computed by applying the statutory federal income tax rate to income before provision for income taxes are as follows:

	Year Ended		
	March 1, 2003	March 2, 2002	March 3, 2001
	(In thousands of dollars)		
Computed expected tax provision	$ **8,154**	$ 14,510	$ 44,672
Increase (decrease) in taxes resulting from:			
State and local taxes, net of federal tax benefit	**617**	900	2,327
Foreign and U.S. tax effects attributable to foreign operations	**(1,387)**	(2,274)	(7,080)
Amortization of intangibles	**-**	549	549
R&D	**(502)**	-	-
Other permanent differences	**(520)**	(689)	(1,323)
Provision for income taxes	$ **6,362**	$ 12,996	$ 39,145

Deferred U.S. income taxes have not been provided on undistributed earnings of foreign subsidiaries as the Company considers such earnings to be permanently reinvested in the businesses as of March 1, 2003. These undistributed foreign earnings could become subject to U.S. income tax if remitted, or deemed remitted, as a dividend. Determination of the deferred U.S. income tax liability on these unremitted earnings is not practical, since such liability, if any, is dependent on circumstances existing at the time of the remittance. The cumulative amount of unremitted earnings from foreign subsidiaries that is expected to be permanently reinvested was approximately $27.8 million on March 1, 2003.

During the year the Company received a refund in the amount of $1.3 million from a foreign tax credit carryback claim that was filed with the Internal Revenue Service and reduced the provision for income taxes. The successful claim resulted from a favorable ruling in a prior tax year.

Taxing authorities periodically challenge positions taken by the Company on its tax returns. On the basis of present information, it is the opinion of the Company's management that any assessments resulting from current tax audits will not have a material adverse effect on the Company's consolidated results of operations or its consolidated financial position.

The components of deferred income tax assets and liabilities are as follows:

	Year Ended	
	March 1, 2003	March 2, 2002
	(In thousands of dollars)	
Deferred income tax assets:		
Provision for estimated losses on sales returns	$ **1,290**	$ 929
Provision for inventory obsolescence	**852**	1,075
Tax assets of thePit.com	**581**	1,937
Total deferred income tax assets*	$ **2,723**	$ 3,941
Deferred income tax liabilities:		
Amortization	$ **1,224**	$ 2,786
Depreciation	**625**	383
Post-retirement benefits	**(1,889)**	(1,593)
Other	**(504)**	(1,978)
Total deferred income tax liabilities*	$ **(544)**	$ (402)

* Net deferred tax assets of $3,267 and $4,343 are presented on the Consolidated Balance Sheet in fiscal 2003 and 2002 respectively.

NOTE 11

Employee Benefit Plans

The Company maintains qualified and non-qualified defined benefit pensions in the U.S. and Ireland as well as a postretirement healthcare plan in the U.S. for all eligible non-bargaining unit personnel. The Company has previously not included information on the Irish pension in this footnote. The Company is also a participant in a multi-employer defined contribution pension plan covering domestic bargaining unit employees.

In addition, the Company sponsors a defined contribution plan, which qualifies under Sections 401(a) and 401(k) of the Internal Revenue Code (the "401(k) Plan"). While all non-bargaining unit employees are eligible to participate in the 401(k) Plan, participation is optional. The Company does not contribute to the 401(k) Plan.

The following tables summarize benefit costs, as well as the benefit obligations, plan assets and funded status associated with the Company's U.S. and Irish pension and U.S. postretirement healthcare benefit plans.

	Pension Benefits		Postretirement Healthcare Benefits	
	March 1, 2003	March 2, 2002	March 1, 2003	March 2, 2002
	(In thousands of dollars)			
Reconciliation of change in benefit obligation				
Benefit obligation at beginning of year	$ 31,662	$ 27,691	$ 6,981	$ 6,836
Service cost	1,184	1,003	225	217
Interest cost	2,316	1,984	514	479
Benefits paid	(1,120)	(1,200)	(546)	(546)
Actuarial (gains) losses	3,376	1,467	2,390	(5)
Plan amendments/Effect of foreign currency	440	717	(46)	-
Benefit obligation at end of year	$ 37,858	$ 31,662	$ 9,518	$ 6,981
Reconciliation of change in the fair value of plan assets				
Fair value of plan assets at beginning of year	$ 20,329	$ 17,101	$ -	$ -
Actual return on plan assets	(2,445)	20	-	-
Employer contributions	689	4,639	546	546
Benefits paid	(1,120)	(1,200)	(546)	(546)
Participant's contributions/Effect of foreign currency	738	(231)	-	-
Fair value of plan assets at end of year	$ 18,191	$ 20,329	$ -	$ -

	Pension Benefits		Postretirement Healthcare Benefits	
	March 1, 2003	March 2, 2002	**March 1, 2003**	March 2, 2002
		(In thousands of dollars)		
Funded status				
Funded status	**$ (19,667)**	$ (11,332)	**$ (9,518)**	$ (6,981)
Unrecognized actuarial (gains) losses	**15,995**	9,486	**1,347**	(915)
Unrecognized prior service cost	**539**	697	**-**	-
Unrecognized initial transition obligation	**(707)**	(608)	**2,298**	2,774
Net amount recognized in the consolidated balance sheets	**$ (3,840)**	$ (1,757)	**$ (5,873)**	$ (5,122)
Components of amounts recognized in the consolidated balance sheets				
Prepaid benefit cost	**$ 1,890**	$ 3,474	**$ -**	$ -
Accrued benefit liability	**(16,879)**	(11,686)	**(5,873)**	(5,122)
Intangible asset	**539**	691	**-**	-
Accumulated other comprehensive expense	**10,610**	5,764	**-**	-
Net amount recognized in the consolidated balance sheets	**$ (3,840)**	$ (1,757)	**$ (5,873)**	$ (5,122)

	Pension Benefits			Postretirement Healthcare Benefits		
	March 1, 2003	March 2, 2002	March 3, 2001	**March 1, 2003**	March 2, 2002	March 3, 2001
			(In thousands of dollars)			
Components of net periodic benefit cost						
Service cost	**$ 1,184**	$ 1,003	$ 817	**$ 225**	$ 217	$ 175
Interest cost	**2,316**	1,984	1,896	**514**	479	474
Expected return on plan assets	**(1,643)**	(1,457)	(1,451)	**-**	-	-
Amortization of initial transition obligation	**(51)**	180	152	**221**	221	221
Prior service cost	**133**	66	(15)	**-**	-	-
Actuarial (gains) losses/Special charges	**875**	491	192	**337**	(22)	(82)
Net periodic benefit cost	**$ 2,814**	$ 2,267	$ 1,591	**$ 1,297**	$ 895	$ 788

As of March 1, 2003 and March 2, 2002, both the qualified and non-qualified pension plans had accumulated benefit obligations in excess of plan assets. Information is as follows:

	Pension Benefits	
	March 1, 2003	March 2, 2002
	(In thousands of dollars)	
Projected benefit obligation	$ **33,990**	$ 29,150
Accumulated benefit obligation	$ **30,495**	$ 25,802
Fair value of plan assets	$ **15,280**	$ 17,420

The weighted-average actuarial assumptions used for the U.S. pension and postretirement healthcare plans are as follows:

	Pension and Postretirement Healthcare Benefits	
	March 1, 2003	March 2, 2002
Discount rate	**6.3%**	7.0%
Expected return on plan assets	**8.0%**	8.5%
Rate of compensation increase	**4.5%**	5.0%

Assumptions for healthcare cost increases are as follows: 10% in fiscal 2003, trending down to a 5.0% increase in fiscal 2008. Increases in healthcare costs could significantly affect the reported postretirement benefits cost and benefit obligations. A one percentage point change in assumed healthcare benefit cost trends would have the following effect:

	1-Percentage Point	
	(In thousands of dollars)	
	Increase	Decrease
On total service and interest cost component	$ 118	$ (97)
On postretirement benefit obligation (APBO)	$ 1,066	$ (914)

Stock Option Plans

The Company has Stock Option Plans that provide for the granting of non-qualified stock options, incentive stock options and stock appreciation rights (SARs) to employees, non-employee directors and consultants within the meaning of Section 422A of the Internal Revenue Code. Options granted generally vest over two or three years and expire ten years after the grant date. The following table summarizes information about the Plans.

Stock Options	March 1, 2003 Shares	Weighted Average Exercise Price	March 2, 2002 Shares	Weighted Average Exercise Price	March 3, 2001 Shares	Weighted Average Exercise Price
Outstanding at beginning of year	3,956,127	$ 6.88	4,309,369	$ 6.34	4,684,052	$ 5.81
Granted	166,000	$ 10.12	599,306	$ 10.55	569,550	$ 9.35
Exercised	(220,750)	$ 6.21	(768,335)	$ 4.93	(587,058)	$ 3.57
Forfeited	(143,400)	$ 15.68	(184,213)	$ 14.24	(357,175)	$ 11.25
Outstanding at end of year	3,757,977	$ 6.73	3,956,127	$ 6.88	4,309,369	$ 6.34
Options exercisable at end of year	3,383,854	$ 6.32	3,181,109	$ 6.08	3,491,735	$ 5.97
Weighted average fair value of options granted during the year	$4.12		$6.86		$5.84	

Summarized information about stock options outstanding and exercisable at March 1, 2003 is as follows:

Exercise Price Ranges	Options Outstanding Outstanding as of 3/1/03	Weighted Average Remaining Contractual Life	Weighted Average Exercise Price	Options Exercisable Exercisable as of 3/1/03	Weighted Average Exercise Price
$1.76 - $3.53	939,984	4.9	$ 2.60	939,984	$ 2.60
$3.54 - $5.29	612,250	5.5	$ 4.55	612,250	$ 4.55
$5.30 - $7.05	246,500	3.6	$ 6.20	246,500	$ 6.20
$7.06 - $8.81	603,500	3.2	$ 7.81	603,500	$ 7.81
$8.82 - $10.57	1,020,493	7.2	$ 9.90	704,495	$ 9.76
$10.58 - $12.34	335,250	5.6	$ 11.10	277,125	$ 11.00
	3,757,977	5.3	$ 6.73	3,383,854	$ 6.32

NOTE 13

Capital Stock

In October 1999, the Board of Directors authorized the Company to purchase up to 5 million shares of stock. In October 2001, purchases against this authorization were completed, and the Board of Directors authorized the purchase of up to an additional 5 million shares of stock. As of March 1, 2003, the Company had purchased 2.6 million shares against this new authorization. During fiscal 2003, the Company purchased a total of 1.6 million shares at an average price per share of $9.01.

NOTE 14

Segment and Geographic Information

Following is the breakdown of industry segments as required by SFAS 131. The Company has two reportable business segments: Confectionery and Entertainment. Consistent with Topps organizational structure and product line similarities, Entertainment now combines the former Sports and Entertainment segments into one.

The Confectionery segment consists of a variety of lollipop products including Ring Pop, Push Pop and Baby Bottle Pop, the Bazooka bubble gum line and other novelty confectioneries including Pokémon products.

The Entertainment segment primarily consists of cards and sticker album products featuring sports and non-sports licenses, including Pokémon.

The Company's management regularly evaluates the performance of each segment based upon its contributed margin, which is profit after cost of goods, product development, advertising and promotional costs and obsolescence, but before unallocated general and administrative expenses and manufacturing overhead, depreciation and amortization, other income, net interest income and income taxes.

The Company does not allocate assets among its business segments and therefore does not include a breakdown of assets or depreciation and amortization by segment.

Business Segments

			Year Ended	
		March 1, 2003	March 2, 2002	March 3, 2001
			(In thousands of dollars)	
Net Sales				
Confectionery		$ **146,865**	$ 152,127	$ 170,700
Entertainment		**143,214**	148,053	266,740
Total Net Sales		$ **290,079**	$ 300,180	$ 437,440
Contributed Margin				
Confectionery		$ **52,101**	$ 54,880	$ 64,390
Entertainment		**39,313**	47,464	119,653
Total Contributed Margin		$ **91,414**	$ 102,344	$ 184,043
Reconciliation of contributed margin to income before provision for income taxes				
Total contributed margin		$ **91,414**	$ 102,344	$ 184,043
Unallocated general and administrative expenses and manufacturing overhead		**(65,778)**	(60,040)	(58,917)
Depreciation & amortization		**(5,038)**	(5,525)	(4,345)
Other income		**184**	(215)	2,964
Income from operations		**20,782**	36,564	121,917
Interest income, net		**2,516**	4,894	5,717
Income before provision for income taxes		$ **23,298**	$ 41,458	$ 127,634

Net sales to unaffiliated customers and income from operations, as presented below, are based on the location of the ultimate customer. Income from operations is defined as contributed margin less unallocated general and administrative expenses and manufacturing overhead, depreciation and amortization, and other income. Identifiable assets, as presented below, are those assets located in each geographic area.

Geographic Areas

		Year Ended	
	March 1, 2003	March 2, 2002	March 3, 2001
		(In thousands of dollars)	
Net Sales			
United States	$ **212,464**	$ 220,368	$ 216,780
Europe	**48,555**	48,387	180,419
Other	**29,060**	31,425	40,241
Total Net Sales	$ **290,079**	$ 300,180	$ 437,440
Income from Operations			
United States	$ **12,306**	$ 22,579	$ 32,591
Europe	**5,406**	11,216	80,132
Other	**3,070**	2,769	9,194
Total Income from Operations	$ **20,782**	$ 36,564	$ 121,917
Identifiable Assets			
United States	$ **213,840**	$ 216,170	$ 171,385
Europe	**41,020**	35,271	101,819
Other	**6,768**	6,509	7,068
Total Identifiable Assets	$ **261,628**	$ 257,950	$ 280,272

NOTE 15

Acquisition of thePit.com, Inc.

On August 26, 2001, the Company acquired all of the outstanding common stock of thePit.com, Inc., which operates a sports card exchange, for a net $5.7 million in cash. The acquisition was accounted for using the purchase method of accounting. The financial statements of thePit.com, Inc. have been consolidated into the financial statements of the Company. As part of the purchase price allocation, $780,000 ($470,000 for technology and $310,000 for marketing agreements) was reclassified from goodwill to intangibles and is being amortized over 5 years. The amount of goodwill remaining after the reclassification was $4.1 million.

NOTE 16

Fair Value of Financial Instruments

The carrying value of cash, accounts receivable, accounts payable and accrued liabilities approximates fair value due to their short-term nature.

The Company enters into foreign currency forward contracts to hedge its foreign currency exposure. As of March 1, 2003, the Company had outstanding foreign currency forward contracts, which will mature at various dates, in the amount of $27,286,000, with over 60% of the contracts maturing within six months, as compared to $12,504,000 as of March 2, 2002. The fair value of these forward contracts is the amount the Company would receive or pay to terminate the contracts. The approximate pre-tax impact on earnings to the Company to terminate these agreements as of March 1, 2003 and March 2, 2002 was $(400,000) and $519,000, respectively. The Company believes there is no significant credit risk of non-performance by counter parties of the foreign currency forward contracts.

NOTE 17

Quarterly Results of Operations (Unaudited)

	2003				2002			
	1st	2nd	3rd	4th	1st	2nd	3rd	4th
	(In thousands of dollars, except share data)							
Net sales	$ 87,739	$ 69,999	$ 66,656	$ 65,685	$ 86,892	$ 81,214	$ 72,052	$ 60,022
Gross profit on sales	32,635	25,296	21,649	22,154	37,702	36,207	22,259	17,673
Income from operations	10,665	6,311	813	2,993	16,993	12,295	5,917	1,359
Net income	7,341	4,692	2,910	1,993	11,629	8,852	6,532	1,449
Net income per share								
- basic	$ 0.17	$ 0.11	$ 0.07	$ 0.05	$ 0.27	$ 0.20	$ 0.15	$ 0.03
- diluted	$ 0.17	$ 0.11	$ 0.07	$ 0.05	$ 0.26	$ 0.20	$ 0.15	$ 0.03

NOTE 18

Commitments and Contingencies

Future minimum payments under non-cancelable leases which extend into the year 2014 are $1,531,000 (2004), $1,531,000 (2005), $1,531,000 (2006), $1,454,000 (2007), $1,400,000 (2008) and $2,980,000 thereafter.

Future minimum payments required under the Company's existing sports and entertainment contracts, with various expiration dates extending into the year 2004, are estimated to be $12,162,000.

Total royalty expense under the Company's sports and entertainment licensing contracts was $25,344,000 (2003), $25,669,000 (2002) and $46,727,000 (2001).

Advertising and marketing expenses (which encompass media spending and consumer promotions costs) included in selling, general and administrative expenses amounted to $20,145,000 (2003), $18,790,000 (2002) and $21,514,000 (2001).

The Company transacts business in many countries, utilizing many different currencies. It is thus exposed to the effect of exchange rate fluctuations on sales and purchase transactions. The Company enters into both foreign currency forward contracts and options on currency forward contracts to manage these exposures and to minimize the effects of foreign currency transactions on cash flow. Such contracts are entered into primarily to hedge against future commitments. The Company does not engage in foreign currency speculation. The Company may be exposed to credit losses in the event of non-performance by counterparties to these instruments. Management believes, however, the risk of incurring such losses is remote as the contracts are entered into with major financial institutions.

Report of Independent Public Accountants

Board of Directors and Stockholders
The Topps Company, Inc.:

We have audited the accompanying consolidated balance sheets of The Topps Company, Inc. and Subsidiaries as of March 1, 2003 and March 2, 2002, and the related consolidated statements of operations, stockholders' equity and cash flows for each of the three years in the period ended March 1, 2003. These financial statements are the responsibility of the Company's management. Our responsibility is to express an opinion on these financial statements based on our audits.

We conducted our audits in accordance with auditing standards generally accepted in the United States of America. Those standards require that we plan and perform the audit to obtain reasonable assurance about whether the financial statements are free of material misstatement. An audit includes examining, on a test basis, evidence supporting the amounts and disclosures in the financial statements. An audit also includes assessing the accounting principles used and significant estimates made by management, as well as evaluating the overall financial statement presentation. We believe that our audits provide a reasonable basis for our opinion.

In our opinion, such financial statements present fairly, in all material respects, the financial position of The Topps Company, Inc. and Subsidiaries as of March 1, 2003 and March 2, 2002 and the results of their operations and cash flows for each of the three years in the period ended March 1, 2003 in conformity with accounting principles generally accepted in the United States of America.

As discussed in Note 6 of the notes to the consolidated financial statements, in 2003 the Company changed its method of accounting for goodwill and other intangible assets to conform to Statement of Financial Accounting Standards ("SFAS") No. 142.

Deloitte & Touche LLP

DELOITTE & TOUCHE LLP
New York, New York
April 4, 2003

Market and Dividend Information

The Company's common stock is traded on the Nasdaq National Market under the symbol TOPP. The following table sets forth, for the periods indicated, the high and low sales price for the common stock during the last two fiscal years as reported on the Nasdaq National Market. As of March 1, 2003, there were approximately 4,500 holders of record.

	Fiscal year ended March 1, 2003		Fiscal year ended March 2, 2002	
	High Price	Low Price	High Price	Low Price
First quarter	$ 11.06	$ 9.35	$ 10.40	$ 8.78
Second quarter	$ 10.57	$ 8.20	$ 12.29	$ 9.60
Third quarter	$ 9.93	$ 7.36	$ 12.16	$ 9.05
Fourth quarter	$ 9.97	$ 7.79	$ 12.49	$ 9.06

The Company did not pay a dividend in fiscal 2003, and any future dividend payments, should they occur, would require an amendment of the Company's Credit Agreement. See "Management's Discussion and Analysis of Financial Condition and Results of Operations - Liquidity and Capital Resources" and "Notes to Consolidated Financial Statements - Note 9."

selected consolidated financial data

	2003	2002	2001	2000	1999
			(In thousands of dollars, except share data, unaudited)		
OPERATING DATA:					
Net sales	$ 290,079	$ 300,180	$ 437,440	$ 374,193	$ 229,414
Gross profit on sales	101,734	113,841	199,911	166,895	93,037
Selling, general and administrative expenses	81,136	77,062	80,958	72,798	70,534
Income from operations	20,782	36,564	121,917	94,852	26,658
Interest income (expense), net	2,516	4,894	5,717	1,712	(454)
Net income	16,936	28,462	88,489	59,215	15,571
Income from operations per share					
- basic	$ 0.50	$ 0.85	$ 2.71	$ 2.04	$ 0.57
- diluted	$ 0.49	$ 0.83	$ 2.63	$ 2.00	$ 0.57
Net income per share					
- basic	$ 0.41	$ 0.66	$ 1.97	$ 1.28	$ 0.34
- diluted	$ 0.40	$ 0.64	$ 1.91	$ 1.25	$ 0.33
Cash dividends	-	-	-	-	-
Wtd. avg. shares outstanding					
- basic	41,353,000	43,073,000	45,011,000	46,398,000	46,415,000
- diluted	42,065,000	44,276,000	46,366,000	47,463,000	46,678,000
BALANCE SHEET DATA:					
Cash and equivalents	$ 114,259	$ 121,057	$ 158,741	$ 75,853	$ 41,728
Working capital	141,484	136,389	140,487	71,952	24,919
Net property, plant and equipment	14,606	14,606	11,181	9,181	7,429
Long-term debt, less current portion	-	-	-	-	5,158
Total assets	261,628	257,950	280,272	203,313	151,453
Stockholders' equity	$ 196,768	$ 194,054	$ 196,542	$ 129,175	$ 77,224

Certain items in the prior years' financial statements have been reclassified to conform with the current year's presentation.

Fiscal 2000 and 1999 Net sales and SG&A do not reflect the reclassification of slotting expenses included in the figures for fiscal 2001, 2002 and 2003.

Fiscal 1999 Income from operations includes non-recurring income of $3.5 million related to the sale of the Company's manufacturing facility in Cork, Ireland and of equipment in Cork, Ireland and Duryea, Pennsylvania.

Board of Directors

Arthur T. Shorin*
Chairman, Chief Executive Officer
and President

Allan A. Feder
Independent Business Consultant

Stephen D. Greenberg
Managing Director
Allen & Company, LLC

Ann Kirschner
President, Comma International

David Mauer
Chief Executive Officer
E & B Giftware, LLC

Edward D. Miller*
Senior Advisor
Former President and CEO
AXA Financial, Inc.

Jack H. Nusbaum
Senior Partner and Chairman
Willkie Farr & Gallagher

Richard Tarlow
Chairman
Carlson & Partners

Stanley Tulchin*
Chairman
Stanley Tulchin
Associates, Inc.

*Nominated to stand for re-election to the Company's Board of Directors at the 2003 Annual Meeting of Stockholders.

Officers

Arthur T. Shorin
Chairman, Chief Executive
Officer and President

Scott Silverstein
Executive Vice President

Ronald L. Boyum
Vice President - Marketing
and Sales and General
Manager Confectionery

Edward P. Camp
Vice President and President
-Hobby Division

Michael P. Clancy
Vice President - International
and Managing Director,
Topps International Limited

Michael J. Drewniak
Vice President -
Manufacturing

Ira Friedman
Vice President -
Publishing and New
Product Development

Warren Friss
Vice President - Internet
Business and General
Counsel

Leon J. Gutmann
Assistant Treasurer and
Assistant Secretary

Catherine K. Jessup
Vice President - Chief
Financial Officer

William G. O'Connor
Vice President -
Administration

John Perillo
Vice President - Operations

Subsidiaries

Topps Argentina, SRL
Managing Director -
Juan P. Georgalos

Topps UK Limited
Managing Director -
Jeremy Charter

Topps Italia, SRL
Managing Director
Furio Cicogna

Topps Canada, Inc.
General Manager -
Michael Pearl

Topps International Limited
Managing Director -
Michael P. Clancy

Topps Europe Limited
Managing Director
Christopher Rodman

Topps Enterprises, Inc.

Topps Finance, Inc.

Corporate Information

Annual Meeting
Thursday, June 26, 2003
10:30 A.M.
J.P. Morgan Chase & Co.
270 Park Avenue
New York, NY 10017

Investor Relations
Brod Group LLC
445 Park Avenue
New York, NY 10036

Corporate Counsel
Willkie Farr & Gallagher
787 Seventh Avenue
New York, NY 10019

Independent Auditors
Deloitte & Touche LLP
Two World Financial Center
New York, NY 10281

Registrar and Transfer Agent
American Stock Transfer &
Trust Company
59 Maiden Lane
New York, NY 10038
877-777-0800 ext 6820

Form 10-K — A copy of the Company's Annual Report on Form 10-K as filed with the Securities and Exchange Commission will be available at the Topps website www.topps.com or upon written request to the Assistant Treasurer.

Summary of Financial Ratios

Chapter 1
Price-earnings Ratio

The price-earnings ratio (P/E ratio) gives an indication of how optimistic the financial markets are about a company's future earnings. The higher a company's P/E ratio is, the more investors are willing to pay for each dollar of earnings that the company generates. Typically investors are willing to pay this higher price because they think the company will grow in the future. Lower P/E ratios indicate investors are less optimistic about the company's future growth. The price-earnings ratio is defined as:

$$\frac{\text{Market price of one share of stock}}{\text{Earnings per share}}$$

Earnings per Share Ratio

The earnings per share ratio (EPS) provides an indication of the amount of a company's earnings that are attributable to each share of common stock outstanding. Obviously, the higher this ratio is the better. In companies that have complex equity structures, such as convertible preferred stock and stock option plans, the computation of EPS can be very complex, but in its simplest form, EPS is defined as:

$$\frac{\text{Net earnings}}{\text{Outstanding shares of common stock}}$$

Chapter 3
Debt to Assets Ratio

The debt to assets ratio reveals the percentage of a company's assets that is financed with borrowed money. The higher the debt to assets ratio is, the greater its financial risk, other things being equal. The debt to assets ratio is defined as:

$$\frac{\text{Total debt}}{\text{Total assets}}$$

Return on Assets Ratio

The return on assets ratio (ROA) helps measure how well a company is using the assets available to it. The greater the amount of earnings that can be obtained for a given amount of assets, the better a company is doing at utilizing its assets, so, in general, the higher a company's ROA, the better. The ROA ratio is defined as:

$$\frac{\text{Net income}}{\text{Total assets}}$$

Return on Equity Ratio

The return on equity ratio (ROE) helps to measure how much the owners of a company are earning on the money they have invested in the business. The higher a company's ROE, the better. The ROE is defined as:

$$\frac{\text{Net income}}{\text{Equity}}$$

Chapter 5

Gross Margin Percentage

The gross margin percentage helps explain a company's pricing strategy. It compares the amount a company pays for the goods it sells to the price the company is able to charge for those goods. The more a company marks up its goods, the higher the gross margin percentage will be. Specialty shops tend to have higher gross margin percentages while discount stores tend to have lower percentages. This ratio is sometimes called the gross profit percentage. The gross margin percentage is defined as:

$$\frac{\text{Gross margin}}{\text{Sales}}$$

Return on Sales Ratio

The return on sales ratio, expressed as a percentage, indicates how much of each dollar of sales remains as profit after all expenses have been deducted. Discount stores do not necessarily have lower return on sales percentages than specialty shops. The higher the return on sales ratio percentage, the better. The return on sales ratio is defined as:

$$\frac{\text{Net income}}{\text{Sales}}$$

Chapter 6

Current Ratio

Liquidity refers to how quickly noncash assets can be converted into cash. The more quickly assets can be converted into cash, the more liquid they are, and the more useful they are for paying liabilities that must be paid in the near future. The current ratio provides a measure of how much liquidity a company has. Specifically, it compares a company's more liquid assets (current assets) to its current liabilities. Other things being equal, the higher a company's current ratio, the easier it can pay its currently maturing debts. The current ratio is defined as:

$$\frac{\text{Current assets}}{\text{Current liabilities}}$$

Chapter 7

Accounts Receivable Turnover Ratio and Average Days to Collect Receivables

The accounts receivable turnover ratio and the average days to collect receivables ratio indicate how long a company takes to collect its accounts receivable. The first ratio, accounts receivable turnover, explains how many times per year a company's receivables are collected, or "turned over"; generally, the *higher* this ratio is, the better. Because the accounts receivable turnover ratios are not easily understood by everyone, the second ratio, average days to collect receivables, is often used. However, the average days to collect receivables ratio cannot be computed without first computing the accounts receivable turnover ratio. Generally, the *lower* the average days to collect receivables ratio is, the better. The accounts receivable turnover ratio is defined as:

$$\frac{\text{Sales}}{\text{Accounts receivable}}$$

The average days to collect receivables ratio is defined as:

$$\frac{\text{365 days}}{\text{Accounts receivable turnover}}$$

Chapter 8

Inventory Turnover Ratio and Average Days to Sell Inventory

The inventory turnover ratio and the average days to sell inventory ratio indicate how long a company takes to sell the goods it has in merchandise inventory. The first ratio, inventory turnover, explains how many times per year a company's inventory is sold, or "turned over"; generally, the *higher* this ratio is the better. Because the inventory turnover ratio is not easily understood by everyone, the second ratio, average days to sell inventory, is often used. However, the average days to sell inventory ratio cannot be computed without first computing the inventory turnover ratio. Generally, the *lower* the average days to sell inventory ratio is, the better. The inventory turnover ratio is defined as:

$$\frac{\text{Cost of goods sold}}{\text{Inventory}}$$

The average days to sell inventory ratio is defined as:

$$\frac{\text{365 days}}{\text{Inventory turnover}}$$

A company's operating cycle is the time it takes it to convert cash into inventory, sell the inventory, and collect the cash from accounts receivable that resulted from the sale of the inventory. The time it takes a business to do this can be computed by adding the *average days to sell inventory* and the *average days to collect accounts receivable.*

Chapter 10
Times Interest Earned Ratio

The times interest earned ratio helps assess a company's ability to make interest payments on its debt. Failure to make interest (or principal) payments can cause a company to be forced into bankruptcy. Other things being equal, a company with a higher times interest earned ratio is considered to have lower financial risk than a company with a lower ratio.

EBIT is an acronym for "earnings before interest and taxes." In other words, it is what net earnings would have been if the company had had no interest expense or income tax expense. Because net earnings are calculated after interest has been subtracted, a company might have $0 of earnings and still have been able to make its interest payments. Thus, the times interest earned ratio is based on EBIT, and is defined as follows:

$$\frac{\text{EBIT}}{\text{Interest expense}}$$

Return on Assets Ratio (refined)

As discussed in detail in Chapter 3, the return on assets ratio (ROA) helps measure how well a company is using the assets available to it. The greater the amount of earnings that can be obtained for a given amount of assets, the better a company is doing at utilizing its assets, so the higher this ratio is, the better. Throughout most of this textbook, ROA has been based on net earnings. However, the use of net earnings creates an ROA that is biased against companies with relatively more debt versus equity financing. Since the ROA ratio is intended to help assess how efficiently a company is using its assets, not how it is financed, the ROA that is used in the business world is often defined as follows:

$$\frac{\text{EBIT}}{\text{Total assets}}$$

Annual Report and Financial Statement Analysis Projects

Annual Report Project for The Topps Company, Inc.

Management's Discussion and Analysis

The annual report for The Topps Company, Inc. opens with a letter to the stockholders that describes the company's mission, products and services, customers, past performance, and future prospects. The letter is followed by a section called "Management's Discussion and Analysis" in which management talks about financial results and trends, liquidity, risk factors, and other matters deemed necessary to provide adequate disclosure to users of the report. Read The Topps Company Stockholders' Letter and Management's Discussion and Analysis on pages 1 through 11 to answer questions 1–6.

1. What are the company's two reportable business segments?
2. What were company's goals for each segment in 2003? What specific achievements resulted from these goals?
3. What percentage of the company's total sales came from the Entertainment segment?
4. What effect has inflation had on the company's operations?
5. What is management's view of the company's liquidity status for the foreseeable future? How does the company plan to meet its cash needs?
6. What caused the changes between the company's fiscal year 2003 and 2002 net sales, gross margin, and selling, general and administrative expenses?

Income Statement—Vertical Analysis

7. Using Excel, compute common-size income statements for all three fiscal years. In common-size income statements, net sales is 100% and every other number is a percentage of sales. Attach the spreadsheet to the end of this project.
8. Using the common-size income statements, identify the significant trends.
9. What was the gross margin (gross profit) and the gross margin percentage for fiscal year-end 2003, 2002, and 2001?
10. If the gross margin changed over the three-year period, what caused the change? (The change in the two components of gross margin will reveal what caused any change in the gross margin.)
11. What was the percentage return on sales for fiscal year-end 2003, 2002, and 2001? What do these ratios indicate about Topps?

Income Statement—Horizontal Analysis

12. What were the absolute dollar and the percentage changes in revenues between fiscal 2003 and 2002 and between 2002 and 2001?
13. Describe the trend in revenues. Be specific (e.g., slight/steady/drastic increase or decrease each year, or fluctuating with an initial modest/significant increase or decrease followed by a modest/significant increase or decrease, etc.) to precisely describe the company's situation.

14. What were the absolute dollar and the percentage changes in cost of sales (cost of goods sold) between fiscal 2003 and 2002 and between 2002 and 2001?

15. Describe the trend in cost of goods sold (cost of sales). Be specific (e.g., slight/steady/ drastic increase or decrease each year, or fluctuating with an initial modest/significant increase or decrease followed by a modest/significant increase or decrease, etc.) to precisely describe the company's situation.

16. What were the absolute dollar and the percentage changes in selling, general and administrative expenses (operating expenses) between fiscal 2003 and 2002 and between 2002 to 2001?

17. Describe the trend in selling, general and administrative expenses. Be specific (e.g., slight/steady/drastic increase or decrease each year, or fluctuating with an initial modest/ significant increase or decrease followed by a modest/significant increase or decrease, etc.) to precisely describe the company's situation.

18. What were the absolute dollar and the percentage changes in net income between fiscal 2003 to 2002 and 2002 to 2001?

19. How would you describe the trend for net income? Be specific (e.g., slight/steady/drastic increase or decrease each year, or fluctuating with an initial modest/significant increase or decrease followed by a modest/significant increase or decrease, etc.) to precisely describe the company's situation. Do you expect the trend to continue?

20. Which items had the largest percentage change between fiscal 2003 and 2001, revenues or expenses (selling, general and administrative expenses and cost of goods sold)?

21. Summarize what is causing the changes in net income from fiscal 2001 to 2002 and 2002 to 2003 based on the percentages computed in questions 12 through 20. Do you expect the trend to continue?

Balance Sheet—Vertical Analysis

22. Using Excel, compute common-size balance sheets at the end of fiscal 2002 and 2003. In common-size balance sheets, total assets is 100% and every other number is a percentage of total assets. Attach the spreadsheet to the end of this project.

23. What percentage were current assets of total assets at the end of fiscal 2003 and 2002?

24. What percentage were long-term assets of total assets at the end of fiscal 2003 and 2002?

25. What percentage was inventory of current assets at the end of fiscal 2003 and 2002?

26. Which current asset had the largest balance at the end of fiscal 2003 and 2002?

27. What percentages were current liabilities of total liabilities and long-term debt of total liabilities at the end of fiscal 2003 and 2002? Comment on the trend and the possible impact on interest expense and net income.

Balance Sheet—Horizontal Analysis

28. What was the absolute dollar and the percentage change between the year-end 2003 and year-end 2002 net accounts receivable balance? Was the change an increase or decrease?

29. What was the absolute dollar and the percentage change between year-end 2003 and year-end 2002 inventory? Was the change an increase or decrease?

30. Compared to year-end 2002, did the amounts reported for the following long-term assets increase or decrease? By how much? Include dollar amounts for each item.

	Year-end 2003	
	Dollar amount	Increase or decrease
Property, plant and equipment, net		
Goodwill, intangibles, and other		
Total long-term assets		

31. What was the amount of the change in the balance in retained earnings between year-end 2003 and 2002? What caused this change?

Balance Sheet—Ratio Analysis

32. Compute the current ratio at the end of fiscal 2003 and 2002. What does this ratio indicate about Topps?

33. Calculate the accounts receivable turnover and the average number of days to collect accounts receivable for fiscal 2003 and 2002. In which year was the turnover and days to collect more favorable?

34. What was the absolute dollar and the percentage change between year-end 2003 and year-end 2002 inventory? Was the change an increase or decrease?

35. Calculate the inventory turnover ratios and the average number of days to sell inventory for fiscal 2003 and 2002. In which year was the turnover and days to sell inventory more favorable?

36. Calculate the ratio of debt to total assets for fiscal year-end 2003 and 2002.

37. Calculate the ratio of stockholders' equity to total assets for fiscal year-end 2003 and 2002. (Recall: 100% Assets = 100% (Liabilities + Stockholders' Equity). Percentages for questions 35 and 36 should total 100% each year.)

Balance Sheet—Stockholders' Equity section

38. Does the company's common stock have a par value? _____ If so, how much was the par value per share? _____

39. How many shares of common stock were issued at the end of fiscal 2003 and 2002?

40. How many shares of treasury stock did the company have at the end of fiscal 2002 and 2003? How were the treasury stock purchases reflected on the statement of cash flows? Include the type of cash flow activity.

41. What percentage of stockholders' equity do the following items represent at year-end?

	2003	2002
Total paid-in capital		
Retained earnings		
Other items		
	100%	100%

Statement of Cash Flows

42. Does the company report cash flows from operating activities using the direct or the indirect method? Describe how you can tell.

43. Did the company pay cash to purchase treasury stock in 2003? If so, what was the amount of the cash outflow?

44. What was the dollar amount of the increase or decrease in cash and cash equivalents for the fiscal years ended 2003, 2002, and 2001?

45. Does the ending balance of cash and cash equivalents agree with the amount reported on the balance sheet?

	2003	2002
Balance Sheet	$	$
Statement of Cash Flows	$	$

46. For each of the following revenue and expense items on the income statement, identify the related current asset or current liability item (working capital item) on the balance sheet.

Revenue or expense item	Related current asset or current liability
Sales Cost of sales Selling, general and administrative expenses Provision for income taxes	

47. Calculate the net increase or decrease in each following working capital items. Do your calculations agree with the amounts reported on the statement of cash flows?

Working capital item	Increase or decrease
Accounts receivable, net Inventories Income tax receivable Prepaid expenses and other current assets Accounts payable, accrued expenses and other liabilities, and Income taxes payable	

48. On what statement(s) would you expect to find information regarding the declaration and payment of dividends? Did the company declare or pay dividends in 2003?

Notes to the Financial Statements

49. In your own words, briefly summarize two significant accounting policies.

50. How much is the estimated allowance for discounts and doubtful accounts for fiscal 2003?

51. What is the net realizable value of receivables at the end of fiscal 2003?

52. How much is accumulated depreciation and amortization at the end of fiscal 2003? For fiscal 2003, what percent of selling, general and administrative expenses is depreciation and amortization expense?

53. What is the book value of property, plant and equipment at the end of fiscal 2003?

54. How does the company expense goodwill?

55. Identify three different accrued expenses in addition to "other" liabilities.

56. Comment on Topps' long-term debt agreement. Name the financial institution extending the credit. What kinds of credit restrictions apply to the long-term debt agreement? Identify at least two restrictions. What is the amount of available credit as of March 1, 2003?

57. Identify two kinds of commitments and contingencies.

58. What are the estimated useful lives of the company's depreciable assets?

59. In addition to goodwill, what kinds of intangible assets does the company have? What are their estimated lives?

60. Complete the following schedule contrasting the effect the three inventory cost flow assumptions have on the balance sheet and income statement dollar amounts. Specify for each financial statement the account that is affected by the sale of inventory. Insert the most appropriate term (High, Middle, or Low) to indicate how the specified account would be affected by each of the given cost flow assumptions. Assume an inflationary environment.

	Cost Flow Assumptions		
Account affected	**FIFO**	**AVG**	**LIFO**
1. Balance Sheet: 2. Income Statement:			

61. What inventory cost flow method does Topps use?

62. Complete the following schedule contrasting the effect the two types of depreciation methods have on the balance sheet and income statement dollar amounts. Specify for each financial statement the account affected by recording depreciation expense. Designate with an X the method (accelerated or straight-line) that would result in the higher balance in the specified account in the early years of the asset's life.

Account affected	Depreciation Methods	
	Accelerated	Straight-line
1. Balance Sheet:		
2. Income Statement:	(Higher balance early in asset's life)	

63. What method of depreciation does Topps use?

Other Information

64. Topps' financial statements are consolidated. Explain the meaning of the term consolidated. Identify two of the company's subsidiaries. (Hint: You can find the definition of consolidated statements in your textbook. The subsidiary companies are shown on page 33 of the Topps report.)
65. On what exchange is the company's stock traded?

Report of Independent Public Accountants (Auditors)

66. What is the name of the company's independent auditors?
67. Who is responsible for the financial statements?
68. What is the outside auditors' responsibility?
69. What type of opinion did the independent auditors issue on the financial statements (unqualified, qualified, adverse, or disclaimer)? What does this opinion mean?
70. The auditors' report indicates the audit was concerned with material misstatements rather than absolute accuracy in the financial statements. What does "material" mean?

Performance Measures

71. Compute the return on assets ratio (use net income rather than EBIT in the numerator) for fiscal years 2003 and 2002.
72. Compute the return on equity ratio for fiscal years 2003 and 2002.
73. For fiscal 2003, was the return on equity ratio greater than the return on assets ratio? Explain why.
74. What was Topps' basic earnings per share (EPS) for fiscal 2003 and 2002?
75. Given an average market price per share of $9.28 for fiscal 2003 and $10.48 for fiscal 2002, calculate the price-earnings (P/E) ratio. What does the P/E ratio mean?
76. Suggest why the company's stock price fell between fiscal 2003 and 2002 while its P/E ratio increased during the same period.

Annual Report Project for Harley-Davidson, Inc.
Management's Discussion and Analysis

In addition to financial statements and related footnotes, most corporate annual reports describe the company's mission, products and services, customers, past performance, and future prospects. In Harley-Davidson's annual report[1] this type of information is presented on pages 1 through 35. Annual reports also typically include a section called "Management's Discussion and Analysis (MD&A)" in which management discusses financial results and trends, liquidity, risk factors, and other matters deemed necessary to provide adequate disclosure to users of the reports. Harley-Davidson's MD&A information is included in pages 42 through 56.

1. Read pages 1–11 of the report. What is management's mission for Harley-Davidson?
2. Read the Chairman's letter to shareholders on pages 5 through 8. Assume you own Harley-Davidson stock. Write a brief statement identifying specific details about the company's performance as described by the chairman that impress you favorably or unfavorably. Explain why the items you identify give you a positive or a negative impression.
3. What is the nature of Harley-Davidson's business? What products or services does it produce and sell? *(Hint: footnote 11 on page 88 also provides information pertinent to this question.)*

Income Statement

4. Locate Harley-Davidson's income statements. Are they presented in the single-step or the multi-step format?
5. Use the income statement figures to calculate the percentage growth in net income from 2002 to 2003 and from 2001 to 2002.
6. Is it likely that Harley-Davidson can maintain the rate of net income growth you computed in question 5? *(Hint: The financial performance summary on pages 37 through 42 provides information pertinent to this question.)*
7. Calculate Harley-Davidson's gross margin (profit) percentage for 2002 and 2003.
8. Did Harley-Davidson's gross margin percentage increase or decrease between 2002 and 2003? What caused the change? *(Hint: Information on pages 44 and 45 of the report is pertinent to these questions).*
9. Calculate the percentage change in Harley-Davidson's gross margin (profit) between 2002 and 2003. What caused this change?
10. Use the information in footnote 11 on page 89 of the annual report to answer the following questions.
    a. What percent of income from operations is provided by Motorcycles versus Financial Services for the years 2003, 2002, and 2001 (ignore general corporate expenses)? Identify any trend present in the data.
    b. With respect to income from operations, which segment (Motorcycles or Financial Services) grew more rapidly for the two years between 2001 and 2003?
    c. Do you expect the trends you identified in parts a and b to continue?
11. Based on the information in footnote 11 on page 89, the Financial Services segment had more identifiable assets ($1,821,142) than the Motorcycles segment ($1,778,566). Yet the Financial Services segment has significantly less depreciation ($5,555) than the Motorcycles segment ($191,118). Explain this apparent contradiction.
12. Use the income statement figures on page 57 to calculate the percentage change in Financial Services income and Financial Services expense for the two years between 2001 and 2003.

---

[1]A Harley-Davidson annual report is packaged with new textbooks. If the annual report is misplaced, you can access it online at www.harley-davidson.com. Because companies change website interfaces from time to time, we cannot provide exact instructions for finding the annual report on the Harley-Davidson web site. Explore the website and follow links such as "Investor Relations" to locate the annual report. This project uses the 2003 report.

13. The percentage changes calculated in response to question 12 show that Financial Services income (revenue) grew much faster than Financial Services expense. In fact, between 2001 and 2002, Financial Services expense declined at the same time that income increased. Explain how Harley-Davidson could have significantly increased revenue while at the same time decreasing expenses. *(Hint: Footnote 3 on page 70 provides information pertinent to this question.)*

Balance Sheet

14. The current asset section of the balance sheets includes the caption "Cash and cash equivalents." What does Harley-Davidson mean by the term "cash equivalents"? *(Hint: cash equivalents are defined in footnote 1 on page 62)*

15. What is the amount of the "At beginning of year" balance of "Cash and cash equivalents" reported on the 2003 statement of cash flows? Where is this amount reported on the consolidated balance sheets?

16. The largest current asset reported on the balance sheets is labeled "Current portion of finance receivables, net." *(Hint: footnote 3 on page 71 and footnote 1 on page 63 provide information pertinent to parts a through d of this question.)*

　a. What is the difference between finance receivables and accounts receivable?

　b. What do the words "current portion" in the asset description mean?

　c. What does the term "net" in the asset description mean?

　d. At what point does Harley-Davidson consider finance receivables (retail loans) to be uncollectible?

17. Calculate the percentage change in the current asset "Current portion of finance receivables, net" between year-end 2002 and year-end 2003. Explain the likely reason for the increase or decrease.

18. What is the total net realizable value of all receivables reported on Harley-Davidson's December 31, 2003 balance sheet?

19. Do the balance sheets report any intangible assets? If so, identify them.

20. Read the section of footnote 1 on page 65 that describes product warranty. The footnote reports an ending warranty balance of $30,475. What caption on the balance sheet most likely includes this amount? Do you expect warranty expense to increase or decrease in 2004?

Statement of Cash Flows

21. How does net income compare to cash flows from operating activities for 2003?

22. Does Harley-Davidson report cash flows from operating activities using the direct or the indirect method?

23. In the presentation of cash flows from operating activities, did Harley-Davidson add depreciation expense to net income or subtract it?

24. Does Harley-Davidson have a pattern of paying cash dividends?

25. What percentage of net income did Harley-Davidson pay out in cash dividends during 2003?

26. The percentage computed in question 15 is less than 10%. Provide an explanation for why Harley-Davidson did not pay a greater amount of dividends.

27. In 2003 Harley-Davidson generated nearly $936 million in cash from operating activities. What did the company do with all that cash?

28. What are the two largest items reported in the "Cash flows from investing activities" section of the 2003 statement of cash flows? Do you expect these cash flows to recur regularly?

29. What is the total amount of finance debt reported on the balance sheet at December 31, 2003? What individual components are included in the finance debt category? Identify the interest rates and terms to maturity for each debt component. *(Hint: footnote 3, page 75 provides information pertinent to this question.)*

More on Equity

(Hint: footnote 7 on page 83 provides information pertinent to questions 30–37.)

30. How many shares of common stock was Harley-Davidson authorized to issue as of December 31, 2003?

31. How many shares of common stock had Harley-Davidson issued as of December 31, 2003?

32. How many shares of common stock did Harley-Davidson have outstanding as of December 31, 2003?

33. What is the par value of the common stock as of December 31, 2003?

34. How many shares of preferred stock was Harley-Davidson authorized to issue as of December 31, 2003?

35. How many shares of preferred stock had Harley-Davidson issued as of December 31, 2003?

36. How many shares of preferred stock were outstanding as of December 31, 2003?

37. What is the par value of the preferred stock as of December 31, 2003?

38. What amount of cash did Harley-Davidson spend to purchase treasury stock during 2003?

Report of Independent Auditors

Hint: The report of the independent auditors is presented on page 91 of the annual report. The report of management is presented on page 92. These reports provide information pertinent to questions 39 through 44.

39. Who is responsible for preparing the financial statements?

40. What is the independent auditors' responsibility?

41. What type of opinion did the independent auditors issue on the financial statements (unqualified, qualified, adverse, or disclaimer)? Assume you own shares of Harley-Davidson stock. Does the auditors' opinion indicate the company is a good investment?

42. Who establishes GAAP? Do you trust the organization that establishes accounting standards (GAAP)? Why? Answers to these questions do not appear in the Harley-Davidson annual report. Look for answers in your textbook or do a Web search to answer the questions. If you search online, we suggest you begin with the following website: www.fasb.org.

43. The auditors' report indicates the audit was concerned with material misstatements rather than absolute accuracy in the financial statements. What does "material" mean?

44. Identify the name of the company's independent auditors. Perform a Web search to assess the reputation of the audit firm. Assume you own shares of Harley-Davidson stock. Do you feel positive or negative about the audit firm's reputation? Why?

Ratio Analysis

Average ratios computed for the 30 companies that make up the Dow Jones Industrial Average are presented below. The underlying data were drawn from the Compact Disclosure Data Base. Calculate each ratio based on Harley-Davidson's 2003 fiscal year and comment on how Harley-Davidson's ratio compares to the Dow average. Indicate specifically whether Harley-Davidson's ratios are more or less favorable than the Dow average.

Ratio	Dow 30
45. Current ratio	1.34 to 1
46. Average days to collect accounts receivable	241 days for all firms, 61 days for all firms except financial institutions
47. Average days to sell inventory	30 days
48. Debt to assets	.64 to 1
49. Return on equity	19%
50. Price-earnings ratio*	20

*Base your computations for Harley-Davidson on a market price per share of $44.27 and use the basic earnings per common share reported on Harley-Davidson's income statement

Financial Statements Project (Selection of Company to be Decided by Instructor)

Date Due: _____

Required

Based on the annual report of the company you are reviewing, answer the following questions. If you cannot answer a particular question, briefly explain why. If the question is not applicable to your company's financial statements answer "N/A."

Show all necessary computations in good form. Label all numbers in your computations. If relevant, reference your answers to page(s) in the annual report.

"Current year" means the most recent fiscal year in the company's annual report. "Prior year" means the fiscal year immediately preceding the current year.

1. What products or services does the company sell? Be specific.
2. What do you think the outlook is for these products or services? Why do you think so?
3. By what percentage have sales increased or decreased in each of the last two fiscal years?
4. If the company reported sales by segments, which segment had the largest percentage of total sales? Which segment had the smallest percentage of total sales? **Show computations of the relevant percentages.**

    Largest segment_____   Percentage of total sales _____
    Smallest segment_____   Percentage of total sales _____

5. What is net income for the current year? _____
6. Did the current year's net income increase or decrease since the prior year? By how much? What caused the change?
7. If the company reported earnings by segments, which segment had the largest percentage of total earnings? Which segment had the smallest percentage of total earnings? **Show computations of the relevant percentages.**

    Largest segment_____   Percentage of total earnings _____
    Smallest segment_____   Percentage of total earnings _____

8. Did the company report any special, unusual, or otherwise nonroutine items in either current or prior year net income? If so, explain the item(s).
9. For the current year, how does net income compare to net cash provided (used) by operating activities?
10. For the current year, what one or two items were most responsible for the difference between net income and net cash provided (used) by operating activities?
11. Did the company pay cash dividends during the current year? If so, how much were they?
12. If the company paid cash dividends, what percentage of net income were the cash dividends? If the company did not pay cash dividends, why do you think it did not?
13. Which of the following is the company's largest asset category: accounts receivable, inventory, or land? What is the amount of that asset category?
14. If the company reported assets by segments, which segment had the largest percentage of total assets? Which segment had the smallest percentage of total assets? **Show computations of the relevant percentages.**

    Largest segment_____   Percentage of total assets _____
    Smallest segment_____   Percentage of total assets _____

15. How much **cash** did the company invest in property, plant, and equipment during the current year?
16. Which inventory method(s) did the company use?
17. Which depreciation method(s) did the company use?
18. If the company has any intangible assets, what kind are they?
19. Did the company report any contingent liabilities ("contingencies")? If so, briefly explain.
20. Does the company have any preferred stock authorized? If so, how many shares were authorized?

21. Does the company's common stock have a par value? If so, what was it?
22. In what price range was the company's common stock trading during the last quarter of the current year?
23. What was the market price of the company's common stock on DD/MM/Year?
24. Where (on what stock exchange) is the company's stock traded?
25. Who was the company's independent auditor?
26. Develop one question about the company's financial report that you do not know how to answer.
27. Compute the following ratios for the current year and the prior year. Show the appropriate formulas in the first column. Show all supporting computations in the second and third columns.

Ratio	Current Year	Prior Year
Gross Profit Formula:		
Inventory Turnover Formula:		
Current Ratio Formula:		
Debt to Equity Formula:		
Return on Assets Formula:		
Return on Equity Formula:		

Chapter 1

p. 3 Bob Daemmrich. **p. 8** Bob Daemmrich/Stock Boston. **p. 22** Royalty-Free/CORBIS. **p. 23** PhotoLink/Getty Images. **p. 23** Joseph Nettis/Stock Boston. **p. 23** Kim Steele/Getty Images.

Chapter 2

p. 55 Royalty-Free/CORBIS. **p. 64** William Taufic/CORBIS. **p. 69** Rudi Von Briel/PhotoEdit. **p. 72** Reuters/CORBIS. **p. 73** Phyllis Picardi/Stock Boston.

Chapter 3

p. 109 Lon Diehl/Photo Edit. **p. 110** Michael Newman/PhotoEdit. **p. 125** Ralph Mercer/Tony Stone/Getty Images. **p. 126** J. Luke/PhotoLink/Getty.

Chapter 4

p. 155 David Young-Wolff/PhotoEdit. **p. 169** Bob Daemmrich. **p. 175** Chad Rachman/AP Photo. **p. 176** Archivo Icongrafico, S.A./Corbis. **p. 177** Ralf-Finn Hestoft/CORBIS.

Chapter 5

p. 217 Joel W. Rogers/CORBIS. **p. 231** John S. Reid. **p. 233** Syracuse Newspapers/C.W. McKeen/The Image Works. **p. 237** Ovark Arslanian. **p. 218** Ryan McVay/Getty Images.

Chapter 6

p. 267 Royalty-Free/CORBIS. **p. 275** Spencer Grant/PhotoEdit. **p. 277** Royalty-Free/CORBIS. **p. 282** Charles O'Rear/CORBIS. **p. 279** Ryan McVay/Getty Images.

Chapter 7

p. 315 D.RENTAS/N.Y.POST/CORBIS SYGMA. **p. 317** Courtesy of Nordstrom. **p. 320** Super Stock. **p. 323** Keith Brofsky/Getty. **p. 332** ALAIN NOGUES/CORBIS SYGMA.

Chapter 8

p. 359 Derk R. Kuyper. **p. 369** Janis Christie/Getty Images. **p. 375** William Whitehurst/CORBIS. **p. 373** Rick Friedman/Corbis.

Chapter 9

p. 407 PhotoDisc/Getty. **p. 424** PhotoDisc/Getty. **p. 425** Reuters/CORBIS. **p. 429** Susan Van Etten/PhotoEdit.

Chapter 10

p. 459 STONE LES/CORBIS SYGMA. **p. 465** AP Photo. **p. 477** David Young-Wolff/PhotoEdit.

Chapter 11

p. 513 Najlah Feanny/Corbis. **p. 515** Steve Allen/Getty. **p. 517** Courtesy of AT&T. **p. 520** Jeff Smith/Image Bank/Getty. **p. 530** BD Lanphere/Stock Boston.

Chapter 12

p. 561 Richard Levine. **p. 571** Steve Cole/Getty. **p. 574** Royalty-Free/CORBIS. **p. 578** Susan Van Etten/PhotoEdit.

GLOSSARY

accelerated depreciation methods   Depreciation methods that recognize depreciation expense more rapidly in the early stages of an asset's life than in the later stages of its life. *p. 413*

account   Record used for the classification and summary of transaction data. *p. 9*

account balance   Difference between total debits and total credits in an account. *p. 181*

account groups   Self-balancing entities that account for a governmental unit's general fixed assets and the outstanding principal of its general long-term liabilities. *p. 535*

accounting   Service-based profession that provides reliable and relevant financial information useful in making decisions. *p. 3*

accounting controls   Procedures designed to safeguard assets and to ensure accuracy and reliability of the accounting records and reports. *p. 316*

accounting cycle   A cycle consisting of these stages: recording accounting data, adjusting the accounts, preparing the financial statements, and closing the nominal accounts; when one accounting cycle ends, a new one begins. *p. 61*

accounting equation   Expression of the relationship between the assets and the claims on those assets. *p. 10*

accounting event   Economic occurrence that causes changes in an enterprise's assets, liabilities, or equity. *p. 11*

accounting period   Span of time covered by the financial statements, normally one year, but may be a quarter, a month or some other time span. *p. 17*

accounts receivable   Expected future cash receipts arising from permitting customers to *buy now and pay later;* usually are small with a short term to maturity. *pp. 56, 359*

accounts receivable turnover ratio   Financial ratio that measures how fast accounts receivable are turned into cash; computed by dividing sales by accounts receivable. *p. 373*

accrual   Recognition of events before exchanging cash. *p. 56*

accrual accounting   Method of accounting that records the effects of accounting events in the period in which such events occur regardless of when cash is exchanged. *p. 55*

accumulated depreciation   Contra asset account that indicates the sum of all depreciation expense recognized for an asset since the date of acquisition. *pp. 112, 412*

adjusting entry   Entry that updates account balances prior to preparing financial statements. *p. 64*

administrative controls   Procedures designed to evaluate performance and the degree of compliance with a firm's policies and public laws. *p. 316*

adverse opinion   Audit opinion for a set of financial statements issued by a certified public accountant that means that part of or all of the financial statements are not in compliance with GAAP and the auditors believe this noncompliance would be material to the average prudent investor. *p. 72*

allocation   Recognition of expense by systematic assignment of the cost of an asset to periods of use. *p. 109*

allowance   Reduction in the selling price of goods extended to the buyer because the goods are defective or of lower quality than the buyer ordered to encourage a buyer to keep merchandise that would otherwise be returned. *p. 223*

Allowance for Doubtful Accounts   Contra asset account that contains an amount equal to the accounts receivable that are expected to be uncollectible. *p. 361*

allowance method of accounting for bad debts   Method of accounting for bad debts in which bad debts are estimated and expensed in the same period in which the corresponding sales are recognized. The receivables are reported in the financial statements at net realizable value (the amount expected to be collected in cash). *p. 360*

American Institute of Certified Public Accountants' Code of Professional Conduct   Set of ethical rules and guidelines above and beyond the requirements of laws and regulations that certified public accountants must follow. *p. 74*

amortization   Method of systematically allocating the costs of intangible assets to expense over their useful lives; also term for converting the discount on a note or a bond to interest expense over a designated period. *pp. 378, 408*

amortization of loan   Systematic repayment of principal and interest over the life of a loan. *p. 459*

annual report   Document in which an organization provides information to stockholders, usually on an annual basis. *p. 23*

annuity   Series of equal payments made over a specified number of periods. *p. 480*

appropriated retained earnings   Retained earnings restricted by the board of directors for a specific purpose (e.g., to repay debt or for future expansion); although a part of total retained earnings, not available for distribution as dividends. *p. 528*

articles of incorporation   Items on an application filed with a state agency for the formation of a corporation; contains such information as the corporation's name, its purpose, its location, its expected life, provisions for its capital stock, and a list of the members of its board of directors. *p. 514*

asset   Economic resource used by a business for the production of revenue. *p. 10*

asset exchange transaction   A transaction that decreases one asset while increasing another asset so that total assets do not change; for example, the purchase of land with cash. *p. 56*

asset source transaction   Transaction that increases an asset and a claim on assets; three types of asset source transactions are acquisitions from owners (equity), borrowings from creditors (liabilities), or earnings from operations (revenues). *pp. 12, 56*

asset use transaction   Transaction that decreases an asset and a claim on assets; the three types are distributions (transfers to owners), liability payments (to creditors), or expenses (used to operate the business). *p. 57*

audit   Detailed examination of a company's financial statements and the documents that support the information presented in those statements. *p. 71*

authority manual   A document that outlines the chain of command for authority and responsibility. The authority manual provides guidelines for specific positions such as personnel officer as well a general authority such as all vice presidents are authorized to spend up to a designated limit. *p. 317*

authorized stock   Number of shares that the corporation is approved by the state to issue. *p. 520*

available-for-sale securities   Marketable securities that are not properly classified as held-to-maturity or trading securities. *p. 284*

average days in inventory ratio (sometimes called **average number of days to sell inventory ratio**)   Financial ratio that measures the average number of days that inventory stays in stock before being sold. *p. 281*

average number of days to collect accounts receivable   Length of the average collection period for accounts receivable; computed by dividing 365 (or 366) by the accounts receivable turnover ratio. *p. 374*

bad debts expense   Expense associated with uncollectible accounts receivable; amount recognized may be estimated using the allowance method, or actual losses may be recorded using the direct write-off method. *p. 361*

balance sheet   Statement that lists the assets of a business and the corresponding claims (liabilities and equity) on those assets. *p. 18*

balloon payment   Large final payment due at the maturity of a debt that otherwise requires systematic smaller payments over the term of the loan prior to maturity. *p. 460*

bank reconciliation   Schedule that identifies and explains differences between the cash balance reported by the bank and the cash balance in the firm's accounting records. *p. 322*

bank statement   Statement issued by a bank (usually monthly) that denotes all activity in the bank account for that period. *p. 321*

bank statement credit memo   Memo that describes an increase in the account balance. *p. 321*

bank statement debit memo   Memo that describes a decrease in the account balance. *p. 321*

basket purchase   Acquisition of several assets in a single transaction with no specific cost attributed to each asset. *p. 409*

board of directors   Group of individuals elected by the stockholders of a corporation to oversee its operations. *p. 517*

bond   Debt security used to obtain long-term financing in which a company borrows funds from a number of lenders, called *bondholders;* usually issued in denominations of $1,000. *p. 464*

bond discount   Difference between the selling price and the face amount of a bond sold for less than the face amount. *p. 468*

bond premium   Difference between the selling price and the face amount of a bond that is sold for more than the face amount. *p. 473*

book value   Historical (original) cost of an asset minus the accumulated depreciation; alternatively, undepreciated amount to date. *pp. 112, 414*

book value per share   Value of stock determined by dividing the total stockholders' equity by the number of shares of stock. *p. 520*

books of original entry   Journals in which a transaction is first recorded. *p. 169*

call premium   Difference between the call price (the price that must be paid for a called bond) and the face amount of the bond. *p. 465*

call price   Specified price that must be paid for bonds that are called; usually higher than the face amount of the bonds. *p. 465*

callable bonds   Bonds that include a feature allowing the issuer to pay them off prior to maturity. *p. 465*

capital expenditures (on an existing asset)   Substantial amounts of funds spent to improve an asset's quality or to extend its life. *p. 420*

capitalized   Recorded cost in an asset account until the item is used to produce revenue. *p. 127*

carrying value   Face amount of a bond liability less any unamortized bond discount or plus any unamortized bond premium. *p. 470*

cash   Coins, currency, checks, balances in checking and certain savings accounts, money orders, bank drafts, certificates of deposit, and other items that are payable on demand. *p. 319*

cash discount   Discount offered on merchandise sold to encourage prompt payment; offered by sellers of merchandise and represent sales discounts to the seller when they are used and purchase discounts to the purchaser of the merchandise. *p. 223*

cash inflows   Sources of cash. *p. 561*

cash outflows   Uses of cash. *p. 561*

Cash Short and Over   Account used to record the amount of cash shortages or overages; shortages are considered expenses and overages are considered revenues. *p. 327*

certified check   Check guaranteed by a bank to be drawn on an account having funds sufficient to pay the check. *p. 324*

certified public accountant (CPA)   Accountant who has met certain educational and experiential requirements and is licensed by the state government to provide audit services to the public. *p. 71*

chart of accounts   List of all ledger accounts and their corresponding account numbers. *p. 169*

checks   Prenumbered forms, sometimes multicopy, with the name of the business issuing them preprinted on the face, indicating to whom they are paid, the amount of the payment, and the transaction date. *p. 321*

claims   Owners' and creditors' interests in a business's assets. *p. 10*

claims exchange transaction   Transaction that decreases one claim and increases another so that total claims do not change. For example, the accrual of interest expense is a claims exchange transaction; liabilities increase, and the recognition of the expense causes retained earnings to decrease. *p. 57*

classified balance sheet   Balance sheet that distinguishes between current and noncurrent items. *p. 330*

closely held corporation   Corporation whose stock is exchanged between a limited number of individuals. *p. 515*

closing entries   Entries used to transfer the balances in the Revenue, Expense, and Dividends accounts to the Retained Earnings account at the end of the accounting period. *pp. 172*

closing the books or **closing**   Process of transferring balances from nominal accounts (Revenue, Expense, and Dividends) to the permanent account (Retained Earnings). *p. 61*

code of professional conduct   A set of guidelines established by the American Institute of Certified Public Accountants (AICPA) to promote high ethical conduct among its membership. *p. 74*

collateral for loans   Assets pledged as security for a loan. *p. 461*

common size financial statements Financial statements in which amounts are converted to percentages to allow a better comparison of period-to-period and company-to-company financial data since all information is placed on a common basis. *p. 232*

common stock Basic class of corporate stock that carries no preferences as to claims on assets or dividends; certificates that evidence ownership in a company. *pp. 10, 521*

compound interest Practice of reinvesting interest so that interest is earned on interest as well as on the initial principal. *p. 478*

compounding Earning interest on interest. *p. 478*

comprehensive annual financial report (CAFR) An annual report that provides information regarding all funds and account groups under the jurisdiction of a government reporting entity. *p. 535*

comprehensive income Net income plus or minus unrealized gains or losses.

consolidated financial statements Financial statements that represent the combined operations of a parent company and its subsidiaries. *p. 288*

continuity Concept that describes the fact that a corporation's life may extend well beyond the time at which any particular shareholder decides to retire or to sell his or her stock. *p. 517*

contra account Account that normally has a balance opposite to that of the other accounts in a particular category (e.g., Accumulated Depreciation is classified as an asset, but it normally has a credit balance). *p. 165*

contra asset account Account subtracted from another account with which it is associated; has the effect of reducing the asset account with which it is associated. *pp. 112, 412*

contra liability account Account reported in the liability section of the balance sheet that has a debit balance; reduces total liabilities. A discount on a Note Payable is an example of a contra liability account. *p. 377*

contributed capital Balance sheet term used to designate the portion of assets contributed to a business by its owners.

convertible bonds Bonds that can be converted (exchanged) to an ownership interest (stock) in the corporation. *p. 465*

copyright Legal protection of writings, musical compositions, and other intellectual property for the exclusive use of the creator or persons assigned the right by the creator. *p. 423*

corporation Legal entity separate from its owners; formed when a group of individuals with a common purpose join together in an organization according to state laws. *p. 514*

cost method of accounting for treasury stock Method of accounting for treasury stock in which the purchase of treasury stock is recorded at its cost to the firm but does not consider the original issue price or par value. *p. 525*

cost of goods available for sale Total costs paid to obtain goods and to make them ready for sale, including the cost of beginning inventory plus purchases and transportation-in costs, less purchase returns and allowances and purchase discounts. *p. 218*

cost of goods sold Total cost incurred for the goods sold during a specific accounting period. *p. 218*

credit Entry that increases liability and equity accounts or decreases asset accounts. *p. 156*

creditor Individual or institution that has loaned goods or services to a business. *p. 5*

cumulative dividends Preferred dividends that accumulate from year to year until paid. *p. 521*

current (short-term) asset Asset that will be converted to cash or consumed within one year or an operating cycle, whichever is longer. *pp. 330, 407*

current (short-term) liability Obligation due within one year or an operating cycle, whichever is longer. *p. 330*

current ratio Financial ratio that measures the relationship between current assets and current liabilities; determined by dividing current assets by current liabilities, with the result expressed in decimal format. *p. 331*

date of record Date that establishes who will receive the dividend payment: shareholders who actually own the stock on the record date will be paid the dividend even if the stock is sold before the dividend is paid. *p. 526*

debenture Unsecured bond issued based on the general credit of the organization. *p. 464*

debit Entry that increases asset accounts or decreases liability and equity accounts. *p. 156*

debt security Type of security acquired by loaning assets to the investee company. *p. 283*

debt to assets ratio Financial ratio that measures a company's level of risk. *p. 124*

declaration date Date on which the board of directors actually declares a dividend. *p. 526*

deferral Recognition of revenue or expense in a period after the cash is exchanged. *p. 109*

deferral transactions Accounting transactions in which cash payments or receipts occur before the associated expense or revenue is recognized. *p. 566*

deferred tax liability Taxes not paid until future years because of the difference in accounting methods selected for financial statements and methods required for tax purposes (e.g., a company may select straight-line depreciation for financial statement reporting but will be required to use MACRS for tax reporting). *p. 419*

demand Consumer preferences expressed by offering money for goods or services.

depletion Method of systematically allocating the costs of natural resources to expense as the resources are removed from the land. *p. 408*

deposit ticket Bank form that accompanies checks and cash deposited into a bank account; normally specifies the account number, name of the account, and a record of the checks and cash being deposited. *p. 321*

deposits in transit Deposits recorded in a depositor's books but not received and recorded by the bank. *p. 323*

depreciable cost *p. 414*

depreciation Method of systematically allocating the costs of long-term tangible assets to expense over their useful lives. *p. 408*

depreciation expense Portion of the original cost of a long-term tangible asset allocated to an expense account in a given period. *p. 112*

direct method Method of preparing the statement of cash flows that reports the total cash receipts and cash payments from each of the major categories of activities (collections from customers, payment to suppliers). *p. 575*

direct write-off method   Method of recognizing bad debts expense only when accounts are determined to be uncollectible. *p. 368*

disclaimer of audit opinion   Position that an auditor can take with respect to financial statements when there is not enough information to confirm compliance or noncompliance with GAAP; is neither positive nor negative. *p. 73*

discount   Amount of interest included in the face of a note; the discount (interest) is subtracted from the face amount of the note to determine the principal amount of cash borrowed. *p. 377*

discount notes   Notes that have the interest included in their face value. *p. 376*

Discount on Bonds Payable   Contra liability account used to record the amount of discount on a bond issue. *p. 470*

Discount on Notes Payable   Contra liability account subtracted from the Notes Payable account to determine the carrying value of the liability. *p. 377*

dividend   Transfer of wealth from a business to its owners. *pp. 13, 285*

dividends in arrears   Cumulative dividends on preferred stock that have not been paid; must be paid prior to paying dividends to common stockholders. *p. 521*

double taxation   Policy to tax corporate profits distributed to owners twice, once when the income is reported on the corporation's income tax return and again when the dividends are reported on the individual's return. *p. 516*

double-declining-balance depreciation   Depreciation method that recognizes larger amounts of depreciation in the early stages of an asset's life and progressively smaller amounts as the asset ages. *p. 410*

double-entry accounting (bookkeeping)   Method of keeping records that provides a system of checks and balances by recording transactions in a dual format. *pp. 12, 156*

earnings   The difference between revenues and expenses. Same as net income or profit *p. 4*

effective interest rate   Yield rate of bonds, which is usually equal to the market rate of interest on the day the bonds are sold. *p. 469*

effective interest rate method   Method of amortizing bond discounts and premiums that computes interest based on the carrying value of liability. As the liability increases or decreases, the amount of interest expense also increases or decreases. *p. 482*

elements   Primary components of financial statements including assets, liabilities, equity, contributions, revenue, expenses, distributions, and net income. *p. 5*

entity   Specific unit (individual, business, or institution) for which the accountant records and reports economic information; has boundaries that are distinct and separate from those of the owners, creditors, managers, and employees. *p. 23*

entrenched management   Management that may have become ineffective but because of political implications may be difficult to remove. *p. 517*

equity Portion of assets remaining after the creditors' claims have been satisfied (i.e., Assets − Liabilities = Equity); also called *residual interest* or *net assets. p. 10*

equity method   Method of accounting for investments in marketable equity securities; is required when the investor owns more than 20 percent of the investee company. The amount of investments carried under the equity method represents a measure of the book value of the investee rather than the cost or market value of the investment security. *p. 288*

equity security   An equity security is certificate that evidences an ownership interest in a company. An example is a common stock certificate. *p. 283*

estimated useful life   Time for which an asset is expected to be used by a business. *p. 410*

ex-dividend   Stock traded after the date of record but before the payment date; does not receive the benefit of the upcoming dividend. *p. 526*

expense   An economic sacrifice (decrease in assets or increase in liabilities) that is incurred in the process of generating revenue. *pp. 13, 59, 76*

expense transactions   Transactions completed in the process of operating a business that decrease assets or increase liabilities. *p. 564*

face value   Amount of the bond to be paid back (to the bondholders) at maturity. *p. 464*

fair value   The price at which securities or other assets sell in free markets. Also called market value. *p. 284*

fidelity bond   Insurance policy that a company buys to insure itself against loss due to employee dishonesty. *p. 316*

financial accounting   Accounting information designed to satisfy the needs of an organization's external users, including business owners, creditors, and government agencies. *p. 6*

Financial Accounting Standards Board (FASB)   Privately funded organization with the primary authority for the establishment of accounting standards in the United States. *p. 9*

financial audit   Detailed examination of a company's financial statements and the documents that support the information presented in those statements; includes a verification process that tests the reliability of the underlying accounting system used to produce the financial reports. *p. 71*

financial leverage   Concept of increasing earnings through debt financing; investment of money at a higher rate than that paid to borrow the money. *pp. 126, 475*

financial resources   Money or credit arrangements supplied to a business by investors (owners) and creditors. *p. 5*

financial statements   Primary means of communicating the financial information of an organization to the external users. The four general-purpose financial statements are the income statement, statement of changes in equity, balance sheet, and statement of cash flows. *p. 8*

financing activities   Cash transactions associated with owners and creditors; also one of the three categories of cash inflows and outflows shown on the statement of cash flows. This category of cash activities shows the amount of cash provided by these resource providers and the amount of cash that is returned to them. *pp. 18, 562*

first-in, first-out (FIFO) cost flow method   Inventory cost flow method that treats the first items purchased as the first items sold for the purpose of computing cost of goods sold. *p. 268*

fiscal year   Year for which a company's accounting records are kept. *p. 155*

fixed interest rate   Interest rate (charge for the use of money) that does not change over the life of the loan. *p. 459*

FOB (free on board) destination Term that designates the seller as the responsible party for freight costs (transportation-in costs). *p. 224*

FOB (free on board) shipping point Term that designates the buyer as the responsible party for freight costs (transportation-in costs). *p. 224*

footnotes to the financial statements Explanations of the information in the financial statements such as estimates used and options allowable under GAAP that have been chosen. *p. 174*

franchise Exclusive right to sell products or perform services in certain geographic areas. *p. 423*

fund Independent accounting entity with a self-balancing set of accounts segregated for the purposes of carrying on specific activities. *p. 535*

fund accounting Type of accounting used by governmental entities. *p. 535*

future value Amount an investment will be worth at some point in the future, assuming a specified interest rate and the reinvestment of interest each period that it is earned. *p. 479*

gains Increases in assets or decreases in liabilities that result from peripheral or incidental transactions. *p. 121*

general authority Policies and procedures that apply across different levels of a company's management, such as everyone flies coach class. *p. 317*

general journal Journal in which all types of accounting transactions can be entered but which is commonly used to record adjusting and closing entries and unusual types of transactions. *p. 169*

general ledger Complete set of accounts used in accounting systems. *p. 14*

generally accepted accounting principles (GAAP) Rules and regulations that accountants agree to follow when preparing financial reports for public distribution. *p. 8*

going concern assumption Assumption that a company will continue to operate indefinitely, will pay its obligations and should therefore report those obligations at their full face value in the financial statements. *p. 360*

goodwill Added value of a successful business that is attributable to factors—reputation, location, and superior products—that enable the business to earn above-average profits; stated differently, the excess paid for an existing business over the appraised value of the net assets. *p. 424*

gross margin (gross profit) Difference between sales revenue and cost of goods sold; the amount a company makes from selling goods before subtracting operating expenses. *p. 218*

gross margin method Method of estimating ending inventory that assumes that the percentage of gross margin to sales remains relatively stable from one accounting period to the next. *p. 279*

gross margin percentage Expression of gross margin as a percentage of sales computed by dividing gross margin by net sales; the amount of each dollar of sales that is profit before deducting any operating expenses. *p. 232*

half-year convention Tax rule that requires six months of depreciation expense to be taken in the year of purchase of the asset and the year of disposal regardless of the purchase date. *p. 418*

held-to-maturity securities Debt securities intended to be held until maturity. *p. 284*

historical cost concept Actual price paid for an asset when it was purchased. *pp. 14, 73, 409*

horizontal statements model Arrangement of a set of financial statements horizontally across a sheet of paper. *p. 19*

imprest basis Description of the periodic replenishment of a fund to maintain it at its specified original amount. *p. 327*

income Added value created in transforming resources into more desirable states. *p. 4*

income statement Statement that measures the difference between the asset increases and the asset decreases associated with running a business. This definition is expanded in subsequent chapters as additional relationships among the elements of the financial statements are introduced. *p. 17*

independent auditor Certified public accountant licensed to perform audits who is independent of the company being audited. *p. 71*

indirect method Method of preparing the statement of cash flows that uses the net income from the income statement as a starting point for the reporting of cash flow from operating activities. The adjustments necessary to convert accrual-based net income to a cash-equivalent basis are shown in the operating activities section of the statement of cash flows. *p. 575*

intangible assets Assets that may be represented by pieces of paper or contracts that appear tangible; however, the true value of an intangible asset lies in the rights and privileges extended to its owners. *p. 408*

interest Fee paid for the use of borrowed funds; also refers to revenue from debt securities. *pp. 6, 285*

interest-bearing notes Notes that require the payment of the face value plus accrued interest at maturity. *p. 376*

internal controls A company's policies and procedures designed to reduce the opportunity for fraud and to provide reasonable assurance that its objectives will be accomplished. *pp. 75, 316*

inventory Supply of goods that is in the process of being made or is finished and ready for sale; also describes stockpiles of goods used in the business (office supplies, cleaning supplies). *p. 217*

inventory cost flow methods Methods used to allocate the cost of goods available for sale between cost of goods sold and inventory. *p. 267*

inventory turnover Ratio of cost of goods sold to inventory that indicates how many times a year the average inventory is sold (turned over). *p. 281*

investee Company that receives assets or services in exchange for a debt or equity security. *p. 283*

investing activities One of the three categories of cash inflows and outflows shown on the statement of cash flows; includes cash received and spent by the business on productive assets and investments in the debt and equity of other companies. *pp. 18, 562*

investment Commitment of assets (usually cash) by a business to acquire other assets that will be used to produce revenue. *p. 63*

investment securities Certificates that describe the rights and privileges that investors receive when they loan or give assets or services to investees. *p. 283*

investor Company or individual who gives assets or services and receives a security certificate in exchange. *pp. 5, 283*

issued stock Stock sold to the public. *p. 520*

issuer of a bond Party that issues the bond (the borrower). *p. 68*

issuer of a note Individual or business borrowing funds (the party receiving the cash when a note is issued). *p. 377*

journal Book of original entry in which accounting data are entered chronologically before posting to the ledger accounts. *p. 169*

labor resources Both intellectual and physical labor used in the process of converting goods and services to products of greater value. *p. 6*

last-in, first-out (LIFO) cost flow method Inventory cost flow method that treats the last items purchased as the first items sold for the purpose of computing cost of goods sold. *p. 268*

ledger Collection of all accounts used by a business; primary information source for the financial statements. *p. 168*

legal capital Amount of assets that should be maintained as protection for creditors; the number of shares multiplied by the par value. *p. 519*

liabilities Obligations of a business to relinquish assets, provide services, or accept other obligations. *p. 10*

limited liability Concept that investors in a corporation may not be held personally liable for the actions of the corporation (the creditors cannot lay claim to the owners' personal assets as payment for the corporation's debts). *p. 516*

limited liability company (LLC) Organizational form offering many of the best features of corporations and partnerships and with many legal benefits of a corporation (e.g., limited liability and centralized management) but permitted by the Internal Revenue Service to be taxed as a partnership, thereby avoiding double taxation of profits. *p. 516*

line of credit Preapproved credit arrangement with a lending institution in which a business can borrow money by simply writing a check up to the approved limit. *p. 462*

liquidation Process of dividing up the assets and returning them to the resource providers. Creditors normally receive first priority in business liquidations; in other words, assets are distributed to creditors first. After creditor claims have been satisfied, the remaining assets are distributed to the investors (owners) of the business. *p. 5*

liquidity Ability to convert assets to cash quickly and meet short-term obligations. *pp. 18, 330*

long-term operational assets Assets used by a business to generate revenue; condition of being used distinguishes them from assets that are sold (inventory) and assets that are held (investments). *p. 407*

losses Decreases in assets or increases in liabilities that result from peripheral or incidental transactions. *p. 120*

lower-of-cost-or-market rule Accounting principle of reporting inventories at market value if their value declined below their cost, regardless of the cause. *p. 277*

Management's Discussion and Analysis (MD&A) Section of the annual report that management uses to explain many different aspects of the company's past performance and future plans. *p. 175*

managerial accounting Branch of accounting that provides information useful to internal decision makers and managers in operating an organization. *p. 6*

manufacturing businesses Makers of goods sold to customers. *p. 23*

market Gathering of people or organizations for the purpose of buying and selling resources. *p. 4*

market interest rate Current interest rate available on a wide range of alternative investments. *p. 474*

market value Value at which securities sell in the secondary market; also called *fair value*. *pp. 284, 520*

marketable securities Securities that are readily traded in the secondary securities market. *p. 284*

matching concept Process of matching expenses with the revenues they produce; three ways to match expenses with revenues include matching expenses directly to revenues, matching expenses to the period in which they are incurred, and matching expenses systematically with revenues. *pp. 64, 114*

material error Error or other reporting problem that, if known, would have influenced the decision of an average prudent investor. *p. 71*

materiality Concept that recognizes practical limits in financial reporting by allowing flexible handling of matters not considered material; information is considered material if the decisions of a reasonable person would be influenced by its omission or misstatement. *p. 116*

merchandise inventory Supply of finished goods held for resale to customers. *p. 217*

merchandising businesses Companies that buy and sell merchandise inventory. *pp. 23, 217*

Modified Accelerated Cost Recovery System (MACRS) Prescribed method of depreciation for tax purposes that provides the maximum depreciation expense deduction permitted under tax law. *p. 418*

mortgage bond Type of secured bond that conditionally transfers title of a designated piece of property to the bondholder until the bond is paid. *p. 464*

multistep income statement Income statement format that matches particular revenue items with related expense items and distinguishes between recurring operating activities and nonoperating items such as gains and losses. *p. 228*

natural resources Mineral deposits, oil and gas reserves, and reserves of timber, mines, and quarries are examples; sometimes called *wasting assets* because their value wastes away as the resources are removed. *p. 408*

net assets Portion of the assets remaining after the creditors' claims have been satisfied (i.e., Assets − Liabilities = Net assets); also called *equity* or *residual interest*. *p. 10*

net income Increase in net assets resulting from operating the business. *p. 17*

net income percentage Another term for *return on sales*. Refer to *return on sales* for the definition. *p. 232*

net loss Decrease in net assets resulting from operating the business. *p. 17*

net method A method of accounting for cash discounts that records inventory purchases at the net price (the list price minus the purchase discount). *p. 223*

net realizable value Face amount of receivables less an allowance for accounts whose collection is doubtful (amount actually expected to be collected). *pp. 360, 361*

net sales Sales less returns from customers and allowances or cash discounts given to customers. *p. 232*

nominal accounts Accounts that contain information applicable to a single accounting period (Revenues, Expenses and Dividends); sometimes called *temporary accounts*. *p. 61*

noncash investing and financing activities Business transactions that do not directly affect cash, such as exchanging stock for land or purchasing property by using a mortgage and that are reported as both an inflow and outflow in a separate section of the statement of cash flows. *p. 562*

non-sufficient-funds (NSF) check   Customer's check deposited but returned by the bank on which it was drawn because the customer did not have enough funds in its account to pay the check. *p. 323*

note payable   Liability that results from the execution of a legal document called a *note* that describes technical terms, including interest charges, maturity date, collateral, and so on. *p. 67*

notes receivable   Notes that evidence rights to receive cash in the future; usually specify the maturity date, rate of interest, and other credit terms. *p. 359*

not-for-profit entities   Organizations (also called *nonprofit* or *nonbusiness entities*) whose primary motive is something other than making a profit, such as providing goods and services for the social good. Examples include state-supported universities and colleges, hospitals, public libraries, and public charities. *p. 7*

operating activities   One of the three categories of cash inflows and outflows shown on the statement of cash flows; show the amount of cash generated by revenue and the amount of cash spent for expenses. *pp. 18, 562*

operating cycle   Time required to turn cash into inventory, inventory into receivables, and receivables back to cash. *pp. 330, 375*

operating income   Income determined by subtracting operating expenses from operating revenues. Gains and losses and other peripheral activities are added to or subtracted from operating income to determine net income or loss. *p. 121*

opportunity cost   Income given up by choosing one alternative over another; for example, the wage a working student forgoes to attend class. *p. 234*

outstanding checks   Checks deducted from the depositor's cash account balance but not yet presented to the bank for payment. *p. 323*

outstanding stock   Stock owned by outside parties; normally the amount of stock issued less the amount of treasury stock. *p. 521*

Paid-in Capital in Excess of Par Value account   Account used to record any amount received above the par or stated value of stock when stock is issued. *p. 522*

par value   Arbitrary value assigned to stock by the board of directors. *p. 519*

parent company   Company that holds a controlling interest (more than 50 percent ownership) in another company. *p. 288*

partnership   Business entity owned by at least two people who share talents, capital, and the risks of the business. *p. 514*

partnership agreement   Legal document that defines the responsibilities of each partner and describes the division of income and losses. *p. 514*

patent   Legal right granted by the U.S. Patent Office ensuring a company or an individual the exclusive right to a product or process. *pp. 408, 423*

payables   Obligations to make future economic sacrifices, usually cash payments. *p. 359*

payment date   Date on which a dividend is actually paid. *p. 526*

period costs   Expenses matched to the period in which they are incurred regardless of when cash payments for them are made; costs that cannot be directly traced to products but are usually

recognized as expenses in the period in which they are incurred. *pp. 102, 218*

periodic inventory system   Method of accounting for changes in the Inventory account only at the end of the accounting period. *p. 236*

peripheral (incidental) transactions   Transactions that do not arise from ordinary business operations. *p. 120*

permanent accounts   Accounts that contain information transferred from one accounting period to the next. *p. 61*

perpetual inventory system   Method of accounting for inventories that increases the Inventory account each time merchandise is purchased and decreases it each time merchandise is sold. *p. 220*

petty cash fund   Small amount of cash set aside in a fund to pay for small outflows for which writing checks is not practical. *p. 327*

petty cash voucher   A document prepared by the petty cash custodian that evidences a petty cash disbursement. The person who receives the cash signs the voucher as evidence of receiving the money. Supporting documents, such as an invoice, restaurant bill, or parking fee receipt, should be attached to the petty cash voucher. *p. 328*

physical flow of goods   Physical movement of goods through the business; normally a FIFO flow so that the first goods purchased are the first goods delivered to customers, thereby reducing the likelihood of obsolete inventory. *p. 268*

physical resources   Natural resources used in the transformation process to create resources of more value. *p. 6*

posting   Process of copying information from journals to ledgers. *p. 169*

preferred stock   Stock that receives some form of preferential treatment (usually as to dividends) over common stock; normally has no voting rights. *p. 521*

present value   Current value of some investment amount that is expected to be received at some specified future time. *p. 479*

price-earnings (P/E) ratio   Ratio of the selling price per share to the earnings per share; generally, a higher P/E ratio indicates that investors are optimistic about a company's future. *p. 20*

primary securities market   Market made up of transactions between the investor and investee. *p. 284*

principal   Amount of cash actually borrowed. *p. 377*

procedures manual   Manual that sets forth the accounting procedures to be followed. *p. 317*

product costs   Inventory costs directly traceable to the product including the cost to acquire goods or make them ready for sale. *p. 218*

productive assets   Assets used to operate the business; frequently called *long-term assets*. *p. 18*

profit   Value created by transforming goods and services to more desirable states. *p. 4*

property, plant, and equipment   Category of assets, sometimes called *plant assets*, used to produce products or to carry on the administrative and selling functions of a business; includes machinery and equipment, buildings, and land. *p. 408*

purchase discount   Reduction in the gross price of merchandise extended under the condition that the purchaser pay cash for the merchandise within a stated time (usually within 10 days of the date of the sale). *p. 223*

qualified opinion Opinion issued by a CPA that falls between an unqualified opinion (see later definition) and an adverse opinion; means that for the most part, the company's financial statements are in compliance with GAAP, but the auditors have reservations about something in the statements or have other reasons not to give a fully unqualified opinion; reasons that a qualified opinion is being issued are explained in the auditor's report. *p. 73*

realization A term that usually refers to transactions that involve the collection or payment of cash. *p. 55*

recognition Reporting an accounting event in the financial statements. *p. 55*

relative fair market value method Method of assigning value to individual assets acquired in a basket purchase in which each asset is assigned a percentage of the total price paid for all assets. The percentage assigned equals the market value of a particular asset divided by the total of the market values of all assets acquired in the basket purchase. *p. 409*

reliability concept Information is reliable if it can be independently verified. Reliable information is factual rather than subjective. *p. 14*

reporting entities Particular businesses or other organizations for which financial statements are prepared. *p. 8*

residual interest Portion of the assets remaining after the creditors' claims have been satisfied (Assets − Liabilities = Residual Interest); also called *equity* or *net assets*. *p. 10*

restrictive covenants Special provisions specified in the loan contract that are designed to prohibit management from taking certain actions that place creditors at risk. *p. 462*

retail companies Companies that sell goods to consumers. *p. 217*

retained earnings Increase in equity that results from the retention of assets obtained through the operation of the business. *p. 11*

return on assets ratio Ratio that measures the relationship between the level of net income and the size of the investment in assets. *p. 124*

return on equity ratio Ratio that measures the relationship between the amount of net income and the stockholders' equity of a company. *p. 126*

return on sales Percent of net income generated by each $1 of sales; computed by dividing net income by net sales. *p. 232*

revenue An economic benefit (an increase in assets or a decrease in liabilities) that is gained by providing goods and services to customers. *pp. 13, 76*

revenue transactions Transactions completed in the process of operating a business that increase assets or decrease liabilities. *p. 564*

salaries payable Amounts of future cash payments owed to employees for services that have already been performed. *p. 57*

sales discount Cash discount extended by the seller of goods to encourage prompt payment. When the buyer of the goods takes advantage of the discount and pays less than the original selling price, the difference between the selling price and the cash collected is the sales discount. *p. 223*

salvage value Expected selling price of an asset at the end of its useful life. *p. 410*

Sarbanes-Oxley Act of 2002 An act of Congress that was established to promote ethical behavior in corporate governance and fairness in financial reporting. Key provisions of the act include a requirement that a company's chief executive officer (CEO) and chief financial officer (CFO) must certify in writing that they have reviewed the financial reports being issued, and that the reports present fairly the company's financial status. An executive who falsely certifies the company's financial reports is subject to significant fines and imprisonment. The act also establishes the Public Company Accounting Oversight Board (PCAOB). This Board assumes the primary responsibility for developing and enforcing auditing standards for CPAs who audit SEC companies. The Sarbanes-Oxley Act also prohibits auditors from providing most types of non-audit services to companies they audit. *p. 515*

schedule of cost of goods sold Schedule that reflects the computation of the amount of the cost of goods sold under the periodic inventory system; an internal report not shown in the formal financial statements. *p. 236*

secondary securities market Market in which securities are exchanged between investors. *p. 284*

secured bonds Bonds secured by specific identifiable assets. *p. 464*

Securities Act of 1933 and Securities Exchange Act of 1934 Acts passed after the stock market crash of 1929 designed to regulate the issuance of stock and govern the stock exchanges; created the Securities and Exchange Commission (SEC), which has the authority to establish accounting policies for companies registered on the stock exchanges. *p. 515*

Securities and Exchange Commission (SEC) Government organization responsible for overseeing the accounting rules to be followed by companies required to be registered with it. *p. 176*

selling and administrative costs Costs that cannot be directly traced to products that are recognized as expenses in the period in which they are incurred. Examples include advertising expense and rent expense. *p. 218*

separation of duties Internal control feature of, whenever possible, assigning the functions of authorization, recording, and custody to different individuals. *p. 316*

serial bonds Bonds that mature at specified intervals throughout the life of the total issue. *p. 464*

service businesses Organizations—accountants, lawyers, and dry cleaners—that provide services to consumers. *p. 23*

service charges Fees charged by a bank for services performed or a penalty for the depositor's failing to maintain a specified minimum cash balance throughout the period. *p. 323*

shrinkage A term that reflects decreases in inventory for reasons other than sales to customers. *p. 230*

signature card Bank form that records the bank account number and the signatures of the people authorized to write checks on an account. *p. 321*

simple interest Interest computed by multiplying the principal by the interest rate by the number of periods. Interest earned in a period is not added to the principal, so that no interest is earned on the interest of previous periods. *p. 478*

single-step income statement Single comparison between total revenues and total expenses. *p. 228*

sinking fund Fund to which the bond issuer annually contributes to ensure the availability of cash for the payment of the face amount on the maturity date. *p. 464*

sole proprietorship Business (usually small) owned by one person. *p. 514*

solvency Ability of a business to pay liabilities in the long run. *p. 330*

source document Document such as a cash register tape, invoice, time card, or check stub that provides accounting information to be recorded in the accounting journals and ledgers. *p. 169*

special journals Journals designed to improve the efficiency of recording specific types of repetitive transactions. *p. 169*

specific authorizations Policies and procedures that apply to designated levels of management, such as the policy that the right to approve overtime pay may apply only to the plant manager. *p. 317*

specific identification Inventory method that allocates costs between cost of goods sold and ending inventory using the cost of the specific goods sold or retained in the business. *p. 268*

spread Difference between the rate a bank pays to obtain money (e.g., interest paid on savings accounts) and the rate that the bank earns on money it lends to borrowers. *p. 475*

stakeholders Parties interested in the operations of a business, including owners, lenders, employees, suppliers, customers, and government agencies. *p. 3*

stated interest rate Rate of interest specified in the bond contract that will be paid at specified intervals over the life of the bond. *p. 464*

stated value Arbitrary value assigned to stock by the board of directors. *p. 520*

statement of activities Statement that reports the revenues, expenses, gains, and losses that increase or decrease the net assets of a not-for-profit organization. *p. 533*

statement of cash flows Statement that explains how a business obtained and used cash during an accounting period. *pp. 18, 533*

statement of changes in stockholders' equity Statement that summarizes the transactions occurring during the accounting period that affected the owners' equity *p. 17*

statement of financial position Statement that reports the assets, liabilities, and net assets of a not-for-profit organization. *p. 533*

statements model Simultaneous representation of a set of financial statements. *p. 14*

stock certificate Evidence of ownership interest issued when an investor contributes assets to a corporation; describes the rights and privileges that accompany ownership. *p. 514*

stock dividend Proportionate distribution of additional shares of the declaring corporation's stock. *p. 527*

stockholders Owners of a corporation. *pp. 11, 517*

stockholders' equity Stockholders' equity represents the portion of the assets that is owned by the stockholders. *p. 11*

stock split Proportionate increase in the number of outstanding shares; designed to reduce the market value of the stock and its par value. *p. 527*

straight-line amortization Method of amortization that allocates bond discount or premium in equal amounts to each period over the life of the bond. *p. 471*

straight-line depreciation Method of computing depreciation that allocates the cost of an asset to expense in equal amounts over its life. *p. 410*

straight-line method Allocation method computed by subtracting the salvage value from the cost and then dividing by the number of years of useful life. *p. 112*

subordinated debentures Unsecured bonds that have a lower priority than general creditors, that is, are paid off after the general creditors are paid in the case of liquidation. *p. 464*

subsidiary company Company controlled (more than 50 percent owned) by another company. *p. 288*

systematic allocation of cost Process of spreading the cost of an asset over several accounting periods in an orderly manner. *p. 114*

T-account Simplified account form, named for its shape, with the account title placed at the top of a horizontal bar, debit entries listed on the left side of the vertical bar, and credit entries shown on the right side. *p. 156*

T-account method Method of determining net cash flows by analyzing beginning and ending balances on the balance sheet and inferring the period's transactions from the income statement. *p. 564*

tangible assets Assets that can be touched, such as equipment, machinery, natural resources, and land. *p. 408*

temporary accounts Accounts used to collect information for a single accounting period (usually revenue, expense, and distribution accounts). *p. 61*

term bonds Bonds in an issue that mature on a specified date in the future. *p. 464*

time value of money Recognition that the present value of a promise to receive a dollar some time in the future is worth less than a dollar. For example, a person may be willing to pay $0.90 today for the right to receive $1.00 one year from today. *p. 478*

times interest earned ratio Ratio that computes how many times a company would be able to pay its interest by using the amount of earnings available to make interest payments; amount of earnings is net income before interest and income taxes. *p. 477*

trademark Name or symbol that identifies a company or an individual product. *p. 423*

trading securities Securities bought and sold to generate profit from short-term appreciation in stock and bond prices. *p. 284*

transaction Particular event that involves the transfer of something of value between two entities. *p. 11*

transferability Concept referring to the practice of dividing the ownership of corporations into small units that are represented by shares of stock, which permits the easy exchange of ownership interests. *p. 517*

transportation-in (freight-in) Cost of freight on goods purchased under terms FOB shipping point that is usually added to the cost of inventory and is a product cost. *p. 224*

transportation-out (freight-out) Freight cost for goods delivered to customers under terms FOB destination; a period cost expensed when it is incurred. *p. 224*

treasury stock Stock first issued to the public and then bought back by the corporation. *p. 520*

trial balance List of ledger accounts and their balances that provides a check on the mathematical accuracy of the recording process. *p. 173*

true cash balance Actual balance of cash owned by a company at the close of business on the date of the bank statement. *p. 322*

2/10, n/30 Term indicating that the seller will give the purchaser a 2 percent discount on the gross invoice price if the purchaser pays cash for the merchandise within 10 days from the date of purchase. *p. 223*

unadjusted bank balance Ending cash balance reported by the bank as of the date of the bank statement. *p. 322*

unadjusted book balance Balance of the Cash account as of the date of the reconciliation before making any adjustments. *p. 322*

unearned revenue Revenue for which cash has been collected but the service has not yet been performed. *p. 110*

units-of-production depreciation Depreciation method based on a measure of production rather than a measure of time; for example, an automobile may be depreciated based on the expected miles to be driven rather than on a specific number of years. *pp. 410, 416*

unqualified opinion Opinion on financial statements audited by a CPA that means the auditor believes the financial statements are in compliance with GAAP. *p. 72*

unrealized gain or loss Paper gain or loss on investment securities that has not yet been realized and is not realized until the securities are sold or otherwise disposed of. *p. 285*

unsecured bonds Also known as *debentures*, bonds issued on the general credit of the organization. *p. 464*

unsubordinated debentures Unsecured bonds that have equal claims with the general creditors. *p. 464*

users Individuals or organizations that use financial information for decision making. *p. 3*

variable interest rate Interest rate that fluctuates (may change) from period to period over the life of the loan. *p. 459*

vertical statements model Arrangement of a full set of financial statements on a single page with account titles arranged from the top to the bottom of the page. *p. 69*

voluntarily disclosing Professional responsibility to clients that forbids CPAs from voluntarily disclosing information obtained as a result of their client–accountant relationships. *p. 73*

warranty Promise to correct a deficiency or dissatisfaction in quality, quantity, or performance of a product or service sold. *p. 370*

weighted-average cost flow method Inventory cost flow method in which the cost allocated between inventory and cost of goods sold is based on the average cost per unit, which is determined by dividing total costs of goods available for sale during the accounting period by total units available for sale during the period. If the average is recomputed each time a purchase is made, the result is called a *moving average*. *p. 268*

wholesale companies Companies that sell goods to other businesses. *p. 217*

withdrawals Distributions to the owners of proprietorships and partnerships. *p. 518*

INDEX

Financial audits—(Cont.)
materiality and, 71–72
types of opinions, 72–73
Financial leverage, 126, 475–476
Financial ratios
accounts receivable turnover ratio, 373–374, 641
average days in inventory ratio, 281, 282
current ratio, 331–332, 641
debt to assets ratio, 124–125, 127, 640
earnings before interest and taxes (EBIT), 476
earnings per share (EPS) ratio, 20–21, 640
effect of cost flow analysis on, 282–283
financial leverage, 126, 475–476
gross margin percentage, 232, 233, 234, 641
inventory turnover, 281, 641–642
net income percentage, 232–233
price-earnings (P/E) ratio, 20–21, 530–531, 640
return on assets ratio (ROA), 124, 127, 476, 640, 642
return on equity (ROE), 126, 127, 640
return on sales ratio, 220, 232–233, 234, 641
times interest earned ratio, 477, 642
Financial resources
defined, 5
market-based allocation of, 5–6
Financial statements. See also names of specific financial statements
accounts in, 9
capital structure in, 518–519
certification of, 75
common size, 231–232
deferrals and, 113, 114, 118, 119, 122
depreciation and, 412, 414–416, 417
elements of, 8–10
footnotes, 174–175
general ledger as basis of, 171–172
horizontal statements model, 19–20
independent auditors and, 23, 71–72, 175–176
investment securities and, 286–288
long-term debt and, 461, 467–468, 471–473
long-term operational assets and, 427
management's discussion and analysis (MD&A), 23, 175
of merchandising businesses, 222–226, 228–229, 269–270, 273–274
of non-U.S. companies, 332, 375
preparing, 15–19
receivables on, 367–368
special terms in, 23–24
types of, 8–9
Financing activities
cash flows from, 573–574
converting accruals to cash, 567–568
defined, 18, 562
noncash, 562

Financing activities—(Cont.)
and statement of cash flows, 18, 19, 562, 567–568, 573–574
First-in, first-out (FIFO) inventory cost flow method, 268, 271, 272–274, 275–276
Fiscal year, 155
Fixed assets. See Property, plant, and equipment
Fixed interest rates, 459
Florida Power and Light (FPL), 574
FOB destination, 224, 225
FOB shipping point, 224
Footnotes to the financial statements, 174–175
Ford Motor Company, 309, 401
Franchises, 423–424
Frank, W. G., 125
Fraud detection and avoidance. See also Accounting for cash; Financial audits; Internal controls
in merchandising businesses, 278–279
required absences and, 316–317
Sarbanes-Oxley Act of 2002, 74–75, 177, 515
Fund accounting, 535
Funds, 535
Future value, 478–479, 483
Future value annuities, 480, 485

G

GAAP. See Generally accepted accounting principles (GAAP)
Gains
accounting for, 120–121
defined, 121
unrealized, 285–286
Gap, The, 155
Gap Company, 311
GEICO Insurance, 12
General authority, 317
General Electric, 70–71
General journal, 169–171
General ledger
as basis of financial statements, 171–172
closing entries, 61, 67, 172–173
defined, 14–15
sample accrual transaction data in, 58–59
sample deferral transaction data in, 112–113
sample double-entry accounting data in, 168–169
sample inventory data in, 221–222, 227–228
trial balance, 173–174
Generally accepted accounting principles (GAAP)
accounting equation and, 10
defined, 8

Generally accepted accounting principles (GAAP)—(Cont.)
as international issue, 22, 125, 176, 275, 332, 375, 424
General Motors, 4, 120, 123, 124, 315
Going concern assumption, 360
Goodwill, 424–426
calculating, 425–426
competitive advantage and, 424
Governmental accounting, 533–535
Governmental Accounting Standards Board (GASB), 533–535
Grant Thornton, 515
Gross margin, 218
Gross margin method, 279–280
Gross margin percentage, 232, 233, 234, 641
Gross profit, 218

H

Half-year conventions, 418
Harley-Davidson, Inc., 48, 148, 210, 259, 308, 352, 400, 451, 504, 552, 553, 648–650
Hartford, 126, 127
Haverty's, 401
Held-to-maturity securities, 284
Hewlett-Packard Company (HP), 425
Historical cost principle, 14, 73, 409
Home Depot, 332
Horizontal statements model
defined, 19–20
illustration, 20

I

IBM Corporation, 4, 120, 578
Identifiable useful life, 408, 426
Imprest basis, 327
Incidental (peripheral) transactions, 120–121
Income, 4
Income statement, 8–9
under accrual accounting, 59, 60, 65–66
deferrals and, 113, 114, 119, 122
defined, 17
depreciation and, 412, 415, 417
in horizontal statements model, 19–20
long-term debt and, 461, 468, 472
matching concept and, 16–17
of merchandising business, 228–229, 269, 273
percentage analysis, 21–22
preparing, 16–17
in vertical statements model, 69, 70
Indefinite useful life, 409, 426–427
Independent auditors, 23, 71–72, 175–176
Indirect method, of presenting statement of cash flows, 575–577
Industry characteristics, 429–430